The Palgrave Handbook of Popular Culture as Philosophy

David Kyle Johnson
Editor-in-Chief

Dean A. Kowalski • Chris Lay • Kimberly S. Engels
Editors

The Palgrave Handbook of Popular Culture as Philosophy

Volume 3

With 1 Figure and 2 Tables

Editor-in-Chief
David Kyle Johnson
King's College
Wilkes Barre, PA
USA

Editors
Dean A. Kowalski
University School of Milwaukee
Waukesha, WI, USA

Chris Lay
Young Harris College
Young Harris, GA, USA

Kimberly S. Engels
Molloy University
Rockville Centre, NewYork, NY, USA

ISBN 978-3-031-24684-5   ISBN 978-3-031-24685-2 (eBook)
https://doi.org/10.1007/978-3-031-24685-2

© Springer Nature Switzerland AG 2024

This work is subject to copyright. All rights are reserved by the Publisher, whether the whole or part of the material is concerned, specifically the rights of translation, reprinting, reuse of illustrations, recitation, broadcasting, reproduction on microfilms or in any other physical way, and transmission or information storage and retrieval, electronic adaptation, computer software, or by similar or dissimilar methodology now known or hereafter developed.

The use of general descriptive names, registered names, trademarks, service marks, etc. in this publication does not imply, even in the absence of a specific statement, that such names are exempt from the relevant protective laws and regulations and therefore free for general use.

The publisher, the authors, and the editors are safe to assume that the advice and information in this book are believed to be true and accurate at the date of publication. Neither the publisher nor the authors or the editors give a warranty, expressed or implied, with respect to the material contained herein or for any errors or omissions that may have been made. The publisher remains neutral with regard to jurisdictional claims in published maps and institutional affiliations.

This Palgrave Macmillan imprint is published by the registered company Springer Nature Switzerland AG.
The registered company address is: Gewerbestrasse 11, 6330 Cham, Switzerland

If disposing of this product, please recycle the paper.

For my wife and son, who demonstrated exceptional patience with me during the five years this project took to complete.

Preface: A Brief Defense of Pop Culture as Philosophy

If you want to tell people the truth, make them laugh, otherwise they'll kill you.
—George Bernard Shaw[1]

Abstract

This introductory chapter articulates the overarching objectives and methodology of the Palgrave Handbook of Popular Culture as Philosophy. Its primary aim is to treat works of popular culture as philosophical works, essentially considering them to be works of art that aspire to articulate philosophical arguments or provoke profound philosophical inquiries. The chapter also defends the concept that creative works, including but not limited to films, possess the capacity to do philosophy – an idea characterized by Paisley Livingston as the "Bold Thesis." A persuasive case in favor of the Bold Thesis is articulated and objections to it are considered and answered.

Introduction

William Irwin started the "Pop Culture and Philosophy" craze with *Seinfeld and Philosophy* in 1999; the second volume of the series, *The Simpsons and Philosophy (2001)*, ended up selling over 200,000 copies. (Because it was published in 2001, at the time it might have been the best-selling philosophy book of the twenty-first century.) Later volumes, like *The Matrix and Philosophy* (2002) and *The Lord of the Rings and Philosophy* (2003), were also highly successful (and impeccably timed with popular movie sequels). And it was around that time, at a point when Irwin started to bring in other editors to help with the workload (Eric Bronson and Greg Bassham were volume editors of the *Lord of the Rings* book), that the series really took off. Regardless of how you count, to date, there are at least 200 "pop and phil" books.

Although I had taught a "Simpsons, South Park, and Philosophy" class at the University of Oklahoma as a graduate student ca. 2004, my first published chapter was in Robert Arp's *South Park and Philosophy* in 2006; the first words I ever published were "Cartman is an ass." I went on to write almost 30 pop culture chapters, attend multiple pop-culture conferences, and edit three books in Irwin's

Blackwell *Philosophy and Pop Culture* series: *Heroes and Philosophy* (2009), *Inception and Philosophy* (2011), and *Black Mirror and Philosophy* (2019). Irwin also graciously asked me to co-edit his textbook *Introducing Philosophy Through Pop Culture* (2010), which is a collection of select chapters from his Blackwell series, organized by subject so that it can be used in the classroom. We published an updated edition in 2022, and I have used chapters from it, and other chapters from the series, in my classroom for many years.

I mention all this not to demonstrate my "bona fides" (others have certainly edited and published on pop culture more) but to emphasize that this current project – *The Palgrave Handbook of Popular Culture as Philosophy* – is *NOT* a continuation of that series. As should be obvious, I am a big fan of the "pop and phil" approach; but it is decidedly not the approach that this handbook takes. The astute reader might have noticed the difference in its title – it's "*as*" philosophy, not "and." It's subtle, but that "as" makes a lot of difference.

The Difference Between "As" and "And"

The goal of the "pop *and* phil" approach is to use popular culture as a kind of springboard to introduce and discuss philosophical concepts and arguments. If the show has an android – like *Data* from *Star Trek* – we can introduce the reader to the philosophical debate about artificial intelligence by discussing whether Data has a mind. If the show has characters waging war and vying for political power – like *Game of Thrones* – we can examine their actions to introduce the reader to just war theory and political philosophy. *The Matrix* can be used to explain Descartes' dream problem, *Inception* can be used to discuss the acceptability of faith, and *The Good Place* can be used to explore ethical theories and the possibility of an afterlife. I'm oversimplifying, of course, and the number of philosophical issues explored in any one "pop and phil" book is broad and diverse. But the "and philosophy" approach treats the pop culture it engages as a kind of thought experiment – one that is already known and loved and so makes the task of introducing the reader to philosophy easier. As Irwin has often said about his series, "A spoonful of sugar helps the medicine go down" (Written Voices n.d.).

The "as philosophy" approach is different. The basic idea is that the creators of popular culture – the directors, the writers – can actually *do* philosophy while playing at their craft. They can not only be inspired by philosophy, or use ideas they learned in philosophy class, but they can convey philosophical points, raise philosophical questions, and even make philosophical arguments.[2] Consequently, the works they produce can *be* philosophy, and as a result are worth philosophical examination. Ruppert Read and Jerry Goodenough's *Film as Philosophy: Essays on Cinema after Wittgenstein and Cavell* (2005), Murry Smith and Thomas Wartenberg's *Thinking through Cinema: Film as Philosophy* (2006), Thomas Wartenberg's *Thinking on Screen: Film as Philosophy* (2007), and Bernd Herzogenrath's *Film as Philosophy* (2017), all embrace the "as philosophy" approach.

Of course, not all pop culture is philosophy; but quite a bit is, with some examples greatly standing out in this respect – like *The Matrix* and *Inception*. In fact, these two movies are perfect examples. While both movies could be used to explain Descartes' dream problem, they seem to argue for completely different conclusions. *The Matrix*, by making a villain out of the one character (Cypher) who willfully embraces ignorance, seems to be arguing that one should care for and strive to embrace reality – to obtain objectively true beliefs. *Inception* on the other hand, by having Cobb turn away from his spinning top (his test of reality) in the final scene and instead choose to believe that his children are real, seems to suggest that, in the end, it is only "your truth" that matters. Other examples of obviously philosophical films include *2001: A Space Odyssey, Lord of the Rings, Star Wars, Blade Runner, Groundhog Day, The Shawshank Redemption, Tenet, Ex Machina, Don't Look Up, AI: Artificial Intelligence, Fight Club,* and *Gattaca*, all of which (and much more) are covered in this handbook.

Going Beyond Films

It's not only films, of course. Most people recognize that series (what used to be relegated to television but now also exist on streaming services) like *Star Trek, South Park, Black Mirror, House of Cards, Doctor Who, The Handmaid's Tale,* and *The Good Place* can do something similar. (All of these and more are also covered in this handbook.) But one thing that generally goes unappreciated, even by philosophers, is that other kinds of popular culture can be philosophy as well – like graphic novels and video games. Both have long since ceased being "for kids only," and the creators of both enjoy certain kinds of creative freedom that make them an especially welcome medium for philosophical reflection. The graphic novel *V for Vendetta*, for example, does a much better job of articulating exactly when violent political rebellion is warranted than the movie it inspired. And modern video games, with their interactive features and story-telling, can make points about, say, political choice and free will that their strictly scripted movie counterparts cannot. (The game *Papers Please*, where you choose whether to cooperate with a fascist regime or resist it – and can "win" the game either way – is most notable in this regard.) What's more, while common wisdom will tell you that graphic novels and video games aren't as "popular" as TV series and films, graphic novels serve as the groundwork for some of the most popular movies and TV of all time (*The Avengers, X-Men, Justice League, Watchmen, 300, The Walking Dead,* etc.) and the video game industry dwarfs all other entertainment industries in terms of profit (grossing $160 billion in 2020).

Because of its reliance on spoken word, another medium that is prime for the doing of philosophy is stand-up comedy. On the *Comedy Gold Minds* podcast (2021), Hasan Minhaj elaborated on how his experience with competitive debate – the same thing that helped prepare me for a career in philosophy – helped prepare him for his career as a comedian. "Comedians," he says, are "just normal philosophers," tasked with turning "coffee into espresso" (i.e., taking what's difficult to understand and compressing it into something comprehensible). In an interview with Khan Academy (2020), he elaborated a bit more: "Stand-up comedy is just funny speech and debate . . . The most important thing for comedy is the argument. You are making a funny joke, but at the core, what is your argument? So great jokes at their essence are great philosophical positions said in a funny way."

Some comedians, like Jerry Seinfeld, shy away from this responsibility. "Ok, fine, fine." he said on the HBO special *George Carlin's American Dream*, "you want the comedian to be your lens on society. Go…enjoy it. But, for me, I never heard a comic bit that changed my opinion on anything" (Apatow & Bonfiglo 2022). But the promotional featurette for the very special in which Seinfeld speaks these words begins with multiple comedians not only saying that George Carlin was the smartest man they ever met, but that he was also a "genius at making you laugh and *changing your mind*" (HBO 2022). In the special itself, Chris Rock was more specific.

> I remember one time Carlin said to me, "I'm not in show business, I'm a comedian." . . . I took it to mean that comedians were thinkers. But, when you think about the history of [hu]man[ity], [hu]man[ity] used to love philosophers. We don't really have philosophers anymore. But we have comedians. So, Carlin encompassed all those things; that's what he meant. Like, this is what we do, this is the life we've chosen, we're, you know, a kind a secret society in a sense. (Apatow & Bonfiglo 2022)

In his last comedy special, "Nothing Special," Norm McDonald (2022) was a bit more kind to living philosophers.

> Like nowadays, I've heard . . . "The comedian is the modern-day philosopher," you know? Which, first of all, it always makes me feel sad for the actual modern-day philosophers, who exist, you know.

Thanks for the shout-out Norm; indeed, we do exist. But what Rock was getting at still stands: the public doesn't listen to philosophers anymore – at least not like they used to. Don't get me wrong, philosophers still influence society; but the public doesn't crowd event halls to go listen to philosophers speak, as they used to do with academics in the past. But they *do* watch comedians; and many comedians – from George Carlin and Dave Chappell to Amy Schumer and Hannah Gadsby – are presenting philosophical arguments that change people's minds. (Sometimes they are explicit, like Carlin's arguments against religion; other times they are implicit, like Schumer's arguments about feminism. But the arguments are there.) They may not always mean to. Carlin himself said that "try[ing] to make people think . . . would be the kiss of death" for a comedian; he only aims "to let them know I'm thinking." But they are doing it, nonetheless – comedians are making people think. And so, it should be worth the real-world (existing) modern philosopher's time to examine what comedians are saying, and the arguments they are making, to see whether they are onto something – or whether they are full of (sh)it.

The same holds for philosophy that is being done in movies, television/streaming series, graphic novels, and video games. While the people who make these things are doing philosophy, they usually are not professional philosophers; they don't always have a philosophy degree; they might not have even had a philosophy class. So, they

Preface: A Brief Defense of Pop Culture as Philosophy   xi

may be getting things wrong.[3] They might also be getting them right; but how can we know unless those who know the subject best take a closer look, identify what argument being made, and evaluate whether it is any good – or identify the question being raised and explore the answers it might have? That is what I tried to do in my course for *The Great Courses* (now known as *Wondrium*) *Sci-Phi: Science Fiction as Philosophy*, and that's what I tried to have my authors do in *Exploring The Orville* (which I edited with Michael Berry) and in *Black Mirror and Philosophy* (even though it was in an "and philosophy" series). And that is what this handbook aims to do: identify and evaluate the philosophy that is being done in and by popular culture.

This is important to do not only because pop culture can be very influential, but because it can be easily misinterpreted and misused. Think of how the term "snowflake" has become ubiquitous in right–wing political circles, to describe those who they think are easily offended. They stole the term from the mouth of Tyler Durden in *Fight Club*; but those who use it today don't seem to recognize that (a) Durden is the villain of the film, not the hero and (b) he uses the term to solidify obedience in his communistic commune – and communism is something that the right decries. (For more on *Fight Club*, see Alberto Oya's magnificent chapter in this volume. For more on how snowflakey (easily offended) many in right-wing political circles are, see the second half of my chapter on *South Park*.)

Speaking of *South Park*, almost every episode of *South Park* is some kind of argument on some social or political issue – and a lot of young impressionable viewers think Matt Stone and Trey Parker make good points. And sometimes they do. *South Park: Bigger, Longer, and Uncut* effectively argues that parents skirt responsibility for their children's behavior by blaming cartoons, and their film *Team America: World Police* effectively criticizes America's militaristic role as "world police" (while also arguing, through a very vulgar (but seemingly accurate) analogy, that it is sometimes necessary). When I was younger, Matt and Trey definitely changed my view about a few things. But Matt and Trey also get things very wrong. In season 10's *ManBearPig* (2006) they made fun of Al Gore (and his 2006 film *An Inconvenient Truth*) and equated his concerns about climate change with concerns about a mythical creature called ManBearPig that didn't actually exist. Their argument was that Gore just wanted attention. But in Season 22, Stone and Parker admitted they were wrong with two episodes, "Time to Get Cereal" and "Nobody Got Cereal?," that revealed that ManBearPig was indeed real, is now murdering and destroying the town, and thus that Al Gore was right (about climate change) all along (see Miller 2018).

Perhaps one might argue that this is more of a scientific, rather than a philosophic, issue. But a scene in "Time to Get Cereal" makes clear that they have a philosophical point in mind. A patron at Red Lobster tries to mansplain to his wife why ManBearPig is not real – "What you need to understand, Susan, is that everyone has an agenda, mmmkay?" – as ManBearPig actively kills the other patrons in the restaurant and his wife yells "he's real!" The patron eventually turns around – yet when he sees ManBearPig with his own eyes, he only begrudgingly admits he was wrong and immediately shifts to "What are we going to do about it now, huh? What are we going to do that's going to make any difference now, Susan? What can we do that everyone else will also do?," only to then be eaten alive by ManBearPig.[4] Matt and Trey go on to show townhall meetings where, as ManBearPig destroys the town, the people calmly agree that, perhaps, they should, maybe, begin to consider thinking about possibly being worried. And when it's revealed that ManBearPig is attacking because Stan's grandpa and his generation made a deal with ManBearPig (for cars and premium boutique ice cream because they "didn't think they would have to live with the consequences"), and Stan tries to renegotiate the contract, Stan goes to the townspeople with the new terms of the deal:

Stan (to the townspeople)　Um, [ManBearPig] says he'll never come back again, but, we have to give up soy sauce and *Red Dead Redemption 2*.
Townspeople (in unison, disappointed)　Ohhh. . . .
A single townsperson　A long silence
　　Just plain rice?
Stan (pauses, but is unsurprised)　Yeah, that's what I thought.

The scene is hilarious and so on the nose that it's depressing. Stan has to strike another deal.

Lawyer　Sign here that ManBearPig has rights to the lives of all children in third world countries.
Stan　Ok, got it.
Lawyer　And you agree to ignore ManBearPig until he returns in five years, in which time the carnage will be a thousand-fold.
Stan　Ok, where do I sign that?

Parker and Stone are not known for being subtle, and clearly they are making a philosophical point; yet one might still struggle to put it into words so that it can be examined – hence the need for professional philosophers to step in. A chapter on these episodes would show that the Red Lobster scene is making a philosophical point about how climate change denial is epistemically bankrupt; no matter how obvious the evidence is, or how imminent the threat, their denial and excuses will continue. Such a chapter would point out that the townhall meeting scene is making the point that, because of people's epistemic tendency toward self-denial when it comes to things so overwhelmingly unpleasant, even those who recognize the severity of the threat are afraid to say that people should be even worried for fear of being labeled "alarmist." And it would point out that the negotiation scene shows how human selfishness makes us collectively incapable of giving up even the most basic comforts for the good of others (like children in third world countries), future generations, or even ourselves five years from now. (My chapter on *South Park* in this volume covers a different topic, but check out this handbook's chapter on *Don't Look Up* to see that Parker and Stone are essentially right on these topics.)

The Handbook's Approach

I've divided the handbook into five sections – cinema, series, comedians, video games, and graphic novels – but the basic approach of each chapter will be similar.

1. A short introduction to the pop culture work and the philosophical issue it raises
2. A quick summary of the work itself
3. An attempt to identify exactly what argument the work is making or what question it is raising
4. An evaluation of that argument or an attempt to answer the relevant philosophical question

Now, there is a lot of variation; I tried to give the author of each chapter the freedom to evaluate the philosophy being done by their selected piece of pop culture in the most appropriate way. But each has the goal of treating the pop culture in question as philosophy – or, in the case of a comedian, as a philosopher.

Another thing I tried to make consistent throughout is the writing style. Each author, of course, has their own flair and approach – but while this handbook is more academic in nature, and some of its chapters are quite long, I intended the handbook for classroom use. So, each chapter is written with the goal of being understandable to the average college student. (If the chapter is long, its sections make it divisible into readable parts.) What's more, the reason that I made sure that each chapter contains a summary of the pop culture in question is so the instructor does not have to assign it or spend valuable class time screening it. That's not to say that doing so wouldn't enhance the student's experience; but a familiarity with the pop culture in question is not required to understand, learn from, or enjoy any chapter.

Defending a Bold Thesis

Despite the popularity of viewing films as philosophy, the notion that films can do philosophy, which of course would entail that popular culture (e.g., TV, graphic novels, etc.) can do philosophy, has its detractors. I, however, have never found the arguments against the notion very convincing. After all, my guess is that most readers would agree that the novels *To Kill a Mockingbird* and *1984* are arguments against racism and fascism – so why can't the movies based on them be the same? And why couldn't something that is even more overtly philosophical, like *The Matrix*, be presenting an argument?

Bruce Russell (2000) would argue that *The Matrix* (and *To Kill a Mockingbird* and *1984* for that matter) doesn't do philosophy but merely inspires viewers (or readers) to do their own philosophy – to construct their own arguments and raise their own questions. I have three responses to this charge. First, even if Russell's claim is true and pop culture can't do philosophy (but instead merely inspires people to do philosophy), this handbook is still warranted, as it essentially contains the philosophy that pop culture inspired professional philosophers to do. Second, inspiring others to do philosophy can be (and often is) philosophy itself. Philosophy is often aimed at simply changing our perspective, making us think about the world or a situation in a way that we have not before. As any philosophy instructor will tell you, that is the goal of nearly every philosophy class. So, even if inspiring others to do philosophy is all a piece of popular culture does, that work of popular culture is still doing philosophy.

The third response is that this claim is simply false. Films can do more than inspire philosophy; they can do philosophy. To take a rather obvious example (anticipated by Smuts 2009), suppose someone took one of Plato's dialogues and turned it into a movie – which, of course, could be done because they are dialogues complete with characters and settings. Wouldn't it undeniably be philosophy? And couldn't the story of Plato's cave be made into a movie; and if it was, wouldn't it have just as much of a philosophical point as the story does in Plato's *Republic*? Or take the article, "A Debate Between a Theist and a Santa Clausist," that Ruth Tallman and I divided into two "acts" and published in the journal *Think* in 2015. It was written (and originally delivered at a conference) as a sketch, and could easily be turned into a short film that has the express purpose of convincing the audience that many of the arguments given in favor of theism could be given in defense in Santa Claus – and thus that theistic belief is on shaky ground. The quality of such a film might be questionable, but such a film would undoubtedly be philosophy.

In reply, skeptics might insist that a film can't be philosophy by simply putting philosophical arguments in the mouths of characters. But, again, I would object. First, why not? I mean, it would be one thing for a painter to say that he had a painting that "did philosophy," only to find out that he had just written a philosophical treatise on a canvas with a paint brush. That's not a painting. In the same way, just recording a video of someone giving a philosophy lecture wouldn't count as an example of "film as philosophy." That's not really a film; it's not cinema. (A recorded lecture lacks certain defining features of cinema at both an aesthetic and technical level.) But to have a character give a philosophical argument at a crucial moment that delivers the film's philosophical message doesn't disqualify a piece of media from being cinema. Take the film *God's Not Dead* for example. It not only contains a student – on three separate occasions – presenting formal arguments for God's existence, but it has the conclusion the movie is arguing for in the damn title! It may have lazy writing and be a really bad movie – and as one chapter in this handbook will show, the arguments it presents are pretty bad – but that doesn't mean it's not philosophy. (Bad philosophy is still philosophy.)

At this point in the debate, skeptics might argue that *good* film can't be philosophy. "Without just putting arguments in characters' mouths, films can't do philosophy. A *real* film would be able to show the argument without having a character 'spell it out' for the audience." There are two problems with claims like this. First, such a line of argument would be fallacious, something akin to the no-true-Scotsman fallacy. If I say that no Scotsmen lie, and then you produce a clear, obvious example of a lying Scotsman, I can't refute your counter example by simply claiming "he's not a *true* Scotsman." That's a fallacy. That's just me claiming, arbitrarily, that your example doesn't count so I don't have to admit I'm wrong. In the same way, those skeptical of the idea that films can be philosophy can't just say that movies like *My Dinner with Andre,* which involves two people having a philosophical dinner conversation, don't count "as philosophical films" because they contain people bluntly making philosophical arguments and thus aren't *true* films. In fact, *My Dinner with Andre* is frequently regarded as a masterpiece of a film – in part *because* of its philosophical content.

What's more, there seem to be clear examples of films, even very good films, doing philosophy without simply putting the argument for the film's thesis in the mouths of its characters. My favorite example might be *Contact*, the movie based on Carl Sagan's novel of the same name, in which aliens (seem to) make contact with Earth and give us instructions for building a device to visit them. Carl Sagan was a famous skeptic and science communicator who was labeled as an atheist by religious conservatives but who was, in reality, merely agnostic. In 2021, in chapter six of William Anderson's *Film, Philosophy and Religion*, I showed how *Contact* is an argument for a thesis that Sagan often defended in public: science and religion are compatible. The film has Dr. Arroway dismiss Rev. Palmer's belief in God because it is based solely on his personal experience, only to have Dr. Arroway turn around and believe that she visited aliens based solely on her personal experience. The argument Dr. Arroway uses against Rev. Palmer (based in Occam's razor) is turned back on her, and she answers it in almost the same way he answered her: "Everything I am tells me it was real. It changed me forever." The movie is an argument from analogy that it never formally states: if Arroway's beliefs based in her personal experience about aliens are justified, and they are, then Palmer's beliefs (and the beliefs of those like him in the real world) in God, based in personal experience, are justified as well. And such beliefs are as compatible with science as Dr. Arroway's are. As I try to explain in my aforementioned chapter, it's not a good argument – Dr. Arraoways' belief is not scientific and science and religion are not compatible in the way that Sagan or the movie suggests – but it is an argument, the kind that are made by philosophers every day. To deny that *Contact* is doing philosophy seems ludicrous.

Or take an even better example: *No Exit*, the play by Jean Paul Sartre that everyone agrees conveys very clearly his intended message: "Hell is other people." Although those words are spoken by the character Garcin, no formal argument for that thesis is put forth; yet the message is clearly there and the play (and thus the movie based on it) is very clearly doing philosophy. A film must do more than just illustrate a position or worldview to be philosophy; after all, mysticism and religion can merely state positions. But when films actually argue for a position, whether it be directly or indirectly, they seem to be doing philosophy.

Now, to be fair, pop culture may not be able to explore every nuance philosophers can in print; but (a) that is what projects like this handbook are for and (b) they might be able to explore other nuances in a way that philosophers can't in print. Think of how *Contact* is able to make the viewer experience Dr. Arroway's contact with her deceased "father" (or the alien she believes is taking his form) and thereby make them feel the same emotions she does – all to make the analogy stick in a way that the mere printed word can't. Or think of how a videogame – because of its immersive qualities and choice-making – can provide the player with a phenomenological experience that reading an argument simply cannot.

When Paisley Livingston (2006) entered the debate on this issue, he argued that doing philosophy in film required some very specific conditions. For film to really be considered philosophy, it must make an innovative, independent contribution to philosophy using only means "exclusive to the cinematic medium" – sounds, images, camera angles, visual setting, and the like – no spoken words (at least, not to convey the philosophical message). He called the idea that films could do this the "Bold Thesis." Since it seems that arguments and questions can only be made and raised with words, it seems that the Bold Thesis is false; film doing philosophy, in the way that Livingston says is must, would seem to be an impossible task. But, again, I have objections.

First, even if pop culture isn't making independent, innovative contributions to philosophy and instead is just putting already existing philosophical arguments into another form, so what? Pop culture has brought those arguments to the public's attention, so the arguments are still worth identifying and evaluating. Even if that's all this handbook does, it's still something that needs to be done.

Second, why use the restrictive definition that Livingston demands? Why must film be making *innovative, independent* contributions to philosophy to be doing philosophy? My introduction to philosophy course doesn't do that, yet I and my students are still doing philosophy. If a film makes an argument, then it is doing philosophy, even if someone else made that argument first. Further, why must a film only use elements unique to film to do philosophy? Yes, one might argue that there is no good way to disentangle the language from the cinema-exclusive elements, so there's no way to determine if the philosophy we find in a film gets its philosophical worth from the language the film uses or from its specifically cinematic elements. So, one might argue, the film isn't doing the philosophical work – it's just a delivery vehicle for language to do philosophy. But language is still an essential part of film; so why must language be excluded as a means by which filmmakers can do philosophy? Wouldn't that be like demanding that, if a song is going to rhyme (like poetry rhymes), it has to do with only with musical notes? "It can't use lyrics to rhyme, since notes are unique to songs but words are not!" That's ridiculous. Sure, musical notes can't rhyme, but musical notes are not all that is essential to a song. In the same way, maybe camera angles can't do philosophy – but that is just one element of a film.

Or think of it this way: Are comedians not doing philosophy when they use words to tell a joke with a philosophical point because words are not unique to comedy? Wouldn't this be like saying that philosophers can't make jokes while doing philosophy because jokes are not something unique to philosophy? Comedians aren't the only ones who get to use jokes to make people laugh, so why are philosophers the only ones who get to use language to do philosophy?

What's more, it seems that Livingston's burden can be met. In his defense of the bold thesis in his book *Joss Whedon as Philosopher*, Dean Kowalski (2017) persuasively argues that the *Buffy the Vampire* episode "Hush" coveys a message about the limitations inherent in propositional knowledge while containing not only no formal argument but almost no dialogue at all (p. 144-8). Now Livingston might object because the philosophical message of the episode can be put into words (e.g., "there are inherent limitations to propositional knowledge"), and (Livingston would argue) it is only once an argument is put into words that it has any value, or is even an argument to begin with. But notice that I have only been able to put the conclusion of the argument into words, not its premises. If the episode can make a conclusion arise within my mind without using language or any articulable premises, this seems to not only be a prime example of a film doing philosophy well, but doing it in exactly the way that Livingston says it must (to be philosophy). If Livingston would still insist that it "doesn't count" simply because I can understand the episode's non-linguistic argument well enough to put its conclusion into words, he has arbitrarily selected standards that would make film doing philosophy impossible. (This is something Livingston seemed to later acknowledge, in that he eventually admitted that Ingmar Bergman's films do philosophy; see Livingston 2009.)

Other criticisms of the "film as philosophy" thesis are answerable as well. Does the fact that works of popular culture are open to interpretation mean that they can't be doing philosophy? Why would it? The works of continental philosophers (such as Hegel, Schopenhauer, Nietzsche, Sartre, Foucault, and Deleuze) are definitely open to interpretation – as are the works of, say, Kant and Spinoza. But even as frustrating as some (like myself) find their works to be, no one will say that they aren't philosophy. Even if film always does its philosophy implicitly, rather than explicitly, well, so do a lot of philosophers. Does the fact that films are fictional while philosophy is supposed to reveal truth about the world mean that films can't do philosophy? Again, why would it? Philosophical thought experiments are fictional, but philosophers use them all the time – not only to reveal our intuitions but also philosophical truths about the world. Nozick's experience machine thought experiment, for example, is thought to be an effective refutation of hedonism. And wouldn't that mean that famous written philosophical works like *No Exit*, *The Stranger,* or *The Metamorphosis* are not philosophy just because they are works of fiction?

What's more, while the arguments against pop culture being philosophy seem to be aimed at preserving the integrity of philosophy, in reality they seem to undercut it. Consider *Saving Private Ryan*, Steven Spielberg's World War II movie that preceded his creation of the landmark HBO series *Band of Brothers*. After depicting the horrors of the war, including D-Day, and how a band of soldiers sacrificed themselves to save another – Private Ryan (Matt Damon), whose three brothers have all died in the war – Spielberg has Capt. Miller (Tom Hanks) simply give Ryan two dying words: "Earn this." An elderly Ryan then stands above Miller's grave in the present day and asks his wife to assure him that he led a good life. It's an obvious ethical call for Americans to (better) appreciate "the greatest generation," because of the sacrifices it made in its fight against fascism, and to better appreciate the life free of the influences of fascism that they earned us – to appreciate it both intellectually and emotionally and also in how they live. Given the rise of fascism in America and around the world more than 20 years later, the film takes on a new significance. But in 1998, it fundamentally changed my perspective on, and my appreciation of (and my relationship with), my (now) late grandfather, who earned a bronze star serving in the war's European theater. To insist that the ethical argument the movie makes is not actually a case of Spielberg doing philosophy seems to suggest that film can do better what philosophy is supposed to do best: affect people's beliefs and change the way they live.

Let me put it another way; this is an important point. Since the time of the ancients, the stated goal of philosophy has been to lead those who do it to "the good life" and an appreciation of what really matters. And philosophy is supposed to do this like nothing else; it is unique in that respect. But as Julian Baggini (2003) points out, fictional stories can and do accomplish this as well (p. 18). If film can do this without doing or being philosophy, then philosophy not only fails to be unique, it is superfluous: it's not really needed. If, instead, we recognize that when films do this, they are doing philosophy, then the uniqueness and indispensability of philosophy are preserved. Films can only change people's lives in this way because they can do philosophy. Yes, they can change my life in a raw, phenomenological way, by appealing to my emotions. But what makes media like film, games, and graphic novels so beautiful is that they can combine that kind of affective response with an intellectual (philosophical) one, so as to have a more genuine and long-lasting effect.

In the end, those who deny works of popular culture can be philosophy may simply have too rigid and inflexible a view of what philosophy is. Just like there are many ways for something to be a religion, and no one definition of religion captures them all, there are many different ways to do philosophy, many of which popular culture can and does engage in. How a piece of pop culture is philosophy may not always be obvious, but we can discern whether and how it is by taking a closer look at what is being conveyed – which is exactly what this handbook intends to do with nearly 100 pieces of pop culture that, I think, most readers will come to agree, are obviously doing philosophy.

"Let's Go to Work"

My goal here is not to give a detailed review of the debate surrounding the bold thesis or even a full defense of it. Christopher Falzon (n.d.) already has a well-informed overview of the debate on *The Internet Encyclopedia of Philosophy*, and much more knowledgeable philosophers than myself – like Stephen Mulhall (2008) and Dean Kowalski (2017), the latter of whom helped edit numerous chapters in this handbook – have elsewhere done a much better job of defending it. Instead, my goal here is to merely defend the idea that pop culture can be philosophy enough to justify the existence of this handbook. If you remain unconvinced, I highly recommend Mulhall (2008) and chapters six and seven of Kowalski's 2017 book. If you still remain unconvinced, I guess this handbook is not for you. But if you are – or if you didn't need convincing in the first place – you will find this handbook worthwhile. At least I hope so. While it was a labor of love, it took over five years to complete!

But before we begin, many thanks are in order. I'd like to thank Ruth Lefevre and Rekha Sukumar at Palgrave, the former of which set up this little project, and the latter of which helped with the logistics of pulling it off. I'd like to thank the other editors of the project – Chris Lay, Kimberly S. Engels, and Dean Kowalski – who helped out with the enormous workload, especially in the latter years of the project (after I finally realized that, without help, I couldn't complete it). You are all wonderful philosophers, careful editors, and great persons; the handbook is ten times better thanks to your involvement. I can't express enough my gratitude for your time, wisdom, and efforts. I'd also like to thank numerous colleagues that I roped into giving feedback on certain chapters, as well as many student aides and others who helped with formatting and proofing over the years. I'd also like to thank King's College for granting me a sabbatical to finally complete the project. I couldn't be more thankful to work at such a wonderful institution.

Finally, but most importantly, I'd like to thank every last one of the authors who contributed to this handbook, for their tireless efforts and for their patience in putting up with me as their editor. Much of the work on this handbook was done during the COVID pandemic; COVID even cost it a few chapters, as the pressures the pandemic brought made it impossible for some potential authors to complete their work. Indeed, even though the handbook has nearly 100 chapters, there are countless pieces of pop culture and comedians that I wanted covered but couldn't find an author for. But to those who did contribute, you all have my heartfelt thanks. Your work was fantastic! Although I know it took a long time to finally see the handbook in print, I hope that it was worth the wait.

Notes

1. The original source of this quote is debatable, but it is credibly attributed to Shaw. See https://quoteinvestigator.com/2016/03/17/truth-laugh/.
2. They can even take you on confusing but potentially enlightening philosophical journeys, like the continental philosophers Deleuze or Derrida do in their works. Admittedly, this volume does not deal with continental philosophy to a large degree. Perhaps that topic deserves its own volume.
3. I don't mean to imply that professional philosophers always get things right; only that non-professional philosophers doing philosophy are more likely to make philosophical mistakes, and thus the philosophical works of non-philosophers deserve an expert eye.
4. You can watch the clip here – and you should: https://southpark.cc.com/video-clips/mqwfxt/south-park-it-s-right-there

April 2024 — David Kyle Johnson

References

Apatow, Judd, and Michael Bonfiglo. 2022. *George Carlin's American Dream*. HBO.
Arp, Robert. 2006. South Park and philosophy. Wiley-Blackwell.
Baggini, Julian. 2003. Alien ways of thinking: Muhall's on film. *Film-Philosophy* 7 (24).
Basham, Greg, and Eric Bronson. 2003. *The Lord of the rings and philosophy*. Open Court.
Comedy Gold Minds (podcast, hosted by Kevin Hart). 2021. Hasan Minhaj. 18 Feb. https://comedy-gold-minds-with-kevin-hart.simplecast.com/episodes/hasan-minhaj-Lb_YEYiw
Falzon, Christopher. n.d. Philosophy through film. *Internet Encyclopedia of Philosophy*. https://iep.utm.edu/phi-film/
HBO (YouTube). 2022. *George Carlin's American dream: What George meant to me, featurette*. 20 May. https://www.youtube.com/watch?v=T_L3mDG9r4I
Herzogenrath, Bernd. 2017. *Film as philosophy*. Minneapolis/London: University of Minnesota Press.
Irwin, William, ed. 1999. *Seinfeld and philosophy*. Open Court.
———, ed. 2001. *The Simpsons and philosophy*. Open Court.
——— (ed.) 2002. The matrix and philosophy.
Irwin, William, and David Kyle Johnson, eds. 2022. *Introducing philosophy through pop culture: From socrates to star wars and beyond*. 2nd ed Wiley-Blackwell.
Johnson, David Kyle. 2009. *Heroes and philosophy*. Wiley-Blackwell.
———. 2011. *Inception and philosophy*. Wiley-Blackwell.
———. 2019. *Black mirror and philosophy.*. Wiley-Blackwell.
———. 2021. Contact and the incompatibility of science and religion. In *Film, philosophy and religion*, ed. William Anderson's. Vernon Press.
Khan Academy. 30 July 2020. Hasan Minhaj on finding your gifts, being authentic, & understanding yourself, Homeroom with Sal. YouTube video, 32:26. https://youtu.be/mm0Y3ym-JUg.
Kowalski, Dean. 2017. *Joss Whedon as philosopher*. Lexington Books.
Livingston, Paisley. 2006. Thesis on cinema as philosophy. In *Thinking through Cinema: Film as philosophy*, ed. Murry Smith and Thomas E. Wartenberg, 11–18. Hoboken: Wiley-Blackwell.
———. 2009. *Cinema, philosophy, Bergman: On film as philosophy*. 1st ed. Oxford University Press.
MacDonald, Norm. 2022. Nothing special. *Netflix*.
Miller, M. 2018. In a rare move, South Park admits it was wrong about climate change. *Esquire*, 15 Nov. https://www.esquire.com/entertainment/tv/a25127458/south-park-climate-change-manbearpig-apology-season-22-episode-7/
Mulhall, Stephen. 2008. *On Film*. New York: Routledge.
Read, Ruppert, and Jerry Goodenough. 2005. *Film as Philosophy: Essays on Cinema after Wittgenstien and Cavell*. Palgrave Macmillan.
Russell, Bruce. 2000. The philosophical limits of film. *Film and philosophy* (special edition): pp. 163–167.

Smith, Murry, and Thomas E. Wartenberg, eds. 2006. *Thinking through cinema: Film as philosophy*. Hoboken: Wiley-Blackwell.

Smuts, Aaron. 2009. Film as philosophy: In defense of a bold thesis. *The Journal of Aesthetics and Art Criticism* 67 (4): 409–420.

Tallman, Ruth, and David Kyle Johnson. 2015a. A debate between a theist and a Santa Clausist: Act I (co-authored with Ruth Tallman). *Think* 14 (40): 9–25. https://doi.org/10.1017/s147717561500010x.

Tallman, R., and D.K. Johnson. 2015b. A debate between a theist and a Santa Clausist: Act II (co-authored with Ruth Tallman). *Think* 14 (40): 27–41. https://doi.org/10.1017/s1477175615000111.

Wartenberg, Thomas. 2007. *Thinking on screen: Film as philosophy*. Routledge.

Written Voices. (n.d.) *About William Irwin with George A. Dunn and Rebecca Housel*. http://mail.writtenvoices.com/author_display.php?auth_id=Dunn

Contents

Volume 1

Part I Television and Streaming 1

1 *The Good Place* as Philosophy: Moral Adventures in the Afterlife 3
Kimberly S. Engels

2 Twilight Zone as Philosophy 101 23
Mimi Marinucci

3 *Star Trek* as Philosophy: Spock as Stoic Sage 41
Massimo Pigliucci

4 *Star Trek: The Next Generation* as Philosophy: Gene Roddenberry's Argument for Humanism 65
Kevin S. Decker

5 *Battlestar Galactica* as Philosophy: Breaking the Biopolitical Cycle 93
Jason T. Eberl and Jeffrey P. Bishop

6 *Black Sails* as Philosophy: Pirates and Political Discourse 113
Clint Jones

7 *Doctor Who* as Philosophy: Four-Dimensionalism and Time Travel 135
Kevin S. Decker

8 *Breaking Bad* as Philosophy: The Moral Aesthetics of the Anti-hero's Journey 163
David Koepsell

9 *The Handmaid's Tale* as Philosophy: Autonomy and Reproductive Freedom 185
Rachel Robison-Greene

10 *Mister Rogers' Neighborhood* as Philosophy: Children as
    Philosophers 211
    David Baggett

11 *Futurama* as Philosophy: Wisdom from the Ignorance of a
    Delivery Boy 233
    Courtland D. Lewis

12 *Firefly* as Philosophy: Social Contracts, Political Dissent, and
    Virtuous Communities 259
    Dean A. Kowalski

13 *Arrested Development* as Philosophy:
    Family First? What We Owe Our Parents 283
    Kristopher G. Phillips

14 The Doctor as Philosopher: The Collectivist-Realist Pacifism of the
    Doctor and the Quest for Social Justice 311
    Paula Smithka

15 *Grey's Anatomy* as Philosophy: Ethical Ambiguity in Shades
    of Grey 341
    Kimberly S. Engels and Katie Becker

16 *House of Cards* as Philosophy: Democracy on Trial 361
    Brendan Shea

17 *Last Week Tonight* as Philosophy: The Importance of Jokalism ... 383
    Christelle Paré

18 *Russian Doll* as Philosophy: Life Is Like a Box of Timelines ... 407
    Richard Greene

19 *The Orville* as Philosophy: The Dangers of Religion 425
    Darren M. Slade and David Kyle Johnson

20 *Westworld* as Philosophy: A Commentary on Colonialism 453
    Matthew P. Meyer

21 *Black Mirror* as Philosophy: A Dark Reflection of Human
    Nature 479
    Chris Lay

22 *Rick & Morty* as Philosophy: Nihilism in the Multiverse 503
    Sergio Genovesi

23 *The X-Files* as Philosophy: Navigating the "Truth Out There" ... 519
    Dean A. Kowalski

24 *Game of Thrones* as Philosophy: Cynical Realpolitiks 541
    Eric J. Silverman and William Riordan

25	*The Mandalorian* as Philosophy: "This Is the Way" 555
	Lance Belluomini
26	*Midnight Mass* as Philosophy: The Problems with Religion 581
	David Kyle Johnson
27	*Squid Game* as Philosophy: The Myths of Democracy 609
	Leander Penaso Marquez and Rola Palalon Ombao
28	*South Park* as Philosophy: Blasphemy, Mockery, and (Absolute?) Freedom of Speech 633
	David Kyle Johnson
29	*Frank Herbert's Dune* as Philosophy: The Need to Think for Yourself 673
	Greg Littmann
30	*The Boys* as Philosophy: Superheroes, Fascism, and the American Right 703
	David Kyle Johnson

Volume 2

Part II   Films 751

31	*Inception* as Philosophy: Choose Your Dreams or Seek Reality ... 753
	David Kyle Johnson
32	*Okja* as Philosophy: Why Animals Matter 773
	Randall M. Jensen
33	*2001* as Philosophy: A Technological Odyssey 795
	Jerold J. Abrams
34	*The Lord of the Rings* as Philosophy: Environmental Enchantment and Resistance in Peter Jackson and J.R.R. Tolkien 827
	John F. Whitmire Jr and David G. Henderson
35	*Star Wars* as Philosophy: A Genealogy of the Force 855
	Jason T. Eberl
36	*The Godfather* as Philosophy: Honor, Power, Family, and Evil ... 873
	Raymond Angelo Belliotti
37	*Groundhog Day* as Philosophy: Phil Connors Says "No" to Eternal Return 897
	Kimberly Blessing

38	*The Big Lebowski*: Nihilism, Masculinity, and Abiding Virtue .... Peter S. Fosl	917
39	*Harry Potter* as Philosophy: Five Types of Friendship .... James M. Okapal	951
40	*Deadpool* as Philosophy: Using Humor to Rebel Against the System .... Matthew Brake	967
41	*Blade Runner* as Philosophy: What Does It Mean to Be Human? .... Timothy Shanahan	983
42	*Up in the Air* as Philosophy: Buddhism and the Middle Path .... Leigh Duffy	1005
43	*Ex Machina* as Philosophy: Mendacia *Ex Machina* (Lies from a Machine) .... Jason David Grinnell	1025
44	*Gattaca* as Philosophy: Genoism and Justice .... Jason David Grinnell	1043
45	*A.I.: Artificial Intelligence* as Philosophy: Machine Consciousness and Intelligence .... David Gamez	1061
46	*The Shawshank Redemption* as Philosophy: Freedom and Panopticism .... Alexander E. Hooke	1091
47	*Snowpiercer* as Philosophy: The Danger to Humanity .... Leander Penaso Marquez	1109
48	*The Matrix* as Philosophy: Understanding Knowledge, Belief, Choice, and Reality .... Edwardo Pérez	1131
49	*A Serious Man* as Philosophy: The Elusiveness of Moral Knowledge .... Shai Biderman	1151
50	*The Cabin in the Woods* as Philosophy: Cinematic Reflections on Ethical Complexity, Human Nature, and Worthwhile Horror .... Dean A. Kowalski	1169
51	*Magnolia* As Philosophy: Meaning and Coincidence .... Bart Engelen	1193

52	*Fight Club* as Philosophy: I Am Jack's Existential Struggle Alberto Oya	1217
53	Tarantino as Philosopher: Vengeance – Unfettered, Uncensored, but Not Unjustified David Kyle Johnson	1235
54	*The Man from Earth* as Philosophy: The Desirability of Immortality Kiki Berk	1271
55	*Avatar* as Philosophy: The Metaphysics of Switching Bodies Joshua L. Tepley	1289
56	*Pulp Fiction* as Philosophy: Bad Faith, Authenticity, and the Path of the Righteous Man Bradley Richards	1311
57	*Tenet* as Philosophy: Fatalism Isn't an Excuse to Do Nothing Lance Belluomini	1327
58	Tom Sawyer as Philosopher: Lying and Deception on the Mississippi Don Fallis	1349
59	*Don't Look Up* as Philosophy: Comets, Climate Change, and Why the Snacks Are Not Free Chris Lay and David Kyle Johnson	1373
60	*Little Women* as Philosophy: Death or Marriage and the Meaning of Life Kimberly Blessing	1411
61	*God's Not Dead* as Philosophy: Trying to Prove God Exists David Kyle Johnson	1435

Volume 3

Part III	**Comedians**	**1467**
62	Hannah Gadsby as Philosopher: Is Comedy Really Such a Good Thing? Mark Ralkowski	1469
63	Amy Schumer as Philosopher: Fuck the Feminine Mystique Charlene Elsby	1491
64	George Carlin as Philosopher: It's All Bullshit. Is It Bad for Ya? Kimberly S. Engels	1511

| 65 | **Louis CK as Philosopher: The King and His Fall** 1533
Jennifer Marra Henrigillis |

| 66 | **Marc Maron as Philosopher: Comedy, Therapy, and Identification** 1563
Steven S. Kapica |

| 67 | **Hari Kondabolu as Philosopher: Enacting a Philosophy of Liberation** 1583
Brandyn Heppard |

| 68 | **Richard Pryor as Philosopher: Stand-Up Comedy and Gramsci's Organic Intellectual** 1603
Cori Hall Healy |

| 69 | **Larry David as Philosopher: Interrogating Convention** 1619
Noël Carroll |

| 70 | **Jerry Seinfeld as Philosopher: The Assimilated Sage of New Chelm** 1631
Stephen Stern and Steven Gimbel |

| 71 | **Dave Chappelle as Philosopher: Standing Up to Racism** 1643
Steven A. Benko and Reagan Scout Burch |

| 72 | **Ricky Gervais as Philosopher: The Comedy of Alienation** 1669
Catherine Villanueva Gardner |

| 73 | **Hasan Minhaj as Philosopher: Navigating the Struggles of Identity** 1685
Pankaj Singh |

| 74 | **Stephen Fry as Philosopher: The Manic Socrates** 1701
Christopher M. Innes |

| 75 | **Phoebe Waller-Bridge as Philosopher: Conscious Women Making Choices** 1719
Neha Pande and Kimberly S. Engels |

Part IV Video Games **1739**

| 76 | *The Last of Us* **as Moral Philosophy: Teleological Particularism and Why Joel Is Not a Villain** 1741
Charles Joshua Horn |

| 77 | *Journey* **as Philosophy: Meaning, Connection, and the Sublime** 1757
Russ Hamer |

| 78 | *The Witness* **as Philosophy: How Knowledge Is Constructed** 1771
Luke Cuddy |

79 *Cyberpunk 2077* as Philosophy: Balancing the (Mystical) Ghost in the (Transhuman) Machine 1789
Chris Lay

80 *Detroit Become Human* as Philosophy: Moral Reasoning Through Gameplay 1811
Kimberly S. Engels and Sarah Evans

81 *Papers, Please* as Philosophy: Playing with the Relations between Politics and Morality 1833
Juliele Maria Sievers

82 *Planescape: Torment* as Philosophy: Regret Can Change the Nature of a Man 1847
Steven Gubka

83 *Disco Elysium* as Philosophy: Solipsism, Existentialism, and Simulacra 1865
Diana Khamis

84 *The Legend of Zelda: Breath of the Wild* as Philosophy: Teaching the Player to Be Comfortable Being Alone 1883
Chris Lay

85 *Persona 5 Royal* as Philosophy: Unmasking (Persona)l Identity and Reality 1907
Alexander Atrio L. Lopez and Leander Penaso Marquez

86 *God of War* as Philosophy: Prophecy, Fate, and Freedom 1929
Charles Joshua Horn

Part V Graphic Novels **1947**

87 Frank Miller's Batman as Philosophy: "The World Only Makes Sense When You Force It To" 1949
Steve Bein

88 *Watchmen* as Philosophy: Illustrating Time and Free Will 1969
Nathaniel Goldberg and Chris Gavaler

89 The Joker as Philosopher: Killing Jokes 1987
Matthew Brake

90 *From Hell* as Philosophy: Ripping Through Structural Violence 2003
James Rocha and Mona Rocha

91 *Deadpool's* Killogy as Philosophy: The Metaphysics of a Homicidal Journey Through Possible Worlds 2025
Tuomas W. Manninen

| 92 | *V for Vendetta* as Philosophy: Victory Through the Virtues of Anarchy .... | 2043 |

Clara Nisley

| 93 | *Asterios Polyp* as Philosophy: Master of Two Worlds .... | 2065 |

Bradley Richards

| 94 | *Yes, Roya* and Philosophy: The Art of Submission .... | 2085 |

Nathaniel Goldberg, Chris Gavaler, and Maria Chavez

| 95 | *The Walking Dead* as Philosophy: Rick Grimes and Community Building in an Apocalypse .... | 2103 |

Clint Jones

Index 2119

About the Editor-in-Chief

David Kyle Johnson is Professor of Philosophy at King's College (PA) who earned his Ph.D. at the University of Oklahoma and specializes in metaphysics, philosophy of religion, and scientific/critical reasoning. He also produces lecture series for Wondrium's *The Great Courses* (such as *Sci-Phi: Science Fiction as Philosophy*, *The Big Questions of Philosophy*, and *Exploring Metaphysics*) and has published in journals such as *Sophia*, *Religious Studies*, *Think*, *Philo*, *Religions*, *SHERM (Socio-Historical Examination of Religion and Ministry)*, and *Science, Religion, and Culture*. In addition to other duties, he regularly contributes chapters to and edits volumes for Blackwell's Philosophy and Pop Culture series (such as *Black Mirror and Philosophy: Dark Reflections*), and also co-edited *Introducing Philosophy Through Popular Culture* with the series editor William Irwin. He maintains two blogs for *Psychology Today: Plato on Pop* and *A Logical Take*.

About the Editors

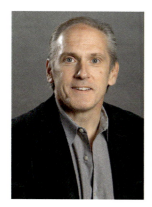

Dean A. Kowalski is Professor of Philosophy and Chair of the Arts and Humanities Department in the College of General Studies at the University of Wisconsin-Milwaukee. He earned his Ph.D. in Philosophy from the University of Wisconsin-Madison. He specializes in the Philosophy of Religion and Metaphysics and has published articles in such academic journals as *Religious Studies* and *Philosophy and Theology*. He regularly teaches philosophy of religion, Asian philosophy, and ethics.

Prof. Dean has written extensively on philosophy and popular culture – both philosophy in popular culture and popular culture as philosophy – specializing in film and television. He has published articles in *The Journal of Whedon Studies* and *Film and Philosophy*, and more than 30 book chapters in volumes dedicated to popular culture. He is the author of *Joss Whedon as Philosopher* (2017), *Classic Questions and Contemporary Film*, 2nd edition (2016), and *Moral Theory at the Movies* (2012). He is the editor of *Indiana Jones and Philosophy* (2023), *The Big Bang Theory and Philosophy* (2012), *The Philosophy of The X-Files*, revised edition (2009), and *Steven Spielberg and Philosophy* (2008), and he is the co-editor of *The Philosophy of Joss Whedon* (2011).

Chris Lay earned his Ph.D. from the University of Georgia in 2018 and has held teaching positions at UGA, the University of Texas at El Paso, and Young Harris College in northeast Georgia. Currently, he runs the YHC philosophy program as Assistant Professor of Philosophy, offering courses like Science Fiction and Philosophy, Video Games as Philosophy, and Feminism in Horror Films. Professor Lay specializes in metaphysics – especially issues of personal identity and mereology – and the philosophy of popular culture generally, and he has published numerous "pop culture" volumes that bring the two subjects together.

Kimberly S. Engels is Associate Professor of Philosophy at Molloy University. She received her Ph.D. in Philosophy from Marquette University in 2017. Her research interests include existentialism, Native American philosophy, philosophy and pop culture, and UAP studies. She is the editor of *The Good Place and Philosophy: Everything Is Forking Fine!* and co-editor of *Westworld and Philosophy: If You Go Looking for the Truth, Get the Whole Thing.*

Contributors

Jerold J. Abrams Creighton University, Omaha, NE, USA

David Baggett School of Christian Thought, Houston Baptist University, Houston, TX, USA

Katie Becker Greensboro, NC, USA

Steve Bein Philosophy Department, University of Dayton, Dayton, OH, USA

Raymond Angelo Belliotti The State University of New York, Emeritus, Fredonia, NY, USA

Lance Belluomini San Francisco Bay Area, CA, USA

Steven A. Benko Meredith College, Raleigh, NC, USA

Kiki Berk Southern New Hampshire University, Manchester, NH, USA

Shai Biderman Beit-Berl College, Kfar Saba, Israel
Tel Aviv University, Tel Aviv, Israel

Jeffrey P. Bishop Center for Health Care Ethics and Department of Philosophy, Saint Louis University, St Louis, MO, USA

Kimberly Blessing Philosophy, SUNY Buffalo State, Buffalo, NY, USA

Matthew Brake Northern Virginia Community College, Manassas, VA, USA

Reagan Scout Burch Meredith College, Raleigh, NC, USA

Noël Carroll Philosophy Program, The Graduate Center, City University of New York, New York, NY, USA

Maria Chavez Charlottesville, VA, USA

Luke Cuddy Southwestern College, Chula Vista, CA, USA

Kevin S. Decker Eastern Washington University, Cheney, WA, USA

Leigh Duffy SUNY Buffalo State College, Buffalo, NY, USA

Jason T. Eberl Center for Health Care Ethics, Saint Louis University, St Louis, MO, USA

Charlene Elsby University of Ottawa, Ottawa, ON, Canada

Bart Engelen Tilburg Center for Moral Philosophy, Epistemology and Philosophy of Science (TiLPS), Tilburg University, Tilburg, The Netherlands

Kimberly S. Engels Molloy University, Rockville Centre, NY, USA

Sarah Evans Molloy University, Rockville, NY, USA

Don Fallis Philosophy, Northeastern University, Boston, MA, USA

Peter S. Fosl Transylvania University, Lexington, KY, USA

David Gamez Department of Computer Science, Middlesex University, London, UK

Catherine Villanueva Gardner University of Massachusetts Dartmouth, North Dartmouth, MA, USA

Chris Gavaler W&L University, Lexington, VA, USA

Sergio Genovesi University of Bonn, Bonn, Germany

Steven Gimbel Gettysburg College, Gettysburg, PA, USA

Nathaniel Goldberg W&L University, Lexington, VA, USA

Richard Greene Weber State University, Ogden, UT, USA

Jason David Grinnell Philosophy Department, SUNY Buffalo State, Buffalo, NY, USA

Steven Gubka Florida Atlantic University, Boca Raton, Florida, United States

Cori Hall Healy Bowling Green State University, Bowling Green, OH, USA

Russ Hamer Mount St. Mary's University, Emmitsburg, MD, USA

David G. Henderson Western Carolina University, Cullowhee, NC, USA

Brandyn Heppard Raritan Valley Community College, Somerville, NJ, USA

Alexander E. Hooke Stevenson University, Stevenson, MD, USA

Charles Joshua Horn University of Wisconsin-Stevens Point, Stevens Point, WI, USA

Christopher M. Innes Philosophy Department, Boise State University, ID, Boise, USA

Randall M. Jensen Northwestern College, Orange City, IA, USA

David Kyle Johnson Department of Philosophy, King's College, Wilkes-Barre, PA, USA

Clint Jones Plover, WI, USA
Capital University, Columbus, OH, USA

Steven S. Kapica Keuka College, Keuka Park, NY, USA

Diana Khamis Nijmegen, Netherlands

David Koepsell Department of Philosophy, Texas A&M, College Station, TX, USA

Dean A. Kowalski Arts and Humanities Department, University of Wisconsin-Milwaukee, College of General Studies, Waukesha, WI, USA

Chris Lay Young Harris College, Young Harris, GA, USA

Courtland D. Lewis Philosophy, Pellissippi State Community College, Knoxville, TN, USA

Greg Littmann Southern Illinois University Edwardsville, Edwardsville, IL, USA

Alexander Atrio L. Lopez University of the Philippines Diliman, Quezon City, Philippines

Tuomas W. Manninen Arizona State University, Glendale, AZ, USA

Mimi Marinucci Eastern Washington University, Cheney, WA, USA

Leander Penaso Marquez College of Social Sciences and Philosophy, University of the Philippines Diliman, Quezon City, Philippines

Jennifer Marra Henrigillis St. Norbert College, De Pere, WI, USA

Matthew P. Meyer University of Wisconsin–Eau Claire, Eau Claire, WI, USA

Clara Nisley Atlanta, GA, USA

James M. Okapal Missouri Western State University, Saint Joseph, MO, USA

Rola Palalon Ombao College of Social Sciences and Philosophy, University of the Philippines Diliman, Quezon City, Philippines

Alberto Oya IFILNOVA – Instituto de Filosofia da Nova (Universidade Nova de Lisboa), Lisboa, Portugal

Neha Pande Royal Roads University, Victoria, BC, Canada

Christelle Paré Department of Communication, University of Ottawa, Ottawa, ON, Canada
École nationale de l'humour, Montréal, Québec, Canada

Edwardo Pérez Tarrant County College, Fort Worth, TX, USA
The University of Texas at Arlington, Arlington, TX, USA

Kristopher G. Phillips Southern Utah University, Cedar City, UT, USA
Eastern Michigan University, Ypsilanti, MI, USA

Massimo Pigliucci Department of Philosophy, The City College of New York, New York, NY, USA

Mark Ralkowski George Washington University, Washington, DC, USA

Bradley Richards Department of Philosophy, York University, Toronto, ON, Canada

William Riordan Christopher Newport University, Newport News, VA, USA

Rachel Robison-Greene Utah State University, Logan, UT, USA

James Rocha California State University, Fresno, CA, USA

Mona Rocha Clovis Community College, Clovis, CA, USA

Timothy Shanahan Department of Philosophy, Loyola Marymount University, Los Angeles, CA, USA

Brendan Shea Rochester Community and Technical College, Rochester, MN, USA

Juliele Maria Sievers Federal University of Alagoas, Maceió, Brazil

Eric J. Silverman Christopher Newport University, Newport News, VA, USA

Pankaj Singh School for Life (SFL), University of Petroleum and Energy Studies, Dehradun, India

Darren M. Slade Global Center for Religious Research (GCRR), Denver, CO, USA

Paula Smithka University of Southern Mississippi, Hattiesburg, MS, USA

Stephen Stern Gettysburg College, Gettysburg, PA, USA

Joshua L. Tepley Saint Anselm College, Manchester, NH, USA

John F. Whitmire Jr Western Carolina University, Cullowhee, NC, USA

Part III

Comedians

Hannah Gadsby as Philosopher: Is Comedy Really Such a Good Thing? 62

Mark Ralkowski

Contents

Introduction	1470
Self-Deprecating Humor	1472
The Problem with Jokes	1478
Humor and Catharsis	1481
Conclusion: Anger and Justice	1487
End Notes	1489
References	1489

Abstract

Hannah Gadsby announces in *Nanette* that she must quit comedy because it has been unhealthy for her and her audiences. She provides four reasons for thinking this, which include criticisms of self-deprecation, jokes in general, comic relief, and anger. She argues that self-deprecation is humiliating and unhealthy for marginalized people like her; she suggests that jokes cannot provide the comic relief we hope for because of their logical structure; she says that comic relief is not good for us when we look for relief from challenging subjects; and she argues that comedy is bad for everyone when it is based in anger because anger only spreads blind hatred. This chapter makes a case for and against each of Gadsby's arguments, and it concludes that she can be wrong on any or all these points while nevertheless being one of the most philosophical comedians in the world.

Keywords

Hannah Gadsby · Nanette · Douglas · Ten Steps to Nanette: A Memoir Situation · Self-deprecation · Jokes · Relief humor · Freud · Neo-Stoicism · Feminism · Catharsis · Anger

---

M. Ralkowski (✉)
George Washington University, Washington, DC, USA
e-mail: mralkow@gwu.edu

© Springer Nature Switzerland AG 2024
D. K. Johnson et al. (eds.), *The Palgrave Handbook of Popular Culture as Philosophy*,
https://doi.org/10.1007/978-3-031-24685-2_13

Introduction

Hannah Gadsby might be the most philosophical comedian in the world. Not everyone will agree with such a strong claim, but there are some good reasons for giving her this distinction. Comedians have always talked about the most pressing issues of their time, and their fans have often seen them as critics of culture who speak truth to power and as therapists of the soul who help us triumph over tragedy. At least since Socrates and the Buddha, the philosopher has fulfilled similar roles in society: the Buddha presented himself as a healer of suffering, and Socrates called himself a gadfly on the neck of man, sent to Athens by a god to wake Athenians up and make them think. One of the most compelling statements of the therapeutic view of humor is in Viktor Frankl's *Man's Search for Meaning*. In that book, Frankl, a Holocaust survivor and influential psychiatrist, describes humor as one of "the soul's weapons in the fight for self-preservation. It is well known that humor, more than anything else in the human make-up, can afford an aloofness and an ability to rise above any situation" (Frankl 2006, p. 43). Simon Critchley captures the idea that humor's most important function is to serve as a critic of culture. In his book *On Humour*, he argues that jokes "return us to a common, familiar world of shared practices, the background meanings implicit in a culture ... and indicate how those practices might be transformed or perfected, how things might be otherwise. Humour both reveals the situation, and indicates how that situation might be changed" (Critchley 2002, p. 16).

Hannah Gadsby's work is in this tradition of cultural critique and existential therapy. She is famous for denying that humor has a therapeutic capacity. But, as this chapter shows, her views about the powers of humor to remove tension and provide relief are more nuanced than it seems. She insists in her 2018 comedy special *Nanette* that comedy cannot be "our medicine" and that storytelling is where true healing occurs. She even uses this show to announce that she must quit comedy because of its contributions to her marginalization. However, she has also said that "laughter serves the purpose of catharsis"; that with *Nanette*, she "lanced a boil, to use really lovely language"; and that comedy in general "has been a lifeline for me" (Fox 2020). In her memoir, she says that if she were pushed to categorize *Nanette*, "I would call her stand-up catharsis," and she writes straightforwardly that "I owe stand-up comedy my life" (Gadsby 2022, pp. 21–24). These are the views of a comedian who finds therapeutic potential in humor. Cultural critique is much easier to identify in her work. Gadsby's comedy addresses a wide range of current issues, from gender presentation and the harms of heteropatriarchy to neurodiversity and a feminist critique of art history. She is not as well known as more mainstream comedians like Tina Fey and Dave Chappelle, but since the summer of 2018, Gadsby has been one of the most influential voices in the world of comedy. Her show *Nanette*, for example, which felt like it came straight from the beating heart of the #MeToo movement, has helped feminist academics revise our understanding of humor theory (Willett and Willett 2019, pp. 149–153), while comedy journalists have recognized it as "the most discussed comedy special in ages" (Berman 2018). Jesse David Fox called it simply "the biggest special ever" because of its unparalleled cultural impact (Fox 2020).

But what truly sets Hannah Gadsby apart from other comedians is her critique of *comedy itself*. She does not just make insightful observations about life and make us laugh; she also invites us to think about why we laugh, what we laugh at, and whether our laughter is good or bad for us. The fact that she does this *within* an extremely successful comedy special is comedic genius.

Hannah Gadsby's *Nanette* first appeared on Netflix in June 2018. She had been working in comedy since 2006 and had performed *Nanette* in Australia and the UK since 2017, winning awards for it from the Melbourne International Comedy Festival (2017), the Edinburgh Festival Fringe (2018), and the Adelaide Fringe (2019). But the Netflix release of her show was an even bigger international breakthrough moment, earning her a Peabody (2019) and an Emmy (2019). "Few stars have exploded on the comedy landscape like Hannah Gadsby did with her 2018 special 'Nanette'" (Kozlowski 2022). There are a few things that account for this sudden global success. The first and most obvious is that Hannah Gadsby is a brilliant and hilarious comedian, and *Nanette* is a good example of her talents – she just needed the right platform, which Netflix provided. The second is its timing: *Nanette* addresses the issues of cancel culture and the harms of patriarchy, and it was released on Netflix at a time when the #MeToo movement was gaining momentum all around the world. It captured the *Zeitgeist* of the time and thus provided many audiences with powerful experiences of identification and catharsis. Four years later, its raw emotional content remains almost overwhelmingly powerful. As Gadsby has noted on her Facebook page, fans regularly write to her with gratitude for sharing her story – of being a victim of sexual violence, of growing up gay in a part of Australia where homosexuality was illegal until 1997, of identifying as "gender not normal," and of living with autism in a world that still struggles appropriately to accommodate individuals who are neurodivergent – and for telling this story with feminist swagger and without a happy ending.[1]

These two factors – Gadsby's exceptional talents and the timing of *Nanette's* release in the summer of 2018 – probably do the most to account for her rising star. But there is at least one more factor to consider: *Nanette* is also famous because it includes a philosophical critique of jokes and a suggestion from Gadsby that she is quitting comedy after reassessing the value of her humor. In this critique, Gadsby argues for four big ideas. The first is that self-deprecating humor is unhealthy for people on the margins because it makes others laugh at the expense of the marginalized joke teller. As she says famously, this is humiliating, not humility. The second is that, because of their structure, jokes cannot tell complete stories of trauma, and humor therefore cannot do the work of healing that is often attributed to it – if it gives us any relief, it is a kind of relief by distraction. This can give us a momentary break from pain but not genuine healing. The third is that humor is unhealthy for joke tellers and for audiences because jokes require *immediate* tension relief. The premise of a joke creates the tension, and the surprise punchline sets us free from it. This is a problem when jokes are about important matters, such as homophobia or the harms of patriarchy, because it lets audiences off the hook by allowing them to avoid uncomfortable realities, and over time it can lead to self-deception and the erasure of memory in joke tellers. In Gadsby's case, joke versions of stories replaced actual memories. The fourth is that while she is angry and has every right to be angry, she does not have a right to spread her anger, which is "a toxic, infectious tension [that] knows no other purpose than to spread blind hatred." And since the tension that her humor relieves depends on anger, it is ultimately poisonous for her and for her audiences. These are the reasons she provides in *Nanette* for saying she must quit comedy. Humor and anger can connect a room full of strangers, but they are dead ends. "Laughter is not our medicine. Stories are our cure. Laughter is just the honey that sweetens the bitter medicine. I don't want to unite you with anger or laughter." This case against comedy was a third contributor to Gadsby's sudden celebrity. Her feminist fans celebrated her as a comedic hero, while critics asked whether her show really was comedy at all (Fox 2018a).

There is so much more to *Nanette* than these reasons for quitting comedy, and there is more to Hannah Gadsby's career than *Nanette*. She released *Douglas* in 2020 after touring it around the world, and in summer 2021, she started to perform *Body of Work*, her forthcoming comedy special, in Australia, New Zealand, Europe, the UK, and the United States. Her memoir, *Ten Steps to Nanette: A Memoir Situation*, was released in March 2022. And during the many years before she became a global celebrity, Gadsby performed standup and held a variety of roles in Australian television, as a writer and as an actor and performer. In these comedy specials and in *Ten Steps to Nanette*, Gadsby famously has a lot to say about a wide range of current social and political issues. However, because this is a chapter and not a book, and because Gadsby's claims about humor and anger are so interesting from a philosophical perspective, this essay will focus on her four reasons for quitting comedy. Is humor as unhealthy as she says it is? Does anger have no purpose other than to spread blind hatred? This chapter will make the best case for and against Gadsby's ideas on these points.

Self-Deprecating Humor

Gadsby's case against self-deprecating humor is one of the best-known and most frequently quoted parts of *Nanette*. She tells her audience that she is quitting comedy after taking time to reassess her career and the material she used to build it. She did not mean this literally; it was part of the performance and its rhetorical force. We know this for a fact because she released *Douglas* two years after *Nanette*, and she has been touring a new show in 2021 and 2022 called *Body of Work*, which is likely to be released as a special in 2023. As she says in her 2019 TED Talk, "quitting launched my comedy career. Like, really launched it, to the point that after quitting comedy I became the most talked-about comedian on the planet." Later in the talk she clarifies that she did not literally quit comedy; she "broke it." And "the point was not simply to break comedy. The point was to break comedy so I could rebuild it and reshape it, reform it into something that could better hold everything that I needed to share. That is what I meant when I said I quit comedy." The result is a kind of comedic Frankenstein: "I took everything I knew about comedy, then I pulled it all apart and built a monster out of its corpse" (Gadsby 2022, p. 21). It also is not clear that she means what she literally says about the harms of self-deprecating humor because she uses it throughout *Nanette* and in most of her public appearances, whether comedy specials, her memoir, or interviews. Nevertheless, it is worth looking closely at her "argument" because philosophers of humor have taken an interest in self-deprecation, especially when it is performed by female comedians and others who have marginalized identities:

> I do think I have to quit comedy, though. And seriously. I know it's probably not the forum ... to make such an announcement, is it? In the middle of a comedy show. But I have been questioning ... you know, this whole comedy thing. I don't feel very comfortable with it anymore ... I built a career out of self-deprecating humor. That's what I've built my career on. And ... I don't want to do that anymore. Because, do you understand ... do you understand what self-deprecation means when it comes from somebody who already exists in the margins? It's not humility. It's humiliation. I put myself down in order to speak, in order to seek permission ... to speak. And I simply will not do that anymore. Not to myself or anybody who identifies with me. And if that means that my comedy career is over, then so be it. (*Nanette*)

To be fair to Hannah Gadsby, she says this in the middle of a comedy show, not a journal article on the philosophy of humor. So it is probably unfair to treat her as making a universal claim here, a point about every single instance of a marginalized person using self-deprecating humor. It is especially important to be charitable on this point since she uses self-deprecating jokes so often: she makes fun of her home state of Tasmania and the gene pool in her family; she mocks herself for not being a good lesbian or having enough "lesbian content" in her shows; she makes fun of her career for having no social or political impact – "I told lots of cool jokes about homophobia. Really solved that problem. Tick"; she makes fun of her body and general appearance and jokes about her gender presentation, for looking like a "good bloke." In her memoir, she calls herself "a financially insecure autistic Australian genderqueer vagina-wielding situation who does not have a bird-like skeletal system" (Gadsby 2022, p. 15). And just a few pages later, she compares herself to a dog because she is a "trusting adult with devastatingly simple needs": she likes to be told she is good; she does not like loud noises; she feels much better after a walk; and she is easily bribed with the promise of food (p. 36).

Judging from these and countless other related jokes in her work, it is impossible to believe that Hannah Gadsby is opposed to marginalized people using *any kind of* self-deprecating humor. However, it is useful to read these lines from *Nanette* literally because it will help distinguish between four different kinds of self-deprecating humor – "ethical," "existential," "ironic," and "self-lacerating" – and clarify the kind that she is against and why. In the end, it should be clear that when Gadsby criticizes self-deprecating humor, she is really talking about *self-lacerating* humor. These kinds of jokes are *especially bad* for marginalized people, but they are bad for everyone else as well because they involve genuine self-denigration, which can be unhealthy for anyone. This explains why Gadsby herself is so comfortable telling self-deprecating jokes in her comedy, even in the show where she subjects it to such withering criticism. There are three kinds of self-deprecating humor that do not (or need not) lead to humiliation. In fact, these kinds of jokes often serve the invaluable function of bringing people together across identities in a shared humanity. So while Gadsby argues that all self-deprecating humor is bad for marginalized people, this section shows that some forms of self-deprecation are not (or need not be) bad for anyone, and some can be good for everyone.

First, some self-deprecating humor is aimed at moral improvement, self-promotion, or self-satisfaction. For shorthand, these kinds of self-deprecating jokes will be called "ethical." The point is not that every instance of this kind of joke is morally praiseworthy. The cases involving self-promotion and self-satisfaction often deserve criticism or moral condemnation. The point is just that these jokes have moral significance. There is an additional type that fits into this category; it is the kind of self-deprecation that is common in workspaces, and it usually involves someone in a position of power making fun of herself for the sake of group cohesion. These cases involve a suspension of power – or at least the appearance of it and at least for a short time (such as the duration of a meeting or a presentation) – to level up power differentials or restore an original or expected power dynamic. The fictional character Ted Lasso, played by Jason Sudeikis on an Apple TV series that has won 11 Emmy Awards for its first two seasons, is an "all-time great" with this style of power-suspending self-deprecation (Baldoni 2020). He uses it memorably at his first press conference as the new football coach for AFC Richmond: "you could fill two internets with what I don't know about football," he says, as he acknowledges that he has never coached the sport and does not really know the rules. Lasso was ingratiating himself in this moment, handing power back to the local press and the fans who were skeptical about him because of his inexperience. In each of these cases, self-deprecation does not need to be rooted in self-loathing or self-denigration, and it does not need to involve humiliation or marginalization. When these jokes are aimed at moral improvement, we are the butts of our jokes, and for good reason. We identify character flaws that we can and should change, and we use self-deprecation, with others as our witness, to put pressure on ourselves to do better or be better. It is a way of holding ourselves accountable in public. In these cases, the aim truly is to improve ourselves. In other cases, the intention can be less clear without it changing this analysis: our aim might be to virtue signal by feigning humility, or it might be simply to take pleasure in our moral failings. The basis of the humor in these cases also does not need to be self-loathing. It might even be an excess of self-satisfaction. This can be a moral problem as well, though for a different reason.

Comedian Louis CK became famous by writing this kind of self-deprecating humor. A lot of his jokes make fun of his own moral failings, such as entitlement, moral weakness, and sexual perversion. In *Live at Beacon Theater* (2011), he does a famous bit on what he calls his "believies":

> I have a lot of beliefs and I live by none of them. That's just the way I am. They're just my beliefs. I just like believing them. I like that part. They're my little believies. They make me feel good about who I am. But if they get in the way of a thing I want . . . I fucking do that.

Louis develops this concept with an example. He says that whenever he sees a soldier on a plane, he thinks about offering him his seat in first class. But he does not act on this belief. It is just one of his many "believies," something he enjoys believing despite it never impacting his actions. "I've never done it once. I've had so many opportunities. I've never even really come close. And here's the worst part: I still just enjoy the fantasy for myself. I was actually proud of myself for having thought of it. I was proud. 'Ah, I am such a sweet man. That is so nice of me to think of that and then totally never do it.'" There is an irony in using an example from Louis CK in a book chapter on Hannah Gadsby. Not only is her joke about him in her 2020 special *Douglas* her "mic drop" moment, but it is important to acknowledge that Louis CK is a man with many moral failings that have not improved, so far as we know, thanks to his mastery of self-deprecating humor. (For more on Louis CK, see Ralkowski 2016 and Jennifer Marra Henrigillis' ▶ Chap. 65, "Louis CK as Philosopher: The King and His Fall," in this handbook.) Nevertheless, this kind of joke is an important counterexample to Gadsby's broad claim in *Nanette* that all self-deprecating humor is humiliating for people who exist on the margins. This clearly does not need to be the case since at least some kinds of self-deprecating humor are aimed at needed moral improvement, a burden that all of us share in life. And one of the virtues of this kind of joke specifically – the kind that points out common moral failings, such as weakness of will – is that it can provide moments of recognition in audiences ("I do that too! I've felt proud of myself for merely holding a belief"), bringing joke tellers *closer to their audiences*, rather than marginalizing them in alienating self-denigration.

A second kind of self-deprecating humor is self-critical about something trivial, or inevitable and universal. These jokes can be called "existential" because they are about ineluctable facts of the human condition, i.e., shortcomings we have in virtue of being human, not because of our choices or character. Like the "ethical" kind, these jokes make the self the butt of the joke without being self-denigrating, but they also do not aim at moral improvement or self-promotion or self-satisfaction. For example, consider jokes about things like aging or having a messy office or hitting the snooze button too often. Gadsby is a master of this kind of self-deprecation as well. She uses it in this famous bit about gay pride parades. She isn't quite up to all that they demand of her:

> My people, flaunting their lifestyle in a parade. I used to watch it, going, "There they are, my people. They're busy, aren't they? Gosh. Don't they love to dance and party?" I used to sit there and watch it and go, "Where . . . where do the quiet gays go? Where are the quiet gays supposed to go?" I still do. I'm just like, the pressure on my people to express our identity and pride through the metaphor of a party is very intense. Don't get me wrong. I love the spectacle, I really do, but I've never felt compelled to get amongst it. Do you know? I'm a quiet soul. My favorite sound in the whole world is the sound of a teacup finding its place on a saucer. Oh, it's very difficult to flaunt that lifestyle in a parade. (*Nanette*)

People with different identities will have different lists of what counts as trivial, and some people will have much shorter lists than others because we are not all equally free in social spaces. But the general point applies just the same: at least in some cases, there are things we mock ourselves for without any hope of self-improvement or change; these jokes are not self-promoting (we do not gain an obvious social advantage from admitting that we have trouble waking up in the morning), and they are not sources of self-satisfaction relating to moral failings – if there is self-satisfaction in these cases, it is more of a pleasure taken in recognizing the inevitability of our imperfections.

In these cases of self-deprecating humor, the traits or circumstances that we mock are either universal and inevitable, or they belong to a class of traits or circumstances that we all draw from in some way – if we do not have trouble waking up in the morning, maybe we go to bed at an unusually early time; if we are not anxious about aging, maybe we are naïve about life's finitude or coolly detached from mere mortals thanks to our spiritual enlightenment; if we do not have messy offices, maybe we are neurotic in our orderliness. There is always a perspective we can take on ourselves that can make us appear ridiculous and laughable. Another thing these jokes have in common, with each other and with the "ethical" kind, is that sharing them with others can drop people's guards and help them relate. Instead of pushing us to the margins, this kind of humor can serve the function of connecting people in a common humanity. As Simon Critchley suggests in *On Humour*, from this perspective, we are all laughably inauthentic: "I would argue that humour recalls us to the modesty and limitedness of the human condition, a limitedness that calls not for tragic-heroic affirmation but comic *acknowledgement*, not Promethean authenticity but a laughable inauthenticity." In our weakness of will and quiet souls, most of us are as good as we can be, "doing our best." And that often means we are not as good as we would like to be, or not doing as well as we had hoped. However, this is "not an occasion for moroseness but mirth" (Critchley 2002, p. 102). Self-deprecation of this kind is what we are asked to do when wise people encourage us to laugh at ourselves and not take ourselves too seriously (McGhee 2010a). We might even call it a virtue that is conducive to wisdom because it counters an inclination toward self-importance, focuses our attention on truths about the world and ourselves that we tend to ignore, and connects us with others. It would certainly count as moral improvement if one attained wisdom! But the difference here is that self-improvement is not what is aimed at in these jokes. If wisdom is attained or sustained at all thanks to them, that is a fortuitous coincidence.

A third kind of self-deprecating humor is "ironic." Like the "ethical" and "existential" types discussed above, ironic self-deprecation can be done without self-denigration or marginalization. It is often used by comedians as a device to expose the ignorance or bigotry of audiences (Lintott 2020, p. 9), employing or embodying racial or other stereotypes without endorsing or promoting them. In special cases, such as in the comedy of Margaret Cho or the early comedy of Dave Chappelle, ironic self-deprecation is intended to enlarge stereotypes to the point that they seem ridiculous, making those who genuinely endorse them look bad (Willett and Willett 2019, p. 43). Gadsby is also master of this kind of self-deprecation. In one famous case, she uses it effectively to address stereotypes about lesbians being humorless and the trope that women are not funny, all in one go:

What sort of comedian can't even make lesbians laugh? Every comedian ever. That's a good joke, isn't it? Classic. It's bulletproof, too. Very clever because it's funny . . . because it's true. The only people who don't think it's funny . . . are us lezzers . . . But we've got to laugh . . . because if we don't . . . proves the point. Checkmate. Very clever joke. I didn't write that. That is not my joke. It's an old . . . an oldie. Oldie but a goldie. A classic. It was written, you know, well before even women were funny. And back then, in the good old days, "lesbian" meant something different than it does now. Back then, "lesbian" wasn't about sexuality; a lesbian was just any woman not laughing at a man. (*Nanette*)

As Sheila Lintott points out, this kind of self-deprecation can be done playfully or strategically, "even from the margins," and instead of being a sign of humiliation, it can be a means of claiming one's voice and speaking one's truth (Lintott 2020, pp. 9–10). Ironic self-deprecation, like the "ethical" and "existential" kinds, can also bring an audience and a performer closer together, in this case as members of a shared tribe that feels superior to – and so takes pleasure in laughing at – the ignorant and bigoted tribe or tribes that really do believe or act on a stereotype. Of course, ironic self-deprecation does not always go as planned, as Dave Chappelle learned while working on *Chappelle's Show* with Comedy Central in the early 2000s. He got to a point where he was not sure whether he was "exploding stereotypes or merely reinforcing them," and eventually this uncertainty led him to walk away from a $50 million offer to do a third and fourth season of the show (Haggins 2007, p. 228). (For more on Chappelle, see Ralkowski 2021 and Steve Benko and Scout Burch's ▶ Chap. 71, "Dave Chappelle as Philosopher: Standing Up to Racism," in this handbook.) Gadsby does not talk about having her irony misunderstood, but she does focus on a fourth kind of self-deprecation that is problematic for performers and joke tellers.

This fourth kind of self-deprecating humor is "self-lacerating." It *does* involve self-loathing and self-denigration, and recent studies have suggested that it is "detrimental to well-being when used excessively" (Martin et al. 2003, pp. 52–54). When a joke teller "repeatedly puts themselves down" and does so without any of the healthy intentions noted above but rather from "genuine shame," it leads its audience to *feel for* rather than *connect with* the joke teller (Lintott 2020, p. 5). Meantime, the joke teller suffers doubly, first from the cruelty of the world and second from the self-deprecating jokes. Instead of connecting her with others in the shared absurdity of human life or the ethical project of self-overcoming, and instead of taking pleasure in one's moral failings (the way Louis CK can), the self-lacerating kind of self-deprecation is isolating and cutting. At best, it elicits pity from an audience. In worse cases, it lets people laugh at the joke teller, amplifying her trauma. Gadsby shares an example of this in her memoir. First, she explains some of her experiences with body shame:

I got told I was a lesbian only because I was so fat and ugly that no man would want to touch me. I got told to kill myself because I was too fat and ugly to be alive. I got told that I was not funny because I was too fat and ugly. I got told that I was so fat and ugly that I wouldn't even get raped in a men's prison. As you would expect, I sometimes struggled to feel good about my success. (Gadsby 2022, pp. 219–220)

A few paragraphs later, she confesses that these experiences led her to become "way better at fat jokes than anybody who thinks they're funny" (p. 221). She would make fun of the way she looked every time she walked on stage, and *she became good at it*. It was not until she learned to share her story in different ways that she could tell people were not laughing *at* her anymore: "they were laughing with me, connecting through their own version of adolescent body image trauma. I had a glimpse of what it felt like to be just like everybody else, instead of the fat ugly spectacle I always felt I had been" (p. 225).

Before getting to this point in her career, Gadsby's experiences on stage were unhealthy for her. She told jokes about her wide hips, small breasts, and large thighs: "I didn't get visited by the breast fairy. I got a visit from the thigh fairy, and she had a trigger finger"; she made fun of her mental health: "I'm not acting when I act. I played a fat, depressed lesbian called Hannah"; and she made fun of her sexuality and appearance: "Of course I'm a lesbian. Look at this haircut. What else am I gonna do? The thing about this haircut is I've always had it. I've always had it and I have never, ever asked for it. It's as if every hairdresser I've ever walked into has just taken one look and gone, 'Oh yeah. She looks a little bit lesbian. Why don't we just clear up any confusion?'" (Burford 2018). These are the kinds of jokes that began to weigh on Gadsby and make her reassess the purpose of her humor (Gadsby 2019). As she says in *Nanette*, for someone who "already exists on the margins," it is not virtuous to tell the oppressor's jokes about oneself. She put herself down "in order to speak, in order to seek permission to speak." *Nanette* is the result of her decision that she could not do this anymore. It was time for her "Frankenstein" version of comedy to provide us with "stand-up catharsis."

The Problem with Jokes

When Gadsby explains why she needs to quit comedy, she does not just make a case against self-lacerating humor. She also discusses a problem with jokes in general. In *Nanette* and in her 2019 TED Talk, "Three Ideas. Three Contradictions. Or Not," she argues that jokes are a problem for someone with her experiences in life because they are structurally unable to provide the "cohesive narrative" that is needed for proper healing from trauma (Gadsby 2019). During a long period of reflection after her grandmother's death, Gadsby realized that she felt alienated by her own work. Comedy was not helping her connect with others. It was having the opposite effect, and this had been the case for years without her knowing it. She realized that she had been telling her life stories – of rape and abuse and social isolation – for other people's entertainment, for laughs. "I'd been trimming away the darkness, cutting away the pain, and holding on to my trauma for the comfort of my audience. I was connecting other people through laughs, yet I remained profoundly disconnected." This was not just how she had built her comedy career. She had been telling jokes about her traumas throughout her life in a misguided effort to process her pain. In these early days, humor was not a job or a hobby. It was a "survival tactic." But jokes could not do what she asked of them – they could not heal her wounds – because of how they are structured: unlike stories, which have a cohesive narrative arc that includes a beginning, middle, and end, "jokes only need two parts: a beginning and a middle."

Gadsby's famous point here is that jokes consist of setups and punchlines and that this prevents them from telling people's complete stories. But complete stories must be told for a person to heal from trauma, and so jokes inhibit healing from trauma. To generate laughs, comedians mask their personal truths and manipulate the emotions of the people in their audiences. They create tension with the joke's setup and then release that tension with a clever punchline:

> It is essentially a question with a surprise answer. Right? But in this context, what a joke is, is a question that I have artificially inseminated with tension. I do that, that's my job. I make you all feel tense, and then I make you laugh. And you are like, "Thanks for that, I was feeling tense." I made you tense! This is an abusive relationship. (*Nanette*)

Gadsby is not just saying that comics are emotionally manipulative. Her point is that jokes function by leading us away from pain and the most important parts of people's stories. The mundane example that she uses to illustrate this in her TED Talk is the "rule of three," where a joke teller introduces a concept, such as the idea that Gadsby's entire family has palindromic names; she then provides two examples: "Mum, Dad, Nan, Pop," which establish a pattern, and this pattern creates an expectation that she upends when she mentions her brother "Kayak." This "third [example]—bam!—Kayak. What? That's the rule of three: One, two, surprise! Ha ha." Comedians create and release tension because that is how they get laughs. This tension can come from setting expectations with a simple pattern, or it can come from an emotionally charged subject. However, when it comes from a charged subject, Gadsby thinks it can negatively impact the mental health of the joke teller because jokes cut stories short. In her own experience with comedy, Gadsby says this practice created a habit of ending her stories at punchlines and freezing "an incredibly formative experience at its trauma point and sealed it off with jokes," suspending her in "a perpetual state of adolescence." The joke versions of her stories became a routine, and the repetition of her routine caused the jokes to become "fused with my actual memory of what happened. But unfortunately, that joke version was not nearly sophisticated enough to help me undo the damage done to me in reality." Gadsby says she did this – she masked her truth and led others away from her pain– because that's what comedy requires: it either deals directly with the trivial and unimportant or it takes what is important and makes it trivial.

There are a few unforgettable examples of this in *Nanette*. One involves a story about being beaten savagely by a homophobic man in front of others who did nothing to help her, and she did not report the incident to the police or take herself to the hospital because she did not feel her life was worth anything. As fodder for comedy, this story gets revised. There is no beating and no need for medical treatment; it is just a hilarious encounter in which Gadsby triumphantly disparages the man for being a moron who thinks gay men are attracted to women: he had mistaken her for a gay man, and he was upset with her for flirting with his girlfriend.

"Now I understand I have a responsibility to help lead people out of ignorance at every opportunity I can, but I left him there, people. Safety first." This is revisionist history, with Gadsby as condescending victor instead of severely traumatized victim. Another example is the story of coming out to her mother. This was the "centerpiece" of Gadsby's earlier show, *Kiss Me Quick I'm Full of Jubes*. "Her response to me coming out, when I told her I was a little bit lesbian ... was ... 'Oh, Hannah. Why did you have to tell me that? That's not something I need to know. I mean, what if I told you I was a murderer?' It's still funny. And it's a fair call. Murderer. Murderer. You would hope that's a phase" (*Nanette*). In *Kiss Me Quick I'm Full of Jubes*, Gadsby neglected to share "the best part" of this story: that her relationship with her mom was better than ever and that they had become friends who trusted each other. She omitted this part because there is nothing funny about it. As she tells this part of the story in *Nanette* to illustrate what is wrong with comedy, she imagines her audience thinking, "Good on you. Got a good relationship with your mom, have you? Can you go back to the tension? That was hilarious."

Gadsby describes other examples of this practice in *Nanette*, and she explains that she has been rewriting her past for humor's sake her whole life, on and off stage. It was never difficult for her to build tension in her jokes. "I *was* the tension. And I'm tired of tension. Tension is making me sick. It is time I stopped comedy." With this habit of rewriting her stories of trauma, Gadsby was getting laughs at a cost to her own mental health. She was not being honest about her own life; she was reimagining it. She was not processing pain; she was distracting herself from it. She was not telling her story; she was trivializing it and distorting her own memories. And she was not connecting with her audiences at all; she was making them laugh, connecting them with each other, all while she suffered by herself in silence. By the time she wrote *Nanette*, she had reached a breaking point:

> I wrote a comedy show that did not respect the punchline, that line where comedians are expected and trusted to pull their punches and turn them into tickles. I did not stop. I punched through that line into the metaphorical guts of my audience. I did not want to make them laugh. I wanted to take their breath away, to shock them, so they could listen to my story and hold my pain as individuals, not as a mindless, laughing mob. (Gadsby 2019)

This was what called for the invention of a new form of comedy, Gadsby's "stand-up catharsis," which did not aim for laughter and refused to let audiences off the hook. "If I wanted to share the literal, visceral pain of my trauma, I knew I had to invent something new.... I was going to repurpose comedy into something that could allow me to express the heat of my anger and the pain of my trauma, but without transferring it" (Gadsby 2022, p. 331). The result was *Nanette*.

Did Hannah Gadsby need to break comedy? Is it unhealthy in the ways she suggests? Sheila Lintott has pointed out that comedy sets often have the narrative structure that jokes lack and that not all comedy fits into the joke structure that Gadsby singles out for criticism. This is not just a matter of telling a lot of jokes over the course of an hour-long set. Comedians include things in their shows that are not funny at all, e.g., to give an audience time to catch their breath, and they develop funny material that is not presented in joke form. The best comedians think carefully about which topics to cover and when, how the parts of a set relate to one another and create a cohesive whole, when to present their most challenging or taboo material, and how they can establish a connection and then push boundaries with an audience. "The structure of a comedy set does, in fact, have a beginning, middle, and end," and Gadsby's *Nanette* is a masterful example of this (Lintott 2020, pp. 15–17). These are valid points about comedy specials, humor, and jokes. But one might also question Gadsby's premise: why would anyone expect humor to have the power to heal wounds from traumatic experiences like rape, body dysmorphia, and homophobic abuse? Gadsby tells us that she hurt herself by transfiguring her pain into popular comedy in Australia, and in *Nanette* she blames comedy for the fact that she is socially isolated and underdeveloped emotionally. But wasn't she just wrong to think that she could heal her life's wounds with jokes? Why would anyone expect so much from humor?

Humor and Catharsis

Hannah Gadsby is not the only person who has had great expectations for comedy. And for good reason: recent studies in psychology have shown humor to be effective for reducing clinical depression and anxiety and for building resilience and well-being (McGhee 2010b), while philosophers have argued that "the sting of ridicule" and "the contagion of joyous laughter" are among the best "weapons for social change" (Willett and Willett 2019, p. 22). In the philosophy of humor, there are different theories about how humor performs these and related functions. Simon Critchley presents one of them in his *On Humour*. According to his Freudian "neo-Stoic" view, humor allows the super-ego to observe the ego from "an inflated position, which makes the ego itself look trivial and ridiculous." This self-mockery is not depressing or unhealthy for the joke teller; on the contrary, it "gives us a sense of emancipation, consolation and childlike elevation" (Critchley 2002, pp. 94–95). Julie and Cynthia Willett, who are critical of Critchley's neo-Stoic theory, present an alternative view in *Uproarious: How Feminists and Other Subversive Comics Speak Truth*, which builds on the ideas of Audre Lorde, a variety of studies in empirical psychology, and many other feminist writers to develop a feminist understanding of humor's capacity to effect social and political change. As they put the point, "the primary aim is not to transcend life's eternal absurdities with Stoic resolve. We engage the humor of eros—that deceptively subversive Greek word for life and love" (Willett and Willett 2019, p. 18), the aim of which is to "overturn oppressive ideals" (p. 114), "connecting mind to body and self to other" (p. 105). Each of these views is worth considering here. What does humor do? How does it work? What does this mean for Gadsby's case *against* comedy in *Nanette*, as well as her case *for* comedy elsewhere?

In *On Humour*, Critchley argues for a version of what this chapter has called "existential" self-deprecation. It is a form of self-ridicule that liberates us from the ego's unrealistic expectations of ourselves and the world, and it offers us the consolation that as imperfect as we are, and as unjust as the world is, it is all as good as it gets, and life remains worth living in our laughable inauthenticity, mortality, and finitude. This is the kind of humor that Viktor Frankl celebrates in *Man's Search for Meaning*. It is an approach to life that functions a lot like Stoicism and cognitive behavioral therapy, changing our judgments, correcting unhealthy habits of thought, and helping us cope with pain and suffering. As the ancient Greek Stoic Epictetus says in his *Enchiridion*, "what upsets people is not the things themselves but their judgments about the things" (§5). For Freud, this change of judgment involves a shift from the ego's point of view, which is narrow and self-absorbed, to the wiser perspective of the super-ego, which sees beyond the ego's preoccupations the way a parent sees beyond the troubles of a child. While the ego suffers through life's ups and downs, the super-ego looks at life and says, "Look! Here is the world, which seems so dangerous! It is nothing but a game for children, just worth making a jest about" (Freud 1990, p. 166). This shift of perspective is what allows us to laugh at ourselves for expecting too much from life. As Louis CK says in a bit on *Late Night with Conan O'Brien* that made him famous overnight, "everything is amazing and nobody is happy." If we are miserable on a flight that is taking too long, we should just remember that we are "sitting in a chair in the sky," participating in "the miracle of human flight." It is only the entitled ego that expects more in these moments, while the wise super-ego reminds us that we would be considered mythical beings by ancient civilizations if they could see us flying. Julie and Cynthia Willett call this view "neo-Stoic" because it promotes resignation to the world's imperfections – at most, it encourages us to "keep calm and carry on" – and it assumes there is a perspective equally available to all of us, regardless of our experiences and identities, that makes our troubles seem trivial and ridiculous.

Would this Freudian neo-Stoic attitude help Hannah Gadsby? It is possible. If it worked for someone like Viktor Frankl, a survivor of Auschwitz who used humor and other tools to develop a new model of psychotherapy called logotherapy, how can anyone say that, in principle, it cannot help others who suffer from oppression? However, it is hard to imagine that there is a perspective available to Hannah Gadsby that would allow her to see her experiences with homophobia and sexual assault as trivial and unimportant. Moreover, even if there were such a perspective, it is not clear that it would be healthy for her to take it up. As she says in *Nanette*, she needs to tell her life story and process her pain directly. This chapter has shown that Gadsby's case against self-deprecation applies specifically to "self-lacerating" humor and that the "existential" style of self-deprecation is different in kind and in effect: it is not cutting or isolating; it brings people together in a common, flawed humanity. However, Gadsby's life has been defined by traumas that are not part of a universal human condition, and so "existential" self-deprecation will not always be a live option for her the way it is for others, at least not without self-*erasure*, which could cause further harm. For example, Critchley can find humor in the incongruity that everyone experiences in relation to their embodiment: we are not fully integrated with our bodies the way animals are; we *have* our bodies – we distance ourselves from them, reflect on them, wish they were different, try to change them, suffer from their imperfections, etc.

> Humour functions by exploiting [this] gap between being a body and having a body, between—let us say—the *physical* and the *metaphysical* aspects of being human. What makes us laugh, I would wager, is the return of the physical into the metaphysical, where the pretended sublimity of the human collapses into a comic ridiculousness which is perhaps even more tragic. (Critchley 2002, p. 43)

Hannah Gadsby is not deluded by any "pretended sublimity of the human," and so there isn't any relief for her in having her life "collapsed into comic ridiculousness." Critchley thinks human beings are "defined by the continual failure to coincide with themselves," and he finds humor in this: our identity consists in a lack of self-identity (2002, p. 43). But this metaphysical sense of failing to coincide with one's body cannot be a source of healthy self-deprecation for Hannah Gadsby. Her relationship with her body, throughout her life, has been defined by an incongruity that goes well beyond ordinary disconnects between human minds and their animal bodies. She has spent most of her life feeling marginalized and dehumanized because of her failure to coincide with herself and her own experiences with lacking self-identity. What she needs, she says, is a new kind of humor that will help her feel more connected to herself, to the body she has been taught to hate, and to others.

Julie and Cynthia Willett present a theoretical framework for this kind of humor in *Uproarious*. They begin by rejecting the neo-Stoic style of humor because of (i) its "fatalism," which does nothing to "challenge abusive forms of social power" (p. 109), and (ii) the mind-body dualism implicit in its recommendation that we elevate ourselves above the absurdities of life (p. 120). In place of this "turtle-like" stance, they argue for a style of humor that connects the body to the mind and people to each other with belly laughter (p. 106). To help explain their view, they distinguish between "homeopathic," "allopathic," and "collective" forms of catharsis. "Homeopathic catharsis" is a byproduct of humor that functions like a traditional vaccine: one injects a small amount of a disease to build up an immunity. This is the idea behind "ironic" self-deprecation and other practices where people appropriate what might otherwise harm them, such as a stereotype or slur, to inoculate themselves against hatred. As Hannah Gadsby says in *Douglas*, "You have worked out why I do that, yeah? Why I snack on hate? It's how I build up immunity. It's called microdosing. Your hate is my vaccine." "Allopathic catharsis" works differently. Instead of micro-dosing on hate, it uses comic ridicule to correct vices like entitlement, arrogance, and unchecked privilege, calling "the target back to common social ideals" (p. 113). Former President Obama was always very skilled with this style of humor. At the 2011 White House Correspondents' Dinner, for example, he famously roasted Donald Trump:

> Donald Trump is here tonight. Now I know that he's taken some flak lately, but no one is happier, no one is prouder to put this birth certificate matter to rest than the Donald. And that's because he can get back to focusing on the issues that matter, like did we fake the moon landing? What really happened in Roswell? And where are Biggie and Tupac? All kidding aside, obviously we all know about your credentials and breadth of experience [laughter]. For example—no, seriously, just recently in an episode of *Celebrity Apprentice* at the steakhouse the men's cooking team did not impress the judges from Omaha Steaks. And

there was a lot of blame to go around, but you Mr. Trump recognized that the real problem was a lack of leadership and so ultimately you didn't blame Lil John or Meat Loaf. You fired Gary Busey. These are the kinds of decisions that would keep me up at night.

The next day, Seal Team 6 flew into Pakistan and killed Osama bin Laden. Obama's jokes at Trump's expense were relentless enough on their own. But the contrast between the reality of the Presidency and the trivialities of Donald Trump's life made the roast even more devastating in hindsight. This roast was partly about getting revenge against Trump for his racist birtherism, but it was also aimed at the mostly white media elite that had failed to contain or condemn the birth certificate story on their networks, instead giving Trump a platform to peddle his lies (Rhodes 2018). Obama's ridicule in the bit was supposed to diminish Trump in public, disempowering him politically (he had flirted with running for President in 2012), playfully scold the White House press correspondents for failing to do their job, and return everyone's attention to the far more serious matters of the Presidency. It did this for a short time. Trump's flirtation with running for President in 2012 ended shortly after this humiliation. But as one commenter on YouTube writes, "this legitimately feels like we're watching a villain origin story." The ridicule backfired in one of its aims. Many friends and associates of Trump's say that this was the moment he decided to run for President in 2016. It also did nothing to seriously question the problem of misinformation in our media. The same media elite in the room that night went on to give Trump a platform to peddle his lies for many years to come.

For feminists like the Willetts, a humor that merely returns us to shared values is not enough: "our question has been how to bring down warped social ideals, not live with them" (p. 114). What we need, the Willetts say, is an emancipatory humor that identifies and dismantles abusive forms of social power. Amber Rose's SlutWalk movement is one of the examples they discuss at length. It began in 2001 as a protest after a Toronto police officer recommended that women "avoid dressing like sluts in order not to be victimized," and in 2015, it developed into a norm-changing global movement that takes on issues like victim blaming and sexual violence, empowering women to feel good about their bodies and take back control of their sexuality. These demonstrations use the kind of carnival humor that has always been featured in the gay pride movement to encourage women to dress however they want and behave however they wish in public, and the women in the SlutWalk movement hoped to convert "the sickly feeling of isolation and shame into head-held-high pride and a fervent sense of belonging on altered terms" (p. 116). They playfully mixed homeopathic and allopathic styles of humor, prominently using the word "slut," proudly celebrating female sexual pleasure, and joyfully displaying "tits and ass." This kind of humor challenges the status quo by "marking as contemptible the social norms themselves," redirecting shame away from women toward misogynistic social structures.

Gadsby often uses this kind of humor in her work to "needle" patriarchy and gender norms:

> Look, I don't identify as transgender, but I'm partial to a holiday. I love being mistaken for a man, 'cause just for a few moments, life gets a hell of a lot easier. I'm top-shelf normal, king of the humans. I'm a straight white man. I'm about to get good service for no fucking effort! (*Nanette*)

The Willetts describe it as a "communal sloughing off of old norms for a renewal and revitalization of the mind, body, and collective animal spirits" (117). It is not just a psychological process "but also a biosocial one" that does more than cultivate elevated Stoic tranquility. Belly-deep laughter shared with others in the face of oppressive systems "regenerates pride in the self and body," exchanges the "rational" for the "relational" self, reconnecting us with ourselves and with others, and changes the world by transforming attitudes and dispositions (116). This is "collective catharsis."

Gadsby tells her audience in *Nanette* that "homeopathic catharsis" did not work for her because she already had the "disease"; she could not inoculate herself against homophobia or misogyny because she had already internalized both. Her "ironic" self-deprecation was self-lacerating rather than self-strengthening. When she realized this, she stopped what she was doing and reinvented her comedy. This reinvention did not mean using "allopathic catharsis" in her shows, however. As the Willetts say, for feminists like Gadsby, the point is to change social norms, not to endure them stoically. Gadsby herself calls *Nanette* "stand-up catharsis," and in her memoir, she says straightforwardly that her "intention was to ultimately create something of a healing catharsis" (Gadsby 2022, p. 339).

But is it an example of what the Willetts call "collective catharsis"? The answer seems to be both yes and no, just as one would expect from Hannah Gadsby. It shares two of the goals, social change and connection, "to feel less alone, to feel connected" (*Nanette*). However, it does not use the same means to produce these effects as collective catharsis. Gadsby does not build connection through infectious, norm-altering belly laughter. She hits her audience in the guts with the "dysphoric ... literal, visceral pain of [her] trauma." She never pulls her punches to "turn them into tickles," and there is none of the triumphant carnival style that characterizes SlutWalk marches. Instead, Gadsby gives us "a comedy show that was not funny," and she leaves us with tension rather than providing comic relief (Gadsby 2022, p. 331).

Catharsis but not relief, it is an important distinction for Hannah Gadsby. "Catharsis" is the Latinized form of the Greek *katharsis*, which means "purging, cleansing." It is also associated with bodily purging and bowel movements, the clearing away of dirt, shame, and guilt. The ancient Greeks associated it with "social menstruation," a cyclical cleansing of the social organism during annual tragedy festivals (McCumber 1988, pp. 61–62). For Hannah Gadsby, the catharsis in *Nanette* is partly a byproduct of the fact that the show refuses to provide audiences with relief. Her stories and jokes create tension, and she amplifies that tension by sharing her own feelings about the traumatic experiences she has had in life. Gadsby thinks it is precisely because she tells these complete stories, without pulling punches and while sharing her worst traumas, that she can produce cathartic experiences for herself and her audiences. Her audiences need to hear her story and feel her pain; she needs to share it all directly and honestly, and the audience needs that tension to linger with them as they leave the venue or change the channel because there is so much to learn from it:

> This tension, it's yours. I am not helping you anymore. You need to learn what this feels like because this tension is what not-normals carry inside of them all of the time ... What I would have done to have heard a story like mine. Not for blame. Not for reputation, not for money. But to feel less alone. To feel connected. I want my story heard. (*Nanette*)

People with similar experiences might feel less alone; others will be pushed to reflect on their own lives and become aware of their participation in systems of oppression; some will be defensive but open to conversation, and they might be persuadable to change their minds in ways that make a difference; some will be angry enough to take action, and Gadsby can heal from facing her traumas and sharing her story with others: "I ... managed to take the worst of the sting out of my own trauma through performing *Nanette* over and over again" (Gadsby 2022, p. 353). In each of these cases, Gadsby will feel that catharsis has been achieved, a toxin will have been purged either from herself (shame, isolation, self-loathing) or from the hearts and minds of others (ignorance, apathy, defensiveness), or both. But this is not comic relief! According to Gadsby, comic relief involves creating and dispelling tension, and she is no longer willing to be responsible for the tension she creates when she shares her story. Catharsis is different. The relief it affords us comes from confronting and releasing repressed emotions, not from erasing them with jokes and punchlines. Gadsby compares it to "lancing a boil," cutting open an abscess and draining the bacteria to allow for healing.

Gadsby writes in her memoir that comedy has been a lifeline for her. But it has also caused her harm: self-deprecation turned into self-laceration; the logic of jokes caused her to distort the truth of her story, and the comedian's responsibility to relieve tension felt irresponsible, to her and to others. But if *Nanette* does nothing else, it proves without any ambiguity that *Hannah Gadsby* does not need to worry that she lets her audiences off the hook. She seems to understand this: "my goal was to simulate a feeling in the room that was akin to trauma, because I wanted to see if I could create an experience of communal empathy in a room full of strangers ... I needed my audience to trust me because I needed my audience to feel safe, and I needed my audience to feel safe so that I could take that safety away and not give it back" (Gadsby 2022, pp. 22–23).

These are not the intentions of an ordinary comedian. It is much more likely for people to feel triggered by *Nanette* (Fury 2018), as Gadsby knows quite well after triggering *herself* on stage with her own "rape joke that was not a joke" while she was performing earlier versions of *Nanette*. "I am ashamed to admit that this was when I first truly understood that what I was attempting to do was quite dangerous, not just for my audience but also for me" (Gadsby 2022, pp. 335–336). She just isn't in the business of pulling punches and providing tickles. In fact, *Nanette* was so different from a conventional comedy show that many critics questioned whether it was comedy at all. *The New York Times* called it "stand-up tragedy" (Kahn 2018); others said it was more of a TED Talk than a comedy special (Fox 2018b), and even Gadsby says that "*Nanette* is arguably the most deliberately miserable, unfunny hour of comedy ever made" (Gadsby 2022, p. 15).

It is not hard to understand why some people would deny that *Nanette* is a comedy special. If comedy has any necessary conditions, a commonsense thought is that intentional amusement is one of them (Deen et al. 2024). And since *Nanette* (i) deliberately simulates trauma, (ii) with the intention of eliciting empathy, and since (iii) this goal is the centerpiece of the show *and* (iv) is accompanied by an innovative philosophical deconstruction of comedy as a cause of humiliation, repression, and isolation, it is surprising that anyone objects when critics ask this question (Krefting 2019). But it is also clear that *Nanette* is a comedy show. Most importantly, she says it is. Second, it is full of jokes, and many of these jokes are paradigm examples of "collective catharsis," which is arguably the highest form of humor. Third, one of Gadsby's primary intentions in *Nanette* is to amuse her audience. This is not her only intention, but most of the show is composed of jokes, so there is a math argument in here as well. The fact that she also provides a theory of humor and how it harms us, while deliberately and flagrantly violating some of humor's most basic logical rules, is not enough to disqualify it as a comedy show. Every piece of the show is part of her larger effort to make us *think about comedy under the banner of comedy, while performing comedy.* It is as if Gadsby is a stunt performer whose high-wire act was to do comedy without doing comedy. Maybe that makes *Nanette* a magic show instead of a comedy special?

Conclusion: Anger and Justice

> I love angry white man comedy. It's so funny, it's hilarious. They're adorable. Why are they angry? What's up, little fella? What are they angry about? . . . They're like the canaries in the mine, aren't they? If they're having a tough time, the rest of us are goners.
> —Hanhah Gadsby (*Nanette*)

As Gadsby concludes *Nanette*, she says she is angry and has every right to be angry. But she worries about spreading her anger, which she calls a "toxic, infectious tension" that *cannot be* constructive because "it knows no other purpose than to spread blind hatred, and I want no part of it." Her story expresses and evokes anger; her humor depends on it, and the tension she leaves for her audience to process is partly a feeling of anger, which is "why I must quit comedy. Because the only way I can tell my truth and put tension in the room is with anger." Earlier versions of *Nanette* did not end this way. Jesse David Fox and Rebecca Krefting were both disappointed by the change. They preferred the more "punk rock" ending of the original shows, which ended without this reflection on the dangers of anger and the importance of being constructive (Fox 2020). However, Gadsby explains in *Nanette* that for her, what is at stake is "connection." She can bring people together in anger, but that is not the communion she longs for. What she wanted most was for her story to be heard and to be connected to the world. The "punk rock" endings of earlier shows left her feeling alone.

It would be a mistake to question the validity of Gadsby's lived experience. If anger made her feel isolated or connected in an unhealthy way, it is important to accept that as true for her. At the same time, one can question the philosophical claims she makes about anger. She does not merely say that anger is bad for her; the point she makes in *Nanette* is about anger in general. Is Gadsby right to think that anger cannot be constructive and that its only purpose is to spread blind hatred? In her book *Anger and Forgiveness*, Martha Nussbaum argues for a position that resembles Gadsby's. She argues that anger is misguided when it aims at payback, since we cannot undo harm by causing more harm, and morally flawed when it aims at correcting status injuries, because these corrections involve humiliating and downranking others, which are not a part of justice. What we must learn to do is transition "from anger to constructive thinking about future good" (Nussbaum 2016, p. 31). This sounds a lot like Gadsby's view that anger *cannot* be constructive.

But is it true that anger is always aimed at revenge? As Amia Srinivasan points out, "many of us experience anger that calls not for revenge but for something else: for the wrongdoer to see just what he has done." There is nothing incoherent or morally problematic in wanting "to be heard and seen by those who racially abuse you, or to have the full horror of their actions publicly registered" (Srinivasan 2016). *In Sister Outsider*, Audre Lorde argues that "anger expressed and translated into action in the service of our vision and our future is a liberating and strengthening act of clarification, for it is in the painful process of this translation that we identify who are our allies[,] with whom we have grave differences, and who are our genuine enemies" (Lorde 2007, p. 127). Frederick Douglas connects anger with rekindling "the few expiring embers of freedom." For him, anger was "the only way of recovering a lost sense of agency … Sometimes, for some people, it can be the only way of registering the full injustice of the world" (Srinivasan 2016).

Far from spreading hatred, anger on these accounts is instrumental in recovering one's humanity and fighting for justice. Neither of these goals is sought as payback, and both are compatible with Gadsby's stated aims in *Nanette*. She does not call for marching in the streets, but her show is a kind of activism that attempts to change our minds about comedy, patriarchy, gender normativity, cancel culture, art history, and more. It also provides Gadsby with an opportunity to reclaim her own humanity by telling her story, being heard, and reinventing her craft. Having her anger heard seems to be one of the main reasons her show feels cathartic, to her and to countless fans. It is the misogynistic ancient Greeks and Romans who counsel us to beware of our anger, to control and silence it, so that reason can govern our public and private lives (Srinivasan 2016). One wonders whether the "boil" that Gadsby lances with *Nanette* was partly formed by this view of anger that we have inherited from the ancients and built into the patriarchal structures of our world. The issue with the end of *Nanette* is not that it is not "punk rock," which makes Krefting and Fox sound like "trauma tourists" (Fury 2018). It is that it undermines the "collective catharsis" of the show.

In *Nanette*, Hannah Gadsby provides four reasons for quitting comedy. Her point about self-deprecating humor was too strong since there are many forms of self-deprecation, and not all of them are based on self-loathing; her point about jokes was overstated because comedy sets provide plenty of space for storytelling and also because the comedy stage probably is not the best space for seeking healing from trauma; her point about comic relief can be valid while we celebrate comedic catharsis for self-strengthening and the critique of culture; and her point about anger may be rooted in a misogynistic view of the emotions that Hannah Gadsby herself finds abhorrent. Nevertheless, there is so much to learn from thinking philosophically about Gadsby's comedy. She is a great example of an artist who can teach us through disagreement. Her work invites us to think with her, not just to accept each of her claims as dogmas. Besides, many of them are meant in jest.

When Simon Critchley describes the emancipatory nature of humor, he talks about returning "us to a common, familiar world of shared practices ... and indicat[ing] how those practices might be transformed or perfected, how things might be otherwise" (Critchley 2002, p. 16). If Gadsby's comedy does nothing else, it is this. She is constantly returning us to our common, familiar world of shared practices, values, attitudes, and beliefs so that she can help us imagine how they might be otherwise. Her comedy makes us reflect all over again about what comedy is, how it works, and what it can do. Feminists have called for us to rethink the entire history of humor theory (Willett and Willett 2019), and Hannah Gadsby is one of the most powerful recent change agents. There are many others: Amy Schumer, Tina Fey, Sarah Silverman, Margaret Cho, Wanda Sykes, and Tig Notaro. But Gadsby is a truly revolutionary figure. We often talk about what comedy can do to change the world and make it better. Gadsby helps us see that comedy first must change itself. That is the only way for it to provide us with the allopathic and homeopathic medicine we need for collective catharsis.

End Notes

1. You can see such comments here: https://www.facebook.com/hannahgadsbycomedy/photos/a.10151349829668000/10156612541818000/?type=3.

References

Baldoni, John. Watching 'Ted Lasso' can make you a better manager. *Forbes*, October 21, 2020. https://www.forbes.com/sites/johnbaldoni/2020/10/21/watching-ted-lasso-can-make-you-a-better-manager/?sh=46be0a1f51b5. Accessed 25 Sept 2022.

Berman, Judy. Nanette' is the most discussed comedy special in ages. Here's what to read about it. *The New York Times*, July 13, 2018. https://www.nytimes.com/2018/07/13/arts/television/nanette-hannah-gadsby-netflix-roundup.html. Acccssed 10 Aug 2022.

Burford, Corinna. 2018. A guide to Hannah Gadsby's pre-Nanette work. *Vulture*, June 28, 2018. https://www.vulture.com/2018/06/a-guide-to-hannah-gadsbys-pre-nanette-work.html. Accessed 10 Aug 2022.

Critchley, Simon. 2002. *On humour*. New York: Routledge.

Deen, Phillip, Lauren Olin, and Mark Ralkowski. Untitled manuscript. Manuscript in preparation, expected 2024.

Fox, Jesse David. How funny does comedy need to be? *Vulture*, September 4, 2018a. https://www.vulture.com/2018/09/post-comedy-how-funny-does-comedy-need-to-be.html

———, host. The specials – Hannah Gadsby's Nanette. *Good One (podcast)*, April 14, 2018b. https://podcasts.apple.com/us/podcast/the-specials-hannah-gadsbys-nanette/id1203393721?i=1000557591236

———, host. Hannah Gadsby's prepositions. *Good One (podcast)*, June 2, 2020. https://podcasts.apple.com/gb/podcast/hannah-gadsbys-prepositions/id1203393721?i=1000476514495

Frankl, Viktor. 2006. *Man's search for meaning*. Boston: Beacon Press.

Freud, Sigmund. 1990. Humour. In *Art and literature*. London: Penguin.

Fury. 2018. Trauma tourism: The complicated comedy of Hannah Gadsby's Nanette. *Metro Magazine*, January 29, 2019. https://metromagazine.com.au/trauma-tourism/. Accessed 10 Aug 2022.

Gadsby, Hannah. 2018. *Hannah Gadsby: Nanette*. Netflix. Sydney. Directed by Old, Jon and Madeleine Parry. https://www.netflix.com/title/80233611ci

———. 2019. Three ideas. Three contradictions. Or not. TED. https://www.youtube.com/watch?v=87qLWFZManA&t=637s. Accessed 10 Aug 2022.

———. 2020. *Hannah Gadsby: Douglas*. Netflix. Sydney. Directed by Madeleine Parry. https://www.netflix.com/title/81054700

———. 2022. *Ten steps to Nanette: A memoir situation*. New York: Ballantine Books.

Haggins, Bambi. 2007. *Laughing mad: The black comic persona in post-soul America*. New Brunswick: Rutgers University Press.

Kahn, Andrew. Stand-up tragedy. *Slate*, July 11, 2018. https://slate.com/culture/2018/07/hannah-gadsbys-netflix-special-nanette-is-powerful-anti-comedy.html. Accessed 10 Aug 2022.

Kozlowski, Carl. Hannah Gadsby moves beyond comedy but promises a 'playful' show in Chicago. *The Sun Times*, July 12, 2022. https://chicago.suntimes.com/2022/7/12/23202970/hannah-gadsby-tour-chicago-theatre-body-of-work. Accessed 10 Aug 2022.

Krefting, Rebecca. 2019. Hannah Gadsby: On the limits of satire. *Studies in American Humor* 5 (1): 93–102. Web.

Lintott, Sheila. 2020. Hannah Gadsby's Nanette: Connection through comedy. *The Southern Journal of Philosophy* 58 (4): 610–631. Web.

Lorde, Audre. 2007. *Sister outsider: Essays and speeches*. Berkeley: Crossing Press.

Louis, CK. 2011. *Louis CK: Live at the Beacon Theater*. louisck.com. New York: Directed by Louis CK https://louisck.com/products/live-at-the-beacon-theater-video-download

Martin, Rod A., Patricia Puhlik-Doris, Gwen Larsen, Jeanette Gray, and Kelly Weir. 2003. Individual differences of the humor styles questionnaire. *Journal of Research in Personality* 37 (1): 48–75.

McCumber, J. 1988. Aristotelian catharsis and the purgation of women. *Diacritics* 18 (4): 53–67.

McGhee, Paul E. 2010a. *Humor as survival training for a stressed-out world: The 7 humor habits program*. Bloomington: Author House.

———. 2010b. *Humor: The lighter path to resilience and health*. Bloomington: Author House.

Nussbaum, Martha. 2016. *Anger and forgiveness: Resentment, generosity, justice*. New York: Oxford University Press.

Ralkowski, Mark, ed. 2016. *Louis CK and philosophy: You don't get to be bored*. Chicago: Open Court Publishing.

———, ed. 2021. *Dave Chappelle and philosophy: When keeping it wrong gets real*. Chicago: Carus Books.

Rhodes, Ben. Behind the scenes the day Osama Bin Laden was killed: Ben Rhodes watches history unfold in the situation room. *Lit Hub*, June 26, 2018. https://lithub.com/behind-the-scenes-the-day-osama-bin-laden-was-killed/. Accessed 10 Aug 2022.

Srinivasan, Amia. Would politics be better off without anger? *The Nation*, December 19–26, 2016. https://www.thenation.com/article/archive/a-righteous-fury/. Accessed 10 Aug 2022.

Willett, Cynthia, and Julie A. Willett. 2019. *Uproarious: How feminists and other subversive comics speak truth*. Minneapolis: University of Minnesota Press.

Amy Schumer as Philosopher: Fuck the Feminine Mystique

Charlene Elsby

Contents

Introduction	1492
Amy Schumer's Work	1492
What Is this Feminine Mystique that Schumer Is Fucking?	1494
Amy Schumer Will Save Us	1498
Honesty About Physical Existence	1501
Honesty About Sexuality	1503
Honesty About Social Expectations	1505
Consequences	1507
Conclusion	1508
References	1509

Abstract

Amy Schumer's feminist revolt is a rejection of the feminine mystique – that is to say, a rejection of the idea that certain aspects of the experiences of women should remain mysterious. Through persistent honesty, Schumer's comedy and other works contribute to the feminist goal of revising patriarchal concepts of femininity by expanding those concepts to include a more complex representation of women and our experience. Her portrayals of women's physicality, women's sexuality, and of woman as a social being demand a reconceptualization of woman as a moral and rational entity (i.e., a full-blown human). Her work laughs at the dehumanizing social constructs that define woman as something less-than, and in doing so reduce woman's alienation by reconciling concepts of women as we are and women as we are perceived.

C. Elsby (✉)
University of Ottawa, Ottawa, ON, Canada

Keywords

Amy Schumer · Simone de Beauvoir · Betty Friedan · Aristotle · Feminine mystique · Honesty · Ethics · Femininity · Masculinity · Gender · The Other · Humor · Comedy · *Trainwreck* · *I Feel Pretty* · *Snatched* · Growing · *Mostly Sex Stuff* · *Live at the Apollo* · *The Leather Special* · *Inside Amy Schumer* · Katherine Ryan · Patriarchal norms · The Girl with the Lower Back Tattoo

Introduction

The days of apologizing for womanhood are over. Or, at least, wouldn't that be nice? The comedy of Amy Schumer delves into the human experience – including the experience of women – always striving toward an honest representation of life as it is. A lot of the jokes she makes depend on the incongruency between what is actually true of the human experience and what is considered appropriate to talk about in civil society. The fact that experiences common to half of humanity are made mysterious and purported to be ineffable to the other half is a depressing but self-evident truth. There are just some lady things you're not supposed to talk about.

When an aspect of women's experience is hidden or made mysterious, that's what I'm calling "the feminine mystique". And Amy Schumer's comedy is a revolt against it. Societal standards have led to a representation of women's experience that is, at best, inaccurate and, at worst, dishonest. (With the latter, there's an explicit intent to deceive.) The effects are insidious and pervasive. By obscuring aspects of women's experience, they become excluded from what our general concept of human experience is. Women are effectively "othered" (differentiated or alienated from the human experience) by our own agreed upon social standards which forbid the expression of certain truths.

Amy Schumer talks about these truths, and she does so publicly and in such a way that people will actually listen – because it's funny *and* it's true. She calls attention to the alienation of women by disparaging, denigrating, and violating social norms – norms that are, despite the fact that they are reinforced by both men and women alike, broadly patriarchal. Thus the feminist aspect of Schumer's comedy serves a particular purpose, even if she doesn't write her jokes with a specific agenda in mind. That purpose is to eliminate the feminine mystique and the alienation of women from the human experience. That is to say, with Schumer running around telling jokes, women everywhere are better off. In what follows, I will elucidate why.

Amy Schumer's Work

Most online biographies of Schumer say that her celebrity started when she was a contestant on *Last Comic Standing* season five in 2007. (She came in fourth.) She has several Netflix specials, the first of which was released five years later (in 2012), and which I would still call "early Schumer." In 2013, her Comedy Central show,

Inside Amy Schumer, aired and lasted four seasons (although she hasn't discounted the possibility of the show continuing at some point). Working on several projects simultaneously, Amy Schumer became an institution of comedy somewhere over the course of that show and contemporaneous specials and films. In 2015, her movie *Trainwreck* (which she wrote and in which she starred) was released to critical acclaim. She also released a standup special, *Live at the Apollo*, in which she discusses filming the movie. *The Leather Special* (stand-up) was released in 2017. And Schumer released two more films, *Snatched* in 2017 and *I Feel Pretty* in 2018.

As evidence that she had become a force to be reckoned with, consider Katherine Ryan's joke about her in her own 2017 comedy special *In Trouble*. Joking about Bill Cosby, Ryan says she understands why women didn't come forward with allegations that would bring down a successful person from a historically disadvantaged demographic: "Tina Fey could be raping me now, and I would tell no one. Amy Schumer could be wearing me like a watch, and I'd just be like… Thank you for everything that you do for women in our industry." It seems Schumer took a brief hiatus sometime after that, but has since returned with a vengeance, with her 2019 special *Growing*, the HBO documentary series *Expecting Amy* depicting her working through her pregnancy (2020), and the series *Amy Schumer Learns to Cook* (2020) on the Food Network. At the time of this writing, she has another show in preproduction.

Schumer's comedy has always played on gender differences and disparities. Notably, she reports on the experiences of women in a way that destroys the mystery of women's internality – what women are thinking. She talks about what sex is like from the woman's point of view, even when she doesn't come off as pretty. We get the impression that the woman's side of the story also matters, that she's not just appealing to the male audience's expectation of what a female comic should say. Her sex jokes aren't sexy. She tells a story where she's drunk and going at it with a fellow, "like two hams." And then there is "Milk, Milk, Lemonade," a sketch from *Inside Amy Schumer*, that went viral for how it made light of how women's bodies are sexualized in music videos.

Schumer's comedy refuses to acknowledge the "feminine mystique" imposed upon us by the patriarchy – the social structures that work to dehumanize women by failing to represent women as conscious beings. This naturally leads to the objectification of women, which includes a host of related subtleties about which most men remain unaware. Now, to be clear, men and the patriarchy are two separate things; just because you're a man doesn't mean you are taking part in the patriarchy, or that you must do so. In this essay, "patriarchy" refers to the conceptual system we are all born into – the system from which men disproportionately benefit and to which people of all genders contribute by propagating its beliefs and/or acting as social enforcers of those beliefs.

Amy Schumer is both a cause and evidence of progress. The fact that she has been able to achieve such success despite the obstacles we've all come to know means that we're getting somewhere. At the same time, she's rolling with it and using that success to erode the oppressive social structures – structures that would not only rather see her fail, but in fact not say anything at all.

What Is this Feminine Mystique that Schumer Is Fucking?

Betty Friedan published a book called *The Feminine Mystique* in 1963. Reading as a less academic version of Simone de Beauvoir's *The Second Sex* (1949) that was instead meant exclusively for American housewives, *The Feminine Mystique* constructed an emaciated definition of "the feminine mystique" that hints at but doesn't touch the feminine mystique that Amy Schumer is fucking.

In an introduction to the 2001 edition of *The Feminine Mystique* called "Metamorphosis, Two Generations Later," Betty Friedan neatly defines what she means by the feminine mystique:

> Consider the terms of women's new empowerment, the startling changes since that time I wrote about, only three decades ago, when women were defined only in sexual relation to men—man's wife, sex object, mother, housewife—and never as persons defining themselves by their own actions in society. That image, which I called "the feminine mystique," was so pervasive, coming at us from the women's magazines, the movies, the television commercials, all the mass media and the textbooks of psychology and sociology, that each woman thought she was alone, it was her personal guilt, if she didn't have an orgasm waxing the family-room floor. (Friedan 2001, p. 18)

Essentially, Friedan's definition of the feminine mystique is limited to the (white, upper-class) housewife. This is the major criticism against second-wave feminism – that is, the circa 1960s feminism that focused on women's right to work outside the home – that makes it seem like a cute little movement that nowhere near reaches the experience of *all of the rest of the* women who don't fit that narrow description (women who aren't confined to the home by social expectations, but perhaps already in the workforce because of financial necessity). What's good about Friedan's definition is that it identifies a relationality to women's existence. It seems that the woman is nothing in and of herself, but defined only in relation to others. What about that do we identify as her "mystique"?

Her mystique is the fact that she *herself* is indefinable *except* in relation to others, a distinction going back to Aristotle's distinction between what exists as a substance and what exists as an accident. If something is a substance, it exists in virtue of itself and does not depend on something else for its existence. Think basically – if a table is blue, the table can exist without its blueness, but the blueness can't exist without the table. So in that example, the table is the substance and the blueness is the accident. If woman is definable only in relation to something else, if she *exists* only in relation, then she too is an accident. (Surely that can't be right.) Imagine if we referred to Amy Schumer only as "Chris Fischer's wife, who's a bit of a performer," or "Gene David's mom." Here, both "mom" and "wife" are relational terms, implying that the person described is who she is only in virtue of somebody else (someone more worthy, like any male toddler). So, despite the narrowness of her definition, Betty Friedan was getting at something, some way in which some women were suffering; she simply shouldn't have limited that observation to women who wax floors at home while their husbands go off to work. It's more basic than that. It is a definition of a certain kind of a mystique – the fact that when some people think of what a woman is, they think child rearer, they think floor waxer, they think something to fuck – but beyond that, *they don't fucking know*. And that's what's mysterious.

That's fucked up, but not as hardcore, fundamentally fucked up as the feminine mystique really is, the feminine mystique which Beauvoir talked about in 1949 and which Amy Schumer is working hard to eliminate. She's not just a comedian who dares to say that maybe women should seek work outside the home. We're past that. She's a comedian who points out the absurdity of the more pervasive, more insidious feminine mystique that continues to ensure that the experience of women is mutated by conceptual forms applied to us since birth and enforced by women and men alike.

In *Expecting Amy*, Schumer expresses how she hates every woman who has lied about what pregnancy is like. "Women don't tell you how hard it is," she says in the *Growing* special. It's something that women are encouraged to do – lie about their experience. It could be to make others more comfortable, or it could be to fulfill some ideal concept of femininity that they feel obligated to fulfill. Schumer, on the other hand, lifts up her dress to reveal her baby bump and the fact that she had to wear two bandages to hold her navel together, and then she announces, "I throw up an exorcist amount every day."

Simone De Beauvoir (1908–1986) is known for her existentialist philosophy, feminism, and literary works. *The Second Sex* is a foundational work of feminist philosophy, applying the existentialist perspective to the problem of gender. The philosophical question in the introduction to *The Second Sex* is genealogical – where have such concepts as "woman" come from, and what are they *for*? Beauvoir takes as assumed the existentialist interpretation of the elimination of absolutes. That is to say, she assumes from the start that there's no absolute definition of what it means to be "woman" or anything else, besides what we humans have created for ourselves. (The first step to feminism is to recognize that "woman" isn't defined by science or religion or psychology, or anything else that's not up to humans, and then to wonder how the definition we choose came about and why we would choose such the particular definition we did.) She says that, "One is not born, but rather becomes, woman" (Beauvoir 2009, p. 283).

One becomes a woman by taking part in the tropes of femininity. Beauvoir writes that, "it is civilization as a whole that elaborates this intermediary product between the male and the eunuch that is called feminine" (Beauvoir 2009, p. 283). But not only has society defined what those tropes are, but they usually change from generation to generation. What's more, "woman" is defined negatively to man – a woman is what a man is not; she is a "not-man" – and the differences are what's important. The point is to take women and to properly differentiate them from humanity, to impose upon women a definition and set of expectations that is meant to exclude us from partaking in humanity itself. It is to dehumanize women. Beauvoir writes,

> No group ever defines itself as One without immediately setting up the Other opposite itself. It only takes three travelers brought together by chance in the same train compartment for the rest of the travelers to become vaguely hostile "others." Village people view anyone not

belonging to the village as suspicious "others." ... For the native of a country inhabitants of other countries are viewed as "foreigners"; Jews are the "others" for anti-Semites, blacks for racist Americans, indigenous people for colonists, proletarians for the propertied classes. (Beauvoir 2009, p. 6)

The consequences are as vast as they are devastating, as is made evident in the terrifying statistics about domestic abuse and spousal homicide rates (Durose et al. 2005). Amy Schumer reports her own story of abuse in *The Girl with the Lower Back Tattoo*, in the chapter called, "The Worst Night of my Life". She writes,

> In the United States, women ages sixteen to twenty-four are three times more likely to be domestic violence victims than women of any other age. Also, every year in the United States, five hundred women in this age bracket are killed by their domestic abuser. A domestic abuser doesn't just have to be someone you live with. It means anyone you are in an intimate relationship with. I was a statistic. (Schumer 2016)

Because if women aren't human, we don't have rights, and if women don't have rights, it's acceptable to hurt and kill us. And it is precisely the idea that women aren't human that allows for such breaches of what our rights should be – from our right to exist (without being raped and murdered) to our right to have our voices heard and respected alongside the rest of the humans with whom we're supposed to exist in civil society.

In Simone de Beauvoir's work, the dehumanizing tendency of social definitions isn't limited to housewives, or women. She points to the Black and Jewish experiences as additional examples. Today, we call people "racialized" precisely because these definitions were imposed by *other people*, other people with an agenda. Someone is "racialized" for a purpose – and the purpose is differentiation. To differentiate any individual from the "real" humans is to instill a variant concept of what their being is, which is intended to justify granting that person an alternative set of rights and privileges. What all oppressed groups have in common is that, at some point, someone decided they shouldn't have the same rights and privileges as others – that the oppression is somehow justified because of the difference between *these humans over here* and *those ones over there*.

Amy Schumer's work touches on the dehumanization of women at all levels. She says, in part three of *Expecting Amy* that "Any woman that talks too long, people get upset," pointing to a fundamental difference in how the stated opinions of one sex tend to be less valued than another. In a more blatant example illustrating the disparity, a sketch called "New Twitter Button" from *Inside Amy Schumer* proposes an "I'm Going to Rape and Kill You" button for men who are tired of having to type out the whole threat when a woman appears to be saying things online. It's funny. It would be less funny if men didn't feel entitled to rape and kill women. According to the sketch, over 120% of comments directed toward women are threats to rape and kill them. If that weren't a slight exaggeration of the truth, the joke wouldn't work. The point is, there's a difference in the way women can expect to be treated on Twitter, by virtue of the fact that they have been defined as "woman." The result is a harmful set of circumstances.

And it's been this way for as long as philosophy has existed. The original differentiation of woman from the rest of humanity rests upon being able to differentiate "woman" from the definition of "human," and that approach was articulated by Aristotle 2400 odd years ago, with his idea of what a human is: a "rational animal." There are two parts to the definition, one "genus" and one "differentia," the idea being that anything can be described according to what kind of thing it is, and what differentiates it from other things of the same genus. Humans are animals, and what differentiates humans from the rest of the animals is that we are rational. *But if women are irrational, that means they are not human*, some people have concluded. And so, we end up with the stereotype of women as irrational, as creatures who are governed by their emotions, somehow less than human, and worthy of being treated as such.

Amy Schumer's sketch "Madame President" from *Inside Amy Schumer* calls out the stereotype of the emotional, irrational woman. In the sketch, she becomes president and can't govern that day because she has her period. She can't be rational, because she's overcome with emotion, crying all over the place and incapable of making any reasoned decisions. We watch this sketch and think of how stupid the situation is. The situation is absurd, and yet it's what a lot of people think would actually happen were a woman ever to inhabit the white house. Schumer plays it up, for sure, but she's playing off of a premise that people do actually believe – that women can't govern society because we'd be overwhelmed by emotion rather than reason. It's a stupid concept of women stretching all the way back to when Aristotle declared that the woman's soul is out of order – that the rational part does not successfully govern the other parts (that woman is a slave to something other than reason).

Before Aristotle, Plato conceived of the soul as having three parts (reason, spirit, appetite), and the virtuous soul kept those three parts in harmony by placing reason in charge of spirit and appetite. Consequently, by questioning the rationality of women, Aristotle not only puts them in prime placement for dehumanization, but also suggests that they are a less moral kind of being. And we see this sentiment echoed today, all the god damned time: This idea that women are meaner, more deceptive, and are so by nature. It all comes from this ancient idea that our souls are out of order. And, again, the effects are devastating; because if someone's soul is out of order, their worth not merely as a human but as a *moral being* is called into question.

This plays out in a couple of ways. If woman is incapable of being a moral being, then she is less responsible for her actions. The modern equivalent of one's soul being out of order is to ascribe mental disorders where none exist. A woman is not responsible for her actions because she is *crazy*, because she's less than human; consequently, she's also not worthy of being treated morally by others. And all this because of a stupid comment from an old Greek guy – a Greek guy whose work everyone is ready to reject as "discredited" when he claims that eels come from rain water, but not when his concepts give us an excuse to hurt someone. Schumer jokes in *Growing* about how she hopes that her baby turns out to be a girl, because, "it's a scary time for men," referring to the idea that some men are now afraid of being accused of abuse – and that it's ironic to be concerned about that, given that women seem to have more to be afraid of (what with all the abuse that's come to light).

The point is, with Beauvoir's concept of the feminine mystique, the feminine is essentially "other." It goes far beyond the fact that we can't conceive of how Betty has made this splendid ham for dinner and the secret for her glaze. It's worse than the fact that Betty claims she just threw it together at the last minute, even though she's been studying up on ham glazes for weeks and then executing the dish all damn day when no one is looking (or cares to look). It's the forced imposition of mystery that allows society as a whole to conceive of woman as something *other than human*, something worthy of less: a not-man.

Amy Schumer Will Save Us

In the language of social justice, "othering" has become a common verb. When you "other" someone, you make them something different, something incomprehensible, and ultimately, something less than. We "other" someone when they do something we don't understand, and instead of trying to understand, we declare their motives incomprehensible and move on. This allows us to attribute all sorts of ulterior motives to that person. For instance, a woman coming forward with a claim of sexual assault is often met with resistance.

Schumer relates her grape (the term she uses for "grey area rape", although the story comes off as pretty damn rapey to me) in her book, *The Girl with the Lower Back Tattoo*. The objections are predictable – they're the same ones applied by *at least someone* to every single woman who has ever made a claim that a man has done something bad. "She misunderstood"; or "she didn't make her intentions clear"; or "she's lying"; or even, "she's lying for attention." This process of othering attributes motives to the woman that aren't even comprehensible (if we were to assume that she is, in fact, a human with comprehensible motives). *Nobody wants to be known as "rape girl."* And yet, through the process of othering – the process according to which we might assume some mysterious and incomprehensible motive that we don't *need* to understand – judgments are made, and people suffer. Somehow or other, Christine Blasey Ford comes forward with a credible witness account of an incident, and instead of being taken seriously, some people are able to conceptually twist themselves into sincerely believing that she's only doing it because *she wants to be known for a sexual assault*. Critics might argue that she had a comprehensible motive – to keep Bret off the supreme court. Then the question becomes, yes, but *why would she want to do that?* Perhaps she decided to finally come forward because her humiliation seemed a lesser cost than what she foresees coming if the country puts a sex offender on the supreme court. And that's what we might assume if we considered her a rational being with comprehensible motives. (Schumer was arrested protesting Kavanaugh's confirmation on October 4, 2018.)

If we were to reflect even for a moment on the fact that the only "reward" for coming forward with a claim of sexual assault is more rape and death threats, we might then conclude that no rational person would do it just for kicks. And there's the kicker – we have to assume that the woman is rational, that she is a human with comprehensible motives, and that's where people seem to have trouble. Because she has been othered – made incomprehensible. She's been granted a form of feminine mystique (to her detriment).

This is why honesty is such a troublesome concept. There are social benefits to be gained by maintaining the feminine mystique. If women are too honest, going around having things to say (about literally anything besides floor waxers) and saying them, there is a form of social punishment that occurs. The patriarchal system that maintains that women can't be trusted because of their inherent dishonesty also encourages and enforces a certain amount of dishonesty. Schumer gives an example in *Growing* about getting her period and the immediate enforcement of a social norm to *hide it at all costs*, which she claims mothers pass to their daughters. She mimics her mother, saying, "You're a woman now! ... And that's disgusting." There are certain things women can't be honest about, like the intricacies of women's bodies, women's sexuality, and of course, the fact that women can't be honest about them. It's forbidden to point to the social expectations that are foisted upon women against our will. (You might come off as – god forbid – feminist.)

But Amy Schumer talks about all these things. Indeed, as her career progresses, she talks about them more and more. If you just watch *Mostly Sex Stuff*, it's easy to dismiss her feminist claims as cute and funny – that which is generally within the allowable guidelines of the patriarchy. For instance, she claims that it's not any harder to be a female comedian than it is to be a male comedian. We understand the logic. The job is the same job, no matter who's doing it. Then she says, "It's harder to be a woman in general," pointing to what now has become a pretty obvious truth. But then she rolls it back, pointing to such difficulties as getting ready to go out – the old trope where men don't put any special efforts into "getting ready," whereas women do (their hair, their makeup, their everything). The fact that Schumer flourished under the patriarchy and then turned against it is one of the reasons so many online trolls have taken to dedicating their lives to giving her one-star reviews wherever the chance allows. She made a joke in *Mostly Sex Stuff* that the hardest part of being a female comedian was "the rape." And then it wasn't a joke anymore.

Schumer's honest realizations serve to eliminate the feminine mystique and the othering of women. And ultimately, the desired effect should be the re-humanization of women. What the feminine mystique aims to hide, precisely, is women's human frailty.

Now to bring these concepts all together, we first have to distinguish between two concepts, both of which we attach to the overarching term "human." One is the rational animal that Aristotle defined, the idea of humanity as something that distinguishes us from the rest of the animals and which grants us a superior moral and intellectual status. This human is a being capable of both rational and moral thinking, and they are afforded all of the attendant rights and privileges in accordance with that capability. This is the definition of humanity from which certain groups of people have been historically excluded. It's the definition of humanity where, if someone doesn't fit that definition, they *don't* get all the same rights and privileges as everyone else. If someone calls a group of individuals "animals," in general it's an attempt to have those people reconceived as not worthy of the consideration we normally afford to full-fledged humans. Take, for instance, when we say that, "All humans are worthy of safe and sanitary conditions," and then someone else says, "But these aren't humans." They say this despite the fact that the people they are discussing meet all of the biological conditions for being defined as human. It's a statement expressly aimed at stripping some people of their human rights.

To combat this dehumanization, women must demonstrate a supreme rationality and moral integrity, to ensure that all involved don't accidentally mistake us for something less than human, where "human" in this sense means a "moral and rational being." Women are held to a higher moral standard, as evidenced by male public figures committing atrocious acts and meeting a societal response akin to "boys will be boys." If a woman were to be uncovered in a similar situation, she would forever be labeled with a scarlet letter in the public discourse.

But equally, or perhaps even more so, when we use the term "human," we're using it to refer to human frailty. "I'm only human" sets our species up against something even better, more perfect (more rational, more moral, etc.). This sense of "human" generally derives from religious sentiments, where the thing against which we're being compared is a deity. Thus to be "only human" is another sense of the term "human" which is connected to (but not the same as) the "rational and moral animal worthy of our consideration" sense of the word defined above.

Depending on how one conceives of an individual, the same action might be taken as evidence of their humanity or their lack of humanity. The moral reprobate, considered charitably, is "only human," whereas another individual who's committed a moral faux pas does so because of their beastly nature. In a super weird way, we've come to a point where to be "only human" is a luxury granted only to some – those who are already assumed to have attained full human status. And this is all a complicated way of saying that, with the growing assumption that women are human (rational and moral actors worthy of consideration), we get to see more complex female characters – flawed, fucked up, hot mess female characters who *get to be that way* – because no one is going to take that behavior as evidence that they're not full humans. So in short, to be a trainwreck, one first has to be conceived of as a human being capable of deliberation and decision.

The way this plays out, being unapologetically flawed is a revolutionary act; it is a demand for recognition and a rehumanization of the mysterious woman (whose motives used to be, I don't know, penis envy and witchcraft). The flawed woman is human in the sense of "relatable," and relatability eliminates mystique. So does machine gun shitting in France while on vacation with your boyfriend, which Schumer jokes about in *The Leather Special*. She assumes, of course, that the relationship is over, for she has demonstrated a human frailty which the patriarchy has deemed unacceptable *for women*. Her honesty defies a social expectation, which is what makes it funny, and at the same time points to a disparity between the sexes, which the joke itself serves to correct.

In the next few sections, I'll outline some of the ways in which Schumer's demand for radical honesty serves to eliminate the feminine mystique. As I've argued, the elimination of the feminine mystique is a key factor in allaying the tendency to *other* women as incomprehensible beings whose ways of existence can't possibly be conceived of or understood. And by reducing the othering of women – given that what we're being othered from is humanity itself – Schumer's comedy actually works toward the purpose of rehumanizing women. In particular, I'll discuss how she works to eliminate the feminine mystique around women's bodies, women's experience in society, and women's experience as sexual beings.

Honesty About Physical Existence

Amy Schumer is a human.

I have an ongoing joke with my cat that when her little torso starts contracting and expanding in such a way that you just know she's about to expel her expensive wet food dinner all over the carpeted section of the floor, that she should, "Choke it back, like a lady." Of course, whether she does or doesn't is up to chance and circumstance. But the point is, if she were ladylike – that is, were she to conform to the externally imposed standards expected of her cat gender, which is female – she would choke it back. Ladies don't vomit.

Amy Schumer doesn't choke it back like a lady. In the promo for her special, *Growing*, she makes a joke of an affliction plaguing some pregnant women (hyperemesis). She talks about her upcoming Netflix special while vomiting like a champ. In *Expecting Amy*, we get some of the possible scientific explanations for this disorder espoused through history. Maybe the mother doesn't want the baby, and that's what's causing the excessive vomiting. Maybe it could be cured – with the appropriate punishment for her obvious *moral* failing. Maybe if she sat in the vomit long enough, she'd become an ideal mother.

Maybe if women were thought of as not inherently evil but rather as persons, we wouldn't be subject to such stupid theories. Medical disorders would be interpreted as medical disorders (as opposed to moral disorders). Women would get treatment instead of mistreatment. Life in general would improve.

But only if we eliminate the feminine mystique.

Women are complicit in perpetuating the feminine mystique, because they're the ones who lied about what pregnancy is really like. Men are complicit, because they're the ones who expect the women to lie. The underlying assumption that women are deceptive *isn't all wrong*. It is merely wrong to think that women will lie because they're less than human inherently evil creatures unworthy of human treatment. The feminine mystique comes into play when we think that Schumer's promo is gross. Because we all know that women are *expected* to lie. Because otherwise, men will think it's gross. Women will think it's gross, because we're raised with the same conceptual apparatus as the men are. Women are gross and need to lie about the human parts if we want to be allowed to exist. The social enforcement of the rule is insidious. People say things like, "It's fine if you do it, I just don't want to see it." But the take home is that it's *not* fine if you do it, because nobody wants to see that.

It's a theme that for Schumer has become a refrain. Men aren't ashamed when their sex organs spew hot goo all over the damn place. You wouldn't find any of them apologizing. This is in direct contradiction to the expectations imposed upon women, which Schumer refuses to propagate. As she says in *The Leather Special*,

> On its best day my pussy smells like a small barnyard animal... That's fine. That's the nature of a pussy. ... Guys are not like that. They don't come in your mouth and ask if they taste O.K. ... I wish we were raised more like men.

Because it seems that there's a disparity between how women and men are raised, that lends itself to the general conclusion that women's bodily functions are gross and men's bodies are fine. And we have to ask ourselves what the point of that is. What's the point of convincing all women that their physical form and all of its activities are disgusting and must be hidden, altered, mutated, or at least a source of constant shame? It's a method for oppressing one gender while at the same time making it impossible to escape that oppression. It's literally impossible to escape one's physical form, and so if that's what's given as the reason for one's oppression, it seems that the oppression is also inescapable. You deserve to be treated badly, because you're ugly, says the patriarchy to *all women*. In *I Feel Pretty*, Amy Schumer does a scene with an actual model whose internalization of patriarchal standards has led her to believe that despite all of the objective evidence to the contrary, she is in fact ugly and also probably fat. The fact that she is also idolized as being one among those whose physicality sets the unattainable beauty standard we know to be perpetrated through advertising and women's magazines has no bearing on her internalized self-evaluation. Because it doesn't matter if you're Rosario Dawson, there's still going to be some dude in a trucker hat out there thinking that his opinion – "meh, she's OK I guess" – matters more than it should. It sounds absurd – but recognizing its absurdity is step one to eliminating this harmful attitude.

Absurdity is one of the methods Schumer uses to point to these social standards. Absurdity is both funny and gut wrenching, because it's true and *it's true*. Like in the sketch "Last Fuckable Day," in which actresses Tina Fey, Patricia Arquette, and Julia Louis-Dreyfus are having lunch in the woods to celebrate Louis-Dreyfus' "last fuckable day," the joke is that there is a point in a woman's life at which, like a switch being turned from on to off, a woman turns from fuckable to unfuckable. From then on, she might play the mother, if anyone, but never the love interest, because she's become incurably unfuckable. It's not the same day for all women, but you know when it happens, and the women discuss how it varies from person to person. And it's absurd, not because it's so outside of the realm of the believable, but because it is so inside the realm of the believable. We recognize the phenomenon immediately; it's just not talked about (except in comedy sketches). No one has ever been bold enough to give it a name.

The point is, one of Amy Schumer's primary demands is that you recognize that she does exist in a human body – a human physical form that has been subject to so much distortion that by the time a woman is an adult, she's expected to be ashamed and to lie about the basic functions of her human body. The feminine mystique is maintained, because if we can't trust the first-person report of the person whose body this is, we can't possibly know what it does. The body becomes mysterious, unknown, unknowable. And the mystery is harmful. There's still a bevy of terrible medical science that is only just now being corrected. All of a sudden, society realized that medical science as it applies to women has been perverted by both men and women's tendencies not to talk about certain aspects of the female experience, because "*that's gross*," or because medical science has always assumed some kind of "default human" which is actually a white male human and therefore doesn't represent all the people who are in fact humans. (An example of how this skews medical knowledge was recently revealed by Malone Mukwende, the fellow who created a handbook for how to recognize skin disorders as they appear for people of color, contrary to what appears in the medical textbooks, which only teach medical students how to diagnose white patients.)

Schumer's "gross-out" comedy combats the dishonesty that pervades women's experience and corrupts the proper functioning of our scientific institutions just by honestly reporting on the female body's form and functions. What used to be "women things" come to be "people things," and we're all better off.

Honesty About Sexuality

"Aren't you the girl from television who talks about her pussy all the time?" says Julia Louis-Dreyfus in "Last Fuckable Day." Amy Schumer's sex comedy has evolved. In *Mostly Sex Stuff* from 2012 (which, you'll be shocked to hear, has some sexual content), she seems to be playing a character. That character is a little less intelligent than Schumer's more recent (and I'd say, more honest) incarnations. She's talking about sex, but she's still somewhat conforming to how women (scandalous women, at least) are allowed to talk about sex. She says she's not that slutty, because she's only been with four guys – and that was a fun night. She talks about how one of her friends changes when she gets into a relationship – but Amy remembers helping her get come out of her hair. She talks about using Plan B as Plan A. And it seems the idea is to break out of our normal concepts of how women should behave by presenting a character who fails to conform to the moral ideal for women – by having sex. The implication she's playing off of (the underlying concept that this character defies) is that women don't have sex or talk about sex – or at least, good women don't. By negating that expectation and then exaggerating to what extent she defies it, the character becomes funny – a caricature.

By the time she released *Live at the Apollo*, Schumer's sex comedy has definitely matured, and by matured, I mean it seems more honest. She's less of a character and more of a human, and by implication, has become more feminist in nature. She talks about how she can always catch a D in New York City (but not in Los Angeles), whereas the character from *Mostly Sex Stuff* was expectedly modest – obviously pretty but still ashamed of her looks in all of the expected ways. (She remarks on how her build is sturdier than some socially defined ideal woman's might be.) It plays into this narrative that the patriarchal system propagates: the idea that only the most attractive women will be accepted as possible love interests and sex objects. It's the underlying premise of women's magazines, the idea that everything about you could possibly be improved, and if it isn't, that's a fault, and wherever there's a fault, it's blameworthy.

Schumer also deals with this theme in the movie *I Feel Pretty*. In *I Feel Pretty*, Schumer's character has self-esteem issues, gets a bump on the head during a spin class, and wakes up with the evidently delusional belief that she's gorgeous. It affects every aspect of her life – her romantic relations, her career, the ways she interacts with the world in just about every situation. It's an illustration of how pervasive this one premise is (the premise that a woman's inclusion in society is and should be predicated on her looks). It's the premise that changes most obviously between Schumer's concept of how sexual relations work, from the early work to the later work.

In *Mostly Sex Stuff*, she can only catch a dick at closing time. In *Live at the Apollo*, and by the time of the *Leather Special*, she's reconceived the part she plays in sexual social relations entirely. She says she loves men because of just how low their standards really are. She says the average male "would fuck you if your head were a ballet slipper." The jokes about getting ready are no longer about the disparity between how long it takes for men and women. They're about how you come to realize that it doesn't fucking matter, because men could literally give zero fucks about what you look like, you still get to fuck. As she says in *The Leather Special*:

> I gained weight. I'm like, Oh my God. Are men gonna still be attracted to me? And that's when I remembered – I always forget this – it's another reason I love men so much. Men, each day, have a thought that goes through their head where they're like. . . "I don't know why, but I want to put my penis right in your butthole." A couple times a day, someone walks by. "Huh". You know, just. . . They're like, "Look it doesn't make sense to me either, but I know for a fact that I want to take the most sensitive, intimate part of myself and just, like ram it right where you poop. Just like, ram it." They're thinking that, and I'm over here like, "Oh, should I get highlights?" He doesn't care! He doesn't care.

And in that progression, she overturns the latent hatred that the patriarchy has towards women (which definitely has roots in a capitalist society hell bent on selling you products to cure your every flaw – see the work of Sandra Lee Bartky) and reveals something much more honest. While *the patriarchy* would have you believe that your hair is an inch too long to be fuckable, *men* actually don't care.

By *Live at the Apollo*, she's joking about a UTI. She reveals honest and accurate information through comedy. *"You know how I got it."* She comes off as human as she recounts how she was too lazy to get up and pee after sex and that's how you end up with a UTI. The way she's talking about sex is honest and human. She talks about how there's no dignity in taking a load. She drives the point home with an image of Michelle Obama carefully walking to the bathroom once a week with her knees together. She explicitly points to the social expectation that, "Men love sex, and women just deal with it." She mocks the way women are supposed to think about sex – "You know I hate your dick, laundry laundry." It's funny, because it's true, and *it's true*. But such expectations are propagated only if the feminine mystique remains intact. She says honestly, "You're made to feel really disgusting and weird if you're a girl and you like to have sex."

She pleads with the men in the audience to make women come during sex. Because there is an orgasm disparity in contemporary society. She points out how absurd it is to think that the woman is there "to witness your process." She says, "It's crazy that we get guilted about this. Women want to come." And it seems that for a while, there are no jokes, because she's just saying things that are true. The funny part is that people walk around really believing that the women in their lives hate sex and orgasms. But by pointing it out, and by making the implication that maybe women are human too and also enjoy the same kinds of human things as men do, she's working to destroy the feminine mystique that allows these assumptions to exist. At the same time, she's integrating women with the overall concept of "human" and hinting that maybe, you can assume what a woman is thinking based on an idea of what any reasonable human might think. Hint – it's not, "I hate your dick, laundry laundry."

So it is ironic that she might be labeled a sex comic when what she's doing is enacting a sex-positive feminism through comedy. She makes a joke about how she's labeled a sex comic, whereas a guy could pull his dick out on stage and people would say, "He's a thinker." But it's just because our vision of women doesn't allow for both concepts to exist at once – that a woman both thinks and fucks. It's a concept we've always had for men, but not for women, and it's alienating. But more on that later.

The longer Schumer talks about sex, the more honest she gets. Now it seems like she's just talking about sex not for a laugh, but out of a moral duty to spread accurate information. In *Amy Schumer Learns to Cook* (in which her husband, Chris Fischer, kind of attempts to teach her how to cook), she just out and recommends that you have sex with your partner once a week. It's not even a joke anymore that women have sex like men do. And it's all right to talk about it, too.

Honesty About Social Expectations

Calling out the differences between men's and women's experiences is one thing, but calling out the differences between how men's and women's experiences differ according to the confines of the limiting concepts of the patriarchy is another. When you point out the differences between gendered experiences, there's one kind of blowback. When you point out that the differences result in inequities, you get next level blowback.

Amy Schumer points to the disparities between the treatment of men and women in a number of ways. One of the most obvious is her use of gender swapping to illustrate those disparities. (Gerald Brown writes about this in the volume I edited with Rob Luzecky, *Amy Schumer and Philosophy: Brainwreck!*) For example, the second episode of *Inside Amy Schumer* includes a sketch where two female colleagues take their male friend out after a bad breakup to a restaurant called O'Nutters, which is Hooters but reversed. Balls protrude from the servers' uniforms, and the male friend is treated like a party pooper for not enjoying the so-called festive atmosphere. By the end of the sketch, though, he learns through social indoctrination that he must enjoy the objectification of men the sketch portrays – or else.

The same phenomenon is under critique in the sketch, "Cool with It," except in this scenario, it's the female character who's expected to go along with the men she works with – in attitude and in behavior. She goes to the strip club and takes conformity to the extreme by being "cool with it" beyond any reasonable measure – trying to make a show of how "cool with it" she is by getting creepily *into* it. This is an example of how, in another way, Schumer's work points to the absurdity of the expectations we place upon women by exaggerating them. In another *Inside Amy Schumer* sketch, agents Crossbolt and Butterface must engage in a mission where the male agent's tasks are those typical of agents (use the gadgets, fight the bad guys), whereas Butterface's task is to distract the perpetrator with a blowjob, under the watchful eye of the entire organization, including her own father. She's provided a scrunchie for equipment.

In another sketch, she outlines how the expectations placed upon women are explicitly contradictory, and thus brings to light their absurdity. In "Madonna vs. Whore," we see a confused Schumer trying to fit the contradictory expectations of a casual hookup who expects her to be sexy but not sexy, experienced but inexperienced, etc. The point is that the social expectations placed on women are contradictory for a reason. There's no way to meet them. The law of non-contradiction that philosophy has recognized since Aristotle (with obviously some disagreement, because philosophers) is that you can't be both something and its opposite in the same way and at the same time. The contradictory expectations placed upon women are there in order to guarantee that *no one* ever meets them. And the idea is that you should feel bad about not being able to meet an impossible standard. And Amy Schumer doesn't.

Sometimes it's like she's revealing secrets that everyone already knows. In *Live at the Apollo*, she reveals the secret of how everyone in Hollywood stays thin. She's been tapped to play the lead role in *Trainwreck*, and whoever's in charge of making sure leads are thin asks her to drop a bunch of weight, and Schumer reveals that, "Hollywood's secret is that they don't put food in their faces." It's not so much a reveal as it is a recognition. You're not supposed to think about the suffering people go through to meet your expectations. If no one talks about it, we can pretend that everything is as it is according to its nature – that the Hollywood elite are effortlessly whatever they are, and that they aren't in fact in anguish, trying to meet an expectation imposed upon them, by us, because of a preference instilled in us by the same system into which we're born and which we propagate without thinking about it.

This is the nefarious feminine mystique acting on a second level. Not only is Schumer expected to lose thirty pounds to star as what seems to be a character (at least somewhat) based on herself, in order to become an attractive enough woman to gain the attention of Bill Hader, she's also not supposed to talk about how that happened. It's an act of defiance to go on stage and reveal that she's a human who puts food in her face, when it flies in the face of an expectation we all know is there but don't acknowledge – that we expect certain people not to put food in their face. The social expectation that we not reveal the methods according to which we meet another social expectation lends an inception-like intricacy to the feminine mystique which, nevertheless, becomes obvious the second it's pointed out.

It's not a *secret* so much as it is just not talked about. A secret isn't told for any number of reasons, usually because of some negative effect that might befall the holder of the secret. But this is a secret because of an implicit social premise that we don't make other people uncomfortable with our sufferings. Schumer and all other Hollywood-ites are supposed not to reveal their methods for keeping their figures, because it would be rude to come out and say, "I'm starving myself because you won't watch a movie with an extra ten pounds in it." That's not a secret so much as it is another form of oppression aimed at maintaining the feminine mystique. But we should be asking, who's the asshole in this situation? The person calling out society in general for having an unreasonable expectation, or society for imposing the unreasonable expectation and then asking, in addition, that we not talk about the expectation, so that we don't all feel bad about the starving people in *Hollywood*? It sounds absurd when you say it that way.

Consequences

Thinking for a moment in the most general sense – we all have a set of concepts which we use to interpret the world as it is. Sometimes it's accurate to think of them as shortcuts. When there are too many individuals in the world to conceive of as individuals, we take shortcuts by ascribing labels to them, labels which refer to general concepts or the type of thing someone is. And "woman" is one of those concepts.

When we encounter something that doesn't fit our concept of what it is, there are two options: we either declare it not to be something of that type, or we have to alter our concept to accommodate the new thing we want to interpret according to that concept. Basically, when Amy Schumer defies our concept of what a woman is or should be, and that concept comes under question, we have two options, both of which I think actually happen. We have to look at Schumer and say, "That's not a woman," something which people would probably say under the guise of something less obviously incorrect, like, "That's not a proper lady." Thus their inaccurate definition of "woman" remains intact, and Schumer is explained away. (Done and done!) Or – and this is the better option – we reconceive of what a woman is or should be, in order to accommodate Schumer's honest representation of it. Because we value accuracy more than we value retaining some outmoded values that, in the end, hurt all women.

We can integrate disparities and create more complex concepts that are both more accurate and healthier. It just means having to do away with some old, malformed concepts that you probably don't even know you're walking around with. One of them is that women can't exist as sexual beings and also as humans with opinions. It turns out, you can be both. It turns out, you have been all along.

I've seen instances of people insisting that comedy stay away from political statements. But that's easier said than done. Existing and behaving in a way that doesn't fit with a political concept of woman is one way of being political. Explicitly expressing opinions on policy is another. One of the prejudices we're working with is that Amy Schumer is a sex comic who shouldn't have opinions. But that goes against all of our experiences of what a human is – the weird thing is that people can have opinions *and* fuck. What's weird about it is that it's not weird at all. As Schumer says, in *The Leather Special*, "What's crazy is that you can catch a hot load all over your titties and still not want your loved ones to get shot in a theatre." The statement is a reference to the 2015 Lafayette shooting. During a screening of her film *Trainwreck*, a mentally ill man whose anti-semitic, racist, and misogynistic views were well-documented, shot eleven people, killing Jillian Johnson and Mayci Breaux. Lorena O'Neil in *The Hollywood Reporter* questioned whether the shooter targeted Schumer's film because of his anti-semitism or his anti-feminism. According to the host of a talk show on which the shooter appeared, the shooter, "was opposed to women having a say in anything."

The fact that there are people running around with these notions is a problem. Are they working with an inaccurate concept of what a woman is or should be? Does that concept include the idea that maybe women are for fucking and shouldn't have opinions? Chances are, yes. So yeah, Amy Schumer is doing something for the general concept of woman just by existing contrary to that notion.

And sometimes just existing is hard. Schumer isn't just existing but *shamelessly* existing, in the face of all who would have her submit to the concepts we thrust upon women from birth to death, concepts which you really have to *shake off* and which come at you in all sorts of nefarious forms through most moments of every day. They are concepts which, if you conform to them, will get you some smiles and an invitation to tea – concepts which, if you don't conform to them, you'll be trolled on Twitter and threatened with rape and death on the daily. And that, I think, is fucking brave.

Conclusion

Amy Schumer's representation of women's experience works toward the elimination of the feminine mystique, which is the harmful idea that women are mysterious creatures whose existence and experience are, by their nature, inexplicable. Her honest portrayals of women's embodiment, sexuality, and oppressive patriarchal social structures enhance our understanding of women as rational and moral beings – i.e., humans. By presenting women's experience and not sparing us the details, Schumer's work encourages a more complex understanding of "woman" – a better and more accurate understanding, which should have positive social and political implications.

References

Bartky, Sandra Lee. 1990. *Femininity and domination: Studies in the phenomenology of Oppression*. New York: Routledge.
De Beauvoir, Simone. 2009. *The second sex*. Trans. Constance Borde and Sheila Malovany-Chevallier. New York: Random House. p. 6.
Durose, Matthew R., Caroline Wolf Harlow, Ph.D., Patrick A. Langan, Ph.D., Mark A. Motivans, Ph.D., Ramona R. Rantala, and Erica L. Smith. 2005. Family violence statistics: Including statistics on strangers and acquaintances. *Bureau of Justice Statistics* June 12. NCJ 207846. https://www.bjs.gov/content/pub/pdf/fvs02.pdf
Friedan, Betty. 2001. *The feminine Mystique*. New York: W.W. Norton.
Schumer, Amy. 2016. *The girl with the lower back tattoo*. New York: Simon & Schuster.

George Carlin as Philosopher: It's All Bullshit. Is It Bad for Ya?

64

Kimberly S. Engels

Contents

Introduction	1512
Part I: Summary	1513
Part II: The Value of Truth Over Ignorance	1517
Plato's Allegory of the Cave	1517
Part III: It's Bad for Ya	1519
Nozick and the Experience Machine	1526
The Ethics of Illusions	1528
Conclusion	1530
References	1531

Abstract

This chapter explores the comedy of George Carlin (1937–2008) as a powerful statement about the value of truth over ignorance. Carlin challenged his audience to confront the truth, regularly using clever rhetorical strategies to force viewers to grapple with inconvenient realities about the world in which they lived. This chapter examines historical and contemporary philosophical arguments for the importance of the pursuing truth over comforting fictions. I begin with Plato's Allegory of the Cave, which argues it is preferable to know reality as it truly is over appearances of the truth, even when it's painful or difficult. I then discuss Nozick's argument that humans would not want to plug into a pleasurable experience machine. Last, I examine contemporary arguments that there are distinctly moral reasons for pursuing the truth. I show how there are examples of all three arguments in Carlin's comedic work, and suggest we can consider Carlin's work a critical commentary that reveals multiple reasons for valuing truth over enticing fictions.

K. S. Engels (✉)
Molloy University, Rockville Centre, NY, USA
e-mail: kengels@molloy.edu

© Springer Nature Switzerland AG 2024
D. K. Johnson et al. (eds.), *The Palgrave Handbook of Popular Culture as Philosophy*,
https://doi.org/10.1007/978-3-031-24685-2_38

Keywords

Carlin · Plato · Nozick · Truth illusion

Introduction

George Carlin (1937–2008) entertained audiences for decades with his vulgar, unapologetic, in-your-face brand of humor. Over the years, Carlin appeared more and more as a grumpy old man, presenting monologues that were essentially long lists of things that pissed him off. Sometimes he tackled the absurdity of the mundane, dirty words you can't say on TV, and the silliness of phrases used when riding on an airplane. At his best, he provided scathing social commentary that forced his audience to confront uncomfortable truths about the world in which they lived. Over the years he repeatedly forced his audience to reflect on the hypocrisies, paradoxes, and absurdity of the United States' social, moral, and political landscape. With a sharp tongue that pulled no punches, Carlin got his audience to laugh while forcing them to confront the contradictions and injustices of the world around them.

A consistent theme throughout Carlin's comedic work is the tension between appearances and reality. He prompted his audience to examine commonly held religious, political, and cultural beliefs, and then exposed the uncertain foundations upon which they rested. Whether it's preferable to live in a world of appearances and illusions (instead of the world as it actually is) is a question that always interested philosophers. From Plato's Allegory of the Cave and Robert Nozick's Experience Machine, to more contemporary work on the ethics of belief, philosophers have explored the tension between the way things appear and the way things are and questioned the value of acknowledging uncomfortable truths over comforting fictions. While philosophers have, for the most part, come down firmly on the side of truth over ignorance, the question of what, if anything makes truth preferable to fiction remains unsettled.

Throughout his decades of complaints and grievances, Carlin examined commonly held beliefs such as the immortality of the soul, the American Dream, the existence of rights, the value of voting, the function of the police, and child worship, and forces his audience to submit them to scrutiny. This often revealed an uncomfortable truth about them, either by appealing to clear counterexamples or revealing absurd conclusions by fleshing out the logical implications of the views. Carlin called out the colonialism, imperialism, and blatant hypocrisy in the actions of the leaders of the United States, both past and present, as well as illuminated the corporate control of almost every detail of modern life, from politicians to media, to our cultural values. He challenged common assumptions regarding moral values Americans hold dear such as "rights," and mocked Americans' paradoxical desire for a "balanced budget" amidst an entire culture dedicated to spending money they don't have on things they don't need. His audience was forced, at least temporarily, to sit in the reality behind their deeply valued illusions.

In this chapter, I will explore some of the common ways philosophers have dealt with the tension between appearances and reality, and the value of pursuing knowledge over comforting fictions. I will explore the question of what, precisely, makes truth more valuable than illusion or fiction and whether it is ever preferable to believe in a comforting fiction over the truth. I will then show how Carlin's comedy sketches elucidated this tension by forcing his audience to confront the full scope of the illusions and hypocrisies of modern life, and whether confronting these illusions head-on is preferable to living in illusions we collectively tell ourselves.

Part I: Summary

Carlin's early comedy sketches focused on pointing out the irony and paradoxes of the mundane, as well as questioning everyday social norms and language. In his early stand-up specials, he comically emphasized what he described as little things we all experience but no one talks about: going to shake hands with someone and they don't notice, going up or down the stairs and thinking there's one more stair than there is, almost putting your groceries in the wrong cart, your dog licking its genitals in front of company ("On Location," 1977). Carlin was able to create a sense of shared experience and community with his audience, as everyone realized that yes, they had these experiences, and there is both humor and comfort in poking fun at things we all do.

But even in his earliest stand-up specials, he coupled his observations of the absurdity of the mundane with social commentary that emphasized the paradoxes of our social conventions, including our use of language. One of the most famous bits from his early career focused on "dirty" words you weren't allowed to say on TV. Carlin questioned why there were words that you could only say sometimes, and never say on TV. He pointed out that children don't know what the banned words are and often find out only by being hit when they say a dirty word. Some words, like "ass" you could use when referring to a donkey, but not to your anatomy. Other, more "vulgar" words were off the table all the time. Carlin prompted his audience to ask why, suggesting there is nothing inherently good or bad about a word, it is only the context that makes it good or bad. He also pointed out the irony that you could not say "fuck" or "fart" on TV, but you could refer to fucking (love scenes, romantic plots) but couldn't even *refer* to farts on TV. Why do we construct a TV world in which no one experiences a daily, normal bodily function? ("On Location," 1977).

Throughout his 40-year career, his stand-up routines continued to consist primarily of these two elements: everyday observations and social commentary. However, over time, his social commentary grew more explicit, more complex, and into more of a center point of his routines. Carlin no longer limited himself to commenting on the language we used; he drew attention to the paradoxes and hypocrisies of our entire cultural landscape. He criticized religion, which he called "the greatest bullshit story ever told," and offered political commentary, with several bits on the corporate control of our politicians, corporate-sponsored America, and how it is corporations (not "the people") who control our political landscape and govern modern life.

He criticized our criminal justice system, our cultural love for violence, the illusion of the American Dream, and our often inconsistent consumerist beliefs.

To highlight the nature of the paradoxes while getting his audience to laugh, Carlin employed at least four rhetorical strategies. First, he would point out obvious counterexamples to a societal belief or value. Second, he would employ the exercise of assuming a premise as true and then drawing out the absurd conclusions, a strategy that originates in the Socratic method. Third, he would conjure up a seemingly absurd scenario, and once he got his audience laughing, point out the scenario is really not that different from what is going on right now. And last, he would often point out how the language we use is deceptive, contrived to sugar-coat things that should be bitter.

As an example of his first method, in which he appeals to obvious counterexamples of commonly held beliefs, in his final HBO special titled "It's Bad for Ya" he delivered a scathing monologue on the American obsession with rights. "Boy, everyone in this country is always running around yammering about their fucking rights. I have a right, you have no right, we have a right, they don't have a right. . .. Rights are an idea, they're just imaginary, they are a cute idea, cute. . . but that's all, cute, and fictional" ("It's Bad for Ya," 2008). Carlin continued with a thought experiment, asking: if rights are real, where do they come from, and if they come from God, what does that mean? "The Bill of Rights of this country has ten stipulations...And apparently God was doing sloppy work that week, because we've had to amend the bill of rights an additional seventeen times. So God forgot a couple of things, like...SLAVERY."

Moving beyond where rights originate if they are real, Carlin prompted his audience to think about Japanese American citizens being put into internment camps during World War II. They were denied any right to an attorney, no right to due process at all, the only right they had was "Right this way!" Just when these American citizens needed their rights the most, they were taken away. And, Carlin says, rights aren't rights if someone can take them away. He concludes that all we have ever had in the United States is a bill of temporary privileges, and the list of privileges we have gets smaller every year. US citizens tend to believe that rights protect them. Carlin is pointing out that often they do not. While Carlin seemed to confuse legal and civil rights, and human and natural rights (which are supposed to exist independent of whether they are protected by social institutions), Carlin forced his audience to confront whether the legal rights they often assert actually protect them the way we often believe they do.

As a second example of this first method, consider how Carlin examined the belief in the "sanctity of life" that is commonly cited by anti-abortion activists in his 1996 HBO special "Back in Town." While the supposed sanctity of life is often appealed to as a value that would morally prohibit abortion, Carlin pointed out the many counterexamples to the idea that we hold life as sacred. He pointed out that the state is interested in the life of babies so they can become dead soldiers. Does a society as committed to war as the United States truly believe life is sacred? Carlin pointed out the number of "crack babies" waiting to be adopted. Aren't their lives sacred? He pointed out that "life" is a continuous process, billions of years old. If we really want to be consistent, we shouldn't be burning coal because we need the carbon for life. What about all the fertilized eggs that don't become successful pregnancies? Aren't those lives sacred? Is any woman who's had more than one period a serial killer? He pointed out the broad support for capital punishment and the fact that millions of people have been killed in the name of religion. In short, "Sanctity of life? Bullshit." We constructed the concept because we're alive. We get to choose which life is sacred and which isn't because we, according to Carlin, "made the whole thing up" ("Back in Town," 1996).

The second method he used was to accept a premise for the sake of argument and then draw out the logical conclusions of accepting the view. In "It's Bad for Ya," he examined the religious belief expressed by some people that their dead parents "up there" help support them in their lives. Carlin, for the sake of argument, agreed to accept this idea as true and then elaborated on the implications of actually embracing it. What if your children are also dead? Do you go into retirement? What if you were adopted? Which set of parents helps you? What happens to dead people who don't have any living relatives to help? Do they help strangers?

In "You Are All Diseased," he referred to religion as the greatest bullshit story ever told and prompted the audience to consider the implications of common religious views. Religion has posited the idea that there is an invisible man who can see everything you do, and has a special list of 10 things you aren't supposed to do, and if you do those things, he sends you to a fiery world of torture and pain ... "But, he loves you." He pointed out that three out of four people in the United States believe in angels. Carlin asked, why draw the line at angels? Why not then also believe in goblins and zombies? Isn't there equal evidence for all of these mythical creatures? Carlin said he really tried to believe in God, but the more he looked at the world, the more he could see that it couldn't possibly be the result of divine planning. If God is real, he is "either incompetent or doesn't give a shit" ("You Are All Diseased," 1999). This is actually a formulation of the philosophical problem of evil, in which the following question is explored: why, if God is all-good and all-powerful, does evil exist? If God is all-powerful, he should be able to prevent evil, and if he is all good, he should want to. So either we are wrong about God, and he doesn't want (or is unable) to prevent evil from happening, or he doesn't exist.

A third method Carlin used was to prompt his audience to imagine an absurd, comedic scenario, and once his audience was laughing, suggest that the scenario was not all that different from things going on in society. This is essentially a philosophical thought experiment: prompting the listener to imagine a hypothetical world or situation that, while fictional, is designed to test our intuitions or assumptions. For example, in "Back in Town," Carlin asked why we don't profit off our country's support of capital punishment. Why not, year-round, broadcast capital punishment, and develop more and more creative means of executing people? Crucifixions, beheadings, shooting someone from a cannon against a brick wall. People could bet on the outcomes and the profits could help balance the budget. He gave another bit about fencing off four rectangular states, one for drug addicts, one for sex offenders, one for the seriously criminally insane, and one for violent offenders. Every 50 miles there would be a small door that is only 10 in wide and open for 7 s a month. Corporations could sponsor the different groups of people. People could watch it on TV or pay-per-view and the profits would lead to a balanced budget. The scenario is meant to be funny because it is so absurd, but Carlin reminded his audience it's not so unlike what things are like right now. "Everyone would have a gun, everyone would be on drugs, and no one would be in charge. Just like now! But at least we'd have a balanced budget" ("Back in Town," 1996). In a country with a serious criminal violence problem that has more guns than people, Carlin forced his audience to question whether this scenario is that absurd after all. The United States criminalizes more behavior and incarcerates more people than any other country in the world (Wagner and Sawyer 2018) and we have a culture that valorizes and profits off violence whenever possible. We also have a capitalist, corporate-controlled culture where people love to spend money they don't have, yet repeatedly express that they want a balanced federal budget. People also love to watch real live criminal shows like *Cops* and *To Catch a Predator*. Is the scenario Carlin presented to the audience, in which the undesirables are removed from society and (through corporate sponsors and customers who pay to see it) brutalize each other in order to balance the budget, really that much different from what we have now? Even if the practices seem different, aren't the underlying values the same? And what does this ultimately say about the worthiness of our cultural practices and values?

A fourth method he used was to point out our tendency to make things sound better than they are with the words we assign to them. He said this is a method we use when we have trouble facing the truth. For example, in "Doin it Again," Carlin discussed how World War II veterans (who were so traumatized by the horror of war that they couldn't function) were referred to as having "shellshock." This transitioned into "battle fatigue" which then became "operational exhaustion." This different way of labeling the condition made it seem less awful. "Sounds like something that happens to your car." Finally, we now refer to the condition as post-traumatic stress disorder or PTSD. Carlin pointed out the pain had been buried under jargon. We introduced a long, eight syllable word to mask reality. "Shell-shocked" sounds brutal because they were suffering from a brutal and horrific experience ("Doin it Again," 1990).

Carlin clearly liked his audience to reflect on the truth behind the masks. Using a blend of comedy and intellectual questioning, Carlin's monologues serve as a form of philosophy in which the audience is prompted to ponder whether their words and beliefs represent reality. This includes the consistency of cultural values, and metaphysical beliefs about the nature of our world. Carlin rarely appears to be calling his audience into any kind of action; often, to the contrary, he forces them to confront truths about which they can really do nothing about. The title of his final HBO special "It's Bad for Ya" is a reference to the line he repeated multiple times in the monologue. "It's all bullshit, and it's bad for ya." The bullshit he referred to are the long list of religious, political, and cultural lies we tell ourselves. Carlin also made a normative claim: this bullshit is bad for you. But why? Why is it bad for us to dwell in illusions instead of reality, especially if we cannot do anything to change it?

Carlin is not alone. Philosophers in particular, going all the way back to Socrates and Plato, have argued that pursuing and advocating for truth is better than believing in comforting fictions, even when confronting the truth doesn't result in any concrete action or change. In the next section, we will explore some classic and contemporary philosophical arguments in favor of pursuing and promoting truth rather than, as Carlin calls it, bullshit.

Part II: The Value of Truth Over Ignorance

Plato's Allegory of the Cave

The value that philosophers place in affirming the pursuit of truth over comforting fictions is found as early as ancient philosopher Plato (428–347 BCE). One of the most often discussed philosophical thought experiments ever is found in his *Republic*. In the dialogue, Socrates, who conveys Plato's views, prompts his interlocutor Glaucon to consider the possibility of people who have lived their entire lives shackled inside of a cave. These people are shackled so they can only see what is right in front of them; they cannot turn their heads. Behind them there is a fire and a half-wall upon which townspeople carry statues, carvings, and artifacts. The prisoners see the shadows of these artifacts on the cave wall in front of them like a puppet show. Because they have been shackled this way their entire lives, they believe that the shadows of objects they see in front of them are the objects themselves. If they heard a voice coming from a person of whom they could only see their shadow, they would assume the voice was coming from the shadow. When Glaucon tells Socrates that this is a highly unusual scenario he has constructed, Socrates replies that we are not so unlike the prisoners in the cave (just as Carlin reminds his audience, we are not so removed from a society of watching criminals kill each other on TV) (Plato 1985, 514–515, pp. 209–210).

If the prisoners were to be released from their shackles, their eyes would be so used to viewing the shadows that they would intuitively turn away from the fire and back at the familiar wall of shadows. The flickering lights would hurt the prisoner's eyes and make them unable to look directly at the objects. If the prisoner was forced to look directly in the fire, it would hurt their eyes so much that they would turn back to the shadows and see them even more clearly. If the prisoner was dragged completely out of the cave and up into the sun, they would feel pain and rage. They would not be able to see the world as it really was, because they were used to viewing the world of shadows. Eventually their eyes would adjust and they would be able to look at actual beings in the world. Eventually the prisoner would reach a state where they could look directly at the sun itself and try to contemplate what it is.

SOCRATES: It is at this stage that he would be able to conclude that the sun is the cause of the seasons and of the year's turning, that it governs all the visible world and is in some sense also the cause of all visible things. (Plato 1985, 516b-c, pp. 210–211)

Socrates then asks Glaucon to consider what the prisoner would want. Would the prisoner, at this point understanding the nature of the sun, envy the people in the cave? Would the prisoner prefer an existence in which they only saw shadows of what is, now that they had gone through the uncomfortable process of learning there was so much more to the world? Glaucon says the prisoner would not wish to become that type of human being. Socrates poses one last question: if the prisoner did return to the cave, his eyes would take time to adjust to be able to see the shadows again, and those still shackled would use him as proof that it is better to remain shackled in the cave, as one is never forced to adjust their eyes. The once freed prisoner, however, knows that those who remain shackled do not see the world as it truly is (Plato 1985, 516c-e, p. 211).

Plato ponders the realm of ideas, or forms: abstracting from the particular into the universal. Plato wants us to examine the meaning behind appearances – that the full truth about things is actually much more than their surface appearances. The world of appearances is one of change, imperfection, and deception. The realm of forms is permanent and perfect. While a beautiful white and blue bird with a sharp beak exists at the level of the physical world, the concepts of "beauty," "whiteness," "blueness," and "sharpness" exist in the realm of forms. Someone who truly knows the realm of forms understands how the concepts of beauty, whiteness, blueness, and sharpness can be abstracted from an individual instantiation and applied in other contexts (see for example 1985, Book VI). At the heart of Plato's conceptions of forms is the ability to abstract deeper universal meanings from our everyday interactions with the world of appearances. To give an example from Carlin, someone could experience his skit on the seven dirty words as funny because of its vulgarity and the way it bucked social norms at the time. At the deeper level, "Seven Dirty Words" is about revealing the inconsistencies in our understanding of language and approach to censorship.

Plato's Allegory of the Cave is used to illustrate how difficult it can be to realize that your reality is not its surface appearance, especially if this is all you have ever known. While almost no one today accepts Plato's conception of the forms, the allegory still demonstrates the value of knowledge over false belief. The prisoners chained in the cave do not know they see only shadows, thus they do not know what they are missing. The freed prisoner goes through a very difficult process of adjusting their eyes to acquire this new-found knowledge, but Plato clearly believes that once they have come up from the cave and seen the sun, they would never wish to return to their previous way of life. Thus while obtaining truth over fictions and seeing the true foundations of your everyday appearances can be difficult and uncomfortable, Plato argues that the affirmation of the truth is preferable to a life chained in a cave, believing the world consists only of shadows. Plato clearly thinks it is not a fully human life to accept the surface world of appearances as the complete representation of the world as it is. The fully human life, outside the cave, emphasizes the importance of objectively understanding how the world works rather than being comfortable with being deceived. The fact that the prisoner who sees the world as it truly is would not want to return to a life of being fooled shows the fully human life pursues the truth even when it is difficult to confront.

Part III: It's Bad for Ya

In his final special, Carlin repeatedly made the statement that holding false beliefs or illusions is bad for you. "It's all bullshit, and it's bad for ya." Why? Is it because someone who knows the truth, however difficult, would never want to return to a life of illusion? Is it because part of seeking true human happiness is having real experiences that connect us with ultimate reality? Is it because it is potentially harmful and therefore unethical to hold false beliefs? In short, yes.

First, let's consider Carlin's comedy in light of Plato's Allegory of the Cave. Plato's prisoners thought that shadows of objects were the real world. Little did they know the real world contained so much more. The world of shadows was simple, one dimensional, and easy to understand. Being dragged outside the cave and exposed to the world as it truly is was extremely painful for the prisoners; but upon making the adjustment, Plato argues they would never want to return to the life of believing in mere shadows.

As a comedian can take many routes to humor, Carlin clearly considered the exposure of truth to be an important component of the purpose of his comedy. Unpacking the deeper concepts and ideas behind surface appearances is an ongoing theme of his comedic work. I think it's clear that Carlin himself considered his perceptions to be preferable to illusions and would not want to live a life that fails to critically examine our societal values. In his first HBO special, "On Location" in 1977, Carlin suggested there ought to be more truth in names, especially in advertising.

> They've tried to clean up, to clean up advertising claims, let them clean up some of the names, like Excello and Acme and Ace and Top. Bullshit. Things should be called what they are. I'd like to bring out a new car, the 1977 Piece of Shit. A Division of United Consumer Fuckers. ("On Location")

Rather than describe the capitalist process that uses deception to maximize profit at the expense of quality, Carlin suggested calling it exactly what it is. Behind the shiny appearances of how products are manufactured lies the essence of advertising: trying to get people to buy things for more than they're worth in order to maximize profits. The person who ultimately loses out is the consumer.

In "Doin' It Again," he examined the concept of prostitution, questioning why it is illegal.

> Selling is legal, fucking is legal. Why isn't selling fucking legal? You know, why should it be illegal to sell something that's perfectly legal to give away? I can't follow the logic on that at all. Of all the things you can do to a person, giving someone an orgasm is hardly the worst thing in the world. In the Army, they give you a medal for spraying Napalm on people. Civilian life, you go to jail for giving someone an orgasm. Maybe I'm not supposed to understand it. (Doin' it Again)

On the surface, we assume prostitution is illegal because there is something morally wrong with it. Carlin asks his listeners precisely what that is. It is not illegal to have sex nor is it illegal to sell things. Yet we've banned selling sex as an unacceptable social activity. He pointed out how we regularly do much worse things that are legal, and are even often rewarded for doing them. Carlin used the Socratic method to try to tease out the concept behind the practice. If something is morally wrong, there must be a reason why. Is it wrong because someone is being harmed? But Carlin showed that it's not clear what the harm is in prostitution: many of the harms that come to prostitutes are a result of its criminalization. Additionally, there are behaviors that are obviously much more harmful that the state has designated are perfectly fine in some contexts. Carlin fails to find an essence of "badness" in prostitution – further he sees no consistent standards for badness in our cultural norms at all.

In his 1992 special "Jamming in New York," Carlin opined about the United States' obsession with war and violence. "We have to declare war on everything," he says, "the war on poverty, the war on litter, the war on cancer, the war on drugs, but did you ever notice we got no war on homelessness?" Carlin asks the viewer to ponder why, then concludes that there is no money to be made off of solving the problem of homelessness. "If you can find a solution to homelessness where the corporate swine and the politicians could steal a couple of million dollars each, you'll see the streets of America begin to clear up pretty goddamn quick, I'll guarantee you that!" Carlin exposes a deeper truth behind the American obsession with war: the wars we wage, whether literal wars motivated by politicians' ties to fossil fuels, the military industrial complex and weapons industry, or figurative wars like the war on drugs that fund the private prison industry, the wars we choose to wage are financially motivated. We declare a war when the powerful stand to financially profit from the results. The surface appearance is that we wage wars for justified, morally sound reasons. Politicians will go to great lengths to make militaristic intervention appear justified. George W. Bush insisted Saddam Hussein had weapons of mass destruction and must be stopped, but the evidence he provided was proven false. The War on Drugs, it was claimed, was morally necessary due to harmful effects of drugs on youth and the criminal behavior of those who used them. In reality, the War on Drugs led to the United States having the largest prison population in the world, benefitting the private prison industry which has spent tens of millions in lobbying, while having no effect in actually decreasing drug use (Global Commission on Drug Policy 2011). We now see increasing legalization of marijuana in multiple states as well as small amounts of cocaine and heroin in Oregon (Fuller 2020). The essence of what is considered a necessary war in the United States, at least in Carlin's view, is who stands to profit from waging it.

In his continued musings on homelessness, Carlin suggests there is further deception in the way the concept functions in societal discourse.

> I got an idea about homelessness. You know what they ought to do? Change the name of it. Change the name! It's not homelessness, it's houselessness! It's houses these people need! A home is an abstract idea, a home is a setting, it's a state of mind. These people need houses; physical, tangible structures.

Why is this distinction important? Because a home, as he says, is a state of mind, an abstract concept that no one can easily provide to someone else. But what the homeless need is much simpler: they need a physical place to live. This is a solvable problem, if we chose to solve it. The heart of the issue, according to Carlin, is that we don't want to.

> They need low-cost housing but where're you gonna put it? Nobody wants you to build low-cost housing near their house. People don't want it near 'em! We've got something in this country – you've heard of it – it's called NIMBY, N-I-M-B-Y, "Not In My BackYard!" People don't want anything, any kind of social help, located anywhere near 'em!

He slams America's supposed spirit of generosity, which he, of course, believes is an illusion. Carlin proposes his own solution to houselessness: build the low-cost housing on golf courses. Golf is a sport that only the wealthy can afford and takes up way too much space: build some houses on it, house the homeless, and the problem is solved. In this monologue, Carlin takes the surface appearance of homelessness: a problem we as a society have decided is not solvable because of our inability to provide the concept of "a home" and because we believe it the unfortunate workings of the economy that will always render some people without a home, and reveals the deeper, true essence behind it: we don't have enough affordable houses, we could have affordable houses, but we choose not to. We choose not to because we are not actually a generous society, and because the wealthy and powerful do not stand to profit from solving this particular problem.

In "Back in Town," Carlin explored another surface belief that is quite common among the American public: the idea that "politicians suck." People of all religions, political affiliations, classes, and racial demographics will feel comfortable agreeing that our politicians suck. But Carlin asks his listener to consider what we truly mean when we say this.

> But where do people think these politicians come from? They don't fall out of the sky. They don't pass through a membrane from another reality. No, they come from American homes, American families, American schools, American churches, American businesses, and they're elected by American voters. This is the best we can do, folks. It's what our system produces: Garbage in, garbage out.

Carlin tells his viewers to look in the mirror. Our politicians are elected from among our citizens and are a product of our society. "When you have selfish ignorant citizens you're going to have selfish ignorant politicians," he opines. "So maybe it's not the politicians who suck. Maybe something else sucks around here. Like, the public?" Behind the surface appearance of the truism that "politicians suck," Carlin forces his audiences to confront the true nature of the issue. Our politicians are us. If the politicians suck, so do we. Many people were surprised by the election of Donald Trump in 2016, and that he managed to get even more votes in 2020 (although he still lost). It is likely Carlin would not have been surprised at all. In a society that encourages and rewards selfishness, greed, consumerism, and ignorance, the election and popularity of a narcissistic billionaire reality TV star is a predictable result.

Like Plato's prisoner who comes up out of the cave, Carlin takes the shadows: "prostitution is immoral" "our wars are justified" and "politicians suck" and exposes the deeper truth behind them. His listeners are brought up out of the metaphorical cave and confronted with the true essences. And like Plato, Carlin is firm that he would not want to return to the cave of shadows after the painful process of being dragged up to see the light. "I don't like language that conceals reality. Americans have trouble facing the truth" (Doin' it Again).

> "I'm not a good American because I form my own opinions. I have certain rules I live by; my first rule: I don't believe anything the government tells me... nothing, zero, no, and I don't take very seriously, the media or the press in this country...I don't really believe in my country and I gotta tell you folks, I don't get all choked up about yellow ribbons and American flags. I consider them to be symbols and I leave symbols to the symbol-minded. (Jamming in New York)"

With the play on words of "simple-minded" Carlin expresses that he sees the world of shadows as an inferior mental space. A truly human life utilizes our intellect to reflect on the real foundational concepts behind our fictional platitudes.

What about Nozick and his experience machine? Does Carlin think humans ultimately desire a true connection with reality? Is happiness only true happiness if it is justifiable and based on real experiences? Again, I think the answer is yes.

In "It's Bad for Ya," Carlin attacked the common phrase "Proud to be an American." Pride, he said, should be reserved for something you achieve or earn. No one achieved or earned simply being born in the United States.

> I've never understood ethnic pride. ...I'm fully Irish. And when I was a kid, I would go to the St. Patrick's Day parade, and I noticed that they sold a button that said "Proud to be Irish"...And I could never understand ethnic or national pride because, to me, pride should be reserved for something you achieve or attain on your own, not something that happens by accident of birth. Being Irish, being Irish isn't a skill. It's a fucking genetic accident. You wouldn't say, "I'm proud to be 5'11". I'm proud to have a predisposition for colon cancer. So, why the fuck would you be proud to be Irish or proud to be Italian or American or anything?

Here Carlin emphasizes the importance of justifiability in what we take pride in. What's the point of being proud if it's not something you earned? He also attacks the self-esteem movement that tells us that every child is special.

> Boy, they said it over and over and over, as if to convince themselves. Every child is special. And I kept saying fuck you. Every child is clearly not special. Did you ever look at one of them?...Now, PT Barnum might think they're special, but not me, I have standards. But let's say it's true. Let's grant this. I'm in a generous mood...Let's say it's true as somehow all...every child is special. What about every adult? Isn't every adult special, too? And if not, if not then at what age do you go from being special to being not-so-special? And if every adult is special then that means we're all special, and the whole idea loses all its fucking meaning.

If everyone is special, then simply put, no one is. Carlin asks, what is the point of being considered special if the concept has no meaning? As humans we crave not just to be called special, but for that statement to have a connection with reality: we want to actually *be* special. Carlin believes the self-esteem movement has made the concept meaningless. What good is a belief that a child is special if it does not have an actual connection with reality? Is it any different from an experience machine where you could plug in and be the type of person you wanted to be?

In "You Are All Diseased," Carlin shared that he really tried to believe in God. But the longer he lived, the more he realized that something was wrong. Looking around at the world he realized this was simply not good work and should not be on the resume of a divine being. If God were real, he must be either incompetent or simply not care. Carlin says he looked for something else. So he became a sun worshipper. He worships the sun because he can see it. He knows it is a real thing to worship.

> So every day, I can see the sun as it gives me everything I need... heat, light, food, flowers in the park, reflections on the lake... and occasional skin cancer but hey, at least there are no crucifixions and we're not setting people on fire simply because they don't agree with us. Sun worship is fairly simple. There's no mysteries, no miracles, no pageantry, no one asks for money, there are no songs to learn, and we don't have a special building where we all gather once a week to compare clothing. And the best thing about the sun, it never tells me I'm unworthy, doesn't tell me I'm a bad person who needs to be saved, hasn't said an unkind word, treats me fine.

Carlin wanted a connection with true reality, not a fabricated experience. While believing in God may have been fancier, with songs and miracles and a shiny afterlife, Carlin didn't find it credible and thus not worth believing in. Instead, he chose a much simpler object of worship, one that is much less flashy and doesn't promise him a potential eternity in heaven or a divine plan, but is, importantly, *real*. Nozick argued that we don't just want pleasure, experiences, results, or to be a certain way. We want our beliefs to be true and to interact with the world as it actually is. We want our emotions, whether happy or sad, to be based on facts. Carlin believes his semi-religious relationship with the sun is preferable because it is at least based on a real experience and on facts: the sun is real and it provides for his basic needs: his need for food, light, warmth, and life itself. Like Nozick, Carlin argues that it is better to have true beliefs, real experiences, and justified emotions than simulations, hallucinations, or illusions of good experiences.

Last, are false beliefs and their promotion unethical? Do false beliefs risk causing harm to others and society at large? It's a resounding yes.

For example, let's return to his monologue on rights. Carlin asks what a right is, and where rights come from. He points out that different countries have different numbers of rights. In moral and political philosophy, there is a distinction between moral and legal rights. Carlin is talking about rights that are granted to you by a government, so he is talking about legal rights. Moral rights, sometimes called human rights, are rights that every person is entitled to irrespective of where they live and the laws of their country. Carlin is looking for a source of legal rights, and criticizes the common belief that legal rights come from God.

But let's say God gave us the original ten. He gave the British 13. The British Bill of Rights has 13 stipulations. The Germans have 29. The Belgians have 25. The Swedish have only 6. And some people in the world have no rights at all. What kind of a fucking, goddamn, God-given deal is that? No rights at all? Why would God give different people in different countries different numbers of different rights? Boredom? Amusement? Bad arithmetic? Do we find out at long last after all this time that God is weak in math skills? Doesn't sound like divine planning to me. Sounds more like human planning. Sounds more like one group trying to control another group. In other words, business as usual in America. ("It's Bad for Ya")

Carlin compares the belief that our rights come from God to a form of social control. If the rights we have are "God-given," it bestows a sense of security or comfort, much like Beauvoir's serious world. It is also, like Beauvoir's serious world, illusory. Believing that "God" backs the legal rights that we have leads to a complacency and lack of reflection on the rights we and others do or do not have. This is, ultimately, harmful to society at large.

Personally, folks, I believe that if your rights came from God, he would have given you the right to some food every day, and he would have given you the right to a roof over your head. God would have been looking out for you. God would have been looking out for you, you know that? He wouldn't have been worrying about making sure you have a gun so you can get drunk on Sunday night and kill your girlfriend's parents.

The belief that our legal rights are part of the serious world and thus inherent, God-given, leads to the acceptance of barely regulated gun ownership as a "God-given" right, because it was granted in the original constitution, but the right to a shelter is not. There is a strong correlation between a large number of recipients of gun lobbyist funds and voting records against gun control. Politicians who receive donations from gun lobbies reject attempts to regulate guns (OpenSecrets.org 2020) and states with gun restrictions have less gun violence than states which have enacted gun control measures (Committee on the Judiciary 2019). Meanwhile thousands of people live without access to housing and nutrition, and the problem goes largely ignored. Further, a belief that legal rights are backed by the authority of the serious world can make people less questioning when these rights are gradually taken away. With lack of critical reflection on the rights we have and why, we often assume there is a good, morally and legally sound reason that our rights to privacy or against unnecessary search and seizure are suspended. Or, as Carlin points out, many sat silently while Japanese citizens had almost all legal rights suspended after the Pearl Harbor attack and were put in internment camps.

Just when these American citizens needed their rights the most, their government took them away, and rights aren't rights if someone can take them away. They're privileges. That's all we've ever had in this country is a bill of temporary privileges. And if you read the news even badly, you know that every year, the list gets shorter and shorter and shorter. You see how silly that is? Yeah. Sooner or later, the people in this country are going to realize the government does not give a fuck about them.

The false belief that the government is enforcing God-given rights is harmful on multiple accounts, in Carlin's view. It leads to beliefs that being denied rights to health care, housing, or nutrition are justified because that's just "how things are." It leads to unreflective acceptance of policies such as gun ownership with very few restrictions, even though that legal right was established at a time when weapons and society in general were very different. Last, it leads to a belief that those enforcing the rights are backed by a God-given moral authority, of which our government officials are enforcers, which makes people more complacent when their legal rights are restricted or taken away.

Clifford argued that a society that promotes or accepts false beliefs ultimately accepts a sense of complacency and stops the curious and rigorous questioning needed for societal progress. In one of Carlin's most famous bits in "Life is Worth Losing," he attacks the illusion of the American Dream. He begins with the common complaint that education in the United States "sucks" compared to many other advanced countries. Carlin says there is a reason the education system is the way it is and will never improve: the big wealthy business interests that control things simply don't want that.

> Forget the politicians. They are irrelevant. The politicians are put there to give you the idea that you have freedom of choice. You don't. You have no choice! You have OWNERS! They OWN YOU. They own everything. They own all the important land. They own and control the corporations. They've long since bought, and paid for the Senate, the Congress, the state houses, the city halls, they got the judges in their back pockets and they own all the big media companies, so they control just about all of the news and information you get to hear. They got you by the balls.

These owners spend billions in lobbying making sure they get what they want – which is more for themselves and less for everyone else. But, Carlin says, there is one thing they definitely don't want:

> They don't want a population of citizens capable of critical thinking. They don't want well informed, well educated people capable of critical thinking. They're not interested in that. That doesn't help them. That's against their interests…..You know what they want? They want obedient workers. Obedient workers, people who are just smart enough to run the machines and do the paperwork. And just dumb enough to passively accept all these increasingly shitty jobs with the lower pay, the longer hours, the reduced benefits, the end of overtime and vanishing pension that disappears the minute you go to collect it, and now they're coming for your Social Security money.

It is in the interest of the wealthy capitalist class to have workers who accept their lot. Lacking a critical consciousness of their situation, they are more complacent to accept worse and worse positions and to have more and more of their benefits taken away. The American Dream is the illusion that working hard can result in the accumulation of wealth and social mobility. But when you are not the primary beneficiary of your own labor and the capitalist owners reap the benefits of your hard work, the accumulation of wealth is not possible. The illusion, however, is enough to keep people complacent.

> Good honest hard-working people continue, these are people of modest means, continue to elect these rich cock suckers who don't give a fuck about you....they don't give a fuck about you... they don't give a FUCK about you. They don't care about you at all... at all... AT ALL. And nobody seems to notice. Nobody seems to care. That's what the owners count on. The fact that Americans will probably remain willfully ignorant of the big red, white and blue dick that's being jammed up their assholes every day, because the owners of this country know the truth: It's called the American Dream, because you have to be asleep to believe it.

More to Clifford's point, Carlin argues the lack of education makes citizens credulous, easily manipulated, and prevents their own progress. It also prevents them from critiquing the political and economic system that each year makes it more and more difficult for them to flourish, thus thwarting overall societal progress.

We can also read this in light of Beauvoir's concept of the serious world. The American Dream is comforting; it instills in people a sense of certainty and knowledge of what they need to do: work hard, and you will be successful. The paths are clearly laid out for them, the world makes sense. But like all aspects of the serious world, it is illusory. Believing in the American Dream prevents people from seeing the ways this concept stifles their freedom and leads to an undesirable situation in which the benefits of their work are transferred to the capitalist class. Further they accept this situation as "just the way things are" so they do not see the situation as one that they can potentially transform. They do not see themselves as creative, free meaning-givers who could potentially create a more fair and just system. Instead, constrained by the comfort of the black and white spirit of seriousness, they are content to go about their lives and accept a system that gradually takes away the benefits extended to the middle class.

Thus it is clear that Carlin thinks false beliefs and their promotion are morally harmful. Not only do the ideas themselves risk harm to others, but they lead to a less critically reflective and inquisitive attitude, leading to complacency, lack of progress, and thwarting our potential to conceive of ourselves as meaningful creators of our social world.

Nozick and the Experience Machine

One reason it can be argued that illusions or appearances are preferable to the truth is that believing in comforting fictions can bring happiness or pleasure. Believing in guardian angels, a loving creator God, or a heavenly afterlife, for example, brings people happiness and helps them deal with grief and death. A more contemporary philosopher who argued that humans should ultimately prefer reality over fiction, even when those fictions are enticing and pleasurable, is Robert Nozick. In Nozick's 1974 work *Anarchy, State, and Utopia,* he poses a thought experiment called The Experience Machine:

> Superduper neuropsychologists could stimulate your brain so that you would think and feel you were writing a great novel, or making a friend, or reading an interesting book.

All the time you would be floating in a tank, with electrodes attached to your brain. Should you plug into this machine for life, preprogramming your life's experiences? (Nozick 1974, pp. 42–43)

While plugged into the machine, you wouldn't know that you were actually floating in a tank, you would think that the things were really happening. Every 2 years, Nozick says you could come out of the tank for 10 minutes or 10 hours and reprogram the next 2 years' worth of experiences. Would you do it? Should you do it?

Nozick thinks we wouldn't and shouldn't for three reasons. First, he says humans seek to do certain things, not just experience things. We don't want to experience writing a novel, we want to actually write a novel. Second, we want to be a certain type of person. A person floating in a tank is an indeterminate blob, not a person. Third, and most importantly, the experience machine exposes you to a human made, constructed reality, but not the *true one*. "There is no actual contact with any deeper reality, though the experience of it can be simulated" (Nozick 1974, p. 43). Nozick compares the process to being on hallucinogenic drugs. While we may enjoy the experiences we have on them, we ultimately know they are not real. And humans ultimately crave real, true experiences in the world as it *really is*, rather than simulated ones.

This is because humans crave more out of life than just pleasure. Nozick poses the possibility that the machine could be a transformation machine that would transform you into whatever sort of person we'd like to be, or a results machine that produces any result we would want to produce in the world in order to make a difference. Nozick says that what is undesirable and disturbing about all these machines is that they would be living our lives for us and denying us contact with reality (Nozick 1974, p. 44). In Nozick's view, we don't just want pleasure, experiences, results, or to be a certain way. We want our beliefs to be true and to interact with the world as it actually is.

Nozick argues that we care about more than just internal feelings or happy mental states. We want our beliefs to be true, for our emotions, whether happy or sad, to be based on facts. In short, we seek a connection with reality itself.

> To focus on external reality, with your beliefs, evaluations, and emotions, is valuable in itself not just as a means to more pleasure or happiness...And if we want to connect to reality by knowing it, and not simply to have true beliefs, then if knowledge involves tracking the facts...this involves a direct and explicit external connection. We do not, of course, simply want contact with reality; we want contact of certain kinds: exploring reality and responding, altering it and creating new actuality ourselves. (Nozick 1989, p. 106)

While we ultimately desire to be happy, we care about the source of our happiness and how it is produced. We want actual experiences, real relationships with other people, to be moved by the awesome or the tragic, to actually create something new, to create a life that we are proud of. "What we want, in short, is a life and a self that happiness is a fitting response to—and then to give it that response." While we ultimately seek happiness, we seek a justified happiness: one that has a connection with an external reality and is based on events and experiences we can call our own. We would not plug into the Experience Machine, because it ultimately denies us a basic connection with external reality that is necessary for true, justified happiness.

The Ethics of Illusions

So far we've considered whether seeking truth over ignorance is part of living a fulfilling human life, and whether experience with the truth leads to a deeper sense of happiness. Another question is if there are distinctly *moral* reasons, we should seek the truth. Is it not only undesirable to hold false beliefs, but actually morally wrong to do so?

One way to evaluate that question is to consider the *effects* of holding or promoting false beliefs. Work that explores this angle of the issue comes from William Clifford, and more recently, from David Kyle Johnson and Simone De Beauvoir. In "The Ethics of Belief," Clifford argues that all beliefs with insufficient evidence ultimately risk causing harm to others. First, the false belief could itself cause harm, as in the example of someone who chooses to believe that something is safe when it is not (Clifford 1999, pp. 70–71). NASA was warned the night before the Challenger exploded that the shuttle was unsafe to launch in frigid January temperatures but officials chose to believe the illusion that the evidence was inconclusive, leading to the deaths of everyone on board (McDonald and Hansen 2012). Or, citizens could believe the Covid-19 pandemic is not that serious and thus refuse to social distance and wear masks, contributing to higher rates of transmission and more deaths.

Clifford thinks the ethics of beliefs goes even further: even if one particular false belief does not harm other people, a general attitude of credulity is ultimately harmful for humankind. False beliefs discourage the critical, inquisitive attitude of pursuing the truth that is necessary for society to progress.

> The danger to society is not merely that it should believe wrong things, though that is great enough; but that it should become credulous, and lose the habit of testing things and inquiring into them; for then it must sink back into savagery. (Clifford 1999, p. 75)

This warning could not be more prescient. There is a culture in the United States that takes pride in ignorance, touting not only unsubstantiated religious beliefs that they want forced on other people, but government conspiracies and rejection of scientific evidence. This has led to a revival of the belief that the world is flat, and the rejection of the results of free and fair elections, despite all evidence to the contrary. This pride in ignorance and beliefs without justification was amplified by the Trump administration, which openly appealed to "alternative facts" and blasted his critics as "fake news," and created a culture that denies the existence of climate change and the seriousness of the Covid-19 pandemic. This not only has caused harm to others, but has hindered vital societal progress in developing more sustainable habits and creating innovative solutions to contemporary challenges. Disregard for scientific expertise became a proud standard of the Trump administration, as they disbanded the nation's pandemic response team in 2018 (Riechmann 2020). They also cut funding for scientific research ranging from the prevention of invasive insects to the effects of certain chemicals on pregnant women (Plumer and Davenport 2019). While this anti-science agenda may be partially fueled by the Trump administration's ties to oil and fossil fuels, as well as wanting to free businesses of environmental regulations, the United States' culture of glorified ignorance has lent support for simply giving up on caring about the truth. This attitude, as Clifford points out, hinders vital societal progress.

More recent work on the ethics of truth and ignorance comes from David Kyle Johnson's work on the Santa Lie. Johnson argues that what many view as a harmless, fun holiday practice – telling children that Santa is real – can actually be morally harmful. As part of this argument, he introduces potential reasons we could argue in favor of promoting a fantasy. One reason is of course consequential: telling people stories often prompts them to change or control their behavior. We see this strategy with the Santa Lie. The myth of Santa is used to control the behavior of small children. If they do not behave, of course, Santa will not bring them any presents. But is this a morally desirable way to get children to behave? Isn't it preferable to teach children why a behavior is undesirable than to use an illusion based on reward to get them to behave? In the same vein, many religious people behave in certain ways because they want an eternal reward – Heaven – after death. Is this a *good* reason to be good? Shouldn't you do the right thing for the right thing's sake, not because you want a reward for yourself? The Santa Lie, Johnson argues, discourages instilling good reasons for moral behavior in children, and instead promotes behaving morally for the sake of personal reward (Johnson 2010).

Another reason someone may promote a false belief such as Santa is that it creates a sense of security or comfort. Believing in Santa, or believing in God, or the goodness of the police, is comforting to many people. It helps them create a world in which there are definite rules and following those rules leads to a reward. It's a simple world. Simone De Beauvoir called this simple world the "serious world." It is a world in which right and wrong are black and white, institutions are there to protect us, adults know what they are talking about, and what your parents and teachers tell you is true. Beauvoir thought the serious world was very comforting. She also thought it was an illusion, and ultimately a harmful one. Beauvoir thought that belief in the serious world, a world of moral black and whites and absolute values, stifled creative freedom and led to the continuation of harmful institutions and practices. It is the belief that these institutions are inherent, God-given, and self-evidently good that fuels resistance to change as well as a failure for individuals to embrace their own freedom to create. It also leads to disrespecting the freedom of others, and choosing alleged pre-given ideals over concrete human lives.

> But the serious man puts nothing into question. For the military man, the army is useful; for the colonial administrator, the highway; for the serious revolutionary, the revolution – army, highway, revolution, productions becoming inhuman idols to which one will not hesitate to

sacrifice man himself. Therefore, the serious man is dangerous. It is natural that he makes himself a tyrant... Dishonestly ignoring the subjectivity of his choice, he pretends that the unconditioned value of the object is being asserted through him; and by the same token he also ignores the value of the subjectivity and the freedom of others, to such an extent that, sacrificing them to the thing, he persuades himself that what he sacrifices is nothing. The colonial administrator who has raised the highway to the stature of an idol will have no scruple about assuring its construction at the price of a great number of lives of the natives; for, what value has the life of a native who is incompetent, lazy, and clumsy when it comes to building highways? (De Beauvoir 1980, p. 49)

The sense of security that the illusory serious world offers discourages critical reflection on our social norms and leads to becoming wrapped up in harmful social causes. It further stifles individuals, hindering them from embracing their ability to create change and transformation in our social world.

This leads directly into the overall argument of the ethics of promoting false belief: even if there were some allegedly positive consequences of promoting false beliefs, such as the control or modification of behavior or an illusion of security, aren't those outweighed by negative effects? Clifford, Johnson, and Beauvoir ultimately argue that it, indeed, is. The promotion of false beliefs discourages critical thinking, distorts our ability to distinguish between good and bad evidence, and ultimately risks harm to others. Further, it can make us resistant to change and creativity, and lead to getting wrapped up in immoral causes. As emphasized by Johnson, while potentially false beliefs such as belief in ghosts or angels may not seem like that big of a deal, false beliefs that the government is responsible for 911, that the Newtown school shooting was a hoax, or that Covid-19 is a government conspiracy are less benign. When individuals get used to accepting beliefs without solid evidence, they are more prone to fantasies that have the potential to cause harm to others and to society at large.

Conclusion

A true philosopher of comedy, Carlin joins a long tradition of philosophers arguing that truth is preferable to illusion. Like Plato, he searched for the true essences behind the realm of shadows, and would never want to return to a world of surface appearances. Like Nozick, he believed that real experiences and a happiness based on justified, true circumstances are preferable to a life of pre-programmed, pleasurable illusions. And like Clifford, Johnson, and Beauvoir, he argued that false beliefs have the potential to cause harm to others and stifle societal progress, thus there are distinctly moral reasons for pursuing the truth. Carlin was a true comedic visionary who entertained his audiences for over 40 years while forcing them to confront uncomfortable truths about religion, politics, and our societal values. A master at pairing ancient philosophical truth with modern comedy, he offered us a true gift: a critical examination of our society's civil and moral contradictions and absurdities, elegantly wrapped in humor.

References

Clifford, William. 1999. *The ethics of belief and other essays*. Edited by Timothy Madigan. New York: Prometheus Books.

De Beauvoir, Simone. 1980. *The ethics of ambiguity*. Trans. Bernard Frechtman. Secaucus: Citadel Press.

Fuller, Thomas. Oregon decriminalizes small amounts of heroin and cocaine; four states legalize marijuana. *The New York Times*, November 4, 2020. https://www.nytimes.com/2020/11/04/us/ballot-measures-propositions-2020.html.

"Gun Control." 2020. *OpenSecrets.Org center for responsive politics*. https://www.opensecrets.org/industries/indus.php?ind=q12.

Johnson, David Kyle. 2010. Against the Santa-Claus-Lie: The truth we should tell our children. In *Christmas and philosophy: Better than a lump of coal*, ed. Scott Lowe, 137–150. Malden: Wiley-Blackwell.

McDonald, Allan, and James Hansen. 2012. *Truth, lies, and O-rings: Inside the space shuttle challenger disaster*. Gainesville: University Press of Florida.

Nozick, Robert. 1974. *Anarchy, state, and utopia*. Oxford: Blackwell.

———. 1989. *The examined life: Philosophical meditations*. New York: Simon and Schuster.

Plato. 1985. *The Republic*. Trans. Richard Sterling and William Scott. New York: Norton and Company.

Plumer, Brad, and Coral Davenport. Science under attack: How Trump is sidelining researchers and their work. *New York Times*, December 28th, 2019. https://www.nytimes.com/2019/12/28/climate/trump-administration-war-on-science.html.

Reichmann, Deb. "Trump disbanded NSC pandemic unit that experts had praised." March 14, 2020. https://apnews.com/article/ce014d94b64e98b7203b873e56f80e9a

"States With Weak Gun Laws Suffer From More Gun Violence." *The Committee on the judiciary*, September 24, 2019. https://www.judiciary.senate.gov/press/dem/releases/states-with-weak-gun-laws-suffer-from-more-gun-violence

"The War on Drugs." 2011. *Global Commission on Drug Policy*. https://www.globalcommissionondrugs.org/reports/the-war-on-drugs

Wagner, Peter, and Wendy Sawyer. *States of incarceration: The global context 2018*. Prison Policy Initiative, June 2018. https://www.prisonpolicy.org/global/2018.html

Louis CK as Philosopher: The King and His Fall

65

Jennifer Marra Henrigillis

Contents

Introduction	1534
The Rise of the Philosopher King of Comedy	1535
CK's History	1535
Louis CK as Philosopher	1536
That Breakout Episode of *Louie*	1542
The Fall and the Return	1543
The Accusations	1543
The Fallout	1544
Tiptoeing Toward a Return	1546
The Two Most Important Questions	1548
Conclusion	1558
References	1559

Abstract

In 2014, Louis CK was unquestionably the philosopher king of comedy, a commercial, cultural, and creative icon who dared to explore the most vulnerable parts of society, culture, and himself. His jokes raised philosophical issues in epistemology and mirrored the philosophy of some of the greats: Quine, Augustine, Aristotle, Schopenhauer, and Buddha just to name a few. Then, with the revelation of sexual misconduct in 2017, CK was dethroned overnight. Many were shocked, confused, and angry that CK, whom they had come to know as an advocate for women, a loving father, and a thoughtful ally to the feminist movement, would abuse his position of power for sexual gratification. Many believed that CK's actions forfeit his access to the cultural marketplace – the only way to truly show disgust and disapproval of CK would be to ban him from comedy clubs, remove him from creative roles, cancel the release of his films, and strip his work from streaming archives.

J. Marra Henrigillis (✉)
St. Norbert College, De Pere, WI, USA
e-mail: jemhenrigillis@gmail.com

© Springer Nature Switzerland AG 2024
D. K. Johnson et al. (eds.), *The Palgrave Handbook of Popular Culture as Philosophy*,
https://doi.org/10.1007/978-3-031-24685-2_51

There is stark disagreement on what has been, and ought to be, done with Louis CK. Some comedians and commentators have understood CK as a sexual predator whose continued presence in the comedy world would only serve to reinforce rape culture, effectively telling victims that they don't matter and men that assault is forgivable. Other comedians and comedy audiences rejoice at the return of CK, believing that his comedy remains entertaining and worthwhile despite his behavior.

There are several philosophical layers of this case to unravel, but after exploring the ways in which CK was the philosopher king of comedy before his fall, the present study focuses on the following two questions: (1) was the industry response to CK's actions the correct one? and (2) should CK be allowed to return to comedy?

Keywords

Louis CK · Cancel culture · Rape culture · Stand-up comedy · Virtue ethics · Libertarianism · Censorship · Feminism

Introduction

In 2014, Louis CK was unquestionably the philosopher king of comedy, a powerhouse of the entertainment industry and a commercial, cultural, and creative icon who dared to explore the most vulnerable parts of society, culture, and himself. As will be shown, his jokes raised philosophical issues in epistemology and mirrored the philosophy of some of the greats: Quine, Augustine, Aristotle, Schopenhauer, and Buddha just to name a few. But then, with the revelation of sexual misconduct in 2017, CK was dethroned overnight. Many were shocked, confused, and angry that CK, whom they had come to know as an advocate for women, a loving father, and a thoughtful ally to the feminist movement, would abuse his position of power for sexual gratification. The default response that many felt, which was subsequently enforced by producers and critics, was that CK's actions forfeit his access to the cultural marketplace – in other words, the only way to truly show disgust and disapproval of CK would be to ban him from comedy clubs, remove him from creative roles in TV shows, cancel the release of his films, and strip his work from streaming archives.

There is stark disagreement between audiences, commentators, and fellow comedians on what has been, and ought to be, done with Louis CK. On the one hand, some comedians (such as Tig Notaro and Hannah Gadsby) and commentators have understood CK as a sexual predator whose continued presence in the comedy world would only serve to reinforce rape culture, effectively telling victims that they don't matter and men that assault is forgivable. Other comedians (such as Dave Chappelle, Joe Rogan, and Christina Pazsitzky) as well as comedy audiences rejoice at the return of CK, believing that his comedy remains entertaining and worthwhile despite his behavior.

There are several philosophical layers of this case to unravel, but after exploring the ways in which CK was the philosopher king of comedy before his fall, the present study focuses on the following two questions: (1) was the industry response to CK's actions the correct one? and (2) should CK be allowed to return to comedy?

The Rise of the Philosopher King of Comedy

CK's History

Louis CK was born Louis Szekely in Washington, D.C. on September 12, 1967. He was raised Catholic and spent his early years in his father's home country of Mexico. The family moved back to the United States when Louis was 7 and settled in Boston, where he spent the remainder of his childhood.

CK's media education began after he graduated from high school and worked for a public access television station. He directed his first short film in 1984 and performed his first stand-up set at an open mic night in 1985. He got his first writing job for Conan O'Brien in 1993 and wrote for several comedy programs through 1999. His first feature film, *Pootie Tang*, was released in 2001. He focused on his stand-up career in the early 2000s and recorded his first hour-long special, *Shameless*, in 2007.

While CK was successful, his career was in plateau. What broke him through the ceiling was the wisdom of comedy legend and CK's personal hero George Carlin. Carlin would write and release a comedy special every year. Early on, he would hone the material in comedy clubs and on his tour, and would release a polished, composed work of entirely new material at the end (Bliss 2016, p. 279). CK decided to do the same thing; he would stop depending on bits that he knew would work, and, in what is a bold and terrifying move for any comedian, threw them out of his set (Ralkowski 2016, p. xv). His 2005 HBO special *One Night Stand* was the first entirely new hour of stand-up, and he has written new hours for every special since (Bliss 2016, p. 277). CK explains that Carlin taught him to go beyond jokes about airplanes and dogs and "dig deeper. Start talking about, you know, your feelings, and who you are...dig deeper. So then you start thinking about your fears and your nightmares and doing jokes about that...And then you just start going into *weird shit*" (*Tribute to George Carlin* 2010).

CK describes this writing process to Charlie Rose in 2014 as painstaking trial and error that he hones and perfects through performing at small comedy clubs, where he "get[s] rid of all the impurities and all the bad stuff," folding and squeezing and banging like a blacksmith making a samurai sword (*Charlie Rose* May 6 2014). Rejecting the temptation to rely on the success of old bits, CK explained on the 2011 HBO special *Talking Funny* that "I would take my closing bit and I would open with it, just to fuck myself, because then I have to follow my strongest bit...because then the end of your act cauterizes it. It gets stronger because you don't have a choice...You get rid of all of your best weapons" (*Talking Funny* 2011).

Louis CK as Philosopher

Louis CK's breakthrough stand-up special, *Hilarious*, was filmed in 2009 and released in 2011. In it, he jokes about cell phones, his divorce, white people problems, and "weird shit" like how most people are dead. Some of the most poignant bits in this special have to do with the way adults in America treat their children:

> Kids can't even taste- Apples are like paper to them. Because we fill 'em, we force them to eat- People force their kids to eat fast food. I was in this hamburger- This woman's, like, just shoving french fries in the- "Eat it!" The kid's, like, "Mom, it's salty. It hurts. I can't eat anymore." "Shut up. Have a soda." We give them MSG, sugar, and caffeine. And, weirdly, they react to those chemicals. And so they yell, "AHHHH." And then we hit them. What fucking chance does a kid have? We pump the stuff in there. "Aah!" "Shut up!" "Stop it. Why are you like this?" "Cause I haven't had actual nutrition in eight years, mom. I'm dehydrated. Give me water. Pepsi's not water, you cunt. Give me a glass of water. I'm dying. I have sores on my tongue all the time. And stop hitting me. You're huge. How could you hit me? That's crazy. You're a giant. And I can't defend myself." (CK 2011)

The argument here is one of instant gratification and epistemic access. The former will be discussed later in this chapter, as the inability to deal with discomfort and the impulse to escape it immediately is a key issue for CK. The latter, explored here, is a recurrent theme in CK's work as well. Epistemic access refers to the limitations of possible knowledge. One has epistemic access – direct knowledge – of one's own thoughts, feelings, experiences, and memories. But she does not have access to the thoughts, feelings, experiences, and memories of others. The only way she can "know" these things is to be told by others what their thoughts, feelings, experiences, and memories are, and even so, she can only know them secondhand, and never as well, or as vividly, as the Other. In the above bit, CK admonishes the parent who does not understand why her child reacts to chemicals – not because the parent lacks the impossible firsthand knowledge of what it is like to be the Other, but because the parent does not bother to consider the child *as* an Other. He offers insight – or epistemic access – to the child through speaking as him: "I haven't had actual nutrition in eight years, mom." This is an argument for empathy. While the parent can never know the child's inner world as well as she can know her own, she can place herself in the position of the child and empathize with him.

Reading the jokes out of context of a comedy show, without an accompanying performance, showcase how deeply sad much of CK's content is. How awful it is that so many children experience what this hypothetical child experiences, and how important it is for CK to address it. How is he able to do it? By acknowledging, as a parent, how hard it is to be a good one. As he put it in an interview with Terry Gross on NPR in 2015, "The greatest thing about having a child is putting yourself second in your own life. It's a massive gift to be able to say you're not the most important person to yourself" (Gross 2015). Putting oneself second is hard. But it's the only way to be a good parent.

Children turn their parents into philosophers, too, with their constant asking "why?". If a parent answers these questions honestly, rather than ignoring the question, they go somewhere profound. As CK put it in *One Night Stand,*

> More questions. "Why?" "Why?" "Why?" Until you don't even know who the fuck you are anymore at the end of the conversation. It's an insane deconstruction...it gets so weird and abstract. In the end it's like "Why?" Well because some things *are* and some things *are not.* "Why?" Well because things that are *not* can't be! "Why?" Because then *nothing* wouldn't be. You can't have fucking "Nothing *isn't,* everything *is!*" "Why?" Because if nothing *wasn't* there'd be fucking all kinds of shit that we don't – like giant ants with top hats dancing around! There's no room for all that shit! (CK 2005)

"There's no room for all that shit" echoes W.V.O. Quine's argument against ontologizing subjects and predicates. In the roughest of terms, Quine argued that it is unnecessary to make beings out of the linguistic terms that are used to describe the world and experience. A sign can exist as a word without that word corresponding to an actual being. In this sense, Quine objects to any metaphysical system which includes entities that science cannot, in principle, study. It is possible, sure, that there are ants with top hats and a possible twin sister, but it is impossible to subject these ideas to scientific analysis, and therefore ridiculous to assume their ontological reality (Quine 1948). Too many ants with top hats make for a crowded metaphysics, just as CK describes here, and not only is there no room for it all, but there's no scientific purpose for it either.

These are just a few examples of the sort of philosophical arguments CK makes in his work, and they have not gone unnoticed. CK has been praised by countless critics and scholars for his philosophical acuity. Max Elder describes CK's work as perfect representations of Nietzschean duality (Elder 2016). He's been likened to Schopenhauer (Heany 2016), Epicurus and Marcus Aurelius (Ralkowski 2016, p. 48), Epictetus (Williams 2016), and Parmenides and Aristotle (Kirkland 2016), just to name a few. Take the philosophical insight of Louie (the character based on CK in his TV show *Louie*) chastising his daughter on a road trip for repeating how bored she is:

> I'm bored is a useless thing to say. I mean, you live in a great, big, vast world that you've seen none percent of. Even the inside of your own mind is endless; it goes on forever, inwardly, do you understand? *The fact that you're alive is amazing.* So you don't get to be bored. (*Louie,*"Country Drive")

This message is consistent throughout CK's work – the things that make people angry, or frustrated, or bored, are really just a matter of limited perspective – of not being able to sit in a moment, of taking for granted the luxuries of modern life, of needing a panacea for every slightly unpleasant feeling that might tickle up the back of a neck. This is an argument from both Stoicism and Buddhist philosophy. The Buddhists argued that it is simply a fact that human beings suffer. Instead of clinging to the idea that one can avoid or prevent that suffering, or craving an impossible world where there is no suffering, the Buddhists argue that happiness can only come from letting go. The reason people are so miserable all the time is because they have a mistaken idea that they can avoid suffering through artificial means, like money or stuff or other people. This comes from a sort of selfishness, in the strictest sense of the term. The preoccupation with One's Self is what makes one suffer: "I" do not like this; "I" deserve better; this is "mine," "my" friend, "my" partner, "my" house, "my" stuff. The "I, me, mine" is at the root of craving and clinging, and this is what leads to suffering. Freedom from suffering, some Buddhist argue, can only be achieved by relinquishing the self. Once this obsession and preoccupation with self is abandoned, the suffering can end. Nirvana, the state in which there is no suffering, is simply a matter of having the Right Ideas about oneself and the world.

Saint Augustine makes a very similar argument, though from a Catholic perspective. He argues in *On Free Choice of the Will* that all sin comes from inordinate desire, which is most simply understood as the desire to control things that one cannot control (Augustine 2010). The pursuit of control – control over one's livelihood, friendships, families, city, belongings, health – is what seduces people into doing evil things for what they may believe to be good reasons. "I know it's wrong to lie," one might say, "but if I tell the truth about this action then my spouse will leave me, so I *have* to lie." This is how human beings fall, again and again, even while knowing better. Augustine argues that the only thing that is within one's control is their own actions.

For both philosophers, it is the pursuit of control over that which makes one uncomfortable that is the root of unhappiness, and people will do just about anything to avoid unhappiness. While explaining to Conan O'Brien why he won't buy his daughters cell phones, CK makes this very argument:

> You need to build an ability to just be yourself and not be doing something. That's what the phones are taking away...Because, y'know, underneath everything in your life, there's that thing – that empty, forever empty, y'know what I'm talking about? Just that knowledge that it's all for nothing and you're alone, y'know it's down there. And sometimes when things clear away, and you're not watching anything, you're in your car, and you start going 'Ohhh no, here it comes! That I'm alone!"...Just be sad. Just let the sadness – stand in the way of it, and let it hit you like a truck. And I let it come, and I started to feel, oh my God. And I pulled over and I just cried like a bitch. I cried so much. And it was beautiful. Sadness is poetic, you're lucky to live sad moments...So I was grateful to feel sad, and then I met it with true profound happiness...And the thing is, because we don't want that first bit of sad, we push it away. (Zimmerman 2013)

Being able to sit with loneliness, without constant stimulation and instant gratification, is a skill he insists his children learn. Confronting the Forever Alone, and bringing it to an audience, is scary but important. CK describes his choice to go to "scary places" as necessary for growth, both for himself and his audience:

> The areas I'm going into ... are touchy...You feel a little sweat on the back of your neck when you get there, but if you stay there for a second, you can find something joyful and funny in it. And it's such a great thing to go to a scary place and laugh...I'm not afraid if I go somewhere and I upset everybody...I got in trouble a lot as a kid, so I got used to it. When you're never in trouble, you can never go to places like that...So when I started going on

stage, I realized if I talk about this stuff I might upset people in the room, but it's worth it because maybe there's something there. (Gross 2014)

What made *Hilarious* so successful was CK's honesty, a characteristic that would propel him to sell out Madison Square Garden eight times. This honesty isn't the typical "telling truth to power" sort that is so common in comedy today, but rather an honesty about the darker thoughts and feelings that hijack his day, thoughts and feelings that many find ashamedly relatable. CK doesn't just tell on himself when he jokes about, for example, how if a kid *can* die from a nut allergy, maybe they *should* die of a nut allergy. He tells on the audience as well. In *Oh My God*, shortly after the nut allergy joke, CK begins an argument that perhaps slavery isn't a *completely* bad thing. When the audience gasps, he chides, "Listen, listen. You all clapped for dead kids with the nuts, for kids dying from nuts. You applauded. So you're in this with me now. Do you understand? You don't get to cherry pick. Those kids did nothing to you" (*Oh My God* C.K. 2013). This is what Duncan Reyburn calls CK's "brutal truth telling," which he likens to a psychoanalyst bearing the unconscious (Reyburn 2016, p. 275).

In addition to talking about the terror of being a parent (*Hilarious* C.K. 2010), CK does a great deal of material on race. His bits on how lucky he is to be white (*Chewed Up* C.K. 2008) and how the machines people want are "all made from the same Asian suffering" (*Louie*, "Late Show Part 1") display a keen understanding of privilege and social hierarchy. Long before "woke" was a popular phrase, CK was presenting argument after argument about the sociohistorical privileges of being a white man. Scholars Myisha Cherry and Chris Kramer, to name only two, have praised these bits extensively (see Ralkowski 2016). Take this bit from *Chewed Up*:

> I love being white. Seriously, I really do. If you're not white, you're missing out. 'Cuz this shit is thoroughly good. Let me clear this up by the way: I'm not saying white people are better. I'm saying that *being* white is clearly better. Who could even argue? If it was an option I would re-up every year! "Oh yeah, I'll take white again. Absolutely." Here's how great it is to be white: I could get in a time machine and go to any time and it would be fuckin' awesome when I get there. That is exclusively a white privilege. Black people can't fuck with time machines. A black guy in a time machine is like, "hey anything before 1980 no thank you, I don't want to go." But I can go to any time. The year 2? I don't even know what was happening then, but I know when I get there, "Welcome! We have a table right here for you sir." (CK 2008)

Here CK argues that it is unquestionably true that white people have had better, more privileged experiences than others. This isn't a very controversial or interesting argument, of course, as it doesn't take very long to roll out a list of historical evidence to support it. What makes this argument unique is CK's subtle chastisement of the white liberal who wishes she were Black – the "Rachel Dolezals" of the world. This bit is an indirect confrontation of those "well-meaning" white folks who ally themselves with Black people due to exoticism. Such white people do not escape racist thinking just because they do not engage in explicitly racist actions. It is just as racist to love a group of people based solely on their skin color as it is to hate that group for their skin color. And it is just as racist to want to be a part of a movement or community because they represent an Exotic Other. CK is not arguing that Black people are better than white people, or the reverse. But neither is he pretending that he would want it any other way given his own racial identity. He does not want to be Black, and other white-passing people shouldn't want to either. If they really understood what it meant to be Black, CK argues, and what it means to be racist, they wouldn't fetishize and fantasize.

It is also worthwhile to note CK was writing, thinking, and performing about these issues long before everyone from politicians to retailers like Wal-Mart and Amazon were promoting Black Lives Matter. And unlike the politicians and retailers, CK didn't stand to make huge financial gains off riding a sociopolitical wave. No, CK's arguments regarding race came from those same scary places that he had always managed to find and spin into relatable material.

Perhaps the scariest, most personally vulnerable place that CK goes in his comedy is his own sexuality. CK's comedy has always had a preoccupation with sex. He tells jokes about his own obsession with masturbation regularly. John Heany (2016) wrote an entire article on the philosophical merit of CK's discourse on sexuality. In it, he argues that CK, like Arthur Schopenhauer, vacillates between "sexual arousal and suicidal despair" (p. 12). CK's jokes about being controlled by sexual thoughts and how these thoughts destroy every normal interaction he has with women are part of the brutal truth-telling that Reyburn and others praise CK for daring to speak out loud. He describes the difference between the way he is controlled by sex versus the way women think about sex in *Live at the Beacon Theater*: "You *get* to have those feelings; I *have* to have them. You're a *tourist* in sexual perversion; I'm a *prisoner* there" (CK 2011).

Perhaps because of men's pathological perversion, CK argues, with statistical evidence, that "men are the number one threat to women":

> A woman saying 'yes' to a date with a man is literally insane and ill-advised, and the whole species' existence counts on them doing it…How do women still go out with guys when you consider the fact that there is no greater threat to women than men? We're the number one threat to women. Globally and historically, we're the number one cause of injury and mayhem to women. We're the worst thing that ever happens to them. That's true! You know what our number one threat is? Heart disease. (*Oh My God* C.K. 2013)

Not only does CK address the hush-hush reality of spousal and stranger abuse, but he understands the struggles facing women in their historical context. In a stand-up bit from his TV show, he says:

> Women are really kept down, even today. A lot of people like to argue that things are equal, but they're really not, and American history hasn't been kind to women. Women couldn't vote until 1920. How crazy is that…which means America wasn't really a democracy until 1920. You can't call it a democracy if the whole sex of women can't vote. (*Louie*, "Pamela Part 1")

CK's understanding of the plight of women is likely influenced by being a father of daughters, but it is also the consequence of being a person who finds dialogue to be extremely important. In 2012, CK found himself caught up in a heated debate when he tweeted a compliment to comedian Daniel Tosh. People were calling for Tosh's show, *Tosh.0*, to be cancelled because of rape jokes Tosh had told on tour. Of the subsequent outrage, CK said:

> All dialogue is positive... I think you should listen. If someone has the opposite feeling from me, I want to hear it so I can add to mine. I don't want to obliterate theirs with mine – that's how I feel...I've read some blogs during this whole thing that have made me enlightened to things I didn't know. This woman said how rape is something that polices women's lives. They have a narrow corridor; they can't go out late, they can't go to certain neighborhoods, they can't dress a certain way. That's part of me now that wasn't before. (*The Daily Show with Jon Stewart* July 16, 2012)

But one ought not confuse his understanding of the hardships women face with an unrealistic idea that women are perfect: "I don't think women are better than men, but I do think men are worse than women." Men and women are simply different creatures, CK argues, and this is seen clearly in children. Boys, he says, are physically aggressive, whereas girls are manipulative: "Girls like leave scars in your psyche that you find later, like a genocide or an atrocity...it becomes the difference between men and women. Because a man will, like, steal your car or burn your house down or beat the shit out of you, but a woman will ruin your fucking life." He continues, "A man will cut off your arm and throw it in a river, but he'll leave you as a human being intact... Women are nonviolent, but they will shit inside of your heart" (*Chewed Up* C.K. 2008).

Part of what makes CK such an effective feminist philosopher is that he is not a perfect representation of a feminist. As I have argued elsewhere, if CK only ever said the "right things," if he only ever praised women and spoke of their woes, his audience would be much smaller (Marra 2016, p. 244). It is precisely because he appeals to a broad audience that his feminist arguments are heard by more than just those who already agree with him. Comics like Hari Kondabolu and Samantha Bee, while brilliant and massively talented, draw exclusively like-minded crowds and thus simply "preach to the choir." CK's ability to draw politically and socioeconomically diverse crowds gives him the opportunity to expose audiences to new ideas that they would not actively seek out.

This, too, is part of the philosophy of CK. CK is not a Sophist on high telling others how to live, how to think, or how to know. Rather, he offers the sticky, contradictory realities of what it is to be a human being in the world and insists that those realities be explored. In this way, CK is a contemporary Socrates – the unexamined life is truly *not* worth living. People *ought* to think about how they raise their children, rather than just doing what their parents did or what they see other parents do. People *ought* to consider why it is that they can't have a bowel movement without using a smartphone. People *ought* to consider how awesome it is to be flying in an airplane instead of complaining about being stuck on the runway for awhile (*Hilarious* C.K. 2010).

From 2011 to 2017, CK's career skyrocketed. His stand-up specials were consistently hailed by critics and audiences, his comedy tours sold out within the first day of ticket sales, he had an Emmy-winning television show, and he was releasing a new feature film that he wrote and directed (Ryzik et al. 2017). Fans had the sense that

CK cared about their wellbeing – not that he wanted to spend time with his fans, of course – but rather that he wanted to do material that his fans could relate to, and perhaps, learn from. On the business end, CK did something few comics would dare to attempt – he sold tickets and digital downloads of his comedy specials through his website. While one could buy DVDs in stores at much higher prices, tickets to see CK perform live were exclusively available through CK himself, rather than venues acting as the middleman. This kept costs low, providing more access to those fans who could not afford to spend hundreds of dollars on a comedy show. Articles like "How Louis CK Helps the Domestic Workers' Movement by showing that Parenting is Work" by Sheila Bapat (published by the online newspaper Feministing in January of 2014) began a rapid-fire level of praise for CK's socioeconomic enlightenment. This was several months before a breakout episode of his show *Louie* titled "So Did The Fat Lady" made CK everyone's favorite feminist comedian.

That Breakout Episode of *Louie*

Louie, which premiered in 2010, was a remarkable show, if only for the level of creative control CK was given. CK explained to Howard Stern that "the greatest deal I ever made in my life" was giving up hundreds of thousands of dollars every year in exchange for full creative control: "FX doesn't even read the scripts. They don't know what the show is until they watch it" (Ralkowski 2016, p. xvii).

"So Did The Fat Lady" originally aired on May 12, 2014. The plot follows Louie, a fictional version of CK himself, as he continually declines dates with an overweight woman, Vanessa, who works at the comedy club where he performs. The episode begins with Louie and his brother going out for a "bang bang" (eating two full meals one after the other from two separate eateries). The men relish what is portrayed as a gluttonous conquest moments before Louie declines a date from Vanessa. Eventually Vanessa's persistence pays off and Louie accepts her offer to join her for a hockey game, though he spends the date making sure that Vanessa knows that he is not interested in pursuing a relationship, despite the fact that they are extremely compatible.

When Vanessa casually mentions the fact that she's fat, Louie feigns shock and disagreement. "You know what the meanest thing is you can say to a fat girl?" Vanessa asks. "'You're not fat.'" This powerful line confronts the nasty little secret of a size-obsessed culture. It admits that, whether society will admit it or not, being fat is the worst thing a woman can be. Vanessa says that if she acknowledges that she's fat, "they call a suicide hotline on me." As if admitting to being a fat woman means that she hates herself, hates her life, and might as well end it, because being a fat woman *is* a reason to hate oneself, hate ones' life, and want to end it. As if being a fat woman is *a good reason* to commit suicide. This reveals the underlying truth behind it all: that fat women are *hated* by society in general and men in particular: "Why do you hate us so much?" Vanessa asks (*Louie*, "So Did The Fat Lady").

CK's argument in this monologue is as uncomfortable as it is direct: society treats fat women as either pitiable and/or defective, but when the ugly truth is spoken, they cannot bear to admit it. People will treat fat women badly *because they are fat*, then deny that fatness is the reason that they are doing so. Further, it is even, and often especially, those who discriminate against women for being fat that *know that this behavior is immoral* and so will deny it when it is called out. Louie *knows* that denying Vanessa because she's fat is wrong, while at the same time knowing that *it is* the only reason he's denying her. Somehow not heavy handedly, somehow delicately yet explicitly, CK exposes the shame one feels when they are called out on this obvious discriminatory behavior. Louie *knows* that it is a superficial double standard that he is using against Vanessa, but the fact that *she* knows it makes him, and the audience, confront the shame they do and ought to feel about it.

But it is not simply a matter of double standards that CK is bringing into focus here, though these are addressed both directly and indirectly in the episode. It is certainly true that fat men, like Louie himself, do not suffer from the same mistreatment as fat women. And it is certainly true that even and often it is fat men, like Louie, who are doing the mistreating. CK is also exposing the more complex, cognitive dissonance of it all. Louie knows he's fat, admits he's fat, and yet still believes that he is "worthy" of a thin woman, that his life is fine enough, that being fat is something that he's not proud of but not something that makes him any less of a human being or partner. But he cannot fathom that a fat woman could feel the same way. This reveals both what society thinks about fat women, and how individuals in society are so calcified in those thinking patterns that they cannot grant fat women the same complex inner world, the same humanity, that they grant themselves.

The nearly 7-min, uninterrupted monologue by Vanessa (actress Sarah Baker), while CK as Louie simply stands there, looking ashamed and uncomfortable, is tense and honest. As the writer and director, CK wrote himself as the deserving target – not of a rage-fueled feminist – but of an intelligent, funny woman deeply hurt by the way the world, and men, and this man in particular, treat her, all because of her size. The raw vulnerability displayed through the monologue, and CK's choice to direct it at himself, are quintessential of why audiences and critics love CK's work.

A flurry of stories praising CK followed the airing of "So Did The Fat Lady." NPR published a story titled "Louis CK Takes On TV Hypocrisy, Aiming Scrutiny Back At Himself" on May 12, 2014 (Deegans 2014). The next day, Emily Yahr of The Washington Post authored "Here's that epic, mesmerizing 'fat girl' speech from Monday night's 'Louie'" on May 13, 2014 (Yahr 2014). Madeleine Davies cited the episode as proof that CK is "one of the greatest comic minds of our generation" (Davies 2014). On May 14, GQ's Andrew Corsello published an interview with CK titled, "Louis CK Is America's Undisputed King of Comedy" (Corsello 2014).

The Fall and the Return

The Accusations

Then, on November 9, 2017, the *New York Times* published a disturbing story: "Louis CK Is Accused by 5 Women of Sexual Misconduct" (Ryzik et al. 2017). Women had come forward to accuse Louis CK of masturbating in front of them without their full consent. This came as a shock to those who hailed CK as a man who truly understood the fear and difficulties of being a woman.

In each case, CK asked a fellow comedian if he could masturbate in front of her. If the woman agreed, CK would proceed. The first woman who came forward reported that the incident happened in the late 1990s. Choosing to remain anonymous, she explains that she agreed to his request because "It was something that I knew was wrong... I think the big piece of why I said yes was because of the culture. He abused his power" (Ryzik et al. 2017).

The next report came from two comedians, Dana Min Goodman and Julia Wolov, over an incident in 2002. Again, CK asked if he could perform the sex act in front of them, and according to them, they agreed, thinking that he was joking.

A fourth woman, Abby Schachner, reports that in 2003, CK began masturbating while on the phone with her. In 2009, CK wrote Schachner a Facebook message apologizing for the incident, stating that it was a bad time in his life and that he was a repulsive person (Ryzik et al. 2017).

The last woman, Rebecca Corry, reported that CK made the same proposition to her in 2005 after shoving her into a bathroom. She declined. He sent her an email apologizing to her for the proposition, stating "I used to misread people back then," but continues to deny that he ever shoved her into a bathroom (Ryzik et al. 2017).

It is worth keeping in mind, however, that rumors of CK's fetish for masturbating in front of women had been a not-so-well-kept secret around the comedy scene for years. A website called Defamer published such rumors about CK in 2015. Comedians Jen Kirkman and Rosanne Barr also mentioned the rumors in 2015; Kirkman by insinuation, Barr by name (Yamato 2016). (Barr later met with a fate similar to CK's as she was kicked off her own television show in 2018 for posting on Twitter what many understood as a racial attack.)

The Fallout

CK's accusers reported that speaking out about the incidents had severe consequences. Goodman and Wolov reported that CK's manager, Dave Becky, threatened their careers. Schachner left comedy altogether, and Corry was taunted with death threats (Aggeler 2018). Speaking out about what CK had done had not only harmed their careers and desires to pursue comedy at the time of the events, but continued years later when the NYT article was published.

As a result of the allegations, CK reported that he lost "35 million dollars in an hour" (Maglio 2018). FX, the channel that hosted *Louie*, banned him from their network and Netflix pulled out of the comedy special they were set to distribute. CK was replaced as a voice actor for two television series and a feature film, and HBO removed all of his content from their on-demand services (Hipes 2017). A film he was just set to release, *I Love You, Daddy*, was dropped by its distributor (D'Alessandro 2017). Lead actors Chloe Grace Moretz and Charlie Day refused to promote the film (Yamato 2017).

CK's once beloved comedy was now being viewed through the lens of the allegations. What had been praised as brave and honest bits about ego and sexual insecurity were interpreted by critics and bloggers as sinister, foreboding, and vile. What was once understood as the vulnerable unveiling of deep yet universal anxieties had become perverse apologetics from a predator. While CK's policy in the past had been to ignore the rumors, this time he released an official statement, reproduced here in its entirety:

> I want to address the stories told to The New York Times by five women named Abby, Rebecca, Dana, Julia who felt able to name themselves and one who did not.
>
> These stories are true. At the time, I said to myself that what I did was O.K. because I never showed a woman my dick without asking first, which is also true. But what I learned later in life, too late, is that when you have power over another person, asking them to look at your dick isn't a question. It's a predicament for them. The power I had over these women is that they admired me. And I wielded that power irresponsibly. I have been remorseful of my actions. And I've tried to learn from them. And run from them. Now I'm aware of the extent of the impact of my actions. I learned yesterday the extent to which I left these women who admired me feeling badly about themselves and cautious around other men who would never have put them in that position. I also took advantage of the fact that I was widely admired in my and their community, which disabled them from sharing their story and brought hardship to them when they tried because people who look up to me didn't want to hear it. I didn't think that I was doing any of that because my position allowed me not to think about it. There is nothing about this that I forgive myself for. And I have to reconcile it with who I am. Which is nothing compared to the task I left them with. I wish I had reacted to their admiration of me by being a good example to them as a man and given them some guidance as a comedian, including because I admired their work.
>
> The hardest regret to live with is what you've done to hurt someone else. And I can hardly wrap my head around the scope of hurt I brought on them. I'd be remiss to exclude the hurt that I've brought on people who I work with and have worked with who's [sic] professional and personal lives have been impacted by all of this, including projects currently in production: the cast and crew of *Better Things*, *Baskets*, *The Cops*, *One Mississippi*, and *I Love You, Daddy*. I deeply regret that this has brought negative attention to my manager Dave Becky who only tried to mediate a situation that I caused. I've brought anguish and hardship to the people at FX who have given me so much, The Orchard who took a chance on my movie and every other entity that has bet on me through the years. I've brought pain to my family, my friends, my children and their mother.
>
> I have spent my long and lucky career talking and saying anything I want. I will now step back and take a long time to listen. Thank you for reading. (CNN 2017)

CK received even more criticism after the apology was published. Some commentators said it wasn't even an apology because at no point does he say the words "sorry" or "apologize." They claimed that the statement was too little too late, as he could have taken ownership for his behavior years before when the rumors first surfaced. He is only confessing his guilt now, they argued, because he is losing money. Still others said that while the apology was fine in and of itself, it did not erase the harm done from his actions (Respers France 2017). Jesse Joho wrote a scathing piece the same day the apology was published, arguing that CK deserves no praise for "doing the bare minimum" of admitting fault (Joho 2017).

Tiptoeing Toward a Return

Following his statement, CK was neither seen nor heard from for almost a year. Then, in August 2018, CK made an unannounced appearance at his old stomping grounds, the Comedy Cellar in Manhattan. The audience was thrilled to see him, greeting him with enthusiastic cries of "Louie!" when he came to the stage.

The set itself is an interesting one. CK goes straight into addressing the fallout of the scandal, saying that every day of the past year has been "absolutely fucking terrible," and that it started to become funny how he "lost 35 million dollars in one day." He makes fun of how excessive he was with his money before, and how horrible it was to "find out who his real friends are." He laments that his mother, not fully understanding the situation, continues to send him articles about himself from the Times, not realizing that the articles are unfavorable toward him. The room does become audibly tense as CK begins a joke about a sick woman who put a thermometer down her pants in front of him to take her temperature anally. He navigates the moments carefully and moves the room back into ease – then suggests she put it in "her pussy" instead. Again, the audience is quiet. He tells a joke about how he likes when the doctor touches him "it's my favorite part." Tense again, but for a short pause before he delivers the punchline that it's because he needs fatherly care and approval.

Probably the most countercultural material in this set is a "kids today" bit. Kids today are boring, he says. They're all about telling people not to do things, how they demand to be addressed by they/them pronouns "like royalty." Addressing the surviving students of the Parkland High School shootings who testified in front of Congress in pursuit of gun control legislation he exclaims, "What are you doing? You're young, you should be crazy, you should be unhinged!... You're not interesting because you went to a high school where kids got shot - you didn't get shot, you pushed some fat kid in the way and now I have to listen to you talking?" In classic CK fashion, he caps this most controversial bit by acknowledging the audiences' squeamishness saying, "You can get offended, I don't care, my life is over." As far as the audience in the room is concerned, the set absolutely kills (CK 2018).

The content of this unannounced set is only known because an audience member recorded it and released the audio (the set has since been removed from YouTube). Even under the best of circumstances with uncontroversial comedians, the first time one tries out a new set with new jokes is never something that they intend to reach a wide audience – such a set is, for all intents and purposes, a field test. From what CK has said about his process, he is likely embarrassed for anyone outside of the club to hear such unpolished material. Unfortunately for CK, the leaked set drew even more criticism.

Matt Wilstein of the Daily Beast wrote a piece titled "Louis CK's 'Comeback' to Female Comedians: 'Ridiculous', 'Depressing' and 'Not Surprising.'" Ironically, Wilstein reports that the biggest disappoint for Comedy Cellar owner Noam Dworman was that CK's set was "typical Louis CK stuff" that didn't address the scandal. Comedian Jackie Kashian told Wilstein that if he had truly made amends and understood why what he did was wrong, he would have included it in his set.

"[He's] smart enough to know that writing a bit about how 'it's not that big a deal' isn't going to work with most of the crowd" (Wilstein 2018). Worse yet, Kevin Fallon writes that CK has reinvented himself as an "alt-right" comedian. His overall impression of the set: "At face value, it's a rather lazy comedy set. A 'kids these days' joke related to gender identity is phoned in, and, more, adds nothing to any cultural discourse besides an expressed intent to undermine it" (Fallon 2018).

Aware of the criticisms, CK made changes to his set as he continued to try new material. In San Jose on January 16, 2019, he opened with: "I like to jerk off, and I don't like being alone…You've read the worst possible things you could read about a person, about me, and you're here" (Sharf 2019). He also replaced the bit about the Parkland shooting victims with the line: "If you ever need people to forget that you jerked off, what you do is make a joke about kids that got shot" (Robinson 2019).

CK began touring again internationally in October 2019. His US dates avoided the big liberal cities like New York and Los Angeles – as he explained in his set in Tel Aviv, "I'd rather be in Auschwitz than New York City. I mean now, not when it was open" (Trock 2019). (The crowd loved the joke.) Like the rest of the entertainment industry, his performing schedule was suspended in 2020 due to the COVID-19 pandemic. He released a new comedy special, *Sincerely, Louis CK*, on April 4, 2020 (CK 2020). The special is the "samurai sword" of material he had honed in the small comedy clubs and is the proper target of analysis. To judge CK based on the leaked set – the first pass of new jokes at a small club – is tantamount to judging an oil painting by the base coat.

Like much of his previous work, in the completed special, CK does what he has always done: goes to those touchy areas, those scary places. He talks about the word "retarded" and what it used to mean, how unfair it is that so much more is expected of people with disabilities than the average person (they have to be exceptional at everything they do, *and* inspirational, *and* have a good attitude), how he had to escape the United States and do shows in Poland "because I had to go to Poland to do shows," and about his new French girlfriend (CK 2020). It is, for all intents and purposes, a pretty average Louis CK set. It is brave in that it remains sexually preoccupied, but safe in that the sexual bits are the easiest and least controversial of the material.

It is clear in *Sincerely, Louis CK* that CK imagines a world in which he could return, and because of that, he continues to play by his old rules: he positions himself as a sad sack, adds a wink at the end of every dirty joke, implicates the audience in his more controversial bits, and asks the audience to consider cultural presuppositions that are accepted by default. In all, CK presents a bit more desperate, less free version of his former self in an otherwise very CK hour of comedy.

The special received mixed reviews from critics and fellow comedians but was nominated for, and won, a Grammy Award for Best Comedy Album in 2021 (Horton 2021). Stand-up comedian Amy Schumer said of the special, "I laughed at a lot of it. But it's hard not to think of what he has done, what he has and hasn't learned, but I definitely laughed" (Zinoman 2020).

CK toured internationally in 2021 and, as of this writing, has tour dates in 2022 which include New York City and other big cities that he had previously avoided or had refused to book him. His live appearances have thrilled audiences and upset activists. Take, for example, the Madison, Wisconsin, appearances in July 2021. According to Lindsay Nejedlo, a cocktail waitress for the club who worked all three nights of the show, CK mostly "kept to himself," not really socializing with the staff or fans, in a manner Nejedlo read as "cautious" (Nejedlo 2021). There were a few protesters outside of the comedy club, but the show was sold out all three nights and the audience thoroughly enjoyed themselves. This appears to have been a trend in his live shows since returning to the stage (Levy 2021).

As time passes, CK is slowly returning to the stage and screen, though he has maintained, necessarily or not, the direct-to-consumer model of distribution. It is unclear if big production studios have any interest in collaborating. In December 2021, CK released his most recent stand-up special titled *Sorry* exclusively through his website (CK 2021).

The Two Most Important Questions

There are several interesting philosophical questions that arise in the Louis CK case. On the one hand, CK is unquestionably a major cultural contributor, and his work has done a lot of good to bring light to marginalized and forgotten voices, particularly women. On the other hand, he committed acts which marginalize, victimize, and undermine the careers of women. What ought to be done with Louis CK? The answer is not as simple to determine as one might imagine.

It is unnecessary to ask whether CK's actions were wrong – they were immoral, plain and simple. Although it will be addressed, below, why CK asking permission first did not make what he did morally permissible, there is no real question about CK's guilt. Rather, this study will ask more complex questions which will yield, as will be shown, a variety of complex answers. The focus will be twofold: first, was the industry response to CK's actions the correct one? Second, should CK be allowed to return to comedy? These questions, while focused on CK specifically, are broader in implication. The first is really asking, Should the work of immoral actors be erased from cultural consumption? The second, Are some actions so unacceptable that one "forfeits" their right to public contribution? A range of philosophical responses to these more universal questions follow.

1. Was the industry response to the CK's actions the correct one? Should the work of immoral actors be erased from cultural consumption?

The feminist answer to this question is often a simple yes. This viewpoint argues that Louis CK used his position and power to coerce women into silence after committing a nonconsensual sexual act in their presence. This position takes very seriously the difficulty faced by women in the comedy industry.

Comedy is a small, incestuous world where women still struggle to get stage time and be treated as equal to men. This is due in large part to the idea that women are not funny, which received a formal defense in the form of an evolutionary argument. In a now infamous article for *Vanity Fair*, Christopher Hitchens argues not that women are somehow incapable of being funny or of creating humor, but rather that the evolutionary survival mechanisms developed by the human species required men to be funny in order to attract a mate. Hitchens argues that reproduction is a biological force, and, like any other animal, human beings engage in mating rituals. Men, he argues, developed the ability to be funny as a means to beat out the competition. Women have no need to develop any such techniques, and thus simply have not. This required men to develop, hone, and perfect the ability to be funny, for the survival of the species, resulting in an abundance of necessarily funny men and, due to the lack of necessity, unfunny women (Hitchens 2007).

While the argument behind Hitchens's position is more recent, the conclusion has been part of the struggle of female comedians since stand-up's inception in America. For one, as Yael Kohen's research acknowledges, until 1957 female comedians not only had to be funny enough to get to the stage, they also had to sing and dance (Kohen 2012, p. 7). Women have always faced discrimination from booking agents, fellow comedians, and audiences alike. According to Joanne Gilbert, women who do comedy must fall into one of the following comedic postures: a kid (e.g., Ellen DeGeneres), a bawd (e.g., Mae West), a bitch (e.g., Joan Rivers), a whiner (e.g., Lucille Ball), or a reporter (e.g., Janeane Garofalo) (Gilbert 2004, p. 96). Even if a comic is more complex than the category allows, she will still be shoved into one of these postures. They represent a cage for women in comedy, one that keeps them confined to a formula that is easy for bookers and audiences to understand.

Louis CK was a highly respected comedian even before his big break. He played comedy clubs, got along with the owners and bookers, and was loved by audiences. A good word from CK regarding a woman's comedy was a shoo-in for stage time, and a bad word was tantamount to a banishment from the club. A shining example of this reality is Tig Notaro, who owes her career to CK's active endorsements.

When CK asked comediennes if he could perform a sex act in front of them, the women were forced to consider how their response would inevitably affect their careers. If they said no, there was a high chance that CK wouldn't put in a good word for them at clubs, or actively tell bookers not to give them time. If they told others about the incidents or complained to clubs directly, they would certainly be looked at as troublemakers, not worth anyone's time, and easily replaceable by any number of eager new comedians quick to fill their spot. The moment CK asked the question, he put his colleagues in an impossible position. If they said yes, as many of them did, they would become responsible for the event. It would be "their fault." After all, CK is not a mind reader – if they didn't want him to do it, they could have just said no. But if they said no, CK might take it personally and could, if he wished, end their careers. And if they told others in the comedy community what was going on (as some of them did), they also risked ending their careers, as they would be (and, as reported by the women, were) labeled as trouble, dangerous, a liability not worth the risk (Ryzik et al. 2017).

This is exemplary of what sociologists and philosophers have called "rape culture," a term dating back to 1988 when it was coined by Dianne Herman. Rape culture describes the ways in which individuals, systems, and institutions blame women for being victims of sexual assault and downplay the seriousness of rape in culture (Herman 1989). The catch-22 of the comediennes propositioned by CK was that all possible options would result in their victimization, either in terms of experiencing the sexual misconduct or fear that they would likely be exiled from the comedy community.

Rape culture and other forms of societal misogyny will not end if society does not take a bold and definitive stand against those who perpetuate it. Banning CK from the comedy scene, taking away his access to the cultural marketplace, removing his specials from cultural consumption, and no longer supporting projects in which he is involved sends a clear message to comedians, bookers, club owners, and audiences that one's behavior has consequences, no matter how popular or powerful the offender.

What would philosophers say about this response? The philosopher Plato would agree that CK should be censored, although not because of anything that he did; Plato would want him censored simply for the content of his material. To ensure a society is Good, Plato argues in *The Republic*, it must aggrandize virtuous things and condemn vicious things. Culture influences character. A culture which allows vicious things to be idolized will create vicious character, while a society which praises virtuous things will encourage virtuous character. For this reason, in Plato's ideal society, only virtuous art is allowed. Plato argues that immoral art is essentially a cancer to the moral development of the citizenry and should be banned.

Insofar as not all of CK's work is morally exemplary, it shouldn't be allowed in a good society to begin with, regardless of what its author has done. Speaking specifically of jokes, Plato writes, "...the effect [of laughter] is similar [to pity] when you enjoy on stage – or even in ordinary life – a joke that you would be ashamed to make yourself, instead of detesting their vulgarity...bad taste in the theatre may insensibly lead you into becoming a buffoon at home" (*Plato* 606c). Plato would disagree, however, with any actions taken against CK in response to public demand. Democracy is no more than mob rule, he argues, and the mob should not be in charge of policy or the cultural marketplace. Even the decisions about what counts as moral and immoral art are not simply a matter of societal determination. The decisions regarding what should and should not be censored are to be made only by philosopher kings who truly know the difference, regardless of whether the public is in agreement (Plato 555b-592b).

John Stuart Mill and, more contemporarily, Greg Lukianoff and Jonathan Haidt, would agree with Plato that public pressure should have no bearing on decisions to ban, censor, or otherwise remove actors from the public sphere. In fact, in stark contrast to the culturally prominent feminist position and in complete disagreement with Plato, these thinkers would disagree with the response to CK and would in fact argue that *no one* should *ever* be censored, banned, or otherwise removed from the public discourse – even in response to immoral actions.

On a societal level, Mill argues from a utilitarian position that free speech and expression have greater overall benefit to society, even if that speech or expression is morally bankrupt: "If all mankind were of one opinion, and only one person were of the contrary opinion, mankind would be no more justified in silencing that one person, than he...would be justified in silencing all of mankind" (Mill 2018, p. 255). According to Mill, we need liberty of expression for the greater happiness of a society for four reasons. First, to assume one is right and another is wrong is to assert infallibility, and of course, human beings are not infallible. To be certain that one's position is the right one without bothering to listen to the alternative is to take the position that one cannot possibly be wrong. This is what José Medina would call the vice of "epistemic arrogance" (Medina 2013, p. 31).

Second, wrong ideas or expressions must be challenged for truth to come to light. If these expressions are censored formally, it doesn't prevent them from being spread informally. Rather than, for example, pull all CK material from streaming platforms, Mill would argue that society benefits from allowing such expressions to remain and serve as fodder for discussion. CK's material, especially the material that was recorded around the time of the incidents, may be worthwhile to study for the sake of understanding why it is that some men choose to act in similar ways. In fact, Mill would argue, even if no fruit can come of mining his material for clues, it is still for the greater good of society not to erase him from culture. While it can be agreed that what CK did was wrong, even by CK, it is crucially important, according to Mill, that it is understood precisely *why* what he did was wrong. This is something that cannot be done if CK, and his work, is vanished and banished from society. This idea echoes what CK himself said of the Tosh scandal: it was the occasion for him to learn something important.

Third, Mill argues that allowing wrong ideas and expressions to remain uncensored is necessary for strengthening the right ones. If an idea is never challenged, it grows stale. This is closely related to the fourth and final reason, which is that dogmatic beliefs, such as that the Earth is round, lose meaning and importance if they are not revisited. That the Earth is round is a "right idea" that is simply taken for granted. No one bothers to explore *why* she believes the Earth is round. Why would she? She has no reason to know, let alone explore, why she thinks this idea is right. Not until, that is, the emergence of the Flat Earthers. Flat Earthers are people who argue that the Earth is flat, and they have a host of compelling arguments for why. While the idea is wrong, Mill would say that allowing the ideas to be freely expressed is necessary for the right idea to become "lively" once again. So much of what people think is "given" and "obvious" that it is accepted without any reflection or discernment. Wrong ideas, Mill argues, present the occasion to revisit those neglected presuppositions. In other words, Mill would say that even those who spout off obvious nontruths should be at liberty to spout them, for the greater good of all. If a society is not challenged by untruths, truth will never have the occasion to be revealed and will simply fade into meaninglessness. "If the opinion is right," Mill writes, "they are deprived of the opportunity of exchanging error for truth: if wrong, they lose, what is almost as great a benefit, the clearer perception and livelier impression of truth, produced by its collision with error" (Mill 2018, p. 255).

But what of public pressure to censor based on the greater good? Mill is a utilitarian, after all, so he would have to favor the action that creates the most happiness and prevents the least pain. Could censoring CK lead to a utilitarian benefit? There are two ways to understand this worry.

First, would the fact that the majority of people want him banned entail that the utilitarian calculus favors banning him? In a word, no. The majority of people may want something, Mill would argue, but that does not mean that the thing that they want is truly what will create the greatest good for the greatest number. He has already given four reasons why CK shouldn't be censored, and those reasons stand even if the majority of people think he should be. That's not to say that if a person finds CK offensive, they shouldn't be allowed to argue that he ought to be censored. Insisting on the freedom to express ideas cuts both ways and includes the freedom to encourage others to agree with one's ideas. And if such a person was successful, it could, for example, create enough public pressure on Netflix to pull his specials and cancel his future projects. But that doesn't mean such an action would promote overall happiness. Public *opinion* is not the same as the public *good*.

The second way to understand this worry begins by drawing a distinction between censoring his work because of its content and censoring it simply to make him pay a price for what he did – to send a message that the relevant kind of "off stage" behavior will not be tolerated. Someone taking the latter position might not even object to the anything CK says in any stand-up routine; on this view, the content of his work is not harmful to society. But making clear that inappropriate behavior like his will be met with such dire consequences, one might argue, will deter CK and others from repeating it – and that generates a greater good. But, again, Mill would not likely agree. For Mill, the freedom of expression is essential for societal good, and thus no one's should be violated – even if it could deter some harmful behavior. Indeed, the only limit Mill puts on expression is of the old "yelling fire in a crowded theater" type (Mill 2018, p. 268). If one's free expression will cause *immediate* harm, then it cannot be tolerated. Of course, the question then becomes, how do we understand immediate harm? Mill understood it in the explicit sense exclusively, pointing out the person that the angry mob wants to kill and telling them to make sure he suffers is immediate harm. So, according to Mill, since the content of CK's stand-up does not cause anyone direct immediate harm, it should not be censored. If it directly called on men to harm women, that would be different. But since his stand-up does not do that, Mill would argue it should not be censored.

But, of course, contemporary American culture does not understand immediate harm in the same way as Mill. Might other understandings generate a different conclusion?

Take, for example, the microaggression. A microaggression is an action that may not be intended to harm but is nonetheless considered violent or harmful to an individual or group (Lukianoff and Haidt 2018, p. 279). For many, allowing CK's material to remain on streaming platforms, his movies to be released into theaters, his television shows to air, and his stand-up shows to continue to tour, bringing in millions of dollars of revenue, could constitute a microaggression in that CK himself is triggering for those who have been victims of sexual misconduct. While not intending to harm those who have been victimized, one could argue that this state of affairs sends a clear, violent, and harmful message to victims that they don't matter. It could cause immediate harm by reminding them of traumatic experiences, further their depression, and, as a result, impede their recovery.

Greg Lukianoff and Jonathan Haidt, however, disagree that microaggressions count as immediate harm, and, even if they were, they should not be dealt with punitively. In their study of microaggressions on college campuses, Lukianoff (a lawyer and the president/CEO of the Foundation for Individual Rights in Education) and Haidt (a respected scholar and social psychologist) argue that policies banning or censoring speech or material that some find microaggressive is actually *more* harmful than the microaggression itself. They argue that punishing and censoring microaggressive content creates oversensitivity and entitlement in students and does psychological harm. Such paternalism on the part of an institute of higher education fails to prepare students for the real world, a world which cannot possibly accommodate them. It teaches students to think pathologically by *validating* anxieties rather than teaching them coping strategies to deal with those anxieties. This results in a learned helplessness with no strategies for how to manage in the world (Lukianoff and Haidt 2018, p. 287).

Given their position, Lukianoff and Haidt would perhaps have the most explicit objection to the aftermath of the CK scandal. They would argue that CK is a victim of "cancel culture." "Cancel culture" is a newly invented term for the practice of mass withdrawal of financial and social support from an individual in response to a perceived injustice. (One may think the practice itself is new, but it is not; consider what happened to Sinead O'Connor when she tore up a picture of The Pope on Saturday Night Live in 1992.) Cancel culture can describe the myriad responses to public figures like CK, or retaliation against private individuals, such as the public pressure on corporations to fire employees for things like culturally unacceptable social media posts.

Lukianoff and Haidt would consider cancel culture a form of social coddling. Individuals with anxieties, traumas, and PTSD who would be triggered by CK's material or career are helped more by exposure therapy than by avoiding the trigger entirely. Exposure therapy is a cognitive behavioral therapy technique which purports to reduce anxiety and PTSD episodes by slowly and gradually exposing a person to their fear rather than encouraging them to run from it. Since the world cannot possibly be sanitized to remove all triggers for all people at all times, the best thing that can be done, they argue, is to teach people how to manage their emotional responses when confronted by a trigger. Attempts to remove triggers from possible exposure rob people of opportunities to learn these strategies and instead deepen their pathologies (Lukianoff and Haidt 2018, p. 287). Lukianoff and Haidt would argue that canceling future CK projects is a fine enough punishment for CK, but removing all traces of him from culture is a paternalistic overreach. Such coddling only serves to harm the public, not protect it.

The degrees of agreement or disagreement with the response to CK notwithstanding, as of this writing, 5 years have passed since the NYT article broke the CK scandal and dethroned the king. And 5 years later, CK has slowly but surely tiptoed back into the public sphere, quietly active, releasing content exclusively on his website and gradually adding cities to comedy tours. But ought he?

2. Should CK be allowed to return to comedy? Are some actions so unacceptable that one "forfeits" his right to public contribution?

There are a host of celebrities that have done horrible things, condemned by the court of public opinion and exiled from the cultural marketplace for a time, who have returned stronger and more popular, not to mention commercially successful, than they were before. Robert Downy Jr., Chris Brown, Michael Jackson, and Aziz Ansari have been accused of alcoholism, violence against women, child molestation, and sexual assault, respectively, and, after some time, have been forgiven, or their offenses forgotten, in the public consciousness. For some, this required a court hearing, while others simply waited for enough time to pass for the culture to forget. And there are others whose actions and ideas have been condemned by feminists who continue to consume and enjoy their work, such as J.K. Rowling, the trans-exclusionist author of *Harry Potter*, and Joss Whedon, the emotionally abusive creator of the *Buffy the Vampire Slayer* television show. In some cases, it may be that an artist's overall contribution to society can outweigh his sins. Take Richard Pryor, for example. It is no secret that Pryor brutally and consistently abused his wives (Henry and Henry 2013, p. 218). His crimes are well known, yet even today he is considered a civil rights hero and a trailblazer in comedy (see Hall Healy's ▶ Chap. 68, "Richard Pryor as Philosopher: Stand-Up Comedy and Gramsci's Organic Intellectual," in this handbook). His work is considered by critics, audiences, and fellow comedians to be some of the best stand-up comedy in history. Neither his work nor his reputation have been tarnished by the sins of his personal life.

CK has not been so lucky. Perhaps this is due to the betrayal felt by those who held him as a moral exemplar. Not only did CK commit an immoral action, but he committed it against one of the very groups whom he used his comedy to help. The feminists, comedians, academics, and reporters who wrote piece after piece about how more comics (and more men) should be like CK surely felt personally offended that they had been, for lack of a better description, duped, and that, in his personal life, it turns out that CK was "just like the rest."

Should CK be allowed to return to comedy? Five positions are summarized here. The first position is that CK must remain exiled from the marketplace of cultural contribution. This position is based on the feminist argument detailed above and would simply conclude that, given power dynamics and rape culture, CK must remain in exile for the protection of women and in service of the dismantling of patriarchal and misogynistic systems and institutions. A second position would be Mill's position, that no expression should be banned from public discourse, for the sake of the greater good. If wrong ideas and people are indefinitely banned from culture, they cannot be learned from, and consequently, society itself will be lulled into ambivalence when it comes to truth.

A third position argues that there is no need to block CK from returning to the stage – if the public doesn't want him there, they won't support him. This is a natural consequence of Robert Nozick's free market. This "market morality" requires that the market be truly free, of course, which Nozick insists is the only way to economically organize a just society (Nozick 2018, p. 592). When the market is free from cultural interference and government control, one can see clearly what a society accepts and endorses by what people spend their money on. In other words, there is nothing to be "done" when it comes to Louis CK; simply let the market decide whether he finds renewed success. Justice will play out through the pocketbook. Rather than banning him from comedy clubs, he ought to continue to book and see if people buy tickets. If club owners can't sell enough tickets to make a profit, they won't book him anymore. But if they do, then clearly the moral issues the public have with him are not serious enough for people to refuse financial support.

This laissez-faire position is a libertarian one. It argues that the fair exchange of money justly acquired is between only the persons involved in the transactions, and that any interference from any other person, government, or public pressure is an infringement on personal liberty (Nozick 2018, p. 596). Threatening Netflix with financial ruin through a hashtag boycott, for example, and inciting a mob against the company, is interference with the market. Bookers are individuals who can choose whether to invite CK to their clubs, and audience members are individuals who can choose whether to buy tickets. If no bookers want to work with CK, no clubs want to host him, no studios want to produce him, and no comics want to tour with him, then no one has any right to interfere. But the same is true of the reverse – no one has any right to interfere if any of those parties *do* want to collaborate with CK. People will "spend their conscience"; if CK's actions truly offend them, they will not financially support him, and there is nothing that ought to be done about it one way or another.

One contemporary comedian who would agree with this position, at least when it comes to the performance of comedy itself, is feminist blogger Lindy West. In a May 30th, 2013 discussion regarding rape jokes (inspired by the same incident with Daniel Tosh referenced above) with W. Kamau Bell and Jim Norton on the television show *Totally Biased with W. Kamau Bell*, West argues that while comedians have the right to tell whatever sort of jokes they wish, she (and anyone else who takes exception to the content) has the right to withdraw her financial support from that comedian. If enough people withdraw their support from a comedian, and that comedian loses their sponsorships and other corporate support to the degree that they can no longer perform comedy, then so be it. Echoing Plato, West argues that cultural artifacts contribute to cultural attitudes, and comedy with intolerant content (rape jokes, racist jokes, etc.) contributes to intolerant cultural attitudes. Rape jokes, she argues, contribute to rape culture. Comedians should not tell these jokes, but it's their choice to ignore this moral obligation and tell them anyway. Her choice is to withdraw her financial support from such comedians (Totally Biased: Extended Talk with Jim Norton and Lindy West).

There is a question, though, regarding whether one's choice to withdraw her support ought to rise to the level of actively encouraging others to do the same. Mill and Nozick had no concept of the power of the internet and how it could be used to get masses of people to come together instantaneously to rally for or against an individual or business. For Nozick, if consumers decide en masse to abandon a product, that's just the free market. But Nozick would draw the line at a product or service no longer being available at all because of the demands of the loud minority who position themselves as moral arbiters of the market. One may find it immoral to pay for a Louis CK special, but that moral opinion should have no impact on whether someone else *has the option* to spend their money purchasing a Louis CK special.

Removing the special from the marketplace entirely because of public pressure, rather than due to a lack of consumer interest, is market interference. If there are still plenty of customers willing to pay for a product, it is an infringement on the liberty of those consumers to pull that product for sociopolitical reasons. A product should only be pulled from the market, Nozick would say, if consumers no longer want that product. Any other reason – including public pressure – is considered market interference. One is, of course, free to call for a boycott, and use her social media presence to do so, but this is beside the point for Nozick. For Nozick, a product not selling would be the only reason to remove it from the marketplace. In the case of Netflix and other streaming services, unless a boycott convinces enough people and thus carrying CK's specials becomes a financial burden – either because they don't get enough views or it makes too many people leave the platform – Netflix should not purge CK from their site. Any other reason manipulates the market and therefore infringes on the freedom of consumers to spend their justly acquired earnings as they please.

The fourth position is that CK is hardly perfect, but neither is anyone else. Condemning a person for a lifetime based on a morally immature past is to misunderstand how human beings learn. This position insists on exploring the evolution of CK's moral character and is based on traditions of virtue ethics. Virtue ethics argues that morality is not about what a person *does*, but rather who a person *is*, and has its roots in Aristotle, the most famous student of Plato.

Virtue ethicists argue that the development of moral character is a process that takes a great deal of time. It requires developing virtue, "practicing" moral activity until it has calcified into automaticity. In other words, becoming a virtuous person requires developing virtuous habits (Aristotle 1103a23–25). Because the development of habits takes time, Aristotle argued that it is not possible to judge a person's character until the end of their life (Aristotle 1098a15–20). Once a life is over, one can look back and see the "whole moral journey," from start to finish. From this perspective, one could see that if a person gradually became more virtuous over time, if they became better at the end than they were at the beginning of their moral life, if they died with a more virtuous than vicious character. Of course, it's impractical to withhold judgment about a person's character while they are alive, but the idea remains merely that there is a past, present, and future in a human life, and judging an action in isolation is, for Aristotle, a mistake.

Aristotle would argue that CK's past behavior, while certainly vicious, does not mean that he cannot become virtuous in the future – or that he could take steps forward and then revert back, ending up more vicious than he was before. This doesn't seem to be the case, though, as far as his sins are known to the public. From what was reported by the women who chose to speak out, the most recent incident with CK was in 2005, 12 years before the 2017 NYT article ran. CK wrote an apology email to Schachner in 2009, long before reports of rumors would have spooked him into confessing, and long before his behavior or exposure of his behavior would pose any threat to his career. In it he says, "Last time I talked to you ended in a sordid fashion... That was a bad time in my life and I'm sorry... I remember thinking what a repulsive person I was being" (Ryzik et al. 2017). If it is true that CK had reevaluated his actions and recognized that his character was deeply morally flawed, was in the process of trying to make amends, and, most importantly, *no longer engaged in the vicious behavior that was previously his habit*, then Aristotle would argue that CK was becoming a better person. Aristotle would argue that it is a misunderstanding of the nature of morality to retroactively punish someone for who he was in the past.

CK's work, both on stage and screen, displays clearly that he wrestles with demons, specifically those surrounding sexual impulses; his exorcising of these demons was once praised as brave and profound insights into the human psyche. He is aware of his weaknesses, his vices, and it seems that he tries, often unsuccessfully, to do the right thing despite them. If he is to be taken at his word that Louie is a pretty accurate portrayal of himself, "although I let myself make huge, terrible mistakes that I wouldn't make in real life. And I let myself have worse judgment," then the show itself can be understood as an exercise on repentance, both through confession (having Louie "get caught") and punishment (making Louie "face the consequences") (CK 2010, quoted in Ralkowski 2016, p. xi). For example, in an episode titled "Come on, God," Louie is confronted by and argues with a Christian woman precisely for his obsession with masturbation. She says, "That's what's so sad. That you don't know the darkness you live in." To which Louie replies, "Oh no. I know the darkness" (*Louie*, "Come on, God").

But, one may object, shouldn't people be judged by their past? It was still CK, after all, and not some imposter who victimized those women. He was not forced or coerced into his actions. CK ought to be considered a criminal, and criminals must pay for their crimes, even if legal action cannot be taken. Compared to his victims, has enough yet been paid? Has CK "done his time"? Is there a "right amount" of time (and money) to right the wrongs he has done? What could count as "enough" for justice to have been served?

Even if CK is understood as a criminal who committed crimes against women, there are still those who would argue that those crimes do not forfeit his right to be a contributing member of society. The Inside Out Prison Exchange Program, started by Lori Pompa in 1997, is a Temple University education project grounded in the philosophy that no one, even the worst of criminals, is beyond redemption or unworthy of humane treatment. The program takes university students into prisons, from minimum security to supermax, to have college-level classes side by side with incarcerated students. Pompa argues that nothing a person has done makes what they have to say lack value, meaning, or importance. Everyone ought to be able to learn, and to be learned from, listened to, and given opportunities to grow.

Pompa does not make this claim under the assumption that most of the incarcerated individuals in her program are victims of wrongful conviction, mistaken identity, shoddy police work, or racial profiling. In almost all cases, her students admit that they are guilty of the crimes for which they are behind bars. Pompa says that it's quite easy to define a person by their worst actions, but this does not mean that one should. She explains, "take the worst thing you've ever done in your life, and imagine yourself defined by that one act, possibly for the rest of your life" (Pompa and Crabbe 2016, p. 2). Those "worst things," whether they are rape, murder, child abuse, or any other atrocity, do not make anyone less human or less worthy of being treated with dignity.

Pompa believes that the worst of a society – the rapists and murderers and child pornographers – ought to be treated with the same respect due to all human beings, and as such, they ought to be granted access to the cultural and intellectual marketplace. If such persons ought to be understood as full human beings rather than as "the worst thing [they've] ever done," surely CK ought to be as well. If such persons have a right to contribute to society – artistically, intellectually, or culturally – surely CK ought to have that right as well.

As has been shown, the spectrum of philosophical responses to wrongdoing is deeply complex. Whether CK has been appropriately punished and whether he ought to be permitted to return are moral questions. The answers will depend entirely on how one understands the nature of human beings and the metaphysics of morality.

Conclusion

Louis CK is a powerhouse comedian, a brilliant writer, and a talented director. He also used his power and position in the comedy world to repeatedly victimize women. What CK did was wrong. There is no excuse for his behavior, and even he admits that his actions were perverted and disgusting. His victims have suffered long-term consequences, personally and professionally. It seems only just that CK should suffer as well. He knew what he was doing was wrong, yet he continued for years. For years, then, he should endure the consequences of his actions, personally and professionally.

In a 2014 NPR interview, CK said, "I know I can survive everybody being pissed off at me" (Gross 2014). He has shown, indeed, that he can survive. His slow return to comedy and film has been guarded, timid, and unannounced. As of this writing, he has just released a new film, *Fourth of July*, which will run for a night or two in several cities across the United States and Canada. His return is welcomed by fans and fellow comedians, which is revolting to some and alarming to many.

"The way CK's flirtations with the offensive and the taboo work, at least historically, is by making himself a temporary stand-in for the bad guy," writes Lili Loofbourow (2021). But he can no longer *stand in* for the bad guy if he *is* the bad guy. His comedy, while following the same formulas and going into the same dangerous places as it always has, has taken on a more melancholic tone. It could be that his new material can only be viewed through an interpretative lens that takes his actions and their consequences seriously. CK has always had a bitterness to his comedy; this was once understood as relatable and honest. To some, that bitterness now reads as a disgruntled response to his fall from grace. It is understood as a bitterness about facing the consequences of his actions, of losing millions of dollars, a career, and a reputation overnight. It is a bitterness that taints his work. Whether it is a bitterness that comes from within CK or a bitterness imposed by critics, the lens through which CK is interpreted has certainly become distorted by his actions. And that is his own fault; he is entirely to blame.

Perhaps enough time has passed and society has gone through enough collective trauma in the years since the scandal broke that people no longer have the energy or emotional bandwidth to trouble themselves with being troubled by CK. Perhaps CK has been forgiven, or forgotten, in the public consciousness. Between COVID-19, lockdowns, curfews, George Floyd, Donald Trump, wars, inflation, the Supreme Court, and Jeffrey Epstein, it would be unlikely that one would find themselves preoccupied with Louis CK.

A large portion of the public has already made up their mind about CK, either for or against. Some will always think of CK in terms of his crimes. Others will remain diehard fans, continuing to attend his shows and buy his content. Perhaps CK will see broad commercial success again, or perhaps he will remain "underground." He may never again be recrowned the Philosopher King of Comedy.

The fall of this king, while particular, brings forward universal questions about what ought to be done when a hero turns out to be a villain. Cancel culture argues alongside its feminist allies that CK, and men like him, ought to be made into examples which will dissuade other men from similar behavior. Anything less would be to actively perpetuate cultural and systemic misogyny. For too long, men in power have gotten away with abusing women with mere slaps on the wrist, or no consequences at all. A hard line must be drawn if the cycle of violence is ever to stop, and it is finally time that society no longer tolerates crimes against women.

Libertarian positions suggest that the fallen hero be subject to the free market, and that liberty requires consumers be given the opportunity to reveal their moral standing through their hard-earned dollar. Utilitarian and contemporary scholars argue that censorship in any form, for any reason, is detrimental to society as a whole and to individual persons. The Ancient Greeks speak of both censoring all immoral art and the evolution of moral character over time, while prison educators argue that no one should be banished from society, no matter how deviant or horrific their crimes. Abstract or concrete, right or wrong, the array of responses provides fruitful food for thought.

References

Aggeler, Madeleine. 2018. What happened to the women Louis C.K. Harassed? *The Cut*, August 30. https://www.thecut.com/2018/08/what-about-the-careers-of-louis-ck-victims.html
Aristotle. 2014. *Nicomachean ethics*. Trans. C.D.C. Reeve. Indianapolis: Hackett Publishing.
Augustine. 2010. On the free choice of the will. In P. King (ed., trans.) *On the free choice of the will, on grace and free choice, and other writings*. Cambridge University Press. https://philonew.files.wordpress.com/2016/08/augustine-augustine-on-the-free-choice-of-the-will-on-grace-and-free-choice-and-other-writings-2010.pdf
Bliss, James. 2016. An hour. In *Louis CK and philosophy: You don't get to be bored*, ed. Mark Ralkowski. Chicago: Open Court.
CK, Louis. 2005. *Louis C.K.: One night stand*. HBO.
———. 2007. *Louis C.K.: Shameless*. HBO.
———. 2008. *Louis C.K.: Chewed up*. Showtime.
———. 2010. *Louis C.K.: Hilarious*. Comedy Central.
———. 2010-2015. *Louie*. FX.

———. 2011. *Louis C.K.: Live at the beacon theater*. Pig Newton.
———. 2013. *Louis C.K.: Oh my god*. Pig Newton.
———. 2015. *Louis C.K.: Live at the comedy store*. Pig Newton.
———. 2017. *Louis C.K.: 2017*. Netflix.
———. 2020. *Sincerely Louis C.K.* Pig Newton.
———. 2021. *Sorry.* Pig Newton.
CNN. 2017. Louis C.K.'s full statement. *Cnn.com* (Entertainment). November 10. https://www.cnn.com/2017/11/10/entertainment/louis-ck-full-statement/index.html
Corsello, Andrew. 2014. Louis C.K. is America's undisputed king of comedy. *GQ*, May 13. https://www.gq.com/story/louis-ck-cover-story-may-2014
D'Alessandro, Anthony. 2017. The orchard no longer moving forward with release of Louis C.K.'s 'I Love You, Daddy'. *Deadline*, November 10. https://deadline.com/2017/11/the-orchard-no-longer-moving-forward-with-release-of-louis-c-k-s-i-love-you-daddy-1202205610/
Davies, Madeleine. 2014. Louis C.K.'s Rant on fat girls is absolutely magnificent. *Jezebel*, May 13. https://jezebel.com/louis-c-k-s-rant-on-fat-girls-is-absolutely-magnificent-1575653738
Deggans, Eric. 2014. Louis C.K. takes on TV hypocrisy, aiming scrutiny back at himself. *All Things Considered*: NPR, May 12. https://www.npr.org/2014/05/12/311897008/louis-c-k-takes-on-tv-hypocrisy-aiming-scrutiny-back-at-himself
Elder, Max. 2016. Everything's amazing and nobody's happy. In *Louis CK and philosophy: You don't get to be bored*, ed. Mark Ralkowski. Chicago: Open Court.
Fallon, Kevin. 2018. Louis C.K.'s leaked comedy set panders to the alt-right. *The Daily Beast*, December 31. https://www.thedailybeast.com/louis-cks-leaked-comedy-set-panders-to-the-alt-right
Gilbert, Joanne R. 2004. *Performing marginality: Humor, gender, and cultural critique*. Detroit: Wayne State University Press.
Gross, Terry. 2014. Louis C.K. on his 'Louie' Hiatus: 'I Wanted the Show to Feel New Again'. *Fresh Air* (NPR), December 30. https://www.npr.org/2014/12/30/373985972/louis-c-k-on-his-louie-hiatus-i-wanted-the-show-to-feel-new-again
———. 2015. Louis C.K. on life and stand-up: 'I Live in Service for My Kids'. *Fresh Air* (NPR), April 28. https://www.npr.org/2015/04/28/402560343/louis-c-k-on-life-and-standup-i-live-in-service-for-my-kids
Heany, John. 2016. Sex has something behind it. In *Louis CK and philosophy: You don't get to be bored*, ed. Mark Ralkowski. Chicago: Open Court.
Henry, David, and Joe Henry. 2013. *Furious cool: Richard Pryor and the world that made him*. Chapel Hill: Algonquin Books.
Herman, Dianne. 1989. The rape culture. In *Women: A feminist perspective*, ed. J. Freeman, 4th ed., 20–44. Mountain View: Mayfield.
Hipes, Patrick. 2017. Louis C.K. dropped from HBO's 'A Night of Too Many Stars' special, on-demand offerings. November 9. https://deadline.com/2017/11/louis-c-k-dropped-a-night-of-too-many-stars-special-sexual-harassment-scandal-1202205375/
Hitchens, Christopher. 2007. Why women aren't funny. *Vanity Fair*, January 2007.
Horton, Adrian. 2021. Grammy awards: Controversial comedians Dave Chappelle and Louis CK receive nominations. *The Guardian*, November 24. https://www.theguardian.com/music/2021/nov/23/dave-chappelle-louis-ck-grammy-nominations
Joho, Jess. 2017. Please stop applauding Louis C.K. for doing the bare minimum. *Mashable*, November 10.
Kirkland, Joseph R. 2016. Because nothing can't be! In *Louis CK and philosophy: You don't get to be bored*, ed. Mark Ralkowski. Chicago: Open Court.
Kohen, Yael. 2012. *We killed: A very oral history*. New York: Picador.
Levy, Piet. 2021. Disgraced comedian Louis C.K. is playing Madison's comedy on state, selling out shows and drawing backlash. *Milwaukee Journal Sentinel,* July 14. https://www.jsonline.com/story/entertainment/2021/07/14/disgraced-comedian-louis-c-k-playing-madisons-comedy-state-selling-out-shows-and-drawing-backlash/7961927002/

Loofbourow, Lili. 2021. What Louis C.K. has really lost. Slate.com, December 23. https://slate.com/culture/2021/12/louis-ck-new-special-sorry-what-is-missing.html?via=rss_socialflow_facebook&fbclid=IwAR29tSI1UdeoxxtVBjTjigo04TrZKypaNzAUVLbUA2S8-w5CcJkurI-kpZI

Lukianhoff, Greg, and Jonathan Haidt. 2018. The coddling of the American mind. In *Readings in moral philosophy*, ed. Jonathan Wolff. New York: Norton.

Maglio, Tony. 2018. "Louis CK says he lost '$35 Million in an Hour' over his sexual misconduct (report). *The Wrap*, October 17. https://www.thewrap.com/louis-ck-lost-35-million-in-an-hour-over-sexual-misconduct/

Marra, Jennifer. 2016. Feminists *can* take a joke. In *Louis CK and philosophy: You don't get to be bored*, ed. Mark Ralkowski. Chicago: Open Court.

Medina, José. 2013. *The epistemology of resistance: Gender and racial oppression, epistemic injustice, and resistant imaginations*. New York: Oxford University Press.

Mill, John Stuart. 2018. On liberty of expression. In *Readings in moral philosophy*, ed. Jonathan Wolff. New York: Norton.

Mills, Ethan. 2016. You're gonna die. In *Louis CK and philosophy: You don't get to be bored*, ed. Mark Ralkowski. Chicago: Open Court.

Nejedlo, Lindsay. 2021. Personal interview with author. August 1, 2021.

Nozick, Robert. 2018. The entitlement theory of justice. In *Readings in moral philosophy*, ed. Jonathan Wolff. New York: Norton.

Plato. 1987. *The republic*. Trans. Desmond Lee. 2nd edn. Penguin Books.

Pompa, Lori, and Melissa Crabbe. 2016. *The inside out prison exchange program instructors' manual*. Temple University.

Quine, W.V.O. 1948. On what there is. *The Review of Metaphysics* 2 (5): 21–38. https://www.jstor.org/stable/20123117?origin=JSTOR-pdf.

Ralkowski, Mark. 2016. *Louis CK and philosophy: You don't get to be bored*. Chicago: Open Court.

Respers France, Lisa. 2017. Was that Louis C.K. apology really one at all? *Cnn.com* (Entertainment), November 11. https://www.cnn.com/2017/11/10/entertainment/louis-ck-apology-reaction/index.html

Reyburn, Duncan. 2016. Louis C.K. meets the unconscious. In *Louis CK and philosophy: You don't get to be bored*, ed. Mark Ralkowski. Chicago: Open Court.

Robinson, Joanna. 2019. Louis C.K. is doubling down on jokes that will enrage his critics. *Vanity Fair*, January 17. https://www.vanityfair.com/hollywood/2019/01/louis-ck-stand-up-9-11-masturbation-jokes

Ryzik, Melena, Cara Buckly, and Jodi Kantor. 2017. Louis C.K. is accused by 5 women of sexual misconduct. *The New York Times*, November 9. https://www.nytimes.com/2017/11/09/arts/television/louis-ck-sexual-misconduct.html?smid=tw-share&_r=0. Accessed 28 July 2019.

Sharf, Zack. 2019. Louis C.K. reacts to parkland shooting joke controversy, jokes about masturbation in new set. *IndieWire*, January 17. https://www.indiewire.com/2019/01/louis-ck-jokes-about-jerking-off-parkland-schooting-comment-1202036287/

Talking Funny. 2011. Dir. John Moffit. HBO. (posted by Ken Jones at https://www.youtube.com/watch?v=OKY6BGcx37k).

Totally Biased: Extended Talk with Jim Norton and Lindy West – Video Dailymotion. n.d. *Dailymotion*. https://www.dailymotion.com/video/x2nuz3m. Accessed 13 July 2018.

Tribute to George Carlin. 2010. New York Public Library. https://www.nypl.org/audiovideo/conversation-portrait-tribute-george-carlin

Trock, Gary. 2019. Louis CK dropped a holocaust joke in Israel and the crowd went wild. *Yahoo! Entertainment*, November 29. https://www.yahoo.com/entertainment/louis-ck-dropped-holocaust-joke-223123752.html

Williams, Bekka. 2016. Just want a shitty body. In *Louis CK and philosophy: You don't get to be bored*, ed. Mark Ralkowski. Chicago: Open Court.

Wilstein, Matt. 2018. Louis C.K.'s 'Comeback' to female comedians: 'Ridiculous,' 'Depressing' and 'Not Surprising'. *The Daily Beast,* August 28. www.thedailybeast.com/louis-cks-comeback-to-female-comedians-ridiculous-depressing-and-not-surprising

Yahr, Emily. 2014. Here's that epic, mesmerizing 'fat girl' speech from Monday night's 'Louie'. *The Washington Post*, May 13. https://www.washingtonpost.com/news/arts-and-entertainment/wp/2014/05/13/heres-that-epic-mesmerizing-fat-girl-speech-from-monday-nights-louie/

Yamato, Jen. 2016. Roseanne Barr calls out Louis C.K.: 'I've heard so many stories'. *The Daily Beast*, June 30. https://www.thedailybeast.com/roseanne-barr-calls-out-louis-ck-ive-heard-so-many-stories

———. 2017. 'I Love You, Daddy' stars drop out of film promotion after Louis C.K. allegations; FX, HBO weigh in. *LA Times*, November 9. https://www.latimes.com/entertainment/la-et-entertainment-news-updates-november-2017-htmlstory.html#i-love-you-daddy-stars-drop-out-of-film-promotion-after-louis-c-k-allegations-fx-hbo-weigh-in

Zimmerman, Neetzan. 2013. Louis C.K.'s explanation of why he hates smartphones is sad, brilliant. Gawker.com, September 20. https://www.gawker.com/louis-c-k-s-explanation-of-why-he-hates-smartphones-is-1354954625

Zinoman, Jason. 2020. Amy Schumer misses stand-up. ('I Should Have Said My Dad, but That's Not the Truth.') *New York Times*, May 25. https://www.nytimes.com/2020/05/25/arts/television/amy-schumer.html

Marc Maron as Philosopher: Comedy, Therapy, and Identification

66

Steven S. Kapica

Contents

Introduction: Lock the Gates 1564
Making "My Clown" 1566
The Philosophy of WTF?! 1569
Consubstantiality and Catharsis 1574
Conclusion: Comedy as Equipment for Living 1577
References 1580

Abstract

Comedian Marc Maron spent decades under the radar, working the comedy club circuit, scoring gigs at fledgling network *Comedy Central*, doing spots on *Late Night with Conan O'Brien*, and wrestling with drug addiction (before getting sober in 2004). On the verge of being fired (again) from liberal radio network, *Air America*, Maron conceived of and recorded the first episodes of his landmark podcast *WTF with Marc Maron*. This chapter explicates Maron's philosophy through his work as a stand-up comedian and podcaster. Maron's "what the fuck" comedic philosophy reflects the central tenets of Kenneth Burke's theory of identification, and Maron's work serves as compelling proof of the essential consubstantiality of comedy. Maron cracks open the common tropes of the "sad clown" and "comedy as therapy" and, through his stand-up routines and extensive catalog of interviews with comedians, proves the extent to which a philosophy grounded in collective, comedic catharsis provides an effective "equipment for living."

S. S. Kapica (✉)
Keuka College, Keuka Park, NY, USA
e-mail: skapica@keuka.edu

© Springer Nature Switzerland AG 2024
D. K. Johnson et al. (eds.), *The Palgrave Handbook of Popular Culture as Philosophy*,
https://doi.org/10.1007/978-3-031-24685-2_52

Keywords

Consubstantiality · Identification · Therapy · Stand-up comedy · Wtf · Marc Maron

Introduction: Lock the Gates

The 1983 film *Risky Business* opens with its main character, Joel Goodsen (Tom Cruise), breaking free from his clean cut, "good son" persona so he can descend into an underworld of "adult" life centered on prostitution and pimping. Joel's friend, Miles (Curtis Armstrong), provides the philosophy that pushes Goodsen past the protective barriers of his childhood: "Sometimes you gotta say 'What the fuck,' make your move. Joel, every now and then, saying 'What the fuck,' brings freedom. Freedom brings opportunity, opportunity makes your future." "What the fuck" (WTF), then, is a stance, a position – an invitation to break with convention. WTF is also a supplication to the void – a curse that exposes inequity and absurdity, and acts as a vocalization of momentary despair before catharsis. Each of these positions aligns with Miles's insistence on "freedom." Through WTF, Joel is given license to freely determine his life's path.

While a WTF attitude can (and often does) lead to a release from social constraints, vocalization of the phrase is, first and foremost, a rhetorical act. It's one thing to come to a personal realization – to despair in private. It's quite another thing to audibly mark that realization in the presence of others, or, in the case of stand-up comedians, during a performance in front of an audience. The laughter elicited by stand-up comedy is proof of its persuasive effect; the comic wins laughs the way a politician wins votes. What separates comedic and political rhetoric, however, is comedy's affective nature– its ability to not only provoke laughter but to produce collective identification that often manifests in comic relief. A WTF philosophy in the hands of a stand-up comedian, then, has the power to produce more than laughter; it has the potential for catharsis.

In 2009, when stand-up comedian turned radio host Marc Maron was fired from liberal radio network *Air America*, he was sober but broken. Twenty-five years into his career as a comedian, he had little success to show for his effort. This was particularly frustrating for Maron as his lack of success sharply contrasted the cultural (and financial) rise of fellow "alternative" comedians, like former roommate David Cross and former friend Louis CK.

Into this moment of despair was born groundbreaking podcast, *WTF with Marc Maron*. "When I started [*WTF with Marc Maron*], it was bleak," Maron admits in his 1000th episode. He continues,

> A thousand episodes later, I have to say the effect it's had on my life, my heart, my mind, my spirit. Everything, everything is different because of a desperate act, in a way, to try to keep something going. Started out in the old garage, with no expectations, not much money, very bleak disposition, and slowly but surely, on a personal level, it opened me up to my peers, it

opened up my heart to the ability to possess some sort of empathy, to engage my empathy, to laugh with other people, to get out of myself, to just move through life in a way that wasn't horrible. (Maron 2019)

Maron titled his podcast *WTF*, but the phrase is also the cornerstone of his comedic philosophy. His invocation of "what the fuck" serves as a rhetorical act of comedic catharsis. Through *WTF*, Maron engages his empathy and gets out of himself, and his performance serves a therapeutic function. *WTF* is not just about Maron finding a way through life that isn't "horrible," it is a performance for his audience's benefit. It is an invitation for us to identify, say WTF, and embrace a WTF philosophy.

While popular innocuous stand-up sells lots of tickets, the brand of stand-up that has come to be viewed as a progressive, countercultural art form has taken "comedy is therapy" to heart and pushed it front and center. "Comedy is therapy" is a problematic trope, however. Edward David Naessens (2020) writes, "Modern stand-up comedy and celebrity are synonymous with personal revelation" (p. 226). According to Naessens, comedians' real lives are often conflated with their carefully constructed personas; they are "sad clowns," rather than articulate purveyors of comedic performances. When the sad clown performance is mistaken as "real," the line between "real" and performance is blurred and encourages identification – and identification invites comedy's connection to therapy. Do comedians use the stage as a therapist's couch? Do comedians' performances act as revealing sessions wherein audiences are surrogates for therapists? Or are comedians the therapists, leading their audiences in group therapy sessions, addressing common psychological problems and using comedy as a form of experiential medication?

Rebecca Krefting (2014) writes, "Identification is not prerequisite for appreciation or commercial success by any account, but for comics whose personae bear greater verisimilitude with actual lived experience, identification is a key factor in engaging viewers" (5). Stand-up is a cultural release valve – providing us a place to air our grievances against the tyranny of capitalism and patriarchy, even offering us a site of resistance and the foment of revolution. Krefting calls this "charged humor," "humor that seeks to represent the underrepresented, to empower and affirm marginalized communities and identities, and to edify and mobilize their audiences" (p. 21). For this brand of stand-up, the therapeutic value of comedy is often taken as a given. "Charged humor" does something more (mentally; psychologically) to/for its audiences than does comedy devoid of political or revelatory bent.

While scholars like Krefting are drawn to the politically subversive qualities of "charged humor," there is no denying the psychological dimension of stand-up. Kenneth Burke (1969) writes, "Identification is affirmed with earnestness precisely because there is division" (Burke, p. 22). Identification occurs because there is a need to bridge diversity and difference. Because we are different, we must enter a world of language and symbols wherein meaningful connection occurs through points of linguistic/symbolic identification. Rhetoric is the means by which we bridge difference to establish identification. Burke writes, "often we must think of rhetoric not in terms of some one particular address, but as a general body of identifications" (p. 26).

This "body of identifications" is a key component of stand-up comedy, which requires an audience that collectively comes to identify with the comedian's worldview and whose laughter is premised on the points of identification the comedian is able to establish and activate.

While Marc Maron is not the only comedy-as-therapy purveyor, he is certainly the most self-conscious and prolific, having made his career using the comedy club stage and his podcast microphone for therapy, working as both doctor and patient. Maron is an exemplar of Burke's "comic frame," and his comedy and podcast provide compelling evidence for how comedy can, in fact, be therapeutic. "The comic frame," Burke explains, "should enable people to be observers of themselves, while acting... One would 'transcend' himself by noting his own foibles" (p. 171). Maron's "what the fuck" comedic philosophy reflects Burke's insistence that the comic frame's prime function is to "enable people to be observers of themselves, while acting" (Burke, p. 171). While Burke's use of "while acting" here refers to a kind of real time self-assessment, wherein the mistaken moment becomes a *corrective* moment for positive change, it also works as an analogue to "acting" as performance. Maron uses the stage (and his podcast) as a site for identification and correction. "The comic frame," Burke writes, "in making a man the student of himself, makes it possible for him to 'transcend' occasions when he has been tricked or cheated, since he can readily put such discouragements in his 'assets' column, under the head of 'experience'" (p. 171). Maron cracks open the common tropes of the "sad clown" and comedy as therapy, and, through his stand-up routines and extensive catalog of interviews with comedians, proves the extent to which a philosophy grounded in collective, comedic catharsis provides effective "equipment for living."

Making "My Clown"

As of this writing, *WTF with Marc Maron* has logged over 1200 episodes. And while Maron has interviewed writers, actors, musicians – and even the former President of the United States, Barack Obama – the lion's share of his earliest interviews were with stand-up comedians. In fact, *WTF* is a veritable treasure trove and archive of stand-up history and lore. Maron's countless hours of interviews with comedians – from pioneers like Shelley Berman to contemporary talents like Byron Bowers – may well serve as his most lasting contribution to American culture. In his June 2020 episode with Jerry Seinfeld, Maron soberly explains why he got into comedy: "For me... I got into it for the pursuit of a certain personal truth, of a way to be seen, as a way to express myself. And I tried a lot of different stuff, man... But from when I was eleven or twelve years old, in my heart, it was like comics are, that's the noble profession."

Born and raised in Albuquerque, New Mexico, Maron attended Boston University where he majored in English and made his first forays into stand-up comedy. In a piece for the university's daily website, *BU Today*, Maron admits that those first attempts were a disaster. "I couldn't hack it," he confesses (Clark 2013). After he graduated, moved to Los Angeles, and started working the door at legendary stand-up club the Comedy Store, he decided to give comedy another try. It was his tenure at the Comedy Store that solidified his resolve to pursue comedy and, in 1988, he returned to Boston and started performing regularly – not only in Boston, but also in New York and on the road. Then, "in the early 1990s, he moved to New York City and became part of the city's nascent alternative comedy scene, performing alongside Louis C.K., David Cross, and Sarah Silverman" (Kapica 2019, p. 537).

While Maron was a fixture on the scene, working comedy clubs and taping spots and specials for *Comedy Central*, bouncing back and forth between the east and west coasts, he could never quite dial in his act for a breakout moment. He struggled with drugs and alcohol, married and divorced, and let his anxiety, anger, and resentment take center stage. As Kapica (2019) notes, "A tour through Maron's first 20 years in comedy reveal [sic] the push and pull of emotional turmoil and identity crises... His career has always been defined by his raw energy and hair-trigger anger and his commitment to, even obsession with, using the stage and microphone as his confessional space" (p. 537).

In his 2011 keynote address to the Montreal *Just For Laughs Comedy Festival*, Maron (2013) confesses, "I've put more than half my life into building my clown. That's how I see it. Comics keep getting up onstage and in time the part of them that lives and thrives up there is their clown. My clown was fueled by jealousy and spite for most of my career" (p. 197). He adds, "Three years ago my clown was broke *[sic]*, on many levels, and according to my manager at the time, unbookable and without options" (Maron, p. 197). Maron's "building my clown" is an unmistakable nod to an intentionally crafted stage persona. As Ian Brodie (2008) observes, "Most stand-up comedy implies a level of performed autobiography. At first one gives some of that biography through an explicit introduction... but over a comedian's career some form of persona is established, mostly concerning the life lived offstage or off the road" (Brodie, p. 174). Naessens similarly observes, "Good comedians intuit and understand that one of the most effective ways to win an audience over is to share stories of personal setbacks, vulnerability, and incompetence... comedians learn how and who to be on stage..." (p. 224). Maron's "clown," then, is a crafted extension of himself, a version of himself that is keyed toward laughter at his foibles. That his "clown was fueled by jealousy and spite" speaks to his attunement to how his comedic persona is/was shaped by both his personal life and how he opted to amplify that personal life in comedic terms.

Maron opens his first full length comedy album, 2002's *Not Sold Out*, by referencing a cold sore. The bit cleverly clues his audience in to his "clown's" personality: "All right, we have to address a couple of things right off the bat because I just can't fucking live with it... this thing on my face? I didn't get hit. It's a big, stinking, fucking cold sore... I just wanted to get that out. I want to share that. Do you understand?" (Maron 2002). That Maron opens his set with this seemingly impromptu, embarrassing admittance speaks to both his cleverness as a stand-up (his ability to read a room and adapt given the circumstances of the performance) and his neuroticism. His "personality" won't let him *not* address his obvious and distracting cold sore. His confession of "I just can't fucking live with it" sets the tone for his set and for his audience. Maron's performed vulnerability (and obsession) quickly establishes identification between him and his audience. After drawing the audience's attention to his "goiter," he doubles back and asks himself, rhetorically, "Is that any way to open a show, Marc?" The answer to his question is, given the worldview and persona building needed to establish clear lines of identification from which laughter occurs, yes. Maron's comedic persona relies on this extreme self-deprecation.

And the line of identification becomes clear as Maron constructs his persona: The universal truth – the through-line between Maron, comic persona, and audience identification – is the mundane frustration and anxiety that such moments cause all members in his audience. The cold sore is a collective representation of when audience members experienced similar moments of cruel irony – when everything needs to be "perfect," coincidental imperfections become fated. *Of course* Maron would get an ugly cold sore on the night he records his first full length comedy album – an album a decade in the making.

Maron continues, referencing his younger self,

> And I try to be optimistic... because I just don't want to be as fucking angry as I used to be. I don't have the energy to be as angry as I used to be. You know why? Because I don't drink anymore, and I don't do drugs anymore. And you know what's amazing about sobriety? Is how clearly you can see your disappointment. (2002)

The clever reversal here again reinforces the world-building Maron is able to do within the first 5 minutes of his set. Sobriety is generally considered to be a positive – overcoming an addiction is rewarded by polite society. The "joke" here is that Maron's sobriety, while welcomed (his referencing of "optimism" and not wanting to be "as fucking angry as I used to be"), actually exhibits a depressing, hard truth. Being sober allows the comedic persona to take control of its life; however, the "payment" for being sober is recognizing in broad daylight the disappointment that addiction sought to overcome and/or bury.

What this clown building does for Maron, and for his audience, is establish trust and a sense of authenticity. By drawing humor from direct, visible, personal examples, Maron convinces his audience of his authenticity, and thereby creates solid ground for an acting-together. The work that results from this rhetorical move is the therapeutic work of comedic catharsis. The audience not only laughs at Maron's misfortune; it identifies and is ultimately comforted by that identification.

Returning to Maron's comments to the Montreal *Just For Laughs* audience, the comedian opines,

> When I was a kid watching comedians on TV and listening to their records, they were the only ones that could make it all seem okay. They seemed to cut through the bullshit and disarm fears and horror by being clever and funny. I don't think I could have survived my childhood without watching stand-up comics. When I started doing comedy, I didn't understand show business. I just wanted to be a comedian. Now, after twenty-five years of doing stand-up and the last two years of having long conversations with over two hundred comics, I can honestly say they are some of the most thoughtful, philosophical, open-minded, sensitive, insightful, talented, self-centered, neurotic, compulsive, angry, fucked-up, sweet, creative people in the world. (p. 201)

Maron's cold sore and sobriety bits do this very thing. They immediately cut through the bullshit and disarm fears and horror by giving voice to the irrational fears that come with coincidental misfortune. Without comedy, a cold sore is an irritating, even debilitating embarrassment; with comedy, it becomes a point of resignation to the chaos of life that then turns to laughter.

The same can be said about Maron's reference to his sobriety. The comedian is clearly still angry, still fueled by spite – though to a demonstrably lesser degree. His confession that he doesn't want to be as angry as he used to be sets up the invocation of a logical fallacy associated with sobriety. The joke turns on a false dichotomy, wherein being sober is a positive thing that makes one's life better – when, in fact, those recovering from addiction are likely to view sobriety as an uncomfortable reckoning with the disappointments that instigated addiction in the first place. While an addictive personality does not need an excuse to initiate the addiction ("I drink because I am a failure"), the two are often closely associated, especially in the mind of the addict. For Maron to turn this on its head for laughter reveals the truth, the pain that an addict feels upon achieving sobriety.

Based on his observations to the *Just For Laughs* audience, the conclusion that Maron's comedic persona is deeply entwined with his personal, lived experiences (misfortunes) seems not only fair but correct. Furthermore, his identification with "thoughtful, philosophical, open-minded, sensitive, insightful, talented, self-centered, neurotic, compulsive, angry, fucked-up, sweet, creative people" is more than a simple affinity; it is a choice and compulsion. Maron is a champion of the medium, and his deep commitment to stand-up and its purveyors is, ultimately, a rhetorical act, a deliberate acting-together. The driving force behind this acting-together is Maron's comedic philosophy, which is characterized through the phrase "what the fuck" and its dual meaning/use value.

The Philosophy of WTF?!

Maron succinctly articulates the WTF philosophy for his podcast – and, it can safely be inferred, his approach to stand-up comedy, and even his life – at the beginning of his very first WTF episode:

> I'll go ahead and say it, what the fuck? That is the question. That is the eternal question. You know, in life, and in the history of mankind, the philosophical question, the great philosophical question needs to be "What is the meaning of life? And then I think it evolved into how am I being used and being okay with that. And now I think we are at a different juncture in the history of culture, and the eternal, philosophical question is "What the fuck?! Seriously. Really? What the fuck?" I mean, that's a question I ask myself a lot. About a lot of things. But also we want to deal with the lighter side of WTF, which is, "What the fuck?" So you got both sides. You got righteous indignation and why not live a little. It's an expressive type of saying. WTF. (2009)

The sentiments expressed in the phrase WTF are not new, of course; that the phrase effectively shuttles between and combines two perspectives, however, is remarkable. On the one hand, outrage and indignation are common responses to unforeseen and distressing situations, real and perceived slights, etc. On the other hand, WTF as a liberatory invocation is arguably a postmodern analogue to carpe diem.

Combining the two – exasperation and liberation – for the purposes of comedic catharsis situates Maron's theory of the joke squarely in Burke's comic frame. Burke observes, "The progress of humane enlightenment can go no further than in picturing people not as vicious, but as mistaken. When you add that people are necessarily mistaken, that all people are exposed to situations in which they must act as fools, that every insight contains its own special kind of blindness, you complete the comic circle" (Burke [1959] 1984, p. 41). Maron's use of the double-meaning of the WTF phrase reveals his particular approach to comedy to be a performance-based analog to mistakenness as enlightenment.

This is most clear in Maron's turn from the general question, "What is the meaning of life?" to "How am I being used?" Richard Taylor ([1970] 2016) observes, "the question whether life has meaning is difficult to interpret... And yet I think any reflective person recognizes that the question... ought to have a significant answer" (p. 21). Maron opens his podcast by invoking "the great philosophical question" and thereby situates the show within the stream of the philosophical – an interesting choice for a fledgling podcast about stand-up comedy. The goal of *WTF*, then, is to chip away at the "meaning of life" through comedy; though, an appropriate subquestion to "What is the meaning of life?" would be "What is the use value of comedy?"

Maron's shift, however, from "What is the meaning of life?" to "How am I being used?" situates his personal (and comedic) philosophy outside the topical, arguably superficial, frame of the existential. For Maron, the question of life's meaning is a loaded one. It is a potential trap wherein he might be hoodwinked – tricked or cheated – by the question's answer. Notably, Maron's choice of "evolved" alludes to a dialectical evolution wherein an isolated metaphysical approach to the question of life's meaning gives way to a shrewd, Marxist, culturally situated approach. This critical shift calls into question the use value of the metaphysical wherein the answer(s) to life's meaning are revealed as paradigmatic dictates. Accepting a certain answer to the question leads to a certain brand of subjugation.

Maron's use of "evolved" also indicates personal growth. His experiences have led him to a point where life's meaning is necessarily contingent on how life has treated him – his lack of success, his general misfortune, and his tendency toward paranoia and self-deprecation all taint the metaphysical. Maron's answer to the question isn't a crass "What's in it for me?", nor is it a self-revelatory invitation to personal achievement (carpe diem); instead, it's a cynical, distrustful, "How am I being used?" If meaning is contingent on external forces, then one's life is necessarily consubstantial to those forces. Put another way, meaning only exists as a use function for subjugation; accepting a certain answer to the question of life's meaning means subscribing to its paradigm. Separated from ideological influence (something it can never be), then, life becomes meaningless.

Taylor observes, "meaninglessness is essentially endless pointlessness, and meaningfulness is therefore the opposite. Activity, and even long, drawn out and repetitive activity, has a meaning if it has some significant culmination, some more or less lasting end that can be considered to have been the direction and purpose of the activity" (p. 25). For Maron, the "long, drawn out and repetitive activity" is essentially his career, his life; that his own logical progression brings him to "How am I being used?" speaks to his worldview and state of mind. When he started his podcast, Maron was 25 years into a career in comedy that resulted in yet another disappointment (failure, firing, etc.). The indignant side of *WTF* is fitting given the spiral of disappointment that led to Maron's separation from *Air America*. (Though, to be fair, Maron has been clear that he was not happy at *Air America*; he felt his involvement in overtly political comedy was not his true calling.) It is easy to imagine Maron throwing his hands up in frustration and pondering "What the fuck?" with regard to the time and energy he had expended in pursuit of comedy. His financial and use-value-laden failures arguably prove his cynical reading of the eternal question. In 2009, Maron was Sisyphus – endlessly pushing a boulder up a hill, only to have it fall down the other side.

Taylor, like Albert Camus, uses the myth of Sisyphus to explicate his view of meaning and concludes that "an existence that is objectively meaningless, in this sense, can nevertheless acquire a meaning for him whose existence it is." Camus's ([1955] 1991) conclusion that "One must imagine Sisyphus happy," speaks to the meaning-making that occurs at the individual level (p. 123). Life takes on meaning as we search for that very meaning. For Maron, WTF – in both instantiations – becomes the point at which life (and work) becomes meaningful. Resignation to the void does not result in a WTF attitude. Resignation is acquiescence. WTF is license to invent meaning, to make one's life meaningful for one's self. Here again, WTF is postmodern carpe diem in that meaning is necessarily filtered through social and economic paradigms. One does not seize the day out of a desire to forward the progress of humanity; rather, one seizes the day because, well, why the fuck not?

Maron's move, then, from "What is the meaning of life?" to "Am I being used?" is both funny and apropos. One might imagine Sisyphus pausing in his eternal task and asking, "What the fuck?!" For Maron, the possibility that life is *not* meaningless leads to the logical conclusion that one is being used – and, furthermore, upon recognizing the paradigmatic power of being used, resistance to cultural appropriation through indignation and liberation is achieved through the comic, through comedy.

Revelation/resignation is less a matter of choice or of navigating circumstances than it is a response to a perceived threat, a survival instinct that places the world in the role of aggressor. Maron looks at the sum total of his accomplishments (circa 2009) and can't, from his particular vantage point, understand why his career has been less than successful (though "success" here might need to be defined). His conclusion – at least as represented by the progression of questions at the top of the first *WTF* episode – is that there are forces at work against him. "How am I being used?" is both an invocation to paranoia and a clear question regarding the (post) modern condition. Consumer culture has subjugated us to a paradigm wherein stand-up comedy is dependent on economic forces; the production and promotion of stand-up reveals a power dynamic of supplication. Comedians must, on some level, cater to their audiences' needs.

This progression – from the classical, metaphysical question of life's meaning, through a Marxist rendering of life's use value – is confirmed by Maron's final move to "What the fuck?! Seriously. Really? What the fuck?" While there is a baseline of paranoia performed for comedy, Maron's appeal speaks to his personal distrust of the powers that be; he is clearly a postmodernist. However, and more importantly, his trust in speech – through mic to audience, through long-form interview in podcast – demonstrates his belief in the unique power/value of comedy. His comedy gives voice to his paranoia in order to dismantle it. Furthermore, by performing a carefully articulated version of his paranoia (anger, indignation, frustration, self-deprecation, etc.), he turns his pain into a rhetorical act whereby his audience can learn, laugh, and come to a better understanding of life.

Maron uses to the power of comedy to dismantle fear, anxiety, frustration, and mistakenness. He vocalizes the power of a WTF philosophy: "You got righteous indignation and why not live a little." This phrase acknowledges the right to be indignant in the face of life's absurdities and inequities. While the phrase WTF implies a certain level of righteousness – or, put another way, a certain acknowledgment of being wronged – absurdity and inequity, actions without meaning, give license to a liberatory, *subversive* impulse. One does not say WTF unprovoked. The provocation is a means to counteraction.

The WTF philosophy, then, hinges on turning indignation into comedy, in recognizing comedy's ability to remix anger into laughter. Maron's early stand-up is curious in its palpable desperation. On the one hand, his innocuous bit about his cold sore might be viewed as topical comedy at its most mundane – and, in the hands of a different comic, it might have been. Maron's energy and mastery, however, turns a seemingly insignificant personal obsession into a raw comedic experience. In his early performances, the comedian was likely not aware of his own comedic philosophy's evolution; but looking at his early material through the lens of the WTF philosophy exposes its emotional intelligence. Maron was desperate, but the performance of his desperation was expert, edgy, and, at times, uncomfortable.

To praise early Maron is arguably anachronistic and/or may run counter to prevailing opinion. If Maron was that good, that expert at his craft, then why did success elude him? Why did his contemporaries – like Louis CK – succeed where he couldn't? Maron, of course, blames himself for his lack of success (or, rather, his near constant expressions of resentment and anger acted as self-sabotage). However, divorced of context, comparing Maron's early material to that of CK's reveals its content, tone, and delivery to be very, very different. CK's performance of personal failures and obsessions were edgy but not truly uncomfortable. CK wrote material that hewed close to home, to the personal, but it never felt real and/or desperate the way Maron's material did. CK's material was not angry or desperate the way Maron's was. And while comparing the two comedians arguably sets up a false dichotomy, the comparison does serve as proof of difference: Maron's comedy was both funny and uncomfortable – and for some audiences, it may have been too personal.

However, separating the comedian from the comedic persona reinforces the claim that Maron's comedic philosophy draws its power from tapping into a deeply personal pain and repurposing that pain for collective acknowledgment, identification, and laughter. Interestingly, Maron's podcast success suggests his level of personal affiliation with his comedic persona (his clown) was better suited to the long-form interview and confessional-based medium. While his stand-up is edgy and masterful (his work ethic and commitment is evidenced in his professional delivery), its inability to reach a wider audience arguably says more about the audience than it does the comedian. However, Maron's breakout success with his podcast raises the question: If his podcast is so successful, why was he unable to breakout as a stand-up comedian? The answer lies in Maron's level of personal engagement/performance. His ability to tap into vulnerability and authenticity may have been too much for comedy club audiences; however, those same characteristics proved vital to Maron's approach to interviewing comedians.

A curious by-product of Maron's philosophy (and his lack of breakout success on the comedy club stage) is its ability to peel back stand-up comedy's crass exterior and reveal heart and vulnerability; this is something for which the *WTF* podcast is particularly well-suited. A significant portion of Maron's interviews for *WTF* hinge on his ability to get his guests to open up: to expose their own vulnerabilities and operational philosophies. In 2020, Maron interviewed sitcom star and stand-up comedian Jerry Seinfeld. In the interview, Seinfeld comes off as clearly beholden to stand-up. Seinfeld's love for comedy is palpable and Maron is able to dial into the heart of Seinfeld's own comedic philosophy. Seinfeld's observes, "if you're funny and you love to be funny... there you go" (2020). This revealing, simple pragmatism is the starting point for all of Seinfeld's comedy. A comedian (the material) is either funny or it isn't. For Seinfeld, all of the rest of the apparatus (the lifestyle, the approach, the motivation, etc.) is inconsequential to the value of the joke itself.

When Maron presses Seinfeld about the "reason" a comedian is funny, observing "The reason that you're funny is... that it's part of your ability to deflect, to charm," Seinfeld cuts him off. "I'm going to stop you at 'the reason,'" he says. "There's no reason" (2020). Seinfeld's insistence that reasons don't matter exposes his comedic philosophy to be an antithesis to Maron's. In so many ways, Maron's primary motivator *is* the reason.

In his truncated interview with watermelon smashing comedian, Gallagher, Maron presents some of his most salient views on comedy. In a heated moment, Gallagher asks Maron, "What is the use of humor? What is the use of humor in our society?" Maron responds clearly and concisely, "To disarm and educate.... But if you just said to me that your job is to release aggression and disarm prejudice of the audience... Then you're a therapist" (2020). I sincerely doubt that many other comedians approach stand-up with the perspective that their role as comedian is synonymous with that of the therapist. It is implicit, sure enough, but Maron says it, affirms it, and thereby clearly explicates his comedic philosophy.

Maron expresses similar sentiments in an interview with Scott Timberg. In response to Timberg's question about comedy based on discomfort, Maron notes, "A lot of people want to think that comics are all unhappy. I don't think that's necessarily true. But there is a level of struggle and discomfort, there is a kind of irritation... I think it's about the struggle for me and definitely about discomfort and panic and anxiety and whatnot" (Timberg 2015). Seinfeld is beholden to the joke for the joke's sake; Maron, however, is beholden to the illustrative power of comedy. The reason one laughs is almost as important as the laugh itself.

Consubstantiality and Catharsis

Stand-up comedians draw laughter from performing carefully crafted versions of their experiences. The work of (good) comedians is drawing lines of identification from their unique, personal, even odd experiences to the experiences of their audiences. The mistake that many make, however, is thinking that comedians simply have a knack for explicating the universal. Conventional wisdom regarding comedy tells us that we laugh because, deep down, we are all the same. Burke writes, however, "Identification is affirmed with earnestness precisely because there is division... If men were not apart from one another, there would be no need for the rhetorician to proclaim their unity" (p. 22). We are not all the same. This is why rhetoric is needed.

Burke explains, quite plainly, "A is not identical with his colleague, B. But insofar as their interests are joined, A is identified with B" (p. 20). A rhetorical situation, then, is founded on the basic premise that because A is not B, A must invent points of identification by which B identifies with A. When comedians perform versions of their experiences, they distort and misdirect; however, it is through distortion and misdirection that comedians arrive at the potential for identification and laughter. One need look no further than observational humor to see this simple premise at work. Consider this excerpt from George Carlin's (1992) "Little Things We Share" routine:

> ...these little things we have in common. Little universal moments that we share separately. The things that make us the same. They're so small we hardly ever talk about them. Do you ever look at your watch, and then you don't know what time it is? And you have to look again, and you still don't know the time. So you look a third time, and somebody says "What time is it?" You say, "I don't know."

The laughter elicited by this bit is the result of B (audience) identifying with A (Carlin). Most stand-up comedy, arguably, is built on this basic joke premise: a comedian points out shared, common, universal moments that we don't normally think about. This particular brand of joke beautifully illustrates Burke's points. Where "interests are joined," identification occurs. A rhetorician's job, then, is to establish (build, create) these points of identification. Good comedians, like expert rhetoricians, bridge division, establish common ground, and from that common ground make audiences laugh (affirmation of joined interest and identification).

But the question remains: How?

Burke writes, "To identify A with B is to make A 'consubstantial' with B." Furthermore,

> In being identified with B, A is "substantially one" with a person other than himself. Yet at the same time he remains unique, an individual locus of motives. Thus he is both joined and separate, at once a distinct substance and consubstantial with another. (p. 21)

The important distinction here (other than A finding ways to achieve identification with – and thereby persuasion of – B) is that "two persons may be identified in terms of some principle they share in common, an 'identification' that does not deny their distinctness" (Burke, p. 21). This is important because Burke's understanding of rhetorical motives has less to do with sameness than with our ability to identify and remain distinct.

Consider again the material from Carlin above. In order for Carlin's audience to "laugh" at his observation, it has to have had a similar experience – or so it would seem. Carlin prefaces his observation about looking at his watch with a set up. He is about to share experiences (for laughter) that "we have in common." These are "universal moments," and they "make us the same." The rhetorical effect of these lead-in phrases is to set up his audience to agree. Alternatively, if he had chosen incongruity, the phrases might have acted as misdirection and produced the opposite effect; this would still allow us to achieve identification. Comedians can either rely on a sense of sameness, or they can "other" themselves. Both approaches position the audience, either as "same" or "other" and establish a collective identification with or against the other. Agreement is likely produced even if an audience member doesn't explicitly identify.

Stand-up comedians are effective rhetoricians because comedy itself is built on the consubstantial. "For substance," Burke writes, "in the old philosophies, was an act; and a way of life is an acting-together; and in acting together, [people] have common sensations, concepts, images, ideas, [and] attitudes that make them consubstantial" (p. 21). We are all different (individual/divided); however, our "acting-together" produces the potential for common sensations, concepts, etc. We may (and do) experience situations differently, but our shared language puts us in constant conversation by which we find/make common ground. Stand-up comedy can only work because of consubstantiality – acting-together is the space/place from which comedy can be made.

In *Stand-up Comedy in Theory, or Abjection in America*, John Limon (2000) tackles stand-up comedy as a scholarly subject and presents a theoretical foundation for thinking about how stand-up comedy works on us. Limon writes,

> [The] collective experience of humor, like the personal experience of pain, fills its moment and perishes; reflection misprizes it of necessity. (Laughter may be the social equivalent of pain, the *group* incorrigible.)... To criticize a joke is to miss it, because the joke, as Freud demonstrates, is, in the first instance, an escape from criticism to a prior happiness. (pp. 11–12)

Limon relies a bit too much on Freud's understanding of humor; however, Limon's "collective experience of humor" dovetails rhetorician D. Diane Davis's (2000) observation, "[Laughter] is not human, not logical, yet is capable of overtaking human beings—of *laughing us* even when we choose not to laugh" (pp. 22–23). Davis's point is that laughter is (often) beyond our control. Think about surprised laughter, those moments when something unexpected strikes a listener as funny – especially when it shouldn't or when it's inappropriate to laugh. The laughter escapes before it can be stopped. These moments of laughter push listeners beyond control. This is what Davis means when she says laughter is not logical (that it can be elicited without our conscious consent; that we can't contain it), or that the laugh *laughs* us – the laughter takes us over, and sometimes we start and literally can't stop.

If we accept the basic notion that comedy can provoke us (often beyond our control) to laughter, and that this provocation is often experienced collectively, then we have the clear makings of a provocative rhetorical situation. Stephen A. Smith (1993) writes, "Aristotle's distinction between poetic form and rhetorical function seems to be joined in humor, making it one of the most effective means of argument and persuasion in popular culture" (p. 51). This is especially true with regard to stand-up comedy and the role a comedian plays in guiding an entire room of individuals toward laughter. The comedy club scene is uncanny in its nearly direct parody of the political arena. A political speaker draws upon the available means of persuasion to gain hearers' confidence and acquiescence; a stand-up comedian draws upon the available means of persuasion to provoke an audience to laughter. Comedians, arguably, are in the more enviable power position in that they can move the members of their audience *beyond* their control, something that is less likely to happen in a political arena.

While Smith rightly observes that "humor is a unique form of communication, and it can have important social functions for both resistance and control," in the hands of "charged" comedians like Marc Maron it also has an important psychological function and can result in comedic catharsis (p. 51). When Maron successfully guides his audience to collective laughter – via his WTF philosophy – the end result is demonstrably therapeutic.

Marc Maron's early comedy is marked mostly by anger and frustration – and, to an extent, failure. He came of comedic age amidst the alternative comedy scene of the late 1980s and early 1990s, and his early comedy is indicative of a general opposition to the wildly popular observational stand-up of the 1980s. In some ways, the revolutionary turn stand-up took in the 1960s – thanks to pioneer Lenny Bruce – folded back in on itself by the time the opulence of the 1980s hit the comedy clubs and television screen. The advent of cable television saw the rise of comedians like watermelon smashing nutcase Gallagher, everyman Tim Allen, and redneck Jeff Foxworthy. The alternative comedy scene turned its bitter back on popular comedy and returned to the deeply personal, often political comedy of Bruce, Mort Sahl, and Richard Pryor.

What's most notable in the shift from popular to alternative, especially with regard to Maron's humor, is the personal – is the turn inward. For Maron, the comedy club stage became the therapist's couch. And it is Maron's commitment to "comedy as therapy" that separates him from most of his peers. Indeed, as Naessens claims, "stand-up comedians translate thoughts and personal anecdotes for audiences" (p. 235). He adds, however, that such translation is misprized if we don't recognize comedians' "pragmatic use of darkness" (p. 236). Again, comedians are not their personae. For Naessens, this means that their comedy cannot be termed "therapy," nor can stand-up comedy's effect be cathartic.

However, Naessens's blanket dismissal of the therapeutic potential of stand-up (which is warranted given the overwhelming evidence he presents for popular misunderstandings and journalistic misrepresentations of comedy and comedians) seems over-determined, especially in relation to the operational motives of Marc Maron. Naessens insists, "The stand-up-comedy-as-catharsis/therapy trope should be seen as self-evidently false" (p. 240). Furthermore, he notes, "while catharsis may well be an unintentional consequence of telling jokes... it is wrong to suggest that stand-up comedy is a form of therapy or catharsis" (Naessens, 240). Naessens bases his conclusion(s) on an understanding similar to Limon, who insists "a joke is funny if and only if you laugh at it... Your laughter is the single end of stand-up" (p. 12). "[The] primary objective of comedy," Naessens concurs, "is the generation of laughter and mirth, not catharsis of therapy" (p. 240).

Like Limon, however, Naessens is speaking in terms of *absolutes* – and this is, ultimately, problematic with regard to laughter's association with, and its reliance upon, the audience. Limon and Naessens both view laughter as terminal, as the end result of a joke, and neither venture far beyond what that laughter represents with regard to collective *affect*. This is not to say that laughter can (or should) be uncritical, that legions of comedians and audiences are wrong to not reflect on what a collective experience of a joke does to/for those who share in the comedic appraisal of common worldview; rather, the point here is that an audience that laughs together is an audience that, following Burke, participates in an acting-together established by/through the rhetorical joke work of the comedian. Laughter cannot exist without an audience. Limon rightly notes this: "no audience, no joke... an untransmitted joke is not, structurally, a joke" (p. 12). However, the points of identification by which a comedian comes to build and organize an audience's experience suggest that while a joke's end point is laughter, that laughter is something *more than* ephemera (p. 12). While laughter "fills its moment and perishes," it is certainly not spoiled by reflection. Instead, by recognizing the comedian's role in harnessing rhetorical forces to bind an audience together and push an audience into a collective experience of laughter, we can begin to believe that catharsis (and/or therapy) can be more than "an unintentional consequence" of a joke.

It is into this speculative space – where the consubstantiality of comedy opens the door to comedic catharsis and/or gradations of therapy – that Marc Maron has taken up residence. His stand-up is articulated through a carefully crafted comedic stage persona. That persona is built on a philosophy (WTF) that derives much of its power and humor from the therapeutic potential of comedy. As therapist and patient, as indignant and liberated, Maron's stand-up persona serves as exemplar of how comedy can do more than just elicit uncritical laughter. *WTF with Marc Maron* further elevates the use value of stand-up comedy to a point where both therapy and catharsis are a possibility.

Conclusion: Comedy as Equipment for Living

Brodie (2008) writes, "The purpose – if not the function – of stand-up is entertainment... Countless theorists identify the phenomenon of the humorous as the revelation of (by the performer) or a reaction to (by audiences) a physical, intellectual, social, moral, or emotional incongruity" (p. 154). That the humorous is both reaction and revelation aligns with the WTF philosophy, where "What the fuck?!" acts as both an exasperated statement/reaction to incongruity, and as a statement of revelation, an acceptance of (or resignation to) the moment. It is in the *performance* of the WTF philosophy by a comedian where both of these functions turn toward a collective experience and rhetorical action, and result in a patterned response (action): reaction > revelation > reaction > revelation. A comedian reacts to a situation (What the fuck?!) and comes to a revelation about the situation (What the fuck.). A comedian then performs the revelation (stand-up/ act) and provides a collective space from within which the comedian's (re)presentation of the original situation (the performed version of the reaction) for an audience primed via identification. Performance re-enacts and thereby elicits a version of the original reaction (What the fuck?!). Finally – if successful – a comedian persuades the audience through laughter and shared revelation (What the fuck).

It is in the turn toward performance that philosophy becomes rhetoric. Brodie adds, "What critics often leave unsaid is that the identification of the incongruous implies a more or less shared worldview" (p. 154). Humor, comedy – laughter – is contingent upon performance, where the comedian mines the incongruities of life and then invokes the consubstantial so that "acting-together" results in persuasion (laughter). Successful performance requires and relies on identification. Comedy generally serves two ends: the comedian either establishes identification in order to laugh away incongruity, and thereby confirm a shared worldview; or/and identification is established in order to critique a shared experience or system. In the first case, comedy does not necessarily serve as social critique; rather, it serves to reinforce the shared worldview. Laughter reifies paradigm.

Conversely, a goal of "charged comedy" is to call upon a shared worldview in order to criticize it; in this vein, identification allows the comedian to call upon humor's "unique form," as Smith suggests, in order to facilitate resistance. However, as David Gillota (2015) observes, "stand-up comedy... reflects the contours of contemporary identify politics" (p. 104). Stand-up comedians often perform to audiences with pre-existing points of identification; in many instances, comedians cater to specific audiences, and/or audiences are drawn to comedians based on perceived affiliations. "Regardless of ethnicity, gender, sexual orientation, class, or political affiliation," Gillota continues, "consumers can find stand-up geared toward them" (p. 104). Through humor, though, the shared worldview(s) of comedian/ audience can be called into question and challenged. As Joanne Gilbert (2004) notes, "Drawing on their shared history of oppression, marginal comics serve as licensed social critics, using rhetorical strategies such as self-deprecation to critique and sometimes subvert the status quo" (p. 17). Performance of self-deprecation allows for resistance and subversion.

Marc Maron's comedy provides us with a third option: It turns the tropes of "comedy is therapy" and "laughter is the best medicine" into points wherein identification leads to comedic catharsis. In this, Maron shares affinity with George Carlin; both comedians offer their audiences more than just an easy laugh; their humor attempts to provide real change in their audience's worldviews. In discussing the extreme humor of George Carlin's "I Kinda Like it When A Lotta People Die,"

Kapica (2020) observes, "Carlin deftly used the rhetorical act of stand-up performance to serve us a powerful, communal—comedic—experience of catharsis (identification), one that ultimately finds value—and transformative power—in darkness, incongruity, and disaster" (p. 65). While Carlin was interested in exposing the arbitrariness of the capitalist apparatus to awaken his audiences to the beauty of an unmistaken life, Maron's goal is, arguably, more personal. For Maron, catharsis is an essential function of comedy. Unlike Carlin's worldview-breaking agenda, Maron's goal is, ultimately, psychological health. It is therapy.

In his address to the *Montreal Just for Laughs Festival*, Maron observes, "despite whatever drives us toward this profession—insecurity, need for attention, megalomania, poor parenting, anger, a mixture of all the above whatever it is, we comics are out there on the front lines of our sanity" (p. 201). Maron's appeal here is to comics; he is reflecting his experience(s) and his psychological need for comedy back to fellow purveyors of the joke. To be "on the front lines of our sanity" is to appeal to the therapeutic value of comedy, its sense-making power. This recalls Burke's observation about the comic frame's transcendent function, its ability to help us "'transcend' occasions when [we have] been tricked or cheated" (p. 171). WTF finds humor in despair, and performance of that humor for an audience serves as a deeply affective rhetorical act, an act of sanity-making that functions as collective revelation and opens the audience up to its own transcendence (comedic catharsis).

In the same speech, Maron reveals the therapeutic impetus behind *WTF with Marc Maron*:

> I started talking about myself on the mic with no one telling me what I could or couldn't say. I started to reach out to comics. I needed help. Personal help. Professional help. Help. I needed to talk. So I reached out to my peers and talked to them. I started to feel better about life, comedy, creativity, community. I started to understand who I was by talking to other comics and sharing it with you. I started to laugh at things again. I was excited to be alive. Doing the podcast and listening to comics was saving my life. I realized that is what comedy can do for people. (pp. 198–199)

While the notion that comedy is therapeutic is rote – just as the "sad clown" label necessarily flattens the concept/role of the comedian – Maron's rhetorical agenda is particularly unique. Maron doesn't present his psychological and sociological traumas so that we can either marvel at his revelations or identify (superficially) with his trauma, the way we might laugh in the face of absurd despair. Instead, his revelations are deeply personal, and through their exposure his audience serves as both a mute though attendant therapist, and as an understanding co-conspirator. When Maron (2011), in *WTF* episode 145, rebukes Gallagher's insistence that "it's a night club... it's not therapy," he does so by insisting, "Yes it is therapy on some level." What this chapter reveals is that for Maron, there is (and always has been) a therapeutic dimension to stand-up.

Naessens rightly observes, "the primary objective of comedy is the generation of laughter and mirth, not catharsis or therapy" (p. 240). What careful perusal of Maron's comedy and podcast interviews ultimately reveals, however, is that comedy has saved, and continues to save, Maron's life. Near the end of his long *WTF* interview with Jerry Seinfeld, Maron half-jokingly asks, "Does comedy save you from the darkness, Jerry?" Seinfeld doesn't miss a beat, responding – almost immediately – "Yes. It does." Stand-up comedy clearly has saved more than just Maron's life (though, he might argue, it certainly complicated it as well). However, while this therapeutic value of stand-up is of import, what is more valuable with regard to Maron's contribution to the medium(s) is his embrace and explication of the WTF philosophy.

References

Brodie, Ian. 2008. Stand-up comedy as a genre of intimacy. *Ethnologies* 30 (2): 153–180.
Burke, Kenneth. 1959. *Attitudes toward history.* Berkeley: University of California Press.
―――. 1969. *A rhetoric of motives.* Berkeley: University of California Press.
Camus, Albert. 1991. *The myth of Sisyphus and other essays.* New York: Vintage International. First published 1955.
Carlin, George. 1992. "The little things we share." Recorded April 24–25, 1992. Track 2 on *Jammin' in New York.* Eardrum/Atlantic, compact disc.
Clark, Andrew. 2013. "Marc Maron does television too." BU Today. http://www.bu.edu/articles/2013/marc-maron-does-television-too/
Davis, D. Diane. 2000. *Breaking up (at) totality: A rhetoric of laughter.* Carbondale: Southern Illinois University Press.
Gilbert, Joanne R. 2004. *Performing marginality: Humor, gender, and cultural critique.* Detroit: Wayne State University Press.
Gillota, David. 2015. Stand-up nation: Humor and American identity. *Journal of American Culture* 38 (2): 102–112.
Kapica, Steven S. 2019. Marc Maron. In American Political Humor: Masters of Satire, ed. Jody Baumgartner, 536–540. Santa Barbara: ABC-CLIO.
―――. 2020. 'I Kinda like it when a Lotta people die': George Carlin's comedic catharsis. In *The dark side of stand-up comedy*, ed. Patrice Oppliger and Eric Shouse, 51–70. Cham: Palgrave Macmillan.
Krefting, Rebecca. 2014. *All joking aside: American humor and its discontents.* Baltimore: Johns Hopkins University Press.
Limon, John. 2000. *Stand-up comedy in theory, or, abjection in America.* Durham: Duke University Press.
Maron, Marc. 2002. "Introducing my cold sore/sobriety, disappointment and suicide/the bishop kid and John Walker." Recorded Jan. 22, 2002. Track 1 on *not sold out.* Stand Up Records, compact disc.
―――. 2009. "Jeff Ross." WTF with Marc Maron (podcast). September 1, 2009. http://www.wtfpod.com/podcast/episodes/episode_1_jeff_ross?rq=jeff%20ross. Accessed 14 Oct 2020.
―――. 2011. Gallagher. WTF with Marc Maron (podcast). January 31, 2011. http://www.wtfpod.com/podcast/episodes/episode_145_-_gallagher?rq=gallagher. Accessed 14 Oct 2020.
―――. 2013. *Attempting normal.* New York: Spiegel & Grau.
―――. 2019. "Episode 1000." WTF with Marc Maron (podcast). March 11, 2019. http://www.wtfpod.com/podcast/episode-1000?rq=1000. Accessed 14 Oct 2020.
―――. 2020. "Jerry Seinfeld." WTF with Marc Maron (podcast). June 8, 2020. http://www.wtfpod.com/podcast/episode-1129-jerry-seinfeld?rq=jerry%20seinfeld. Accessed 14 Oct 2020.
Naessens, Edward David. 2020. Busting the sad clown myth: From Cliché to comic stage persona. In *The dark side of stand-up comedy*, ed. Patrice Oppliger and Eric Shouse, 223–246. Cham: Palgrave Macmillan.

Smith, Stephen A. 1993. Humor as rhetoric and cultural argument. *Journal of American Culture* 16 (2): 51–64.

Taylor, Richard. 2016. The meaning of life. In *Life, death, and meaning: Key philosophical readings on the big questions*, ed. David Benatar, 21–30. Lanham: Rowman & Littlefield. First published 1970.

Timberg, Scott. 2015. "Marc Maron won't talk politics anymore." Salon. https://www.salon.com/2015/05/05/marc_maron_wont_talk_politics_anymore_now_i%E2%80%99d_rather_deal_with_the_source_of_that_anger/

Hari Kondabolu as Philosopher: Enacting a Philosophy of Liberation

67

Brandyn Heppard

Contents

Introduction	1584
Summary: Eat the Rich – 'A little meal I call justice'	1585
Barbarian Philosophy	1587
Rethinking Comedy	1591
Rethinking Liberation	1598
Conclusion	1602
References	1602

Abstract

Comedian Hari Kondabolu likes to remind audiences and critics alike that he is not a political comic or an Indian comic, just a very talented comic. Kondabolu's reluctance to being labeled as a political comic forces those interested in comedy to rethink its relation to the political, as well as those interested in liberation to rethink its relation to the comic. For those interested in comedy, the tension between Kondabolu's political content and his reluctance to being labeled as a political comic forces a recognition that there is, and has always been, an inherently political dimension to comedy. For those interested in liberation, Kondabolu's work is a reminder that although artists are not political figures, the aesthetic must still play a vital role within liberatory struggles. In other words, although comedians are not revolutionaries, the revolution must nevertheless be funny! In this light, it is possible to situate Kondabolu within a long-standing tradition of comedians as critical outsiders. However, as an artist and comedian, Kondabolu should not be considered a political figure. Instead, his comedy can be

B. Heppard (✉)
Raritan Valley Community College, Somerville, NJ, USA
e-mail: Brandyn.Heppard@raritanval.edu

© Springer Nature Switzerland AG 2024
D. K. Johnson et al. (eds.), *The Palgrave Handbook of Popular Culture as Philosophy*,
https://doi.org/10.1007/978-3-031-24685-2_53

understood as enacting a liberatory philosophy, which ruptures his audiences' ability to identify with the prevailing systems of domination and oppression, while also exercising the radical imagination by offering transcendent alternatives that extend far beyond the current situation.

Keywords

Hari Kondabolu · *Waiting for 2042* · Mainstream American Comic · Jonathan Swift · *A Modest Proposal* · Herbert Marcuse · Enrique Dussel · *Philosophy of Liberation* · Bobby Jindal · Columbus Day · Tracy Morgan · Weezer · Andy Warhol · Cy Twombly · Etymology of comedy · Origins of comedy · Aesthetics · Political philosophy · Comedy · Liberation · Revolution

Introduction

Although he has been a nationally headlining comic for well over a decade, many people, including fans of comedy, may not be familiar with Hari Kondabolu. Kondabolu made his first national TV appearance in 2007 on *The Jimmy Kimmel Show*, and then went on to perform on *The Late Show with David Lettermen*, *Conan*, and Comedy Central, among other high profile gigs for up-and-coming comedians. In 2014, Kondabolu released his debut album, *Waiting for 2042*, followed by several other releases, including a Netflix special, *Warn Your Relatives* (2018), and an unexpected surprise album, *New Material Night: Volume 2* in 2020. Although Kondabolu is neither a celebrity, nor a household name, some readers may recognize him from his break-out role playing the "Crossword Businessman" in the 2009 film *All About Steve*, starring Sandra Bullock and Bradley Cooper (heavy sarcasm intended). However, you may also recognize him from the 2017 documentary he wrote and starred in about the character Apu from *The Simpsons*, entitled *The Problem with Apu*.

Although Kondabolu's work extends beyond the world of stand-up, including forays into acting and writing, as well as co-hosting podcasts ("Politically Reactive" with W. Kamau Bell and "The Kondabolu Brothers Podcast" with his brother Ashok), the scope of this chapter will focus on Kondabolu's stand-up. On the one hand, since Kondabolu's comedy regularly confronts the ways in which systems oppress in everyday life, including and especially issues of race and representation, it's not surprising that Kondabolu's work outside of the sphere of stand-up takes on an expressly more political tone. On the other hand, the seemingly overt political nature of Kondabolu's comedy makes his resistance to being labeled a political comic quite curious, especially since his work shows him to be a student of comedy and politics. Kondabolu's resistance to such labels leads us then to wonder why he is so resistant to being labeled a political comic and if there may be some merit to his resistance. If so, what might this reveal about the nature of comedy and/or the relation between the spheres of comedy and politics?

Summary: Eat the Rich – 'A little meal I call justice'

The title of Kondabolu's 2014 debut album, *Waiting for 2042*, is a reference to the year in which census figures predict non-white people will outnumber white people in the United States, making them, in one sense, a minority. When discussing the album title, Kondabolu points out that, in his experience, racial and ethnic minorities are not the ones most concerned with this date. Rather, it is a source of anxiety for some white people who are worried about losing power and privilege. For those white people who are uncomfortable about this statistic, Kondabolu remarks, "Don't worry white people, you were the minority when you came to this country, things seemed to have worked out for you" (Kondabolu 2014). Kondabolu then goes on to explain that being 49% of the population does not make white people the minority. As he states, "That's not how math works, right. 49% white is only the minority if you think the other 51% is exactly the same. It only works if you think, 'Well, it's 49% white people and 51% *you* people'" (Kondabolu 2014).

Like this joke, most of the content on Kondabolu's debut album carries with it some political implications. In one bit on the album, Kondabolu reflects back on some of his hopes and disappointments regarding the Obama presidency. In this bit, he recalls downsizing his dreams from universal health care to a public health insurance option. Then, speaking with exasperated clarity, Kondabolu concedes,

> But of course we weren't going to get that, right? This country doesn't work like that. 'Cause if you've got a reasonable idea and it goes through the legislative system, it gets negotiated back and forth, you end up with far less than you wanted. We started out with the public option, went through the system, what do we have now? Like, echinacea, prayer, and a hug? And the Republicans are trying to take the hug away. They like the prayer, oh they like the prayer. (Kondabolu 2014)

Then, in classic Kondabolu form, he counters with his own strategy.

> The public option was criticized for being a redistribution of wealth... That's why I wish we started with my health care proposal. "Cause my health care proposal wasn't about a redistribution of wealth. My health care proposal was about a redistribution—of organs, right, from rich to poor. And you're thinking, 'Oh, you mean after rich people die, we would take the organs from them?" Yes, after rich people die, and after—we kill them, like a bunch of scalpel wielding Robin Hoods in the night. (Kondabolu 2014)

Doubling down on this proposal, Kondabolu continues, "We would kill these rich people and take the organs from them. 'Cause there's a lot of poor people who need those organs, for transplants and of course—for food" (Kondabolu 2014).

Those unfamiliar with the *Swift*ian satirical legacy may hear Kondabolu's *eat the rich* proposal as crude and barbaric; however Kondabolu's proposal is actually an erudite reimagining of Jonathan Swift's work, *A Modest Proposal*, in which Swift satirically proposes that the children of the poor be eaten so that they are no longer a burden on society. Kondabolu's rendition flips this on its head and satirically proposes eating the rich in order to make them, to borrow Swift's phrase, "beneficial to the public." Kondabolu's joke continues,

> And as we all know, rich people's organs are a delicacy. We would force feed them organic grains, get them all plump and fat, their organs juicy and succulent like foie gras, right. And then we'd have them walk around their very large estates. They'd be free range, they'd be free range rich people. And very humanely we'd kill them. Because they're human beings dammit. Let us not forget their humanity. We'd electrocute their anuses, rip out their entrails, and pull out their organs, and we'd feast. We'd eat a little meal I call justice. (Kondabolu 2014)

Keenly aware of the shock value of his eat the rich proposal, Kondabolu's punchline concludes, "Now some of you might be thinking, 'Hari Kondabolu, that proposal sounds so unreasonable.' Yes. And if we'd started with it, we'd have the public option by now. That's all I'm saying. It's a modest proposal" (Kondabolu 2014). In one sense, it literally is *A Modest Proposal*, just reprised for a contemporary scenario. Much like Swift, Kondabolu's proposal is not an attempt to rally support for an actual policy, but instead, a way to illuminate the current system as an object of ridicule through his use of satire, while also creating some critical distance between that system and his audience.

Kondabolu's modest proposal is no outlier in his body of comedic work. He routinely addresses systems of oppression and domination, including but not limited to white supremacy, patriarchy, heterosexism, xenophobia, classism, and even liberal hypocrisy. However, when critics and fans alike refer to Kondabolu's comedy as political, he frequently demurs. To this end, Kondabolu's follow-up album, *Mainstream American Comic*, is an ironic nod to his reputation as a political comic, as well as an attempt to overcome the label. On the album, Kondabolu quips,

> I know a lot of people are here because they like my jokes against racism and sexism. I know you love that shit. That shit's not going to pay the bills, okay. Alright, cum jokes–cum jokes are mainstream America, okay! Yeah, I know it's beneath me… Do you know what's not beneath me? Health care, okay? Cum jokes for America! Now back to our regularly scheduled programming. (Kondabolu 2016)

Despite his protests to the contrary, the majority of the content on *Mainstream American Comic* further reinforces Kondabolu's reputation as a political comic. Still, Kondabolu makes it clear that political persuasion is not the goal of his craft. In a 2018 article, Kondabolu states,

> When I create art, I don't think about that. You can't think about that. Then you're going to make something that might be righteous politically but not funny and therefore ineffective. Art is as political and persuasive as it is effective. If it's not good art, it's not effective for any purpose. So if I have that in my head, I'm not going to create the best work. (Van Der Werff 2018)

As Kondabolu rightly points out, his work is not political in the sense of organizing, amassing power, or attempting to affect policy. As Marcuse puts it, "Art remains alien to the revolutionary praxis by virtue of the artist's commitment to Form" (Marcuse 1969). This means that the artist remains fixed on aesthetic aims as opposed to political ones. And yet, even without express political aims, his comedy is nevertheless politically potent. Through his comedy, he is able to rupture the audience's identification with the prevailing systems of oppression, often by showing their complicity, as well as exercise their radical imagination by creating an awareness of transcendent possibilities beyond the current situation. So, instead of considering Kondabolu's work political, it is perhaps more helpful to frame his work as philosophical.

Building on this, it is precisely in his role as an artist and comedian that Kondabolu enacts a liberatory philosophy. And yet, his reluctance to being labeled as a political comic forces those interested in comedy to rethink its relation to the political sphere, as well as those interested in liberation to rethink its relation to the comic. For those interested in comedy, the tension between Kondabolu's political content and his reluctance to being labeled as a political comic forces a recognition that there is, and has always been, an inherently political dimension to comedy. For those interested in liberation, Kondabolu's work is a reminder that although artists are not political figures, the aesthetic must still play a vital role within liberatory struggles. In other words, although comedians are not revolutionaries, the revolution must nevertheless be funny!

Barbarian Philosophy

Two thinkers that are particularly helpful for understanding liberation philosophy are Herbert Marcuse, of the Frankfurt School and author of *On Liberation*, and Latin-American philosopher Enrique Dussel, author of *Philosophy of Liberation*. While Marcuse offers a clear prescription for liberation, Dussel views the work of Marcuse and other European left thinkers as both an entry point for thinking about liberation, as well as a point of critique. Dussel contends, "Against the classic ontology of the center, from Hegel to Marcuse—to name the most brilliant from Europe and North America—a philosophy of liberation is rising from the periphery, from the oppressed, from the shadow that the light of Being has not been able to illumine" (Dussel 1985). In Dussel's estimation, a true philosophy of liberation must begin from a position of "otherness," and therefore outside the dominant systems.

One the one hand, this positioning allows for a critical distance from the hegemony of traditional Western thought. On the other hand, philosophy of liberation appears untamed and unintelligible from the viewpoint of the dominant tradition. This leads Dussel to describe it as a "barbarian" philosophy (Dussel 1985). The word "barbarian" was originally used in ancient Greece as an onomatopoeic insult describing the sound of non-Greek speakers to the Greek ear: "bar bar bar." The ancient Romans, who were themselves barbarians by definition, later transformed the term to mean all foreigners who lacked Greek and Roman traditions, with particular attention to those perceived as enemies just outside of Rome's borders. From there, many scholars have generalized the term to refer to those outside of a given civilization that don't share the same traditions. Accordingly, from the viewpoint of the dominant system, philosophy of liberation is indeed barbarian philosophy, particularly because of its exteriority to and hostility toward the hegemony of Western thought.

In one sense, we might regard all comedy as barbarian philosophy. One reason for this is because of its position of "otherness" in relation to traditional logic and reason. From this position of otherness, the comic spirit repeatedly demonstrates a recurring desire to subvert social norms and hierarchies. As one might expect, this makes comedy appear irrational from the standpoint of traditional reason. And yet, there remains a method to its madness. Comedy is not irrational, but rather contra-rational. It has a logic of its own which flies in the face of traditional logic. In sharp contrast to notions of traditional common sense, not only does comedy have its own comic sense, but comic sense works outside of the traditional structures of logic and thrives on confounding them.

Although these features hold true for comedy in general, Kondabolu's comedy, in particular, enacts barbarian philosophy par excellence. Kondabolu uses comic sense as a means of confronting the "common sense" logics that perpetuate the systems that dominate society and the people in it. Further, much like Dussel's notion of philosophy of liberation, Kondabolu's comedy also arises from a position of exteriority and demonstrates a fundamental hostility toward the prevailing systems which reproduce reality in ways that seem inevitable.

In terms of exteriority, Kondabolu draws heavily on his own experiences as a first-generation Indian-American. Kondabolu regularly jokes about the paucity of famous Indian-American voices in popular American culture. For instance, after Mindy Kaling's sitcom, *The Mindy Project*, was green-lit, he joked, "This is huge. We've had an amazing run the last few years with more Indians in the public eye than ever before. There's like fourteen of us now... There's now enough Indian people where I don't need to like you just because you're Indian" (Kondabolu 2015a). Similarly, on his Netflix special, *Warn Your Relatives*, he jokes, "I would start a mango podcast if I could. It would just be me and famous Indian-Americans, all 15 of us, just eating mangoes and talking about how great they are" (Kondabolu 2018).

On the one hand, the limited number of Indian-American voices throughout the media landscape positions Kondabolu's viewpoint squarely on the margins. On the other hand, however, Kondabolu is a native New Yorker, hailing from Queens, with a liberal arts background from Bowdoin in Maine and later receiving a Master's Degree in Human Rights from the London School of Economics. As a result, his view point is as cosmopolitan as it is scholarly, which he plays up for his nerdy-intellectual stage persona. For example, on his *Mainstream American Comic* album, Kondabolu jokes that it surprises people when he tells them he's a huge sports fan, "Because—come on. Look at me. Why would I root for my natural predator?" (Kondabolu 2016). He then goes on to clarify that his favorite sport is, "of course," chess. Not lost in all of this, however, is a performance of masculinity that stands in contrast to the dominant performances throughout the media landscape, moving him even further to the periphery.

Kondabolu further enacts philosophy of liberation in his comedy by using his lenses of otherness to disrupt the mundane ways in which the dominant systems shape our everyday experiences through un-thought clichés, expressions, and icons. One example of this can be found in his critique of the expression "boys will be boys." Kondabolu describes the expression as "the worst thing ever," arguing that "nothing good has ever come before that phrase" (Kondabolu 2016). Kondabolu begins by using the phrase ironically in ways that it typically would not be used. In so doing, he presents a series of alternative performances of masculinity that directly confront more toxic and homophobic performances. As he explains,

> It's never like, "Hey, did you hear that Obama signed a nuclear deal with Iran?" "Psst, boys will be boys. Using non-violence means to end conflict." It's never that. It's never that. It's never like, "Hey, did you see Channing Tatum dance at a gay pride parade?" "Yeah, boys will be boys. Being so comfortable with your sexuality that you support the sexuality of others." It's never that. It's never that. (Kondabolu 2016)

Then, Kondabolu again draws on his own experiences, saying, "It's never like, 'Hey Hari, did I see you under a tree with your headphones on crying?' 'Boys will be boys. I was listening to The Cure and their hit song, *Boys Sometimes Cry*.' It's never that" (Kondabolu 2016).

Another helpful example of Kondabolu using his lenses of otherness to disrupt the mundane ways in which the dominant systems shape our everyday experiences can be found in the case he makes against Columbus Day. Kondabolu begins, "Christopher Columbus was a demon. He was a fraud who murdered and enslaved thousands of Native Americans. But that's not the only reason I hate him, it's also personal" (Kondabolu 2015b). While first acknowledging Columbus' most notorious acts, Kondabolu then draws on his firsthand experience as an Indian-American to shape his critique of Columbus.

> Columbus is why I have to tell people that I'm Indian from India. I mean, come on, for real, of course I am. That's where Indians originally come from... but if you're Columbus they apparently can come from the Caribbean, New England, South America, Staten Island, an abandoned warehouse, or anywhere else you mistake for India. Because of Columbus, I had to deal with kids in school asking me where my bow and arrow and feathers were. First of all, that's racist. Secondly, that's racist. (Kondabolu 2015b)

Just as Dussel argues that philosophy of liberation very often appropriates the language of the "center" to enact liberation, Kondabolu then appeals to another cultural icon in order to turn the cultural mythos in on itself. Kondabolu continues,

> So, I know a lot of Italian-Americans love Columbus because he's their dude. But Italians, you got a lotta' dudes. I mean, why not have Joe DiMaggio day instead, right? He was a Hall of Fame baseball player with a record 56 game hitting streak. Look at his stats: Career .325 batting average, seven straight seasons of over 100 RBI, and most importantly, no career genocides. The only Indians Joe DiMaggio ever slaughtered were from Cleveland. (Kondabolu 2015b)

It's important to note that appropriating the language of the dominant culture does not also mean appropriating their values, bringing to mind Audre Lorde's argument that *the master's tools will never dismantle the master's house*. In Lorde's case, she was specifically arguing that the racism and homophobia of patriarchy, which led to a culture of silencing difference, would not help women achieve liberation. Dussel similarly argues that the hegemonic, totalizing approach of Western thought, which also silences difference in favor of homogeneity, should not be replicated by philosophy of liberation. However, Dussel also recognizes that appealing to the language of the dominant culture is very often a necessary step in the process of enacting one's liberation. So, although Kondabolu appeals to iconography that resonates within the dominant culture, he also uses it in a way that allows for some critical distance. Ultimately he punctuates the joke, concluding, "So screw Christopher Columbus and long live Joe DiMaggio" (Kondabolu 2015b).

As a form of barbarian philosophy, Kondabolu's comedy serves as a sort of insurrection against the hegemonic nature of, to borrow a phrase from bell hooks, "imperialist, white supremacist, capitalist patriarchy" (hooks 2000). At the same time, however, he also offers a liberatory vision, which gives the audience the opportunity to begin imagining worthy alternatives. In fact, Kondabolu regularly uses his comedy to show that the way things are is not the way they must be; that new and better futures are possible if the audience is willing to sever their relations with the dominant systems, which also hurt those they purport to help.

The value in framing Kondabolu's comedy as enacting a philosophy of liberation is that it illuminates his work as philosophical, as opposed to ideological or political. As Dussel states in *Philosophy of Liberation*, "The philosophy that knows how to ponder this reality, the de facto world reality, not from the perspective of the center of political, economic, or military power but from beyond the frontiers of that world, from the periphery—this philosophy will not be ideological" (Dussel p. 9). In like fashion, Kondabolu's comedy is not advocating for the advancement of a particular party, policy, or politics, but instead, helps to make sense of the world as it is currently constituted.

Instead of making political arguments, Kondabolu's comedy invites us to a different way of knowing and understanding, providing his own life, and the lives of those around him, as evidence to the contrary of the logics used to perpetuate the dominant systems. This directly opposes the ways in which the dominant culture tends to silence and erase those with less power. Instead, from the viewpoint of philosophy of liberation, the lives and experiences of those outside of these systems can no longer be excluded from our understanding of reality. As Dussel says in *Philosophy of Liberation*, "'The wretched of the earth' (who are not nonbeing) are also real" (p. 10). The same holds true in Kondabolu's comedy. This means that in Kondabolu's comedy, black lives matter, queer lives matter, the poor, women, immigrants, non-Americans, as well as all those who have been victimized by oppressive systems.

Rethinking Comedy

Although Kondabolu frequently draws on personal experience, the overt political nature of his comedy raises questions about his reluctance to embrace the label of political comedian. On the surface, Kondabolu's resistance to this label could simply be dismissed as a desire to remain commercially viable, perhaps just not wanting to be pigeon-holed in such a way that would limit his work opportunities. And yet, Kondabolu is readily aware that his comedy has a very particular niche, as he remarks after a bit on abstract art: "those are the jokes that keep me on NPR and off television. I'm a *Jeopardy* man in a *Wheel of Fortune* world" (Kondabolu 2016).

Kondabolu frequently makes mention of how his comedy doesn't play in some parts of the country. He is also not shy about discussing the many "bad" shows he has suffered through, which have included audience members walking out on his set. In one bit, Kondabolu shares hate mail he received after a show from a person named "Thad." In Thad's email, he writes,

> I came to see your show at the Neptune last night in Seattle. I want to let you know that you have become the cliché that you seem to be trying to avoid. You talked a lot about how you want to be a comic, rather than an Indian comic. For reference, please refer to your curry sauce joke. (Kondabolu 2016)

In response, Kondabolu quips, "I know my own jokes. I don't need to refer to my own jokes, alright. I'm familiar with my material" (Kondabolu 2016). Kondabolu then continues reading Thad's email. "Instead, you have become just another non-white comic who makes fun of white people. There are plenty of these. Look it up" (Kondabolu 2016). Kondabolu interjects again, saying, "Will you stop giving me research assignments in this hate mail, please! Just get on with it. I like my hate mail straight forward. Just tell me you hate me already" (Kondabolu 2016). Thad continues, "You are the non-white comic standing on the stage talking about white power," to which Kondabolu remarks, "Yeah! It's kinda' my thing" (Kondabolu 2016). Thad's email continues by explaining how offended he was as a white male listening to the show, telling Kondabolu, "It took all my strength to not get up and walk out" (Kondabolu 2016).

In another bit, Kondabolu recounts hate mail he received after an NPR appearance. Kondabolu remarks, "By the way, NPR hate mail is very unique. The grammar is perfect" (Kondabolu 2016). Kondabolu then reads the email, which begins, "Just got through listening to an interview on 90.5 about your album *2042* and was very offended by your comments. It seems we have some reverse racial discrimination going on," to which Kondabolu responds, "Sorry sir, don't believe in magic" (Kondabolu 2016). Continuing to read, he says, "Don't forget, once the Obama dollar becomes even more devalued... no one will be the winner and you will not be able to grin and say 'I've made it.' By the way, I listened to your music and you are a disgusting, no-talent, little shit" (Kondabolu 2016). Kondabolu then hits back, saying, "Now, to be fair, if you listened to my album thinking it was music, then—you have every right to be disappointed" (Kondabolu 2016).

I cite these examples just to point out that even though Kondabolu would certainly like to keep his career options open, he also understands that his material isn't for everyone. Aware of this, Kondabolu remarks, "That's fine... that's why it's good" (Kondabolu 2018).

Kondabolu's reluctance to identify as a political comic could also be dismissed as a lack of self-awareness; perhaps he's not in touch with his own brand. Yet, Kondabolu's comedy is painfully and hilariously self-aware. For instance, Kondabolu closes *Waiting for 2042* with a list of imaginary movie roles for which he would be perfectly type-cast. The list includes "a young sociology professor at a small liberal arts school in Vermont," "a mutant that has Pooh's body, Piglet's anxiety, Owl's insomnia, and Eeyore's depression," and finally, "a former radical leftist activist who has compromised and is now living a life as a middle class, middle aged, father of three in suburban New York" (Kondabolu 2014).

Another example of Kondabolu's self-awareness occurs on his Netflix special, *Warn Your Relatives*. Kondabolu recounts a story of an encounter he had with fellow comedian Tracy Morgan after the comedian heckled him at a show. Kondabolu remembers Morgan offering him this advice: "You're too smart. These people aren't geniuses. They're not rocket scientists. You need to keep it simple. Elementary my dear, Watson. El-e-men-try. I mean, look at you. Look at what you look like. Look at you" (Kondabolu 2018). Kondabolu responds,

> And I knew what he meant. I know what I look like. You know, I look like a Muppet getting his Ph.D. I'm familiar with my aesthetic. I have very big features. If someone was to draw a caricature of me it would just look like me. I get it, I look like a Muppet, a handsome Muppet, but a Muppet nonetheless. (Kondabolu 2018)

In the same bit, Kondabolu recounts how Morgan chided him for his intellectual, high-brow style, suggesting, "If you walked out on stage and talked about licking a girl's asshole, that would be hilarious" (Kondabolu 2018). Kondabolu then remarks to the audience, "And that's where I figured out that Tracy Morgan definitely writes his own material" (Kondabolu 2018). In classic comic fashion, Kondabolu later does a call back to this memory, exhorting, "Hari Kondabolu doesn't tell dirty jokes just to tell dirty jokes. There's a reason for all this. So I was licking this girl's asshole—I don't know Tracy. I don't know. It doesn't feel like me, Tracy. It's not consistent with the brand" (Kondabolu 2018). Kondabolu routinely jokes about his own aesthetic and affect, which further undermines the idea that he is unaware of his brand.

Although Kondabolu's self-awareness makes it surprising that he resists being labeled as a political comic, his resistance becomes all the more curious when we also factor in that he is a student of comedy, as evidenced by his Jonathan Swift allusion. Kondabolu frequently delivers meta-jokes about the nature of comedy and joke-writing, which also points to an underlying philosophy of comedy. One such joke is his Weezer joke. Kondabolu concludes the joke, saying,

> Now audience, look, we can be honest about this... The end of that joke was very disappointing. I mean, it was a very long way to go for very little. I mean the beginning of the joke had a couple of big punchlines, right, and then it plateaued for a really long time, really living off the early part of the joke. And then it ended really disappointing. And, you might be wondering, "Hari Kondabolu, why would you write a joke like that?" I'll tell you why. I wanted to write a joke that echoed the trajectory of Weezer's career. (Kondabolu 2014)

Another example of Kondabolu's meta-joke telling is in a bit he does about abstract art. Kondabolu begins the joke, saying,

> Stand-up comedy is such a beautiful art form. And it frustrates me because people don't really consider it art, right. Which begs the question, what gets considered art? And what gets considered art is whatever rich people say is art, right. Whatever rich people will fund and finance and buy and put in museums, that's what gets considered art, right. Like abstract art. I fucking hate abstract art, but rich people like it so it's art, right. (Kondabolu 2016)

Kondabolu then holds up the artist Cy Twombly as an example of what he hates most about abstract art.

> My least favorite artist of all time is Cy Twombly. I fucking hate Cy Twombly, right. The first Cy Twombly painting I ever saw was on a canvas, a bunch of pencil scratches, a splotch of red paint, the word "Leda" and the word "swan." And the name of the painting was *Leda and the Swan*. No it's not! It's *Scratchy Scratchy Splotch*. Why are you lying to us? You are lying right now. This other exhibit was five canvases all painted red, all labeled untitled. Try, at least, try! And this other exhibit was his shit bronzed. He bronzed his feces! And people paid to see this because rich people say its art. (Kondabolu 2016)

Kondabolu then turns his gaze to Andy Warhol, of whom he is a self-described fan. Kondabolu states,

> I fucking love Andy Warhol but Andy Warhol was a dick, man. He was in New York in the 60s, 70s, and 80s, part of that art scene, right. He had his gallery, the factory, right. He had tons of money. He hung out with rich and famous people. Everyone said he was a genius. I mean, he was full of himself. He wasn't humble and you have to be humble, right. Andy Warhol wasn't even from New York. He was from Pittsburgh. That's less impressive to me, alright. (Kondabolu 2016)

Kondabolu continues the bit by imagining Warhol's embarrassment when his old friends from Pittsburgh show up unannounced at his gallery. In the midst of a winding imaginary exchange between Warhol and an old friend from Pittsburgh named Jim, who Kondabolu dreams up, he imagines Warhol saying to Jim: "Let me ask you a question. Where the fuck is this joke going?" (Kondabolu 2016). To which the imaginary character of Jim responds, "I have no idea what Hari's doing right now, Andy. I think the biggest problem is that he only knows three things about you and he's already used them in the joke. Because he didn't even finish the Wikipedia entry, the most basic form of research" (Kondabolu 2016). Kondabolu then concludes the joke with a surprise punchline. "'Oh yeah, yeah this is terribly disappointing. Just a bunch of random ideas and facts, strewn together pretending to make some kind of nuanced point. Is this a joke?' 'No, it's abstract art'" (Kondabolu 2016).

Not only does Kondabolu demonstrate a nuanced understanding of the nature of comedy, he also demonstrates a strong grasp of the political, as evidenced by his equal opportunity lampooning of politicians on both sides of the aisle. He also uses contemporary political issues as the premises for many of his jokes. So, in some ways, Kondabolu's steadfast stance against being labeled as a political comic challenges us to clarify our understanding of the comic and its relation to the political. If comedy contains an inherent political dimension, then perhaps Kondabolu is correct to identify himself as just a comedian.

Although comedy has a long and winding history, as Alexander Leggatt argues, it is "our most consistent and relatively stable literary form" (Stott 2005). So despite the diversity of comedy, as well as its desire for novelty, there is a recurring spirit of comedy that has remained roughly intact for millennia. If we examine the etymology of comedy, it suggests that it has held political implications since its origins. Some traditions understand the root of comedy as komos. As Dmitri Nikulin, author of *Comedy Seriously*, explains, "A komos was traditionally a revel, celebrated in many cities and often accompanied by 'a festival of Dionysus in which a phallus was carried in procession' and by the singing of phallic songs" (Nikulin 2014). If you then added the suffix "ody," meaning song in ancient Greek, then "a picture emerges of a boozed-up bunch making a song and dance about things" (Bevis 2013).

Others, however, argue that comedy is derived from the ancient Greek word "kome," or "komai," meaning country village. Andrew Stott, author of *Comedy*, argues that Aristotle, for instance, preferred this derivation of comedy. Stott goes on to argue that comedy's origins lie not in the komos, but rather in the exteriority of the comedians, "because they toured the villages when expelled from the town in disgrace" (Stott 4). Tracing comedy's etymological origins to the rural kome represents not only a geographical distancing, but also as a class distinction, aligning comedy with the rural peasants outside of the city, on the socio-economic margins of society. Following this origin story, "The rural 'kome' reveals a communal activity in which peasants sing songs that mock their fellow citizens for wrongdoings—a spontaneous dialogical exchange within a critical, reflective community" (Nikulin 3). Moreover, as Nikulin goes on to explain, this origin story also carries with it the implication that rivalries were brought down "from the level of war and legal action to the level of carnival, where justice was accomplished without bloodshed and without much resentment" (Nikulin 3–4). Over time, the "critical lampooning and personal attack" that were largely improvised and informal before comedy's formal integration into the state became stalwart features of comedy. As a result, the sublimation of violence "to the level of carnival" becomes a trademark of comedy, infusing it with an ethical, political, and communal sensibility.

Moreover, not only is comedy inherently political, it is also politically progressive. As the truism goes, comedy punches up. It takes aim at centers of authority, power, and tradition, in order to achieve freedom and equality. So, the sublimated violence of comedy is not random or arbitrary, but instead directed from margin to center, from those with less power at those with more power. Even comedy that is not overtly political relies on comic humor that is subversive and anarchic. As Nikulin notes, "it signifies an (anarchic) fight against authority and thus both liberates from oppression and establishes the superiority of the right against the wrong" (Nikulin p. 99). This allows us to understand Kondabolu as belonging to a long tradition of comedy in which the comedian acts as a critical outsider.

Further, if we examine Kondabolu's most overtly political content, often about elected officials in both the Democratic and Republican parties, it becomes apparent that the humor of these bits falls back on more personal ground. One glaring example of this is Kondabolu's extensive bit on Bobby Jindal, the former governor of Louisiana. In his trademark style, Kondabolu first lays out Jindal's most notorious attributes, explaining,

> He's against gay rights, he's against immigrant rights, he's against women's rights. I can't support that dude and it hurts me because he looks like my uncle—Tom. I can't support him. I just can't. Bobby Jindal's an assimilationist. He believes in assimilation. I don't believe in assimilation, right. Assimilation to me means that people of color and immigrants have to pander to the white majority and become who they're told to be. I don't believe in that. (Kondabolu 2016)

Following this, Kondabolu then gets into his more personal reasons for "hating" Jindal. He explains,

> It's personal for me, man, because my name is Hari. That's been an issue my whole life. I always have a conversation with people. "My name is Hari." "Hurry?" "Hari." "Hāri?" "Hari." "Harry?" Meanwhile, this guy, "Oh, what's your name?" "Piyush." "What?" "Bobby." Are you kidding me? No spine whatsoever. (Kondabolu 2016)

Kondabolu then continues,

> Bobby Jindal is the type of dude that wouldn't give you a minority head nod. You guys know the minority head nod? Yeah, like, when you're in a real white place and you see another person of color, you give 'em the head nod, right... Not Bobby Jindal, though, not Bobby Jindal. You give that dude the head nod, he'd put his head right back down. "Stop it, you're going to blow my cover. Stop it." I don't respect that dude. I do not respect Bobby Jindal, man. (Kondabolu 2016).

Kondabolu then goes on to discuss how he created a trending hashtag on Twitter called #BobbyJindalIsSoWhite, which he argues was not done to belittle Jindal's racial identity but rather to express his disdain for his assimilationist beliefs. Kondabolu describes his anger as based on a sense of personal and cultural betrayal, which he largely attributes to Jindal turning his back on the Indian-American community after embracing their cultural and financial support in order to get into office. Kondabolu specifically cites Jindal's rebuke of "hyphenated identities," like Indian-American, further brandishing the assimilationist beliefs that Kondabolu finds so repugnant. Accordingly, in his act, Kondabolu proceeds to read a series of tweets that he wrote directed at Jindal, each one more vicious than the last, which began to trend under the hashtag #BobbyJindalIsSoWhite. Some of the tweets were so vicious that Kondabolu's mom scolds him and convinces him to take them down.

In response to the tweets, Jindal's presidential campaign launched a fundraiser "in response to the liberal media's race baiting," to which a bemused Kondabolu remarks: "Liberal media? You mean me? I'm the liberal media? Some Indian dude with his pants off in his apartment in Brooklyn tweeting is the liberal media? I tell cum jokes for health care, what are you talking about?" (Kondabolu 2016). Finally, Kondabolu concludes his bit, saying, "As some of you might know, Bobby Jindal ended his campaign for the presidency months ago, right. Which of course marks the second time that Bobby Jindal quit a race" (Kondabolu 2016).

So, although it is clear that Kondabolu doesn't agree with Jindal's political beliefs, the comedy of Kondabolu's jokes about Jindal arises from a personal sense of betrayal. Kondabolu felt so personally enraged by Jindal that at one point during his twitter beef with Jindal, he tells his mom, "I'm at war," to which his mother replies, "War? You're not at war Hari, you don't even have pants on" (Kondabolu 2016).

Of course, in the era of Trump, Kondabolu also had choice words for the candidate turned president. But again, most of Kondabolu's jabs at Trump are more personal than political. On *Mainstream American Comic*, Kondabolu jokes,

> A lot of comics who make fun of Donald Trump make fun of his hair. That's low hanging fruit, man. I'm not going to do that. I think I'm more clever than that. I'm not going to make fun of his hair, you know. His hair looks like it was drawn by a child—while sneezing. It felt good. (Kondabolu 2016)

Even after Trump's election, although expressing his clear dislike for his politics, much of Kondabolu's Trump material still remained more in the personal realm. For instance, Kondabolu jokes about how many people assumed Trump's election would be a boon to his comedy, to which Kondabolu responds, "No it's not. If you read his tweets, if you hear what he says, he does all the work already. There's nothing you can add to that. Like CNN is basically Comedy Central at this point" (Kondabolu 2018). So again, although Kondabolu's comedy frequently draws on the political, the comedy is derived from its very personal nature. The intent of these jokes isn't political persuasion, but rather comic relief.

Despite the fact that Kondabolu's comedy is politically progressive—or rather, because it is politically progressive—he is also quite critical of liberal politicians. Biden, Clinton, Obama, Sanders, none of the preeminent figures in Democratic Party politics remain unscathed. Perhaps more worthy of attention than Kondabolu's lampooning of liberal politicians are his frequent critiques of (white) liberals more generally, which make up a considerable portion of his audience.

In one bit, Kondabolu recalls discussing his anxiety about an upcoming gig in North Carolina with a friend. As Kondabolu tells it,

> My friend's from North Carolina and he's like, "Hari, you're being ridiculous. You're performing in Asheville. Asheville's the most liberal part of North Carolina." And I'm

like, I don't know what the fuck that means. Does that mean they call the ambulance after the hate-crime? What does that mean? What does *liberal* mean for me? Does that mean I'm going to be hit over the head with a bottle of Kombucha? What does that mean? What does liberal mean for me? (Kondabolu 2018)

Kondabolu's exteriority allows a moment where liberalism must take a look at itself from the eyes of the other.

Kondabolu's critiques of liberalism also highlight liberal hypocrisy. In one bit on *Waiting for 2042*, Kondabolu lambastes liberals for their empty threats to move to Canada every time the political winds shift in ways that make them uncomfortable. As Kondabolu remarks, "Canada doesn't have a special visa for American liberal cowards" (Kondabolu 2014). He then goes on to critique Canada for its own history of colonization and oppression, saying, "Canada's not even that fucking great... They killed a bunch of indigenous people to steal that land, too!" (Kondabolu 2014). He goes on to say,

> The only reason why people think Canada is so fucking great to begin with is because the US happens to be the biggest asshole in the world. So, in comparison, Canada looks good. It's like being in high school, right, and there's a dude that's punching you in your face every single day against your locker, right. Then his friend shows up and starts laughing. And as the two of them walk away, the dude that was laughing turns around and says, "Dude, I'm so sorry." That's Canada! [But] they do have healthcare, that's pretty great. (Kondabolu 2014)

In another bit critiquing President Obama, Kondabolu cuts right to the core of his critique of liberalism, implicating himself and much of his audience.

> Some of you might be thinking, "Hari Kondabolu, if you're so critical of this president, then why did you accept an invitation to meet Vice President Joe Biden in his house in Washington DC last year?" I'll tell you why I accepted that invitation. I. Am. A. Hypocrite. But I'm self-aware so that makes everything okay. That's how liberalism works. (Kondabolu 2016)

Kondabolu's criticism of liberal hypocrisy also extends to liberal silence and silencing. In another story, Kondabolu recounts an incident he experienced in a coffee shop in Seattle, "a town full of white liberals" (Kondabolu 2018). As Kondabolu notes, "the white liberals in this coffee shop did what white liberals tend to do when there's a confrontation. They put their heads down and pretended that nothing was happening" (Kondabolu 2018). In another bit, Kondabolu challenges liberals not to fall back on old forms of diminishing and silencing those on the margins. He states, "If we want racial justice in this country, we're gonna' need white allies" (Kondabolu 2018). Then, in his next breath he cautions, "But we don't need a certain kind of white liberal that says stuff like, 'Well, I know things are bad right now but we've come a long way.' 'Well, you have to admit, we've come a long way'" (Kondabolu 2018). As he retorts, "I don't give a fuck how far we've come. I wasn't alive then, I'm not going to be alive later. I'd like to enjoy the shit now please. I mean, that's how this should work" (Kondabolu 2018).

The way Kondabolu excoriates liberalism makes clear that his aims are neither ideological, nor overtly political in the traditional sense. The goal of his comedy is not to vote liberal politicians out of office or pass more progressive legislation. Instead, in classic comic fashion, Kondabolu is merely "punching up" at the prevailing systems that shape his life, as well as our own. His comedy holds a mirror up to liberalism, which allows his audience to see its flaws and hypocrisy. And, just as he does with other systems, Kondabolu disrupts the audience's ability to easily identify with them, thereby creating some critical distance. It is this ability which makes a further inquiry into the liberatory dimension of comedy, and Kondabolu's work in particular, worthwhile.

Rethinking Liberation

Kondabolu's comedy not only forces us to rethink the relation between comedy and the political, but also, how it specifically relates to liberation. By drawing on the best of liberatory philosophy, we begin to recognize that there is an important role for the aesthetic, including comedy, within a holistic framework of liberatory activism. Although many conceive of liberation only in the negative sense of freedom, as a breaking-away-from, the liberatory philosophies espoused by Dussel and Marcuse recognize that truly revolutionary forms of liberation will require a positive notion of freedom, in the sense of creating and founding, in addition to enacting the traditional negative notions of freedom, or else face the risk of being fatally ineffective and temporary. As the saying goes, sometimes you find your way out of the frying pan and into the proverbial fire. In other words, the liberatory philosophies of Dussel and Marcuse both recognize that liberation is a precarious endeavor. Therefore, both thinkers recognize that aside from any considerations of whether or not the liberatory process of breaking-away-from necessarily entails violence, there must also be some consideration of the role of the aesthetic, which is essential to the positive freedoms of creating and founding.

It is, however, worth noting that this does not mean that art alone is capable of achieving liberation. Nor does it resolve questions about the role of violence in liberation and/or revolutionary struggles; questions which extend well beyond the scope of this chapter. But, by taking comedy seriously as an art form, specifically its liberatory and revolutionary force, it allows us to rethink the relationship between comedy and liberation anew.

Beyond the negative freedom (the breaking-away-from) entailed in liberation, Marcuse describes the aesthetic as playing a dual role in the positive freedom required for liberation. As Marcuse explains, the dual role of the aesthetic "may serve to designate the quality of the productive-creative process in an environment of freedom" (Marcuse 24). Marcuse describes the dual role of the aesthetic as, on the one hand, "pertaining to the senses," while on the other hand, "pertaining to art" (Marcuse 24). In regard to the senses, liberation must have an aesthetic component which is literally pleasing to the senses and conducive to the good life. As Marcuse argues, the aesthetic sensibility required for liberation would express "the ascent of the life instincts over aggressiveness and guilt, would foster, on a social scale, the vital need for the abolition of injustice and misery and would shape the further evolution of the 'standard of living'" (Marcuse pp. 23–24). As Marcuse goes on to explain, the revolution "can and ought to be light, pretty, playful" and that "these qualities are essential elements of freedom" (Marcuse p. 26). To quote Emma Goldman, "If I can't dance I don't want to be in your revolution." The same must be said for laughter.

Marcuse argues that the other role of the aesthetic in liberation pertains to art and its commitment to beauty. In the aesthetic realm, the "aesthetic necessity of art supersedes the terrible necessity of reality" (Marcuse p. 44). In other words, the artist is not committed to making an accurate representation but rather to an artistic form. As Marcuse explains, "It is precisely the Form by virtue of which art transcends the given reality, works within the established reality against the established reality" (Marcuse p. 40). Beauty is, therefore, the achievement of form's triumph over its content. Accordingly, as Marcuse states, "When the horror of reality tends to become total and blocks political action, where else than in the radical imagination, as refusal of reality, can the rebellion and its uncompromised goals be remembered?" (Marcuse pp. 44–45). The aesthetic, which includes comedy, provides a field in which the radical imagination can be exercised and stretched. Therefore, although this means that comedians are neither political actors nor revolutionaries, the revolution must nevertheless still be funny!

What makes Kondabolu's comedy so liberatory is his ability as an artist and comedian to enact both the negative and positive forms of freedom which are required for revolution. In terms of negative freedom, which entails a breaking-away-from, Marcuse makes clear that a new aesthetic sensibility must be cultivated which would lead people to reject their identification with the systems that have continually perpetrated the world's atrocities. In Marcuse's estimation, people must learn

> ...not to identify themselves with the false fathers who have built and tolerated and forgotten the Auschwitzs and Vietnams of history, the torture chambers of all the secular and ecclesiastical inquisitions and interrogations, the ghettos and the monumental temples of the corporations, and who have worshipped the higher culture of reality...If and when men and women act and think free from this identification, they will have broken the chain which linked the fathers and sons from generation to generation. They will not have redeemed the crimes against humanity, but they will have become free to stop them and to prevent their recommencement. (Marcuse pp. 24–25)

Building on this, Marcuse concludes, "The rupture with the continuum of aggression and exploitation would also break with the sensibility geared to this universe. Today's rebels want to see, hear, and feel new things in a new way: they link liberation with the dissolution of ordinary and orderly perception" (Marcuse p. 37).

In this light, Kondabolu's comedy can be read as enacting this type of negative freedom. Kondabolu not only names the prevailing systems of oppression, but also uses his comedy to rupture the audience's identification with them. One of Kondabolu's most frequent targets is white supremacy. In one bit Kondabolu states,

> I can't believe we still have to talk about white supremacy; that we have to deal with this shit man. 'Cause you see, here's the thing: Race is made up bullshit. Racism is real. The stuff that, you know, happens because of the made up bullshit. Race is made-up bullshit. Think about it: I'm black. I'm Asian. I'm a color. I'm a land-mass. Like, it doesn't even equate, man. Like, white people. White people is not a real thing. White people is made up. There was a time when the Polish weren't white, when the Italians weren't white, when the Jews weren't white, when the Irish weren't white. There used to be signs like: "No Irish. No Blacks. No dogs." No dogs! Do you know what that means? Cats are white people. And of course they are. (Kondabolu 2018)

Another example of Kondabolu comically confronting white supremacy can be found in the opening bit on his debut album which he refers to as his "White Chocolate Joke."

> I, of course, love chocolate for political reasons, right. Because in America, white is still the default. Despite how diverse this country is, the average American is still seen as white. We see that in television, we see that in film, we see that in media, the average American is seen as white. That's why I like chocolate. Because when you first think of chocolate, you think of something brown. And if you think of white chocolate first, you're a fucking racist. I mean, honestly, who's thinking of white chocolate in that situation? And that brings up the bigger issue, why do we need white chocolate to begin with? It's chocolate, man. It's great! Why would you need to make white chocolate? "Do you love the taste of chocolate but can't stand looking at it? Well, then, try some white chocolate. It's from the people that brought you white Jesus." (Kondabolu 2014)

Directly following Kondabolu's "White Chocolate Joke," he seamlessly transitions into a bit addressing sexism, which he titles his "Feminist Dick Joke." The joke takes aim at sexist tropes which argue against the idea of a woman becoming president for fears that her hormones would inhibit her judgment during menstruation. Following this (il)logic, Kondabolu points out that if we are going to accept the premise that someone's judgment becomes inhibited because of their hormones, then the same premise would apply to him as a man "who happens to have a penis and hormones," in which case his judgment is impaired "every 5-7 min" (Kondabolu 2014). The apparent punchline concludes, "Sometimes I admit, I wake up in the morning with my judgment impaired. And that joke answers the question: 'Hari Kondabolu, can you write a feminist dick joke?' Yes, it can be done" (Kondabolu 2014).

This is only the "apparent" punchline, however, because Kondabolu then continues with a post-script to address transphobia. He continues,

> "But can you write a joke that doesn't reinforce gender-binaries, Hari?" Look, I'm doing the best I can. I mean, I did say "happens to have a penis and testicles," which implies that not all men do have a penis and testicles. I mean, perhaps I could write a post-script at the end of the joke which acknowledges the Trans community in some small way. And maybe, perhaps in the future, I could write a joke that is truly more inclusive. (Kondabolu 2014)

This joke is an example of how Kondabolu finds ways to call out these systems while also revealing his own complicity, as well as the complicity of the audience.

In another bit about homophobia on his Netflix special, *Warn Your Relatives*, Kondabolu describes himself as growing up as homophobic even though his mom was a staunch supporter of the Queer community. Kondabolu remarks,

> My mom has supported gay rights forever. My mom had gay friends in conservative Southern India before that seemed possible. And that's because my mom has a really open heart and people can share their truth with her, right... Love my mom. I have this mom that supports gay rights but I was homophobic as a kid, right. Because I went to middle school. That's where this stuff gets incubated. (Kondabolu 2018)

He then goes on to describe the ways in which homophobia was wielded against him in middle school, stating,

> I was called gay all the time in middle school. It didn't even make sense, right. I made an abbreviated list of all the reasons I was called gay. Again, this list is abbreviated. A list of reasons I was called gay in middle school: Because I had earmuffs. Because I had a handkerchief. Because my favorite ninja turtle was Donatello. Because I had a pink backpack. Because I claimed my pink backpack was magenta. Because I knew the color magenta. Because one time I ate a nectarine. And because of my use of the phrase salutations. It doesn't make sense. It's not going to make sense. (Kondabolu 2018)

Kondabolu uses his comedy in a way which creates distance between the objects of his comedy, which are very often systems of oppression, and his audience. Furthermore, by showing our complicity in these systems, not only does his comedy create a critical distance between the audience and the prevailing systems but it also generates a desire to no-longer be complicit; to be on the right side of the joke. And as demonstrated above, the objects of Kondabolu's comedy are frequently systems of oppression, including but not limited to white supremacy, patriarchy, heterosexism, capitalism, nationalism, and imperialism.

Building on this, as Marcuse makes clear, revolutionary forms of liberation are not just subtractive, but additive. A liberatory praxis becomes truly revolutionary by coupling its negative freedom, in terms of breaking-away-from the prevailing systems of oppression, with the positive freedom of building, creating, and/or founding. As Marcuse states, "the awareness of the transcendent possibilities of freedom must become a driving force in the consciousness and the imagination which prepare the soil for this revolution" (Marcuse p. 23). This means that liberation must do more than simply reject the old systems. Truly revolutionary forms of liberation must also entail the awareness and cultivation of alternative possibilities.

Accordingly, another reason why Kondabolu can be read as enacting liberatory philosophy is because his comedy not only ridicules the current systems, but it also opens the door to creative alternatives. Examples abound in his work, including but not limited to Kondabolu's Swiftian health care proposal, his reclamation of the expression "boys will be boys," and his proposal to replace Columbus Day with Joe DiMaggio day. Another example of this is a joke that Kondabolu makes about racial profiling. He remarks,

It's been 16 years since 9-11, so I think it's time that all airport security be done by Muslims and Sikh men. Because if you're the expert on being harassed, it's time that you do the harassing, right. That's why I also think all cops should be black and all convenience stores should be run by teenagers. Justice! (Kondabolu 2018)

Many, if not most, of Kondabolu's proposed alternatives are ridiculous, and therefore a source of comedy, but they nonetheless exercise the radical imagination, giving his audience a framework to think beyond the current situation.

Conclusion

As Kondabolu frequently reminds his audiences, he is not a political comic or an Indian comic, but just a very talented comic. As he puts it, "I don't like being niched as a thing. I'm a mainstream American comic, man. I've been on Letterman, Conan, Kimmel, Comedy Central. I've been in a shitty Sandra Bullock movie. Nothing is more mainstream than a shitty Sandra Bullock movie" (Kondabolu 2016). Kondabolu's repeated reluctance to being labeled as a political comedian challenges critics and fans alike not to see him as anything other than a mainstream American comic. It also puts forth a challenge to those interested in comedy to rethink its relation to the political. And yet, it is precisely within his role as an artist and comedian that he is able to alter our aesthetic sensibility, which is a necessary precondition for the possibility of a revolutionary liberatory praxis. Therefore, not only does his work force us to rethink comedy's relation to the political, but it also forces those interested in liberation to rethink its relation to comedy. Despite the fact that Kondabolu is neither a political figure nor a revolutionary, as an artist, his work is a worthy reminder that the revolution must be funny.

References

Bevis, Matthew. 2013. *Comedy: A very short introduction*. Cambridge: Oxford University Press.
Dussel, Enrique. 1985. *Philosophy of liberation*. Eugene: Wipf and Stock Publishers.
Hooks, Bell. 2000. *Feminist theory from margin to center*. Cambridge: South End Press.
Kondabolu, Hari. *Waiting for 2042*. Kill Rock Stars, 2014, LP.
———. 2015a. "Mindy Kaling, Apu & Indian-Americans by Hari Kondabolu." Nov 9, 2015. YouTube video. 5:30. https://youtu.be/ktQH78FNCfs.
———. 2015b. "Christopher Columbus Was A Demon by Hari Kondabolu." Dec 24, 2015. YouTube video. 4:06. https://youtu.be/TzJp43NOzXc.
———. *Mainstream American Comic*. Kill Rock Stars, 2016, LP.
———. *Warn Your Relatives*. Aired May 8, 2018, on Netflix.
Marcuse, Herbert. 1969. *An essay on liberation*. Boston: Beacon Press.
Nikulin, Dmitri. 2014. *Comedy, seriously: A philosophical study*. New York: Palgrave Macmillan.
Stott, Andrew. 2005. *Comedy: The new critical idiom*. New York: Routledge.
Van Der Werff, Emily. "Comedian Hari Kondabolu on the response to his documentary The Problem With Apu." *Vox* website, June 21, 2018. https://www.vox.com/2018/6/21/17488564/hari-kondabolu-podcast-the-problem-with-apu-interview.

Richard Pryor as Philosopher: Stand-Up Comedy and Gramsci's Organic Intellectual

68

Cori Hall Healy

Contents

Introduction	1604
Getting to Know Gramsci	1605
What Is Gramsci's Organic Intellectual?	1606
The Great Crossover Star	1607
Example 1: Cops Don't Kill Cars	1609
Example 2: When You Hear "Yee Haw"	1611
Example 3: Mudbone	1613
Example 4: Motif	1614
Conclusions	1617
References	1618

Abstract

Names like Richard Pryor (1940–2005) and Antonio Gramsci (1891–1937) are not often seen together. Pryor is a famous African American stand-up comedian. He is widely regarded as one of the greatest performers of the twentieth century. He won five Grammy awards, an Emmy, and starred in some of Hollywood's biggest blockbusters. Gramsci is an Italian Marxist philosopher known for the writings he produced during his long imprisonment under the Fascist regime of Benito Mussolini. On the surface, a stand-up comedian like Pryor and a Marxist philosopher like Gramsci may appear to create an unlikely connection. However, upon close inspection, a carefully crafted stand-up comedy routine can illustrate ideas and concepts found within the field of philosophy. Pryor, for example, often used his artistic and creative acumen to illustrate the concept of the "Organic Intellectual," one of Gramsci's most well-known philosophical concepts.

C. Hall Healy (✉)
Bowling Green State University, Bowling Green, OH, USA
e-mail: chealy@bgsu.edu

© Springer Nature Switzerland AG 2024
D. K. Johnson et al. (eds.), *The Palgrave Handbook of Popular Culture as Philosophy*,
https://doi.org/10.1007/978-3-031-24685-2_64

Keywords

Richard Pryor · Antonio Gramsci · Richard Pryor biography · Stand-up comedy · Antonio Gramsci · Organic intellectual · Solo performance · Comedy · Humor · Authenticity · Stand-up comedy film · Comedy and philosophy · Cultural theory · Performance studies · Comedy studies

Introduction

In the grand scheme of intellectual inquiry, stand-up comedy does not often come to mind as a medium by which important theories or serious commentary are conveyed. The term "stand-up" is enough to conjure images of a nightclub performer hunched over a smoky bar microphone – a scene where tasteless, crude jokes fly as fast as the cheap whiskey. After all, some of the most popular standup comedians of the modern era crafted their personas around highly sexualized one-liners. The works of Andrew Dice Clay and Rodney Dangerfield illustrate that, even as adults, the average American has the capacity to appreciate the most immature, base, and crude aspects of human nature.

On the other hand, stand-up, in its most potent form, can be insightful and provocative and also explore complex ideas. Richard Pryor often used his comedic talents to openly address social issues. He did not shy away from topics that challenged his audiences and forced them to think about uncomfortable subjects. In some of his most iconic stand-up performances, he used the comedic stage to illustrate the racial divide between black and white Americans. In the late 1970s and early 1980s, Pryor produced a series of three concert films: *Live in Concert* (Margolis 1979) *Live on the Sunset Strip* (Layton 1982), and *Here and Now* (Pryor 1983). These films not only moved stand-up comedy forward as an art form; they showcased Pryor's ability to create funny characters and tell stories that brought attention to systematic oppression, drug addiction, and racism. In these concert films, Pryor directly addressed police brutality, racial profiling, and white privilege. As one of the most successful crossover stars of the 1970s, Pryor used his talent and celebrity status to expose white audiences to aspects of the black experience. Pryor's comedy, through virtue of his immense popularity among white audiences, served as a conduit by which these white audiences became aware of issues facing the African American community.

But does Pryor's ability to translate elements of the black experience to white audiences have a name? What is it called when a member from an oppressed group finds a way to influence the thoughts and actions of the dominant group? The answers to these questions are found when Pryor's comedy is analyzed in reference to philosophical concepts. For instance, philosopher Antonio Gramsci predicted scenarios in which individuals called "Organic Intellectuals" would cultivate specialized knowledge that, in turn, could be used to challenge the views of a ruling class. Pryor, through his career, did just that. Pryor cultivated his knowledge of the black experience and used art to translate it to a dominant class. Examining the works of Pryor through the lens of Gramsci yields a deeper understanding of the connection between Pryor and philosophy. Further, it reveals Pryor himself to be an organic intellectual, and thus, a philosopher.

Getting to Know Gramsci

Before delving into the comedy routines from Pryor's three concert films, it is first important to discuss the philosophical construct taking center stage. In other words, what is an organic intellectual? To understand this concept, one must understand its author, Italian philosopher Antonio Gramsci. Born in Sardinia Italy in 1891, Gramsci discovered his talent for writing and politics as a student at the University of Turin. After abandoning his studies, he became heavily involved in Italian politics. By today's standards, Gramsci could be described as a political activist. He staged walkouts, started newspapers, and founded political parties. Eventually, he would lead the Italian Communist Party from 1924 to 1926. He was a champion of workers' rights and strong labor unions. When Benito Mussolini took power in Italy, Gramsci was arrested and imprisoned. During his trial, Gramsci's prosecutor (acting on behalf of the fascists) famously said, "For twenty years, we must stop this brain from functioning" (Crehan 2002, p. 17). Gramsci would go on to die in jail in 1937 at the age of 46.

During his years of confinement, Gramsci wrote *The Prison Notebooks*, which is a series of essays and political thoughts. They were first published in the late 1940s, long after Gramsci's death, and have since become some of the most influential writings in the field of cultural studies, politics, and philosophy. Building on the foundation left by Marx, Gramsci continued to discuss social class, working conditions, and elements of the "superstructure." Like Marx, Gramsci saw society as dominated by a capitalist hegemony, in which one group holds the influence, power, and control. In the United States, for example, white people's experiences and culture dominate and are supported by the ruling class. However, Gramsci is known for his break with the traditional Marxist philosophy as it applies to agency. Where Marx saw an unyielding class system, Gramsci saw pockets of agency and argued that hegemony can change over time. Gramsci believed individual "intellectuals" could make the difference. Consider this passage from the *Prison Notebooks*:

> What are the "maximum" limits of acceptance of the term "intellectual"? Can one find a unitary criterion to characterise equally all the diverse and disparate activities of intellectuals and to distinguish these at the same time and in an essential way from the activities of other social groupings? The most widespread error of method seems to me that of having looked for this criterion of distinction in the intrinsic nature of intellectual activities, rather than in the ensemble of the system of relations in which these activities (and therefore the intellectual groups who personify them) have their place within the general complex of social relations. Indeed, the worker or proletarian, for example, is not specifically characterised by his manual or instrumental work, but by performing this work in specific conditions and in specific social relations [...]: is a metaphor to indicate a limit in a certain direction: in any

physical work, even the most degraded and mechanical, there exists a minimum of technical qualification, that is, a minimum of creative intellectual activity. (1971, p. 8)

In this passage, Gramsci puts forth the idea that there is a certain amount of creativity associated with even the most degrading of jobs. And labor does not have to be confined to acts that simply perpetuate a structure that is only to the benefit of the wealthy. Gramsci goes on to say:

> Each man, finally, outside his professional activities, carries on some form of intellectual activity, that is, he is a "philosopher", an artist, a man of taste, he participates in a particular conception of the world, has a conscious line of moral conduct, and therefore contributes to sustain a conception of the world or to modify it. . . .. (1971, p. 9)

Gramsci expands on Marxism by allowing the possibility for an "intellectual" to exist outside the confines of his or her job. In Gramsci's view, people can have meaningful ideas, artistic inclinations, and morality despite the fact that a capitalist ideology seeks to separate the worker from his or her humanity. Moreover, an individual can "modify" a conception of the world by virtue of his own experience.

What Is Gramsci's Organic Intellectual?

The "intellectual" plays such a large part in Gramsci's ideas on power and position that he places them in categories and describes, in detail, how each of them functions in society. He called the first category "traditional intellectuals." Doctors, lawyers, and clergy fall into this category. Traditional intellectuals acquire their knowledge through formal avenues like schools, the church, and universities. Furthermore, they feel connected to the dominant (capitalist) system that educated them. The second category is "organic intellectuals." This latter group acquires knowledge through informal means and uses it to represent segments of society that have been overlooked or marginalized by a capitalist hegemony. In other words, Gramsci's organic intellectual gains knowledge through lived experience.

Pryor's concert films demonstrate how he used his artistic acumen to relay aspects of his own life and, in doing so, positioned the comedy stage itself as a mechanism by which he challenged hegemonic structures and advocated for new ways of thinking, which is a major function of Gramsci's organic intellectual:

> Every social group, coming into existence on the original terrain of an essential function in the world of economic production, creates together with itself, organically, one or more strata of intellectuals which give it homogeneity and an awareness of its own function not only in the economic but also in the social and political fields. The capitalist entrepreneur creates alongside himself the industrial technician, the specialist in political economy, the organizers of a new culture, of a new legal system etc. (1971, p. 5)

Gramsci argued that an organic intellectual had a significant role to play in political revolutions and the reorganization of oppressive systems.

It is important to note that Gramsci did not write about race or racism in a way that would make his work relevant to the world in which Richard Pryor lived. In actuality, it is difficult to divorce Gramsci's ideas from 1920s Italy and the European political landscape that led to WWII. In short, Gramsci wrote about a specific sliver of history. He was inspired by the October Revolution in 1917. In 1920, he witnessed unrest as "strikes and factory occupations broke out across Italy. In Turin alone 185 metal-working factories were occupied, including the main vehicle producing plants" (Schecter 1994, p. 94). He also saw the rise of Mussolini. Gramsci's writings are tethered to specific historical times and events.

However, Gramsci's work also touches on larger ideas. For example, as the *Prison Notebooks* progresses, Gramsci speculates on the mechanisms by which revolutions can occur. He is concerned with strategy, political alliances, and how a ruling class can be subverted. In other words, Gramsci wants to know how those metal factory workers in Turin can take more control of their own lives and move to a position of power, however difficult or unlikely doing so may be. He writes extensively about the processes in which intellectuals use knowledge to challenge hegemony. If it is accepted that Pryor used the stage to confront an oppressive structure (racism or otherwise), then the application of Gramsci's theories is appropriate if not ideal.

The Great Crossover Star

For many black entertainers in the twentieth century, fame and fortune meant crossover success. Richard Pryor was no different. By the mid-1970s, he had established himself as a major box office headliner. In 1976, he starred alongside Gene Wilder in *Silver Streak* (Hiller 1976), a financially and critically successful action comedy that propelled Pryor into the spotlight. After the success of *Silver Streak*, Pryor went on to play lead roles in a string of hits like *Stir Crazy* (Poitier 1980), *Bustin' Loose* (Scott 1981), *Some Kind of Hero* (Pressman 1982), *Superan III* (Lester 1983), and *See No Evil, Hear No Evil* (Dark 1989). His film career pushed the sale of his comedy records, which sold millions and won him several Grammy Awards. Pryor also starred in two television series, *The Richard Pryor Show* in 1977 and *Pryor's Place* in 1984. During the late 1970s and early 1980s, Pryor was a cultural fixture in mainstream American entertainment. And mainstream meant he had the adoration and attention of white audiences.

It was during this time, at the height of Pryor's mainstream popularity, that he recorded three concert films. The first one was called *Richard Pryor: Live in Concert*, which was shot at *Terrace Theater* in Long Beach California in 1978. The second was *Live on the Sunset Strip*, which was recorded over two nights at the Hollywood Palladium in 1981. The third concert film was *Here and Now* filmed at the Saenger Theater in New Orleans in 1983. These three films are significant for several reasons. One is the way Pryor chooses to relay aspects of the black experience to an audience comprised of multiple races. Pryor takes great care and effort to explain, as Gramsci might say, a "specialized knowledge" of the world. But what is this "specialized knowledge" and why did Pryor choose the comedy stage as his platform?

Pryor does possess a specific kind of knowledge; an American experience filtered through a life of pain, brutal encounters with racism, and drug addiction – examples of which can be found in Pryor's 1995 autobiography *Pryor Convictions*. Racial slurs and sexually explicit descriptions of Pryor's sexual encounters are found throughout the book. However, the explicit nature of the language is positioned as an extension of Pryor's rough childhood. For instance, Pryor goes into great detail regarding the unjust treatment of African Americans that he witnessed as a young man. He describes the rampant discrimination and the racially charged violence he saw in his hometown of Peoria, Illinois:

> Even the best days in Peoria were tainted by gloom, a murky darkness that hung over people the same way smog lays flat over a city as pretty as L.A. It just fucks up the picture. I saw shit that would cause an adult nightmares. Heard tales about hangings and murders that happened just because a man happened to be black. (2005, p. 17)

In an effort to detail his world and circumstances, Pryor chose to use harsh language, just as he experienced it.

Pryor was born in Peoria in 1940, a time when the city was known for vice and rampant corruption. Pryor's mother was a prostitute. His father was a bouncer in the brothel where his mother worked. They married but eventually divorced after only a few years. After the separation, Pryor's paternal grandmother, Marie Carter, took responsibility for raising him. By all accounts, Pryor loved his grandmother, who he called "Mama." Pryor's father, LeRoy "Buck" Carter, continued to play a role in his life. However, Marie Carter was Pryor's primary caregiver, disciplinarian, and the only real parent he would ever have. It should also be noted that Carter was the owner of the brothel in which Pryor's parents met. He grew up in this brothel watching all kinds of depravity, later recalling memories of such things from his childhood in various interviews and books. He explained how he remembered seeing his mother perform sex acts on a stranger through a keyhole in his grandmother's brothel. According to a 1977 interview with the New York Times, Pryor says that "I saw my mother turn tricks for some drunk white man when I was a kid. I saw my father take the money, and I saw what it did to them" (Saul 2014). Pryor also witnessed drug abuse, domestic violence, and street violence.

In Pryor's case, as in the case of all black people in America, the mere act of existing in racist society provides intimate knowledge of a dangerous political imbalance. If this rare knowledge could be weaponized in some way, it would be the key to siphoning power and influence from the dominant class. Pryor is the personification of Gramsci's "organic intellectual" because Pryor was able to authentically and *profoundly* understand the issues of inequality, racism, and prejudice that were plaguing his community. In turn, Pryor was able to convey his understanding through his mastery of the stand-up form and, in doing so, politicize his knowledge and advocate for (what Gramsci would call) a subaltern class.

Example 1: Cops Don't Kill Cars

To begin, let us examine a segment from *Richard Pryor: Live in Concert* that places a spotlight on racial inequality in America. *Live in Concert* is the first of Pryor's three aforementioned concert films. It was recorded in December of 1978 in California and went on to be the "first successful film of its kind" (Kantor and Maslon 2008.) The film begins with images of Pryor arriving at the theater, exiting his car, and walking through a series of backstage passages. As Pryor gets closer to the stage, the sounds of the buzzing crowd get louder and louder. Finally, Pryor takes the stage and the crowd erupts into applause.

Pryor grabs the microphone and thanks everyone for coming out to see him. At this point in the show, many attendees are scrambling to get back in their seats. Patti LaBelle, Pryor's opening act, had just finished her set and many attendees took a brief intermission. Pryor makes a joke about the situation. He says, "Wait for the people to get from the bathroom. People in there pissin'. 'Wait. The shit done started, Damn." Then, Pryor calls attention to the mixed nature of the audience:

> Jesus Christ. Look at this. White people rushing back. [laughter]. White people don't care Jack. [They] just come out anyways. [...]. You niggas taking a chance being in Long Beach though Jack. I saw the police had some brother jacked up when we was coming in here. Nigga's hands way up here.

Pryor sticks his hands up. He acts out being frisked by the police. The crowd laughs as Pryor remarks that he "bets" the black man was taken away to jail. Then Pryor makes a couple jokes about how black audience members should be careful not to get arrested in Long Beach because it is, presumably, a white part of town. Pryor tops off these opening remarks by saying, "White people, this is [the] fun part for me, when the white people come back after intermission and find out niggas done stole their seats." So, within the first 3 min of the show, Pryor has already addressed the fact that his audience is a mixture of black and white people.

His next few bits also surround the differences between black and white people at large events and concerts. He says, "White people be funny. And you ever notice like, you be the only nigga someplace, and you go where white people [are], and they be funky. Right?" Pryor then launches into his "white voice," one his comedic signatures. The voice is an accent free, flat, semi-nasal sound that is remnant of a generic, male midwestern newscaster. In the white voice, Pryor says, "You want to move out of the way fella? Excuse me. Thank you, every much. Takin' up all the fucking area, Jesus Christ." As Pryor delivers these lines, he acts out a white man walking through a crowd of black people. Pryor's "white walk" is similar to his "white voice." It is rigid, flat-footed, and uptight. And although the crowd appears to be predominately white, as seen in cutaway shots from Pryor's point of view, the bits lampooning white people are met with uproarious laughter. Thus, white people are laughing at Pryor even when he is making fun of white people.

Pryor capitalizes on his rapport with his white audience when he eases into a bit about police brutality. He starts by recounting a story in which cops showed up to his house to investigate a domestic disturbance. He says, "I don't want to never see no more police in my life, at my house, takin' my ass to jail, for killin' my car." Pryor explains that his wife wanted to leave him, so he used a magnum pistol to shoot the tires out of her car and the police eventually showed up. Although this bit, like most of Pryor's bits, involves complicated and disturbing subjects, the audience laughs. Pryor's presentation is full of lively expressions, deliberate cadence, and comedic sound effects that bring levity to the scene. For example, when he acts out drunkenly shooting his wife's car, he makes a high-pitched sound that imitates the sound of air escaping the tires. He also anthropomorphizes the bottle of vodka he was drinking during the incident. He also makes fun of himself. He is not afraid to make himself look foolish or diminutive. The bit ends when Pryor, aware of his own blackness and lack of advantage, tells the audience that when the cops arrived, "I went in the house. Cause [the cops] got magnums too. And they don't kill cars. They kill nig-gars." In his delivery, he rhymes the word car with "gar," which results in a huge laugh from the audience.

As unnerving as it is to think about police shootings, Pryor manages to guide his white audience through it. He uses humor, his comedic abilities, and his celebrity status to go even further. Pryor's next comments confront police brutality with more direct language. He says:

> Police got a choke hold they use out here though, man. They choke niggas to death. I mean you be dead when they though. Did you know that? Niggas goin, "yeah, we knew." White folks, "No! I had no idea!"

In this example, Pryor calls attention to the fact that the black members of the audience knew what he was talking about without any further explanation. However, the white audiences had no idea that such injustice and violence was happening. Although the white audience is laughing, the bit manages to make them aware that there are aspects of the African American experience of which they have the privilege of ignorance.

He continues by describing the hold.

> Two grab your legs, one grab your head, and [mimics the hold] *snap*. [In his white man voice.] 'Oh, shit, he broke. Can you break a nigger? Is it ok? Let's check the manual. Yep, page eight. *"You can break a nigger."* Right there. See. Let's drag him downtown. Ok.

Long before the deaths of Rodney King, George Floyd, Dante Wright, Tyre Nichols, and countless others, Pryor was warning his white audience that the police can beat, "break," and even kill black men with impunity.

Then Pryor goes even further. As the bit continues, he tells the audience about more instances of police brutality. For example, he acts out a story in which he saw black men being chased by police dogs. Pryor mentions he has seen chases with both German Shepherds and Doberman Pinscher. He says:

> I saw [the cops] letting [a Doberman] loose on a young brother, about sixteen, in an alley. The police jumped out the car and sicced the Doberman loose on him. And the brother was low running. I mean he was down in here.

Now, Pryor acts out the way the young man was running. He crouches down towards the stage and makes a flapping motion with his hands. This flapping motion, in an almost cartoonish way, indicates the wind passing by quickly as the young man ran to avoid being hurt by the vicious animal. Pryor adds to the scene by creating sound effects with his voice. He imitates the terrifying growling sound the dog made as it edged closer and closer to the man.

Finally, Pryor ends the bit by telling the audience that the young man got away. Pryor indicates that the man was simply too fast for the dog. Pryor, in a moment that gets one of the bit's biggest laughs, tells the audience that the young man outran the dog, essentially by turning his hat around backwards as if it was a switch that made him run faster. "[H]e shifted into overdrive on the dog. Yeah. The brother had a cap on, he just went..." and Pryor uses his hand to indicate that the boy turned the hat around backwards. The entire bit is met with uproarious laughter from the audience, which seems odd given the grotesque subject matter. After all, Pryor is recounting a completely horrifying instance in which a young black man is chased by a large, aggressive, police dog.

Pryor's ability to elicit laughter while discussing the most depressing topics is an obvious indication that he has reached a level of success usually reserved for rock stars. The fans in the audience cheer, snap pictures, and wave profusely and are ready to laugh at almost anything that comes out of Pryor's mouth. Although it is argued that he ultimately uses his comedic prowess to, in philosophical terms used by Gramsci, function as an organic intellectual, his presentation is still in keeping with that of a superstar stand-up comedian. In other words, even though Pryor is about to discuss police brutality and the oppression of black men with a predominately white audience, he does not come across as a politician or as a man engaged in a lecture. Instead, Pryor's points are disguised as comedy bits. He is an entertainer. The jokes invite audience members (especially those who are white) to let down their guard and listen to the point of view of a member outside their hegemonic class.

In terms of specialized knowledge and the connection to Gramsci's organic intellectual, it should be noted that in 1940, the year of Pryor's birth, "a full two-thirds of black Pretorians reported [...] the persistence of police brutality" (Saul 2014, p. 24). When Pryor acts out scenes in which a young black man has to run from a police dog, he is sharing his own lived experience. As a result, white audience members are being exposed to ideas, concepts, and realities to which they would not otherwise be exposed.

Example 2: When You Hear "Yee Haw"

Pryor continues to share his specialized knowledge in *Live on the Sunset Strip*, his 1982 follow-up to *Live in Concert*. In *Live on the Sunset Strip*, Pryor takes the stage dressed in his iconic red tuxedo. Throughout the special he tackles personal topics. For example, *Live on the Sunset Strip* was taped after Pryor's widely publicized brush with death. In 1980, police were called to Pryor's home after reports that the comedian was on fire. At the time, the incident was attributed to Pryor's drug abuse and his preference for freebasing cocaine (People Staff 1980). However, in the years that followed, Pryor explained that the fire was in fact a suicide attempt. In *Live on the Sunset Strip*, Pryor goes into the gory details of his hospital stay and recovery. As a performer, Pryor was always willing to bring his pain on stage.

This willingness extends to more offerings about the African American experience as well. As a matter of fact, early on in *Live on the Sunset Strip*, Pryor takes a moment to directly address racism. At the show's 30-min mark, almost immediately after his opening bit, Pryor goes into a routine about his new home in Hawaii. He says:

> There's 500 people live where I live. And they are brown. And I like that because you can sleep at night. You know, cause you live around white people in the country and anything can happen. [Laughter]. Not that I don't trust white people. It's just that, in the night, you know what I mean? [Laughter]. I don't know, something happens to white when you start drinking and when you hear one of them mother fuckers go "Yee Haw!" [...] It makes the hair on the back of my neck stand up.

Live on the Sunset Strip, like all of Pryor's concert films, is filmed in front of a mixed crowd. B-Roll shots of the audience reveal, what appears to be, an equal number of black and white people. Thus, Pryor is constantly having to walk a fine line. He must take care not to alienate the white half of the crowd. Case in point, he couches the setup to this particular bit by saying that "not that I don't trust white people." Pryor's word choices indicate that he understands he is addressing a group of people that are part of the hegemonic class. And, in order to convey his point, he has to maintain his likability. He must keep them laughing even as he brings the bit into a darker territory. And darker territory is coming. Pryor eventually says, "Cause I know what's next. After 'Yee Haw,' [white people] get a rope and a black mother fucker."

Once again, Pryor's subject matter is not something typically found in a comedy show. In this example, he is talking about lynching black people: something devasting, macabre, and completely devoid of humor. Nonetheless, Pryor finds a place for it. He finds a way to discuss it and place it in the minds of white audiences. As improbable as it sounds, it is important to remember that when *Live on the Sunset Strip* was taped, Pryor was a huge crossover star. He was absolutely adored by white and black audiences. He is in a unique position to bridge a gap between both communities. Instead of backing away from the opportunity to share the black experience, Pryor embraces it.

After this bit about lynching, Pryor makes a rare declaration. He comes out and tells the audience directly that "racism is a bitch." He then tells white people what he wants them to know. Pryor says:

> White people, you gotta know. It [racism] fucks you up. But what it does to black people is a bitch. . . . It's hard enough being a human being. It's really fucking hard enough just to be

> that –like, just to go through everyday life without murdering a motherfucker; it's hard enough to walk through life, decent, as a person. [But there is] another element added to it when you are black . . .

In this example, Pryor is directly explaining his perspective to the audience. He is using his status as a celebrity and world class performer to share his lived experience with a white audience. As this bit continues, Pryor details the humiliation and pain associated with being called a "nigger." He explains that the word "nigger" makes a person feel less than human. Pryor says that once he is called that word, he is not "a man anymore." He is, in effect, something subhuman.

Example 3: Mudbone

Live on the Sunset Strip also features an appearance by Mudbone, one of Pryor's most famous stage characters. In short, Mudbone is an old African American man who Pryor knew from his youth in Peoria, Illinois. Mudbone spits tobacco into a coffee can and tells stories to anyone who will listen. He appears on several of Pryor's comedy records and television shows. His backstory was revealed in detail during a stand-up segment of *The Richard Pryor Show* in 1977. Before beginning his monologue as Mudbone, Pryor explains:

> Mudbone is a person born in Mississippi. And I knowed him well, you know? And he dipped snuff, you know?. And he [would] sit around in front of the pool hall or barbeque pit and he'd spit in a can. [. . .]. He had an old Maxwell House Coffee can with the top cut off it, and he'd spit in it, see? (Pryor 1977)

Pryor goes on to tell the audience that although Mudbone was originally from Tupelo Mississippi, he traveled to Peoria to find work. However, when Pryor met Mudbone in Peoria, he was retired and spent his time "hanging" in front of local establishments telling stories to the locals.

When Pryor performs as Mudbone, he completely transforms his body and voice. He sits on a stool and makes a subtle but noticeable change to his posture by raising his shoulders. The move gives Pryor an older, more sunken look. Pryor also changes his voice and accent. Mudbone's voice is slightly higher pitched and comes out like a quick whisper. Mudbone also has a decisively more southern accent. Pryor maintains these aesthetic elements throughout his performance as Mudbone. He even takes time from his monologues to mime spitting into a coffee can. Mudbone's many appearances on Pryor's records and concert films typically involve telling dirty jokes or recounting stories from Mudbone's life.

Mudbone makes an appearance in *Live on the Sunset Strip* when a fan yells out. "Do Mudbone Richie!" After a few moments and encouragement from the audience, Pryor finally agrees to transform into Mudbone and perform a monologue. As Mudbone, Pryor says, "I know that boy. See, he fucked up. See, that fire got on his ass, and it fucked him up, upstairs. Fried up what little brains he had." At this point, the audience is completely onboard with the bit. They are laughing hysterically as it becomes clear Mudbone is making fun of Pryor's hospitalization after burning himself.

As Mudbone continues his monologue, he uses phrases and exaggerations that are typical of his storytelling style. In this excerpt, Mudbone makes light of all the "hard times" he has seen in his life. Mudbone says:

> See, I lived through hard times before. Like, people talkin' about, "these is hard times." Hard times was way back. And they didn't even have a year for it, just called it hard times. [Laughter]. It was dark all the time. I think the sun came out on Wednesday. [Laughter]. And if you didn't have your ass up early, you missed it. [Laughter]

Mudbone's world was tempered by his experiences in the deep south. His background provides a sense of gravitas and perspective that he can readily adapt to the situation.

Although Mudbone is a fictional character, the details of his life align with the plight of many ex-slaves born in the Deep South. More specifically, Mudbone's story echoes what historians have called the Great Migration. As Ronald Takaki summarizes in the 2008 edition of his book *A Different Mirror: A History of Multicultural America*:

> An exodus was under way. "The Afro-American population of the large cities of the North and West," the *New York Age* reported in 1907, "is being constantly fed by a steady stream of new people from Southern States." Between 1910 and 1920, the black population jumped from 5,700 to 48,000 in Detroit, 8,400 to 34,400 in Cleveland, 44,000 to 109,400 in Chicago. (2008, p. 312)

When examined in relation to the historical perspective, Mudbone appears to be an ex-slave or a child of ex-slaves who heard about opportunities in the North and traveled there. Takaki goes on to cite a letter written by a black man working, like Mudbone, at a packing plant in Chicago. The letter says, "I work in Swifts packing Co., in the sausage department.... We get $1.50 a day.... Tell your husband work is plentiful here and he won't have to loaf if he want work" (2008, p. 314). When Pryor brings Mudbone to the stage, he brings a piece of African American history to white audiences.

Example 4: Motif

Finally, we come to Motif, one of Pryor's many characters. Simply put, Motif is a drug addict from Pryor's past in Peoria. Motif appears in the last half hour of 1983s *Here and Now*. At this point in the show, Pryor has done a number of bits about his sobriety. In the late 1970s, Pryor had a very public battle with cocaine addiction. At the height of his substance abuse, he was spending $30,000 a day on drugs. The culmination of his addiction occurred when Pryor lit himself on fire.

By the time *Here and Now* was filmed Pryor had stopped using drugs. Before introducing Motif, he recaps his own battle. Pryor says, "I haven't done any drugs, now. It's been seven months." The audience responds with applause. Pryor continues, "And that's a lot for me, you know, 'cause I done—I think I done drugs since I was fourteen." He goes on to tell the audience that when he was 19, he became a heavy drug user and now is the first time in his life that he is completely sober. He uses the announcement as a segue to explain how sobriety has changed his life. For example, Pryor goes into a bit about how funny it is to have people come up to you and tell you things you did when you were drunk – things that you didn't even remember doing. After a couple more bits, Pryor comes back to the more serious issue. He hints that he ultimately regrets how much time he spent addicted to drugs that that he "should have learned from people that I knew that would get fucked up when I was little."

At this point, Pryor is ready to show Motif to the audience. They are still laughing from the previous bits and Pryor seizes the opportunity to explore a topic that is a little more serious. Pryor explains that he failed to notice the horrors of drug addictions because, when he was a child, as he puts it, "I didn't think [drug addicts] were on dope or nothin'. I thought they were cool. 'Cause I had friends like—I had a friend, Motif. The motherfucker, he just sounded so cool. Anything—he took his time to answer." Pryor uses the prompt "Hi Motif," to bring Motif to the stage. For his transformation, Pryor stands still. He hangs his head by pushing his chin into his neck. Finally, after several beats Motif answers "What's happening." Motif's line gets a huge laugh. The scene plays out just as Pryor has described. Motif takes a long time to answer questions. Pryor points out, to a child, this delay is seen as "cool." Pryor says, "I was young, I thought that was cool."

Pryor goes on to tell the audience that he and his childhood friends thought Motif's reactions were not only cool, but hilarious. They would urge each other to "say something" to Motif so that he could provide another delayed response that young Pryor and his young friends found so amusing. Pryor acts out how one of the neighbor kids would yell out "Hey Motif!" Once again, Pryor changes his posture and expression. His eyelids get heavy. He slowly bobs his head up and down. At a glacial pace, Motif turns his head towards the boys and finally says, "hey." Once again, Pryor tells the audience he thought Motif's delayed reaction and short answers were cool. Then, Pryor hits the audience with the truth. "I didn't know [Motif] had shot his brains out." At this point, Pryor has kept the atmosphere light enough that the audience laughs at the revelation that Motif is a drug addict.

Now, Pryor moves the bit into decisively darker territory. He tells the audience more about Motif. Pryor begins "But [Motif] liked to talk to me sometimes, you know?" At this point, Pryor goes into a full-fledged embodiment of Motif, similar to the way he embodies Mudbone. The result is a monologue that, at times, feels like it may be better suited for a Broadway production. For almost 12 min, Pryor (as Motif) talks to a young Pryor. Motif asks him to take a bag of watches "down the street." Motif says he "can't carry 'em 'cause the police are looking for me." Young Pryor expresses hesitation because he suspects they are stolen. Motif responds by saying:

> No, [the police are] not looking for me. You know who they looking for, man? They're looking for my brother Bobby. No, "cause the bitch up the street talking about, I broke in her

house. She said I broke in there and stole some of her shit. But I didn't do it" cause I told her, you know. I said, "Look, I want your shit, I just come in here and take it." You know, I ain't got to break in. I'm bold. You know, I walk in the door.

As Motif continues, it becomes clear that his explanations do not make any sense. (Notice he says that the police are both looking and not looking for him.) The monologue goes back and forth between trying to convince young Pryor that he didn't break into anyone's house and recounting an incident in which his brother Bobby robbed a liquor store with a pistol. Motif then starts to talk about how he doesn't want to go back to prison.

Eventually, Motif's ramblings are halted when he is approached by a friend named Les that he hasn't seen in a long time. Motif catches up with Les. They have a short exchange about the liquor store robbery. At this juncture in the bit, the audience is still laughing at Motif's antics and speech pattern. After all, Pryor portrays him vividly and, at this point, the entire scene could still be interpreted as a rendition of the funny things people say and do when they are high on drugs. However, Motif's monologue takes another dark turn. It is revealed that Les has heroin. Motif immediately pulls out a tourniquet and wraps it around his upper arm. He looks for a vein by aggressively tapping on his elbow crease. He finds it and proclaims, "there it is." Then, Motif's friend injects the drugs into Motif's newly found vein. As the drugs take effect, Motif wobbles. His eye droop and wander. He mumbles profanities. Motif, as he goes deeper and deeper into the drug, lets his body be pulled over. He eventually hunches over completely and is unable to do anything other than silently look at the ground. After a few moments pass, Motif lifts himself up again, stands straight up, and lets his head fall back.

Now, it becomes completely apparent that Motif is a junkie. For the next couple minutes, Motif twitches, shakes, speaks incoherently, and makes a series of sounds remnant of echolalia. As the monologue concludes, Motif (still heavily under the influence) relays his experience of trying to get a job.

> Check the logic. Check the logic. I went downtown, right? Now, this is me, right? I'm gonna try to get the job. A motherfucker tell me I can't have the job, but I can take an application. Are you ready for that? I say "Well, what's the logic? What is the logical conclusion of the logic of it?" I just wanted to know. I figured it was something wrong with the logic. Yeah, motherfucker tell me I ain't dependable. Shit. Say, baby, I got a $200 a day habit. I ain't missed a payment. Shit. Is that dependable?

Motif finally explains that he would like to have "The job as the town junkie." He proposes that he could stand on the street corner and get high for the tourists. This line gets a big laugh from the audience. Motif continues with some final comments about his own mortality. "I'm not going to heaven or hell. I'm just going." After these words, Motif takes out his tourniquet again and ties off another vein. Before shooting up, Motif appears to directly implicate the audience when he says, "You weren't sensitive, you motherfuckers. You weren't sensitive. You just– Well, you just didn't like a motherfucker sensitive, man. You run over people. You put 'em – you put 'em in a position that they can't do nothing in it. Then when they can't, you all say, 'See?' That, that wasn't right." Motif then shoots up, drops to the floor, and rolls over onto his back. The stage lights go out and the entire audience is left in darkness, a moment that signals Motif's death by heroin overdose.

Pryor does not close *Here and Now* with Motif's death, however. When the lights come back on, Pryor goes directly into a lighthearted, crowd pleasing bit. His show ultimately ends on a more traditional, high note. However, Pryor had already used the comedy stage to relay his specialized knowledge. In other words, Motif is not a fictitious character. He is, as Pryor suggests with his own words, someone he knew when he was young. After all, the Peoria of Pryor's youth was a city of vice. According to Scott Saul's 2014 book *Becoming Richard Pryor*:

> Peoria of the 1930's was "wide open as the gateway to hell," wrote the *Peoria Journal* twenty years later – "a city where every sordid passion had its willing handmaidens." This was not just vivid hyperbole. (p. 22)

And Pryor was born in the heart of the red-light district on North Washington Street, where his family's brothel was located.

Once again, Pryor is using the comedy stage to illustrate the plights of the drug addicts and wayward souls he saw as a child. He is acting out his "specialized knowledge" for audiences that likely never saw a black man overdose on heroin or listen to his thoughts about racial injustice as his life fades away. In this instance, Pryor has done something remarkable. He has managed to transport a white audience to the streets of 1940s Peoria to watch the drug-induced death of a black man.

Conclusions

When Antonio Gramsci wrote about organic intellectuals in the *Prison Notebooks*, it is safe to say that he was not thinking about stand-up comedians. His writings were largely inspired by the political situation in Italy during his imprisonment. Nonetheless, Gramsci's ideas are adaptable. It is clear that he felt the working classes (those outside the dominant class) could produce their own leaders – intellectuals who communicate the lived experience of their particular class. Because Pryor took such great care to share the African American experience with the white world through his comedy, he is an example of what Gramsci's organic intellectual can be. Pryor was, in effect, a teacher and a philosopher.

After years in prison left him weak and suffering from a variety of painful ailments, Gramsci died at age 46. He spent the last years of his life being moved in and out of hospitals. He sadly would not live to see the publication of his prison notebooks or their effect on the world. In many ways, he reexamined Marx in a way that allowed subsequent philosophers to ask a poignant question, "who manufactures idea and consent?" For Marx, the question was secondary to the superstructure. There was the proletariat, the bourgeoisie, and the petit bourgeoisie. Furthermore, for Marx, the changes to the capitalist system would come by way of technological advances that are applied to the means of production. In other words, the capitalist system could not produce any kind of organically created equilibrium between the working class and the ruling class. Instead, the arc of history and technology served as the great equalizer. Gramsci took this argument to a new place by suggesting that there are instances in which the lesser class can have an influence on the ruling class by means of simply communicating a story or a lived experience. Pryor was a living example of a member of a disadvantaged class influencing the dominant white class through his recounting of his lived experiences, in a format that they were receptive to.

In the end, Pryor's comedy does not feel like a lesson. When he discusses issues relating to the black community, the routines do not morph into lectures or rants. The opposite is true. Pryor keeps the audience laughing even when the subject matter turns dark and unsettling for white audiences to hear. In effect, Pryor's humor functions as a Trojan Horse. The jokes invite audiences (especially white audiences) to let down their guards, listen, and learn. The process is as perplexing as it is fascinating. And although Gramsci did not specifically address comedy in his philosophical writings, his work did focus on how an individual can use his or her lived experience to disrupt or defy hegemony. Richard Pryor, in many ways, is philosophy in action, an illustration of political progress.

References

Crehan, Kate. 2002. *Gramsci, culture, and anthropology*. University of California Press.
Gramsci, Antonio. 1971. *Selections from the prison notebooks*. Translated and edited by Quintin Hoare and Geoffrey Nowell Smith. International Publishers New York.
Kantor, Michael, and Laurence Maslon. 2008. *Make 'Em laugh: The funny business of America*. Hachette Book Group, New York, NY.
People Staff. 1980. Richard Pryor's tragic accident spotlights a dangerous drug craze: Freebasing. *People Magazine*, 30 June 1980. https://people.com/archive/richard-pryors-tragic-accident-spotlights-a-dangerous-drug-craze-freebasing-vol-13-no-26/
Pryor, Richard. 1977. *The Richard Pryor show*. Transcript of the relevant routine can be found at https://joescanlan.biz/dicks-last-stand/)
———. 1979. *Richard Pryor: Live in concert*. Directed by Jeff Margolis. Filmed at the Terrace Theater, Long Beach, CA, 28 December 1978. Warner Brothers Records. Released on DVD, 1998.
———. 1982. *Richard Pryor: Live on the Sunset Strip*. Directed by Joe Layton. Filmed at the Hollywood Palladium, 22–23 October, 1981. Columbia Pictures. Released on DVD, 2000.
———. 1983. *Richard Pryor: Here and now*. Delphi Films, Columbia Pictures, 1983.
———. 2005. *Pryor convictions and other life sentences*. Revolver Books.
Saul, Scott. 2014. *Becoming Richard Pryor*. Harper Collins.
Schecter, Darrow. 1994. *Radical theories: Paths beyond Marxism and social democracy*. Manchester University Press, Manchester and New York.
Takaki, Ronald. 2008. *A different mirror: A history of multicultural America*, Revised edition. Back Bay Books, New York, NY.

Larry David as Philosopher: Interrogating Convention

69

Noël Carroll

Contents

Introduction	1620
On Critique	1621
Incongruity	1622
Larry David's Philosophical Thesis	1625
Qualifications	1627
Addressing the Skeptic	1628
Concluding Summary	1630
References	1630

Abstract

In this chapter, we treat Larry David's television series, *Curb Your Enthusiasm* as, in large measure, a philosophical exercise. We argue that it presents a critique of our norms, practices, and conventions of social behavior, notably those that pertain primarily to civility rather than to morality. This critique identifies certain essential features of such behavior including: the typical unspoken-ness of its governing norms, and their non-necessity, despite appearances to the contrary, due to our intense emotional investment in them. In *Curb Your Enthusiasm*, the ostensible justification that "This is just how we do things" comes in for merciless, satirical interrogation, most often by Larry David but sometimes by others, at Larry David's expense. This chapter relies heavily on Mary Douglas's discussion of jokes, but parts company with it in crucial respects. The chapter will also situate Larry David's brand of humor in the context of the philosophy of comic amusement in terms of the notion of incongruity. Special emphasis will be played on the importance Larry David assigns to emotions in the maintenance of the relevant social norms.

N. Carroll (✉)
Philosophy Program, The Graduate Center, City University of New York, New York, NY, USA

Keywords

Incongruity · Henri Bergson · Mary Douglas · Ludwig Wittgenstein · Jokes · Etiquette · Critique · Simon Critchley · Socrates · Maieutic method · Plato · *Meno* · Anti-rites · Emotions

Introduction

> A serious and good philosophical work could be written entirely consisting of jokes.
> —Ludwig Wittgenstein (Malcolm 1958)

The scene opens as a car pulls into a lot and parks. Larry David and his manager, Jeff Greene, are walking across the lot, chatting, as the driver of the car steps out of the vehicle. Larry stops, staring at the driver, and says: "Hey, that's a handicapped spot." The driver, looking at Larry, truculently demands "What?"

Larry	"What's with the walking?"
Driver	"F…k you. I have a stutter."
Larry	"Yeah but you can walk."
Driver (stuttering somewhat)	"Lo'ok at my lic'ense plate. I have permission."

This encounter occurs in an episode entitled "The Bowtie" (Season 5, Episode 2) of the long-running HBO comedy series *Curb Your Enthusiasm*. As we will see, it is an exemplary sample of the way in which Larry David, the star of the program, articulates his philosophical take on the structures of everyday life.

Curb Your Enthusiasm first broadcast on October 15, 2000; it is now in its eleventh season. The show is a fictionalized version of the life of Larry David, famous from the beginning of the show onward as a co-creator of the sit-com *Seinfeld*, and, as such, he is a fabulously wealthy man. And it's exactly because it's a fictionalized version of David's life – and also that he's the primary creative force behind the series – that *Curb Your Enthusiasm* is the ideal way to examine David's philosophy in this chapter.

As the title of the program proclaims, the fictionalized Larry David has a recurring problem: he has no impulse control. Nothing, it seems, can come into his purview without being subjected to obsessive query and comment. For example, he can't resist remarking upon the behavior of the aforementioned driver. Tim Gibbons, the executive producer of the sixth season of *Curb Your Enthusiasm,* maintained that David "just doesn't know when to stop, and he always pushes it farther than any of us in real life would do it" (Clewis 2012, p. 206).

In short, he just cannot *curb his enthusiasm*.

It seems that nothing is below the fictional Larry David's testy attention. And this personality trait – or defect, if you will – supplies the actual Larry David, the creator of the show, with the perfect optic with which to interrogate the vicissitudes of day-to-day social intercourse and its assumptions.

Prior to the success of *Seinfeld*, the actual Larry David earned a modest living doing stand-up comedy (not always successfully), some acting, and writing for television. For instance, he wrote comedy routines for *Saturday Night Live* (although he quit after a year because none of his skits ever made it to the screen). At around the same time, Jerry Seinfeld, an acquaintance of David's and an admirer, was having a much more fortunate career as a comic and, as a result, Seinfeld was approached by NBC with an invitation to develop a sit-com. Since Seinfeld felt that he and Larry David shared an approach to comedy – notably a wry appreciation of quotidian absurdities – Seinfeld suggested that they collaborate. The result was the TV triumph *Seinfeld*, where for seven seasons (and for the show's finale in its ninth season), David was both the show runner and its principal writer.

Larry David emerged from the experience a very rich man, a fact sometimes seen as the occasion for some reflexive humor on *Curb Your Enthusiasm*. In an episode in which he accuses a TV executive of stealing some of the shrimp from his Chinese take-out order, the executive shouts back, "You know what, Larry? Take your $475 million dollars and buy yourself some f…king shrimp" (Levine 2010, p. 2).

But David did not only profit financially from *Seinfeld*. It also enabled him to hone to perfection his comico-philosophical critique of the microanatomy of the practices we live by in *Curb Your Enthusiasm*.

On Critique

I have just claimed that *Curb Your Enthusiasm* offers us a *critique*. Although the word "critique" has invaded ordinary language – where it operates as a fancy synonym for "criticism" – it has a more technical, philosophical meaning. In philosophical jargon, a *critique* is first and foremost an examination of the conditions of possibility of some practice. Immanuel Kant's monumental *Critique of Pure Reason* is an illumination of what makes a certain kind of reason possible – namely, reasoning of this sort: "All men are mortal. Barack Obama is a man. Therefore, Barack Obama is mortal." Likewise, when Karl Marx wrote his *Critique of Political Economy*, he was asking "What makes capitalism possible?" His answer was *surplus value*, which enabled the capitalist to make a profit on his investments.

By maintaining that *Curb Your Enthusiasm* presents viewers with a *critique*, I am asserting that at least part of the aim of the show is to say something about the nature of certain aspects of our everyday behaviors. Of course, Larry David's philosophical critique proceeds comically, not by jokes as Wittgenstein would have had it, but by means of humorous, largely improvised sketches. So, one way in which to plumb the nature of Larry David's critique is to probe his comic *modus operandi*.

Incongruity

What is funny about the scene with which I began this article – the one involving the parking lot and the man with the stutter? Surely, it is the idea that stuttering is a disability that calls for the provision of handicapped parking spaces. After all, as Larry points out, the stutterer can walk. Given that, the very notion of handicapped spaces for mere stutters is absurd. And that the stutterer has an official permit for use of a handicapped space just compounds the ludicrousness. (I do not know whether there is anywhere in the world where there are actually handicapped parking permits being issued for stutters, but no matter; it is just the sort of nonsensical misapplication of the law that one can imagine some benighted bureaucrat enforcing.)

The philosophical term for this kind of humor is *incongruity*. Incongruity humor is based upon the perception that the representation involves a breach in the way things are or should be. Of course, this is only a necessary condition for incongruity humor – that is, something is an example of incongruity humor *only if* it involves a perception of a breach in how things are or should be since not every appearance of incongruity or absurdity will engender comic amusement. But, for present purposes, that is all we need in order to approach Larry David's line of attack (Carroll 2014).

We have already noted that perhaps the most obvious personal trait of the fictional Larry David is his lack of impulse control. For example, in the episode "Meet the Blacks" (Season 6, Episode 1), Larry and his wife Cheryl go to the airport to pick up a family, the Blacks, whom the David family has offered to house, since the Black family's home was destroyed by Hurricane Edna. The Blacks are African Americans. This leads Larry to observe the coincidence that their surname is "Black" and that they are black, which, Larry goes on to say, would be like his name being "Larry Jew" because he is Jewish. This observation is greeted with a look of suppressed disgruntlement by Loretta Black, head of the Black family. But as if this breach of etiquette was not enough, Larry proceeds to repeat it, thereby managing to be even more annoying.

As these two brief examples show, the incongruities that the actual Larry David gravitates towards are breaches in the way society has arranged things or the way things should, by presumed social consensus, be arranged. In contrast to slapstick comedy, which focuses on how things are or should be physically (preferably upright, rather than slipping on banana peels), the primary subjects of Larry David's comedy are social norms and conventions. Social norms are a natural topic for comedy since they stipulate how most of us behave most of the time because that is assumed to be how we *should* behave. But comedy may take at least two different and contrasting stances toward social norms and conventions. Comedy may function to support such standards, or, alternatively, it may endorse their subversion.

The philosopher Henri Bergson (1911) argued that the function of comedy was to enforce what should be. The absent-minded professor, for example, is the perfect butt of comic laughter since one should be alert to one's surroundings. Slipping on the banana peel likewise is the result of inattention; the comic butts are not, as the saying goes, "looking where they are going." In both these cases, the pertinent people are functioning on automatic pilot. For Bergson, this is the antithesis of what it is to be human: it is robotic in its inelasticity – machinelike. And ridicule in the form of comic laughter is the penalty the comic butt must suffer for being inattentive. In this way, comedy functions to discipline us, to keep us in line, as it is said.

However, even though this is one function of comedy, it is not the only one – for comedy can also derive from subverting norms and conventions. And that is the form that is explored by a very large number of the incongruities in *Curb Your Enthusiasm*. Larry David interrogates implicit or taken-for-granted social norms and conventions in several different ways in *Curb Your Enthusiasm*. Here are a few overlapping and non-exhaustive examples.

Sometimes, Larry David ignores the norm or convention outright, often to the demonstrative consternation of others. For example, at synagogue, he cleans his glasses with his yarmulke ("The Larry David Sandwich," Season 5, Episode 1). Or he eats while delivering an apology over the telephone, causing his outraged interlocutor to feel further insulted ("Kamikaze Bingo," Season 5, Episode 4). Or he argues with children (children!), demanding his money back for what he claims is their overpriced, foul-tasting lemonade ("Officer Krupke," Season 7, Episode 8). Once, upon greeting Ben Stiller, he rebuffs Stiller's offer of a handshake because Stiller has just covered his nose with his hand when he sneezed ("Mel's Offer," Season 4, Episode 1). Larry, an inveterate germophobe, feels justified, but Stiller is nevertheless visibly offended.

Indeed, with many of these *faux pas,* Larry David does not regard his behavior as amiss and says so (with typical insistence), thus at least raising questions about the authority of certain norms. In "The Hot Towel" (Season 7, Episode 4) Larry's doctor upbraids him for using the telephone in the examining room; but Larry pushes back, insinuating that his doctor is a "prick." Larry David is the natural-born enemy of given social protocols whose best defense is "That's just the way it's done." Likewise, Larry turns down the ritual new-house tour when Susie Greene, as a matter of customary exchange, offers such a walk-around, thereby catapulting Susie into a torrential rage ("Krazee-EyezKilla," Season S, Episode 8). In both of these examples, Larry David pushes back against what he regards as mere social protocols bereft of any defensible rationale with his own version of practical commonsense. Like the perennial child who persists in asking "Why?" Larry David will not take "Because I (or society) say so" for an answer.

In some cases, Larry David has very good reasons to break the rules. For instance, in "The 5 Wood" (Season 4, Episode 5), Larry attends the open-casket wake of Marty Funkhouser's Uncle Leo. Uncle Leo is being buried with his favorite golf club – a five wood. But this particular five wood is a club that Uncle Leo borrowed from Larry and never returned. The club is irreplaceable; the model is no longer being made. Larry protests: "Why should this guy be buried for all eternity with my club. That's not fair." So, Larry takes matters into his own hands. He retakes possession of the five wood and replaces it in the casket with another different type of club. Of course, Larry is right. It isn't fair Petranovich (2012). But equally, it is common knowledge that you don't appropriate something from a casket, especially in defiance of the last wishes of the deceased. So, Larry, his manager, and their wives are banished from the country club of which they had been members.

Much of the humor in *Curb Your Enthusiasm* gravitates around Larry David's refusal to be bound by "what everyone knows." For example, he doesn't give Ben Stiller a birthday present because the invitation to the party explicitly instructed that the guests bring no gifts ("Ben's Birthday Party," Season 4, Episode 2). But Stiller is nevertheless offended on the grounds that everyone knows that that instruction is not to be taken seriously. Once again, David's reasonable protests are defeated – at least by the court of social opinion – by the implicit rules of the game. In fact, the presumed etiquette of gifting and re-gifting is recurring satiric quarry in *Curb Your Enthusiasm*.

As has already been mentioned, Larry David consistently gives voice to thoughts that might occur to us but which we would never express out loud. I have alluded to his meeting with the Black family. But when he learns that the living father of one of his acquaintances had been a kamikaze pilot, Larry can't resist querying how one can be a kamikaze pilot and still be alive – an embarrassing question that most of us would keep to ourselves ("Kamikaze Bingo," Season 5, Episode 4). But Larry persists. Likewise, when visiting a woman in mourning, Larry notices and admires the shirt her dead husband is wearing in a photo and, thus, wants to know where her husband got it ("Chet's Shirt," Season 3, Episode 1). No matter how taken you were by a shirt in such circumstances, anyone of minimal acculturation would know to keep that to themselves.

Larry David is willing to make arguments by taking literally sayings that we know are just a way of speaking, as we saw regarding Ben Stiller's birthday present. Thus, when discussing reaffirming his marriage vows with Cheryl, David bridles at pledging faithfulness for eternity, having, he thought, only signed on "for death do us part" ("The Survivor," Season 4, Episode 9). (Apparently, he was planning on seeing other people in the afterlife, even though he's a nonbeliever.)

Debates about social etiquette occur with regularity on *Curb Your Enthusiasm*. On some occasions, Larry David, constitutionally prone to selfish and egoistic behavior, is not above trying to fabricate rules to serve his own purposes. One evening, he wants to telephone Jeff, but Cheryl says he can't because it's 10:20 PM and everyone knows that 10:00 PM is the cut-off hour for late-night phone calls ("The Wire," Season 1, Episode 6). No, Larry asserts; the cut-off is 10:30, as "everyone" supposedly now knows. When he calls, he predictably gets into trouble with Jeff's wife Susie, who flails him verbally. The issue of phone etiquette comes up more than once for comic effect in *Curb Your Enthusiasm*, and this repetition at least raises the question of why the rule is 10 PM. Isn't that somewhat arbitrary?

Arguments about the appropriate time to call or to visit or to start eating recur frequently in *Curb Your Enthusiasm*. See, for example, "The Car Salesman" (Season 2, Episode 1), which implicitly alludes to the episode "The Wire," reprising the phone debate launched there, while "The Thong" (Season 2, Episode 5) stages one of many protracted and querulous restaurant discussions over etiquette. These sketches all reinforce the theme of the arbitrariness of so many of our social practices.

Larry David is not always the subverter of social conventions. Sometimes he is as staunch a defender of the rules of the game as anyone else. When some teenagers show up on Halloween trick-or-treating, Larry refuses to give them anything on the grounds that they are not costumed ("Trick or Treat," Season 2, Episode 3). Even though the social contract merely stipulates an exchange of a treat for a trick, Larry invokes the unwritten understanding that a costume is also a requirement, and he does it with the same high dudgeon that others level at Larry David's own rule breaking.

Larry David's Philosophical Thesis

As the preceding examples indicate, everyday cultural norms or conventions of behavior for carrying on social intercourse are one of the presiding themes, if not *the* presiding theme, of Larry David's comedy in *Curb Your Enthusiasm*. But they are not only a recurring subject of the series. Larry David presents a certain perspective on that subject matter – a thesis, if you will. Through various strategies, such as the ones compiled above, norms of social behavior are routinely disrupted either by Larry David himself or by others.

The fictional Larry David violates unwritten behavioral expectations, such as taking the tour of the new house or singing "Happy Birthday" at Ben Stiller's party, while also arguing in defense of his actions, as he does with the doctor whose phone he's expropriated. Or he attempts to "rewrite" the rules for his own purposes, sometimes compulsively offering alternatives that are no less arbitrary than the existing ones. Or he takes obsessive umbrage when others break the rules. In short, as David is the creator of the *Curb Your Enthusiasm* and its many cringe-inducing scenarios like these, we can surmise that worrying the often-unspoken norms of civility is an abiding concern of the actual Larry David (Svolba and Flanders 2012).

Following the anthropologist Mary Douglas (2003), we may note that Larry David's comic sketches afford the "opportunity for realizing that an accepted pattern has no necessity. Its excitement lies in the suggestion that any particular ordering of experience may be arbitrary and subjective" (150-1). The realization of the contingency of the conventions of social life grants the viewer a momentary release from their grip as well as an occasion to laugh at the seriousness with which we invest them, as the characters hurl themselves into emotional apoplexies when they are breached. Susie Greene and the fictional Larry David are especially expert in this regard. Indeed, Susie Greene's expression of her ire is virtually operatic.

Earlier I hypothesized that *Curb Your Enthusiasm* could be interpreted as developing a critique of social manners – indeed social manners as such. I say, "as such," because the insistent recurrence of these disruptions of the implicit rules of the social game is so frequent, that one surmises that the actual Larry David's target is not this or that social folkway, but the micro-social contract of everyday life in general, a social contract he problematizes at every turn.

Moreover, if a critique is a matter of examining the conditions of possibility of a practice, then the substance of David's critique is that most of these norms of social behavior – especially those we refer to as manners (as distinct from mores, a.k.a. ethical imperatives) – are (1) not necessary (they could have very easily been otherwise) and (2) sustained by little more than the feeling of fundamentally unsupported emotional outrage that itself is comically amusing when the viewer recognizes it is ultimately groundless. Of course, insofar as he often offers alternative ways of ordering affairs, the fictional Larry David admits that *some* rules of the game must obtain; however, ironically, for the most part, none of them are necessary, even though for them to work, most of us need to be emotionally committed to them – that is, we must be utterly convinced in our hearts of their authority. What makes the operation of these social norms of decorum possible, in other words, us our blind, uncritical emotional commitment to them (a.k.a. our *enthusiasm*).

Another feature of the structures of everyday, polite behavior that the actual Larry David is so adept at disclosing is that for the most part, they go unspoken – at least unspoken until defied. Who has ever explicitly ordained the commandment that bourgeois civility requires one to accept an invitation to tour a new house, even if one has been through the same boring polite ritual a hundred times before? Nevertheless, Susie's "uncurbed" emotional outburst when the fictional Larry David demurs unmistakably alerts us that a tacit norm of suburban etiquette has been flouted. Indeed, the very fact that these norms are standardly unwritten or unspoken means that they typically escape the sort of scrutiny that would make their "non-necessity" transparent.

For the most part, this unspoken knowledge is knowledge of how to navigate the social world we live in. It is operational know-how. It is inculcated wordlessly as we observe and fall into step with our "fellow citizens," starting with our parents and our peers. In this way, we assimilate "what everyone knows" and proceed likewise. *Curb Your Enthusiasm* is very good at drawing attention to these assumed ordinances and their patent contingency via the various imaginative ways in which the comedy upsets them. The actual Larry David by means of his sketches regularly reveals the degree to which generally unspoken norms of civility – norms that are at root arbitrary, but which appear, emotionally to us, to be necessary – govern everyday social behavior. In this, he offers viewers philosophical insight into certain essential features of social know-how which is what we also call *savoir faire*.

Perhaps as signaled by the title of the series, especially as underlined by the invocation of the concept of "enthusiasm," the most important insight that the real Larry David, the creator of the series, offers the viewer is his emphasis upon emotion as the real glue that holds our norms of civility, including etiquette, in place. Although reason recommends that some convention should be in place in order to regulate this or that collective behavior, typically the choice of the convention is arbitrary. Larry David's comedy not only underscores this, but stresses that what is actually holding the convention in place is primarily our unthinking feeling that this must be the right way to do things. Perhaps the very intensity with which characters react to breaches of norms and conventions in *Curb Your Enthusiasm* is testimony to Larry David's conviction that our attachment to the presumption that this just is the way we do it is ultimately supported by little more than a gut reaction. That is, we ramp of the ferocity of our response as we become – maybe unconsciously – alert to the fact that we are operating on little more than spleen. Surely something like this best explains Susie Greene's glorious arias of outrage.

Of course, it is not only the victims of Larry David's breaches of decorum who should recognize that the source of their responses to Larry is finally emotional and that, in consequence, they should curb or modify their enthusiasm. Larry David's own defiance of the various norms of civility themselves belie an excess of feeling on his part that is beyond whatever might be at stake in his recurring confrontations. Thus, Larry David, the character, ought to consider curbing his own enthusiasm, although obviously Larry David the creator knows this antic, "over the top," inappropriate (and in that sense irrational) behavior is as ridiculous as the enraged bafflement of the character's rule-following comic butts. That is, Larry David the character invests as much passion in attempting to establishing his "rules," as they do in defending theirs (and this is intended by Larry David the comedian/creator).

Yes, reason dictates that there be a coordinated, communal rule. But reason rarely establishes that *this* rule is the only way to go. That is a job for the emotions. And given this insight into the indispensable role that feeling plays in facilitating social commerce, it may be that Larry David the creator of the show is recommending that in matters of social civility, we should consider curbing our enthusiasm, relax, and just "lighten up."

Qualifications

In attempting to explicate *Curb Your Enthusiasm*, I have invoked Mary Douglas' account of jokes. However, I should add that, although I find Douglas' remarks highly suggestive, I do not endorse her view in its entirety. One reason for my reluctance is that her view seems overly general. She appears to think that it accounts for all jokes, and, by extension, to all humor. Specifically, she asserts that all jokes are potentially subversive (Douglas 2003, p. 152). This is very questionable. When I was growing up in the 1950s, sexist jokes about housewives' preoccupations, shopping habits, and driving were quite common – the stuff of many a stand-up comedy routine. This scarcely affronted the social norm. It was hardly subversive; it was a way of keeping women in their place. Moreover, this is a common error in comic theorizing: the tendency to forget the dark side of humor – its Hobbesian capacity to be nasty and brutish in the service of the powers that be.

Furthermore, although I came to my Douglasian analysis of *Curb Your Enthusiasm* on my own, as I later discovered, I am not the only philosopher to have done so. Mark Ralkowski (2012) emphasizes the importance of Larry David's violation of the social contract and accepts Mary Douglas' notion of jokes as anti-rites that reveal the lack of necessity of the accepted ways of living and behaving – the rituals, so to speak, of everyday life. However, he then goes on to claim that this is the basis of the viewer's identification with the fictional Larry David. I am suspicious of this. It seems to me that for the most part we are laughing *at* the fictional Larry David, not with him. Phenomenologically, identification would require us to be laughing *with* the character at the idiocy he sees the "normals" to be embracing. And I do not think most viewers do this while watching *Curb Your Enthusiasm*. More often it is the character Larry David's resistance to the norm that entertains us – *his* lack of impulse control.

Though Simon Critchley (2002) does not mention *Curb Your Enthusiasm*, he does seem to accept Douglas's theory of jokes as focusing on "shared life-world practices, the background meaning implicit in a culture..." He goes on to claim that "humour also indicates, or maybe just adumbrates, how those practices might be transformed or perfected, how things might be otherwise..." (p. 90). Here I think that Critchley goes beyond Douglas. I do not believe that she holds that jokes literally suggest *how* practices might be "transformed and perfected."

Critchley says that jokes might adumbrate "how things might be otherwise." That locution – "how things might be otherwise" – is a progressive cypher for changing the social order. But I think that it is a logical non sequitur to jump from Douglas' idea that jokes unmask the non-necessity of codes of civility to envisioning some version of utopia. Here again we find the philosophical tendency to presuppose that humor is inherently on the side of history, whereas it is just as frequently of lever of reactionary control.

One need not only think of sexist humor to support this observation. Racist, ethnic, homophobic, antisemitic, and scores of anti-Otherness jokes and cartoons have been a recurring adjunct of social domination for an untold number of years. Patently, humor can serve demons as well as angels.

Addressing the Skeptic

This chapter has proceeded on the assumption that situation comedy could be a vehicle for philosophizing. However, is that credible? We offered the epigraph from Wittgenstein. But so what? Wittgenstein merely affirmed the possibility that jokes could constitute philosophy. On what grounds should we accept his bold assertion?

Clearly challenging Wittgenstein's contention involves presupposing some view of what philosophy is to which things like *Curb Your Enthusiasm* fail to accord. What might the skeptics of the possibility of comedy-made-philosophy have in mind? If the skeptics are what are called analytic philosophers, it is likely that they will say that *Curb Your Enthusiasm*, like most comparable comedies, lacks explicit argumentation. They will demand to learn: how does one get from the sketches that the actual Larry David presents to the conclusion that everyday norms and practices lack necessity, despite our typically strong emotional conviction that said norms of behavior are not arbitrary, but instead are what everybody should do? Look and listen as closely as you will, you won't find a demonstration – or even an attempted demonstration – of that verdict on the television screen.

Although, given his view of philosophy, Wittgenstein would probably not be fazed by this objection, it is a concern that those of us drawn to the notion of humor-made philosophy need to address by meeting the skeptics on their own terms. That is, we should try to convince them that the arguments they press us for are available. To that end, let us begin by asking: is the skeptic asking us to look for the argument in the right place? Admittedly, the requested reasoning is not to be found in the television monitor. Instead, it is to be found in the mind of the reflective viewer – in what Peter Kivy (1997) calls "the laboratory of fictional truth." The actual Larry David presents us with the kinds of disruptions of the codes of civility enumerated above. As a result, especially given the kinds of repetitions emphasized, the attentive viewer is nudged to ask, "What is going on here?" Why does the actual Larry David insistently return to just these kinds of cases? What exactly does he intend to show us?

That is, the very structure of *Curb Your Enthusiasm* invites an interpretation which points to the non-necessity of these typically unspoken norms of behavior. The "argument" is an inference to the best explanation that occurs in the mind of the reflective viewer either alone or in concert with other reflective viewers, while watching the program or in what Kivy (1997) calls its "afterlife." Audience members mull over and think about the thematic point or significance of the program not only while watching it, but afterwards – either by themselves or in discussion with similarly interested viewers.

In this regard, it is helpful to think of Plato's *Meno*. In that dialogue, Socrates through a series of questions prompts a slave boy to deliver a geometrical proof. This is frequently Socrates' *modus operandi*. It is why he calls himself a midwife; he draws the argument from his interlocutor by means of raising question. In honor of this sort of intellectual midwifery, the method is called "maieutic" (from the Greek word "maieutikos," meaning "of midwifery").

We may think of what the actual Larry David is doing in *Curb Your Enthusiasm* as maieutic. The repeating motifs of disrupted social conventions pose a hermeneutical puzzle. What is he trying to say? What is his intention? And in answering that, the audience comes to a putative insight about the nature of a large body of social practices which they, the audience, can confirm on the basis of their observation of their own social behavior and the behaviors of others.

The idea that the audience is doing the work of articulating, filling-out, and substantiating in their own experience the argument of *Curb Your Enthusiasm* should not strike the reader as strange. Readers of nonfiction arguments, in such things as op-ed articles, often have to complete the claims the author advances by supplementing the what the author presents with evidence from readers own store of knowledge in combination with their own reasoning. Even when presented with an argument in a philosophy paper, the readers must run it through their own mind to assess it for its validity and soundness. In short, audiences must always engage the presentation with their own cognitive and affective resources. How large the audience's share comprises is merely a matter of degree.

Where the work is maieutic, the audience's contribution is substantial. But that does not mean that there is no argument or evidence with respect to a work structured in this way. As with arguments such as rhetorical questions, the argument is worked out in the mind of the reader, viewer, and/or listener. Consequently, even if there is no explicit, step-by-step demonstration of its thesis in *Curb Your Enthusiasm,* that does not entail that its claims are without argument and/or evidence. Rather the comedy is structured in such a way as to prompt its philosophy from its reflective viewers, by guiding them into coming to its conclusions on their own, by using their own powers of reasoning and knowledge of the world.

Concluding Summary

In this chapter, we have approached Larry David's comedy – by way of his series, *Curb Your Enthusiasm* – as a philosophical exercise composed not of jokes, as Wittgenstein suggested, but of comic sketches – mostly improvised routines typically aimed at disrupting social codes of civilized behavior in contemporary American culture. Larry David targets these specific folkways in order to initiate a critique of the features that govern such behaviors in general. By means of his distinctive presentation of these comic episodes, Larry David manages to reveal to reflective viewers that these usually unspoken rules of the game are not necessary despite our often intense (enthusiastic) emotional attachment to them – which itself is the source of their hold upon our behavior. This is something that reflective viewers can see, if they curb their enthusiasm and adopt the kind of philosophical distance that Wittgenstein suggests also belongs to comedy.

References

Bergson, Henri. 1911. *Laughter*. New York: Macmillan.
Carroll, Noël. 2014. *Humour: A Very Short Introduction*. Oxford: Oxford University Press.
Clewis, Robert R. 2012. Should We Curb Our Enthusiasm? In *Curb Your Enthusiasm and Philosophy: Awaken the Social Assasin Within*, ed. Mark Ralkowski, 205–220. Chicago and LaSalle: Open Court – a division of Carus Publishing Company.
Critchley, Simon. 2002. *On humour*. London and New York: Routledge.
Douglas, Mary. 2003. Jokes. In *Implicit Meanings: Selected Essays in Anthropology*. London and New York: Routhledge.
Kivy, Peter. 1997. Laboratory of Fictional Truth. In *Philosophies of Art: An Essay in Differences*, 121–139. New York: Cambridge University Press.
Levine, Josh. 2010. *Pretty, Pretty, Pretty Good: Larry David and the Making of Seinfeld and Curb Your Enthusiasm*. Toronto: ECW Press.
Malcolm, Norman. 1958. *Wittgenstein: A Memoir*. Oxford: Oxford University Press.
Petranovich, Sean. 2012. How to Philosophize with a 5 Wood. In *Curb Your Enthusiasm and Philosophy*, 173–186. New York: Open Court.
Ralkowski, Mark. 2012. Deep Inside You Know You're Him. In *Curb Your Enthusiasm and Philosophy*, 3–23. New York: Open Court.
Svolba, David, and Chad Flanders. 2012. People Just Don't Do That. In *Curb Your Enthusiasm and Philosophy*, 59–71. New York: Open Court.

Jerry Seinfeld as Philosopher: The Assimilated Sage of New Chelm

70

Stephen Stern and Steven Gimbel

Contents

Introduction	1632
Why Jewish Epistemology Is Largely Excluded from Western Philosophy	1632
Jewish Epistemology	1634
Summary 1	1636
Jerry Seinfeld as a Secular Talmudist	1636
Summary 2	1638
Chelm	1638
Summary 3	1640
Seinfeld as the New Chelm	1640
Conclusion	1641
References	1641

Abstract

The epistemic foundation of Hellenic-Christian thought is based on a correspondence between thought and a single reality, but the epistemic foundation of Jewish thought stresses the creative act of perspectival interpretation of an absolute text. This stress on wisdom from extracting a multiplicity of contextualized understandings of an absolute can be seen in the writings of the great rabbis, but also in the work of Jerry Seinfeld. Where Talmudic thought takes as its basis, passages of the Torah as its source of truth to interpret, Seinfeld's stand-up is neo-Talmudic in using a different source – phenomenological commonalty (our shared experience) – as its basis. The move from the stage to the small screen changed the comedy of Seinfeld as his eponymous television program now lampoons the sort of neo-Talmudic thought of his stand-up material just as the classic rabbis of Chelm jokes mock Talmudic thought.

S. Stern · S. Gimbel (✉)
Gettysburg College, Gettysburg, PA, USA
e-mail: sstern@gettysburg.edu; sgimbel@gettysburg.edu

© Springer Nature Switzerland AG 2024
D. K. Johnson et al. (eds.), *The Palgrave Handbook of Popular Culture as Philosophy*,
https://doi.org/10.1007/978-3-031-24685-2_50

Keywords

Jerry Seinfeld · Jewish · Neo-Talmudic thought · Chelm

Introduction

Jerry Seinfeld is a comedian. Jerry Seinfeld is Jewish. But is Jerry Seinfeld a philosopher? If you understand that notion of "philosopher" in terms of Jewish philosophy, he is. Take his classic joke about fear, "According to most studies, people's number one fear is public speaking. Number two is death. Death is number two. Does that sound right? This means to the average person, if you go to a funeral, you're better off in the casket than doing the eulogy." The construction of this joke is based upon what we call "neo-Talmudic thought," that is, like the ancient rabbis, Seinfeld starts with an absolute truth and develops a novel interpretation that generates wisdom by seeing the truth from an unusual angle.

Unlike the ancient rabbis, Seinfeld's text is not the Torah, but phenomenological commonality – our shared experience. But as the master of observational comedy, we can see Seinfeld's work as an embodiment of the Jewish style of epistemology, wherein wisdom and understanding emerge from knowledge when knowledge is viewed contextually. In this chapter, we will develop this notion of neo-Talmudic thought through an exploration of traditional Talmudic thought and see that, while Seinfeld's stand-up material is neo-Talmudic, the comedy of his television show is different. It is a parody of neo-Talmudic thought much like the classic Eastern European Jewish jokes about the Talmudic thought of the rabbis from the Polish town of Chelm.

Why Jewish Epistemology Is Largely Excluded from Western Philosophy

There are two ways of making something invisible. The obvious way is to remove it from the line of sight. If it is not there to be seen, then no one sees it. The second is to make it always seen. As Nietzsche says of the slave revolt in morality, it remains unseen because it has triumphed so completely. If something is everywhere, then the lack of differentiation from anything else you look at makes it invisible. The erasure of Jewish philosophy from Western philosophy is a case of the first masquerading as the second. Despite the wealth of both secular and religiously influenced Jewish philosophers, a Jewish approach to philosophy has been effectively removed from virtually all of contemporary philosophy. But this trick was accomplished by claiming its ubiquity. Western philosophy, we are told, is shot through with Judeo-Christian methods and presuppositions.

Christian, yes. Judaic, no. The proper citation should be Hellenic-Christian. The fundamental epistemology inherent in Jewish philosophy was largely stricken from Western thought by merging questions arising from theological issues arising from the Christian tradition with Greek epistemology. Greek thought arises in the context of Athenian democracy. (The philosophy from this democracy found its present footing about a thousand years ago when medieval Christian theologians began reading their own theistic understanding of God into these texts' explanations of eternal truths from which some tried to substantiate knowledge of God.) If government is the result of popular belief, then rhetoric becomes a crucial skill. Rhetorical capacity, however, becomes suspect to the early philosophers because it is possible to be quite effective in convincing others even when you do not possess the truth. Hence, the distinction between knowledge and belief becomes central to Greek epistemology. The Sophists become the villains of the story for championing belief full stop, whereas the offspring of Socrates become the heroes for their indefatigable defense of truth as rationally justified belief. Because there is only one reality, there is only one truth. Those who hold that there is much to be learned from a multiplicity of views of reality are resorting to dangerous sophistry and must be eliminated.

For Christians, who are told that they have the Way and the Truth and the Light, this Greek dichotomy between inferior multifaceted sophistry and legitimate, rational philosophy is deeply appealing. This is in part because it undermines the Jewish approach to (or understanding of) knowledge and wisdom, according to which there is always a multiplicity of viewpoints from which to gain knowledge. By reducing Jewish tradition, or Jewish thought, Talmudic reasoning, to sophistry, Jewish epistemology can – and has – been largely eliminated from philosophy.

The Hellenic-Christian approach to philosophy starts from a fundamental problem – which should be primary: the knower or the known, the subject, or the object? The object of knowledge is truth, reality, God, and therefore surely should be primary. But the point of that which is theological is to spread the good news, to convince the unbeliever. Faith, belief is the central goal. From Rene Descartes through Kant and Hegel, the central problem of Hellenic-Christian philosophy has been to elucidate the relationship between the subjective and objective. This question is irrelevant to the Jewish approach and so when philosophical discourse is based upon it, Jewishness is displaced. From the modern period through contemporary thought, this is the fundamental problem of Western philosophy.

The second way that the Jewish influence was eradicated from Western philosophical methodology comes through the Enlightenment figures that give us the canonical treatments of the subject/object relationship debate. Twentieth-century historians of thought, including Nathan Rosenstreich and David Nirenberg, have shown the way that major Western figures, such as Immanuel Kant and Friedrich Hegel, succeeded in creating a straw Jew that was guaranteed to fail the tests of Enlightenment rationality.

Following on the arguments of Moses Mendelssohn, Kant and Hegel argued that the heart of Jewish thought is a slavish dedication to absolute laws. They correctly set out that at the core of Jewish thought is an acceptance of basic inviolable principles. There are absolute moral principles that must be taken as immutable. But they were wrong about the source of the authority underlying these truths. Kant and Hegel argued that it is faith, but it is actually tradition. They also thought that Jews believed that these commands came from God – which, when they wrote, was generally assumed by Jewish tradition(s). But while Kant also wanted us to believe in absolute moral rules and thought the key to discovering them was reason, he also wrongly assumed that the Jewish approach is grounded in an acceptance of rules without reason. Jewish tradition also uses reason too, but it also suggests that one must not venture too far into metaphysical explanations in coming to understand how one is to conduct oneself because one loses sight of the community from which one is bound in such pursuits. Kant doesn't understand the Jewish epistemic orientation of biblical Hebrew, which assumes an epistemic orientation toward the other that begins with hearing the other – an orientation that is opposed to the Hellenic-Christian approach of figuring out how the subject knows there is something more than oneself.

In other words, neither Kant nor Hegel understood that Jewish epistemology is pluralistic. For example, in biblical Hebrew the word for "other" has the same root as responsibility (my responsibility) for the always differing other, who in the Bible, calls one into identity. Response is thus not known in advance, and thus Jewish knowledge is indeterminate in its reliance on the other who is never beyond context. Here, one hears what Jewish thought is at its core and why Kant found Judaism unreasonable and slavishly bound to this unreasonableness. By insisting on a transcendental deduction of the rules from the principles of pure reason itself, Kant was able to preserve the absolute rules but strip them of their problematic Jewish association.

So, Jewish thought gets squeezed from both sides. On the one hand, it is sophistic in its lack of absolutism in its never-ending demand for pluralism. On the other side, it is irrational in its reasonless insistence on absolutism. Jewish philosophy finds itself in the same sort of position that Socrates did in being accused of both atheism and believing in false gods. And like Socrates, in the end, it was left to die.

Jewish Epistemology

These arguments historically explain why Jewish epistemology has largely been excluded from philosophy. They do not, of course, justify that exclusion. As thinkers like Jacques Derrida point out, there is much to be gained by reintegrating Jewish epistemology into Western philosophy. Indeed, one can see his understanding of what he called *differance* as him integrating Jewish epistemology into Western philosophy. But what exactly is meant by "Jewish epistemology"?

Jews are called "The People of the Book," but a more accurate appellation would be "The People of the Books" because there are two central texts at the heart of traditional Jewish thought. One is the *Torah*, that is, the first 5 books of the 24 books making up the Hebrew Bible, or, as the goyim call it, the *Old Testament*. It is taken to be true, at least those parts that can be true. But central to the Jewish reading of this text are the parts that can be neither true nor false. These are the mitzvot, the commands. The Rabbinic tradition reads 613 mitzvot (blessings) or commandments for Jews to fulfill in the Torah. To be a Jew is traditionally to be bound by these 613 laws.

How can they not be true, you ask? Because truth is a property only attributable to declarative sentences. Commands are imperative sentences and therefore not capable of truth or falsity. For example, if one were to give a true/false quiz to a philosophy class with the only question being, "True or false?: Stand up," the assessment would be met with complete confusion.

Because the center of Torah are laws that cannot be true or false, the epistemological questions that form the heart of the Hellenic-Christian approach to philosophy simply do not arise for traditional Jewish thought. Since the origin is a set of commands that are jointly accepted, the centrality of the two problems of the justification of truth and of the relation of subject and object are not questions relevant to the Jewish style of thought. This is largely because there is no word for "is" in biblical Hebrew. The text cannot grammatically equate one thing with another. "This" can never be equated with "that." But there is Hebrew word for "and." And that word is the hinge of plurality in biblical Hebrew.

The word "and" is a root of Jewish philosophy. From here, one may hear a question that informs Jewish modes of philosophy. It is, "How do we apply these laws to the real world?" Or, "What is required of me here, right now?" In other words, the application always begins with a question: How am I to respond? My response is never outside a relation, never beyond relating to something other. My response will always move me toward or away from the other. Kant is so far away from here that he can no longer see or hear the other in his work.

Jewish thought will not consider and will thus not conclude knowledge of the law to be abstract knowledge; it grammatically cannot play this language-game when it comes to ethics or the laws or comedy. The Jewish question is always about application, or how it applies practically. How am I to apply wisdom in my response so that it is always necessitated by something other than me, e.g., the other. In other words, the Jewish question never absents the other; the other cannot be substituted with abstraction. The world is a complex, messy place. How ought we make sense of the laws in light of the intricacies of the world?

Addressing this question is the focus of the second book crucial to Judaism, the *Talmud*. The *Talmud* records interpretations and debates concerning the law. When laws bump up against one another or when it is unclear how to apply the law in a strange circumstance, there must be expansive interpretation. Accepting the law does not answer all of the questions concerning the law. The *Talmud* sets out and explains such interpretations, including those of contrasting scholars, and gives arguments in support of them.

The supposition is that all of these interpretations contain elements of wisdom. None deny the starting point of the law. It is not a disagreement concerning fact, but rather a matter of finding and applying a principal that gives the law a hinge, so to speak – something to move on. This allows different moves, and, in Jewish thought, understanding these different moves gives rise to insights.

Talmudic reasoning is thus a very different model of philosophical discourse than we find in the Hellenic-Christian model. It proceeds in two steps: Step 1: find a common set of principles that will be taken as given; and Step 2: find ways of interpreting and thus applying the principles in terms of different contexts of lived human experience that allow aspects of the given to give meaning to the given. Even if contrasting results come from Step 2, they both still fully accept the given and hence are not mutually exclusive. Indeed, we may derive a number of very different insights from the same element of the given when viewed in different contexts from different perspectives.

Consider the commandment "thou shalt not steal." It is immutable. It is accepted without condition. But what does it mean to steal? If you look down and see a $100 bill that was never yours and you pick it up and put it in your pocket, did you steal it? You can only steal something that belongs to someone else. Does the $100 bill belong to anyone? The rabbis tell us that it depends on the context: "Is the thing identifiable?" "Where and when you find it?" If you step on it on the ground in a busy mall parking lot on Christmas Eve and you see no one looking for it, then it is not stealing. It is just a found object. On the other hand, if you see it on the floor while visiting your friend's house, then, yes, it is stealing. One principle, never denied, but applied differently based upon the facts on the ground – literally "on the ground" in this case.

Is this Jewish approach to philosophy objective or subjective? Yes. Step 1 involves what we can call the question of knowledge and can be seen as requiring objectivity, in that the process requires general agreement with that from which the process originates. Step 2 involves what we can call the question of wisdom and can be seen as intersubjective in its pluralistic or perspectival orientation and can lead in a multitude of different directions. This multitude is dialogic, and the result is insight.

This picture can be used to complicate the contemporary division in academic philosophy. Analytic philosophy is concerned with Step 1. What ought we put in the universal basis? Continental philosophy can be seen as focusing on Step 2. How ought we include the phenomenological experience of different consciousnesses in different social-political contexts in the search for wisdom? To a Jewish thinker, the analytic/continental divide is not a problem.

Summary 1

While Hellenic-Christian epistemology is based on questions of determining objective truth which is uniquely contained in certain propositions, Jewish epistemology is different. It accepts certain basic commands (that are neither true nor false) and then seeks insight and wisdom from them through interpretations. While the Hellenic-Christian model is unitary (there is only one truth), the Jewish picture is dialogical, allowing different insights to remain in discussion with one another.

Jerry Seinfeld as a Secular Talmudist

Jerry Seinfeld's comedy makes use of the same structure of reasoning as we see in the *Talmud*. As an observational comedian, he starts with the given, that which is accepted by all as a necessary principle. In Seinfeld's case, this is cultural phenomenological commonality. He starts from shared experiences (intersubjective) that will be universal among those in the social group who are his audience. There is no disagreement of fact in Seinfeld's set ups. He refers to that which is well-known to all.

But what he then does with it is show it to us from a different angle. The glory of Seinfeld's philosophy is that when he places the mundane in front of us at an oblique angle, he derives novel, surprising insights that enlighten us. The contrast between this insight and the mundanity of the given is the incongruity that generates the humor. We now see something normal in a completely new way. We have wisdom from normality.

Talmudic approaches or discourse begins with the given of the Torah. Non-Talmudic Jewish thought must find some other source of the given, that is, a distinct set of universally accepted beliefs or practices to use as a starting point. Seinfeld, like all other observational comedians, mines the shared cultural phenomenological for this. We, as members of a sociohistorical context at a place at a time, share certain lived experiences. There is a common intersubjective reality that comes with being a cultural being.

As a Jew, Seinfeld has an advantage. Jewishness lives on the boundary of Otherness in the current American context. Jews are separate, while they are assimilated. If one were fully part of those with the social power, then one would be blind to alternative ways of being. Members of minority groups, as W.E.B. Dubois points out, are forced to live with a double consciousness. When one is in a group that lacks the capital necessary to control the society, you have to live in the world constructed by those with the power. You learn to talk their talk. But you also have the perspective and accompanying conceptual categories that come from your home culture. Outsiders are forced to always look at the world through two different lenses at all times.

And so, as a Jew, Jerry Seinfeld sees the world in different ways simultaneously. The majority of American Jews are white-ish compared to non-European Jews. European Jews or their descendents are known as Ashkenazi. Their Otherness has been diminished in certain ways through assimilation. This allows the distinct ways of seeing to be more easily translated into the language of the mainstream. The second lens may warp the image in certain ways, but it does not radically transform it. As such, reporting the image of the given in the second lens to those who only see it through the first lens allows the audience to easily absorb the new perspective and the differences it contains. The insight, the wisdom, is light and accessible.

Consider Seinfeld's bit about milk.

> Milk is a big problem for people in the supermarket. They're never quite sure if they have it, if they need it. They bury it way in the back of the supermarket. You have to find it. You have to hack your way through all the displays. "There it is. There's the milk. Do we have any milk?"

People are never sure if they have milk. 'I think we have milk. We might have milk. I know there's a carton in there. I don't know how much is in it. Well, what should we do?'

'Cause you want to be sure. There's nothing worse than thinking you have milk and not having it. You know, you have the bowl set up, the cereal, the spoon, the napkin, the tv, the newspaper, everything's ready to go. You go to lift up the carton and it's too light. 'Aaaah. Oh, no. Too light.'

Or sometimes you think you need milk. 'Hey, we better pick up some milk.' Like many of you are thinking right now. 'You know, he's right. Maybe we should pick up some milk.' So, you'll pick up some milk on the way home and then you'll discover that you already have milk. Now you've got way too much milk. That's no good either.

Now, it's a race against time with the expiration date. Now, you're eating giant punch bowls of cereal three times a day. You're washing your face with milk. You're bringing in cats from all over the neighborhood. 'Hurry up and drink it. C'mon, it's almost time.'

It starts from an immutable command that is universally accepted among his audience. In this case, it is "Have milk in your refrigerator." For those living a standard American lifestyle, this is a way of being in the same sort of way that the 613 mitzvot are to Jews. It is contested by no one and the opening of the bit describing the search for milk in the supermarket is designed to manufacture the universal consent needed to make the command part of the given. Once we have the law, the given, then we interpret and apply it to specific contexts. How ought one act when one is unsure of the existence of milk within one's fridge? It depends.

There could be the context in which one has too little milk. We see the lived consequences of this violation of the law. There could be the context in which one has too much milk. Different and unexpected, but universally recognized consequences follow from this context. What you see in this sort of discursive observational humor is a contextualization of a universally accepted given. It is comedy created through the use of the Talmudic approach when applied to the phenomenological cultural given instead of the theologically given.

Summary 2

Talmudic thinking starts with the commandments of the Torah and, through creative acts of interpretation, gives us insight. Neo-Talmudic thought uses the same epistemic approach, but replaces the sacred text with some other foundation. Jerry Seinfeld replaces the central text with phenomenological commonalities experienced by everyone in modern life and, through creative acts of interpretation, allows us insight into the mundane.

Chelm

There is a long tradition in Jewish culture of mocking everything, even that which is sacred. Talmudic thought is lampooned in a joke cycle about the rabbis from Chelm. These jokes, we will argue below are to Talmudic thought, what the comedy in the television show *Seinfeld* is to the neo-Talmudic thought of the stand-up of Seinfeld.

The Talmudic approach opens up the possibility of multiple interpretations generating wisdom. As such, one must be open to the possibility of new, different, even contrasting views in order to expand one's understanding. This pluralism gives rise to the fear of subjectivism. What's the difference between pluralism and subjectivism? Pluralism allows for multiple valid ways of seeing something, where subjectivism forces one to accept all interpretations as equally valid. Pluralism allows for one to constrain the set of possibilities without privileging a single perspective, where subjectivism leaves the gates wide open for all comers, even those that are absurd. As Franz Rosenzweig quipped in his book the Star of Redemption, [Hellenic-Christian or Western] Philosophy is "selficating."

It is by playing on this line between subjectivism and pluralism that the Talmudic approach has been lampooned within the Jewish community. Wisdom often seems absurd at first, so we can put in the mouth of fictional rabbis that appear to be wise while actually being absurd. This is the basis for a long-lasting joke cycle involving the residents of Chelm.

Chelm is a real town in Poland, and hence Chelm jokes are a Jewish form of Pollock joke which demonstrates the prejudices that Western German-speaking Jews held concerning their Ostjuden cousins. The east was the province of the provincial. These jokes allowed many Jews to make fun of that which is central to their way of seeing the world without challenging the way of seeing the world.

The citizens of Chelm strive to live what are recognizably Jewish lives, facing recognizably mundane challenges. They seek to meet these challenges using the sort of reasoning one expects from Jews, at least prima facie. But when one thinks one step further, the reasoning falls to pieces.

Consider a couple of classics.

The Rabbis of Chelm decided they had a problem when half the inmates of their prison claimed they had been wrongly convicted. So, they built a second prison. Now they have one for the guilty and one for the innocent.

Two sages of Chelm got involved in a deep philosophical argument.

"Since you're so wise," said one, sarcastically, "try to answer this question: Why is it that when a slice of buttered bread falls to the ground, it's bound to fall on the buttered side?"

But as the other sage was a bit of a scientist he decided to disprove this theory by a practical experiment. He went and buttered a slice of bread. Then he dropped it.

"There you are!" he cried triumphantly. "The bread, as you see, hasn't fallen on its buttered side at all. So where is your theory now?"

"Ho-ho!" laughed the other, derisively. "You think you're smart! You buttered the bread on the wrong side!"

And it is not just the Wise men of Chelm who are fools, but the entire village. The foolishness that is at the heart of the humor infects all since, in the village, the lives of all are interconnected.

The residents of Chelm decided to build a new, larger shul. It would take a lot of lumber, so they sent their strongest men up the mountain to harvest the biggest trees. They carried down massive log after log. The other residents pointed out to the men that the logs are round and that it would be much easier to roll them down the mountain, rather than carry them. They agreed and took them back up the mountain to roll them down.

We laugh at the residents of Chelm for their stupidity. But the stupidity is not ignorance, it is reasoned stupidity. Psychologist of humor Avner Ziv refers to this sort of joke logic as "local logic":

> Like local patriotism, local logic is appropriate only in certain places. In humor, local logic is appropriate in a way, because it brings some kind of explanation to the incongruity. We wait for one thing, and we get another thing that is quite different but that nevertheless has a certain suitability. (p. 90)

Local logic is unexpected and contextual, just like Talmudic reasoning, the difference is that the latter provides insight and wisdom, whereas the former provides none despite the seeming promise to do so. That incongruity between the joke and the Talmudic application of law, in the face of the structural congruity that unites them, is what makes Chelm jokes Jewish.

Summary 3

The wise men of Chelm jokes use Talmudic reasoning as a basis for humor. The rabbis of the Talmud employed complex reasoning that often leads to unexpected insights. By employing absurd reasoning, we also come to unexpected insights. This parallelism makes Talmudic thinking ripe for satirization.

Seinfeld as the New Chelm

If we understand the observational humor in Jerry Seinfeld's stand-up as neo-Talmudic, then we ought to understand the comedy in the television program *Seinfeld* as a revival of the absurdities of Chelm. The show brings together a village with a fictionalized version of Jerry along with his shtetl-mates Elaine, George, and Kramer in which, just like in Chelm, the normal is treated in new ways that seem from one angle to be sensible, but in reality are absurd. Jerry Seinfeld's stand-up material gave us laughs because it allowed us to see *the given* in a broader, multifaceted way, giving us deeper insight into the seeming trivialities of day-to-day life. *Seinfeld*, on the other hand, took the trivialities of day-to-day life and treated them in ways that seemed at first to be reasonable, but which when extended to their logical conclusion, ended up being absurd...just like Chelm.

Contrary to the claim in the episode *The Pitch* in season 4, *Seinfeld* was not a show about nothing. It certainly contrasted to high drama, soap opera, or most sitcoms where to keep the audience the plots tended to become hyperbolic or fantastic. Like Seinfeld's stand-up, the plots of *Seinfeld* would focus on the rules connected with the contexts of the mundane, of real-life experiences within contemporary late twentieth-century American life. The show was Seinfeldian in the Jewish sense in that it would begin, like the Chelm jokes, with the sorts of trials and tribulations that are a part of day-to-day life for the audience. It is an active engagement with the phenomenological cultural given.

But where Seinfeld's stand-up would explore the contextualizations of this given, the show would take it in a different direction, from seeming triviality toward absurdity. We pair a local logic with a slightly altered context and see how the slight change gives rise to absurdity. This mismatch of local and global logic while following the rule joins *Seinfeld* to Chelm.

Consider Elaine getting news of her boyfriend's accident in the lobby of a movie theater. The context of being in a movie theater lobby makes the buying of a box of Jujyfruits to be normal. It fits well with the local logic. But with the altered context of the accident, this seemingly trivial, normal act becomes relationship-ending.

Making out with one's date at the movies is not an unusual occurrence in the normal course of things. It follows the local logic. But if, as with Jerry, that you were seeing *Schindler's List*, the change in context changes the logic.

What we saw in each episode of *Seinfeld* was different from the stand-up of Seinfeld. Where his stand-up makes use of a Talmudic approach, the sitcom mocks it in the same sort of way we saw with the residents of Chelm.

Conclusion

Jerry Seinfeld's comedy can be understood philosophically as deriving from an epistemological foundation different from that of the Hellenic-Christian tradition. His observational humor can be seen as structurally belonging to a Jewish approach to wisdom. This approach has long been parodied within the Jewish community, in a way, just like Seinfeld himself parodies his own insightful stand-up on his eponymous television series.

References

Derrida, Jacques. 1997. Of Grammatology. Baltimore: Johns Hopkins University Press.
Hegel, G.W.F. 1975. The spirit of Christianity and its fate. In *Early theological writings*. Philadelphia: University of Pennsylvania Press.
Kant, Immanuel. 2018. *Religion within the bounds of mere reason*. Cambridge: Cambridge University Press.
Nietzsche, Friedrich. 2013. *On the genealogy of morals*. New York: Penguin.
Niremberg, David. 2013. *Anti-Judaism: The history of a way of thinking*. New York: W.W. Norton.
Rosenstreich, Nathan. 1964. *The recurring pattern: Studies in anti-Judaism in modern thought*. New York: Horizon Press.
Rosenzweig, Franz. 2005. *The star of redemption*. Madison: University of Wisconsin Press.
Seinfeld, Jerry. 1998. *I'm telling you for the last time*. New York: Home Box Office.
Ziv, Avner. 1984. Personality and Sense of Humor. New York: Springer.

Dave Chappelle as Philosopher: Standing Up to Racism

71

Steven A. Benko and Reagan Scout Burch

Contents

Introduction	1644
Race and/As Contradiction	1647
Color-Blind Racism	1657
Conclusion	1664
References	1666

Abstract

Dave Chappelle is one of the most talented and controversial comedians working today. Beginning with *Chappelle's Show* in 2003 and continuing through his more recent stand-up specials on Netflix, Chappelle has worked to infuse laughter with difficult observations about race and identity. Chappelle uses race as a lens to think about representation more generally, using incongruity and contradiction to point out false equivalences and strategies that perpetuate systemic racism. Chappelle's philosophy of race has matured over time: on *Chappelle's Show*, he displayed a more playful, anarchic attitude toward the constructed nature of stereotypes. Chappelle sought to undermine stereotypes not by showing that they were false but by showing that it was ridiculous to give them any weight or consideration to begin with. The more mature Chappelle of *Equanimity* (2017), *The Bird Revelations* (2017), and *Sticks and Stones* (2019) recognizes that revealing the artificial and constructed nature of stereotypes has only made people give them more weight and credibility. Chappelle has responded by adopting a perspective on personal responsibility that repeats the post-racist and color-blind racist attitudes toward freedom, choice, and responsibility that shape the White habitus in which most of his audience exists. Chappelle is not post-racist, but his

S. A. Benko (✉) · R. S. Burch
Meredith College, Raleigh, NC, USA
e-mail: benkos@meredith.edu; rsburch@email.meredith.edu

© Springer Nature Switzerland AG 2024
D. K. Johnson et al. (eds.), *The Palgrave Handbook of Popular Culture as Philosophy*,
https://doi.org/10.1007/978-3-031-24685-2_85

emphasis on choice and responsibility allows him to rank the oppression different marginalized groups suffer, concluding that Black men are always the most oppressed group. This is why Chappelle's more controversial statements about women and transgender individuals can be interpreted through his racial lens. Chappelle wants to use comic misdirection and hyperbole to make larger points about American history and identity, and thus his comedy is the latest, perhaps greatest, example of the way that Black comics have used humor to illuminate cultural contradictions and change their audience's perceptions about the long, violent history of racism in America.

Keywords

Race · Gender · Incongruity · Comedy · Post-racism · Fairness · Transgender

Introduction

Dave Chappelle is one of the most famous and influential comics of his generation. He began his stand-up career as a teenager and has found success in movies (*Robin Hood: Men in Tights*, 1993; *The Nutty Professor*, 1996; *Half Baked*, 1998; *Undercover Brother*, 2002; and, most recently, *A Star is Born*, 2018). Although Chappelle became famous for his eponymously named sketch show, *Chappelle's Show* (2003–2006), he became infamous for walking away from a reported $30 million contract to film a third season. More recently, Chappelle has returned to his stand-up comedy roots with a series of specials for the streaming service Netflix. These specials, *Equanimity* (2017), *The Bird Revelation* (2017), and *Sticks and Stones* (2019) have seen Chappelle return to the themes of race, gender, and identity in America that made *Chappelle's Show* controversial and groundbreaking. In addition to his movies, *Chappelle's Show*, and his stand-up specials, Chappelle has performed or produced other works (*Dave Chappelle's Block Party*, 2006) and performed as a voice actor and made guest appearances on TV shows (*The Larry Sanders Show*, 1998; *Wanda at Large*, 2003). The scope of this chapter will focus on Chappelle's work on *Chappelle's Show* and his stand-up career, as these are the mediums in which his commentary and opinions on race are most evident.

Race is a recurring theme in Dave Chappelle's comedy. Throughout his career, Chappelle has mined racial stereotypes to ask two difficult questions: if stereotypes are untrue, how responsible are people for believing them? Further, if stereotypes are untrue, how responsible are people for performing them? Chappelle's comedy explores these questions as they relate to race, because for him race and the logic of racism are a way of thinking about how and why other social groups face discrimination. Chappelle's understanding of race is situated in an ethics of fairness, specifically, the idea that no one gets to complain about how they are being treated unless race and racism are first taken into account. Race, and the harms that systemic racism has done and continues to do to the Black community, are the lens through which others' harms are compared, ranked, and made sense of.

The concern that frames Chappelle's comedy as a philosophy of race is the relationship between systemic, institutional racism and personal agency and responsibility. Chappelle asks his audience to decide whether those who impose stereotypes on others are wrong for doing so; whether those who are marginalized by being stereotyped have been wronged; and if those who engage these stereotypes either for laughs or in their daily lives are wronging others or themselves. Chappelle's comedy is about rights and wrongs in the sense that he mines the past and the way things were to raise questions about how things are. When he tells stories about himself, friends, family, media figures, or strangers, Chappelle is asking his audience to evaluate what it means to perpetuate, lean into, embrace, or refute things like racial stereotypes. In Chappelle's philosophy of race, some people are more or less free to perpetuate, deny, parody, or embody racial and gender stereotypes. That means that though he believes that current instances of systemic racism are built upon the lingering effects of Jim Crow racism, Chappelle speaks from the same neoliberal logic of choice and personal responsibility for one's situations and actions that perpetuates what Eduardo Bonilla-Silva calls in *Racism Without Racists* "color-blind racism." Color-blind racism is the perspective that minimizes the effects of systemic racism while emphasizing individual agency and responsibility as an explanation for social, political, and economic inequality.

Chappelle's use of stereotypes for comedic effect, along with his emphasis on fairness and personal responsibility (for example, in many of his jokes comparing the Black experience to the Queer rights movement) has led to criticisms, which suggest that Chappelle is not liberating Blacks as much as he is making it easier for Whites to justify their racist and anti-Queer views. Chappelle himself wondered about this. The demise of *Chappelle's Show* is linked to the filming of a sketch that, like many others, played on Black stereotypes. That sketch, titled "The [N-slur-Pixie]," featured Chappelle "clad in the costuming of minstrelsy (blackface, white lips, gloves, red vest, and a Pullman Porter's cap)" standing on the shoulders of prominent African Americans (Chappelle as Tiger Woods and as himself) exhorting them to "react 'naturally' and perform the stereotypical tropes of black masculinity" (Haggins 2007, p. 229). When a White crew member laughed too hard, Chappelle became convinced that people were missing the point of his satire and he abandoned the show before the third season completed filming. He also said, in *Sticks and Stones* (2019), that if he makes fun of a particular group, it is because he sees himself in them; to be available for insult is, in Chappelle's logic, to have achieved a level of acceptance where one can be taken back down a few pegs. So while Chappelle is not color blind, how his understanding of race intersects with his sense of personal responsibility can make him come across as, in his words, a "victim blamer." No matter how strongly Chappelle believes insults humanize, he is still the one on the stage with the microphone while his audience sits, anonymously, in darkness. Chappelle's desire to have it both ways – systemic racism is real but people are responsible for the situations they find themselves in – has made him a polarizing figure.

The first question to ask when thinking about Chappelle as a philosopher of race is what Chappelle hopes to accomplish when he performs exaggerated racial stereotypes that White audiences have long associated with the Black community: is he ridiculing Black people who have not rejected these behaviors in their own community, or is he mocking White people for believing these stereotypes are true in the first place? Complicating Chappelle's philosophy of race is the way he positions himself so that he can critique the contradictions of American society: Chappelle draws from stereotypes about Blacks that are part of a White habitus that casts Blacks as lazy, materialistic, hyper-sexualized, and anti-intellectual. So it becomes necessary to ask a second question: is it right to draw on other stereotypes, most of them harmful, as a way to frame jokes that expose the harm of believing that stereotypes are true while also blaming people for adopting stereotypical attitudes, behaviors, and perspectives? As a comedian, Chappelle is not obligated to "say it straight," though at times he has – or at least, he has played at saying it straight. Chappelle's point is that the constructed (created, authored, or composed; not natural or objective) nature of stereotypes means that they cannot withstand scrutiny. Their constructedness reduces them to a choice that some are more or less free to make: everyone can choose to reject them; some can choose to embrace them, even if only parodically. However, given the pervasiveness of stereotypes, is there blame to be had, and if there is, then who should be blamed, when people act in stereotypical ways?

Any analysis of Dave Chappelle's comedy should not forget that Chappelle is funny. But Chappelle is painfully funny, sometimes telling jokes that the audience member should feel bad about laughing at and sometimes telling jokes that cause other people pain. He ponders this distinction in the opening of *The Bird Revelation*:

> Sometimes, the funniest thing to say is mean. You know what I mean? It's a tough position to be in. So I say a lot of mean things, but you guys got to remember. I'm not saying it to be mean. I'm saying it because it's funny. And everything's funny till it happens to you. (00:00:15–00:00:34)

Chappelle uses laughter as a way to speak hard truths about race, gender, identity, and American culture in an intelligent and compelling way. All of this is to say that Chappelle is a talented and challenging social critic who believes that joking is a way to speak truth to power. He believed that he was committing professional suicide when he left *Chappelle's Show* and fought for 12 years to regain his standing as the defining comedian of his generation – an effort that culminated in being awarded the Mark Twain Prize for American Humor in 2020. Correspondingly, Chappelle believes it is only fair to ask his audience to take the same risks he does: be honest, but be willing to be judged and criticized for what you think, say, and do. But, if the fairness that will bring about racial healing and reconciliation is the goal of Chappelle's comedy, is that goal undermined by being built on a foundation that does not withstand scrutiny?

Race and/As Contradiction

Dave Chappelle's understanding of race rests on four principles: first, racism is America's original sin. Second, contradiction is the root of racism and what makes it impossible to sustain when interrogated logically and with critical thinking. The third principle is that it is wrong to treat people differently than you yourself want to be treated. Fairness demands that people ought to be treated with the same deference and respect they ask from others. For Chappelle, there is nothing worse than the hypocrisy of asking to be treated one way and then not extending that same consideration to others. The second and third principles are intertwined: contradiction at the expense of an individual or group is unfair. The fourth principle is that because of their lack of freedom from the effects of slavery, Jim Crow racism, and anti-Black stereotypes and attitudes, any comparison of suffering between marginalized groups begins and ends with the fact that Black men have suffered more than any other group. Chappelle does not elaborate on this stance, nor does he come across as feeling he has to. From slavery, to Jim Crow, to police brutality, Chappelle approaches the conversation about ranking the suffering of different groups as if the matter is already settled: Black men have suffered the most.

The first principle that undergirds Chappelle's philosophy of race is that racism is a sin that America has not yet fully reckoned with or paid for in full. In a wide-ranging interview on *Inside the Actor's Studio*, Chappelle told host James Lipton that:

> America needs an honest discourse with itself. This is the greatest country in the world by default ... but we could be the greatest country that ever existed if we were just honest about who we are, what we are, where we want to go. And if we learn how to have that discourse. Things like racism are institutionalized, it's systemic. You might not know any bigots, you feel like "well, I don't hate Black people so I'm not a racist." But you benefit from racism just by the merit of the color of your skin. Just by the opportunities that you have. You're privileged in ways you may not even realize because you haven't been deprived in certain ways. We need to talk about these things in order for them to change. I do a show, walk down the street ... it needs to be talked about. It's like the elephant in the living room that nobody says anything about. ("Dave Chappelle" 1:17:21–1:19:00)

What Chappelle says directly on *Inside the Actor's Studio* he says indirectly on *Chappelle's Show* and in his stand-up specials. He turns incongruity and misdirection toward larger social truths about the state of race in America. Chappelle has said that his comedy is "truth in jest" and that he prides himself on his ability to create moments of truth through misdirection and incongruity: "I pride myself on saying real shit that people don't even notice I'm saying. But they feel it ... they can feel it but I don't think they really know" ("Dave Chappelle" 44:59). This places Chappelle squarely in the tradition of Black comedians for whom humor is an act of resistance against negative attitudes and stereotypes about Blacks. Bailey (2012) writes that:

> By conceding to the possibilities that Black comics are doing more than telling jokes, entertaining us, or are otherwise there for our consumption, we endow them with agency so that we can begin to consider ways that analyzing said performances yields new and

insightful commentary about race, class, gender, sexuality, and a host of other conditions endemic to life in America, indeed to life everywhere. (p. 254)

Chappelle's insight is what he shared with Lipton: racism is contrary to American values and we refuse to reckon with the way that sin diminishes America as a nation and as a people. The things that are supposed to make America great are the institutions that promote and protect our freedoms and liberties. The contradiction is the way that those institutions have been turned against people for racist and arbitrary reasons. Chappelle's use of contradiction to explore the contradictions inherent in racist beliefs relies on reiterating and exaggerating stereotypes in order to reveal how ridiculous those stereotypes were to begin with.

The second aspect of Chappelle's understanding of race is contradiction. Contradiction, or more specifically, noncontradiction, is central to Chappelle's attitude toward race and gender: a position on one topic or social issue ought to be logically consistent with – ought not to contradict – another. Chappelle has spoken about how he, like all Black Americans, live the contradiction of what W. E. B. DuBois called "double consciousness" both seeing themselves as themselves and seeing themselves as White people see them. In his appearance on *Inside the Actor's Studio*, Chappelle told host James Lipton that "every Black American is bi-lingual" in that they have a vocabulary and way of speaking for the street and a different way of presenting themselves in job interviews ("Dave Chappelle" 46:24). Chappelle's double consciousness and intertwining of contradiction and fairness are displayed in his 2019 special *Sticks and Stones* in a joke about gun violence:

> I've given this a lot of thought. I don't see any peaceful way to disarm America's whites. There's only one thing that's going to save this country from itself. Same thing that always saves this country from itself, and that is African Americans. Right. And I know the question that a lot of y'all have in your minds is, "Should we do it?" Yeah. Fuck yeah, we should do it. Listen, no matter what they say or how they make you feel, remember, this is your country, too. It is incumbent upon us... to save our country. And you know what we have to do. This is a fuckin' election year. We gotta be serious. Every able-bodied African American must ... register ... for ... a ... legal ... firearm. That's the only way they'll change the law. (40:41–41:48)

Again, Chappelle is using a somber and reflective tone to heighten the incongruity of the punch line. The expectation is that Chappelle will call on people to make themselves heard through democratic representation and vote for the policies that they want to see enacted. The irony in this joke is that the racism that fueled the violence that led to the oppression of Black Americans can be turned to their benefit by scaring Whites into enacting meaningful gun reform laws. Chappelle reaches back to a time when Black gun ownership was restricted because of its link to slave rebellions, self-defense against White supremacists, and political agitating during the Civil Rights movement. Casting himself as reasoned and wise, Chappelle is resigned to the perception held by Whites and perpetuated by the media that Blacks are violent, so violent in fact that if they did try to amass a storehouse of firearms that the fear of political violence would lead Whites to surrender their own right to own guns.

Here, Blacks, who disproportionately suffer violent crime, benefit from racist assumptions. The double-consciousness on display and mined for humor is that Blacks, knowing how they are perceived, know better than Whites how to solve the problem of gun violence. The contradiction is that while it may not be fair to view them this way, they would benefit from the exploitation of this racist attitude.

The third principle of Chappelle's understanding of race is that hypocrisy, specifically the hypocrisy of asking to be treated one way and then not returning it in kind, is the worst kind of unfairness. Fairness becomes intertwined with contradiction through the mechanics of comedy of incongruity, specifically, the fact that humor is elicited by a delightfully surprising deviation from the trajectory in which the narrative was heading. Chappelle, who in *Equanimity* brags that he is so good at telling jokes that he can write them backward by scripting the punch line first and then finding a story to apply it to, has mastered the ability to string a story along and interject the punch line through incongruity at just the right moment. What starts as a bit about finding a joke where "So I kicked her in the pussy" is the punch line, Chappelle meanders through a story about growing up poor, eating dinner at a White friend's house, being offered Stove Top Stuffing, which he had dreamed of eating, and then assaulting the mother when she tells him that they do not have enough Stove Top stuffing for him: "Ladies and gentlemen, I told you I'm dope, [n-slur]. I told you I was gonna say it, and you still didn't see it coming. And that's why I make the big bucks" (00:08:42).

Laughter from incongruity occurs when the joke teller creates a set of expectations about what will come next in a joke/story and frustrates those expectations in a way that is both pleasant and surprising. The audience, thinking that the joke/story is going to be resolved in one way, is pleasantly surprised when it is resolved in a different way; though the joke/story can be resolved in an infinite number of ways, laughter occurs when the particular resolution is both pleasant and surprising. The comedian's task is to resolve the joke/story in a way that aligns with the narrative, but not in the way the listener could have expected or anticipated. If the resolution does not make narrative sense, the resolution could be too disconnected from the narrative to be pleasant and there will be no laughter; this is a hallmark of absurdist humor. If the resolution is too close to the logical trajectory of the joke/story then it is not surprising enough to elicit laughter, though it could be pleasant. Rod Martin (2007), author of *The Psychology of Humor*, describes the cognitive processes of comedy of incongruity this way:

> [W]hile we are hearing the setup of a joke, a schema (or script) is activated to enable us to make sense of the incoming information. However, information in the joke punch line does not fit with the schema, causing us to search for another schema that will make better sense. This second schema typically gives an altogether different (and even contradictory) interpretation of the situation, rather than just a slightly modified perspective. The second script does not completely replace the first one, however, so the two are activated simultaneously. (pp. 86–87)

The notion of schema interruption and replacement raises interesting questions when thinking about a comedian who addresses the topics that Chappelle addresses. On the one hand, at this point in his career, Chappelle is a known quantity: none of his views on race, religion, gender, masculinity, drugs, etc., should be surprising. In this way, Chappelle is able to show the contradictions and illogic of the White perspective by using comic tropes like hyperbole, but especially incongruity, to demonstrate that it is an absurd point of view that cannot survive logical scrutiny. It is likely that there is already schema agreement between Chappelle and his audience. On the other hand, Chappelle still gets his audience to laugh, so he is still saying surprising things. Chappelle does say shocking things, but none of the shocking things he says are so outside the realm of possibility that they fail to elicit laughter. His willingness to provoke and shock has earned him praise for his bravery and truth telling. However, Chappelle has been criticized by a variety of groups who feel that he is being provocative and shocking at their expense. Cisgender women and members of the queer community in particular have expressed their dismay at Chappelle's willingness to trade in stereotypes in order to get a laugh.

Comedians who rely on incongruity to generate laughter have to work from within the audience's conceptual schema. They have to tell stories with premises and a narrative logic that is familiar to the audience. With some exceptions, Chappelle speaks from a perspective that is, essentially, a White fantasy of how a Black man thinks and behaves. Comedians who cannot relate to their audience at this basic conceptual level will not have an audience for long. The question is why schema shifting is a pleasant experience, especially if, upon reflection, the audience realizes that they are being criticized or that the schema that they inhabit positions them on the wrong side of social justice or basic human decency. The easy answer is that the agreement that audiences make with comedians is that when the comedian criticizes a group of people, he is not biting the hand that feeds them; the comedian is criticizing people outside of the venue. For Bambi Haggins, Chappelle's ability to position himself within his audience's perspective "takes some of the sting out of Chappelle's social critique" because "there is never any *direct* blame – at least for the people in the audience." The audience may feel that they are exempt from the criticisms that Chappelle is making: having paid to be entertained, they are not going to ruin their good time by thinking that they are who he is talking about. Additionally, the audience might feel like they agree with what Chappelle is saying. Haggins (2007) believes that Chappelle "always gives the audience a different kind of out: he implies that he *knows* white people ... and that makes it OK" (193). Chappelle is not really talking about those who happen to be in the audience: he is talking about other White people.

This was truer of the stand-up Chappelle did prior to his distribution deal with Netflix. After his Netflix deal, he was no longer content with just identifying contradictions or with simply walking away and letting his audience figure out that they were engaged in a contradiction themselves. Chappelle began to use his humor to interrogate who benefits from the perpetuation of contradictions about race and gender and how it contributes to the continued marginalization of people of color and members of the queer community. It seemed that he began to hope that his audience would come to see things differently by taking the jokes personally.

For example, in the opening of *Sticks and Stones*, Chappelle criticizes the audience for their hypocritical attitude toward laughter and being held responsible for laughing. He begins the joke by saying that he is going to do an impression and wants the audience to guess who it is:

> You gotta guess who it is, though. Okay, here it goes. Uh, duh. Hey! Durr! If you do anything wrong in your life, duh, and I find out about it, I'm gonna try to take everything away from you, and I don't care when I find out. Could be today, tomorrow, 15, 20 years from now. If I find out, you're fucking-duh-finished … Who is that? (pause) That's YOU! That's what the audience sounds like to me. That's why I don't be coming out doing comedy all the time, 'cause y'all [n-slurs] is the worst motherfuckers I've ever tried to entertain in my FUCKING life. (5:42–6:18)

Chappelle wants the audience to hear that joke and feel discomforted by the hypocrisy and privilege that allows them to enjoy something in one moment and then disingenuously criticize Chappelle when it is convenient to do so.

What Chappelle has figured out and is communicating to his audience is that there is something not quite right about the situation he is describing. Chappelle continues to appeal to the typical person's belief that unfairness is always out of place. He posits the question: is the unfairness itself always surprising or is it a Black man's astonishment that something is unfair that is surprising? Whatever the topic is, it has given him pause, confused him, frustrated him, or made him indignant or angry. Chappelle taps into the audience's sense of fairness by implying or outright stating that it is not fair that he, Chappelle, has to feel these negative emotions; as a Black man, he already has enough burdens. The resolution of the joke is the exposure of the contradiction, which shifts the audience to a new way of seeing things. In his impersonation of the audience, Chappelle wants the audience to recognize that if they have come to see their laughter differently – specifically, to see it as problematic – then they should not forget two things. First is the fact that they laughed and no one forced them to laugh. Taking that shame out on the person who provoked the laughter unfairly shifts the responsibility from the audience to the joke-teller. Second is the fact that laughter was provoked by replacing one way of seeing things for a new, maybe better, point of view or perspective. There should be pleasure in seeing things differently if seeing them differently also means seeing them more clearly or more fairly. The pleasure comes from being vindicated; now realizing that something was wrong (surprise), it feels better to be right (delight). Chappelle knows that the most effective incongruity that he can generate in order to make comedy of social critique is comedy of logical contradiction that rests on feelings of unfairness that shift the schema to a state of affairs that is more deserved and therefore fair. This logic of deservedness and fairness is how Chappelle can use the Black experience as the litmus test for claims by other groups that they are treated unfairly.

Chappelle's growth as a comic and artist has been to make more explicit this connection between the unfairness of contradiction and rightness of fairness. On

Chappelle's Show, it was more obvious that this dynamic operated more in the background; unfairness as contradiction animated many of the more race-conscious sketches while leaving the audience to do the work of filling in what would be fair and right. No sketch demonstrates this point more than the one that Chappelle told James Lipton was his manifesto (see "Dave Chappelle" 57:06) and opened the first episode of *Chappelle's Show* in 2003: "Frontline: Clayton Bigsby." Clayton Bigsby was the only Black child in a school for the blind; out of concern for his feelings – as if it were something to feel bad about – the school tells him that he is White. Bigsby grows up to prove the adage that no one is born hating another person because of the color of their skin; they have to be taught to do that – as he apparently is in this school. The sketch relies on three contradictions that prove the social construction of race and hate: first, his friend Jasper is the only person in the KKK who knows Bigsby is Black but refuses to tell him because of their friendship and because Bigsby is too important to the White Supremacist movement. He takes steps to protect Bigsby when he is confronted by racists for being Black and making sure his hood is on so he can preach hate at a gathering of White supremacists. The contradictions are multilayered: if you hate all Blacks then you should hate every Black; if your friend is Black then you should not let them contribute to a movement that would threaten them physically and deny them rights. The second contradiction is the encounter with White teenagers blaring rap music. Bigsby tells them to turn down their music and they are elated when he calls them n-slurs, satisfying their desire to be seen as authentically Black. The contradiction is clear: White people want it both ways, to use the word as a slur against Blacks and as a compliment when they can associate its meaning with an authentically Black "ghetto" experience that they have fetishized. Finally, the conclusion where Bigsby reveals (after he learned he was Black) that he divorced his wife because she is, in his words, a "[n-slur] lover" further reveals the artificiality of the meanings and behaviors attributed to race but also the way that power is layered in society, giving power to some while denying it to others. As a man, Bigsby is able to hold inconsistent and illogical views and act on them while women, in this case Bigsby's wife, suffer those behaviors and are denied a voice. Her interests, perspectives, and sufferings are not considered and are second to Bigsby's. For comedy of incongruity to work the audience has to have a conceptual schema where race is biological, and somewhere in their horizon of meaning there has to be some understanding of, and possibility for, race to be socially constructed. Through hyperbole and exaggeration, Chappelle moves his audience from one schema to another. He shows them another way of seeing race and a vocabulary for explaining race to themselves and others. However, what to do with the notion that race is socially constructed is left vague and what would be right is undefined.

Chappelle is not unique in having to worry about whether his audience "gets" his jokes or if they are hearing something different from what he is intending; all comedians who are also cultural critics have this concern. If he left *Chappelle's Show* because he was suspicious that "some individuals were not understanding his humor as he intended and were instead using his performances to fulfill racist pleasures, even as he worked to conjure stereotypes in order to show their absurdity and inhumanity" then his frequent explanations of his intentions and attitudes in his more recent standup can be read as a desire not to be misunderstood again (Bao 2009, p. 169). As a Black comedian coming from a marginalized group, Chappelle bears this burden as he is more acutely aware of the perception that his voice should be used (ideally) to uplift others and (at least) not to put others down. Lawrence (2009) writes that "given the fact that Chappelle belongs to an ethnic group that has been historically subjugated, it would seem that the comedian would be above participating in the marginalization of another group" (p. 41).

A more explicit connection between the unfairness of contradiction and rightness of fairness is on display in Chappelle's jokes about members of the transgender community. (These are jokes that Chappelle has been criticized for and the following explanation is not meant as a defense of their content.) The setup for this joke is a letter that Chappelle received from a fan who said that Chappelle's jokes hurt them deeply:

> I thought about how I felt. Asked myself a very basic question that I don't think I ever directly contemplated. I said, "Man, Dave, if you're writing all these jokes, do you have a problem with transgender people?" And the answer is absolutely not. The fuck you guys think I am? I don't understand all the choices that people make. But I do understand that life is hard, and that those types of choices do not disqualify you from a life with dignity and happiness and safety in it. But if I'm honest... my problem has never been with transgender people. My problem has always been with the dialogue about transgender people. I just feel like these things should not be discussed in front of the blacks. It's fucking insulting, all this talk about how these people feel inside. Since when has America given a fuck how any of us feel inside? And I cannot shake this awful suspicion that the only reason everybody is talking about transgenders is because white men want to do it. That's right. I just said that. If it was just women that felt that way or black dudes and Mexican dudes being like, "Hey, ya'll, we feel like girls inside." They'd be like, "Shut up, [n-slur]. No one asked you how you felt. Come on, everybody, we have strawberries to pick." It reeks of white privilege. You never asked yourself why it was easier for Bruce Jenner to change his gender than it was for Cassius Clay to change his fucking name? (*Equanimity,* 22:54–24:55)

Several aspects of how Chappelle's understanding of sexual identity intersects with his understanding of race are on display in this joke. First, Chappelle refers to sexual identity generally, and the experience of trans women specifically, as a choice. He presents that identity as a choice he does not understand and then says that even if it is a choice, it is not one that disqualifies a person from a basic level of respect, happiness, and safety. Second, understanding sexual identity, or at least the performance of one's sexual identity, as a choice means that it is something that a person can be judged or evaluated for; because it was a choice they could have chosen otherwise. Third, if it is a choice, it is one that stimulates a sense of entitlement to something (in Chappelle's mind) more than basic dignity, happiness, and safety.

Here the comparison to the Black experience becomes clear and that comparison is the root of Chappelle's frustration: it is unfair for transgender individuals to feel entitled to something based on a choice that they did not have to make, to feel as oppressed as Blacks, because Blacks were not given a choice and yet have been treated with anything but dignity. Gillota (2019) explains this turn toward using the racism experienced by Blacks as Chappelle's on-ramp to talking about other forms of oppression:

> This habit of discussing racism in relation to other social justice issues is fraught with contradictions ... you can't do comparative suffering but only moments before he asks how a white woman could ever yell about discrimination to a black man? In moments like these, Chappelle uses his knowledge and experience of racism as a lens through which to view all other forms of discrimination and as a license to allow him to talk about any form of discrimination that he pleases. (p. 14)

Gillota's conclusion is that Chappelle sees racism, especially racism against Blacks, "as the standard against which all other forms of discrimination should be measured" (16). And that is the fourth principle of Chappelle's philosophy of race. People never cared if Black people felt happy and safe, even though they did not choose to be Black, and discriminated against them accordingly. To Chappelle, demanding that Americans care about the feelings of someone else, especially someone who *did* have the freedom to make a choice (and thus could have avoided the discrimination), is unfair. Chappelle's moral vision is not much more than "do unto others as you have had done unto you." It does not matter if "they" have done it to you; what matters is whether you have suffered an injustice and if people are cutting in line asking for respect, happiness, or safety before you have gotten yours. The audience does not need to know anything about the transgender community or even have a strong opinion about them; that is not the schema that Chappelle is engaging. Rather, Chappelle is engaging his audience's fairness schema: anyone in the audience who has been treated unfairly recognizes the contradiction of someone asking for special treatment, especially when they have chosen the behaviors that have led to them being discriminated against. Two things would be fairer: first, it would be fairer, and therefore right, to recognize the suffering of a group who had no choice in the matter; everyone else can fall in line behind them. Second, it would be fairer, if all those who are discriminated against recognized that White privilege is the common enemy and that if the groups that Whites discriminate against are at odds with each other in their quest for recognition, this will only help perpetuate White hegemony (with very little effort from Whites). Ideally the audience shifts to this schema and welcomes transgender individuals into the moral community. It is just as likely, unfortunately, that the audience will be offended by Chappelle's comments in a way that reinforces their sense of entitlement for recompense for injustices they have suffered and that the groups will thus be more at odds. If so, Chapelle's efforts have backfired.

Chappelle's frequent structuring of his jokes around the illogic, and therefore unfairness, of racism and racist stereotypes is not consistent. Nowhere is this more apparent than in his jokes about transsexual individuals and his frequent use of the word "bitch." Chappelle's audience might not notice how frequently he says the word; however, when he does say it, he is usually referring to women (Hillary Clinton, Rachel Dolezal, and people who have criticized him have all been called "bitch") and only sometimes does he refer to men (Donald Trump, for example).

Chappelle uses the word to signal that he disapproves of the person or their behavior: they have not behaved the way that he thinks they ought to, usually because they have crossed some line in his mind. In his stand-up, "bitch" becomes a term used to put a person, usually a woman, in their place. Calling a man a bitch has the same effect: it puts him in his place, but is even more degrading because he is being placed on the same level with women.

While his use of the n-slur is vaguer – sometimes it is used as a put down and sometimes it is used in a more familiar way – at least Chappelle can claim that he is trying to reclaim the n-slur. There is no similar defense for "bitch" because it is not seen as a racial slur. Andrea Cumbo (2009), in "The Comedian is a 'Man': Gender Performance in the Comedy of Dave Chappelle," argues the opposite point about Chappelle and his use of the word "bitch." Cumbo is confident that the audience knows that the word has multiple meanings and that Chappelle is playing with those multiple meanings as a way of undermining the pejorative use of the term (see 58).

Something more is happening with Chappelle's use of the term "bitch" than what Cumbo argues, however. Chappelle's use of the word "bitch" shows how the connection between the four principles described here (freedom of choice, personal responsibility, contradiction as the source of racism, and fairness as the criteria for assessing claims of deservedness) creates in his mind a racial hierarchy that plays out as if he and others were competing in what can be called the "Oppression Olympics" Here, Oppression Olympics refers to the effort to rank the social inequalities and injustices one has suffered in order to claim a moral high ground; the group that has suffered the most is the most authentic. The group that wins the Oppression Olympics gets to decide how to address injustice and inequality. Chappelle's deployment of the Oppression Olympics logic inverts Orwell's *Animal Farm* logic, in which the pigs maintain that "all animals are equal but some animals are more equal than others"; in other words, all people (except Whites) have been oppressed; some people have been oppressed by Whites more than others; Blacks have been oppressed the most. They are "more equal."

Chappelle's use of the Oppression Olympics can be subtle, but at times is overt. When he plays the Oppression Olympics, Blacks win, but within the Black community, Black men win every time:

> You know, everyone has it hard. But I think, harder than black people and harder than Arabs and Mexicans, you know who has it the worst? Fat black people. It's hard for white people to understand, but what I'm saying is very true. Fat black people have a really rough road, because all manner of things kill white people. But you know what kills more black people than anything, more than police and terrorism? Salt, [n-slur]. Regular-ass table salt. Here, white people are getting Ebola cures and shit, and meanwhile, I'm dying from fucking flavoring. (*Deep in the Heart of Texas* 17:00–17:26)

Chappelle had just finished saying that Blacks used to have it the worst, but after 9/11 Arabs had stepped up and claimed that spot (they have it worse because they cannot even leave their backpacks unattended without being called a terrorist). Chappelle, in the above, quickly reverses course and reasserts that Blacks still have it the worst, and while this observation could apply to Black people of all genders, Chappelle's closing line ("I'm dying from fucking flavoring") reaffirms that it is Black men who are, again, the most disadvantaged. The claim that Black men are the most oppressed class allows Chappelle to position himself, per the logic of the Oppression Olympics, as having a unique and more credible perspective on race in America.

A serious problem with the Oppression Olympics is the way that Chappelle genders the game. "Bitch" is a highly gendered term and it reveals a contradiction in Chappelle's thought: stereotypes are constructed and therefore illusory; gender is biological and therefore real. While there are stereotypes that construct gender, in Chappelle's mind there is a way that women ought to be. In Chappelle's opinion, women are not the same blank slate that men are. A woman is responsible for any conflict between how Chappelle thinks a woman ought to be a woman and how she is a woman. Because it was her choice to behave as she does, she must accept the consequences of performing her gender a particular way; she could have performed it otherwise.

> You can see it! You, you ever have this happen? This is how confusing it is; this is, this is the practical application of what I'm talking about. Like a guy will be out, having a good night, you'd be out at a club, bar, right? Just kicking it with your boys and . . . a girl walks by and man she looks good. She looks good, not good in that classical way. I mean you, you know, I'm talking good like she got half her ass hanging out her skirt, mhmm, her titties are all mashed together popping out the top of her turtleneck and shit. [pause for crowd laughter] And you're with your buddies, right? You're with your buddies, had a couple drinks in you and you see a girl and you might try and talk to her and it might not come out right. I know what you say. "Damn look at them titties" [pause for laughter] The girl gets mad at ya, "Oh, oh uh-uh, oh wait a minute, wait a minute! Just because I'm dressed this way does not make me a whore." Which is true, Gentlemen, that is true. Just because they dress a certain way doesn't mean they are a certain way. Don't even forget it. But ladies, you must understand that is fucking confusing. It just is. Now that would be like me, Dave Chappelle, the comedian, walking down the street in a cop uniform. Somebody might run up on me saying, "Oh, thank God. Officer, help us! Come on. They're over here. Help us!" "Oh-hoh! Just because I'm dressed this way does not make me a police officer!" See what I mean? All right, ladies, fine. You are not a whore. But you are wearing a whore's uniform. ("Dave Chappelle Whore Uniform")

Chappelle's use of the term "bitch" and the entire "whore's uniform" joke shows that most of his comedy is masculine and hierarchical.

Chappelle's use of the term, as well as his depiction of Black women on *Chappelle's Show*, both fit within his philosophy of race and reveals internal contradictions and inconsistencies in it. In Chappelle's racial hierarchy, no one has had it worse than Black men. He seems protective of that position and threatened when someone else might make a legitimate claim to that title. Consider how bell hooks' (2015) analysis, in *Ain't I a Woman?* of the fraught relationships between Black men and women who are jockeying for political and social recognition, applies to Chappelle. Writing on the link between sexism and racism, hooks makes the point that men, Black or White, benefit from the oppression of women. Keeping someone lower than you on the social ladder is one way to gain prestige. As hooks points out, "the black man who had seen himself as the loser in the all-male competitive struggle with white men for status and power could show a trump card – he was the 'real' man because he could control 'his' woman" (96). The struggle against racism, hooks observes, does not prevent one from absorbing "the same sexist socialization white men are inundated with" (102). Much of the way that women have been controlled has been sexual in nature: women have been devalued and degraded as, on the one hand, "loose" and licentious, and, on the other hand, available for male gratification. Chappelle's humor plays out many of these themes and for that reason he can be rightfully accused of denigrating women – and Black women in particular – who would also have a legitimate claim to make. Chappelle gets himself caught in this contradiction because in order to change the schema of his largely White, male audience, he has to position himself within that logic and speak from that position, so that it is easier for his White, male audience to identify with him.

Color-Blind Racism

The fact that Chappelle's audience is largely White gives him ample opportunity to point out that Blacks have had it worse than any other group in America. Quoting Michael Eric Dyson, Novotny Lawrence (2009) writes in "Comic Genius or Con Man?" that comedians like Chappelle who play the role of cultural critic help explore and explain the cultural contradictions of Black culture to the audience. Chappelle does do this but on a larger scale, explaining the contradictions that perpetuate unhealthy relations between different races. This puts Chappelle in the position of not just explaining Black culture to Whites but also the position of explaining aspects of Asian and Hispanic culture to Whites. Chappelle has been able to do this because he has been able to position himself as thoroughly immersed in Black culture, specifically hip-hop culture, but also as having credibility in the Asian community if only for the thin reasons that his wife is Filipina and he is a fan of the Wu Tang Clan.

Chappelle believes that people make choices and therefore have the opportunity to choose otherwise. This vague notion of free will allows Chappelle to mine those decisions for their logical consistencies and contradictions. Choice intersects with racial stereotypes in several ways that reveal another aspect of Chappelle's idea of race as culturally constructed. If behavior is a choice and stereotypes are behaviors that define a group and distinguish it from others, then the decision to perform a stereotype is a choice that the individual is making. Therefore, individuals are responsible for the choice to perform that particular stereotype and have brought the consequences of being seen and understood that way upon themselves. At the same time, the constructedness of race and the stereotypes that flow from it are, precisely because of their social construction, superficial. Chappelle seems to operate from an understanding of social construction that it is something others may believe about you but you do not have to believe about yourself (or perform). This gives him license to play with stereotypes: to mine them for laughter through their reiteration, through exaggeration, and by pointing out the contradiction that a stereotype, as socially constructed, should be taken seriously at all.

The twin ideas of personal responsibility for choice and the social constructedness of race are indicative of a post-racist (the view that society has solved or moved beyond racism) or a color-blind view. To be clear, Dave Chappelle is not post-racist or color-blind; he is the opposite of both. However, the way that he frames his social critique in terms of contradiction, fairness, and personal responsibility overlaps with many of the features of color-blind racism as defined by Eudardo Bonilla-Silva (2017) in *Racism Without Racists*. The overlap between Chappelle's moral worldview and features of color-blind racism are part of what makes Chappelle's comedy so complex and controversial, and this overlap is also how he leaves himself open to charges that he is victim blaming when he is, more often than not, operating on a different register.

Color-blind racism emerged in America in the 1960s with the shift away from the explicit racism of the Jim Crow era. The racism of the Jim Crow era (and before) is based on the belief that biological factors – like skin color – have psychological and moral meanings. For example, having black skin color was equated with low intelligence and aggressive sexual behavior. Color-blind racism shifts the explanation for educational, social, moral, and economic inequalities away from biology to culture, specifically, cultural attitudes toward education, labor, and progress that are internalized by individuals. If the racism of Jim Crow is buttressed by biological myths, color-blind racism is legitimated by cultural generalizations that softly, implicitly, otherize people of color and ultimately blames them for their marginalized social position (see Bonilla-Silva 2017, p. 3). Meghan Burke (2019) writes:

> The final core feature of colorblind racism is its ongoing use of racial stereotypes. This presents a paradox of sorts, given that colorblind racism is meant to deny racism. These stereotypes, however, are often presented as an objective measure of presumed reality (e.g. "Native Americans are alcoholics"), as something to be read positively (e.g. "Asian families teach the value of hard work and academic achievement"), or even sympathetically ... (e.g. "Black children can't succeed because of chaotic home lives"). This core feature allows us to understand how racial myths, racial codes, ... and racial storylines are deployed as a commonsense understanding of the contemporary racial landscape, working together ... to advance racism by denying its legacy in bias and intent. (p. 5)

The shift away from racism rooted in biology is accomplished by the move to view race as socially constructed. When race is a social group, not a biological category or genetic distinction, race becomes plastic but also self-reinforcing, subject to political and social forces (see Lopez 1995, p. 193). Writing in "The Social Construction of Race" Lopez says that "races are categories of difference which exist only in society: they are produced by myriad conflicting social forces; they overlap and inform other social categories; they are fluid rather than static and fixed; and they make sense only in relationship to other racial categories, having no meaningful independent existence" (p. 199).

The movement of race from biology to culture allows the connection between morphological differences and psychology and behavior to take on any meaning that the dominant group wants to ascribe to those differences. This is how stereotypes form, are perpetuated, and change over time: a behavior is attributed to a group not because of what that group looks like but because of how the dominant group is advantaged by perpetuating that stereotype. Those stereotypes shift and change over time, always to the benefit of the dominant group and at the expense of the marginalized group. This is still racism because it fabricates harmful untruths about a class of people that create division, marginalization, and oppression. In Bonilla-Silva's (2017) words, this new racism "reproduces racial domination mostly through subtle and covert practices that are often institutionalized, defended, with coded language ("*those* urban people"), and bonded by the racial ideology of color-blind racism" (p. 206, emphasis in original). Chappelle also seems to embody what Meghan Burke (2019) points out in *Colorblind*: that Black Americans recognize the truth of systemic racism but also tend to adopt "individually focused explanations for success, which is central to colorblindness" because they may "have absorbed some of the biases that are socialized in a skewed media system and its narrow portrayals of Black Americans, and/or may still attribute individual missteps to the influence of culture" (pp. 80, 83).

Color-blind racism is perpetuated by what is considered commonsense understandings of group behaviors and dynamics. These commonsense understandings are ideologies of race that support the status quo. Chappelle's comedy is an interrogation of the White status quo that has marginalized Black men (most of all) and everyone else (to varying degrees). The status quo that Chappelle is challenging is a White habitus, defined by Bonilla-Silva (2017) as "a racialized, uninterrupted socialization process that *conditions* and *creates* whites' racial taste, perceptions, feelings, and emotions and their views on racial matters" (p. 121, emphasis in original). The White habitus consists of (supposed) commonsense attitudes about other races that advantage White people. The form that this advantage takes are, first, claims of cultural, historical, political, social, and religious superiority of traditions and institutions created by White people; second, is the reiteration of these claims through education, law, and culture at the expense of other histories, traditions, religions, philosophies, or ways of knowing. Working from within the White habitus, if only to show its contradictions, Chappelle has adopted one of its dominant features: a belief in liberal individualism that separates the individual from the limitations imposed by their socioeconomic status and location and makes free choice the determining factor in evaluating a person's actions. In the White habitus, every person has an equal opportunity to succeed. Success and failure are not determined by institutional advantages or disadvantages but by individual virtues such as determination and resolve. Nobody can tell anyone else what to do, but having had the freedom to choose otherwise and opportunity to act without hindrances, people can be held accountable for their actions, credited for their successes, and blamed for their failures.

The White habitus that most of his audience exists in is largely free from interracial contact; this means that Chappelle has an outsized influence on how his audience sees and understands Black culture. Segregation in housing, education, and in social experiences means that White people do not engage with people of color at all, or often enough, to understand their experience of racism. Their view – both of themselves and of people of color – becomes how they see the world, and their privileged position allows them to establish the White perspective as the norm while other perspectives are marginalized as abnormal. And as Bonilla-Silva (2017) points out, "the more distant the group in question is from the white 'norm,' other things being equal, the more negative whites will view the group" (p. 140). This logic is on display in Chappelle's joke about celebrity chef and media personality Anthony Bourdain that opens *Sticks and Stones* (see below) and other moments in Chappelle's comedy. Another example is in the opening of *Equanimity* where Chappelle is discussing his upbringing:

> You know, when I was growing up, I was probably about eight years old, and at the time, we were living in Silver Spring. Yeah. Yes. Common misconception about me and DC, a lot of people think I'm from the "hood". That's not true. But I never bothered to correct anybody... because I wanted the streets to embrace me. As a matter of fact, I kept it up as a ruse. Like sometimes I'll hang out with rappers like Nas and them, and these motherfuckers start talking about the projects. "Yo, it was wild in the PJs, yo." And I'll be like, "Word, [n-slur], word." But I don't know. I have no idea. My parents did just well enough so that I could grow up poor around white people. To be honest, when Nas and them talk about the projects, [n-slur], I used to get jealous. Because it sounded fun. Everybody in the projects was poor, and that's fair. But if you were poor in Silver Spring, [n-slur], it felt like it was only happening to you. Nas does not know the pain... of that first sleepover at a white friend's house. When you come back home on Sunday and just look at your parents like... "Y'all need to step your game up. Everything at Timmy's house works." Remember the first time you saw that? The cold winter and to be at a white friend's house and see them motherfuckers in their living room without their coats on? (*Equanimity* 3:38–5:30)

Chappelle will go on to say that after being invited over for dinner, he has to feign calling his mother for permission (when, in reality, he has not seen her for several days because she was busy working multiple jobs). However, missing from that joke and his memory of growing up poor in Maryland is any reference to the structural barriers that created the poverty he grew up in and why his mother, who despite working several jobs, did not earn enough to lift the family out of poverty. Chappelle saying that his parents need to step their game up either repeats or mocks the liberal fantasy that work is available to all who want it; those without work or success just need to try harder; ultimately the audience has to decide which side of the joke Chappelle is on; however, given the repetition of theme of personal responsibility, it is likely that he is repeating the idea that work is available to all who want it.

Similar to how Chappelle's attitude has shifted toward reducing the undecidability in some of his humor by telling his audience how they should feel about a joke, there is an evolution in his comedy from *Chappelle's Show* to his more recent stand-up sketches. In *Chappelle's Show*, the awareness of the constructedness of race is liberating and playful. Since race and the stereotypes that accompany it are not real, no one has to take them seriously; they can be played with, embraced, and exaggerated. The joke is on anyone who thinks that race and stereotypes are still real.

As Bao (2009) points out, Chappelle has been able to demonstrate "both the performative nature of race and the ridiculousness of essentializing race" (p. 175). Several sketches revel in this freedom, but no sketch reveals the fluidity of race more than "The Racial Draft." In this sketch, the arbitrariness of race is revealed and celebrated when Tiger Woods becomes officially Black instead of bi-racial ("So long fried rice, hello fried chicken!"), Colin Powell and Condoleezza Rice can be drafted by the White delegation, OJ Simpson is traded from the Whites and is "Black again," and the Asian delegation drafts the entire Wu Tang Clan. Chappelle's show is what Gamber (2009) calls "a festival of misrule" in which "all of the usual rules that govern racial categorization and interaction is suspended" (p. 158). The racial draft is an example of a younger Chappelle who is more comfortable disrupting stereotypes and social meanings. More contemporary examples show that Chappelle has soured on his idea that stereotypes can be played with; despite his earlier attempts at disrupting them, he sees stereotypes as still unfairly benefitting Whites and marginalizing people of color: he now recognizes that just playfully calling attention to the social constructedness of race is not enough.

The change in Chappelle's attitude over time can be accounted for by resignation: the adoption of the perspective that race is socially constructed did not have the liberating effect that Chappelle thought it would. Despite some progress in media representation and the election of Barack Obama, what Bao (2009) would call the "racial epidermal schema" has never been left behind:

> Occurring within a white supremacist society, this "schema" dictates that a non-white person's skin color is a way of seemingly knowing the individual by simply assigning her to a racial collective and reducing her existence to a host of stereotypes, thereby robbing the individual of their personhood. (p. 172)

Instead, racial stereotypes became more reified and impossible to escape. Chappelle still tells jokes from the perspective that race is constructed, but he is now more upfront and direct in his attitude that it is constructed by, and for the benefit of, Whites. Where Black comedians from previous generations have had a clearer understanding of race, race relations, and racism to work with, the era of colorblind racism that Chappelle navigates requires that he define and explain what racism is, how racism works, and then point out what is wrong with it. So, where Bambi Haggins (2007) writes that Black comedy has always overtly and covertly "explored the trials, tribulations, and triumphs of African American communities," Chappelle has had to work in a context where Blacks are seen as responsible for their own trials and tribulations and where the perception of success is always based on criteria that White people think are meaningful and important to the Black community (p. 2). Chappelle wades into this post-racial era and uses humor to remind his audience that racism is still a pervasive force in society, even if only part of his audience would agree with that sentiment. Those members of his audience who have been racialized as White are more likely to see racism as a thing of the past and wonder why Chappelle (and others) keep bringing it up. For example, *The Cosby Show* portrayed Black success as a Black family achieving the American dream of educational achievement leading to economic security. The possibility of that sort of success, and its representation on television, has been enough to make people believe that racism is no longer a potent force in society. Chappelle takes a different approach. Chappelle uses misdirection and hyperbole to show that racist attitudes and stereotypes are ridiculous and should be given up; anyone who performs them is just playing and anyone who believes them is foolish. No one could logically believe that paying Blacks reparations for slavery would result in 800 record labels being started in 1 hour, the price of oil plummeting to $1.50 a barrel, the price of a bucket of chicken soaring to over $600, and 3 million Escalade trucks being sold in an afternoon. Chappelle's deft use of misdirection and hyperbole make the point better than if he were saying it straight:

> The pleasure of misdirection is twofold: the unanticipated shift from what appears to be positivist rhetoric of self-determination to a blatant assertion of the untenable position for black kids in the ghetto is a tried-and-true Chappelle comic device ... and speaks to the fact that the civil rights era rhetoric (as enunciated by Cosby), on some level, does not and cannot necessarily apply in the lived experiences of black urban youth today ... By forcing audiences to interrogate the interconnectedness of a multiplicity of factors from daily life, from media, from our own long held societal assumptions—about race, class, and ethnicity – Chappelle provokes the audience and puts our own notions of community, identity, and of course, race on the discursive table. (Haggins 2007, pp. 202–204)

Haggins' point is that Chappelle performs this perspective by being "aware of the state of race relations but not necessarily determined by them," which is the attitude displayed by post-racist/color-blind Whites. They too believe that there is racism but, first, that people of color need to move past it, and second, that they have individually risen above whatever societal racism may still exist even if others, or society in general, has not (Haggins 2007, p. 193). But this is a strategy to preserve their privileged social position, one that Chappelle wants to reveal the contradictions of. If color-blind racism rests on liberal ideas (1) of equal opportunity for those willing to work and (2) that every person has equal access to the job market through freely and equally available educational opportunities, then Chappelle wants to turn that logic on its head, revealing how unequal expectations about life, education, and success make claims that America is a post-racist and color-blind society impossible to defend.

One example of the more mature Chappelle tackling the idea that racism is still pervasive in society and that stereotypes remain to the advantage of Whites is the opening of Chappelle's most recent Netflix special, *Sticks and Stones*. The joke reveals that the playful attitude and joy with which he used to approach stereotypes has been replaced by frustration and resentment that these double standards still exist. The joke is a comparison between the suicide of Anthony Bourdain and the persistence of a childhood friend who Chappelle would later learn was a manager at a Foot Locker. He begins with a serious tone and then switches to an incredulous one:

> Good people of Atlanta, we must never forget . . . that Anthony Bourdain . . . Yeah! . . . killed himself. Anthony Bourdain had the greatest job that show business ever produced. This [n-slur] flew around the world . . . and ate delicious meals with outstanding people. That man with that job hung himself in a luxury suite in France. (*Sticks and Stones* 1:25–1:58)

Chappelle continues the joke by telling the story of an academically gifted friend who, despite being from a bad neighborhood, attended college and law school. Chappelle is leaning into audience assumptions about what types of success are available to Black males from bad neighborhoods, an assumption he needs his audience to entertain if he is going to make his point. It was in law school that Chappelle's friend met someone, fell in love, and married her (despite Chappelle's advice to wait until later):

> But he's in love. He didn't listen to me. He married her while he was in law school, and sadly, they got divorced, while he was in law school. He was a street [n-slur] from the hood. This man had nothing . . . and that bitch took half of that. And then, I just never saw him again for years, and then, two years ago, I was home in DC doing some shoppin', tryin' to buy my sons some socks at Foot Locker. I go to Foot Locker. Guess who's the manager? That [n-slur]. Dressed like a referee, the whole shit. This motherfucker is 45 years old! We went out drinking that night just tryin' to catch up, and . . . and he told me. He said he's been living with his mother for, like, ten years, just trying to get back on his feet. But that's not the point of the story. The point of the story is . . . never occurred to this [n-slur] to kill himself. He's alive and well in D.C. I even suggested to him that he should try it out. Like, "I don't know, maybe . . ." (*Sticks and Stones* 2:58–4:24)

If the joke were about his friend, it would be fair to criticize Chappelle for perpetuating stereotypes about what types of successes are available to Black men: having ignored sound, reasonable advice, his friend earned his misfortune. Further, having lost his opportunity to have more, he deserves less and should be happy with what he has. The punch line suggests that having fallen so far, maybe death is a better option! But the joke is not about his friend; the joke is about how Anthony Bourdain's suicide is framed as a tragedy but the decline and struggle of Chappelle's friend is not. Chappelle's perspective (which discounts the role of mental illness in suicide) is that Anthony Bourdain had it all and it was not enough; Chappelle's friend was on his way toward professional, financial, and societal success, lost it, and could never get it back. It is a joke about how the worlds that Whites and Blacks live in have different standards for success and failure. The surface level reading of the joke makes Chappelle's friend the fool for not wanting more; a deeper analysis reveals Chappelle's attitude that there is a double standard that applies to Whites and Blacks: if his friend could find meaning and value as a manager of a Foot Locker, especially after how far that career was from where he was heading, why is Anthony Bourdain's death a tragedy? Shouldn't Bourdain's life have been enough to overcome whatever troubles he had? Chappelle is pointing out the double standard that we hold White and Black lives to. This requires the audience to pause for a second and see the world the way that Chappelle does, something Yates (2009) suggests (in "When Keeping It Real Goes Right") that Chappelle is adept at (see Yates, p. 151). Chappelle wants to negate the White vista as much as he wants to validate a

Black one. By suggesting that his friend consider suicide Chappelle is speaking from inside the White habitus, revealing its disregard for Black lives, holding them back by imposing impossibly high standards they cannot reach.

For those who see Chappelle educating his audiences on the reality of race relations in America, his humor is a window through which to see experiences they do not have access to or avoid. In order to change the White perspective, Chappelle has to operate from inside of the White habitus in order to create exaggerations that defy logic (see Gray et al. 2009, p. 16). Writing in "Black Humor as Self-Affirmation," Bowles (1994) sees it as the role of the Black comedian to "stir audiences into seeing situations which they choose not to want to see" (p. 5). Haggins (2007) sees Chappelle as playing with his audience, almost taunting them, "encouraging, and in some instances demanding that the audience own up to its own complicity in the sociopolitical absurdities of post-civil right era American consciousness" (p. 199). For his Black audience members, Chappelle is providing an opportunity to laugh (maybe laugh so they do not cry) at their situation so that they find solidarity and community in their experiences. Chappelle's jokes about growing up Black and poor are as much catharsis as they are self-defining. At the same time, there is a real risk that Chappelle's audience could miss the point of his joke and leave with the impression that Black people are lazy and have earned their poverty. Constance Bailey (2012) makes the point that even if what Chappelle is doing is an act of resistance against White hegemonic norms, "white audiences have fetishized Chappelle and other Black comics because it reinscribes their own sense of power" (p. 261). So, where Chappelle has been criticized for reiterating harmful stereotypes about Blacks in order to get a laugh from his largely White audience, it is necessary to situate those critiques within the racial frame that he is telling those jokes. Telling them from within the frame of color-blind racism, even to point out the contradictions and illogic of it, runs the risk of reiterating and reinforcing that logic in the audience. Ultimately, as Gray II and Putnam (2009) conclude, "Chappelle's humor reveals that racism is still alive and well in our society. However, the comedian also demonstrates that humor can also exploit this fact and serve as a way to discuss, to analyze, and to critique such ways of thinking" (p. 28).

Conclusion

When accepting the award for the Mark Twain Prize in American Humor, Chappelle extolled the virtues of American stand-up comedy. He is confident that every opinion in the country is represented on the stage. He teases the audience that the comedian telling jokes about racism on the stage has said some racist shit when hanging out with other comedians, saying "that motherfucker means that shit." He redeems comedians by pointing out a trait they possess that Chappelle sees lacking in society at large: the comedian's ability to talk it out with people who have a like-minded attitude about the relationship between comedy and truth-telling:

There's something so true about this genre, when done correctly. That I will fight anybody that gets in a true practitioner of this art form's way because I know you're wrong. This is the truth and you are obstructing it. I'm not talking about the content, I'm talking about the art form. Do you understand? Do we have an agreement? (*Dave Chappelle: The Kennedy Center Mark Twain Prize for American Humor* 1:19:12–1:19:34)

The structure of the joke is one of the reasons why comedians can tell difficult truths. They can speak truth to power because power is the dominant schema and comedy is the contradiction that lets truth in, but with laughter. This is why comedians have the reputation as modern-day prophets, philosophers, or organic intellectuals.

[They] challenge the stereotypes and common sense beliefs held about their respective ethnic groups. At the same time, they communicate to their own communities the worldviews expressed by the ruling class in order to achieve, through parody and satire, a relational equilibrium between both sectors of influence. (Amarasingam 2009, p. 120)

Chappelle's high-wire act is not without risks, as it looks like Chappelle is reiterating harmful stereotypes about Blacks in order to generate laughter. Chappelle might intend that laughter to be painfully funny to the audience; too often that laughter is painful to the butt of the joke. Some critics agree: Katherine Lee (2009), in "When Keeping it Real Goes Wrong," argues that Chappelle is guilty of perpetuating reductive images of Blacks that promote racist ideology. She argues that if Chappelle were sincere in his desire to expose and eliminate these contradictions, his work would more obviously "serve a corrective and emancipatory function, dismantling stereotypes and forwarding socially prescriptive messages" (p. 128).

It was the concern that he was on the wrong side of that conversation, and was perpetuating harmful stereotypes about Blacks, that made him leave *Chappelle's Show*. Bao (2009) sums up Chappelle's concerns about the effects his show was having on race relations: "For those who did not comprehend the message behind the satire, they at best just missed his point and at worst hijacked Chappelle's comedy to reinforce racial hierarchies and reify racist stereotypes" (p. 179). So, when people yelled, "I'm Rick James, bitch!" or "I'm rich, biatch!" or even the n-slur, "without any awareness of its satirical meaning," they were making Chappelle "a racial caricature of his own parody of degrading representations of blackness in order to co-opt the stereotypes" for self-serving purposes (p. 179). Chappelle's decision to reject a reported $30 million contract for the third season of the show has been pored over. Though it took him 12 years to feel like he had come all the way back from that decision, walking away from that much money made Chappelle come across as more authentic and allows him, to this day, to be a more effective truth-teller. For walking away at the height of his fame and turning down that much money, Chappelle is better able to position himself as a truth-teller willing to risk the consequences of saying what he thinks.

Saying that Dave Chappelle has figured out a formula for how to marry moments of incongruity with incisive observations about race and racism is not meant to diminish either his skills as a comedian or as a social critic speaking difficult truths about race. Chappelle has earned his reputation as one of the greatest comedians of all time, placing him in a pantheon with Lenny Bruce, Richard Pryor, Moms Mabley, and Eddie Murphy (to name just a few). As he has grown as a comedian, he has accepted the responsibility as one of America's "grios" – storytellers and keeper of traditions – by reminding his audience that America's stories and traditions are steeped in racism and White privilege. He reminds his audience of the contradictions in the American dream, though he would do better if he were more aware of the contradictions in his own logic regarding women and individuals in other marginalized communities. While he genuinely wants an end to all forms of discrimination and oppression, his neoliberal tendencies make it difficult for him to not blame people for the situation they find themselves in. He does not blame Black men for the situation in which they find themselves, but does not extend the same grace to other groups. Unable to see such contradictions and blindspots in his own thinking, but desperate for a better future for those who have suffered so much, might make Dave Chappelle the most American philosopher of race of all.

The authors would like to thank Ellie Jones and Andrew Ball for their helpful comments on previous versions of this chapter. Also, Dr. Sarah Roth for her comments and feedback and also for creating an encouraging an open atmosphere where these sorts of collaborations can occur and these topics can be researched and discussed. Lastly, the handbook's editors Johnson and Lay; their thoughtful feedback and critiques made this a much better chapter.

References

Amarasingam, Amarnath. 2009. Gramsci, selling out, and the politics of race loyalty. In *The comedy of dave chappelle: Critical essays*, ed. K.A. Wisniewski, 115–126. Jefferson: McFarland & Co.

Bailey, Constance. 2012. Fight the Power: African American Humor as a discourse of resistance. *Western Journal of Black Studies* 36 (4, Winter): 253–263.

Bao, Chiwen. 2009. Haunted: Dave chappelle's radical racial politics in the context of co-opted blackness. In *The comedy of dave chappelle: Critical essays*, ed. K.A. Wisniewski, 167–183. Jefferson: McFarland & Co.

Bonilla-Silva, Eduardo. 2017. *Racism without racists*. Lanham: Rowman & Littlefield Publishers.

Bowles, Dorcas D. "Black humor as self-affirmation." Journal of Multicultural Social Work, vol. 3, no. 2, Mar. 1994, pp. 1–9.

Burke, Meghan. 2019. *Colorblind racism*. Medford: Polity Press.

Cumbo, Andrea. 2009. The comedian is a 'Man': Gender performance in the comedy of dave chappelle. In *The comedy of dave chappelle: Critical essays*, ed. K.A. Wisniewski. Jefferson: McFarland & Co.

"Dave Chappelle." *Inside the Actors Studio*, performance by James Lipton, and Dave Chappelle, season 12, episode 11, 12 Feb. 2006. https://www.metatube.com/en/videos/78229/Inside-The-Actors-Studio-Dave-Chappelle/

Dave Chappelle: The Kennedy center mark twain prize for American humor. Directed by Chris Robinson, Done and Dusted Productions; WETA, 2020. Netflix.

"Dave Chappelle Whore Uniform." *Youtube*, uploaded by Jtoven1, 25 October 2012. https://www.youtube.com/watch?v=J7QNw1LRJv4

Dave Chappelle: Deep in the heart of texas: Dave chappelle live at Austin City limits. Directed by Stan Lathan, performance by Dave Chappelle, Netflix studios. 2017. Netflix.

Dave Chappelle: Equanimity & the bird revelation. Directed by Stan Lathan, performance by Dave Chappelle, Netflix Studios, 2017. Netflix.

Dave Chappelle: Sticks and stones. Directed by Stan Lathan, performance by Dave Chappelle, Pilot Boy Production, 2019. Netflix.

"Frontline: Clayton Bigsby." *Chappelle's Show*. Created by Neal Brennan and Dave Chappelle, season 1, episode 1, Marobru Inc, 2003.

Gamber, Francesca. 2009. White people, run for cover. In *The comedy of dave chappelle: Critical essays*, ed. K.A. Wisniewski, 156–166. Jefferson: McFarland & Co.

Gillota, David. 2019. Reckless talk: Exploration and contradiction in dave chappelle's recent stand-up comedy. *Studies in Popular Culture* 42 (1, Fall): 1–22.

Gray, I.I., J. Richard, et al. 2009. Exploring niggerdom. In *The comedy of dave chappelle: Critical essays*, ed. K.A. Wisniewski, 15–30. Jefferson: McFarland & Co.

Haggins, Bambi. 2007. *Laughing mad: The black comic persona in post-soul America*. Piscataway: Rutgers University Press.

hooks, bell. 2015. *Ain't I a woman: Black women and feminism*. New York: Routledge.

Lawrence, Novotny. 2009. Comic genius or con man? In *The comedy of dave chappelle: Critical essays*, ed. K.A. Wisniewski, 31–46. Jefferson: McFarland & Co.

Lee, Katherine. 2009. When keeping it real goes wrong. In *The comedy of dave chappelle: Critical essays*, ed. K.A. Wisniewski. Jefferson: McFarland & Co.

Lopez, Ian F. Haney. 1995. The social construction of race. In *Critical race theory: The cutting edge*, ed. Richard Delgado, 191–203. Philadelphia: Temple University Press.

Martin, Rod A. 2007. *The psychology of humor: An integrative approach*. Burlington: Elsevier Academic Press.

"Racial Draft." 2004. *Chappelle's Show*. Created by Neal Brennan and Dave Chappelle, season 2, episode 1, Marobru Inc.

"Reparations." 2003. *Chappelle's Show*. Created by Neal Brennan and Dave Chappelle, season 1, episode 4, Marobru Inc.

Wisniewski, K.A., ed. 2009. *The comedy of dave chappelle: Critical essays*. Jefferson: McFarland & Co.

Yates, Kimberley A. 2009. When 'Keeping it real' goes right. In *The comedy of dave chappelle: Critical essays*, ed. K.A. Wisniewski, 139–155. Jefferson: McFarland & Co.

Ricky Gervais as Philosopher: The Comedy of Alienation

72

Catherine Villanueva Gardner

Contents

Introduction	1670
Gervais' Comedy	1670
Marx on Alienation	1671
Aspect One: Alienation from the Product of Labor	1673
Aspect Two: Alienation from the Activity of Labor	1674
Aspect Three: Alienation from the Self or Species	1676
Aspect Four: Alienation from Others	1678
Derek – Transcendence of Alienation	1679
Alienation and Religion	1680
Conclusion	1683
References	1683

Abstract

The humor of the television series (*The Office*, *Extras*, *Derek*, *After Life*) of Ricky Gervais, the British comedian, is often considered an example of the twenty-first century genre of "cringe comedy," which plays on the darkness and anxieties of living in the modern world. I will argue, however, that Gervais' work is best described as "the comedy of alienation," with alienation understood in the Marxist sense – as the estrangement or splintering of humans from their work, themselves, and each other, which is caused by capitalist society. Through each of his comedy series, Gervais uncovers the capitalist roots of society and reveals and criticizes the effects alienation has on the members of that society. Not only does Gervais' work serve to illustrate Marx's account of alienation under capitalism, but Marx's account, in its turn, can show why Gervais' work is funny, even if painfully so.

C. V. Gardner (✉)
University of Massachusetts Dartmouth, North Dartmouth, MA, USA
e-mail: cgardner@umassd.edu

© Springer Nature Switzerland AG 2024
D. K. Johnson et al. (eds.), *The Palgrave Handbook of Popular Culture as Philosophy*,
https://doi.org/10.1007/978-3-031-24685-2_73

Keywords

Alienation · Atheism · Capitalism · Gervais, Ricky (1961–) · Labor/Work · Marx, Karl (1818–1883) · Radical Humor

Introduction

Ricky Gervais (1961–) is a British comedian who studied philosophy at the University of London. Gervais' early comedy television series, such as *The Office* and *Extras*, were initially applauded as cutting-edge examples of the so-called "cringe comedy," alongside *Curb Your Enthusiasm* and *Da Ali G Show*. Even though most comedy finds its roots in humiliation or discomfort (whether it is slapstick or satire), this new comedy genre plays on the darkness and anxieties of living in the modern world, which range from avoiding political incorrectness to acceptance of our own mortality. However, Gervais's comedy is becoming increasingly described as "alienating" for such characters as the intellectually challenged Derek of the television series of the same name, or for Gervais' critique of the audience during his 2020 Golden Globes hosting. For example, at the Golden Globes, Gervais gave an opening speech in which he lampooned individual members of the audience, and he also – and this was where the accusations of alienation came in – burst the pretensions of those award winners who use their acceptance speech as a platform for a political speech: "You're in no position to lecture the public about anything. You know nothing about the real world. Most of you spent less time in school than Greta Thunberg" (Golden Globes, Monologue).

There is certainly no doubt that Gervais's comedy is becoming more painful to watch; *Derek* (in which the main character appears to be developmentally disabled) and *After Life* (in which the protagonist Tony copes with the death of his spouse) are not standard television fodder, and these two series will be explored further later. But is the viewer *being* alienated, whether intentionally or unintentionally? Or, rather, is Gervais's comedy instead *about* alienation, specifically alienation under capitalism? To ask the question another way: Is Gervais alienating his audience, or is he using his comedy to show us how we are alienated in the political sense of the nineteenth-century philosopher Karl Marx? I will argue that it is the latter. Moreover, unlike most of the other chapters here on comedians, I am going to focus on the shows Gervais helped write and produce (as opposed to his standup) as their format – long narrative buildup and character development – allows for an analysis of alienation.

Gervais' Comedy

In order to answer this question, we need first to disentangle and define what is meant by "alienation." In non-philosophical terms, alienation is often used to signal a lack of sympathy or estrangement. This is not the case for Gervais; *surely, it is quite the opposite*. In bringing down Hollywood royalty, Gervais is speaking sympathetically to us: the majority, the people who purchase the cinema tickets. Gervais is instead addressing the Marxist concept of alienation in its different aspects throughout his work. In essence, alienation is the problematic separation of a subject (in this case a self or person) and an object that should belong together. In the case of Marxist alienation – as will be seen in the next section – it has four interconnected aspects.

There have been commentaries on Ricky Gervais's work – especially the television series *The Office* and *Derek* – that identify them as critiques of capitalism; for example, Tony McKenna claims that *Derek* provides "a trenchant critique of capitalism from the purview of a revolutionary humanism" (McKenna 2015, p. 201). However, such commentaries do little to explain *why* Gervais's work is simultaneously both funny and philosophical. Instead, Gervais's major works – *The Office*, *Extras*, *Derek*, and *After Life* – can all be seen as illustrative exemplars of Karl Marx's "theory of alienation." (The focus in this article is only on work written by Gervais.) Moreover, once framed within an understanding of this theory, we can comprehend just why Gervais is so bitterly funny and why his work continues to push accepted social boundaries for comedy.

According to Norman Malcolm in his biography of philosopher Ludwig Wittgenstein, Wittgenstein once said that "a serious and good philosophical work could be written consisting entirely of jokes" (Malcolm 1984, pp. 27–28). This comment has often been misunderstood as an encouragement to hunt for jokes about philosophy or to analyze Wittgenstein's view of humor; however, Wittgenstein's comment should instead be framed within the context of his philosophical work on understanding: if you laugh (get the joke), then you have understood the philosophical issue. Similarly, if you laugh at Gervais' comedy, then you have understood the philosophical issue. Contemporary Marxist philosopher Bertell Ollman's comments on "radical jokes" may help here. To paraphrase Ollman, "radical" means to get at the roots of our capitalist society and thus "radical jokes" are those that uncover previously unrecognized effects of capitalist society on our lives. In this way, Gervais' comedy is not just cringe comedy but "the comedy of alienation": it works to illustrate Marx's account of alienation under capitalism, but also Marx's account of alienation, in its turn, explains why Gervais' works are so funny or – more accurately – tragicomic: a blend of the funny with tragedy. To understand why, we need to first understand what Marx said about alienation, before we go on to see how Gervais' work expresses it.

Marx on Alienation

Many of us have experienced the subjective feeling of alienation: a sense of estrangement from the world we live in. For families, ritualistic shopping at megastores has become a substitution for other forms of social behavior and interaction, with consumers often able to purchase guns, liquor, and patio sets around the clock. During the Covid-19 pandemic, social distancing, quarantines, and remote meetings all but guaranteed this feeling of estrangement. However, alienation for the political philosopher Marx is more than a subjective feeling; for Marx, alienation is a specific kind of social ill that we suffer from under capitalism, in essence, the estrangement of subject and object when they should belong together.

"Alienation," in Marx's writings, is the most familiar of the standard English translations of both *Entfremdung* and *Entäußerung*. Sean Sayers, a twentieth-century interpreter of Marx, states that, according to the Hungarian Marxist philosopher György Lukács, "these terms were originally the German translations of the English eighteenth century word 'alienation' used in an economic or legal sense to mean the sale of a commodity or relinquishment of freedom" (Sayers 2011, p. ix).

The term alienation has become part of our own modern discourse, but more often than not it is used interchangeably with a general sense of meaninglessness or disaffection; for example, "alienation" is used to describe punk rock or other youth movements in Thatcherite Britain. Yet, as Sean Sayers notes, Marx's own theoretical use of the term is "precise and specific" (Sayers 2011, p. x).

We typically think of Marx as focusing on nonhuman elements of life under capitalism, such as mode of production, for the organization of his theory; however, as Bertell Ollman notes in *Alienation: Marx's conception of man in capitalist society*, Marx's "theory of alienation places the acting and acted upon individual in the center of this account" (Ollman 1976, p. xi). Ollman elaborates further in Chapter 18 of *Alienation* that "The theory of alienation is the intellectual construct in which Marx displays the devastating effect of capitalist production on human beings, on their physical and mental states and on the social processes of which they are a part" (Ollman 1976, p. 131). (Although Marx's focus is on the proletariat, the capitalist – as human being – is also subject to alienation, albeit differently from the worker)

Under capitalist production, man is separated from his work and its products. Man works for wages to survive; he does not choose what he does or what happens to the product of his labor. He is also separated from his fellow men, experiencing his relationship to them as one of competition (for wage-work) and hostility (due to that competition). Thus, estranged from these elements of his material world, alienated man becomes little more than an abstraction: "Alienated man is an abstraction because he has lost touch with all human specificity. He has been reduced to performing undifferentiated work on humanly indistinguishable objects among people deprived of their human variety and compassion" (Ollman 1976, p. 134).

In this way, alienation, according to Marx, is not simply a generalized concept or feeling. Rather, alienation is the rupture and separation of human nature. In the *Economic and Philosophical Manuscripts of 1844*, Marx identifies four main, interconnected, aspects of alienation experienced within capitalist society that extend to cover the whole of human existence: man's relations to product, to productive activity, to our species-essence/human essence, and to others. It should be noted that even though alienation is a concept associated with Marx's early work (1840s and 1850s), the concept did not disappear from his philosophy in later years; rather, it became reconceptualized into the themes of commodity fetishism and machine-labor. Alienation is part of capitalism, even if Marx no longer explicitly discusses it in later works.

Aspect One: Alienation from the Product of Labor

The Office (first broadcast in 2001) is perhaps the best known of Gervais' television series. It is a day-to-day "mockumentary" sitcom set in the Wernham Hogg paper company run by David Brent (played by Gervais), a breathtakingly clueless manager desperate for validation from his employees. Even though not all of Gervais's Wernham Hogg workers produce commodities in the classical sense, much of what Marx has to say about production and labor is appropriate and thus the series can be analyzed through the lens of Marxist alienation. *The Office* provides an illustrative example of the first aspect of Marxist alienation: alienation from the product of labor.

Under the capitalist system workers only own their own ability to labor. They do not own the tools, the products, or the materials from the which the products are formed. Indeed, according to Marx, the worker becomes a commodity themselves: "the worker sinks to the level of a commodity and becomes indeed the most wretched of commodities" (Marx 1959, p. 28). Labor produces commodities, but under capitalism it produces both itself and the worker as commodities. The more the worker produces and the more effort they put into this work, the more powerful the alien world of commodities becomes. In tandem, the inner world of the worker becomes increasingly impoverished as they have fewer things they can call their own. "The *alienation* of the worker in his product means not only that his labor becomes an object, an *external* existence, but that it exists *outside him*, independently, as something alien to him...It means that the life which he has conferred on the object confronts him as something hostile and alien" (Marx 1959, p. 29). In this way the worker experiences the product of his/her labor as *"something alien"* (Marx 1959, p. 29).

Most of the main workers at Wernham Hogg sell paper or assist with selling paper (for example, the accountants); they do not actually make the paper. As wage-laborers, they are further alienated from their product in that they cannot use paper to survive (they cannot eat it or wear it) or to generate their own product. In doing this work they are commodified, ultimately reduced to the amount of the sales they generate. In fact, it is no surprise that the top salesman – Chris Finch – is grossly sexist, treating women as trophies and objectifying them, in a reflection of a commodified and competitive world that is all he knows.

The character of David Brent would like to believe he is a (somehow) beloved part of the owner class and that he is also an entertainer-artist, but his internal world is perhaps the most impoverished, with his dreams of being a pop star and his banal attempts at dispensing philosophical wisdom. The character of Tim lives with his parents and is often the butt of the cruel humor of people like alpha male salesman Chris Finch. Tim recognizes how impoverished his own existence is; something brought home to him on his 30th birthday when he receives only two presents, both useless: a hat-radio from his mother and a giant inflatable penis from his fellow workers. Tim works to earn money to spend socializing with the other workers (who are not really friends) in tacky nightclubs in Slough in order to cope with his pointless job. However, Tim does not have the courage to leave Wernham Hogg and change his life. In many ways, Tim is the most crushed by the system, whereas David Brent is so self-deluding that he does not understand how crushed he is.

In this way, *The Office* provides a way of illustrating and explaining one aspect of Marx's account of alienation. But what makes *The Office* so funny? Certainly, the cringe-comedy aspects and the slapstick moments are enjoyable (in a sense!). But Gervais is also encouraging us to laugh at alienated labor under capitalism. In any other show, whether drama or comedy, the character of Tim would simply be portrayed as sweetly endearing, with his unrequited crush on the receptionist Dawn. However, Tim also provides a gently sarcastic "Greek Chorus" of commentary on the alienation of life at Wernham Hogg, mainly for the documentary camera, but sometimes for the private amusement of Dawn and himself. Frequently, Tim functions as a provocateur, encouraging David Brent to go to extremes or taunting his co-worker Gareth Keenan. In so doing, Tim is a puppeteer for our amusement, but it is the alienation of Brent's and Gareth's lives that he is showcasing for our amusement. Tim hides Gareth's desk equipment, a harmless practical joke, but Tim knows that the joke will reinforce Gareth's sense of powerlessness over his work and Gareth's secret concern that he cannot actually do the work. In encouraging Brent to live out his entertainer-artist fantasies, Tim shows us how much Brent needs these fantasies to avoid recognition of his own alienation.

Aspect Two: Alienation from the Activity of Labor

Marx states in the *1844 Manuscripts*:

> First, the fact that labor is *external* to the worker, i.e., it does not belong to his essential being; that in his work, therefore, he does not affirm himself but denies himself, does not feel content but unhappy, does not develop freely his physical and mental energy but mortifies his body and ruins his mind. The worker therefore only feels himself outside his work, and in his work feels outside himself. He is at home when he is not working, and when he is working he is not at home. His labor is therefore not voluntary, but coerced; it's *forced labor.* It is therefore not the satisfaction of a need; it is merely a *means* to satisfy needs external to it. (Marx 1959, p. 30)

Labor under capitalism is external to or separate from the worker: it does not belong to his essential being. We are alienated from the product of our labor and thus the production itself is alienation. This second aspect of alienation is the alienation from the activity of labor, more specifically, this is the activity of labor under capitalism; however, work in itself can be a self-realizing activity. Under capitalism we work for wages; we do not do it to directly meet our own human needs (for food, shelter, etc.) or for its own satisfaction. Working for wages entails that we work for another and this work is not controlled by ourselves. We are denying out nature and limiting both our bodies and our intellects. "The external character of labor for the worker is demonstrated by the fact that it belongs not to him but to another, and that in it he belongs not to himself but to another. . ... The activity of the worker is not his own spontaneous activity. It belongs to another, it is a loss of his self" (Marx 1959, p. 30). The results of such stultifying labor can be seen in *The Office*, with the misshapen "desk-bound" bodies of the workers and the boring conversations in the break room about what they watched on "telly" the night before (with Keith, the accountant, being the main culprit in this regard).

However, the alienation from the activity of our labor is best illustrated using Gervais' television series *Extras* (first broadcast in 2005). Filmed in a more traditional sitcom style, *Extras* takes the audience on the journey of Andy Millman's rise from "background artist" to producer/writer of his own lowest-common-denominator comedy driven by catch phrases: *When the Whistle Blows*. (So *Extras* is about a sitcom within a sitcom.) When we first meet Andy he is an aspiring actor who is supporting himself through working as an "extra," although Andy himself prefers the term "background artist" as it seemingly gives more human dignity to his work. In reality, extras are hired and fired at the whims of the directors or celebrity actors, and they are treated much like the props on the set; indeed, in one instance Andy is simply addressed as "background" by a production worker (S.1 Ep. 4). In one particularly humiliating and dehumanizing scene, Andy's best friend, Maggie, is rejected as not being suitably attractive enough to be in a scene with actor Clive Owen (S.2 Ep.7). (She is supposed to play a prostitute Clive's character hired.) Owen says to the director he is not happy with "this," with "this" meaning Maggie, indicating that he would not pay for such an unattractive prostitute. The director apologizes and says he was sent "an absolute truckload of hogs" and Maggie was the best one. The director and Owen then soothe Owen's ego by having him throw dung in Maggie's face in the scene as a display of contempt at her unattractiveness (instead of paying her). Maggie leaves the set to preserve her pride. She then takes a cleaning job, although it means she has to leave her cozy apartment and live in a grim studio apartment. As for Andy, he eventually finds that success does not give him freedom. His own sitcom is so controlled and rewritten by its main producer that it becomes the dregs of sitcoms much like the real-life series *Are You Being Served?* Whether as an extra or a sitcom star, Andy is just a cog or a tool in the vast machine of cultural production and is dehumanized accordingly.

What makes *Extras* funny? On the surface level, the fact that Gervais persuaded so many famous actors (Patrick Stewart, Kate Winslet, etc.) to laugh at themselves indicates that these actors recognize either their past experiences as struggling actors or are breathing a sigh of relief that they do not share Andy's fate. On a darker, Marxist level, Gervais is showing us how the background artists are shaped by their need for work and the work itself. These performers are not recognized as individuals, but put on costumes to play types – indeed, at one stage Andy is dressed as a SS storm trooper. They often wear uncomfortable, physically restraining costumes and make-up, but remain in the "background"; and they do not get rewarded – either financially or personally – with a speaking part. How far are Andy's and Maggie's experiences from our own work experiences? How much are we stultified and restrained? Gervais is showing that it is a case of *degree, not kind*. And that is what make *Extras* so painfully funny.

Aspect Three: Alienation from the Self or Species

While humans share certain fundamental aspects of their life with animals, such as the need for food, as a species we have a more complex relationship to the natural objects around us. Bertell Ollman explains this aspect in *Alienation: Marx's conception of man in capitalist society*: "This shows in production where...[man]...is able to create things which are not objects of immediate need, a greater range of things, more beautiful things; [man]...can also reproduce the objects he finds in nature" (Ollman 1976, p. 151). Work is the "species activity" or essential activity of humans, it is what distinguishes us from other animals: we are creative beings who can only fulfill ourselves through productive activity. However, estranged labor under capitalism warps what Marx conceptualizes as our "species life." "In tearing away from man the object of his production...estranged labor tears from him his species life...in degrading spontaneous activity, free activity, to a means, estranged labor makes man's species life a means to his physical existence" (Marx 1959, p. 32).

Thus, alienation from both product and activity interconnect with and underpin the third aspect of alienation: an alienation from the self or from the human essence, a loss of self. In pre-capitalist conditions, work directly satisfies our needs: it is "natural." Under capitalism this connection is broken. Thus productive work (our species activity or essential activity) becomes the mere means to earn a wage. And – as such – we become alienated from it and ourselves. Selling our labor as a commodity means that we are estranged from our very self; we become alienated from our human "species-being." Work becomes a means to stay alive instead of life being the opportunity to do work. Estranged from species activity under capitalism, man becomes – what Marx calls – an "abstraction." Our life – separated from the characteristics of our species – has simply become the purpose of work, a reversal of our relation to work that makes us what we are not.

This estrangement from our individual humanity runs throughout Gervais' central works: *The Office, Extras, Derek,* and *After Life*. Tim and Dawn in *The Office* experience a loss of self at Wernham Hogg, with both of them unable to follow their dreams yet accepting of their narrow lot in life. Tim still lives with his parents and appears to have no friends outside work, while Dawn lives with the cloddish Lee, who thinks her dream of being an illustrator will evaporate once she has "squeezed out a couple of kiddies" and she will be content with a part-time cleaning job. In *Extras*, Andy's loss of self is symbolized by the talking plastic "Andy" doll, a useless consumer good made to cash in on the success of his sitcom, that swiftly ends up in bargain bins in stores (S. 2 Ep. 4). However, Gervais does seem to offer the viewers hope through the fate of these characters. Andy eventually seems to recognize that fame and fortune lead to loss of self and the series ends with him walking out of a publicity event with Maggie, while Tim and Dawn finally admit to caring for each other and leave the Wernham Hogg Christmas party together in the final episode of the series.

Alienation from self is not just a central theme in the television series *After Life*, it is often the driving force of the narrative. The series, which Gervais has described as a love story, is about Tony (played by Gervais), a journalist for a free local newspaper: *The Tambury Gazette*. Essentially a vehicle for advertisers of consumer goods and services, the newspaper features laughable and fatuous local news such as the man who got the same birthday card five times (S.1, Ep.1). Most of the people Tony interviews are retired or unemployed, and they are lonely and alienated from themselves, such as the woman who claims that her cat speaks to her.

Tony's wife of 25 years has recently died of cancer, leaving Tony depressed and at a loss. His work, such as it is, does not sustain him; indeed, in the first episode, Tony denies that he is a journalist, that he has actual work. Tony claims that it is only the fact that he needs to feed the dog that prevents him from killing himself (S1. Ep.2). Without his wife, Tony has decided to deliberately alienate others, saying outrageous and hurtful things to keep them at arm's length and to make them feel a fraction of his pain. In Season 2, Episode 3, Tony's co-workers are shocked to find out that the newspaper will close. Sandy, the new reporter, in particular, is devastated, as she says it is the only job she has ever loved. His co-workers are not just working to earn a living, they are working (to paraphrase Marx) as an expression of their own human nature. There is a human relationship to the labor process, best exemplified by the fact that they work together to tell local, human, stories (however silly). Tony promises Sandy that he will find a way to keep the newspaper open. Even though he may not share her feelings, Tony understands how meaningful the work of *The Tambury Gazette* is to her. Eventually, Tony meets the newspaper owner in private and persuades him not to close the paper, and – in fact – the owner of the paper envisions himself in future working in collaboration with the workers to build the newspaper and to make it a meaningful publication.

Tony's snarky comments to and about others are amusing, but what makes a whole television series about death, suicide ideation, and depression a comedy? Gervais himself says "I never doubted a comedy about a suicidal man whose wife dies of cancer could be anything other than hilarious" (Gervais 2019). In many ways, *After Life* is not a comedy series at all, certainly not in any traditional sense of belly laughs or slapstick or catch phrases. However, it is a character-driven series about human life, more satisfying – perhaps – to philosophers who study the human condition. When he is at home, Tony endlessly watches videos of his deceased wife, and here we can see Tony's gentle, kind side. It is that side of Tony that makes him good at interviewing people and writing their stories, fundamentally affirming the importance of these people. And as the series progresses, it is that side of Tony that is brought out by his work at the newspaper. While it would be untrue to say that Tony's work and the people at his work can ever replace Lisa, his wife, the newspaper and his co-workers do fulfill his need to care for someone or something to a great extent: to care about what he does and find it meaningful. When he was married to Lisa, Tony says all he wanted to do was finish work and return home. As the series develops, Tony begins to find meaning in his work, and he matures: through his work he becomes less estranged from his sense of self, although obviously he is still grieving. It is in this way that the series is amusing: a rueful "feel-good" experience like the 1946 film *It's a Wonderful Life*, without that film's maudlin message of self-sacrifice.

Aspect Four: Alienation from Others

Just as we are estranged from our own species-nature, so we are also estranged from each other as humans: the fourth aspect of Marx's account of alienation: "An immediate consequence of the fact that man is estranged from the product of his labor, from his life activity, from his species-being, is the *estrangement of man* from *man*" (Marx 1959, p. 32). Like alienation from self, alienation from others comes out of the worker's alienation from productive activity: "Every self-estrangement of man from himself and from nature appears in the relation in which he places himself and nature to men other than and differentiated from himself" (Marx 1959, p. 33). Under capitalism we are working for wages, estranged from our essential nature and thus from one another: "What applies to a man's relation to his work, to the product of his labor and to himself, also holds of a man's relation to the other man, and to the other man's labor and object of labor. In fact, the proposition that man's species-nature is estranged from him means that one man is estranged from the other, as each of them is from man's essential nature" (Marx 1959, p. 32).

The worker is alienated from the capitalist, but, more importantly, in Marx's account of social alienation, the worker is alienated from, and hostile to, those in his own class. According to Sayers, Marx explicitly describes in his later work, *Das Kapital*, this alienation from others as specific to capitalism and commodity production. Under capitalism we are working for wages: working for ourselves independent of others. Under the conditions of alienated labor, therefore, we experience others as well as ourselves as atomistic individuals. The (expected) hostility between workers and capitalists plays out *throughout* society. We do not recognize the needs of others, nor do we understand how others can help us satisfy our own needs.

This alienation from and hostility to others is demonstrated throughout Gervais' work. There are two particularly telling examples of this experience from *The Office*. In Season 1, Episode 5 David Brent meets some women in a nightclub and says "Anyone of them will do." For Brent, the women are interchangeable – atomistic individuals – just like we think of other workers under capitalism. In Season 2, Episode 5, the workers at *The Office* are collecting money to relieve world hunger. Their supposedly funny – but typically cruel – acts demonstrate how charity is framed under alienation and capitalism; for example, Chris Finch takes the opportunity to sexually harass the receptionist Dawn, treating his interaction with her as one of purchase and commodity, while the others "debag" one of the accountants (supposedly) for the viewing public. As Brent proclaims proudly, "Who says famine has to be depressing?"

As we have seen, Gervais' commentary on the alienation of man from man underpins all his comedy, especially *Extras*, *The Office*, and *After Life*. His work is not simply "cringe comedy," but "the comedy of alienation": the comedy of estranged individuals who do not recognize how others can help with their needs and their sense of isolation. Gervais' comedy is – following Ollman – radical in that it reveals something about the capitalist relations in our society and criticizes the effects of these relations on our lives. While Marx's account of alienation may dovetail with three of Gervais's major works – *The Office*, *Extras*, and *After Life* –

the television series *Derek* (2013–2014) appears to be an apparent anomaly. *Derek* requires a closer inspection, as – ultimately – its titular character (Derek) *transcends* alienation and appears untouched by capitalist society.

Derek – Transcendence of Alienation

Derek is another mockumentary series, this time set in a nursing home, with Gervais starring in the title role as a helper in the home. Gervais has been criticized for creating the role of Derek, who is apparently intellectually impaired or perhaps autistic, although Gervais denies that he is mocking disability. However, Gervais may instead be bringing to our attention a phenomenon that is increasing in Britain: that of the individual who cannot cope well in our increasingly fast-paced and cruel capitalist society. Viewers of Michael Apted's *7 Up* documentary series can see a real-life example of this type of individual in Neil, an intelligent but overly sensitive man, who drifts into homelessness. Such individuals may be designated as mentally ill, but more often they are too vulnerable and are now broken. Certainly it would appear true, as McKenna states, that, "Even the helpers in the care home – such as Derek himself – are people, for the most part, who would struggle to secure conventional employment" (McKenna 2015, p. 201). (Thank you to Tony McKenna for supplying the article on request.)

McKenna claims that *Derek* functions as a critique of capitalism. McKenna writes that the residents of the home in *Derek* live in a capitalist world that is growing ever more ruthless: "This is capitalism mark II: a sleek, refined, steely sharp model that in the pursuit of capital expansion, more and more eliminates from its remit any extraneous, 'unproductive' baggage" (McKenna 2015, p. 201). In this world, it is the elderly who are the most vulnerable as they are no longer "productive" laborers and thus have no value: "In other words, by focusing on a group of elderly people living in a retirement home, *Derek* is drawing attention to those who fall outside the remit of the cycle of capital expansion and are therefore outsiders by the very fact of their social being" (McKenna 2015, p. 201).

McKenna's claims about *Derek* and capitalism are cogent. In addition, McKenna's work leads us to see how *Derek* does, in fact, tie in with the theme of Marxist alienation that runs through Gervais' other work. Both the workers and the residents – as McKenna says – are alienated from the social system. We can see that the secondary characters of Dougie and Kev are estranged from themselves. Kev is unemployed and spends his days at the care home drinking, while Dougie is actively employed at the home. Confined to his windowless workshop, Dougie does not appear to have social connections with anyone but Derek, and he explicitly states he has no interest in a romantic relationship.

However, in contrast, Derek and Hannah (the care home manager) do not experience alienation from their own self or from others. Both of them are happy and fulfilled working at the home; indeed, the line between their own homelife and their work is blurred into nonexistence. Despite the best efforts of the local council to cut costs, Hannah and Derek create a place where the elderly residents can be (to paraphrase Marx) at home like a fish in water. Hannah achieves this through her running of the home and attention to the residents. Derek achieves it through entertaining the residents, in many ways he is like an eternal child, giving them someone to care about and helping to satisfy their emotional needs.

What makes *Derek* funny? Critics are divided as to whether the series is funny at all, but most of the humor in the first season comes from Derek and the care home residents defying the societal expectations of the elderly and social misfits (like Derek). According to the council, Hannah spends too much on staff, without realizing that the staff are not employed just for the work skills they bring. Dougie, the jack-of-all-trades, is underqualified, but he cares about the residents and Hannah. The care workers are a (dysfunctional) family for the residents, who – typically – have been placed in the home because their own families cannot be bothered to look after them. While there are plenty of quirky moments of humor, *Derek* offers the viewer gentle pleasure through seeing the happiness of marginalized others. Even the deaths of residents are surprisingly upbeat without plunging into sentimentality.

What is also interesting is that in Season 2 of *Derek* the show loses its originality and humor while simultaneously losing its account of alienation. Overall, in the second season, there is less emphasis on finding fulfillment through their work and more emphasis on self-awareness and happiness through having Derek as a friend. Moreover, there is an increase in a cloying sentimentality and a decrease in incisive political critique from the first season. The comedy follows suit; for example, Dougie gets electrocuted in a tired slapstick move, while Derek's long-lost father appears, and we are supposed to find humor in the fact that he is the stereotypical drunken lazy Irishman.

Alienation and Religion

Alienated man is therefore alienated from his product, activity, his species-self, and others. Marx calls this being an abstraction: a being estranged from the social mode of human existence. In this way, alienation is "a disease of the entire social body," which "demands a total social cure" (Ollman 1976, p. 226). As we splinter into abstraction, "alienated life elements," notably property and religion, take on an independent life as they develop away from their original foundation in humans (Marx and Engels 1956, p. 157). Eventually, these elements become "'needs,' which the individual is forced to satisfy, and the original connection is all but obliterated" (Ollman 1976, p. 135).

According to traditional Christian theology, humankind is made in the image of their god. Ludwig Feuerbach (1804–1872), in contrast, held that it was humans who created their gods in their own image. Marx followed Feuerbach's inverted picture of the relationship of man and God. Yet Marx also saw that, in projecting their own powers onto an abstract object, religion becomes a form of alienation for humans, as it separates humans from their "species-essence." Marx was able to show why humans fall into this religious alienation. Unlike Feuerbach, who held that religious belief was an intellectual mistake that could therefore admit of resolution, Marx recognized that religion is a created need in response to the alienation of material life. With the transcendence of alienation (*and only with this transcendence*), however, the "needs" apparently satisfied by religion will disappear.

Gervais is famous (or notorious) for being an outspoken atheist, and his philosophical background clearly shows in his logical discussions of religious belief; take, for example, his discussion with Stephen Colbert on *The Late Show* about the existence of the Judeo/Christian god (2/2/2017). As David Kyle Johnson points out, Gervais does offer some strong responses to Colbert, but, ultimately, Gervais does not respond fully to Colbert's original question: "Why is there something rather than nothing?" (Johnson 2017). Unfortunately, as much as philosophers enjoy an argumentative fray, Gervais' critique of religion and religious belief on *The Late Show* does not initially appear to tie in particularly well with Marx's account of religious alienation, but we shall see later that the nonexistence of a god underpins Gervais' demonstration of religion as a lie in the film *The Invention of Lying*.

In Gervais' 2009 film, *The Invention of Lying*, there is a more interesting perspective. Here Gervais is not entering the battle armed with arguments; instead, the film is offering an account of what social life would be like once the notion of a happy afterlife and "the man in the sky" are introduced. In *The Invention of Lying*, the world is just like the modern Anglo-American world, except nobody lies. Indeed, people can be quite brutally honest, such as when the woman Gervais' character loves tells him she has no romantic interest in him because he has no money and is not genetically a good prospect as a father.

The main character – Mark Bellison, played by Gervais – is described as a "chubby, little loser," who works as a screenwriter for "Lecture Films." Given that everyone tells the truth, only historical films are made, and, unfortunately, Mark has been assigned to write on the fourteenth century, a century that is dominated by the plague, a highly unpopular subject. Mark finds his work dull. Moreover, he is unpopular at work, which may be partially due to a more successful screenwriter encouraging others to despise him. Perhaps expectedly, Mark is fired from his miserable job. In order to avoid eviction for non-payment of rent, he goes to the bank to withdraw his savings: $300. He is told the system is down, and the bank teller asks him how much money he has. Mark has an epiphany that honesty is not in his favor and claims that he has $800 (the exact amount he is behind on rent). This is mankind's first lie. Mark then experiments with the power of lying, finding that he is able, for example, to make money at the casino.

Mark's mother is dying, and she tells him she is frightened to die and to go to "an eternity of nothingness." To make her happy, Mark tells her that there is an afterlife where she will be happy and surrounded by the ones she loves. The hospital staff overhear, and when Mark returns home he is mobbed by news crews and people anxious to know more. He is convinced to share "his knowledge" of what "the man in the sky who controls everything" has planned for humans in the afterlife and why this man allows bad things to happen to good people (two central questions debated in philosophy of religion).

The notion of this man does bring a measure of happiness to some people; indeed, some of Mark's "loser" friends become content with their miserable existence now that they believe they will be happy in the afterlife. Here the movie illustrates Marx's best-known dictum on religion from *A Contribution to the Critique of Hegel's Philosophy of Right*: "Religion is the sigh of the oppressed creature, the heart of a heartless world, just as it is the spirit of a spiritless situation. It is the opium of the people" (Marx 1844b). While Marx is critical of the illusions of religion, he also recognizes the necessity of religious belief in a "heartless" – capitalist and oppressive – world. Despite his recognition of the psychological need for religion, Marx understands that religion is the symptom of the cancer of capitalism and thus both cancer and symptom must be excised: "The abolition of religion as the *illusory* happiness of the people is required for their real happiness. The demand to give up the illusion about its condition is the *demand to give up a condition which needs illusions*" (Marx 1844b). In *The Invention of Lying* Gervais offers an illustration of both the need for and a critique of religion in a capitalist society.

What is fascinating about Gervais' illustration of religion is that belief in the existence of this entity does not make people kinder or more compassionate, as religions in all their diverse forms usually claim. In the movie, *society itself does not change*, as people continue to view each other in terms of socioeconomic worth (not as having human worth) and in terms of their genetic potential to produce children who are good physical and intellectual specimens. Indeed, the woman Mark loves asks him if the fact that he is now rich and famous can alter his genes so that any children they have will not be chubby with a button nose. (He tells her the truth and says it won't.) Women still choose partners for their genetic potential to father children and their ability to support them financially. Successful men still choose partners for their looks, even though these will eventually fade. Then, presumably, these men will be able to move on to a younger, newer model.

Thus, *The Invention of Lying*, while providing an amusing critique of religious belief, also provides an explanation of why capitalist society requires a complete overhaul. Most of the people in the film are alienated from their work, especially as there is no room for creativity in this work. Anna, the woman Mark loves, says she enjoys her job, but that is because she earns a lot of money for minimal effort, while, in one repeated vignette, there is a woman who stands outside Mark's job saying she cannot bear to go in to work. The characters portrayed in the film are alienated from their individual species-being as they lack fulfillment from productive activity and only view their worlds through the measure of socioeconomic success. Most of the characters portrayed in the film are isolated, atomistic individuals alienated from each other, treating each other like commodities on the marriage market. Indeed, Anna *nearly* marries the handsome and successful Brad, even though she has grown to love Mark and value their friendship, as Brad is a "win" in this market.

But what of Mark himself? He becomes rich and famous because of his ability to tell lies (writing fantasy history and creating the cult of "the man in the sky"). And here Gervais is certainly tweaking the noses of Christians who believe it is wrong to tell lies; however, there is also a deeper message. If we are uncomfortable in our bourgeois morality in accepting Mark's success, then we need to upend our entire belief system. Moreover, Gervais is telling us that – in lying – Mark has not acted differently from the church. Just like Mark, no matter how well intentioned it is, the church is telling a lie about the existence of its god. And here we can see the relevance of Gervais' atheism to the film. According to Gervais, there is no god and thus church and religion are founded on a lie.

Conclusion

In these ways, Ricky Gervais' television series and the film, *The Invention of Lying*, provide illustrative examples of Karl Marx's account of human alienation under capitalism. In its turn, Marx's theory of alienation gives insight into the laughing discomfort we feel watching Gervais' work. Gervais does push the accepted social boundaries for comedy, but that is not so much because it fits the category of "cringe-comedy," but rather because he is offering what is best called "the comedy of alienation." Following Ollman's account of "radical" humor, Gervais uncovers the capitalist roots of our society, and he reveals the alienation within that society and criticizes the effects alienation has on our lives.

References

Feuerbach, Ludwig. 2012. *The Essence of Christianity*. Trans. George Elliot. Digireads.com Publishing.
Gervais, Ricky. Blog Entry. *Blog 4/13/2019*. https://www.rickygervais.com/. Accessed 2/3/2021.
———. *Golden Globe Monologue*. https://www.hollywoodreporter.com/news/transcript-ricky-gervais-golden-globes-2020-opening-monologue-1266516
Johnson, David Kyle. 2017. Royally Bad Philosophy (A Reply to Craig and Colbert). *Psychology Today*, February 7. https://www.psychologytoday.com/us/blog/logical-take/201702/royally-bad-philosophy-reply-craig-and-colbert
Lawson, Mark. 2013. Ricky Gervais' *Derek*: Cruel or just unusual? *The Guardian*, January 31. https://www.theguardian.com/culture/2013/jan/31/ricky-gervais-derek-cruel-unusual
Malcolm, Norman. 1984. *Ludwig Wittgenstein: A memoir*. New York: Oxford University Press.
Marx, Karl. 1959. *Economic and Philosophic Manuscripts of 1844*. Trans. Martin Milligan, Revised by Dirk J. Struik, Contained in Marx/Engels, *Gesamtausgabe*, Abt. 1, Bd. 3. Moscow: Progress Publishers.
———. 1844b. *A Contribution to the Critique of Hegel's Philosophy of Right*. Deutsch-Französische Jahrbücher, 7 & 10 February 1844 in Paris. Unknown source and date of transcription. Most recent correction by Matthew Carmody in 2009. https://www.marxists.org/archive/marx/works/1843/critique-hpr/intro.htm. Accessed 7/21/2021.
Marx, Karl, and Friedrich Engels. 1956. *The Holy Family*. Trans. R. Dixon. Moscow: Foreign Languages Publishing House.
McKenna, Tony. 2015. *Art, literature, and culture from a Marxist perspective*. London/New York: Palgrave Macmillan.
Ollman, Bertell. 1976. *Alienation: Marx's conception of man in capitalist society*. Cambridge: Cambridge University Press.
Sayers, Sean. 2011. *Marx and alienation: Essays on Hegelian themes*. New York: Palgrave Macmillan.

Hasan Minhaj as Philosopher: Navigating the Struggles of Identity

73

Pankaj Singh

Contents

Introduction	1686
The Dilemma of National Identity	1688
On Ethnic Identity	1691
"Audacity of Equality," Freedom, and Authentic Identity	1695
Conclusion	1699
References	1699

Abstract

Hasan Minhaj uses his craft of comedy both for the laughs and for his takes, points, messages, claims, and arguments. The comedy is driven by his conviction that great comedy routines, in their essence, are great philosophical positions. This, we might say, is his philosophy of humor. When doing comedy, he often attempts to slip in social messages by combining his comedy with arguments, thus presenting his viewpoints (and countering those of others) on several topics through various formats of his work. Drawing his arguments from his own experience of being an Indian-American Muslim, he uses his comedy to forward his arguments about immigrants' struggles and stories, and has also been particularly vocal about issues related to identity. This chapter primarily focuses on highlighting Hasan's philosophy, ideas, claims, and arguments on various identities, from national and ethnic identities to personal identity; however, the chapter will also briefly present and comment on a few other philosophical concepts that can be found in Hasan's work. In the end, we shall see that Hasan provides us with a prime example of how the words of a comedian can also contain deep philosophical insights and messages.

P. Singh (✉)
School for Life (SFL), University of Petroleum and Energy Studies, Dehradun, India

© Springer Nature Switzerland AG 2024
D. K. Johnson et al. (eds.), *The Palgrave Handbook of Popular Culture as Philosophy*,
https://doi.org/10.1007/978-3-031-24685-2_100

Keywords

Hasan Minhaj · Identity · Nation · Existentialism · Freedom

Introduction

> Basically our job [as comedians] is to distill coffee into espresso.... We are just normal philosophers.... That's really what comedians are.
> —Hasan Minhaj (Comedy Gold Minds podcast: Pandora/hosted by Kevin Hart, Feb 18, 2021 (9:00 min))

From a professional identity point of view, Hasan Minhaj is a comedian, writer, producer, political commentator, actor, and television host. At a more personal level of identity, he is an Indian-American Muslim. Although he was first brought to the public's attention as a correspondent at Jon Stewart's *The Daily Show*, he is perhaps best known for his Netflix stand-up special "Homecoming King," his 2017 White House Correspondents Dinner Speech, and his Netflix show "Patriot Act with Hasan Minhaj." In an interview with Sal Khan, the founder of Khan Academy, Sal asks Hasan, "Did you think you are going to be an entertainer?" Hasan replies, "No," but continues to describe how he found his calling for comedy.

> I wasn't a pop culture junkie as a kid, but I was really into speech and debate. That was one of the things I was naturally kind of good at. And I found when I was doing speech and debate tournaments and public speaking tournaments in high school, I just naturally had an inclination to make fun of the prompt. (Khan Academy 2020)

He concludes from his experience, "Stand-up comedy is just funny speech and debate." That was the primary motivation for him to become a comic and he blended his talent for comedy and knack for debate in his correspondent role at Jon Stewart's "The Daily Show." In the interview with Khan, Hasan shares what he learned working with Jon. "I realized that take is more important than jokes ... The most important thing for comedy is the argument. You are making a funny joke, but at the core, what is your argument. So great jokes at their essence are great philosophical positions said in a funny way."

Given his philosophy of humor – that jokes should provide a new take, arguments, and philosophical positions – Hasan Minhaj is perhaps the epitome of the philosophical comedian and the reasons for his inclusion in this work is apparent. He embodies and embraces the philosophy of humor by recognizing that comedians are philosophers; they present arguments, advocate for positions, and change minds. And he took this philosophy of humor to his solo venture, the Netflix series *Patriot Act with Hasan Minhaj*. In the *Patriot Act*, he took rigorous journalistic research on different issues and presented it humorously. Hasan also incorporated audio-video graphics, something he first tried in his Netflix comedy special *Homecoming King*. But he prefers to only talk about issues that he can present comedically.

His motivation for engaging in personalized storytelling only about problems that can be portrayed comically is twofold. First, Hasan wants to bring something new to the table; second, he feels that he can rely on his strength of storytelling and be able to convey the issues in a much more emphatic way. From a journalistic point of view, one could argue that such a personalized approach constrains the type of issues he discusses; and it does. Personalized storytelling limits the scope of the topics covered. But understanding Hasan's perspective on journalism and comedy will help us understand his personalized approach to issues. Hasan is very clear about his approach and the distinction and importance of journalism and comedy.

> In my job, the necessary condition is comedy, and the sufficient condition is news. People come to me all the time, and they are like, 'hey man, you're like the melanin savior, you need to talk about Rohingya'. I'm like, I can't make it funny. That's why real journalism matters because the necessary condition is news, sufficient condition is, is it interesting? The problem is, I think, cable news and a lot of certain sort of click-baiting media, the necessary condition is, is it salacious? People want to click on it, then are we providing information or context? The whole game has been sort of flipped on its head now, which is weird. (92nd Street Y 2019)

His attempt is more about slipping in a thought-provoking idea to people's minds with the help of comedy without compromising the integrity of an important issue.

> I do my due diligence to make sure we're alright in terms of our argumentation. In terms of the jokes, I really do the best that I can with my writers…The thing that is more important to me is the take. There are these very visceral moments when, if you make a really good point, you can just hear it in the room. Like, you can hear those gasps, or you can hear the, like, the nods, or like the "mmmh." Like you can hear people [say] "yeah," sort of understanding. That, to me, is the stuff that's really important. And then layering on jokes afterward is a little bit easier. (92nd Street Y 2019)

He wants to use his philosophy of comedy as an art to connect with people and connect with his true self.

> I think art is a true reflection of the times. I use comedy as an art form to understand myself. And the work that I do is to present my thoughts and my viewpoint of the world to people so that they feel seen. So that I feel seen, and I feel understood. I want to connect with people, and I want to explain the human condition through comedy. And ultimately, I want to say how I really feel in my heart and not be a *darpok*. (Khan Academy 2020)

Darpok is a Hindi language word that means coward; or, as Hasan explains, "scaredy-cat." He feels a responsibility toward his conscience to speak up against the injustice surrounding him without worrying about the consequences. He uses his philosophy of humor by lacing his comedy with arguments and presenting his viewpoints on various topics.

He has been particularly vocal, however, about the issues related to identity. He often draws his arguments from his own experience of being an Indian-American Muslim. He uses his comedy to expose the truth about immigrants' struggles and stories. Through jokes, he weaves counterarguments to opposing opinions in a palatable way. Applying his jokes and arguments, he covers a wide spectrum of identities. It is for this reason that this chapter shall present and examine Hasan's philosophy, ideas, claims, and arguments regarding his identity – his identity as it is conceived from a national point of view, an ethnic point of view, a religious point of view, and from a personal point of view.

The Dilemma of National Identity

Hasan talks about the identity dilemma for immigrants. On the one hand, in the country where they live, they face problems due to their race, color, religion, culture, and language; on the other hand, people from their home country see the immigrants as opportunists who ditched their country of origin for gains. People from their home country do not want their involvement in the serious issues of the country. For example, when Hasan wanted to feature Indian elections in one of his episodes of "Patriot Act," his dear and near ones warned, requested, and even pleaded for him not to ("Indian Election Update and the 1 MDB Scandal" 2019). Instead, they suggested, if Hasan is so keen on doing an episode on India, he should opt for lighter topics like Bollywood, cricket, Indian food, and spices. His conversation with his Uncle and Aunty at the beginning of the episode gives a glimpse of the perception of both sides. Hasan asks them, "Why can't I talk about Indian politics? I'm Indian." Uncle sarcastically replies, "You're an Indian? You didn't even live there. How do you call yourself Indian?" Hasan responds, "My family is from there." His Aunty makes it clear, "People think you're American. You're a white washed." Hasan disagrees, saying, "No, I'm not. You know me and Uncle are brown; you know that." But his Uncle interrupts, "How? But you don't behave like a brown." Hasan wonders, "What does that even mean?" The Uncle clarifies, "You think that you're a smart white dude. Sorry, you're not [an Indian]" ("Indian Election Update and the 1 MDB Scandal" 2019).

The conversation raises profound questions about national identity. But, what is national identity? When asking about a person's identity or group, we try to determine their ethnic group to make an easy distinction. But, philosopher Varun Uberoi notes, "we think and talk about national identity in at least two ways: first as, for example, a person's 'English,' 'British,' 'American' or 'French' identity, and second as England, Britain, America or France's identity" (Uberoi 2018, p. 49, paraphrasing Parekh 2008, p. 56). National entities as India or America are a territory of people sharing values, history, and culture. The culture may consist of beliefs, values, norms, language, traditions, and conventions. Familiarity with the culture of a nation not only shapes people but also makes them comfortable.

Keeping the above rudimentary understanding of national identity in mind, if we rethink Hasan's funny conversation with his Uncle, it raises many difficult questions. Does a person need to carry the national identity of the country he is born in? Or does a person need to maintain the national identity of one's ancestors? The answer to the first question seems obvious from a legal point of view – the country name on your passport defines your national identity. In this sense, we would say that Minhaj is American; he was born in, and is a citizen of, the United States. In regard to the second question, one might say that, yes, Minhaj is Indian, because of his lineage. But taking that argument to its extreme, one could say that – because as a species, we all migrated from Africa – we all carry the national identity of Africa. However, if one says no, and we do not assume the identity of our ancestors, then shall we prevent people from identifying themselves with their ancestral homeland? Can a Caucasian born in America, but who lives in India, say they are not an American? Can that person, without any prior connection to Indian roots, but who gains citizenship, claim the identity of being an Indian?

Hasan circumvents such questions with his pragmatic approach to nationalism. He switches between his Indian and American identities according to context and situation. Sharing one of his childhood memories, Hasan says, "[There are] moments, where I'm like, yeah man, I gotta go back to the motherland. And then, sometimes I go back. I remember going back to go visit [India]. When I was a kid like my cousins, and I was in Delhi, and I had to take a dump, and I had to do squatty potty [squatty potty: popular in the Indian subcontinent, a type of toilet seat on which one has to sit in a squat-like position to excrete], I'm like, man, I'm American" (HOT 97 2018). His unfamiliarity with this method of relieving himself made him realize the American side of identity. However, many times, he feels alienated from American culture and values. He illustrates the point of difference between the two cultures by citing family values. He tells one of his favorite Indian stories when he saw a man cutting the line at an Indian airport due to some family emergency.

> [Concern about] overpopulation is a huge thing [for me], especially coming from America. I go to the airport, I'm just like, god damn, there's too many people, like I'm just becoming an American, right! American side of me coming out, like, yo boundaries, respect my boundaries. And then, here's this long line, and I'm trying to get through, and then this guy runs in, and he goes my father's sick, I need to see my father, and everyone's like hey get out of the way. Man, his dad's sick, and there was that sort of like internal[ly] recognized Family Values like Hey! Family is above everything. (HOT 97 2018)

His distinction is that in terms of family values, in America, individuals come before family, and in India, family comes before the individual. Hasan was simply trying to depict the difference rather than evaluating the ethics of the difference. His example also points toward the incommensurability of cultures, i.e., although he highlights the differences in the culture, he does not consider one culture or nation superior to the other. He acknowledges the differences in nations' values and cultures and proposes a unique philosophy about national identity. He challenges the whole idea of national identity. He argues for getting rid of identifying oneself with any one region or even to any absolutist notion of identifying with one particular group identity.

> The more you travel, you become a little bit less absolutist about the Yankee cap. You love it, but you're not like this is the *be-all and end-all* of everything. You know, you went to high

school with kids, and they're just like this town is everything, and this pizza spot, and you're like, come on man, there's a whole world out there. (HOT 97 2018)

Although, there is no denying that one has a natural affinity to the nation one is born in – to the language one speaks, the food one eats, the clothes one wears, the music one listens to, the game one plays or watches, the political party one supports, or the school or college one attends – there is nothing wrong with being attached to the elements specific to one's identity. However, being comfortable with familiar things is different than thinking that things specific to one's identity are right or best. Hasan's point is that there are many nations, languages, food habits, clothing styles, music, sports, and political parties; and being rigidly confined to one's myopic view is problematic. Opening up to multiple perspectives is the solution to avoid absolutism and extremism.

Hasan cites his own liberating experience of traveling to support his claim, "I did shows in South Africa, and I did shows in London. The cheque cleared, and I'm like, man, if I get my bread, I can get it wherever I need to get it." His claim carries with it an assumption that travel gives a person exposure to different perspectives. Perspective-taking helps in understanding the culture, values, belief systems, and opinions of others. Once people start opening up to a plurality of ideas, the urge to be over-attached to a group identity diminishes. For example, if one identifies with a country, whether with America or India, that does not mean that one becomes an absolute nationalist or that one considers only the values or culture of any particular country to be the best. By a less absolutist approach, one becomes receptive to good things from all over the world. At the same time, one may also become critical of anything terrible happening in the world.

This, however, moves one toward what seems to be Hasan's philosophy of national identity, to consider himself a *global citizen*. To be a global citizen, one does not take oneself to belong to any one nation, and most certainly rejects the idea of the supremacy of one nation over another. And Hasan has certainly practiced what he preaches. For example, when he got his solo show "Patriot Act," he tackled a wide variety of issues worldwide. He not only talked about issues pertaining to America, but also took a dig at other countries such as India, China, Saudi Arabia, and Canada.

Motivated by his philosophy of national identity as a global citizen, he also speculates about the redundancy of the whole idea of nationalism. "The more you travel, I'm just kind of like, yo, nationalism is wack. I'm telling you, I think in 15–20 years, the more people travel, people claiming that I'm from this one place is kind of corny" (HOT 97 2018).

Any detractor of Hasan's philosophy might argue that Hasan can say all these things because he is in a privileged position as a stand-up comedian and getting the opportunity to visit the many countries of the world. What about those who do not have fancy jobs and do not get any chance to liberate themselves by enjoying world tours? There are two things to say in response.

First, what motivated Hasan to be a global citizen is what he learned on his travels; the fact that someone else cannot travel as he has does not negate what he has learned. And it's still true that if someone else were able to travel as he has, they would likely learn what he has learned and adopt the global citizen view. The fact that another person is not able to travel might mean that it is harder for them to adopt the view of a global citizen, but that doesn't mean that they can't, and certainly doesn't mean that they shouldn't. You can't legitimately refuse to accept the conclusion of an argument, and certainly can't say that others shouldn't, by saying that you personally weren't aware of the truth of the argument's premises.

Secondly, there are ways to learn about other cultures without traveling. What traveling did for Hasan was expose him to different cultures, ideas, and belief systems. In the information age, one can acquaint oneself with just about any nation or culture, virtually traveling and interacting with them, by the click of a button. Such research may not lead to a level of knowledge equivalent to what Hasan has gained by traveling, but it should be enough to adopt the view of a global citizen. What's more, one does not have to have grand amounts of information to be able to be open-minded enough to embrace citizens of any nation. Hasan's point is not just about travel, but about opening oneself to the world. His aim is to promote the philosophy of global citizens to make the world an inclusive, tolerant, and less radical place to live. National identity, however, is but one of the identities one assumes in the vast landscape of identities one bestows oneself. The next section would look at Hasan's philosophy on ethnic identities.

On Ethnic Identity

Hasan identifies himself as an Indian as well as an American. Coming from an Indian immigrant family, he also knows the values and culture of India. He likes to talk about the issues related to India. However, he faces lots of resistance for not doing episodes on the serious issues of India. To complicate matters further, Hasan is a Muslim. Although India is a secular nation, and most of the time, members of all the religious minority communities live peacefully with the Hindu majority, politicians still try to create a wedge between the Hindus and Muslims (the largest minority group) to garner political advantage. Hasan humorously illustrates the difference between Hindu and Muslim Indians.

> Hindus don't eat beef. "No beef!" Right? And Muslims, we don't eat pork. "Is that pepperoni pizza? No pepperoni!" And then Hindus, they like statues. They're like, "Oh! This is a statue of an elephant. I'm going to put this in my car." Muslims are like, "No statues! Calligraphy! We're about the alphabet. We put that in our car. We're different." And then Hindus, they like cartoons. They're like, "Oh, this is a cartoon, Ganesh. I'll just put this on the wall." And Muslims... We don't really, uh, like cartoons. We've got to get better about our cartoon policy. (Minhaj 2017)

Despite the peaceful coexistence of the two communities in India, there is still a reluctance to mingle. In Indian culture, interfaith marriages are still considered taboo; an interreligious marriage between a Muslim and a Hindu is definitely an eyebrow-raising matter for all the parties involved. People migrating from India have continued to adhere to the culture of their homeland. For example, when Hasan decided to marry a Hindu girl, it became a big issue. His father was against the marriage. Hasan presented his points to convince his father.

> How many times do we complain about racism in our community? All the time. Now the ball is in our court, we're going to be bigoted? Dad, I promise you, God doesn't like bigotry. God's not like, "You're racist. Good job." No! Number two, you want me to change my life to appease some aunty and uncle I'm never going to see? You want me to change my life for Naila Aunty? Fuck Naila Aunty. Are you fucking kidding me? (Minhaj 2017)

He makes two arguments in his two points. Argument one can be restructured as such: if God is omnibenevolent, why would God promote hatred and bigotry? This argument points out the hypocrisy of using the name of God for committing discrimination, prejudice, bigotry, crimes, or any heinous act. Gods of most of western religions are conceptualized as omnipotent, omniscient, omnipresent, and omnibenevolent. Conceptually speaking, a deity equipped with Omni attributes would not appreciate hate in their name.

His second point can be rephrased as such: just because you are part of a group doesn't mean you should follow the rotten norms of the group, especially due to the fear of how the group members would react to your choices. Hasan's answer is clear: one should not succumb to any peer pressure when it comes to big personal decisions. He further argued against adhering to the cultural prevalence of his ancestors.

> Dad, I love her, she loves me. Isn't there something bigger that unites all of us outside of race, color, creed, class? This is America. We can choose what we want to adhere from the motherland. Isn't life like biryani, where you push the weird shit to the side? Why do we got to adhere to this weird shit from back over there? (Minhaj 2017)

Let's call Hasan's point of choice a biryani argument. For those unfamiliar with the term *biryani*, biryani is cuisine prepared using rice, meat, and spices – but the use of meat, rice, and spices differs a lot depending on the preparation style, and so biryani dishes can differ wildly. Biryani is extremely popular in the Indian subcontinent and among its diaspora. The biryani argument suggests that, just like one has the freedom to choose a variety of meat, spices, and rice when preparing one's favorite dish in the biryani style, one should choose to follow the lifestyle one wants to live irrespective of what is prevalent in one's culture or country.

Hasan's experiences and argument points out the complexity involved in religious identity. Religion is one of the most deeply rooted associations with which many people identify themselves. According to philosophers Elisabeth Arweck and Nesbitt Eleanor, "Religious identity is a specific type of identity formation. Particularly, it is the sense of group membership to a religion and the importance of this group membership as it pertains to one's self-concept" (Arweck and Nesbitt 2010, pp. 67–87). Christianity, Islam, Hinduism, or any other religion, for that matter, is a set of beliefs. Religious beliefs come from various sources – myths, epics, folklore, histories, stories, people, and places. No matter how absurd the elements of one's religious beliefs are, they can become a core to one's identity.

What would happen if one part of your identity is loved and accepted and the other part hated and criticized? This question indicates a continuous identity conflict for Hasan.

> Because I'm Indian and Muslim, it's very weird to be something that people love and then also be something that people do not like. It's like if one half of you was Oreo cookie and then the other half was Muslim. There's no winning. It makes everything so much more complicated and confusing. ("Indian Elections" 2019)

Hasan's complications and confusion get more severe in the cocktail with his national identity. If he speaks about the internal issues of India, he would be termed as a "Pakistani agent" or terrorist just because of his religious identity. On the other hand, he is often asked to hide his religious identity as a Muslim in America. Hasan's father warned him, "Hasan, whatever you do, do not tell people you're Muslim or talk about politics" (Minhaj 2017). The scariest thing about being Muslim is the expectation of proving one's loyalty to one's nation, be it India or America. 9/11 made it more challenging for his religious identity. Speaking about the difficulty of his identity as a Muslim, he shares:

> The Muslim part of my identity was something that now was indicative of me being an enemy of the state. And so, ever since then, and if you look at even political rhetoric here in this country [America] and around the world, there's this idea that if you're a Muslim, you are an anti-national. (Vanity Fair 2019)

Islamophobia is a prevalent covert phenomenon in most non-Islamic nations. Islamophobia is an outcome of many fallacious thoughts. Criticizing the whole community of certain religious practitioners because of instances of violence perpetrated by individual members of that religion invoked the hasty generalization fallacy. Similarly, arguing that the inclusion of people from certain races, religions, nationalities, and ethnicities will ultimately lead to the doom of a country (e.g., a country being taken over by those races, etc.) commits the slippery slope fallacy. People who do not think critically often fall prey to such biases, stereotypes, and fallacies. Sometimes politicians tend to utilize such fallacious tendencies in their favor to gain votes, or rile up their voting base. Such anti-intellectual attempts can escalate the irrational fear of people from a particular class, color, creed, community, religion, and so on and so forth. Hasan terms fear of Muslims as irrational. He believes that people overlook the deeds of the majority of Muslims who have become an integral part of American society, from selling Kebab to driving cabs, medical professionals, grocery store clerks, and many more professions.

> This irrational fear of Muslims in America [is not understandable]. We're already here. And we already control every aspect of your life. Think about New York City, food, transportation, medicine, we have it all on the lock [Muslims are present in all walks of American life].

My mom is a doctor. She works at the VA. She's been there for decades. At every corner, [at any opportunity], she could have poisoned you, [but] she didn't, so you're welcome. So, we're contributing members of society. This is insanity to think that 1.5 billion Muslims want to destroy the Earth. (Breakfast Club Power 105.1 FM 2017)

He credits the mainstream representation of Muslims as one of the reasons for the irrational fear of Muslims. The way Muslims are represented in the mainstream is one of the reasons Hasan provides for the irrational fear many carry. When asked to characterize the mainstream representation of Muslims, he says:

If you look at [programs and shows] like Serial Podcast or The Night Of or Homeland, it's like [viewers of these shows may think]: these crazy brown dudes are radicalizing, and they've come here to kill us. What is going on with these deranged young brown kids? (Breakfast Club Power 105.1 FM 2017)

People come across a lot of narratives throughout their lives. With the information age, there is no dearth of narratives on anything. One can subscribe to any narrative of one's choice. So, if one wants to subscribe to the narrative about Muslims in popular movies, news, or tv series, one is free to do so. Hasan also presents a narrative through his craft of comedy. In his stand-up "Homecoming," Hasan wanted to convey, "What are the 99.9% of Muslims? What do they deal with in the face of insanity? So when a terrorist attack happens, how do they navigate the collateral damage of that?" (Breakfast Club Power 105.1 FM 2017). He is also empathetic to people fed a distorted version of reality.

I'm empathetic to that. You can only make decisions based on what you know, but I think also you got to hold people accountable to say, "Hey, you also have to be open to new information." (Breakfast Club Power 105.1 FM 2017)

Through his narrative, Hasan warns against confirmation bias which is a tendency to confirm one's own beliefs and opinions by selecting the information that fits their narrative. The danger of not opening up to new information is that one would miss the larger picture of someone's religious identity. In his philosophy of religion, Hasan defends a secular private practice of religion.

Coming from a minority background, what's wrong? I think the majority of people are secular-religious people. What I mean by that is that they adhere to the laws of the land. They want a separation of church and state. Still, in the privacy of their own home, they want to pray to God. And why is that a bad thing? To lump every person who believes in God or religion and call them an idiot or stupid, I think that's wack. (Breakfast Club Power 105.1 FM 2017)

Hasan adds that this problem of irrational fear is not limited to just religious identity but to fear of the other. The identity of the other could be reduced to the color of skin, race, or class; and this leads to bigotry.

It's happening to African-Americans to this day. Why is it every time the collateral damage has to be death for us to talk about this? A kid has to get shot 16 times for us to be like, "Maybe we have a race problem." For every Trayvon Martin or Ahmed, the clock kid, there is bigotry that happens every day. (Minhaj 2017)

So, according to Hasan, the attack of someone's identity is not just limited to religious identity. It can be any identity. He mockingly adds the point further, "I also feel like xenophobia and racism has its flavor of the week. It's kind of like Baskin Robbins. So this week we have the migrants that are seeking asylum" (HOT 97 2018). In this example, he talks about the change of narrative with the change in circumstance due to the socio-political atmosphere. The narrative changes according to place and time. Different countries may have other identity-related issues. Hasan points out the real problem beneath all this, "We need to level up the conversation to say Blacks are the problem, Mexicans are the problem, Muslims are the problem. No! It's violent extremism [that is the problem]. So violent extremism has no color or religion."

Hasan wants to emphasize that by being engaged in superficial discussion related to identity, one might lose the focus on the real issues. He believes that the talk should be focused on the group of foolish people spreading violent extremism. They can be found in every community. As Hasan points out, "the majority of people ISIS kills are Muslims" (HOT 97 2018). The conversation should be on gun control, racial violence, police brutality, and anything that promotes violent extremism.

This section emphasized the problems with religious and ethnic identity as pointed out by Hasan through his philosophical lens. The following section will continue the exposition on identity by focusing on personal identity.

"Audacity of Equality," Freedom, and Authentic Identity

Hasan points to an exciting crossroads of national and ethnic identity. The intersection also showcases the conflict for the people carrying multiple identities. In fact, doesn't everyone carry numerous identities? Defining what is meant by "personal identity" is key in determining the answers to these questions.

If by "personal identity" one means to refer to the self or a soul, the unchanging core part of human beings, then no; people do not carry multiple identities. You are one and the same person over time; your 8-year-old self is numerically the same person as you are now. You may not be the same *type* of person you were then, but you are still you. When philosophers discuss this issue, they are careful to delineate between the latter kind of "type-identity" (which can change over time) and "numerical identity" (which can't). And there are numerous theories regarding what preserves numerical identity over time: memory, psychological continuity, physical continuity, etc.

We will not, however, be going down that particular rabbit hole – because that is not the kind of identity that Hasan is concerned about. He is concerned about "personal identity" in the sense that the phrase is used in daily life when one person asks another who they are – a sense akin to the "type" identity just mentioned. By asking who a person is, one is not asking about their soul or unchanging self. Instead, the inquiry is to the ever-changing phenomenon of how one views oneself and the values or qualities with which they identify. And that is an ever-changing phenomenon. As philosopher Eric Olsen puts it,

> One's personal identity in this sense is contingent and temporary: the way I define myself as a person might have been different, and can vary from one time to another. It could happen that being a philosopher and a parent belong to my identity, but not being a man and living in Yorkshire, while someone else has the same four properties but feels differently towards them, so that being a man and living in Yorkshire belong to his identity but not being a philosopher or a parent. And these attitudes are all subject to change. (Olson 2021)

For example, after the World Trade Center attacks in 2001, Hasan's religious identity was impugned and his family experienced various assaults. They were called "sand niggers," received phone calls asking the address of Osama bin Laden, had car windows smashed, and even received death threats. His father, however, never raised his voice in response; indeed, he asked Hasan not to talk about politics in public or tell people about his Muslim identity. When an angry Hasan asked his father why they weren't retaliating against or even saying anything about the attacks, his father replied, "These things happen, and these things will continue to happen. That's the price we pay for being here" (Minhaj 2017). Hasan dubs this idea the "American dream tax," so we can call his father's argument "the American dream tax argument." The idea behind the argument is this: if a person leaves their home country to pursue a better lifestyle and living standard, then one is obligated to endure whatever hardships one must in order to attain that better lifestyle and living standard – even if that includes enduring racism. It's better than the poor conditions back in the home country; the racism is simply the price one must pay to avoid those conditions – a tax on the pursuit of the American dream. "Keep your head down, do your work diligently, make money, and don't delve into the question of identity." That was the mantra of the first generation of immigrants. As Hasan puts it, "My dad did not give a shit about identity stuff."

Hasan traces the origin of the American dream tax argument to the generational gap. He jokingly illustrates first-generation immigrants' mentality, "Every immigrant father feels like they brought you to the US. Happy Birthday. Starbucks, Wi-Fi, freeways, happy birthday. No more birthdays. Go be president." Hasan counters the American dream tax argument by arguing that it is no longer valid for second-generation immigrants. He contends that he need not audition his love and loyalty for the country.

> But for me, I was born here. So, I actually have the audacity of equality. I'm like, I'm in Honors Gov, I have it right here. Life, liberty, pursuit of happiness. All men created equal. It says it right here, I'm equal. I'm equal. I don't deserve this... Now you're like, "Let's be reasonable with the bigots." What? (Minhaj 2017)

He further explains the difference in identity creation for the first generation of immigrants and second generation. For the first generation, "Assimilation was the win"; for the second generation, "Authenticity is the win" (Khan Academy 2020). Authenticity means you are not required to hide your identity for approval or acceptance from anyone else. He claims that authenticity is the true American dream, which does not require any taxation. So, first-generation immigrants also got the meaning of the American dream wrong because it is about unconditional freedom for becoming what one desires to be.

Hasan's call for authentic identity has some philosophical discussions in existentialism. The central proposition of existentialism, *existence precedes essence,* is a good starting point to understand authentic identity (Sartre 2007, p. 345). The celebrated slogan of existentialism means that the consideration of the *existence* of an individual (i.e., recognizing the individual as an independent, acting, responsible being) should happen before assigning their *essence* (i.e., trying to fit the individual in various preconceived labels, roles, definitions, and stereotypes).

Another critical aspect of an individual is acceptance and recognition of what Heidegger called *thrownness,* "An entity of the character of Dasein is its "there" in such a way that, whether explicitly or not, it finds itself in its thrownness" (1996, pp. 135–136). People are thrown into a particular and narrow social milieu, surrounded by rigid attitudes, archaic prejudices, and practical necessities not of their own making. However, in the Heideggerian sense, thrownness is not a limiting deterministic way of life but an indicator of being thrown into the world of possibilities. He wanted to bring forth the *facticity* of being born in a concrete historical situation.

Sartre (2003, pp. 649–656) has also used the term *facticity* to refer to a limitation and condition of freedom. In the conception of limitation, facticity tells about the things one was not free to choose, such as birthplace or parents; a condition of freedom is the acceptance of one's facticity and creating one's own values for oneself in light of it.

But there is a critical distinction between how Heidegger and Sartre conceive of facticity. For Heidegger, the emphasis is on drawing freedom from the possibilities of thrownness into a historical situation; for Sartre, such possibilities undermine one's choice. The question is how one *transcends* from the facticity and thrownness of one's situation? The answer lies in another existential concept of *authenticity.* Heidegger suggested the answer to living an authentic life is moving from *they-self* to *our-selves. They-self* is surrendering oneself to a socialized, superficial mode of living. *Our self* is a mode of living according to one's own free choice. On the other hand, Sartre considered living in *bad faith* as an inauthentic mode of living, where bad faith is a resignation to circumstances however unfavorable and consequently becoming blind to other options. Sartrean authentic living is the exercise of freedom – the freedom with which humans are condemned to live. Behind all these concepts and jargons of existential philosophy lies a simple call to the human being, an ancient aphorism: *know thyself.*

The question is, how can one have an authentic identity and also allow others to express their authentic identities? Hasan proposes two philosophies for dealing with "the identity stuff." First, "May the best argument win" (Breakfast Club Power 105.1 FM 2017). Hasan is a strong advocate of freedom of speech and presenting one's argument. Having a conversation is the starting point of understanding each other's identities comprehensively. Conversations and dialogues may also lead to disagreements; however, conflicts should not prevent people from discussing uncomfortable topics. In the case of a dispute, which is natural in a plural society, the solution is having critical thinking devoid of biases and fallacies. This is much easier said than done, however, because humans do not run on 0s and 1s with logical units. People have their unique worldview and perspective. The attempt shall be on understanding each other's perspectives, respecting the freedom of speech of those involved in the discussion. As Hasan puts it...

> I'm really a proponent of free speech. So to me, I think what's great about freedom of speech is the open marketplace of ideas. Say what you want to say, but I'm a big advocate in presenting the best argument. May the best argument win. (Breakfast Club Power 105.1 FM 2017)

It is important to note the distinction between arguing and fighting. Arguments are collections of statements meant to establish a conclusion; arguments and counterarguments are part of a healthy discussion and there are courteous ways to disagree with another's point of view. Hasan emphasizes that such things are all part of a healthy conversation in which both parties agree to maintain civility.

> We need to figure out how we can disagree with civility. That concept has been completely lost. If you disagree with someone, now people are like, I'm not friends with that person anymore. Or they have this one thing that I don't align with them on this particular political issue or social issue, I can't fuck with them anymore. (HOT 97 2018)

Incivility may seem insignificant, but it could lead to what Hasan considers one of the biggest problems: violent extremism. With the great boom of information in the internet age came the bane of misinformation and fake news, but online anonymity in virtual interactions has also paved the way for negativity toward identity issues as well. If people engage in a disagreement online, the common response has become canceling, trolling, and general toxicity – and often people won't realize the immense negative impact their berating comment has on someone else's mental health and life. That is why Hasan's call for civility and humanity in disagreement is so important. People assuming an inauthentic identity and abusing freedom of speech need a positive response.

The second solution of Hasan is also positive and is apparent from his mantra of "Love is bigger than fear" (Minhaj 2017). According to Hasan, the root cause of hate, racial slurs, and abuse based on identity, stems from fear. Fear of what? Hasan clarifies:

> Because we're too afraid of the Other, someone who's not in our tribe. I wish I could tell 18-year-old me, "Hey, man, don't let this experience define you." It's good people and bad people. Irrespective of creed, class, color, find those people. Because love is bigger than fear. (Minhaj 2017)

Fear of the other compounded with the mentality of "either you are with us or against us" leads to an unhealthy approach to identity. Seeing any group from a myopic view could give rise to biases and prejudices. One should treat people as unique individuals. Hasan reiterates his philosophy of love:

> I just think that love intrinsically being bigger than fear will help end it. And in seeing people as individuals, that's the thing that to me will be one of the many reasons that can end racism. If you stop lumping people as these large monoliths and see people as individuals. Like we're not a monolith, we should have different diverse voices within the community. This idea that one person has to carry the mantle for everybody is insane. There's shades of belief and I think that's awesome. (Breakfast Club Power 105.1 FM 2017)

Hasan hints at respecting the plurality of ideas and opinions. Individuals bring their unique perspective, which furthers the development of civilization. If a person discards someone's idea just because it is not compatible with their own, they can suppress an insight they need to discover the truth and move forward. Many great ideas that later improve the lives begin as anomalies.

Conclusion

Hasan has opinions, claims, philosophy, and arguments toward the question of identities related to nation, race, religion, and person. He not only preaches about identity and other issues pertaining to our society but tries to present the best take possible on an issue. He is not afraid of poking the bear on controversial issues around the world. He notices the dilemma of national identity, the deep-rooted impact of ethnic identity, and the need for authentic identity with freedom. He often captures his life experiences in personalized storytelling to further practical social and identity-related issues. In the self-assessment of his work, drawing from the "Star Wars" analogy, he considers himself a Padawan in the socially sensitive comic force. He wields his lightsaber to cut across biases, fallacies, misconceptions, and stereotypes. He reckons, "I'm still a Padawan, but the best Jedi wield that sword incredibly well. The Chappells, the Carlins, the Stuarts, the Colberts, they're really good at that" (HOT 97 2018). Let's hope Hasan continues the battle against ignorance and gives us more laughs with critical philosophical insights into the human condition. I wish him to join the ranks of Jedi Master. May the force be with him.

References

Arweck, Elisabeth, and Eleanor Nesbitt. 2010. Young people's identity formation in mixed-faith families: Continuity or discontinuity of religious traditions? *Journal of Contemporary Religion* 25 (1): 67–87.

Breakfast Club Power 105.1 FM. 2017, June 8. Hasan Minhaj speaks on America's fear of Muslims, freedom of speech, Bill Maher & more. *YouTube Video*, 36:44. https://youtu.be/gS8W4KRSvRc

Heidegger, Martin. 1996. *Being and time: A translation of Sein und Zeit*. New York: Suny Press.
HOT 97. 2018, November 5. Hasan Minhaj gets real & unfiltered on Kanye West, politics, Amazon & patriot act. *YouTube Video*, 46:01. https://youtu.be/Olo_lQKarXo
Indian Election Update and the 1 MDB Scandal. 2019. Pariot Act with Hasan Minhaj. Netflix, https://www.netflix.com/in/title/80239931
Khan Academy. 2020, July 30. Hasan Minhaj on finding your gifts, being authentic, & understanding yourself | Homeroom with Sal. *YouTube Video*, 32:26. https://youtu.be/mm0Y3ym-JUg
Minhaj, Hasan. 2017. Hasan Minhaj: Homecoming king. *Netflix*. https://www.netflix.com/in/title/80134781
Olson, Eric. 2021. Personal identity. In *The Stanford encyclopedia of philosophy*. Spring, 2021 edition. https://plato.stanford.edu/entries/identity-personal/
Parekh, Bhikhu. 2008. *A new politics of identity: Political principles for an interdependent world*. Basingstoke: Palgrave Macmillan.
Sartre, Jean-Paul. 2003. *Being and nothingness*. Trans. Hazel E. Barnes. London: Routledge.
———. 2007. *Existentialism is a humanism*. New Haven: Yale University Press.
92nd Street Y. 2019, February 11. Hasan Minhaj talks patriot act with The New Yorker's Vinson Cunningham. *YouTube Video*, 1:01:15. https://youtu.be/4RjC1Q-Jli0
Uberoi, Varun. 2018. National identity – A multiculturalist's approach. *Critical Review of International Social and Political Philosophy* 21 (1): 46–64.
Vanity Fair. 2019, October 9. Hasan Minhaj answers increasingly personal questions. *YouTube Video*, 10:50. https://youtu.be/c8XToZCS7Rc

Stephen Fry as Philosopher: The Manic Socrates

74

Christopher M. Innes

Contents

Introduction	1702
Summarizing Stephen Fry	1703
Socrates as a Guide to Fry's Social Criticism	1704
Satire as Socratic Questioning of the Absurd	1705
Hell Is Emma Thompson	1707
Praising the Institutions with Faint Mockery	1709
By Job, Theodicies Are Silly!	1714
Conclusion: Socrates's Voice, Fry's Mania, and the Comforts of Moderate Reform	1716
References	1717

Abstract

Stephen Fry is the thinking person's comedian. Through his talent for satire, he encourages others to consider social, political, and religious matters. Like Socrates, Fry mocks the institutions and those in positions of power who think that their authority alone makes them better than others, and he asks questions that lead to what Socrates believed to be the purpose of inquiry: an examined life. Fry guides his audience by persuading them to think about their absurd surroundings. He mocks everything that deserves to be mocked: the military, the concept of social class with concentration on the upper class, and the absurd notion of an all-powerful God who allows suffering. Fry is what we might call a "manic comedian" because he suffers from bipolar disorder (which is also known as manic depression) and it figures heavily into his subtle comedic process. Middle class by birth, Fry moved to the upper class due to his social influence and celebrity, and yet he mocks the elite for their incompetence; the convert is often the most ferocious critic. He even imagines a sit-down interview with God,

---

C. M. Innes (✉)
Philosophy Department, Boise State University, ID, Boise, USA
e-mail: cinnes@boisestate.edu

© Springer Nature Switzerland AG 2024
D. K. Johnson et al. (eds.), *The Palgrave Handbook of Popular Culture as Philosophy*,
https://doi.org/10.1007/978-3-031-24685-2_103

threatening an egalitarian leveling of the Almighty; that is, Fry wants to point out that God, and those who elevate God to a special status, are not as faultless as they have been presented to the public. This chapter will determine the degree to which Fry, through his comedy, demands actual social change as part of the Socratic principle of the "examined life." It will reveal that, although Fry *does* call for social reform, it is perhaps moderate instead of radical.

Keywords

Stephen Fry · Socrates · Christianity · God · Theodicy · Satire · Social class · Alexei Sayle · Horatian Satire · Juvenalian Satire · Menippean Satire · The Apology · Catholic Church · BBC · Emma Thompson · Jean Paul Sartre · Pierre Bourdieu

Introduction

Stephen Fry is a satirist, and like many comedians he makes fun of things around him that he sees as absurd: the army, the Church, the social class system (especially the pretensions of the upper class), and the idea that cruelty can be justified in the face of an all-powerful God. He would question God if he ever met him just as he questions the ultimate purpose of the above-mentioned institutions of power and authority (hereafter, just "the institutions").

It's all well and good to elicit answers. But for what purpose? Like Socrates, Fry examines the world around him and finds it absurd. The odd thing, though, is that Fry is part and parcel of this absurdity; he is a member of the upper class. This makes his critique difficult to clarify. Now when watching comedians, it is common to take into account their social and political outlook. For example, it is not difficult to identify one of Fry's peers, Alexei Sayle, as a Marxist-leaning comedian because he criticizes the institutions and government with a keen eye on social and political concerns and clearly implies that radical change is needed. Sayle's working class credentials and ideology match his comedy. Fry's objective is more elusive, however. He has a middle-class background and his comments and his jokes don't lean toward Marxism, which might indicate that Fry is up to something other than bringing down the social and political system. So, is he supporting the system he mocks? Does his satire indicate that he merely wants to reform the outdated institutions and a dowdy notion of God rather than replace them?

To answer this, this chapter will look at Fry as a Socratic wanderer – one that is on a mission to point out the absurdity of the contemporary world. Caution is needed in such a quest, however. Sayle wants the system radically changed, but Fry does not make jokes that hint of the need for radical change. So, what does Fry want to happen? It might turn out that Fry is a conservative reformer whose comedy supports the status quo more than it detracts from it. This may sound like an odd use of satire, but one can imagine a teacher that mocks a student's work with the intention of improving it instead of destroying its author. Likewise, Fry's Socratic quest might reveal criticism for something while also supporting it in principle – just with some reform, which is still quite reasonable of any reformer to ask.

Summarizing Stephen Fry

Before addressing this chapter's argument, it would be helpful to say something about Fry's personal history. This will be best done by referring to his character as a comedian. One of the first things that viewers will note about Fry the comedian is that he has a scholarly sense about him. Film studies editor and writer Richard Porton likens Fry's erudition to that which made Oscar Wilde famous many years ago. He is an expressive individual who, like the "Crown Prince of Bohemia," knows what it is to be creative in a world that prevents such freedom. Indeed, Fry played the title role in the 1997 film *Wilde*, saying in an interview in the magazine *Cineaste* that he was born to play it. Like Wilde, Fry wants to express himself, read, and discuss the greats of philosophy and the myths of Greece. He feels that modern life is geared too much toward making a living and not enough toward being interested in philosophy, art, and literature. People often want to conform and just get on with life, but, for Fry, this leads to a very humdrum way of living. For both Wilde and Fry, being authentic is important. All told, Fry gives the impression of being very genuine and concerned with the plight of himself and other people in the modern world.

As part of the middle class, Fry's early days were blessed by the benefit of education and good taste. This is the class between the limited social expectations of the working classes and the excesses of the upper classes. It is like a social no-man's land, where the minefield of social norms and mores might blow up in one's face at any moment. There are behavioral expectations that, when violated, lead to social trouble. Fry noticed this in his school days. Though his manic depression was not diagnosed until later, it first showed itself when he failed to successfully navigate the school rules.

Although Fry has appeared in a number of films and is a prolific writer, he is probably best known for British sketch comedy shows like *A Bit of Fry and Laurie* and *Blackadder*. But in one of his earlier comedic roles, Fry mocked the very same privileged, yet socially fraught life of a university student that he also enjoyed. He appeared with Hugh Laurie and Emma Thompson in an episode of BBC's *The Young Ones* ("Bambi") in a spoof of *University Challenge:* a British quiz show on which Fry had actually competed in 1980 for Cambridge University's Queens College. The sketch was a satire of the class privilege found in university education. Fry played the part of Lord Snot, an entitled, half-witted undergraduate on a team called "Footlights College." The sketch is a double spoof of both his time at Cambridge University and his membership in *Footlights* Dramatic Club, an "elitist" comedy club where Fry's satirical awakening began. The critique of social class is a defining factor of this sketch – something that fits Fry's later comedy. He played a part satirizing the absurd privileges of "class," and he is part of the class he is mocking.

This sort of winking, class satire would become a model for his comedic career. Fry, Laurie, and Thompson continued closely working together – to the point that they gained the reputation in the media and general public of being a bit "clingy" toward one another. Admirers and detractors alike began calling the group "luvvies" (along with other, similarly publicly effusive actors). Their relationship is seen in both intended and unintended parody in the film *Peter's Friends* and later in the satire *Bright Young Things*. Yet, this closeness perhaps proved too suffocating for Fry, who disappeared to Belgium in 1995 in an emotional panic – abandoning a play (*Cell Mates*) in the middle of its run, even though he was both the co-writer and the co-star.

Sadly, this event was not Fry's only encounter with emotional turmoil. He was diagnosed later with bipolar disorder, or manic depression (hereafter the phrase "manic depression" will be exclusively used). The documentary *The Secret Life of a Manic Depressive* makes it clear that Fry suffers from this illness but also sees it as a benefit to his comedic method. On the one hand, he has bouts of sadness that can appear without notice. He has made two suicide attempts and is often thrown into deep depression by comments made by others and situations he hears about. Indeed, while media and others speculated on the reason he dropped out of *Cell Mates*, Fry would eventually admit that his flight was motivated by ceaseless pressure he received from press coverage, including a negative early review of the play. Once diagnosed, he would go on to attribute much of the ordeal to his manic depression. On the other hand, much of Fry's comedy and commentary on the institutions is driven by his mania – an attitude sometimes apparent in the persona he publicly adopts.

Taken together, these snippets from Fry's life may help the reader to see him as very much like a manic Socrates. He is someone who seeks to educate and better himself, who walks alone (as when he fled London for Europe), who asks provocative questions of the institutions around him, but also has no ambition to take over and provide alternative leadership. But to what degree is this Socratic comparison accurate?

Socrates as a Guide to Fry's Social Criticism

The Oracle of Delphi might not have called Fry the wisest person around, as she did with Socrates. Yet, Fry *is* respected as a learned media guru who asks lots of questions that serve an important social purpose. But this is not enough to make him a contemporary Socrates. If Fry is to be compared to one of the most important thinkers in the Western world, it needs to be shown that he is the Socratic gadfly that attempts to wake up the metaphorical lazy horses of his society.

As is depicted in Plato's *Apology*, Socrates was charged with worshipping false gods and of wittingly corrupting the youth of Athens. Curiously, Socrates spends most of his "defense" questioning the jury and his accusers rather than actually defending himself. For instance, Socrates says that it was not he who has corrupted Athens's youth, but the elders of Athens, who are not suited to teaching their children. Moreover, Socrates says that he should be thanked and not blamed for his attempts to enlighten the Athenian people. In the end, Socrates was executed by the Athenian state. His death is shown in Plato's *Phaedo*, where Socrates drinks hemlock in the presence of his friends.

Throughout the *Apology*, there is more than a hint of sarcasm and mockery of those in power. The jury held ultimate control over Socrates's life, just as many of his accusers held important positions in the Athenian state as political figures, poets, and artisans. Socrates would argue that this is too much power for ordinary people to have. They are not skilled in the administration of justice because they are ignorant of what justice really is. So, Socrates mocks them by calling them "men of Athens" and not the accepted title of respect: "gentlemen of the jury." He falls short of calling them morons but more than hints at their lack of ability.

But is Fry's mockery as subversive as Socrates's, or is Fry just making trouble? Socrates was seen by his first group of accusers as a busybody who went around Athens annoying people. This fits Fry very well. He is a satirist, rather than a stand-up comedian, lambasting his targets in sketches, speeches, interviews, and other kinds of work – and nothing and no one is off-limits. For example, in his documentary, *Last Chance to See*, Fry goes through a list of New Zealand bird names, such as the Kākāpō or the Pūkeko, claiming that they have been named by 7-year-olds. Even those who name birds are targets of criticism. Socrates was in search of knowledge and, like Fry, heard that certain groups had this knowledge. Fry is keen to seek out those who think they know about justice. He approaches politicians who claim to be wise, but upon closer examination they not only prove themselves ignorant, but they are not aware of this ignorance. Showing up politicians as ignorant can lead to Fry being perceived as a busybody, too, but of course today this would not lead to capital criminal charges. At any rate, there is a parallel here to the image of the gadfly conjured up by Socrates that is needed to wake up the lazy horse of Athens and its people. For Fry, the "lazy horse" that needs to be roused from its stupor is a combination of social, political, and religious institutions.

Satire as Socratic Questioning of the Absurd

Like Socrates, Fry wants to put his audience in a position to question themselves and the prevailing opinions of their society. To do this, Fry's comedic tool of choice is satire. But what type of satirist is he?

In a comment that is widely attributed to one of Fry's many TV interviews, he claims that comedy should be experienced with an obvious vocal response. He said that to simply say that something is funny without laughing is like saying something is sexy without "getting a stiffy." Jokes aside, though, perhaps one does not need to laugh out loud to appreciate the joke. There is more to comedy: it encourages people to think. Fry knows this, too, and it shows in his satire. By provoking the audience to both laugh *and* think, comedy can be more effective than dryly presenting an argument. Fry points out something that is apparently absurd in a way that makes it *obviously* absurd. For instance, Americans are frequently mocked by the rest of the world for both a tendency to rush into armed conflict and an ignorance about the rest of the world's affairs. So, on his quiz show, *QI*, Fry quotes Ambrose Bierce, saying that "war is God's way of teaching Americans geography."

Like a leading question from a skilled attorney, the exposition of the absurdity involves the audience as though they are going through the thought process – which they are – but it is Fry that leads them. They laugh because they have come to a new understanding. Fry is aware that thought-provoking comedy is difficult, and that the particular satirical tool to elicit a thoughtful response needs to be chosen carefully. He rarely uses less sophisticated humor, like slapstick, and his sexual references are kept to a minimum. When he does include them, they have a purpose, such as to expose sexual hypocrisy. Case in point: in the documentary *Out There*, Fry interviews Dr. Joseph Nicolosi, who holds a clinic to "resolve the conflicts" that he thinks cause homosexual attraction. Fry appears contemplative throughout the interview but closes by suggesting that Nicolosi looks very "Metro-sexual" – hinting that the good doctor is repressing some of the very sexual preferences he seeks to "resolve."

Among the classical types of satire, Horatian satire best describes Fry's comedy. This does not mean, however, that Fry does not keep Juvenalian and Menippean satire in his toolkit, too. But what are Horatian, Juvenalian, and Menippean satire?

Horatian satire differs from other types of satire because it attempts to get people to laugh with the use of dead-pan humor that playfully mocks that which the speaker finds absurd. His derision of Dr. Nicolsi is one example as is his later interview in the same show with a man who coaches gay men to cover up their gayness to get acting jobs. As Fry says, "maybe hiding your sexuality is warranted in Hollywood, because the audience wants to believe that the romantic lead, or action hero, is the real straight deal." The goal is to show the absurdity of Hollywood and its contradictions. It is supposed to be a place where gay men can be openly so in what is supposed to be the free and expressive profession of acting. This is a kind of sarcasm. While sarcasm has been described as the lowest form of wit because it is seen as impolite, sarcastic humor also engages the audience's intellect. One has to think to get the joke, and that thinking involves understanding the intellectual predicament that the speaker presents. The audience is not merely laughing; they are being enlightened.

This fits in nicely with Fry's mockery of social conventions and people's malicious religious, political, and social attitudes. In a sketch on the BBC's *A Bit of Fry and Laurie*, Fry plays a Christian called Arnold who wants to discuss the Book of Genesis with his friend, Glen ("Naked Bible Study"). Glen, instead, wants to discuss the size of Arnold's girlfriend's breasts. This is a satirical prodding of the way that ordinary people might weigh the importance of religion when compared to their sexual desires. Glen, probably like many people, finds sex much more interesting than Arnold's analysis of Genesis. Ignoring Glen's questions and pressing on, Fry plays Arnold with a peculiar lilt in his voice and an awkward, almost creepy presence. The sketch, of course, is making fun of an uptight and out-of-touch Christianity but not particular Christians, and it wouldn't be a surprise to learn that many practicing Christians find the sketch funny and not offensive.

At other times, Fry's satire takes a more aggressive tone. This is a hallmark of Juvenalian satire, where indignant anger is used to alert the audience of a serious wrongdoing. In a 2015 interview with the Irish TV host Gay Byrne, Byrne asks – as part of his regular set of questions for guests – what Fry would say in a meeting with God. His response? "Bone cancer in children? What's that about? How dare you? How dare you create a world in which there is such misery that is not our fault. It's not right. It's utterly, utterly evil." For his part, Fry describes how he would hold the deity accountable for the evil in the world.

Here and elsewhere, Fry savages divine power and authority, at least as it is seen by others, with his fierce criticism of theists and sexual moralists. Even the *Fry and Laurie* Genesis sketch, referenced above, could have a bit of Juvenalian bite. The passage from Genesis that Arnold quotes notes that Adam would not have realized his nakedness "unless you have eaten the fruit of the tree whereof I said thou shouldst not eat." As presented in the sketch, the fact that God withholds knowledge (like nakedness) would imply that God wants people to be ignorant – and worse, that the Church cultivates this belief. So, Fry sometimes gets angry and appears to actively want to upset people with his ideas. In these situations, Fry's aim is less on being funny and more on making a serious point.

At times, Fry invokes a third type of satire – Menippean satire – where character faults and personal obsessions are satirized. Despite a focus on these character flaws, Menippean satire still tends to broadly criticize ideas, attitudes, and dogmatisms rather than the specific individuals who hold them. The use of Menippean satire can be seen in another *Fry and Laurie* sketch ("Censored") through the overbearing personality of Sir William Rees-Mogg, later Lord ReesMogg, the real-life chairman of the "Broadcasting Standards Council" and one-time vice chairman of the BBC. In the sketch, Fry explains that Rees-Mogg did not like a previous version of the sketch that included excessive sex and violence, so a new sketch was produced. (This is part of the joke: there probably really was no specific earlier sketch that Rees-Mogg rejected; Fry and Laurie claim, for instance, that the refused sketch involved the two actors "going to bed together...violently." Instead, the present sketch is likely just a wider dig at British censorship). Laurie, seen on a television screen mounted beside Fry, then states that this kind of censorship is not "so sweeping as to be a kind of government thought police." Rather, the concern is merely with "standards...for the sake of our children." Of course, Fry and Laure *do* in fact see this kind of censorship as "government thought police," and Rees-Mogg is ridiculed for foisting his views onto the viewing public, who are assumed to be unable to decide for themselves what is appropriate to watch. As indicative of Menippean satire, the sketch is really a general message against the harmful effects of censorship, despite referring to Rees-Mogg specifically.

Hell Is Emma Thompson

Challenging institutions of power through sarcasm and satire is certainly a form of troublemaking – but it is not true subversive activity, as subversion aims at drastic change rather than just the personal satisfaction of the troublemaker. Additional work is to be done before Fry can be said to be authentically subversive, like Socrates. In fact, it needs to be established that Fry is authentic in the first place.

To be authentic is to think in a way that is not created by others. For someone so closely involved with other "luvvies" like Hugh Laurie and Emma Thompson, this may have been difficult for Fry. To belong to any group, one often has to adopt that group's way of thinking; it is necessary to get along. This is certainly a handicap for the authentic thinker.

As a lover of philosophy and literature, Fry might well have been aware of French philosopher Jean Paul Sartre's *Huis Clos* (*No Exit*, in English), wherein Sartre presents the claim that individuals should not be emotionally dependent on others for reasons of individual authenticity and freedom. Sartre was an existentialist philosopher who argued for authenticity in all matters, especially relationships with other people. According to Sartre, individuals usually view themselves as an object through the gaze of others; and to view oneself through the gaze of others is to accept their view. So, if a person is told that she is "a scholar who likes pizza," then that is a view she will have to accept if she is going to be friends with those defining her. To tell them that they have got her wrong will cause them to resent her. Therefore, she – and everyone, to Sartre – has a choice: either remain inauthentic and keep her friends, or live authentically, define herself, and have few or no friends. This is not an easy dilemma to resolve. As a public celebrity, Fry's sense of viewing himself through others is arguably even greater, as there are many more people attempting to define him.

Recall that Fry was also viewed and characterized in a certain way by his fellow "luvvies." Take Emma Thompson. Fry was put in the position of accepting Thompson's view of him or rejecting that view. (Whether Thompson's view of him is problematic or not does not really matter; the point for Sartre is simply that it is up to Fry to accept this view – unauthentically – or construct his own, authentic self). To accept Thompson's view would allow a relationship with Thompson, but would diminish his own authentic self-awareness. On a Sartrean view, one way to understand Fry's disappearance to Belgium is that he was rejecting others' views of him while at the same time presumably looking for his true self. However, according to Sartre there is no essential self; if that is right, making such a quest is likely to end with Fry finding a self that is still defined by others like Thompson. The compulsion to accept Thompson's view of him is there – and if he did accept it, he would be doing what Sartre calls in *Being and Nothingness* "acting in Bad Faith." To Sartre, though, it is always Fry's own responsibility to choose whether to reject or accept the characterizations that people like Thompson make. Authenticity demands that he reject the characterizations of others; this will lead him to nothingness but it is where he will be free to choose for himself who he will be.

Fry's predicament is much like the predicament of the three characters in Sartre's play, *No Exit*. They are locked in a room in the afterlife, seemingly waiting to be admitted to Hell. But the characters soon find out that, in essence, the room is Hell, because the company of the others is gained only at the cost of their authenticity. For example, one of the characters, Garcin, finds a way to escape but decides not to leave until he convinces another character, Inèz, that his pacifism in life did not make him a coward. This indicates that Garcin lacks self-worth, and indeed all three captives are in some way dependent on each other for their self-worth. This lack of self-worth leads to lack of authenticity and dooms them all to eternal "punishment."

As was observed above with Fry, authenticity is important for the examined and worthwhile life. This is because people tend to desire the emotional support or admiration of others. They are social beings and as such feel a need for others to like them. But to have someone like you comes with the baggage of why they like you – not to mention that you are confined by how they define your character and your "self." This is why one of the characters in *No Exit* declares, famously, that "hell is other people." For Sartre, each individual – both in the play and the real world – is trapped by the way that other people perceive and define them. In his personal life, Sartre's long-term romantic partner Simone De Beauvoir constantly encouraged him to have an open relationship so neither was dependent solely on the other.

Fry was depressed when he went to Europe. This existential crisis would presumably include doubt about who he is and about people wanting him to be something he is not. In many of his interviews after this emotional episode, Fry said that he felt like his friends and fans wanted him to be available to them. To read Fry's escape to Belgium through a Sartrean lens, Fry believed that others, including friends like Thompson, were projecting their views of Fry as an object – an object of love, emotional support, a source of laughter, etc. – onto him. To accept these views would be in Bad Faith. Acceptance would make Fry into a socially created object. It is, of course, wrong to turn someone into a socially created object simply because it will deny them the authentic, examined life of an independent *subject*. Socrates often discussed the need to live an "examined life." This is an examination of every aspect of one's daily conduct and thought. Part of living this "examined life," then, involves self-reflection and the building of an authentic self. To be a contemporary Socrates, Fry's departure to Europe may have been entirely necessary so that he could examine himself and develop this authenticity in solitude.

Praising the Institutions with Faint Mockery

Like Socrates, Fry is self-aware and craves authentic freedom. One of Fry's most frequent comedic targets remains the absurdity of the class system and the institutions that sustain it. This is seen in another sketch from *A Bit of Fry and Laurie*, where Laurie wants to join the British Army Secret Armed Service, or SAS (the sketch is also called "SAS"). The recruiting officer tells Laurie that the SAS is no longer a fighting force but is instead just "a masturbatory aid for various backbench MPs." In the United Kingdom, "backbenchers" are members of Parliament – MPs – who hold no real government office. So, the sketch argues that the military's role has been reduced to something that props up and preserves the hollowest of political appointments.

Today's social classes were not in place during Socrates's time, but Socrates was certainly critical of the power of the state and those who held their authority within the state, just like Fry. Indeed, Socrates was *so* critical of the state – and so committed to exposing others to this critique – that he was willing to be put to death for it. In the *Apology,* Socrates outright refuses lesser sentences like exile.

Obviously, Fry has not followed Socrates to this radical endpoint. But even if it can be established that Fry is an authentic person, it is not clear whether his comedy calls for genuine change in the institutions he criticizes. Could it be that Fry actually wants to preserve the very institutions he mocks – the government and civil branches, universities, the judiciary, the military, and of course the Church – because he benefits from them in some way? For example, in the above sketch on SAS recruitment, Fry is not saying that the army needs to be abolished, just that it needs to be more self-aware and examine its purpose as an institution. Examining Fry's strange relationship with such institutions is both illuminating and confusing.

Despite his mockery of it, Fry's celebrity at least suggests he has been granted a kind of guest membership to the upper class; although he was not born into it, Fry was given access to it by his work in the media, and then was not kicked out of it by other (born) upper-class members because of his acceptable conduct. That he attended Cambridge University, an expensive and privileged institution, likely plays a major role in this. That is perhaps how he became a member of the Garrick, a theatrical gentleman's club in London that has a 7-year waiting list to which one can only be admitted as a member if one is proposed by an existing member.

Still, Fry mocks the upper-class. For example, Fry (seemingly intentionally) calls the Garrick, "The Garrick *Club*," which is considered a faux pas. But generally, Fry's mockery of upper-class elitism resembles the good, old-fashioned style of British mainstays like Monty Python. For instance, a sketch from *A Bit of Fry and Laurie* includes Laurie as a university physics teacher who, while filming a lecture, makes the mistake of getting his figures wrong ("Open University Bloopers"). When the director points out the error, both of them begin laughing out of control. Of course, the teacher's mistake is not something that would be recognized by most people – and that is the point. As part of an elite group that understands the mistake, the teacher and director have a good laugh at something that ordinary people would find dull, at best.

And yet, he also actively enjoys the advantages of upper-class life and is allowed to remain in that social group. Is there a reason why the upper class allows this mockery? Perhaps the upper class and the institutions are getting something out of it. Indeed, it might be that the kind of mockery that Fry offers helps bolster and reinforce the existence and role of the upper-class and its institutions. How so?

The Marxist philosopher and sociologist Pierre Bourdieu's perspective on socio-economic class shows how individuals such as Fry engage and identify with their respective social class. Bourdieu argues that class membership is not maintained by money alone. Its status and credibility are also maintained by social capital – features of society such as education, fashion, and personality – that also give the individual class member their role and purpose. As the group "on top," members of the upper class obviously benefit the most from class hierarchy. So, part of the "role" of upper-class people will be to maintain the institution of class. Fry's role as a comedian belonging to the upper class is twofold: he is expected to be funny, but he cannot mock the upper class so fiercely that he gets kicked out of it.

To see how Fry's comedy fits his social role, consider this: a normal turn of phrase is to say that a person "damns" something "with faint praise." This means that the person is making a remark that seems praiseworthy when it is actually intended to mock the target in some way. Most students know such remarks well, such as when a professor says that an essay is "well written and interesting" before picking it apart for its lack of insight and other errors. But if we invert the concept of faint praise, we might think in terms of *faint mockery* – where something is seemingly mocked, but the actual intention is to praise.

With this in mind, one might think that Fry is engaged in faint mockery when he makes fun of the institutions, given both that the institutions tolerate his mockery and that he afterward seems to participate in and benefit from those same institutions. When Fry takes part in sketches like the *University Challenge* spoof on *The Young Ones,* he is clearly damning the elitism of upper-class schools like Cambridge; yet, as a Cambridge alumnus, he also has a certain fondness for the very same sort of privileged education he criticizes. Although university education and privilege are mocked, they are mocked so lightly that the people who attend places like Cambridge are also "in on the joke." In this way, faint mockery helps to perpetuate institutions like elite universities.

Why would Fry do this? Whichever class he inhabits, Fry lives by a process that Bourdieu calls "habitus." This is the socially ingrained disposition of attitudes, habits, and skills that individuals gain as members of their social class. It takes a lot of effort to maintain the attributes and physical appearances needed to keep one's class membership. In order to maintain membership of a class one needs to express certain beliefs, speak with a certain accent, and even walk and present oneself in a way that is similar to other members of that class. And Fry's wit and scholarly outlook fit him into a class where he feels comfortable and other class members are comfortable with him.

And yet, Fry also seems to mock the habitus of social class as arbitrary and quite absurd. This happens regularly on *A Bit of Fry and Laurie*, where social class is often mocked for the mannerisms and quirks needed for a person to belong. For instance, consider the recurring appearances of the two businessmen characters, Peter and John, who utter phrases such as "the Boardroom and the Bedroom are two sides of the same agenda." In between downing many tumblers of scotch (already something associated with their social position), the two are seen as mocking the mores and attitudes that make them acceptable in the class of businessmen.

At the same time, these are the very same class mannerisms that Fry maintains in his own field as a culture critic. Granted, like Peter and John, Fry would find belonging difficult without buying in to the "stock" of social norms and mores of his class. But he also criticizes them. One might argue that Fry is perhaps in a better position to meaningfully criticize the institutions by accepting their rules and "speaking their language," but one does not necessarily have to belong to a group to criticize it. And so there seems to be a bit of hypocrisy in Fry's mockery of upper-class habitus. And certainly, simply pointing out the absurdities of the rules of social conduct in, for example, the business class does not genuinely disrupt that class or challenge the class system as a whole.

But perhaps that is the point and Fry's mutual class membership and mockery is not so odd, after all. Perhaps he is not trying to destroy the idea of class and the institutions that support it or even undermine them significantly because he wants to "have his cake" (by enjoying the advantages of his class) and "eat it, too" (by calling attention to its failures, problems, and silliness). This might make him seem less "cutting edge," but it may also be a more accurate representation of him as not only a comedian but as a person.

As a critic, Fry's support of institutions of power and class can be seen by delving deeper into Richard Curtis and Ben Elton's *Blackadder Goes Forth*. This is a BBC historical sitcom based in the trenches of the First World War. In it, Fry plays the childish and incompetent General Melchett and Hugh Laurie plays Lieutenant George. As others have commented, by applying Bourdieu's analysis to *Blackadder*, it is clear that social class is presented in the series as something natural, when in practice it is kept in order by military custom and expectations (Webb et al. 2002). Adherence to values and beliefs is aggressively enforced while the soldiers are not aware that these beliefs are largely arbitrary.

For instance, Captain Blackadder, a middle-class army officer, fulfills his duties as an officer without realizing that they are carried out mostly unconsciously, given Bourdieu's notion of habitus. In order to get out of actual combat, Blackadder secures the position as the new illustrator for the *King and Country* – a propaganda paper printed in Paris – by stealing Lieutenant George's painting and claiming it as his own work ("Captain Cook"). The *King and Country* appointment is revealed to be a ruse; however Blackadder is instead supposed to illustrate the defenses across the enemy's line to better help the British soldiers prepare for their next assault. In another attempt to avoid the fight, Blackadder – with help from Lieutenant George – produces a falsified image showing immense enemy fortifications, up to and including *elephants*. When this plan *also* fails, Blackadder ultimately avoids charging "over the top" by posing as an Italian chef for General Melchett.

Through each of these increasingly outrageous plots, Blackadder's focus is always on saving himself; it does not seem to occur to him to try and stop the war or usurp the chain of command. Indeed, the hierarchical, officer structure is still respected and maintained in peculiar ways. Despite its ridiculousness, consider the rigid and order-like manner in which Blackadder responds to Lieutenant George's question about what to do when stepping on a mine: "Well, normal procedure, Lieutenant, is to jump up 200 feet into the air and scatter yourself over a wide area." For Blackadder, the war (and the roles of officer and subordinate) must go on – just not with him getting killed.

So, the class customs and expectations he abides by are real only in a social sense. This is to say that they are not real in the same sense that food is needed for nourishment or heat is needed to stay warm. Rather, they are fabricated for the purpose of identifying social class membership. It is like playing a game, but the game is deadly serious, and the players have interests in power and politics that motivate them to act the way they do. Deviation is deemed unreasonable or unthinkable because those in power wish to retain their power; the status quo is to be kept at all costs.

Fry's performance as the silly General Melchett illustrates the notion of habitus and Fry's acceptance of it in his daily life. Different members of the British Army in the Great War – WWI – are in a state of constant anxiety about orders to "go over the top," a suicidal strategy that saw soldiers charge out of the trenches and straight into a line of enemy fire. Social class differences are made clear in this scenario. General Melchett and his sidekick, Lieutenant George, are clearly upper-class people. Their many antics and rituals, from a shared school background, are incomprehensible to Captain Blackadder (who is middle class) and Private Baldrick (who is working class). General Melchett is enthusiastic about the war and is not aware of the real dangers it poses; he might be excused because he is not in the trenches and does not see the death and maiming first-hand. But Lieutenant George, who *is* in the trenches and *should* know better, is equally enthusiastic. His obliviousness toward the impending carnage is both hilarious and scary.

Yet, Lieutenant George throws off his upper-class habitus and questions whether the war is actually just when it is time to go over the top. George momentarily enters the habitus of Blackadder and Baldrick and he sees the war and what it demands of its rank-and-file soldiers as absurd. The notion of social "stock," once seen in objective terms, is now useless in explaining that the War has objective meaning for all Britons. Despite this, however, George also has no intention of stopping it or changing the plan of action and returns to the habitus of his own class.

Knowing Lieutenant George's relationship with his habitus helps us better understand Fry's situation and intentions. Just as George both understands the horror of war for the average soldier (however briefly) *and* still accepts his role in the war, Fry's criticism of his class just serves to reinforce his class membership and what he perceives as the importance of the institutions. He has no reason to reject them. He is aware that the rich kids ran the schools he went to as a schoolboy. It was also the rich kids who ran Cambridge. He knows that his access to the upper class is limited, and that his participation is based on his education in their schools and universities; yet he also knows that he can make fun of them while still participating in the game that they have created (because his staying in that class is contingent on him playing the game). He praises the institutions with faint mockery in a way that might appear insincere, but it is satire that even the ruling class needs and even expects in moderate amounts. It's part of the language. Like his permanent membership at the Garrick is based on his previous good conduct, his guest membership in the upper-class would be revoked with immediate effect if he were to be more radical.

Fry definitely plays the "game" of social class and wants to avoid professional estrangement. The only way to do this is to take part. This is shown in an episode of BBC's adult puppet satire program, *Spitting Image*. Stephen Fry and the other "luvvies" like Laurie, Thompson, and others, sit at a dinner party with Anthony Hopkins as their guest. Hopkins is asked where he went to university and replies that he did not attend university, to which Laurie amusingly says, "Oh how droll, you went to Oxford!" Hopkins responds, clarifying that he did not go to *any* university at all. Hearing this socially devastating news, Fry promptly instructs Hopkins to serve drinks once he's cleared up the dining table. One's social class is contingent and Hopkins's membership has just been revoked – as would Fry's if he had not gone to

Cambridge and did not praise the institutions with faint mockery. Keeping full membership of any class takes effort. "Treason" is out of the question because the game must go on. Which means that the social class system might need reform but only a bit at a time. And as long as Fry – unlike Socrates – knows how much dissent is socially acceptable, and it never turns into treason, this dissent may be a hallmark of his class membership. Light mockery is tolerated because it keeps social class, and the institutions that support class, going.

By Job, Theodicies Are Silly!

Fry treads carefully in matters of dissent in some social institutions, so it might be thought that his treatment of the Church would be done with even more care, so as not to offend the powerful too much. Yet, Fry has also publicly referred to himself as an atheist on more than one occasion, such as during a 2009 Spectator Lecture for the Royal Geographical Society. Although Socrates was not an atheist – he considered doing philosophy to be a service to the god Apollo – Socrates did challenge the prevailing religious institutions of his time. In fact, he was in part executed on the charge of "impiety" toward the gods of the state. In this way, Fry's criticism of the Church and the notion of God more generally seem to be perfectly Socratic.

Fry certainly sees theism as philosophically problematic, mostly because many theists accept God as perfect despite the fact that God allows evils like cruelty to children. Explanations of why God allows evil are called theodicies, and most of Fry's critique of religion manifests as an attack on such arguments, especially as they are applied to what is known as the "problem of evil" – the argument which suggests that the evil of the world entails that God does not exist.

Fry states this clearly in his interview with Gay Byrne on RTE, the Irish Public Broadcast station, when Byrne asked Fry what he would say if he ever met God: "Why should I respect a capricious, mean-minded, stupid god who creates a world that is so full of injustice and pain?" Fry's point seems to be that there is great evil and wrong in the world – and so God (an omnipotent deity out for the good of all creation) must not exist; if he did, there would be no such evil. Of course, one might argue that whatever God does is good, by definition. But Fry makes it clear that this would mean that God could decide on a whim what is right or wrong (and then even change his mind about it later), and that Fry would not want to get "into a heaven" on terms that would require him to accept a God that would allow such things as good. Such a God "is, quite clearly, a maniac – utter maniac, totally selfish."

Fry's interview with Byrne evokes shades of another Platonic dialogue, *Euthyphro*. In it, Socrates has a discussion with a priest named Euthyphro about the nature of piety. Famously, Socrates presents what has come to be called the Euthyphro dilemma: is something called pious just because the gods love it, or do the gods love the pious thing because it is already pious? In more contemporary philosophy of religion, the Euthyphro dilemma is used to illustrate problems about God's relationship to moral goodness. Is an act morally good because God commands it, or does God command the act because it is morally good? The worry with the second horn of the dilemma is that it suggests that there is a moral standard outside of God's control. God is bound to call that which is good by that standard, "good." This would entail that God is neither all-powerful nor the final arbiter of right and wrong, and that is contrary to the traditional definition of God as a "perfect, all-powerful" being.

But the worry with the first horn of the dilemma – that an act is good *just because* God commands people to do it – is that it makes morality arbitrary. This is like Fry's criticism about God being a capricious, selfish maniac. Infant murder couldn't and wouldn't suddenly become good if God commanded it. Of course, one might argue that God would never do that, but there are two problems with such an argument. First, he does in the Old Testament (Hosea 13:16, 1 Samuel 15:3, Psalms 137:8–9). Second, the only way it is true that God would never command such a thing is if there is a moral standard, outside of God's control, that entailed infant murder is bad that God would always adhere to. And that brings right back to the "there is a standard outside of God" problem again.

But at the heart of Fry's criticism is the problem of evil. In a televised Intelligence Squared debate in 2009, on whether the Catholic Church is a force for good in the world, Fry argued for the negative. When his opponents made the argument that the Church was a kind of moral model for the world, Fry retorted by pointing out that it is anything but. "[The Church,] for example, thought that slavery was perfectly fine, absolutely okay, and then they didn't. And what is the point of the Catholic Church if it says 'Oh, well we couldn't know better because nobody else did.' Then what are you for?" Likewise, one could argue, if God is not willing to step in to prevent evils like the suffering of children at the hand of bone cancer – and indeed, since he is the author of the laws of nature, which seem to entail that such things are necessary – then, like Fry, one might rightly ask of God: "Then what are you for?"

What Fry demands, then, is an explanation from believers – an explanation for how an all-good God could allow (or even author) such evils – and this is precisely what a theodicy offers. The Biblical book of Job is the traditional target of many theodicy arguments, where God attempts to prove to the devil that his faithful worshiper, Job, will maintain his faith no matter what afflictions are cast upon him. God allows the death of Job's children, among many other ills, but still Job does not stop worshiping God. Just as Fry asks why God would permit bone cancer in children, one might wonder why God would allow such horrible suffering for even his very faithful, like Job and his family.

Among the many theodicies proposed over the years to answer questions like this, two of the most popular involve the notions of free will and character building. In terms of free will, Richard Swinburne (1978) argues that God permits evil to preserve the free choices of human beings. Even natural evils like bone cancer must be permitted so that freely chosen moral evil is possible – such as the choice to steal in order to pay for expensive cancer treatments. It is only because of natural evil that the moral choice presents itself in the first place. Dovetailing nicely with this idea, John Hick (1966) posits a "soul-making" theodicy rooted in the beliefs of the Greek bishop Irenaeus, whereby the adversity of dealing with moral and natural evil builds character.

Given how he responded to Byrne and others, though, it is unlikely that Fry would accept these theodicies. Perhaps, for instance, Fry might be willing to call his mania a "gift from God," as he has admitted it makes him very productive and contributes to his comedy. He has, in a sense, built much of his own character through the adversity of manic depression. But even setting aside the suicidal ideations with which he frequently battles, Fry would likely say that manic depression is one thing, but terminal bone cancer in children is another entirely. This does not improve the character of dying children, and their tremendous suffering is no excuse for the potential character-building of the family members who endure the deaths of their loved ones. Likewise, if such is the cost of "free will," one can expect Fry to say that it is too highly bought.

So, just like Socrates, Fry maintains a robust skepticism of religious institutions and their adherents. Primarily, this is because the adherents too often do not think critically about what they are being asked to believe. For Socrates, this "belief" came in the form of widespread acceptance that the gods were just as petty and jealous as ordinary humans – as he challenges in *Euthyphro*. To Fry, this "belief" is in inadequate theodicies and inconsistencies between God's supposed goodness and the evils of the world. As Socrates would, Fry pushes the faithful to question their beliefs. This is not a demand that the religious prove God's existence to him, as Fry's fellow comedian Ricky Gervais makes. Rather, Fry asks theists to *think* for themselves.

Conclusion: Socrates's Voice, Fry's Mania, and the Comforts of Moderate Reform

In the *Apology*, Socrates talks about an inner "voice" that cautions him against doing wrong. To Socrates, this voice is a kind of divine spirit. Given Fry's comments about his manic depression, perhaps the suggestion in the previous section is not too far off: that his mania is *also* a sort of divine gift. It helps him do his comedy. Still, the lows and highs of manic depression are no laughing matter. Before his diagnosis, Fry has made fun of the disorder on at least one occasion. On an adlib BBC radio program called *Whose Line is it Anyway*, Fry had the task of improvising current affairs as someone who suffers from manic depression. As part of the bit, one moment he was joyous and the next he declared "who really cares." Fry's mania is ever present, and it is a vital motivating force for his comedy and view of the world. This is shown in his documentary *The Secret Life of a Manic Depressive*, where he is now aware of his condition and is thankful that it is what drives him as that person who asks so many questions.

Fry's medium is certainly different from Socrates. Although the Greek philosopher was at times sarcastic, he was no satirist or comedian. The point is the same, though: in the asking of questions that challenge authority, Socrates and Fry both hope to bring others to reflect on themselves and their societies. But he can only call for this kind of societal self-examination because he also examines himself, in an authentic way.

Perhaps Fry really is a manic Socrates – but with a restraint that Socrates never had (nor wanted). Fry's desire for change is genuine, but it is also limited to a conservative, incremental reform that the ruling class can accept and Fry can still say is just. There will be no radical change, but that is Fry's intention. After all, he benefits from most of these institutions, too. In this sense he is a modern-day gadfly to the establishment, its underbelly often exposed for Fry to see. His bite is enough to cause annoyance but not enough to summon a call for his execution. The Democratic and Christian establishment rarely puts its enemies to death, anyway (at least, any more). Should Fry ever be charged with impiety and corrupting youth, the jury will be heavily in favor of acquittal. No hemlock for Stephen Fry! They will restore his freedom to stroll through the hallways, streets, and chambers of the establishment to remind them of what they are doing wrong and that what they say is nonsense, but with little consequence.

References

Hick, John. 1966. *Evil and the god of love*. New York: Harper and Row.
Swinburne, Richard. 1978. Natural evil. *American Philosophical Quarterly* 15 (4): 295–301.
Webb, Jen, Tony Schirato, and Geoff Danaher. 2002. *Understanding Bourdieu*. London: Sage.

Phoebe Waller-Bridge as Philosopher: Conscious Women Making Choices

75

Neha Pande and Kimberly S. Engels

Contents

Introduction	1720
Who Are Lulu and Fleabag?	1721
Phoebe Waller-Bridge's Female Characters and Her Appetite for Transgressive Women	1722
Jean-Paul Sartre's Existentialism	1724
Existentialist Themes in *Fleabag* and *Crashing*	1727
Phoebe Waller-Bridge's Female Characters: Making Choices and Eliminating Bad Faith	1731
Simone De Beauvoir's Existentialism, and Freedom	1733
Conclusion	1736
References	1737

Abstract

Phoebe Waller-Bridge is not an unknown name. The writer, actor, and producer has been a part of various comedy TV series and films. However, she has a pattern in her comedy writing and character creation that is obvious in the TV series – *Fleabag* (2016–2019) and *Crashing* (2016). In both these series, one cannot miss the obvious similarity between the characters she wrote and played – characters who knew what they wanted and did not hesitate to make attempts to achieve it, even when it meant defying the conventional rules of social relationships and breaking out of the gender identities set by society for women. In fact, other characters created around these female characters seem to lack the same courage, which leads to the creation of comical situations but also often results in these characters facing emotional obstacles that they eventually overcome. The women in both shows not only choose to reject predefined gender identities, but also make choices and take risks while being aware of the consequences. Throughout

N. Pande (✉)
Royal Roads University, Victoria, BC, Canada

K. S. Engels
Molloy University, Rockville Centre, NY, USA
e-mail: kengels@molloy.edu

© Springer Nature Switzerland AG 2024
D. K. Johnson et al. (eds.), *The Palgrave Handbook of Popular Culture as Philosophy*,
https://doi.org/10.1007/978-3-031-24685-2_105

their journeys of embracing their free consciousnesses, these characters illustrate Jean Paul Sartre's and Simone de Beauvoir's process of transcending their facticity, thus avoiding bad faith. Implicit in Waller-Bridge's work is the argument that we could do better to be – and encourage other women to be – the types of women that her protagonists are.

Keywords

Phoebe Waller-Bridge · *Fleabag* · *Crashing* · Jean Paul Sartre · Simone de Beauvoir · Conscious women making choices · Bad faith · Being-for-itself · Being-in-itself · Facticity · Transcendence · Fundamental project · Freedom · Feminism · Being and nothingness · The ethics of ambiguity · Transgression · Second sex

Introduction

Phoebe Waller-Bridge is not an unknown name. While not a stand-up comedian (like others in this section of the handbook), her writing and characters have not only represented women's actual experiences but have also validated them on the screen, in contrast to the prevalent tokenistic portrayals of women. The female characters in her stories are what real (authentic) women are like – the way they talk, the way they express their feelings, the way they make their choices, the way they express love and desire, and the manner in which they deal with trauma. This chapter is an attempt to understand the characters created by Phoebe Waller-Bridge and how they represent strong female characters who make their own choices and avoid getting trapped in what existentialist philosopher Jean Paul Sartre called bad faith.

Indeed, implicit throughout the stories of her major characters in both series is an argument about the importance and ability of women to remain outside of bad faith in a society set up for them to fail at doing so. Waller-Bridge's women characters repeatedly demonstrate the path of authenticity more consistently than their male counterparts, acknowledging the very real effects of social roles and conventions while simultaneously remembering that they always have a choice of how to respond. Societal norms, cultural conventions, the pressure of others, and patriarchal standards make producing oneself as a free authentic subject a difficult task. Despite these difficulties, Waller-Bridge gives audiences examples of two women doing just that, suggesting that we would do better to be the kind of women that Fleabag and Lulu are: women who acknowledge social norms but remember they are not bound to them, who are aware of the limitations posed by the expectations of others but aren't controlled by them, and who remain outside of bad faith by accepting what they cannot change – facticity – while embracing their freedom to transcend it. But to build the case that this is what her shows are doing, it will be necessary to begin by briefly summarizing the plots of Phoebe Waller-Bridge's series *Crashing* and *Fleabag*.

Who Are Lulu and Fleabag?

Lulu is the protagonist of *Crashing*, a one season show which follows Lulu as she travels to London in hopes of revealing to her childhood friend Anthony that she loves him. *Crashing* establishes the pattern of Phoebe Waller-Bridge creating independent women characters on the screen. Later she would also create *Fleabag*, and although Lulu has many shades of (the character), Lulu cannot be said to be as complex as the latter. This is likely due to the age difference between the two characters, and the same age difference of Waller-Bridge when she wrote and acted in these shows, along with the length of the series.

Lulu's character is free-spirited, unapologetic, and determined. She can, sometimes, be considered selfish and only conveniently altruistic. Lulu hopes to be romantically involved with Anthony but he is engaged to Kate. Lulu does not have any animosity against Kate, as typically shown in a conventional storyline when two women love the same man. The show concentrates on the desires of a woman who continuously puts forth effort but does not assume that the man/person she loves belongs to her. Lulu does not assume a sense of authority over Anthony, which the conventional understanding of love tends to afford a person. In the last episode, Anthony asks her if she loves him, and wants to be with him, and if she had come to London to end his relationship with Kate. She admits that she loves him and had come to be with him, but she did not have an intention to break them up. It is contradictory, as being with him in a mono-amorous relationship would mean Anthony would have to break up with Kate. However, her choice makes it clear. She knows she wants to be with Anthony and has traveled all the way to express herself; however, she does not want to make a decision on his behalf. In the last episode, after Anthony and Lulu make love, Anthony tells Lulu that Kate still wants to be with him and asks Lulu what he should do; Lulu is taken aback but tells him, passive-aggressively, that he should be with Kate. This is where her choice – that is, to let Anthony make his own decision after she has confessed her feelings to him – establishes the core of her character: she makes her own choices, sometimes knowing the consequences, but does not take away anyone else's right to choose.

The series *Fleabag* has two seasons. Fleabag, though similar, is a more carved character. She is a single woman, in her early 30s, running a failing café in London which she started with her best friend, Boo, who tragically died. She has made her choices in life, some of which were bad, and she is continuously trying to deal with the guilt she feels as a result of those bad decisions. Fleabag has her own dilemmas which come from the choices she makes in the first season. The second season concentrates more on how her life is influenced by the choices made by other people, especially, the Priest whom she falls in love with and who is consistently confused about his choices between her and the priesthood. She does not hesitate to explore further and continues without thinking about the consequences. Moreover, in the show, Fleabag as a character is shown in a certain light, but not always in a positive way; yet her toxicity is not validated by the show making her look like a larger than life, heroic character. She is a human - good, bad, and ugly. However, one quality that Fleabag shares with Lulu is her unapologetic attitude toward life.

Phoebe Waller-Bridge's Female Characters and Her Appetite for Transgressive Women

Phoebe Waller-Bridge tries to present women with a spectrum of qualities, different personalities, and unique characteristics of their own. They make their choices but are also influenced by societal pressures. Both Lulu and Fleabag are different, at least to some extent, than other female characters in their respective shows. Waller-Bridge has continuously shared her perspectives on the characters she has created or has been inspired to create. For example, in a *HuffPost* interview, she said "the conversations about Fleabag, people are saying in a positive way that she is flawed and yet we like her..." "...women are in and that's like..." (She chuckles. The host nods in agreement) (HuffPost 2016, 02:48).

This shows that women can identify with Fleabag and her atypical characteristics. She is not understood by the conventional patriarchal perspectives which portray women especially as shy, indecisive, and only looking for stability. The shows represent an attempt to humanize women, defining them as self-determining subjects – which makes them look transgressive in a patriarchal society – rather than an attempt to understand and define them from the perspective of what *women should be like*.

During an interview with *The Guardian*, Waller-Bridge made clear that, as a writer, she wants to show women indulging their appetites and venting their grievances. "We sexualize women all the time in drama and TV. They are objectified. But an exploration of one woman's creative desire is really exciting. She can be a nice person, but the darker corners of her mind are unusual and fucked up, because everyone's are" (Hattenstone 2018). Waller-Bridge shares an incident about showing an early cut of *Fleabag* to her family. Her brother told her, "I think you're going to scare a lot of men with this show. It's going to freak them out." To which she replied, "Fucking good, it's about bloody time. Again, that narrative of keeping your man satisfied is rammed down our throats forever" (Hattenstone 2018).

During another interview with *The Guardian*, when asked about the "character's preferred method via sex," Waller-Bridge shares that she thinks "there was a certain shock value appeal in a woman expressing her sexual desires so frankly. But it is a faulty connection, and Fleabag's desire is more for the escapism and power than actual physical gratification of sex" (Aitkenhead 2017). Take, for instance, the second episode in season one. (From here on out, we will use the abbreviations like S1E2; the episodes don't have individual titles.) In S1E2 Fleabag says, "I'm not obsessed with sex, I just can't stop thinking about it. The performance of it, the awkwardness of it, the drama of it. The moment you realize someone wants your body. Not so much the feeling of it." Further, she describes the use of sex to escape her loneliness. In S2E2, when the counsellor asks her why she thinks her father gifted her a voucher for a counselling session, Fleabag replies to the therapist, "Um I think... because I spent most of my adult life using sex to deflect the screaming void inside my empty heart."

Moreover, the character of Fleabag has been written by Waller-Bridge to give her a sense of perversion throughout. In S1E5, during the conversation with her doctor while she gets her breasts checked, Fleabag says, "Bet you look forward to seeing Claire. A lot more to touch, if you know what I mean." She then chuckles. The doctor clears his throat. Fleabag, reading the awkwardness in the room, continues, "I'm sorry, it's just that there are worse jobs." To this the doctor (emphatically) replies, "Look... I check for cancerous lumps in mammary glands. Now, any pleasure I derive from that is entirely dependent upon whether or not I am about to save your life." Fleabag, embarrassed, says, "Of course, Doctor."

In the original script this scene was different: the doctor is caught masturbating in his office immediately after. This detail was scrapped via a mutual decision of Amazon and her team. Waller-Bridge emphasized that "Everyone's got to be quite sweet, really, for her twisted mind to work" (Young 2017). This shows an unconventional (sexual) side of a woman which is quite natural for them to have but has not been normalized in the patriarchal society. However, this female character had been deliberately created to be sexually inappropriate, and as one who does not shy away from exploring the consequences of her sexual choices.

Waller-Bridge also talks about how she wanted to eliminate the conventional understanding of a sexual woman as a "slut" that exists in all patriarchal societies. She says,

> You're always being told you're at your peak, you're the most attractive you'll ever be, so get out there and use it. You have a finite amount of time that everyone will want to fuck you. But it's such a weird conflicted message: I must be more promiscuous, I must make the most of this dying, shriveling shell that I've been gifted for this short amount of time, but, at the same time, it's "don't be a slut", you know? I felt really strongly while writing *Fleabag* that there was no such thing as a slut, and I was just going to erase that from the equation. (Aitkenhead 2017)

Waller-Bridge has talked about transgressing the problematic images of women created by/in our patriarchal society. From *The Guardian*: "I write from the point of view of what I'd like to watch. I'm always satisfying my own appetite. So I guess that means transgressive women, friendships, pain. I love pain [and rage]" (Hattenstone 2018). She also talks about the biases and scrutiny women are constantly subjected to.

> Being proper and sweet and nice and pleasing is a fucking nightmare. It's exhausting. As women, we get the message about how to be a good girl – how to be a good, pretty girl – from such an early age. Then, at the same time, we're told that well-behaved girls won't change the world or ever make a splash. So it's sort of like, well, what the fuck am I supposed to be? I'm supposed to be a really polite revolutionary?...It's impossible. (Aitkenhead 2017)

In an interview with Terry Gross, Waller-Bridge talks about how the female body has been used as a commodity in the market. The bodies of women have been sexualized in order to sell things.

> It's just very, very beautiful women on screen and with media and the pressure and adverts. I mean, I went through phases of just - you couldn't open - I couldn't open a newspaper, and it would just be women in their bras, like, advertising mortgage. .... But I just felt like it was

being commodified, like, the female body and the female - and not for our - not in any way that was healthy or made anybody happy. And that really, really frustrated me. (Gross 2019)

In another interview with *The Vulture* she says, "I think that a woman not giving a shit about what people think in a certain moment—being undercutting or self-aware—weirdly means that she's a profoundly unlikable person." She further shares how *Fleabag* shocked people.

It's so funny how shocking - yeah, it is like a secret (women masturbating). And it's like the shock of it. Like, I remember when *Fleabag* first came out, and the idea that she was - 'cause a funny reaction happened to *Fleabag* was - the TV show - was that people were talking about it like there was an awful lot of nudity in it or very gratuitous sex in it. And actually, there's no nudity in it. And you don't see any sex. Like, you don't see it very graphically. But the language is very graphic. And the fact that, I think, I'm looking straight down the barrel of the camera and that you stay on her, she's talking you through these moments. (Gross 2019)

She adds that men in comedy so often use sex or nudity in their content and it goes unnoticed. On the other hand, if women do it, it is seen as a "dirty" or a "transgressive act." Self-pleasure is a "selfish act."

[T]here's a moment when I'm masturbating with my boyfriend next to me, and it just feels, like, really, really intimate, I think, because we held on to it. But then the show was written about like it was the filthiest, most, like, exposing... Like, [reviewers] couldn't [believe] how much nudity there was in it. And I had - kept having to correct everybody like, no, nothing happened. And I can't - like you say, I cannot count on my fingers and toes how many scenes I've seen of, like, men on TV since I can remember ... I mean, especially in comedy. But it just seems like this thing - that it's just, like, an everyday occurrence for men that we all kind of understand and we all kind of see that it's kind of adorable. Like, these poor guys have [to] get on with it. .... And, you know, for women, it's this, yeah, transgressive act of, you know - of something naughty or in some cases something dirty, I think. You know, the - that women pleasuring herself was, like, a deeply selfish act, whereas a man having to do it was just, he had to get something off his chest or wherever else it comes from. (Gross 2019)

Waller-Bridge writes women characters who possess an individuality that affords them the freedom 'to be' and make their choices, even within the confines of a patriarchal society. But she portrays them facing the consequences of doing so. As I will show in the next section, these characters, and Waller-Bridge's approach to creating these characters, can be read using Sartre's and Beauvoir's philosophy of existentialism.

Jean-Paul Sartre's Existentialism

Existentialism, as explained by Sartre, is anchored in the lived experience of the individual. Human beings are both free to build their own essences, and completely responsible for the selves that they construct. The individual is free because through human consciousness we always have the ability to interpret the world and create meaning within it for ourselves, organizing our lives based on the values that we choose. For Sartre, no values are pregiven, and he encourages individuals to recognize themselves as meaning-creators instead of feeling bound to social norms and cultural values.

Sartre's early existentialism is built around the assertion that human existence precedes human essence. There is no formal "blueprint" for being a human. Human beings choose their own essence through their choices, actions, and thoughts. Sartre insisted that human beings do not have pregiven essences in the sense that an object such as a table does. A table is created by a carpenter with a purpose in mind and so its blueprint or essence is fixed. It has key defining properties that make it what it is. Sartre, as an atheist, argues that there is no divine creator of humans, and thus, there is no ideal human being who everyone should be like (Sartre 2007).

In his landmark work *Being and Nothingness,* Sartre introduces the concepts of being in-itself and being for-itself. Being in-itself refers to objects that have a pregiven essence or purpose and are not conscious, like a table, pen, tree, car, or basically any physical object that simply is what it is. Being for-itself, in contrast, refers to human consciousness, which defines itself by differentiating itself from the in-itself. Lacking a predetermined essence, being for-itself comprehends what it is not (the in-itself) and then subsequently constructs its own image of what it is. Being for-itself lacks a pregiven identity, and thus is free to determine its own being through choice. Human beings are, to put it simply, what they make of themselves, either by embracing identities given to them, or refusing to be defined by them. In either case, the choice is theirs (Sartre 1956, pp. 28–30).

Two more important concepts introduced in *Being and Nothingness* are "facticity" and "transcendence." Facticity refers to concrete aspects of our situations that we cannot change, for example, our physical characteristics, our race, country of origin, sexual orientation, socio-economic status at birth, family history, and past actions. For example, a rural agricultural worker may have the freely chosen desire to become the queen of England, but facticity will prevent this from ever becoming a reality – only those born into the royal family could become queen. Transcendence refers to the ability of each person to use our free consciousness to project meaning upon any given aspect of our facticity. So while it is true that she could never become the queen of England, she is still free to choose what *meaning* she gives to that situation. The attitude or perspective we take toward our unchangeable circumstances is always a free choice (Sartre 1956, pp. 131–133, 240–249).

As human beings have indefinite ways to construct their essences through transcendence, this lack of direction and pregiven purpose leads to feelings of anguish. Lacking a creator's plan or grand design for how they should be, the realization that their essence is dependent upon them lead to feelings of dread and anxiety. One reaction to this situation is for humans to shirk responsibility for their choices, falling back into pregiven roles. This leads to what Sartre refers to as "bad faith." Bad faith, a form of self-deception, can take two different forms: denial of our transcendence or denial of our facticity. In the first case, denial of transcendence, one refuses to take responsibility for their own choices, falls back into pregiven identities, and acts as if they have no choice in the matter. In denial of facticity, we fail to acknowledge concrete, real aspects of our situations, telling ourselves that we are simply free when we are inevitably bound by many restraints (Sartre 1956, pp. 97–98). Sartre's famous example is of a waiter in a café. In one sense he *is* a waiter, it is a social role he plays, what he relies on for his income, and a part of his social situation. If he tells himself he is not a waiter, this is a form of bad faith. Simultaneously, he does not exist as a waiter in the same way a table is a table. His transcendence allows him to take up a perspective in regards to his position as a waiter – the amount that it determines key aspects of his identity is up to him (Sartre 1956, pp. 101–105).

Another important concept in *Being and Nothingness* is the Other. There are multiple ways that the Other interacts with our own consciousness. When we encounter another consciousness, we realize ourselves as an object for others. Thus, the meaning of our environment and the meaning of our own actions are subject to the consciousness of another. We realize that the Other's consciousness and perception of us is out of our control. We feel ourselves as seen, which places limitations on our project. Additionally, we realize that as they are Others for us, we too are Others for them. We may become obsessed with the way the Other views and perceives us, although this perception is completely out of our control (Sartre 1956, pp. 341–347).

In *Being and Nothingness* Sartre discusses how the identity of individuals can be heavily influenced or even determined by the gaze of the Other, or what he calls "The Look." To illustrate this concept, Sartre uses the example of an individual looking through a keyhole. He says,

> Let us imagine that moved by jealousy, curiosity, or vice I have just glued my ear to the door and looked through a keyhole. I am alone and on the level of a non-thetic self-consciousness. This means first of all that there is no self to inhabit my consciousness, nothing therefore to which I can refer my acts in order to qualify them. They are in no way known; I am my acts and hence they carry in themselves their whole justification. I am a pure consciousness of things, and things, caught up in the circuit of my selfness, offer to me their potentialities as the proof of my non-thetic consciousness (of) my own possibilities. This means that behind that door a spectacle is presented as "to be seen," a conversation as "to be heard......But all of a sudden I hear footsteps in the hall. Someone is looking at me. What does this mean? It means that I am suddenly affected in my being and that essential modifications appear in my structure...". (Sartre 1956, pp. 347–348)

In this passage Sartre describes the transition from being the one who looks, and thus is in full position as subject, the creator of one's whole conscious experience, into one who is being looked at. When one is looked at, they suddenly realize all of their behavior and choices are subject to interpretation by the Other, and it is no longer solely their consciousness which is creating the conditions for their reality. They realize the environment that was previously there for them to project meaning on to is also there for the other to do the same. Thus, they realize that the Other places direct limits on our transcendence, as we share our social world with them.

Those who remain outside bad faith, or are authentic, recognize themselves as both freedom and facticity. Rather than falling back on social convention to justify their decisions, Sartre's authentic individual embraces their freedom and takes full responsibility for their existence, accepting that they are both facticity and freedom. Authentic individuals acknowledge that we do inhabit a social world in which societal conventions put limitations on us, but at the same time, they accept that we have the ability to transcend them and choose our own values. Authenticity also requires accepting that there will be consequences to rejecting social norms in favor of our freely chosen values. In authenticity, we acknowledge our freedom and our limits simultaneously, and accept the consequences of our choices. We also accept that we are not completely determined by the gaze of the Other, while simultaneously acknowledging that our own freedom is interwoven with the freedom of others, and we exist in a social context with them. Thus, while it would be bad faith to allow the perspective of the Other to define us, it would also be bad faith to believe that the freedom and choices of others do not concern us at all (Sartre 1984, p. 221).

Existentialist Themes in *Fleabag* and *Crashing*

We can see Sartre's ideas reflected in various situations and characters in both *Fleabag* and *Crashing*. For example, there are characters who think they must stick to conventional rules in the way they live their lives in order for them to have established standards of a good life, shirking their responsibility for creating their own values. Take Anthony from *Crashing*, for example, who assumes he must be with Kate, as she is his fiancée, instead of accepting that he loves Lulu. He lets his formal social obligation toward Kate prevent him from acting on his true feelings. Or take Kate who – until she discovers that she only has orgasms if Anthony cries during sex – completely ignores the fact that she has not been able to enjoy sex with Anthony and, indeed, that entire part of their relationship. Similarly, Claire (Fleabag's Sister), in S1E1, says "I have two degrees, a husband and a Burberry coat," to show that she has "made it" in her life. Despite being unhappy with her husband and their marriage, she took a long time to leave the relationship, as she considered being married to be part of a happy life. Similarly, Sam (the housemate of Anthony and Kate), in *Crashing*, is unable to accept his feelings for Fred (housemate of Anthony and Kate), expressing homophobia until the very end, when he finally does. Sam lets the societal norm of heterosexuality delay him walking his true path.

All these characters have perspectives for their lives that are dictated by culturally constructed social systems of gender, sexuality, and marriage/cis-relationships. They also keep reproducing them, as they believe these are the only acceptable ways of life. When they finally come across other perspectives which question their long-held beliefs, this makes them aware that their perspective is singular, not inherent, and leads to emotional and psychological discomfort, or Sartrean anguish. Falling back on cultural constructs to determine their actions relieves them from the burden of freedom – the existential mandate to forge their own paths. But this ultimately amounts to a form of bad faith, as they are letting pregiven cultural norms dictate their journeys instead of their freely chosen values.

It is clear throughout both shows how the free possibilities of the different characters are intertwined with each other, showing how the presence of others affects our own free choices. For example, in *Crashing*, Kate is affected by Lulu's free-spiritedness in such a way that it prompts her to try to get out of her comfort zone. Similarly, Claire in *Fleabag* constantly appreciates Fleabag for being herself. When Fleabag tells Claire that she is going out with the same priest who is officiating their father's and stepmother's wedding, Claire responds, "...it's just you're a genius. You're my fucking hero." Fleabag offers an example of an alternative way to live, showing both Claire and Kate that there are other options than only submitting to the patriarchal blueprints for women.

Fleabag serves as a consistent example of a human being who is perpetually exploring and contemplating herself. She is cis-gendered and queer. She tries to avoid pain and grief in life. But she also yearns for intimacy, and when trying to find it in other people she generally does not emphasize her gender or sexuality. However, when she tries to find validation through sex, it is mostly from men and she even ends up objectifying and narrowing them down to their trivial characteristics, calling them arsehole guy, the bus rodent, and the hot misogynist.

Both Lulu and Fleabag also make their authentic choices being aware and accepting of the consequences that may follow. Lulu decides to come to London to express her feelings to Anthony but then later, shocked and hurt, tells a confused Anthony to be with Kate because he cannot make up his mind. Similarly, Fleabag expresses her feelings to the Priest knowing that it would be difficult to be together with him but does not contact him after he decides to not be a part of the wedding and asks her to never return to his church again. Both Lulu and Fleabag knew that trying to be with the people they desired would be difficult. However, they made their choice regardless, even though it meant being vulnerable and hurt in the end.

Fleabag and Lulu are, to a large extent, able to transcend their facticities. In contrast, the Priest from *Fleabag* makes a choice to keep being a priest and breaks ties with Fleabag whom he confesses he loves. This remains a situation where, despite knowingly making a choice, he could not bring himself to transcend his current identity. He could also make this choice because he had a system to fall back on, a social and cultural (religious) structure to comfort him, while Fleabag had no other option but to accept his decision and try to move on.

Though occasionally being influenced by people around them, Fleabag and Lulu are able to consistently break the gaze of the Other. For example, the core of the story in the second season of *Fleabag* revolves around her romantic inclination toward the priest – who reciprocates her advances but in the end chooses to stick with being a priest over being with her. The scene ends with the song "This Feeling" by Alabama Shakes, with the song playing through the scene (continuing through the closing credits), showing Fleabag's spirit toward her life.

> I just kept hoping, I just kept hoping/ The way would become clear/ I spent all this time Tryna play nice and fight my way here/ See, I've been having me a real hard time /But it feels so nice to know I'm gonna be alright. / So, I just kept dreaming, yeah, I just kept dreamin' / It

wasn't very hard/I spent all this time /Tryna figure out why/Nobody on my side /See, I've been having me a real good time/And it feels so nice to know I'm gonna be alright.

In *Fleabag,* the audience can be seen as the Other, as Fleabag is aware they are watching her and addresses them throughout. In the second season, when the priest confesses his love for Fleabag, but then chooses God over her anyway and leaves, she stops the camera from following her. In this case, Fleabag becomes a character who could have been caught in bad faith but instead decides to act by deliberately distancing herself away from the gaze or "look" of others (the audience). She is conscious of this gaze, and how she is understood by it; she has even been able to manipulate it, but in this final moment, she wants only her own consciousness to give meaning to this situation, not the Other.

One way Sartre expresses the process of building one's essence is through the "fundamental project." The fundamental project is the original choice of oneself in the world, which they use to structure/organize all other choices. It is a goal-oriented end which serves as a guiding thread for further conscious experience. Future value judgments and choices are made in light of the goal or project already chosen. The original fundamental project is chosen without deliberation between options. However, as humans age, they are able to consciously reflect on their chosen projects and direct themselves toward new ones, if they choose. However, a change of fundamental project will result in a substantial change in individual identity (Sartre 1956, pp. 464–468; Engels 2014). For instance, in the context of the shows *Crashing* and *Fleabag*, Lulu and Fleabag are women who make their own choices about their lives, bodies and desires in a patriarchal world where the choices of/for women are restricted culturally and socially. This represents a fundamental project of living as women who challenge societal norms.

In contrast, the Priest is again an interesting character to discuss. After they start making out in the church, a painting falls down and gives the Priest second thoughts about his relationship with Fleabag. He decides not to officiate the wedding. He also tells Fleabag to never return to his church. However, he later comes to meet her at her home. He walks around anxiously and tells her that he has decided to officiate the wedding. Eventually he calms down and says, "I sacrificed a lot for this life. You know? I've given a lot of things up." The scene is interrupted by the arrival of the Hot Misogynist, who, after a conversation with Fleabag, leaves. The Priest continues, "I can't be physical with you." Fleabag quips, "What, we can't even wrestle?" The Priest laughs. Fleabag, in an explanatory tone, says "No, priests have sex, you know. A lot of them actually do. They don't burst into flames, I Googled it." The Priest replies in a calm tone, "I can't have sex with you because I'll fall in love with you. And if I fall in love with you, I won't burst into flames, but... . . .my life will be fucked." Fleabag then looks at the camera, "We're going to have sex." The Priest, pointing his finger upwards, says "I'm supposed to love one thing. . ." Fleabag again looks at the camera, "Oh, my God, we're gonna have sex. . ." She is taken aback as The Priest shouts, "For fuck's sake! Stop that! I don't think you want to be told what to do at all. I think you know exactly what you want to do. If you really wanted to be told what to do, you'd be wearing one of these [the priest's cassock]." Fleabag tries to reply, "Women aren't actually allowed to. . ." He again shouts, "Oh, fuck off, I know!" She chuckles and then stops. He pauses. "We're going to have sex, aren't we?" Fleabag looking at him with a straight face, nods, "Yeah." "Yeah." "Okay." And they have sex.

At the end of the series, however, when Fleabag and the Priest are waiting for the bus after the wedding, and both are fondly smiling at each other, Fleabag asks in an emotional tone "It's God, isn't it?" He smiles, "Yeah." Fleabag smiles. "Damn," she says, "You know, the worst thing is...that I fucking love you." She is almost on the verge of crying. "I love you." The Priest is about to say something. "No, no, don't." She laughs nervously. "No, let's just leave that out there just for a second on its own. I love you." The Priest puts his hand on hers, and they hold hands. "It'll pass." She looks at him and smiles, and they both remain quiet. Fleabag then breaks the silence and says, "This bus is not magically coming." "I think I'll walk," the priest says. "Okay." The Priest stands up to leave, walks a little and then turns around, "Uh, see you Sunday? I'm joking. You're never ever allowed in my church again." Fleabag smiles while holding her tears back. The Priest says, ". . .I love you, too." Fleabag starts crying and nods. He is emotional, "Okay." And he walks away.

Although the Priest was romantically inclined toward Fleabag, he continuously found himself bound to playing the role of the priest. Thus, he was confused about being a lover. While he had told Fleabag to not visit his church, his confusion is clear as he comes back to her place to tell her that he is not allowed to fall in love with her but ends up having sex with her (even though he feared ruining his life if he fell in love with her). However, even after accepting that he loves her, he chose being a priest over her even though it meant hurting her. Thus, the Priest could have decided to be with her, but because he would be "fucked' as a result (assuming both socially and emotionally), and because he has made sacrifices to be a priest, he decides to walk away from the relationship and consoles her with the idea that her feelings shall pass.

This scene illustrates how the social and cultural norms and roles prompt people to create their identities to fit into these systems, and simultaneously tend to rob people of even exploring the possibility of being someone different. One can argue that the Priest deliberately chose his priesthood and made sacrifices/choices around this decision and thus that became his fundamental project. However, during his conversation with Fleabag he also shows that one of the reasons he chose the priesthood is because he is not sure about how to navigate through life. On the other hand, he was sure about his feelings for Fleabag, and yet he decided to continue with his priesthood; after being with her for some time. So one can ask, is his choice truly based on a genuine commitment to God? Or did he fear that his past sacrifices would become meaningless, and feel uncertain with what the future held with Fleabag? The priesthood offered him a life role with very certain, set expectations. Giving up the priesthood to pursue a relationship with Fleabag would have forced him to take a real risk, and the anguish is too much for him to bear.

In this context, knowing that if he decides to be with Fleabag he would put his priesthood in jeopardy, he disrupted his fundamental project of being a priest and made the choice of becoming romantically involved with Fleabag. However, within a few hours of making this decision, he reversed his position, incapable of fully devoting himself to a new project.

Phoebe Waller-Bridge's Female Characters: Making Choices and Eliminating Bad Faith

The culturally and socially conventional images of women often portray them as passive and shy. They are not expected to take many risks in life, and often play complementary roles in society, rather than active ones. Men, on the contrary, are expected to be dynamic, and to assert themselves as subjects. They must make decisions and women must accept them. Lulu and Fleabag do exactly the opposite. Lulu visits Anthony to express her love knowing he is dating someone else. Similarly, Fleabag expresses her love to a priest knowing that he has taken a vow of celibacy and will likely be rejected. These characters take risks and put themselves in the vulnerable position of being humiliated, which – in social and cultural expectations – women are not expected to do. On the other hand, while, socially and culturally, men are expected to make decisions, not only for themselves but for their female counterparts, Anthony and the priest are confused about their feelings. They want validation from Lulu and Fleabag to be able to accept their feelings and to act upon them.

Both Lulu and Fleabag can be seen as authentic individuals as they have a streak of independence and personal freedom and try to live their lives, make choices, and take actions to make those come true. They do not have a life plan ready regarding what their lives should be like as women; instead they decide spontaneously and move with the current. While most of those decisions are driven by love and pleasure, they are not always perceived as "correct" – socially or morally. Lulu and Fleabag also accept the consequences that follow from their actions and take responsibility for them, demonstrating acknowledgement of their facticity. In the first season of *Fleabag*, the consequence is guilt that she feels because her desire for pleasure resulted in her betraying her best friend, Boo (by sleeping with Boo's boyfriend), which eventually resulted in her accidental death. In the second season, the consequence is falling in love with the priest who chooses priesthood over her. And in *Crashing*, it's Anthony's constant confusion about choosing between Kate and Lulu. Both Lulu and Fleabag are also realistic about the facticity of the situations of their romantic interests: Lulu has full knowledge that Anthony may choose to stay with Kate, and Fleabag knows that the priest is unlikely to leave the priesthood. They both choose to proceed anyway, accepting the consequences that will follow.

That is not to say, however, that Lulu and Fleabag are perfect examples of authentic individuals. Fleabag, in particular, constantly swings between being her authentic-self and being caught in bad faith. In the first season, although she seemingly shares all her innermost thoughts with the audience, she does not reveal that she played a role in Boo's death. She, thus, may not be her authentic self until the final scene where this secret is revealed. Claire decides to stay married to Martin, who kissed Fleabag but instead accuses her of kissing him, and Claire believes him over Fleabag because, Claire now tells us, Fleabag had betrayed Boo. At this moment, Fleabag realizes that she may have lost the support of her audience and tries to run away from the camera. One might say that Fleabag had manipulated the audience to be on her side, and the moment the truth is revealed, she decides to distance herself from them.

Despite these setbacks, she finds her way back to a path of authenticity. In S1E6 – during her breakdown in front of the bank manager, she accepts her authentic self – when she says,

> I fucked up my family... And I fucked my friend by fucking her boyfriend... And sometimes I wish I didn't even know that fucking existed. And I know that my body, as it is now, really is the only thing I have left, and when that gets old and unfuckable I may as well just kill it. And somehow there isn't anything worse... than someone who doesn't want to fuck me. I fuck everything ...You know, everyone feels like this a little bit, and they're just not talking about it, or I'm completely fucking alone... which isn't fucking funny.

In this monologue we see Fleabag accepting that her choices are her own; she is not trying to shirk the blame or make excuses for the way she is or what she has done. She acknowledges that she has freedom to do otherwise, and has regret for not doing otherwise, but is honest with herself about her path.

In *Crashing* S1E6, before they become intimate, Anthony (who thinks that Kate likes women) asks Lulu, "Do you fucking love me, Lulu?" Lulu nods in a yes. He then asks, "Did you come all the way here to break me and Kate up?" Lulu shakes her head saying no. "Do you want to be with me?" Lulu (smiling and emotional) nods yes. "Fuck! This is going to be a disaster isn't it?" Lulu nods again. They kiss and have sex. In the morning Lulu wakes up to find herself alone in the bed. She stares blankly at the ceiling. Later, Lulu is sitting next to the window, smoking. Anthony comes back to talk to her as he again feels confused. "Kate's not a lesbian," Anthony says, "and she doesn't want to break up." Lulu looks disappointed but replies "OK . . . Just say it." Lulu smiles softly. Anthony replies, "What should I do? Should I get back with her, or. . ." Lulu's smile disappears, "Or. . .?" Anthony, unable to verbalize the other option of "Be with you, Lulu" just repeats, "What should I do?" Lulu is taken aback, "Get back with her," she replies sarcastically, "100%." Anthony is still confused. "But. . ." "100%," Lulu replies. The moment starts to get tense. "Yeah. Yeah. I guess, thanks." Lulu smiling with sad eyes, "No worries." Anthony turns around to leave, then stops and turns toward Lulu again and says, "Can we just... Keep this between us?" Lulu assures him "OK, cool." Lulu watches him leave with a sad face.

Lulu knows what she wants and is not afraid to accept it. She acknowledges her desire and acts on it. However, Anthony is constantly confused about his feelings for both Kate and Lulu and continues his relationship with Kate until he thinks she is into other women. He never makes the decision confidently. Even when he feels confused about his feelings for both women, he tries to escape from having to make the decision. Finally, even after Lulu and he have sex, and Kate tells him that she wants to continue the relationship, instead of accepting his feelings for Lulu, he asks

Lulu to get him out of the dilemma and make the choice for him. Further, he asks her to hide the truth from Kate because he does not want to accept the consequences. In this case, he finds lying to Kate and hurting Lulu easier than accepting his true feelings toward both of them. Lulu, on the other hand, is consistently conscious of her underlying desire to be with Anthony. She is conscious of what she wants, makes a decision, and thus, does not slip into bad faith.

When Anthony – either due to social pressure or the fear of telling the truth – refused to accept his true feelings for Lulu and chose not to make a decision about whether to accept Lulu, he slipped into bad faith. The Priest also swings between his desire and emotions, between the sacrifices he has made to become a priest and how falling in love with Fleabag would affect it. Anthony and the Priest's confusion make things difficult for Lulu and Fleabag, while both the women make up their minds. And because they do not depend on the decisions taken by other people for them about how they want to act, and accept the results even if these are not desirable, Lulu and Fleabag avoid bad faith and demonstrate Sartrean authenticity.

In her portrayal of these two women's authentic paths, Waller-Bridge entices the audience to sympathize and relate to the paths of both Lulu and Fleabag. This suggests Waller-Bridge thinks we could all do better to be the kinds of authentic people that both Lulu and Fleabag are.

Simone De Beauvoir's Existentialism, and Freedom

Simone De Beauvoir, another major existentialist thinker, focused more specifically on how the social situations of individuals affect the ability to create a free project. Beauvoir's thought also takes a distinctly ethical approach, focusing on the relationships between individuals and how the meaning of our projects are intertwined with the projects others. The existence of the other is, thus, an opportunity to extend our project to others by inviting their participation. As she wrote, "[M]y freedom, in order to fulfil itself, requires that it emerge into an open future: it is other men who open the future to me" (De Beauvoir 1980, p. 82).

Beauvoir's existentialism focused in particular on the situations of women in patriarchal society. In her landmark text *The Second Sex,* Beauvoir explores how society has set up men as the default, standard human being, and thus made women the ultimate Other. Historically, women were seen to belong first to their fathers and then to their husbands, always being defined in relation to a man (De Beauvoir 1974, pp. xviii–xix). To give modern examples, evolution posters showing the progression of species from water dwellers to modern humans almost always present a male at the end of the evolution chart. Safety equipment in cars has been designed and tailored around men's bodies. TV channels like *Lifetime* are advertised as "television for women" because by default all other channels are directed toward men. Then there is the distinction made between the basketball leagues the NBA and the WNBA: while the women's league is specified as a league for women, the generic "National Basketball Association" is assumed to be for men, no designation needed.

In short, according to Beauvoir, when discussing human beings we assume we are discussing males, unless it is directly specified to the contrary.

Historically women have been expected to talk, walk, dress, behave, and even think in specifically "feminine" ways. This is what makes the work of Phoebe Waller-Bridge so "existential." Lulu and Fleabag through their personal choices fracture the social ideals of a *perfect woman*. Waller-Bridge's characters normalize women as human beings with self-determined characteristics, instead of reproducing patriarchal images of women.

It is crucial to note, however, that although Lulu and Fleabag make unconventional choices in their day to day lives – including their sexual choices – their social positions of being white, upper class, (mostly) heterosexual women gives them a social advantage in comparison to those in the working class, racial minorities, or people in the LGBTQ+ community. Although Fleabag touches upon the conventionally non-normative sexuality since she is queer and gender fluid, she is still not affected by many violent consequences that other people have had to suffer due to their race, gender identity, class, or marginalized background. For example, black trans women are far more likely to experience gender-based violence and lose their lives than women like Lulu and Fleabag. Beauvoir's work reminds us that social situations are substantial parts of the existential project, and that forms of oppression that affect others should be of concern to everyone.

An important aspect of Beauvoir's idea of human freedom is that it requires the realization of other's freedom alongside one's own. Beauvoir emphasized that only people with an authentic moral attitude can understand that the freedom of self also needs other people's freedom. To act alone, with no regard for others, is not to be free. "[T]o be free is not to have the power to do anything you like; it is to be able to surpass the given toward an open future; the existence of others as a freedom defines my situation and is even the condition of my own freedom" (De Beauvoir 1980, p. 91). In *Fleabag*, we see it when Fleabag continuously encourages Claire to leave her toxic relationship with her husband and be with the man she loves (instead of thinking about the consequences of her choice). Similarly, it can be seen (indirectly) in *Crashing* when Lulu's sense of freedom affects Kate too. Although Kate dislikes Lulu's free-spiritedness and expressivity about her thoughts and feelings, it is for these characteristics that Kate envies Lulu. This inspires Kate, when relaxed after drinking wine, to admit to Anthony that she is pretending to be in love with him. Finally, although she says that she wants to continue the relationship with Anthony, when Kate knows that Lulu and Anthony like each other, she confronts them, and, presumably, breaks up with Anthony.

Further, Beauvoir emphasized that human freedom is ambiguous. This ambiguity stems from the fact that we have a free consciousness, hence, a sense of inner freedom, but are simultaneously bound by many constraints. An ethical, authentic attitude requires embracing this ambiguity rather than trying to flee from it (De Beauvoir 1980, pp. 129–131). Beauvoir does admit, however, that doing so will lead to dilemmas in human life. For example, a woman brought up in a patriarchal world faces the dilemma of either living with the patriarchal values that she is given and accepting them, or questioning those values, navigating through the discomfort doing so causes, finding herself as a human being, and exploring the other potential identities. Waller-Bridge talks about this kind of dilemma when she discusses how women are forced to become conscious of their bodies in ways men are not. She says,

> I feel rage about casual and systemic sexism......I feel rage at how quickly the double standards could be balanced if men gave women the backup they need to stop us having to shout into our own vaginas all the time. I feel rage about how many times I've Googled before and afters of chemical peels when I could have been working, when I know I've just been programmed to do that . . . and how redefining this image and changing these perspectives can also lead to dilemma and conflict for women as well...But mainly I rage at myself for my own ability to let things slide because I'd rather be "nice" than stand up for myself in an uncomfortable situation. My characters have streaks of fearlessness. I get a rush writing women who don't care what you think. Probably to help me grow into being one. (Hattenstone 2018)

Similarly, in the first episode of *Fleabag*, Claire and Fleabag go to a feminist lecture. The speaker asks the participants: "So I pose the question to the women in this room today. Please raise your hands if you would trade five years of your life for the so-called perfect body." Claire and Fleabag are the only people in the room who raise their hands. In the same episode when Fleabag feels lonely, she goes to her father's house late at night to talk, and tells him, "I have a horrible feeling that I'm a greedy, perverted, selfish, apathetic, cynical, depraved, morally bankrupt woman, who can't even call herself a feminist." This constant fight to push away the social and cultural structures of the patriarchal world, and accept the more human feminist perspective toward life, is shown frequently throughout the show. While Fleabag knows that she wants to be a feminist, she finds it difficult to give up on her patriarchal socialization completely. Her freedom is ambiguous – she has a free, transcendent consciousness, yet she is never completely free of social pressures.

In *The Second Sex*, Beauvoir argues that women's bodies themselves contribute to feelings of ambiguity. She writes about the ways in which women's attitudes change toward their bodies over time, and how society influences this. Beauvoir emphasizes the primary question in this social and cultural context: Are the alleged disadvantages of the female body actual disadvantages which exist objectively in all societies, or are they merely interpreted to be disadvantages by our society? In other words, are the disadvantages women face inherent or created? She answers this by using case studies of the various stages of female life; the positive as well as the negative aspects of the female body – showing women as both oppressed as well as free – and by observing that a woman's body is a site of ambiguity. Her body is the vehicle through which she expresses her freedom; simultaneously, being born into a female body leads to various forms of oppression. Thus, the body is caught in a conflict between freedom and constraint. Attempts to utilize her body as a site of transcendence are often thwarted by patriarchal prohibitions (formal or informal) regarding what women are allowed to do (De Beauvoir 1974, pp. 301–450).

Vicky Jones, Director of *Fleabag*, shares in their interview (Edinburgh Festival) that she and Waller-Bridge would talk to each other about giving up 5 years of their lives in exchange for a perfect body, and then later feel guilty about it. So they tried to find out if theirs was a kind of feminism which was relatable to young women in the world they live in; perhaps they could assuage women of the guilt they feel for being a (sometimes conventional) women while simultaneously striving to be a feminist. For instance, in S2E3, Belinda says profound lines, as a woman, when she talks about the pain associated with menstruation. She says,

> I've been longing to say this out loud. Women are born with pain built in. It's our physical destiny: period pains, sore boobs, childbirth. We carry it within ourselves throughout our lives. Men don't. They have to seek it out. They invent all these gods and demons so they can feel guilty about things, which is something we do very well on our own. And then they create wars so they can feel things and touch each other, and when there aren't any wars they can play rugby. We have it all going on in here, inside. We have pain on a cycle for years and years and years, and then just when you feel you are making peace with it all, what happens? The menopause comes. The fucking menopause comes and it is the most wonderful fucking thing in the world. Yes, your entire pelvic floor crumbles and you get fucking hot and no one cares, but then you're free. No longer a slave, no longer a machine with parts. You're just a person. In business.

This is not every woman's or feminist's perspective on menstruation, but it is important to note that the experiences shared related to this bodily function (which is not restricted to a woman's body but is socially, culturally and 'naturally' attached to them) is not commonly discussed in culturally patriarchal media, even though it's an experience 50% of the population has. Belinda expresses feeling limited by menstruation, however, her grievance seems to be equally about the way patriarchal society reacts to menstruation as it is about the bodily process itself.

In *The Second Sex*, Beauvoir illustrates how women have always been written about, spoken about, and thought about only from the perspectives of men. This makes it difficult for women to view themselves through their own lenses and their own standards. However, Waller-Bridge's characters consistently do the opposite. They clearly know what they want, have created a language for that, explain it well, make decisions, and are also ready to accept the consequences of their actions. Thus, they continuously claim their freedom by making decisions that women might not be expected to make. Thus, they disrupt the status of women as Other and complimentary to a man, positioning themselves as self-determining subjects.

Conclusion

Characters created by Phoebe Waller-Bridge are constantly aware of making their own choices and do not hesitate to try to fulfil them. Along the way, they defy the conventional rules, especially those attached to their genders and create images of self-determined women who challenge the status quo. As the characters are conscious of their choices and the reasons behind them, they are able to balance their freedom and facticity and avoid bad faith. While doing this, they also influence other women around them, encouraging them to transcend their facticities, rejecting pregiven social roles. Finally, these characters embrace themselves as they are, and continuously create their own individual *essence of being* instead of choosing to become what is socially and culturally expected of them. Thus, these characters provide examples of ways for women to be that are different from conventionally re/produced images of women and encourage women to embrace their own freedom.

In modern society there are many challenges pushing us constantly toward attitudes of bad faith. We feel a constant pressure to fall back to the comfort of pre given social roles, or to make excuses for ourselves that fail to acknowledge the ability of our consciousness to choose and transcend. That Waller-Bridge sets up both her protagonists as women who manage to navigate a path of authenticity in spite of this reflects an argument that we ought to be the type of women – and people – that Fleabag and Lulu are. That is, we ought to express our feelings, be willing to push back against social conventions, take responsibility for our own choices, accept any and all consequences for acting, reject patriarchal restrictions, acknowledge the Other while not being defined by them, and make decisions that embrace ourselves as free meaning-givers in the world.

References

Aitkenhead, Decca. 2017. Phoebe Waller-Bridge: 'I felt strongly there was no such thing as a slut'. *The Guardian*. July 17. https://www.theguardian.com/tv-and-radio/2017/jul/31/phoebe-waller-bridge-i-felt-strongly-there-was-no-such-thing-as-a-slut. Accessed 28 Sept 2021.
De Beauvoir, Simone. 1974. H.M. Parshley (trans. and ed.) 1974. *The second sex*. New York: First Vintage Books.
———. 1980. Bernard Frechtman (trans.) 1980. *The ethics of ambiguity*. Secaucus: Citadel Press.
Engels, Kimberly S. 2014. Schopenhauer's intelligible character and Sartre's fundamental project. *Idealistic Studies* 44: 101–118.
Gross, Terry. 2019. 'Fleabag' and 'Killing Eve' Creator Phoebe Waller-Bridge is full of surprises. *Delaware Public Media*. August 27. https://www.delawarepublic.org/post/fleabag-and-killing-eve-creator-phoebe-waller-bridge-full-surprises-0. Accessed 22 Feb 2021.
Hattenstone, Simon. 2018. Phoebe Waller-Bridge: 'I have an appetite for transgressive women'. *The Guardian*. September 8. https://www.theguardian.com/tv-and-radio/2018/sep/08/phoebe-waller-bridge-fleabag-killing-eve-transgressive-women. Accessed 27 Nov 2020.
HuffPost. 2016. Phoebe Waller-Bridge On Shocking "Fleabag" Sex Scenes. YouTube video, 3, 12. https://youtu.be/-aAQexS62e4
Is *Fleabag* a Feminist Show? Phoebe Waller-Bridge on women in comedy and More|Edinburg TV Festival, YouTube video, 12:27. "Edinburg Television Festival," February 29, 2020. https://youtu.be/L56eLJhoE9w, https://philosophynow.org/issues/69/Becoming_A_Woman_Simone_de_Beauvoir_onFemale_Embodiment. Accessed 14 Feb 2021.
Sartre, Jean-Paul. 1956. Hazel Barnes (trans.) 1956. *Being and nothingness*. New York: Washington Square Press.
———. 1984. Quintin Hoare (trans.) 1984. *War diaries: Notebooks from a phoney war, November 1939–March 1940*. London: Verso.
———. 2007. Carol MacComber (trans.) 2007. *Existentialism is a humanism*. New Haven: Yale University Press.
Young, Sage. 2017. Why 'Fleabag' Creator Phoebe Waller-Bridge Isn't Interested In Writing "Aspirational" Women. *Bustle*. July 12. https://www.bustle.com/p/why-fleabag-creator-phoebe-waller-bridge-isnt-interested-in-writing-aspirational-women-63003. Accessed 13 Feb 2021.

Part IV
Video Games

The Last of Us as Moral Philosophy: Teleological Particularism and Why Joel Is Not a Villain

76

Charles Joshua Horn

Contents

Introduction	1742
The Last of Us Narrative	1743
Joel, the Villain	1746
Teleological Particularism	1751
Concluding Remarks	1754
References	1756

Abstract

The protagonist of the wildly popular recent video game, *The Last of Us*, makes a difficult decision at the end of the game by refusing to sacrifice his surrogate daughter so that scientists could try to find a cure for a disease that has devastated humanity for decades. I will take seriously *The Last of Us* as a piece of moral philosophy and argue that Joel has been interpreted as a villain primarily because many understand morality in terms of a consequentialist or deontological framework. On those frameworks, Joel could be interpreted as a villain because he is not acting in a way that maximizes the good on the one hand or not acting in a way consistent with the universal moral law on the other. Against this interpretation, I argue that Joel's actions are morally justified based on a view articulated here called teleological particularism. On this view, an agent is morally justified in their actions if and only if the action is in conformity with a role they occupy. It is teleological because it demands that we consider the roles, goals, and purposes of each individual, and it is particularist because it recognizes that those very roles, goals, and purposes can change from subject to subject, time to time, and culture to culture. The role of "father" demands that he protect and provide for the child, and that the father helps the child become autonomous. Joel's role then demands that he put his child's interests even above the interests of the rest of humanity,

C. J. Horn (✉)
University of Wisconsin-Stevens Point, Stevens Point, WI, USA
e-mail: jhorn@uwsp.edu

even if those interests are absolutely dire. According to teleological particularism then, Joel is not a villain and his actions in defense of Ellie are permissible.

Keywords

Video games · Philosophy · Last of Us · Ethics · Teleological particularism · Naughty dog · Roles · Obligations

Introduction

The Last of Us is one of the most critically and commercially acclaimed video games ever created. In general terms, the game tells a harrowing story of a disease that devastates humanity, turning everyone exposed into something very much like traditional zombies. On a much smaller scale, the game is about how two characters, Joel and Ellie, survive after the outbreak. More than just a video game though, *The Last of Us* can be understood as a piece of moral philosophy that attempts to help us understand what, if any, moral obligations we have to each other. *The Last of Us* is a significant game for many reasons, each worth a great deal of discussion, but in this chapter, I want to focus on one element that came up from the reception of the game. After it was released, there was a great deal of conversation regarding whether Joel was the villain of the game. In fact, the voice actor for Joel, Troy Baker, claimed that Joel would even consider *himself* to be the villain (Fischer 2019). Baker stated,

> Joel, I don't think deals in those terms at all. I don't think Joel believes he's a hero. If he was to lean anywhere I think that Joel would consider himself a villain, which is why he can say that he's been on both sides. Like he can say "I'm just a guy trying to get by. I'm not here to save anybody, I'm not here to upset anyone's plans. I'm just trying to live one day at a time."

What was amazing is not that the main character was a villain – many games have the protagonist and gamer do awful, reprehensible, and deeply immoral actions in sometimes very visceral ways (I am looking directly at you Grand Theft Auto series, God of War series, and Shadow of Colossus, in particular). The amazing thing was that nobody seemed to notice that, in this game, they were playing as the villain. How could this be? How could it be that most people playing the game did not recognize that Joel's actions were unethical? I contend that there are two reasons for such confusion. On the one hand, there is the ambiguity and complicated nature of Joel's actions, and on the other hand, there is the fact that most people have shifting moral views. Perhaps the most important reason that Joel was considered a villain though was because many assume that either a consequentialist or deontological moral framework is correct. And since Joel's actions are incompatible with these frameworks, he is a villain.

While there is some plausibility to the position that Joel is a villain, my contention is that *The Last of Us* is presenting a much more complicated and nuanced view of morality – one where Joel's actions are morally permissible. In this chapter, my goal is to take seriously *The Last of Us* not just as a video game, but as a piece of philosophy making a case for a nuanced moral theory. More specifically, I will argue that the game presents a moral theory that I call teleological particularism – on this view, an agent acts morally if and only if their action is in conformity with their role. The result of this moral view is that despite plenty of evidence suggesting that he is morally blameworthy for his unethical actions, Joel is *not* a villain and his actions throughout the game were morally defensible.

The Last of Us Narrative

The Last of Us begins just as a disease breaks out, and the story follows Joel and his daughter, Sarah, as they try to escape their home in Austin, Texas. The city has begun quarantine procedures to control the spread of the disease, and law enforcement personnel have been instructed to kill anyone that is infected or suspected of infection. During the escape, Joel and Sarah get into a car accident and Joel is forced to carry his injured daughter to safety. The two come across someone from the military helping to enforce the quarantine. Despite their protests that they were not infected, the officer is instructed to kill Joel and Sarah. The officer opens fire and despite Joel trying to jump in front of the gunfire, he shoots Sarah in the abdomen. She bleeds out in her father's arms. As he loses his daughter, Joel weeps. "Sarah... Baby... Don't do this to me, baby. Don't do this to me baby girl. Come on... No. no. Oh no, no, no... Please. Oh. God. Please, please, don't do this. Please, God..." (Druckmann et al. 2013). This is devastating to the player, and it is even more devastating to Joel. And it all takes place during the prologue to the game.

The story then jumps forward in time 20 years, and Joel is understandably portrayed as a broken man. He is angry, sad, and detached from everyone. Society has crumbled into separate quarantine zones with strictly rationed resources for survival. Joel's friend, Tess, eventually tasks him with smuggling a young girl, Ellie, out of the quarantine zone to a group of revolutionaries. Initially, it is unclear what the reason for her importance to the revolutionaries is, but it is later revealed that Ellie is immune to the fungus causing the disease. It is believed that the revolutionary group, the Fireflies, can use Ellie to create a vaccine that will protect humans from the disease. The consequences for Ellie reaching the Fireflies cannot be overstated. Everyone would not only be able to survive in this landscape, but they would be able to thrive outside of quarantines. Life would return to some semblance of normalcy after decades of living like a hamster in a cage – relatively safe with limited rations. Although some humans have survived, they have not really lived.

Joel reluctantly agrees to help smuggle Ellie, to the Fireflies, but initially acts very coldly to her, treating her essentially like other kinds of property that he must smuggle in and out of the quarantine zones. After they run into military personnel trying to impose the quarantine and combat the infected, Joel asks Tess, "What are we doing here? This is not us." Tess responds, "What do you know about us? About me?" Joel continues: "I know that you are smarter than this." Tess retorts and explicitly tells Joel (and the gamer) in the opening hours of the game, "Really? Guess what, we're shitty people, Joel. It's been that way for a long time." Joel rejects this characterization in anger, "No, we are survivors!" (Druckmann et al. 2013). At least in Joel's mind, there is no room for heroes or villains in this new world – just survivors. And anything done in the name of survival is morally legitimate.

In most postapocalyptic dystopian narratives (and possibly even outside of these narratives), Joel's mindset is completely understandable – that which is done for the sake of necessity is morally justified and permissible. In the state of nature, the state of perfect freedom, morality is meaningless. *The Last of Us* will ultimately subvert this trope though. By the end of the game, it will become clear that Joel is not a nihilist who thinks that morality is meaningless. And he is not simply a villain that does unethical actions out of ignorance or malice.

Cornered in an abandoned building, Tess confesses that she was recently bitten during their escape from the quarantine zone. She compels Joel to continue their journey to help Ellie reach the Fireflies. After Tess's death, Joel snaps at Ellie as she tries to apologize for her death. Ellie says, "Hey, look, um... about Tess...I don't even know what to—" Joel responds, "Here's how this thing's gonna play out. You don't bring up Tess—ever. Matter of fact; we can just keep our histories to ourselves?" (Druckmann et al. 2013). If Joel was distant with Ellie before, then at this point the relationship is purely transactional. Ellie is, simply put, nothing to Joel – property to be smuggled and nothing more.

The most important arc of the story though is that along their journey, Joel grows to love and protect Ellie as if she were his own daughter. And Ellie grows to love and protect Joel as if he were her father. The first part of the game where the player starts to see a shift in Joel's disposition toward Ellie is when they are separated for the first time. Joel and Ellie come across two other survivors, Sam and Henry, also trying to escape the quarantine zone. They get split up in a sewer with Joel and Sam on one side of a gate and Ellie and Henry on the other side of the gate. Joel seems genuinely worried about Ellie for the first time because he is not there to protect her. If Ellie was still truly nothing to Joel, then he would not be afraid and anxious after the separation. When they reunite, Joel appears to be genuinely relieved and thankful that they are together again – even if he does not explicitly relay those feelings to Ellie. Even though he does not verbally make it known to Ellie, his attachment to her is palpable.

Joel and Ellie eventually find Tommy in a small community of survivors. Tommy is Joel's brother and knows the location of the Fireflies, so Joel tries to convince him to finish taking Ellie the rest of the way. When Ellie finds out about Joel trying to pawn her off to someone else, she takes a horse and leaves the community without saying goodbye. Joel's actions have made it clear to her that he does not genuinely care about her, but rather sees her as a burden. Joel and Tommy search and eventually find Ellie in an abandoned house. Joel finds her in an upstairs bedroom reading through a journal from a young girl before the outbreak happened. In this scene, we get a very explicit account of how Joel *seems* to feel about Ellie. He tells her, sounding very much like her father, "Do you even realize what your life means? Huh? Running off like that. Putting yourself at risk. It's pretty goddamn stupid." Ellie responds, "Well I guess we're both disappointed with each other then." Joel says, "What do you want from me?" Ellie, exasperated that he does not understand why she ran off says, "Admit that you wanted to get rid of me the whole time." Joel tries and fails to justify his actions, saying "Tommy knows this area better than—" Ellie interrupts to reject this justification, "Agh fuck that—" she says. Joel continues, "Well, I'm sorry. I trust him better than I trust myself." Ellie finally calls him on his bad excuse, saying "Stop with the bullshit. What are you so afraid of? That I'm going to end up like Sam? I *can't* get infected. I can take care of myself." Joel tries to help her understand that they have just been very lucky so far. "How many close calls have we had?" he asks. Ellie responds, "Well we seem to be doing alright so far." Joel raises his voice, clearly exhausted at trying to explain to a teenager what it will mean to keep her safe. "And now you'll be doing even better with Tommy." And then, Ellie cuts right through Joel's bad defense and strong façade, "I'm not her, you know." Joel says, "What?" Ellie responds, "Maria told me about Sarah. And I—." This is the first time that the connection between Sarah and Ellie has been made explicit to the player, even though it has been lingering right beneath the surface for the entire game. Joel says very sharply, "Ellie. You are treading on some mighty thin ice here." Ellie, thinking that she understands his reluctance to protect another young girl says, "I'm sorry about your daughter, Joel, but I have lost people too." Joel rightfully admonishes this line of thought. "You have no idea what loss is." Ellie continues, "Everyone I have cared for has either died or left me. Everyone—fucking except you. So don't tell me that I would be safer with someone else—because the truth is I would just be more scared." At last, Joel explicitly rejects Ellie. He says, "You're right…You're not my daughter and I sure as hell ain't your dad. And we are going our separate ways" (Druckmann et al. 2013). Joel, Ellie, and Tommy then travel back to the community in silence.

Despite Joel insisting that they are moving apart and that he could not care about Ellie, and especially care about her as if she were his daughter, he agrees to help her continue out west. In arguably the most iconic scene in the game, Joel and Ellie are searching for the fireflies at Eastern Colorado University and they find giraffes roaming the empty campus. While they are having a quiet moment of reflection, Joel tells Ellie, "We don't have to do this. You know that right?" Ellie replies, "What's the other option?" Joel says, "Go back to Tommy's. Just…be done with this whole damn thing." Ellie rejects this selfish attitude saying, "After all we've been through. Everything that I've done. It can't be for nothing. Look I know you mean well…but there's no half-way with this. Once we're done, we'll go wherever you want. Okay?" Joel responds, "Well, I ain't leavin' without ya, so let's go wrap this up" (Druckmann et al. 2013).

Eventually, Joel and Ellie finally reach the Fireflies and their long and arduous journey is almost complete. Joel says to Marlene, the leader of the Fireflies, "Take me to her." She responds, "You don't have to worry about her anymore. We'll take care of—" Joel responds, "I worry. Just let me see her. Please." Marlene responds, "You can't. She's being prepped for surgery." Joel is confused, "The hell you mean, surgery?" Marlene informs Joel that the only way to fully reverse engineer a cure for the disease is to extract it from Ellie's brain while she is still alive. The result, of course, is that Ellie will die. Marlene tries to explain, "The doctors tell me that the cordyceps, the growth inside her, has somehow mutated. It's why she's immune. Once they remove it, they'll be able to reverse engineer a vaccine. *A vaccine.*" Joel begins to understand, responding, "But it grows all over the brain." She quietly responds to Joel, "It does." Without the slightest hesitation, Joel orders her, "Find someone else." Marlene continues, defending her choice to do the surgery, "There is no one else." Joel insists angrily, "Listen, you are gonna show me where—." Joel is interrupted, getting hit with a gun to the back of the head. Marlene, sounding both thoroughly rational, deeply caring, and yet, exceedingly villainous. "Stop. I get it. But whatever it is you think you're going through right now is nothing to what I have been through. I knew her since she was born. I promised her mother I would look after her." Joel pleads, "Then why are you letting this happen?" Exasperated, Marlene tries to justify her actions, "Because this isn't about me. Or even her. There is no other choice here." Not accepting the argument that the ends justify the means, Joel retorts, "Yeah...You keep telling yourself that bullshit" (Druckmann et al. 2013).

It is perhaps clearest here that the game may be understood as an attempt to present a consequentialist moral view. Marlene and the Fireflies are justified in killing one person to save millions. The consequences would be better if the Fireflies sacrificed one for the many. This scenario presents the most significant moral dilemma in the game for Joel – should he allow this group of revolutionaries to kill a child for the hope of a vaccine for humanity, or should he try to protect his surrogate daughter at any cost?

Despite his initial resistance to Ellie, Joel chooses the latter option without hesitation. He kills numerous guards and doctors to free Ellie from the facility. In short, Joel sacrificed humanity to protect one little girl – importantly, *his* little girl – at least in his mind. As he escapes the facility holding her in his arms, we hear him crying to the still unconscious Ellie, "Come on, baby girl. I gotcha...I'm getting you outta here girl. I got you. I got you" (Druckmann et al. 2013). Not only is Joel carrying Ellie to safety in exactly the same fashion that he did with his own daughter, Sarah, in the opening of the game, he is even calling Ellie "baby girl," just as he did with Sarah. It could not be clearer that in this moment, Ellie is being protected just as Joel tried to protect his daughter, Sarah. Joel has taken on the role, not of a smuggler, but a father. And that role carries moral obligations.

In the final scene of the game, Ellie wakes from the anesthesia, and Joel commits his last seemingly unethical action. She asks Joel what had happened while she was unconscious, not knowing herself that the Fireflies were going to kill her in hopes of finding a cure. And because of their conversation earlier in the game while they watched the giraffes, Joel knows that Ellie would have gladly sacrificed herself so that her life would have meaning. So he does the only thing that will stop Ellie from returning on her own to the Fireflies. Joel lies. He tells Ellie that the group had other subjects with immunity to the fungus, that none of the attempted vaccines had been successful, and that they have stopped looking for a cure.

Joel, the Villain

Perhaps the two most central questions in ethics are "how can I live the good life?" and "what does it mean to do the right thing or be a good person?" By far and away, two of the most popular and influential moral theories in the west are consequentialism and deontology, and these theories are attempts to answers to those fundamental questions. Part of the confusion with respect to whether Joel is a villain is primarily because philosophers and nonphilosophers alike tend to think of morality in these terms. As a result, it will be helpful to have a short primer on how these theories provide guidance on how we ought to live, so that we can better understand the moral permissibility of Joel's actions throughout *The Last of Us*.

According to both major modern ethical theories, lying, stealing, and killing are usually immoral. Whether one is convinced by the veracity of the argumentation or whether the moral framework simply coheres with one's own moral intuitions, the result is often the same – Joel's actions throughout the game are typically considered morally impermissible on both consequentialist and deontological terms. Joel commits many seemingly immoral actions in the game. He lied. He stole. He killed. He sacrificed the good of the whole human race so that he may protect one little girl. And it is for these reasons that many argued, very plausibly, that *The Last of Us* was presenting a strictly consequentialist moral theory that Joel actively works against, and thus that Joel is the villain of the game.

The most famous version of consequentialism is utilitarianism, the moral view associated with Jeremy Bentham and John Stuart Mill. According to their system, the feature we should be concerned with in our moral deliberations are the consequences of actions. More specifically, our concern should be solely on the utility of an action, which they equated with pleasure, advantage, or even goodness itself. Bentham writes,

> By utility is meant that property in any object, whereby it tends to produce benefit, advantage, pleasure, good, or happiness, (all this in the present case comes to the same thing) or (what comes again to the same thing) to prevent the happening of mischief, pain, evil, or unhappiness to the party whose interest is considered.... (Bentham 1907, p. 2)

Put simply, according to utilitarianism, an action is morally right if it maximizes utility, that is, an action is good if it brings about the greatest utility or good to the greatest amount of people.

Mill describes how the principle of utility implies a larger moral framework.

> The creed which accepts as the foundation of morals "utility" or the "greatest happiness principle" holds that actions are right in proportion as they tend to promote happiness; wrong as they tend to produce the reverse of happiness. By happiness is intended pleasure and the absence of pain; by unhappiness, pain and the privation of pleasure. (Mill 2001, p. 7)

In order to make a correct moral deliberation, we ought to consider a variety of features that are related to the utility of an action. This hedonistic calculus compels us to consider things like how long the utility lasts, whether it will bring any associated pain, the intensity of the pleasure, and so on (Bentham 1907, pp. 29–32).

Intuitively, consequentialism makes a great deal of sense – it is unselfish since it is concerned with the good of the whole, and it is flexible, in that what is morally permissible may change from case to case when the variables related to utility change. Killing, stealing, and lying may all be permissible in certain circumstances and impermissible in others. For instance, if killing one person were to save thousand lives, then many would consider that death as morally justified. If stealing a loaf of bread from an international multibillion-dollar big box store will save a young child from starving to death, many would consider that theft as morally justified. And if someone lies to relieve another's suffering, then many would consider that deception as morally justified. But there are other circumstances where the same actions would be impermissible. Considering consequences in our moral deliberations allows us to smuggle in the flexibility that many believe a coherent ethical system demands.

One problem with these sorts of moral justifications though is that because the moral worth of the action is contingent only on its consequences, its capacity to promote utility, there is no action that is intrinsically morally wrong – *anything* can be justified so long as it will produce an overall net good. Even morally reprehensible things such as genocide and slavery have been justified on consequentialist terms. While an individual or group may suffer, their suffering could be justified for the good of the whole. To be clear, consequentialism would not simply say that it is acceptable to commit things like genocide or maintain a system of slavery, but it would insist that we are morally obligated to do these things if they maximize utility. And when we have an ethical framework that tells us that we are *required* to exterminate a people or enslave others, surely the framework must be mistaken.

One plausible reason why gamers might have considered Joel's actions throughout the game to be morally acceptable is because they considered his actions on consequentialist grounds. One might believe that when Joel kills soldiers, steals resources such as bandages and scissors from abandoned homes, or lies to Ellie that he is doing so for the benefit of the whole. But while these actions may benefit others, it would be a mistake to think that he could justify these actions on consequentialist terms. When he kills soldiers and doctors at the end of the game, he does so to protect Ellie. And while her welfare is a good, so is the good of the people that he kills to protect her. Put differently, by killing many to protect one, Joel is not maximizing utility – in fact, he is doing the furthest thing possible from maximizing utility. When Joel steals resources on the journey out west, he does so to provide for Ellie. And while providing for himself and Ellie is surely a good thing, it is unclear how much harm will be produced by the theft. Perhaps in stealing the bandages and scissors to heal Ellie, he is taking those resources from a family that could have used them to heal parents who are protecting their three children. The player and the characters in the game simply do not have enough information. It might be the case that the resources that they steal would have produced more good if they had left the resources alone. And finally, when he lies about the possibility of a vaccine, he does so to benefit Ellie. And while saving Ellie's life is a good thing, it is not the greatest good in this instance because it does not maximize utility. Without the lie, Ellie would return to the facility to sacrifice herself for the common good. And while her sacrifice may be justified in consequentialist terms as a good thing, Joel's lie cannot. To protect the one, Joel has sacrificed the good of the whole. And he did so throughout the game, again and again.

Perhaps, our moral intuition is that Joel is a villain not because of assumptions about consequentialism though, but instead because actions such as killing, stealing, and lying are wrong in themselves. The belief according to which there are some actions that are intrinsically wrong because they violate our duties is called deontology. According to deontology, the good life is attained by identifying these correct moral principles and fulfilling our duties out of respect for those principles. Most commonly associated with the German philosopher, Immanuel Kant, his version of deontology imposes rules for morality which cannot be violated under any circumstance. Not only are actions such as killing, stealing, and lying morally impermissible, they are *always* morally impermissible. Nothing could possibly justify making an immoral action moral, especially the context of a particular situation or the consequences that would come from it. For instance, one might think that there are exceptions to certain moral rules, like prohibitions against killing, stealing, and lying, and yet Kant is adamant that this intuition is misguided.

One might believe that an individual should be able to kill in self-defense or times of war, steal a loaf of bread if they are starving to death, or tell a white lie to prevent suffering brought on as a result of the truth. But for Kant, the consequences of an action are irrelevant to the intrinsic nature of the action itself, and the particular circumstances of an action can often help us justify immoral behavior. He writes, "the moral worth of an action does not lie in the effect expected from it and so too does not lie in any principle of action that needs to borrow its motive from this expected effect" (Kant 1900, 4:401; 14). In other words, while our moral intuition might tell us that killing, stealing, and lying might sometimes be morally acceptable and excusable, Kant insists that this moral intuition is not grounded on reason. The moral law must be universally applied – if actions are immoral in some cases, then they are immoral in all cases. Kant's moral law, the categorical imperative, is a universal command, dictated from reason, and compels us to act purely for the sake of our duty and out of respect for the moral law itself. Nevertheless, many philosophers find Kant's deontological system far too demanding for morality. We may agree that certain kinds of actions are blameworthy, but surely it is counterintuitive to think that those rules can *never* be violated under any circumstance.

For Kant, actions such as killing, stealing, and lying are always morally impermissible because they violate our duty to the moral law. And they violate our duties because the actions cannot be universalized – they cannot be applied to everyone at all times. Put differently, it is just a violation of basic logic and fairness to insist that one kind of action is acceptable for one person and unacceptable for another, or acceptable in one case and unacceptable in another. If killing is blameworthy, then it is always blameworthy. If stealing is blameworthy, then it is always blameworthy. If lying is blameworthy, then it is always blameworthy.

Kant describes the moral duty in terms of universalizability, writing, "I ought never to act except in such a way that I could also will that my maxim should become a universal law" (Kant 1900, 4: 402; 15). Later in the same text, Kant argues that this is also the simplest moral framework. He writes,

Inexperienced in the course of the world, incapable of being prepared for whatever might come to pass in it, I ask myself only: can you also will that your maxim become a universal law? If not, then it is to be repudiated, and that not because of a disadvantage to you or even to others forthcoming from it but because it cannot fit as a principle into a possible giving of universal law, for which lawgiving reason, however, forces from me immediate respect. (Kant 1900, 4:403; 16)

If we try to think of our actions in terms of how good the consequences would be, then we would be forced to consider far too many variables that we could very reasonably misjudge. It is much simpler to rationally consider whether the action could be universalized. If the action can be applied to everyone at all times, then the action is moral; if it cannot, then the action is immoral.

Kant is clear that our moral obligations must be derived from the respect for the moral law itself and the respect for each other as rational beings who can legislate that moral law. Part of the motivation for considering morality divorced from the particular circumstances and consequences of our actions is that we have a disposition to harshly judge others and excuse our own actions, even when those actions are equivalent. This concern is the problem of self-deception. How can we hope to do good if we do not first recognize that our own actions might be wrong? For example, we may agree that stealing is morally blameworthy, but then try to justify our own actions when it is convenient. If ethics is just a complicated system of justifying our own behavior, then Kant argues that it becomes meaningless. Not only is that framework false, Kant insists it is also dangerous.

Whereas consequentialism focuses entirely on the results of actions, deontology focuses purely on the intrinsic nature of moral rules. Put differently, consequentialism accepts that the world is gray and our ethical system should match that grayness, whereas deontology considers moral principles in black and white terms that are universally applicable.

In *The Last of Us*, it is clear that Joel's actions throughout the game would be considered blameworthy on Kantian deontological grounds. The very same thing that makes killing, stealing, and lying morally impermissible before the disease breaks out is the thing that makes killing, stealing, and lying morally impermissible afterward. Put differently, while it is a common trope in postapocalyptic narratives that morality becomes meaningless outside of a society, Kant is clear that morality is the same in a state of nature or in a political state with laws and a system of authority to enforce those laws. Universality and necessity are the only relevant marks for morality on the Kantian moral framework.

At least on the face of it then, it appears as if there is a good case to be made that in *The Last of Us*, Joel is indeed the villain. After all, his actions cannot be defended on consequentialist grounds since his actions are often directly at odds with the good of the whole. And it also appears that his actions cannot be justified on deontological grounds because he violates many of the most fundamental moral obligations that we have to others. Even though it is reasonable that *The Last of Us* was presenting a view that Joel is a villain, either on consequentialist or deontological grounds, the view is mistaken. I contend that the game is offering a more nuanced ethical theory according to which our moral obligations are derived from our roles, and given that Joel had assumed the role of Ellie's father and protector, his actions in that capacity supersede the moral responsibilities that he has to others. As a result, Joel is not a villain and his actions are morally permissible.

Teleological Particularism

A former professor and mentor once told me that the history of philosophy is littered with bad moral theories. There is an obvious sense in which what he was saying was certainly true. History abounds in insidious justifications for war, imperialism, colonialism, slavery, oppression, violence, and just about every kind of inequality imaginable. While it may be obvious that moral arguments supporting these systems of injustice are clearly faulty, even well-respected and influential, moral theories such as consequentialism and deontology are flawed as well.

Consequentialist theories of ethics are rightfully criticized for being far too flexible and ambiguous. Any action, no matter how heinous, could not only be permissible, but morally obligatory should it maximize the good. By contrast, deontological theories of ethics have been rightfully criticized as being too strict and inflexible. While killing, stealing, and lying might intuitively appear to be morally impermissible, it is simply too much to insist that these moral imperatives can never be bent or broken. For Kant though, this inflexibility is a feature of the system – not a flaw. If morality allowed for exceptions and ambiguity, then we could use it to justify any, and perhaps all, of our actions, instead of using the moral code to guide our moral considerations and actions.

Although it may be conceivable that another ethical theory could both capture our moral intuitions and be defensible, my contention is that the best way to conceive of our moral obligations is to think of at least some of them as contingent on the roles that we inhabit. Considering our moral obligations as dependent on our roles allows us to navigate the middle ground between having utterly flexible commands such as they are in consequentialism and utterly inflexible moral commands such as how they are in deontology.

Roles at least partially define our identities and are almost always relational. My identity is shaped by being a father, husband, professor, neighbor, citizen, human, and so on. On the view defended here, my moral obligations are at least partly shaped by these roles – these roles dictate what I should and should not do. Others have different roles, and as a result they may have distinct moral obligations. My wife's identity is shaped by being a mother, wife, bookstore manager, neighbor, citizen, human, and so on. While some of our moral obligations are the same (such as protecting and providing for our children), some of our moral obligations are distinct (she is not required to protect my student's privacy, for instance). Put simply, many of our moral responsibilities are derived from the roles that we inhabit, so the more imbedded we are in communities where we occupy more roles, the more obligations and responsibilities we have to others.

Teleological particularism holds that some of an individual's moral obligations are derived from their roles – roles which are typically socially constructed. Teleological particularism is plausible given our intuition that the more imbedded we are into a community, the more responsibilities we have to others. While some of our moral obligations will be fairly straightforward because our roles are straightforward, other obligations are less obvious because the relata are less obvious. Consider three examples.

The moral obligations easiest to understand are those in relation to other *persons*, such as my role to protect my children or keep confidential my student's privacy. But we can also occupy roles wherein we do not stand in relation to other persons. I have moral obligations to the environment, for instance, because I may occupy a role as something like a steward of the Earth. In this case, the relation is between me and a *place* (or thing, depending on your ontology). We may also occupy a role in relation to *ourselves*. In this case, we may have duties to care for our own physical, mental, emotional, and spiritual health. We may also occupy a role in relation to *God*. Here, we may have obligations to follow God's commands, show reverence for creation, and perform certain religious acts such as pray and fast. Each of these relations imposes different moral obligations depending on whether we occupy that role. Even an individual alone on an island may still have obligations because they still occupy roles, albeit not to other people, but to the environment, themself, or God, for instance.

Conceiving of moral obligations in terms of our roles helps to explain why many agree that there are distinct moral rules for the military, police officers, lawyers, reporters, and so on. The codes of conduct governing these roles range from when it is permissible to kill, hold people against their will, withhold information, and so on. On the teleological particularist framework offered here, some of an agent's moral obligations are derived from their roles. It is teleological because it demands that we consider the roles, goals, and purpose of each individual, and it is particularist because it recognizes that those very roles, goals, and purposes can change from subject to subject, time to time, and culture to culture.

Some might contend that the moral view defended here is just a version of moral particularism. Moral particularism is the view according to which moral principles do not exist, and as a result, the morality of an action cannot be determined by any moral principles. Instead, the morality of an action is determined by the particular context of a given situation. But it would be a mistake to conflate teleological particularism with moral particularism. While teleological particularism draws on the same intuition that moral principles often require exceptions to be tenable, it does not deny them altogether. Instead, teleological particularism accepts that there are moral principles but denies that they are universal and objective. Instead, teleological particularism contends that some moral principles are relative to the roles that we inhabit and that some of our duties are contingent on those roles. In Joel's case, he has taken on the role of Ellie's father and because that role demands that he protect for Ellie's well-being, the actions taken acting in that role such as killing, stealing, and lying are morally defensible.

Moral dilemmas in applied ethics are often the result of having conflicting moral obligations. Very often, it appears that there are conflicting moral obligations because we are trying to understand the dilemma with a framework that is, on the one hand, either too flexible and consequentialist or, on the other hand, too strict and deontological. Consider, for instance, the case of a doctor who not only has a moral obligation to protect the privacy and confidentiality of his patients, but also has a moral obligation to protect the safety of his family, friends, and neighbors. Suppose that the doctor has a patient with a highly contagious disease and is being careless about infecting others and secretive so that their family, friends, and neighbors do not know the risks. Further suppose that the patient is going to encounter the doctor's family, friends, and neighbors. On the one hand, the doctor has a moral obligation not to reveal the diagnosis to preserve privacy and confidentiality, and a separate moral obligation to reveal the diagnosis to protect the safety of his family, friends, and neighbors.

Cases with conflicting moral obligations are common in applied ethics. Traditionally, these kinds of dilemmas get wrapped up in questions such as whether lying is equally morally blameworthy to withholding truth or whether we can maximize happiness, goodness, or utility by revealing the relevant information. But the moral dilemma is very easily addressed when we consider that the problem arises because of conflicting obligations brought on by conflicting roles. The solution to the problem comes from those same conflicting roles. To address the apparent moral conflict, we need only to consider which roles have priority over others. If the role of the individual as a doctor has priority, then the obligations associated with that role are more important. In this case, he would be obligated to protect the privacy and confidentiality of his patient. And if the role of the individual as a family member, friend, and neighbor has priority, then the obligations associated with that role are more important. In this case, he would be obligated to preserve the safety of his family, friends, and neighbors.

The reader may have different moral intuitions and insist that Joel is a villain even within the context of teleological particularism. One might object that while it may be true that Joel has competing obligations, that is, while it may be true that he has an obligation to protect Ellie as her surrogate father and true that he has an obligation to protect humanity as a fellow member of that community, his obligations to humanity at large supersede those obligations to Ellie. The problem though is that this objection rests on an underlying assumption that consequentialism is the correct moral theory, that is, that the right action is the one that maximizes the good. In this case, because there are competing moral obligations with responsibilities pulling in opposing directions, the right action is the one that will maximize the good. Such an interpretation is plausible, but it assumes the thing that it is trying to prove, namely, that consequentialism is a preferable moral framework to teleological particularism.

The root of the objection is that there is a "fact of the matter" about what is morally required, one course of action that is necessitated. But there is no objective judge to decide what is required. There is no impartial and omniscient jury of which to appeal so that Joel can decide what he should do. A jury of the rest of the humanity would argue that it is better to sacrifice the one because they would benefit. Importantly, nothing would be wrong about that interpretation, but it is just one interpretation.

There is a different sort of response to the previous objection though. The primary conclusion of teleological particularism is that some of our moral obligations are derived from our roles. This claim still stands even if we grant that Joel's obligation is to the rest of humanity and not Ellie. Where the disagreement comes is which role has priority – not *whether* the moral obligation is derived from a role. It is plausible that two rational agents could come to different conclusions about which role has priority and the nature of the obligation that is demanded. Put differently, it has not been argued here that the interpretation of Joel's actions according to which he is a villain is *necessarily* wrong – only that there is a competing interpretation where his actions are defensible, based primarily on his role as Ellie's surrogate father. In other words, on the view defended here, there is a range of options that could be justified, defended, and permitted. In short, there is less of a focus on what is morally *commanded*, and more of a focus on what is morally *permitted*. Importantly, the shift of focus does not mean that what is permitted is relative. In most cases, our moral obligations are derived from the roles we occupy, but the roles are subject to change.

In the context of *The Last of Us*, there is confusion about Joel's moral character because it seems that he justifiably broke certain moral commands (meaning his actions were not justified on deontological grounds), but did not do so for the benefit of the whole (meaning that his actions were not justified on consequentialist grounds either). His actions become much clearer when considering them from a framework grounded on roles. Put simply, Joel's actions are defensible because he has taken on the role of Ellie's father. According to teleological particularism, Joel's actions are morally permissible because the role that he has designated for himself is that he is, in effect, Ellie's father. It does not matter in the least that he is not her biological father any more than it matters that parents who adopt or foster children are not the biological parents. While being a parent is sometimes biological, it is not always a matter of biology. And while some roles may be based on biology, certainly not all roles are based on biology.

Concluding Remarks

Video games have the capacity to delight and entertain us in different ways. But the best games can do more than just entertain; they can invite us to consider them as art and compel us to ask questions about the nature of reality, knowledge, and values. In short, just as great works of art and literature can be treated as philosophical works, so too can some of the best video games. *The Last of Us* is an exemplary narrative about loss, grief, survival, and redemption. In dealing with these themes, the game raises the question of whether Joel is a villain whose actions are morally blameworthy. In fact, it invites us to reflect on what it truly means to be a villain in the first place. While there is a very plausible interpretation according to which Joel is indeed a villain, I have argued that there is a competing interpretation of his actions. According to the alternative interpretation, Joel's apparently vicious actions are morally defensible because of the role he has taken on as Ellie's surrogate father. Joel's role as a father demands that he protect and provide for Ellie, and that he help her to become autonomous and flourish. Joel's role demands that he put his child's interests even above the interests of the rest of humanity, even if those interests are utterly dire. Therefore, it is a mistake to believe that Joel is a villain and that his actions are morally blameworthy.

There are lingering questions related to teleological particularism. How do we choose which course of action is morally required given that roles can have conflicting obligations? All that has been shown here is that *some* of our moral obligations are derived from the roles that we occupy, but there has not been a defense of the priority of roles or an account of whether moral obligations may be derived beyond our roles. And there is also a lingering question regarding what to say about conflicting moral obligations *within* the same role. These are great questions worthy of further inquiry, but they go beyond the scope of the paper. The focus here has been an attempt to show that Joel's actions in *The Last of Us* are morally defensible given that he interprets his moral obligation to protect Ellie as more important than his moral obligations to the rest of humanity.

Our identities are shaped by many different features – history, education, culture, and family and friends all help to define who we are. The roles that we occupy also fundamentally shape our identity in profound ways. There is an important sense in which when we lose one of our roles, we lose a part of our identity. When my students graduate, it is bittersweet because one role is changing, and another role is beginning. When we retire from our careers, we also lose part of our identity. For Joel, perhaps the most heartbreaking thing imaginable happens when he loses his daughter, Sarah. It is in this context that we should consider what it would mean for him to lose yet another daughter in Ellie. Joel was already broken by the time that his journey with Ellie began decades after the disease started infecting humanity. Were he to also lose Ellie, Joel would simply become nonexistent – his identity would be completely lost – he would be an amorphous husk, not unlike the infected he has spent decades fighting. Indeed, in *The Last of Us 2*, Joel fulfills his promise to teach Ellie to play guitar and, in one memorable scene, sings "Future Days" by Pearl Jam. The very first lyric to the song is "If I ever were to lose you, I'd surely lose myself." The song, and this lyric in particular, clearly indicates that his identity is very much wrapped up in Ellie. Joel's actions are defensible precisely because his identity has become defined by his relationship with Ellie. Losing her, especially after losing Sarah, would amount to losing himself. Fiercely protecting one's child at any cost is not a mark of villainy – it is the mark of parenthood.

Acknowledgments I am grateful for the opportunity to present my work there and am appreciative of the comments and feedback from the conference participants. I am also thankful to the

Philosophy Club at the University of Wisconsin Stevens Point for their feedback on earlier versions of the paper. And, of course, I am especially thankful for the very helpful suggestions from the editor of this handbook, David Kyle Johnson.

A version of this paper was given at the "Science Fictions, Popular Cultures" conference, in conjunction with HawaiiCon, in 2018.

References

Bentham, Jeremy. 1907. *An introduction to the principles of morals and legislation*. Dover.
Druckmann, Neil, et al. 2013. *The last of us*. Sony Computer Entertainment.
Fischer, Tyler. The last of us: Joel is more villain than hero, says voice actor. *Comicbook*, August 15, 2019. https://comicbook.com/gaming/news/the-last-of-us-part-ii-ps4-joel/
Kant, Immanuel. 1900–. *Gesammelte Schriften*. Academy of Sciences; Kant, Immanuel. 1997. *Groundwork of the metaphysics of morals*. Cambridge University Press. Passages of Kant are cited by the volume and page number, given by Arabic numerals in the standard edition of Kant's works, Kant's gesammelte Schriften, edited by Academy of Sciences, 29 volumes.
Mill, John Stuart. 2001. *Utilitarianism*. Hackett.

Journey as Philosophy: Meaning, Connection, and the Sublime

77

Russ Hamer

Contents

Introduction	1758
Summary of *Journey*	1758
Analysis of *Journey*	1761
Journey and the Sublime	1762
Journey and Meaning	1765
Commentary	1767
Conclusion	1768
References	1769

Abstract

Journey is a game famous for its visuals and sound design, along with the emotional experience of playing. While the game eschews standard practices in video games, like having strategy, complex gameplay mechanics, or dialogue, it is nonetheless able to leave a deep impression on its players. This impression is due to a number of factors, but some of the big ones are the interplay between meaning, connection, and the sublime. In *Journey,* you play with other players who you can't talk to as you wander around a desolate, yet beautiful, landscape. There is a massive mountain in the distance that you're wandering towards, and so you and the other players that you encounter have a shared experience of the sublime. This experience creates connections with other players, despite your inability to talk to them or message them in any way. The game's narrative is rather straightforward, but the storytelling, world-building, and overall game design are done in such a way that you cannot help but consider the problem of meaning. Your journey to the top of the mountain accomplishes nothing, yet you

R. Hamer (✉)
Mount St. Mary's University, Emmitsburg, MD, USA
e-mail: r.a.hamer@msmary.edu

© Springer Nature Switzerland AG 2024
D. K. Johnson et al. (eds.), *The Palgrave Handbook of Popular Culture as Philosophy,*
https://doi.org/10.1007/978-3-031-24685-2_36

are compelled to do it over and over. By playing with these different themes, and weaving them into each other, *Journey* creates an unforgettable experience.

Keywords

Journey · Sublime · Kant · Burke · Aesthetics · Meaning · Existentialism · Camus · Myth of Sisyphus · Emotion · Connection · Fear · Beauty

Introduction

In 2012, thatgamecompany released *Journey* to much critical acclaim. Building on their successes with *Flow* and *Flower*, thatgamecompany further pushed the argument that games can indeed be art. *Journey* went on to be a critical and commercial success, winning a plethora of awards; its musical score was even nominated for a Grammy – the first such nomination for a video game. Reviewers consistently commented on the beauty of the game and the emotional experience of playing. Jenova Chen, the director of the game, said that he knew *Journey* was ready when multiple play-testers were crying at the end of the game. The game itself is rather short, it is beat-able in 2 hours, and only takes 4 hours or so for you to fully explore the entire game. Despite the short length, the game holds a score of 92 on Metacritic and continues to sell to this day.

Journey is a rather simple game in a genre that has come to be called "walking simulators." In *Journey*, you only have two real actions that you can take outside of basic movement. You can jump/fly, and you can make a musical chirp. In view of these simplistic mechanics and the short length of the game, it's surprising how replayable the game is. This replay value, and the reason the game was reviewed so well and is considered such an excellent game, is because of the way that the game makes you feel. *Journey* does not challenge the player in terms of gameplay or mechanics; instead, it challenges the player to share a sense of meaning and awe with strangers, and by doing so to create an emotional journey for the player.

Summary of *Journey*

In *Journey*, you play as a character called the Traveler. However, your character is never named in the game and you are intentionally designed to be rather nondescript. You have pointy legs and are wearing a giant shawl-like robe that obscures your entire body except for your eyes. There is no dialogue in the game and no text of any kind. Instead, the game begins in a vast desert. You see a star-like object shoot through the sky and then you come upon the Traveler sitting in the sand. You stand up and walk towards a dune in front of you. As you crest the dune, you see a giant mountain in the distance with a shining light at its peak, reaching higher into the sky than the sun currently sits. The mountain is clearly very far away and the visual and auditory cues signify to you that it is of some importance. Traveling forward, you walk through what appears to be, and what you later find out is, a graveyard. There are graves everywhere in the sand and you eventually come upon the old, decrepit ruins of various buildings. All of them are in states of decay, with the sand covering up their bases. This is your introduction to the world of *Journey*, a vast desert filled with the remnants of some old civilization, and a massive mountain in the distance that beckons you.

Outside of two very short moments, there isn't a tutorial, and you are left to your own devices to figure out how to move forward. You unlock the ability to fly short distances almost right away by finding a glowing glyph on one of the buildings and with that, you move through the ruins. There are numerous similar glyphs hidden throughout the levels, all of which extend your flight ability. Some of the ruins are inhabited by small creatures that look like pieces of cloth. If you chirp near them, they will swirl around you and propel you into the air, creating the basis for some of the game's basic puzzles. These ruins will also power up your flight ability, which has limited use before needing to be powered again.

The desert that you're in is quite massive. Your flight ability makes it easier and faster to navigate, but the size of your character against the dunes and the ruins leaves you with a continual impression of the breadth of the landscape. Eventually you come to a larger set of ruins and a small shrine that the ruins all point towards. You maneuver your way through the ruins to the shrine, which you proceed to sit and meditate at. You have a vision of a giant character like yourself, but dressed in all white. They reveal a scene to you which plays out the history of your people. Each level in the game ends with another such vision, revealing your history over time. In the first vision, you see characters much like yourself surrounding the mountain. They grow crops and seem to prosper in an area that is not yet a desert. Your vision ends and the door opens before you leading to the second area.

This is the general flow of the game. You play through an area, each one centered around a theme or idea, get to the end and have a vision of your ancestors, and then move to the next area, all the while getting closer and closer to the mountain. In the next area, there is a giant stone bridge across a chasm, but the bridge is broken in multiple locations. Because of this, you run around on the ground below the bridge and you find the skeletons of giant stone serpents. When you chirp next to these skeletons, you bring large pieces of cloth to life, and that fabric stretches across the bridge for you. Once you have done this a few times, you complete the bridge and you can cross it. Upon crossing the bridge and meditating at the altar you once again have a vision of the giant white character who reveals the history of your people to you. This time you see your ancestors building the bridges and giant cities around them. They are using the cloth to assist in much of what they are doing as if the cloth is a power source. This vision seems to also imply that the cloth might be alive in one way or another. You then realize that what you've been doing so far is bringing this dead cloth back to life by chirping near it, and that's how you rebuilt the bridge.

Next, you move on to an area that's full of giant dunes. These dunes are massive, some taking 30 seconds to walk up, and there are hundreds of them. Despite the size of these dunes, the mountain looms in the distance, towering over everything. In this area, if you stop and watch, you can see stars shooting off the top of the mountain.

Some of them land as glyphs near you, which extend your flying time, and some shoot past you towards where you came from. You also stumble across more stone serpent skeletons, though this time when you chirp near them you bring cloth creatures to life. This confirms that the cloth at least has some ability to be alive, and these cloth creatures guide you through the level. You find a large number of these creatures trapped in a machine, and you can have another vision which sets them all free. In this vision, you see your ancestors building the city larger and higher. They leave behind their lives of agriculture and build a magnificent city powered by cloth.

You next enter an area where you are skiing through the sand. You move through the entirety of a massive city in a level that requires very little thinking and thus the experience of speed is evoked and you are able to spend your time soaking in the beauty of the city and the music. Despite the size of the city and its majesty, and the joy of moving through it, the mountain dwarfs it all. At the end of this, you descend into the under-city, an area that is dark and which expresses none of the joy of the previous level. This is accompanied with a vision of your ancestors fighting with one another. They use the cloth to power the stone serpents and go to war.

The under-city creates a feeling of being underwater, with the cloth creatures here even looking like jellyfish. You come across your first living stone serpent, and if it sees you, it will attack you by ramming its body into you. You eventually run into multiple serpents who all chase you to the end of the area where a shrine is protected by the glyphs you have seen throughout the game. They keep the serpents at bay, and you are given another vision. Here you see your civilization fall apart. The city is destroyed, your people are all dead, and the desert overcomes the city. The stars are full of glyphs, and you see one of these glyphs descend from the sky and turn into a creature like yourself.

The next area is like an elevator shaft running back to the surface. You progress by activating paintings that tell the story of your journey thus far. You see yourself playing through the levels as you ascend through the elevator shaft, with a vision waiting for you at the top. Here you see all the things you just saw, the story of your journey, but you also see one image that wasn't previously shown. You see yourself on your knees, in defeat, at the foot of the mountain. Despite this, you travel forward, entering the final area. The peak of the mountain is very close, and everything is white with snow. The cold takes away your ability to fly, and stone serpents fly in the sky above you. The world becomes harsher the closer you get to the peak. The wind pushes against you and serpents try to attack you. You walk through a graveyard of your people and eventually get close to the peak. However, the wind is too much. You push forward but eventually drop to your knees, collapse, and die.

You have a final vision. You are surrounded by the giant white figures who you have seen before. You come back to life and shoot through into the sky, breaking through it and the storm that was there a moment prior. You are pure light as you come to the peak of the mountain. You are surrounded by numerous cloth creatures and you can fly almost indefinitely. You are free, fast, and alive. The cold of the mountain has been transformed, with warm springs dotting the landscape. Death has become life. You fly to the very peak and walk into the light that it shines. You keep walking until you become transformed into a star, and you shoot back through the landscape, landing exactly where you started so that you can begin the journey anew.

Analysis of *Journey*

There is a lot going on in *Journey* that isn't revealed to the player, partially because no words are ever spoken in the game. The visions that you receive paint the general picture of the history of your ancestors, or at least, your assumed ancestors. As you continue the journey, you learn that they were an agricultural people who were able to harness the power of the magic cloth and use it to build a massive city at the foot of the mountain. Over time, they began to fight over the cloth and war erupted. This war ended up killing many of them and eventually ensured the destruction of all of them and their works. All that is left behind is an empty and broken city full of graves. Yet, there are clues all throughout the game that something more is going on here. As you play through the game, you can come across wall paintings that you have to chirp next to in order to reveal. These wall paintings tell much the same story as your visions do, but they flesh things out a bit more. One of them shows an ancestor of yours dying and releasing a glyph into the air. Thus, there's an implication that the glyphs are potentially the souls or spirits of your ancestors, helping you along your path. They protect you from the stone serpents in the under-city and empower you to fly further.

Similarly, when the game ends, the mountain fires off a star that flies through the air until it lands right where the game began, and you can start all over. In the dunes level, you see this happen; however, you also see one of the stars land near you and turn into a glyph. So, it seems that you do indeed die at the top of the mountain, but then you are reborn back in the desert so that you may begin the journey anew. *Journey* is a short and quite easy game, and this feeds into the cyclical nature of the story. Experience the world of the game for a little bit, beat it, and then come back later for another experience. Nothing changes, and there are very few secrets to find throughout the game, but nonetheless it invites multiple play-throughs.

Part of this invitation is tied into something that hasn't yet been mentioned: *Journey* is a multiplayer game. The game is always online, assuming you are connected to the internet. You can meet other travelers that may join you in the game. You do not see their usernames, nor are their characters at all different from yours. The only difference between the two of you is your chirp, which is a slightly different tone. When you chirp, a glyph appears above your head, and every user also receives a slightly different glyph. However, the only interaction that's possible between you and other players is to chirp at them. Chirping is your only form of communication and other than that, you can only run around with the other player and hope that they understand. These interactions very often take the form of more seasoned players guiding newer players. The game randomly gives you another traveler to journey with, and if you do not stay with your assigned traveler, they will exit your game and a little bit later a new one will pop into your game. You do not need to interact with these players at all, but oftentimes players will travel together, at least for a time.

The director of the game, Jenova Chen, said that he wanted to create a game where the multiplayer was "just the relationship and the connection between two genuine human beings" (Chen 2013). In most multiplayer games, you can learn a lot about the person that you're playing with by the way their avatar looks, by communicating with them via text or voice, and by watching their game play decisions. In *Journey*, none of these things are possible. Chen wanted to strip all of that away so that individuals had the opportunity to simply connect with one another. He claims that he "want[ed] the interaction [between players] to be about the exchange of emotion, of feelings" (Chen 2013).

Journey achieves this very well. It is very common for you and the player that you are paired with to simply sit and look at some of the beautiful vistas that the game presents you with. These traveling companions of yours do not make the game any easier, generally speaking. The game is designed such that you should always be able to figure out where you should go, and the puzzles are all quite straightforward. While another player might help you find a secret or two, they likely do not lower the difficulty of the game. So, despite them not offering any real advantage, it's not uncommon for players to stick with their traveling companion for the entirety of the game. In this, Chen seems to have succeeded at creating a game where an emotional connection is made between players, despite their complete inability to talk with each other.

So, when we examine *Journey*, we see that much of the game is about human connection. The story of your character and their ancestors is one in which greed and conflict caused mutually assured destruction. Your ancestors' inability to work together, to value each other more than their ambitions, ended them. You are then given other players that you can work with. It is impossible to impede or harm other players in any way. At most, you can choose to ignore them, but you will soon run into other players, so it's hard to do that entirely. Thus, you travel through the levels learning what your ancestors did not. You learn how to connect to one another and how to value that connection. *Journey* is a game about sharing emotional experiences with complete strangers and being entirely unable to talk to them about what you're feeling. Instead, you can only lead them to a beautiful vista, look at it with them, and hope that they feel what you feel. This hope, this desire to connect, is made all the stronger and all the more successful by the stripped-down systems in the game. Since you cannot merely type out to another player "go through the waterfall," you instead must go to them, chirp, and lead them to something beautiful. The necessity of you being present with the other player deepens the connection that you feel with them. This connection is further deepened by the content of the emotion that the game constantly sets up: the sublime.

Journey and the Sublime

Most people, when they play through *Journey*, are struck by the artistic nature of the game. The game prompts you to take your time, to observe, to simply sit and watch. Many of the environments are vast and the mountain is massive, always looming in front of you. All of this leads many players to experience a feeling of awe as they play the game. Edmund Burke, an eighteenth century philosopher, wrote about the experience of the sublime. Burke separated the sublime from the beautiful, a separation that has since become foundational in the study of art and beauty. Burke considered the sublime to be something akin to a pleasurable experience of terror. He found that the sublime had its roots in pain and terror, which he thought to be the strongest of emotions. He argued that pleasure is almost never found in pain alone and that pain is far stronger than pleasure. However, when pain can be distanced from us so that it doesn't threaten us with immediate danger, we can sometimes find those pains pleasurable.

Burke uses the example of a horse. When we consider a horse as a working creature, it doesn't elicit much fear from us. A horse pulling a carriage down a busy street isn't very frightening, and thus it also doesn't elicit the sublime. However, a large horse running powerfully through the wild, the sound of its hooves echoing in our ears – that might cause a little fear. We recognize the power within the creature, that it has the power to run us over and grind us into the dirt. Yet we also feel awe when we see this. Although that horse has the power to harm us, it is not currently about to harm us. This, for Burke, would be a situation that might elicit the sublime. We feel a kind of pleasurable fear when we see the power of the creature set loose. If we imagine that this horse is sprinting directly at us and is about to hit us, we are likely no longer experiencing the sublime, for the threat is no longer distant from us. We only experience dread and horror and we take no pleasure in it.

Burke tied the sublime to the experience of astonishment. When we experience the sublime, we are astonished at the object that gives us this feeling of pleasurable fear. Burke writes, "astonishment is that state of the soul in which all its motions are suspended, with some degree of horror" (Burke 2005). This feeling of astonishment, and thus an experience of the sublime, is a pleasurable experience, but it differs quite greatly from beauty, as beauty does not have the accompanying horror. Thus, things like power, vastness, the infinite, magnitude, and greatness are all listed as sources of the sublime by Burke. We see something great and powerful and we recognize that under different circumstances it could threaten us, even destroy us. However, since we are not under those circumstances, we gain a kind of pleasure from the distant horror of the object, and for Burke, this is the sublime.

Another eighteenth century philosopher followed Burke and wrote extensively on the sublime, Immanuel Kant. Kant initially connects the sublime with magnitude, writing, "That is sublime in comparison with which everything else is small" (Kant 2010). For Kant, when we perceive something immense, we end up having a bit of a conflict between our faculty of imagination and our faculty of reason. When I see a huge waterfall, my imagination struggles to comprehend what I'm seeing. Water is everywhere; there's so much of it that it seems almost infinite. It makes such a loud noise and yet it just keeps coming. Yet, I understand what the waterfall is and I'm able to grasp it through reason. I know that millions of gallons of water are flowing through it at a specific speed. I know where the water is coming from and where it's going. I know how water erodes rock over time and thus creates these phenomena. Despite knowing all of those things, I nonetheless struggle to imagine them. My mind is unable to picture a million gallons of water, it's just too much for me to imagine. Similarly, I can't very well imagine a stream wearing down the rock on the face of a cliff over hundreds of millions of years. So, while I'm able to grasp all of these things through reason, I seem unable to grasp them through imagination.

For Kant, this victory of reason over imagination is the mathematical sublime. Normally, possessing an inadequate faculty, like that of our imagination in this situation, would bother us. However, because reason succeeds Kant thinks that "this inadequacy [of imagination] is the arousal in us of the feeling that we have within us a supersensible power... Hence what is to be called sublime is not the object, but the attunement that the intellect [gets] through a certain presentation that occupies reflective judgment" (Kant 2010). Kant thinks that our experience of the sublime isn't rooted in the thing we are observing but in the failure of our imagination where our intellect or reason succeeds. Thus, we are made to feel quite small in relation to the object, for our imagination cannot even grasp the thing, yet we understand it completely and thus gain a sense of pleasure. In this way, Kant experiences a similar mix of pleasure and pain as does Burke. Being made absolutely small in relation to something isn't a great feeling, as it's an experience of powerlessness. However, our reason being able to comprehend the thing that is so massive provides us with a kind of pleasure.

Kant also outlines a second kind of the sublime, the dynamically sublime. The dynamically sublime comes from an experience in which nature should overpower us and yet we are nonetheless safe from the power of nature. An example of such an experience would be watching a powerful thunderstorm from the safety of your home. We recognize the power and vastness of nature, and yet, because of human ingenuity, nature poses no threat to us. Kant writes,

> Compared to the might of any of these, our ability to resist becomes an insignificant trifle. Yet the sight of them becomes all the more attractive the more fearful it is, provided we are in a safe place... [this] allows us to discover in ourselves an ability to resist which is of a quite different kind, and which gives us the courage [to believe] that we could be a match for nature's seeming omnipotence. (Kant 2010)

We know that nature has the ability to destroy us, yet experiencing it safely gives us a feeling of power over nature. So, just as with the mathematically sublime, we have both a feeling of smallness and fear, as well as a feeling of power.

Kant and Burke take slightly different approaches to the sublime, but their accounts share quite a bit in common. Both involve perceiving something larger or more powerful than us but perceiving it in such a way that it is no longer a threat to us. We are astounded at our smallness, and this brings a feeling of fear and apprehension, but a pleasurable one. The experience of playing *Journey* is the experience of feeling small. The game does a great job of varying each level such that you are constantly made to feel small by new things. The mountain is a constant, towering above everything else in a way that's hard to imagine. You spend hours walking and flying towards the mountain and yet it seems the same size. As you play you are completely unable to imagine the actual size of the mountain or its distance from you. Yet, you understand the mountain, you can grasp it as a concept. This experience of your reason succeeding where your imagination has failed gives us both fear in our failure and elation in our victory.

In *Journey*, the mountain is always in the distance, towering over you. As you move through the levels, everything towers over you. The sand dunes, the stone serpents, the cloth, the ruins, the sun, the mountain, everything is exponentially larger than you. This provides the setting for a sublime experience. You don't experience it right away, and likely not through the first level. But as you move closer and closer to the halfway point of the game, you become more and more aware of how small you are. Everything dwarfs you, and as you ski down the sand throughout the city, you finally grasp the size of it all. However, none of it poses a threat to you. The magnitude is there, and thus the cause of fear; however, you cannot die in Journey. It is impossible to ever fail and have to start over. Because of this, despite the magnitude and size of everything, you feel safe. You are small and insignificant and normally would be in harm's way, but the game makes you safe, which allows you to then have a sublime experience. Were death or failure possible, you would only chance upon the sublime in moments where you were safe, and the rest of the time you would just be fearful. You might still find the game beautiful and enjoy the soundtrack, but the sublime wouldn't be as constant as it is. However, as you get close to the top of the mountain, it seems like the mountain is indeed hurting you. You start to walk slower and you lose the ability to fly. Eventually the wind and the cold overcome you. In these moments, you no longer experience the sublime for the threat has become real.

Despite that, after you die, an amazing experience awaits you. Kant describes the dynamically sublime as a feeling of power over nature when nature is unable to harm us. When you die in *Journey*, you are reborn as you shoot through the clouds with amazing speed and can fly nearly indefinitely as you work towards the peak. In this moment, you feel larger than the mountain. Certainly, you are not physically larger, but the experience of speed and flight endows you with the power to clearly conquer the mountain. While this is no longer a sublime experience, as it lacks the necessary fear or horror that the sublime contains, it contains the joyful feeling of power that we have in the dynamically sublime. At first, we were safe from the mountain and it towered over us and we felt the sublime. But then our safety was taken away, and with it, our sublime experience was removed. At the end though our safety is returned, and we are empowered to feel larger than the mountain. In the dynamically sublime, we feel powerful because we are safe, but in *Journey*, we are actually made powerful. We surpass the sublime and enter into joy.

Journey and Meaning

When the game ends, you reach the peak and are turned into a star that shoots through all the levels while the credits roll. When it finishes you are back at the beginning of the game, ready to start anew. There is no piece of the story that's learned; there is no conclusion. You do not save your civilization or somehow protect the souls of your ancestors. You accomplish nothing, and now you get to do it again. Why? Why make the journey to the mountain a second time? Why even do it the first time? What was the point?

Albert Camus, a twentieth century philosopher described a similar situation in his book *The Myth of Sisyphus*. Camus begins by examining the Greek myth of Sisyphus. Sisyphus was punished by the gods for tricking them. He was made to push a boulder up a mountain, yet as soon as he reached the peak of the mountain, the boulder would slip out of his hands and roll back down to the bottom. Sisyphus then had to walk back down, get the boulder, and try all over again. Many of us would find this task challenging, and certainly Sisyphus is described by various Greek and Roman authors as having to toil and sweat to complete his task. However, the real punishment here is that this task is unending and unrewarding. Sisyphus must push this rock up the mountain and have it roll back down forever. Not only is this task unending, it's also pointless. Sisyphus accomplishes nothing by pushing the rock. Atlas, who in Greek mythology held the world aloft, had a very difficult and perpetual task. However, at least this had meaning. He kept the earth in the sky, something that was very important to everyone living on the earth. Sisyphus, on the other hand, must toil at something meaningless.

It is this meaninglessness that Camus focuses on. Camus compares Sisyphus to the workman of his day. Every day we wake up, we get dressed, we go to work, we come home, we eat dinner, we watch TV, we go to sleep, and then we do it all over again the next day. None of us are accomplishing anything, we're all trapped in the same cycle that Sisyphus is, a cycle of repetition and meaninglessness. We even see the fruits of this in our society with things like the mid-life crisis and now also the quarter-life crisis. Camus thought that our fate was the same as that of Sisyphus, we just weren't always aware of it.

Despite this, Camus argues that we can and that we must imagine that Sisyphus is happy. Camus writes, "All of Sisyphus' silent joy is contained therein. His fate belongs to him. His rock is his thing" and later,

> Sisyphus teaches the higher fidelity that negates the gods and raises rocks. He too concludes that all is well. This universe henceforth without a master seems to him neither sterile nor futile. Each atom of that stone, each mineral flake of that night-filled mountain, in itself forms a world. The struggle itself toward the heights is enough to fill a man's heart. (Camus 1991)

For Camus, Sisyphus is free to decide his fate, as are we. In a world where meaning has been taken away, we are freed to fill the world with meaning. Sisyphus can choose to ignore the gods and instead push his rock because he desires it, he can create meaning and give it to his actions. This choice is also available to us. Despite our lives being full of repetition, we can choose to give them meaning. We can grasp what we have been given, like Sisyphus grasps his rock, and make it our own.

Journey deals quite heavily with many of the same themes as Sisyphus. Not only are both faced with a literal mountain and a task that requires climbing it, but both can never end their journey. Both Sisyphus and the traveler must get to the top of the mountain only to be sent back to the bottom and told to do it again. One might imagine this repetition would make us feel the hopelessness and meaninglessness that we see in Sisyphus, yet the game is often replayed. When other travelers join you on your journey up the mountain, you can tell how many times they've beaten the game based on their clothing. Each time you beat the game, your shawl gets a small pattern added near the hem. It's not much, and you'd probably only notice it if you were looking for it, but you can nonetheless discern if you're playing with a new player or one that is more experienced. It is quite common to play with other travelers who are on their fourth or higher play-through, which is as high as the patterns will show. Despite it being a repetitive task, players put in the time and effort to travel up the mountain again and again.

Journey thus embraces Camus' solution to the problem of meaninglessness. Recognize that the game is repetitive. Recognize that it's just the same path over and over. Once you've done that, you're free to choose what you want to do with your play time. Maybe you're playing through the game to listen to the score, maybe you just want to experience the sublime, or maybe you just want to connect with other players. Whatever your purpose, *Journey* invites you to choose for yourself. The game is very open about its repetition. It does not try to hide a repetitive task around some sort of experience point or collectible system. There are certainly hidden things that you can find in the game, but they serve to allow you to create a meaningful experience of play more than anything else. The lack of dialogue, the general lack of any tracking of your accomplishments, and the length of the game all contribute to a situation where you play *Journey* simply because you wish to experience the journey to the top one more time.

Commentary

Journey creates a wonderful experience of play. It is not a game full of excitement and action, but instead a slower, thoughtful game. You connect with others, experience the beautiful and the sublime, and are tasked with considering the question of meaning and purpose, all while you reflect on the greed that caused the downfall of the traveler's ancestors. Yet some of the concepts within the game struggle against each other, and even against the concept of a game itself.

The aforementioned meaninglessness of your journey is somewhat premised on the fact that you accomplish nothing. At the end, you are shot right back to the beginning to start all over, just like Sisyphus. However, unlike Sisyphus, there are in-game accomplishments. As was mentioned, the pattern on your shawl evolves as you beat the game more, and the game also has trophies. The implementation of trophies is likely a requirement from Sony for the game to exist on the Playstation platform, but nonetheless, trophies exist. This makes it so that each time you play through the game, as long as you haven't yet unlocked every trophy, there is a specific thing that you can aim for. You can find all the glyphs or all the paintings, or a number of other trophies that denote certain in-game achievements. While none of this takes away from the narrative of meaninglessness, the nature of being a game on the Playstation takes some force away from the impact of the game.

Another issue that we run into is that the sublime is what provides that feeling of astonishment. This mix of fear and joy, this pleasure at being able to comprehend something massive that could destroy us, is all predicated on the thing which feels threatening to us. The hugeness of the mountain, or the city, or the waterfall, or the stone serpents all make an impression on you when you first run into them. However, they don't make quite as strong of an impression on your third or fourth playthrough. What was once sublime simply becomes beautiful over time. The mountain no longer instills fear, nor does the cold or the wind. The hugeness of the city or the stone serpents chasing you in the under-city all become slightly banal when you've experienced them multiple times. Eventually the sublime fades. The beautiful remains, for the beautiful is not premised on this feeling of fear, but the sublime is. In nature, fear can remain constant. No matter how many times I've walked a mountain path, the vastness of the mountain still exceeds my imagination, and the threat of something so vast is always present. At any moment, a rockslide could take my life, for instance. But in *Journey*, no such event can occur. Eventually the dynamic sublime fades entirely, for no threats exist, and the mathematical challenge also fades a bit, as we can imagine and remember each level that we play through. This change is premised on familiarity. Certainly, we can replay games after longer periods of time such that we have become unfamiliar with them, and thus have the sublime experience all over again. However, to the extent that the creators of *Journey* intend for it to be replayed consistently, it begins to lose some of its power.

Thus, what ends up happening is that two of the core concepts present in the game are at odds with one another. The sublime wants to make an astounding impression on us, but the question of meaning wants us to engage in repetition and learn to make the repetition meaningful. Yet, the more we repeat, the less the sublime is present, and to fully engage with the sublime is to not engage in repetition. The two concepts work in opposite directions and thus likely do not ever engage us at the same time. This isn't necessarily problematic, but it's certain a tension that's present in the game. By working against one another, we first focus on the sublime, as it makes an immediate impression on us. As the sublime fades and the beautiful remains, we repeat the journey again and again, contemplating the meaninglessness of the repetition, but engaging with such a beautiful world that we are constantly prompted to make the beautiful meaningful. Where Sisyphus only had his rock, thatgamecompany has given us a world of beauty to make our own.

Conclusion

Journey leaves us at the foot of the mountain. It teaches us to stop and observe, to allow ourselves to be overcome with awe. It asks us to connect with other players and to share our feelings of awe with them. It is a game designed to provide a specific experience more so than it is a game designed to force the player to overcome a challenge. All of the challenges in the game are quite simple, and all abilities have been stripped away except using one button to fly, and another to chirp. To try to beat the game as efficiently as possible is to miss the point. So, play through *Journey*, be astonished, and connect with others. Ponder the question of repetition and meaning. Make each grain of sand, each mineral flake of the mountain, each ray of sun shining down on us, a world of our own. The journey to the top is what fills our hearts. We must imagine the traveler happy to take up their task again, and so too, we must imagine ourselves happy.

References

Burke, Edmund. 2005. *A philosophical inquiry into the origin of our ideas of the sublime and beautiful with an introductory discourse concerning taste, and several other additions*. Project Gutenberg. https://www.gutenberg.org/files/15043/15043-h/15043-h.htm#A_PHILOSOPHICAL_INQUIRY.
Camus, Albert. 1991. *The Myth of Sisyphus and Other Essays*. Trans. J. O'Brien. Vintage Books. New York.
Chen, Jeonva. 2013. "Emotion oriented interactive entertainment - inspirations and theories behind journey." Youtube. D.I.C.E. Summit, 15 June 2020, www.youtube.com/watch?v=S684RQHzmGA.
Kant, Immanuel. 2010. *Critique of judgment*. Trans. W.S. Pluhar. Hackett. Indianapolis, Indiana.

The Witness as Philosophy: How Knowledge Is Constructed

78

Luke Cuddy

Contents

Introduction	1772
Summarizing *The Witness*	1773
What about the Tape Recorder Messages?	1775
Those Windmill Videos	1775
James Burke	1775
Richard Feynman	1775
Tarkovsky's Nostalghia	1776
Brian Moriarty	1776
Rupert Spira	1777
Gangaji	1778
The Witness' Argument?	1778
Possible Argument 1: Knowledge Depends on the Observer	1779
Possible Argument 2: Realism Leads to Knowledge	1780
Possible Argument 3: Scientific Realism	1782
Possible Argument 4: Knowledge is Dependent on Paradigms	1783
Conclusion	1786
References	1786

Abstract

When innovative game designer Jonathan Blow released his second game, *The Witness*, after a roughly 7-year development process, it was to instant critical acclaim. The few critics who were less impressed said nothing about any serious flaw in the game design; they just said it was too *hard*. Indeed, as a puzzle game in which the player must solve increasingly sophisticated puzzles that test the limits of her deductive and inductive reasoning abilities, *The Witness* is incredibly frustrating. But why? Perhaps the frustration results from a theory of knowledge (or epistemology) that Blow built into the game, both explicitly and implicitly.

L. Cuddy (✉)
Southwestern College, Chula Vista, CA, USA
e-mail: lcuddy@swccd.edu

© Springer Nature Switzerland AG 2024
D. K. Johnson et al. (eds.), *The Palgrave Handbook of Popular Culture as Philosophy*,
https://doi.org/10.1007/978-3-031-24685-2_48

Perhaps the game is making an argument about knowledge construction that incorporates this frustration. After carefully examining the game itself (with special attention to the windmill videos), the most plausible epistemological arguments the game could be making will be examined, on both a subjective and species-wide level. A frustrated critic might think that the game isn't making an argument at all, or that, if anything, it represents some version of epistemological relativism: the view that what we define as knowledge/truth is dependent upon perception. A case will be made, however, that the game argues that true knowledge is attainable, both individually and collectively, even if it is difficult to acquire.

Keywords

The Witness · Jonathan Blow · Socrates · Plato · Sophists · Knowledge acquisition · Thomas Kuhn · Paradigms · Objective knowledge · Epistemological relativism · Realism · Video games · Scientific realism · Nondualism · Hilary Putnam

Introduction

Jonathan Blow's first major game was *Braid*, an innovative and widely praised indie game allowing players to manipulate the flow of time to solve puzzles. When you play it, the game at first appears to be a standard side-scroller (think Mario jumping on platforms from left to right while disposing of turtles), but it quickly reveals itself to be more complex. For one, the player can rewind and "go back in time" after making a mistake, even after dying. And there are parts of the game world that remain the same, even while the player goes back, leading to intricate puzzle solutions that require nonlinear, creative thinking.

Braid made Blow a bit of a celebrity in the gaming community, and he was even featured in the 2012 documentary *Indie Game: The Movie*, which went behind the scenes on the development of three games (the other two being *Super Meat Boy* and *Fez*).

Blow used the revenue and fame from *Braid* – it did pretty well – to fund his next game, which took him and his small development team about 7 years to finalize. That game, of course, is *The Witness*, a 3D puzzle game set in an incredibly beautiful and immersive open world that was released in 2016.

And it's a masterpiece. Not only is *The Witness* largely critically acclaimed (except for those, presumably with less patience, who found it too hard), but it includes mysterious audio recordings from people like Albert Einstein and Douglas Hofstadter that players can find throughout the game world. There are also six longer videos that, in some cases, present extended arguments. These are clips from actual talks and lectures, including from physicist Richard Feynman and nondualist teacher Rupert Spira (who was the student of my spiritual teacher, Francis Lucille!). These media clips don't exactly tell a traditional story (as would be the case in some video games), but together with an understanding of the puzzles and game mechanics, they can help us understand the arguments being made. (By *mechanics* in this context, I mean the objective rules of the game that dictate and limit the player's ability to interact with the game world. For example, one common mechanic in *The Witness* involves the tracing of a line around a grid/maze by depressing the proper direction on the game controller.)

All in all, *The Witness* is an incredible achievement for video game design and, I would argue, art. Gone are the days when video games connoted prepubescent, aggressive teens yelling at each other over *Mortal Kombat* (not that that doesn't still happen...). But even in today's gaming culture with movie-like development teams for titles like *Grand Theft Auto V* or *Assassin's Creed Odyssey*, The Witness stands out as perhaps the pinnacle achievement of a visionary artist, Jonathan Blow.

Summarizing *The Witness*

The Witness has no guidebook, no tutorials. The game starts with the player, from a first-person perspective, staring down a long, cylindrical hallway with a door at the end. Unlike other games where the identity of the avatar (the character onscreen controlled by the player) is clear, it's never really clear who you are in *The Witness*. This is quite the contrast to games like *World of Warcraft* where the player not only chooses a race (like a Night Elf or Dwarf), but can customize her appearance. Other games, like *Uncharted*, give your avatar a clear, fixed identity.

As the player progresses down the hallway, she soon sees that the door at the end has a yellow square on it, which eventually reveals itself to be the first puzzle of the game. Once this very basic puzzle is solved, the door opens, and the player moves on to the next, only slightly more complicated puzzle, before entering the courtyard of a strange castle, repletes with luminescent green, blue, yellow, and purple vegetation.

However, if the player at this point infers that the game will be a series of increasingly difficult puzzles of this type (as many other puzzle games are), she will be sadly mistaken. It does appear that way for a while, as the player solves the requisite puzzles to leave the castle area. At first, each new puzzle does appear to build directly on the mechanics of the prior puzzles. However, it becomes very clear that the gamer will have to do a lot more creative thinking as subsequent puzzles appear.

Also, as the player exits the castle area, she quickly realizes that this is going to be a more difficult, and wonderful, game than she initially imagined. Winding down a green forest path the player, if she turns right, is led to a ledge where she can see what first appears to be a still lake, but upon closer inspection connects to the ocean: the game takes place on an island. If she goes left at that point on the path instead, she comes across a significantly more complex puzzle on a door sealing a mountain bunker. At this point it would be almost impossible to solve this puzzle as it involves puzzle mechanics that she has not encountered and won't for a while, and this inability will be revealed quickly if she tries.

For now, at this early point in the game, the player must trudge forward on the forest path, eventually leading to a forest glen of sorts, and more puzzles. These puzzles are different from the ones in the castle, but in some ways have similar mechanics. The player begins to understand that the puzzles here build off of the previous puzzles while gradually adding new mechanics. For example, the puzzles thus far in the game appear on rectangular grids with lines that the player must trace properly to solve. Now, added to the lines are different colored squares, and the player has to figure out how these squares are integrated with the lines to solve them.

But again, the player will be sadly mistaken if she infers that the puzzles will increase in complexity in *this* way throughout the game – that is, that the increasing complexity will be based on the puzzles gradually incorporating new, similar mechanics *directly* into the old ones. While this integration of new mechanics into the old does happen, it's not *all* that happens, and it becomes much less direct as the game progresses. There are new puzzle sets whose mechanics at first seem to mimic those of previous puzzles, but actually do not. Also, some puzzles are completely different. Some require environmental cues to solve (i.e., cues that can *only* be found outside of the actual grid that makes up the puzzle). These environmental cues can sometimes be based on sound; so unlike many other games, you can't play this one with the volume turned down.

As the player exits the forest area outside the castle, the true complexity of the island is revealed in steps. For one, after each series of puzzles is solved, a laser opens up and points to a large mountain at the center of the island. It becomes clear that unlocking these lasers will be integral to progressing in the game and ultimately beating it.

Along the way the player encounters an incredible open world: underwater bunkers, boat rides, sunken ships, tree forts, and greenhouses with every color of the rainbow. Drawing from the *2001: A Space Odyssey* playbook, there are even mysterious, black monoliths scattered around the island. It likely takes most gamers (and I'm no exception) quite some playing time to realize that these monoliths, though unconnected to the main progression of puzzles, are puzzles of a sort themselves.

Once the player unlocks all the lasers, she is ready to head up to the mountain to tackle the final set of puzzles *within* the mountain. When she completes them, the game ends, sending her on a flight over the island, then back into the dark tunnel where it all started. Toward the end of the flight, a voice can be heard saying "a phantom," then "and a dream" three times.

However, there is a secret ending as well that can be accessed when the game is restarted. This ending takes the player through what seems to be a fancy apartment where there are nice paintings of some of the places around the island, including the windmill. There are balconies with God's-eye views of the island as well as computers that seem to be monitoring different locations. Ultimately, the player follows a dark path to eventually be shown a live-action, first-person video of someone (Blow himself?) who is coming out of virtual reality (VR). The player can only observe as this awakened person explores an apartment with framed puzzles on the walls, among other things, interacting with his environment as though he has been in VR for a very long time.

What about the Tape Recorder Messages?

Throughout the game in various locations (some more obvious than others), the player finds messages on tape recorders that, when accessed, are played aloud. Most are brief quotes from people like Albert Einstein or Douglas Hofstadter. But some are longer, like a famous passage from Arthur Eddington where he describes entering a room from a physicist's perspective. When the player reaches the aforementioned secret ending, some of the messages just give credit to programmers and others who worked on the game.

Although the purpose of and continuity between the audio tapes is less clear, the windmill videos present some longer arguments and are, therefore, worth considering in more depth.

Those Windmill Videos...

The six windmill videos in the game are to some degree in dialogue with each other. They are only unlocked after solving difficult puzzles that themselves can be hard to locate in the game world. One even involves a timed challenge in which the player must find solutions that are randomized on each playthrough over Grieg's "Anitra's Dance" and "In the Hall of the Mountain King." This challenge is arguably the hardest part of the entire game. The audio tapes, on the other hand, are often in plain sight, and even the ones that are harder to find do not directly require puzzle-solving. Therefore, perhaps Blow was sending a message about the significance of the content of these videos. Why choose these particular six?

I will number the six videos from the way the puzzles that unlock them appear on the grids under the windmill, left to right.

James Burke

The first is a clip of James Burke, television personality and science historian. Burke ponders the question of what drives the advancement of human knowledge, arguing that while it may have been different in the past, today it is scientists who are the primary drivers. He dismisses things like art and philosophy – which he calls "products of emotion" – as being, at best, interpretations of the world. He presents a strict scientific realism in which art is "easier to take," while science is "harder to take" because the latter "removes the reassuring crutches of opinion, ideology" (Blow 2016).

Richard Feynman

The second video begins with a black and white lecture of the late, famed physicist Richard Feynman. Feynman explains a "hierarchy of ideas" in our scientific knowledge, in which "higher" levels are built on "lower." He points out that, on one end of the hierarchy, we have the fundamental laws of physics. But...

> ... then we invent other terms for concepts which are approximate who have, we believe, their ultimate explanation in terms of the fundamental laws. For instance, heat. Heat is supposed to be the jiggling and it's just a word for... a hot thing is just a word for a mass of atoms that are jiggling. (Blow 2016)

Feynman goes on to point out that when we're talking at one level, we often forget about the others: that is, we don't think of atoms jiggling around when we say that something is hot. And the levels of explanation get higher, too, when we talk about "storms" or "stars," then "man" or "history" or "beauty." Finally he poses the question, using a religious metaphor, as to which end of the hierarchy is nearer to God – that is, nearer to the ultimate explanation for everything. Feynman argues that the task of intellectuals (not just scientists) is to draw connections between the levels, ultimately claiming that neither end is nearer to God and implying that there is a certain degree of hubris in believing that one level is superior to the others.

This video also contains a second clip from Feynman in a one-on-one interview when he's older where he says:

> People say to me, "Are you looking for the ultimate laws of physics"? No I'm not, I'm just looking to find out more about the world...When we go to investigate we shouldn't prejudge what we're trying to do except find out more about it. (Blow 2016)

Feynman here suggests that if we prejudge the answers we expect to find in terms of *anything*, we may not actually discover the truth. He goes on to say: "I think it's much more interesting to live with doubt than to find answers that might be wrong." He admits that he has hunches and approximate answers to many questions, but also says that "I don't have to know an answer. I am not frightened by not knowing" (Blow 2016).

Tarkovsky's Nostalghia

The third video is a scene from Russian director Andrei Tarkovsky's film *Nostalghia*. The film touches on a few existential themes, but especially the sense of loneliness or lack of a foundation/center in one's life. The majority of the clip Blow used is one where the main character, a Russian writer in Italy who longs to return to his homeland, carries a lit candle through an empty pool.

Brian Moriarty

The fourth video is a long lecture by game designer Brian Moriarty, which is played over the slow unfolding of an eclipse. This lecture has achieved a degree of fame in the gaming community since it was given in 2002. Moriarty says quite a bit in the lecture, and it's tough to do it all justice here. But I think it's fair to say that a central theme is the concept of an *Easter egg*, or a hidden feature/secret within a video game that was intentionally put there by the designer. He mentions the early Atari game *Adventure*, one of the first games to include an Easter egg, along with the creator Warren Robinett's name.

Moriarty points out that there have been Easter eggs of a sort in many other art forms for hundreds of years. He mentions Kit Williams' *Masquerade*, a children's book that supposedly gave readers clues to the location of various treasures hidden around England. Some people became so obsessed with the search that they needed psychological help. Moriarty discusses a number of historical examples of hidden messages in art, including those in Disney movies, the letter "n" in Thomas Kinkade paintings, and Bach's obsession with gematria, or assigning numeric values to letters of the alphabet.

He goes on to discuss the perils of numerology, relating the story of someone he met on a discussion board in the early 1990s who tried to connect Biblical passages to Santa Claus. Finding these sorts of Easter eggs in *The Bible*, he points out, has been a pastime of many a historical figure in the West. The same goes for determining who Shakespeare really was, and he spends some time investigating accounts of the origin of the great playwright as well.

Moriarty claims that the contemplation of works like *The Bible* and those of Shakespeare can lead to an incredible human emotion that is the pinnacle of art that of awe. But he immediately makes clear that his lecture should *not* be interpreted as suggesting that the key to game design is the installation of Easter eggs. He argues that "awesome things don't hold anything back" (Blow 2016). In other words, if as a designer you are proud of your creation and want players to experience it, why not just put it all in plain sight? Why make it hidden or more difficult for the player to find?

He ends by pointing out that video games are a historically recent art form with great potential:

> Someday soon, perhaps even in our lifetime, a game design will appear that will flash across our culture like lightning. It will be easy to recognize. It will be generous, giddy with exuberant inventiveness. Scholars will pick it apart for decades, perhaps centuries. It will be something wonderful, something terrifying, something *awe*-ful. (Blow 2016)

Rupert Spira

The next video is one with Rupert Spira, a teacher of nonduality – a belief system drawing from Hinduism called *Advaita Vedanta*. Similar to Buddhism in some ways, Advaita suggests that much of our personal suffering comes from identifying with a false self. However, Advaita emphasizes that we have a true self beneath all that, which usually gets cashed out as a deeper awareness or consciousness. (Some strands of Buddhism emphasize liberated consciousness, which is arguably the same idea.)

Touching on these themes, in sometimes dense language, Spira emphasizes the subtle nature of human subjective experience. From the level of subjective experience, consciousness is the backbone, the everlasting awareness behind everything else. All else only *appears* in consciousness: thoughts, the sense of time, feelings, and so forth. At one point he describes getting lost in thought at an airport, and then coming back to presence to realize that he had never really left the physical place he was in.

He describes our consciousness/awareness as imperturbable. He distinguishes the separate self (our desires, wants, sense of being a body, etc.) from the true self (consciousness). He uses a metaphor of a moth and a flame. The flame is all the moth wants, but it can't have it. When it touches the flame, it dies. It becomes the flame, that is the separate self's way of finding love, by dying. The experience of love is the separate self-dying, which can give rise to consciousness, our true self.

Gangaji

Although coming from a similar, nondual perspective, the shorter Gangaji video seems to be an antidote of sorts to the Spira video in the sense that the message is more straightforward. Gangaji, a spiritual teacher based in Oregon, asks us to stop looking. Stop looking for what we think we want in the next thought, the next experience, and the next person. More than what we wanted, she tells us, is already what we are. Like Spira, she is referring to the difference between the false self of ego and the true self of conscious awareness. She emphasizes that her message is not a teaching or belief system, but a way to live your life. Unlike Spira who seems to exude intensity, Gangaji exudes a deep love and compassion.

The Witness' Argument?

Considering some of the points made in the Moriarty video, it's reasonable to wonder whether the game is making an argument at all – or whether, like the numerologists, we're going to fall prey to our own imagination in trying to determine the message.

As philosophers know well, it's easy to find apparent meaning in an information set, regardless of whether there is any meaning or not. This is why we teach our students in introductory classes about logical fallacies, like the *false cause* fallacy which reminds us that a mere correlation between events does not necessarily entail a causal relationship between them. These considerations, however, do not prevent plausible arguments from being inferred.

I won't be inferring anything here about the ultimate purpose of *The Witness*. For example, I won't be connecting it to numerology, or *The Bible*, or Shakespeare. But there are a couple of plausible arguments that the game may be making in the philosophical branch of epistemology, or the theory of knowledge. These arguments touch both on the individual acquisition of knowledge as well as a more species-wide acquisition of knowledge.

Possible Argument 1: Knowledge Depends on the Observer

To return to a question posed earlier: why is *The Witness* so frustrating sometimes? Perhaps an argument Blow is making is that knowledge, at the subjective level, is dependent upon the observer. It may seem as though we're learning new things, finding new puzzle solutions and so forth, but there is no true knowledge being acquired, just the manipulation of knowledge based on the individual's perspective. This gap in our expectations might explain the frustration. Indeed, in the timed challenge, the puzzles regenerate on each playthrough, leading even the same player to get a different set of puzzles, and thus a different perspective, every time.

This line of argument is also supported by the repetition of the phrase "and a dream" at the end of the game as well as by the secret ending where the person on the couch wakes up from VR. Maybe the implication is that every player has a different subjective experience with the game and, therefore, a slightly different subjective acquisition of knowledge? Inside the mountain in particular, the player sees maps and drawings of various places and objects around the island, perhaps suggesting a constructed reality.

The group of thinkers from ancient Greece, who generally believed that both knowledge and morality are dependent upon the observer, were the sophists. One of their core views is famously encapsulated by Protagoras' quote: "man is the measure of all things" (Guthrie 1971). Frustrating many, these folks were known to argue passionately for one point of view, then just as passionately for the opposite view. If knowledge is merely a matter of perspective, then why not?

A few considerations about *The Witness*, however, show us why it is implausible to see the game as making this argument. First of all, although the puzzles in the challenge section change, most of the puzzles in the game do not; they have objective solutions that will be the same for every player. Most puzzles in the game, then, are not a matter of perspective – at least in one sense. (In another sense, though, they are, which I will touch on later.)

Also, the puzzles make use of inductive and deductive reasoning, which have been identified as core elements of knowledge by philosophers and other academics for years. Inductive knowledge is based on probability, whereas deductive knowledge is based on certainty. If I know that most of my friends like puzzle video games, and I have a friend named Jose, then it's not unreasonable to think that Jose will like a puzzle game like *The Witness*. This is inductive reasoning since my conclusion about my friend is reasonable based on the evidence given, but could still be wrong. Inductive arguments, then, can have broader and more potential conclusions. However, if I know that all women are mortal, and I also know that Hilary Clinton is a woman, then I know with certainty that she must be mortal. This conclusion *must* be true given the evidence – this is deductive reasoning.

Many puzzles in *The Witness* are deductive in that there is only one possible solution given the puzzle mechanics known by the player. Some of the early maze and black and white square puzzles are strictly deductive in this sense. However, as the game goes on inductive mechanics are incorporated, sometimes environmental. For example, although the basic mechanics for the *Tetris* puzzles may be understood, there are multiple ways to solve some of them. Some puzzles also involve an incredible synthesis of inductive and deductive reasoning in which the player must search for a probable clue in the environment around the puzzle grid, but once that clue is found, the puzzle must be solved deductively according to the previously understood rules.

The bunker is a great example of this synthesis. In the bunker, the player faces multicolored square puzzles in which different colored squares must be isolated from other colors by tracing a line around them properly. At a certain point in this area of the game, the player realizes that one of the puzzles simply cannot be solved no matter how hard she tries – she has to look to the environment for solutions. Eventually she realizes (spoiler alert) that she has to look through yellow-tinted glass at the puzzle in order to solve it, which then changes the colored squares in such a way that makes the puzzle solvable.

To make such heavy use of knowledge types (inductive and deductive) that were developed historically with the assumption of some level of objectivity suggests that *The Witness* is making an argument closer to that of Plato and Socrates, the sophists' biggest critics.

Possible Argument 2: Realism Leads to Knowledge

In his seminal work *The Republic*, through the mouthpiece of Socrates its central character, Plato presents the now famous allegory of the cave (Plato 2008). The allegory tells the story of prisoners in a cave who are, unbeknownst to them, chained up and staring at shadows on a wall. The shadows, which they take to be real, are being cast by puppeteers behind the prisoners holding up shapes in front of a fire.

In this metaphor, the prisoners are often aligned with sophists. Like sophists, the prisoners are stuck in a limited reality, never arriving at true, objective knowledge. Indeed, this limitation leads them to believe that relative knowledge is all there is. However, in the allegory, one of the prisoners escapes the cave and realizes his prior ignorance, which paves the way for an objective understanding of reality.

Considering *The Witness'* ending, especially the secret VR ending, it's tempting to see the entire game as a metaphorical shadow. The person who takes off the VR headset and gets off the couch even stumbles to the ground at one point, just like the escaped prisoner in the allegory takes some time to adjust to the real world once he exits the cave. And I don't deny that some points of this comparison make sense. But the detail Blow puts into the game itself (which on this interpretation would merely be a shadow on the wall) suggests that the comparison is lacking. There is also a link between the primary game world and the apartment explored by the person that suggests more than a distinction between appearance and reality. For example, although there are pictures of puzzles from the game on the wall of the apartment, these are just pictures, and the puzzles themselves in the game world are actually much more complex. It is the real puzzles that require that sophisticated mix of inductive and deductive reasoning. If the puzzles within the game were just an appearance, an image, we'd expect the opposite.

But more importantly, the puzzles themselves have objective solutions, gradually get more complex, incorporate new mechanics, and lead to an ultimate ending to the game. While it may seem obvious that a puzzle game like this would have these features, it's also easy to see how Blow could have designed the game without them if he'd been coming from a different epistemological perspective. He could have created the same island, for example, but then simply spread out random puzzles to solve that were not connected with each other at all and that did not progress in terms of difficulty. As Blow himself puts it on the podcast *Adam Explains Everything* (which is hosted by Adam Conover, the star of *Adam Ruins Everything*, a TV show that debunks common misconceptions in an attempt to better understand the world):

> Part of what the game is trying to do is be an exploration of... hey if we're really just trying to look at the world and understand the world, how do you even do that? How do you take these little things and put them together into a bigger picture? And how do you do that without just being a wacko and going off and believing some random thing that's totally wrong and dumb, which is something that a lot of people do. (Blow and Conover 2017)

If Blow cares about understanding the world and developing a bigger picture, this suggests that he cares about more than just appearance. But a deeper reason for thinking that Blow intends the game to represent a more robust theory of knowledge is his use of aporia. Aporia, a Greek word referring to a state of puzzlement, goes back to the Socratic dialogues as well, the end of which often left Socrates' interlocutors in such a state. In one of the most famous, *The Meno*, Socrates teaches a slave boy geometry by drawing figures in the sand (Plato 2006). At one point, the boy answers incorrectly regarding the area of a shape based on the length of the sides. Before employing his characteristic cross-examination technique to bring the boy to the right answer, Socrates addresses his main interlocutor in the dialogue, Meno, regarding the boy's state of mind:

> At first he did not know... and he does not know yet; but he thought he knew then, and boldly answered as if he did know, and did not think there was any doubt; now he thinks there is a doubt, and as he does not know, so he does not think he does know. (Plato 2006)

Socrates goes on to make the point that if the boy's ignorance had not been exposed then...

> ... do you think he would have tried to find out or learn what he thought he knew, not knowing, until he tumbled into a difficulty by thinking he did not know, and longed to know? ... So he gained by being numbed? (Plato 2006)

Like most who talk with Socrates, Meno wholeheartedly agrees. The boy gained by being "numbed," by being exposed to the state of not knowing, puzzlement, or aporia. Aporia puts one in a state where one's ignorance can be corrected, where true knowledge can be gained. Once this knowledge is gained, as happens with the slave boy, there is often an accompanying sense of epiphany or resolution.

Some of the puzzles in *The Witness* are very good at generating aporia in the player. Indeed, some puzzles are so hard that the state of puzzlement I experienced was almost painful. I would try one strategy after another, then more, finally believing that I reached the solution. But then, it didn't solve the puzzle. Sometimes I was incredulous. How could that not be it? Is there anything else that is even possible?

Of course, there always was something else. And once I discovered the solution, it was always an *ah-ha* moment – sometimes it seemed obvious and I couldn't believe I hadn't seen it before. Here is Blow from that same interview touching on aporia (though not by that term) and epiphany:

> What happens very often with this game is that people are stuck, they don't have any idea what to do, and they go just take a break, they go do whatever they're doing in life, or they go to sleep and wake up the next morning, and then they just suddenly know the answer to the problem. That happens a lot to many people who play the game... I don't know exactly how to invoke that experience for sure but from a design standpoint there are criteria that I stick by to try and encourage the possibility of that, right. And that to me is a really interesting experience... there's almost this feeling of epiphany that happens where it's just like, bam, right away you understand something, and it's like an instantaneous transition where a minute ago you really had no idea and now you know. (Blow and Conover 2017)

It seems clear that Blow, like Socrates and Plato before him, sees the construction of at least individual knowledge as being sometimes difficult, but certainly possible. This contrasts him, like the two Greeks, with the sophistic theory in which knowledge is dependent upon the observer alone.

But then, does the above analysis suggest that *The Witness* ultimately represents a more straightforward theory of objective knowledge in which science is the primary, or only, driver of truth? I don't think so, but to investigate we have to go back to that James Burke video.

Possible Argument 3: Scientific Realism

Recall that in that video, Burke rejected things like art and philosophy and suggested that objective, opinion-less science is what truly advances human knowledge. Burke's view seems to align with scientific realism, the idea that scientific theories closely mirror and describe the way reality actually is. Realism tends to view science as a cumulative, linear process.

American philosopher Hilary Putnam penned one of the most famous defenses of this sort of realism, which became known as the *no miracles* argument (Putnam 1975). This argument is a type of inference to the best explanation, where one compares multiple possible explanations and accepts the best one. As an example of such an argument, suppose I turn on my Xbox One to see that my saved game has been erased, and I want to know what happened. What's the best explanation? It could have been foul play (like from an evil roommate), but the best explanation is probably some sort of hardware or software failure with the console. Formally, in science, one appeals to criteria like parsimony and explanatory power to determine which among the available explanations is the best. But here, this kind of basic common sense reasoning, to determine which is the best explanation, will do.

Instead of explaining an erased game file, what Putnam is trying to explain with the no miracles argument is why science has been so successful. Why has it led to so many empirically verified predictions, allowing us to manipulate the laws of nature to build amazing stuff like vaccines, skyscrapers, and, yes, video games like *The Witness*? Because, Putnam argues, science is describing reality. If it wasn't, its success would just be a coincidence – a big giant miracle. In other words, science must really be working to find actual, real truth. That is the best explanation. It would be a miracle if science *wasn't* finding truth and yet still led us to so many successful predictions and inventions. The success of science wouldn't make any sense if scientific theories didn't at least approximately describe reality as it is.

If we stop with the Burke video, it's tempting to interpret *The Witness* as representing a similar sort of realism, in which the puzzles contain objective rules that players must figure out to advance. Yes, the puzzles are exceedingly complicated, this argument goes, but with the requisite understanding, they can be solved objectively – that is, without reference to the perception of the player, as a scientific realist like Burke or Putnam would have it. (It should be noted, however, that Putnam later changed his mind about this, as he did with many other ideas.)

However, if we interpret *The Witness* as an argument for strict scientific realism, it's not clear why it's fundamentally different than any other puzzle game like, say, *Tetris*. So if this was the game's argument, why weren't the puzzles just presented on grids sequentially, rather than being placed strategically as part of an intricate open world that players can explore? One might respond: because it's more fun that way. But then that ignores that fact that some of the puzzles, even when the internal rules are understood, still require a shift in perspective (sometimes literally moving to a different viewpoint in the game world to see the solution) and other times require an even deeper shift in one's logical assumptions about the puzzle mechanics.

It therefore seems that Blow included the Burke video not as a representation of *his* argument, but as *one possible* argument for the construction of knowledge. Indeed, the very next video from Feynman presents a challenge to scientific realism.

But first, it is important to note that aporia, as discussed in the previous section, is not necessarily incompatible with scientific realism. Although Socrates and Plato were not exactly scientific realists in the modern sense, they did believe in objective truth – they just thought it existed in some abstract world of universals (called *forms*). However, I am less concerned with compatibility and more concerned with plausibility. In other words, I think it's more plausible to pair aporia with a different theory of knowledge, which I'll turn to now.

Possible Argument 4: Knowledge is Dependent on Paradigms

Whereas Burke argues that enterprises like art and philosophy are *only* interpretation, Feynman suggests that they are higher levels of analysis that are equally important in helping us to understand our world. Feynman's view of knowledge is therefore more expansive than Burke's. Feynman also reminds us not to prejudge in our search for knowledge, except to say that we want to find out more about the world. In Burke's claims about science, philosophy, and art, of course, he was prejudging that the proper method for the development of human knowledge *is* scientific realism.

A more plausible theory of knowledge being advanced in *The Witness* will take us from Putnam to that other great American philosopher, Thomas Kuhn, and will also have us considering those pesky nondualist videos along the way.

Kuhn rocked the scientific and academic community when he published one of the most important books of the twentieth century: *The Structure of Scientific Revolutions* (Kuhn 1962). The book presents an extended argument against scientific realism in favor of a less linear model that involves *paradigm shifts*. Rather than science being the strict truth-finding project that realists envision, Kuhn argues that scientific progress is largely a social game in which, during periods of what he calls *revolutionary science*, the old gatekeepers engage in a struggle with younger scientists. The struggle occurs not due to any serious disagreement over actual scientific evidence, but due to the interpretation of that evidence through different paradigms – the accepted assumptions, concepts, and experimental practices adopted and accepted by a particular group of scientists.

As an example, consider a paradigm shift of sorts that is happening in health sciences right now. For years, the calorie model of health has held sway: we get fat and unhealthy because we eat too many calories and don't burn them off by exercising. However, more and more health researchers in recent years have challenged the calorie paradigm, calling it, among other things, too simplistic and not consistent with controlled scientific experiments. Perhaps the clearest articulation of the argument against the model can be seen in science journalist Gary Taubes' book *Why We Get Fat* (Taubes 2011). Taubes was joined by biologist Gary Dunn in his criticisms of the calorie model in an issue of *Scientific American* devoted specifically to food (Dunn 2013).

These disagreements are the source of the recent carbohydrate revolution. Sometimes called the hormone hypothesis, Taubes is one of a growing body of researchers who believe weight gain to be a hormonal problem in which eating the wrong carbs sets off a response in the body that leads to fat accumulation. The crucial thing to notice is that if the hormonal view is correct, then it's not the overall *amount* of calories you eat that matters (as in the calorie model) but the quality or nature of the food that you're eating. For example, if the hormonal view is correct, then you can eat all the calories-worth of eggs that you want, because eggs are a low carb food that do not start the process of fat accumulation. This may seem strange to many people who have internalized the calorie model, but as these researchers have pointed out, some controlled experiments have found that health measures improve, including weight loss, regardless of calorie intake (Gardner et al. 2007).

In line with Kuhn, these assumptions about health are not logically compatible and make sense only within their respective paradigms. Kuhn labeled paradigms like this (two paradigms that contradict one another) as *incommensurable*. This incommensurability is precisely why researchers in these different paradigms will take the same scientific study (the same evidence) and interpret it in different ways to support one particular paradigm (theirs) over the other.

It's easy to see how Kuhn's view here might lead us back to a sophisticated version of epistemological relativism, and many of his critics did interpret his argument that way. After all, if the truth depends on the paradigm, and the paradigm depends on a set of assumptions, then doesn't the truth also depend on those assumptions? So in other words, isn't the truth just determined by dogmatism, by the scientists with the most clout in the community?

A more charitable reading of Kuhn's argument suggests that it allows for some degree of objective truth. His argument just highlights a much less linear and direct route to truth than Putnam's *no miracles argument* would suggest.

But let's return to *The Witness* before following up with those last points. In the aforementioned interview with Blow, he and his interviewer, podcaster Adam Conover, discuss the roles of expectation and perspective in solving puzzles in the game:

> *Blow*: Part of what happens is you have to engage in a little bit of a preliminary experimentation to try to figure out what works. So the puzzles start off very simple where there are only a few things that you could possibly do, and you maybe try them and one of them is right and the other ones are wrong and then you start to engage a sort of pattern understanding kind of mind of like why was that one right and why were the other ones wrong? And you maybe form an idea. Then you see if that idea holds up for the next few and it might hold up for a couple and then turn wrong and you're like "wait, I thought I understood what is going on." It's a process of developing an understanding from something very simple to something very complex actually. And in some of these sequences in the game there are sort of hard left turns where you think you've fully got it and then just something totally random is in there out of left field and you have to sort of change your understanding of the system.
>
> *Conover*: Talking to friends about the game, that's one of the biggest frustration points or one of the experiences that I think stands out to people is that you can go through, sometimes almost half of a puzzle section thinking "I understand how these work" and get to a point where you're like "wait a second I understand this, this isn't working, this puzzle is wrong!" And you are confronted with the fact that the puzzle cannot be wrong. (Blow and Conover 2017)

Interpreting these remarks about the game makes much more sense in light of paradigm shifts rather than strict scientific realism. Recall that the realism of Burke, for example, completely discounts the role of philosophy. And yet, Kuhn reminds us of the significance of philosophical assumptions within paradigms to the progression of science. In the quotes above, Blow and Conover both consistently represent the idea that the player must change her perspective while playing. But their points go beyond visual perspective because they are talking about more than just, say, adjusting your eyes to see an optical illusion. They are talking about adjusting your entire understanding (or paradigm), even after being completely convinced that your prior understanding was accurate.

Recall Feynman's point about prejudging. When we have an idea of what we expect to find, as Burke does regarding realism and as players do while solving puzzles in *The Witness*, that idea itself can influence what we do, or do not, find. So we have to step back and think more creatively, in both science and in the game.

Just as it is less plausible to interpret Kuhn's view as epistemological relativism, it is less plausible to interpret *The Witness* as representing that view. First of all, as I already noted, the primary puzzles in the game have objective solutions and, when all the appropriate puzzle sections are completed, will lead the player to finish the game. But secondly, even if there is a lot of paradigm-shifting required to advance in the game, beneath all that are puzzles with objective solutions, and a game with an objective ending.

Conclusion

Let me first address the elephant in these pages. What about those nondualist videos? If Blow included them as the final two videos of the six, and they were included after Feynman, isn't he suggesting that they trump the prior videos? First of all, Blow says in the aforementioned interview that he included those videos partly because some of them present very different views and don't agree with each other. So it doesn't seem he included the latter videos as corrections to the prior.

Secondly, as a practitioner of a fairly secular form of nondualism myself, I know that Advaita Vedanta in particular does not deny the objectivity of science. I recall one meditation group I attended with my teacher (Francis Lucille, as noted above) where a questioner was challenging him on this very point. The questioner was pointing to psychological theories, noting that some had been verified by scientific studies. Lucille responded that he agreed that those theories were likely true. He even tapped on the table and said that some of those theories were as real as the table. However, he did add that the theories were still "only as true as that." His point is that there is a deeper truth, namely, that of the true self or consciousness, as discussed above.

It's possible that Blow was trying to make a deeper point with the game than I've discussed here. By starting with the *Nostalghia* clip and transitioning into the nondualist videos, maybe he was presenting an argument about how we should live our lives and what we should care about. That may be, but as noted above, I am not concerned with the overall point or moral of the game, but with the potential epistemological argument being made from an individual and species-wide level. And my case will stand regardless of any spiritual point Blow may have intended.

References

Blow, Jonathan. 2016. *The Witness*. Thekla, Inc.
Blow, Jonathan and Adam Conover. 2017. *Adam ruins everything*. "Game Designer Jonathan Blow unpacks *the witness*".
Dunn, R. 2013. Science reveals why calorie counts are all wrong. *Scientific American* 309 (3): 56–59.

Gardner, C.D., A. Kiazand, and S. Alhassan. 2007. Comparison of the Atkins, Zone, Ornish, and LEARN diets for change in weight and related risk factors among overweight premenopausal women: The A to Z weight loss study: A randomized trial. *Journal of the American Medical Association* 297 (9): 921–1022.

Guthrie, W.K.C. 1971. *The sophists*. Cambridge: Cambridge University Press.

Kuhn, Thomas. 1962. *The structure of scientific revolutions*. Chicago: The University of Chicago Press.

Plato. 2006. *The Meno*. Digireads.com.

———. 2008. *The Republic.* Digireads.com.

Putnam, Hilary. 1975. *Mathematics, matter and method*. Cambridge: Cambridge University Press.

Taubes, Gary. 2011. *Why we get fat*. New York: Random House.

Cyberpunk 2077 as Philosophy: Balancing the (Mystical) Ghost in the (Transhuman) Machine

79

Chris Lay

Contents

Introduction: Welcome to Night City – Transhuman Life in 2077	1790
"Transcending" to a Better Human?	1791
Enhancing Ourselves to Death, Part 1: The Loss of Personal Identity	1795
Enhancing Ourselves to Death, Part 2: Transhuman or Posthuman?	1799
Transhuman Corporatism and Buddhism as Resistance	1803
Conclusion: Relation to Others and Spiritual Balance	1807
References	1809

Abstract

Philosophically, human enhancement is often discussed in terms of *transhumanism*: transcending the normal biological limits of human physical and cognitive abilities. Despite obvious advantages to transhuman enhancement in the form of longer lives, healthier immune systems, and enriched capacity for learning, many people foresee problematic consequences, too. Transhuman enhancement poses risks to personal identity and the ability of humans to live meaningful, autonomous lives – assuming that those who enhance themselves even remain human. This chapter will examine the way that transhumanism – the "cyber" in cyberpunk fiction – is portrayed in *Cyberpunk 2077*. Although the video game's narrative and world do engage with the threat transhumanism poses to identity and living an authentic human life, this chapter's author argues that the real danger of transhuman enhancement in *Cyberpunk* is how easily enhancement has been exploited to maintain corporate control over society. Yet, *Cyberpunk* mostly recommends against violent, revolutionary resistance. Curiously, the "punk" in *Cyberpunk 2077* seems to be a call to reprioritize one's life, pivoting away from self-interested consumerism towards spiritual health and communal

C. Lay (✉)
Young Harris College, Young Harris, GA, USA
e-mail: cmlay@yhc.edu

© Springer Nature Switzerland AG 2024
D. K. Johnson et al. (eds.), *The Palgrave Handbook of Popular Culture as Philosophy*,
https://doi.org/10.1007/978-3-031-24685-2_72

relationships. To that end, this chapter reframes transhumanism in *Cyberpunk* as a social problem with a solution in interpersonal mysticism found in Buddhism and the philosophies of thinkers like Simone Weil and Martin Buber.

Keywords

Cyberpunk 2077 · Transhumanism · Human enhancement · Singularity · Extended mind · Feminist posthumanism · Personal identity · Persistence · Physiological continuity · Psychological continuity · Fission/fusion · Authenticity · Genetic determinism · Critical theory · Buddhism · Power · Philosophy of dialogue · Mysticism

Introduction: Welcome to Night City – Transhuman Life in 2077

> Almost nobody remembers when a person wasn't just a meat bag full of secondhand implants.
> —Johnny Silverhand

Cyberpunk 2077 is a videogame about bodies. Night City – the main setting of the game – is choked with holographic advertisements that stretch into the evening sky, towering above the tallest skyscraper; even the most benign of these ads are hypercharged with an exploitative sexuality, whether the bodies in question are female, male, or transgender. *Cyberpunk* is also a video game about minds. The driving force behind the game's critical path – the quests that compose the main story threads – is the idea that a digitized construct copied from the brain of anarchist musician Johnny Silverhand gradually overwrites the player's character and protagonist V's mind into nonexistence. Most often, bodies and minds in Night City converge in the (so-called) ripperdoc's chair. Effectively pawn brokers with a surgeon's skill set and a tattoo artist's flair, ripperdocs replace or enhance a patient's biological limbs, organs, and cognitive abilities with complicated technological surrogates. Whether a street kid scraping by on petty crime or a corpo-rat skittering up the corporate ladder, almost everyone needs the advantage a ripperdoc can provide – ordinary human bodies and minds just are not enough to succeed in Night City. Philosophers and futurists call this kind of physical and mental human modification, which exceeds or redefines normal human limits, *transhumanism*. Night City is then a transhuman city, and *Cyberpunk* is a game about particularly transhuman bodies and minds.

Cyberpunk's main plot (and many side stories), its aesthetic, and even many principal game mechanics all depend on transhumanist themes. Plot discussion will be seeded throughout the chapter, so we shall consider mechanics and appearance here. As a role-playing game (RPG), progressive development of the player character's statistics is a central feature of the experience. The game includes traditional leveling for stat increases, like improving one's "Body" or "Reflex" attribute, as well as a "Street Cred" level that represents the player's perceived social status in Night City. Both of these levels place restrictions on what kind of body and brain implants a character can install from the ripperdoc. In this sense, access to ever-more-impressive transhuman enhancements is another form of character advancement. Of course, these enhancements increasingly widen the suite of abilities available to the player and dramatically improve combat abilities, traversal, technical skills, and so on. As such, modification and enhancement are a planned part of *Cyberpunk*'s systems; enhanced characters are simply better equipped to deal with steadily more difficult opponents in each of Night City's distinctive districts. Most players that don't enhance will quickly find themselves outmatched. At the same time, a character's "chrome" and cyberware – the transhuman modifications they have – are as much cosmetic as they are functional. That is, particular colors and styles of enhancement are expressions of how Night City's inhabitants project themselves and their personalities into the world, often to impress their chooms (friends).

Clearly, transhuman enhancement is integral to *Cyberpunk* and is pervasive in its world. Part of this is due to both its involvement in the wider cyberpunk genre and the source material on which the game is based: the tabletop RPG *Cyberpunk*. Yet, it would be unfair to attribute the transhumanism commentary in *Cyberpunk* purely to these influences. The rest of this chapter will attempt to situate *Cyberpunk 2077*'s unique take on transhuman enhancement in the ongoing philosophical debate about the viability and moral permissibility of transhumanism.

"Transcending" to a Better Human?

The biologist Julian Huxley (1957) was the first person to use the term "transhumanism" (or is regularly attributed to be the first), so his account is a good place to start. To Huxley, normal human existence is enfeebled by physical and mental limitations that result in lives full of disease, unhappiness, and ignorance. He calls for humanity to "transcend itself" through the use of scientific enhancement that can redraw the boundaries of what is humanly possible. To be clear, Huxley sees this transcendence as something closer to humans reaching their full potential as a species – it is not transcendence from humanity to, say, a further and more developed link on the evolutionary chain.

Although Huxley optimistically viewed human transcendence as a future goal, more contemporary thinkers see transhuman results as more immediate (and inevitable). This is perhaps best represented in the views of futurist Ray Kurzweil. Originally responsible for advancements in tech fields like optical character recognition and text-to-speech software, Kurzweil has, in more recent years, turned his attention toward what mathematician John Von Neumann referred to as the *technological singularity*. In *The Singularity is Near*, Kurzweil (2005) defines the singularity as "a future period during which the pace of technological change will be so rapid, its impact so deep, that human life will be irreversibly transformed" (2005, p. 7). What makes this transformation so certain to Kurzweil is the *law of accelerating returns*. In terms of technological progress, both technological advancements and their technological effects increase exponentially; this generates a feedback loop whereby the creation of things like faster chip speeds reciprocally leads back to an increased rate of technological development. In other words, better tech results in better means to produce tech (and vice versa). What was once a linear and gradual slope of technological progress quickly becomes a vertical wall.

Night City – and the wider world of *Cyberpunk 2077* – has collided headfirst into the exponential technological increase of the singularity. Ripperdocs sell cyberware that enables users to interface with computers and light their enemies on fire, all *with only the power of their (enhanced) minds*. Body implants modify musculature to allow users to double jump (a physics-defying second jump once the user is already airborne) and convert their arms into swords or missile launchers. Perceptual enhancements let users "scroll," or record, their perceptual field and all somatosensory and emotional responses in the form of a "virtu." Virtus can then be repacked as "braindances", virtual reality programs that allow one to experience someone else's inner life firsthand. Expectedly, this has dramatic effects on *Cyberpunk*'s entertainment industry, but braindances have also opened new opportunities for therapy and how individuals share life experiences (or revisit their own memories). Similarly, self-image and beauty standards are upended by transhuman changes. During the side quest "Raymond Chandler Evening," V follows a woman who had a "full bodysculpt" such that *all* of her external features were transformed; as part of the same quest, the player can read a ripperdoc's notes, which contain references to everyday procedures like the above "full phenotype change" and "eye color change, spine-stretching and strengthening, [and] skin dyeing."

Some among those who take transhumanism seriously welcome the singularity and its projected changes to human life. Indeed, there are many foreseeable benefits to transcending current human biology. The philosopher Nick Bostrom is an outspoken advocate of transhumanism and its positive consequences. As such, Bostrom (2003) argues that human enhancement is overwhelmingly good for society by providing advancements that are both obvious – increased learning aptitudes, the eradication of many genetic diseases, general improvements to health and lifespan – and less plainly evident – the possible discovery of new means of pleasure, new categories of cultural and ethical valuations, and greater possibilities for self-actualization. Moreover, Bostrom believes that the many means of realizing human enhancement encourage interdisciplinary cooperation among scientific communities, including genetic research, cybernetics, AI, and possible future fields like nanotechnology. Others, like Ingmar Persson and Julian Savulescu (2012) in their book *Unfit for the Future: The Need for Moral Enhancement*, see transhuman enhancement as an ethical imperative. Extravagant consumption and self-interest tend to dominate, even in liberal democratic societies. Persson and Savulescu contend that the best way to ensure proper concern for future generations of humans and the entire nonhuman ecosystem is through transhuman enhancement that produces more sustainable moral motivations.

Most of the above benefits of transhuman enhancement are the results of transhuman changes to the individual. But there might also be advantages at the level of institutions and social structures. In her "Cyborg Manifesto," feminist theorist Donna Haraway (1991) considers the notion of a cybernetic organism, or cyborg, as something that is neither purely "natural" nor artificial. Rather, the cyborg is simultaneously *both* biological and mechanical and cannot be *essentially* categorized as one or the other. By contrast, societies in the Western world are largely organized around essential categorizations – that is, categorizations that claim that individuals belonging to certain groups have group-specific traits that form their *essence*. These traits draw rigid boundaries between groups so that groups themselves can be called largely homogenous. Essentialism about groups also brings about many harmful sexist, racist, and otherwise problematic assumptions. Haraway argues that categorization and boundary-drawing is rooted in creating "antagonistic dualisms" between the self and the abstract Other. By applying the notions of a cyborg-self to society at large, Haraway posits that social relationships can be reframed around a boundary-blurring conception of difference as complementary – just as the natural and artificial within the cyborg complement one another. For these reasons, Haraway's theory has often been called "posthuman feminism," as it seeks to secure a kind of social equality by blending the human being with something more.

Cyberpunk undeniably takes transhuman enhancement as a benefit. Most reading in Night City is done through "shards," data storage devices that can be slotted into a user's brain-based "deck" and read like a normal article. While representative of the possible benefits of transhumanism in their own right, this chapter will mostly discuss shards for the way that they build out the lore of *Cyberpunk,* and what they reveal about philosophically relevant Night City individuals and happenings. One shard, "75 Years of Cyberware," speaks favorably of the elimination of disability bias in hiring due to easy access to limb replacement. On an elevator ride while headed to V's apartment, the player might overhear a random newscast praising the effectiveness of transhuman enhancement at improving human health, as the broadcaster affirms that "MS (multiple sclerosis) is one of the few remaining diseases that cannot be cured by replacing the affected tissue with implant technology." In line with Bostrom's suggestion, braindances (and the technology to privately play them) appear to provide transhumans in *Cyberpunk*'s world with opportunities for richer categories of emotional and creative experience. Judy Alvarez, a prominent side-character and possible romantic interest for players who created a female V, is a braindance "editor." She manipulates the raw collections of percepts and feelings into a virtual experience that tells a kind of narrative to the user: the narrative of another person's intimate emotional life. To Judy, this is surely a form of artistry. This same technology permits individuals to mentally link themselves and share the emotional resonance of particular memories and even present experiences. Judy's emotive responses to childhood relics she finds bleed into V's experience while the two explore Judy's sunken hometown. Even more pointedly, a mind-linked sexual encounter between V and Panam Palmer (another side-character and romantic interest for male V) is amplified precisely because the two can each feel the other's pleasure.

Likewise, the side quest "Dream On" demonstrates Persson and Savulescu's claim that transhuman moral enhancement is a necessary condition for a future-oriented society motivated by more than self-interest. Politicians in Night City are notoriously corrupt and primarily serve corporate agendas. However, mayoral candidate Jefferson Peralez and his wife Elizabeth, a prominent attorney, both notably refuse corpo graft. The player learns that this is not due to the inherent virtues of either Peralez. Rather, their mental states – beliefs, desires, memories, personality, and character traits – are being directly overwritten by an unknown transmission which is being beamed into their apartment. Without this external moral enhancement, it is heavily implied that the Peralezes would be just as susceptible to political misconduct as anyone else in Night City.

It is less clear that Haraway's notion of complementary cyborg difference plays its part in *Cyberpunk*. Substantial inequalities persist in Night City that suggest that at least some essentialisms remain. As with much of the cyberpunk genre more generally, there is a sense of Orientalism about *Cyberpunk*'s world that depicts Asian otherness. For instance, much of Night City's aesthetic is built out of the sort of neon-soaked signage common to many East Asian countries. And organizations like Arasaka Corporation – including narratively vital characters such as CEO and patriarch Saburo Arasaka and his bodyguard Goro Takemura – follow well-established Japanese tropes of ruthless business practices underpinned by a commitment to family honor.

While the game has a more trans-friendly character generation system than that featured in similar games, like *The Elder Scrolls* series or more recent *Fallout* titles, beyond Claire Russell (an extremely nuanced trans bartender at Night City's night club Afterlife), transgender people have limited representation in Night City. A soft drink called Chromanticore provides what is probably the most visible transgender depiction in the game. Advertisements invite the consumer to "Mix It Up" while displaying a trans woman with an erection so exaggerated that its outline beneath her leotard can be traced halfway up her stomach. Clearly there continue to be groups in *Cyberpunk* that are represented as a kind of Other, despite near-universal transhuman enhancement. Still, there is at the same time a broad acceptance of the transhuman marriage of self with what is explicitly *not* the self, as body modification to even the most extreme degree is as normal as shopping for new clothes. As will be argued in a later section, it is possible that most "antagonistic dualisms" in Night City can be reduced to a single dualism: the class dualism of wealthy versus poor. In this sense, Haraway's cyborg theory is still at play in Night City, as at least some features of the social structure have changed due to transhuman enhancement.

With this in mind, it might seem like the shard "Rewiring Synaptic Pathways" sums up *Cyberpunk*'s view towards transhumanism: "We, as a society, can no longer image (sic) an existence without technologically heightened senses, enhanced memory capacity, and pain modulators." Yet, just because society can no longer be conceived of without drastic transhuman enhancements does not mean that *Cyberpunk*'s portrayal of transhumanism is uniformly positive.

Despite substantially longer lifespans (in theory), improved immune systems, and technologies that enable novel kinds of experiences, just about no one in Night City is happy. To the contrary: it is shown to be an oppressive place ruled by rapacious corps and (lightly) organized criminals. Because the police force is as corrupt as the political caste, ordinary people are hired by "fixers" to curb gang violence – but only when they are not also contributing to it. Moreover, the transhuman enhancement on display in *Cyberpunk* is disproportionately engineered to do harm to others. It is hardly a stretch to say that very few people's lives are improved by ready access to brain-melting cyberware or hulking Gorilla Arms at the local gas station. Despite clear benefits, *Cyberpunk 2077* is much more pessimistic about what is *lost* by so eagerly adopting transhuman enhancement.

Enhancing Ourselves to Death, Part 1: The Loss of Personal Identity

Bostrom (2005) and others distinguish between those who advocate for transhuman enhancement and those who, for varying reasons, resist it. The latter he calls "bioconservatives." One reason that more philosophically-minded bioconservatives might fear transhuman enhancement is this: if you submit to repeated or extreme enhancement or modification, eventually there may be a point where the person being modified is no longer you but someone else. Just as (in *Star Wars*) Obi-Wan says of Darth Vader that "He's more machine now than man," the opponent to transhumanism might worry that a person could enhance themselves out of existence while bringing another, different, being *into* existence. This is just one facet of the thorny philosophical problem of personal identity; more specifically, the concept in question is about persistence – what makes someone persist as numerically the same individual over time. How could enhancement threaten an individual's persistence? That depends on the method of enhancement.

Suppose that "enhancement" just means the replacing of one's parts with shinier, newer ones. This would include both physical enhancement and cognitive enhancement – even conditioning that replaced mental states, like what happened to the Peralezes in the "Dream On" side quest (where the couple is having their mental states overwritten by a mysterious signal beaming into their apartment). An example will help to illustrate the problem this replacement poses. Though first credited to the Greek historian Plutarch, the Ship of Theseus is a philosophical puzzle that has more or less entered the lexicon of common knowledge. A wooden ship that belonged to Theseus is preserved by the Athenians (let's say in a museum). To keep it in show condition, its planks are replaced as they rot; eventually, *all* of the planks of the ship are replaced. Is the "repaired" ship with all new planks still one and the same ship that once belonged to Theseus? Is it still Theseus' ship? Note that this *isn't* a question about qualitative or type identity; "Is it the same kind of ship? Does it look the same?" Neither is it just a question of legal ownership: "Does Theseus own the ship that is in the museum?" Instead, it is a question of numerical identity. Is the ship that now stands in the museum one and the same ship as before? Is it the same object, the same entity? If so, what distinguishes that repaired ship from another ship made of completely different material? Neither has any of the parts or material from the *original* ship, after all. So why would the original ship and the repaired ship be numerically the same? If the repaired ship is not the same ship, why not? When did it cease being Theseus' ship? After the removal of which plank of wood. For most philosophers, the answers to these questions are not clear.

One way that has been proposed to answer questions like this appeals to the notion of *continuity*. Derek Parfit (1984), in his *Reasons and Persons*, suggests two relevant and distinct senses of continuity: physiological and psychological. In both cases, the idea is that a subject can persist through change so long as that change is gradual and causally connected – somewhat like the links in a chain. Although the first link and the last aren't directly connected, both endpoint links are held together by intermediate connectors. If too much changes all at once, though, continuity is severed and the individual ceases to be – and, importantly, another individual takes their place. Whether one should prefer physiological or psychological continuity (and thus physiological or psychological parts) is not important right now. What matters is that causal continuity preserves identity. If Theseus' ship is given new parts over a long period of time, then the parts are gradually integrated into the whole and it is evident how the parts relate to the continuous spatio-temporal chain that is Theseus' ship. Theseus' ship survives. On the other hand, if a terrible storm swallowed up Theseus's ship and only its foremast floated to shore, it seems far-fetched to say that Theseus' ship persisted through the storm – even if a skilled shipbuilder replaced the parts quickly.

On the continuity view, someone could persist through even radical enhancement if parts were exchanged gradually – like Theseus' ship if it were slowly given new parts, one at a time. This seems to be the stance taken by several characters in *Cyberpunk*, too. The Kabuki ripperdoc warns V of a mind/body disconnect if too much chrome gets swapped out. During the side quest "Cyberpsycho Sighting: Six Feet Under," a Valentino gang member who was forcibly augmented is said to have "turned psycho" because the body "didn't have time to adjust to the 'ware'." But the most overt mention of continuity and persistence comes during the main story quest "Automatic Love" when V talks to the dolls Skye or Angel at *Clouds*, a sex club. As the doll questions V about the fear of "becoming someone else," V responds that there is a feeling of connection to the person one is today and yesterday, even if that person qualitatively changes from day to day. But there is no connection to Johnny, whose thoughts and desires are alien to V – they are not causally connected to the thoughts and desires that came before them but seem to intrude from the outside. This causes discontinuity between V and the new, enhanced person that V is "becoming."

Cyberpunk, however, also includes certain examples that are uniquely challenging to continuity approaches to identity: where one entity becomes two (fission) or two become one (fusion). The Ship of Theseus is something of a fission case, and we can consider it further to understand the issue. Suppose all the planks of the original that were removed were set aside in a warehouse, and then years they were restored (the rot was removed and their holes filled) and a new ship was built from them, with all the original planks in all the same places as they were. So now there is a *repaired* ship that has none of the original planks sitting in the museum, but then also a *restored* ship that has the same (restored) planks, but that just came into existence in a warehouse. Which is the original? Which is Theseus' ship? As a product of the process of gradual replacement over time, the former is causally continuous with the original. But so is the latter, given that it is made of much of the same material. It appears that we have two candidates for Theseus' ship, both of which seem to fit the requirement for being Theseus' ship, even though they are not numerically identical to each other. Things get even worse when you consider: If the restored ship in the warehouse is the original, did Theseus' ship just pop back into existence after a long period of time? If so, when did the repaired ship in the museum stop being the original? Was it the moment the restored ship was completed? That doesn't make sense; nothing changed about the repaired ship at *that* moment – only the parts composing the restored ship changed. Perhaps the repaired ship stopped being the original some time before the other ship was restored? If so, which single, restored plank of wood made the repaired vessel stop being Theseus' ship? Any answer one gives to these questions seems to be ludicrous, and for most philosophers, it is not obvious which, if either, of the two ships actually is the original.

To show how this relates to the identity of persons, David Wiggins (1967) conceives of a peculiar situation where a man named Brown has each of his brain hemispheres placed into different bodies. By hypothesis, Wiggins stipulates that each hemisphere will have the same psychological features – memories, beliefs, and so on. Further, both hemispheres have the right kind of continuous causal history. That is, the mental states in both hemispheres follow a sensible causal chain; the present states are what they are exactly because of previous mental states. Both resulting people, Brown I and Brown II, are continuous with Brown. So, if we follow Parfit's rule about identity, we must conclude that Brown I and Brown II are the same person. Clearly, though, this conclusion must be rejected: Brown was one person, so Brown I and Brown II cannot both be Brown. As both have equal claim to being Brown, it also seems as arbitrary as flipping a coin to say that one of the two is the real Brown and the other is a mere copy. Worse still, there *also* seems to be something wrong with saying that neither is Brown. Part of the earlier problem is that there appeared to be *too many Browns*, so suggesting that Brown somehow did not survive is absurd. And so, again, it seems that any answer that one gives is ludicrous.

Roderick Chisholm (1979) presents an even more bizarre example of fission, but it can be adapted to illuminate the related problems of fusion. Rather than splitting brains, suppose there is a person who can replicate like an amoeba. Upon spontaneously dividing, it becomes impossible to tell which was the original and which is the offspring. Now, consider that the situation might be inverted: there are two people (who need not be qualitatively identical) that merge into one, like a reverse-amoeba. We can stipulate that the fused person has a roughly equal number of physical and psychological characteristics from both pre-merge people. Is the composite being one person or two? As with the fission case, there is continuity with both pre-merge people. And, just as in that previous case, choosing simply one seems unprincipled, and to say "neither persists" appears to fly in the face of the obvious fact that both pre-merge people seem to have survived in some way.

Cyberpunk has more than its share of fission and fusion cases, and these can tell the careful player much about the game's view of persistence problems. Taking examples of identity fusion first: the street-fighting side quest "Beat on the Brat: Kabuki" has V fight a set of twin brothers, Certo and Esquerdo, who have installed a joint neural implant that synchronizes their thoughts and felt states. Alt Cunningham, a netrunner (hacker) and one of Johnny's former flames, has her consciousness "uploaded" to the Net and plans to assimilate all uploaded people in Arasaka's servers *into her* to free them from imprisonment. The dynamic between the Johnny construct and V is also a kind of fusion. As Arasaka bioengineer Anders Hellman says, "It's not like hearing voices – you're both yourself and Silverhand, simultaneously...It's not as if one of you wins the debate. The scale simply shifts, slowly but surely."

Analogously, V's separation from Johnny is, in a majority of the game's several endings, viewed as a sort of fission. In the ending where Johnny remains in V's body and V is uploaded to the Net to join Alt, Johnny seems melancholy without V. If V sides with Arasaka and Johnny instead disappears into Cyberspace, the sense of absence is even more pronounced. Arasaka doctors are unable to prevent V's body and brain from deteriorating, and V feels incomplete. Notably, part of the battery of tests that V is subjected to involves responding to narratives about the Ship of Theseus (!) and dicephalic twinning – real-world cases where a single body is born with two distinct heads.

Like Johnny and V, Delamain (Del), the AI cabbie who assists V in an early mission, can be seen as both a case of fission and fusion. During the side quest "Epistrophy," the player is tasked with tracking down a series of rogue AIs that are both somehow part of Del and distinct entities in their own right. The follow-up quest "Don't Lose Your Mind" gives the player a choice: destroy the rogue AIs by deleting and rebooting Del's personality, free them into the Net, or (if the player's stats are high enough), merge the AIs into the Del master program. Perhaps mirroring the way that Johnny and V gradually become "fused," Johnny strongly recommends merging the AIs and suggests that they are all just aspects of a single Del.

Taken together, these varied cases of fission and fusion certainly do not offer answers to the problems of persistence found in the Ship of Theseus, Wiggins's multi-hemisphere brain transplant, or Chisholm's amoeba person. Johnny and V, Certo and Esquerdo, and the various Delamain AIs sometimes seem to be *both* distinct entities and also a single, conjoint being different from the individuals that constitute their parts. *Cyberpunk*'s silence about a sure answer to these identity questions is telling, though. Again, Parfit (1984) provides a helpful explanation. He suggests that it is possible that identity is sometimes indeterminate. In other words, there are fringe cases where there are no clear answers to whether or not a given individual is you or someone else, despite apparent continuity. To Parfit, this is okay: it turns out that identity is not what matters. All that is important is that *someone* is able to continue your projects, fulfill your desires, and care for those who matter to you. If this is right, transhumanism might still pose a legitimate threat to personal persistence, but the threat is really toothless because a loss of personal identity is not a meaningful loss. Bostrom (2003) says as much when he both concedes that transhuman enhancement could prevent someone from persisting and argues that many people might prefer that the most important parts of themselves survive, even if "they" (the actual people) do not.

To carry this notion further, once strict commitments to identity and persistence are let go of, it becomes possible to see once problematic aspects of transhuman enhancement as quite good. In an influential paper called "The Extended Mind," Andy Clark and David Chalmers (1998) propose that artificial things external to the body and brain can still be incorporated into thought processes so long as they function like run-of-the-mill internal thinking. This is part of a wider thesis in the philosophy of mind known as *functionalism*, which states that what makes something count as "mind" or "mental" is that it acts like a mind. On this view, minds are defined by what they do, not what they are made of. To Clark and Chalmers, both artificial and biological things can equally be part of cognitive processes and – more strongly – *part of the mind itself*. This is good for humans. Calculators can work math problems effortlessly, and a phone's GPS is much more skillful at navigating an unfamiliar place than a biological person alone. Moreover, if the mind is no longer preoccupied with more mundane operations like calculation and navigation, it is freed to focus on more sophisticated, creative thought. Whether or not transhuman enhancement eliminates the individual, the resulting "extended" entity surely seems to function better in the world.

The unimportance of identity and the idea that transhuman enhancement extends identity into the world both seem consistent with *Cyberpunk*. The shard "New Release Braindances" claims that "[t]he body is everything…It is you, but it is also just a tool for your mind to interact with the world." How can the body be both everything that is "you" and also just a "tool"? Given a second look, this apparent contradiction makes sense in light of the "identity does not matter" and "extended identity" views. In the world of *Cyberpunk*, there is no single "thing" that is you; nor is there a clear border between you and the world. Nothing is more routine in Night City than merging the world and the self through transhuman enhancement. So, there is little use in trying to determine whether or not a person could persist as herself through radical enhancement. This is clear to the doll at Clouds who talks V down from a crisis of personal identity, remarking "Not a single thing in this world isn't in the process of becoming something else." Personal identity is therefore fluid. The real worry is, as Misty says to V just before the major, culminating choice in "Nocturne OP55N1": "We shouldn't fear change itself – only who we might change into."

Enhancing Ourselves to Death, Part 2: Transhuman or Posthuman?

For many bioconservatives, the real threat of transhuman enhancement is exactly this fear of changing into *something* else, not someone else. To transhumanists like Huxley, enhancement is merely a way to fulfill latent human potential. Transhumanism may transcend human limits, but these limits are really limits of sociohistorical time and place. The language of Haraway's posthuman feminism suggests enhancement that transcends the limits of the human *species*, though. Bostrom (2009) welcomes this *posthumanism*, whereby enhancement modifies physical or mental capacities so far beyond what is biologically possible that they no longer even reasonably qualify as human anymore. Most bioconservatives see the posthuman project as the endpoint of transhumanism generally, and they argue that this is disastrous for the human species. This section will consider how enhancing the "human" out of the human person might severely impoverish the meaningfulness, agency/autonomy, and dignity uniquely afforded to human lives. Does *Cyberpunk* share this view?

Considering meaningfulness first, it is reasonable to ask, "What makes a human life meaningful or authentically human, and how might transhuman enhancement deny this meaning?" One of the earliest discussions of the potential shortfalls of transhuman enhancement was articulated by the bioethicist Erik Parens (1995). Parens objects to enhancement on the grounds that the drive to eliminate disease and prolong life will strip human life of experiences of personal vulnerability and the care for vulnerable others. Enhancing away what he calls human "fragility" risks diminishing empathy for others and all but erases forms of "excellence" that depend on overcoming human limitation, including appreciation for sport and other achievements. Parens is far from alone with this concern. According to the political scientist Francis Fukuyama (2002), confronting pain, death, and so-called bad emotions like grief and sadness are crucial to human character-building. Attempts to enhance away these experiences in favor of a blanket, utilitarian reduction of suffering may bankrupt the value of transhuman life. Likewise, the political and moral philosopher Michael Sandel (2007) argues that transhumanism threatens traits like humility, responsibility, and solidarity with others by encouraging a "mastery" outlook on the world. To Sandel, recognition of limitation – namely, that humans cannot do *everything* they want or can think of – is an enriching feature of life. If particular aptitudes can be genetically or technologically engineered into humans, they are no longer mere "gifts" of biological nature to be celebrated. Rather, the motive becomes "perfecting" the human being in order to overpower the world (and others).

Cyberpunk does seem to accept at least some part of the claim that transhuman enhancement devalues life. Players can overhear a female actor at a busy party beaming about how she is easily able to play male roles: "Wardrobe swapped out everything – including my voice." Because implants and cyberware in *Cyberpunk* are so modular, completely overhauling how one looks, sounds, and behaves is hardly different from a costume change. Surely, this blunts some of the accomplishment of superior acting in a nontrivial way. Instead of practicing at affecting a particular accent or way of moving, the actor can install an implant that immediately does this work for her. At the same time, ubiquitous enhancement clearly has not divested Night City's residents of the ability to have caring relationships, experience loss, or grow into people of substantial character. The player's relationships with people like Claire, Judy, Kerry, Panam, and River each hinge on the player helping other characters cope with various traumas. Claire and Judy grieve over the loss of their respective romantic partners, Kerry struggles with feeling creatively stunted, Panam ambivalently seeks to reconnect with her estranged, extended family, and River is overwhelmed by both the guilt of his nephew's disappearance and the impossibility of being a righteous police officer in a city where corruption impedes justice.

This evaluation of meaning in transhumanism relies on the ability of the enhanced person to act freely. To this end, other critics of transhumanism charge enhancement with restricting the free agency of the enhanced person. Some threats to agency/ autonomy come in the form of genetic tinkering to predetermine a child's traits and dispositions, as philosopher and sociologist Jurgen Habermas (2003) discusses. While genetic modification might seem scarcely different from carefully manipulating a child's environment to ensure success – say, by fostering musical talent through regular lessons and forced study – Habermas notes that there is a substantial difference. Namely, the child who is genetically modified cannot "contest" his conditioning, as it is programmed into him beforehand. Like a parent preselecting the child's genetic layout, Hans Jonas (1985) sees permissiveness toward transhuman enhancement as an exercise of social power whereby present generations deny future people the ability to refuse enhancement. By simply being born into a society that has already embraced widespread transhuman enhancement, there is no choice to assent to either genetic modifications made before one's birth or technological enhancements that form the centerpiece of society's functioning. Still other opponents of transhumanism suggest an inevitable limiting of specifically political agency/autonomy. The ethicist Robert Sparrow (2014) fears that transhuman enhancement could lead to political inequality between enhanced and unenhanced populations. Due to their massively improved capacities for intellectual and possibly moral reasoning (recall the initiative to "morally enhance" suggested by Persson and Savulescu), the enhanced would have a plausible claim to rule or at least receive additional representation in societies where outright enhanced takeover would seem profoundly undemocratic. Furthermore, Sparrow (2016) foresees the unwelcome possibility that governments may adopt mandatory enhancement agendas that serve the "national interest."

Resistance to authority – and by extension, preservation of autonomy – is at the heart of cyberpunk fiction. *Cyberpunk 2077* is no different in this regard. But *Cyberpunk*'s statements on agency/autonomy are largely unrelated to the restrictions these authors see in transhumanism. Though it is plausible to assume that there is a degree of eugenics-style genetic modification in the world of *Cyberpunk*, the type of enhancement that players see in-game is mostly enhancement that informed adults *choose* for themselves. There are, of course, exceptions: Maelstrom gang members sometimes kidnap and forcibly augment unwilling people, such as in the side quest "Losing My Religion." And neither V nor Johnny wanted to share mental space, especially in such a way that their thoughts, desires, and other states begin to overlap into a fused person. On the whole, though, this is not how most enhancement in *Cyberpunk* occurs. In addition, enhancement is not depicted as central to a political or social divide between enhanced transhumans and unenhanced "normals." Apart from a few religious sects, there is almost no opposition to transhuman enhancement in *Cyberpunk*. The enhanced do not compose an oppressive regime of rulers, and governments appear to matter very little in determining what individuals in Night City can and cannot do. In fact, much governmental authority has been ceded to corporations like Militech and Arasaka. So, it seems that transhuman enhancement does not threaten human agency/autonomy in the world of *Cyberpunk 2077* – at least, not in the ways described by Habermas, Jonas, and Sparrow.

There remains, however, a final objection that transhuman enhancement might dehumanize the enhanced. One way to understand the fear of dehumanization is as a special concern for the species of which one is a member. In the book *Humanity's End*, philosopher Nicholas Agar (2010) calls this concern a type of "species-relative" reasoning and explains that this is not the same as privileging humans above other species. Instead, he argues that species-relative reasons are those reasons that make sense within the context of membership to a given species (but not others). Agar states that radical transhuman enhancement may irrevocably change fundamental features in the wide "cluster" of biological characteristics normally associated with being human. Enhancements like increased life spans and incredible intellectual gains would in all likelihood completely change the character of an individual's desires, motivations, and valuations. Like the fictional Charlie Gordon in Daniel Keyes's (1994) *Flowers for Algernon* – the story of a mentally disabled man who receives a treatment that enhances his intellect to transhuman levels – such a profound cognitive leap would isolate transhuman people from both human society and themselves. Past desires are now pointless, dwarfed in scope by the desires and values of a towering mind. Many impressive human goals are made trivial to achieve by enhanced physical and mental abilities. Worst of all, it would be all but impossible to have mutually satisfying relationships with unenhanced people – even those about whom one once cared greatly. Their interests, desires, and intellects would diverge too much to find common ground or even communicate meaningfully without a severe "dumbing down" by the transhuman. (This also suggests reproductive isolation between transhumans and humans. Even if genetic compatibility is assumed after radical enhancement, humans probably would not make for attractive mates.)

Despite any benefits enhancement might have, there are species-relative reasons that might justifiably keep a human from willingly alienating herself from others and abandoning human desires, motivations, and values. This is true even if the human knows that, once she becomes enhanced, she would not miss these things. Agar (2014) illustrates with an example inspired by the film *Invasion of the Body Snatchers* (applicable to both the 1956 original and the 1978 remake). Following Agar, assume that those who have been body-snatched and subsequently turned into pod-people are no longer human and yet also persist as the same individual through the pod-person transformation. To a pod-person, being freed of distractions like human emotion is exceedingly good! From a species-relative point of view, it would be quite bad for the pod-person to become human again. In the same way, the species-relative view can simultaneously accept that a human-turned-pod-person would approve of the transformation and that the transformation is still bad *for the human when she is still a human*. Comparably, it would clearly be bad for an enhanced person to be somehow "unenhanced" and become human again. Too much that the enhanced person values – his enhanced capacities, for instance – would be lost. But it is also bad for a human to become enhanced in the first place, as the individual would lose those relationships, desires, and goals that *humans* value.

Transhuman enhancement in *Cyberpunk* does not alienate the individual from himself or others. First, this is because there is no rigid social separation between the enhanced and the unenhanced. Second, though, enhancement does not appear to have resulted in a posthuman age of staggering intellects and abnormal desires, unrecognizable to humans. People in Night City want new cars, better jobs, companionship, sex, prestige – said another way, people in Night City seem to have many desires common to ordinary humans today. While playing *Cyberpunk*, there is no sense that the player's character and regular folk who inhabit the world have transcended humanity and are a new, uplifted species. Perhaps this is because *Cyberpunk*'s view of "being human" is much closer to philosopher Andy Clark's. Clark (2003) says that humans have a distinctly cyborg nature. That is, it is simply part of being human to adapt other things – especially artificial things – into parts of themselves. If this is correct, the transhuman enhancement that Agar and others worry dehumanizes users is actually the purest possible expression of being human.

Transhuman Corporatism and Buddhism as Resistance

Cyberpunk 2077 does not seem to take transhuman enhancement to be harmful to either individual or human species identity. People can survive enhancement, and it might even make them *more* human – or at least a *better* kind of human. That said, it would be pretty gonk (stupid) to assume that means there is no downside to enhancement in Night City. Proponents like Bostrom (2003) suggest that democratic policy will ultimately prevail and increase universal access to enhancement. While stopping short of advising legal intervention, Bostrom thinks that sufficient social regulatory practices will minimize any inimical effects on the economically disadvantaged. Given analogies to the patchwork American healthcare system, there is little confidence that Bostrom has it right and that market forces and social pressure alone can make for a more egalitarian, enhanced world. Though *Cyberpunk* may not emphasize much of a gap between specifically transhuman haves and have-nots, its depiction of an aggressively corporate transhuman future poses as a scathing rebuke to Bostrom's claim. In Night City, corpos turn enhancement into a particularly nasty way of exploiting the enhanced and subduing free thought – all for a tidy profit of eddies (Eurodollars, the relevant currency in *Cyberpunk 2077*).

Corpos in *Cyberpunk* are certainly the authority, but they are not a threat to autonomy by traditional, political means. Rights, political representation, and governmental mandates barely get any mention in Night City because corpos (and the drive for market share) are really what call the shots. Corporate authority is exercised through structural limitation rather than direct political fiat. Instead of directly prohibiting certain behaviors, corpos control the people of Night City by creating a public narrative that emphasizes immediate pleasure and promotes consumption as the path to the good life. In the essay "Free Time," the philosopher and sociologist Theodore Adorno (1991) explains this as a social cycle that reproduces itself as a byproduct of a capitalistic economics similarly organized around reproduction. It goes like this: if the goal of capitalism is the accumulation of capital, this is best accomplished by producing more of the things that generate capital. As more capital is made, yet more things can be produced – so, production and capital self-perpetuate. To Adorno, the notion of having "free time" in which people do what they please is the result of a culture that prioritizes most time as "work time." Free time exists to make work time *more* productive. It is both an opportunity to recharge for the return to work and consume what has been produced – free time must be filled with something, after all. The need to fill free time appeals to existing impulses and desires that people already have, but it repackages them so that they contribute to the system of reproduction. In other words, free time simultaneously creates a need for consumer desires and a means to satisfy them.

This consumption-production cycle and its social impact are at the heart of *Cyberupnk 2077,* and it also explains the way that transhumanism is portrayed. Transhumans in Night City seem able to live authentic, *human* lives. Likewise, there is no harsh class dichotomy between the enhanced and unenhanced. However, transhuman enhancement is inextricably tied to corporate exploitation of human bodies and desires. Every implant and piece of cyberware that the player can purchase is manufactured by a corpo to fulfill a specific need. Many are stamped with names like Kiroshi Optics or Biodyne, uncomfortably suggesting that users' bodies are in part owned – or at least branded – by corpos. The needs that implants target are often created by those same corpos, too. For instance, the shard "75 years of Cyberware" observes an increasing tendency for corpos to pressure employees to enhance themselves in order to increase productivity. Doc Paradox, an underground publisher of anti-corporate media in *Cyberpunk*, summarizes the corporate influence nicely:

> Corps want to destroy nature, 'cause it doesn't give them IPs or copyright ownership! So, we eat test tube chicken, plants that grow in labs – hell, even photosynthesis has been trademarked...What about our bodies? There's no chunk of 'em that can't be cut, improved, and modified so that every breath we take, every heartbeat generates profit.

Part of Adorno's point in distinguishing between free and work time is to illustrate how exploitative reproduction can reshape thinking. It seeps into how people view the world, making it nearly impossible to imagine an alternative to reproduction-based society. This is why a *Cyberpunk* radio report, casts a "pension-restorer" as a criminal and radical recommended for "braindance rehabilitation therapy." It is simply an accepted part of the social narrative that corpos ought to have no pension obligations, as these interfere with profit. Yet, visits to the movies and engagement in hobbies during free time also serves as a kind of escape – another need that reproduction-based society both creates and fills. Garry the Prophet, a tin-foil-hat type, shouts at passerby about conspiracies led by powerful vampires and reptilians. A side quest, "The Prophet's Song," ends with Garry's disappearance – implied because he overheard too many corporate secrets while being otherwise ignored on his street corner. Johnny remarks that fairy overblown conspiracies are easier to stomach than the mundane reality of "twisted corps pulling the strings...skezzed out on their own power fantasies." There is comfort in the belief that something monstrous is behind the evil in the world. But, like the political theorist Hannah Arendt (1963) demonstrates in her coverage of Nazi officer Adolf Eichmann's trial, evil is rarely so exotic. Eichmann's part in the extermination of

German Jews was more as a small-minded office drone than a malicious puppeteer. To drift with Garry into wild fantasies about alien takeover is just another way of failing to confront corpo control – and thus another way of contributing to its reproduction.

Despite its hostility towards transhuman corporatism, *Cyberpunk 2077*'s messaging is not aimed at dismantling reproduction-based society. Sure, Johnny constantly demands explosive, revolutionary moves toward corpos (especially Arasaka); players even experience some of his corporate insurgency firsthand in a series of Johnny-flavored flashbacks. But the major takeaway from these scenes is often what Johnny's violence has cost him – his friendships, his lover, his freedom, and his life. None of the game's endings deal major blows to corporate culture, either. In some, Arasaka is all but burned to the ground, but news reports indicate that other corpos have immediately begun to fill the void. Just like Johnny's bombing of Arasaka Tower over 50 years prior, acts of violent resistance seem to be swallowed up by the enormity of corporate authority. Violent resistance is not the only form of resistance, though, and *Cyberpunk* is not telling the player to give up. In the ending where Johnny joins Alt in Cyberspace, his last words before returning V to the "real world" are: "Goodbye V. And never stop fightin'."

To see how *Cyberpunk* might recommend that one fight corporatism without the guns, swords, and cyberware to which the player is accustomed, consider the various Buddhists V meets in Night City. Few Buddhist beliefs are explicitly mentioned, but much can be gleaned from a handful of specific encounters. The shard "Buddhism and Cyberware: A Perspective" makes it clear that Buddhists reject enhancement as a barrier to Enlightenment, here described as "inner peace." Enhancement serves as an attachment to the world – a distraction from attaining peace of mind. During the side quest "Losing My Religion," V encounters a Bhikku monk – a monk of the more conservative Theravada school – who was forcibly enhanced. Although the enhanced monk now feels detached from the Buddhist way, he nonetheless insists that V refrain from violence when rescuing his captured brother. Another questline, which begins with the quest "Imagine," involves braindance meditation. V is guided by a mysterious monk called the Zen Master, who teaches V to achieve calm through contemplation of the interconnectedness of nature.

Though particular schools of thought differ within Buddhism – and so interpretations of concepts and practices are quite varied – the founder of the madhyamaka school of Buddhist philosophy, Nagarjuna, proves especially salient for discussing *Cyberpunk*. In *The Fundamental Wisdom of the Middle Way*, Nagarjuna (1995) argues that things exist only in the mutual dependence of activity. For instance, there is no activity of movement without both an act of moving and a mover that moves. Outside of the activity, though, there is no mover or moving. The mover might still exist as a living thing while motionless – but she is not a mover at that time. (And life is, of course, another activity). If things exist only in activity, they do not exist *essentially* but are instead impermanent.

Generally, Buddhists find attachment problematic because of its relation to desire. To be attached to something is to desire it, and if this desire is frustrated, there is suffering. Yet, if things are impermanent, then both the objects that one attaches to and the person herself (and her desires) are only temporary. This ought to mean that there is less incentive to attach – or grasp – to worldly things. Recognizing activity as mutually dependent also highlights the interdependence of people and the world. The world is not a place full of things to be owned but is instead a lattice of intertwined relationships. Nagarjuna's ultimate conclusion is that one can overcome the suffering of the world only by pacifying activity completely. This is Nirvana (Enlightenment), and it extricates the practitioner from the cycle of rebirth, whereby the unenlightened return to the world to which they have shown so much attachment.

Nagarjuna's philosophy includes all of the principles valued by *Cyberpunk*'s Bhikkus: attachment as an impediment to peace, the commitment to minimize suffering in the world, and the belief that all of the elements of reality are interconnected. To its advantage, Nagarjuna's account also jibes with other philosophical ideas present in the game, including Haraway's anti-essentialism and Parfit's claim that identity/self does not matter. Besides the Bhikkus, Nagarjuna's argument that pacification of activity leads to Enlightenment receives unexpected support from another in-game place. The claim is echoed in a shard containing an excerpt from Arthur Schopenhauer's *The Word as Will and Idea*. In the passage, Schopenhauer ([1819], 1909) states that death – perplexingly – is the only place in which an individual can truly be free, going on to claim that there is no freedom in *Operari* (work). What Schopenhauer seems to mean is that the work or activity an individual does is always determined by their character – and nothing determined is free. Put in Nagarjuna's words, the activity of life is always *dependent*. It is only in death, the pacification of the activity of life, that attachment to the world is truly severed. A part of the passage omitted from *Cyberpunk*'s shard reveals that Schopenhauer shares Nagarjuna's opposition to attachment, calling death a remedy for the egoism whereby people see reality as existing for themselves alone. The links to Buddhism are surely intentional. In the closing of the section – also left out of the shard – Schopenhauer directly references Nirvana, which he translates as "extinction."

Reproduction-based society is a continuous cycle of creating and satisfying consumer needs. As the foundations of such a society are built around exploiting desire for profit, it is no stretch to say reproduction-based societies are *saturated* with attachment. Pacification of worldly activity and the ego therefore represent the antithesis of a society obsessed with "getting what is mine" and thus are a kind of genuine resistance. To this end, each of *Cyberpunk*'s main endings engages with pacification or its absence in some way.

This is most obvious in the ending where V is uploaded to Cyberspace as an AI construct and joins Alt, leaving Johnny to stay in V's body ("New Dawn Fades"). Most of the impetus for V's journey in the main storyline is a desperate attempt to stave off erasure by Johnny's construct. Although the player can choose the degree to which V is comfortable with Johnny's presence throughout, the goal is still to separate Johnny and V so that V can go on to fulfill the late Jackie's wish and become a Night City Legend. When Johnny's chip revives V after a bullet to the head, V is not yet able to pacify worldly desire and so is reborn, now with Johnny in tow. By choosing to upload forever and abandon their body, V then chooses to pacify the attachment to prestige at the Afterlife (the premier club for doing shady biz), relationships made throughout the game, and all of the other desires that Night City dangles in front of the player. Unlike V, Johnny – now left alone in V's body – does not escape the Buddhist cycle of rebirth. Yet, he has also pacified many of his revolutionary desires and instead carves out a simpler life, mending his friendship with Kerry and mentoring his abused but musically gifted neighbor, Steve.

The other endings can likewise be read in terms of pacification and attachment. Leaving with Panam and the Aldecados in "All Along the Watchtower" still involves some attachment to the world, but it is also a clear rejection of the consumerism of Night City. There is also little hope that V will survive, given the damage that Johnny's construct has unintentionally done; in that sense, V simply detaches at a slower rate here than in "New Dawn Fades." The "Path to Glory" ending sees V inherit Rogue's status at the Afterlife and become the Legend Jackie always wanted to be. Even so, V also appears remarkably unfulfilled – in spite of limitless wealth and riches. In concluding with a brash raid on the independent corpo space station Crystal Palace, V's story is punctuated by the sense of one permanently chasing a "bigger high." Similarly, the Arasaka ending, "Where is My Mind," banks hard on the importance of identity and attachment to the self. In perfect alignment with Buddhist ideas, this results in what is plainly the bleakest ending. The player abandons Johnny and has Arasaka remove the chip that's devouring V's brain, but V cannot be cured. Isolated in the Arasaka lab, V is alienated from every friendship forged over the course of the game, treated like a test subject, and then ejected back into the world to salvage a few remaining months of miserable life. In each ending, the message is clear: pacification of desire leads to tranquility, while attachment causes suffering.

Conclusion: Relation to Others and Spiritual Balance

These are good reasons to think that Buddhist-like opposition to transhuman corporatism best explains *Cyberpunk*'s position. But this explanation may not fit as neatly as it first appears. Buddhist nonattachment is not limited to simple consumerism. Suffering is dependent on desire, and grasping in *any* form might foster desire. Whereas most people would find value in dedication to righteous causes or passionate love for a partner, the Buddhist sees a harmful desire to hold onto impermanent things. Because of this, many Buddhists withdraw from the world, living as recluses among only other committed Buddhists. Seclusion from others does not square with the above endings or with *Cyberpunk* on the whole.

Even if *Cyberpunk 2077* endorses Buddhist nonattachment as a kind of passive resistance, it does not appear to accept withdrawal from the world entirely. Regardless of the ending, the credits sequence always includes video messages from the many characters important to V throughout the game – everyone from Vik Vektor, V's personal ripperdoc (and sometimes therapist, it seems) to Ma Welles, Jackie's mother. "New Dawn Fades" is hopeful because Johnny is starting to re-engage with others in the world and start forming non-selfish relationships. "All Along the

Watchtower" offers V brief respite in their last months alive through acceptance into communal, nomadic Aldecado living. "Path to Glory" and "Where is My Mind" are empty because they dismiss the interpersonal relationships and resultant sweet, vulnerable moments that have been the keystone of the player's previous hours of gameplay in Night City. Arguably, *Cyberpunk*'s plot is grounded by two primary relationships that overshadow this or that particular narrative event. The game opens by establishing the player's close friendship with former Valentino-banger Jackie Welles. Then, the player spends the rest of the game *inseparable* from Johnny. No adequate explanation of *Cyberpunk*'s answer to the problem of corporate transhumanism can leave out relation.

Two philosophers seem to each capture important elements of *Cyberpunk*'s emphasis on purposeful relationships with others while preserving other ideas from the entry: Simone Weil and Martin Buber. Weil ([1955], 2001) identifies power (in later writings, force) as a defining and exceptionally negative social relation. It is mutually damaging to both the wielder and those oppressed by it. How the oppressed are harmed is obvious, but the wielder also becomes "enslaved" the more that power determines the actions he will take. In light of this view of power, Weil is critical of the State and other institutions of power. Yet, she also disapproves of revolution as merely a reversal of who has and exercises power – revolution does not address the fact that power is itself the problem. As an alternative relation, Weil ([1949], 2002) proposes obligations of compassion. She argues both that only individuals (not collectives or institutions) can have such obligations to one another and that these obligations are universally binding on all persons. Ultimately, Weil is motivated by a Christian mysticism and regards interpersonal relation as a necessary way to meet the "needs of the soul" and to combat what she calls social "uprootedness" – a spiritual displacement caused by selfish individualism and the desires for money and prestige.

Like Weil, Martin Buber (1937) views interpersonal relationships to be fundamental to understanding the world. Using the word-pairs "I-Thou" and "I-It," Buber distinguishes between two ways individuals can relate to the world. I-Thou acknowledges the subjectivity in other things and people, but at the cost of knowing them. Conversely, I-It relates to a world of objects. In I-It, someone can experience things and know, say, their properties; at the same time, things seen as "it" cannot truly be the subject of mutually worthwhile relationships. To Buber, there can be no "unity of the soul" if one denies either I-Thou or I-It – lives lived purely in either relation are incomplete. Moreover, through mutual relation in I-Thou, Buber believes that people can uniquely feel the presence of the eternal Thou, God. In an extended discussion of Buddhism, Buber claims that the Buddha nearly got things right by proposing interconnectedness between self and world. Yet, the Buddha also rejected the unity of the soul by denouncing attachment so fully, as this amounts to a disregard of I-It entirely. By seeking the pacification of life and cessation of rebirth, the Buddha failed to see the mystical connection to the eternal evinced by I-Thou.

Between Weil and Buber, one can now form an accurate image of how *Cyberpunk* treats the problem of transhuman corporatism. From Weil, *Cyberpunk* adopts the oppressive nature of power and the futility of violent resistance in overcoming it. From Buber, *Cyberpunk* takes the analysis of Buddhism's mistake in rejecting the Thou in the world. In considering both philosophers together, one can also pinpoint something about *Cyberpunk* that has been present all along but has not been visible: its mysticism. Though its transhuman technology is most often front and center, mysticism and the spiritual are never far removed from anything that happens in the game. At its most important junction points – both when V first struggles with the prospect of being killed by Johnny's chip and again just prior to the fateful choice in "Nocturne OP55N1" – Misty and her tarot cards appear. Most of all, though, Misty is really there to listen to V and offer a feeling, personal connection that contrasts with the cold alienation of Night City. Though Buddhism is also certainly mystical, its mysticism does not arise out of this specific connection to other people. Like Weil and Buber, *Cyberpunk* seems to see interpersonal relation as spiritual nourishment. It does not bother to take time defining what this "spirituality" is, but this is also consistent with Buber's Thou. The other person is not something to be understood – the other is simply met in mutual relation.

Cyberpunk 2077's final word on transhumanism thus becomes this: people must reject a suffocating consumerism that seeks to repackage individuality as profit and instead refocus on relationships of dependence. Transhuman enhancement is a brute fact of Night City, and there are many benefits to having access to enhancement. All the same, it sharply reflects a wider problem of the society in which it is embedded – the ease with which bodies and minds can be exploited by institutions within that society. To *Cyberpunk*, this exploitation succeeds in dehumanizing the individual, even if enhancement itself does not. In reproduction-based society, other people are a means to make more eddies and reinforce the reproductive structure. This is, to use Buber's terminology, a focus on the I-It to the neglect of the I-Thou, leading to incomplete lives. Johnny's nemesis, Adam Smasher, represents this idea nicely. Smasher's enhancement is brutish, robotic, and near total – he looks vaguely like a Transformer with a squishy bald head. Likewise, his catcall at Evelyn Parker reveals his entire view of the world when he says that she looks "like a cut of fuckable meat." He has surrendered himself entirely to a world that contains only objects to be used or possessed, not people with whom to share relations. Smasher is the final boss-enemy in *Cyberpunk* because he is the inversion of the game's message. Yes, *Cyberpunk* is a game about transhuman bodies and minds that transcend traditional biological boundaries. But *Cyberpunk* just wants to remind the player that one of the boundaries to be transcended is the one between "me" and "you."

References

Adorno, Theodore. 1991. Free time. In *The culture industry: Selected essays on mass culture*, ed. J.M. Bernstein. London: Routledge.
Agar, Nicholas. 2010. *Humanity's end: Why we should reject radical enhancement*. Cambridge: MIT Press.
———. 2014. *Truly human enhancement: A philosophical defense of limits*. Cambridge: MIT Press.

Arendt, Hannah. 1963. *Eichmann in Jerusalem: A report on the banality of evil*. New York: Viking Press.
Bostrom, Nick. 2003. Human genetic enhancement: A transhumanist perspective. *Journal of Value Inquiry* 37 (4): 493–506.
———. 2005. In defense of posthuman dignity. *Bioethics* 19 (3): 202–214.
———. 2009. Why I want to be a posthuman when I grow up. In *Medical enhancement and posthumanity*, ed. Bert Gordijn and Ruth Chadwick. Dordrecht: Springer.
Buber, Martin. 1937. *I and thou*. Trans. Ronald Gregor Smith. Edinburgh: T&T Clark.
Chisholm, Roderick. 1979. *Person and object: A metaphysical study*. Chicago: Open Court.
Clark, Andy. 2003. *Natural born cyborgs*. New York: Oxford University Press.
Clark, Andy, and David Chalmers. 1998. The extended mind. *Analysis* 58 (1): 7–19.
Fukuyama, Francis. 2002. *Our posthuman future: Consequences of the biotechnology revolution*. New York: Farrar, Strauss, and Giroux.
Habermas, Jurgen. 2003. *The future of human nature*. Boston: Polity Press.
Haraway, Donna. 1991. A cyborg manifesto: Science, technology, and socialist-feminism in the late twentieth century. In *Simians, cyborgs, and women: The reinvention of nature*. New York: Routledge.
Huxley, Julian. 1957. Transhumanism. In *New bottles for new wine*. London: Chatto & Windus.
Jonas, Hans. 1985. *Technik, medizin, und ethik: Zur praxis des prinzips verantwortung*. Frankfurt am Main: Suhrkamp.
Keyes, Daniel. 1994. *Flowers for Algernon*. Orlando: Harcourt.
Kurzweil, Ray. 2005. *The singularity is near: When humans transcend biology*. London: Penguin.
Nagarjuna. 1995. *The fundamental wisdom of the middle way*. Trans. Jay L Garfield. Oxford: Oxford University Press.
Parens, Erik. 1995. The goodness of fragility: On the prospect of genetic technologies aimed at the enhancement of human capacities. *Kennedy Institute of Ethics Journal* 5 (2): 141–153.
Parfit, Derek. 1984. *Reasons and persons*. Oxford: Oxford University Press.
Persson, Ingmar, and Julian Savulescu. 2012. *Unfit for the future: The need for moral enhancement*. Oxford: Oxford University Press.
Sandel, Michael. 2007. *The case against perfection: Ethics in the age of genetic engineering*. Cambridge: Harvard University Press.
Schopenhauer, Arthur. (1819) 1909. *The world as will and idea, vol. III*. Trans. R.B. Haldane and J. Kemp. London: Kegan Paul, Trench, Trübner and Co.
Sparrow, Robert. 2014. Egalitarianism and moral bioenhancement. *American Journal of Bioethics* 14 (4): 20–28.
———. 2016. Human enhancement for whom? In *The ethics of human enhancement: Understanding the debate*, ed. Steve Clarke, Savulescu Julian, C.A.J. Coady, Alberto Giubilini, and Sagar Sanyal. Oxford: Oxford University Press.
Weil, Simone. (1955) 2001. Reflections concerning the causes of liberty and social oppression. In *Oppression and liberty*. Trans. Arthur Wills and John Petrie. New York: Routledge.
———. (1949) 2002. *The need for roots: Prelude to a declaration of duties towards mankind*. Trans. Arthur Wills. New York: Routledge.
Wiggins, David. 1967. *Identity and spatio-temporal continuity*. Oxford: Blackwell.

Detroit Become Human as Philosophy: Moral Reasoning Through Gameplay

80

Kimberly S. Engels and Sarah Evans

Contents

Introduction	1812
Summary and Overview of the Game	1814
Moral Reasoning	1816
Analysis: *Detroit Become Human* and What We Owe to Androids	1822
Moral Reasoning Through Game Play	1828
Conclusion	1830
References	1831

Abstract

Detroit Become Human (DBH) offers a stunningly visual gameplay experience that both tells a philosophical story and stimulates the moral reasoning process in players. The game features a futuristic world where highly intelligent androids are bought and sold as workers who take on menial labor tasks for humans. In this chapter, we explore three dimensions of moral reasoning: accounts of moral agency, ethical theories or frameworks, and accounts of moral patiency. We then explore how DBH addresses all of these philosophical issues in its narrative and gameplay scenarios. Issues of moral agency are explored through some of the androids gaining consciousness and autonomy. Ethical theory is explored through various ethical dilemmas that emerge in the gameplay. Moral patiency is explored by questioning if the androids, conscious and unconscious, are worthy of moral concern and why. We then show how the gameplay structure offers a unique interactive opportunity for players to engage in the moral reasoning process. Additionally, through the questions it raises and scenarios it poses, DBH makes an implicit anti-speciesist argument regarding moral patiency. Additionally, it makes a secondary argument that suffering and struggle are necessary to develop the possibility of second-order desires and true freedom and agency. The

K. S. Engels (✉) · S. Evans
Molloy University, Rockville Centre, NY, USA
e-mail: kengels@molloy.edu; sevans@molloy.edu

© Springer Nature Switzerland AG 2024
D. K. Johnson et al. (eds.), *The Palgrave Handbook of Popular Culture as Philosophy*, https://doi.org/10.1007/978-3-031-24685-2_83

interactive structure of the game, in which players' choices have more weight than in many gameplay experiences, makes DBH a unique work of contemporary philosophical pop culture.

Keywords

Detroit Become Human · Consciousness · Free will · Moral reasoning · Moral agency · Ethical theory · Moral patiency · Immanuel Kant · Noumenal self · Harry Frankfurt · "Wanton" · Second-order desires · Utilitarianism · Aristotle · Virtue ethics · Carol Gilligan · Care ethics · Peter Singer · Speciesism · Video game

Introduction

Video games are a standard element in the contemporary media landscape. The 2021 Entertainment Software Association's annual report found that 76% of children (defined as age 18 and under) and 67% of adults play video games, bringing the total number of US video game players to 226.6 million (ESA, 2021). Video games primarily function as entertainment, but they are also vehicles for expressing aspects of culture, including moral and ethical norms. In particular, video games that tell stories can facilitate contemplation on philosophical and moral reasoning. While pop culture functions as a powerful medium for exploring philosophical ideas in the contemporary world, the gameplay format offers an interactive experience in which players are not just spectators, but themselves contribute to the stories that are told. Because players have some agency within the game and make choices about what to do, realistic games like *Detroit Become Human* (DBH) allow for a more immersive experience with moral reasoning processes than watching a TV show or movie. This immersive experience, in turn, allows an attentive player to engage the philosophical process in a novel way.

DBH is a graphically realistic video game set in a futuristic, but relatable society. The storylines in the game tell the tale of advanced androids who are bought and sold as workers and replace humans in many menial labor and caretaking positions. Gradually some of the androids achieve consciousness and the ability to act according to their own wills rather than according to their programming. The storylines present moral and philosophical dilemmas to the players, immersing players in an ambiguous moral realm where they are not just spectators, but active participants.

The immersive narrative of DBH offers a game experience where choices affect the actual outcome. Some games offer the illusion of choice, but all choices eventually lead to the same end. However, in DBH, the decisions a player makes have consequences that affect both the playable and nonplayable characters (NPCs) and can lead to different possible endings for the game. The game also offers players a flow chart of the decisions made throughout the game that help facilitate the moral reasoning process and prompts players to reflect on their decisions. While the setting is a fictional world, it is not a fantasy world, but presented as a realistic possibility for our future. This combination makes DBH stand out as a powerful work of pop culture that not only tells stories with philosophical themes, but builds an interactive and realistic philosophical experience.

DBH is one of many video games to utilize morally difficult decision-making as a core part of the game's narrative. Past games such as *Mass Effect*, for example, offer players moral quandaries, the answers of which contribute toward filling either side of a binarized good vs. evil morality meter. But morality meters have been criticized for encouraging players to think in black and white terms like good and evil and to assign definitive values to morally gray contexts (Babij, 2013). A more recent study of player perceptions of the role of a morality meter in their in-game decision-making processes found that the meter was used in a variety of ways, but overall "many players reject or ignore the meter...because they want to make decisions on their own merits and for their own reasons and not because the game rewards or penalizes them" (Formosa et al., 2021, p. 10). Therefore, while the stories in video games inherently express values as products of culture, a straightforward, in-game measure of morality such as a meter fails to produce an outcome of more typical or aberrant morality during play. A game that offers choices but leaves the moral judgment up to the individual is a more effective experimentation space for grappling with matters of moral reasoning.

The process of moral reasoning, a key component of the philosophical field of ethics, requires moral agents (decision-makers), moral patients (those who are morally considerable), and a set of values for judging actions as right or wrong. DBH poses questions related to all three of these areas of moral reasoning. Through the process of gaining consciousness, questions about the requirements for moral agency and personhood are explored. By asking if the androids, even those who have not reached consciousness, are worthy of moral concern, the player is prompted to reflect on conceptions of moral patiency or considerability. And by posing various moral scenarios throughout the game that offer different outcomes, players are prompted to ponder competing values or frameworks through which to judge our moral decisions. Through the scenarios posed for gameplay, DBH makes an antispeciesist argument regarding moral patiency, in which it seems clearly wrong to exclude the androids from moral concern based merely on the fact that they are not biologically human. Additionally, through the painful process of androids gaining consciousness or freedom, the game argues that personhood and moral agency require at least a capacity to reflect on and change one's own desires, and this capacity is developed through struggle and suffering.

Throughout this chapter, we will present an overview of the stories told in the game and the choices offered to players. We will explore the key components of moral reasoning in the field of ethics, including requirements for moral agency, requirements for moral patiency, and a value-based theoretical framework. We will show that the setting, stories, and structure of DBH offer a unique, interactive pop culture experience that prompts players to think carefully about who is responsible, who is considerable, and what it means to do the right thing. Through this process, the game presents an antispeciesist conception of moral patiency and suggests that developing the autonomy and reflection necessary for true personhood and moral responsibility requires suffering and struggle.

Summary and Overview of the Game

DBH is a Sony Playstation and PC adventure game released in 2018 by Quantic Dream, a studio known for creating gripping narrative games. The game takes place on Earth in 2038 and follows the stories of three playable characters, Connor, Markus, and Kara, who are advanced androids. In this world, androids are visually indistinguishable from humans and replace humans in many menial and/or caretaking positions such as store clerks, nurses, babysitters, and more. These intelligent machines presumably do not feel pain and are bound to obey the commands of their human owners, no matter how menial or potentially self-destructive to the android a command may be.

DBH contains readable, in-game newspapers or magazines that offer perspective into the larger world of the characters. News articles recount occurrences like android astronauts exploring Jupiter's moon Io for NASA or Canada voting against the use of androids. Further glimpses into the generally negative attitudes toward androids in this world are provided by walking past an anti-android protest, the participants of which cite them stealing jobs as a primary reason for hating them. Players also catch glimpses of the attitudes of some android owners and service workers who say things like "don't leave that here" (indicating the android is an "it" rather than a person) and signage outside particular locations articulating "No androids allowed." The general attitude toward androids in this world ranges from resigned acceptance to outright hatred as indicated by various NPCs discriminatory language and rough treatment toward androids.

DBH contains 32 "chapters" of gameplay, defined here as discrete playable scenes, each ending in a flowchart depicting the player's chosen narrative path as well as the paths that they did not choose – which will play an important role in the opportunities for moral reasoning offered by the game. To explore these scenes, players take turns between the perspectives of Connor, Markus, and Kara to interact with the visually realistic game world via an over the shoulder, third person perspective. This means the player views the game world from behind and slightly above the character they are controlling, allowing players both a perspectival field of view and the ability to cinematically witness their character within the game environment.

A key plot point in the game is the existence of "deviants" or androids who have gained their own consciousness and thereby have the free will to act against their programmed commands. Connor is the most advanced android in existence, though he is still under the control of his programming (until a possibility to overcome his programming in a scenario very late in gameplay) and is hired by the Detroit City Police Department to help track down and capture these rogue, conscious androids. These deviants often commit crimes as part of their escape or afterward in an effort to survive a world that is generally hostile to their kind. In Connor's first scene, there is real possibility for him to die and be out of play (showing the higher stakes introduced in the game), but when he lives, his plotline revolves around being partnered with an android-hating detective named Hank. The two work together to apprehend deviant androids and solve the larger mystery of why so many are gaining consciousness.

Kara is a housemaid android charged with taking care of the home and child (named Alice) of an alcoholic and abusive man named Todd Williams. Early in her story arc, players witness Todd belligerently threatening his daughter, and the player, as Kara, must make a choice about whether to obey his command and not interfere or to rescue Alice and run away with her to safety. So long as Kara survives this encounter (with or without succeeding in saving Alice), the rest of her gameplay focuses on trying to flee the country to Canada. During the abusive scene, players have the opportunity for Kara to deviate from her programming and gain consciousness and freedom.

Markus is a domestic android who primarily cares for an aging famous painter named Carl Manfred by helping him around and doing tasks and chores for him. In Markus's fourth chapter, Carl's estranged son, Leo, gets into a confrontation with Carl that results in either Markus injuring Leo as he defends Carl or Markus being blamed for Carl's unexpected death. Markus is dismantled and must rebuild himself to fulfill the rest of his journey, becoming free in the process to lead the android revolution that would seek equal rights between androids and humans. Markus could be understood as the main character since his storyline is the only one that cannot be ended within the first three chapters. The stories of the three protagonists are distinct from one another and offer players glimpses into the lived experiences of several different living contexts for androids. Players have opportunities for the three characters to cross paths with one another and interact with each other at various moments in their plot lines. This becomes particularly important since Connor is on the oppositional side of the android revolution compared to Markus and Kara.

Typical to the interactive drama genre, gameplay experiences largely consist of exploring settings, interacting with NPCs through dialogue options, and solving problems or mysteries. Timed button sequences and cut scenes fill out the game with the context for the players to react to and operate within. In this game, choices and actions, even seemingly insignificant ones, can have a substantial impact on the outcomes both within a discrete chapter and also lasting throughout the duration of the story. The game boasts more than 85 different endings where various playable and NPCs live or die according to choices the player makes. Unlike some other interactive fiction games like the *Mass Effect* series or some Telltale games which contain fewer truly impactful decisions, even minor decisions in DBH can lead to drastically different outcomes. Since there are three protagonists who all have multiple opportunities to make narrative progress or die, it is possible to play through the game with only Markus's story because Connor and Kara died in their first and third chapters, respectively. These radically different outcomes contribute to making the exploratory potentials of this game for philosophical ideas so worthwhile. When characters whose stories we become familiar with can actually die (and not be immediately reborn Mario-style) and leave the game, choices made in the game have an additional level of seriousness to them. This can prompt a reflection on one's choices and actions as well as reflection upon how the characters are treated. With these possibilities, the point that there is a lot at stake when navigating the moral realm is clearer.

Moral Reasoning

There are many philosophical themes present in DBH, but one that stands out as a staple of the stories told and the options presented to players is the process of moral reasoning. DBH explores moral reasoning from the viewpoint of the characters in the game as well as offering unique possibilities for the moral reasoning process in the player. Moral reasoning contains at least three components: a *moral agent* making the moral decisions, a *moral framework* or set of values for judging the right thing to do, and a conception of *moral patiency*, or who or what should be morally considered in judgments. As we will see, through gameplay, DBH suggests the androids should be morally considerable and (implicitly) argues that reflection on one's actions and desires is necessary for autonomy and moral agency.

While there are competing accounts of the requirements for moral agency, philosophers seem to generally agree that to be held morally responsible, persons must have had some control over their behavior, be capable of acting with intention, and be capable of rational reflection on their actions. Some accounts of moral agency require that in order to be held responsible for a decision, the decision-maker must have had the opportunity to do otherwise. This means that there were multiple possibilities for action, and the agent chose from among them. For example, while we may morally blame a drone operator who presses a button releasing hellfire missiles on a village, we would not blame the drone itself. This is because the drone itself is not a decision-maker; it merely obeyed its programming and did what it was programmed to do. It could not have done otherwise; therefore, we do not judge the action of a drone. Further, the drone is incapable of having desires or reflecting on them.

A firm proponent of the "could have done otherwise" account comes from classic moral philosopher Immanuel Kant. Kant argues that in order to be held responsible for our actions, we must be truly free, meaning at the time of our actions, we had the genuine possibility of doing otherwise. Kant argues that what matters is whether our actions are under our control *now*. While Kant acknowledges that the causal laws of nature seem to indicate our actions are predetermined (by genetics, social conditioning, and physical causality), he posits the existence of a "noumenal self," or, a self that exists outside the traditional causal laws of time and space. The noumenal self exists at the level of the Kantian "thing in itself," meaning the world as it is before it is processed by the categories of our human intellect (space, time, and causality). This higher self is not subject to the causal laws of nature and thus always has control of its reasoning and behavior (Kant, 1998, pp. 539–543). If this seems a bit ambiguous, it is because it is. We are ultimately incapable of comprehending the higher noumenal self through our intellect, so it leaves a mystery at the heart of Kant's account of agency.

This is partially because the compatibility of genuine human freedom with a purely causal determinism is not an easily solvable philosophical problem.

Not everyone is convinced by Kant's mysterious metaphysical noumenal self and some argue that it introduces far more questions than it answers. If the noumenal self exists outside the causal world of nature, it seems at the very least ambiguous how a self with no physical properties could interact with the moral realm, which exists in the physical realm. Similar problems arise for accounts of "soul" that argue the soul is purely nonphysical, with no extension or mass that could produce a causal effect on the physical world. Additionally, it seems that time and space are key components to the moral realm and all of our moral decisions are implicated in the traditional dimensions of space-time.

Harry Frankfurt avoids these difficulties by arguing that the key requirement for moral agency and responsibility is not the genuine metaphysical possibility of doing otherwise, but whether someone *acts in accordance with their desires.* In order to show that moral responsibility is possible even if scientific determinism is true, Frankfurt argued that all that is required for moral agency is that the actor is acting in a way that they *want to.* Frankfurt appeals to common sense examples such as the difference between self-defense and murder. We generally do not consider killing in genuine self-defense wrong, because while the agent may have killed someone, they did not do it because they wanted to, they did it because they *had to.* A husband who kills his cheating wife, on the contrary, does not do it because he had to, but does it in accordance with his *own desires.* Frankfurt argues that the key moral question is only whether a person is capable of reasoning morally and is acting according to their own will rather than out of coercion (Frankfurt, 1969, pp. 830–831).

A key part of Frankfurt's argument for moral agency comes with his distinction between *wantons* and *persons.* Only persons, in Frankfurt's view, can be truly free. Persons, unlike wantons, can have second-order desires. A first-order desire is simply to want something: for example, I want to eat ice cream for breakfast. A second-order desire is a desire about a desire. Frankfurt says someone has a second-order desire when "[H]e wants simply to have a certain desire or when he wants another desire to be his will" (Frankfurt, 1971, p. 10). In other words, I can reflect on my desire to eat ice cream for breakfast and wish that I desired something differently. I can override my desire and choose something healthier, based on my ability to reflect on my own desires. An implication of Frankfurt's view is that people who are unable to overcome their first-order desires, such as addicts or kleptomaniacs, cannot be considered free. If addictions or phobias prevent a person from truly being able to override a first-order desire based on a second-order desire, that person is not truly free.

Someone who has all of their desires programmed and is incapable of reflecting on them or overriding them is not truly free and would meet Frankfurt's definition of a wanton. A wanton cannot be considered a true moral agent, because they do not have the ability to want anything else. Frankfurt says of wantons, "His desires move him to do certain things, without it being true of him either that he wants to be moved by those desires or that he prefers to be moved by other desires" (Frankfurt, 1971, p. 11). In order for genuine moral responsibility in Frankfurt's view, the agent must have the ability to have wanted something different, to reflect on the desires they have and potentially change them. People who truly do not have the ability to act on their second-order desires, because of addiction, phobias, etc., would not be considered free and responsible. Similarly, the androids who act only according to their programming in DBH can be considered wantons, while those who reach consciousness and can reflect on their programming would be considered persons, and thus, moral agents.

In both accounts of moral agency, the intentions must emerge from agents themselves. Thus, a programmed android that does not have any of its own formulated desires, or can make only automated decisions, would not be considered a moral agent. We would not blame androids for acting the way they were programmed to act, just like we would not blame the drone itself for dropping the missiles. We introduce moral blame when we judge that agents act of their own accord, and should be held responsible for doing so, either because they had the genuine metaphysical possibility of doing otherwise (Kant) *or* were capable of formulating, reflecting, and acting upon their own desires (Frankurt).

A truly autonomous choice emerges from the desires of the agent – the agent's decision is *self-caused.* This means the agent is not reacting, or acting as an effect, but making a choice that emerges from the agent's own decision-making process. Some have even argued that many people never reach this true state of autonomous decision-making and are content more or less to be told what to do, or to let others shape their intentions and desires. Becoming truly autonomous is a state of higher order reasoning, a capacity to direct one's behavior based on one's own chosen values, rather than on programming. While the androids are programmed by their designers, most people are programmed by our parents, our peers, and society. The truly autonomous person is able and willing to make choices that go against their social programming, to reflect on and potentially change their own desires.

The second key component to the moral reasoning process is theories or frameworks for supporting moral judgments. Four common frameworks are Kantianism, which focuses on universalizability and inherent respect for the individual person; utilitarianism, which focuses on consequences and the production of maximum welfare for all those involved; virtue ethics, which focuses on the development of desirable character traits in the individual; and care ethics, which focuses on the fostering of caring relationships.

Kantianism is guided by two key imperatives: to act only in a way that you can will something to be a universal law and to not treat any person as means only, but always as an end in themselves. Kant argues that what distinguishes human beings as human beings is our capacity to reason. It is reason, then – not empirical observation – that should guide our moral deliberations. To reason morally, an agent must ask two questions: Can I reasonably will that everyone act this way? And am I treating anyone as a means only, rather than as a decision-maker who deserves respect? (Kant, 1997, pp. 31, 38). Suppose a businesswoman was considering not honoring her contract with her supplier. Kant would say she must ask if she could rationally want everyone to act in the same way. Would a rational person endorse the maxim "Do not honor your business contracts"? Kant thinks they would not, as that would make the contracts meaningless. The whole point of having a business contract is that you should honor them. If everyone failed to honor their agreements in a contract, there would be no point of entering into them, as they would be self-defeating. Thus, if a person defaults on a contract, she is making an exception for herself that she would not make for others. Additionally, considering Kant's second imperative, failing to honor her contract with her supplier would constitute treating the supplier as a means only: Assuming he held up his end of the contract, defaulting on their agreement is treating him like an object or means to her own ends, rather than respecting him as a person who entered into an agreement with her.

A second common theory for helping guide moral decision-making is utilitarianism or consequentialism. Unlike Kantianism that bases morality on reason, utilitarianism bases it on the consequences produced by an action or rule. For utilitarianism, whether an action is rationally universalizable is not what's important, all that is important is whether the action produces more welfare or harm for everyone affected, with everyone's interests counting equally (Mill, 2001, p. 53). In terms of the businesswoman's decision about whether to honor her contract with her supplier, she would ask whether honoring the contract would produce more positive or negative consequences for all considered. She would have to consider the harms caused to the supplier as well as potential repercussions for her own business if it gains a reputation for not honoring her contracts. She must consider the welfare of her own employees as well as the welfare of the supplier's employees. For utilitarianism, it is important that no one's interests count more than anyone else's.

The third common framework for evaluating moral decisions is virtue ethics, which was founded by Aristotle. Virtue theory focuses on each person's moral character rather than the evaluation of individual actions. Virtue theory thus focuses on the habitual development of desirable character traits. For example, loyalty, honesty, patience, generosity, and courage are considered desirable states of character. Aristotle argued that developing virtuous character traits is a matter of finding a balance between excess and deficiency. Persons could be overly honest, for example, if they spoke the truth when unnecessary or in a time that it could bring great harm (Aristotle, 1999, pp. 20–33). They could also be deficient in honesty if they deceived a friend or cheated in class. Hitting the right balance between excess and deficiency through habituation is a matter of finding the golden mean, or middle point. In the case of the businesswoman's decision, the businesswoman would ask what an honest and just person would do. She would likely conclude that the virtuous thing to do in this case would be to honor the contract. Failing to do so would not meet the right balance for the golden means of being just and honest. Rather than looking at the honoring of contracts in isolation, virtue ethics evaluates the character traits of a person who would fail to uphold them. Thus, the question is not "is honoring business contracts right or wrong?" Rather, it is "Would an honest and just person uphold their business contracts?"

A fourth framework that has been introduced in the past half century is care ethics, which was founded by Carol Gilligan. Care ethics focuses on elements of moral reasoning that were neglected historically, partially because they are moral reasoning traits more likely to be associated with women. Care ethics grounds moral reasoning in the fundamental human concept of taking care of one another. It focuses on relationships, especially relationships of interdependency between people that are close to us. Care ethics takes the natural care-taking of children, the elderly, etc., and argues that we all have a basic human need to care for each other. Asking what kind of care the relationships in our lives require is part of living a moral life. For example, from a care ethics perspective, someone who follows Kantian universals about not lying or not stealing or seeks the utilitarian goal of ensuring their actions result in the greatest good for the greatest number, would still be failing morally if they were cold and uncaring to the people around them, especially those who are closest to them in their lives. Further, care ethics argues that empathy and sympathy are key components of the moral realm and should influence our moral decision-making. While care ethics lacks the rigorous structure of some of the other theories, it adds an important and arguably often-overlooked dimension to ethics and emphasizes that fostering caring relationships is part of living a moral life (Gilligan, 1982).

The last key component to the moral reasoning process to be explored are debates about moral patiency, that is to say, who or what should be morally considerable. There are scenarios in the game in which the player is prompted to consider whether the androids are morally considerable, that is, whether we should be concerned for their well-being. The question of moral patiency has been answered in many ways throughout the history of philosophy. Philosophers have used criteria such as human DNA, rationality, and sentience, to argue for who or what should count in our moral deliberations.

The most common argument for moral considerability made among ordinary people is that one must be a member of the species *Homo sapiens* in order to be morally considerable. The basic idea is that morality is a human construct, and thus, only other human beings are owed moral treatment. Anthropocentric accounts are often rooted in religious beliefs that human beings are specially made in the image of a deity and thus are superior to other species. In this framework, being a member of the species *Homo sapiens* is both necessary and sufficient for possessing moral status. This means all humans: Fetuses, infants, children, adults, the cognitively disabled, the elderly, the comatose, etc., are morally considerable. Notice, however, who is *not* morally considerable: nonhuman animals, plants, and artificial intelligence such as androids (Beauchamp and Childress, 2013, pp. 65–69).

Those who support anthropocentric accounts will often argue that it is inclusive and protects all humans. But critics argue that it is unnecessarily exclusive: Why, for example, should infants or severely cognitively disabled humans be morally considerable, but highly intelligent mammals such as chimpanzees or dolphins are not? Philosophers such as Peter Singer have argued that is nothing short of discrimination to exclude certain beings from the moral realm based on the species to which they belong. Singer calls this speciesism and compares it to racism or sexism: While racism and sexism focus on giving unjustified preference to one sex or race, speciesism involves giving unjustified preference to members of our own species. Singer thinks anthropocentric accounts of moral patiency are, thus, woefully inadequate (Singer, 1975, pp. 1–23). Another problem with anthropocentric accounts of moral patiency is that they do not seem to be grounded in any morally relevant characteristic. Why is human DNA a necessary and sufficient condition for moral patiency? What is the relevance of species alone for how one should be treated? Many philosophers argue that unless we accept a faith-based religious account in which human beings are special because we are made in the image of a higher power, there seems to be no good reason to limit moral treatment to human beings alone.

Kant argued that it is not the possession of human DNA that is important, but the possession of *rationality*. Kant argues that the ability to reason morally and make moral decisions is necessary for you being worthy of moral treatment. Morality in this framework is a contract between rational agents. For Kant, any being that can make decisions has a special dignity and is owed respect. They are not things or objects, but decision makers, and thus, it is wrong for us to treat them like objects (Kant, 1997, p. 38). Kant's framework includes all rational human beings, but also leaves moral status available to rational aliens who could visit us and to artificial intelligence as well. For the androids who have been awakened to consciousness and are able to make decisions based on their own volition, it would be equally wrong to treat them as a means only as it would be to treat a human who can make decisions.

But Kant's criteria also possess serious shortcomings. In particular, it has been argued that Kant's criteria are *too* exclusive. Infants, toddlers, the intellectually disabled, those with dementia, and other human beings who are not rational decision makers are excluded from his framework. Additionally, *all* living things or systems that do not possess rationality would be excluded. The androids who have not reached consciousness would also be excluded from moral consideration, as they would be seen as mere objects or tools. While Kant's approach to moral patiency seems to solve some of the problems of the anthropocentric account, it also seems to introduce substantial new problems as well (Beauchamp and Childress, 2013, pp. 72–73).

Another approach to moral patiency is based on sentience. Let us return to Peter Singer. Singer argues that it is not the possession of human DNA that is important nor the possession of rationality, but having interests and the capacity to suffer. Singer argues that all beings that have the capacity to suffer have interests, and if a being can suffer, there is no good reason not to take that being's suffering into account. Different beings with different cognitive capacities will obviously experience different types of suffering. For example, the suffering of a human child is certainly different from the potential suffering of a lobster, but Singer does not think we have good reason to not consider the ways a lobster could suffer. If a being has the capacity to suffer, it has interests, and disregarding those interests for no good reason is a form of discrimination (Singer, 1975, pp. 8–9). In Singer's framework, if the androids can suffer, there is no good reason for not taking their suffering into account. While the androids supposedly cannot feel physical pain, they appear capable of mental and emotional pain, such as sadness and fear, and thus have the capacity to suffer. Under this account, all androids, those who are awakened and those who are not, would still be morally considerable.

While this overview of moral agency, moral theories, and moral patiency cannot do full justice to the entire scope of philosophy and process of moral reasoning, it is sufficient for understanding some of the key themes in DBH, both in terms of the scenarios and stories told in the game, as well as the moral reasoning options for the player that are presented through game play.

Analysis: *Detroit Become Human* and What We Owe to Androids

DBH presents the player with a vivid, interactive experience of intelligent androids who exist to serve the interests of humans and can be bought and sold as household workers. Throughout the stories and outcomes in the game, themes of moral agency, moral justification, and moral patiency emerge.

The theme of moral agency is most dramatically explored through the possibility of the androids gaining true consciousness, or the ability to stray from their given programming. We saw above that accounts of moral agency require, at minimum, the ability to reflect on our desires and potential to choose from alternative paths. Competing accounts require that the actor has the genuine metaphysical possibility of doing otherwise. According to both mainstream accounts of moral agency, the androids who have not reached consciousness act only according to their programming and cannot be considered free, nor are they capable of reflection on their programming, and thus cannot be considered moral agents. This would be true only of the deviants who are able to stray from their programming. The game's narrative eventually explains that some androids have a unique software mutation that allows them to overwhelm their programmed instructions. Throughout the stories of Kara, Connor, and Markus, in moments of self-preservation or protection of their charges, players are given the option to go against the android characters' respective programming. Importantly, players are in no way systematically obligated to resist their programming. Players are fully free to obey the androids' owners' given orders and face the consequences of these choices. When the initial choice to deviate from their human owner and/or innate programming is presented, it is distinguished as such in a dramatic interactive scene. The process of deviating from programmed instructions is visually and haptically represented by asking the player to hit a button on the controller repeatedly in order to break through a transparent visual barrier, representing the achievement of free will.

The idea here is that some sort of struggle and overcoming is a key part of choice-making and the emergence of true autonomy: It is in moments of fear and desire to save oneself or those they care about that the androids develop the ability to question and reflect on how they have been programmed. Without the sense of urgency bestowed upon them by self-preservation, the androids remain at the level of a Frankfurtian wanton. It is by being forced to consider the possibility of nonexistence or harm to those they are charged to care for that they are capable of making a true choice, of rising to the level of a person. This is because it is in decisions with high stakes in which we are forced to find the strength and reflection inside ourselves to make a self-directed decision.

For example, in an early Markus scene, he observes as his owner (Carl) is threatened by Carl's son Leo. Depending on what choices are made (intervening or not), Markus ends up either attacking Leo or, if the player chooses not to intervene, being blamed for Carl's death at Leo's hands. Markus is then apprehended by the law and dismantled before being deposited into what is presumably a junkyard for broken and decommissioned androids. Markus, not quite "dead" yet, runs a diagnostic on himself and identifies that parts of himself are missing or broken beyond repair: his legs, his right eye, his audio processor, and a thirium pump regulator (a part of his "heart"). While searching among the bodies of other androids for compatible replacement parts, Markus is faced with two androids who are not yet dead. One of them grabs him and tells him to find a place called Jericho, a refuge for deviants. This becomes Markus's objective once he leaves the landfill. However, before that happens he attempts to grab a pump regulator from a presumably dead android before she opens her eyes and starts begging for her life. The player is then faced with sparing her life or killing her so that Markus might replace his broken pump. Through this scenario, Markus not only goes through a process of suffering that allows him to begin to reach consciousness, but he also becomes capable of second-order desires for the first time. Markus has a clearly moral choice to make in the scene: He can choose his own self-interest, and perhaps the utilitarian greater good, by taking the pump from the android; however, he is also prompted to reflect on the suffering of the android and whether that suffering should overrule his own desires. Markus begins the true moral reasoning process for the first time – he not only has a desire to survive but must weigh his desire to survive against other moral concerns. Later, when Markus reaches Jericho, the underground city composed of deviant androids, he says "There's something inside me that knows I'm more than what they say. I am alive, and they're not going to take that from me anymore...we are people. We are alive. We are free." In this quote, Markus identifies some innate feeling of individual personhood, one quality of which, we argue, is illustrated as necessary for achieving true agency.

Regarding suffering, there is a parallel process to the development of true agency in human beings. Most of us assume we have free will by default, but a closer examination reveals that we generally act according to our programming as well. Especially if it serves them, children will act in ways directed by their genetics and social conditioning. It is only through the difficult process and suffering of adolescence and adulthood, of realizing the world is not as simple as it seemed, that we gain the ability to truly reflect on the origins of our social conditioning, beliefs, and desires. Often people who have not experienced much suffering or struggle lack a robust sense of self-determination and are content to follow social conventions and norms. The process of true suffering prompts reflection in the agent, forcing them to question their own beliefs, as well as cultural and social norms and institutions. While humans obviously believe themselves superior to and "more free" than androids, the possibility of true autonomy and moral agency emerges through a similar process. It is only when one has been able to consciously reflect on their first-order desires as well as the world around them that they develop a strong sense of self-determination and freedom.

But when the androids become conscious, and thus Frankfurtian persons, they also become responsible. Consciousness comes not only with opportunity, but with a responsibility for one's behavior. This is reflected in the game through the moral dilemmas presented to the playable conscious androids. Once the androids are free, they have the possibility (and burden) of moral reasoning and choice. They can no longer fall back on their programming as an excuse. For example, Kara is held captive in an attempt to wipe her memory, erase her consciousness, and resell her. In this scenario, she must navigate a large house in order to rescue Alice and escape. She finds other androids that the homeowner had been experimenting on and the player is given the choice to free them. The player is operating as a conscious being with moral obligations who should feel responsible for freeing the androids or not. In another scenario, Kara has the choice to "kill" an android she finds upstairs in an abandoned building after the android says things that lead the player to believe he might expose her location to the police. The player is forced to make a moral decision on Kara's behalf: Should she uphold the Kantian universal of not killing? Does the Kantian universal of not killing apply since the other android is not conscious? Remember, Kantian ethics says one is morally considerable only if they are rational. Should she make the utilitarian choice of killing one android to potentially free others and save Alice, thus producing more happiness and welfare overall? What would the virtuous thing be? Does it meet the golden means of justice, bravery, and loyalty to kill one of her own kind in order to save Alice and facilitate her own escape? These implicit moral questions are relevant because the character (Kara) has achieved moral agency and is responsible for their actions. The game typically does not give explicit feedback on the moral goodness of any decisions (there is nothing like a morality meter except for in one specific scene described in the next paragraph) and there are usually multiple options available in morally ambiguous situations that players must navigate without knowing the outcomes beforehand.

Markus also has to navigate moral decisions when deciding what kind of revolution the androids will wage. When sending a message by taking over Capitol Park as a form of protest, the question is posed whether the revolution should be violent. Again, there is a tension between Kantian and utilitarian principles. Can you universalize the loss of lives? Would the potential loss of life be justified on utilitarian grounds by an appeal to the greater good: A world in which androids are free? In a rare moment for the game, the player is given immediate visual and textual feedback after certain decisions about the protest are made. As players choose to either tag with graffiti or destroy particular structures and objects in the park, the player is given a heads-up display indicating the percentage of violent or pacifist actions they have used during this scene. Although there is no morality information given to the player other than a running percentage of violent/pacifist actions taken, the player is given this information as an opportunity to question the role of violence in producing a potentially better society and consider how this could be justified. Virtue theory seems particularly relevant here. If some violence is inevitable, what is the most appropriate use of force? What is the golden mean? It seems never resorting to violence under any circumstances would be the deficiency – in cases of self-defense or potential conflicts, violence may be necessary. But gratuitous use of force, as well as taking pleasure in the use of force and harm, would constitute the vice of excess. The virtuous person would consider the right amount of force, in the right circumstances, in the right way, at the right time.

In a vivid visual scenario that exemplifies multiple dimensions of DBH's philosophical implications, Markus gives a revolutionary speech to a crowd of free androids and then looks down at his hands. If Markus has killed anyone during that chapter, he will have blood on his hands, an amount relative to the number of "kills" he committed. This stunning visualization exemplifies that Markus is indeed a moral agent capable of reflecting on the blood on his hands, the end result of actions used to achieve his goals. He not only has the desire to lead and win the revolution, but also has the ability to reflect on his desires and his behavior, making him a Frankfurtian person instead of a wanton.

The scene has the potential to cause players to reflect on their own role in those decisions. First, the inclusion of a narrative moment of pause where players watch Markus look at the bloodiness (or not) of his hands is meaningful. Blood on the hands is a common metaphorical saying to indicate responsibility or fault and here the game makes this literal. If players choose to replay the level committing more or fewer murders, they may be able to further recognize the powerful visual rhetoric taking place. And if they have the acumen, players may consider the following: Does the end result of the revolution justify the blood on Markus' hands? Could the same result have been achieved with fewer deaths? While the android revolution overall seems to be driven by utilitarian aims, this scene suggests that end results are not all that matter morally. The blood on Markus' hands suggests that the means we take to achieve a goal are also morally important. It is possible for a player to navigate the game without becoming this intellectually involved or thinking too deeply. However, players who are drawn to this type of emotionally complex gameplay with investment in the feelings/perceptions of the characters will be more likely to use this opportunity for moral reflection. This represents a way in which DBH engages (or distinctively stimulates) the philosophical process.

The third component of moral reasoning, the question of moral patiency, is displayed consistently throughout the chapters. The key question is: Are the androids moral patients? Through the scenarios posed, the philosophical message conveyed by DBH is that we should care, morally, about what happens to the androids. This rejects an anthropocentric account of patiency in which none of the androids, conscious or not, are morally considerable because they lack membership in the species *Homo sapiens*. As Singer points out, it is discriminatory to deny moral consideration based on a morally irrelevant category like species membership. Additionally, the free androids display human properties: They look, think, act, and experience in ways extremely similar and almost identical to human beings. If the androids have human properties and experiences, it would seem they are sufficiently similar to human beings to matter morally. That is, if they have the capacity to suffer, emotionally and mentally, as scenes in the game suggest they do, then they have interests, which is evidence that they are due moral consideration. The game is thus in agreement with Singer's view that if a being has interests, there is no good reason not to take those interests into account.

This key argument is implicitly exemplified in a scene about halfway through the game. Kara eventually travels North and seeks help from Rose, a human who is sympathetic to the androids' plight and has a reputation for helping them cross the border into Canada. During this scene, a conversation between Rose and Kara is interrupted by Rose's son urging his mother to come quickly. Rose leaves and Kara can see her pull back a curtain to reveal an android couple: a visibly distressed man with a woman, eyes wide open, laying across his lap. Rose's son informs them that "she just shut down." Players then watch as the widower expresses his grief. He says: "I loved her; I loved her more than anything," as he hugs and rocks her lifeless form. The game dedicates significant time to his grief as Kara turns and sees Alice watching the scene unfold. Players then have a choice to either remove Alice from the situation or let her stay. If she stays, Alice walks up to peer into the tear-streaked face of the android man mourning his recently deceased partner. In this scene, it is clear androids possess distinctive human-like properties including very strong emotions such as love. Because androids have distinctively human characteristics, including morally relevant ones like the capacity to feel loss and grief, there seems to be no good reason for denying them moral consideration. While the game does leave the choice up to the player, the strong display of grief and emotional pain from the androids suggests we should indeed care what happens to them.

If we demand some kind of rationality as the criteria for patiency, then the free androids are morally considerable. By becoming familiar with the androids' stories, personalities, fears, and desires through the many hours of gameplay it takes to finish the game, it seems natural that players would care morally about what happens to the conscious androids, particularly as their fates are tied. If a playable character dies, there is no more gameplay with that character. Additionally, while playing as Markus, players are working toward achieving a successful android revolution. Therefore, it is understandable and expected that players become invested in the playable characters' storylines if not their feelings.

The question of the unfree androids is less obvious, however. If we are using Singer's account, we must consider that the androids, even the unawakened, can experience discomfort, fear, and pain. Although they are presumably coded not to experience physical pain, they clearly show other types of suffering, expressing sorrow, fear, guilt, and shame. Thus, if they have the capacity to suffer, even if the suffering is not like ours, then they have interests, and those interests should be taken into consideration. While the unfree androids may not have second-order desires, they still seem to have the capacity to suffer. A parallel could be drawn with some animals: While most nonhuman animals, such as cows, do not have second-order desires or the ability to reason, they still have the capacity to suffer and thus have interests. Similarly, an android that can suffer has interests.

All of the protagonist androids make personally dangerous, difficult, and/or self-sacrificing decisions to achieve their respective goals. In particular, there are multiple opportunities throughout the game for Kara or Alice (or both) to die as a result of their escape journey. Throughout the entire game, players presumably care about protecting Alice, insofar as Kara's primary drive dictates such. In one of the last chapters, players, through the eyes of Kara, discover that Alice had been an android all along. Therefore, throughout the entire journey when Alice was hungry or complained of the discomfort of being cold, she was communicating human needs. However, players never explicitly learn the consciousness status of Alice. Since we clearly have cared about Alice all along under the premise that she was human, when we realize she is an android, and we do not know whether she was truly a rational moral agent or not, players are prompted to simultaneously consider the strengths and weaknesses of different accounts of moral patiency. Further, building a connection with Alice throughout gameplay, then having it revealed that she is an android, sends the clear message that if we cannot tell the difference, there seems to be no good reason to exclude the androids from moral concern. At this point, players have been prompted to care about an android and her seemingly human experiences. Thus, DBH presents an implicit argument against both anthropocentrism and rationality accounts – players don't know if Alice is free and conscious but are still prompted to care about her interests.

In other scenarios, androids are pitted against other androids, prompting the player to question if they should care about the interests of the unawakened androids as much as they do the conscious, playable ones. For example, virtually all of Connor's play experience is focused on him being a highly intelligent, skilled, and yet unawakened android working against the deviants. Many times throughout his story, players are faced with either following his, and thereby the government's orders, or looking for ways to undermine his investigation to benefit the android liberation led by Markus. By asking players to take the perspective of both deviant and nondeviant androids, players can act as androids who "just follow orders" and as those who make choices through their own free will. This can lead to an uncomfortable choice for the player who is forced to consider who or what matters more – an awakened or unawakened android. This shows a tension between a sentience–/suffering-based account of patiency and a rationality-based account. It also poses the question if there is a moral hierarchy of interests that prioritizes those of autonomous beings. In other words, perhaps all androids are considerable, but do the interests of some androids matter more when there is conflict?

There is not necessarily a clear stand taken on this issue from the structure of the game, as players become familiar with the storylines of both free and unfree androids. A prime example of this friction occurs near the end of Connor's storyline when Hank and the Detroit City Police Department raid Jericho. In this scene, characters who players have roleplayed for the entirety of the game are now potential head-to-head opponents. Players can actively choose decisions for either character that benefits the aims of Markus or Connor since they have details about and have spent time playing through the perspectives of both. Here players are asked to weigh the moral interests of both free and unfree androids: In this scene, Connor is still unfree, working to reign in deviant androids with which most players have come to sympathize. Since players likely do sympathize with the deviant androids at this point, an implicit argument could be made that there is some preference given to the interests of rational and free beings.

A comparable tension between who or what matters more is present throughout Kara's story. Kara gains the ability to make free choices during an intense experience with Alice's abusive father, Todd. In defending Alice's interests, players are given an option to transcend Kara's programming in order to save and protect Alice. If they do not make this choice, then Todd may kill Kara, ending her storyline in the game. Thus, players who wish to continue playing Kara's storyline will be obligated to help her become free and to become a person. Through scenes involving Todd, Alice, and Kara, the player can make choices that are in the interest of Kara as well as those in the interest of Alice, but making those decisions requires an evaluation of who is more important. At this point in the gameplay, players are under the impression that Alice is a human being while Kara is a free android. Kara is clearly capable of rationality, suffering, and experiencing basic emotions, making her a person. Because she has these capacities, the gameplay prompts the user to ponder why the android's interests should be of less concern than the other characters. The only justification for giving Kara less moral consideration is that she is not human – which matters for anthropocentric accounts of patiency. The domestic violence scenario makes this moral tension explicit: When playing the game, it seems clear that we should be concerned about the welfare of the android. It is only after assuming a speciesist, discriminatory account of patiency that her interests become unimportant. Thus, DBH takes an implicit stand that speciesist accounts of moral patiency are unsatisfactory.

In another antispeciesist scene in the game, during the protest in Capitol Park, players are given the opportunity (through Markus) to choose different slogans of graffiti. One of the choices is "I think, therefore I am." This play on Descartes' assertion that he could not deny the fact that he exists as long as he is thinking suggests a comparison between androids and human beings. If both can think, then they both *are,* and what makes us assume that human consciousness or thinking warrants more moral consideration than android thinking?

We see all dimensions of moral reasoning illustrated throughout the gameplay scenarios, offering the player an exercise in the moral reasoning process, even if they may not explicitly realize all the questions implicit in each decision. DBH also offers scenarios with high stakes, because the androids can actually die in some storylines. As a video game, DBH offers an interactive experience not offered through other platforms by making the player an active participant and co-creator of the story. But DBH goes even further than other video games in key ways that make it a unique philosophical experience. It engenders moral reflection and contemplation throughout the game and makes implicit arguments regarding moral agency and moral patiency.

Moral Reasoning Through Game Play

In short, games model systems. Throughout gameplay, players get a glimpse into the way a system works: its inner processes, cause/effect relationships, and procedures. Since the player is given a semblance of control over the actions and outcomes of the story, they are asked to engage in a more interactive way than television or movies. In the game format, the experiencer is prompted to contemplate and reflect on the context in a more direct manner, since the playable characters experience the consequences of your actions. While the consequences are obviously predetermined and manmade, the dilemmas considered and the decisions made in any particular situation simulate a real-world experience of moral decision-making. Thus, while television and movies may prompt the viewer to think philosophically or ponder the moral implications of the plot, video games such as DBH force the player to actually make morally significant decisions as part of the experience. This interactive philosophical experience allows the player to see and weigh the consequences of different choices. There is a difference between game play and the real world, and one could argue that the video game characters are not "real," and thus, no actual harm comes to anyone through playing the game. However, the fact that the player is prompted to care about the various androids and their storylines and that these storylines can end by the androids "dying," this can at least simulate a process of moral reasoning in those players who genuinely engage the narrative and full dimensions of the game. While this may not necessarily mirror a direct one on one correlation with life scenarios outside the game, it offers players the possibility to practice the moral deliberation process.

At the end of each chapter, players are shown a decision tree that displays the choices they made and the consequences of those choices, including what new paths were opened and the alternative possibilities not explored. By showing players the decision tree, and therefore the way their choices had consequences that prevented and opened distinctive paths, the game offers a moment for players to reflect both on the consequences of their decisions and on the fact that there were other options that may have led to better outcomes. Reflection is identified by Nicholson as a key component in creating opportunities for players to learn from in-game experiences; he says, "reflection creates the situation where a learner can connect what happened in the game to elements in his or her own life" (2015, p. 11). Nicholson further explains that the power of these reflections is more efficacious when shared with others. The fact that DBH shows what percentage of players chose each path allows another moment for learning so that the player can think about how their choices compared to the choices of others – was it more or less commonly chosen? Choosing something less often chosen by others might cause a reflective player to consider why their choice deviated so much from the norm. This offers both the possibility of social pressure to conform more with the choices of others and the possibility of critiquing normalized ethical choices within mainstream culture. Which direction the player takes their reflection is up to them, but the tools provided by the game enable these connections to be drawn, which provides the player novel opportunity to engage the philosophical process.

The social and reflection elements that influence moral decision-making are also present in DBH during "quick-time events" in which players have a limited time frame to hit a sequence of buttons to achieve an outcome or make a choice. For example, when Connor (who does not become free in all storylines but has the possibility of becoming free in some of them late in the game) is chasing a deviant android across rooftops, there comes a moment when the deviant pushes Hank off the roof. Players, as Connor, have a very limited amount of time (around 5 seconds) to hit either the square or circle button on the PS4 controller to pursue the deviant or help Hank off the ledge respectively. If Connor chooses not to save Hank, his relationship with Hank suffers. Once certain decisions are made in the presence of companion characters like Hank or Alice, an icon in the corner of the screen indicates an increase or decrease in friendship as a result of the decision. This works to simulate the type of social pressure that can exist when we must make difficult choices that other people immediately around us or even more broadly within our culture may disagree with. There is immediate feedback about the strength or weakness of the relationship as impacted by particular decisions and actions. This brings us directly to the concerns of the care ethics framework, which argues that relationships are an important component of the moral realm. By seeing how their decisions affect their friendships with other key characters in the game, players are prompted to reflect on how decisions with moral stakes affect their relationships with those closest to them, and players are given the opportunity to reflect on how the effect on relationships should be weighed against other moral concerns.

The ability to participate in time-sensitive decision-making is a media experience unique to digitally interactive fiction such as video games. Television or movies do not allow real time input in the story and even one of video game's closest analog counterparts – choose your own adventure novels – cannot enforce a time limit on making choices for protagonists. While there will always be a gap between playing a game and making decisions in "real life," the elements of DBH's structure result in a compelling simulation of navigating a realistic moral realm. Additionally, the fact that this game *isn't* "real life" and players can see things like a decision tree or play the game multiple times offers more opportunity to practice thinking through various scenarios and their differing moral implications. While the game can never directly force the player into the process of moral reflection, the scenarios and opportunities of the game offer a rich landscape for the critically engaged player. Additionally, all available storylines make the implicit argument against antispeciesist accounts of patiency and argue that suffering and the capacity to reflect are key for developing moral agency and responsibility.

Conclusion

Through a stunningly realistic visual landscape, varied gameplay choices, a philosophically rich narrative, a range of decisions for players, and higher stakes than many games (key characters who we grow to care about can die), *Detroit Become Human* offers a unique, interactive philosophical experience. It prompts players to consider moral agency and responsibility, ethical frameworks, and ultimately grapple with who or what is worthy of moral concern. It asks questions about who is responsible and how we become responsible, as well as whose interests matter and whose interests take precedence. It poses moral dilemmas with no obvious right answer in which the players must weigh the concerns and criteria of classic moral frameworks. It implicitly argues for an account of moral agency that emerges through the possession of second-order desires and the ability of reflect on one's own view and the world itself. Because it stimulates players to care about the androids, both free and unfree, it challenges anthropocentric accounts of patiency and suggests we should care about all beings who can suffer.

By exploring the process of becoming a moral agent, as well as a range of scenarios for exercising one's moral reasoning faculties, and introducing a futuristic world that while fictional, is still realistic, DBH offers players an extraordinary moral reasoning experience. It blends the classic philosophical concerns that emerge with ever-advancing artificial intelligence with the ongoing social issues of contemporary life. Players are prompted to not only go on an intriguing narrative experience with the playable characters, but to empathize, critically reflect, and trace and critique both their decisions and their consequences. By offering the player a chance to reflect on the consequences and limitations of different paths, DBH provides opportunities to practice and develop a careful critical examination of competing moral concerns. Because of this, *Detroit Become Human* stands out as a distinctive and innovative philosophical work of contemporary pop culture, one that facilitates novel engagement in the philosophical process.

References

Aristototle. 1999. Terrence Irwin (trans.) 1999. *Nicomachean ethics,* 2nd ed. Indianapolis: Hackett.

Babij, K. 2013. The good, the bad, and the neutral: Problems with the ethical constructions of video and computer games. In *Ctrl-alt-play: Essays on control in video gaming*, ed. M. Wysocki, 158–168. Jefferson, North Carolina: McFarland. Print.

Beauchamp, Thomas, and James Childress. 2013. *The principles of biomedical ethics.* 7th ed. Oxford: Oxford University Press.

Entertainment Software Association. 2021. *Essential facts about the computer and video game industry.* https://www.theesa.com/wp-content/uploads/2021/08/2021-Essential-Facts-About-the-Video-Game-Industry-1.pdf.

Formosa, P., Ryan, M., Howarth, S., Messer, J., & McEwan, M. 2021. "Morality meters and their impacts on moral choices in videogames: A qualitative study." Games and Culture, 0.0, pp. 1–33.

Frankfurt, Harry. 1969. Alternate possibilities and moral responsibility. *Journal of Philosophy* 66 (23): 829–839.

———. 1971. Freedom of the will and the concept of a person. *Journal of Philosophy* 68 (1): 5–20.

Gee, J.P. 2003. *What video games have to teach us about learning and literacy.* Palgrave Macmillan.

Gilligan, Carol. 1982. *In a different voice: Psychological theory and women's development.* Cambridge: Harvard University Press.

Kant, Immanuel. 1997. Mary Gregor, (trans/ed.) 1997. Grounding for the metaphysics of morals. Cambridge: Cambridge University Press.

———. 1998. Paul Guyer and Allen Wood (eds.) 1998. A critique of pure reason. Cambridge: Cambridge University Press.

Mill, John Stuart. 2001. George Sher (ed.) 2001. *Utilitarianism.* Indianapolis: Hackett.

Nicholson, Scott. 2015. A recipe for meaningful gamification. In *Gamification in education and business*, 1–20. Cham: Springer.

Singer, Peter. 1975. *Animal liberation: A new ethics for our treatment of animals.* New York: New York Review.

Papers, Please as Philosophy: Playing with the Relations between Politics and Morality

81

Juliele Maria Sievers

Contents

Introduction 1834
Summarizing *Papers, Please* 1835
The Immigration Inspector: Hannah Arendt's Banality of Evil 1837
Immigrants, Citizens, and Refugees: Judith Butler's Precarious Lives 1842
Conclusion 1845
References 1846

Abstract

One of the most interesting characteristics of the *Papers, Please* game lies in the fact that it actually makes the player seriously engage in the repetitive and monotonous task of checking official documents of visa candidates. In the "glorious country of Arstotzka" – a totalitarian nation surrounded by enemies somewhere in Eastern Europe during the 1980s – the work as an immigration inspector at a border checkpoint is reduced to checking for inconsistent numbers, expiration dates, altered photos, interrogatory sheets, and then stamping "approved" or "refused" in the candidates' passports. The player's work each day earns a paycheck from which he will have to choose which household expenses he can satisfy. No matter how many tasks the player completes, the paycheck is almost never enough to cover all bills: rent, heating, food, and medicine for his son. The consequences will be devastating for the character and, in a certain manner, for the player as well. As such, *Papers, Please* provides the perfect opportunity to explore Hannah Arendt's notion of "banality of evil." In a place like Arstotzka, under the shadow of an excessively rigid rule system and

J. M. Sievers (✉)
Federal University of Alagoas, Maceió, Brazil

© Springer Nature Switzerland AG 2024
D. K. Johnson et al. (eds.), *The Palgrave Handbook of Popular Culture as Philosophy*,
https://doi.org/10.1007/978-3-031-24685-2_88

an oppressive and authoritarian form of government, where bureaucratic emptiness of everyday tasks is no longer questioned and actions become mechanical, the worker is refrained from "thinking from the standpoint of somebody else." Judith Butler's notion of "precarious lives" will also be explored and help us understand the biopolitics involved in the forms of violence against immigrants, refugees, and other individuals whose lives themselves are in constant wait for validation, in constant suspension between "approval" and "refusal."

Keywords

Papers, Please · Dystopia · Totalitarianism · Hannah Arendt · Banality of evil · Judith Butler · Precarious lives · Biopolitics

Introduction

> Beware of anything that you hear yourself saying often.
> —Susan Sontag

Papers, Please is an independent single-player video game first released in 2013, created by American game developer Lucas Pope. It presents a dystopian reality – somewhere in Eastern Europe during the Cold War – where the player is faced with the social, economic, and political abuses of a totalitarian regime that surveys and distrusts every individual's action and behavior. The player is inserted in this context into the skin of an unnamed character that performs an extremely limited and specific task: checking passports in an immigration office.

While the concept deviates from most "adventurous" or "action" gameplays, Pope experienced lots of success with the release of the game, winning many prizes and having great numbers on sales. It is actually difficult to explain the high level of engagement generated by the plot: as a player, one feels actually fully committed with such a bureaucratic undertaking: standing behind a desk doing paperwork. As many "empathy games," *Papers, Please* puts you in someone else's shoes: an immigration officer who cannot put himself in someone else's shoes – someone who must rather simply obey strict orders and work mechanically. The player accepts the immigration candidates that have all the correct papers, and denies entrance to all others, no matter how desperate they are or how legitimate their excuses might be. Not doing so will lead to different outcomes: the game has 20 different endings, according to the lines of action chosen by the player. The paradox is that, while the gamer clearly enjoys playing the game, he is left wondering whether he should ever admit *having fun* while playing it. It seems that this would be... wrong. But even if playing *Papers, Please* doesn't seem to be a "joyful" undertaking in that sense, it certainly is – I will argue here – a meaningful philosophical experience.

Summarizing *Papers, Please*

> There are no right answers to wrong questions.
> —Ursula K. Le Guin

The game takes place in the fictional dystopian country of Arstotzka, located somewhere in eastern Europe, during the 1980s. The player works in the Ministry Of Admission, as an immigration inspector at a border checkpoint, in charge of letting people cross the border into the country. Every day the candidates, whether citizens or foreigners, will form a line by the office door and wait to have their papers examined. Every day, the player will check and compare different documents, permits, visas, IDs, searching for inconsistencies, typos, expiration dates, declarations, photos, and many other details. As the days pass by, the absurdity of everyday life is expressed in the monotonous and mechanical tasks the player repeats: stamping "approved" or "refused" in people's passports, for as many times as he can, since the paycheck of the day will depend on his efficacy in diminishing the line of candidates.

However, the player gets a fine for any mistakes in the process, for every discrepancy he lets pass or any legal candidate that gets interdicted. As the game advances and gets more complex, he will eventually be facing bribes and menaces from the candidates and must choose if he will accept the promised benefits from the criminals and dissidents, and also face the terrible consequences that might come up. If the bills at the end of the day surpass the paycheck, the player will be much more tempted to change his "perfect" mechanical behavior. If not, he can keep working with strict adherence to the rules, and eventually realize, coming home one night after his shift is finished, that his young son has just died from cold, since the money was not enough for paying the heat bill.

Despite the constant messages concerning the greatness and gloriousness of Arstotzka – "Glory to Arstotzka" can be heard or read countless times during the game, – it is easy to realize that poverty and scarcity strike, and anyone should be content to simply have a job, even if the paycheck barely covers their most basic expenses. Back home, the player's family strive in hunger, sickness and cold, and wait for the money he'll bring every day. This detail builds up a constant sense of responsibility in the gamer, who is the only provider for this family in a State that will not supply for their most basic needs. Neither the well-being of the family nor their lack of elementary care seems to matter to the State: they only matter to the player, since he's the only one responsible. The pressure is overwhelming. Along all this, the work reveals the absurdity of everyday life, denouncing the repetition of meaningless gestures that don't allow the gamer's character to feel content or accomplished in his job. Actually, the monotony of the mindless gests are eventually interrupted by a bomb attack, and with the development of the plot, the player will see that he will eventually become responsible for also trying to prevent those: he now has a gun and can use it to kill the attackers. But until those sudden events happen, the work is stressful and doesn't involve creativity, only reproduction and replication of mechanical gestures. The player feels exploited, dehumanized, isolated, and the money is never enough.

In addition, there's the relationships the player engages in with the many characters that come and go. And in this totalitarian country, the oppression is visible on their faces – as is the precariousness he has witnessed every night when retuning home. But why do some of those lives seem to matter more than others? Some are just passing through, while others are seeking a better life, or even a way to survive. They have been abandoned and they are neglected. In fact, some of them would seem to be a burden on the State. Sometimes, the player might even feel like he is simply another source of their oppression. He has the power to allow them a better life, and while the player reads the papers, they stand in front of him, looking tired, a sad glance in their pixelated eyes while they wait for the final sentence only the player can deliver. "Glory to Arstotzka," say the lucky approved ones before entering the country.

In one specific event early in the game, the player meets a candidate who claims she is trying to go home to rejoin her son. She is anxious to see him after 6 years apart, but she is missing one of the papers. There, the player starts to understand the effect his decisions have on those people's lives: "Too bad... she will not pass," "Rules are rules," the player probably thinks to himself. Actually, those are the moments the player realizes that there are no moral dilemmas in his work, because he starts feeling like he doesn't really have a choice to make. He starts feeling that there is no place for empathy, compassion, or emotions: it is a simple matter of rationally manipulating paperwork. After all, the player doesn't make the rules, he only applies them. If he would care for every person here, he'll go mad. He has his own family to worry about. "Next!"

Later in the game, another woman arrives and, as she presents her papers, the player sees that she's from Kolechia – Arstotzka's worst enemy. The rules he must enforce say she must go through an x-ray inspection, simply because she's a Kolechian. She must strip naked in a small room and the player will soon receive the images of her vulnerable naked body. There's nothing wrong, no hidden weapon or bomb, no menaces. The player is sorry and disconcerted that she has to face this embarrassment, but there's nothing he can do. As players, we learn to know that the work performed here is sometimes, somehow, wrong, maybe even evil. Not the "evil" of some villain in a story, but a banal evil that one doesn't really know how to explain. After all, the player is simply following very clear orders. It's not that he starts to hate Kolechians. He's even trying to help them! The player is just a piece of the engine: he is just doing his job.

As the game gets more complex, the player gets the power to detain the candidates that don't meet the requirements. While there's no certainty about what will happen to those detained, the player receives a small bribe from his fellow officer for every refused candidate he chooses to detain (instead of letting go). Further in the game, when the player receives a key to a drawer keeping two loaded guns – one with regular bullets, the other with a tranquilizer – he realizes his decisions have become more serious. Should he aim to shoot those dissidents and criminals who are themselves trying to kill other people? After all, killing them instead of letting some innocents be killed by them seems like the right thing to do. This is when the player realizes he is no longer doing the job he was initially doing. He is no longer putting to himself the same questions and reflections he was at the beginning of the game; and he doesn't know when, at what point in the game he stopped being a bureaucrat and started being a killer.

Papers, Please cleverly finds a way to blur those lines, and in doing so, exposes how we (the gamers) might behave with some amount of power in our hands. How far into the game's plot will we go using excuses like "I did that because my family needed money" or "I was only following orders," or even "I don't make the rules, I only apply them?" We have already seen throughout history the real-world implications for these lines of reasoning. The very justifications listed above can easily connect with abominable events such as slavery, Jim Crow laws, Nazism, the Crusades, or any sort of class-based oppression. And when you are put in the position of the player, it becomes much more difficult to make the choice you always assumed you'd make, given the opportunity. The relationship between political power and morality explored in this game might show us exactly what side of history we would have found ourselves on. And that can be profoundly disturbing.

The Immigration Inspector: Hannah Arendt's Banality of Evil

> All sorrows can be borne if you put them into a story or tell a story about them.
> —Isak Dinesen

The odd feeling experienced by gamers once they get acquainted with their function and daily duties in *Papers, Please* also shows the bizarre sense hidden behind the repeated motto the player hears multiple times a day: "Glory to Arstotzka." Not an exclamation point on it. Just... period. It's as cold and strict as the weather of those days in Arstotzka. Actually, there seems to be nothing glorious about it. The first clue to this perception is the general feeling that surrounds mostly any aspect of the game: the underlying sentiment of fear. The candidates fear refusal, the player fears he won't make enough money to pay the daily bills, the people in the line at the door fear some random suicidal bomb attack, the player fears the fine he'll get if he makes any mistake because it might end up costing the lives of those he loves at home. Depending on how badly he screws things up, it could cost him his life too. So, that's the general feeling everywhere he turns: diffused, pervasive, omnipresent fear. Politically, however, fear is a valuable element in government regimes that use it as a means of control. Historically, mankind has witnessed how fear, nationalism and violence lead to the horrors of totalitarianism.

Hannah Arendt (1906–1975) was the most prominent author aiming to investigate the history behind the elements which made possible the formation of this political alignment, in a process she named the "origins" of totalitarianism. Her discussion focuses primarily on the developments of anti-Semitism in Europe in the beginnings of the twentieth century. The author pointed to the fact that the Jewish people were in a precarious position where they were never completely assimilated or integrated in terms of political rights (even for the economically privileged parcel of the Jewish population). Although the latency of anti-Semitism was present in Europe already in the end of the nineteenth century as the *Dreyfus affair* testifies, it only culminated in the full collapse of basic civil liberties of minorities later, in the genocidal politics constituting the subsequent Nazi ideology. According to Arendt, it was historically possible to notice the transition of racism as a social practice tied to colonialism toward a genocidal political ideology, where the State openly promoted practices of extermination of social minorities. The increasing racism toward Jewish people, foreigners, and others was encouraged by the scenario of the economic, political, and social damages of WWI, where the increasing inflation and unemployment rates were used to stimulate a brutal hostility toward them, openly promoting anti-Semitism as a specific political agenda, culminating in the Holocaust.

Despite tracing an historical line of thought concerning the development of the elements that marked the reinforcement of totalitarian beliefs and purposes, Hannah Arendt pointed to the fact that there were no means to "scientifically" or "theoretically" identify and classify all the motivations and reasons that led the political context and the politic agents to the rising of totalitarianism. To assume the possibility of a definition and demarcation is to assume an essentialism toward the concept of totalitarianism. According to Arendt, if we can define and fully diagnose such political extremism, it implies we have a clear means to understand and rationally explain the horrific deeds the regime promoted, so we can avoid them in the future. Arendt suggests we cannot. We have no means to completely "prevent" the reappearing of totalitarianism because we cannot fully identify its origin nor its complete features: the evil emerged and spread there as a kind of *fungus*, with no clear source or specific moment of identification, and we must remain constantly alert against it.

This is exactly where *Papers, Please* seizes the opportunity to demonstrate how diffuse our moral beliefs are when we face the fear imposed by a totalitarian country. The game explores the level of empathy and compassion the gamer feels – or does not feel – according to different cases, different situations and stories that are presented by the candidates. At the same time, the player is constantly confronted with his fear in facing the consequences of his acts, in a context full of high stakes for everybody involved.

Papers, Please is a game about normativity: about following rules but also about having authority. Those candidates following the rules should be "covered" and pass by the border with no further complications. However, that is not the case for a great part of the population, especially in the geopolitical area of eastern-Europe during the 1980s. Hannah Arendt also notices that, in the political context of the promotion of nationalism under totalitarianism, human rights – which are normally claimed to be universal – were guaranteed only to those who belonged to the State. An individual who didn't was considered "*unimportant in himself, apparently just a legal freak*" (Arendt 1962, p. 278). In that manner, citizenship was a condition to basic human rights. Arendt discussed this issue conceiving it as an enigma: the right to have rights, which should be guaranteed to any human being, but which was denied to those without a "formal" nationality. What is also noticeably clear, in this context, is the identification of those not belonging to the State as an ideological target, as the "enemy."

The verdict that the loss of civil rights implies the loss of human rights is a fundamental aspect of the game *Papers, Please*. In Arstotzka, the visa candidates who do not have a means to prove that they belong to a specific citizenship are granted no requests: they do not "exist," neither politically nor socially. Any demand, any right, must be preceded by the presentation of valid papers, and the candidate must personify the clear correlation of the trinity "State-people-territory." In the same way, the figure of an "enemy" is symbolized by the Kolechians: the members of the "rival" Kolechia must be especially checked, detained and, above all, particularly distrusted in every one of their intentions.

According to Arendt, another important feature of totalitarian regimes is the bureaucracy of the government segments that exist without communication or relation to one another: there is no clear hierarchy, but instead numerous sectors and levels of administration, completely isolated from one another, with flexible and changeable positions of power which can be altered as it might be opportune. According to her, the duplication and multiplication of offices is a fundamental tool of totalitarianism; it destroys all sense of responsibility and competence while at the same time making the power of the bureaucrat unlimited.

So, in that system, every official can achieve higher positions or status, and they do so by showing respect and providing unquestionable protection for the main leader. Consequently, acts of violence are not only tolerated but encouraged; all disagreements must be resolved by force, thus generating terror. Isolation, censorship, general distrust and the feeling of paranoia, and conspiracy mark the work relations and are extended even beyond the work frame.

> While isolation concerns only the political realm of life, loneliness concerns human life as a whole. Totalitarian government, like all tyrannies, certainly could not exist without destroying the public realm of life, that is, without destroying, by isolating men, their political capacities. But totalitarian domination as a form of government is new in that it is not content with this isolation and destroys private life as well. It bases itself on loneliness, on the experience of not belonging to the world at all, which is among the most radical and desperate experiences of man. (Arendt 1962, p. 475)

In *Papers, Please*, one can observe the same dynamics: the job is unstable, the player is constantly being watched, audited, and evaluated, and a bad performance can lead to dismissal from the job and the whole family being evicted without further notice. The player must work alone, isolated, aiming only for minor improvements in his workplace. The constant contact with people trying to bribe him, and even colleagues trying to benefit from his work, asking favors and offering obscure deals, puts him in constant alert against "enemies" and people trying to undermine his daily efforts.

According to Hannah Arendt, the element of violence is important given its close relation to responsibility: in totalitarian regimes, the individual's moral decisions are subverted, replaced by the prompt following of strict orders. Violent actions, when they are required, are not seen as individual actions; therefore no sense of moral responsibility is felt. So, an association with the regime comes with the suppression of any capability of thinking, judging, or questioning.

That is the aspect of totalitarianism explored by the game when the player gets access to a drawer that contains two types of guns: one with tranquilizers, the other with regular lethal bullets. The player is encouraged to make use of violence to prevent attacks: he gets money for every time he succeeds in preventing an attack or putting down an attacker – a terrorist. This moment is carefully explored during the plot: if the player doesn't do anything, he might see a guard putting down the attacker, but he might also see the attacker killing every guard, and eventually himself too. He sees the whole scene taking place by his window, and must decide fast: knowing that every violent action he takes will not only not be judged but actually rewarded by the government of Arstotzka which he now represents in its "full glory."

According to Arendt, the commitment to the ideology is reinforced precisely as a lack of regard for individuals is promoted. The individuals are considered superfluous in their singularity and are no longer relevant political subjects with singular identities; instead they are regarded as mere animals whose behavior must be conditioned by strict orders. Their lives are disposable and abolishable.

This is an element of totalitarianism that *Papers, Please* explores very well on different levels: narratives, complaints, and personal stories told by the candidates seem to be a great distraction from the efficacy aimed for in the player's work. There is no place for a meaningful conversation: anything which is not written down in the documents is not relevant. Questioning, if needed, must be direct and objective, and answers must be short and clear. The player must simply follow the script and pay attention to the directions. Any mistake in that sense will be punished by a citation at first, and eventually by a fine for each mistake. And the player quickly understands the destructive effect of a fine in his paycheck: every small amount will have a great impact on his savings. For this reason, there is no interest in hearing or trying to figure out the candidates' intentions and excuses: communication is limited to data processing. If the outcome is morally dubious or reprehensible, that's not the gamer's fault. After all, as he knows very well by now: he did not write the rules, he only applies them as they are.

In her book "Eichmann in Jerusalem" (1963), Arendt explores the motivations and even the psychological features of those who had the power in their hands during the Nazi regime. The author describes her impressions as she personally attended, as a journalist working for the *New Yorker* magazine, the trial of Nazi officer Adolf Eichmann, accused of war crimes and crimes against humanity. Eichmann was directly responsible for transporting prisoners to concentration camps and dealing with immigration matters. For Arendt, it was disturbing to be confronted in court with the impression that Eichmann was a "normal" individual, an average person, a simple bureaucrat, a law-abiding citizen. She was expecting to see somewhat of a horrific, diabolical monster; instead, she faced an elderly man, physically weakened by the circumstances of the trial. This was an opportunity for Arendt to investigate how totalitarianism impacted and affected the decisions of one specific individual entrusted with power.

In the game, we do not know exactly what is happening in Arstotzka. The player can read the newspaper – issued by the government – every morning before work, then he will work all day in his booth and go back home to his family. There are no friends, no social life: there's only work. He works his immediate tasks: he doesn't question why there should be a border checkpoint, armed guards everywhere, or walls around the country. The player is fully committed to his mechanical, simple, immediate tasks of stamping passports.

Hannah Arendt, when facing Eichmann's declarations about his deeds and crimes, elaborated on her famous notion of the *banality of evil*. According to her, the agents of totalitarian regimes such as the Nazi were not examples of the radical evil she described in her previous book, *The Origins of Totalitarianism* (1951), but were rather people who were "covered" by the authority of the regime, who were incapable of critical thinking, unable to understand the horrible consequences of their actions, and blind to their own responsibility. This lack of thinking and judgment, this superficial understanding of the horrors of violence, were manifestations of the "*word-and-thought-defying banality of evil*" (Arendt 1963, p. 118) promoted by totalitarian societies. The working agents of totalitarianism were, like Eichmann, deluded by the idea that they were, as he himself attested, just doing their job. This transmission of the responsibility to the system "as a whole" was used as a mechanism to erase their agency and their influence as individuals with power in their hands.

> The trouble with Eichmann was precisely that so many were like him, and that the many were neither perverted nor sadistic, that they were and still are, terribly and terrifyingly normal. From the viewpoint of our legal institutions and of our moral standards of judgment this normality was much more terrifying than all the atrocities put together for it implied – as had been said at Nuremberg over and over again by the defendants and their counsels – that this new type of criminal, who is in actual act *hostis generis humani*, commits his crime – under circumstances that make it well-nigh impossible for him to know or to feel that he is doing wrong. (Arendt 1963, p. 129)

As Arendt describes, Eichmann is somewhat a dull man, incapable of an articulated conversation, and, more important, incapable of putting himself in the place of another human being. This lack of empathy was directly related to his readiness to commit the brutal and hateful actions characteristic of the Nazi regime. The motivation for the actions Eichmann committed were always tied to his loyalty and obedience to the law, as a perfect bureaucrat. In his own perspective, he wasn't culpable of anything: he even declared he had nothing against the Jewish people.

This terrifying scenario narrated by Arendt invites us to reflect upon the human capability of doing evil actions. The point is that evil (political) actions can be performed by "normal" people, and forces us to wonder whether this kind of behavior can occur in contemporary times as well, particularly in times of political instability and crisis. According to Arendt, totalitarianism is a particularly suited political context for the emergence of those kinds of actions, for promoting the banality of evil – but so is any kind of political extremism which promotes censorship, attacks civil rights, generates a sense of fear, and disapproves of critical thinking. This is an invitation to be constantly aware of and promote humanistic values, to reinforce the value of empathy and freedom, to cultivate the development of critical thinking, and to respect difference and diversity.

Immigrants, Citizens, and Refugees: Judith Butler's Precarious Lives

> If they come for me in the morning, they will come for you in the night
> —Angela Davis

In *Papers, Please*, if we take the point of view, not of the player but instead of the candidates, other interesting philosophical issues arise. Of particular interest are those raised by Judith Butler, in her essay "Can one lead a good life in a bad life?", which is a transcription of the lecture she gave upon her winning the Adorno Prize in Frankfurt, Germany, on September 11, 2012. It invites us to wonder whether those living politically repressed and terrorized lives can pursue a moral life. How can such persons be autonomous in their decisions about how to lead their life, instead of being led by their circumstances, especially when their existence is being effaced by so many forms of exploitation and neglect? Butler recognizes this is no easy question to answer, but gives us a clue to the answer when she quotes Adorno's *Minima Moralia* (1974). "[A] wrong life cannot be lived rightly." At the same time, Butler also questions whether anyone can lead a "good" life knowing how many of their fellow human beings live in such precarious situations.

Actually, this question can be raised by any individual: how can we personally seek a good life in a world marked by inequality, poverty, and violence? And how can we do so also knowing that many aspects of what constitutes a so-called good life depend on things like the exploitation of the poor and the perpetuation of other inequalities, both social and economic?

As Butler puts it herself, "there are many different views on what 'the good life' (*das Richtige Leben*) might be" (2012, p. 9). Even if she refrains from providing a closed definition on what the "good life" might be, Butler stresses the importance of confronting the individualistic forms of moral conduct – the Aristotelian pursuit of happiness, for example – with the social and economic aspects that traverse our moral thoughts. According to her, even the most private questions like "how best should I live this life of mine" are fundamentally accompanied by the recognition that not all persons are able to take this kind of autonomy over their lives. Other people's lives are conditioned upon social and economic constraints – lack of freedom, extreme poverty, loss of rights and protections – which characterize those lives as "bad." Moreover, for Butler, a good life must not rely on the existence of bad lives: it cannot depend on them or be caused by them. She says:

> When Adorno queries whether it is possible to lead a good life in a bad life, he is asking about the relation of moral conduct to social conditions, but more broadly about the relation of morality to social theory; indeed, he is also asking how the broader operations of power

and domination enter into, or disrupt, our individual reflections on how best to live. (Butler 2012, p. 9)

In *Papers, Please*, the player is confronted with a plurality of different forms of life, which are presented by means of short descriptions: nationality, work, some physical characteristics, and not much else. Their existence is defined and determined based on limited qualifications which the player operates according to his function. But he can still compare, evaluate, and quickly understand how politics operate in the determination of the value of the individual's lives: the difference of treatment the player performs is determined by rules arbitrarily posited by the authoritative government of Arstotzka. For example, at some point, it is only the Kolechians who have to be stripped naked in a private X-ray room, and have their bodies uncovered to the eyes of a stranger, because those specific individuals coming from there are portrayed as the enemy, and that is all they are.

That capability of politics to organize individuals' lives in that manner, imposing different treatments, constraints, and intimidations by acts of power actually determines, according to Butler, the value of the lives involved, performing differentiations among them. This political administration of human life is an expression of the notion of *biopower*, proposed by French philosopher Michel Foucault, where the State promotes "an explosion of numerous and diverse techniques for achieving the subjugations of bodies and the control of populations" (1976, p. 140). Judith Butler explores this aspect of the biopower and biopolitics and proposes another criterion for evaluating those lives: grief. Protected lives are worthy of collective grief once they end, but those targeted lives, the precarious lives, already have the status of non-lives, of non-existence: in the game, anyone without a passport is abandoned and forgotten, already dead.

The grief addressed by Butler is not the personal grief of family and friends, but the collective grief concerning the absence of social and economic structures necessary for the maintenance and development of a life worth living, and without which life becomes precarious. If life in those terms has no worth, death becomes trivial and, consequently, is not grievable.

We can take as an example one particular aspect present in the game: the fact that one or another of the player's family members is constantly sick, because he cannot afford the payment of heating, food, or medicine all at once. That life is grievable for the family and for the player's character. But not for the government, who won't provide even the most basic means to sustain life.

In the face of that problem, the original question splits: how can a person with a non-grievable life have a good life? And how can a person with a grievable life have a good life if they know about the bad life of others? Or, as Butler puts it:

> When the life that I lead is unlivable, a rather searing paradox follows, for the question, how do I lead a good life? presumes that there are lives to be led; that is, that there are lives recognized as living and that mine is among them. (...) In other words, this life that is mine reflects back to me a problem of equality and power and, more broadly, the justice or injustice of the allocation of value. (Butler 2012, p. 11)

To Butler, being aware of the precarity of non-grievable lives demands that we condemn the mechanisms that promote such a differentiation of values. The authority and any means of power that promotes the distinctions and inequalities we are analyzing here must be objects of criticism.

In *Papers, Please*, not only immigrants, but the player himself might observe his life in the game as disposable, unprotected, and precarious. The lack of confidence in a stable future, the fear of not being able to provide the most basic needs of his family, the feeling of not being empowered to decide about his own life, are some of the many aspects of this kind of experience. If with Hannah Arendt we investigated how the political oppression of totalitarianism defined forms of life completely detached from most humanistic moral principles, with Judith Butler we recognize how social, economic, and political determinations of whose lives are valuable constitute an essential feature of current neoliberalism.

In the context of neoliberalism, Butler defends the idea that our bodies can act politically. We can use our bodies to morally react to political devaluations of lives or entire populations. In that sense, Butler defends the idea that in order to live a good life, one must show resistance to the bad life by protests and interventions, both social and collective, and also private and reflexive. Since in *Papers, Please* the political scenario is much more authoritative, words or acts of resistance cannot be freely expressed. But they exist, although in a rather concealed way, when the player is confronted with what is presented as *The Order of The Ezic Star*. There is no clear explanation of what this organization might be, except for its clear opposition to the political regime – and some aspects of the game's plot might indicate that the political beliefs of *Ezic* are not completely distant from totalitarianism itself.

So, at some point in the game, the player is "invited" to join the resistance, and the choices he makes will directly determine the way the game will end. In the game's alternative endings, depending on the player's level of commitment to *Ezic* group, several outcomes can be reached. In one outcome, for example, by collaborating with *Ezic*, he might be caught by his superiors and be sent to death penalty for treason and betrayal, and his family sent back to their village without any support whatsoever. Performing most tasks leads to an ending where *Ezic* gains power, the border is destroyed and the player becomes an official member of the order, receiving a better apartment for him and his family. But even then, the player is not free and must simply follow new orders, while declaring loyalty to "New Arstotzka." Ignoring all *Ezic* recommendations will lead to an end where Arstotzka's government praises his good work and overlooks his small transgressions. The player comes back to work under the same conditions and even unlocks the "endless mode." His obedience allows him an infinite future of loyalty to Arstotzka.

Those situations demonstrate the limitations of political mobility in Arstotzka. The signs of opposition are themselves radical and violent. In other iterations, the game ends abruptly because someone sent the player a bomb that explodes in his face. Many times during the game the workday is cut short because of a "terrorist" attempt to explode the wall. The choice of resisting the government and joining the "resistance" will imply betrayal and be susceptible to State retaliation. The choice of loyalty to the job will imply betrayal to the resistance and be susceptible to retaliation from the attackers.

Those details show how limited the forms of resistance and protesting are under a totalitarian government system. If, while Hannah Arendt spoke about the horrors of a regime that nowadays seems to us far in time, Judith Butler calls our attention to the cruel social and economic discriminations that neoliberalism promotes – the precarious lives that are invisible, invalidated, not grievable. To conform to it is to accept the cancelling of our most basic human rights, and not to conform to it must lead to resistance and to the constant defense of democracy and democratic values. As Adorno says:

> Anything that we can call morality today merges into the question of the organization of the world ... we might even say that the quest for the good life is the quest for the right form of politics, if indeed such a right form of politics lay within the realm of what can be achieved today. (Adorno 2000, p. 138)

Conclusion

> No borders, just horizons – only freedom.
> —Amelia Earhart

In this chapter, we proposed a discussion about the relations between morality and politics in the context of repressive governments. *Papers, Please* presents us with such a fruitful scenario representing these relations that many philosophical questions arise. Among them, we have chosen two to investigate more deeply: "can one regular individual – a normal citizen – entrusted with political power, perform such evil actions to the point that they become banal?" and "how can one live a good life knowing that there is a political distinction between the lives that matter and those that don't?"

Of course, gamers can finish *Papers, Please* without caring for those questions: they can enjoy detaining as many Kolechians as possible, killing as many terrorists as they are able, and being the best immigration inspector Arstotzka has ever witnessed. Such a gamer will obtain every reward possible and might experience a lot of accomplishment at every achievement they unlock. They will have played their game, and played it very well. But is playing "technically" well the best decisions one can make? In a place like Arstotzka, is there a way of being good, of leading a "good life"? At what point does the gamer stop seeing their actions as simply required of them and start seeing them as bad?

The philosophical problems we put forward here present us with those same questions. In our current political and social reality, are we playing our game well or are we playing a good game? Within our possibilities of action, what are our responsibilities given the political context we face today? Are we ready to assume any responsibilities or to present resistance when needed? We do not need to be philosophers to raise and try to answer those questions. Actually, Hannah Arendt herself denied the "title" of philosopher, because she said she was interested in simply understanding what had happened to humanity to let things like the horrors of totalitarianism she experienced in Europe happen. In her book *The Human Condition* (1958), she expresses this very well by saying: "What I propose, therefore, is very simple: it is nothing more than to think what we are doing."

That is also the important message that a game as unpretentious yet profound as *Papers, Please* delivers. When everything that is demanded from us is to perform mechanical and repetitive tasks that do not seem relevant at first glance, we should give a little thought to the true meaning of such tasks, and their influence on others – on how they might affect lives beyond mine. Judith Butler has called our attention to the real meaning of this confrontation between my life and the life of others, especially regarding the unjust distinctions and limitations that might come into sight.

Attentive thinking leads to a better comprehension of our social reality and locates ourselves outside the point of view of our personal needs and interests. To think beyond them is to be able to put ourselves in the shoes of others. Video Games like *Papers, Please* achieve that in a very effective way: we can see the world from the perspective of another person, in another country, in another time. And we can learn a lot from it – like we should have learned from our past.

References

Adorno, Theodor W. 1974. *Minima moralia: Reflections from damaged life*. London: New Left Books.
———. *Problems of moral philosophy*. Trans. Rodney Livingstone. Cambridge: Polity Press, 2000.
Arendt, Hannah. 1958. *The human condition*. Chicago: University of Chicago Press.
———. 1962. *The origins of totalitarianism*. Cleveland: The World Publishing Company.
———. 1963. *Eichmann in Jerusalem – A report on the banality of evil*. New York: The Viking Press.
Butler, Judith. 2012. Can one lead a good life in a bad life? *Radical Philosophy Archive*. https://www.radicalphilosophy.com/article/can-one-lead-a-good-life-in-a-bad-life
Foucault, Michel. 1976. *The history of sexuality*. Vol. 1. Paris: Hachette.

Planescape: Torment as Philosophy: Regret Can Change the Nature of a Man

82

Steven Gubka

Contents

Introduction	1848
Summarizing *Planescape: Torment*	1849
Ravel's Question and the Nature of Virtue	1851
Are People Irredeemably Selfish by Nature?	1854
How Does Regret Help Develop Virtue?	1857
Philosophical Challenges to Regret	1860
Conclusion: Moving Past Torment	1862
End Notes	1863
References	1864

Abstract

In *Planescape: Torment*, players assume the role of the Nameless One, an immortal being who suffers from amnesia. By making choices for the Nameless One, players decide not only what happens to the Nameless One but also the development of his moral character. In this way, *Planescape: Torment* invites its players to consider "what can change the nature of a man." In the game's canonical ending, the Nameless One regrets the great harm he inflicted on others, and he gives up his immortality to amend his wrongdoing. Thus, the game holds that it is regret that can change someone's moral character for the better. A defense of this claim about regret can be found in Aristotle's view that one must practice virtuous actions in order to develop the moral virtues. The alignment system of *Planescape: Torment* demonstrates a similar connection between action and character: the Nameless One improves his moral character by taking selfless actions. Since regret motivates one to practice virtuous action to make amends for one's wrongdoing, regret enables one to develop virtue, and so better

S. Gubka (✉)
Florida Atlantic University, Boca Raton, Florida, United States
e-mail: sgubka@fau.edu

© Springer Nature Switzerland AG 2024
D. K. Johnson et al. (eds.), *The Palgrave Handbook of Popular Culture as Philosophy*,
https://doi.org/10.1007/978-3-031-24685-2_94

moral character. Although Spinoza argues that we should avoid feeling regret because it makes us miserable, *Planescape: Torment* suggests that the painfulness of regret is what makes it an effective source of motivation to practice virtuous actions.

Keywords

Aristotle · Hobbes · Moral character · *Planescape: Torment* · Psychological Egoism · Regret · Spinoza · Virtue

Introduction

> You are nameless. You awoke on a slab in the Mortuary in Sigil, covered in scars and tattoos, your memory gone. Who has done this to you, and why? You don't know... yet. But you're going to find out.
> —Journal of the Nameless One (*Planescape: Torment*)

We strive to live without the burden of regret. We carefully choose what to do – and what not to do – to prevent ourselves from regretting our actions (or inaction) in the future. This is especially common when we deliberate about choices that substantially affect our lives, such as picking a career, starting or ending a relationship, or deciding where to live. In addition to choosing our actions carefully to avoid future regret, we also try to avoid thinking about the regrets that we already have. Regrets can feel painful in their uselessness – a deep heartache about what one did or did not do that is now too late to change. In this way, regrets are often felt to be unpleasant distractions from the present moment.

The fantasy roleplaying video game *Planescape: Torment* (PST) challenges the seeming uselessness of regret. PST takes place in Sigil, the sprawling quasimedieval city at the center of the planar multiverse, where ideological factions fight for influence.[1] The player assumes the role of the Nameless One (TNO). TNO is an immortal amnesiac on a journey to remember his past and discover why he is immortal. Unfortunately, he learns that he has done much worthy of regret. He has abused and betrayed his loyal companions for his own gain. Moreover, to sustain his immortality, others must die in his place. In the canonical version of PST's story, TNO comes to regret his actions and thereby strives to remedy the harm that he has caused.[2]

PST explicitly focuses on a philosophical question that we will examine at length: "What can change the nature of a man?" Interpreted as a work of philosophy, PST uses TNO to illustrate that regret can ultimately change one's nature or lead to moral improvement. This path to moral improvement requires that one feel regret to the right extent – not feeling too regretful or not feeling regretful enough – about one's misdeeds, which motivates one to address the harm caused by one's actions. To that end, one ought to embrace their regrets as potential sources of moral improvement, as painful as that may be.

Along the way, we will see that PST's approach to moral character and moral improvement broadly resembles the ethical framework of the ancient Greek philosopher Aristotle. PST uses an alignment system to describe someone's moral outlook, which can change for the better or worse depending on whether one performs moral or immoral actions. Similarly, Aristotle's virtue ethics conceives of positive character traits as virtues, and he advises us to practice virtuous action in order to develop virtuous character. Despite this support from Aristotle, PST also faces difficult challenges to its view: How does regret motivate us to address our misdeeds? And is regret a worthwhile way to pursue moral improvement given its painfulness? In response, PST demonstrates that the very painfulness of regret makes regret conducive to moral improvement: PST's story concerns suffering as much as it concerns redemption.

Summarizing *Planescape: Torment*

> I know you feel like you've been drinking a few kegs of Styx wash, but you need to CENTER yourself. Among your possessions is a journal that'll shed some light on the dark of the matter. Pharod can fill you in on the rest of the chant, if he's not in the dead-book already... Don't lose the journal or we'll be up the Styx again. And whatever you do, DO NOT tell anyone WHO you are or WHAT happens to you, or they'll put you on a quick pilgrimage to the crematorium.
> —The Tattoo on the back of the Nameless One

At the beginning of PST, TNO awakens on a mortuary slab. He does not remember anything about his past, let alone how he got there. Here he meets Morte, a floating and talking skull who also wants to escape the mortuary. With Morte's assistance, TNO is able to read the tattoo on his back, and he learns of a journal that will help explain his identity. Unfortunately, this journal is nowhere to be found in the mortuary. TNO must seek out others to learn about his past. Before long, TNO discovers something unusual about himself: He is immortal and cannot be slain through ordinary injury. He was mistaken for a corpse and brought to the mortuary because he *was* dead – at least in physical appearance. Moreover, he learns that he often suffers from amnesia after such deaths, which explains his current predicament.

The player assumes the role of TNO on his journey to uncover the mysteries of his identity and immortality. The game gives the player an overhead graphical perspective of TNO and his surroundings, and they can direct TNO to travel to anywhere that they can see on their screen and interact with any displayed objects. In this way, the player can explore Sigil, the city that TNO finds himself in. People crowd the cobblestone streets of the city, and the player overhears snippets of their conversation as TNO passes by them. The city is packed also with buildings, some dilapidated, some reduced to rubble, and some under construction. The activity in the city creates a sense of urgency for the player, and TNO himself will complain if the player leaves him standing idle while everything moves around him. In these ways, Sigil feels alive and active to the player even before TNO interacts with its denizens.

The player can direct TNO to talk to displayed nonplayer characters (NPCs), which initiates a text dialogue that appears at the bottom of the screen. Most dialogues present the player with choices for how TNO responds to that NPC's words. A player that chooses wisely might find out a valuable clue or gain an ally, but a misstep may lead to hostility or combat, even from a former ally. (Short of reloading an earlier save file, there is no undoing one's choices.) The player's choices for TNO's dialogue are sometimes dependent on TNO's attributes, which the player sets at the beginning of the game. For example, if the player allocates enough points to TNO's Intelligence, TNO might have a dialogue option to solve a NPC's riddle that would have otherwise been unavailable. Similarly, if the player allocates enough points to TNO's Charisma, TNO is more likely to be able to persuade someone to let him pass peacefully through an area (otherwise he may be attacked or captured).

TNO may recruit several companions through the player's dialogue choices, each with their own reasons for joining his journey, and some of which have a history with TNO. In addition to Morte, TNO may recruit Dak'kon, who swore an oath to serve TNO at some point before the events of PST; Annah, a tiefling (a kind of human with fiendish ancestors) who falls in love with TNO; Fall-From-Grace, a succubus (a kind of demon that tempts others with sexual pleasure) who has renounced her evil nature; Ignus, a powerful Mage whom TNO tortured in a past life; and others. Each companion offers further unique dialogues that enable TNO to learn more about himself and the strange new world that he finds himself in.

Alternatively, the player can direct TNO to attack or use abilities on NPCs, which often results in a combat between TNO and that NPC. If the player does nothing when combat begins, TNO and his companions will respond with scripted actions in real time. But the player can also select TNO or one of his companions and manually choose an action for them to perform. Since the player can also pause the game and queue up their desired actions, they can engage with combat at their own pace. TNO's available actions in combat depend on his class, which the player can change during the game. For example, if he is a Fighter, he is likely to be using weapons like maces or clubs, but if he is a Mage, he is likely to be casting spells like Magic Missile instead. TNO can attempt to fight almost any NPC in the game if the player directs him to do so. Except in rare cases, the player can continue to play and finish the game even if they kill an NPC that would have otherwise been important to the story. However, TNO can also avoid most fights if the player chooses specific dialogue options, even for NPCs that are initially hostile to TNO.

The breadth of choices in dialogue and the option to avoid harming most NPCs (even hostile ones) make PST a unique roleplaying game that encourages players to think carefully about who TNO is (or who they want him to be). Does he help others freely or only if there is something in it for him? Is he honest or willing to tell lies to get what he wants? When there is a conflict, does he prefer peaceful resolutions or violent ones? As we will see, the player's choices for TNO affect his alignment, which describes what kind of person TNO is.

These choices become especially pressing as TNO begins to unravel the mysteries of his past. He learns that, during his previous lifetimes or incarnations that he cannot remember, he was cruel and selfish to others, including his loyal companions. One particularly grievous betrayal concerns TNO's former companion, Deionarra. TNO meets the ghost of Deionarra in the early stages of his journey and, although he does not recognize her, some memory of her stirs within him, and Deionarra gives him guidance. Later, TNO learns that in a past lifetime, he used Deionarra's affection for him to manipulate her into serving his purposes. He allowed Deionarra to die horribly and alone, foreseeing that her soul would linger because of her love for him, and thereby act as a guide for him in the future.

TNO also learns more about how and why he became immortal. At some point in the past, TNO committed an atrocity (though the specifics are not revealed). TNO's actions meant that, if he were to die, he would be condemned to a gruesome afterlife of fighting a futile war in the Lower Planes. (Planes are distinct realms of existence, and the Lower Planes are miserable places inhabited by all manner of fiends.) Eager to escape this punishment, TNO sought out Ravel Puzzlewell, a night hag with terrifying magical power. TNO asked Ravel to make him immortal so that he would never have an afterlife. However, Ravel's magic had two unforeseen side effects. First, TNO may lose his memories when he dies. Second, Ravel's magic resurrects TNO by killing someone else on the planes each time he dies. These innocents are transformed into shadows that seek murderous vengeance against him.

In the canonical ending of PST, TNO is regretful of what he has done, and fearful of what will happen if his immortality continues. For these reasons, he travels to the Fortress of Regrets to reclaim his mortality, which has become a mysterious being known as the Transcendent One. But after all this time, TNO's reclamation of his mortality results in his true death. In the final scene of the game, hellfire engulfs TNO and he is dragged down into the Lower Planes. When TNO awakens, he sees a massive battle unfolding on a great plateau. Accepting responsibility for his actions and so his punishment here, he grabs a flail and joins the fight.

Ravel's Question and the Nature of Virtue

> The tale of Ravel Puzzlewell, frightener of children, begins and ends with a question: "What can change the nature of a man?" Many were the times she posed this riddle to those who approached her, those who sought to glean from her the strange magics that she alone seemed to possess. All attempted to answer her query, but to no avail... and they found the price of their wrong answer to be some horrible fate, always more terrible than the last victim's. To recount their various torments would be to speak of things that nightmares are woven from.
> —Yvas the Storyteller

To understand PST's position on regret, we can begin with Ravel, the night hag who helped TNO achieve immortality. During his journey, TNO hears the foregoing tale of Ravel and the question that she puts to others: What can change the nature of a man? But Ravel's question is ambiguous in various ways: What does she mean by nature? What is a man? And which changes in nature are relevant?

Ravel construes someone's nature as their character – psychological traits like being humorous, stubborn, or gentle. To truly be part of one's character, these psychological traits must be stable and help drive one's actions. Someone who is humorous does not merely make a joke now or then – they are reliably disposed to find situations amusing and joke accordingly. In support of this focus on character, consider what TNO learns from listening to the skull of someone known as Ocean-Before-the-Storm, who met a grisly death after his encounter with Ravel:

> [Ravel's question] was: How does one change the nature of a man? I thought hard on her answer, and said, "With love." She said all people love themselves too much to be changed by something as simple as love. And then she... she... I must rest now.

If love were capable of changing a person's nature, it seems that love would change someone's character for the better by making them more selfless. However, Ravel refuses the idea that love can change someone's nature. She appeals to the excessive love that people have for themselves in support of this claim. This excessive self-love is itself plausibly a character trait – perhaps a type of narcissism. This exchange makes it clear that Ravel is interested in what can change someone's character, rather than in some other understanding of someone's nature.

Furthermore, it is clear that Ravel is asking about the character of persons, regardless of their sex, gender, or species. In one philosophical sense, a *person* is just a rational agent capable of reasoning about their actions. For example, TNO's companion Morte is a person, even though he is a floating skull and not a human being. This is because Morte can reason and make decisions, though perhaps he reasons poorly when he decides to deceive and mock others. On the other hand, stones are not persons because they cannot reason, decide, or act. Because many creatures throughout the planes are persons in this sense, we can appreciate the broad relevance of Ravel's question when it is framed in this way.

Perhaps another reason why Ravel focuses on the nature of persons is that only persons have the ability to consider and act on reasons to change their nature. Arguably, such reasoning is required for an authentic change in character. If one cast an enchantment spell that compelled Morte to tell the truth, that would not count as a change in Morte's nature, since Morte does not decide for himself to perform those actions. For Morte to decide for himself would require that he consider and respond to his own reasons to tell the truth.

Moreover, we are naturally interested in learning about the character of others because a person's character influences their motivation for action. A kind person is likely to decide to help a suffering stranger just for the sake of that stranger's well-being. However, a selfish person is likely to help a suffering stranger only if their helping would benefit themselves in some way, perhaps by improving their reputation. We tend to evaluate someone's action based on their motivation for that action, often excusing actions that cause harm so long as someone acted for the right reasons. Sometimes knowledge of someone's character can help us predict their future actions. For example, a trustworthy person is likely to keep their promises.

Finally, Ravel's question is about a change of moral character for the better. Ravel's concern that people love themselves too much reveals her concern about immoral character traits like selfishness. Indeed, Ravel's preoccupation with TNO suggests that it is his "ungrateful" character that she is really interested in changing! Moreover, PST's narrative focuses on TNO's attempts to understand and rectify the terrible consequences of his actions, reflecting TNO's struggle to change his own moral character for the better.

To understand more about what it means to have (good) moral character, consider what Aristotle said about moral character traits or virtues:

> I am speaking of virtue of character, since it is concerned with feelings and actions. . . To feel such things when we should, though, about the things we should, in relation to the people we should, for the sake of what we should, and as we should is a mean and best and precisely what is characteristic of virtue. (2014: II.6, p. 28)

Following Aristotle, a *virtue* is a stable tendency for an appropriate emotional response in a specific type of situation. Courage is a classic example of a virtue: It is the tendency to feel brave in response to a dangerous situation, despite one's fear of the danger. However, virtue does not merely produce idle feelings on Aristotle's view. In having the appropriate emotional response to a situation, one thereby feels inclined to perform the right actions in the right way and for the right reasons. For example, TNO's companions demonstrate courage when they follow him to find Ravel. Even though they risk death or imprisonment to do so, they are steadfast in their decision to help TNO find answers about his immortality and loss of memories. They feel brave despite their fears, and thus are inclined to act without excessive regard for their own safety or well-being, but instead to help TNO as needed.

Virtue is treasured but rare. In fact, Aristotle held that cultivating and exercising virtues was an essential part of a good life. But few of us are as virtuous as we would like to be. On the contrary, we are riddled with vices that prompt us to perform actions that we ultimately regret. Aristotle construes vices as tendencies for excessive or deficient responses in contrast to virtue, which finds the appropriate response somewhere between these extremes:

> [Virtue] is a medial condition between two vices, one of excess and the other of deficiency. Further, it is also such a condition because some vices are deficient in relation to what the relevant feelings and actions should be and others are excessive, but virtue both finds the mean and chooses it. (2014: II.6, pp. 28–29)

We can illustrate this point by returning to our previous example of courage as a virtue. Since courage is a virtue, there are two corresponding vices. Whereas courage itself is the virtue that manifests as an appropriate response to danger, cowardice is the vice that manifests as a deficient response to danger and recklessness is the vice that manifests as an excessive response to danger. A cowardly person has a deficient response to danger because they tend not to feel any bravery in response to danger, and, as a result, they are uninclined to face danger even when it would be reasonable for them to do so. A reckless person has an excessive response to danger because they tend to feel excessive bravery in response to danger, and, as a result, they are inclined to put themselves into danger even when it is unreasonable for them to do so. The claim that there is a vice of excess and a vice of deficiency for every virtue is sometimes known as the "doctrine of the golden mean" because every virtue manifests as a correct response between two extremes.

Another example of a virtue is good temper, which corresponds to the vices of irascibility and lack of spirit. Someone with good temper tends to be angry to a fitting extent given a situation that calls for anger. They will not fly into a rage at a minor offense against them or react calmly at a major transgression of their rights. Instead, they will be angry at the right times, to the right extent, for the right reasons, and act accordingly.

PST provides some helpful examples of characters who suffer from vices of temper. One of TNO's companions, Annah, exhibits the excessive vice of irascibility. She is hot-headed and easily provoked to anger, even in otherwise peaceful conversations. As a result of her anger, she feels inclined to verbally lash out with insults and threats, and she often does. In contrast to Annah, the Dustmen of Sigil believe that strong emotions are detrimental and thus avoid emotions like anger. Aristotle would say that the Dustmen have the deficient vice of a lack of spirit. People with a lack of spirit tend to feel little or no anger even when they are wronged, which normally calls for a moderate amount of anger in response. As a result, they may fail to speak out against or resist the wrongdoing of others, even though it would be correct to do so.

With the help of Aristotle and a close reading of PST, we can state Ravel's question without its initial ambiguities: "How can a person improve their moral character, such that they lose their vices and develop virtues?" In this formulation, the importance of Ravel's question is laid bare. It is not hard to imagine why someone may wish to undergo moral improvement. The virtuous person is admirable and seemingly happy with their lives, whereas our vices demonstrably cause excessive suffering to ourselves and others. But moral improvement requires more than the mere preference for virtue instead of vice. In the next section, we will understand how TNO comes to reckon with the consequences of his actions and reflect on his character. Then we will explore the pessimistic view that it is impossible for us to become more virtuous, even when we want to change.

Are People Irredeemably Selfish by Nature?

> Then this is my answer, and you are the proof. Nothing can change the nature of a man.
> —The Transcendent One

TNO and his companions search for Ravel to learn about his past: Why is he immortal? What kind of person was he? Why do these shadows seek his death? During his journey, TNO learns that he became immortal to escape justice in the afterlife; that he betrayed and abused his companions, especially Deionarra, in his prior incarnations; and that every time he avoids death, an innocent person dies in his place and becomes a shadow.

After these discoveries, TNO strives to amend himself and become a better person than his prior incarnations. But self-improvement is not easily accomplished. As much as one wants to, changing oneself often seems difficult or insurmountable. Our vices are often ingrained in us because they help us manage pressing problems, even if they exacerbate those problems or introduce new ones in the long run. For example, one may seek pleasure from sensory experiences, like listening to harmonious music or eating chocolate, to help manage or blunt unpleasant emotions like anger or fear. Though people with the virtue of temperance enjoy such pleasures in moderation, the pursuit of pleasure in excess can develop into the vice of self-indulgence, which distracts one from everything else of value in one's life, such as one's relationships with others. Even the Society of Sensation in Sigil stands against *hedonism*, the view that only pleasure is ultimately valuable, and eschews self-indulgence: instead, its members strive for novel experiences of all kinds, whether pleasant or unpleasant.

We can also consider one of TNO's companions on this point. Recall that Fall-From-Grace is a succubus. As a type of demon, succubi are cruel creatures, arguably by definition. (If a succubus ceased to be cruel, then perhaps that creature is no longer a succubus.) But Fall-From-Grace has reformed herself, and her words and actions demonstrate compassion to TNO and others. Nevertheless, she gives TNO the following insight about her change in character:

> Ravel sees much with her black-brambled eyes, some things which are hidden to other's eyes, even things about their own natures... Sometimes, the pain makes itself known. I have learned it is a *difficult* thing to turn on one's nature.

Fall-From-Grace has turned from her nature in attempting to be compassionate rather than cruel. Perhaps her pain indicates that she is still actively resisting her vices, suggesting that she is not yet virtuous, but merely attempting to be. If it is merely an attempt, Fall-From-Grace performs admirably in face of her difficulties. But sometimes we attempt to resist our vices (presumably the first step to overcoming them entirely) and fail. In these moments, it can seem to us that changing ourselves for the better is impossible.

PST acknowledges this pessimism about moral improvement. In the Fortress of Regrets, TNO engages in a battle of wits against the Transcendent One, who has observed TNO's actions throughout his lifetimes. When TNO poses Ravel's question to the Transcendent One, the Transcendent One replies that TNO himself demonstrates that it is impossible for someone to change their nature. The Transcendent One thus claims that it is impossible for one to become a more virtuous and less vicious person.

Perhaps this bold claim seems obviously false. After all, Fall-From-Grace has succeeded in avoiding cruelty to others, despite her nature as a succubus. But the Transcendent One only claims that it is impossible to truly change one's nature, not that it is impossible to refrain from acting in accordance with one's nature. Perhaps the Transcendent One would say that Fall-From-Grace will never be truly compassionate (and thereby virtuous in that way) until it becomes a part of her character. This seems correct given our understanding of virtue. To be compassionate is not just to help others sometimes, but instead to have a stable tendency for a specific emotional response. The compassionate person tends to feel sympathetic toward others in situations where those people need one's help. In light of this emotion, a compassionate person feels inclined to help others for its own sake. Still, why should we believe that it is impossible for Fall-From-Grace (or anyone else) to become compassionate, even if they were once cruel?

There is a philosophical view underlying this pessimism about improving one's character. Recall Ravel's claim that people love themselves too much, suggesting that excessive self-love is an obstacle for improving one's character. Taking this idea even further, the seventeenth-century English philosopher Thomas Hobbes argued that self-love (or at least self-interest) is the ultimate explanation for why we perform all of our actions. "No man giveth but with intention of good to himself; because gift is voluntary; and of all voluntary acts the object to every man is his own pleasure" (1998: I.16, p. 100).

We can refer to Hobbes' view as *Psychological Egoism*, which says that our own self-interest is the fundamental motivation for all of our actions. In other words, all actions are egotistical because we aim to benefit ourselves with every action that we take. It follows that genuinely altruistic action is impossible: Such actions would aim to benefit someone other than oneself. Psychological Egoism is an attractively simple theory because it posits a single source of motivation for all actions. The view also seems to enjoy some empirical support: It is natural for us to pursue what is pleasurable to us and to avoid what is painful to us. Moreover, one can have an intimate understanding of what benefits oneself but lack such understanding of what benefits others, suggesting that our own view of the good is the only basis we could have for action. Perhaps for these reasons, Psychological Egoism has been an influential view in modeling human behavior in fields such as behavioral economics.[3]

If Psychological Egoism were true, it would help explain why we are prone to specific vices and why it is impossible for us to develop specific virtues. Exercising cruelty toward someone involves an attempt to harm them (or at least to let them come to harm) for one's own benefit, such as the satisfaction of a sadistic desire. On the other hand, exercising compassion toward someone involves helping them for their sake, even at some cost to oneself. Psychological Egoism entails that it is perfectly coherent to exercise cruelty and other vices that prioritize personal benefit, but incoherent to exercise compassion and other virtues that prioritize the benefit of others. Such virtues would require the genuinely altruistic actions ruled out by Psychological Egoism. Thus, this view vindicates the Transcendent One's admonishment that moral improvement is impossible, despite our aspirations to change our character for the better.

But is Psychological Egoism true? It often seems like some of our actions are motivated by the fact that they benefit other people. Moreover, these actions typically come at some cost to us. For example, TNO helps Mebbeth, a wise woman that lives in the Ragpicker's Square. In doing so, he uses his valuable time to run her errands instead of pursuing his desire to learn more about his past, thereby incurring a cost to himself. But the defender of Psychological Egoism has a strategy for responding to such cases. They can attempt to redescribe the motivations for an apparently altruistic action as ultimately aimed at the benefit of the person who performed that action. In the case of TNO helping Mebbeth, they would remind us that TNO wants to learn magic from Mebbeth. Perhaps he only helps her at some cost to himself because becoming a Mage is more beneficial to him than the cost of the time that he used to help her. Using this strategy, the defender of Psychological Egoism can concede that people sometimes help others, though only when helping would benefit their self-interest.

However, it is generally considered implausible that every apparently altruistic action is ultimately aimed at the benefit of the person who performs that action. The conclusion of PST offers an excellent example of a genuinely altruistic action: TNO chooses to give up his immortality, thereby preventing his resurrections from taking any future innocent lives. TNO does this at incalculable cost to himself: He truly dies and enters the afterlife to accept his punishment, which is conscription in an endless war on the Lower Planes.

To respond to this example, the defender of Psychological Egoism must claim that either TNO mistakenly believes that his actions are in his self-interest or TNO's actions are in fact in his self-interest. But both of these positions seem untenable in this case. TNO chooses to give up his immortality knowing what awaits him because it is the only way to prevent death and suffering for others. And if one's self-interest is understood in terms of one's pleasure, it is clear that TNO does not choose on the basis of what will be most pleasurable to him, since fighting a futile war will be frustrating and painful on the whole. Instead, he chooses to give up his immortality for the sake of others.

Ultimately, Psychological Egoism does not seem true under closer scrutiny. Perhaps its initial plausibility is because self-interest is a common motivation for action. But human nature (as well as the nature of persons generally) is not constrained by self-interest: People are sometimes motivated to act for the sake of other's interests. Even so, how does one become the kind of person that cares for the interests of others? In the next section, we will see how PST focuses on regret as a way of changing one's character for the better.

How Does Regret Help Develop Virtue?

It is regret that may change the nature of a man. But it was too late. I was already damned. I found that changing my nature was not enough. I needed more time, and I needed more life. So I came to [Ravel] and asked her for a boon — to try and help me live long enough to rectify all the damage I had done. To make me immortal.
—A Prior Incarnation of the Nameless One

TNO searches for Ravel to help answer questions about himself. But Ravel refuses to help TNO until he answers her questions. The most important of these questions is the same one that she puts to everyone else: What can change the nature of a man? Or as we might now put it: How can a person improve their moral character, such that they lose their vices and develop virtues? Although players can select TNO's response to Ravel's question, the canonical answer is regret. PST illustrates its view of regret primarily through TNO's redemption narrative.

After Ravel tells TNO the horrible truth – that each time he is resurrected, an innocent person somewhere in the planes dies instead of him – TNO begins to search for a way to reclaim his mortality. TNO discovers that he can give up his immortality at the Fortress of Regrets, and that the secret to opening the portal to this place is a sincere regret. In order to access the Fortress of Regrets, TNO expresses his regret for his wrongful actions directly: "I regret the deaths I've caused, here and across the multiverse."

In addition to this regret, TNO demonstrates regret for his betrayal of his current and former companions. When TNO finds the ghost of Deionarra in the Fortress of Regrets, he confesses his betrayal to her and asks for her forgiveness. Moreover, these expressions of regret are not simply outpourings of guilt or token gestures at doing the right thing. Ultimately, TNO gives up his immortality to prevent his resurrections from killing others. In contrast to the selfishness of his prior incarnations, including the betrayal of Deionarra and the choice to become immortal to escape his punishment in the afterlife, TNO has improved his moral character and become more virtuous than his predecessors at the end of PST.

Regret helps motivate TNO's redemptive actions. With his apology to Deionarra, TNO aims to repair the harm of his betrayal, perhaps with the hope that Deionarra will move on to the afterlife once she learns the truth. In giving up his immortality, TNO aims to prevent himself from causing more harm to innocent people who might lose their lives in his place. Given its role in TNO's redemptive narrative, PST understands regret as an emotional response to one's wrongful actions. This emotional response inclines one to repair the harm caused by one's actions or to prevent oneself from causing similar harm in the future.

How exactly do TNO's regrets and redemptive actions make him more virtuous? PST offers an answer to this question in terms of the alignment system that the game uses to describe TNO's moral character (as well as the moral character of NPCs). Simplifying somewhat, TNO is either Good, Evil, or Neutral (with respect to Good and Evil).[4] However, TNO's alignment is not a static description of his moral character. Instead, TNO's alignment changes depending on his actions. TNO begins his journey as Neutral with respect to Good and Evil. But when TNO helps people without asking for a reward, his alignment shifts toward Good, and when TNO simply kills someone to take what he wants, his alignment shifts toward Evil.

Thus, the alignment system helps explain how TNO can undertake moral improvement through regret. Here I will substitute virtuous and vicious for Good and Evil, respectively. When TNO regrets the deaths that he has caused, he is motivated to repair the harm or prevent similar harm from happening again in the future. Although TNO is not initially virtuous, his regret prompts him to do what a virtuous person would do if they wronged someone else. Given that TNO's alignment changes if he performs enough actions of the right type, TNO can develop virtuous character in this way. Thus, PST uses the alignment system to propose that one becomes virtuous by performing virtuous actions. (Conversely, one becomes vicious by performing vicious actions.)

PST's view on moral improvement broadly resembles Aristotle's view on the development of virtue. Aristotle writes that:

> ... the virtues come about in us neither by nature nor against nature, rather we are naturally receptive of them and are brought to completion through habit... we become just people by doing just actions, temperate people by doing temperate actions, and courageous people by doing courageous ones. (2014: II.1, p. 20)

Consider a specific virtue such as generosity. The generous person has a stable tendency to feel giving toward others in situations where those people need material help such as wealth. Aristotle would advise that to become a generous person, one must perform generous actions, such as giving some of one's fortune to others. But the habitual performance of generous actions does not by itself transform one into a generous person. It is also crucial that one develop the right motivation for generous actions, as well as the right emotional responses. On this point, consider how Aristotle characterizes the generous person:

> And a generous person will give for the sake of what is noble and will do so correctly. He will give to the people he should, in the amount he should, when he should, and so on for all the other things that correct giving entails. And he will do it with pleasure or without pain, since what is in accord with virtue is pleasant or without pain, and least of all is it painful. (2014: IV.1, p. 58)

For TNO to become generous requires that he perform generous actions for his own sake and that he enjoys (or at least not find unpleasant) acting generously. Accordingly, Aristotle would wonder if TNO is learning to perform virtuous actions for the right reasons or if TNO is developing the emotional responses that a virtuous person would. Although TNO practices the actions that a virtuous person would perform, at least in part because of his regret for his wrongful actions, it is implausible that this is sufficient for becoming virtuous. If TNO performs generous actions like giving away his wealth because he wants to improve his reputation, or if it is unpleasant for him to part with his wealth, TNO will fail to develop generosity.

Perhaps the best way to become virtuous on Aristotle's view would involve finding and learning from a virtuous teacher. Consider an analogy between virtue and other skills on this point. Suppose that one wants to learn a new skill, such as playing the piano. Typically, one will identify someone who can already play piano, undergo their instruction and demonstration of the right actions to play piano, and then practice those actions oneself. With a skilled teacher, one's playing of piano will reflect understanding of the reasons for one's method of playing. Likewise, if one wants to be virtuous, one will identify a virtuous person, undergo their instruction and demonstration of virtuous action, and then practice those actions oneself. With a virtuous teacher, one's virtuous actions will reflect understanding of the reasons for one's virtuous actions.

Unfortunately, TNO does not have a virtuous teacher. Nonetheless, PST does seem to indicate that one's motivational and emotional development is part of one's moral development, though without saying directly that these components are necessary for moral development in the way that Aristotle seems to say they are. For example, TNO seems to apologize to Deionarra because apologizing is the right thing to do, and not because he wants to assuage his guilt. And given the cost of giving up his immortality, it is difficult to imagine why TNO would choose to do so if not because it is the right thing to do. But how exactly does regret motivate one to address one's wrongdoing? In addressing challenges to PST's view of regret, we will see how PST uses the painfulness of regret to help explain its role in moral development.

Philosophical Challenges to Regret

> I think there would have been many others who, when subjected to the experiences you were, would have crumbled. You learned from it, and you became stronger. It shows great strength of will and of character... and I admire that about you. Not only the strength, but the ability to see such horrors as a way of becoming a better person takes a strength few possess.
> —TNO, to Fall-From-Grace

This section evaluates whether PST succeeds in defending its view that regret can help one's moral development. Unsurprisingly, philosophers have examined regret before, and some of their conclusions disagree with PST about regret. Consider the following warning against regret from influential seventeenth-century Dutch philosopher Baruch Spinoza: "He who repents what he has done is twice wretched..." (1994: IV.54, p. 228).

According to Spinoza, someone who performs a wrongful action suffers from some wretchedness or misfortune. But to regret that error is to increase that misfortune.[5] For example, TNO caused significant misfortune for himself through his decision to become immortal. The possibility of losing his memories upon his deaths and resurrections make him hostage to the whims of future incarnations, and he must contend with the shadows that hunt and inevitably find him. Given that TNO holds others dear to him, TNO is also misfortunate when his actions cause harm to his loved ones.

These actions seem worthy of regret on the grounds of their harmfulness to TNO and others. But here Spinoza would say that TNO should not regret these actions because that would only cause him additional misfortune, not improve his situation. Thus, Spinoza seems to understand regret as an unpleasant rumination of one's past mistakes. Absent powerful magic, the past is unchangeable: Once one has made a mistake, it will always be true that one has made that mistake. If regret is only concerned with the past and facing the misfortune of our errors is enough, why should anyone increase that misfortune with regret?

The following hypothetical scenario may help illustrate Spinoza's view. Suppose one could take a pill that prevents one from feeling any regret for one's actions for a short time. (Imagine that this pill is cheap and widely available.) Should one take this pill whenever one starts to feel regretful or anticipates an episode of regret? If Spinoza is correct that regret is misfortune without benefit, then one should resort to such means to alleviate regret.

In light of our previous discussion, PST clearly disputes Spinoza on regret. PST contends that regret does have an important benefit – it motivates us to perform actions to repair or prevent harm. In performing virtuous actions, such as helping those we have harmed, we may begin to develop virtues. PST adds support to this view with TNO's redemptive narrative and the alignment system, and we find additional support from Aristotle's view of the development of virtue. But is it psychologically plausible that regret motivates us in this way?

In support of Spinoza on this point, contemporary philosopher Rüdiger Bittner argues against connections between regret and doing better in the future. First, he claims that someone who does not regret their mistakes may still attempt to do better in the future. For example, if I forget your birthday, I can attempt to remember it next year, even if I do not regret my mistake. Second, Bittner claims that regret does not necessarily make it more likely that one will do better in the future. Perhaps I regret forgetting your birthday so intensely that I put myself down about it. Caught up in this self-punishment at my mistake, I do nothing to ensure that I will not forget birthdays in the future. Thus, Bittner argues that it is possible to fail to regret but do better, and it is possible to regret but fail to do better.

However, PST can respond to Bittner's concerns about regret. Consider that TNO could have felt too little or too much regret about his wrongful actions. If TNO felt too little regret or none at all, he might not have had adequate motivation to do better in the future. Unrepentant, TNO could make the most of his immortality in Sigil by hiding from the shadows and living a life of pleasure for as long as possible. If TNO felt too much regret, he might have felt hopeless about the prospect of doing better in the future. Overwhelmed by regret, TNO could decide to incapacitate himself with the Blade of the Immortal, a magic item that he can acquire to end his own life. In actuality, TNO feels the appropriate amount of regret for what he has done, and it sufficiently motivates him to repair and prevent harm.

The foregoing discussion suggests that an apt sense of regret is itself a virtue. Recall Aristotle's claim that for every virtue, there is a vice of excess and a vice of deficiency. A deficiency of regret is remorselessness, and an excess of regret is self-condemnation. An apt sense of regret represents the "golden mean" between these extremes. Thus, PST can concede that regret is not always a pathway for moral development. One who is remorseless or self-condemning will fail to act virtuously because they feel too little or too much regret. But one who feels the appropriate amount of regret will be motivated to act virtuously and thereby find themselves at the beginning of a path toward developing a virtuous character.

Likewise, PST can concede to Bittner that doing better in the future does not necessarily require regret. However, PST makes the case that the painfulness of regret is a potent source of motivation. PST illustrates that regret is painful through TNO's revelations. When TNO learns about the cost of immortality, he is repulsed. When he discovers his betrayal of Deionarra, he is overcome by grief. It is the painfulness of regret that is an effective source of motivation. Pain itself motivates in characteristic ways: One naturally seeks to lessen existing pain and avoid sources of future pain.

Moreover, pain motivates us more effectively than our intellectual grasp of what we ought to do. In support of this point, consider the actions of children with a congenital insensitivity to pain. Since these children do not experience pain upon bodily injury, they must be explicitly told to avoid actions that will damage their bodies. However, this sometimes fails to motivate them adequately, and these children typically suffer more injuries and exhibit riskier behavior than children who have normal pain responses. In other words, pain that occurs in tandem with bodily damage motivates us more effectively and more consistently than a mere intellectual grasp on what will damage one's body.

Likewise, regretting a mistake is a painful feeling that will motivate one to lessen that pain (by trying to repair the harm that has been done) and avoid increasing that pain (by trying to avoid making that mistake in the future). Thus, feelings of regret are more likely to motivate us because of their painfulness than a merely intellectual grasp of our mistakes. In addition to explaining why the remorseless person is less likely to be motivated to do better in the future, this also explains why the self-condemning person is likely to be too overwhelmed to act appropriately. When regret is too painful because one blames oneself too much for what has happened, one is bound to focus on alleviating the painfulness of regret through means other than addressing the harm of one's actions.

Spinoza and Bittner argue that the apparent benefit of regret comes at a high cost – the painfulness of regret. But painfulness is what makes regret an effective means of motivation for doing better in the future. Recognizing this, PST can maintain that regret enables moral development, so long as regret is felt in appropriate amounts, and that the painfulness of regret is more likely to improve our actions and ourselves than a merely intellectual grasp of one's mistakes.[6]

Conclusion: Moving Past Torment

> The symbol – the symbol of torment – seems brittle somehow, as if it is only barely holding itself to your skin. Unconsciously, you reach out and peel it from your arm. It gives way with a slight resistance, like pulling off a scab. As you hold the symbol, you know you can harness its power. It no longer rules you.
> —PST, describing TNO's redemption

During the events of PST, TNO discovers that he has done much worthy of regret. These regrets help motivate him to make amends to Deionarra and sacrifice his immortality for the sake of others. In this way, PST demonstrates that regret helps motivate us to perform virtuous actions. What follows from this about how one should live one's life? In particular, what should one do when one performs actions worthy of regret?

Even though regret is painful, one should not deaden oneself to one's regrets. This would risk making one into a remorseless person who does not care whether one's actions have caused or will cause harm. But neither one should ruminate on one's regrets. This would risk making one into a self-condemning person who feels helpless to repair or prevent harm via one's actions. Fine-tuning one's sense of regret to feel regret to the right extent will likely require deliberate emotion regulation. Such techniques can help increase or decrease the duration and intensity of regret, ensuring that one's regrets reflect the severity of one's wrongdoing.

Instead, one ought to face up to one's regrets because regret motivates one to repair and prevent the harm caused by one's wrongful actions. It is in this way that regret motivates virtuous action. Moreover, the practice of virtuous action is itself part of developing virtue. Thus, PST instructs that regrets are not futile heartaches, but opportunities to shed vices and develop virtues, thereby changing oneself for the better.

End Notes

1. PST relies on the tabletop fantasy roleplaying game *Dungeons and Dragons* for its basic game mechanics and setting. See Cook (1989) and (1994).
2. Players can make choices in PST that produce a playthrough with a narrative that deviates significantly from what I refer to as the canonical version of PST's story. Nonetheless, the overarching theme of regret and a special ending reserved for playthroughs that reflect that theme arguably indicate a canonical version of events. Ultimately, whether this playthrough is actually canonical does not undermine the philosophical views that are present in at least some playthroughs of PST.
3. For discussion and criticism of this approach to behavioral economics, see Kahneman (2011).
4. Most approaches to alignment in *Dungeons and Dragons* also include Chaotic and Lawful alignments. However, it is controversial whether Chaotic and Lawful are *moral* alignments. As such, I omit discussion of them to focus on Good and Evil, since these alignments more clearly reflect moral virtues.
5. Although the quoted passage refers to repentance rather than regret, Spinoza's understanding of repentance is closer to our contemporary understanding of regret – feeling pained by one's actions. See Bittner (1992).
6. See Brady (2018) for a more comprehensive discussion of these issues. On Brady's view, the capacity for some kinds of suffering (such as the emotional pain of regret) are a requirement for some moral virtues.

References

Aristotle. 2014. In *Nicomachean ethics*, ed. C.D.C. Reeve. Indianapolis: Hackett Publishing.
Bittner, Rüdiger. 1992. Is it reasonable to regret things one did? *The Journal of Philosophy* 89 (5): 262–273.
Brady, Michael. 2018. *Suffering and virtue*. Oxford: Oxford University Press.
Cook, Zeb. 1989. *Advanced dungeons and dragons*, Player's handbook. 2nd ed. Lake Genova: Tactical Studies Rules.
———. 1994. *Planescape campaign setting*. Lake Genova: Tactical Studies Rules.
Hobbes, T. 1998. *Leviathan,* ed. Gaskin J. C. A. Oxford: Oxford University Press.
Kahneman, Daniel. 2011. *Thinking, fast and slow.* New York: Farrar, Straus and Giroux.
Spinoza, Baruch. 1994. In *The ethics and other works*, ed. E.M. Curley. Princeton: Princeton University Press.

Disco Elysium as Philosophy: Solipsism, Existentialism, and Simulacra

83

Diana Khamis

Contents

Introduction 1866
Summary of Main Story 1866
Analysis 1870
    Subjective Idealism 1870
    Transcendental Idealism 1873
    Semiological Idealism 1876
Conclusion 1880
References 1880

Abstract

The quest-rpg *Disco Elysium* is set in a peculiar world: in it, the various continents are separated from each other by what is called "the Pale," a rarefied medium devoid of any properties. This "Pale" is constantly expanding, threatening to consume reality, and is apparently caused into existence by the human mind. This raises the worry: if humans have brought the Pale into existence, then maybe they can make reality disappear altogether. In this manner, the game explores some ideas pertaining to idealism – the belief that reality is inextricably intertwined with the operations of mental faculties. To help make sense of the idealist implications of this game, this chapter will focus on the Pale. First of all, the game's approach to the Pale reminds us of Berkeleyan subjective idealism. Berkeley argues that objects are sets of ideas and that God is the ultimate source of these ideas. It we keep examining the claims of the game, we are led towards transcendental idealism, especially the way it was approached by Schelling: cognitive agents produce knowledge over and above the "thing-in-itself." But the game presents its idealism particularly negatively, and we can spot a

D. Khamis (✉)
Nijmegen, Netherlands

Department of Philosophy, Texas A&M, College Station, TX, USA

© Springer Nature Switzerland AG 2024
D. K. Johnson et al. (eds.), *The Palgrave Handbook of Popular Culture as Philosophy*,
https://doi.org/10.1007/978-3-031-24685-2_102

semiological idealism in its stance – one that is similar to that of Baudrillard, with the Pale serving as a decaying hyperreality which produces informational "noise." In this sinister context, the amnesiac protagonist of the game is new to the symbolic order and can potentially find a new approach to it.

Keywords

Berkeley · Schelling · Baudrilliard · *Disco Elysium* · Transcendental idealism · Subjective idealism · Hyperreality

Introduction

Disco Elysium is a role-playing/quest game by the Estonian studio ZA/UM, which was released in October 2019. Since then, it has received wide critical acclaim and a loyal following. It is a unique game, aesthetically stunning, narratively brilliant, and philosophically rich. Portraying a murder investigation – but also an investigation into the mind of a deeply troubled man – the game takes its player on an existential journey through trauma, self-destruction, solipsistic doubts, and attempts to reforge a disintegrating personality into a living whole. While not explicitly aiming to make a philosophical point, *Disco Elysium* ends up being a cornucopia of philosophical concepts, which are briefly picked up and playfully explored. In the course of the police investigation it portrays, it raises (among others) ethical and political issues pertaining to policing, distribution of wealth, revolution, the prospects of communism, and potential for its abuse. Moreover, through the mental operations of its protagonist, the game also invokes a mind-boggling network of ontologically and epistemologically relevant topics and questions – from solipsism to simulacra. This chapter is meant to look at these ontological and epistemological issues, sorting through this network and making sense of the game's philosophical trajectory. I will begin with a summary of the game, to make sure that its storyline and atmosphere come across before its philosophical explorations and conclusions are examined.

Summary of Main Story

Disco Elysium opens to a scene of its unfortunate protagonist on the floor of his trashed hotel room, naked, sore, and with a monstrous hangover. After he finally gets up, he realizes: he remembers nothing about himself and his past. Some blanks are filled in quickly: he is told that he has gone on an alcohol and amphetamine binge for several days and trashed parts of the hostel he is staying in, annoying everyone in that hostel in the process. He is also greeted by a *partner* – a police officer called Kim Kitsuragi, who claims that he has come to assist the protagonist with his *murder investigation*. All this comes as a surprise to our protagonist, who has descended so deep into his amnesia that he does not realize what country he lives in or even recognize his own face in the mirror. Gradually, however, he has to get his bearings and begin investigating that murder, questioning witnesses and suspects, and generally gathering information about the area he is in. In the process, he gradually remembers and rediscovers information about himself.

The picture painted as a result is somewhat disconcerting. The events of *Disco Elysium* unfold in a world similar to ours, but with a different history and geography. The planet of *Disco Elysium* has several continents, called isolas. These isolas are separated not by water, but by a rarefied substance called only "the Pale" – an odd *non-substance* without properties. It is the most common geological feature of the planet and has been pictured from upper layers of atmosphere, looking like a grayish corona radiating from the isolas. Completely obscure in nature, it seems to be the closest possible thing to nothingness. It is furthermore able to consume matter, as its reach constantly grows and Pale appears where previously there was land. As a final disconcerting touch, it is also harmful for human beings, as people who spend a long time in the Pale gradually lose their mind.

More specifically, the events of *Disco Elysium* unfold on the Insulindian Isola, in the city of Revachol. Founded by colonists from other isolas who had managed to cross the Pale, it was an initially prosperous kingdom that gradually declined, after which the Revolution struck and Revachol ultimately became a communist state. Partly reformist and partly repressive, it existed for several years until a coalition of other nations formed to destroy the Commune of Revachol. Although devoted, soldiers of the commune were no match for combined armies of several countries. Eventually, under severe bombardment, the Commune fell. At the time of the game, corporate capitalism reigns in the *Disco* world as a whole – in addition to several strong governments, powerful multinational corporations control policy and trade among the isolas, and have many interests in the Revachol. The game takes place a couple of decades after the city's division in a slum called Martinaise – a district struck by poverty and violence. Martinaise was the seat of the Revachol Commune, and as such it was heavily damaged in the war. It has a number of damaged houses, a few shops, mostly closed, and a hostel. To the south of it, there is a tiny and almost deserted fishing village. Rather importantly, Martinaise is home to Revachol's large docks, with plenty of dockworkers and truck drivers constantly around. This is the Elysium the protagonist has to deal with.

The gameplay of *Disco Elysium* is almost entirely reduced to reading substantial volumes of well-written text, followed by choosing an action or response from a list of available ones. The narrative, however, is not done by some omniscient unbiased narrator. Instead, around half of the text is "uttered" by twenty-four "voices" within the protagonist – loosely personified skills, determining his capabilities. Due to his rather unfortunate mental state, his fragmented ego sounds almost cacophonic. Different abilities within him constantly offer suggestions as to what to do next and, the protagonist can either follow the advice of these "voices" or try to act like a unitary subject, taking a decision over and above those suggestions. The suggestions can be helpful or utterly ruinous, and it is through – or despite – them that the protagonist generally advances through the world.

The protagonist himself – named, as we soon learn, Harry DuBois, is indeed a police detective. He has a problem: many years ago his wife left him, and every night his subconscious forces him to relive the abandonment in his dreams. To cope, Harry takes amphetamines to delay sleep and then drinks until he blacks out. Nevertheless, he has managed to remain a cop in relatively good standing. It is in this condition that he is sent to Martinaise to investigate a strange, politically fraught murder. A burly, tattooed man from out of town had been killed after staying in the town for a few days; his body was found hanging from a tree in the hostel's backyard. After arriving in Martinaise, Harry turns to binge-drinking and partying instead of investigating, which is what brings him (along with the player) to the beginning of the game in quite a sorry state: hungover, in pain, without his uniform, gun, or badge. Fortunately, he is assisted by Kim – a cop every bit as organized and competent as Harry is an alcoholic wreck. They must now find a way to take the body off the tree and question the many suspicious people around Martinaise. This is no small task, given that none of them want to cooperate with the police. Police mistrust is, Harry will discover, a common phenomenon on the streets of Martinaise, which has been de facto left without official policing. This, in turn, has made a group of seven dockworkers – the Hardy Boys – collectively take the mantle of "the sheriff." They think that police is good for nothing and that they can hold law and justice in their own hands. They are also prime suspects in the case – it seems that the dead newcomer had done some questionable things and was punished for his transgressions.

In order to make the dockworkers talk to him, Harry must speak with the head of the Dockworker Union, Evrart Claire. Evrart is a corpulent, hideous man with vast power and absolutely no scruples. Having ascended to head of the trade union by allegedly killing his predecessor, he now treats the union as his personal mob. True enough, he seems to care for the well-being of his workers/mobsters far more than the multinational corporations which book the docks, but he demands Harry run shady errands for him. Claire's assistance is, however, necessary to get the Hardy Boys to talk. At first, they claim that the dead man had raped a woman at the hostel, and that they had punished the rapist; but their story falls apart upon closer questioning. It turns out, as Harry presses them, that they don't know what truly happened between the woman and the victim, and that they hung the victim after he was already dead.

Upon questioning the allegedly raped woman, Harry learns that she and the dead man had been partying together before his death, regularly taking drugs and having sex. During one such night, the woman says, the man was shot dead in the back of the head by someone she could not see. Mortified, she asks for help and the Hardy Boys decide that they will take the responsibility and present the murder as a lynching.

But these are not all the shady things *Disco Elysium* presents to the player. Harry learns that the dead man was no chance visitor to Martinaise, but belonged to a brutal private military contractor, Krenel. He was in Revachol as part of a small squad, sent by a multinational corporation to break a strike which the dockworkers have organized, using lethal force if necessary. The dead man was the leader of the squad; and with their leader gone, the squad is likely to organize a manhunt after his suspected killer. This is much to the dismay of the Hardy Boys, who spent a good deal of time convincing people that they lynched the man for rape. A volatile situation arises and eventually Krenel employees, somewhat drunk, decide to attack and kill the Hardy Boys. Kim and Harry defend the dockworkers, and a shootout ensues, where all hell breaks loose and Harry gets injured.

In even more physical pain than before, he limps towards the resolution of the game – to explore his very last lead and check the very last place he hasn't examined – a potentially inhabited bunker in the sea, on a small island, from which Martinaise could be easily viewed through the scope of a sniper rifle. It is there that he finds the real murderer: an old communard deserter, Iosef Lilianovich Dros. Dros, by now deathly ill and apparently somewhat deranged, deserted from his unit, escaped Martinaise when it was bombed, and hid out on the abandoned islands around Revachol for decades. He watched Martinaise from his bunker through his rifle scope: he developed an unhealthy voyeuristic interest in the woman Ellis had sex with, and one night, as he watched them have sex through his rifle scope, he shot Ellis. After that, he remained on the island – apathetic, dying, used up – until Harry found him and finally solved the case.

This, in a nutshell, is the plot of Disco Elysium – and yet, before our idea of the game is complete, we need to address one more in-game event. At the beginning of the game, Harry learns that cryptozoologists are in Martinaise, looking for an elusive giant stick insect that is supposed to live around Revachol. During investigation, Harry can choose to generally watch out for signs of the phasmid. If the player does this, they of course will not find any trace of the cryptid. And yet, at the very end of the game, when the murderer is found, a gigantic reed-like shape will rise from the water next to Harry, and he would discover it: the Insulindian phasmid. Indeed, if Harry has the requisite skills, he can even enter into a prolonged conversation with it. That conversation is the culmination of Harry's simmering doubt and existential angst, culled throughout the game with tasks and drugs. At this point in the endgame, Harry has been shot, remembered that his wife had left him, solved the murder, and helped everyone he can help in Martinaise. And now, finally, in front of this unexpected, almost impossible sight, he is confronted with all the uncertainty and confusion that plague his life in general.

The conversation with the phasmid begins cautiously at first. And yet, like anyone confronted with a wondrous, seemingly supernatural being, Harry quickly turns fully existential. He asks the insect where the world comes from and whether there is any point to it at all. He laments that his life is terrible. But the phasmid, or whoever it is that speaks to Harry through the phasmid, tells him that, while it may be very confusing to be a human, humans are very special precisely for that reason. Their nervous systems, their vast consciousnesses are new to the planet – no one before has had anything resembling the human mental faculties. And, astonishingly, the phasmid tells Harry that the Pale has only appeared in the world with the advent of human beings and their active minds. All the animals, says the phasmid, are aware of the Pale, but no one remembers it preexisting humans. This has made every life form on the planet conclude that humans will eventually destroy everything through this ever-growing onslaught of the Pale. Here we finally receive a definition of this elusive substance: "[i]t is a nervous shadow cast into the world by you, eating away at reality" (Kurvitz 2019). This coincides with certain theories on the Pale which

Harry can find out about in the beginning of the game – namely, that the Pale is degrading past information, everything that has ever been thought and is now no longer, which is why it is growing in scope and corrupting the minds of those it touches. The phasmid begs Harry not to blink, not to lose sight of her and the world, lest everything vanish from existence through the degradation of its idea. At this point, near the end of the game, Harry and Kim can take a picture of the elusive cryptid, exchange a few words, and take Iosef Dros into custody.

Analysis

While the story of *Disco Elysium* is exquisite and full of interesting political undertones, this chapter will largely be focused around the last part of my summary – Harry's encounter with the phasmid and the game's theories of the Pale. In the course of this analysis, I will attempt to make sense of the epistemology of this game and its implications through three various idealisms: the subjective idealism of George Berkeley, the transcendental idealism of Immanuel Kant and Friedrich Schelling, and the semiological idealism of Jean Baudrillard.

Subjective Idealism

From Harry's conversation with the phasmid, we learn that she is worried that if Harry blinks, or if mankind collectively falls asleep on one fine night, the world will disappear. This implies that, according to the phasmid, in order to guarantee that the world not disappear, someone – at least a single human – has to keep thinking it. Theories of the Pale advanced by Elysium scientists suggest that the Pale may be decaying thoughts. If we accept this hypothesis, we would have to accept that what we call "matter" and what we call "thoughts" are of the same nature, since they can interact with each other. On this view as well, maintaining the world would entail maintaining thoughts, as much as possible, and not letting them decay. This stance is reminiscent of the subjective idealist view embraced by George Berkeley.

Berkeley was a leading figure of eighteenth-century British empiricism. Like all empiricists, he holds that experience is the primary source of human knowledge. Beyond that, however, his views on the world and the human mind are remarkably unlike what might be expected from an empiricist. He holds, namely, that what we know from our experience – i.e., what our experience gives us access to – are *ideas*. These ideas are the only objects of our knowledge and they are formed through several mechanisms (Berkeley 1949, p. 41). First there are the ideas of table, cup, sun, and other extended objects, on which we then bestow the name of "material things." These are ideas we do not in any way control – they appear to us independent of our will and are not a product of our minds. Secondly, we also arrive at ideas through reflecting on "the passions of our mind" – on our anger, sadness, and joy, and thus form the ideas of those emotions and any other mental states we might have. Finally, there are ideas which are formed with the help of memory and imagination.

This, in turn, can go two ways. We could combine ideas with which we have familiarized ourselves in the past and which are now fixed in our memory to create an idea of an imaginary thing – coupling, for instance, the idea of a beautiful maiden and a fish tail to create the idea of a mermaid. We could also divide the ideas of certain things in order to arrive at their "component parts" – analyzing, for instance, the idea of an apple into an abstraction of its shape (roundness) and its color (red). Like a good empiricist, Berkeley of course denies the existence of abstract ideas like "roundness," "redness," "motion," or "extension." They do not correspond to anything separately existing in reality, but are merely bits and pieces, cut out from ideas of concrete things (Berkeley 1949, pp. 30–31). Roundness, he would have it, cannot exist by itself, without a certain definite extension and color; there is no such thing as pure roundness, and the same applies for all abstract concepts.

However, there is one more kind of idea which, for Berkeley, is merely a product of our minds. Since ideas are the objects of our knowledge, and since ideas are always coupled with and dependent on the activity of our mind, we do not and could not have an idea of anything existing independent of the mind. The notion is itself incoherent – something being an idea is incompatible with it being mind-independent. Thus, for Berkeley, we have no evidence of mind-independence. We could, of course, derive by reason the notion that some objects could exist beyond our mind, but the mind will deliver to us no proof or necessary connection between this idea and the actual mind-independent existence of such objects. Hence, for Berkeley, the notion of a substratum underlying the ideas of extension, color, motion, temperature, smell, and texture of an object is itself an abstraction, derived from putting together the many ideas of extended, material objects and deriving from them a kind of commonality of nature. This abstract commonality of nature Berkeley calls the "material substratum," but it does not correspond to anything outside our mind (Berkeley 1949, pp. 43–44).

This, coupled with the above insistence on the abstract character of the individual qualities of a thing, make for an interesting contribution to the early modern ontological and epistemological debate about primary and secondary qualities. It was argued by Descartes, and then by Locke after him, that certain qualities of material things, called secondary qualities, are subjective and "in the mind" of the perceiver, while some others – primary qualities – are objective and inhere in the perceived substance (Descartes 2008, pp. 22–23; Locke 1997, pp. 135–136). Commonly, qualities like smell, taste, color, sound, heat, and cold were taken to be secondary because their perception was taken to depend on the perceiving subject. Someone could find that Gruyere cheese smells like dirty feet, while another perceiver could find it deliciously fragrant. To someone, coriander could taste like soap, while to another perceiver it could taste like a delicious herb. Sounds are similarly affected by what appears melodic to a listener and what doesn't, while color is affected by the ability of the perceiver to see color, and heat/cold, among other things, by the body temperature of the perceiver. Primary qualities, on the other hand, were taken to be in the perceived thing (Locke 1997, p. 141) – they are, commonly, extension, solidity, figure, and mobility. These are perceived by all observers and are, supposedly, inseparable from the object they inhere in.

Berkeley casts doubt on this distinction: for him, color, heat, sound, and other secondary qualities are just as inseparable from the objects as the primary qualities. In his *Three Dialogues between Hylas and Philonous,* Berkeley, using the character Philonous as a mouthpiece, invites the readers to imagine an extension entirely devoid of any color, of any certain hotness or coldness, of the capacity to generate sound, etc. This, Philonous concludes, is impossible. Furthermore, just as human experiences with secondary qualities differ from observer to observer, our experiences with primary qualities differ according to perspective and distance: the shape of a thing looks different depending on our angle of view and distance from it. These same experiences vary even more vastly if we use tools to aid our perception. Berkeley uses the example of microscopes to illustrate his argument – they magnify viewed objects, showing something utterly tiny as something big. Motion does not escape as well – being merely a succession of images in one's mind, it can hardly be called "objective" (Berkeley 1949, pp. 181–186). Thus Berkeley aims to convince his readers that we do not have evidence for any mind-independent or "objective" quality, which reinforces his claim that all the objects of our knowledge are ideas.

From here Berkeley furthermore derives his well-known and controversial claim of "esse est percipi": to be is to be perceived. This claim, as we have seen in the foregoing, applies to all qualities and all ideas of things, including the much-discussed idea of substance or substratum. We only have access to our objects of knowledge as existing in our minds. We could have no evidence – which for Berkeley, since he is an empiricist, means sensory evidence – for the mind-independent existence of these ideas, since sensory evidence is all mind-dependent. This means that the objects of our knowledge only exist in minds. Despite the fact that this sounds like solipsism, Berkeley vehemently denies this: pointing to how most of our ideas appear to us without us exercising any control over them, he suggests that the human mind is not the source of the ideas. When human minds produce ideas on their own, the result is ideas of imagination, which are far less vivid and far more intuitively controllable by the human will; so the solipsist view, according to Berkeley, is false. The ideas, according to Berkeley, are also not a copy of some non-ideal external things; no idea can be a copy of an extended thing entirely unlike it. Berkeley takes his view to be quite advantageous for thinking. For starters, since both ideas and what was taken to be "material objects" turn out to be of the same nature on this view, the question of how material things could possibly affect the mind vanishes. This is useful not only because it deals with the problem of mind-body interaction but also because it deals a blow to the skeptic; on this view, the problem of immaterial mind interacting with the material world dissolves (Berkeley 1949, pp. 211–212).

With finite spirits and external objects out of the window as potential sources of ideas, Berkeley turns to a spirit infinite: to God. God is the source of our ideas: he has "kept" them in his own mind eternally and has made human beings experience them so that they can survive in the world and know his creation (Berkeley 1949, pp. 231–232). It is here that Berkeley's subjective idealism is relatable to *Disco Elysium.* In the game, the insect's awe before mankind's cognitive superiority is such that she also takes man to have a spirit potent enough (if not infinite) to be the ultimate source of everything everyone perceives. However, the game suggests a far more solipsistic twist on subjective idealism than Berkeley has in mind. Berkeley, of course, took himself to handily solve the problem of reality eluding the human subject trying to grasp it – for him, it is all in the mind of God and God serves as a guarantor of the truth-aptness of our ideas. Short of being a solipsist, Berkeley staves solipsism off. In game, on the other hand, idealism takes a more precarious turn. It is highly likely that the "vision" Harry had when talking to the insect was a vision entirely within his head, i.e., the fictional insect is not actually capable of telepathic communication with the protagonist. Thus, if we take the insect's thoughts to be a projection of Harry's thoughts, the conversation translates into Harry being genuinely worried, at least at the periphery of his mind, that human beings are indeed the source of all there is in the world. Recall: if the Pale interacts with matter, and if the Pale is rarefied thoughts, then thoughts and matter are of the same nature, i.e., matter is, in some sense, thought. If true, all that surrounds everyone in Elysium is ideas, and the extinction of human mind – "blinking," sleep, death, especially on a massive scale – could wipe Elysium out. Human minds are not infinite like the mind of God, and the ideas produced by them could not be sustained for eternity. Along with the physical fragility of the town in the game – shelled time after time in wars and revolutions – the game suggests the fragility of the world and everything in it. It is all the more poignant because of the fragility of our protagonist, who gets shot and punched, and suffers heartbreak, hangover, and withdrawal. Towards the end, he is also drawn closer to a kind of existential crisis, a subjective idealism without the firm foundation of God: if humans disappear, perhaps everything will.

Transcendental Idealism

The dialogue with the phasmid at the end of *Disco Elysium* is heavily suggestive of subjective idealism. And yet if we think carefully about what the insect communicated to Harry, we realize that in Elysium, human beings do not cause reality into existence. The insect says that while creatures – other insects, birds, beasts – remember existing before humankind, they do not remember the Pale. Thus the insect – or Harry's projection – is, at another level, not *really* concerned about solipsism, but rather about the imprint human beings leave on the world. Human beings produce the Pale, or to be more precise: they produce information or ideas about reality which can – apparently – contribute to reality, but then decay and take away from reality, consuming parts of it and perhaps even destroying it. This leads us to a second kind of idealism: transcendental idealism.

Transcendental idealism, a philosophy first developed by Immanuel Kant, arose in no small part as a reply to skepticism. The specific skeptical problem Kant highlights in his *Critique of Pure Reason* is the Humean problem of causation – namely, how we know that a certain phenomenon does indeed produce an effect if we do not perceive a necessary connection between the two (Hume 2007, pp. 45–46). In order to tackle this problem, Kant decided to change the terms of approaching it. It was true, he accepted, that we do not have knowledge of cause and effect (and some other very fundamental things) *from experience*. We do, however, still have this knowledge, and so it must be a priori – obtained before access to any experience. But this is problematic: the standard epistemological assumption states that in knowledge our cognition must conform to its objects. If there is some a priori knowledge, then it would be groundless, as it would seem to conform to nothing. In order to break this stalemate and win back the concept of causation and its necessity, Kant chooses to invert the persistent assumption: what if, he proposes, it is the case that the objects of our cognition conform to it? (Kant 1998, p. 110). This proves to be revolutionary: if it is the objects that conform to our cognition, we do not have to doubt our a priori knowledge.

Kant conducts his philosophical deliberations in a very innovative fashion: he starts from the fact of our experience, dissects it to identify its a priori elements, and then elaborates how these elements fit together into the general structure of our cognitive faculties. It turns out, on this investigation, that the spatial and temporal ordering of experience, as well as fundamental concepts (Kant calls them categories) like cause and effect, substance and attribute, reciprocity, quantity, quality, and modality are a priori (Kant 1998, p. 212). This leads Kant to embrace a peculiar view of the objects of our experience. These are, he claims, nothing but phenomena – they appear to us only ever conforming to the forms of spatial and temporal intuition and at least some of the above categories. Beyond that, we can have no conception of objects of experience as somehow independent of our experience, because it is only in our experience that they are the object that we take them to be. To simplify: when we look at a tree sway in a breeze, our cognitive faculties process what appears to us in a certain way. It is thanks to this processing that we see the spatial position of the tree and how its leaves move over time. We also understand, thanks to this processing, that it is a *single* tree, that the trunk, branches, and leaves form a *totality*, that the tree is a *substance* with a number of *attributes*, that the wind *causes* the twigs and leaves to move, etc. If we are to wonder what there is beyond our experience of all these things, we would have to conclude, according to Kant, that it is unknowable. To refer to this unknowability, Kant uses the expression "things as they are in themselves," often shortened in Kant scholarship as "thing-in-itself." Knowledge, for Kant, is thus of phenomena, and "below" phenomena there is no deeper level, except, perhaps, for the unknowable thing-in-itself. This is an idealism because, just like in Berkeleyan idealism, there are no "objects" outside our experience, but merely this unknowable in-itself which, moreover, is (at least for Kant himself) nothing but a postulate, an abstract concept posited to mark our ignorance (Kant 1998, p. 350).

Although knowledge, for Kant, is not (at least not obviously) rooted in some determining external object, independent from our mind, it is systematic through the operations of the faculty of reason. Reason is the faculty of syllogism; it is what makes sure that our knowledge coheres together into a whole. It is because of reason that we make generalizations and arrange our knowledge into a system, a feature which Kant called the "architectonic." Through the systematicity of our knowledge, we can gradually determine the world, forging new concepts and determinations and engaging in science (Kant 1998, p. 502). This is easily understood if we look at the work of a scientist: we can partly, but not fully, understand a certain phenomenon – for instance, we can know what results from crossing differently-colored pea plants, although we would not know how the inheritance process works. Nevertheless, we must, owing to the systematicity of the world, hypothesize mechanisms for transmitting inherited traits. This is what scientists did after Mendel, eventually discovering DNA, and this was possible because there were certain systematic patterns they could discern in the objects of their experience.

What we have so far, with Kant, is a set-up quite unlike *Disco Elysium:* human cognition produces knowledge and we do not know what exists above and beyond that. In order to go a little further with transcendental idealism, we will move to another transcendental idealist: F. W. J. Schelling. Schelling has had a long, productive, and varied philosophical carrier in which he experimented with various philosophical hypotheses. Nevertheless, throughout the entirety of his career, he largely accepted Kant's general premise about how objects correspond to our cognition, also accepting Kant's division of the faculties and their powers. Yet, also throughout his career, Schelling remained dissatisfied with how Kant declined to address the generation and emergence of our faculties.

Influenced by the booming natural sciences, Schelling viewed human beings as creatures that emerge from nature and believed our minds to also be, at least in part, products of nature. For Kant, we could not even talk of the emergence of our faculties, as we are unable to conceptualize any state prior to their complete emergence. On this view, nature is just the sum of all phenomena. Schelling, however, not satisfied with this limitation, proposes in a series of texts belonging to what he calls "philosophy of nature," that since human beings are products of nature, nature and human beings obey similar general rules (Hogrebe 1989, p. 43). The details of these rules are not important here, but the schema of human beings' relationship to nature which emerges from Schelling's works is as follows: nature – with at least some of its products, like rocks, birds and phasmids – pre-exists human beings (Schelling 2004). After the emergence of the human mind with its faculties and powers, this mind began to theorize and conceptualize the nature from which it emerged. Thus, it produces a layer of "second nature" over the "first nature" over which it theorizes (Grant 2013, p. 27). This "second nature" is the conceptual image of nature as formed by the mind, and it is as systematic as the architectonic of reason in Kant. Since Schelling does not want to reject the Kantian hypothesis of objects conforming to our cognition, even though he does postulate a commonality between the two above and beyond our cognition, he still does not claim that we have access to the producing "first nature."

Thus, For Schelling, there is still a "thing-in-itself" and we are still unable to grasp it for what it is, only having access to how it appears to us with the help of our faculties. Our mind shapes the experiences we receive, and we are thus always beholden to our conditions of access. All we can do when it comes to nature is produce reflections of it. These reflections can pile upon each other, layer upon layer, forming levels of abstraction. For instance, describing a collision of two balls using concepts such as "ball" and "collision" is already somewhat abstract, insofar as we are using concepts. A higher level would be talking about balls as point-masses and applying Newton's laws of motion and laws of the conservation of momentum. An even higher level would be treating the molecular structure of the colliding balls or the collision of two atoms. Human thinking constantly produces new levels of abstraction to better understand what happens in the world, both coming closer to nature and ironically distancing itself from the first level from which it emerged.

It is here that we come close to *Disco Elysium* and the layers of decaying information floating – or perhaps simply existing – around all its continents. These layers – if the leading theory on the Pale is correct – are all the mental images, all the representations, and all the abstract constructions which human beings have made of Elysium for centuries; they are the second nature surrounding Elysium. The game even takes the premise of second nature further than Schelling himself, allowing the produced ideas or information to interact directly with matter – after all, mind and world are continuous and of the same nature. If we accept this scheme of things, the insect – or again, that part of Harry projected onto the insect – is right: with the disappearance of human beings, some part of reality will inevitably disappear. With humans gone, physics as a body of knowledge will cease to exist, without negating any physical laws. Christianity or vegetarianism will all cease to exist as a series of beliefs and customs, as will all ideas and conceptual apparatuses humans created.

And yet, this idealism is not entirely satisfying when it comes to dealing with *Disco Elysium*'s Pale. The second nature is generally, whether in Kant or in Schelling, seen as something good – as an advancement for humanity, an ever-growing and potentially infinite store of systematic knowledge. It is what our faculties are meant to do. It is true that, at least for Schelling, we can go too deep in abstraction and lose sight of the real world and its history (Schelling 2008, p. 211), engaging in endless thought experiments and neglecting life. Yet even simple thinking about life is already "second nature." In other words: nowhere in transcendental idealism is the process of producing knowledge and/or information colored as negatively as the encroaching of the Pale in *Disco Elysium*. We need a third idealism to make sense of this.

Semiological Idealism

In order to find an idealism which could help us with interpreting the Pale's encroachment on the world, we need to change registers and talk of producing signs and signification instead of producing ideas or concepts. If we take seriously the in-game hypothesis that the world of *Disco Elysium* is threatened by information whose status as meaningful has been decaying, we could, potentially, view it as a decaying network of signs losing their signification. In order to ground this view and assume a theoretical stance towards this topic, we would have to look at the work of two French philosophers, Ferdinand Saussure and Jean Baudrillard, and use their concepts of signification and hyperreality to reach some final conclusions about the Pale and the world of *Disco Elysium*.

Ferdinand Saussure, a prominent linguist and philosopher of language, was one of the fathers of contemporary semiotics – the study of signs. In his *Course on*

General Linguistics, Saussure defines the linguistic sign as a dual entity uniting a concept, which he calls the "signified," and a certain sound-image – not a sound itself, but the "psychological imprint" of a sound, which Saussure calls the "signifier" (Saussure 1959, pp. 65–66). So, for Saussure, the sign "tree" unites the concept of a tree and the sound-image "tree" (i.e., how the word "tree" sounds to us). All linguistic signs, for Saussure, are arbitrary: there is no necessary connection whatsoever between the signifier and the signified (Saussure 1959, pp. 67–69). Signs are not mandated by God or some other power; there is no reason for the word "tree" or "horse" to mean what it does other than a social convention. And every member of the society participating in the convention has their own, slightly different version of the concept "tree" or "horse" in their mind because of different experiences with trees and horses. This makes all signs "float," i.e., be underdefined, where the signifiers have only a *likely* coupling with the signifieds, not a certain one. This might seem like a skeptical point, and to some extent it is, but it is not only so. It does entail that when a certain person says "pass me the salt," they might in fact be speaking an alternative private language, transparent only to them, and mean "the cat is on the mat." But that is not the interesting feature of floating signification. It is also the case that certain signs – "democracy," "value," "virtue," a symbolist poem – are floating even without supposing a private language; the signifier is a lot more flexible and ambivalent. This remarkable ambivalence makes it impossible to decode the sign using a straightforward mental "codebook."

Having looked at the basic principles of Saussure's theory of signification, we now turn to Baudrillard. Saussure's theory is of crucial importance for Baudrillard's thought. To give some, albeit simplified, context: Baudrillard, in a collection of essays entitled *For a Critique of the Political Economy of the Sign*, sets out to criticize the way production of and relation to commodities is generally thought about in economics. For Baudrillard, classic economic theory – which focuses on the consumption and production of objects as primarily useful, so that they are prioritized based on the use-value of the object – is false. In truth, the production and consumption of objects are prioritized to produce signification, i.e., to uphold or demonstrate a certain status. This does not mean that nothing is ever produced or consumed because it is a need, vital or otherwise: certainly, even things consumed largely "for status," like the latest cell phone models, are fulfilling a need in a certain sense. It does mean, however, that, at least in contemporary economic systems, a large part of why a certain item is produced or consumed pertains to the signification of these items, where, contemporarily, use is less and less relevant and signs are more and more important.

To give a concrete example, Baudrillard talks about the middle-class bourgeois in France in the 1970s, with meticulously organized houses, lots of porcelain, with lace doilies under every cup: the bourgeois, in this case, would be consuming these kinds of objects (porcelain, lace, antiques) in order to emulate being upper-class, to correspond to their desired self-image (Baudrillard 1981, p. 34). Perhaps more relevant now, Baudrillard also gives the example of environmentalism: the production and consumption of "green" energy and "natural" or "bio" commodities are *en vogue* right now (they already were in the 1970s and 1980s, when he produced his main writings) because they send a certain signal and project a certain image of the producer or the consumer (Baudrillard 2017, p. 53). If we look more closely at production and adopt a historical lens, as examined in Baudrillard's book *Symbolic Exchange and Death*, we see that while signification has always been central to production, consumption, and the exchange of goods (Baudrillard 1981, p. 30), there has been a certain qualitative change in signification in society.

Baudrillard here proposes four regimes. The first is that of feudal or archaic caste societies, where signs are limited in number and their circulation is restricted. (A medieval peasant does not have the option to signify except in his or her religious devotion and loyalty to their feudal lord.) In the Renaissance, signs begin to proliferate and begin to simulate that which they are not, while still maintaining an obligatory reference to the original. Baudrillard sees this in the appearance of fashion as a phenomenon and the ubiquity of stucco in construction (Baudrillard 2017, pp. 71–72) – a kind of very versatile plaster which can be used to imitate practically any desired material or texture (most notoriously, marble). This is how Baudrillard's famous concept of "simulation" makes its entrance: stucco simulates other materials. With fashion, people get more leeway to simulate the image of themselves they want. The industrial revolution brought forth the next stage of this development of production and simulation, where production unfolded on a giant scale, with series of identical objects churned out by the machine, so that there no longer were any "originals" to point to. Plastic became the new stucco: undegradable and able to simulate everything, with even greater versatility to signify whatever its producers or consumers desired. Finally, at the last stage, this indeterminability of the original in mass-production is taken even further, towards the dominance of the model taking place of the original (Baudrillard 2017, p. 77).

The latter is the hallmark of the current socioeconomic system, where the economy is largely based around services, and for each service provision, there is a model to be followed. There are models involved in knowledge production, where, for example, if a researcher wants to investigate something empirically, they are likely to simulate the circumstances they want to research according to a certain model. There are models in politics: models predicting voter behavior and polling results, models proposed by the media for public opinion, and none of these are rooted in the real (Baudrillard 2017, pp. 86–87). Baudrillard's point here is not that models never work or are "bad," but rather that these models do not correspond to a certain state of affairs, i.e., they are not a map of a territory, but simultaneously the map and the territory itself. If we take the polling model that a political party looks at to plan a campaign, that model is not the reality of their voters; it is precisely a model, a hyperreality, and simulation. Models are backed by conjecture, by the fact that they are supposed to work, although we begin with the presupposition that they would. This is nowhere more evident than in the current structure of the financial markets, with trading on derivatives – contracts involving obligation dependent on future conditions pertaining to a certain financial asset. With contemporary financial trading involving derivatives on derivatives, the use-value of the object of trade has become virtually nil; the entire trading is based on the exchange-value of objects – how certain derivatives and securities relate to others. The entire structure of the market is based on models and conventions which are not backed by anything except the (usually) good faith of the actors involved in the trade and the immense complexity of the system (which is sometimes the very thing that fails it). This is at least one instance where, although there are signs, there is no signification – just floating "signals" with no referentials. This is what Baudrillard calls "pure simulacra," copies with no originals, models with nothing for them to be a model of. Baudriallard sees this tendency towards hyperreality and creating simulacra also in mass media and communication, in art and art markets, in international politics and contemporary warfare. Where systems of exchange were governed by utility first and productivity afterwards, postindustrial revolution, there is now just floating signification.

The world of *Disco Elysium,* haunted by the Pale, is a hyperbolic vision of this state. Its events are set against the backdrop of in-game communism's failure to emancipate the proletariat (just like the developments of late capitalism are set across the backdrop of the various failures of Marxism). Labor – both in our world and in that of *Disco Elysium*, short of undergoing a revolution by the exploited worker class – became a sign. In *Disco Elysium*, the dockworker labor force exists to uphold the power of the corrupt union leader Evrart Claire. In our world, according to Baudrillard, unions became subject to a crisis of representation, where the issue was no longer that of workers against capitalism, but that of who speaks for whom. Eventually labor became a sign of belonging to a system or "having a place," so that the work of women and immigrants (just as, if not more exploitative than the work of men) came to be viewed as an improvement of the lots of the women and immigrants involved. Labor became a sign of being "non-useless" (Baudrillard 2017, p. 35). In *Disco Elysium* as well, the dockworkers are "not useless," although in-game they do nothing but stand around in the hostel bar and drink beer, striking a "tough guy" pose. They are nothing but a signifier, and this signifier is moreover vacuous: they, after all, fail to keep order, and the order they purport to keep is only the order of Evrart Claire's whim, posturing against oppressive corporate rule.

Most interesting, however, is the Pale itself. In Baudrillard's book *Simulacra and Simulation,* he puts forth a diagnosis: there is more and more information but less and less meaning (Baudrillard 2010, pp. 79–80). His hypothesis for why this is the case is as follows: information, its profusion and proliferation, actively destroy meaning. His own position comes from his analysis of mass media. Mass media does not create communication, it creates merely a setting for communication by telling everyone that they can participate in that communication which is focused on them. But, in reality, that is merely a lure, because no meaningful exchange takes place within the auspices of mass media. The surplus of information created as a result is thus not innovative, it is chaotic. The Pale is also information that has become chaotic and come to destroy meaning. The Pale, this "second nature" network of ideas and signs, is a hyperreality blanket thrown over reality, full of vanishing, obsolete signifiers that signify nothing – the link to the long-gone signified is cut. The Pale is the decayed symbolic order, potentially encroaching on the intact elements of symbolic order around it.

Conclusion

Disco Elysium is set in a world of profound political failure and corporate rule. Coupled with the no less profound personal failure of the protagonist, it sets out to explore a number of ideological and personal conflicts between inhabitants of this world through the eyes of an amnesiac – someone who can act as a newcomer to this world. With such a newcomer for a protagonist, the game also manages to explore the problematic relationship between human beings on the one hand and ideas, information, and meaning on the other. The game namely comes into the vicinity of three different idealisms: the subjective idealism of George Berkeley, the transcendental idealism as presented by F. W. J. Schelling, and the semiological idealism of Jean Baudrillard. At a first glance, it suggests, to the protagonist, the possibility that things in the world might exist only as being thought by human beings (subjective idealism). It then turns out that the suggested view is closer to the idea of human beings creating a conceptual second nature over the first nature (Schelling's transcendental idealism). Finally, if more elements about the game world are taken into account, we are left with an idealism of hyperreality and signs without signification. This emptiness and loss of signification is interestingly paralleled by the protagonist's own "emptiness" and loss of signification (as an amnesiac, he has to rediscover or re-create some significance anew).

Whether this is a hopeful, potentially liberating radical move on behalf of the game is open to interpretation. Be that as it may, at the end the protagonist has rediscovered some of his meaning by getting in touch with his lost past and reinvented some more by forming new connections, some transgressive to the order of signification he found himself in. In *Disco Elysium*, there is no moment of truth at the end, and no great happy or tragic endings. After the game is finished, we, just like the protagonist, have not necessarily discovered more insights about the world; but we have been exposed to ideas, meanings, and significations – also about our ideas, meanings, and significations – and are free to carry on with that knowledge, having, hopefully, been rendered more thoughtful as a result. After all, producing signification "must be incredibly hard," as the phasmid says, professing her "silent and meaningless awe." Although her and her kin's awe is meaningless, just like most of the signification that surrounds you, it is not quite empty. "Know that we are watching – when you're tired, when the vision spins out of control. The insects will be looking on. Rooting for you. And when you fall we will come to raise you up, bud from you, banner-like, blossom from you and carry you apart in a sky funeral. In honour of your passing" (Kurvitz 2019). That has to count for something.

References

Baudrillard, J. 1981. *For a critique of the political economy of the sign*. Trans. Charles Levin. Candor: Telos Press.

———. 2010. *Simulacra and simulation*. Trans. Sheila Faria Glaser. Ann Arbor: University of Michigan Press.

———. 2017. *Symbolic exchange and death*. Revised edition. Trans. Iain Hamilton Grant. Los Angeles: Sage Publications.

Berkeley, G. 1949. *The works of George Berkeley, Bishop of Cloyne*. Vol. 2. London: Thomas Nelson and Sons.
Descartes, R. 2008. *Meditations on first philosophy.* Trans. Michael Moriarty. Oxford: Oxford University Press.
Grant, I.H. 2013. How nature came to be thought. Schelling's paradox and the problem of location. *Journal of the British Society for Phenomenology* 44 (1): 24–43.
Hogrebe, W. 1989. *Prädikation und Genesis. Metaphysik als Fundamentalheuristik im Ausgang von Schellings „Die Weltalter"*. Frankfurt/Main: Suhrkamp.
Hume, D. 2007. *An enquiry concerning human understanding*. Oxford: Oxford University Press.
Kant, I. 1998. *Critique of pure reason.* Trans. Paul Guyer and Allen W. Wood. Cambridge: Cambridge University Press.
Kurvitz, R. 2019. *Disco Elysium.* London, UK: ZA/UM Studio.
Locke, J. 1997. *An essay concerning human understanding*. London: Penguin.
Saussure, F. 1959. *Course in general linguistics.* Trans. Wade Baskin. New York: Columbia University Press.
Schelling, F. W. J. 2004. *First outline for a system of the philosophy of nature.* Trans. Keith R. Peterson. New York: SUNY Press.
———. 2008. *The grounding of positive philosophy: The Berlin lectures.* Trans. Bruce Matthews. New York: SUNY Press.

The Legend of Zelda: Breath of the Wild as Philosophy: Teaching the Player to Be Comfortable Being Alone

84

Chris Lay

Contents

Introduction: Pandemic Guidelines in Hyrule	1884
Summary: How *Breath of the Wild* Redefines What It Is to Be a *Zelda* Game	1886
"My Hate Never Perishes...I Will Rise Again!"	1888
Absolute Freedom to Make Meaning from *BotW*'s Open World	1890
Two Repetitions: Fatigue from Meaningless Choices and Remaking the Individual	1894
Solitary, But Not Isolated: Finding the Self as Part of the Natural World	1896
Conclusion: Sequence Breaking as the Path to Human Flourishing	1902
References	1905

Abstract

Although many philosophers have historically regarded solitude as character-building, the popular conception is that solitude and isolation from other people are indistinct – being alone *just is* the same thing as loneliness. This became even more evident during lockdown and quarantine procedures during the early days of the global 2020 COVID-19 pandemic. As many people found themselves unable to enjoy face-to-face interpersonal contact for weeks or even months at a time, virtual means of socialization, such as video calls and multiplayer video games, became quite popular. This makes sense, of course. What was curious, though, was that certain single-player video games also started trending; among these was the 2017 Nintendo game *The Legend of Zelda: Breath of the Wild*. Why would experiences that ask players to withdraw even more deeply into seclusion prove to be so welcome during a time when so many people already feel isolated and lonely? This chapter argues that, at least in the case of *Breath of the Wild*, part of what players found so attractive is that the game suggests a view of being alone that teaches players to be more comfortable with both solitude and with them-

---

C. Lay (✉)
Young Harris College, Young Harris, GA, USA
e-mail: cmlay@yhc.edu

© Springer Nature Switzerland AG 2024
D. K. Johnson et al. (eds.), *The Palgrave Handbook of Popular Culture as Philosophy*,
https://doi.org/10.1007/978-3-031-24685-2_107

selves. In this chapter, in the context of the game's plot, objectives, and underlying mechanics, existentialist themes of eternal return, absolute freedom, the anxiety of choice, and Kierkegaardian repetition will all be considered. While these ideas may be present in *Breath of the Wild* to varying degrees, the chapter ultimately concludes that the game's central philosophical message is one of self-realization – and possibly human flourishing – through solitude.

Keywords

The Legend of Zelda · Solitude · Boredom · Existentialism · Absolute freedom · Choice · Eternal return · Repetition · Stoicism · Kierkegaard · Nietzsche · Sartre · Schopenhauer · Mill · Aristotle · Marx · Flourishing

Introduction: Pandemic Guidelines in Hyrule

By the time the COVID-19 pandemic hit most of the world in full force, *The Legend of Zelda: Breath of the Wild* was very nearly three years old and had already (seemingly) had its moment. Launching with Nintendo's hybrid console/handheld in March 2017, *Breath of the Wild* (*BotW*) was met with near universal acclaim – both from professional critics and ordinary gamers. Yet, the games industry thrives on a regular cycle of high-profile releases. Soon, titles like *Super Mario Odyssey, God of War*, and *Red Dead Redemption 2* would be along to captivate popular attention. *BotW* would certainly remain a uniquely important game for completionists, speed runners, and sequence breakers (players who attempt to skip required events and actions or access them out of the expected, linear order – often through glitches that break regular game boundaries). Even at the time of this chapter's writing, articles are still being published about the discovery of new secrets or techniques in the game (Price 2021). But, for the most part, people stopped talking about *BotW* as a videogame that *you need to play right now* and focused instead on how it would influence the industry going forward with its innovative mechanics.

Then, the pandemic happened. Many countries began issuing lockdown orders and shelter-in-place recommendations, and people suddenly found themselves walled off in their homes or apartments, with only their pets and devices to keep them company. As a salve for social isolation, a great number of people turned to multiplayer video games like Nintendo's *Animal Crossing: New Horizons* – fortuitously released in March 2020, as quarantine rules were at their peak. The simple charm of visiting a friend's island and running around together, catching fish and bugs, served as a stand-in for actual human contact. Curiously, however, others found solace in decidedly single-player gaming experiences. On its surface, this might appear strange. What help could something played exclusively alone provide to those already suffering from loneliness and social seclusion? Even more bizarrely, social media feeds were filled not just with people absorbed into newly released single-player titles – like *Doom Eternal*, which launched on the same day as *Animal Crossing* – but with those returning to old favorites, too. While *BotW* surely has a fetching look, owed to some impeccable art design, Nintendo's hybrid Switch lacks the flashier visuals and raw horsepower of both dedicated gaming PCs and competing machines from Sony and Microsoft. Likewise, the game does not offer players the most expansive or densely packed world to explore – released a year after *BotW* in 2018, both *Red Dead Redemption 2* and *Assassin's Creed: Odyssey* touted bigger maps with more to do, collect, and see.

Despite this, *BotW*, a three-year-old video game that was not even the most recent release in the *Legend of Zelda Series* (the *Link's Awakening* remake came out in the fall of 2019), was suddenly like new again. Pandemic players found something peculiarly beautiful in *BotW*'s portrayal of nature (Anderson 2020). Some argued that the simple plot, hefty length, and familiarity of its characters – *The Legend of Zelda* series has been going strong since 1986 – made the game a gentle comfort amidst the fear and confusion of the pandemic (Salam 2020). As the pandemic dragged on, lockdowns lifted, and people starting to have to navigate normal society again, still others found parallels in *BotW*'s depiction of communities trying to recover from disaster (Warner 2021). Like the villainous Calamity Ganon, the COVID-19 pandemic has been a nasty force that brought mass death, upended lives, and, at least for a time, left "civilized" spaces barren and ghostly.

There are multifarious reasons that explain *BotW*'s renewed popularity during the pandemic – many more than those described above. This chapter will attempt to make sense of this popularity, both in and out of quarantine, through an examination of what *BotW* appears to teach the player. Unlike films, television, and even other contemporary videogames, *BotW* does not philosophize through its story and characters; or, at least, it does not use narrative as its primary means of delivering a philosophical message. Rather, the game demonstrates an argument to the player through its structure, mechanics, and bold design choices.

Players spend dozens, and in many cases, *hundreds*, of hours trekking through *BotW*'s gorgeous world, working out solutions to slick environmental puzzles, taming wild horses, discovering new cooking recipes with varying status effects, and more – and the overwhelming majority of this time is spent alone. Yet, the experience importantly never feels *lonely*. (Contrast this with how the vast wastelands of the more recent *Fallout* titles feel desolate and suffocating.) Although *BotW* depicts a postapocalyptic world, its solitude encourages creativity and reflection instead of regret and loss. This chapter will argue that this is an intentional function of *BotW*'s design: Just as philosophers like John Stuart Mill and Arthur Schopenhauer do, *BotW* advocates solitude as something that is *good for* people because it allows them to flourish as human beings. If this claim is right, it also explains the renewed interest in the game through the pandemic. During a time where outside circumstances often forced people into social isolation, *BotW* showed them a way to be okay with being alone.

Summary: How *Breath of the Wild* Redefines What It Is to Be a *Zelda* Game

Part of *BotW*'s appeal comes from its radical changes to the venerable *Legend of Zelda* formula. Most *Zelda* games follow a similar gameplay template: as Link, the Chosen Hero, players navigate a large "overworld" map and periodically descend into perilous dungeons – complex, multitiered puzzle boxes that usually contain an especially useful item, such as bombs or the grappling-hook-like "hookshot," and one or more tough "boss" enemies. There is usually a healthy balance between combat, exploration, and puzzle-solving, and nearly all *Zelda* games share a similar, mythical story (these repeated themes will be discussed in the next section).

Outside of plot similarities and a map full of familiar locations – like the irrationally long Great Bridge of Hylia or the volcanic Death Mountain, belching smoke in the distance – *BotW* becomes a tremendous departure from roughly 40 years of tried-and-true *Zelda* mechanics. It is perhaps best to let series producer Eiji Aonuma introduce these differences. First, in a 2013 Nintendo Direct video describing the then in-production title, he teased:

> Our mission in developing this new *Zelda* game...is quite plainly to rethink the conventions of *Zelda*. I'm referring to things like the expectation that the player is supposed to complete dungeons in a certain order...The things that we've come to take for granted recently. We want to set aside these "conventions", get back to basics and create a newborn Zelda game so that the players today can best enjoy the real essence of the franchise.

Then, at the official Electronic Entertainment Expo (E3) reveal of *BotW* in 2014, he elaborated:

> It's quite a vast world isn't it? You can even reach those mountains in the distance, if you walk far enough. We couldn't create such a wide world like this in the past. As far as what you can do with such a vast field to explore, as soon as those boundaries are removed, it means you can enter any area from any direction. So the puzzle solving in this game begins the moment the player starts to think about where they want to go, how will they get there, and what they will do when they arrive. This...departure will create opportunities for new game-play that have not been experienced in previous Zelda games.

Despite some mild experimentation in past entries, such as the item shop in *A Link Between Worlds* that allowed players to tackle dungeons out of sequence, *Zelda* games had always been a linear experience. That is, dungeons were typically designed in escalating difficulty, areas of the world map were gated off until very specific items were obtained to "unlock" them, and game design carefully ferried players through an intentional "path" through the game.

By contrast, what characterizes *BotW* is its openness in nearly every aspect of design. Taking cues from "open-world" games like *The Elder Scrolls V: Skyrim* or *The Witcher III* – titles that drop players into massive, freely traversable game worlds – *BotW*'s Hyrule is a single, giant, continuous map, uninterrupted by loading screens. Players navigate this huge world via a map screen, gradually revealing obscured areas on the map by climbing towers dotted across Hyrule. This recalls a similar mechanic used by game publisher/developer Ubisoft in its *Assassin's Creed* and *Far Cry* franchises. Dungeon order does not matter anymore, as there are *no dungeons whatsoever*. (The Divine Beasts in *BotW* could be described as mini-dungeons, but even these are extremely nonlinear; players have a set of consoles that must be activated in each Beast, and this may be done in whatever order the player pleases.) Outside of the starting region of the Great Plateau – which is really just a large tutorial space that eases players into *BotW*'s new mechanics – nearly every part of the map is instantly accessible. Indeed, an especially skilled player can stroll right up to Hyrule Castle and challenge the final boss immediately after the tutorial zone.

This openness extends to the tools and abilities afforded to the player. Without dungeons to reward essential items, and with the removal of item-based "gates" in the overworld, players are now given all of Link's necessary abilities after the meaty tutorial is over. A new stamina meter, paired with a clever climbing ability, means that Link can scale any nonsmooth surface – unless his stamina runs out. Getting back down from those high places is also a cinch. Although usually a deterrent against free exploration of the world, fall damage is hardly a concern for *BotW* players; at any point in the air, Link can deploy a paraglider and float safely to the ground. A slew of color-dyeing options and an array of both weapons and armor sets, each with unique properties, give players the chance to customize Link like never before.

In addition to items and equipment, multiple complex systems are baked into the world to empower player choices. For instance, a day-night cycle regulates both weather/temperature mechanics and nonplayer character (NPC) behavior. And a robust physics system governs everything from item weights to magnetic charge to electric conductivity. Puzzles remain intricately designed, of course. However, immediate access to a full suite of abilities, large experimental spaces within which to move, and detailed systems that determine behind-the-scenes rules mean that players can approach puzzles from a multiplicity of directions. There is no longer just *one* way to solve them.

This is best seen in the new "shrines." While these enclosed areas sometimes serve as combat trials for the player, they are more often than not unique puzzle rooms designed around a single theme – such as using the Switch's gyroscopic controller to rotate a huge platform in order to guide a large ball through a stone maze. Moreover, shrines also subvert the traditional method by which *Zelda* players increase their health pool. Normally, players acquire "pieces of heart" from quests, chests, and particularly devious puzzles that gradually add "hearts" to their health meter. Conversely, *BotW*'s shrines award Spirit Orbs that can be exchanged for health or stamina upgrades at specific statues of the goddess Hylia found in the game world.

"My Hate Never Perishes...I Will Rise Again!"

Amidst all of this talk about how *BotW* plays, not much has been said about its plot. This is partly because most mainline entries in the *Zelda* series share certain story beats. The kingdom of Hyrule, populated by both humans and fantasy creatures such as the aquatic Zora and the gregarious, boulder-munching Gorons, is threatened by an ancient evil called Ganon. To defeat Ganon – who typically commands the Triforce of Power, one part of a triadic artifact – Link and the eponymous Princess Zelda must use the Triforces of Courage and Wisdom to banish Ganon and restore peace to the land. There have been variations on these general themes; for instance, Ganon does not even appear in the entries *Link's Awakening*, *Majora's Mask*, *The Minish Cap*, and *Phantom Hourglass*, among others. However, recurring characters, places, and events are common, and the *Zelda* game *Skyward Sword* even provides a canonical explanation for this repetition within the series' lore (which will be discussed below).

For its part, *BotW* does little to alter the narrative of the *Zelda* series. Ganon, now Calamity Ganon, has returned to terrorize Hyrule. Anticipating his arrival, King Rhoam enlists Champions from Hyrule's various races to each pilot one of four enormous machines called Divine Beasts and lead an assembly of "guardians" – smaller, autonomous machines created by the Sheikah, a tribe charged with protecting Hyrule and opposing Ganon throughout the ages. The four Champions are joined by Link, a skilled sword fighter who has been given the legendary Master Sword, and the scholarly Princess Zelda, who struggles to unlock her family's hereditary power. Before the Hylians can fully prepare, Calamity Ganon appears, defeating the Champions and securing control over the Divine Beasts and the guardians (in *BotW*'s fictional history of Hyrule, this event is known as the Great Calamity). Mortally wounded while defending Zelda, Link is placed in the Shrine of Resurrection to recover for 100 years while Zelda contains the spread of Calamity Ganon with her sealing magic – though this traps her with him. The player steps in as Link, who is suffering from amnesia after his century-long sleep. He must learn the history and purpose of his quest, reclaim the Master Sword, free the spirits of the slain Champions in their Divine Beasts, and recover enough of his former power to challenge Ganon in Hyrule Castle (in no particular order).

The above sketch of *BotW*'s story would appear to have next to nothing to do with this chapter's claim: that *BotW* sees solitude as central to human flourishing. If the reader's focus is restricted to only the details of the plot – its *contents* – this is surely true. Link does not succeed in banishing Ganon on his own. Even those players daring enough to fight Calamity Ganon without first rescuing the Champions still only succeed with Zelda's help. Likewise, the amnesiac Link would never have been able to set foot outside of the Great Plateau without King Rhoam's advice. In terms of its storytelling structure, though – the plot's *form* – the groundwork is laid for the necessity of solitude.

To see why, consider the philosophical notion of *eternal return* (sometimes also called *eternal recurrence*). One of the earliest versions of this idea can be found in the beliefs of the ancient Greek Stoics: The philosopher and historian Plutarch (1878) specifically attributes the view to Chrysippus, though it is named "ekpyrosis" there. Many Stoics – Chrysippus included – were famously fatalistic. They held that at least certain events were fated to occur and simply could not be avoided. Worse, these events recur continuously throughout time. The universe is destroyed in a great, purifying conflagration – the ekpyrosis – then restored anew, only for the same fated events to happen again before another cleansing fire continues the process, ad infinitum.

Friedrich Nietzsche revisits eternal return in several of his works, too. In *The Gay Science* ([1882] 1974), he develops the concept alongside a belief in *amor fati*, or the love of fate. It is unclear whether Nietzsche actually thinks that all of the events and actions of a person's life will repeat, given an infinite amount of time. Unlike the Stoics, he invokes the idea in the service of self-affirmation, not a cosmology of the universe. To Nietzsche, one must welcome the eternal recurrence of everything within one's life, both good and bad, becoming a "Yes-sayer" to whatever is fated. Doing so allows one to assert themselves as an individual in an act of claiming "fate" for themselves rather than just being a passive victim of it.

BotW is one instance in an overall structure of narrative repetition that permeates the entire *Zelda* series. Given this and the above descriptions from the Stoics and Nietzsche, *BotW* could fit as a case of eternal return. In the admittedly convoluted chronology of the franchise, each game represents one among an infinity of possible ways that the same events play out. Specific details might differ – Hyrule is submerged under a vast ocean in *The Wind Waker*, and the world of *BotW* is so technologically rich that Link can (if the player completes a certain quest) ride an actual motorcycle. Yet, the same core events seem to recur: Ganon rises with an ancient power, and both a Zelda and a Link appear to oppose him. In fact, Ganon is described in *BotW* in exactly this way when he is said to be the "Pure embodiment of ancient evil, reborn again and again." Sometimes, even smaller events on the periphery of the Ganon-Zelda-Link interaction repeat themselves. Mipha, the Zora princess (and Champion) in *BotW*, plainly loves Link – she even created a custom-made piece of aquatic armor for him, described in the item index as "Custom armor painstakingly crafted by each generation's Zora princess for her future husband." This echoes the relationship between Princess Ruto and Young Link in *Ocarina of Time* (though it is played for laughs there). In that earlier game, the haughty royal demands Link's affection and sneakily gifts him the Zora's Sapphire he needs to open the Door of Time. Of course, Link has no idea that the stone *also* serves as a Zora engagement ring!

Crucially, these multiple Hyrules seen across each *Zelda* game are not disconnected possible worlds, separated by the fact that some are actualized and others are not. No, like the Stoic ekpyrosis, at least some of the recurring events in the *Zelda* series fall within a linear timeline where Ganon's threat is purged, then repeated. (According to the official *Hyrule Historia*, published by Nintendo in 2011, there are actually *two* distinct timelines that branch off of a certain divergence point; each of the games fall somewhere along these two lines.) This is clear because some titles reference events and characters unique to others – like Zelda's claim in *BotW*, as she entrusts Link with the Master Sword, that "Whether skyward bound, adrift in time, or steeped in the glowing embers of twilight, the sacred blade is forever bound to the soul of the Hero." The phrases "skyward bound," "adrift in time," and "steeped in...twilight" indicate that the *Zelda* games *Skyward Sword*, *Ocarina of Time*, and *Twilight Princess* all precede *BotW* in the cycle of eternal recurrence.

Skyward Sword, the earliest title in the series' official chronology (so far), is unique among *Zelda* games in that it builds the eternal return of the conflict between Ganon, Zelda, and Link directly into the franchise's lore. Rather than Ganon, the terrible Demon King Demise imperils the kingdom. Upon his defeat by Zelda and Link, Demise threatens that "My Hate Never Perishes...I Will Rise Again!" Demise's design and color palette – including his gray skin, fiery red/orange hair, bulky physique, and general attitude of malice – suggest that the similar-looking Ganon is the recurring embodiment of his evil. (Of note: Ganon is *also* called the Demon King in various *Zelda* titles.) It is precisely Demise's curse that binds Hyrule, and some version of both Zelda and Link to a cycle of eternal return.

Even if *BotW* could be said to rest firmly within a cycle of eternal return that encompasses the whole series, this does not establish solitude as good for the player. Nietzsche's attempt to ground eternal return in self-affirmation may be a step in the right direction, but there is much more work to be done. More problematically, the open, choice-focused gameplay of *BotW* emphatically does not support the idea of an inescapable, repeated cycle. If anything, *BotW* breaks *Zelda* tradition with its incredibly nonlinear structure and thereby transcends this cycle. Perhaps this sense of free choice will offer a better inroad to finding a beneficial notion of solitude.

Absolute Freedom to Make Meaning from *BotW*'s Open World

BotW is an open-world video game, but the phrase "open-world video game" may mean less than it used to. While not an explicit genre unto itself, open-world structural elements began to be widely incorporated into mainstream games in the seventh console generation, which included the Xbox 360, Playstation 3, and Nintendo Wii. Of course, there had been examples of open-world design prior to this; *Grand Theft Auto III* and its successors popularized the open-world concept in a very narrow way in the early 2000s, but even the very first *Legend of Zelda* game in 1986 was remarkably "open-world" for its time. However, as advancements in gaming technology in the seventh and eighth console generations allowed for dynamic, increasingly expansive play spaces filled to the brim with characters and activities, open-world features became a standard part of nearly every designer's toolkit. For a time, "open-world" picked out a particular type of game with expected gameplay mechanics in much the same way as the phrase "role-playing game" (RPG) did. Eventually, though, RPG elements like leveling and character advancement crept into titles not otherwise associated with traditional RPGs. Similarly, large, freely roamable environments started to appear in the 2010s in games that could not neatly be sorted into the open-world category.

Though what open-world exactly means is somewhat up for grabs, the term generally describes a kind of nonlinear design where player objectives are spread out over a large area and can be approached in a variety of ways. Sometimes, open-world games include gobs of collectible items tucked into every corner of the game environment, like the more recent *Tomb Raider* entries. In others, players can take part in time-wasting side activities that seem completely tangential to normal gameplay (consider *Spider-Man 2*'s pizza delivery missions or the absurd number of money-making minigames in *No More Heroes*). Often, traversal mechanics are a major focus – whether one travels by vehicle (the *Saints Row* series), horse (*Ghost of Tsushima*), or some sort of superpower (*Infamous*). Above all, open-world design is defined by the enormity of the game world and players' freedom to choose how they will take part in it. To this end, most open-world games encourage "emergent" game experiences by layering mechanics into the world that make it appear to be "alive" – like *BotW*'s weather and day/night cycles, NPC behavior patterns, and other rules that govern how things operate in its world. Linear games ferry players through intricately crafted set pieces where everything that happens is intentional; by contrast, open-world design allows things to simply *happen* to players, given the systems in place.

On the whole, then, open-world games like *BotW* allow players to go wherever they want and do whatever they want – within the constrictions of a given title's rules for the world. But does this freedom of action as a design philosophy translate to a proper philosophy about free action? One might be tempted to draw similarities to Jean Paul Sartre's notion of *absolute freedom*. In *Being and Nothingness* (1956), Sartre acknowledges a difference between the popular conception of freedom and its reality in active human agents. Most people consider "freedom" to be the ability to do what one wants. This almost never accords with reality; however, the conditions in which each person is situated limit what actions one can take. Unlike the overwhelming majority of birds, no human can fly without significant technological aid (note that jumping and falling from a great height does not constitute flight). More realistically, someone confined to a hospital bed with a terminal illness is not free to leap out of bed and cartwheel out the door, even if they were an accomplished gymnast when not bedridden.

So, the freedom to do anything whatsoever, in stark defiance of social and physical restrictions, cannot be what Sartre means when he claims that humans are absolutely free. No, the freedom that humans actually enjoy is a freedom in meaning-making. The terminally ill person may be unable to simply choose to be healthy, but he/she can choose what importance his/her disease holds to him/her. Indeed, to say that humans *can* choose is to undersell Sartre's point. The freedom to confer meaning is unique to conscious beings, who are thereby made into a unique kind of thing: being-for-itself. Anyone who rejects this freedom acts in "bad faith" by believing themselves to be no different than ordinary objects, which possess only being-in-itself. Sartre says that being-for-itself – the active choice of meaning – is the negation of being-in-itself – a thing that simply is. In other words, being-for-itself is no thing at all (it is "nothing") but is instead *activity* or a mode of existing. People who believe that they cannot choose meaning for themselves thus misunderstand their own being, failing to recognize that this peculiar freedom is part and parcel of human existence.

In line with Sartre's observation, the player's choices in *BotW* are distinctly limited by the situation in which Link finds himself. Unlike the avian Rito – another of Hyrule's races – Link cannot fly unassisted. Nor can players "choose" to not take cold damage should they trudge through the snow in the mountainous Hebra region without the appropriate gear. To progress the main story of *BotW*, certain objectives *must* be completed – again, players cannot just decide not to follow them and still see the full narrative. There are no branching story options whereby player decisions can drastically change the trajectory of the game's events or the fates of its central characters, *a la* the *Mass Effect* franchise. And, in contrast to many other open-world games, there are few distraction-type activities in Hyrule; yes, players can go snowball bowling or challenge characters to a footrace, but there are no dedicated minigames like taxi driving or pizza delivery. In fact, some unsatisfied players criticized *BotW* as a sparse world with a lack of things to do.

Yet, the player *does* seem encouraged to invest his own meaning in the experience of playing *BotW*. Puzzles and objectives have intended solutions, but the complexity of the game's overlapping systems (like rules about, say, electric conductivity) and its nonlinear structure mean that nearly any obstacle can be successfully approached in multiple ways. The combat mechanics alone accommodate myriad styles of play, including stealth, mounted combat, ranged attacks, magic rods, and both one- and two-handed weapons. Enemy behaviors are nuanced enough – and the environments cleverly designed enough – that difficult fights can be rendered trivial by something as simple as rolling a large boulder down a hill onto a group of unaware enemies. Even apparently puzzle-oriented powers like the Magnesis Rune are surprisingly useful (and hilarious) in combat: It is difficult to suppress a manic cackle once players discover that they can gently smack a lumbering, cyclopic Hinox in the face – from a reliably safe distance – with a magnetically charged metal box until it dies (evidently from shame). The point is that gameplay options permit players to determine for themselves how they will play *BotW* and which types of play are meaningful, as there is no single playstyle that dominates.

There is, in fact, very little that *BotW* overtly tells players that they must value or find meaningful. Like other open-world games, there is nothing stopping players from ignoring the main questline altogether and passing the time with side quests – say, helping a Goron get the perfect cut of rock roast to revive his injured brother. A player may desire to master cooking or photography and so attempt to discover every recipe or photograph every item, creature, and major character to fill the in-game compendium. One could take this further, as Richard Taylor ([1970] 2000) might suggest, and generate meaning out of the most mundane of activities. Just as Sisyphus's boulder-pushing could have meaning if the activity were accompanied by an inner desire to push boulders, players could, for instance, choose to devote their time in Hyrule to chopping down every visible tree or by collecting every sneaky river snail they come across – all and only because this is what they want to do. At no point does the game discourage any activity within the world that the player could decide has meaning (save, perhaps, violence against innocent NPCs, which is simply not allowed).

This kind of self-directed gameplay is standard for open-world gaming. Where *BotW* distinguishes itself from its open-world peers, though, is in the way it handles the attachment of external – or game-defined – meaning to certain important activities. There are precious few collectibles in *BotW*. Scattered chests might contain rupees (*Zelda*'s longstanding currency) or rare weapons, but most "hidden" items in the world are either Spirit Orbs or golden Korok Seeds, and both of these are normally obtained through puzzle solving. Recall that Spirit Orbs are used to increase the player's health or stamina pool and are acquired from shrines – often complex combat or puzzle rooms. Korok Seeds are rewards given by tiny, friendly, tree-like creatures for completing minor environmental puzzles or feats of skill, like shooting down moving target balloons. These seeds can be exchanged with the giant Korok, Hetsu, for an improved weapon and shield capacity.

Now, in most games, hunting down all of a given collectible confers some additional reward on the player. This counts as external incentivization; with the promise of a unique prize dangled in front of players, collectibles are given meaning by the game itself. *BotW* actively does not provide this external incentivization for its collectibles, however. For completing all 120 shrines in the base game, players receive the "Wild" armor set, which resembles Link's iconic green cap and tunic from other games in the *Zelda* series. At the same time, even with the additional four Spirit Orbs provided by the Champions' Ballad expansion chapter, it is impossible to fully upgrade both Link's health and stamina pools at the same time. Players must decide which feature – health or stamina – is more meaningful to their playthrough. Things are different with Korok Seeds. The item description for the seeds cryptically suggests that "If you gather a bunch of them, you never know what may happen..." Should the player do this and give Hetsu all 900 seeds – even though only 441 are needed for full inventory capacity upgrade – the player receives a huge seed in return called Hetsu's Gift. If the player has not realized it already, it finally becomes obvious that Korok Seeds are actually Korok droppings; Hetsu's "gift of friendship" is then an *especially big* swirl of Korok dung. (Unsurprisingly, Hetsu's Gift "smells pretty bad" and is useless.)

For completionist players who feel compelled to do everything a game has to offer, these "rewards" are likely infuriating. Yet, both seem to express the Sartrean idea of absolute freedom, whereby the individual's greatest freedom is the ability to determine what counts as meaningful. By preventing players from fully upgrading Link – the normal incentive games provide for collecting upgrade items – *BotW* deliberately declines to attach external meaning to the task of collecting things. This is reinforced even more strongly by rewarding the dedicated Korok Seed collector with a massive handful of golden excrement. From a design perspective, the endpoints of Spirit Orb and Korok Seed collection communicate a specific message to the player: If these activities are to be meaningful, it is only because individual players infuse them with meaning. Although players are restricted by both the rules governing *BotW* and the range of possible activities programmed into the game, *BotW* also appears to be designed in such a way as to allow players to freely decide which of these activities are important.

Two Repetitions: Fatigue from Meaningless Choices and Remaking the Individual

Absolute freedom cannot be the whole story. Even setting aside the fact that the connection between solitude—the focus for this chapter—and absolute freedom is not immediately clear, this account leaves out something key to Sartre's theory: the fact that freedom is sometimes dreadful. In "Existentialism is a Humanism," Sartre ([1946] 2007) famously claims that human freedom is a state of condemnation. Fellow existentialist Soren Kierkegaard carries the notion further, cashing out the problematic nature of choice as a feeling of stifling anxiety or angst – most explicitly in *The Concept of Anxiety* ([1844] 2013). Every choice presents the chooser with a set of mutually exclusive options; committing to one option obliterates the possibility of ever choosing the other. The irreversibility of the choice, the unknowability of the consequences, and the simultaneous repulsion and attraction to having to choose force the individual into a state of anxiety. But, to Kierkegaard, it is only in this state that individual freedom is realized. The experience of anxiety is a response to the possibility of freely choosing, and the actualization of a possible choice in a single moment of choosing is also the becoming of a distinct self.

It is sometimes said that open-world games in particular foster a sort of anxiety in players (though this is not unique to gaming) – called decision paralysis – around the lack of external direction and extreme player agency in making gameplay decisions (Slack 2015). For many open-world games, this is because of their content. Designers of giant play spaces feel the need to stuff those spaces with activities, mission objectives, side events, and all manner of trinkets to keep players engaged and exploring for dozens of hours. As a result, map screens in games like the *Assassin's Creed* series and *The Witcher III* are so saturated with icons – indicating everything from high-priority enemy targets to treasure stashes – that the player seemingly needs a sophisticated search engine just to decipher what everything on the map legend means. Some games even incorporate frequent, repeated prompts, in the form of both video and audio cues, to complete unfinished quests and objectives. Of course, this adds further pressure to commit to a choice as if an unseen authority is monitoring the player's every move.

Here is where *BotW* breaks both from the existentialist account of freedom and from many other open-world games. *BotW*'s world is expressly not bloated with superfluous side activities and collectibles. Vast swaths of its landscape are empty; again, this was a critique from some players who expected a more standard open-world experience. For the most part, *BotW*'s map screen includes only unlocked fast-travel locations (visited landmarks to which a player can instantly teleport). Other map icons can be manually added by the player, either by directly appending "stamps" to the map or by marking waypoints using the Sheikah Slate – a ubiquitous, tablet-like piece of technology that allows the player to manage inventory items, view the compendium, and more – as a viewfinder. Choice is simply not anxiety-inducing in the way of most open-world titles, as players of *BotW* are not constantly bombarded with competing activity options or reminders of outstanding tasks that the game insists must be completed.

To get a more precise picture of how *BotW* presents freedom to the player – and to bridge the gap from freedom to solitude – it will be necessary to revisit the notion of eternal return, though this time by a different name. While Nietzsche already characterizes the acceptance of eternal return as the self-affirmation of fatalistic events, this chapter's detour into absolute freedom and the anxiety of choice informs discussion of a new phenomenon, also drawn from Kierkegaard. Writing under the appropriately repetitive pseudonym "Constantine Constantius," Kierkegaard ([1843] 1983) examines the possibility of *repetition* in a book of the same name. Unfortunately, neither Kierkegaard nor Constantine do the reader the service of cleanly defining what repetition *is*. (Indeed, to truly decipher it would require a lengthy aside on the ways that *Repetition* intersects with other writings in Kierkegaard's body of work.)

Constantine does claim that repetition is the same "movement" as recollection, just in the opposite direction. Recollecting allows one to bring the wonder and intensity of a past pleasure back into the present moment where it might be experienced in perpetuity; however, recollection also seems to separate one from that which is desired, as it is a backward movement that represents retreat into the past. For instance, *BotW*'s "Captured Memories" side quest sends the amnesiac Link all around Hyrule to recover meaningful memories of his work with Zelda before the Great Calamity occurred. In revisiting the locations where these events happened, though, what is important is not the act of recalling them. Rather, the significance of the repeated memories is in how they inform Link's future actions and better position him to save Hyrule. Repetition is then preferred to recollection. It is a way of eternalizing the pleasurable but with a forward movement. Yet, Constantine's search for repetition ends up frustrated, though the young man he advises in the book appears to encounter a second, more fulfilling type of repetition.

Spurred by a critic's remarks, Kierkegaard ([1909] 1975) does attempt in some of his personal journals to explain his meaning further. Here, as in the book, he outlines two repetitions – but he importantly ties both to freedom and the actualization of the individual. The first repetition is freedom at the level of choosing and experiencing external pleasure; here, repetition spoils freedom in the way that a lack of novelty inspires boredom. One may attempt to recapture past pleasures that were deeply satisfying, as Constantine does when he returns to Berlin to replicate a prior trip and all of its pleasures. But there is no way for him to exactly repeat what has already happened with the newness it originally held.

Instead, Kierkegaard suggests a second repetition that is focused inwardly rather than at the temporary objects of the external world. As in other works by Kierkegaard, there is a transcendent and religious character to this inwardness. In the context of this chapter, though, it is best to understand the inward repetition as freedom that relates only to itself instead of to what is outside of it. In other words, what gets repeated are not particular experiences but the self as a meaning-making individual.

Kierkegaard's two repetitions exemplify the differences between more standard open-world videogames and *BotW*. In normal open-world games, the glut of same-y activities and collectibles quickly becomes repetitive and monotonous for many players. By inundating the player with too much to do – evidently following an "if players liked doing this once, they'll love it 100 times" theory of game design – the fun of playing the game eventually feels like simply checking off boxes on a completion list. What was once open-world decision paralysis becomes *decision fatigue* with doing the same thing, again and again.

This is especially true for titles like Ubisoft's long-running *Assassin's Creed* and *Far Cry* series, but also the company's more recent – and decidedly *BotW*-inspired – *Immortals: Fenyx Rising*. For instance, 2020's *Assassin's Creed: Valhalla* casts the player as a Viking leader intent on conquering medieval England. Seeing the story to its end requires a lengthy grind whereby the player weakens and eventually topples the existing authority in a given region of the world map, usually culminating in an intense raid/assault on the enemy's keep. While doing this once or twice can be incredibly exciting, repeating the same actions in *five* distinct regions might become a chore for some players. And this is to say nothing of the treasure, collectibles, and side activities like drinking mini-games or flyting – the Viking equivalent of a rap battle. Likewise, *Immortals*, which ostensibly takes its cues from *BotW* with the inclusion of a recharging stamina meter, shrines, gliding, and a "climb-nearly-anything" mechanic, misses much of the point of *BotW*. Rather than leaving exploration and collecting decisions up to the player, the map is once again overloaded with icons for gems and other currencies to collect.

These gameplay decisions are all clearly in-line with Kierkegaard's outwardly oriented, pleasure-seeking repetition. By avoiding the "checklist-style" gameplay loop and placing the determination of meaning in the hands of the player, as described in the previous section, *BotW* seems to instead encourage the *other* repetition: the inward expression of the individual as an active agent. (Note: many players seem to very much enjoy these repeated actions – this chapter is not making a value judgment about the quality of other open-world games or players' experiences with them. The point is just that the type of repetition employed by those games can uniquely lead to boredom and dissatisfaction in a way that *BotW* does not.)

Solitary, But Not Isolated: Finding the Self as Part of the Natural World

Here at last, in the kind of inwardly turned repetition that creates a distinct individual opposed to the external, is the connection to solitude as something good for the player. The chapter can now explore its thesis: that *BotW* argues – given the time and opportunity to reflect on themselves in solitude – players can truly learn and grow in a way prevented by preoccupation with outside things. This belief is not universally held among philosophers, of course. For one, David Hume ([1751] 1989) notably refers to solitude as a "monkish virtue" that atrophies the genuine development of the person. All the same, there is a considerable philosophical history in favor of the intellectual advantage and necessity of solitude.

To start with someone already mentioned, one of Sartre's (1955) most repeated – and misunderstood – philosophical points is the claim in the play *No Exit* that "Hell is other people." Writing in an introduction to a long-unpublished novel by Sartre's frequent philosophical collaborator and lover Simone de Beauvoir (2021), celebrated author Margaret Atwood notes that the proper corollary to Sartre's claim must be "Heaven is solitude." Whether or not Sartre would accept his corollary himself is immaterial. Atwood's inversion of his quote represents a philosophical stance toward solitude rooted in the ancients. (These few examples are not meant to be exhaustive – neither for philosophical antiquity nor for the broader history of philosophy, most of which is left out completely. Rather, they serve here only as a baseline for the long-standing belief among philosophers that solitude is good for the mind.)

In the *Nicomachean Ethics*, Aristotle (2009) writes of the best sort of life as one involving contemplation. "Best" here refers both to a life's quality and its potential for virtue or moral excellence, and both of these are only achievable alone. As part of his defense of *anamnesis*—the idea that individual knowledge is recollected from the immortal soul's previous experience—in Plato's *Phaedo*, Socrates tells his audience that "the soul reasons best...when it is most by itself" (2002, p. 102). To Plato, even the basic capacities for bodily sense perception are just distractions from the sort of intellectual solitude needed to achieve wisdom. Laozi, in verse 42 of the *Tao Te Ching*, remarks that "Ordinary men hate solitude. But the Master makes use of it, embracing his aloneness, realizing he is one with the whole universe" (1988). Solitude thereby empowers a sense of philosophical discovery and a path to truth that are both impossible in its absence, and this is something that the adept thinker understands.

Nonetheless, simply being alone is not enough for the sort of solitude that is character-building and self-affirming. As Aristotle observes in the *Politics*, "He who is unable to live in society, or who has no need because he is sufficient for himself, must be either a beast or a god" (1996, p. 14). The latter option – that one is so self-sufficient to be a god – is not really a live possibility for Aristotle. So, his implication is that being isolated from others in society is in fact quite bad for the intellect; it reduces human reason to the incapacity for thought of a beast. If *BotW* is to propose solitude as something advantageous, solitude will need to be conceptually distinguished from more harmful forms of isolation from others.

To this end, the remainder of this section will highlight two particular philosophical treatments of solitude that best accord with solitude's depiction in *BotW*, from John Stuart Mill and Arthur Schopenhauer. Beginning with Mill, there is an emphasis in his discussion of solitude on contact with the nonhuman world. In Book IV, Chapter VI of his *Principles of Political Economy* ([1848] 1909), he states:

> It is not good for man to be kept perforce at all times in the presence of his species. A world from which solitude is extirpated is a very poor ideal. Solitude, in the sense of being often alone, is essential to any depth of meditation or of character; and solitude in the presence of natural beauty and grandeur, is the cradle of thoughts and aspirations which are not only good for the individual, but which society could ill do without. Nor is there much satisfaction in contemplating the world with nothing left to the spontaneous activity of nature; with every rood of land brought into cultivation, which is capable of growing food for human beings; every flowery waste or natural pasture ploughed up, all quadrupeds or birds which are not

domesticated for man's use exterminated as his rivals for food, every hedgerow or superfluous tree rooted out, and scarcely a place left where a wild shrub or flower could grow without being eradicated as a weed in the name of improved agriculture.

There is little to analyze here that Mill has not already said for himself. He defines solitude as a mental space within which one "contemplates the world." Presumably, this space is the locus of growth and "depth of character" for the individual because it forces one to retreat from the myopic considerations of purely human society and recognize that humans are just one part of a larger ecosystem. Mill laments the possibility of a world in which all so-called "natural" elements have been brought to serve purely human purposes, like the razing of land for agriculture and industry, the elimination of "pest" species, or the domestication of wildlife. Without nature, there is no longer a genuine "world" to contemplate – just an extension of individual humans and human society. So, despite closing one off from other people in thought, solitude is decidedly not an isolating experience for Mill. To the contrary: Solitude *opens* the agent to a type of thinking that goes beyond narrow, selfish concerns.

Mill's claim seems to be that solitude engenders an appreciation for nature and affords the individual a clearer understanding of his place in a world where he is not really the sovereign. In the player's solitary wanderings through the scope, beauty, and wonder of Hyrule, *BotW* also appears to be making this claim. Almost all of the game is spent alone; short of tamed horses to call to Link's side, there are no companion characters to accompany the player (as in, say, *Fallout 3* or *The Outer Worlds*), and encounters with the rules, structures, and people in "civilized society" are quite brief. The chief cities and lived spaces for the various races – Gorons, Zora, Rito, Gerudo, and Koroks – are each visually memorable and full of activity. Yet, no sooner do players enter one of these areas than they are pushed out into nature again. Sometimes, this is because an NPC in town assigns the player a side quest with an objective that requires leaving. Often, though, players just feel the call of the wild.

It is no coincidence that the game's title alludes to this notion: the wild spaces, apart from civilization, have a certain "breath" to them. In other words, *BotW*'s world feels *alive*. The world – with its idiosyncratic weather patterns, varied biomes, and rich wildlife – is a character unto itself. In many titles, most features of the game world feel premade specifically for the player. This is obvious in linear experiences that funnel the player through successions of carefully designed moments, but also in open-world games where "gamified" elements reshape the world into a playground for player decisions. For instance, in *Bioshock*, players might come across enemies standing in a puddle of water – perfect fodder for the player's Electro Bolt plasmid (a power that allows the player character to discharge electricity from his hand). Games train players to see parts of the game world in this way: Every character, item, and piece of level geometry is first and foremost assessed in terms of its utility for player actions.

This "gamification" is exactly what Mill warns against when he worries that, without solitude, nature will be reduced to its use-value for humans. Importantly, *BotW* avoids these gamified elements precisely because its world seems to get on just fine without the player's involvement. Perched atop a nearby hill, Link can observe as a group of enemy Bokoblins and Moblins spend hours chasing horses or goats before they eventually settle down for a nap. While scaling a sheer cliffside, the player might be passed by a flock of birds that lands nearby. Unlike some games, these birds are not background features but are actual character models that can be interacted with. A few arrows later, Link has a set of bird drumsticks to roast over the fire. Sat by that same campfire while admiring the night sky, Link may trace a meteor's path to where it hits the ground in a shimmering flash – if he's quick enough, he can collect an exceedingly rare "star fragment" from the point of impact! None of these events are scripted: that is, programmed to happen *exactly this way*. Rather, they occur naturally given the constant interaction of all of *BotW*'s overlapping systems. This further lends the feeling that the player has been invited to take part in a game world whose existence does not depend solely on the player and their actions – the "spontaneous activity of nature" that Mill describes.

Reaching harmony with the vicissitudes of the natural world is a key part of several gameplay mechanics. Excessive heat and cold will gradually whittle down the player's health and must be protected against with clothing, potion, or food medleys that offer heat/cold resistance. The aforementioned cooking system allows players to brew potions or concoct meals that heal, improve Link's character statistics (like strength, speed, and defense), or provide stamina buffs. However, the effects of food and item combinations must be discovered by the player through experimentation with both ingredients and cooking methods – an apple broiled in a pot has different properties than one dropped to bake beside the fire. Success in *BotW*'s world demands that the player come not just to understand but also to *appreciate* how the parts of that world work together.

Appreciation for the world looks to be an intentional part of *BotW*'s design. Rotate the camera in just about any direction while playing, and the screen will be filled, frame to frame, with a marvelous vista. Fields of long grass sway in the wind in Hyrule Field. Smoke rings hover around Death Mountain's imposing figure. Rays of golden light pierce the thick canopy of the Lost Woods. The incredible art direction that gives the game its distinctive, cel-shaded style and bright, pastel colors seems tailor-made to force the player to periodically stop and just gape at the world. *BotW*'s impressive scale adds to the awe-struck relationship players have with Hyrule's geography. Looking out from one of the Sheikah Towers used to uncover hidden parts of the map, the game's massive draw-distance lets the player see just how tiny Link is by comparison. And yet, seeing the world spread out so widely is simultaneously encouraging, as players realize that everything they see is also accessible – given the right combination of gliding, climbing, running, and riding.

Admiration for the natural world in the way that Mill discusses – and that *BotW* builds neatly into its design – can only come by being apart from other people. This may not be immediately clear from Mill's short remarks, so this section now shifts to Schopenhauer. Schopenhauer's account of solitude is far more systematic than Mill's – or indeed than most philosophers, who often seem to take the intellectual benefit of solitude to be self-evident. Across two volumes of his *Parerga and Paralipomena*, which include short essays on a number of topics, a clear understanding of solitude comes into focus.

In the first volume, Schopenhauer (2014) connects solitude with the same sort of self-actualization seen in Kierkegaard's inward repetition. He argues:

> We can only be entirely ourselves as long as we are alone; therefore, whoever does not love solitude, also does not love freedom; for only when we are alone, are we free...Accordingly, we will flee, tolerate, or love solitude in exact proportion to the value of our own self. In solitude the wretched person feels his whole wretchedness and the great mind the full extent of its greatness; in short, everyone becomes aware of himself as what he is. (p. 447)

In the most literal sense, solitude is "freeing" because there is no other authority or source of obligation beyond the individual himself/herself. However, solitude also gives the mind its best opportunity to contemplate, reflect, and seek satisfaction in its own activity. Just as choice might, to existentialists like Kierkegaard or Sartre, force the chooser into a kind of crisis, solitude is horrifying to the undeveloped mind – or to the person unused to thinking for itself. Stripped of both the social affectations that people publicly adopt and the safety net of other people's advice, solitude forces the individual to confront itself and discover what beliefs he/*she* holds. So, solitude is also freeing by cordoning off the individual from the social environment in order to permit an authentic self to express itself.

To Schopenhauer, the difference between the person delighted by solitude and the person terrified by it is really the difference between the distinct states of solitude and isolation/loneliness. Someone with a mature sense of self – whose sense of self is *internally* defined – and a reflective attitude finds separation from other people to be often helpful. As Schopenhauer puts it, "For the more somebody has in himself, the less he needs from the outside and the less others can be to him" (2014, p. 351). In solitude, such an autonomous individual relates only to himself/herself and can think without distraction. But "being alone" turns into "being isolated/lonely" for those individuals whose self-perception is heavily dependent on others, since being alone cuts them off from other people – the external sources of their sense of self. For this reason, Schopenhauer sees these individuals as nonautonomous; and because they are inexperienced in thinking for themselves, nonautonomous people tend to become bored easily due to repetitive or "monotonous" thoughts.

If Schopenhauer is right, then boredom is not as benign a condition as it is perhaps taken to be today. Conversely, boredom is one of the greatest harms to free thought and the development of the individual, as the bored person seeks simply to "kill time" – typically through sensuous pleasures or the company of other people. The problem with "time killing" activities is that their effect is just to distract the mind rather than to improve the intellect or character and thereby lead to the creation of an autonomous self. Solitude does not produce boredom, as the solitary individual is an autonomous self and is comfortable being alone. By contrast, isolated/lonely individuals cannot tolerate themselves and flee into socialization to avoid having to introspect (whether they are directly aware of this or not).

To be clear, Schopenhauer does not demonize interpersonal interaction in principle. Indeed, he admits that humans have social needs as a matter of biological fact, adding that human youth and adolescence are periods where socialization is the basis for learning anything at all. Moreover, Schopenhauer concedes that excessive time alone can be inimical to the individual; too much distance from other people can make one ignorant of social cues to the point of regularly misinterpreting what others say as hostile or mean. Nonetheless, he is adamant that solitude is altogether necessary for intellectual and personal growth and that, as one gets experience with reflection-in-solitude, mature individuals withdraw from society as they age.

Schopenhauer thus more fully explains Mill's claim that the appreciation of nature requires genuine separation from other people. The active, contemplative state of mind needed to view the natural world as anything more than something with a use-value is (to Schopenhauer) suppressed when dealing with others. That *BotW* presents the player with this view of solitude in nature has already been argued. But there is more from Schopenhauer that the game appears to support – in particular, the distinction between isolation/loneliness and solitude.

In *BotW*, the player is alone but not lonely. Despite taking place in an apocalypse, exploring Hyrule is a tranquil experience. Much has already been said about the game's visuals in this regard, but *BotW*'s music also contributes to the muted, pleasant atmosphere. A soundtrack of peaceful and relaxing piano chords accompanies the player while roaming the hills, fields, and valleys; interestingly, the music never descends into the melancholic as in the similarly piano-heavy *I Am Setsuna*. This is because the world of *BotW*, though shattered by Calamity Ganon's spreading malice, is meant to be viewed as a place of promise and possibility for what the player can accomplish – not hopelessness because Link is alone.

As with Schopenhauer, there is also an expectation in *BotW* of at least temporarily breaking solitude and associating with others. Whether to complete and begin quests or to rest and resupply, it does sometimes happen that players have to enter society. Yet, towns and cities – as places where players are surrounded by other characters – simply have little for the player to do. They are spaces where players can talk to people, certainly, but there is not much more to be gained from the interaction than a bit of information about the region. The excitement in *BotW* is to be found in the solitude of the open world, such as the thrill of being met with a challenging group of enemies or a particular head-scratcher of a shrine puzzle, then coming up with a novel way to overcome these obstacles.

The distinction between solitude and isolation/loneliness is reflected in a majority of *BotW*'s mechanics, too. The structure of the game compels the player toward self-sufficiency in thought by asking the player to internalize the rules that govern the use of abilities, items, and all of the overlapping systems in the game world. Then, the player must constantly apply these rules by approaching problems with creative solutions. Nearly all gameplay decisions are player-directed; in general, there is no more explicit, tutorial-style guidance once the player floats down from the Great Plateau. Players set objectives on the world map for themselves, discover potion and food recipes through trial and error, and receive no hints at all when trying to solve complicated shrine puzzles. Even the in-game item compendium must be manually filled in, entry by entry, by photographing every weapon, item, and creature. In this way, *BotW*'s player-directed gameplay mechanics nicely capture Schopenhauer's belief that solitude builds an intellectually autonomous self. One can surely "kill time" in *BotW*, but this hardly seems to be the goal of the game's design. "Killing time" is, on Schopenhauer's definition, a mindless kind of activity. Were this something that *BotW* promoted, one would expect less self-directed gameplay and more of the very guided, checklist-style activities found in other open-world titles.

Conclusion: Sequence Breaking as the Path to Human Flourishing

Though *Zelda*'s overarching, series-spanning plot might invoke eternal return, any repetition in its gameplay is not simply doing the same thing, again and again – it is instead the inward repetition of affirming and empowering oneself to make meaning of Hyrule's open world. And, despite giving the player this freedom to make meaning for itself, the absolute freedom of *BotW* is not the terrible burden that Sartre and Kierkegaard conceive. This chapter has argued that *BotW*'s emphasis on player agency as part of a living, natural world is best explained by different (though related) philosophical notions of solitude found in Mill and Schopenhauer. Part of the chapter's argument is that *BotW* depicts solitude as *good for the player*. While this has somewhat been resolved in the previous section, what if solitude could be intimately connected to human flourishing – the kind of life where a human most fulfills their potential? In other words, could *BotW* be saying not just that solitude is good but that it is also a path to what philosophers have called *the good life*?

In the second volume of *Parerga and Paralipomena*, Schopenhauer (2015) returns briefly to the concept of boredom and suggests something that the nonautonomous person plainly lacks by refusing to introspect: imagination. He calls boredom a sudden awareness that existence is "empty." People then attempt to fill this emptiness with activities that are, at best, trivial and, at worst, self-destructive: gambling, alcoholism, frivolous spending, and gossip, among others. By way of what was said above, one sense in which boredom signifies emptiness is that the nonautonomous individual has an underdeveloped sense of self that is grounded in external sources. Yet, Schopenhauer also seems to see the nonautonomous person as "empty" in imagination. Though imagination requires sensory experience for the material out of which imagination generates its objects of thought, imagination is only active in solitude and for those capable of reflecting in solitude – when external stimuli, including other people, have been shut out. So, the nonautonomous individual – who can only think repeated, monotonous thoughts – also lacks imagination, which is creative in character.

Now, creativity also features in Marx's account of human flourishing, and Marx's account owes a debt to Aristotle. As part of the virtue-based ethic that he advances in the *Nicomachean Ethics*, Aristotle (2009) describes *eudaimonia* – the condition of living well. In short, achieving *eudaimonia* and living the best kind of human life means fulfilling the human function as excellently as possible. Since Aristotle defines the human function as rational thought, the very best kind of human life will be one that is both guided by rationality and that allows one's rational capacity to develop more fully. Though Marx (1964) agrees that rationality is an important component of the well-lived human life, he adds to Aristotle's claim that it is *spontaneous and creative* rational activity that is essential to humans. So, Marx argues in his essay "Estranged Labour," in repetitive, monotonous labor which requires no thought – like factory work – humans become alienated from the creative, rational core of human flourishing.

Taken together, Schopenhauer's notion of imagination and Marx's theory of human-function-as-creative-rationality suggest that an autonomous individual, engaged in imaginative solitude, is fulfilling human flourishing. For all of the inwardly directed creative thought that *BotW*'s gameplay inspires, it probably seems like a stretch to claim that figuring out a nonstandard solution to a shrine puzzle represents the best way of living. In fairness to Marx, though, this sort of problem-solving likely would not count as the spontaneous creativity that he had in mind. Namely, just supplying a nonstandard solution would fail to count because its creativity is still bound by the fairly narrow, established rules of *BotW*'s play space. True spontaneous creativity would likely have to subvert the existing rules and invent an entirely new method of approaching the problem.

As it turns out, this sort of rule-breaking creativity *is* regularly practiced in *BotW* (and in the wider gaming community more generally) in the form of sequence breaking. Often used to improve player completion times in speed runs, sequence breaks exploit glitches and other game errors to bypass rules and boundaries in order to complete events out of the expected sequence. Sometimes, sequence breaks involve actually breaking boundaries: A popular method is to discover a means of "clipping" through level geometry to move the player character outside the normal regions in which the character can move. There are far too many sequence breaks and other exploits used by *BotW* players to mention here, but hopefully a single, illustrative example will serve present purposes.

The first DLC expansion for *BotW*, called Trial of the Sword, is a 51 "floor" series of successive combat rooms, increasing in enemy difficulty and divided into three independent sections. Link also starts each of the three sections with no weapons or armor at all. The Trial of the Sword is no joke! As might be expected, this level of challenge proved restrictive for many players, so some in the community discovered a very clever (and still rather difficult to pull off, in its own right) sequence break. Sparing the grittier details, the sequence break allows the player to travel outside of the first combat room in a given section by exploiting a movement glitch to clip through the room's wall. During a normal run through the Trial of the Sword, the player teleports from room to room and never sees beyond the walls. By sequence breaking, though, players find out that all of the rooms are actually placed on a single, giant map. So, by clipping through the wall of the first combat room, the player can determine the location of the final combat room in the sequence, clip through *that* wall using the same glitch, and bypass all of the other rooms.

Arguably, the sort of creativity expressed by this complex sequence break fits Marx's idea of spontaneous, creative rational thought. These sequence breakers did not merely work within the existing system of rules to solve a problem – they discovered unique ways to bypass those rules and thereby create a new kind of solution. Crafting this solution could also be said to satisfy Schopenhauer's definition of imagination and autonomy. Surely the sequence breakers could not have been thinking only repetitive, monotonous thoughts; otherwise, they would have been unable to conceive of such a novel solution. Even if one provisionally accepts that *BotW* sequences breaks like this *do* show that creative displays of imagination (by Schopenhauer's definition) represent solitude-as-flourishing, the goal of the chapter is to demonstrate that *BotW* makes this argument. And, at first glance, it seems like the actions of a group of players to work outside the boundaries deliberately designed into the game have nothing to do with an argument that *BotW* makes. These players had no authorial input in the making of the game, after all.

Yet, *BotW* is a four-year-old game, at the time of writing. Like any contemporary game, it has received various stability patches over its lifespan. Glitches/exploits that enable sequence breaks are frequently "patched out" when developers are made aware of them, if those glitches/exploits somehow deviate from their vision for the game. For just one very small example, games like *Borderlands 3*, *Diablo III*, *Dragon Age: Inquisition*, and *Dying Light* all removed item duplication glitches in patches and game updates. But the above sequence break – and countless other *BotW* glitches/exploits – have not been touched. This seems to imply that *BotW*'s developers at least see these sequence breaks as harmless to their intended way of experiencing the game. However, game developers take their work quite seriously, and Nintendo is notorious in the videogame industry for releasing highly polished, glitch-free titles. It seems reasonable that even an innocuous glitch/exploit would be removed if it failed to align with the experience that developers have painstakingly designed for the player.

More likely, then, is that the developers regard creative sequence breaks as an extension of *BotW*'s design philosophy. Given the direction of this chapter, this would make sense. The chapter has argued that, mostly through its design, *BotW* actively encourages a particular kind of self-affirming decision-making from the player. To make use of the very skills that the game teaches in order to bypass the rules of the game would appear to be the ultimate application of self-affirming decision-making.

(There is a tangential concern that lies somewhat outside the scope of this chapter about whether or not sequence breaks and exploits constitute "cheating." It is worth mentioning that the above claims still apply – if *BotW*'s developers saw these activities as "cheating" or deviating from the intended experience in an otherwise dishonest way, one would expect that they would hurry to correct the problem in patches/updates. At the same time, one must note that video games have a long history of developer-included "cheat codes" that alter gameplay substantially, often by *over*powering the player. And, as many players within sequence-break communities point out, as long as glitches/exploits exist in a purely single-player game where there is no competitive advantage to be gained and other players are not affected whatsoever, making use of glitches/exploits is left to individual player choice. If this chapter's argument is correct, it hardly matters whether sequence breaking is "cheating" because the player's choice to do so – or not – is paramount.)

So, solitude is good for players because it allows them to reflect inwardly, eventually causing them to see the game world differently and become autonomous thinkers. It is clear that *BotW* endorses this view because these are the success conditions for the game; contemplating situations and devising creative solutions is the best way to "win" things like enemy encounters and puzzle rooms. Ganon can be challenged any time after the player leaves the Great Plateau, but defeating Ganon – the stated object of the game's plot, by all accounts – is far from the "end" of the game. Loading up a "cleared" save file just sees the player returned to Ganon's throne room, immediately prior to the boss fight. A new completion percentage tracker, among a few other additions, encourages players to keep exploring Hyrule. Again, this is because the real point of *BotW* is fostering creative player agency, not "beating the game" in the traditional sense. By accepting that this same autonomous thought can be used to *transcend* the game's boundaries, though, *BotW* claims that solitude is similarly transcendent. To Schopenhauer, there is comfort in solitude because only then can one be a self. *BotW* does him one better: The comfort in solitude is that it teaches one to be their *best* self.

References

Anderson, Cade. 2020. The pandemic is proof that video games are good for you. *The Daily Utah Chronicle*, November 14, 2020. https://dailyutahchronicle.com/2020/11/14/the-pandemic-is-proof-that-video-games-are-good-for-you/

Aristotle. 1996. The politics. In *The complete works of Aristotle*. Edited by Johnathan Barnes and Stephen Everson. Cambridge: Cambridge University Press.

———. 2009. *The Nicomachean ethics*. Trans. by David Ross. Ed. by Lesley Brown. Oxford: Oxford University Press.

De Beauvoir, Simone. 2021. *Inseparable: A never-before-published novel*. Trans. by Sandra Smith. New York: Harper Collins.

Hume, David. (1751) 1989. *Enquiries concerning human understanding and concerning the principles of morals*. Ed. by P. H. Nidditch. Oxford: Oxford University Press.

Kierkegaard, Soren. (1909) 1975. *Søren Kierkegaard's journals and papers*, vol. 4: s-z. Trans. by Howard V. Hong and Edna H. Hong. Indianapolis: Indiana University Press.

———. (1843) 1983. *Fear and trembling/repetition*. Trans. by Howard V. Hong and Edna H. Hong. Princeton: Princeton University Press.

———. (1844) 2013. *The concept of anxiety: A simple psychologically orienting deliberation on the dogmatic issue of hereditary sin*. Trans. by Reidar Thomte. Princeton: Princeton University Press.

Laozi. 1988. *Tao te ching: A new English version*. Trans. by Stephen Mitchell. New York: Harper & Row.

Marx, Karl. 1964. *Economic and philosophic manuscripts of 1844*. New York: International Publishers.

Mill, John Stuart. (1848) 1909. *Principles of political economy, with some of their applications to social philosophy*. Ed. by William James Ashley. London: Longmans, Green, and Co.

Nietzsche, Friedrich. (1882) 1974. *The gay science*. Trans. by Walter Kaufmann. New York: Vintage Books.

Plato. 2002. *Five dialogues*. Trans. by G.M.A. Grube. Indianapolis: Hackett Pub.

Plutarch. 1878. *Plutarch's morals*, vol. 4. Ed. by William W. Goodwin. Boston: Little, Brown.

Price, Renata. 2021. Somehow we're still learning new things about BotW in 2021. *Kotaku*, September 1, 2021. https://kotaku.com/somehow-we-re-still-learning-new-things-about-BotW-in-2-1847598286/amp

Salam, Maya. 2020. The video games that got us through 2020. *The New York Times*, December 17, 2020. https://www.nytimes.com/2020/12/17/arts/video-games-pandemic.html

Sartre, Jean-Paul. 1955. *No exit, and three other plays*. New York: Vintage Books.

———. 1956. *Being and nothingness: An essay on phenomenological ontology*. Trans. by Hazel E. Barnes. New York: Philosophical Library.

———. (1946) 2007. *Existentialism is a humanism*. Trans. by Carol Macomber. New Haven: Yale University Press.

Schopenhauer, Arthur. 2014. *Parerga and paralipomena: Short philosophical essays*, vol. 1. Trans. by Sabine Roehr. Ed. by Christopher Janaway. Cambridge: Cambridge University Press.

———. 2015. *Parerga and paralipomena: Short philosophical essays*, vol. 2. Trans. by Adrian Del Caro. Ed. by Christopher Janaway. Cambridge: Cambridge University Press.

Slack, James. 2015. Is decision paralysis really the problem? Fanatical take. *Game Fanatics*, December 7, 2015. https://thegamefanatics.com/decision-paralysis-really-enemy-fanatical-take/

Taylor, R. (1970) 2000. The meaning of life. In *Good and evil*. Amherst: Prometheus Books.

Warner, Noelle. 2021. *Zelda: Breath of the Wild* cured my media burnout. *Destructoid*, May 23, 2021. https://www.destructoid.com/zelda-breath-of-the-wild-cured-my-media-burnout/?_gl=1*w7xlea*_ga*YW1wLVZBeWxwdlA3QXdjSV9aejRPek5wSk1OS1NPTE5MRmhFcndtdjJEX1J5YnMwY2FWNmZHbl9PTnFNWmtTbkhneTc

Persona 5 Royal as Philosophy: Unmasking (Persona)l Identity and Reality

Alexander Atrio L. Lopez and Leander Penaso Marquez

Contents

Introduction: *Persona 5 Royal* and the Characterization Question of Personal Identity	1908
The Discovery of Identities and Realities: Summarizing *Persona 5 Royal*	1909
The Mystery of Qualia: How It Is to Feel Like One's Self/Persona	1911
The Mystery of Qualia: Privacy and Difficulty	1912
The Mystery of Qualia: Public Real World Versus Private Metaverse	1913
The Certainty of Hinge Propositions	1915
The Language-Game of Creating Characterization Identity: Language-Game Characteristics	1918
The Language-Game of Creating Characterization Identity: Personal Identity Characteristics	1920
Stealing the "Identity of Reality"	1922
Conclusion	1925
References	1927

Abstract

The video game *Persona 5 Royal* revolves around the Phantom Thieves of Hearts, high schoolers who navigate the cognitive world or Metaverse to change the hearts of corrupt individuals using power sources called "Personas." Central to the struggles of the Phantom Thieves inside and outside the Metaverse is how to answer the characterization question of personal identity – or the question of "Who am I?" The Thieves figure out which experiences and attributes constitute their personal identities within a corrupt society in the real world; they also have

---

A. A. L. Lopez (✉)
University of the Philippines Diliman, Quezon City, Philippines
e-mail: allopez1@up.edu.ph

L. P. Marquez
College of Social Sciences and Philosophy, University of the Philippines Diliman, Quezon City, Philippines
e-mail: lpmarquez@up.edu.ph

to assert who they are as Persona-wielders in the Metaverse. Unmasking these identities is crucial in their quest for justice and truth.

To unmask these identities, this chapter attempts to offer three different bases of characterization identity: qualia, Wittgensteinian hinge propositions, and Wittgensteinian language-games. Qualia – conscious experiences that are qualitatively distinct for each individual subject – can form the basis of what personally matters to one's identity. These qualia can be expressed via foundation-bearing Wittgensteinian hinge propositions. These expressions can be realized via the mechanics of Wittgensteinian language-games. The Thieves can create their own identities because they can invent new language-games.

Not only do these characterization identity issues matter theoretically, they also matter practically. Personal identity is important in relation to collected individual identities and realities dramatically presented through *Persona 5 Royal*'s new characters, Kasumi Yoshizawa and Takuto Maruki. These characters' story arcs compel *Persona 5 Royal*'s players to face the question of whether it is not only preferable but also correct to either live in a blissful dream or a painful reality.

Keywords

Personal identity · Characterization · Qualia · Gilbert Ryle · Ludwig Wittgenstein · Hinge proposition · Language-game · Plato · Utilitarianism · Jeremy Bentham · Pragmatism · William James · Jean Baudrillard · Simulacrum · Hyperreality

Introduction: *Persona 5 Royal* and the Characterization Question of Personal Identity

Persona 5 Royal immediately puts the player in the thick of action and mystery with an unnamed character infiltrating a casino. The character's domino mask, his black-caped costume that heavily covers his body, and the several unnamed voices that communicate with him via radio-like sounds, all these details heighten the player's desire to answer the question: Who is the boy called Joker?

When Joker gets caught by the police and his torture starts, the player finally gets to see his face. Once the lawyer, Sae Nijima, begins to interrogate him, more personal details about Joker get divulged: He is a high school sophomore, a teenager, etc. These bits of information can answer the question "Who is Joker?" But in another important sense, it may take not only the events of the entire game but also the player's playthrough choices to satisfactorily define the characterization of Joker's personal identity. In philosophy, characterization is a problem within the discourse of personal identity. Marya Schechtman defines this problem as "the question of which actions, experiences, and traits are rightly attributable to a person" (2014, p. 100).

To better illustrate this concern, in contemporary society, there are different ways of answering the question "Who are you?" How will some of the characters of *Persona 5 Royal* answer this question? Sae may reply that she is a lawyer on her way to the top of the judicial bureaucracy. Morgana may answer that he is NOT a cat.

It is typically thought that an individual or a person gets to define who oneself is. The abovementioned characters clearly show how they define themselves in the words that they use and the actions that they exhibit, especially in the Confidant portion of the game. People define themselves according to the considerations they deem most important.

Self-definition, however, may clash with how the self is defined by others. Morgana may keep on insisting that he is not a cat, but that may not be how he is defined or identified by the rest of the party. Fittingly, Schechtman mentions how the characterization question of who one is "can be asked from either a first-person or third-person perspective" (1996, p. 74). So, what makes more sense: identification by oneself or by others? Are there more specific guidelines that can help one come up with criteria for characterization identity?

As mentioned, characterization is just one topic under the "personal identity" heading. Olson (2019) gives a handy classification of related issues, such as identity over time or diachronic identity. Diachronic identity looks into the more specific concern of providing criteria to determine whether an entity or person at one point in time is the same one at another point in time. This discourse corresponds to the issue of personal identity over time. This latter problem is discussed more in this book's ▶ Chap. 55, "*Avatar* as Philosophy: The Metaphysics of Switching Bodies." This chapter, on the other hand, will focus on characterization.

The Discovery of Identities and Realities: Summarizing *Persona 5 Royal*

Before delving into how *Persona 5 Royal* explores the characterization identity of its characters, it will be useful to summarize some of the major events and figures of the game. Tokyo is abuzz with the news of recent, widespread mental shutdowns and psychotic breakdowns causing massive accidents, like a fatal subway train derailment. Against this backdrop, 16-year-old Ren Amamiya starts living in the Yongen-Jaya cafe, Leblanc, owned by his new legal guardian and his parents' friend, Sojiro Sakura. Ren also starts his second year of high school in Shujin Academy as a transferee. Teachers and students gossip about Ren's background and call him "the delinquent"; his move to Yongen-Jaya is because he has a criminal record of physical assault. Unbeknownst to the public, Ren defended a woman from being sexually harassed by a politician, and the politician pulled strings to convict Ren and bury the case. Ren was eventually sent to Yongen-Jaya as part of his probation.

Ren becomes friends with two Shujin sophomores terrorized by the volleyball coach, Suguru Kamoshida. The first is Ryuji Sakamoto, an ex-Shujin track and field runner who suffered a leg injury under the command of Kamoshida. The second, Ann Takamaki, is a student and model against whom Kamoshida is making unwanted sexual advances.

Ren, Ryuji, and Ann discover the sudden appearance of the Metaverse Navigator or Meta-Nav app in their smartphones. The Meta-Nav allows them to access the Metaverse, a realm constituted from the subconscious thoughts and feelings of humans. In the Metaverse, they also meet Morgana, a talking, anthropomorphized cat who is trying to regain his memories about his origin and his true non-cat form.

Morgana explains the nature of the Metaverse: It contains Palaces, representations of the psyche of individuals with powerful distorted desires like criminal or strong emotional desires. These desires manifest as the Palace ruler's Treasure. Another kind of Palace is Mementos, the collective Palace or collective subconscious of multiple individuals at once, whose desires are not strongly distorted. In the Metaverse, Ren, Ryuji, and Ann awaken their Personas, entities that give them various powers. They steal the Treasure of Kamoshida, making him have a change of heart in the real world where he confesses his crimes. Ren and company decide to use the Meta-Nav in looking for Palaces and stealing Treasures to produce a change of heart among corrupt individuals. They call themselves the Phantom Thieves of Hearts.

In this quest to uphold justice, other highschoolers join the Thieves. Yusuke Kitagawa is a painter who discovers that his mentor, benefactor, and father-figure Ichiryusai Madarame indirectly killed his mother and sells counterfeit copies of his mother's masterpiece as his own. Makoto Nijima, an academic overachiever and Shujin's Student Council President, resolves to balance her own needs and desires with the unjust high demands of the adults around her. The anxious shut-in Futaba Sakura, Sojiro's daughter, reintegrates into society after unearthing the coordinated efforts to kill her mother and steal her research on the Metaverse. Haru Okumura is a business tycoon's heir who escapes his father's arranged marriage with a sexual harasser and finds her own footing in the business world after her father gets murdered. Goro Akechi is a celebrity ace detective trying to prove himself to his father who abandoned him and his dead mother. Kasumi Yoshizawa, the pressured gymnast honor student, struggles to achieve medals for Shujin while overcoming her depression and the accidental death of her twin sister.

The Thieves are also eventually aided by what the game labels "Confidants." Some of them include Sojiro, who warms up to Ren. Sae, Makoto's sister, becomes an invaluable legal aid. Confidants also include the mysterious Metaverse residents Igor, Caroline, and Justine. Ren strengthens his relationship with these Confidants, and, in turn, they give Ren and the Thieves additional powers.

As the Phantom Thieves infiltrate Palaces and defeat Palace Rulers, they encounter a masked killer within the Metaverse. They soon discover that this killer is Akechi, who has been working with the powerful, well-connected politician, Masayoshi Shido. Ren figures out that Shido was the harasser who led him to a criminal conviction. Shido is the mastermind behind using Akechi, the Metaverse, and other government pawns in causing mental shutdowns to cause chaos in Japan. Shido pins these shutdowns to the Thieves and runs for Prime Minister as Japan's new savior.

The Thieves successfully steal Shido's heart. However, even after Shido confesses to the public, the majority still "worship" him. The Thieves discover that deep in Mementos, influencing all of these events, is the God of Control, Yaldabaoth. Yaldabaoth attempts to fuse the real world and the Metaverse with the goal of satiating the desires of the people to have saviors that will take care of all their problems: the Phantom Thieves. The Thieves' Confidants help to persuade the people to support the Phantom Thieves in defeating Yaldabaoth and rejecting the alteration of a reality fused with the Metaverse.

After Yaldabaoth's defeat, all seems well, but Ren realizes that this sense of calm is illusory. Ren discovers that in the attempted fusion of the real world and the Metaverse, Takuto Maruki fully awakens his Persona's power to "change the cognition" of people in the real world, and he is expanding the scope of this power to cover the whole world. (Note: "changing someone's cognition" is how *Persona 5* refers to manipulating the mental states of subjects, like memories, beliefs, desires, etc.; Maruki's power is also labeled in-game as "actualization.") Ren wakes up the other Thieves, one by one, from this fake utopian cognition where all their desires are fulfilled. Kasumi, after waking up, realizes that she is actually Sumire, and Kasumi is her twin who died. Partly to relieve survivor's guilt, Maruki changed her cognition, so she started living the life of Kasumi.

At the end, the Thieves reject Maruki's offer of a false utopia and steal his heart. Tokyo citizens' cognitions are restored.

The Mystery of Qualia: How It Is to Feel Like One's Self/Persona

The Thieves' act of digging deep within themselves to make sense of their individual characterization is essential to overcoming the adversities they faced. One key to understanding this endeavor is the philosophical concept of qualia. A quale (plural, qualia) is the distinct qualitative feeling of a conscious experience. For instance, one can consider the feeling of listening to *Beneath the Mask* (2017), the background music that plays in Sojiro's cafe and the game's Tokyo locations at night. One may feel a certain relaxing, comforting, or homey effect. These are qualities of the listening experience. These qualitative experiences are distinct, especially in contrast with the experience of listening to *Rivers in the Desert* (2017), the upbeat, bass-heavy, cymbal-filled boss theme against Shadow Shido.

A quale can also refer to one's feeling regarding which qualities define oneself. This characterization quale is extremely intuitive and intensely, intimately felt. This quale can form the basis of answering the question "Who am I?" To illustrate a response to this question, in a battle against Shadow Kamoshida's henchman right after Ryuji forms a pact with his Persona, Captain Kidd, Ryuji says: "I'll act like the troublemaker I am."

"I am" is a statement of self-identification. Here, the subject both identifies himself and characterizes himself as a troublemaker. Preceding this scene, one can unquestionably sense the pain and shock expressed by Ryuji writhing viscerally as he unleashes his Persona for the first time. As such, "I'll act like the troublemaker I am" is uttered within a background of an intensely felt qualitative, subjective experience of what it is like to be one's self: a characterization identity quale. Feelings, more specifically qualia, can form the bases of how one self-identifies or characterizes oneself. Ryuji, then, forcefully expresses his troublemaker identity quale by vanquishing the henchman and escalating the impending troubles and eventual downfall of Kamoshida.

Captain Kidd, like other Personas, is an expression of one's characterization identity by embodying certain attributes that people could ascribe to themselves – like Ryuji's assertion that he's a "troublemaker." Various in-game depictions attest to such a description. The establishment of a new Confidant bond comes with the utterance: "I am thou, thou art I..." This "I" can be the Persona, like Captain Kidd, and "thou" can be interpreted as the Persona owner, like Ryuji.

The same line appears when Ren makes a pact with his first Persona, Arsène. Ren is suddenly shown as wearing a domino mask that he bloodily removes from his face, as if this mask is a natural extension of his skin, supplied by his own blood, like the rest of his organs. It is as if Ren is mutilating himself to finally show the world what he is like inside. Arsène further adds: "I am the rebel's soul that resides within you." In other words, Arsène, the Persona, represents a rebellious attribute that Ren would use to characterize himself.

The Mystery of Qualia: Privacy and Difficulty

From these various explanations of what characterization identity qualia are, especially in relation to Personas, it makes sense that one important characteristic of qualia is that they are privately felt. That is, one can never completely experience another person's quale. One may explain to another how one feels something, and someone may try to empathize with what another person feels, but both of these are different from the unique, subjective experience that each person has.

A specific illustration is how *Persona 5 Royal* players may recall the first time that they enter the section of Kunikazu Okumura's Palace. They can explain to someone else how they may have been overwhelmed with awe: the feeling of being inside what seems like a gargantuan futuristic space station with sleek interiors, flashing LED panels, and the arresting holographic letters "BIG BANG BURGER" floating in midair. It is one thing to provide this explanation, but it is another to actually feel what the words pertain to. A simpler illustration of the privacy of qualia is the difficulty of explaining to another how one feels the experience of seeing a certain color.

If qualia are private, then the experience or quale of one's characterization identity is also private. This privacy makes sense especially because the quale corresponding to one's characterization identity is something that allows one to perceive one's being separate or distinct from other selves. There is a distinctness to how one feels that will never be felt by another self that feels another specific, distinct quale of their own personal identity.

One may empathize as best as one could with another's feelings via interviewing the other self or researching scientific information about what one feels in certain contexts. However, these endeavors will not result in the full feeling of another's exact quale. A drastic and summative illustration is Thomas Nagel's statement of how a human will never feel like what it is like to be a bat ([1974] 2002). It is quite easy to realize how different the anatomy, physiology, and life cycle of a bat is compared to a human, so it makes sense how a human may never fully understand how it is to be a bat and vice versa. Even an attempt to imagine what a bat feels like will fall short – this is to imagine what it's like for *you* or *me*, as human persons, to be a bat. This tells us nothing of what it's like for a *bat to be a bat*.

It is the private nature of qualia that makes the existence of this entity quite controversial among certain philosophers. Gilbert Ryle vehemently denies the alleged "privileged access" one has to one's own feelings ([1949] 2009, p. 99). Substitute "qualia" for "feelings" and the privacy of qualia for "privileged access," and it will be easy to see how Ryle's concern applies to the present argument. Ryle maintains how it is the set of gestures shown and words used by someone within a specific context that allows people to determine how one feels. The identification of feelings is not done via the invocation of private qualia; instead, feelings are identified by publicly verifiable criteria such as gestures, words, and contexts.

Ludwig Wittgenstein ([1953] 2009) attests to something similar. It is through someone's behavior that someone's feelings are elucidated. What Wittgenstein and Ryle mention makes sense given the depictions of Ren's and Ryuji's Persona awakenings, which are typical of how Personas are awakened. *Persona 5 Royal* players become aware of how Ren and Ryuji are specifically feeling from how their Personas talk to them and from Ryuji's own utterance, which identifies himself as a troublemaker. Other striking indicators are the new Phantom Thieves' picaresque, sleuthy clothes, which seem to suddenly materialize when a Persona is awakened. Pertaining to this attire, Morgana mentions: "Your appearance reflects your inner self. It's the rebel that slumbers within."

Both Wittgenstein and Ryle stress the importance of intersubjective communication, which seems precluded by the existence of private qualia. In Wittgenstein-speak, the existence of thoughts and emotions that can only be accessed by one's self means a private language exists. A private language is one that only the inventor and user can understand. How can people communicate with such a kind of language? However, there may be value in thinking about the fact that these two philosophers seem to be oblivious of the fact that even the saddest people can present themselves to others with a smile, and many cases of suicide involve individuals who were moments earlier laughing their hearts out. In other words, one's external behavior and internal feelings may not always match up, providing further evidence of just how challenging it is to bridge public and private language (assuming a private language exists).

The communication difficulties arising from a private language are carried over in discourse regarding characterization identity. It is a running joke how Morgana, in every initial encounter with a party member, asserts that he is NOT a cat. He emphasizes to Ryuji: "I am NOT a cat! Say that again and I'll make you regret it!"

In contrast, party members repeatedly refer to him as one. From Morgana's private qualia, he identifies as something aside from a cat, specifically: "I'm a human – an honest-to-god human!" From how the party members perceive Morgana from what are publicly available cues (appearance, purrs, and uncontrollable catnip frenzy over Palace Treasures), he seems like a cat.

The Mystery of Qualia: Public Real World Versus Private Metaverse

Given these complications, there are different philosophical reactions to antiprivate language sentiments. Prominent philosophers of mind like David Chalmers (1996) are dismissive and mention the intuitive, fundamental feelings of private qualia among other argumentative support. Followers of Wittgenstein and Ryle cling to the need for the public nature of language for effective communication among other reasons.

Persona 5 Royal and the use of private qualia as bases for characterization identity can illustrate vividly the clash between both poles of the public/private dichotomy. The public domain can be regarded as what is referred to in-game as the "real world." The private, privilege-accessed individual domain can be seen in the Metaverse, with its varied sections like Palaces and Mementos.

Morgana describes a Palace as a cognitive world that reflects Palace rulers' desires and how the rulers see themselves. Palace rulers are referred to as Shadow versions of themselves. Morgana explains a Shadow as "the true self that is suppressed – a side of one's personality they [the Palace ruler] don't want to see." In other words, the Palace represents the inner experiences or qualia of an individual, out of which they construct a characterization identity of themselves.

In the real world, Kamoshida sees himself as king of Shujin Academy. Here, he subjects his volleyball team to physical abuse and sexual harassment. He calls individual volleyball team members to his office and tortures them physically whenever he feels upset. He even claims that everyone knows what he does: the students, the teachers, and the parents. No one stops him because he brings prestige to the high school through the competition victories resulting from his coaching of the volleyball team. From these achievements, the recommendation letters that he can write for his students can be life changing. Thus, his Metaverse Palace is a castle, one wherein Shadow Kamoshida, a king, treats the volleyball team members as slaves and certain female members as sex objects.

When party members step into a Palace (or into Mementos) using the Meta-Nav, it is like they are able to access the qualia of the Palace ruler. The fact that they can do so starkly presents the possibilities of public-private language interaction. While party members refer to the real word as differentiated from the Metaverse, their actions in the Metaverse have real-life implications. If the Phantom Thieves die in the Metaverse, they also die in the real world. If they steal the Palace ruler's Treasure, the ruler will have a change of heart and confess their sins. Morgana explains this event as a Treasure being the "material" manifestation of the ruler's desires. Once the desires are stolen or gone, the ruler, in the real world, also loses their desires. The desires are gone, but the past actions (and public consequences) from the evil or distorted desires remain. As such, immense guilt sets in.

It is noteworthy how Morgana uses the term "material" to designate something from the Metaverse. This "material" description actually works in a literal sense. When the Phantom Thieves steal the Treasure, they can take this back to the real world, and the Treasure is an actual physical object. Similar to the use of "material," Yusuke describes the Metaverse location Mementos as "the physical embodiment of the desires of the heart."

So, while the navigation of the Metaverse can be seen as a figurative way of illustrating how private qualia can be accessed, there are real-world, material implications. Maruki comments further on how the Metaverse covers nonfigurative aspects: "[The Phantom Thieves'] 'theft of desire' is not metaphorical, but something more direct."

Such dynamic interaction between the public, literal real world and the private, metaphorical Metaverse provides avenues to argue for the possibility that yes qualia can exist, and they are private, but this existence does not automatically mean that chaos in communication completely ensues. Access to Palaces in the Metaverse means that, at least to the Thieves, qualia aren't *completely* private.

Morgana arguing with the rest of the Phantom Thieves over his identity provides much-needed comic relief to punctuate the Thieves' struggle in the assertion of their identities against an oppressive, corrupt society. However, as the 100+ h story progresses, the player and the Thieves laugh less at Morgana and begin to understand the gravity of his struggle to definitively know who or what he is and to assert this identity. Morgana's private qualia exist, and the Thieves perceive publicly available cues, but it is also through these cues that the privacy, even if not completely pierced, becomes progressively peeled away. In this intersubjective unshelling, the player and the Thieves get to empathize more deeply with Morgana and even root for his self-discovery and self-assertion, all without Morgana having a Palace or the Thieves encountering a Shadow version of him in Mementos. Qualia and effective, liberating communication can coexist.

This kind of communication is especially liberating because, as one knows other people better, one knows oneself better as well: One is liberated from self-doubt. The Confidant system exemplifies this notion. As Ren spends more time knowing each Confidant, Confidants level up, Ren gets more powers in the Metaverse, and fusing Personas together lead to higher-level Personas. The increase in Metaverse and Persona power can be likened to an increase in self-knowledge. After all, a Persona is a version of the self. A higher-level Persona can mean a deeper knowledge of oneself, and this deeper knowledge manifests as more Persona abilities. Similarly, as one knows oneself better, one can show more aspects or powers of one's self to others. In the language of *Persona 5 Royal* and this chapter, getting to know Confidants and leveling-up Personas helps a person to better characterize themselves and to form a self-identity more fully.

While discussions on qualia highlight how one's own feelings are essential in shaping one's own characterization identity, it is not only one's personal emotions that can have an impact on one's identity. In characterizing and expressing one's identity, the concept of hinge propositions can also help bridge the personal and social aspects.

The Certainty of Hinge Propositions

To understand what a hinge proposition is, it is useful to briefly talk about its origin in Wittgenstein's *On Certainty* (1969). In this work, Wittgenstein attempts to find out the possible bases of certain foundational beliefs that humans have; for instance, that the Earth exists (together with the things and beings on the Earth) or that the two hands that one possesses are real. Can it be proven with certainty that the existence of the Earth or one's two hands are indeed real, instead of say, merely dreaming these or being deceived by some mischievous entity?

Wittgenstein concludes that there are statements like "the Earth exists" and "these two hands are real" that cannot be sufficiently proven with complete assurance. Despite this insufficiency, these statements have to be assumed to be correct. Wittgensteinian scholars have labeled such statements "hinge propositions." This label follows from Wittgenstein's explanation of how one's comprehensive set of beliefs depends on or hinges on such propositions.

To illustrate, for Yusuke to believe that he should go along with his usual routine from going to school to improving his art to maintaining his relationships with the rest of the Phantom Thieves, he has to assume that the planet in which he lives on is real. If Yusuke is living in some kind of false reality like a dream or an illusion, then his efforts of trying to live his life may just not make sense. His whole life is anchored on the notion that the Earth and the structures and beings on it are real.

This illustration highlights how hinge propositions form the background of other beliefs: One cannot have these other beliefs without the anchors or hinges. These other beliefs cannot make sense without the underlying beliefs on which they hinge. As such, hinge propositions are crucial for the justification of all these other beliefs.

Said another way, hinge propositions can be understood as basic beliefs. These are beliefs that are self-evident to the believer, and, thus, are basic and foundational such as the belief in God, equality among humans, or human freedom, among others (Marquez 2014). From these basic beliefs, one can formulate other beliefs, for instance, that a higher power created the world, that all humans are entitled to the same rights, or that humans are free to choose and decide for themselves.

The secondary literature presents different ways of classifying hinge propositions, but to help unmask characterization identity, what can be most useful is Danièle Moyal-Sharrock's notion of a "personal hinge," which has intersections with Hans-Johann Glock's personal hinge propositions. Moyal-Sharrock's example of a personal hinge is "*I come from such and such a city*" (2003, p. 129). Glock's examples of personal hinge propositions include "My name is N. N." and "I have spent most of my life in Germany" (1996, p. 78). For this chapter, the usage of the phrase "personal hinge proposition" covers commonalities between Moyal-Sharrock's and Glock's ways of defining personal hinge propositions.

Personal hinge propositions are part of an individual's "subjective world-picture" (Glock 1996, p. 78). As an explanation, Yusuke can have a personal hinge proposition of "I will use my art to paint over the blackness of this world." This hinge was born from the tragic death of his mother, a uniquely talented painter, when he was young, resulting in Madarame raising him. Madarame has become his substitute parent and art mentor. Yusuke is devastated when he hears from Shadow Madarame how Madarame actually let his mother die by not giving her medicine while she was having a severe seizure. This hinge has affected drastically how he sees the world and how he acts in it; he tries to see what is beautiful within humanity despite the cruelty he has suffered. Fueled by this search for the aesthetic, he strives to create a one-of-a-kind masterpiece like his mother's painting *Sayuri*.

From this illustration, it is not a far jump to use a personal hinge proposition as a basis for characterization identity. The term "*ch*aracterization *i*dentity hinge *p*roposition" or CHIP is now introduced to refer to hinges that are crucial for the certainty of one's identity.

For example, Yusuke can have a CHIP of "I'm striving to become an artist." Yusuke utters this when he introduces himself to Ann, Ren, and Ryuji in their first meeting. Aside from defining Yusuke's subjective world picture, this CHIP is also responsible for making sense of Yusuke's other beliefs or propositions, such as "I'm Madarame-sensei's pupil." Even after the party learns all of Madarame's crimes from Shadow Madarame's own confessions, Yusuke cannot shirk the feeling that his sensei is not purely evil. After all, he took care of Yusuke. This belief is further reinforced when Yusuke learns from Akiko Kawanabe how Madarame was extremely worried when young Yusuke had a fever and all the nearby clinics were closed. Madarame took in Yusuke even if he did not like children. Yusuke's link with Madarame is tied to his CHIP or lifelong quest of becoming an artist.

Because the way a person characterizes their identity can be expressed and explained by their conviction with their CHIP, it is important to stress how certain Wittgenstein thought they were. Because a hinge proposition is a basic belief, its certainty lends a strong foundation for the rest of the beliefs that it supports. Such a firm anchor is also important for characterization identity. One can feel a certain comfort and security when one is confident with one's self-identification. The more robust this self-identification is, the more it can withstand attacks from others. For an in-game illustration, Confidants and their abilities level up as they become more certain of who they are. More dramatically, upon maximizing party members' Confidant levels and fully resolving their characterization struggles, their Personas evolve into stronger ones, even gaining evade skills against their weaknesses.

However, how unshakeable are hinge propositions really? Wittgenstein gives different examples of hinge propositions in *On Certainty*. One example is that it is impossible for man to go to or be on the moon. That is, one can be certain that one is not on the moon. Such a hinge can also be labeled as a nonpersonal hinge proposition. (Of course, history has proven repeatedly that such a proposition is false.) It is probably safer to mention how Wittgenstein says that hinge propositions can change, but regardless of the exact ramifications of this characterization of hinge propositions, one interpretation is that he truly holds that it would never be possible for humans to go to the moon. Assuming this interpretation is correct, it is fair to say that an opening is made for the certainty of hinge propositions to be attacked. (Again, hinge propositions like "humans will never go to the moon" can obviously be false, which means they can't have the certainty of something like unshakable knowledge and that people may be able to stop holding hinge propositions as true.) Wittgenstein does mention how one's background (like how one has grown up and the surroundings where this growth is situated) influences which hinge propositions individuals hold. This explanation obviously aids in the understanding of which specific personal hinges are held by individuals.

However, it can still be pushed that perhaps biases and milieu can also influence the alleged certainty of other kinds of hinge propositions, in particular those that cover more the public, intersubjective character of people's lives (nonpersonal hinges). Perhaps it can be said that Wittgenstein's milieu influenced his views on what science can accomplish and whether it can allow humans to step on the moon or not. Within the universe of *Persona 5 Royal*, these paradigm-altering changes in hinge propositions do occur. People in the real world anchor their beliefs on the hinge that it is impossible to enter one's psyche. Of course, this hinge changed when the Meta-Nav allowed the Phantom Thieves to explore Palaces and Mementos.

An example closer to characterization identity is how Morgana and Igor are shocked to discover how Ren can possess and use multiple Personas. Morgana mentions how it makes sense for someone to only have one Persona because a human only has one heart. One may interpret "heart" here as one's characterization identity. Of course, the party discovers that Akechi can also wield more than one Persona.

These illustrations in *Persona 5 Royal* and outside the game depict how it is not only personal but also nonpersonal hinge propositions that can change. This characterization of hinges is pointed out to further stress the dynamic relationship between the private and public dimensions of characterization identity. The biases and milieu that mold one's personal hinges can also affect other people's or society's publicly held hinges. The discussion can be linked to the private/public concerns about qualia. Characterization identity can have private aspects (qualia, personal hinges) and public aspects (discourse about qualia and personal hinges, nonpersonal hinges). The private and public domains can be traversed to facilitate meaningful discourse. To further demonstrate the mechanisms behind this meaningful, interpersonal discourse, Wittgenstein's language-games can help.

The Language-Game of Creating Characterization Identity: Language-Game Characteristics

In *Philosophical Investigations*, Wittgenstein ([1953] 2009) roughly describes a language-game as any activity that involves language. Examples extrapolated from this definition include writing a paper, talking via instant messaging, and the Phantom Thieves sending a calling card to a Palace ruler. What may be unusual is that Wittgenstein defines language as anything that transmits meaning. By this definition, a picture that does not use words is still language. A stop light that only uses three colors is still language. The silence that one replies with, in an exchange, is also language.

With such an expansive characterization of language, the examples of language-games also diversify. Practically any activity can probably involve the transmission of meaning. Playing charades is a language-game. Others include Ann modeling to sell products and the Phantom Thieves infiltrating Palaces and Mementos to send a message to both the real world and the Metaverse that justice will ultimately prevail.

This assortment of what language-games can cover is accounted for by Wittgenstein's concept of family resemblance. In a family, two members may be tall or share a liking for pancakes. Other members may not. A resemblance may be shared by some family members but not all. Similarly, language-game X may exhibit features P, Q, and R; language-game Y may exhibit features Q, R, and S; and language-game Z may exhibit features R, S, and T. As such, Wittgenstein explicitly states that a language-game has no one definition. To clarify, it can be stated that while one can generally characterize language-games as any activity involving language and sporting other features, technically, a language-game cannot be defined.

Speaking of features of language-games, an important one is that language-games have rules. Much like the game of chess has rules to guide its players, language-games have rules to guide its players or participants. Thus, in the language-game of modeling, there are rules of how to be an effective model. These rules are mentioned by different industry insiders; a popular source is supermodel Tyra Banks's *America's Next Top Model* series (Mok et al. 2003–2018). With the example set by her modeling rival Mika, Ann learns some of these rules along the way: "She worked out, watched her diet, made friends with everyone...!"

The rules of language-games are also important because they determine the meaning of a word. For example, in the game of basketball, "traveling" gets its meaning from the rules of basketball. A referee can call traveling when a player in possession of the ball does not dribble the ball for a few steps. Different language-games are made up of different rules. "Traveling" means something else in the language-game of world travel or taking a vacation. "Traveling" is spelled the same and is pronounced the same in both basketball and in vacationing, but the same word gets different meanings according to which language-game "traveling" belongs. In Wittgenstein's language-game view, a word gets its meaning from how it is used – more technically, how the word is used in a given language-game.

An important in-game illustration of how a word gets its meaning through use is how "justice" gets its meaning in *Persona 5 Royal*'s language-games of upholding justice. At different moments in the game, characters, especially Phantom Thieves-haters, repeatedly mention how a "just" response to crime requires a set of rules. Ignoring these rules is unjust. To quote Akechi regarding his comments on the Thieves' stealing Madarame's heart: "They are taking the law into their own hands by judging him. It is far from justice."

On the other hand, the Thieves discuss why what they do can be considered just. In an instant messaging exchange:

Yusuke   I doubt everyone would forgive us for what we did to Madarame.
Yusuke   Yet, I still decided that it was a necessary act.
Ryuji   Kamoshida too. We weren't gonna do shit to him through any kinda normal methods.
         ...
Yusuke   Hm. I believe our best path forward is sticking to our justice, not that of the law.

This tension between justice as a language-game of following the law and as a language-game of doing what is necessary to benefit people is succinctly expressed by this exchange between Makoto and Sae:

Makoto   ...Is it a crime to manipulate someone's heart?
Sae   ...Depending on the means, yes. He's [Akechi] absolutely right.
Makoto   Even if it makes someone admit their evil deeds and helps make them pay for their crimes?

These exchanges show how the rules and language-games of justice are defined by the Thieves in one sense and the Thieves' opponents in another sense. Morgana captures the language-game characteristic of being an invention or creation: "[Akechi] can say whatever he wants. The justice of it all is something we can decide for ourselves."

However, language-games cannot only be invented but also discovered. Ancient humans probably discovered rules of the language-game of eating plants to survive. Rules that they discovered include not eating poisonous plants and which ones are indeed poisonous. On the other hand, there was a time when basketball was not yet invented. James Naismith invented the game in 1891.

These two aspects of the discovery and creation of language-games also point out how language or thought affects reality and vice versa, a classic dichotomy in philosophy of language. To explain, thought or language can affect reality because the words that people use (after thinking about which words to use) can produce visibly perceptible effects. As an illustration, the game developers thought about which words to use in the script of *Persona 5 Royal*. They made Akechi utter "pancakes" in a key exchange with the Thieves that ultimately lead the Thieves to discover that Akechi is actually the Metaverse mass murderer. The effect of "pancakes" in the reality of *Persona 5* players is that several memes have been created in the fandom illustrating Akechi and his love of pancakes.

Another dramatic example of how language can affect reality is how entering a Palace requires the input of several keywords: the Palace ruler's full name, the Palace location, and the Palace distortion. With these words, the Thieves gain access to the inner reality of the Palace ruler and alter this reality: The ruler's heart can be stolen.

On the flip side, reality can also affect thought or language. The reality is that the *Persona 5 Royal* game exists. Because of this game, this book chapter with its words thought of by the authors now exist. An in-game example is that after the Thieves' reality alteration of stealing a Palace ruler's heart, in the real world, the Palace ruler confesses their crimes, and they use language to do so.

The creation of the game, the writing of this chapter, the infiltration of a Palace, and the confession of a Palace ruler are all language-games. Each uses language and has rules that determine word use and meaning; each exhibits the diversity of what a language-game could be or the family resemblance concept; each also shows discovery and invention or creation.

The Language-Game of Creating Characterization Identity: Personal Identity Characteristics

All these features of a language-game also apply to characterization identity. That is, the determination of identity can be construed as a language-game. And this seems to be one of the best ways to understand how *Persona 5 Royal* makes its case for characterization identity. Like the way that the Thieves use language-games to define what "justice" means, one can reconstruct Akechi's probable answers to "who am I" according to the features of a language-game. In answering this question, language is involved in different stages. After being abandoned by his father Shido, Akechi uses language while thinking what to make of himself. He eventually decides to present himself as someone perfect for his goals: "I was extremely particular about my life, my grades, my public image, so someone would want me around!" This facade of perfection effectively disguises the deeper side of him – the one seeking revenge through deceit and mass murder. He will make Shido notice and accept how supremely great his abandoned kid has become. To successfully realize this self-identification, Akechi learns the rules of leading a double life. He learns how to be a celebrity ace detective in public and how to manipulate and kill in the Metaverse in private. How fitting that he has two Personas; to quote Futaba: "But you trusted no one, so you only got two Personas, one for your lies [Robin Hood], and one for your hate [Loki]."

Akechi, depending on which qualia he feels most intensely at the moment, can swap which Persona to use as an expression of his self-characterization, but the language-game of personal identity also involves how others identify him. When the Phantom Thieves discover Akechi's past and finally confront him, they try their best to persuade him to change. Yes, he can self-identify as a mass murderer, but he can still stop and aid the Phantom Thieves in their crusade for justice, too. Like every Phantom Thief, he is a victim who can channel personal pain for this crusade. Haru points out the complexity of this scenario: "I have no intention of forgiving you for what you did to my father, but. . . I sympathize with you."

In the process of identification, the meaning of the words "Goro Akechi" – who these words identify – becomes clearer according to how Akechi uses his own name and how others use his name. After all, meaning is determined according to use in a language-game. Within the varying contexts or language-games that one finds oneself in, the language-game of characterization identity becomes highly diverse as well – an expected conclusion given the family resemblance illustration of language-games. Akechi's characterization identity language-game involves defining himself through abandonment, revenge, and the crucial decision of accepting or rejecting the possibility of change amidst the weight of all his crimes. How different these contexts are from the characterization identity language-games of Ren, Morgana, Ryuji, and Ann as illustrated previously, and with the other Phantom Thieves as well.

Through all these circumstances that the Thieves encounter, some aspects of their characterization identity language-game are discovered and some are invented. Alternatively, one may say that characterization identity language-games involve other language-games, some of which are discovered and some of which are invented.

For instance, upon stumbling into the Metaverse through the sudden appearance of the Meta-Nav in his phone, one can imagine Akechi discovering the Metaverse rules: When he is hurt inside the Metaverse, the wounds remain when he goes back to the real world; he can kill someone in the Metaverse resulting in that Shadow's death in the real world; he can use his Personas while in the Metaverse, etc. However, Akechi does not discover his honor student, ace detective personality in the real world – he creates it. He finds this disguise essential for the fruition of his plans and the realization of his revenge-seeking identity to enable him to cooperate with the police and access secret information and government channels.

Though inventing language-games is evidently possible, there are certain limitations. Wittgenstein mentions the form of life or the natural characteristics that humans share and how these characteristics restrict what can be done as humans interact with their environment. The form of life tips back the scale to the discovery aspect of language-games. Akechi and the Phantom Thieves, as teens growing up, discover the form of life of finding and expressing their identities in contemporary Japan. They have to develop their minds through studying at school, their bodies through training at the gym or spending time at the batting cages, and their social skills via Confidants and navigating the struggles of each.

The human form of life also covers the Metaverse. The Palace and Mementos have their own rules that Morgana explains. The Velvet Room also has a gamut of rules that Igor, Caroline, and Justine teach: Persona fusion via guillotine or group guillotine, Persona strengthening via hanging, Persona training via solitary confinement, and Persona itemization via electric chair execution. A succinct reminder that much like language-games can be discovered or invented/created, characterization identity language-games can similarly be discovered or invented/created is that Personas – as aspects of an individual's self-characterization – can be discovered during their initial awakening, and Personas can also be created in the Velvet Room.

Stealing the "Identity of Reality"

This chapter has already framed the distinction between public and private identity characterization in the context of *Persona 5 Royal*'s division between the real world and the Metaverse. Even though the video game – or so this chapter has argued – takes this understanding of personal identity to be constructed, the identity that is the result of public and private characterization is still very much *real*. Because features of the game's real world and its Metaverse help to shape the real identity of characters, it is important to also discuss the nature of *Persona 5 Royal*'s reality – or the "identity" of its reality.

Part of the reason why the nature or truth of reality matters is because humans seem to have an unshakeable yearning for the truth. The truth is often useful. For example, one way that science is understood is that scientists study how the universe works to predict phenomena and produce concrete applications like drugs and therapies. An inaccurate theory may produce predictions that fail to occur and drugs that fail to cure. So, in a scientific sense, having knowledge of the truth of reality enables one to manipulate this reality to improve lives and better understand the world.

But what if knowing the truth of reality is not useful? In Plato's *Apology* (1997a) and *Phaedo* (1997b), Socrates dies for the truth. He is convicted by political enemies of crimes he did not commit, and he is given a chance to escape from capital punishment. However, he reasons that by escaping he concedes to the false allegations charged against him. He drinks up the truth, a fatal dose of hemlock.

Socrates is usually depicted as the philosopher par excellence. He is a model thinker in search of the truth no matter what. Plato, in *Phaedrus* (1997c), further entrenches truth as the essence of philosophy. As opposed to rhetoric that can be used to spew lies, the role of philosophy is the study of truths. However, rhetoric can also be used to disseminate the discoveries of philosophy.

This conviction of the supreme value of the truth is not shared by Maruki. Even before the formation of the Phantom Thieves, Maruki discovers the power of his Persona, Azathoth, to change the cognition of his patients in a counseling session. One of his patients is Kasumi.

Kasumi is actually Sumire, an identical twin. Both are gymnasts. Sumire looks at herself as inferior compared to Kasumi, who usually wins competitions. Sumire considers Kasumi her role model. This comparison exacerbates Sumire's depressive symptoms, which Kasumi seems to dismiss. In a heated argument over this tension, Sumire runs off to a high-traffic road where, just before a vehicle is about to hit her, Kasumi pushes her out of the way, resulting in Kasumi's death.

Sumire then starts to see Maruki for counseling, who takes note of Sumire's survivor's guilt and her stance that if she could somehow be Kasumi, everything would be better. Maruki changes Sumire's cognition of how she sees reality and also how she characterizes herself. Sumire begins to see herself as Kasumi and acts and presents herself as Kasumi would, even taking her name.

It would seem that upon this change in cognition, things would truly become better for Sumire. However, as Ren becomes closer to Sumire even before discovering her true identity, Sumire worries over confusing events like failing to consistently perform certain gymnastics moves and getting easily tired from lifting weights, despite being a top-tier gymnast. Sumire also suddenly feels drastic changes in her mood like being depressed or irritated.

Furthermore, unbeknownst to Sumire, the people around her are puzzled as to why she started pretending to be Kasumi. While this puzzlement is not an issue to Shujin students, since Sumire is a recent transferee like Ren, it is an issue for people close to her like her father. In Sumire's head, she is Kasumi, but Maruki's power changes only Kasumi's cognition and not the cognition of those around her.

The limitations of Maruki's power as manifested in Sumire's case are a further reminder of the clash of the private and public aspects of characterization identity. Sumire has certain qualia manifested via personal hinge propositions (i.e., "I am Kasumi") operating within different language-games (the language-games of being Kasumi, of being a gymnast honor student, and of being a Phantom Thief in the pursuit of justice). However, others identify Sumire as Sumire via these mechanisms as well.

What complicates the scenario – and what bridges discussion of characterization identity with this section's focus, the nature of reality – is Yaldabaoth's attempts to fuse the real world with Mementos. In this attempt, Maruki fully awakens his Persona, and his cognitive distortion or actualization power massively increases in scope. When the Phantom Thieves defeat Yaldabaoth, Maruki takes it upon himself to be the new god of humanity. He uses Mementos to start changing the cognition of the masses, starting with people in Tokyo. Maruki's mental manipulation altered

Sumire's characterization of herself and her perception of reality, but others were unaffected. By changing the cognition of all of Tokyo – and beyond – Maruki could rewrite how reality is experienced at a collective level, effectively changing the truth of reality (and, of course, impacting how all of these people characterize themselves in their new "reality").

One of Maruki's hinge propositions is that "pain shouldn't exist at all." His goal is to heal mental trauma at any cost. This hinge or goal makes sense given both that he has a sense of empathy one would expect of a school counselor and that he witnessed his girlfriend's crippling psychopathology. Maruki has taken a paternalistic stance, depriving his patients (Kasumi and eventually Tokyo residents) of a chance to say no to actualization. At a sociopolitical level, this paternalistic stance shares features of totalitarianism. Maruki himself talks about totalitarianism in Ren's class:

> It's a governmental structure that unites its people under a single ideology and authoritarian control of the masses... That definitely comes with logistical benefits... But it also means forcing ideals on people. Assimilating the unwilling. And that's how wars get started.

When Yaldabaoth was defeated, Maruki assumed the stance of the authoritarian god. His Palace Shadow inhabitants share this view:

Shadow's Voice   Accept yourself.... Our lord laments the foolishness birthed from your pain.
Monstrous Entity   You dare to spurn our lord's mercy...

Aside from espousing paternalism and totalitarianism, Maruki's power also imbalances the private/public dynamic interaction that molds characterization identity. Maruki is now completely deciding how people see themselves. Yes, he bases the cognitive distortion on people's actual desires, but people's what-ifs are different from Maruki's new reality. That is, one's attitude toward a wish may be different when they know that this wish may become true. They may reconsider their initial desires. On the other hand, one may judge that, even without consent, a pain-free fake reality is still preferable to a truth filled with misery. Perhaps, borrowing from the Monstrous Entity's line above, this fake reality is actually a form of divine mercy that people should be thankful for.

Different philosophies can support this beneficial lie in different ways. Consequentialist ethical theories like Jeremy Bentham's utilitarianism ([1780] 2007) may be invoked. In an ethical dilemma, the action that generates the greatest net pleasure (usually cashed out as the greatest pleasure for the most people) is the most ethical. Maruki's distorted reality may be fake, and he may have been paternalistic and totalitarian, but because this new reality is free of pain, it may be regarded as a Benthamite moral utopia. The utilitarian take on Maruki's goal can be exemplified by one of the Thieves' targets in Mementos, Shadow Fukurai, who says, "People want to be deceived! Don't you see? They're all desperate to feel safe!" (A parallel line of reasoning can hold for the Phantom Thieves' consequentialist disregard of the rules of the law to help the oppressed. After all, the Thieves justify their actions as bringing about the best consequences for people, even if they have to defy society's rules and norms to do so.)

The deception that Fukurai talks about may not even be an issue for certain philosophies. Pragmatism, a school of thought famously espoused by William James ([1907] 1987), teaches that what is real is what is useful, practical, or pragmatic. Maruki's new reality can be seen as more useful than the old one in different ways: It is certainly useful for Maruki's attainment of his own ends of eliminating pain from the world, and (at least for Maruki) it is useful for people who do not want to experience pain anymore. After all, the Shadow's Voice mentions how foolishness comes from pain (perhaps because people do foolish things to avoid pain).

This reframing of the truth of reality is also evident in Jean Baudrillard ([1981] 1994). Baudrillard argues that people now live in what he terms "hyperreality." In this hyperreality, it is irrelevant to try to determine which is a simulacrum, copy, or image and which is the referent or origin of the image. This philosophy seems intuitive today: "pix or it didn't happen!" Pictures, especially in social media, are sometimes considered definitive proof of an event happening. Once people see the pictures or simulacra, some don't care anymore how accurate these images represent what happened in reality. The image or simulacrum, which is supposed to be a representation or copy of an actual event or referent, becomes more valued than the actual happening that is merely captured by the picture. Maruki's new reality can be regarded as a simulacrum of the referent of the undistorted reality. For Maruki, this simulacrum trumps the value of the truth of the preactualized reality. Indeed, the simulacrum becomes the new "truth" for those who embrace it.

Conclusion

But what do Ren and Akechi think of this new reality – and, through them, what does *Persona 5 Royal* really have to say about it? These two are less affected by Maruki's cognitive distortion, probably as a side effect of their unusual powers of being able to use multiple Personas. They are actually given a choice by Maruki whether they want to live in this pain-free world. Of course, the answer also depends on what the player chooses. Will the player choose to live in a blissful dream (where one's characterization is largely formed by external forces) or a painful reality (where one can, at least in part, determine "who they are" for themselves)?

The word "dream" is appropriate. Even the characters who are already engulfed by the blissful new world have moments where they feel like something is wrong or uncanny about the world. Regardless of whether a certain situation is pain free, pragmatic, or muddled in a hyperreality, people cannot shake the feeling that there is another, true reality out there. Maruki's victims feel it. People having dreams, especially lucid dreams, feel it. A child reared in sheltered privilege feels it and eventually desires to know what is outside their parents' mansion's buttressed walls.

A perfect example of this child is in Futaba, even before Maruki's cognitive distortion. Futaba was fed lies that her mother, Wakaba Isshiki, committed suicide partly because taking care of Futaba meant time away from Wakaba's groundbreaking cognitive psience research (in the game, "cognitive psience" refers to the study of mental worlds, like the Metaverse). Futaba's Palace is a reaction to these events. In her Palace, her mother is still alive as a Shadow. As the Phantom Thieves are losing against Shadow Wakaba, Futaba finally makes a choice to give up her illusory shelter, saying "I'll never live a life where everything gets decided by someone else! That's why I'll live in the real world, even if she's not there with me anymore!"

The light of truth – the true reality – finally fully pierced Futaba's Palace. Such piercing is a culmination of the Phantom Thieves' infiltration of Futaba's dark room in real life and her dark pyramid Palace in the Metaverse. This Palace infiltration is accomplished by reorienting cannons that shatter the walls of the pyramid, allowing in more light.

A grander example of the sheltered child rebelling to know the truth is a possible take on Maruki's Palace. The final part of his Palace seems like an interpretation of the Garden of Eden (in game, the place is labeled "Psientific Model Eden"). In this Garden, those who have fully received Maruki's cognitive distortion therapy live worry free, frolicking amidst the verdant grounds glistened by golden rays of light. Such tranquility is foreshadowed by the peace-symbolizing white doves at the base of Maruki's Palace.

The centerpiece of this Garden is a towering tree bearing big red apples. This tree seems similar in stature to the Biblical Tree of Knowledge. In the Bible, eating the fruit means gaining complete knowledge of the world. God forbids the eating of this fruit and the gaining of this knowledge. In Maruki's Garden, as the Thieves ascend the Tree, they are on their way to get hold of full knowledge of the true reality without any trace of Maruki's cognitive distortion. Maruki is effectively God, replacing Yaldabaoth, and worshiped by the Shadows in his Palace.

The Phantom Thieves rebel one more time. They rebelled against corrupt authority figures (Kamoshida and Shido, to name a few) and Yaldabaoth, and they are rebelling against Maruki to not only recover the true reality but to assert their choice of their true identities: individual maturing teenagers and defenders of the just and the true. The Thieves are rebelling against falsity – however pleasant it seems. This lie is also an injustice, an affront to truth-seeking humans. The Phantom Thief rebellion is therefore a struggle not only against social injustice but also metaphysical injustice. The affinity with justice and truth are part of the Phantom Thief and human form of life.

By the end of the game, this kind of "rebel" characterization is hopefully not only something that the Phantom Thieves ascribe to themselves but also part of the *Persona 5 Royal* player's identity. It is with good reason that what is labeled as the game's "true ending" is the one that involves revealing the truth of reality. Much like qualia feel fundamental to self-identity, hinge propositions feel fundamental to world views, and language-games feel fundamental to understanding the rules of social identity, knowing the true "identity of reality" feels fundamental to the totality of how a person should characterize their identity. It is from their private experience of this reality that people form a self-identity; at the same time, other people who publicly share this reality socially attribute other characteristics that form a complete answer to the question of "Who am I?"

The private and public domains of existence are part of the human form of life. Yaldabaoth tried to fuse (private) Mementos and the (public) real world – an injustice that the Thieves rebelled against. Such a world is fake, and life is not that simple; humans have lived their lives one way within their hearts, Palaces, or Mementos, and another way within the real world. Though one is private and another public, both are real. Such is the reality of characterization identity, and such is the truth of the reality in which all these personas or Personas exist. *Persona 5 Royal* is counting not just on the Phantom Thieves but on all players to choose the truth of reality to best actualize our identities. There is a Phantom Thief in each of us.

References

Baudrillard, Jean. [1981] 1994. *Simulacra and simulation*. Trans. Sheila Faria Glaser. Ann Arbor: University of Michigan Press.
Bentham, Jeremy. [1780] 2007. *An introduction to the principles of morals and legislation*. New York: Dover Publications.
Chalmers, David J. 1996. *The conscious mind in search of a fundamental theory*. New York: Oxford University Press.
Glock, Hans-Johann. 1996. *A Wittgenstein dictionary*. Oxford, UK: Blackwell Publishers.
James, William. [1907] 1987. Pragmatism: A new name for some old ways of thinking. In *William James writings 1902–1910*. New York: Library of America.
Marquez, Leander P. 2014. Belief as an evaluative and affective attitude: Some implications on religious belief. *Social Science Diliman* 10(1): 28–52. https://journals.upd.edu.ph/index.php/socialsciencediliman/article/view/4332/3932
Mok, Ken, Tyra Banks, and Kenya Barris, creators. 2003–2018. *America's next top model*. 10 by 10 Entertainment; Anisa Productions; Bankable Productions; Pottle Productions; Ty Ty Baby Productions.
Moyal-Sharrock, Danièle. 2003. Logic in action: Wittgenstein's logical pragmatism and the impotence of scepticism. *Philosophical Investigations* 26 (2): 125–148.
Nagel, Thomas. [1974] 2002. What is it like to be a bat? In *Philosophy of mind: Classical and contemporary readings*, ed. David J. Chalmers. New York: Oxford University Press.
Olson, Eric T. 2019. Personal identity. In *Stanford encyclopedia of philosophy*. https://plato.stanford.edu/archives/sum2022/entries/identity-personal
Plato. 1997a. Apology. In *Plato complete works*. Trans. G. M. A. Grube and ed. John M. Cooper. Indianapolis/Cambridge, MA: Hackett Publishing Company.
———. 1997b. Phaedo. In *Plato complete works*. Trans. G. M. A. Grube and ed. John M. Cooper. Indianapolis/Cambridge, MA: Hackett Publishing Company.
———. 1997c. Phaedrus. In *Plato complete works*. Trans. Alexander Nehamas, and Paul Woodruff and ed. John M. Cooper. Indianapolis/Cambridge, MA: Hackett Publishing Company.
Ryle, Gilbert. [1949] 2009. *The concept of mind 60th anniversary edition*. London: Routledge.
Schechtman, Marya. 1996. *The constitution of selves*. New York: Cornell University Press.
———. 2014. *Staying alive: Personal identity, practical concerns, and the unity of a life*. Oxford, UK: Oxford University Press.
Wittgenstein, Ludwig. 1969. *On certainty*. Trans. Denis Paul, and G. E. M. Anscombe and ed. G. E. M. Anscombe, and G. H. von Wright. Oxford, UK: Basil Blackwell.
———. [1953] 2009. *Philosophical investigations*. Trans. G. E. M. Anscombe, P. M. S. Hacker, and Joachim Schulte. Revised 4th ed. P. M. S. Hacker, and Joachim Schulte. West Sussex: Wiley-Blackwell.

God of War as Philosophy: Prophecy, Fate, and Freedom

86

Charles Joshua Horn

Contents

Introduction	1930
The Problem of Prophecy in *God of War*	1930
Four Solutions to the Problem of Prophecy	1933
Determinism and Indeterminism	1937
Conclusion	1943
End Notes	1943
Bibliography	1944

Abstract

Prophecies and fate are heavily thematized throughout the *God of War* video game series. In the original trilogy, prophecies are given to Kratos, Zeus, Kronos, and others by a range of beings with purported foreknowledge including the Fates and Oracles In the Norse duology, the Norns, Giants, and others also provide prophecies. In line with the common trope of Greek tragedies, Kratos, Zeus, and Kronos' actions, in trying to avoid their fates, created the very conditions by which those fates came to pass. In the duology set within Norse mythology, the themes of prophecy and fate are also thematized. However, in these games, it is shown that prophecy can be overcome, and that fate is flexible. This chapter considers some of the historical solutions to the problem of prophecy within classical theism and evaluates their applicability in the *God of War* series. It will also be argued that the two sets of *God of War* games present different accounts for the way in which prophecy operates. More specifically, it will be shown that the Greek Trilogy uses prophecy to maintain a deterministic understanding of the universe. In contrast, the Norse Duology uses prophecy to maintain an indeterministic account of the universe.

C. J. Horn (✉)
University of Wisconsin Stevens Point, Stevens Point, WI, USA
e-mail: jhorn@uwsp.edu

© Springer Nature Switzerland AG 2024
D. K. Johnson et al. (eds.), *The Palgrave Handbook of Popular Culture as Philosophy*,
https://doi.org/10.1007/978-3-031-24685-2_119

Keywords

Fate · Freedom · Free will · Foreknowledge · God · Prophecy

Introduction

Prophecies are important philosophical and religious phenomena that raise questions related to fate and freedom. Prophecies are true accounts of future events that are yet to be. They are often given through language by an individual or group of individuals. In some cases, prophecies need not be given through language and can be provided in other mediums such as visual representations of the future. In the *God of War* video game series, both kinds of prophecies are prevalent. There are prophecies given by beings with purported foreknowledge of the future, including the Oracle and the Fates in the original trilogy and the Giants and Norns in the sequel duology, using both written and oral mediums, as well as visual representations of the future in the form of paintings and murals. The very possibility of prophecies, which by their nature give true accounts about the future, present a prima facie problem for free agency. After all, it seems that if a prophecy conveys that Kratos will overthrow Olympus, for example, then it appears that he must, with certainty, do so, that is, Kratos is not free to not overthrow Olympus. If he does not overthrow Olympus, then it was not really a prophecy to begin with, but instead just a prediction that turned out to be false. Even well-founded predictions about the future are not problematic for freedom; prophecies are.

Philosophers and theologians have considered the nature of prophecy and developed complex solutions to the problem it suggests: the apparent incompatibility between freedom and foreknowledge. In this chapter, I consider the *God of War* franchise as a piece of philosophy which offers metaphysical views about freedom and theological views about prophecy. Interestingly, and perhaps unique in this volume though, I contend that the series offers two incompatible views of prophecy and freedom. In Part II, I give a brief account of the way in which the *God of War* franchise thematizes prophecy and freedom throughout the series with particular attention to the mainline games in the Greek Trilogy and Norse Duology. In Part III, I analyze several philosophical solutions for how to deal with the problem of prophecy and consider the degree to which they are applicable for addressing the threat to freedom in the *God of War* series. And finally, in Part IV, I defend the claim that the Greek Trilogy accepts a deterministic view of the universe which is later rejected in the Norse Duology.

The Problem of Prophecy in *God of War*

The *God of War* video game series has five mainline games released over the better part of the last two decades that tell the story of the Spartan warrior, Kratos. In chronological order of the events as they are depicted in the life of Kratos, the games are *God of War* (2005), *God of War II* (2007), *God of War III* (2010), *God of War* (2018), and *God of War Ragnarök* (2022).[1] There is not enough space in this chapter to properly summarize the detailed events of the life of Kratos, so attention will be restricted to only the parts of the games most relevant to the themes of prophecy, fate, and freedom. More specifically, I will focus on three prophecies throughout the series: the prophecy of the Marked Warrior in the original *God of War*, the prophecies given by the Sisters of Fate in *God of War II*, and the prophecy depicting Kratos' future at the end of *God of War Ragnarök*. The games released from 2005 through 2010 (*God of War I*, *II*, and *III*) describe the events set against the backdrop of Greek mythology. Throughout the chapter, I will refer to these games as the Greek Trilogy. The games released in 2018 and 2022 describe the events set against the backdrop of Norse mythology. In the chapter, I will refer to these games as the Norse Duology.

In the Greek Trilogy, the protagonist, Kratos, is a vicious Spartan warrior on the verge of defeat in battle. Kratos begs Ares, the god of war, to defeat his enemies in exchange for a pledge of fealty. Ares agrees to Kratos' bargain, destroys his enemies, and places the Spartan warrior in bondage. During his service to Ares, Kratos is commanded to destroy a village who worships the rival goddess, Athena. Kratos serves Ares and kills everyone in the village, including, unknown to Kratos, his wife and child, who Ares had brought to the village. Ares believed that if Kratos killed his family, then he would have no other mortal ties that would make him vulnerable and susceptible to disobedience. Unfortunately, when Kratos learns of this plot, he renounces his oath of fealty to Ares and seeks to murder him. Eventually, Kratos receives the power to defeat and kill Ares, does so, and is crowned the new god of war.

While serving as the new god of war, Kratos is eventually stripped of his powers by Zeus. Zeus tells Kratos that he will not be forgiven for killing his family, nor will Kratos' power be restored, unless he swears obedience to him. Kratos refuses the ultimatum so as to not be in service to another god, and Zeus kills him, or so it seems. Kratos' life is spared by the Titan, Gaia, so that she can gain his help in killing Zeus. She narrates to the player, "Kratos was destined to bring about change so severe that it would shake the very pillars of Mt. Olympus. His death was simply something that I could not allow...Fight spartan. You are not meant to die here" (*God of War II*). Kratos awakens in the underworld and plots his vengeance against Zeus and by extension, Olympus. To kill Zeus, Kratos must gain the power of the Titans, the forebears of the Olympian gods. He then must find the Sisters of Fate, and attempt to undo the events where he initially loses to Zeus. When the Fates refuse to help Kratos undo his destiny, he kills the sisters and uses their power to return to the moment where Zeus kills him. As it turns out, the moment that Kratos returns to is exactly the moment that he originally died. Kratos realizes that he is not undoing his fate after all, but bringing about the events that always occurred. At the beginning of the game, when Kratos "dies" we follow his perspective when he wakes up in the underworld. But in reality, the future Kratos arrived just as the past Kratos "died." In short, the past did not change – the past set up the events of the future, and the future protected the past.[2] It is clear that Kratos is not changing the past and simply completing a closed circle because when he gains the Loom of Fate that allows him to go back in time, he visits Gaia during The Great War between the Titans and the Olympians and saves them from Zeus using the Blade of Olympus, a mystical weapon with the power to kill a god. But earlier in the game when Gaia is communicating the events of the Great War to Kratos, the player can clearly see that even in the past the Titans are saved by a blue energy that is later revealed to be caused by Kratos wielding the Blade of Olympus. Again, time is a closed circle here and Kratos is bringing about the events that had happened previously.

Kratos overpowers Zeus and nearly kills the king of the gods in battle, but then Athena intervenes. Athena dies protecting Zeus, but before she does, she reveals several things. First, Kratos is Zeus' son and the Oracle had told Zeus the "Prophecy of the Marked Warrior," a prophecy that a marked warrior (who turns out to be Kratos) would destroy the Olympian gods.[3] What is more, because Zeus had overthrown his father, Kronos, Zeus tried to prevent his son, Kratos, from overthrowing him. Thus, we learn that, in trying to stop his fate, Zeus brings it about that he is overthrown by his son, Kratos, in the same way that Kronos was overthrown by his son, Zeus. In other words, in trying to change their respective fates, the actions of Kronos, Zeus, and Kratos fulfilled their destinies. In recounting the events of the Greek Trilogy to Mimir in *God of War Ragnarök*, Kratos explains how even the Oracle's actions brought about the future that she foresaw.

Mimir   "She had visions of Olympus being brought down...?"
Kratos   "Yes – by the God of War. Therefore, she helped me, intending to undermine Ares and protect her realm. She did not foresee that I would kill him and take his office. In the end, I proved her vision of doom correct."
Mimir   "So the Oracle herself brought about the very future she hoped to avoid."
(God of War Ragnarök)

The Norse duology also raises and emphasizes the same themes of fate and freedom, but in a way that is substantially different than the treatment in the Greek trilogy. Set years after the Greek Trilogy, *God of War* (2018) serves as a continuation of Kratos' story. The basic plot of the narrative is that Kratos and his son, Atreus, must reach the highest peak in all the nine realms to scatter the ashes of his mother, Faye. In the conclusion of the game, Kratos and Atreus find murals painted by the Giants depicting their journey throughout the game along with a hidden mural of a future yet to pass. In this hidden mural, Kratos appears to be dying in Atreus' arms. The implication here is that the Giants had foreknowledge since they created the art long before the depicted events took place, and that Atreus will continue the cycle of patricide started by Kronos. In *God of War Ragnarök*, prophecies are also plentiful. Kratos and Atreus see visual representations of Sköll and Hati, the Wolf-Giants who chase the sun and moon and signal the beginning of *Ragnarök*. They also discover that Odin was given a prophecy by the Frost Giant, Gróa, which foretold of his demise during *Ragnarök*. The primary driving part of the plot is Odin trying to find the Mask of Creation, which he thinks will help him avoid his own death at the events of Ragnarök.

Four Solutions to the Problem of Prophecy

In this section, I will contend that the *God of War* series presents a slightly different version of what is often called Theological Fatalism, the argument which shows that a being's foreknowledge threatens human free action. While the series does not include the God of classical theism, the series nevertheless demonstrates a version of the problem. After the problem is explained as it manifests with beings such as the Oracle, Fates, Norns, Giants, and so on, I examine some historical solutions[4] to the problem to evaluate the extent to which they are successful.

Philosophers typically try to understand the problem that prophecy raises by analyzing it in terms of the God of classical theism, the God that is omnipotent (God can do anything that can be done), omnibenevolent, (God loves things as much as possible), and (most relevant to our purposes) omniscient (God knows everything which can be known). And while there are gods throughout the *God of War* series, none of these gods, not even the supreme deities of their respective pantheons like Zeus or Odin, possess the identical properties of the deity of classical theism. Regardless, the fact that some beings possess some knowledge of the future still potentially undermines the freedom related to the individuals. It need not matter that all these beings lack omniscience. They do not need to possess perfect knowledge of *everything* for the problem to manifest. It is sufficient for the problem that if the beings have some actual knowledge of some future event, then the event must happen. Of course, their knowledge does not cause the events future occurrence, but their knowledge does entail the events. Put simply, knowledge of some future events is sufficient to motivate the problem at least some of the time. It is in these fated events of individuals with apparent freedom that the problem arises.

To be precise and motivate the problem, below is a rendering of what has commonly been called "The Argument from Theological Fatalism" which is adapted to the *God of War* series to take account of the difference between the God of classical theism and the beings with foreknowledge in the games. The threat of theological fatalism is only going to be problematic as it relates to libertarian freedom, the account which demands that freedom requires the ability to do otherwise. A compatibilist who accepts freedom and determinism will not be troubled by the argument since they can insist that one can be free in the meaningful sense despite being determined and prophecies being true.

1. The Oracle (or another being with foreknowledge of the event) believed yesterday that Kratos will kill Zeus tomorrow.
2. Nothing can be done now about the fact that the Oracle believed yesterday that Kratos will kill Zeus tomorrow, that is, we cannot change the past or the Oracle's true belief about the future.
3. Nothing can be done now about the fact that if the Oracle infallibly believed yesterday that Kratos will kill Zeus tomorrow, then Kratos will kill Zeus tomorrow.

4. It follows then that nothing can be done now about the fact that Kratos will kill Zeus tomorrow.
5. So, Kratos will not kill Zeus freely.

The first solution, developed by Boethius in the sixth century and made even more popular by Thomas Aquinas, denies the first premise of the above argument. The solution of Boethius and Aquinas is to insist that God does not *foreknow* anything because God exists from the perspective of timeless eternity. In other words, God does not know the future because the past and future are indistinguishable from God's perspective of timeless eternity. Although it is difficult to conceive of timeless eternity, Boethius describes this perspective as if God is at the peak of a mountain surveying events at bottom. While the events at the bottom of the mountain take place in time, God perceives and understands them from his perspective as happening all at once. Boethius writes, "Since God has a condition of ever-present eternity, His knowledge, which passes over every change of time, embracing infinite lengths of past and future, views in its own direct comprehension everything as though it were taking place in the present" (Boethius, *Consolation*, p. 117).

While the solution of timeless eternity is popular among philosophers and theologians in their attempt to solve the problem of foreknowledge, many insist that timeless eternity is incoherent. Insofar as we are beings in time, the best that we can do to explain timeless eternity is via analogies like God on the mountaintop. At the very least, we should be mindful that insofar as analogies are all deviations from what is the case, we do not know exactly what it means to perceive from the perspective of timeless eternity.

Even if we ignore this problem though, there is another which is arguably more pressing and more relevant for the *God of War* franchise: Many religious traditions depict God, not as timeless, but as acting *in* time. God performs miracles, answers prayers, and most importantly for the present purposes, offers prophecies. This is true for the Biblical God, but it is also true for the mystical beings in the video game series. Some perform miracles, some answer prayers, and some offer prophecies. But prophecies are true statements about the future. So, it is at least intuitively unclear how a being *outside* of time could say something about the future at all. Eleonore Stump and Norman Kretzmann, two contemporary advocates of the timeless eternity view, insist that God can still provide prophecies because they are often vague and subject to interpretation (see Stump and Kretzmann 1991). Mimir reflects this philosophical position in the games, insisting that "Prophecies are slippery by nature. Although some are more obvious than others" (God of War: *Ragnarök*).

While the timeless eternity view may or may not be successful within the context of classical theism, it cannot be a solution to the way that foreknowledge works in the *God of War* series. All the entities which possess foreknowledge in the series, Fates, Norns, and so on, exist *in time*, and so a different way to understand prophecy is needed. In one sense then, explaining prophecy with the God of classical theism is more difficult than within the context of the *God of War* series because we have some empirical information about the beings in the games which possess foreknowledge, but this is not obviously the case with the God of classical theism. At the very least, we know that the beings which possess foreknowledge in the games do not exist from the perspective of timeless eternity; they exist in time and space and interact directly with Kratos.

The second solution to the problem of foreknowledge was developed by the Spanish Jesuit, Luis de Molina, in the sixteenth century. Molina developed an account of what he called "middle knowledge" to explain God's providential control of the universe.[6] Molina divided God's knowledge into three different types. The first type of knowledge is "natural knowledge" and constitutes God's knowledge of necessary truths which are beyond the scope of God's will; although omnipotent, God cannot alter these truths. The second type of knowledge is "free knowledge" and constitutes God's knowledge of contingent truths that are within the scope of God's will. These propositions are true because of God's will. Molina referred to the third kind of knowledge as "middle knowledge" because it combined elements of both natural and free knowledge. God's middle knowledge is like natural knowledge in the sense that it is beyond God's control, but like free knowledge in the sense that it is contingent.

Examples of middle knowledge are often referred to as "counterfactuals of freedom" – middle knowledge is God's knowledge of what human free agents would do if left free in any fully specified set of possible circumstances. There are prophecies in the Bible, some defenders of middle knowledge insist, which suggest that God has knowledge not only of what will be done, but also what would be done under different circumstances in the way described by Molina. For instance, consider the prophecy depicted in the Book of Jeremiah, "If at any time I announce that a nation or kingdom is to be uprooted, torn down and destroyed, and if that nation I warned repents of its evil, then I will relent and not inflict on it the disaster I had planned. And if at another time I announce that a nation or kingdom is to be built up and planted, and if it is evil in my sight and does not obey me, then I will reconsider the good I had intended to do for it" (Jeremiah 18:7–10). The prophecy in Jeremiah seemingly indicates that God knows what would happen if a nation were to obey or disobey the desires of God. God does not just know his own actions, but he knows his own actions in relation to the kingdom.[7]

Because God knows what every human free agent would do in any possible circumstance, God also knows, Molina argues, what every human free agent is going to do in the future. Even though God has foreknowledge, human free actions remain contingent because there are possible worlds where those individuals behave differently. Applied to the game series, Molina would contend that even though God knew that Kratos would murder Zeus before it happened, Kratos' actions remain free and contingent. Moreover, God knew what Kratos *would have done* if he were to choose not to murder Zeus in those circumstances. God knows the truth of every future possible state of affairs, including the future in the actual state of affairs.

Molina's middle knowledge solution is particularly important for the problem of prophecy because it allowed him to make sense of a robust view of freedom that preserved God's foreknowledge and maintain a strong view of providence. For example, at the last supper, Jesus gives a prophecy that one of his disciples will betray him (Matthew 26: 20–21). Of course, Judas later betrays Jesus, fulfilling the prophecy. According to Molina, Judas' action is free and contingent and part of God's middle knowledge because God knew not only that Judas would betray Jesus, but also that if Judas were in different circumstances, then he (probably) would have done something else instead. Molina's solution is especially advantageous in the sense that, if it works, it preserves the moral responsibility of individuals such as Judas or Kratos.

Unfortunately, middle knowledge is difficult to classify in the *God of War* series. Although prophecies are vague in the Greek Trilogy, none of them seem to be conditional in nature. And except for the ending of *God of War Ragnarök*, the Norse Duology consists only of unconditional prophecies as well. One key exception is Faye's final mural depicting a "possible path" which indicates that something like middle knowledge may be true. Faye apparently possessed knowledge not only of actual events, but also of genuinely possible events. And she knows those other possible events because Kratos can freely choose otherwise. And it also would not follow that just because Faye knew one possible path for Kratos, that she knew all of them.

On the face of it, Molina's solution has much to offer in the sense that it preserves many of the things that classical theists often desire: a strong view of providence, a robust view of human freedom, and God's foreknowledge. And there are circumstances in the Norse Duology, in particular, where Molinism is an especially enticing interpretation of events. But there are issues with middle knowledge that may make it untenable both for classical theism and for the *God of War* series.

The main advantage of Molinism is the preservation of divine providence, and yet, none of the characters in the lore of the games are provident. Even the Fates which create, measure, and cut the thread of life of every mortal, god, and Titan in existence are not provident over all of creation in the way that the God of classical theism is provident. Rather, the governance of the world is divided by the relevant deities, which serve as sovereign over the different parts of creation. So, the main advantage of Molinism is completely lost in the context of the games. Of course, Molinism may still be correct even if it does not preserve divine providence. Middle knowledge has other benefits aside from the preservation of divine providence; it provides a robust theory of freedom and an explanation for foreknowledge and prophecy. So, while Molinism is a possible interpretation of how to deal with the threat of theological fatalism in the *God of War* series, the evidence for it is confined to only one prophecy in the climax of the final game.

The final historical solution to the problem of foreknowledge is to reject the second premise of the above argument. The second premise is that nothing can be done now about the fact that the Oracle believed yesterday that Kratos will kill Zeus tomorrow, that is, we cannot change the past or the Oracle's true belief about the future. Developed most notably by William of Ockham in the fourteenth century, this position holds that something can be done now about the fact that the Oracle believed yesterday that Kratos will kill Zeus tomorrow. The reason why the Oracle held the belief that she did in the past is *because* of Kratos' actions tomorrow. And importantly, if Kratos were to freely decide *not* to kill Zeus tomorrow, then the past would be different – the past beliefs of the Oracle would be other than they are. There is nothing incoherent about the counterfactual power over the past. In other words, nobody can do anything to *change* the past, but there is nothing incoherent, Ockham insists, about *causing* the past. Put simply, Ockham's solution works, defenders argue because God's past beliefs are only accidentally necessary, and they are not immutable "hard facts" (see Plantinga 1986). Rather, God's past belief about Kratos' future free action would be different depending on the free actions of Kratos. And if Ockham's account is true, then premise 2 above is false – something *can* be done now about the fact that the Oracle believed yesterday that Kratos will kill Zeus tomorrow, that is, we can change the past or the Oracle's true belief about the future. And if something can be done, then the conclusion of the argument from theological fatalism does not follow.[8]

Boethius' timeless eternity view, Molina's middle knowledge view, and Ockham's asymmetry of the past and future view offer compelling explanations for foreknowledge in the case of God. However, only Ockham's solution makes sense within the mythology of the entire *God of War* series. Insofar as Ockham's solution to the foreknowledge problem preserves God's existence in time (unlike Boethius' timeless eternity view) and more closely reflects the way providence is depicted in the games' beings with foreknowledge (unlike Molina's middle knowledge view), it is preferable for how we should understand prophecy in the *God of War* series. Boethius' solution is inconsistent with beings existing in time, Molina's solution is inconsistent with beings which are not provident, and although there is nothing to indicate that the beings with foreknowledge have their past knowledge caused by future actions, it is the only traditional solution that *could* work across both the Greek Trilogy and Norse Duology.

Determinism and Indeterminism

While Ockham's solution is the only viable solution that might work across the entire series, it will be defended that the Greek Trilogy and Norse Duology offer competing accounts of determinism based on the different kinds of prophecies depicted in the games. More specifically, I will argue that the Greek Trilogy offers a deterministic view of the universe, and the Norse Duology holds an indeterministic view of reality. Determinism is used here to indicate roughly the same thing as fate or destiny. On this view, fated events must happen, they cannot fail to happen. I am not using fate or determinism here to be the view that "whatever is going to happen is going to happen, no matter what" as if our choices are immaterial to the future. Rather, fated events are those that must occur. By contrast, the Norse Duology denies that there are fated or determined events which must occur. In this sense, the prophecies depicted in the Norse Duology are such that they might be false – the future is open and could be otherwise.

One of the major themes throughout the series is the dialectic that many of the characters share in their attempt to either contest or accept their perceived inevitable fates. Kratos' attitude throughout the Greek Trilogy is to accept the reality of fate, but to insist that it can be changed through force of will. In the Norse Duology, Tyr and

Odin represent Kratos' attitude from the Greek Trilogy. Odin's attention is focused almost exclusively on obtaining and unlocking the powers of the Mask of Creation, an artifact which he believes will give him unlimited knowledge, including knowledge of how to stop Ragnarök and prevent his own death. Odin tells Kratos that Atreus is "the key to peace in our age, to break free from all this fate and prophecy" (*God of War Ragnarök*). Upon seeing his future in one of the prophecies of the Giants in *God of War Ragnarök*, Tyr tells Atreus in a way closely mirroring Kratos' actions from the Greek Trilogy, "I won't allow prophecy to define my choices" (*God of War Ragnarök*). Angrboda, one of the Giants who has foreknowledge of at least some future events insists not just on the reality of fate, but on the proper attitude being one of acquiescence. She tells Atreus after he learns of the prophecy that his actions will lead to his father's death, "Look, this is the only way things turn out. The sooner you accept that the better" (*God of War Ragnarök*). Of course, Angrboda will be shown to be wrong in her beliefs here from early in the game. Atreus' actions do not lead to his father's death. And the final mural that Kratos sees which depicts "another path" shows that she is wrong when she suggests that "this is the *only* way things turn out" (*God of War Ragnarök*).

In addition to the Prophecy of the Marked Warrior described earlier, which shows Kratos becoming the "Ghost of Sparta" and bringing about the death of Zeus, the Greek Trilogy also draws heavily on mythological figures depicted by Greek authors like Hesiod and Orpheus, including the Fates. In Greek mythology and religion, the Fates (or Moirai) were three sisters named Clotho, Lachesis, and Atropos. They were regularly depicted, like they are in the Greek Trilogy, as beings who create, control, and destroy the thread of life that represents each individual. Clotho is the spinner who creates the thread of an individual like Kratos. Lachesis is the fate who decides how long Kratos' thread should be. And Atropos cuts the thread to end the life of an individual at the appropriate time. Importantly, and exactly the way they are depicted in Greek mythology, the Fates are beings which have authority over not just humans, but the Olympians and Titans as well. Hesiod, for instance, writes, "And Night bore hateful Doom and black Fate…And she generated the Destinies and the merciless, avenging Fates, Clotho, Lachesis, and Atropos, who give mortals at birth good and evil to have, and prosecute transgressions of mortals and gods" (Hesiod, *Theogony*). Gaia narrates a similar account to the player, "Clotho weaves the thread of life for every mortal, god, and Titan" (*God of War II*). The clear implication as it is depicted in both Hesiod and the game is that every individual's actions are mandated by the Fates.

In *God of War II*, Kratos seeks an audience with the Fates to undo what he thinks was his past. And the journey to the Fates signals as much to the player. In the Temple of the Fates, Kratos has one of the temple translators read from a book blocking his path, "Hear me noble sisters, who forge our destinies. Another seeks an audience to change their fate" (*God of War II*). Upon meeting them though, they insist that changing one's fate is not possible. Lachesis tell him, "None can change their destiny, Kratos. We sisters determine the fates of all. It was I who deemed the Titans to lose the Great War and I who have allowed you to come this far. It is not your destiny to kill Zeus…You do not defy fate, Kratos. For we have woven the events of your life...We control your destiny, foolish mortal. With a whim we can end your life or allow you to live" (*God of War II*).

One might think that Kratos proves the Fates wrong here, thereby showing that determinism is false even in the Greek Trilogy. After all, he ultimately kills Zeus in *God of War III* (2010). There are two plausible ways to deal with the apparent contradiction. In terms of the logical space, the only options are that the Fates have infallible knowledge of Kratos' future or they do not. If they have infallible knowledge of Kratos' future, then there must be some other reason that they are misleading him. There could be a lot of reasons for their deception, so I only offer one possible explanation. In the context of the Greek Trilogy, the Fates, like Zeus and Ares, are using Kratos' destiny as a means of control. Put simply, the Fates are lying to Kratos when they insist that his destiny is not to kill Zeus because they know that once he does, creation will be destroyed. As *God of War III* shows, the death of the Olympians results in the universe falling into chaos. There is no Poseidon to calm and control the seas. There is no Hades to oversee the realm of the dead. And the death of Zeus plunges the entire world into darkness. Indeed, the Fates know that if Kratos believes himself capable of killing Zeus, then he must kill them first in that pursuit. And he does. So, lying to Kratos was a final effort to preserve themselves and the Greek world.

If the Fates do not have infallible knowledge of the future, then there is a clear way to explain their apparent premonitions to Kratos – they are simply mistaken. On this interpretation, the Fates would be ill-named and be fallible just like every other being. If this interpretation is true, then perhaps the Greek Trilogy is just as indeterministic as the Norse Duology and the lesson is that strength of will is even more powerful than fate. But there are some strong reasons against this interpretation. First, if the universe is indeterministic, then we are giving preference for one prophecy which suggests indeterminism against every other which suggests determinism. Even if the statements of the Fates to Kratos indicate that the future is open, all the other prophecies throughout the Greek Trilogy indicate that the future must unfold in only one way. Second, if the universe is indeterministic and open and the Norse Duology is indeed indeterministic as well, then both series have the same depiction of reality and the developers are treading the same narrative ground as they did before. But if this is the case, then Kratos does not gain any new insight in the culmination of *God of War Ragnarök*. He does not realize that fate can be undone, for he already knew this fact years earlier when he encountered the Sisters of Fate. None of these reasons provide certain evidence that the second interpretation is weaker, of course, but the totality of the evidence slightly favors the first interpretation.

Although prophecies remain a key element in the Norse duology, *God of War Ragnarök* shows that the future is open and subject to change. In the Norse Duology, the Norse Sisters of Fate, the Norns, state that the way in which they have knowledge of the future is because of Kratos' predictability.[9] In knowing Kratos' past actions, they have a *very* good sense of what he will do in the future. And since they justifiably believe that he cannot change his character because nothing in his past actions has indicated that he will change his behavior, they know with a high degree of likelihood what he will do in future situations. Consider the exchange between Kratos and Freya with the Norns:

Norns "You come to us, piteous archetypes, seeking freedom from your scripts as if knowing your lines would grant you power to rewrite them...You will die, Kratos of Sparta."
Mimir "But you called him the destroyer of fate. There must be a way to subvert destiny."
Norns "There is no destiny. There is no grand design. No script. Only the choices you make. That your choices are so predictable merely make us seem prescient."
Freya "When my son was born...Your prophecy said he would die a needless death."
Norns "And he did. Because YOU could not let him go. Because HE thirsted for revenge. And because you (pointing to Kratos) kill gods...You are the sum of your choices, nothing more. And because your choices never change, you will learn that Heimdall intends to kill your son in Asgard, and you will do what you do best. And then Ragnarök. The skies burn. The curtains fall." (*God of War Ragnarök*)

The best interpretation of this exchange is that the Norns have knowledge of the future in a way similar to God on the view of Open Theism. Open Theism is the view according to which God does not know the future with complete certainty (see Pinnock et al. 1994). God does not know the future not because he operates from the perspective of timeless eternity, but because God has either freely limited his own knowledge in such a way to preserve the free actions of human agents or because the future, at least in part, does not yet exist. What does not yet exist are our future free choices. Open Theists insist that God still knows with an exceedingly high degree of likelihood what we will freely do in the future because God knows our character and history completely. While God does not know the (complete) future on this model, this need not mean that God is not omniscient. Rather, God's omniscience simply means that God knows all there is to know or all that there is that is worth knowing (depending on the interpretation of Open Theism). The future cannot be known with certainty – it is "open."

Strictly speaking, Kratos' future contingent actions are open and subject to change, so their "knowledge" of the future is more like very sophisticated probabilistic judgments. For all intents and purposes, on Open Theism, God has a very good sense of what human future actions probably will be, but nevertheless, God's very good sense of the future could turn out to be false. And that is exactly what happens to the Norns in the Norse Duology. They suggest to Kratos that they know what he will do because of the nature of his character and their knowledge of the past, but when Kratos' character changes in the climax of *Ragnarok* and he does something outside of his character and in a way inconsistent with his past experiences, there is good reason to think that they would not have seen such a change coming. After all, they tell Kratos that "He *will* die" and "he *will* do what he does best (kill other gods)."[10] But they are wrong in their predictions. Their knowledge was fallible – not only does Kratos survive, but also he stops himself from killing Thor, and ultimately shows mercy to Odin by not killing him, too. In short, the Norns would be surprised by Kratos' actions because they do not know with certainty what he will do in the future in the same way that Open Theists insist that God's infinite knowledge does not extend to the future with complete certainty. And if it was not for the final mural that Kratos finds at the end of the game, we would have good reason to think that the Norse Duology is following the exact same pattern as the Greek Trilogy; the respective Fates think they have infallible knowledge of the fixed future and are shown to be mistaken. But the existence of the mural depicting a possible alternative path for Kratos shows that each set of games is offering a unique perspective to the player. Atreus succinctly captures this new lesson when he tells Angrboda, "This looks an awful lot like defying destiny...I'm rewriting my story" (*God of War Ragnarök*).

Narratively, it would make sense that the young Atreus reflects the young Kratos in rejecting the fixed nature of reality. It is surprising then that in the game's conclusion, Kratos learns that his entire worldview about fate from the Greek Trilogy all the way up to the climax of the Norse Duology is mistaken and Atreus is correct – we can rewrite our story. Up until the point where Kratos tells Atreus that they can open their hearts to suffering, indicating that his character can change and that he is not locked into the necessity of violent deicide, Kratos wholeheartedly believed in destiny. The Greek Trilogy finds Kratos fighting tooth and nail against his fate only to realize that he cannot escape it. In the Norse Duology before his epiphany and change of heart, Kratos still accepted the reality of fate but chose to accept it instead. When Kratos sees his fate on the reverse mural at the end of *God of War Ragnarök*, Mimir asks, "What did you see in there, brother?" Kratos responds, "A path. One I had never imagined" (*God of War Ragnarök*). We can change our fate after all.

Perhaps the best narrative arc in the entire two-decade-long series is Kratos changing his attitude in the Greek Trilogy from one that mirrors the rebellious Tyr to the accepting attitude of Angrboda in the Norse Duology. The Greek Trilogy is full to the brim of examples of Kratos learning that he is fated to do something and responding with violence to stop those events from occurring. In contrast, in the Norse Duology we find Kratos teaching his son, Atreus, to not protest our fate. Instead, they should accept their violent natures. In *God of War* (2018), after Atreus kills someone for the first time and is understandably upset and in tears, Kratos tells his son, "Close your heart to it." Kratos is passing down to Atreus the moral lesson that he learned during his decades of war – do not sympathize with those who suffer. The world is violent, and the only rational attitude in a violent world is to be violent. Animals do not feel guilty for destroying their enemies any more than they should.

But in the climax to *God of War Ragnarök*, Kratos acts in a way that even the Norns could not foresee – he acts in such a way as to effectively change his fate. Contrary to the beliefs he held in the Greek Trilogy, Kratos realizes that we are not just animals and that we may respond to suffering not with resignation, but with empathy. The God of War has learned not just to defeat his enemies, but to protect those that cannot protect themselves. This is important not just because he is showing empathy, but because Kratos is acting in a way inconsistent with his past and character. When Atreus witnesses Sindri, the dwarf and blacksmith who has helped them on their journey, harming Midgardians who are dying during the battle of Ragnarök, Atreus repeats to himself the lesson that he learned from his father. Atreus mutters to himself, "Close your heart to it. Close your heart" (*God of War Ragnarök*). But in this pivotal moment, Kratos realizes that he was wrong, acts out of character, and changes his fate. Kratos tells Atreus that he was wrong to show apathy to suffering. He tells his son, "Son, listen closely. You feel their pain because that is who you are. And you must never sacrifice that. Ever. Not for anyone. I was wrong, Atreus. I was wrong. Open your heart. Open your heart to their suffering. That is your mother's wish…And mine as well. Today…today. We will be better" (*God of War Ragnarök*). "Being better" is not just Kratos becoming morally better – he is changing his fate.

But how is it possible for Kratos to change his fate? In the Greek Trilogy, he tried, unsuccessfully, to change his fate through sheer force of will. Even when he killed the personifications of fate themselves, he did nothing more than bring about the future that was destined to occur. Kratos thought that the only way to break free from the prophecies depicting his actions was to change everything external to him. But in the climax of the Norse Duology, he realizes that the only way to change fate is to change his own actions. Kratos must conquer his greatest enemy, himself. Kratos must destroy the old vengeful Ghost of Sparta, metaphorically speaking, and become a better father. And he does. Kratos changes his fate by changing himself. In short then, the Greek Trilogy finds Kratos constantly trying to subvert his fate to no avail. It is for this reason that we find him teaching Atreus early in the Norse Duology that our only option is to accept fate. But in the resolution to the Norse Duology, Kratos realizes that we can change our fate by changing ourselves. Fate itself is not as determined as he initially thought; the future is open.

Remarkably, when Kratos changes his fate at the end of *God of War Ragnarök*, it does not render the hidden mural at the end of *God of War* (2018) false. The hidden mural depicted what appeared to be Atreus' father dying in his arms. And this still turns out to be somewhat true. In the climax of the game, Atreus begs for his surrogate father, Odin, to cease his quest for changing fate. Odin tells Atreus, "This was our chance Loki [Atreus's other name]. I could have had my answers. I could have learned the truth. You took that away from me! I could have made things better. We could have made the Nine Realms better." Atreus responds, "This was never about the realms, or me – it was about you." Odin fires back, "You destroyed everything. My home, my family, my kingdom." Atreus corrects, "YOU did those things. Your choices. You killed your own son." And Odin persists that he is just a pawn to fate. He responds, "It wasn't my choice. I had no choice." Atreus retorts and tries to teach him what he has learned from his father, "There's always a choice. You have to stop. You can choose to be better." But Odin denies the mercy and the lesson, insisting that his fate is unavoidable. He responds, "No. I can't. I have to know what happens next. I will never stop" (*God of War Ragnarök*). Odin dies in Atreus' arms following the same path of Kratos in the Greek Trilogy, relentlessly and ceaselessly trying to avoid his fate by any means necessary. The mural was true, from a certain point of view.

Conclusion

We can see then that prophecies are prevalent in both the Greek Trilogy and Norse Duology, and both introduce and problematize fate and freedom for the player. But they do so in very different ways. On the face of it, it appears that the Greek Trilogy and Norse Duology raise the very same problem with respect to prophecy. If someone has knowledge of a future event, then those events must come to pass. And if they must come to pass, then the individuals depicted in the future event *must* act in such a way that those future facts come to pass. Although both the Greek Trilogy and the Norse Duology maintain that our choices determine the future, the Greek Trilogy suggests that some of our actions are determined and could not be otherwise. But the Norse Duology has a more complicated lesson. The vast majority of the Norse Duology has Kratos continue his beliefs about determinism, fate, and freedom from the Greek Trilogy, namely, that our fates are set in stone, and we can fight against it to no avail or accept it. But regardless of our own attitudes, the Greek Trilogy maintains that the future is fixed. On the view of the conclusion of the Norse Duology, however, the future is not determined; rather, it is genuinely open and could be otherwise. In short, Kratos can change his fate in the Norse Duology in a way that was never possible in the Greek Trilogy.

In this chapter, it has been argued that the traditional solutions to the problem of foreknowledge exemplified in prophecies are mostly unsuccessful because the God of classical theism is so fundamentally different than the deities and beings with foreknowledge represented in the games. Moreover, it has been argued that the Greek Trilogy and Norse Duology endorse different views with respect to determinism. More specifically, the Greek Trilogy holds that determinism is true and we are nevertheless free, embracing a view of determinism consistent with many Greek writers. Although prophecies are ambiguous, fate is not malleable, and the future is fixed. The Norse Duology, on the other hand, holds that determinism is false. Our future is open, and our fates are not set in stone. While our past and our character shapes who we are, they do not determine it. Prophecies remain ambiguous, but fate is malleable, and the future is open. The *God of War* series has been problematizing the relationship between prophecy, fate, and freedom and attempting to provide the player with some philosophical and religious views about these notions. And although there are currently different accounts of determinism between the Greek and Norse narratives, they are each uniquely compelling, inviting the player to consider these themes time and time again.

End Notes

1. Not included here are a few spin-off games, mobile games, table-top car games, text-based games, and graphic novels. These are left out in the interest of brevity.
2. In this sense, the time travel is similar to the way it is depicted in *Terminator* (1984) when Kyle Reese is sent to the past to protect Sarah Connor and ends up impregnating her with John Connor, who in the future sends him to the past to

protect his mother. This is not the time travel of *Back to the Future* (1985) where Marty McFly's shenanigans in the past create a different future that he returns to.
3. In *God of War: Ghost of Sparta (2010)*, it is revealed that Zeus initially thought that Kratos' younger brother, Deimos, was the marked warrior and set up the events for his death. Deimos' death provided even more motivation for Kratos to kill Zeus.
4. I use "solution" here not because these are all successful ways to deal with the problem, but because this is the common way in the secondary literature to discuss these views.
5. Although it might for Thomists. See *Summa Theologica*. Question 14, Article 8: "Now it is manifest that God causes things by His intellect, since His being is His act of understanding; and hence His knowledge must be the cause of things, in so far as His will is joined to it."
6. Kyle Johnson maintains that Molina's solution is not really a solution to the freedom and foreknowledge problem because Molina is merely stipulating that God can have foreknowledge of free actions. As a result, the objection is that middle knowledge is more of a theological view rather than a philosophical solution to the problem at hand.
7. One might insist that the conditional prophecy depicted in Jeremiah is too vague to refer to anything in particular. Again though, prophecies are often vague in nature and remain prophecies so long as they are true depictions about the future. Nevertheless, a more specific conditional prophecy can be found in the Book of Jonah when God commands Jonah to give a message to the people of Ninevah. See Jonah 3:3.
8. It might be objected here that it is unclear what it means to say that something *can* be done to change God's past beliefs. The compatibilist and incompatibilist analyze "can" very differently. I set aside this complication here as it would take the chapter too far afield.
9. Thanks to Ethan Walker for reminding me of this important conversation.
10. My emphasis in both cases.

Bibliography

Adams, Robert M. 1977. Middle knowledge and the problem of evil. *American Philosophical Quarterly* 14: 109–117; reprinted in *The virtue of faith and other essays*. Oxford: Oxford University Press, 1987.

An enquiry concerning human understanding, edited by Tom L. Beauchamp. Oxford/New York: Oxford University Press, 1999.

Boethius. 1981. *The consolation of philosophy*. Trans. W.V. Cooper. Chicago: Regnery Gateway.

Corabi, Joseph, and Rebecca Germino. 2013. Prophecy, foreknowledge, and middle knowledge. *Faith and Philosophy* 30 (1): 72–92.

Craig, William Lane. 1990. *Divine foreknowledge and human freedom*, Brill's studies in intellectual history 19. Leiden: EJ Brill.

Davison, Scott A. 1991. Foreknowledge, middle knowledge, and 'nearby' worlds. *International Journal for Philosophy of Religion* 30 (1): 29–44.

Finch, Alicia, and Michael Rea. 2008. Presentism and Ockham's way out. In *Oxford studies in philosophy of religion*, ed. Jonathan Kvanvig, vol. 1, 1–17. Oxford: Oxford University Press.

Fischer, John Martin. 1983. Freedom and foreknowledge. *Philosophical Review* 92: 67–79.

———, ed. 1989. *God, freedom, and foreknowledge*. Stanford: Stanford University Press.

———. Ockhamism. *Philosophical Review* 94: 81–100.

Flint, Thomas. 1998. *Divine providence: The molinist account*. Ithaca: Cornell University Press.

Freddoso, Alfred. 1983. Accidental necessity and logical determinism. *Journal of Philosophy* 80: 257–278.

Hasker, William. 1989. *God, time, and knowledge*. Ithaca: Cornell University Press.

Hesiod. 2011. *Theogony and works and days*. Oxford: Oxford University Press.

Hobbes, T. 1651/1994. Leviathan. In *Leviathan, with selected variants from the Latin edition of 1668*, ed. E. Curley. Indianapolis: Hackett.

Kreisel, Howard. 2003. *Prophecy: The history of an idea in medieval Jewish philosophy*. Amsterdam: Springer Publishing Company.

Kvanvig, Jonathan. 1986. *The possibility of an all-knowing god*. New York: St. Martin's Press.

Merricks, Trenton. 2011. Truth and molinism. In *Molinism: The contemporary debate*, ed. Ken Perszyk, 50–72. Oxford: Oxford University Press.

de Molina, Luis. 1588/1988. *On divine foreknowledge (De liberi arbitri cum gratiae donis, divina praescientia, providentia, praedestinatione et reprobatione concordia*, 47–53. Trans. Alfred J. Freddoso). Ithaca: Cornell University Press.

Ockham, William. 1983. *Predestination, god's foreknowledge, and future contingents*, 2nd ed. Trans. M.M. Adams and N. Kretzmann. Indianapolis: Hackett Publishing Company.

Pinnock, Clark H., Richard Rice, John Sanders, William Hasker, and David Basinger. 1994. *The openness of god: A biblical challenge to the traditional understanding of god*. Downers Grove: InterVarsity.

Plantinga, Alvin. 1986. On Ockham's way out. *Faith and Philosophy* 3 (3): 235–269.

Pruss, Alexander. 2007. Prophecy without middle knowledge. *Faith and Philosophy* 24 (4): 433–457.

Sony Santa Monica. 2005. *God of War*. Sony computer entertainment. PlayStation 2.

———. 2007. *God of War II*. Sony computer entertainment. PlayStation 2.

———. 2010. *God of War III*. Sony computer entertainment. PlayStation 3.

———. 2018. *God of War*. Sony computer entertainment. PlayStation 4.

———. 2022. *God of War: Ragnarök*. Sony computer entertainment. PlayStation 5.

Stump, Eleonore, and Norman Kretzmann. 1991. Prophecy, past truth, and eternity. In *Philosophical perspectives 5: Philosophy of religion*, ed. James Tomberlin. Atascadero: Ridgeview Press.

Warfield, Ted A. 2009. Ockhamism and molinism – Foreknowledge and prophecy, Oxford studies in philosophy of religion: Volume 2, ed. Jonathan L. Kvanvig, 317–32. Oxford: Oxford University Press.

Widerker, David. 1990. Troubles with Ockhamism. *Journal of Philosophy* 87 (9): 462–480.

Wierenga, Edward. 1989. *The nature of god*. Ithaca: Cornell University Press.

———. 1991. Prophecy, freedom, and the necessity of the past. In *Philosophical perspectives 5: Philosophy of religion*, ed. James Tomberlin. Atascadeo: Ridgeview Press.

Zagzebski, Linda. 1991. *The dilemma of freedom and foreknowledge*. New York: Oxford University Press.

Part V
Graphic Novels

Frank Miller's Batman as Philosophy: "The World Only Makes Sense When You Force It To"

87

Steve Bein

Contents

Introduction	1949
Frank Miller's Batman: A Summary	1951
The Ethics of Vigilantism	1953
The Joker Problem	1955
Batman and the Will to Power	1957
Libertarianism and Bat-Libertarianism	1961
The Frank Miller Problem	1964
Conclusion: Good and Scary	1966
References	1967

Abstract

Comics writer and artist Frank Miller reinvented Batman, bringing greater emotional, moral, and political depth to the character. This chapter considers Batman's ethics and politics, examining his rejection of utilitarianism, his embrace of the will to power, his Kantian dilemma when dealing with the Joker, and the distinction to be drawn between Miller's own libertarianism and Bruce Wayne's Bat-Libertarianism.

Keywords

Frank Miller · Batman · Liberalism · Libertarianism · Utilitarianism · Will to power · Kant · Bentham · Nietzsche · Nozick

---

S. Bein (✉)
Philosophy Department, University of Dayton, Dayton, OH, USA
e-mail: sbein1@udayton.edu

© Springer Nature Switzerland AG 2024
D. K. Johnson et al. (eds.), *The Palgrave Handbook of Popular Culture as Philosophy*,
https://doi.org/10.1007/978-3-031-24685-2_15

Introduction

1986 was the year everything changed in comics. Two short series – just 16 issues between them – ushered the term "graphic novel" into public consciousness and prompted publishers to reimagine who their target audience could be. The first was Frank Miller's *The Dark Knight Returns* with artistic efforts from Lynn Varley, Klaus Janson, and Miller himself. Miller transformed Batman from a playful, quip-tossing crimefighter to a dark, brooding menace who frightened criminals, civilians, and even other superheroes. The second was *Watchmen*, illustrated by Dave Gibbons and written by Alan Moore, whose heroes were more realistic – indeed, more *human* – than any before. Miller and Moore made readers think about what a world with superheroes would really be like – heroes with curse words and genitalia and sex lives, heroes whose vices are as great as their virtues, heroes with the kinds of personal problems that might actually prompt someone to put on tights and seek out fistfights with street gangs. Because of Miller and Moore, comic books weren't just for children anymore.

Watchmen has already gotten its share of philosophical attention (White 2009), but for the most part Miller's work has escaped philosophers' notice. Frank Miller (1957–) is a living legend in the comics industry. Arriving at Marvel Comics' New York headquarters in 1979, he became a personal favorite of Stan Lee, arguably the most influential figure in comics history. Miller took one-dimensional B-list characters and turned them into some of today's best known (and most lucrative) stars, including such characters as Wolverine, Daredevil, and the Punisher. At DC Comics, he brought new depth to all the flagship heroes of the Justice League, and at Dark Horse he created era-defining work like *Sin City*, *Hard Boiled*, and *Give Me Liberty*. But Miller is also a polarizing figure. For instance, he drew international ire with *Holy Terror*, a violent post-9/11 rant that he himself has since disavowed. This chapter will not whitewash his personal history; it will consider the artist warts and all.

Because Miller's work is so wide-ranging, this chapter will focus only on the character he's best known for, the character that allowed him to write his own ticket for the rest of his career: Batman. The principal focus will be Miller's most philosophically robust work, *The Dark Knight Returns* (1986–1987, hereafter abbreviated *DKR*) and *Batman: Year One* (1987, hereafter abbreviated *Year One*), with passing references to the Dark Knight sequel series *The Dark Knight Strikes Again* (2001–2002, hereafter abbreviated DK2) and *Dark Knight III: The Master Race* (2015–2017, hereafter abbreviated DK3).

The following chapter contains as few spoilers as possible, but any philosophical analysis of Miller's Batman necessarily includes some discussion of what he does and what happens to him. Because of this, and because *DKR* and *Year One* are among the best Batman books ever written, I recommend that you read them first if you don't want the plots spoiled. DK2 and DK3 are easier to discuss without spoilers, so if you're already familiar with *DKR* and *Year One* (or you don't mind them being spoiled), read on.

Of course the first thing to say about Frank Miller's Batman is that he isn't just Frank Miller's. Comics, are a collaborative art, and without the sparse noir pencils of

David Mazzucchelli (*Year One*) or the flowing watercolors of Lynne Varley (*DKR*), Miller's scripts could never have come to life. Moreover, Miller was standing on the shoulders of giants – namely, all the other writers, artists, and editors who have worked on Batman, going all the way back to Bob Kane in 1939. So Miller's Batman wasn't born out of nothing; he's an interpretation, a response to everyone who went before. He's also a product of his time; *DKR* is set during the Reagan Administration, and that's not a random choice. So the subject of this chapter isn't Batman as philosophy and it isn't Frank Miller's personal philosophy, it's Frank Miller's Batman – that is, the artwork, the scripts, the historical context, and how the author's philosophy and the character's philosophy are intertwined.

Frank Miller's Batman: A Summary

Miller's Batman was born in the first issue of *The Dark Knight Returns*. There, Bruce Wayne is not the dashing billionaire playboy of comic fame but a broken, angry, 55-year-old recluse with a death wish. Long since retired as the Batman, Bruce now struggles to make sense of a world that's willing to let television tell it what to think, let corporate interests tell it what to want, and let street gangs tell it when it's safe to go outside. The cape and cowl call to him but he knows he's past his prime. The spirit is willing but the flesh is weak: his next heart attack is only a matter of time. When at last he dons the Bat-mantle again, gone are the comic antics and witty quips of the Adam West era. Gone, too, is the Greek god's physique; this Batman is blocky, even ugly. Brimming with anger and riddled with self-doubt, this is a Batman the world had never seen. He's not as fast or as strong as he needs to be, and he berates himself constantly for being too old, too sluggish, and too reliant on luck.

We meet another diminished Batman in *Year One*, this time at the opposite end of his career: too naïve, too amateur, and (again) too reliant on luck. Bruce Wayne, age 25, returns to Gotham City after spending the last 12 years abroad. Miller doesn't tell us what he's been up to because we already know: he's sought out the masters of every skill he needs, honing his body and mind into the perfect weapons for fighting crime. His first round in that fight goes poorly: armed with nothing but a cheap disguise (he has yet to create the Batman persona, so he doesn't have the costume or gadgets yet), he winds up handcuffed and bleeding out in the back of a squad car. After a narrow escape he contemplates whether he should ring for his trusty butler (it was Miller who first gave Alfred his training in combat medicine) or just let himself bleed to death. It's been 18 years since his parents were murdered, and so after 18 years of preparation to avenge them he says, "I have everything but patience. I'd rather die than wait another hour" (*Year One*, p. 20). But you already know who rescues him. A bat crashes in on his meditations, and just like that he knows how he's going to inspire fear in Gotham's criminals.

In *Year One* there are no costumed supervillains to fight, because for Miller it's a kook like Batman that inspires kooks like Penguin or the Riddler. (In fact, in *DKR* Batman's retirement costs the Joker his smile. As soon as Batman disappeared, the Joker became a model citizen of Arkham Asylum, just staring blankly at the television. Only when Batman returns does the smile – and the murder and mayhem – come back.) Instead, Batman's enemy is corruption. He has an uneasy ally in the fight: a police lieutenant by the name of James Gordon, who's equally vexed by corrupt cops and politicians but who's also tasked with bringing down the city's mysterious caped vigilante. As Batman works his way up the police department's command structure, Gordon has to defend himself from within. Police Commissioner Loeb uses blackmail and extortion against Gordon, but against Batman he sends his ultraviolent SWAT commander. In the end, Batman and Gordon come to realize they're each other's best bet for getting through all of this alive – which, of course, is the only way *Year One* could possibly end. Their roles were already written: Batman breaks the law; the Gotham City Police Department tolerates it under Gordon's supervision.

As Miller sees it, Batman's ending is as inevitable as his beginning. Bruce Wayne is not a guy to go gracefully into that good night; he's going to go down fighting. And since Batman is one of the longest-running, most iconic characters in comics history, that fight has to be epic. In *DKR*, Miller sets the stakes as high as they can go: a one-on-one fistfight with Superman himself.

The US government illegalized superheroes years ago, but it kept Superman on its payroll. He agreed to do the government's dirty work, and in exchange, the feds allowed his fellow heroes to live so long as Superman could make them quit their heroics. (If this sounds a bit like Dr. Manhattan's role in *Watchmen* to you, you're right. The excesses of the police state is a theme in both Alan Moore's and Frank Miller's writing, and not just in *Watchmen* and *DKR*.) Superman wasn't always gentle about it; he forced Green Arrow's retirement by cutting off his arm. But when a gang called the Mutants arises in Gotham, Bruce Wayne finds he can no longer stand by and watch. These Mutants aren't like the criminals he and Robin used to fight; these are "a purer breed" (*DKR*, no. 1, p. 5), committing their crimes not for profit but for the sheer sadistic joy of it. Batman tries to bring them down, but in a one-on-one fight with the Mutant leader he meets his match. More than his match, in fact; he only survives by the intervention of a teenage girl in a home-made Robin costume.

This is Carrie Kelley, who was inspired by Batman's return and decided she'd try her hand at being a costumed crimefighter. Others are inspired by him too, even including the Mutants, who, after Batman defeats their leader with especially brutal tactics, declare themselves the Sons of the Batman and wage their own war on crime. The Joker, too, gets back in the game, killing hundreds on live television. Batman tries to stop him, but the new police commissioner isn't as forgiving of vigilantes as Jim Gordon was, and Batman has to fight his way through an army of cops to get to the Joker. It doesn't go as well for him as it did in *Year One*; once again Carrie Kelley – now officially the new Robin – saves his hide.

Batman blames himself for the Joker's many murders, and he knows their final confrontation is coming, the one where only one of them will walk away. He knows another confrontation is coming too: if he kills the Joker, it'll be impossible for Superman to turn a blind eye. The result is two of the most legendary battles in all of comicdom: Batman and the Joker in their final duel, followed by the aging Bruce

Wayne versus the invincible Clark Kent. I won't give away the ending here, but it's epic.

Miller has done more Bat-work since then, including the two Dark Knight sequel series (DK2 and DK3) and a third sequel series reportedly in the works (Rogers 2015). With artist Jim Lee, he wrote *All Star Batman and Robin, the Boy Wonder* (2005–2008), a ten-issue series that re-envisioned Dick Grayson as a force to be reckoned with even for Batman. None of that work has proved as philosophically rich as *DKR* and *Year One*, so let us take those two as our focus as we start to unpack the philosophy of Frank Miller's Batman.

The Ethics of Vigilantism

Every superhero deserves an origin story, but the first question to ask these superheroes isn't how they got their fantastic abilities but why they feel justified in taking the law into their own hands. It's easy to see why a character like Batman has such staying power: we sympathize with him, and when the world treats us cruelly we wish we had power like his to do something about it. But Batman himself doesn't think that way. Other authors have had Bruce Wayne pursue a career in law enforcement only to drop out, but in *Year One* there's no hint that Bruce gave any thought to working within the law. Right from the start he plans to fight crime by becoming a criminal.

This must have been the plan for many authors' renditions of Batman, but Miller's Batman doesn't even bother to apologize for it. To the other heroes he laughs and says, "Sure we're criminals. We've always been criminals. We *have* to be criminals" (*DKR*, no. 3, p. 30). Presumably he means that "*have* to be" in the moral sense, not the metaphysical sense: he's a criminal because it's the right thing to do, not because he has no free will and the universe predestined him to be a criminal. But if putting on tights and breaking the law is the right thing to do, *why* is it the right thing to do?

The most straightforward answer is that when law enforcement fails, the only people left to defend the law are ordinary citizens. But this is a flimsy premise, and it's also the justification used by the sort of people Batman fights. Countless comic book villains seek power because they think things would run a lot better if they were the ones in control. And in the real world, criminal syndicates think of themselves as the police for people who can't go to the police. When the United States denigrated Italians as second-class citizens, when its law enforcement wouldn't defend their interests, the mafia touted itself as the only organization that would protect them. (For a price, of course.) Yakuzas in Japan see themselves in the same role. So if Batman is to be more than a gangster, this line of argument won't work.

A better argument is grounded in utilitarianism, the moral theory that defines right and wrong in terms of positive and negative consequences. A utilitarian says an action is right to the extent that it maximizes the greatest good for the greatest number, and wrong to the extent that it fails to do that. For example, in the movie *Superman* (Donner 1978) Lex Luthor fires two nuclear missiles, one at the San Andreas Fault and one at Hackensack, New Jersey. Superman is strong enough to stop either missile but not fast enough to stop both; he has to choose. As Frank Miller envisions him, Superman is a utilitarian, and as a utilitarian he ought to evaluate his options and see which generates the greatest benefit for the greatest number:

Option one: Stop the eastbound missile. Benefit: Saves the population of Hackensack (which today is about 45,000 people). Cost: Allows everything west of the San Andreas to collapse into the sea, including most of the population of California (Los Angeles alone being about four million people).

Option two: Stop the westbound missile. Benefit: Saves everyone west of the San Andreas Fault. Cost: Allows Hackensack to be consumed in nuclear fire.

Option three: Come up with some cool Supermannish feat that will stop both missiles. Benefit: Saves everyone and also wins big on style points. Cost: None.

If Superman's a utilitarian, then he should never choose option one and should only choose option two if he can't come up with a whiz-bang idea necessary for option three.

A lot of people find utilitarianism quite appealing. It aligns with many of our basic intuitions, not just about ethics but about decision-making in general. (Jeremy Bentham (1748–1832), one of the founding fathers of utilitarianism, said this was one of the big benefits of the theory: we already follow it routinely (Bentham 1789, p. 1).) It also has a built-in mechanism for fairness. Superman shouldn't make his decision based on whether Lois Lane is in Los Angeles or Hackensack, because despite the fact that he's sweet on her, she's just one voice among many. He's not allowed to give her preferential treatment – or, to put it in the words of Bentham's successor, John Stuart Mill (1806–1873), "Everybody to count for one, nobody for more than one" (Mill 1993, p. 208).

But Batman has never been a utilitarian. Throughout his countless authors, his overarching motivation has always been justice. And Frank Miller's Batman is downright scornful of utilitarian thinking. He'll say utilitarianism is built to compromise, and compromise allows the supervillains to run the world. Consider the following choice:

Option one: Superman detonates a nuclear bomb in Los Angeles.

Option two: Superman refuses to detonate it, in which case Lex Luthor detonates a nuclear bomb in Los Angeles and New York.

If these really are the only two options – if Superman can't come up with some clever option three – then utilitarianism doesn't just tell Superman to blow up Los Angeles. It says blowing up Los Angeles is *morally right*. In fact, there is no crime Superman shouldn't commit, provided that he could prevent two of that crime by committing it once.

Batman doesn't agree. In fact, he thinks Superman's a sellout. In DK2 Brainiac holds hostage the bottle city of Kandor, which is the last refuge of the Kryptonian people. He can make Superman do just about anything, because whenever he refuses, Brainiac kills a Kryptonian family. But Batman, who is *never* willing to compromise his principles, can't be manipulated that way.

That puts Batman closer to Immanuel Kant (1724–1804), an enormously influential philosopher who first turned his attention to ethics because he thought the utilitarians were completely wrong. Like Batman, Kant saw that people could use consequences to "justify" even the most reprehensible acts. On top of that, human beings aren't all that good at predicting consequences. Batman's buddy Martian Manhunter can see the future, but the rest of us rely on guesswork, and Kant thinks it's dangerous to base your moral thinking on guesswork. Instead, he says you can tell right from wrong using reason alone. But things get tricky when you start dealing with the unreasonable, and Batman's greatest nemesis is the living embodiment of the unreasonable.

The Joker Problem

Right from his first appearance, in the very first issue of *Batman* (Finger 1940), the Joker was on a killing spree. (Four murders and three attempted murders in just ten pages!) He would go on to kill hundreds, of course – he is Batman's most iconic, most enduring foe – and in *DKR* Batman repeatedly blames himself for the countless deaths at the Joker's hands. After all, if he'd murdered the Joker when he first had the chance, those people would still be alive. Many of the TV personalities in the book agree, including the Joker's own psychologist. From a strictly utilitarian point of view, their reasoning isn't half bad. If what defines right and wrong is consequences, then it doesn't really matter who does what; the only thing that matters is the end result.

But Kant rejects this line of thinking. You probably do too, unless you see Batman and the Joker as moral equals. Kant explains the difference by saying ethics isn't a matter of consequences, it's a matter of intent. Batman starts with the will to do good, the Joker starts with the will to make mayhem, and that difference is what makes one a hero and the other a villain.

But having the will to do good isn't much use by itself; without some direction, the will won't know what to do. The young Bruce Wayne has this problem in *Year One*: he's got all the skills he needs but he doesn't know what to do with them. In *DKR*, Batman faces a different brand of uncertainty when it comes to handling the Joker. Sending the Joker to Arkham Asylum never works – he always escapes again – but killing him crosses the one line Batman vowed he'd never cross. It's a good thing Bruce Wayne studied the classics, so he's familiar with what Kant would tell him about this dilemma.

Bruce is well aware of the *categorical imperative*, Kant's famous formula for discerning right from wrong. Kant phrases the formula in several ways, but the most relevant for Batman as he pursues the Joker is what Kant calls the "second formulation," which says one must "treat humanity, whether in your own person or in the person of another, always at the same time as an end and never simply as a means" (Kant 1981, p. 36). That means it's acceptable in some circumstances to use people as a means to an end, but it's never acceptable to use them *solely* as a means to an end. You always have to respect the fact that they have ends of their own. For example, if I want Frank Miller's next Batman comic, I have to pay whatever the owner of my local comic shop wants to charge me; if I steal it, I'm treating him like his profit margin isn't important.

From the second formulation you'd think it follows that Kant would deem the death penalty immoral, since it treats the condemned merely as a means to society's end. And you'd be half right: *if* the point of executing the Joker is to make Gotham City safer, then for Kant that's a clear case of abusing him for the benefit of others. But there's a big *if* there. Astute student that he is, Bruce will not have forgotten that Kant himself was actually a big fan of the death penalty, arguing that executions ought to be carried out even if they have no utilitarian benefit whatsoever. His only concern was whether they were deserved – that is, whether the criminal did something so heinous that death was the appropriate punishment (Kant 1996, pp. 106–107). So for Kant, the state shouldn't execute the Joker in order to make Gotham safer; it should only execute him if he deserves it.

In fact, Kant can be interpreted as going even further, suggesting that someone who violates the categorical imperative is no longer protected by it. To put it more simply, Kant might tell us that those who behave immorally no longer need to be treated morally. If this interpretation is right, then Kant is on a slippery slope (albeit it is an appealing slope, and one that lots of people want to join him on). Standing on that slope you easily can justify things that seem intuitive from a utilitarian standpoint, such as killing in self-defense. And for a guy whose idea of a normal Saturday night is clubbing people in the head with bat-shaped boomerangs, this logic will certainly justify a lot of his nocturnal behavior. But as we'll see in a moment, this slippery slope leads to some disturbing conclusions.

If Bruce wants to avoid the slippery slope, he might focus instead on the question of what punishment the Joker *deserves*. People only deserve punishment for the things they're responsible for, and let's not forget, the Joker is criminally insane. If he's truly incapable of knowing right from wrong, then he isn't fully responsible for his crimes. In that case, he doesn't deserve to be executed. However, this opens up a final Kantian argument for Bruce to consider. If the Joker really isn't a rational being capable of moral deliberation, then he may be treated more like an aggressive predator than a human being possessed of inherent dignity. (It goes without saying, I hope, that by today's standards Kant's position on the mentally ill is seriously problematic.) If the Joker is morally on par with a wild animal, then presumably Batman is allowed to kill him before he hurts someone.

At this point, it's not looking good for the Joker. Either he is a rational moral agent or he is not. If he's not, then he's not protected by the moral respect and dignity that Kant says all rational moral agents deserve. If he is, then according to the interpretation of Kant we considered earlier, he gave up his right to moral respect as soon as he murdered his first victim. So either way, it looks like killing him is okay. But notice that we've crossed a dangerous line here. We've ventured out onto that slippery slope. If the moral rules that protect the rest of us don't protect the Joker, then it looks like Batman is permitted not only to kill him but also to behead him and have his stuffed head mounted on the wall of stately Wayne manor. If people can do that with wild animals, why not with human beings who behave like wild animals?

Luckily there is a Kantian counterargument to such a monstrous conclusion: he speaks of certain duties we have to ourselves, which include abstaining from cruelty. If Batman were to kill the Joker, he would sully not the Joker's dignity but his own. He owes it to *himself* not to use his great physical power against a very sick man in need of hospitalization. If we're right to read Kant as being out on that moral slippery slope, then this duty to maintain his own moral dignity might be the Bat-rope he can cling to in order to keep from sliding all the way down.

In the end, we're still left with a burning moral question: what is Batman's moral responsibility regarding the Joker? An easy utilitarian answer is to kill him, sparing countless victims in the future. But Kant shows us you can use that logic to justify any crime you can imagine. A more complex utilitarian answer is don't kill him, because things like human rights maximize the greater good but they can only do so if those rights are sacrosanct. Kant's probably on board with that – Kantian philosophy thoroughly permeates today's human rights laws – but he'll add that Batman's moral duties go beyond not killing him. In fact, Kantians and utilitarians can both make a strong argument that Batman ought to treat the Joker as humanely as possible while still preventing him from being inhumane to anyone else. They'll just differ on *why* Batman should do that. Utilitarians will appeal to consequences while Kantians will appeal to more abstract ideals like dignity, abuse, and reason.

The odd thing is, Batman has no interest in such arguments – or at least Miller's Batman doesn't. He shows his true colors in the first issue of *DKR* when he deals with some of Two-Face's henchmen. "I smell their fear," he thinks, "and it is sweet" (p. 27). Later, when one of the henchmen is about to get the drop on a rookie policeman, Batman strikes preemptively. "There are seven working defenses from this position," he tells us. "Three of them disarm with minimal contact. Three of them kill. The other one – *hurts*." Batman uses the latter, of course, and the cop, who's too young to have seen him before, says, "You're under arrest, mister. You've crippled that man!" Batman's reply is flippant: "He's young. He'll probably walk again. But he'll stay scared" (p. 31).

So Batman agrees with Kant that utilitarianism is a theory of moral compromise, and he agrees with Kant that killing the Joker is morally wrong. Yet somehow he reaches the conclusion that killing is the *only* line he shouldn't cross. Intimidating people, beating them senseless, even crippling them – none of these give him pause so long as the person he's hurting deserves it. To make sense of why, we'll have to turn to a philosopher who knew a thing or two about pain and suffering: Friedrich Nietzsche (1844–1900).

Batman and the Will to Power

One of Nietzsche's most important ideas, perhaps the idea he's most known for, is the *will to power*. To understand what he's talking about, it helps to know that he was a contemporary of Charles Darwin (1809–1882) and a young man when Darwin published his famous *On the Origin of Species* (1859) and *The Descent of Man* (1871). Nietzsche was writing philosophy in an era of "biologism," a widespread intellectual trend that sought to explain elements of human psychology and behavior by means of biological variables. It's worth mentioning that much of this work is nonsensical – phrenology comes out of biologism, for example – but at least one idea from biologism has extraordinary explanatory power: the basic will to survive is a powerful instinct that can overcome many hardships.

Nietzsche saw this Darwinian instinct not as a primary motivator but a derivative effect of something both greater and more fundamental: the will to exert one's own power. This so-called will to power is present in many of Nietzsche's works, often in the subtext, so let us consider a passage from *Daybreak* where he describes it directly and succinctly:

> *The demon of power.* – Not of necessity, not desire – no, the love of power is the demon of men. Let them have everything – health, food, a place to live, entertainment – they are and remain unhappy and low-spirited: for the demon waits and waits and will be satisfied. Take everything from them and satisfy this, and they are almost happy – as happy as men and demons can be. (Nietzsche 1997, §262)

This describes Bruce Wayne perfectly. He lives in the lap of luxury; there is no material good he cannot afford. Yet there is something he wants – only one thing, and it's the one thing even a billionaire can't buy: his parents' lives. To be "almost happy – as happy as men and demons can be," he must deprive himself of every physical comfort, risking his life every night in the vain hope of cleansing Gotham City of criminality.

As fate would have it, Frank Miller's path to Batman wasn't so different from Bruce Wayne's. By 1983, he was already a successful writer and artist, making good on Stan Lee's prediction that "Lanky Frank Miller" was "a truly great new artist [who] will explode upon the Marvel scene like a bombshell" (*Daredevil*, no. 158, p. 1). Lee was half right: everything Miller put his pencil to turned to gold, but the real bombshell was his vision. Before Miller, the Punisher was a B-list Spider-Man villain, Daredevil was a Spider-Man knockoff, and Wolverine was a one-dimensional psychopath. After Miller, the Punisher got his own title, Daredevil gained new life as a gritty noir crime drama (a theme Miller would return to in *Sin City*) and Wolverine became the complex, conflicted antihero we know today as one of Marvel's most popular characters. So like Bruce Wayne, Miller could spend his career however he wanted, writing and drawing whatever took his fancy.

Then Miller got mugged. More than once. These attacks made him feel helpless and angry, and from these attacks *DKR* was born. His description of the experience is in effect an appeal to the will to power:

> There's something demeaning about the first time you're knocked to the ground and punched in the stomach and have a gun waved in your face and realize that you're completely at somebody's mercy. And they can take your life. And at that point, you'll do anything. There's something so humiliating about that. And to me that made me realize that Batman was the most potent symbol [DC Comics] had in its hands. Sure, Superman can fly, but

Batman turns me back into that guy who is scared and at the same time the guy who can come and save him. It's a perfect myth. (Kit 2016)

Notice who he wishes to be: "the guy who is scared" *and* "the guy who can come and save him." Miller was powerless and the experience humiliated him. This gave him a new sympathy for Bruce Wayne, who, like Miller, suffered a loss of innocence because of a random act of violence.

This is why Miller's Batman is grim, brooding, and scary, and why he's so much more compelling than the campy, playful Batman of the 1950s and 1960s. That Batman seemed to fight crime for the sport of it. This Batman has a very different view of the world, a Nietzschean view: "The world only makes sense when you force it to" (*DKR*, no. 4, p. 40).

This, perhaps, is why Superman has always been the Big Blue Boy Scout to Miller, with simplistic morals and little understanding of his own power. As the strongest and hardiest being on the planet, he's never "the guy who is scared." He's the guy who can rescue the one who's scared. This is especially interesting in the context of Nietzsche, for two reasons. First, as the mightiest superhero, Superman is more capable of exercising the will to power than anyone else, and that's what makes him boring (or at least tough to write) as a character. Second, Nietzsche himself wrote of the Superman – specifically, the *Übermensch*, also translated as "Beyond-Man" and "overman" – as a higher moral goal for the brave and the bold to strive for.

Nietzsche had great scorn for the Christian morality of his day, which he saw as simultaneously sycophantic and parasitic. In a book none-too-subtly titled *The Antichrist*, he argues that Christian morality is incompatible with the will to power: "Christianity is called the religion of pity. Pity stands in antithesis to the tonic emotions which enhance the energy of the feeling of life: it has a depressive effect. One loses force when one pities" (Nietzsche 1968, §7). He despises pity and being pitied, perhaps because he himself suffered a great deal. His body was a constant source of pain to him, demanding opium in ever-increasing dosages if he was to function. If we see enduring such trials an expression the will of power, we should not wonder that it was Nietzsche of all people who said, "That which does not kill me makes me stronger" (Nietzsche 1968, p. 33).

That maxim epitomizes Frank Miller's Batman. He too has scorn for the morality that surrounds him, be it the utilitarianism of Superman and other heroes (all too willing to sacrifice principles just to prevent pain) or the complacency of Gotham's citizens (all too willing to let corrupt politicians and violent street gangs rule the city). Whether it's his naïveté in *Year One* or his advancing age in *DKR*, his internal enemies are more formidable than anything the villains can throw at him – but if they don't kill him they'll make him stronger. Batman and Nietzsche both value trial and hardship for their own sake; they value the worthy opponent; they value fighting the good fight even when defeat is all but certain.

However, there remains a looming question: to what extent does the will to power permit overpowering other people? Batman overcomes his own personal limitations, but he also overcomes the personal limitations of other people – the limits of their pain tolerance, for instance, or the limits of their courage. If human beings are centers of the will to power, as Nietzsche suggests, we must still ask what these people are allowed to do to each other in the name of exerting that will.

Consider Batman's fights against Superman in *DKR* and DK2. Both combatants know Superman is physically superior in every respect, so both fighters know Batman can only win through dirty tricks. His arsenal of tricks is dirty indeed: missiles activated by x-ray vision, Kryptonite weaponized into napalm, sneak attacks prepared in advance so other heroes can wear Superman down before Batman joins the fight in earnest. Batman cannot win by fighting fair; he can only win by exploiting every vulnerability Superman has. And let us not forget, he discovered some of these vulnerabilities through the course of a friendship. However dark and cynical Bruce Wayne may be, Clark Kent still considers him a friend. If the will to power includes premeditating which weapon is best for stabbing a friend in the back, then surely this is a moral precept for villains, not heroes.

But Nietzsche draws an important distinction between the will to *power* and the will to *force*. (In German, the difference is between *Macht* and *Kraft*.) Force, or *Kraft*, is the strength Frank Miller's muggers used against him when they made him a victim. Power, or *Macht*, is the inner strength Miller called upon to turn that terrifying experience into art. Nietzsche has little regard for force, and in fact ordinary experience tells us that people often use force because they feel powerless. It isn't self-control that enables schoolyard bullies to pick on other children; it's the absence of self-control. When the Nazis held up Nietzsche as their philosophical forbear, and when today's white supremacists do the same, they can only do so by failing to understand (or worse, willfully ignoring) the difference between power and force.

With that distinction in mind, let us reexamine Batman. It was the will to power that drove him to earn all the black belts, master the skills of criminology, and become the Caped Crusader. Once he dons the cowl and starts pelting people with batarangs, he has given up on power and resorted to force. He uses force against Superman – staggering amounts of it, in the form of missiles, Kryptonite napalm, and all the rest. But the only way he can face Superman at all – the only way *any* human being could voluntarily duke it out with a Kryptonian – is through the indomitable will to power.

It's still not clear that Batman is doing the right thing, though, in waging his war against crime. We've now reviewed utilitarianism, Kantian ethics, and the Nietzschean will to power, so let's consider what all of them have to say about using force to corral criminals.

For the utilitarian, Batman's history of violence is only justifiable if there's no better option for bringing more overall happiness into the world. But this doesn't seem to be the case. A billionaire like Bruce Wayne could presumably eliminate the financial inequity in Gotham that leads to so much criminality in the first place. He could also finance his own police academy, to better train officers in law enforcement ethics, nonviolent interventions, and how to be good whistleblowers when they see corruption. It wouldn't make for thrilling comic books, but it would be better at maximizing overall utility.

For the Kantian, Batman faces a dilemma. Criminals either deserve to be treated like the rest of us or they do not. If they are like the rest of us, they can be used as a means to an end but only when their own ends are also respected. That precludes punching them in the face (unless of course they give their consent first). So if Batman catches bank robbers in the act, he can ask them to put the money back, or he can propose a boxing match where the winner gets the money (and whenever Batman wins he just puts the money back), but he can't just start whacking them with Batarangs.

On the other hand, if they are *not* like the rest of us, then he has very few moral duties concerning them. His more pressing moral duties are directed toward himself – most importantly, the duty to maintain his own moral dignity. This includes abstaining from cruelty, which leaves Frank Miller's Batman with very few options. (Adam West's Batman is a different story; in the episode "Surf's Up, Joker's Under" he foils the Joker's villainous scheme by beating him in a surfing contest.) Kant's fondness for the death penalty sits better with Miller's rendition of the Punisher or Wolverine, or with Dwight McCarthy or John Hartigan of *Sin City*, since none of these characters have qualms about killing people who deserve it. But Batman won't cross that line, and it's hard to give a Kantian justification for Batman's delight in seeing just how close he can get to that line without crossing it.

For the Nietzschean, Batman epitomizes the will to power but is much too liberal in using the will to force. *Maybe* we can justify that with Superman. Since facing a Kryptonian *mano a mano* isn't a fair fight, the only way to make it fair is to resort to force. (And lots of it.) But using force against a street gang like the Mutants is entirely different. Batman has black belts galore, he's armed with outlandish weapons, and he wears bulletproof armor. A frightened Mutant teenager with a machinegun is hopelessly out of his depth. Dangerous, yes, but hardly an obstacle to Batman's will to power.

Miller's critics have a more straightforward reading: there is no morality here, just macho revenge fantasies. And there's no question that Miller's characters – men and women alike – tend to be macho and vengeful. But if that's all there is to Batman, then he's just another costumed villain, and surely that is a false equivalency. There is another possibility, however: Batman is neither a villain nor a straightforward hero, but rather a figurative *Übermensch*. In the later issues of *DKR*, and especially in DK2, Batman wants to usher in a new morality, a higher code than the people of Gotham (and in fact the United States) are comfortable with. What if, as he sees it, comfort isn't relevant in morality? (Nietzsche felt the same way: in a scathing rebuke of the utilitarians he said, "Man does not strive after happiness; only the Englishman does that" (Nietzsche 1968, p. 33).) What if what interests Batman is not happiness but liberty?

Libertarianism and Bat-Libertarianism

Let us begin with a thought experiment from the philosopher Robert Nozick (1938–2002), but let's fold it into Christopher Nolan's *The Dark Knight Rises* (2012, based in part on *DKR*). Bruce Wayne escapes an underground prison in a desert, but for our thought experiment we'll send another prisoner along with him, one who knows the terrain. Each of them manages to scrounge a canteen from the prison, and the prisoner tells Bruce that if they ration their water carefully, one canteen each will be enough to get them through the desert and back to civilization. So Bruce decides he will drink no more than half of his water in the first half of the trek, but as they go he sees his new hiking partner hasn't got the same self-control.

When they reach the halfway point, Bruce has been conservative enough that he's only drunk a third of his water, while his partner has foolishly run out. It's now late afternoon and they have reached the highest point of the trail, so from here onward it will be downhill in cooler temperatures. Thus the math is clear: each of them only needs one-third of a canteen to safely reach the far trailhead. Bruce has two-thirds of a canteen, and his partner has no water at all. Of course we know what Bruce will do – he's a hero, after all – but there is a more pressing question: is it wrong not to share his water?

The difference between what he *would* do and what he *should* do is critical here. The *would* only describes a preference, and that preference might have nothing to do with morality. (Bruce might just want a hot shower at the end of their ordeal, and the prisoner's house might be the first place they get back to.) But what he *should* do is a moral question. The prisoner will die if he doesn't share his water, but does that entail any moral obligation for Bruce to share it?

Kant and the utilitarians say the answer is an obvious yes, since it costs Bruce almost nothing and in return he saves a life. But a libertarian like Robert Nozick will point out that we usually conceive of rights and duties as having a logical relationship, such that when someone has a duty to do X or to not do Y, that entails someone else having a right to not-X or a right to Y. For example, if it was wrong to murder Thomas and Martha Wayne, then the Waynes had a right not to be murdered. That's simple enough. But from this principle it follows that if you have a moral obligation to share your water, then I have a right to your water. Libertarians say this completely perverts what it means for the water to be *your* water.

In political philosophy (as opposed to metaphysics, where the term means something quite different), *libertarianism* is the view that the role of government is to stay out of the way to the greatest extent possible, allowing citizens to make their own choices as freely as possible. Government's only job is to provide for citizens what they cannot even theoretically provide for themselves. For instance, even a billionaire like Bruce Wayne could not build an entire interstate highway system. He can hire a metaphorical army of personal bodyguards but he cannot finance an actual military. Even if he could, he'd have no legal standing to do so. For libertarians, this should be a government's sole function: to provide what the people cannot do without and cannot do for themselves.

On the surface it doesn't sound like a controversial position. In fact, it sounds a bit like the basic principle underpinning western democracy. But democracy as we know it is founded not on *libertarianism* but *liberalism*. In this context "liberal" has nothing to do with modern political parties; it only refers to the principle that citizens should have as much liberty as possible, compatible with the maximal liberty of all other citizens. And that's not a libertarian principle.

To understand why, consider seat belt laws. In the US, 49 out of 50 states require drivers to wear a seat belt. (The state motto of New Hampshire, "Live Free or Die," includes the freedom to go flying through your own windshield.) It's often supposed that seat belt laws are for the driver's own benefit, which a libertarian will put in the same category as parents forcing children to eat their vegetables. Libertarianism says the government ought not to treat citizens like children, and no one has any business forcing adults to eat anything they don't want to eat – *especially* if what's on the menu is more expensive than it needs to be. Seat belts aren't free, so when the government says cars need seat belts, that means consumers have to pay more for their cars. For the libertarian, that's government coercion.

But it turns out that seat belt laws aren't for protecting drivers, they're for protecting everyone else. As liberalism sees it, we have a limited number of emergency rooms and a perpetual shortage of blood for transfusions, and these are services provided to the public at large. Seat belts are especially good at preventing head wounds, which, because they're especially complex and especially bloody, require a lot of emergency room attention and a lot of donated blood. So apart from New Hampshire, every legislature in the United States says drivers don't have the right to put limited public goods like emergency medical care at unnecessary risk. Drivers can still exercise their liberty to drive without a seatbelt, but the state can fine them for doing it, and set the fine high enough that they'll freely choose to buckle up.

So returning to Bruce Wayne in the desert, is the water in his canteen like emergency room access – namely, a public good? Or is the water more like the Batmobile – namely, a thing he owns, a thing no one else has any plausible claim to? If it's the former, then sharing the water is like putting on a seat belt: a tiny personal inconvenience in service of a greater public good. But libertarianism says it's the latter, and so regardless of whether Bruce *would* share the water, it's not morally wrong to leave the prisoner to die in the desert, because no one has any right to the water other than Bruce himself.

To be sure, there's plenty of internal dissent within both theories. For instance, within liberalism there's debate about which firearms to ban (I know of no democracy where any and all firearms are legal) and within libertarianism there's debate about which government services really are absolutely necessary (for example, whether fire departments ought to be a private enterprise or a taxpayer expense). What matters for present purposes is that Frank Miller is an avowed libertarian and his Batman seems to be one too.

Batman's detractors in *DKR* find his actions outrageous, and accuse him not of libertarianism but fascism. After all, this is a man who behaves as though he's above the law, enforces his own vision of what the law should be, and has no concern at all for due process. That is exactly how fascist dictators behave. His brand of justice is shockingly violent, and fascism is associated with especially harsh treatment of criminals. But his critics in the book overlook one crucial factor: Batman only forces his will on criminals. Fascism is oppressive to *all* resistance, which means that if Batman really were a fascist, he'd also come after the commentators who call him a fascist.

As Frank Miller conceives of him, Batman isn't interested in controlling the general population. His primary interest is in getting criminals out of the way so that everyone else can be free to pursue their lives as they see fit. His second interest, which we see hints of in *Year One* and which drives the plot of DK2, is wresting power from government and corporate elites and returning it to the people. He behaves like a Nietzschean libertarian, an overman who rallies the people to overthrow their oppressors – to become superheroes in their own right. As he tells his grassroots army in DK2, "Children, pull on your tights and give them hell" (no. 2, p. 78).

But the libertarian will have serious qualms about Batman's will to force as opposed to the will to power. Libertarians are generally in favor of legalizing consumer goods of just about any description, including some of the drugs and guns that Batman beats people up for possessing. Thus we might better describe him not as a libertarian per se but a Bat-libertarian. And as we've seen, the difference between Nietzschean Bat-libertarianism and macho revenge fantasy is pretty slim.

Even if he were an ordinary libertarian, however, he would still face some pressing objections. It's one thing to say no one has a right to the water in your canteen; it's quite another to say there's nothing wrong with leaving someone to die in the desert. We can test the theory with another thought experiment. Suppose Bruce Wayne, standing on the deck of his yacht, sees someone drowning in Gotham Harbor. Hanging on a nearby hook is one of the yacht's life preservers, and Bruce has the strength and skill to throw the life preserver to the drowning person. The libertarian, of course, will say that Bruce is free to throw the life preserver if he so chooses, but only one person in the world can say he has a *right* to the life preserver, and that is Bruce himself, the legal owner of the yacht.

Keep in mind that Bruce has no conceivable need of the life preserver. (The yacht isn't sinking, and even if it were, he can swim.) It won't even cost him anything to throw it; he can put the life preserver right back on its hook. The question is this: if Bruce is a libertarian (or Bat-libertarian, as the case may be), can he plausibly adhere to his libertarianism if he switches places with the drowning person? That is, if he were the one floundering in the water, moments from death, could he plausibly look up at a wealthy yachtsman standing next to a life preserver and affirm, "If that fellow chooses not to throw me the life preserver, he has done nothing wrong"? If not – if in fact he would see the yacht owner's inaction as adding insult to injury – then it looks like libertarianism is deeply hypocritical. If Bruce is a libertarian while aboard his yacht but a sudden convert to utilitarianism when in the water, then libertarianism is a philosophy people can only affirm while in a position of power and privilege. In other words, it is little more than a sophisticated argument for oppression.

The Frank Miller Problem

Let us consider a final moral question, and that is what to do with a writer and artist whose personal politics sometimes get him into hot water. A New Yorker for most of his adult life, Frank Miller was shaken to the core by the 9/11 attacks. His response was to write a book where Batman and Catwoman go to Afghanistan to torture and kill terrorists. The original title was *Holy Terror, Batman!* (oddly lighthearted given the dark subject matter), but when DC balked at it he revised it, replacing Batman with a character called the Fixer and publishing the book with Legendary Comics in 2011. In the newly titled *Holy Terror*, the Fixer and his ersatz Catwoman use tactics exactly in keeping with al Qaeda's: they refuse to discriminate between military and civilian targets. As a result, the book fails to distinguish between the world's 1.8 billion Muslims and the infinitesimal minority of militants who twist Islam to fit their political ends.

This was deliberate; Miller described the book as "a propaganda comic." But it certainly was not tongue-in-cheek. *Holy Terror* was widely lambasted as an Islamophobic screed – *WIRED* summed it up aptly as "a vulgar, one-dimensional revenge fantasy" (Ackerman 2011) – and Miller's personal response didn't earn him much sympathy: "I can tell you squat about Islam. I don't know anything about it. But I know a goddamn lot about al-Qaeda and I want them to burn in hell" (Pappademas 2019). Ten years after the 9/11 attacks, and given 10 years of widespread media coverage on Islam and Islamism, to know "squat" about Islam suggests willful ignorance.

Shortly after *Holy Terror* was released, Miller published an angry tirade on his website deriding Occupy Wall Street, a left-wing protest movement that demonstrated against income inequality, corruption, and corporate control of government. It was an odd choice of targets for Miller, given that the wealthy, the politically corrupt, and the corporations that manipulate governments are all villains in his comics. (In DK2, he even foresees an Exxon oil executive as the Secretary of State, 15 years before Donald Trump would appoint ExxonMobil CEO Rex Tillerson to that office. Batman takes particular relish in attacking him, saying, "God, I love my job" (DK2, no. 2, p. 14).) Given Miller's naked contempt for the very entities Occupy Wall Street was born to combat, it was easy for critics to blast Miller as bitter, confused, and obsolete – a "right-wing loon" (Barnett 2011).

Miller has been apologetic since. He took down the anti-Occupy essay, saying, "I wasn't thinking right when I said those things" (Thielman 2018). Of *Holy Terror* he now says, "When I look at [it], which I really don't do all that often, I can really feel the anger ripple out of the pages. There are places where it is bloodthirsty beyond belief. [...] I'm not capable of that book again." But apology is not erasure, and holding adults accountable for their actions is at the heart of libertarianism. So we must ask the question: should any of us still read Frank Miller? Or does a writer/artist prone to angry outbursts, including a decade of outspoken vitriol directed at 1.8 billion people based on their religion, deserve to be boycotted as a right-wing loon?

It is a pressing question of our time. People who were once untouchable – think Harvey Weinstein, Bill Cosby, Bill O'Reilly, and so many others – are being held accountable for their actions, many of them for the very first time. Whether to forgive public figures for their misdeeds, and how to forgive them, and how long to wait before that forgiveness: these are questions the general public is asking in a way it has not asked before. The questions are new not because the behavior is new but because the public has newfound power to hold the mighty to account for their misbehavior. In the realm of comics, Frank Miller certainly ranks among the mighty.

And he is accused of more than Islamophobia. There is evidence of misogyny, as his female characters are overwhelmingly sex workers, temptresses, or the victims of violence. Nearly all of his most famous characters are white, which may have been unavoidable in his early career (the Marvel and DC stables were hardly Meccas of diversity) but was entirely voluntary when he ventured out into original works like *Sin City*. His characters who aren't white are almost invariably villains. Martha Washington stands out as a striking counterexample – she is one of the most well-developed, compelling, self-reliant African American women anywhere in comics – but for him she's a paragon of libertarianism, which, as we've seen, offers an argument for oppression masked as an argument for individual freedom.

But his critics today often leave out important counterevidence. From the outset of his career Miller actively fought the right-wing Comics Code Authority and supported the Comic Book Legal Defense Fund, which protects First Amendment rights. Long before he was demonized by the left, he was demonized by the right, for his portrayal in *DKR* of Ronald Reagan as a doddering old fool stumbling carelessly into nuclear war. This wasn't a young man's liberalism to be cast off in middle age: the first thing Batman does in DK3 is attack two policemen just before they can gun down an unarmed African American teenager. And Miller's caricature of Ronald Reagan is positively docile compared to his critique of Donald Trump: "This president is an opportunity for cartoonists. The buffoons usually are. But this one has a particular range of exceptionally cartoony characteristics" (DeVega 2017). Thus the accusation of being a "right-wing loon" misses the mark. If he is a loon, he's one whose politics don't align neatly with modern American notions of left and right.

A more careful reading reveals that Miller's Batman books are deliberately structured to deliver political punditry, through the television talking heads who deliver both storytelling and commentary on the story. Through them Miller argues forcefully for both liberal and conservative positions, and he lampoons liberals and conservatives without fear or favor. He is especially critical of his own position, for the nastiest of the civilians in *DKR* are also the closest to Ayn Rand's philosophy, which Miller has cited as an inspiration (Miller 2010, p. 385). To write Batman as a mirror for his own politics and then deride him as a fascist reveals a political complexity that Miller's critics often overlook.

None of this excuses "a propaganda comic" rightly decried as "a vulgar, one-dimensional revenge fantasy," of course. What it does mean is that it's disingenuous to cherry-pick from an artist's body of work in order to cast that artist as one's political enemy. In Miller's case, the cherry-picking is especially easy – his body of work is massive and varied – but that's all the more reason not to take the disingenuous approach. Better to take the artist as he really is: complex, flawed, given to anger and to being ashamed of his anger, a product of his era and a defiant rebel against it, capable of genius and capable of dreck.

Conclusion: Good and Scary

There are those who boycott Miller because of *Holy Terror*. It's easy to be sympathetic to that position, if not for the fact that those who argue for blacklisting authors are rarely seen favorably in the hindsight of history. I will take no position on Miller or his personal politics here, except to say that if you feel uneasy as you sort out whether to forgive, how to forgive, and how long to wait before forgiving, you're not alone. So with that out of the way, let's return our attention to the Caped Crusader.

Batman's ethics and politics have always been complex. He was never the Big Blue Boy Scout that Superman is, never a stand-in for the oppressed that the X-Men are, never the struggling big-hearted do-gooder that Spider-Man is. When Miller finally got his chance to write Batman, he'd already used many of the moral tropes associated with him on other characters: Daredevil seeks those who slip through the loopholes of the justice system, the Punisher rains vengeance upon the guilty, Wolverine the loner crosses the lines other heroes can't bring themselves to cross. Batman had to be something new.

Miller's greatest gift as a creator of comics is transforming the familiar into something novel yet true to the original. For him the Batman of the Adam West era was novel but it wasn't authentic. ("For me Batman was never funny," Miller said. Even at the age of 8, what he liked about Batman was that "the artwork…looked good and scary" (Miller 1989).) "Good and scary" is exactly the right description of Bob Kane's original vision of the Batman: a mysterious figure in the shadows, feared by criminals yet hunted by the police.

Miller's Batman is a gestalt of Daredevil's justice, the Punisher's vengeance, Wolverine's lonerism, Bob Kane's mystery man, Lynn Varley's bloody watercolors, and Miller's own powerless, humiliated rage. Channel all of that into a 7-year-old boy looking down at his murdered parents and the lesson they have to teach him is clear: "The world only makes sense when you force it to." There was Batman's new moral code: a Nietzschean Bat-liberalism incapable of compromise and immune to corruption and manipulation. Good and scary indeed.

To be sure, Miller added other flourishes too. He was the first to give Batman a good reason to put a big yellow target on his chest (he can't bulletproof his head), the first to give the Joker a personal psychologist (prefiguring Harley Quinn by 6 years), the first to depict Arkham as the deeply dysfunctional place it must be (setting the stage for Grant Morrison's *Arkham Asylum: A Serious House on Serious Earth*), and the list goes on. But what sets his Batman apart from that of previous storytellers, what makes Miller's interpretation of the character so frightening and so compelling, is his novel yet authentic moral psychology.

References

Ackerman, Spencer. 2011. Frank Miller's holy terror is fodder for anti-Islam set. *Wired*. https://www.wired.com/2011/09/holy-terror-frank-miller/

Barnett, David. 2011. Are Frank Miller's politics visible in his comics? *The Guardian*. November 15. https://www.theguardian.com/books/booksblog/2011/nov/15/frank-miller-politics-visible-comics

Bentham, Jeremy. 1789. *An introduction to morals and legislation*. London: T. Payne and Son.

Darwin, Charles. 1859. *On the origin of species*. London: John Murray.

Darwin, Charles. 1871. *The descent of man*. London: John Murray.

DeVega, Chauncey. 2017. Comics icon Frank Miller on "Batman," his career and Donald Trump. https://www.salon.com/2017/10/01/comics-icon-frank-miller-on-batman-his-career-and-donald-trump/

Donner, Richard. 1978. *Superman*. Distributed by Warner Bros. and Columbia-EMI.

Finger, Bill, with Bob Kane. 1940. *Batman*, no. 1. New York: Detective Comics.

Kant, Immanuel. 1981. *Groundwork for the metaphysics of morals*. Indianapolis: Hackett Publishing Company.
Kant, Immanuel. 1996. *The metaphysics of morals*. Cambridge: Cambridge University Press.
Kit, Borys. 2016. A rare interview with Frank Miller: "Dark Knight," the unmade Darren Aronofsky Batman movie, and Donald Trump. *The Hollywood Reporter*. March 3. https://www.hollywoodreporter.com/heat-vision/a-rare-interview-frank-miller-871654
McKenzie, Roger, with Frank Miller, et al. 1979. *Daredevil*, no. 158. New York: Marvel Comics Group.
Mill, John Stuart. 1993. *On liberty and utilitarianism*. New York: Bantam Books.
Miller, Frank. 1989. *The complete frank Miller batman*. Stamford: Longmeadow Press.
Miller, Frank, with Dave Gibbons. 2010. *The life and times of Martha Washington in the twenty-first century*. Madison: Dark Horse Comics.
Miller, Frank, with Jim Lee. 2005–2008. *All Star Batman and Robin, the Boy Wonder*, nos. 1–10. New York: DC Comics.
Miller, Frank, with David Mazzucchelli. 1987. *Batman: Year one*, nos. 1–4. New York: DC Comics.
Miller, Frank, with Lynne Varley. 2001–2002. *The Dark Knight strikes back*, nos. 1–3. New York: DC Comics.
Miller, Frank, with Lynne Varley, and Klaus Janson. 1986–1987. *The Dark Knight returns*, nos. 1–4. New York: DC Comics.
Miller, Frank, with Brian Azzarello, et al. 2015–2017. *Dark Knight III: The master race*, nos. 1–9. New York: DC Comics.
Moore, Alan, and Dave Gibbons. 1989. *Watchmen*. New York: Warner Books.
Nietzsche, Friedrich. 1968. *Twilight of the idols and the antichrist*. New York: Penguin Classics.
Nietzsche, Friedrich. 1997. *Daybreak*. Cambridge: Cambridge University Press.
Nolan, Christopher. 2012. *The Dark Knight rises*. Distributed by Warner Bros. Pictures.
Pappademas, Alex. 2019. Frank Miller's Dark Night. https://grantland.com/features/frank-miller-sin-city-dame-to-kill-for-batman-dark-knight-holy-terror-comic-books/
Rogers, Vaneta. 2015. Frank Miller to return for the Dark Knight IV. https://www.newsarama.com/26831-frank-miller-to-return-for-the-dark-knight-iv.html
Rudolph, Oscar. 1967. *Surf's up, joker's under. Batman*.
Thielman, Sam. 2018. Frank Miller: "I wasn't thinking clearly when I said those things." *The Guardian*. April 27. https://www.theguardian.com/books/2018/apr/27/frank-miller-xerxes-cursed-sin-city-the-dark-knight-returns. Accessed 1 July 2019.
White, Mark D., ed. 2009. *Watchmen and philosophy: A Rorschach test*. Hoboken: Wiley.

Watchmen as Philosophy: Illustrating Time and Free Will

88

Nathaniel Goldberg and Chris Gavaler

Contents

Introduction	1970
Summarizing *Watchmen*	1970
Nature of Time	1972
Existence of Free Will	1976
Eternalism – and Compatibilism or Determinism?	1980
"You Know I Can't"	1983
Conclusion: Who Watches the Watchmen?	1985
References	1986

Abstract

Alan Moore and Dave Gibbons' *Watchmen* may be the most acclaimed graphic novel of the twentieth century. This chapter examines how it explores two metaphysical questions: What is the nature of time? Does free will exist? Moore and Gibbons explore these questions together, illuminating connections between time and free will through connections between the graphic novel's form and content. The chapter introduces three views of the nature of time: *presentism*, the view that only the present exists; *growing-universe theory*, the view that only the present and past exist; and e*ternalism,* the view that past, present, and future exist. Because of Moore and Gibbons' distinct use of images and words within the visual structure and their depiction of a character who is simultaneously aware of past, present, and future events, the chapter deduces that the operative view in *Watchmen* is eternalism. After discussing three views of the existence of free will, the chapter then argues that eternalism entails that people could not have acted otherwise than they actually acted. Hence the operative view in *Watchmen* is either *determinism*, according to which no one has free will because no one could

---

N. Goldberg (✉) · C. Gavaler
W&L University, Lexington, VA, USA
e-mail: goldbergn@wlu.edu; gavalerc@wlu.edu

© Springer Nature Switzerland AG 2024
D. K. Johnson et al. (eds.), *The Palgrave Handbook of Popular Culture as Philosophy*,
https://doi.org/10.1007/978-3-031-24685-2_89

have done otherwise, or *compatibilism*, according to which people can have free will because having it merely requires having acted. The chapter concludes that the operative view is compatibilism. Finally it responds to the objection that compatibilism is mistaken. If no one could have done otherwise, then determinism must be true.

Keywords

Comics · Compatibilism · Determinism · Eternalism · Free Will · Growing-Universe Theory · Libertarianism · Presentism

Introduction

Alan Moore and Dave Gibbons' (1987) *Watchmen*, published by DC Comics as a "maxi-series" of 12 issues in 1986 and 1987 and as a single volume in 1987, may be the most acclaimed graphic novel of the twentieth century. It is the only graphic novel included in *Time* magazine's "Top 100 All-*Time* Novels" published between 1922 and 2005, in which Lev Grossman describes it as "a watershed in the evolution of a young medium" (2010). Adapted into a 2009 film directed by Zach Snyder, a 37-issue set of limited-series comic-book prequels by DC Comics in 2012, and an HBO live-action sequel series created by Dam Lindelof in 2019, *Watchmen* explores many philosophical questions. Some of the most overt are ethical: Does government-sanctioned violence differ from vigilantism? Do the ends always justify the means – specifically the murder of millions of New Yorkers to prevent the death of billions worldwide from nuclear annihilation?

Other questions are metaphysical: What is the nature of time? Does free will exist? This chapter examines how the graphic novel explores those questions. Examining this is worthwhile for two reasons. First, Moore and Gibbons explore the questions together, illuminating the connection between time and free will. So *Watchmen* presents a lesson in both areas of metaphysics. Second, Moore and Gibbons explore the questions by appealing to the graphic novel's distinct use of images and words within its visual structure, illuminating the connection between the graphic novel's form and content. Thus, *Watchmen* can be read as presenting a lesson in how graphic novels and comics generally communicate. In short, Moore and Gibbons figuratively illustrate the connection between time and free will in philosophy by literally illustrating it in ink.

Summarizing *Watchmen*

Charlton Comics, a competitor of DC and Marvel, published a roster of superhero characters beginning with Captain Atom in 1960 and a rebooted 1964 version of Blue Beetle, a superhero originally published by Fox Comics in the 1940s. When Fox Comics went out of business the following decade, Charlton acquired the

Golden Age Blue Beetle, and when Charlton went out of business, DC acquired both Blue Beetle characters along with the rest of the Charlton heroes in 1983. DC hired Alan Moore to write *Saga of the Swamp Thing* the same year. Moore and artist Dave Gibbons began experimenting with the Charlton cast, submitting a proposal focused on the murder mystery of one of the heroes, Peacemaker. DC liked the proposal but, wanting to preserve the newly purchased properties, directed Moore and Gibbons to invent new characters and to change the old ones in ways that made them new. Captain Atom became Doctor Manhattan, Blue Beetle became Nite Owl, Nightshade became Silke Spectre, Peacemaker became the Comedian, the Question became Rorschach, and Thunderbolt became Ozymandias. *Watchmen* was born.

The series is set in an alternative 1980s where, having won the Vietnam War with the superhuman aid of Doctor Manhattan and having kept the Watergate break-in secret, Richard Nixon is serving his sixth term as president. *Watchmen* opens with an investigation of the murder of the Comedian, thrown through his skyrise apartment window the night before. The Comedian, along with the original Silke Spectre, had been a member of the 1940s Minutemen superhero team. He later worked with a less formally defined and unnamed group of characters, which was disbanded in 1977 when the US government outlawed superhero vigilantism. Only the increasingly homicidal Rorschach continued as a vigilante. Nite Owl retired into literal impotence, the super genius Ozymandias revealed his identity as Adrian Veidt and franchised into billionaire businesses, and the nihilistic Comedian (until his death) worked secretly as a government assassin. The god-like Doctor Manhattan conducted scientific research in a military facility with the second Silke Spectre, daughter of the original character, at his side as a government-subsidized girlfriend. Doctor Manhattan's previous girlfriend, Janey Slater, who also appears in the graphic novel, was a fellow scientist who had witnessed his transformation into the world's only superpowered being. He was accidentally atomized in an experimental test chamber but eventually able to reconstitute himself; when he did, Doctor Manhattan's abilities included a simultaneous awareness of all his past, present, and future experiences.

As the lone remaining costumed vigilante, and in pursuit of the Comedian's killer, Rorschach investigates his former teammates. With the backdrop of escalating conflict between the USA and the USSR, the doomsday clock marks the increasing likelihood of nuclear holocaust. After leaving Doctor Manhattan, Silke Spectre stays with Nite Owl and the two revive their vigilante roles and begin a new sexual partnership. When the media reports multiple cases of cancer among Doctor Manhattan's oldest contacts, including Janey Slater and his former enemy Moloch, Doctor Manhattan exiles himself to Mars. Meanwhile, an anonymous tip leads the police to arrest the fugitive Rorschach, but he is soon freed from prison by Nite Owl and Silke Spectre. Doctor Manhattan then transports Silke Spectre to Mars where she tries to convince him to aid the team in capturing Ozymandias – who they now suspect murdered the Comedian. She is ultimately successful though only after learning that she is the Comedian's daughter. Doctor Manhattan, despite no longer being able to experience all moments of time, then joins Rorschach, Nite Owl, and Silke Spectre as they confront Ozymandias at his Artic stronghold.

There Ozymandias admits his masterplan: stage the appearance of a deadly alien invasion to unite the United States and Soviet Union against a common enemy to thus prevent Word War III – though at the cost of millions of lives. Because the Comedian had accidentally discovered the plan, Ozymandias murdered him. Ozymandias also gave many of Doctor Manhattan's associates cancer to drive him from the planet, tipped off the police to arrest Rorschach, used a tachyon-admitting machine to suppress Doctor Manhattan's vision of the future, and now – as they face off in the Arctic – tries but fails to kill Doctor Manhattan by replicating the experiment that produced his powers. Regardless, arriving too late to stop Ozymandias and seeing the faux alien attack produce the world peace Ozymandias intended, all but Rorschach agree to keep the secret and save the new American-Soviet alliance and so the world. Believing Rorschach to be a threat, Doctor Manhattan kills him before leaving Earth again. The novel concludes with the discovery of Rorschach's diary and the unresolved possibility of its secrets being published and the conspiracy revealed.

Nature of Time

There are three broad philosophical views about the nature of time:

1. *Presentism* is the view that only the present – this moment, right now – exists. The past did exist but doesn't anymore. The future will exist but doesn't yet. There's something special about today.
2. The *growing-universe theory* is the view that only the present and past exist. Once a moment comes into existence – once it is present – it never goes out of existence, not even after it becomes past. Yesterday is as real as today. The present is that which is coming into existence. Tomorrow however isn't real at all.
3. *Eternalism* is the view that past, present, and future – all moments in time – exist. Yesterday, today, and tomorrow are all equally real. Moments don't "come" into existence. They always – or eternally – exist.

"Presentism" and "eternalism" are more descriptive names of what many philosophers, following John M.E. McTaggart (1908), a turn-of-the-twentieth-century English philosopher, call the "A-theory" and "B-theory," respectively. (Not all philosophers following McTaggart identify presentism with the A-theory, though many who do not have in mind a species of what this chapter would understand as eternalism. Called the "spotlight theory," it is the view all moments in time exist – it is a form of eternalism – though the present is privileged, as if a spotlight were cast on it. And the spotlight moves as the present moves from earlier to later moments. The spotlight theory will not be discussed further.). McTaggart himself talked not about "theories" of time but about time "series" that those theories explain. Specifically, McTaggart argued that the A-series and B-series are the only two candidate time series, and that because the B-series does not permit change – everything that occurs, occurs eternally and so could not have been otherwise – to be a time series, the B-series must reduce to or otherwise depend on the A-series. But since the A-series is self-contradictory, McTaggart argued, there is no viable time series, and so time is not real.

Few find McTaggart's argument persuasive. Whether or not it succeeds, however, McTaggart is wrong that the A-series and B-series are the only candidate time series, because the A-theory and B-theory – at least, if understood as presentism and eternalism – are not the only theories of time. Long before McTaggart, Aristotle, a Greek philosopher of the fourth century BCE, advocated for what above was named the "growing-universe theory." "A sea-fight," wrote Aristotle, "must either take place tomorrow or not, but it is not necessary that it should take place tomorrow, neither is it necessary that it should not take place tomorrow, yet it is necessary that it either should or should not take place tomorrow" (Aristotle 2020, I.9). While the sea-fight must either take place or not take place, neither individually must happen. Unlike the present and past, the future consists only of possibilities. Though logical laws apply to the future as they do to all moments in time, the future itself does not actually exist. The present exists, and every time that was present exists too. As for the future, it is all up in the air.

The growing-universe theory might be the most intuitive of the three views. Presentism captures the intuition that only what is, leaving the past not in the past but nowhere at all, and so denying the existence of remembered events. Eternalism, which treats the universe not as a growing but as a static block (it is sometimes also called the "block-universe" theory), captures the competing intuition that not only what is, but so too is what was and what will be – thereby setting past, present, and future in stone. Because space is understood as having different points existing simultaneously, and eternalism understands time as having different moments existing simultaneously, eternalism is sometimes said to spatialize time.

Interestingly, Moore and Gibbons side with eternalism, embracing rather than dismissing its intuitive challenges. Elsewhere Moore attributes the view to Einstein, who he says

> stated that we exist in a universe that has at least four spatial dimensions, three of which are the height, depth and breadth of things as we ordinarily perceive them, and the fourth of which, while also a spatial dimension, is perceived by a human observer as the passage of time. The fact that this fourth dimension cannot be meaningfully disentangled from the other three is what leads Einstein to refer to our continuum as "spacetime". This leads logically to the notion of what is called a "block universe", an immense hyper-dimensional solid in which every moment that has ever existed or will ever exist, from the beginning to the end of our universe, is coterminous; a vast snow-globe of being in which nothing moves and nothing changes, forever. (Moore and Sassaki 2019)

Moore is echoing McTaggart's point that the B-series does not permit change. That is why McTaggart went on to argue that the B-series must somehow rely on the A-series to be a time series. Moore argues that the correlative theory, the B-theory – eternalism – is not a theory of time; and to do so he cites an authority no less than Einstein and his conclusion that what we think of as time is actually a dimension of space.

In the above quotation, Moore is discussing his 2016 prose novel *Jerusalem*; but there are two reasons to think that the operative view of time in *Watchman* is also eternalism: the graphic novel's formal structure and its character, Doctor Manhattan. First, Moore and Gibson literally illustrate eternalism with the novel's form. Like any graphic novel, every page of *Watchmen* is preestablished. Because the content of each panel depicts one moment, and because each sequence of panels typically depicts a forward progression of moments, each page represents a discreet range of time. Viewers are aware of the page, its layout, and its narrative time range. While readers of prose-only works are equally aware of the formatting of yet-unread-words on a page, the content of comics panels are more easily glimpsed and at least partially gleaned before a viewer apprehends each panel sequentially. Viewers in a sense see both the future and the past every time they focus on the panel representing what for them is the narrative's present. This formal quality of comics page layouts has led Thierry Groensteen, a contemporary Belgian comics theorist, to conclude erroneously that the comic's form necessitates retroactive storytelling, in which all events are past events:

> In truth all comics should be seen, by their nature, as being in the past, on account of the panoptic spread of the images: at the very instant when my attention is focused on one of them, I can already perceive the following frames—I can see the future is *already there* ... it is possible for me to seize, by glancing ahead, events that are yet to come ... (2007, p. 6)

Eternalism however provides a better metaphysical grounding for the comic's form. The narrative content of all panels is unchanging, regardless of whether a viewer or a character experiences them as taking place in the past, present, or future.

Watchmen also features a consistent kind of baseline layout, adding an additional preestablished quality to the novel's formal structure. Most pages feature three rows of three identically sized rectangular panels, creating two full-length vertical and two full-width horizontal gutters. And when it is not overt, such a 3 × 3 grid is implied through variations that either combine or subdivide the standard panels. Groensteen refers to a *Watchmen*-style grid as a "waffle-iron," which

> can be applied strictly (all the pages contain, say, nine or twelve images of an identical format) or more flexibly. Flexibility allows for the inclusion of larger images that are multiples of the standard frame size; the simple "elimination" of one vertical frame division produces an image that is twice as big; the elimination of two will produce a full-width panel, but these multiples fit into the grid without disrupting its geometrical regularity or altering the dimensions of the matrix. (p. 44)

Even with its flexible application, the consistency of the *Watchman* grid is unusual for its time and genre. DC and Marvel comics readers were accustomed to panels varying within a row, rows varying within a page, and pages varying within an issue. Breaking the convention draws further attention to the artistic choice. The page design is already determined, and viewer expectation comes to be too. Viewers know that every yet-unviewed page conforms to some degree to the structure-defining 3 × 3 grid.

Watchmen's rigidity in form – and subsequently in the representation of narrative time as preestablished – also allows Moore's signature cross-cut scenes, in which actions in two locations occur simultaneously in alternating panels. The alterations on a 3 × 3 grid produce a diamond pattern: the second location appears in panel two of the first row, panels one and three in the second row, and panel two in the third row. Cross-cutting 3 × 3 grids appear multiple times in *Watchmen* (pp. 43, 85, 86, 161, 226, 354), as well as other works scripted by Moore but drawn by different artists. In each case, every new panel in a sequence, despite switching to a different physical location, progresses to a next moment in time, synchronizing the cross-cut images chronologically. The synchronizing is most apparent when dialogue from one location appears in caption boxes within panels depicting the other location, and then the dialogue continues in speech balloons pointed at a character in the subsequent panel. The presence of the dialogue in caption boxes establishes the physical and temporal relationship of the initial words and image: the words are being spoken at the same moment as the moment depicted in the image (and from the same reference frame of the reader), but from a location not currently depicted. The locations alternate, but time still precedes forward frame by rigid frame.

In addition to literally illustrating eternalism with their comic's form, Moore and Gibbons also literally and figuratively illustrate it with Doctor Manhattan. Chapter IV, "Watchmaker," illustrates his experience of time through both the form and the content of the graphic novel's 3 × 3 layout grid. The first panel of the first page features a sideview image of his blue hand holding a photograph, with a caption box containing the character's narrated words: "The photograph is in my hand" (p. 111). The words and the image provide essentially identical information. In the second panel, the two diverge. The image features the photograph lying on the ground, with the captioned words: "In twelve seconds time, I drop the photograph to the sand at my feet, walking away. It's already there, twelve seconds into the future. Ten seconds now." The words represent the next partitioned moment in chronological narrative time, while the image represents some later moment after the photograph has dropped. When Doctor Manhattan speaks the words at one time, the image illustrates that his words are already true of an event that happens at a later time. All moments in time exist, and he perceives them as such. The words and images resynchronize for the reader in the third panel. There is an image, similar to the first panel image only from a more distant point of view, that frames his body as he sits looking at the photograph and repeating: "The photograph is in my hand." The fourth panel features his finding the photograph 37 hours before the enclosed narration. The event of the photograph's falling does not occur until the seventh panel, with the caption: "I'm tired of looking at the photograph now. I open my fingers. It falls to the sand at my feet." The image depicts only his open hand and the photograph's beginning to fall, not its landing. The last panel is identical to the second panel, except with different caption boxes, and could be understood as the same moment or as a distinct but ambiguously related moment. What Doctor Manhattan says figuratively illustrates eternalism, while its asynchronocity with Doctor Manhattan's and the photograph's images literally illustrates it.

Like every other page in the graphic novel, each of the above panels references a subsequent moment in time – though in those panels only the captioned narration consistently does so. The images instead may reference a past, present, or future moment relative to the captions. The temporal divergence between words and images is unique to moments narrated by Doctor Manhattan. He experiences time as eternal. But that is because time is eternal. Recalling the impossibility of preventing his father from throwing out the pieces of a clock that he was reassembling as his teenage apprentice, Doctor Manhattan says: "But it's too late, always has been too late, always will be too late" (p. 128). What is, always has been, and always will be.

Existence of Free Will

Hence eternalism is the operative view of time in *Watchmen*. There are also three broad philosophical views about the existence of free will.

1. *Libertarianism* is the view that sometimes people could have done otherwise than how they actually acted. That is the sense in which they sometimes act without being caused to act, and so some of their actions are free.
2. *Determinism* is the view that because people never could have done otherwise than how they actually acted, none of their actions is free. That is the sense in which they always act by being caused to act.
3. *Compatibilism* is the view that even though people never could have done otherwise than how they actually acted, some of their actions are nevertheless free. That is because though they always act by being caused to act, sometimes they are the ones acting. (Because compatibilism agrees with determinism in rejecting libertarian free will, it is sometimes called *Soft Determinism* and determinism is sometimes called *Hard Determinism*.)

Historically, though the descriptive terms came later, the concepts behind libertarianism and determinism have dominated Western philosophy. Plato, a Greek philosopher and Aristotle's mentor, was arguably the first to defend the ideas behind libertarianism. He (1997) argued in the *Republic* that everyone has three parts to their mind or soul – reason, will, and desires – and that only if their reason convinces their will to keep their desires in check do they act freely. Desires, however, or even the will itself, could have controlled them even if reason actually does. And, even if reason actually was not in charge, it could have been. So having free will still involves being able to act otherwise. Even the tyrant – Plato's example of someone whose will sides with desires rather than reason – could have acted otherwise. For Plato, the job of philosophy is to help convince people to have their will side with their reason, whether or not it actually does.

The idea of someone's having free will only if their will sides with reason against desires, when it could have done otherwise, finds its greatest expression in the works of Immanuel Kant, an eighteenth-century German philosopher. In both the *Groundwork for the Metaphysics of Morals* and the *Critique of Practical Reason*, Kant claims that willing based on reason is to be autonomous, or governed by one's true self, and therefore to be free. Willing based on desires is to be heteronomous, or governed not by one's true self but instead by desires, and therefore not to be free. Indeed, for Kant, acting on reason involves the Categorical Imperative, which he claims is the supreme principle of morality. Because morality requires acting on reason, morality and freedom, for him, go together.

Conversely, Leucippus and his student Democritus, also Greek philosophers and the latter Plato's near-contemporary, held that everything – people, as well as their reason, will, and desire – are determined. Though which works are Leucippus's and which are Democritus's is disputed, Aristotle critiqued their ideas. The idea that everything is determined found its greatest expression in Baruch Spinoza, a seventeenth-century Jewish-Dutch philosopher. In his *Ethics*, Spinoza (2020) argues that everything in the universe is made of matter and governed by mechanical laws. He does admit that everything in the universe could instead be understood as aspects of the divine. However, because there is only one universe, Spinoza argues, regardless of how the universe is understood, mechanical laws explain everything. It is just a matter of scientists figuring out what all the laws are. Regardless, because mechanical laws describe how everything in the universe must behave, no one could have done otherwise.

Yet, also starting in the seventeenth-century Europe, many philosophers – including Thomas Hobbes, an English philosopher writing toward the beginning of the century; John Locke, an English philosopher writing toward the middle; and David Hume, a Scottish philosopher writing toward the end – rejected both libertarianism and determinism and argued instead for compatibilism. Each maintained that whether or not one could have done otherwise was not necessary for having free will, so long as one was acting. Compatibilism, however, just like libertarianism, does not require that every way that one behaves is free. One does not circulate one's blood freely. That happens automatically, as long as they are alive. To use Locke's own example in his *Essay Concerning Human Understanding*, someone in a locked room is not free to leave, as long as they do not have the key (1975, II.xxi.10). (See specifically Hobbes's *Of Liberty and Necessity* (1999, §16), Locke's *An Essay Concerning the Human Understanding* (II.xx.8), and Hume's *Enquiries Concerning Human Understanding* (VIII.1).)

Libertarianism might be the most intuitive of the three views. It seems that sometimes people are in charge of what they do. They are not about circulating their blood or getting out of locked rooms. Also, nature and nurture may make someone more likely to make some choices rather than others. Taller people are more likely to choose to play basketball, as are people growing up in areas where basketball is popular. But people still freely choose whether or not to play – or, at least, that is what libertarianism maintains. Determinism captures the intuition that all human "choices" (if they can even be called that) result entirely from nature and nurture. If scientists had full knowledge of each, then (setting aside potential effects of quantum indeterminacy) they could flawlessly predict anyone's behavior. The hardest view to understand may be compatibilism. Just as the growing-universe theory combines elements of presentism and eternalism, compatibilism combines elements of libertarianism and determinism. Compatibilism, like determinism, maintains that everything is caused. There is no free will in the libertarian sense. Yet compatibilism, like libertarianism, permits that sometimes people do act freely. That is because, according to compatibilism, having free will does not require being able to have done otherwise. It merely requires having acted. As long as one is the source, or cause, of what they do, one is free – even if they could not have done otherwise because they were themselves caused to do what they did. Compatibilism is therefore committed to the compatibility of determinism and free will (in the compatibilist sense).

While Moore and Gibson side with eternalism regarding the nature of time, the view with which they side concerning the existence of free will is less clear. Whichever view they embrace, however, they again figuratively and literally illustrate their thoughts with Doctor Manhattan. They figuratively illustrate in Chapter IV when Doctor Manhattan's lover Janey holds a newspaper reporting the Kennedy assassination. Addressing him as "Jon" – short for "Jonathan Osterman," the US government scientist whose accidental exposure to radiation turned him into Doctor Manhattan – Janey asks about the scope of his knowledge and his ability (or lack thereof) to change the future.

Janey   So what you're saying is you knew he'd get shot? Jon, I... I mean if you're serious, I mean, why didn't you do something?
Jon   I can't prevent the future. To me, it's already happening.

To Jon, it is already happening, because it is happening eternally. He does not suggest that eternalism entails determinism, but Janey does.

Janey   Jon, what are you saying? That you know the future? Everything? About us?
Jon   In 1959, I could hear you shouting, here, now, in 1963, soon we make love...
Janey   Just like that? Like I'm a puppet? Jon, you know how everything in this world fits together except people. Your prediction's way off, mister.

To Janey, Jon's awareness of eternalism implies determinism, rendering all people puppets, with causes pulling their strings – and, though Janey does not say this, other causes pulling those causes' strings. No one or thing is free. Janey voices this view to reject it. Though Jon may understand how everything in this world, from the sub-atomic to the astronomic, fits together spatially, she insists that his understanding does not include time as a knowable dimension of Einstein's spacetime. She therefore insists that Jon does not have knowledge of the future, calling it a mere "prediction," to sidestep what she concludes to be the otherwise inevitable deterministic result. Jon however does know the future, as demonstrated by the allegedly unpredictable details of his "prediction" coming true.

Jon   No, we make love right after Wally arrives with the earrings I ordered for you...
Janey   Shut up! You're messing with my mind, Jon! Sometimes I think you're messing everything up! I mean all this new technology, all because of you! Things are happening too fast. Things shouldn't... Was that the doorbell?

Wally   Janey? The mailman delivered this to me by mistake. Sorry I didn't drop it by earlier. Say hi to Jon for me.
Janey   Uh... Uh, sure. Thanks, Wally.

After opening the package and removing the earrings, Janey embraces Jon.

Janey   Jon? I-I'm scared. I feel like there's big invisible things all around me. Will you please hold me? (p. 126)

While Janey is voicing the worry of determinism as a view of free will only to dismiss it, Jon's voicing eternalism as a view of the nature of time could reinforce determinism. Because all moments in time already, eternally, exist, Jon already knows what happens. And, even if Jon does not, those moments already do happen. Because moments of time do not come into existence, they are fixed. That means – as Moore and Gibbon illustrate with the exchange between Jon and Janey – that neither could have done otherwise.

Jon however does not explicitly voice determinism or any claim regarding free will per se. He does not tell Jane that he could not prevent Kennedy's assassination, only that he could not "prevent the future." If he is there when Kennedy is about to be assassinated, presumably he can prevent it – but he never is there. For each moment of time, he can play only the role that he always, eternally, plays. Jon and Janey are in a way speaking past each other. She wants to know why he did not stop the assassination, and Jon could answer that it is because he was not (and, for him, is not) there to stop it. It is not a matter of foreknowledge. From Jon's perspective, her question makes no more sense than asking why he is not currently standing somewhere other than where he is currently standing – on Mars, for example, rather than in their apartment.

But Jon does provide evidence that the nature of time is eternal, which does negate one view of free will. Since libertarianism requires that the times when people acted freely are only those when they could have done otherwise, eternalism is inconsistent with libertarianism. Indeed, eternalism was described above as not permitting change. Everything that occurs occurs eternally and so could not have been otherwise. Hence, if eternalism is true – which in the world of *Watchmen* it is – then libertarianism must be false. The only difference between Jon's and Janey's perspectives is that Jon realizes this while Janey does not. And Jon's making Janey aware of the determined nature of time alters nothing. It never does.

Moore and Gibson literally illustrate the eternal nature of time and its implications for free will by the layout arrangement of Chapter V, "Fearful Symmetry," in which the first 14 pages mirror the last 14. The center spread of pages 14 and 15 features a full-height middle column image that extends across the book spine, with columns of three double panels on each side. Moving simultaneously backward and forward from that center, the pages continue to reflect each other: the next three pages in either direction – 16, 17, and 18 if moving forward, and 13, 12, and 11 if moving backward – all feature standard nine-panel grids; pages 19 and 10 include full-width center panels; and pages 20 and 9 include three alternating double panels. The mirroring continues for the entire chapter, demonstrating that "future" layouts, as much as "past" and "present" ones, are not only determined but also predictably so. Given the symmetrical formal motif (one also featured in Rorschach's constantly changing but always symmetrical mask), they could not have been otherwise. Just as Jon knows that libertarianism is false, the reader of the comic knows that in Jon's world it is false too. Events are literally shaped by a predictable structure. Once set, none of its parts could have been literally illustrated otherwise.

Eternalism – and Compatibilism or Determinism?

If eternalism is true, then no one could have done otherwise. So eternalism is inconsistent with libertarianism. Yet compatibilism and determinism both accept that no one could have done otherwise. According to determinism, no one has free will. According to compatibilism, however, as long as a person is the one who acted – even though they could not have done otherwise – they do.

If eternalism is the operative view of time in *Watchmen*, then whether compatibilism or determinism is the operative view of free will needs answering. Doing so depends on whether compatibilism and determinism are ultimately distinct. If being able to have done otherwise is required for having free will – and both libertarianism and determinism maintain that it is (they just disagree on whether or not we have the ability to do otherwise) – then compatibilism collapses into determinism. Determinism is the operative view of free will in *Watchmen* by default.

Though it may not have been their intent, Moore and Gibbons figuratively illustrate that compatibilism and determinism do not collapse because they are distinct. In the above dialogue between Jon and Janey, Janey voices determinism by describing things as puppets, which she rejects as describing people. Whether or not Jon views people as puppets, he does think that people could not have done otherwise. And the reader sees that Jon is right. If determinism is true, then they do not have free will. If compatibilism is true, then they do. Which does the situation better illustrate?

Jon and Janey do act. When they lovingly embrace, they do so as two consenting adults. There is no coercion, and both are fully aware of what is happening. That supports compatibilism. Yet their embracing results entirely from nature (their attraction to one another) and nurture (Janey's growing up valuing earrings and the ones that Jon had got her just being delivered). If scientists had full knowledge of Jon's and Janey's nature and nurture, then they could have flawlessly predicted their behavior. Of course, one scientist did flawlessly predict their behavior, but not through calculation: Jon. While still supporting compatibilism, described that way intuitions might veer toward determinism. If human behavior is in principle as predictable as the most predictable physical phenomena, then human beings are nothing more than physical phenomena. Since quarks and quasars do not have free will, neither do we.

But human beings are not quarks or quasars, nor are we photographs. Recall the scene of Jon – Doctor Manhattan – and the photograph. Doctor Manhattan's narration might be read as supporting compatibilism. He states first, "I'm tired of looking at the photograph now," and then, "I open my fingers." Though being tired, whether physically or as in the sense of being bored, is (presumably) not something in his control, and though being tired causes him to open his fingers, Doctor Manhattan nevertheless is the one opening them. He causes the photograph to fall, and so ascribing to him free will in the compatibilist sense makes sense. However, read with the next statement, "It falls to the sand at my feet," the total narration might instead support determinism. Doctor Manhattan seems to be narrating three equally determined events: his being tired, his opening his fingers, and the photograph's falling. If so, then there is nothing distinct about the middle event. He is the one opening his fingers, just as the photograph is the one falling. The photograph does not have free will in either the libertarian or the compatibilist sense. That suggests that Doctor Manhattan does not either. But still, we could argue for a difference. The photograph did not cause its own fall; Doctor Manhattan did. But Doctor Manhattan does cause his own fingers to open (even though he could not have done otherwise). So Doctor Manhattan acted while the photograph did not. There is a meaningful distinction between Doctor Manhattan's behavior and the photograph's. Compatibilism identifies the distinction: the former is free, while the latter is not.

There is also a way of reading an exchange between Doctor Manhattan and Adrian Veidt, the now-unmasked former Watchman Ozymandias, as illustrating compatibilism. In the novel's climax, Doctor Manhattan joins the other former team members – Nite Owl, Silke Spectre, and Rorschach – in confronting Veidt in his base in the Arctic. Veidt admits his plan to prevent World War III by convincing the United States and Soviet Union that extraterrestrials have attacked New York, so that the superpowers have to put their differences aside. In reality, Veidt attacked the city, causing millions to die. The next section of this chapter talks about how the others react to Veidt's admission. Relevant here are Veidt and Doctor Manhattan's exchanges. After news reports confirm that the USA and USSR have unified against their perceived common enemy, Veidt seeks Doctor Manhattan's moral approval for killing half the population of New York to save almost all the population of the planet:

Veidt	Jon, wait, before you leave… I did the right thing, didn't I? It all worked out in the end?
Doctor Manhattan	"In the end"? Nothing ends, Adrian. Nothing ever ends. (p. 409)

Given Doctor Manhattan's knowledge of his past, present, and future experiences, he may mean two things by this. First, nothing ever ends in the sense of ceasing to exist, because everything exists eternally. That is how he experiences time; the form of graphic novel underscores this. Second, he wants Veidt to know that Veidt's own actions cause other actions, which cause other actions. The chain of causality never ends, and indeed no actions are uncaused and so no actions are free. Of course, those two are connected. Eternalism entails that no one could have done otherwise. Libertarianism is therefore false, and the novel's form and content show that of the remaining views compatibilism is true.

Their final words to one another however may suggest that libertarianism is not false:

Doctor Manhattan   I'm leaving this galaxy for one less complicated.
Veidt   But you've regained interest in human life . . .
Doctor Manhattan   Yes, I have. I think perhaps I'll create some.

Since this occurs after Doctor Manhattan has regained his view of eternal time, his parting words are intriguing since he "knows" he either will or will not create new human life. Maybe Doctor Manhattan is speaking loosely or colloquially. Or maybe, and perhaps more likely, he is using "I think perhaps" not as a conventional expression of uncertainty but as a conversational indicator that he feels an impulse to do something, or at least he will as soon as he makes up his mind and chooses what to do. The phrase, and the entire exchange, on the surface seems to characterize an unknown future of someone about to make a choice – someone having free will in the libertarian or compatibilist sense. Given eternalism, however, it likely instead characterizes the known future of someone about to make a choice – even though he has already in the future made it, and therefore he could not have done otherwise – and so having free will only in the compatibilist sense.

While *Watchmen* figuratively illustrates that being unable to have done otherwise is not necessary for having free will, it literally illustrates it in an earlier scene between Silke Spectre and Doctor Manhattan. After Silke Spectre realizes that her father was the Comedian, Doctor Manhattan is so moved by the revelation that he reassess his commitment to the human race:

> I don't think your life is meaningless [. . .] I changed my mind [. . .] To distill so specific a form from that chaos of improbability, like air to gold . . . that is the crowning unlikelihood. The thermodynamic miracle. [. . .] But the world is so full of people, so crowded with these miracles that they become common place and we forget . . . I forget. (p. 307)

Literally illustrating the miraculous improbability of any actuality, Doctor Manhattan's monologue is framed by a sequence of images revealing that the Martian crater where he and Silke Spectre are standing has the coincidental appearance of the Comedian's signature icon, a smiley face. Doctor Manhattan no more chooses to be moved by Silke Spectre's revelation than the crater chooses to be so shaped (or, for that matter, Silk Spectre chose to be the Comedian's daughter). Both were impacted, the crater literally by a meteorite and Manhattan figuratively by Silke Spectre's parentage, and, in combination with their unique compositions prior to those moments of impact, each assumed a new shape. The crater's new shape is overtly physical, but, if thoughts and emotions are the manifestation of physical brain activity, then Doctor Manhattan's changed mind is a change in his physical shape too.

"You Know I Can't"

Hence eternalism is the operative view of time and compatibilism the operative view of free will in *Watchmen*. Or at least compatibilism would be the view were it guaranteed not to collapse into determinism. So far this chapter has argued that it does not collapse. But the intuition that free will requires being able to have done otherwise is strong, no matter how the above scenes are read. What is required, then, in the context of *Watchmen*, is a scene in which someone could not have done otherwise yet even a proponent of libertarianism would be hard pressed to convince people that they thereby lacked free will.

That scene comes right before Veidt and Doctor Manhattan's exchanges above, when Doctor Manhattan, Nite Owl, Silke Spectre, and Rorschach all learn what Veidt had done. Realizing that his plan had already succeeded – World War III has been averted – everyone except for Rorschach agrees to keep Veidt's secret.

Nite Owl	How can humans make decisions like this? We're damned if we stay quiet, Earth's damned if we don't. We... Okay. Okay, count me in. We say nothing.
Rorschach	Joking of course.
Nite Owl	Rorschach...? Rorschach, wait! Where are you going? This is too big to be hard-assed about! We have to compromise...
Rorschach	No. Not even in the face of Armageddon. Never compromise. (p. 402)

Veidt is unconcerned, convinced that no one would believe Rorschach. But Doctor Manhattan is concerned and acts on it.

Doctor Manhattan	Where are you going?
Rorschach	Back to Owlship. Back to America. Evil must be punished. People must be told.
Doctor Manhattan	Rorschach... You know I can't let you do that.
Rorschach	Huhhh. Of course. Must protect Veidt's new utopia. One more body amongst foundations makes little difference. Well? What are you waiting for? Do it.
Doctor Manhattan	Rorschach...
Rorschach	Do it! (pp. 405–406)

Doctor Manhattan gestures, and Rorschach's body explodes into a puddle of blood in the snow. Gibbons however first draws several panels in which Doctor Manhattan appears to hesitate. Though his hand is raised and he can kill Rorschach at will, he first engages him in conversation and then continues to pause even after Rorschach has restated his unwavering intentions. Only after Rorschach has fully turned, unmasked, and is drawn in close-up facing Doctor Manhattan and commanding him to fulfill his conflicting moral obligation, does Doctor Manhattan finally act. Extending the sequence across eight panels visually suggests that Doctor Manhattan is struggling to complete the action, one that could be accomplished and depicted in a single frame because for him it would be as simple as a falling photograph obeying the law of gravity. Even so, given eternalism, Doctor Manhattan could not have done otherwise. All the same, his hesitation, literally illustrated over several frames, as well as the decision that he final comes too, are both evidence of free will.

Focusing on Rorschach reveals that the scene also figuratively illustrates that being unable to do otherwise is not required for having free will. That Rorschach believes that evil must be punished and that people must be told does not mean that Rorschach believes that he has no free will. Nor does Rorschach's being the one who must try to tell them mean that. Rorschach could not have done otherwise *because*, given his moral convictions, he has no choice but to try to tell the world. The overpowering strength of his convictions are evidence of free will, not its absence. Indeed, depending on one's ethical outlook, the fact that Rorschach has no choice but to act on those convictions might be reason for moral approbation. People would be less likely to admire Rorschach if he *could* have done otherwise. It would mean that his moral "convictions" were hardly convictions at all. He would be without principle. Acting on principle – even immovable principle – is instead a way of exercising freedom. And even proponents of libertarian might be hard pressed to convince people otherwise.

Whether or not Moore and Gibbons meant to illustrate this, Harry Frankfurt, a contemporary American philosopher, imagined a series of varying cases where individuals wanted to act in one way, did act in that way, and were morally responsible for doing so, even though they could not have done otherwise (because of either external or internal constraint). He did so to argue against what he calls *the principle of alternative possibilities*. "[A] person is morally responsible for what he has done only if he could have done otherwise" (1969, p. 829). The principle of alternative possibilities applies to moral responsibility. Frankfurt is rejecting the claim that people who could not have done otherwise are never morally responsible for what they did, and above Rorschach's decision was put in terms of "moral convictions." Free will and moral responsibility however are strongly connected. People are morally responsible only for things that they do out of their own free will. If someone is thrown off a bridge by someone else, injuring passersby below, the person who threw them off is morally responsible for the injuries, not the person who was thrown. Suppose for a minute that the principle of alternative possibilities is right. It follows from the principle and these considerations about moral responsibility and freedom that people are free (and not merely morally responsible) only if they could have done otherwise. Libertarianism endorses the principle of alternative possibilities, so it is unsurprising that being able to have done otherwise is the libertarian sense of free will. Nonetheless, Frankfurt's examples, and the above example of Doctor Manhattan and Rorschach show that the principle of alternative possibilities is not true. It follows that it is not the case that people are free only if they could have done otherwise. They can still be free even if they could not; as long as they are the ones who acted, in the compatibilist sense, they act freely.

While Frankfurt makes the point only about moral responsibility, Daniel Dennett, another contemporary American philosopher, builds on Frankfurt's work to make the point about free will and particularly to support compatibilism. Dennett describes a case similar to the one of Doctor Manhattan and Rorschach, though he turns to actual history. Martin Luther was a sixteenth-century German theologian whose protests against the Roman Catholic Church helped cause the Protestant Reformation. Asked by the Church to recant his accusations, Dennett explains, Luther responded: "Here I stand. I can do no other" (1984, p. 133). Like Rorschach, Luther's moral convictions forced him to act as he did and prevented him from being able to have done otherwise. As Dennett understands Luther, what was right was right, and Luther had no choice but to act on it. Luther's "conscience made it *impossible* for him to recant." And Dennett takes this to show that the idea "that one has acted freely (and responsibly) only if one could have done otherwise" (p. 131) is false. Rorschach is no Luther, nor do Moore and Gibbons intend him to be. But he does share with Luther the strength of his moral convictions. Rorschach's conscience made it *impossible* for him not to try to tell the world the truth. That Rorschach, like Luther, could not have done otherwise is evidence of free will.

Above it was argued that Moore and Gibson literally illustrate Doctor Manhattan's free will with his hesitation and final decisive act. They also figuratively illustrate it with his words. Doctor Manhattan responds to Rorschach's insistence that evil must be punished, and that people must be told, with: "You know I can't let you do that." Doctor Manhattan's moral convictions make it so that he has to stop Rorschach. His conscience made it *impossible* for him to let him live. Doctor Manhattan cannot, and ultimately could not, have done otherwise – just like Rorschach and Luther.

Conclusion: Who Watches the Watchmen?

Watchmen, the graphic novel, references a group of superhero vigilantes watching, or holding vigil over, America. The novel's name also evokes the question "Who watches the watchmen?," asked by Juvenal, a turn-of-the-second-century Roman poet. The watchmen – *Watchmen* seems to be saying – require watching. *Watchmen* figuratively and literally illustrates the saying throughout its story as graffiti, a curious combination of words and images.

One can also ask of the graphic novel, "Who watches *Watchmen*?" The readers of course do – by watching its words and images. And that reveals to them that Moore and Gibbons figuratively and literally illustrate eternalism and compatibilism. Moore and Gibbons know of course, as do their readers, that the world of *Watchmen* is not the actual world. The nature of time and existence of free will in the actual world remain open questions. In reference to his first graphic novel, *V for Vendetta*, begun before and finished after *Watchmen*, Moore wrote: "I didn't want to tell people what to think. I just wanted to tell people to think and consider some of these admittedly extreme little elements" (2005). "Watching" *Watchmen*, in the sense of reading it, does just that.

References

Aristotle. 2020. *On interpretation*. Trans. E.M. Edghill. *The Internet Classics Archive*. http://classics.mit.edu/Aristotle/interpretation.1.1.html. Accessed 21 Dec 2020.

Dennett, Daniel. 1984. *Elbow room*. New York: Oxford University Press.

Frankfurt, Harry G. 1969. Alternate possibilities and moral responsibility. *The Journal of Philosophy* 66 (23): 829–839.

Groensteen, Thierry. 2007. *The system of comics*. Jackson: University Press of Mississippi.

Grossman, Lev. 2010. "Watchmen." *All-TIME 100 Novels*. https://entertainment.time.com/2005/10/16/all-time-100-novels/slide/watchmen-1986-by-alan-moore-dave-gibbons/. Accessed 21 Dec 2020.

Hobbes, Thomas. 1999. Of liberty and necessity. In *Hobbes and Bramhall on liberty and necessity*, ed. Vere Chappell. New York: Cambridge University Press.

Hume, David. 1975. *Enquiries concerning human understanding and concerning the principles of morals*. 3rd edition. Edited by P. H. Nidditch. New York: Oxford University Press.

Kant, Immanuel. 1999. Critique of practical reason. Trans. Mary J. Gregor. In *Practical philosophy*. Edited by Gregor. New York: Cambridge University Press.

———. 2002. *Groundwork of the metaphysics of morals*. In *Practical philosophy*. Edited by Gregor. New York: Cambridge University Press.

Locke, John. 1975. *An essay concerning the human understanding*. Edited by Peter H. Nidditch. New York: Oxford University Press.

McTaggart, John M.E. 1908. The unreality of time. *Mind* 17: 457–473.

Moore, Alan. 2005. A for Alan. The Beat. The Anarchist Library. https://usa.anarchistlibraries.net/library/the-beat-a-for-alan. Accessed 21 Dec 2020.

Moore, Alan, and Dave Gibbons. 1987. *Watchmen*. New York: DC Comics.

Moore, Alan, and Raphael Sassaki. 2019. Moore on Jerusalem, Eternalism, Anarchy and Herbie! *Alan Moore World*. https://alanmooreworld.blogspot.com/2019/11/moore-on-jerusalem-eternalism-anarchy.html. Accessed 21 Dec 2020.

Plato. 1997. *Republic*. Trans. G. M. A. Grube. Revised by C. D. C. Reeve. In *Plato: complete works*, ed. John M. Cooper. Indianapolis: Hackett Publishing Company.

Spinoza, Baruch. 2020. Ethics. In Edwin Curley, ed., trans. *A Spinoza reader: The ethics and other works*. Princeton: Princeton University Press.

The Joker as Philosopher: Killing Jokes

89

Matthew Brake

Contents

Introduction	1988
Summary and Plot	1989
Absurdity and Injustice	1992
Reason and Memory	1994
The Value of Madness	1998
Conclusion	2000
References	2000

Abstract

Alan Moore and Brian Bolland's *Batman: The Killing Joke* is one of the most popular Batman comic stories, and it is considered one of the greatest Joker stories of all time. The story finds the Joker kidnapping Commissioner Jim Gordon and psychologically torturing him. He does so in order to prove that the world is an absurd and unjust place, and in response to the injustices of the world, one should reject reason and order in favor of irrationality, chaos, and madness. The graphic novel asks readers to consider whether or not the Joker is right – that the only way to live in an absurd world is to be absurd and "go mad" – and whether people like Batman and Gordon are in denial, not only about the world, but about their own ability to remain rational in an absurd world.

Keywords

Alan Moore · Brian Bolland · Batman · Joker · Absurd · Reason · Madness · Albert Camus · Michel Foucault · Friedrich Nietzsche

---

M. Brake (✉)
Northern Virginia Community College, Manassas, VA, USA
e-mail: popandtheology@gmail.com; mbrake@nvcc.edu

Introduction

Written in 1988 by Alan Moore and drawn by Brian Bolland, *Batman: The Killing Joke* is one of the most iconic Joker stories ever written. (Note the pages are unnumbered.) Directors Tim Burton and Christopher Nolan, not insignificant figures in the history of the Batman movie franchise, were both influenced by it, the latter having given it to Heath Ledger as a part of his character research (Collura 2012). The comic is notable for, among other things, the kidnapping and mental torturing of Police Commissioner Jim Gordon and the violent and sexualized maiming of Barbara Gordon (Batgirl). The Joker does this in an attempt to show that every normal, ordinary person, or even the most exceptional person, is only "one bad day" from being driven mad.

Despite the comic's influence on other media portrayals of Batman, Moore himself is not a fan of the work, stating, "I've never really liked my story in *The Killing Joke*. I think it put far too much melodramatic weight upon a character that was never designed to carry it. It was too nasty, it was too physically violent. There were some good things about it, but in terms of my writing, it's not one of my favorite pieces" (Wilber 2016). In a response to a fan on Goodreads, Moore expresses additional disdain for *The Killing Joke* (while praising the art by Brian Bolland), claiming that the story "was far too violent and sexualised a treatment for a simplistic comic book character like Batman and a regrettable misstep on my part"; furthermore, he admits that he has no interest in Batman and that "any influence I may have had upon current portrayals of the character is pretty much lost on me" (Moore 2022). Elsewhere, however, he goes on to say that if, "god forbid, I was ever writing a character like Batman again, I'd probably be setting it squarely in the kind of 'smiley uncle period' where Dick Sprang was drawing it, and where you had Ace the Bat-Hound and Bat-Mite, and the zebra Batman – when it was sillier. Because then, it was brimming with imagination and playful ideas. I don't think that the world needs that many brooding psychopathic avengers. I don't know that we need any" (Wilbur 2016). Moore has become disaffected by the "grim and gritty" take on Batman, and indeed, on all superheroes, that he played a part in inaugurating and which is seen in *The Killing Joke*. He has effectively disowned the book, and instead, this writer known for "realistic" takes on superheroes like *Watchmen* would prefer to write a few "silly" Silver Age stories (Wilbur 2016).

Even though its writer despises the story, *The Killing Joke* is a perennial favorite among comic book fans, and in 2016, it was adapted into an animated film with fan-favorite voice actors Kevin Conroy (Batman) and Mark Hamill (the Joker) reprising their roles from the popular *Batman: The Animated Series.* (In the Goodreads comment, Moore disavowed the adaptation, asked for his name to be removed from it, and refused any royalties for it.) Unfortunately for fans, the film adaptation was not well-received, in part because of poor voice acting direction and animation quality, but also because of added content featuring Barbara Gordon, which consisted of a mediocre prologue before the main story and a post-credits scene featuring the paralyzed heroine adopting the identity of expert computer hacker Oracle. While this material was added in order to pad the time for the movie and give the character greater agency than the original story, its portrayal of Barbara is unflattering, showing her to be incompetent; it also sexualizes her and involves her in an unnecessary sexual relationship with Batman to motivate him in the movie's main storyline. In an attempt to address the sexualization and torture of the character in the original story, it is possible that the film made those problems worse (Mendelson 2016).

In what follows, I will explore what, if anything, the Joker teaches readers. I will first consider the picture that the Joker paints of the world as an inherently absurd and unjust place. Next, I will examine Joker's rejection of reason, reason's connection to memory, and the sense of identity that is created when one rejects reason. Finally, I will consider the value that the Joker places on madness as a viable alternative to reason for living in the world.

This chapter, while primarily drawing from *The Killing Joke*, will also draw on other notable works featuring the Joker, such as *Arkham Asylum: A Serious House on a Serious Earth* (1989) and Christopher Nolan's *The Dark Knight* (2008). *The Killing Joke* will provide the "springboard" for all the ideas allowed for by the action and dialogue from these other works, so that we can examine the argument the Joker makes.

Summary and Plot

The Killing Joke follows a fairly simple premise: the Joker wants to prove that ordinary human beings are not so different from him – they can be driven to madness as easily as he was. It begins with Batman arriving at Arkham Asylum. He goes into the Joker's cell as the villain is playing solitaire. Batman tells the Joker that he came to talk, because he recognizes that the two of them are on a deadly path together. Either Batman will kill the Joker, or the Joker will kill Batman. Batman wants to prevent that from happening and know that he's done everything he can to prevent it; however, the Joker, sitting in the shadows, continues to play cards, causing Batman to grow frustrated that the villain is not taking this matter of "life and death" more seriously. He grabs the Joker's hand, only to see streaks of white makeup on his gloves – he realizes that the Joker in the cell is a fake.

The scene changes to a dilapidated amusement park. The park's co-owner (who for some reason doesn't seem to recognize one of the most wanted men in Gotham) apologizes for the park's disrepair, but the Joker expresses glee at the injuries he can inflict on others with the park's rides. As the Joker agrees to buy the park, he informs the man that he won't be paying, poisoning the owner, leaving him sitting with a hideous smile.

This sequence of the Joker exploring the park and murdering its owner is interspersed with the first of many flashbacks in the story, showing the Joker's life before he became a master criminal. Readers learn that he is a failing comedian, trying to support his loving and pregnant wife. As more flashbacks are shone, the nameless comedian, out of desperation to make ends meet and create a better life for his family, gets involved with a gang of criminals. The comedian was once an employee of a local chemical company; the gang wishes to take advantage of his knowledge to enter the factory undetected so they can, in turn, break into the playing card company next door. The criminals intend to make the comedian wear the mask of the "Red Hood." The Red Hood is the name of a supposed criminal mastermind in Gotham but is in fact a fake identity worn by different members of the same gang, and in the comedian's case, is meant to make him stand out as the fall guy if anything goes wrong.

On the day the crime is supposed to happen, the comedian finds out that his wife has been electrocuted and killed in a freak accident, and he tries to back out of the robbery; however, the criminals don't let him. That night, when they break into the chemical plant, security guards spot them, killing one of the gang members and injuring the other; the injured criminal convinces the guards that the comedian in the Red Hood outfit is the mastermind behind the crime. They chase him until Batman arrives. As Batman reaches out to him, the comedian falls into one of the chemical vats and is flushed out into the river. He emerges with green hair and his skin bleached white, laughing maniacally. Readers have just witnessed the birth of the Joker.

In the present, Commissioner Gordon is at home with Barbara. As she opens the door to leave, she is confronted by the gleaming eyes of the Joker; donning a Hawaiian shirt and with a camera hanging from his neck, he points a gun at her stomach and shoots Barbara through the spine. The Joker's henchmen knock the Commissioner unconscious as the Joker begins to undress Barbara, camera now in hand. Weakened and in pain, she asks why he is doing this. He replies, "To prove a point."

Barbara is taken to the hospital, and Batman learns that she has been permanently paralyzed from the waist down. Meanwhile, Commissioner Gordon wakes up at the Joker's amusement park, surrounded by various carnival freaks, who undress him and chain him up. The Joker puts him on a nightmarish ghost train ride and subjects him to mental torture by showing him pictures of Barbara, naked, mortally wounded, and in pain, all while the Joker sings a song about madness.

Searching for Gordon, Batman is summoned to GCPD, where the police give him a ticket to the Joker's amusement park. Arriving, Batman confronts the Joker, who burns his arm with acid before running into a fun house equipped with numerous booby traps. First, Batman frees Gordon, who tells Batman to bring the Joker in "by the book" in order "to show him that our way works!" As Batman pursues the Joker through the fun house, avoiding the various traps, the Joker speaks to him over a loudspeaker system. Believing he has driven Gordon mad, the Joker wonders why Batman can't acknowledge that the world makes no sense and that everyone is on the verge of madness. He gloats, "I've proved my point. I've demonstrated there's no difference between me and everyone else! All it takes is one bad day to reduce the sanest man alive to lunacy. That's how far the world is from where I am. Just one bad day." Batman, however, informs the Joker that he's wrong – Gordon is still sane. Perhaps, he says, "ordinary people don't always crack.... Maybe it was just you, all the time."

The Joker and Batman continue to fight, until the Joker seems to have the upper hand on Batman, pulling out a gun, which he fires, only to discover that it was a fake. The Joker tells Batman to "kick the hell out of [him]" for what he's done, but Batman refuses. He doesn't want to hurt the Joker. Instead, he offers to help rehabilitate him, returning to the conversation at the beginning of the story. If they don't make things right, they'll end up killing each other. In a moment of empathetic compassion for his murderous archenemy, Batman says, "It doesn't have to end like that. I don't know what it was that bent your life out of shape, but who knows? Maybe I've been there, too. Maybe I can help." The Joker, unfortunately, refuses, saying that it's too late for that, which leads to an ending whose ambiguity has stirred up its own share of controversy.

Standing in the rain, the Joker tells Batman a joke about two men escaping from an insane asylum:

> So, like, they get up onto the roof and there, just across this narrow gap, they see the rooftops of the town...stretching away to freedom. Now, the first guy, he jumps right across with no problem. But his friend...daredn't make the leap. Y'see...he's afraid of falling. So then, the first guy has an idea...he says, "Hey! I have my flashlight with me! I'll shine it across the gap between the buildings. You can walk along the beam and join me!" But the second guy just shakes his head. He says, "What do you think I am? Crazy? You'd turn it off when I was half way across!"

At this, the Joker and Batman both begin to laugh uncontrollably, and in one panel, Batman stretches out his arm to lean on the Joker...or does he? It's also possible that Batman strangles the Joker in this panel. Could this be the "killing joke," Batman killing the Joker in a fit of laughter, finally seeing the world for the absurd joke that the Joker thinks it is? The ending raises a number of questions, not only about the Joker's fate, but about the joke itself.

On the surface, it's possible that the title is simply making a pun. As Julian Darius points out, "A joke is said to 'kill' if it goes over particularly well" (Darius 2012, p. 38). As for the meaning of the joke, Darius says, "Superficially, the joke is simply the Joker saying that he's crazy and can't accept help because of it" (Darius 2012, p. 18). Darius further notes:

> Reading a little deeper, we can see that the lunatic asylum represents the "one bad day" that both men have experienced – symbolizing all the pain of life bundled up in a single day. Batman is the first inmate, who was able to make it across into freedom. The Joker, however, is scared of falling and won't go. (Darius 2012, p. 18)

It may seem like this is a case of Batman being right and the Joker being wrong, but it isn't that simple, as Darius continues:

> This "freedom," however, is hardly a lack of insanity. Indeed, the first inmate still thinks that his friend can walk on a flashlight's beam. If this first inmate is Batman, then Batman is truly insane not for dressing up as a bat and fighting crime in response to personal trauma – an idea Joker raises earlier – but for believing that the Joker can be cured. (Darius 2012, p. 18)

This may shed light on the choice of the joke, but what of the Joker's fate? Since this story wasn't originally supposed to be "canon," was Batman supposed to kill the Joker at the end?

A rather complex picture emerges when trying to answer this question. Brian Bolland, the artist of the work, has coyly implied that there may be more to this scene than a simple laugh between rivals (Johnston 2013). Grant Morrison, Moore's sometimes-rival, has gone on record saying that, indeed, Moore intended for Batman to kill the Joker at the end of the story (Begley 2013). This ending would certainly serve to prove Joker's point that Batman is just as crazy as him and that he can break. However, when one looks at the script (which is available in full online), there is no mention of Batman killing the Joker (Zalben 2013). Moore himself confirms this, highlighting how readers may have made too much of this final scene:

> ...for the record, my intention at the end of that book was to have the two characters simply experiencing a brief moment of lucidity in their ongoing very weird and probably fatal relationship with each other, reaching a moment where they both perceive the hell that they are in, and can only laugh at their preposterous situation. A similar chuckle is shared by the doomed couple at the end of the remarkable Jim Thompson's original novel, *The Getaway*. (Moore 2022)

Moore's actual intent is almost trite compared to the legend that has grown up around the ending of his work. Nevertheless, what readers see at the end are two men, sharing a joke and sharing an appreciation for their absurd situation, an absurd situation that the Joker's own philosophizing may shed some light on.

Absurdity and Injustice

The Joker's greatest contention throughout *The Killing Joke* is that the world is an absurd place. There is no greater plan for the world, and there is nothing that can make all the randomness make sense. As Commissioner Gordon comes to the end of his hellish ghost train ride, the Joker proclaims the insignificance of humanity in light of such a vast cosmos, singing, "Man's so puny, and the universe so big!" Humans merely get lost in the shuffle of random events and try to make sense of them. There's no "consistent whole" that allows them to find "true North." One is reminded of Albert Camus's idea of the absurd as the "confrontation" between the human longing for the world to make sense and "the unreasonable silence of the world" (Camus 1983, p. 28).

Locking Gordon naked in a cage for his minions to see, the Joker misanthropically castigates "the average man" for his attempts to make sense of an inherently irrational and absurd world, noting that human beings are the most "tragic of nature's mistakes!" Particularly, he notes the "bloated sense of humanity's importance" along with values such as "optimism" and having a "social conscience." The Joker especially laments human "notions of order and sanity." Rather than deal with the absurdity of the world, humans try to give the world meaning and purpose, denying their hopeless state. The Joker asserts that these attempts to give the world meaning don't turn out well. In fact, he says, "Faced with the inescapable fact that human existence is mad, random and pointless, one in eight of them crack up and go stark raving buggo!" Any artificial sense of order brings about the opposite of its intended effect for most people. Instead of bringing them peace and comfort, the artificial weight of a false order crushes them. Eventually, the true nature of the world reasserts itself and breaks them.

The Joker brings up the (possibly apocryphal) story about a flock of geese (mistaken on a radar screen for an enemy attack) nearly causing World War III as proof of the world's absurdity. In light of society's false notions of order and security, he uses this story to demonstrate that chaos, death, and destruction can be unleashed at any time and bring ruin to any sense of order people create. If such a thing were to happen, then "everything anybody ever valued or struggled for" may indeed be reduced to ashes, which from the Joker's point of view, would mean that "it's all a monstrous, demented gag!"

Now, one could argue that the prevention of World War III in the face of such a close call is a sign that maybe there is some sort of order keeping things from getting too off track, but that may be little comfort in the face of the other atrocities that have taken place – and continue to occur in the world. The Joker brings up (again, possibly apocryphal) events leading up to and causing World War II as well, a terrible time in human history when six million Jewish people were murdered along with millions of others; and in his song to Gordon, he draws attention to the continuing evils of "rape, starvation [and] war" that continue to plague humanity. It is in these last comments that one can see the reason for Joker's rejection of any grand plan for the universe.

In Camus's case for the absurd, he argues epistemologically that it is simply impossible to know if there's any overarching purpose for the world based on the things he can actually know, and one can only know two things for sure: "This heart within me I can feel, and I judge that it exists. The world I can touch, and I likewise judge that it exists" (Camus 1983, p. 19). One can know that they desire for things to make sense, and one can know the world, which refuses to give any assurance that it all makes sense. But the Joker's problem is not merely epistemological. The Joker's rejection of any grand plan or order for the world is grounded in the experience of injustice.

The Joker connects his claims about the absurdity of the world and the injustices of life in a few different places, but it becomes particularly apparent in his interactions with Gordon. The song he sings ends with "and if life should treat you bad, don't get even, get mad!" Afterwards, he has his minions throw the commissioner in a cell, saying, "Perhaps he'll get a little livelier once he's had a chance to think his situation over…to reflect upon life, and all its random injustice." Because the flashbacks in *The Killing Joke* tell readers about the Joker's origin, Moore and Bolland shed light on why this may be the key to understanding the Joker's insistence upon an absurd, unjust world.

Readers know that the Joker was a nameless comedian, having left his job at the chemical plant in order to follow his dream of becoming a comedian and being able to still provide for his wife and unborn child. Of course, readers know that the comedian is failing at providing for his family. This is why he agrees to help criminals enter the chemical plant he used to work at so they can break into the card company next door. The payout for this job was going to provide the means to give himself and his wife and child a better life. Unfortunately, on the day the break-in was supposed to happen, the comedian's wife and unborn child were randomly electrocuted. Two police officers notify him of this tragedy and one explains, "It was a million to one accident!" Right when events in his life seemed to be coming together purposefully to make his life better, when he tried to gain control of his situation, randomness and chaos broke in and destroyed his plan. Life seemed unfair to him. He was a desperate man going to desperate lengths to help his family, and then he was taken advantage of by gangsters, who forced him to carry out a crime even though his wife died. Perhaps that's why the Joker couldn't accept Batman's help. All the things he himself valued and struggled for came to nothing, so he can't believe for anything else. The Joker asks readers, "Why struggle? Randomness and chaos will always win and take your false hope away and make your struggles meaningless." This leads to the Joker's rejection of reason, for it is reason that tries to make sense of the whole of life and give it coherence.

Reason and Memory

In rejecting the rationality of the world, or the ability of the world to fit together as an ordered and coherent whole, the Joker also rejects rationality as a mode of existence for the individual. If the world is disordered and random, then a person's own self should be disordered and random. But what does it mean for the individual to reject reason and embrace irrationality? One can see the answer to this question when the Joker tortures Gordon. Having broken into Gordon's home and shooting (and paralyzing) Gordon's daughter, the Joker brings him to the carnival grounds, strips the commissioner naked, and loads him onto a horrific ride where he shows Gordon pictures of his naked and badly wounded daughter. Gordon is initially disoriented as he is being stripped and led to the ride, but then as his mind clears, the realization of his current predicament hits him: "Oh no. I...I remember."

The Joker takes this short comment by Gordon and uses it to go on a diatribe about the problem with memories: "Remember? Ohh, I wouldn't do that! Remembering's dangerous." He continues to describe memories as "treacherous" and "filled with the damp, ambiguous shapes of things you'd hoped were forgotten." They can be "vile" and "repulsive." Of course, the Joker's commentary about the pain of memories fits with the tenor of Moore's overall story, which is all about the Joker's origin and the pain that led him to become the Clown Prince of Crime. Rather than remember that heartache, the Joker has disassociated from it and embraced madness. It is here that the Joker reveals what he sees as a key ingredient of rationality itself. Continuing his monologue about memories, the Joker tells Gordon, "But can we live without them? Memories are what our reason is based upon. If we can't face them, we deny reason itself! Although, why not? We aren't contractually tied down to rationality!" Joker draws a direct line from memory to rationality. Joker's comments link the continuity of memory with reason, while the discontinuity of memory is one of the constituting factors of unreason or madness. What is at stake here for reason is a continuity of self.

As ever, Batman resists Joker's plans – the obvious one about Gordon, but also his philosophical aspirations regarding reason, madness, and the self. As Batman pursues the Joker through the fairgrounds, the Joker gloats (mistakenly) that he has driven Gordon mad. This is the specific moment when the Joker proclaims to Batman that all it takes is "one bad day" to drive the sanest person mad. But now, the Joker goes further, inquiring about Batman himself:

> You had a bad day once, am I right? I know I am. I can tell. You had a bad day and everything changed. Why else would you dress up like a flying rat? You had a bad day, and it drove you as crazy as everybody else…only you won't admit it! You have to keep pretending that life makes sense, that there's some point to all this struggling! God, you make me want to puke.

But the Joker isn't done. He continues, "When I saw what a black, awful joke the world was, I went crazy as a coot! I admit it! Why can't you? I mean, you're not unintelligent! You must see the reality of the situation." The Joker acknowledges Batman's intelligence. Batman is strong. Batman is clever. For the Joker, that should have guaranteed that Batman would come around and see things the Joker's way. Of course, Batman is not responsive to the Joker's philosophizing about the senselessness of reality, and when he asks Batman, "Why aren't you laughing?" Batman crashes into the room and responds (probably referring to all his other encounters with the Joker), "Because I've heard it before, and it wasn't funny the first time." Batman is unwilling to acknowledge that the world may indeed be without sense, and has retreated instead to a safer, more confined, structured world. In doing so, he strives to maintain a coherent sense of self – even if sometimes this is a struggle. (And one wonders whether it being a struggle proves Joker's ultimate point.)

Of course, we are supposed to root for Batman. After all, Joker is a fiend. But let's bracket Joker's murderous pathology and explore his view on its own merits, beginning with: What is the logical outflow of the Joker's denial of rationality and ongoing conscious continuity? Might there even be advantages to such an outlook?

To begin answering these questions, the Joker eschews the idea that all of one's experiences should be underwritten by a unity of memory, by a coherent story of how one understands their life; rather, the Joker advocates for a more fragmented understanding of one's sense of self. Joker contrasts rationality with his understanding of madness, consisting of a fragmented sense of self, one that seemingly expresses, if not condones, discontinuity. As he talks to Batman over the speakers in the fairgrounds' Fun House, he tells him that he himself had "one bad day once," saying, "I'm not exactly sure what it was. Sometimes I remember it one way, sometimes another. If I'm going to have a past, I prefer it be multiple choice!"

The emerging view of the Joker – and the one the Joker himself implicitly advocates for here – has become influential. Not surprisingly, one can find it in Christopher Nolan's *The Dark Knight*, in (at least) the following two ways. First,

Nolan's Joker, memorably played by Heath Ledger in an Oscar-winning role, conveys this idea of the Joker's "multiple choice" past by having him tell multiple versions of his origin story ("Wanna know how I got these scars..."), with the viewer never being certain which one is correct. Perhaps the Joker is no longer certain which one is correct? Second, recall Nolan's Joker frequently questions Batman's adherence to his "one rule" to not kill (Polo 2018). In the interrogation scene from *The Dark Knight*, the Joker scolds Batman, saying, "You have all these rules, and you think they'll save you," but the truth, he tells Batman, is that "the only sensible way to live in this world is without rules." Presumably, the Joker would extend his point about "sensibly living without rules" to include any so-called rules that require one to prioritize rationality and maintain a coherent sense of self in an absurd world.

Given its influence in the genre, it's also not unsurprising that multiple authors have explored the idea of there being a multiplicity to the Joker's past and even his identity. One of the more recent efforts was put forth by Geoff Johns and Jason Fabok in their *Batman: The Three Jokers* (2020) story, a follow-up to the revelation from the duo's *Justice League: Darkseid War* (2018) where Batman learns that there is not one Joker, but three. *Three Jokers* attempts to provide an in-canon reason for the different depictions of the Joker's personality throughout the character's publication history.

Long before Johns and Fabok's *Three Jokers*, writer Grant Morrison and artist Dave McKean had offered a more elegant explanation for the Joker's discontinuous self in 1989's *Arkham Asylum: A Serious House on a Serious Earth*. (Note the pages are unnumbered.) Being published just a year after *The Killing Joke*, Morrison seemingly builds on Moore's Joker, which isn't surprising given the two writers' rivalry with one another. Morrison takes the idea of Joker's misremembered past and multiple personalities and runs with it, giving the Joker an "official" diagnosis from Dr. Ruth Adams, who describes the Joker's condition to Batman:

> The Joker's a special case. Some of us feel he may be beyond treatment.... In fact, we're not even sure if he can be properly defined as insane. It's quite possible we may actually be looking at some kind of super-sanity here. A brilliant new modification of human perception, more suited to urban life at the end of the 20th century.... He can only cope with that chaotic barrage of input by going with the flow. That's why some days he's a mischievous clown, others a psychopathic killer. He has no real personality. He creates himself each day.

Not only does Morrison account for the differences in the Joker's personality over the years, but Morrison's explanation also seems to put a positive spin on the Joker's (alleged) psychosis. He is not insane, but "super-sane." In fact, perhaps the Joker's diagnosis is a beneficial and necessary adaptation to life in the postmodern twentieth-century urban environment, which is incessantly bombarded with competing messages via a constant flow of information. It is incredibly taxing to maintain one's sense of self in a world that is ever-changing at a moment's notice (and exacerbated by the twenty-first century's fascination with the Internet and smartphones). The Joker constantly re-creates himself given current environmental inputs.

Morrison's take on the Joker's discontinuous personality and fragmented consciousness is reminiscent of Friedrich Nietzsche's views. In *Ecce Homo*, Nietzsche declares that consciousness itself is only a surface or appearance, and it is thus freed from all metaphysical imperatives (Nietzsche 2005, p. 97). In other words, there is no particular way that the world "has" to be. There is no plan. Nietzsche provides the metaphor of a wave to describe the life of someone freed from all metaphysical considerations of both the world and themselves. He writes, "But already another wave is approaching, still more greedily and savagely than the first, and its soul, too, seems to be full of secrets and the lust to dig up treasures. Thus live waves – thus live we who will – more I shall not say" (Nietzsche 1974, p. 247). As Walter Kaufmann explains, "What he shares with the waves is the overflowing vitality that never comes to a stop – not because it has failed to find what it was looking for but because this constant play is its life" (Kaufman, "Commentary," in Nietzsche 1974, 248 n38). Like the changing of the waves, Nietzsche's life is now typified by the liberation, or the "play," of constantly changing appearances. Nietzsche writes, "Rather has the world become 'infinite' for us all over again, inasmuch as we cannot reject the impossibility that *it may include infinite interpretations*" (Nietzsche 1974, p. 336, original emphasis). This ability to embrace the possibility of infinite interpretations of the world involves "the strength to create for ourselves our own new eyes – and ever again new eyes that are even more our own" (Nietzsche 1974, p. 192). Thus, there is no eternal horizon or perspective for humanity, but only a constantly changing multiplicity of interpretations and perspectives.

What we see here is Nietzsche's understanding of the instability of any stable notion of a "self." Instead, who a person is can change like the waves crashing on the beach: one crashes, then dissipates, then another follows. There is a free play of instincts underneath the surface that allows for the appearance of something "new" on the surface. As it is with the Joker, the self is a constantly reinterpreted, unstable surface appearance below which lies the impenetrable play of instincts. It is also interesting that Dr. Adams mentions that the Joker's condition may be a product of twentieth-century life. Nietzsche himself looked forward to the emergence of a being who would embrace this play of instincts underneath the surface of consciousness and the subsequently changing self, which would emerge after the "modern" with its ordered rationality. Perhaps Nietzsche (and the Joker, despite his flaws) have stumbled on the way to live in an ever-changing and fast-paced world, now driven by technological advancements. Not only can there be "three Jokers," but there can be an infinite number of Jokers (but in one body, not three), emerging and disappearing like waves on the ocean. If the world is irrational without any overarching metaphysical stability, then what other way is there to live? If the universe is absurd, rather than live with the angst of wanting order in an orderless world, he wants the self to be orderless as well. To struggle against as absurd world, as Batman arguably does, only invites more angst. To Camus's earlier point about the absurd being a confrontation between the desire for rational order in the world and the silence of an irrational "universe so big," the Joker's response is to evacuate the desire for order and become as chaotic and irrational as the world itself. Or, as the Joker refers to it, to become "mad."

The Value of Madness

Michel Foucault writes that madness still haunts the modern world through art and the works of thinkers like Nietzsche. They cause the world to question its reason and sanity, to "justify itself before madness" although this question receives no answer (Foucault 1988, pp. 288–289). Foucault contends that madness hasn't always been a remote possibility for a human being. Perhaps we are more susceptible to it than we think. As is stated in Foucault's work: "Do not glory in your state, if you are wise and civilized men; *an instant suffices* to disturb and annihilate that supposed wisdom of which you are so proud; an unexpected event, a sharp sudden emotion of the soul will abruptly change the most reasonable and intelligent man into a raving idiot" (Foucault 1988, pp. 211–212, emphasis added). One could add "Alan Moore" and "Brian Bolland" to the list of artists and writers haunting the modern world with madness. Like those Foucault cites, Moore and Bolland have Joker utter his famous argument, "All it takes is one bad day to reduce the sanest man alive to lunacy. That's how far the world is from where I am. Just one bad day."

The character of the Joker haunts *The Killing Joke* with the specter of madness, and while both Commissioner Gordon and Batman reject the Joker's madness, one might ask the question, "Should they?" Nietzsche would assert that they should not; nevertheless, Gordon tells Batman to bring the Joker in "by the book" because "we have to show him that our way works!" And Batman, in his confrontation with the Joker, seems to reject the Joker's proposition, saying that "he's heard it before" and that "maybe there isn't any need to crawl under a rock with all the other slimey [sic] things when trouble hits...maybe it was just you, all the time."

Yet, upon closer examination, Gordon and Batman both "crack" in ways that show that they themselves recognize, or even give in, to the madness and absurdity of the world. One of the innovations of *The Killing Joke* animated adaptation is an added sequence where Gordon is asked to judge a man who ignores the law and brutalizes others. When Gordon says that he would "throw the book at him," he picks up a book with "Law" written on it and throws it at the Joker, only for a cut out of Batman to spring up and intercept it. While Gordon may resist the Joker's insistence that the world is without order and mad, Jim gives into some of that madness by condoning Batman's extrajudicial actions.

For Batman, Moore establishes in the opening sequence that he and Joker are "two guys in a lunatic asylum," and even though Batman is the figure in Joker's final joke who (somehow) jumps to freedom, in that scenario, he's a desperate escapee from madness at his best. Batman attempts to leap over "the gap between his powers of explanation and the irrationality of the world and of experience" (Camus 1983, p. 33). What's worse, the hope he offers Joker may indeed be illusory, nothing but a flashlight beam that shines brightly, but will end with a fall. As Camus states, hope is one of the ways people try to avoid the world's absurdity, but that hope has no foundation and runs against the course of the way the world actually is (Camus 1983, pp. 8–9). Darius notes that it is Batman's groundless hope that the Joker takes aim at with his joke (Darius 2012, p. 18). The absurd nature of their dilemma is not lost on

Batman, for in his laughing, there may be a brief acknowledgment of the Joker's point, and thus a recognition of his own madness.

And then there's the Joker. While Batman resists the idea that everyone is just like the Joker, it must be admitted that before his dip into a vat of acid, there was nothing particularly distinguishable about the Joker. Batman insists that there's something exceptionally misguided about the Joker for him to go mad like he did, and yet, the character readers see in the flashbacks is unremarkable. He is just an ordinary guy who tragically and unexpectedly loses his wife and unborn child, only to be disfigured by chemical burns. By contrast, although Gordon's daughter is grievously injured, she doesn't die, and one could argue that while Bruce Wayne suffered tragedy, he was insulated by family wealth and by Alfred and he *still* went mad enough to dress like a giant bat (and fall in love with a jewel thief who dresses like a giant cat). *The Killing Joke* readers are left wondering if the Joker is indeed the exception. Why, exactly, is the Joker misguided, especially given all the world's randomness and cruelties – it's absurdity, as Camus would say – that each of us regularly face?

Accordingly, Moore and Bolland's work causes readers to reflect upon the absurd world humans live in, one full of injustice and suffering. The Joker argues that in the face of the injustices that reveal the absurdity of the world, one should embrace madness and adapt one's self to the world's fragmented irrationality rather than going against the grain to establish rational order, which will always crack. Even the proponents of order, Batman and Commissioner Gordon, have moments that reveal that they each dabble with madness. So maybe Gordon and Batman are more mad than they would like to admit.

But is the Joker as mad as he claims, and is he truly being consistent with his own argument? After all, if Joker intends to rationally convince Gordon or Batman that it is better to embrace the absurd via a fragmented self, his implicit argument becomes self-defeating; one cannot consistently use reason to prove irrationality. To avoid that complication, we might interpret Gordon's horrific carnival ride and the final joke to Batman as conveyed along existentialist lines where the most profound insights can be achieved only through truly experiencing the human condition (and not rational discourse).

Still, going back to the end of Joker's song, "Don't get even, get mad!" one must ask if the Joker is indeed mad, or if he's actually getting even with a world that he thinks mistreated him. The Joker's arguments are based on a litany of complaints about the world's unfairness, and his nihilistic destruction of the lives of others could simply be an act of revenge against the world. If it is an act of revenge, then revenge implies a belief in rationality. The logic of "an eye for eye" recognizes a disrupted balance that needs to be restored, some sort of order that has been violated. While it may be true that Gordon and Batman flirt with madness, the Joker may be more rational than he lets on. This is something that Batman's son, Damian Wayne, pointed out about Joker in Grant Morrison's *Batman and Robin* #13: "You say you're a force of chaos and you don't plan anything, it just happens. But I've read your files and everything's a plan. . . . Because I don't think you know what chaos is. . . . They say you're mad, but I say you're not." Before Damian, in *Batman* #649, Batman's resurrected sidekick Jason Todd, who had been killed by the Joker, captured the Joker and was able to wipe the smile off his face with the following comments: "But I know a secret. A good one. You're not nearly as crazy as you'd like us all to believe or even as crazy as you'd like to believe. It just makes it easier to justify every sick, monstrous thing you've ever done when you play the part of the mad clown."

Perhaps the Joker is right about the absurdity of the world, and maybe a Nietzschean-inspired "free play" of one's personality and memory would help humans adapt better to the world and help them embrace Camusian absurdity. But it is questionable whether the Joker himself has done this as much as he claims. There may indeed be a little madness in any attempt to create an order in the world and a sense of stability that people can survive in, but the Joker, through his destructive actions, seems to be getting even with the world. And if he is getting even, has he really embraced madness?

Conclusion

Despite the order and rationality that many may look for in the world, the Joker calls these desires into question in *The Killing Joke* and, indeed, through many instances of his representation(s) across various media. Does the Joker's rejection of reason and stability bring him closer into step with the way reality truly "is"? While some, like Batman, may cling to ideas of order and try to make sense of the world, the Joker, through his unique lens, provides readers with another possibility – perhaps the world is irredeemably absurd. Perhaps looking for an underlying "way of being," rationale, or sense of inherent purpose is a mistake, and maybe all attempts to find those things are worth nothing more than a laugh. (And so: "Why so serious?")

While the Joker claims to embrace absurdity and does so in pathological and harmful ways for others, there exists the possibility that there is a non-pathological means of embracing his insights. Maybe a person does not need to lock themselves into one way of living life, but is able to embrace the playfulness of life and can reinvent themselves. In an ever-changing and absurd world, maybe we all could benefit from a little irrational playfulness.

References

Begley, Chris. 2013. Grant Morrison: Batman kills Joker in the Killing Joke. *Batman News*, August 16, https://batman-news.com/2013/08/16/grant-morrison-batman-kills-joker-in-the-killing-joke/

Camus, Albert. 1983. *The Myth of Sisyphus*. Translated by Justin O'Brien. New York: Vintage Books.

Collura, Scott. 2012. The Dark Knight: Heath Ledger talks Joker. *IGN*. https://www.ign.com/articles/2006/11/08/the-dark-knight-heath-ledger-talks-joker, (Updated) May 16, (Posted November 07, 2006).

Darius, Julian. 2012. *And the universe so big: Understanding Batman: The killing joke*. Edwardsville: Sequart Organization.

Foucault, Michel. 1988. *Madness and civilization: A history of insanity in the age of reason*. Translated by Richard Howard. New York: Vintage House.

Johns, Geoff, and Jason Fabok. 2018. *Justice league: The Darkseid war*. New York: DC Comics.

———. 2020. *Batman: Three jokers*. New York: DC Comics.

Johnston, Rich. 2013. When Brian Bolland revealed what happened between Batman and the Joker – and the full killing joke script. *Bleeding Cool*, August 17, https://bleedingcool.com/comics/when-brian-bolland-revealed-what-happened-between-batman-and-the-joker-and-the-full-killing-joke-script-alan-moore/

Mendelson, Scott. 2016. 'Batman: The Killing Joke' review: The controversial comic is now a terrible movie. *Forbes*, July 27, https://www.forbes.com/sites/scottmendelson/2016/07/27/batman-the-killing-joke-review-the-controversial-comic-is-now-a-terrible-movie/?sh=7845eeec29a3

Moore, Alan. 2022. *Goodreads*. https://www.goodreads.com/questions/572895-hi-alan-how-are-you-to-be-totally. Accessed Dec 21.

Moore, Alan, and Brian Bolland. 1988. *The killing joke*. New York: DC Comics.

Morrison, Grant, and Dave McKean. 1989. *Arkham asylum: A serious house on a serious Earth*. New York: DC Comics.

Nietzsche, Friedrich. 1974. *Gay science: With a prelude in rhymes and an appendix of songs*. Translated by Walter Kaufmann. New York: Vintage Books.

———. 2005. Ecce Homo: How to become what you are. In *The anti-christ, ecce homo, twilight of the idols, and other writings*. Ed. by Aaron Ridley. Trans. by Judith Norman. New York: Cambridge University Press.

Polo, Susana. 2018. The Batman comics that inspired the Dark Knight's hyper-realism: Holy world-building, Batman! *Polygon*, July 17, https://www.polygon.com/comics/2018/7/17/17564454/batman-comics-that-inspired-christopher-nolan-dark-knight

Wilbur, Brock. 2016. Alan Moore has a lot to say about 'The Killing Joke'. *Inverse*, April 28, https://www.inverse.com/article/14967-alan-moore-now-believes-the-killing-joke-was-melodramatic-not-interesting

Zalben, Alex. 2013. Batman didn't kill the Joker in 'The Killing Joke,' pretty much 100% confirms Alan Moore's script. *MTV*, August 22, https://www.mtv.com/news/vbuxr6/the-killing-joke-batman-didnt-kill-the-joker

From Hell as Philosophy: Ripping Through Structural Violence

90

James Rocha and Mona Rocha

Contents

Introduction 2004
Welcome to Whitechapel 2006
Structural Violence and Patriarchy 2007
Sensationalized and Routine: Varieties of Violence 2011
The Corruption of Moral Relations 2014
Hell as the Contemporary Workplace 2018
Conclusion: The Future the Ripper Delivered 2022
References 2023

Abstract

Deep beneath the Jack the Ripper story, Alan Moore and Eddie Campbell use *From Hell* to argue for a philosophical thesis: Although physical violence and structural violence are quite different, they are also interconnected as each causes the other to worsen. William Gull claims that through the Ripper murders, he has "delivered" the twentieth century, as seen in his premonition of the mundane office place. In other words, Gull believes that the Ripper murders somehow played a foundational role in creating twentieth-century life. This premonition suggests that horrific murders like those of the Ripper make structural violence, such as that found in the contemporary office place through wrongs such as sexual harassment, recede into the background of society where it becomes invisible and taken for granted. As Gull sees his violence as particularly

---

J. Rocha (✉)
California State University, Fresno, CA, USA
e-mail: jamesr@mail.fresnostate.edu; jamesr@csufresno.edu

M. Rocha
Clovis Community College, Clovis, CA, USA
e-mail: mona.rocha@cloviscollege.edu

© Springer Nature Switzerland AG 2024
D. K. Johnson et al. (eds.), *The Palgrave Handbook of Popular Culture as Philosophy*,
https://doi.org/10.1007/978-3-031-24685-2_93

connected to his misogynist worldview, *From Hell* makes the clearest case for the connection between physical violence and structural violence through the problem of patriarchy.

Keywords

Structural violence · Patriarchy · Feminism · Violence

Introduction

Jack the Ripper, who killed at least five women in London in 1888, may have been the first serial killer in modern history, but we do not normally think of Jack the Ripper as laying key historical foundations for the twentieth century. Yet, as we will see shortly, Alan Moore and Eddie Campbell, in their graphic novel *From Hell*, suggest this very point, which will raise philosophical issues about the relationship of physical violence and structural violence.

Well over a century after the horrific Ripper murders, we still do not know who Jack the Ripper was, but there have been numerous theories on his identity. In building their fictional account, Moore and Campbell curiously chose to use a discredited theory from Stephen Knight (1976). According to Knight, and also in Moore and Campbell's fictional version, four women blackmailed Queen Victoria and the royal family. The royal family then tasked the Queen's physician, Sir William Gull, with killing the four women, which he did – along with a fifth woman due to a mistaken identity – making him Jack the Ripper.

After Gull murders his last victim in *From Hell*, he has a bizarre vision of the twentieth century that does not otherwise fit within the graphic novel (Moore and Campbell 2020, Chapter 10, pp. 20–23). What is significant is not just that the vision is of the future, but also that the vision is so mundane. Gull foresees an office place from the future, replete with all the visages of modern technology: computers, calculators, a photocopy machine, etc. And this premonition *horrifies* Gull. Gull's horror results from his understanding that the seemingly boring vision indicates that his murders will bring about the "armageddon" of the dull office space, which Gull describes as "indifferent … disinterested [and] 'lustless'" (Moore and Campbell 2020, Chapter 10, p. 22). As Gull portentously explains to his carriage driver, John Netley, "For better or worse, the twentieth century, I have delivered it" (Moore and Campbell 2020, Chapter 10, p. 33).

If the reader could not tell prior to this moment, this scene is a solid indicator that *From Hell* offers something that requires further analysis, critical reflection, and philosophical attention. The scene challenges readers to ask deep questions about the implied linkage between Jack the Ripper's horrendous murders in Victorian England and the apparent ordinariness of the contemporary office space. These seemingly disparate moments in history are connected through the union of structural violence and patriarchy. A society is plagued with structural violence when individuals are unjustly harmed by the mere arrangement of social structures – it is as if violence is constantly being perpetrated against some people just by virtue of how society is arranged.

As an example, consider all of the various pressures that challenge people experiencing homelessness from overcoming their plight. Let us consider just one of the many: the bias that employers have against hiring someone with large gaps in their resume. Some people may leave gaps on their resume because they are hiding something pernicious: Perhaps they wreaked havoc at a previous job. Such gaps can therefore make employers leery. But many other people may have gaps in their resumes for reasons that they cannot share without creating unfair biases. Suppose a person who formerly could not find housing (through no fault of their own, such as a former soldier who was dealing with PTSD) tries to rebuild their life, but the large gap on their resume keeps them from finding work. This person, who is trying their best, could fall back into homelessness, which shows that the social structures are arranged in ways that continue to harm people who have once fallen into significant bad luck.

Such structural violence occurs when an inequitable, hierarchical social system (such as is prevalent in either Victorian England or in many societies across the globe today) oppresses people in an inherently unjust fashion through social structures, which can include the way in which workplaces operate, the legal system functions, how society handles poverty, etc. While structural violence can include physical violence, there can be structural violence that involves unjust harms unrelated to physical violence, but these harms can often be similar to or even worse than harms from physical violence.

Both Jack the Ripper's terrifying physical ferocity and the seemingly safe respite of a lackluster workplace are locales where women are subjected to violence, though in different forms. With *From Hell*, Alan Moore and Eddie Campbell present a philosophical thesis that establishes the connection between overt physical violence against women and more hidden structural violence that makes up the reprehensible underbelly of the patriarchy. The general philosophical point of *From Hell* is that physical and structural violence are interconnected with each causing the other to worsen, which is noteworthy because physical violence is striking while structural violence retracts so deeply into the background of society that it becomes routine and invisible. The more specific claim is that Jack the Ripper's overt, horrendous violence against women is connected to the mundane violence of the standard office place. The structural violence that makes up Whitechapel in the Victorian Age makes possible the work of a serial killer insofar as the residents of Whitechapel have become conditioned to think of the violence of their society as inevitable and unavoidable, as if they even deserve it. Yet, while the terrifying violence of Jack the Ripper shocks law-abiding folks, it also makes these same individuals more inoculated to the structural violence that occurs not only all around the people in Whitechapel, but also that is embedded in the world all around us today. Structural violence, having receded into the background, remains potently dangerous as it manages to corrupt people into becoming morally worse agents themselves, which in turn leads to many of them committing more physical violence. Ultimately,

Whitechapel and the Ripper can be seen as symbolically enabling the structural violence found in the contemporary office place of today.

Consequently, when looking at *From Hell*, physical violence is clearly quite bad, but the graphic novel also shows how poverty and oppression not only lead to an increase in physical violence but can also be themselves a form of violence. Immediately after having the accurate vision of the future that horrifies him, William Gull attempts to rationalize his evil actions by explaining to the corpse of Mary Jane Kelly (also known as "Marie Kelly") that "You'd have all been dead in a year or 2 from liver failure, men, or childbirth. Dead. Forgotten" (Moore and Campbell 2020, Chapter 10, p. 23). In the scene, Gull is pointing out that because a marginalized woman's life was already so difficult in Victorian England, the social structures around her were begetting the same effects as those of real violence. While Gull is problematically trying to legitimize his act of murder, one must acknowledge that the harm he points out is still real.

The tragedy is that this structural violence remains a problem nowadays, even in seemingly mundane locations such as the ordinary office space. For instance, sexual harassment at work can serve as just such a form of structural violence. In one form of sexual harassment, the quid pro quo, someone either threatens another person on the job to obtain sex acts (a person is told they will be fired or demoted if they do not sleep with their boss) or makes a work offer that is conditioned on receiving sex acts (a person is told they will only be hired or promoted if they sleep with their boss). In both cases, people are forced to make sexual choices to protect or improve their jobs, and so the sexual harassment infringes on their feelings of privacy, autonomy, and bodily integrity. Sexual harassment unjustly harms workers, often without any physical violence, and perhaps without any other coworkers even noticing the significant harms. Thus, sexual harassment exhibits structural violence in the workplace.

Alan Moore and Eddie Campbell use *From Hell* to explore the various connections between physical and structural violence, especially as these play out within patriarchy. Ultimately, physical violence, including horrendous murders, provides the gruesome surface of a violent social structure that is inherent to the patriarchy in sexist and misogynistic societies. To see how they do so, it will be helpful to begin with a quick summary of the story.

Welcome to Whitechapel

Alan Moore and Eddie Campbell's *From Hell* revolves around the love affair of Royal Prince Albert with Annie Crook, a poor woman from London. The scandalous and unauthorized love affair – and unlikely marriage – results in a child; as Queen Victoria discovers the affair, she breaks up the lovers and institutionalizes Annie, who did not even know her husband was a prince.

As Annie's friends discover the identity of her husband and child, they decide to blackmail the Queen, threatening to reveal Annie and Prince Albert's marriage (as it would be scandalous for the monarchy). Unfortunately for the blackmailers, the

Queen retaliates violently; taking advantage of the fact that Annie's friends are sex workers, the Queen employs royal physician and prominent Mason Sir William Gull to kill them. Aided by his carriage driver John Netley, Sir William Gull murders these women in Whitechapel, thus creating the lore of Jack the Ripper.

With each murder, Gull loses part of his humanity and his mind. Rationalizing his evil acts, Gull becomes convinced that he is part of a magical, mystical ceremony through which he is ensuring the domination of men over women in an imagined war of the sexes that Gull finds evidence for in the masonry and architecture spread throughout London. Yet, the horrific nature of his crimes eventually causes Gull to lose his grip on reality, causing him to hallucinate a greater connection between himself and the secrets of the universe. Just as he believes he has killed Mary Kelly, his final victim, Gull hallucinates that he has been transported into the future, which places him in the ordinary, twentieth-century office space that horrifies him.

As the police investigate the Ripper murders, Inspector Frederick Abberline stumbles on an alleged psychic informant that leads him to Gull as the culprit, but his superiors at Scotland Yard cover up the reveal. Instead of a public and legal trial, Gull ends up being institutionalized under a fake name after a secret Masonic trial. Prior to Gull's death, at the end of the graphic novel, he has a series of final hallucinations that show Gull future serial killers as well as a possible vision of one of his victims – Mary Kelly – who appears to have somehow escaped the Ripper's brutality.

Structural Violence and Patriarchy

Peace scholar Johan Galtung originally defined "structural violence" as the harm or violence that "is built into the structure and shows up as unequal power and consequently as unequal life chances" (Galtung 1969, p. 171). Hence, for Galtung, structural violence shows up when the social structures that make up society produce an unjust hierarchy of power that leads to people having different opportunities at creating meaningful lives. In other words, due to the specific arrangement of these social structures and/or institutions, some folks are made worse off and end up being marginalized in some fashion, unjustly leading to different life outcomes (Rocha and Rocha 2019, pp. 21–25; Sinha et al. 2017). To start with an easy example, imagine a society with a rigid class hierarchy where the laws prevent social mobility. Further, imagine that membership in a certain class completely determines what one can do with one's life (i.e., lawyers, doctors, management positions, government positions, etc., all come from one class, while work that is much more difficult and less rewarding comes from another class). The fact that one's life is predetermined to be positive or negative based on one's class counts as a kind of violence for Galtung because one is unjustly destined to remain in that lower position. Further, if one attempted to force one's way into a higher position, physical violence would be used to keep one out. Structural violence is upheld by forces, such as threats of physical violence, that enable the structures to continue existing and which intimidate individuals into going along with these structures (Rocha and Rocha 2019, p. 21).

Of course, in this example, the class hierarchy is rigid as law enforces it. In most democratic societies today, hierarchy is not so rigid and instead it is more abstract social structures that enforce the hierarchy through more invisible means. Social structures are the imagined combination of certain institutions or organizations, including the persons who make up those institutions. As a couple of major examples, the economy is the way in which banks, businesses, unions, workers, management, etc., come together to organize how money and commerce operate in a given society; the law is the social structure that involves the creation and the enforcement of the various regulations, which includes legal institutions in legislative bodies, courts, law firms, and more.

Structural violence can thereby exist in more subtle forms than a rigid hierarchy. Galtung noted that structural violence results in "Resources [that] are unevenly distributed, as when income distributions are heavily skewed, literacy/education unevenly distributed, medical services existent in some districts, and for some groups only, and so on. Above all, *the power to decide over the distribution of resources* is unevenly distributed" (Galtung 1969, p. 171). Thereby, the economy can create and maintain a class hierarchy where it is very difficult for the poor to compete, as their schools are worse, they have clothes that expose their class on job interviews, they cannot afford training that may be required for certain jobs, etc. And, of course, the result of this class hierarchy often involves both physical violence and more subtle forms of violence. That is because being poor involves living in more dangerous areas, but also because the chances for meaningful life options are reduced (but not totally eliminated as they are where the hierarchy is rigidly enforced), which Galtung points to as essentially violent as well.

This idea of resources being unevenly distributed so that some groups benefit while others suffer is further complicated by the idea of intersectionality. Coined by Kimberlé Crenshaw, intersectionality refers to how race, class, gender, sexual identity, ability, age, and other factors interlock with one another to affect an individual's life in a distinct fashion (Crenshaw 1991). As such, an individual might be oppressed due to poverty, racism, sexism, homophobia, transphobia, ageism, etc., based on their identity type. These oppressions are imbricated so that an individual might feel multiple effects. Thus, when looking at structural violence from an intersectional perspective, it emerges that the effects of structural violence will be felt in a variety of ways depending on one's complex identity type.

Consider, for instance, the various pressures on the women's lives in *From Hell*. A lot of the women portrayed in the text are poor and marginalized, and they experience pressures that would have been routine for sex workers of that era and unfortunately are not uncommon today. Inspector Frederick Abberline informs the readers about the horrible conditions that sex workers, and everyone else, must live under in Whitechapel when he is discussing things with Inspector George Godley. (Moore confirms that his depiction of these social conditions is based on his own research in Appendix I (pp. 21–22).) Abberline notes that there are 8500 people living in just 250 lodge houses, children can be seen having sex in the streets, and there are at least 1200 sex workers, though Abberline suspects it is much more. As Abberline states, "How do you maintain law and order in a fucking bedlam like this?" (Moore and Campbell 2020, Chapter 6, p. 22). Hence, these sex workers are forced to deal with poverty, intensely overcrowded and unhygienic conditions, the lack of protections for their children, and, of course, constant threats of physical violence, all while living in a world that devalues them for simply being poor and female.

A district in East London, Whitechapel was filled with a great number of destitute individuals, slums, crime, and poverty; it was this poverty that propelled many into sex work (Rumbelow 2004, p. 12); the depiction of it in *From Hell* is unfortunately accurate. Whitechapel hence provides a historical depiction of the structural violence inherent in the patriarchy. Scholars Parul Sinha, Uma Gupta, Jyotsna Singh, and Anand Srivastava note that, "Women are subject to 'structural violence' which results from sexism, rape, domestic violence, psychological violence, and other acts of violence resulting from the social structure" (Sinha et al. 2017, p. 134). In Whitechapel, that structural violence included physical violence from johns, the police, intimate partner violence, and much more. But it also included a violent substructure of society that no women in Whitechapel could escape. That substructure involves the ways in which sexism in general, and misogyny in particular, underwrites the social customs of society such that women have life chances cut off and are much more likely to struggle to even survive. It is not that Whitechapel's structural violence does not impact the men, but that men have somewhat more opportunities available to them as there are more job types available to them, even if these jobs may be quite difficult to obtain.

Let us take a moment to discuss life conditions for women in Victorian England. Due to their patriarchal society, women in Victorian England experienced various challenges in their lives, which oftentimes were exacerbated by class. Lacking the right to vote or hold property, women were legally viewed as their husbands' property (Bailey 2007). Even upper and middle class women were regarded as belonging in the domestic sphere, meaning that they were relegated to performing domestic labor, and were expected to take secondary, submissive roles to the males in their families. Upper class women were meant to manage their households and focus on child rearing, while middle class women, if employed, could work as governesses, teachers, or perform domestic labor within the household of rich women (Perkin 1993; Buckner 2006).

Lower class and working-class women were employed in precarious, low paying jobs, competing with male workers (who were paid a better wage). For example, in mining, women could be employed as hurriers (pushing and pulling coal carts along mine tunnels) until this type of employment for women was outlawed by the Mines and Collieries Act of 1842 (Davies 2006). Additionally, as various so-called protective labor laws were passed (labor laws that purportedly protected female workers in the workplace for their own good), factory work for women became harder to obtain (Oren 1996, pp. 328–330). Women were then relegated to textile mills, needle work at home, or matchbox making. These jobs paid very little, even though female workers were preferred for having more stamina and were seen as less combative than male workers (Perkin 1993, p. 191; Wise 2009). Having to make ends meet – especially if males within a family died or were unable to work – pushed women into other positions, such as hawkers of various goods on the street. With no guaranteed wage, and dependent on what could be sold within a given day, these jobs were inherently precarious (Wojtczak 2021).

The women of Whitechapel were suffering immensely from various causes, such as high rents combined with overcrowded conditions and scarcity of stable employment. Thus, high numbers of them were pressured into sex work. This point is not to judge sex work in general as men and women can freely choose sex work among various options (especially today). The women of Whitechapel were trapped within a social structure where they had few options other than sex work in a way that is both coercive and fails to free them of the various other harms that negatively impacted them. Hence, patriarchy as a form of structural violence trapped women and unjustly harmed them.

Feminist economist Heidi Hartmann defines patriarchy as hierarchal relations where men have solidarity with other men that allows them to control women. She concludes, "Patriarchy is thus the system of male oppression of women" (Hartmann 1976, p. 138, fn. 1). In other words, patriarchy is where men have a sense of shared interests in the oppression of women, which the men then fashion through their various everyday activities. For instance, Gull feels a sense of kinship with his driver Netley – an affinity that should feel very strange given their quite different classes and social groups in that time period. In actuality, men need not recognize their interests as shared; it is sufficient that they act as if they have shared interests by treating women worse just insofar as they are women. That often means cutting off meaningful life opportunities for women, which worsens women's lives – thus patriarchy becomes structural violence.

Patriarchy can work alongside capitalism to suppress women's lives; race and other identity types further complicate the picture. As law scholar Laura Oren explains it, the interplay of gender and class raises institutional barriers for women in the workplace, resulting in oppression and disparate impacts throughout history (Oren 1996). Oren explains that these impacts vary, from women not being hired for certain jobs, and women being paid less for the same jobs, to the creation of a male "breadwinner's wage" which rationalizes eliminating women workers, limiting their pay, etc. (Oren 1996, pp. 322, 330–331, 336). And, in Whitechapel, these types of actions lead women into sex work.

Patriarchy is a system through which women are oppressed, but it interconnects with other systems that likewise spread oppression. Furthermore, as with the idea of intersectionality above, interconnected identities can often create distinct oppressions at the intersection. Therefore, the women of Whitechapel had to deal not only with the patriarchy and with the oppression they faced through poverty, but also with the intersection of the two, which created a third kind of oppression that made it particularly hard to be an impoverished woman. The idea with intersectionality is that one cannot understand this intersectional oppression even if you fully understood the oppression faced by both richer women and poor men, as the women of Whitechapel faced horrors that would seem unimaginable for richer women and poor men. Significantly, this intersection of patriarchy and poverty coerced them into sex work, which exposed them to further physical violence.

Patriarchy and structural violence are not meant to overlap each other in a tight conceptual fashion. There can be forms of sexism that fit within the patriarchy, but do not seem to contribute to structural violence because they may harm women, but not in ways that impact their life chances. Similarly, there can be forms of structural violence that are not part of the patriarchy because they harm people regardless of their sex and gender, such as in a tyranny where everyone, save the tyrant, regularly lives with structural violence (even if the tyrant does not regularly engage in physical violence).

In *From Hell*, Alan Moore and Eddie Campbell provide a philosophical account of how the physical violence of misogynists can connect to the structural violence that women face under patriarchy. The next section explores how physical violence and structural violence differ in *From Hell* especially in the sense that Jack the Ripper's violence is sensationalized, whereas structural violence is largely invisible. Ultimately, the sensationalization of the Ripper's violence leads to the structural violence being taken even more for granted.

Sensationalized and Routine: Varieties of Violence

Structural violence exists within the basic structure of society in a fashion that creates unequal life chances for different individuals in unjustified ways. Structural violence recedes into the background from society insofar as it does not stand out as much as physical violence does. When someone has money stolen off their body through a physical attack, it is quite obvious to everyone who witnesses it how wrong it is. When someone has money taken from them through an unjust system of regressive taxation that targets the poor, most people barely notice as taxes are quite complicated and rarely explained. Structural violence is ubiquitous and yet invisible, which ultimately makes the problem of structural violence much worse.

On the other hand, physical violence can be so sensationalized that it appears to be almost celebrated. While most people rarely acknowledge this highly improper embrace of physical violence as if it were a socially implied vindication of the violence, society's fascination with it is rampant and especially strong when the physical violence is at its most intense and grotesque. Of course, this scenario is exactly how the Jack the Ripper murders play out. Perhaps the earliest sensationalized serial killer of the modern era, Jack the Ripper continues to stand out as a killer whose grisly crimes almost everyone is at least somewhat familiar with. Alan Moore and Eddie Campbell both take part in this sensationalism but also critique it in *From Hell*.

It is perhaps due to this need to critique our society's fascination with a serial killer from over a century ago that Alan Moore and Eddie Campbell chose to portray William Gull as the royal murderer. This point again brings to mind Stephen Knight's infamous and widely discredited story of the murders emanating from England's royal family (Knight 1976). Such a story cannot help but sensationalize the murders by adding an enticing twist through the royal connection. Further, *From*

Hell even brings in various aspects of the occult, freemasonry, history, and much more, interweaving them together to really draw in our attention – making the horrendous murders all the more thrilling.

Alan Moore and Eddie Campbell have provided an exciting tale, but that very excitement exposes how much more concern is raised about the suffering and deaths of others when they are connected to sensationalized physical violence. At the same time, Moore and Campbell work to subvert this sensationalism by regularly depicting the awful conditions of Whitechapel. Campbell's style is especially apt for this characterization as the art is far from lively, colorful, or rich, but is instead dark and even dreary. Even the drawings of sexual activities are not erotic but are instead almost depressing. For example, consider the art when Annie Chapman sexually services Edward Stanley (Moore and Campbell 2020, Chapter 7, pp. 9–10) or when Marie Kelly has intercourse with Joe Barnett, which leads to a huge fight between them (Moore and Campbell 2020, Chapter 9, pp. 38–39). In neither case does the art appear to be erotic or sensual, nor do the participants appear to be experiencing joy or pleasure. (Marie Kelly does appear to enjoy sex with a woman prior to sex with Joe, which emphasizes that the scene with Joe is purely transactional.) The images instead are muted, dark, and somber. This stark depiction portrays the sad reality that Kelly and Chapman experience as coerced sex workers who are routinely and violently objectified. It is important to note that sex work is not inherently problematic, especially when it is chosen freely, but it is likely that many of the sex workers in Whitechapel feel pressured into it. Here, it is as if the style of the comic communicates that the structural violence has robbed Kelly and Chapman not only of their life chances, but also of any pleasure or joy in the act of sex.

Further, the book regularly depicts both poverty and misogyny, two potent sources of structural violence, in manners that detract from the potential glorification of the killings. Consider Marie Kelly performing her job as a sex worker in the early pages of Chapter 3. Alan Moore explains that she does so in the backyard of No. 29 Hanbury Street, where Annie Chapman's body would later be discovered (Moore and Campbell 2020, Appendix I, p. 6). In this scene, Marie is performing a trick by not allowing the john to actually penetrate her but rather have the penis between her upper thighs to simulate penetration (Moore and Campbell 2020, Appendix I, p. 6). But this trick amounts to Marie risking her life to make a small amount of money, while in a dingy, dirty yard, risking exposure, and facing potential violence from her john. The scene ends with the john simply throwing the money on the ground. As such, the john disrespects Marie, having instrumentally objectified her; the entire setting exhibits the dreary nature of her work, and the ever-present underlying current of violence involved therein, as any given john could kill Marie on any given day.

Structural violence and misogyny are essential components of Marie Kelly's daily work. Even were she to escape any physical violence, which would have been unlikely, she would have constantly been dealing with the fear that things could go horribly wrong. Hence, she still would be coerced into taking this life path due to the lack of preferable options, and the men around her would constantly be exploiting her difficult situation and treating her in sexist fashions. Marie's daily life, even prior to the involvement of a serial killer, was essentially one based in patriarchy and structural violence.

Such structural violence would, of course, recede into the background when horrendous physical violence becomes newsworthy, which is what happens when Jack the Ripper became a public spectacle. The problem is that structural violence becomes no better off, and likely much worse off, when it becomes normalized. While their Victorian society appears completely uninterested in the plight of the women of Whitechapel prior to the Ripper murders, they are clearly entranced when the murders become a news item. Consider the beginning of Chapter 9 where Mitre Square is filled with spectators of all types after the double murder in one night of Elizabeth Stride and Catherine Eddowes. One man is depicted as profiting off the crowds gathering the day after the murders by selling souvenirs of other grisly murders from the past (Moore and Campbell 2020, Chapter 9, p. 1). Inspector Abberline responds to this by saying, "Four women get killed and it's like the start of a new industry! Only the start, mind you" (Moore and Campbell 2020, Chapter 9, p. 2). Of course, he is correct. Taking advantage of the double murders of these women, the seller sees his chance for profit; the women are thus exploited in life and death, once by structural violence and misogyny and then by structural violence and capitalism (also see Harris 2003).

The Ripper murders are bringing out audiences, with various people looking to profit, and even the funerals of the unfortunate victims become overcrowded spectacles. Consider the funeral of Mary Ann "Polly" Nichols as depicted in Chapter 6. Campbell has indeed drawn an incredibly large crowd in attendance. Further, Inspector Allison (who Moore explains is a fictional character, Moore and Campbell 2020, Appendix I, p. 21) says that, "You'd think there'd never been a Whitechapel woman cut up before, wouldn't you?" Abberline responds, "That's the newspapers trumping everything up" (Moore and Campbell 2020, Chapter 6, p. 20). This quick exchange points to the idea that the inspectors understand that, on the one hand, this kind of violence is typical for the women of Whitechapel, and yet, on the other hand, the newspapers' handling of the Ripper case has brought out a huge audience of onlookers for this particular violent streak. The murders have become sensationalized, and once again the victims are exploited, even in death.

Once structural violence becomes normalized, people stop caring about it. It is obviously important to sympathize with the victims of physical violence. But it is also necessary to sympathize with the various victims whose fate comes from forces the media fails to glamorize. While the fates of the victims of Jack the Ripper are horrifying, the fates of many other women of Whitechapel were quite terrible as well, but their names, their stories, and their suffering are almost entirely forgotten. Their plight is erased, and their appalling circumstances are rendered as normal, but these women deserve much better.

There are no audiences for the women whose deaths are routine, much less for the women who regularly face threats, internalize real fears, and live in ways that no one should have to endure. The violence of the Ripper pushes structural violence deeper into the background, where it is made invisible, but no less potent. Importantly, and at the same time, that structural violence is leading to the moral corruption of the people touched by it, which can lead to greater physical violence. This will be covered in the next section.

The Corruption of Moral Relations

The previous section examined how physical violence renders structural violence even more invisible, which allows it to have even more power since people do not work as much against what they do not see. This section covers how structural violence worsens physical violence by corrupting the moral relations between people. Once structural violence has receded into the background, people come to treat others as deserving of their fates, which leads to their moral corruption. In the case of patriarchy, this moral corruption occurs as men stop seeing women as fully worthy of respect. Alan Moore and Eddie Campbell depict the male characters as losing sight of the dignity of women, or as never having seen women's dignity in the first place. In this fashion, *From Hell* shows how both physical violence and structural violence lead to moral corruption, especially for men under patriarchy. This trend is exhibited by looking at the stories of the two main male characters, William Gull and Frederick Abberline.

The William Gull case is more straightforward as it should not be controversial to claim that engaging in actual physical violence both amounts to and increases moral corruption. William Gull starts out as a misogynist who is engaging in a Royal mission from the Queen, and through his evil actions, he eventually loses his mind. While he tries to rationalize his horrendous actions initially, they catch up to him as he completely loses touch with his own humanity.

Chapter 4 depicts Gull's original worldview as he gives his driver, John Netley, a tour of London. Gull sees a world in war: "Tis in the war of sun and moon that man steals woman's power; that left brain conquers right... that reason chains insanity" (Moore and Campbell 2020, Chapter 4, p. 21). The heroes, who are the protectors of rationality and science, are the men, while the villains are women, who represent the forces of "magic, art, and madness" (Moore and Campbell 2020, Chapter 4, p. 11). Gull's entire worldview is openly misogynist, with his entire point being driven by the need to remove "wretched women" in an alleged "great work" (Chapter 4, p. 6). Gull feels he must step in and perform his ritualistic killings because, in his twisted worldview, "man's triumph over woman's insecure, the dust of history not yet settled, changing times erase the pattern that constrains society's irrational female side" (Moore and Campbell 2020, Chapter 4, p. 29). So, Gull sees himself as a righteous warrior defending the patriarchy from women potentially securing a small victory over the powers that be. Gull's misogyny is not localized and limited to his personal world but is globalized and demands human sacrifice. Gull sees the patriarchy correctly – as systemized violence of both the physical and structural varieties that works to keep women disempowered with fewer meaningful life chances. Yet, Gull's accurate depiction of the patriarchy comes not with a moral need to rebel against and defeat it, but with an evil need to defend and champion it at all costs.

Gull's defense of the patriarchy ends up corrupting him and taking away his own sense of humanity until he loses his mind, ostensibly over his premonition of future office places. When Abberline and the fake psychic Robert Lees catch up to Gull, he immediately confesses but acknowledges that he lost grip with what was real after the killing in Miller's Court (Moore and Campbell 2020, Chapter 12, p. 12). The Miller's Court killing refers to Gull's murder of Marie Kelly, who was the final victim of Jack the Ripper. So, Gull acknowledges that once he killed Kelly and had his premonition, he lost grip on reality.

As Gull turns mad, his view of the world becomes much more artistic, such as in his mad wanderings through space and time where he envisions himself as becoming meaning, energy, wind, fire, etc. (Moore and Campbell 2020, Chapter 14, pp. 10–11). In fact, this delirious diatribe reveals that Gull sees himself as the tool that makes meaning out of the female spirit of the city and the instrument that renders patriarchal order over London, hunting down women and imposing a violent structural hierarchy upon them. Gull in fact looks down on the city of London and views it as the site of countless historical male wins and female losses, ranging as far back as the war of the Romans against Boadicea, the female leader of a Celtic uprising (Moore and Campbell 2020, Chapter 4, 8), or the disposal of female mother goddesses in favor of male gods (Moore and Campbell 2020, Chapter 4, 10, p. 25). Gull even sees the architecture of London as proclaiming a male world order: He proclaims an obelisk (Hawkmoor's Steeple) as the "symbol of man's ascendancy" (Moore and Campbell 2020, Chapter 4, p. 12) and derides that the poet William Blake rests in its shadow (because Gull believes Blake aligned with women in the war against men).

As previously mentioned, Gull claimed that women's side in the war was the side of "magic, art, and madness" (Moore and Campbell 2020, Chapter 4, p. 11), which Gull fully opposes, and which Blake endorsed. Yet, at the end of the book, in Chapter 14, it is Blake who sees Gull's ghost and casts Gull as a monster in his artistic rendering of him (Moore and Campbell 2020, Chapter 14, pp. 15–17). Moore, in his first appendix, tells us that he intends this artistic rendering to be Blake's *The Ghost of a Flea*, a real painting that depicts a reptilian monster, which in this case is Gull (Moore and Campbell 2020, Appendix I, p. 40). Blake, steeped in the female magic and art of the world, sees Gull for what he is *because* of that art and magic: Gull is a scaly monster bent on upholding the patriarchy. Importantly, the fact that Blake is able to perceive Gull when others cannot would also signify that the patriarchy is losing in Gull's imagined war.

In upholding himself as the embodiment of the patriarchy, Gull has, then, lost the war for his own soul and is rendered useless. Gull upheld a misogynistic dichotomy, where he aligned himself with the side of reason and manhood, which he viewed as opposed to womanhood, with its magic, art, and madness (Moore and Campbell 2020, Chapter 4, p. 11). In showing Gull's end, Moore makes it clear that this misguided dichotomy must be rejected, as feminist philosophers likewise reject Gull's binary of reason as male, emotions as female (Jaggar 1997). For it is in the end that Gull's demise at the hands of the feminine comes about – and the feminine is based on his own terms: Gull descends into violence and has yielded a ghost of himself (through magic), which then leads to him being memorialized in a painting as a monster (through art), and obviously he has gone mad (he associates madness with the right brain and women, see Chapter 4, p. 11). The feminine traits that he has vowed to suppress have overtaken and overpowered him, and he has failed in his task to win the war that "steals woman's power...where left brain conquers right... [and] reason chains insanity" (Moore and Campbell 2020, Chapter 4, p. 21). This point is especially clear in the moment of his final vision, which tellingly appears to be of the real Marie Kelly, whom readers are left to realize he never in fact killed (Moore and Campbell 2020, Chapter 14, p. 23; Moore himself decides to be cryptic and refuses to confirm this point at Appendix I, p. 40). In other words, Gull's warrantless killings did not arrive at the fulfillment of his wretched mission, leaving him not only mad and on the wrong side of his imagined gender war, but also completely unsuccessful.

Another main character who likewise cannot count himself as successful is Inspector Frederick Abberline. While Abberline's moral descent is not nearly as full as Gull's, it is also more insightful for us as it is based in structural violence. Of course, the details are familiar as Abberline spends the book investigating the Ripper murders, carrying with himself the certainty that the main leads the papers are trumpeting are false, and then ultimately learning who the killer is without any ability to bring Gull to justice in the official manner he is used to.

Beyond his direct investigation into the murder though, Abberline is consistently troubled by the structural violence around him, especially in Whitechapel. Abberline's frustrations with the Ripper killings appear to be genuine, but so are his frustrations with the way in which Whitechapel exists – that is, he accurately sees Whitechapel as a haven for structural violence in general and patriarchy in particular. Structural violence most assuredly frustrates and unnerves Abberline.

Consider the innocent connection Abberline develops with Emma in the East End bar (such as at Moore and Campbell 2020, Chapter 6, p. 24, Chapter 7, p. 36, Chapter 9, p. 23). The connection is presented as nonsexual and is instead one of the concerns where Abberline certainly does not wish anything bad to happen to Emma, who of course could 1 day be a victim of the Ripper. She most certainly however will be a victim of the harsh life that both the patriarchy and prevalent structural violence have carved out for women like her on the East End. It is a casual connection, but one that indicates that Abberline cares about the fate of these women in themselves and not just as a case to be solved or as routine work to be done.

Of course, as the case worsens and Abberline gets more sucked into the poverty and despair of Whitechapel, Emma leaves town – which surely is the best choice for her (Moore and Campbell 2020, Chapter 11, p. 14). Yet, Abberline immediately and unfairly lashes out at the very next sex worker who approaches him (Moore and Campbell 2020, Chapter 11, p. 15). What has happened here? Perhaps Abberline saw himself as potentially saving Emma and is upset that she has saved herself. His reaction is borne out of the patriarchy that sees women as lacking agency or initiative and relegates men to the roles of heroes. He was robbed of the chance of becoming her champion and lashes out at the very next woman. But there is also something more here: Abberline seems to realize that he cannot truly save Emma or the other sex worker from the full range of problems that face them. After all, the various women who suffered in Whitechapel suffer distinctly and deeply, whether directly from the Ripper or more generally from the structural violence and patriarchy that constituted their lives as women living in abject poverty. So, instead of facing this truth, Abberline begins to lash out at sex workers – he first feels impotent in abating their suffering, quickly becomes angry, and then ends up blaming them for their own fate and calling them demeaning slurs (Moore and Campbell 2020, Chapter 11, p. 15). Hence, in the flash forward to the future that starts *From Hell*, Moore and Campbell depict Abberline as a hateful misogynist. When Abberline and Lees happen across a sex worker having sex, who is in no way bothering them, Abberline explodes in a tirade of slurs and threatens the sex worker (Moore and Campbell 2020, Prologue, p. 6).

Moreover, Abberline provides an explanation for his drastic change, and he locates his reasoning in Whitechapel itself. Abberline tells his wife, "It's just Whitechapel" (Moore and Campbell 2020, Chapter 11, p. 37). He then walks her through the problem, asking her how he could possibly "threaten someone who's already living with the worst?" (Moore and Campbell 2020, Chapter 11, p. 37). He explains that they do not have morals or codes because "they can't afford them" (Moore and Campbell 2020, Chapter 11, p. 37). This lack, according to Abberline, is because they come from an earlier time, "an animal time," and there is something "in the squalor of 'em, something you can't look away from, and it's dangerous. It sucks you in" (Moore and Campbell 2020, Chapter 11, p. 37). Abberline notes that it is not that the people of Whitechapel are born without morality, but instead that "they can't afford" morality. This point is insightful as the burdens of morality would be much harsher, much less realistic for people whose lives are constantly under attack, whose attempt to find meaning for themselves is nearly hopeless due to their conditions, and who cannot help but to always put their survival first because doing so is absolutely necessary to actually survive. It is also important to note that from his privileged position, Abberline can afford to analyze these unfortunate individuals. In doing so, he also "others" them, that is, he treats them as if they were in some way different and worse than him, as if they were animals. In othering the people of Whitechapel, Abberline not only devalues their humanity, but also reifies the hierarchy of structural violence.

Let us return to Abberline saying that "the squalor of 'em, ... it's dangerous. It sucks you in" (Moore and Campbell 2020, Chapter 11, p. 37). On the one hand, Abberline correctly notices *the dangers* of structural violence, even though he lacks the theoretical terms to identify it as such and even though he does not attack structural violence as the problem, but rather its victims. On the other hand, the structural violence is getting to him as he sees the plight of the people as a threat to himself, which it certainly is, as evidenced by it leading to his own moral corruption. Abberline pathologizes the entirety of Whitechapel, and in doing so becomes a worse moral agent himself. He is seeing the people and their plight as dangerous because he cannot easily solve the problems that they face. He cannot simply lock up a few criminals and have the problems of Whitechapel go away. Instead, he fears that their suffering will become contagious, pass onto him, and cause him to become trapped within the very same structural violence they face.

Given this background, and his complete loss of hope to effect change, Abberline finds no way to help people like Emma, much less to successfully do his job. And this realization of his own hopelessness has eaten away at him and results in making him morally corrupt. He cuts off his feelings for others – especially his moral feelings – because Abberline realizes there is nothing he can do to help. Of course, this decision is not the right one – it cannot be since it is shutting down moral concern for the people who need it the most – but it is almost understandable when one sees how dire being fully immersed in structural violence can be. You give up. And that is, unfortunately, what the Ripper murders in particular, and the structural violence seen in Whitechapel in general, have delivered us in modern-day times.

Hell as the Contemporary Workplace

The problems of structural violence and the patriarchy are relevant today as they have receded into the background of contemporary life. And so, in a sense, Jack the Ripper has delivered the twentieth century just as Gull stated when he said, "For better or worse, the twentieth century, I have delivered it" (Moore and Campbell 2020, Chapter 10, p. 33). This line refers to the premonition that Gull experienced with his final murder of Marie Kelly – a vision of the future office workplace, which horrifies him. It does not horrify him due to some display of physical violence – though at times there is violence in the workplace, Gull does not see that aspect of the future. Instead, at least part of what horrifies Gull is the drudgery clearly experienced by the workers, in spite of the modern, technological advancement they enjoy all around them. Gull asks the workers, who can neither see nor speak to him, "Where comes this dullness in your eyes? How has your century numbed you so? Shall men be given marvels only when he is beyond all wonder?" (Moore and Campbell 2020, Chapter 10, p. 21). They do not answer but instead carry on with their dull tasks, in spite of the many marvels that surround them, such as the fantastic photocopy machine.

This section explores why the contemporary office place could be considered horrific, or even akin to hell. Anthropologist David Graeber makes this connection when he says, "Hell is a collection of individuals who are spending the bulk of their time working on a task they don't like and are not especially good at" (Graeber 2018, Preface). As will become clear, the office is where people feel trapped, lose their autonomy, and have their moral relations corrupted. In other words, the future that the Ripper has brought forth is one where mundane workplaces are the sites of structural violence.

Anarcha-feminist Emma Goldman posited, in the time period when Gull was alive, that institutions where folks do routine, nonproductive work are problematic since they rob individuals of their autonomy. Autonomy is the ideal met when someone lives according to their own standards. One of the results of structural violence is a hindering of autonomy because people lack meaningful options and cannot pursue the options that they would endorse if they were free to do so. Goldman wrote, "those who are placed in positions which demand the surrender of personality, which insist on strict conformity to definite political policies and opinions, must deteriorate, must become mechanical, must lose all capacity to give anything really vital" (Goldman 1996, p. 223). Such workers lose their freedom and are "dead souls" on arrival, trading their independence and autonomy in return for money and stability (Graeber 2018, Preface). Modern office workers still fit this pattern: Workers quietly conform to office policies and politics, giving up portions of their authentic selves to their jobs just by engaging in routine work. In other words, they are limited by the capitalist system that demands they pay their way to live.

Graeber continues the critique of the modern workplace, adding that most such jobs are bullshit jobs, which he defines as any job that is ultimately so pointless that even the person performing the job admits that their work accomplishes nothing (Graeber 2018, Preface). Graeber explains that our overreliance on office work on the fact that "the ruling class has figured out that a happy and productive population with free time on their hands is a mortal danger" (Graeber 2018, Preface). Folks are kept busy "working on a task they don't like and are not especially good at," in service of a paycheck and at the cost of giving up their creativity, autonomy, and free time (Graeber 2018, Preface). In other words, the modern workplace exchanges meaningful life options for repetitive, mind-numbing drudgery. The office place, as we know it today, is a site where structural violence has become completely normalized and taken for granted as if meaningful life options were a fantasy. It is this very drudgery in the face of scientific and technological advancement, which should have left us living lives full of meaning, that leads Gull to think that his terrifying physical violence has created a future where structural violence is not even feared, but is merely accepted.

Graeber also adds that this work structure – which we see as constitutive of structural violence – is stripping people of their moral worth: "in our society, there seems to be a general rule that, the more obviously one's work benefits other people, the less one is likely to be paid for it" (Graeber 2018, Preface). Graeber notes that this state of affairs is not questioned by society, but is rather seen as the correct, if not only, way of organizing labor. He worries that this complacency where "we have collectively acquiesced to our own enslavement" constitutes "a profound psychological violence" (Graeber 2018, Preface). Under this system, everyone becomes a worse moral agent, losing their authentic selves and learning to not challenge authority, resenting fellow workers or those with free time, and not reaching out to help others. In the same way that Abberline blames the unfortunate women of Whitechapel for their misery, Graeber explains that our reliance on the modern workplace has led us "to believe that men and women who do not work harder than they wish at jobs that they do not particularly enjoy are bad people unworthy of love, care, or assistance from their communities" (Graeber 2018, Preface). Just as Gull sees in the contemporary office place, people are not finding human connections with one another but are instead entirely alone even while working in a crowded office group. This contemporary system has taught individuals to prioritize bullshit jobs over helping fellow workers, making everyone worse moral agents in the process.

Within this bleak environment, where worker autonomy is subverted and actual contributions to society are discounted and underpaid, female workers additionally endure the harms that patriarchy brings onto them. As Goldman explains, female workers believe themselves freed of the shackles of the patriarchy (imagining that they escaped both the dictatorial mandates of sexist husbands and the social mores obliging them to a life of domestic labor), only to find themselves disillusioned within their work lives: "the emancipated woman runs away from a stifling home atmosphere, only to rush from employment bureau to the literary worker, and back again" (Goldman 1996, p. 225). Further, working women trade dependence on a husband for dependence on a boss, such as "the city editor, the publisher, or the theatrical manager" (Goldman 1996, p. 225). However, they do not find independence, merely the illusion of it, Goldman argues.

Likewise, Heidi Hartmann examines how the patriarchy works to exploit women's labor. Following up Goldman's train of thought, Hartmann explains, "In the labor market the dominant position of men was maintained by sex-ordered job segregation. Women's jobs were lower paid, considered less skilled, and often involved less exercise of authority or control" (Hartmann 1976, p. 152). As such, women in the workplace are kept economically dependent, are not truly empowered, but rather, are economically exploited.

While there is vast improvement from the time of Whitechapel to the present, the exploitation of working women continues, with access mostly denied to any meaningful life options beyond what society expects and even demands in menial employment. Sylvia Walby sums up this system of economic precarity masquerading as economic independence. She writes that:

> The key feature of patriarchal relations in paid work is that of closure of access by men against women. This involves the exclusion of women from paid work or the segregation of women within it. This leads to a devaluation of women's work and lower wages for women, which itself becomes a social fact with determinate effects, not only on women's paid work, but in other areas including the domestic sphere and other aspects of gender relations. (Walby 1989, pp. 222–223)

Another scholar explicates that, "Men earn more than women even when they are in the same general occupation" (Roscigno 2007, p. 58). In other words, the intersectional influence of patriarchy on capitalism devalues female workers in particular, from Whitechapel to the present day.

As Goldman further explains, within the marketplace, these female workers compete over positions with both one another and male workers and do so to their detriment: "Professional women crowd the offices, sit around for hours, grow weary and faint with the search for employment, and yet deceive themselves with the delusion that they are superior to the working girl [sex worker], or that they are economically independent" (Goldman 1996, p. 225). Not only does Goldman note that women are underpaid due to this competition – as males garner higher wages and the general competition results in lower wages overall for all workers – but she also notes the presence of a false sense of moral superiority in emancipated, professional women over female sex workers (Goldman 1996, p. 226). She notes that when the emancipated woman looks down on the working girl, thinking herself above the misery of the sex worker and as right in devaluing the sex worker, worker solidarity is splintered.

This treatment is akin to Abberline's othering of the sex workers in Whitechapel. Abberline eventually felt as if their plight was of their own making; he ended up pathologizing their condition and not getting involved to help them. Goldman's observation of the self-imposed superiority of the emancipated female worker over the sex worker parallels Abberline's moral decay. Goldman notes that instead of forming an alliance to fight for better working conditions for all, the problem of workers being treated poorly is allowed to continue, as workers are pitted against each other, thereby enabling the structural oppression – and its inherent violence – to remain unchallenged.

The patriarchy is firmly entrenched in the workplace, and the arrangement is so common that it is not really challenged. Patriarchal attitudes in the workplace continue to result in the undervaluing of women's labor, creating challenges for women to find meaning in their work lives and thus showing the impact of structural violence (Adisa et al. 2019, p. 28). In fact, women workers report feeling stressed, intimidated, and even become disinterested in their jobs as a result of working with domineering, patriarchal male bosses (Adisa et al. 2020, pp. 153–157). Additionally, women in leadership positions find themselves challenged by sexist, patriarchal male workers (Adisa et al. 2020, p. 158). For instance, women in leadership experience the common scenario where men "are reluctant to follow instructions because the instructions are coming from a woman. This always causes friction..." (Adisa et al. 2020, p. 154). Under the patriarchy, the work environment becomes toxic for women, bringing about a systematic subjugation of women that William Gull would likely approve of.

One way patriarchy populates office spaces is in the forms of sexual harassment and gender harassment. Sexual harassment has two main forms: quid pro quos (where work performance is connected illicitly and illegally to sex acts) and hostile work environments (where work is sexualized even though the job does not require any sexualization). Gender harassment can be just as intolerable but is less recognized as problematic. Gender harassment occurs when someone is treated worse just because of their gender, regardless of any connection to sexuality.

These two kinds of harassment create an underlying structural violence that leaves some women under very direct and constant threats from their supervisors and sometimes other coworkers. Their workplaces are sexualized in ways that undercut their ability to work free of worry. Their gender is put on display as misogynists and other sexists use it to diminish their accomplishments and skills. Even women who do not face active sexual or gender harassment work under a reasonable fear of it since it is so ubiquitous throughout society (Bergman et al. 2002; Fitzgerald and Cortina 2018; Bongiorno et al. 2019).

Let us remember that Gull not only noted with horror the drudgery of the modern office place in his vision, but he also was dismayed that the alleged sexuality he saw in women's workplace appearances was being ignored; this is implied when he says, "your own flesh is made meaningless to you" (Moore and Campbell 2020, Chapter 10, p. 22). Here, we see Gull's misogyny in action as he only sees his premonition from the perspective of the male gaze (Mulvey 1989). Gull, in this instance, is not the distanced viewer, but he himself still contributes to the patriarchy as a ghost. He simply cannot leave his misogyny behind. While Gull is wrong to think women's workplace appearances are ignored (given how sexual harassers respond to their appearances just as Gull does), his horror is warranted at least in the sense that he points to the structural violence that is redolent in the office place, especially as it impacts women within the patriarchy. In many ways, Gull's vision of bringing about the contemporary office is truly a nightmare, especially for the female workers that are routinely devalued or objectified within it.

Conclusion: The Future the Ripper Delivered

Moore and Campbell use *From Hell* to exhibit a philosophical analysis of the interconnectedness of physical violence and structural violence, especially under patriarchy. The physical violence of the Ripper murders is made possible by the ubiquitous structural violence that makes up Whitechapel of the Victorian Age. It is because poverty is rampant, women are pressured into sex work, life opportunities are extremely limited, etc., that the Ripper can seem to operate with impunity; even though the Ripper's violence is new and surprising, it also is not entirely beyond the spectrum of what is ordinary in Whitechapel.

Yet, at the same time, the Ripper's violence pushes the structural violence more into the background as the extremeness of the former makes the latter seem less bothersome, especially to the onlookers from far away – comfortable in their distance and comparative opulence and shielded by privilege. And as this structural violence recedes into the background, it becomes more potent as less people even think of doing anything about it – any concerns they have dissipate as they simply do not wish to even think about how bad it is, what should be done, how they are complicit in it, etc. The structural violence appears to pale in comparison with the awful murders of the Ripper, but this makes it much worse since almost no one appears to be doing anything about it – and those who are trying to fight structural violence feel alone and helpless.

And, in this way, physical and structural violence lead to a moral degradation of the various people who are touched by it, which is ultimately all of us. Gull loses his mind after all the horrendous crimes he takes part in, but Abberline also slowly gives up on helping as he finds no hope of success. And these problems are exacerbated by the patriarchy. Gull's misogyny allows him to see himself as better and above the women whom he condemns to death, but this morally bankrupt path leads him to lose his humanity insofar as he no longer respects the dignity and absolute worth of other humans. Abberline attempts to feel for the women he is helping but eventually ends up seeing them as distinct from him, far from him, and less deserving of his help. In this way, Abberline too loses grip on his own humanity.

Gull's fears of the drudgery of the contemporary workplace are quite noteworthy. This drudgery shows how far the structural violence has come, and it is fair to connect it to the extreme physical violence of the past. *From Hell* shows that there is a connection between the two: Structural violence morally corrupts people, which can turn them to physical violence, and physical violence allows structural violence to recede into the background, where it becomes normalized and accepted. This is precisely what has happened in Gull's premonition. With viewers seeing so much physical violence on the news, just as it was so sensationally displayed during the Ripper murders, they have lost touch with the ways in which they lost opportunities for joyful and meaningful lives as they give into the routine drudgery of their day jobs. The repetitive motions, the inability to find pleasure in the advances of modern technology, and the lack of genuinely friendly contact with coworkers all show how major life opportunities can systematically diminish. And, according to *From Hell*, this contemporary and gendered structural violence was brought to us by Jack the Ripper.

References

Adisa, Toyin Ajibade, Issa Abdulraheem, and Sulu-Babaita Isiaka. 2019. Patriarchal hegemony: Investigating the impact of patriarchy on women's work-life balance. *Career Development International* 34 (1): 19–33.

Adisa, Toyin Ajibade, Fang Lee Cooke, and Vanessa Iwowo. 2020. Mind your attitude: The impact of patriarchy on women's workplace behavior. *Career Development International* 25 (2): 146–164.

Bailey, Joanne. 2007. English marital violence in litigation, literature, and the press. *Women's History* 19 (4): 144–154.

Bergman, M.E., R.D. Langhout, P.A. Palmieri, L.M. Cortina, and L.F. Fitzgerald. 2002. The (un)reasonableness of reporting: Antecedents and consequences of reporting sexual harassment. *Journal of Applied Psychology* 87: 230–242.

Bongiorno, Renata, Chloe Langbroek, Paul G. Bain, Michelle Ting, and Michelle K. Ryan. 2019. Why women are blamed for being sexually harassed: The effects of empathy for female victims and male perpetrators. *Psychology of Women Quarterly* 44 (1): 11–27.

Buckner, Philip. 2006. *Rediscovering the British world*. Calgary: Calgary University Press.

Crenshaw, Kimberlé. 1991. Mapping the margins: Intersectionality, identity politics, and violence against women of color. *Stanford Law Review* 43 (6): 1241–1299.

Davies, Alan. 2006. *The pit brow women of the Wigan Coalfield*. London: Tempus Books.

Fitzgerald, L.F., and L.M. Cortina. 2018. Sexual harassment in work organizations: A view from the 21st century. In *APA handbook of the psychology of women: Perspectives on women's public and private lives*, ed. C.B. Travis, J.W. White, A. Rutheford, W.S. Williams, S.L. Cook, and K.F. Wyche. Washington, DC: American Psychological Association.

Galtung, Johan. 1969. Violence, peace, and peace research. *Journal of Peace Research* 6 (3): 167–191.

Goldman, Emma. 1996. Intellectual proletarians. In *Red Emma speaks: An Emma Goldman reader*, ed. Alix Kates Shulman. Amherst: Humanity Books.

Graeber, David. 2018. *Bullshit jobs: A theory*. New York: Simon & Schuster. Kindle Edition.

Harris, Alice Kessler. 2003. *Out to work*. Oxford, UK: Oxford University Press.

Hartmann, Heidi. 1976. Capitalism, patriarchy, and job segregation by sex. *Signs* 1 (3): 137–169.

Jaggar, Alison. 1997. Love and knowledge: Emotion in feminist epistemology. In *Feminisms*, ed. Sandra Kemp and Judith Squires, 188–193. Oxford, UK: Oxford University Press.

Knight, Stephen. 1976. *Jack the ripper: The final solution*. Chicago: Academy Chicago Publishers.
Moore, Alan, and Eddie Campbell. 2020. *From hell*. San Diego: Top Shelf Productions.
Mulvey, Laura. 1989. Visual pleasure and narrative cinema. In *Visual and other pleasures*. London: Palgrave Macmillan.
Oren, Laura. 1996. Protection, patriarchy, and capitalism: The politics and theory of gender-specific regulation in the workplace. *UCLA Women's Law Journal* 6 (2): 321–373.
Perkin, Joan. 1993. *Victorian women*. London: John Murray Publishers.
Rocha, James, and Mona Rocha. 2019. *Joss Whedon, anarchist? A unified theory of the films and television series*. Jefferson: McFarland Press.
Roscigno, Vincent J. 2007. *The face of discrimination: How race and gender impact home and work lives*. Lanham: Rowman & Littlefield.
Rumbelow, Donald. 2004. *The complete Jack the ripper*. London: Penguin.
Sinha, Parul, Uma Gupta, Jyotsna Singh, and Anand Srivastava. 2017. Structural violence on women: An impediment to women empowerment. *Indian Journal of Community Medicine* 42: 134–137.
Walby, Sylvia. 1989. Theorizing patriarchy. *Sociology* 23 (2): 213–234.
Wise, Sarah. 2009. *The blackest streets: The life and death of a Victorian slum*. London: Vintage Books.
Wojtczak, Helena. 2021. Women of the lower working class. *The Victorian web: Literature, history, and culture in the age of Victoria*. www.victorianweb.org. Accessed 26 June 2021.

Deadpool's Killogy as Philosophy: The Metaphysics of a Homicidal Journey Through Possible Worlds

91

Tuomas W. Manninen

Contents

Introduction	2026
Synopsis	2027
Deadpool's Master Plan Analyzed	2029
Deadpool as an Anti-Sisyphean Hero	2030
Possible Worlds, Transworld Identities, and Counterparts	2031
The Ontological Status of Possible Worlds	2034
Traversing the Possible Worlds	2035
Fictional Entities as Artifacts	2036
(Dead)Pooling It All Together	2039
Concluding Remarks	2040
References	2042

Abstract

What if the Merc with a Mouth was sent to a psychiatric institution with the intent of helping him, but what came out was something even more disturbing? This is the basic plotline of *Deadpool Kills the Marvel Universe* where Deadpool, well, kills all the characters who make up the Marvel Universe in order to save them from a fate worse than death. Under the gory surface of this story are substantive philosophical questions about the nature of reality, the place we inhabit in it, and the meaning of our seemingly absurd existence. This chapter explores the nature of possibility and the arguments for cashing out the notion of alternate realities in terms of possible worlds.

T. W. Manninen (✉)
Arizona State University, Glendale, AZ, USA
e-mail: tuomas.manninen@asu.edu

Keywords

Deadpool · Marvel Universe · Multiverse · Possible worlds · David Lewis · Genuine modal realism · Ersatz realism · Transworld identity · Counterpart theory · Artifact theory of fiction · Albert Camus · Absurd · Continuity

Introduction

> Don't take it as a matter of course, but as a remarkable fact, that pictures and fictitious narratives give us pleasure, occupy our minds. ("Don't take it as a matter of course" means: find it surprising, as you do some things which disturb you...).
> —Ludwig Wittgenstein (*Philosophical Investigations*, §524)

Scripted by Cullen Bunn, Deadpool's *Killogy* is a trilogy consisting of the graphic novels *Deadpool Kills the Marvel Universe* (Bunn et al. 2012; hereafter DKMU), *Deadpool Killustrated* (Bunn and Lolli 2013; hereafter DK), and *Deadpool Kills Deadpool* (Bunn and Espin 2015; hereafter DKD). The series is situated in an alternate reality from the Marvel Universe – a fact which is capitalized on by the plot of the novels. The *Killogy* can be viewed as a "What if..." story centered on the title question: What if Deadpool killed everyone who makes up the Marvel Universe? The question of why Deadpool would do such a thing requires some attention, and here we will enlist the philosopher Albert Camus and his writings on the Absurd for assistance. Deadpool does not just snap because he loses a loved one (which is the premise of *Punisher Kills the Marvel Universe*). Instead, Deadpool comes to view his own existence – and that of his fellow Marvel heroes and villains – as a comic book character to be absurd, and he wants to liberate everyone from the binds of this continuity by killing them off.

Philosophically speaking, the most substantial question in *Killogy* comes from contemplating the nature of the alternate realities. Deadpool's murderous rampage against the Marvel heroes and villains is not just limited to the actual world: using the Nexus of All Realities, Deadpool wrecks carnage across multiple realities. But how are we to understand the alternate realities and the nature of possibility? Are the alternate realities just parallel universes that are part of a multiverse? Or are they possible worlds, complete with inhabitants who are counterparts of the individuals in the actual world? Although the story in *Killogy* seems to leave this question open, it provides fertile grounds for further exploration. This chapter will present an argument – supported by considerations in the graphic novels – that these alternate realities are best understood to be (what David Lewis called) possible worlds. Using Lewis's theory, called genuine modal realism, I will describe the story of the *Killogy* in the most coherent and consistent manner. But in order to understand the argument for possible worlds, we first need to trace Deadpool's journey through the alternate realities.

Synopsis

In *Deadpool Kills the Marvel Universe*, Deadpool is involuntarily admitted to the Ravencroft Asylum by Professor Xavier, who admits defeat in trying to help Deadpool. Dr. Benjamin Brighton promises to take care of Deadpool, touting his track record in helping other unfortunate souls, even if through unorthodox methods. In reality, Dr. Brighton is the villain Psycho-Man in disguise, and his goal is to recruit Deadpool into his army by brainwashing him. Deadpool resists the attempt which ultimately fails. As a result, Deadpool stops hearing the usual voices in his head – the serious voice and the comic voice – and starts hearing an evil voice instead. This voice goads Deadpool to kill Psycho-Man, which he does in a gruesome manner. The voice then continues: "You've been waiting for me. You've killed one of them... Finish the job" (DKMU). As Deadpool escapes the asylum, he kills the orderlies and sets the place on fire – with the other inmates still locked in their cells. Deadpool does not end his reign of carnage after he escapes, however. Instead, he attacks and kills the Fantastic Four, as well as the Watcher who was narrating the events in the background.

Deadpool continues his murder spree, targeting superheroes and supervillains alike. Some of his victims are killed off-page, only receiving a passing mention of their fate, while others are dispatched in graphic detail. Deadpool's usual banter has taken a more serious tone, and his comments leave many of his victims baffled. All along, Deadpool is revealing bits and pieces of his grand plan – sometimes talking just to corpses. "I'm sorry they don't understand. They always thought I was crazy...but they never realized I saw the world the way it really is. ... They never realized they were puppets, made to dance and love and die and suffer ... just like me" (DKMU). Evil Voice responds to this lamentation just by saying "You're doing them mercy." In his exchange with Professor Xavier, Deadpool states, "So what if I break the fourth wall? It's the fourth wall that's been breaking me... crushing me... crushing each and every one of us... for as long as we've been in existence" (DKMU). In what seems to be a final duel, between Deadpool and Taskmaster, we get a more thorough explanation: "All the senseless deaths... The resurrections only to be killed again... the freak mutations... the cosmic rays... the chemical disasters... the unrequited loves... the secret wars... the secret invasions... the hero's journey is about pain." Deadpool continues, "Don't you get it? We're puppets! And Geppetto's feeding us through the wood-chipper for &#$%# and giggles! I can save us all from this endless cycle of continuity!" (DKMU). Deadpool kills Taskmaster with the help of Man-Thing, the guardian of the Nexus of All Realities. After Man-Thing sacrifices himself, the Nexus opens and Deadpool steps right in. "I thought I could just... y'know... stab creation in the heart or something..." he muses, as he sees the vastness of his task (DKMU). His goal to kill off all superheroes in order to save them is limited to each world: Killing of the Avengers in *this* world does not affect the Avengers who exist in all the *other* worlds – contrary to what Deadpool might have thought. Ultimately, Deadpool navigates the Nexus to reach a world of the comic book authors who created *Deadpool Kills the Marvel Universe*, and in a cliffhanger ending, he sets on them with his characteristic homicidal glee.

After killing all the Marvel heroes and villains in one world, Deadpool moves on with his murderous task and kills the heroes in multiple realities. *Deadpool Killustrated* opens with a frame showing him sitting in the Baxter Building, surrounded by corpses of the heroes; for many heroes, there are several versions of them. Deadpool laments how all the killing has not brought about the desired effect – it has not ended the Continuity: "I kill and I kill and I kill... but it's never enough. There's always another Spider-Man, another Captain America, another Ms. Marvel... I wonder... you think after everything I've done, they'd let me die?" (DK). Deadpool turns to what he calls Plan B: He has formed a think tank composed of all the Marvel scientists who are exploring ways to help Deadpool in his task. Mad Thinker explains a strategy: "We've developed some new theories using your belief that we are all fictional nonentities as a starting point... We are ... designed... by this progenitor species that controls every aspect of our lives for their own voyeuristic amusement. We are trapped in... the continuity, an endless cycle of conflict and victory, death and resurrection" (DK). Mad Thinker continues:

> You can try to scare the progenitors out of their hiding places, but they'll only write more obstacles into your path. And reality has built-in defense mechanisms. It adapts. No two versions of a single entity can be killed in the same way. You've trapped yourself into an interminable cycle of hunting and killing. But we've discovered a fissure. A hidden metaverse. And it is our belief that the nonentities that exist therein represent earlier works of fiction. The classics if you will. ... The "characters" in this Ideaverse in all likelihood served as the inspirational building blocks for the heroes and villains you seek to destroy. (DK)

And Evil Voice completes the thought: "...and if we kill the inspiration, the 'heroes' cease to exist" (DK).

Deadpool uses the Nexus to travel to the Ideaverse with the intent of killing all the characters he encounters. He jumps around times and places in the Ideaverse, leaving carnage behind. As he encounters (and kills) classic literary characters, he is able to see which Marvel hero or villain they inspired: Pinocchio inspired Vision; the characters of *Little Women* inspired Black Widow, Mockingbird, She-Hulk, and Elektra; the headless horseman inspired Ghost Rider and the Green Goblin; and so on. Facing significant resistance from the classic characters, Deadpool decides to interfere with Dr. Frankenstein's experiment, giving part of his own brain to the monster. As a result, Evil Voice becomes incarnate and assists Deadpool in his rampage. Unbeknown to Deadpool, the scientists led by Mad Thinker were able to send messages to the Ideaverse; one of these is intercepted by Sherlock Holmes who assembles a group of heroes to help him stop Deadpool. Holmes's group – using H. G. Wells' time machine – intercepts Deadpool in Paris in 1627. In the final duel between Holmes and Deadpool, Deadpool is cast adrift in the dimension.

Deadpool Kills Deadpool begins with the revelation that the Deadpool who perpetrated all the killings across the possible worlds and who hears Evil Voice is not from the actual Marvel Universe timeline (Earth-616), but from another world altogether. Having survived in the Ideaverse, Deadpool comes to think that he – and by proxy, all Deadpools – is a progenitor to the universes they inhabit. Deadpool's new goal is to eradicate all Deadpools whatsoever from existence, and he takes control of the Evil Deadpool Corps to achieve the goal. The real Deadpool (from Earth-616) sides with the Deadpool Corps, whose members include Lady Deadpool, Pandapool, Dogpool, and a Watcher who has taken interest in all things Deadpool. Ultimately, only Deadpool-616 and Deadpool are left, and in their final battle, Deadpool-616 convinces Deadpool that killing heroes is not the only way to set them free. Deadpool-616 decapitates Deadpool as revenge for killing all his friends, pours universal acid on the corpse to prevent it from regenerating, and walks away as the sole survivor.

Deadpool's Master Plan Analyzed

Having regularly broken the fourth wall to interact with the audience, Deadpool had formulated the thought that he – and all the heroes alike – existed as a fictional character on the pages of a comic book. This existence was burdened by the Continuity, and it is best understood as the continuous narrative that sometimes calls for the hero to die and then to be resurrected. Examples abound – and Deadpool is aware of all these. Deadpool plans to provide release from the continuity to all the heroes – by mercy killing them. At this stage, his thinking seems to presuppose two things: One, the spin-offs/alternate storylines seemingly take place in different realities. And two, the heroes he kills bear an identity relation to heroes in those different realities. That is to say, putting a bullet through Spider-Man's head not only kills Spider-Man in this reality, but it also kills the other versions that occupy different realities.

When Deadpool enters the Nexus of All Realities, he realizes that his second assumption was flawed: Killing the heroes and villains in one world did nothing to the other versions of the heroes and villains. He sees glimpses of worlds where different possibilities have been actualized – all of them involving Deadpool. This realization pushes him to think that there are creators – progenitors, as he calls them – who are responsible for bringing about the heroes and villains. "Finding the centerpoint of existence is no easy task. Even the progenitors of *our* universe may be nothing more than the playthings for other entities" (DKMU). The volume concludes by Deadpool seeming to think that to rid the world of the creation, he needs to kill the progenitors.

In *Deadpool Killustrated*, Deadpool reflects on some newfound problems. His thinking that he can kill the Marvel heroes for good has come to naught; well, it resulted in a big pile of corpses, but still – the final goal eludes him. Killing Iron Man in one reality leaves plenty of counterparts of Iron Man alive in other realities. And Deadpool has been unsuccessful in pursuing the progenitors, who would only write more obstacles to Deadpool, should he get too close to them. But Mad Thinker presents him with the theory of the Ideaverse, a universe populated by classic literary characters, who have served as inspiration to the Marvel heroes and villains. Should Deadpool be successful in eliminating these characters – in destroying the Ideaverse – the inspiration for the Marvel characters would vanish, and so would the characters themselves. Here, Deadpool and Mad Thinker are invoking a version of the artifact theory of fiction, which holds that fictional entities are dependent entities. The dependencies involve the authors: Without Stan Lee, there would be no Marvel heroes or villains; without Cullen Bunn, there would be no Deadpool who kills the Marvel heroes and villains. The artifact theory can also go a long way in explaining the multiple versions of the same character: Each author who adds to the story of, say, Spider-Man starts with a copy of the original character and develops it to their liking. This avoids the problem of inconsistencies, at the cost of establishing new possible worlds. Deadpool's plan to attack the authors was thwarted, so he decides to go after the inspiration the authors had from the classic literary characters.

Deadpool as an Anti-Sisyphean Hero

"There is but one truly serious philosophical problem," Albert Camus wrote, "and that is suicide. Judging whether life is or is not worth living amounts to answering the fundamental question of philosophy" (Camus 1955). For Camus, life is absurd, and he inquires after how exactly one should respond to such absurdity: "Does its absurdity require one to escape it through hope or suicide—this is what must be clarified, hunted down, and elucidated while brushing aside all the rest" (Camus 1955). For Deadpool, the option of suicide is foreclosed due to his ability to regenerate. As he muses in *Deadpool Killustrated*, while putting a gun to his temple and pulling the trigger: "I wonder... you think ... after everything I've done... they'd let me die" (DK). But yet again, Deadpool recovers from his suicide attempt. His plan to deal with the rest of the Marvel Universe heroes and villains can be traced to the question that Camus posed. For Deadpool, the Continuity stands in as a proxy for the Absurd: Continuity is the requirement that the heroes survive all the events where the odds are against them; even after death, they come back: "It's more likely you'll heal... or be cloned... or go into some sort of larval state until you can emerge again, stronger than before... or be raised through black magic...or" Deadpool rattles off the common ways in which Marvel characters have cheated almost certain death.

To illustrate the absurdity of life, and how individuals can find escape through hope, Camus revisits the story of Sisyphus. Condemned for his crimes against the gods, Sisyphus spends eternity rolling a boulder up a hill. Once the boulder reaches the apex, it rolls down, and Sisyphus's task begins anew. For Camus, Sisyphus is an absurd hero: "His scorn of the gods, his hatred of death, and his passion for life won him that unspeakable penalty in which the whole being is exerted toward accomplishing nothing" (Camus 1955). Focusing on Sisyphus's self-reflective journey from the top of the mountain to the bottom between the tasks, Camus argues that there is enough for Sisyphus to find meaning in his existence: "The struggle itself toward the heights is enough to fill a man's heart" (Camus 1955).

Here, Deadpool takes a markedly different approach to the absurd. His goal is to free all the fellow heroes (and villains, too) from the torments of the Continuity, and he sets to accomplish his goal the way he knows best – through homicidal rage. In terms of the myth, Deadpool does not just reject the task of endlessly rolling the boulder up a hill – he engages in terraforming, attempting to wipe out both the boulder and the hill alike.

Possible Worlds, Transworld Identities, and Counterparts

That the *Killogy* takes place in multiple alternate realities seems to be given. But how exactly are we to understand the alternate realities? One way to cash out the notion would be to invoke the structure of possible worlds. The talk about possible worlds may strike one as counterintuitive at first: Surely, there is only one world – the actual world – and to talk about other worlds as existing seems overkill, even if this notion is designed to help solve philosophical problems. However, as Michael Loux (2006) argues, possible world metaphysics is just a formalized notion of something with which we are already familiar in our prephilosophical intuitions.

> We all believe that things could have been otherwise. We believe, that is, that the way things actually are is just one of many different ways things could be. But not only do we believe that there are many different ways things could be; we take the different ways things could be to constitute the truth makers for our prephilosophical modal beliefs. (Loux, p. 159)

Moreover, the readers of Marvel comics have long been acquainted with the notion of different possibilities. Take the *What if...?* series. These stories are set in the Marvel Comics multiverse, depicting how events could have been otherwise; the inaugural issue, published back in 1977, considers what if Spider-Man had joined the Fantastic Four. So there is no great departure from commonplace intuitions or the Marvel Multiverse to the discussion of possible worlds. Loux continues:

> The idea that a proposition, p, is necessary just in case for any possible world, W, p is true in W is simply a formalization of the belief that a proposition is true no matter what; and the idea that a proposition, p, is possible just in case there is a possible world, W, such that p is true in W is nothing more than a rigorous expression of the belief that this or that could have been the case provided there is a way things could have been such that had they been that way, this or that would have been the case. (Loux, p. 159)

Possible worlds, in brief, are representations of different states of affairs. The worlds are causally and spatiotemporally closed, "two individuals are parts of the same world if and only if (iff) they stand in some spatiotemporal relation to one another" (Divers 2009, p. 336). (Here, the fact that, in the *Killogy*, Deadpool freely travels from one world to another is set aside for the moment.) When it comes to the actual world, and how the states of affairs actually are, "actual" is used as an indexical term indicating that actuality is judged with respect to each world: "from the standpoint of any other world, that world is actual and our world is non-actual" (Divers 2009, p. 336).

But what about the entities that populate the different possible worlds? Let us first investigate the question from Deadpool's perspective, assuming that the world in which he begins his murderous rampage is the actual world. The denizens of each possible world are concrete particulars. (Here, I am glossing over some substantial debates in contemporary metaphysics just to get to my point; for an in-depth introduction of what concrete particulars are, see Loux 2006, Chap. 3.) Initially, Deadpool seems to have assumed that the Marvel heroes he sets to kill in the actual world are identical with the heroes in other possible worlds, so killing them in the actual world would spell their demise in other worlds. Put slightly differently, killing the Marvel heroes in the actual world releases them from the Continuity, which means that all the possible worlds in which they continue on further adventures would become impossible worlds.

For Deadpool's assumption to be true, it would have to be the case that entities in one possible world are identical with entities in another possible worlds. In a word, what is needed is a robust notion of transworld identity. But in order to cash this notion out, one needs to get clear on the nature of possible worlds. One popular view about possible worlds is presented by Alvin Plantinga (1974), who advocates for possible world actualism. On Plantinga's view, all possible worlds exist – as abstract entities composed of states of affairs. Michael Loux characterizes Plantinga's position as follows:

> Every state of affairs is a necessary being. Accordingly, every state of affairs exists, exists in the actual world; but some states of affairs fail to obtain. What Plantinga proposes is that possible worlds, all of them, are just states of affairs of a certain kind. Since all states of affairs are necessary beings, all the possible worlds actually exist; they are all among the contents of the actual world. Not all of the possible worlds, however, obtain. Only one among them does—this world, the actual world; and its being actual is just its obtaining. (Loux, 176; see also Plantinga 1979, pp. 257–258)

Against this backdrop of possible worlds, the notion of transworld identity can be spelled out thusly:

> To say that I exist in possible worlds other than this world is just to say that there are possible worlds other than the actual world which are such that had any of them been actual, I would have existed. It is merely to make a counterfactual claim. (Loux, p. 182)

In light of this, consider the Watcher's musings in the beginning of *Deadpool Kills the Marvel Universe*:

> In some worlds, the Psycho-Man would successfully build his army of villains. In some worlds, heroes aligned against his forces and cast them down. In others, Psycho-Man seized dominion of the Earth. But here—in this reality—the machinations of the would-be conqueror awakened a killer... (DKMU)

We find a strikingly similar (and a bit more technical) characterization of Plantinga's actualism here:

> States of affairs are conceived as unstructured entities (no parts or members): a world represents that Socrates is a carpenter, or it is true at a world that Socrates is a carpenter, when the world includes the state of affairs of *Socrates' being a carpenter*. Some such states of affairs are possible (could have obtained) like *Socrates' being a carpenter*; some are impossible (could not have obtained) like *Socrates' being a number*, and among the possible states of affairs some are actualized (do obtain) like *Socrates' being a philosopher.* (Divers, p. 339)

All the possible worlds described in this passage are states of affairs which exist, but only one of them – the last one – obtains. This amounts to saying that each of the states of affairs could have been made to obtain, but only one of them did obtain. Going back to the Watcher's example, the world in which Deadpool becomes a member in Psycho-Man's army is different from the world in which Deadpool becomes a killer, and so on, for all different possibilities. Yet, it is the same Deadpool in all these scenarios.

In light of this, Deadpool's master plan becomes easy to see: By killing the heroes (and villains alike), Deadpool aims to bring about the state of affairs where "X is dead" obtains (for *all* values of X), thereby effectively precluding all possible worlds where X does something different than dying from obtaining.

But there are two reasons for doubting that this view – Plantinga's actualism about possible worlds – can be used to make sense of the story in the *Killogy*.

For one, the view itself suffers from certain philosophical shortcomings, like the problem of representation: It does not provide us with a mechanism that allows distinct possibilities to be represented as distinct. The worry can be stated thusly:

> [The] problem of transworld identification concerns how we know that an individual is (say) Adam rather than Noah. After all, we cannot rely on identifying Adam by looking for an individual who is represented by having all of Adam's actual properties, for the point of the postulation of other worlds is precisely to represent Adam as he could have been otherwise. (Divers, p. 342)

For this reason, David Lewis calls this "magical ersatzism": either the system has "insufficient power to represent, or else sufficient power by means of unwelcome ontology" (Lewis 1986, p. 174).

The second worry is that Plantinga's actualism cannot fully make sense of the story; elements of the story contradict it. Consider the end of *Deadpool Kills the Marvel Universe*, as Deadpool closes in on his goal and enters the Nexus of All Realities. His master plan comes to a grinding halt because he realizes that different possible worlds, along with their inhabitants, actually exist in a concrete way. He thought that killing a hero in one world would end their existence, but all the heroes he has already killed are alive in all these other worlds. This revelation not only contradicts Plantinga's assumption of transworld identity – if Spider-Man was numerally identical to his counterpart in another possible world, killing him in one world would kill the other – but it also shows that, contrary to what Plantinga suggests, other possible worlds do obtain. They are real. By the end, Deadpool has a pile of corpses (containing multiple versions of the same hero) to show that Plantinga's assumptions are false.

The Ontological Status of Possible Worlds

Thus far, the discussion on possible worlds has assumed that the different possible worlds actually exist as abstract entities (states of affairs) which do not obtain in actuality. But Deadpool's realization in the Nexus seems to render the possible worlds concrete. The Plantingan actualism described above cannot account for this – but another theory can. In the philosophical literature, this theory is the position advocated by David Lewis, called genuine modal realism: "The possible worlds (like our universe) are concrete individuals, and the possible individuals are parts of those worlds" (Divers, p. 336). As a payoff for committing to the existence of possible worlds, Lewis argues, we gain an explanatory advantage on possible states of affairs: "If we want the theoretical benefits that talk of *possibilia* brings, the most straightforward way to gain honest title to them is to accept such talk as the literal truth" (Lewis 1986, p. 4). Lewis articulates how the kinds of explanation include conceptual analyses, ontological identifications, and a semantic theory (Divers, p. 337; for details, see Lewis 1986, chapters 1.2 through 1.5).

Somewhat cautiously, Lewis acknowledges that the theoretical benefits to be reaped from accepting the existence of possible worlds may be a deal not worth the ontological cost, for the benefits could be had more cheaply; these views he dubs ersatz modal realism. Needless to say, there are plenty of detractors from his genuine modal realism, Plantinga being among them. What the ersatz theorist hopes is to achieve two goals over Lewis's realism: "the ersatzer hopes his theory will be ontologically a lot cheaper than Lewis's and a whole load easier to believe in" (Melia 2008, p. 136). The parsimonious approach to possible worlds and possibilia can be traced back to Ockham's famous dictum, *do not multiply entities beyond what is necessary*. Thus, if the ersatz theory (which is committed just to the existence of states of affairs) can flesh out the possible worlds, then one ought to opt for the ersatz theory. But Ockham's razor seems to cut against the ersatzist theory here – the ersatz theory cannot account for the possible worlds as concrete entities. Therefore, the principle of parsimony as stated supports adopting the more ontologically costly theory: Because the simple theory does not deliver, one is free to consider a more ontologically costly theory that does deliver.

But even if we accept Lewis's theory and consider the possible worlds as concrete entities, this is not the end to the problems. Rather, one faces the problem with isolation. Each possible world is isolated from each other possible world; Lewis is emphatic on this point: "There are no spatiotemporal relations across the boundary between one world and another" (1986, p. 71). Addressing this problem will have to wait, because if we adopt genuine modal realism and reject ersatz realism, we also need to relinquish the transworld identity. After all, individuals in other possible worlds are not identical to individuals in the actual world, just by virtue of being in different worlds. But surely they bear some relationship to the individuals in the actual world. This relationship between possible world denizens, according to David Lewis, is the counterpart relation, which is similar to the identity relation:

> To say that something here in our actual world is such that it might have done so-and-so is not to say that there is a possible world in which that thing *itself* does so-and-so, but that there is a world in which a *counterpart* of that thing does so-and-so. To say that I am such that I might have been a Republican, but I am not such that I might have been a cockatrice, is to say that in some world I have a counterpart who is a Republican, but in no world do I have a counterpart who is a cockatrice. That is plausible enough, for the counterpart relation is a relation of similarity. (Lewis 1971, p. 205)

Lewis goes on to note how the counterpart relation "serves as a substitute for identity between things in different worlds" (1971, p. 206). The reason for this becomes clear when we consider the identity relation, which is transitive and symmetric; in contrast, the counterpart relation is neither of these. Thus, the counterpart relation allows us to make claims about the various similarities and dissimilarities between a thing (or a person) and its counterpart that identity relation would not allow us to make.

The counterpart relation allows us to cash out Deadpool's rampage across the different possible worlds (granting his ability to traverse different possible worlds) in the following: The gruesome gallery of his kills we see in the opening pages of *Deadpool Killustrated* depicts a pile of Spider-Man corpses. Each of these deceased Spider-Men comes from a different possible world, and they are not identical with one another; they are – or were – counterparts of one another. As Deadpool laments, as many Spider-Men as he has killed, there still remain more counterparts of Spider-Man, in worlds that he has yet to visit.

From Deadpool's perspective – given how he can traverse the different possible worlds, either through magic or comic book logic – the best alternative seems to be to embrace a Lewis-style genuine modal realism and treat the possible worlds as concrete entities. Otherwise, it would be exceedingly difficult to make sense of Deadpool's actions – or the pile of corpses he has amassed in his makeshift headquarters in the Baxter Building: The counterparts of Marvel heroes he killed in the other possible worlds are real persons – not linguistic constructs or states of affairs. This is, essentially, Lewis's pragmatic argument again: It is a serviceable hypothesis, and, as such, this gives us a reason to think it is true.

Traversing the Possible Worlds

Yet, the very possibility of Deadpool's actions – especially traversing to other possible worlds and killing individuals there – militates against some deeply held convictions about possible worlds. On Lewis's analysis of a world, two individuals are worldmates if and only if they are spatiotemporally related to one another. Moreover, he allows for transworld comparisons (employing counterparts) but not transworld spatiotemporal relations: Different possible worlds are isolated from one another. Yet somehow, *per impossibile*, Deadpool manages to have spatiotemporal relations to individuals in other worlds, making his victims to be his worldmates. Instead of glossing this over as mere comic book logic, there is a principled way to respond to this objection. Lewis states that "a world might consist of two or more completely disconnected spacetimes" (Lewis 1986, p. 71). Practically speaking, this would allow Deadpool's actions: The Nexus of All Realities does not connect different genuine possible worlds, but it connects otherwise disconnected spacetimes (that is, universes), which all are yet part of the Nexus. Thus, Lewis says the following:

> I cannot give you disconnected spacetimes within a single world; but I can give you some passable substitutes. One big world, spatiotemporally interrelated, might have many different world-like parts. These are not complete worlds, but they could seem to be. They might be four-dimensional; they might have no boundaries; there might be little or no causal interaction between them. Indeed, each of these world-like parts of one big world might be a duplicate of some genuinely complete world. (Lewis 1986, p. 72)

Here, a new worry arises. If the apparent possible worlds through which Deadpool traverses are not genuine possible worlds, then why bring the apparatus of possible world ontology even to bear on this issue? It appears that the ontological cost of possible world talk does not yield any genuine benefits when it comes to understanding the story in the *Killogy*; moreover, the very notion of possible worlds would be overkill.

This worry persists for Deadpool's actions off the page. Between the first and second installments of the trilogy – that is, between *DKMU* and *DK* – he continues his rampage against the Marvel heroes and populates his makeshift trophy room in the Baxter Building, and for these actions, the world-like parts are seemingly adequate. But as the story continues in *DK*, we see Deadpool entering the Ideaverse to go after the literary characters who inspired the creation of the Marvel heroes and villains. And it is these characters that are better viewed as inhabiting their own concrete possible world. Thus, to account for this part of Deadpool's murderous odyssey, the need for concrete possible worlds returns with a vengeance.

Fictional Entities as Artifacts

Thus far, the discussion has treated Deadpool as if he were an actual person living in the actual world. But besides Deadpool's frequent forays into the real world through his breaking the fourth wall, he yet remains a fictional character whose existence is confined to the pages of comic books. Fictional entities pose an intriguing philosophical problem in that they both exist (at least as characters in literature and in film), yet they do not exist (as entities in the real world).

This problem has garnered plenty of attention from philosophers for the past century or so. Bertrand Russell eschewed the existence of fictional characters on the grounds that their names do not denote anything in the real world. Alexius Meinong, in contrast, held that while fictional objects do not exist either in space-time (as concrete objects do) or outside of it (as ideal abstract entities do) they still subsist. One could be tempted to treat this problem as a pseudoproblem and scuttle fictional entities from existence entirely, save for the fact that we frequently make truth-claims about them. Even worse, we make *true* truth-claims about fictional entities, both within the stories (e.g., it is a fact that Deadpool's name is Wade Wilson) and mixing them with the real world (e.g., it is a fact that Deadpool is a Marvel character created by Fabian Nicieza and Rob Liefeld, or that Deadpool is portrayed in film by Ryan Reynolds). In short, we make all sorts of *true* claims about fictional characters – but if these characters do not exist, what are the truthbearers for all these claims?

Instead of going over the gamut of ontological theories of fictional entities (especially since Hanley 2009 does a great job at this), this section will hone in on one particular theory, namely, the artifact theory of fiction to contrast it with David Lewis's genuine modal realism. Both of these are considered versions of Quinean actualism, but the two diverge from one another in that Lewis considers fictional characters to be concrete, while the artifact theory takes them to be abstract (Hanley, p. 362).

Although one could try to employ Lewis's genuine modal realism for dealing with fictional creations (which is what Lewis himself does, in Lewis 1978), especially since the rest of the *Killogy* seems to presuppose (a version of) this theory, there are some problems with it. As noted above, we want to make truth-claims about fiction (e.g., it is true that Deadpool kills Spider-Man by shooting him in the head, and that it is false that Deadpool kills Spider-Man by decapitating him with a sword), and here Lewis's theory shines by allowing us to make such claims. The truth-maker for the above claim about Spider-Man is, in the world inhabited by Deadpool and Spider-Man, the fact that their duel does end with a bullet lodged in Spider-Man's head. But we also want to make heterogeneous statements – statements which are about fictional characters qua characters, such as "Wolverine's popularity has allowed his character to return from the dead numerous times" or "The character of the Headless Horseman in *The Legend of Sleepy Hollow* was inspiration for Marvel's The Green Goblin" – and here, Lewis's theory runs into problems.

The biggest problem Lewis's theory has with heterogeneous statements about fiction is that his offered analysis is not equipped to handle them at all; Lewis admits as much and passes the heterogeneous statements over in silence (Lewis 1978, p. 38). So clearly, a different theory is needed. While Lewis's view considers fictional characters to be as concrete as the worlds that they inhabit, there is an alternative view: to treat them as abstract entities. But if fictional characters are abstracta, what kind of abstracta are they? Amie Thomasson's answer to this question is that they are abstract *artifacts*:

> According to the Artifactual Theory of fiction, characters are abstract artifacts: created objects dependent on such entities as authors and stories. While they are abstract in the sense that they lack spatio-temporal location, it must be emphasized that fictional characters under this conception differ importantly from abstract entities considered as ideal, necessary,

independent entities as they so often are .... On this view, fictional characters are not necessary entities, but instead are created, *dependent* abstracta. (Thomasson 1996, pp. 301–302)

Per Thomasson's argument, the fictional characters are contingent artifacts in that they depend on their creators for their existence and their features: "indeed they can come into existence only through conscious acts of an author and exist for the first time when first they are created" (1996, p. 302). Their dependence on the author is rigid in nature: Only Stan Lee could have created the Marvel characters that he did. After the creative act of the author, the fictional characters can continue to exist without any further acts by the author; for the fictional characters to persist, "some story about [them] must remain in existence" (1996, p. 303). Thomasson notes that the mere existence of stories is inadequate to guarantee the continued existence of fictional characters: There also need to be conscious beings who can competently read the story (1996, p. 305). This dependence, however, is generic in nature; there does not have to be any specific competent reader, but any competent reader will do. (For more on the nature of the dependencies, see Thomasson 1999, pp. 35–38.)

The reason why this section focuses on the artifact theory of fiction is obvious if we revisit the storyline in the *Killogy*, as Deadpool's master plan to rid the universe of the Marvel heroes initially involves going after the creators of the Marvel characters. As Thomasson notes, "Lucky for us, the residents of Southsea were unusually healthy. For if Arthur Conan Doyle's medical practice had been busier, Sherlock Holmes might have never been created" (1996, p. 296). Thus, if Conan Doyle had never had the chance to start writing his detective stories, the character Sherlock Holmes would never had been created. Here, it bears repeating that the character of Sherlock Holmes is rigidly dependent on Conan Doyle being the author; generalizing the point, much of the Marvel Universe's characters owe their existence to Stan Lee, and so on. According to the artifact theory, the fictional characters are abstract entities, but they are unlike some other abstract entities – like numbers, or states of affairs. The latter types exist in all possible worlds, that is, they exist necessarily. But because the fictional characters depend for their existence on their creators, these characters exist only in those possible worlds where their creators exist. Moreover, they exist in those worlds where their creators did not have an alternative career plan that precluded them from their creative work (Thomasson 1999, pp. 38–40).

But back to the master plan: In *Deadpool Killustrated*, Deadpool has discovered it to be too difficult to go after the creators of the Marvel heroes themselves. As the Mad Scientist advises Deadpool, "You can try to scare the progenitors out of their hiding places... but they'll only write more obstacles into your path" (DK). Here, Deadpool takes the path of least resistance: Instead of eliminating the authors, Deadpool decides to kill off the sources of the creators' inspiration, the archetypes. In brief, had Stan Lee never been exposed to classic literature, chances are that he would not have come up with many of the Marvel characters he did; without knowing about Norse mythology, chances that Stan Lee would have created the character of Thor are minuscule at best. Here, Deadpool is intent on ensuring that Stan Lee will never get acquainted with the classics by eliminating them.

How successful was Deadpool's master plan? In *Deadpool Killustrated*, he successfully eliminates Don Quixote, the crews of both *Nautilus* and *Pequod*, Tom Sawyer, Dracula, the Headless Horseman, the four March sisters, and many others. Yet at the end, he is left stranded in the vortexes of the Ideaverse after struggling with Sherlock Holmes. Holmes, being made privy of Deadpool's plans, tries to stop his plan of carnage and save the characters. After seemingly defeating Deadpool, Holmes takes on not the role of the creator of the characters (after all, the characters are rigidly dependent on their original creator) but that of a competent reader of their stories.

(Dead)Pooling It All Together

At this juncture, it becomes apparent that there is a tension between the theories that have been presented for accounting for Deadpool's exploits in the *Killogy*. On one hand, the possible worlds command for a Lewisian genuine modal realism – or a comparable theory – which would render them concrete. On the other hand, there is the artifact theory of fiction which regards fictional characters (like those in the Ideaverse) as dependent abstract entities. Lest the overall theory becomes inconsistent, one of these elements needs to be adjusted to accommodate the other.

Here, it appears that the most prudent choice is to tweak the artifact theory of fiction, and allow that the characters that populate the Ideaverse start of as abstracta dependent on their respective authors, but that the Ideaverse is a concrete place with concrete denizens. Thus, all the creations by Alcott, Twain, Stoker, Melville, Conan Doyle, and many others exist as concreta; Deadpool's excursion to the Ideaverse, which started off with him getting lanced through the chest by Don Quixote, serves as a point in favor of this contention.

But if the common response to Lewisian genuine modal realism has mostly been incredulous stares, the above contention is bound to receive even more perplexed gazes (Bricker 2008, p. 130). It would seem that there needs to be more said in favor of genuine modal realism than merely doubling down on the theory because it is needed to make the story work. Luckily, arguments abound which support the Lewisian project. The first is the truthmaker argument, based on the truthmaker principle: "for every (positive) truth, there exists something that makes it true, some entity whose existence entails that truth" (Bricker 2008, p. 120). For example, the (true) statement "David Lewis was an eminent American philosopher" has David Lewis as the truthmaker. For modal truths, such as "Deadpool's real name is Wade Wilson," albeit there is no actual truthmaker, there is a possible truthmaker, the fictional character of Deadpool himself, and what is said of them in the fictional story. But this argument alone does not support the view that possible entities are concrete entities, or that possible worlds are concrete worlds akin to the actual world; "perhaps abstract possibilia can meet the demand for truthmakers" after all (Bricker 2008, p. 120). So, although the truthmaker argument can provide further support to the thesis that possible worlds are concrete worlds, this support is far from being conclusive.

Further support for the claim that possible worlds are concrete may be found in considerations of intentionality which, "in the relevant philosophical sense, refers to a feature of certain mental states such as belief and desire' one doesn't *just* believe or desire, one always believes or desires *something*" (Bricker 2008, p. 121). Thus, there seems to be a foundation for concrete possibilia after all: "concrete possibilia are needed to provide the objects of our intentional states, to provide ontological framework for the content of our thought" (2008, p. 121). But again, the foundation is far from being secure: The object of my thought may be just a possible object that does not actually exist. With this in mind, Bricker says:

> Suppose, for example, that I am now thinking about a dodecahedron made of solid gold. I can do this, of course, whether or not any such object actually exists. If there is, unbeknownst to me, an actual gold dodecahedron, then I am related to it in virtue of being in my current intentional state; it is an object of my thought. But what if there is no actual gold dodecahedron? Does that somehow prevent me from thinking about one? Of course not. (2008, p. 121)

Moreover, if concrete existence were a prerequisite for intentional objects, then we would be in dire need of a new account of creativity: Instead of creating new fictional characters – such as Lady Deadpool, or Dogpool, or Motorpool, and so on for the entire cast of *Deadpool Kills Deadpool* – we would be in a position where our creative thoughts do not actually create anything, but they merely link to previously existing objects. Hence, on this account, the artifactual theory of fictional characters would have to be scuttled.

So the question "Why believe in a plurality of worlds?" with which David Lewis began at the outset of his *On the Plurality of Worlds* refuses to go down. The above considerations aside, we seem to be left just with Lewis's initial answer – that the hypothesis is serviceable, which gives a reason to think it is true. Notice, however, that Lewis did not say that this reason was conclusive – which it may not be, because of the ontological cost it commands; the benefits achieved through this hypothesis just may not be worth the costs. But here, Phillip Bricker cautions us that Lewis's claim (that a hypothesis is true if serviceable) is even more precarious than it first seems. After all, it is a rational insight, but a fallible one – so even this foundation turns to be shaky.

Concluding Remarks

In the foregoing, Lewis's argument was explored in the context of Deadpool's *Killogy* with admittedly mixed results. Initially, it appeared that Plantingan (ersatz) realism about possible worlds along with a robust notion of transworld identity was all that was needed to make sense of the story as it initially unfolded. Yet, shortly after Deadpool entered the Nexus of All Realities, it appeared that the story could not be cashed out without resorting to an ontologically more costly theory of genuine modal realism (together with the counterpart theory) after all; as the story in the

Killogy progressed, the need for concrete possible worlds returned. However, the demand for support of concrete possible worlds also increased proportionally, and all that seems to be there is a shaky foundation. Though, as Phillip Bricker notes, "Better a shaky foundation, I say, than no foundation at all" (2008, p. 122). The situation is aptly put in the following:

> [A]rguments for and against Lewisian realism have filled philosophical books and journals. Lewisians have had to develop and revise their position in the light of powerful criticism; non-Lewisian alternatives have sprouted like weeds in the philosophical landscape. The debate goes on; *as with other metaphysical debates, a decisive outcome is not to be expected.* (Bricker 2008, p. 131; my emphasis)

What complicates these considerations is Deadpool's nature as a self-aware fictional character who has the ability to break the fourth wall and interact with the audience instead of remaining confined to the pages of the graphic novels. In brief, although some aspects of the story could be easily accounted for by employing, say, ersatzism, the fact that Deadpool straddles the gap between the real world and the comic book world suggests that only a full-blown modal realism will be adequate for describing the stories. Being a denizen of the comic book world and occasionally poking his head outside through the fourth wall, Deadpool (and his homicidal rampage) presents a formidable philosophical challenge, and not just in terms of ethics. (And if ethics had been the main concern of this piece, then it would have been centered on *Deadpool Kills the Marvel Universe Again*.)

So we seem to be left with the notion that although we live in an actual world, there are potentially innumerable counterparts of each of us who occupy different possible worlds and whose existence – just like ours – is marred with the question about the absurdity of it all. But here, we can find some consolation from a comic book character, analyzed through the lens of philosophy. In the final duel between Deadpool and Deadpool-616, the former laments how the Continuity makes life absurd: "It's the Continuity. The Continuity has us trapped... like flies on a glue strip... abusing us... making us suffer... making us dance like puppets..." (DKD). In response, Deadpool-616 delivers a swift kick that knocks Deadpool off his feet and continues: "And Mama never loved us? I get it. You had a rough life. You know who else had a rough life? Everybody!" (DKD). Deadpool-616 points out that Deadpool's attempt at freeing individuals of the continuity (or the Absurd) is, in itself, an absurd task. The point that Camus is making with the story of Sisyphus was to illustrate that even in the absence of external meaning to one's life, one can still find meaning even in seemingly menial tasks, like rolling a boulder up the hill:

> I leave Sisyphus at the foot of the mountain! One always finds one's burden again. But Sisyphus teaches the higher fidelity that negates the gods and raises rocks. He concludes that all is well.... The struggle itself toward the heights is enough to fill a man's heart. One must imagine Sisyphus happy. (Camus 1955)

In trying to evade the Sisyphean task of rolling up the boulder (or accepting the Continuity), Deadpool committed himself to another task, which turned out equally meaningless. And, as Deadpool-616 sagaciously puts it, "The mind-numbing, soul-crushing realization that nothing's ever going to change . . . that nothing will ever get any better . . . that's how I get girls" (DKD). Well, maybe not so sagaciously, after all, but still. One must imagine Deadpool happy.

References

Bricker, Phillip. 2008. Concrete possible worlds. In *Contemporary debates in metaphysics*, ed. Theodore Sider, John Hawthorne, and Dean W. Zimmerman. Malden: Blackwell.
Bunn, Cullen, and Salva Espin. 2015. *Deadpool kills Deadpool*. New York: Marvel Entertainment.
Bunn, Cullen, and Matteo Lolli. 2013. *Deadpool Killustrated: Butchering stories from literature's finest authors*. New York: Marvel Entertainment.
Bunn, Cullen, Dalibor Talajic, and Loughride Lee. 2012. *Deadpool kills the Marvel Universe*. New York: Marvel Entertainment.
Camus, Albert. 1955. *The myth of Sisyphus and other essays*. Trans. J. O'Brien. New York: Vintage Books.
Divers, John. 2009. Possible worlds and *Possibilia*. In *The Routledge companion to metaphysics*, ed. Robin Le Poidevin, Peter Simons, Andrew McGonical, and Ross Cameron. New York: Routledge.
Hanley, Richard. 2009. Fictional objects. In *The Routledge companion to metaphysics*, ed. Robin Le Poidevin, Peter Simons, Andrew McGonical, and Ross Cameron. New York: Routledge.
Lewis, David. 1971. Counterparts of persons and their bodies. *Journal of Philosophy* 68 (7): 203–211.
———. 1978. Truth in fiction. *American Philosophical Quarterly* 15 (1): 37–46.
———. 1986. *On the plurality of worlds*. Malden: Blackwell Publishing.
Loux, Michael J. 2006. *Metaphysics: A contemporary introduction*. 3rd ed. New York: Routledge.
Melia, Joseph. 2008. Ersatz possible worlds. In *Contemporary debates in metaphysics*, ed. Theodore Sider, John Hawthorne, and Dean W. Zimmerman. Malden: Blackwell.
Plantinga, Alvin. 1974. *The nature of necessity*. Oxford: Clarendon Press.
———. 1979. Actualism and possible worlds. In *The possible and the actual: Readings in the metaphysics of modality*, ed. Michael Loux. Ithaca: Cornell University Press.
Thomasson, Amie. 1996. Fiction, modality, and dependent abstracta. *Philosophical Studies* 84 (2–3): 295–320.
———. 1999. *Fiction and metaphysics*. New York: Cambridge University Press.

V for Vendetta as Philosophy: Victory Through the Virtues of Anarchy

92

Clara Nisley

Contents

Introduction	2044
Summarizing *V for Vendetta*	2045
Aristotle: Correct and Deviant Constitutions	2050
Aristotle and Plato on the Tyrant	2052
The Ties to Tyranny and the Source of Revolution	2053
John Locke	2054
V's Rebellion and Why It Is Justified	2056
V's Right to a Violent Rebellion	2057
Evey's Pacifist Rebellion	2058
Rebuilding from the Rubble	2059
Conclusion: Real-World Connections	2060
References	2063

Abstract

Alan Moore's graphic novel *V for Vendetta* is a political narrative about a country's loss of liberty and freedom. The novel shows how a free society can transform into an authoritarian state after it is ravaged by war and disease. It also demonstrates the lengths to which individuals are willing to tolerate the surrender of their freedoms for the sake of order and unity. *V for Vendetta* questions the rights and duties of the individual and the actions of an anarchist that inspires a revolt to those wrongs. It forces us to look at a society whose individuals are made to conform to the law through the use of surveillance cameras and enforcement officers who gather up people in unmarked vans and place them in concentration camps. This chapter takes a close look at Moore's graphic novel to determine the limitations on the freedoms placed on individuals by a state through a philosophical/ethical lens and examine how its lessons relate to the real world.

C. Nisley (✉)
Atlanta, GA, USA
e-mail: cnisley@alumni.lsu.edu

© Springer Nature Switzerland AG 2024
D. K. Johnson et al. (eds.), *The Palgrave Handbook of Popular Culture as Philosophy*,
https://doi.org/10.1007/978-3-031-24685-2_97

Keywords

Alan Moore · Aristotle · Plato · John Locke · Thomas Hobbes · A. John Simmons · Anarchy · Consent · Freedom · Justice · Rights · Social contract · State of nature · State of war · Tyranny · Virtue

Introduction

> You've been in a Prison all your life.
> —V (V for Vendetta, p. 168)

Alan Moore and David Lloyd's *V for Vendetta* is a graphic novel relevant to our time, especially if we consider political ideas such as freedom, anarchy, and authoritarian regimes that employ the military and police as part of their dictatorial power. It introduces a tyrannical government that limits the freedoms of its citizens and an anarchist who rejects the self-appointed authoritarian regime. In the novel, the Norsefire government has granted security in exchange for restrictions of freedom of action and movement in certain areas. Individual citizens have not chosen but have unknowingly become bound by the unjust government, which controls their lives. The threat of an absolute power hangs over all who live under the threat of a pandemic. What is intriguing is that one man, an anarchist in a Guy Fawkes mask, is not only able to weaken but to subvert the established government through bombings, killing of the top party members, seizing their propaganda machinery, and announcing a call to disobey the tyrannical authority, the Norsefire party.

The graphic novel starts with V blowing up the House of Parliament and the sky alite in a beautiful display of fireworks. "Anarchy must embrace the din of bombs and cannon-fire" (Moore 2005, p. 219). V believes the bombings are the only way to stop the corrupt government that infringes on individual freedom, such as freedom of speech and the freedom of association. V's claim is that the Norsefire government has not only failed to protect the people; it has actually endangered them, and now, the only alternative is violence. V draws the people's attention to how complacent they have become about the corruption in the Norsefire government. They have traded their ostensive security for lack of private life and private choices. It is up to the individual citizens to fight for their freedom and rid themselves of political tyranny. If they decide not to act against the Norsefire regime, they give their consent to the Norsefire government's villainy. On the other hand, however, if they do choose to fight, they might end up with something worse: no government at all. That would guarantee freedom but may lead to a state that is potentially fraught with conflict. So it seems that the citizens have to choose whether to live in their existing conditions by giving consent to an oppressive tyrannical regime, or risk chaotic anarchy by overthrowing it in the name of freedom.

However, for Alan Moore, ethical principles guide individuals pre-politically, so that even if overthrowing an oppressive government leads to the state of nature, there are laws of nature that prevent individuals from harming one another because reason guides us without government interfering in individual freedom. Of course, there will always be some individuals who will violate the law of nature, but Moore believes that injustices are entrenched in a system where leaders exist. Moore, himself, has made the claim "that leaders are mostly of benefit to no one save themselves"; he thus portrays leaders as tyrants (Flood 2019). Moore, himself, does not seem to believe that there are good and bad political societies since they do not have "ethical dimension" (Killjoy 2009). In *V for Vendetta*, Moore demonstrates an oppressive state that violates human freedom and must be toppled, even if doing so leads to anarchy. Moore seems to be concluding that V is justified in his rebellion against the Norsefire government by making V the hero.

It is the purpose of this chapter, therefore, to examine whether Moore, in *V for Vendetta*, makes a strong argument for toppling authoritarian regimes. I will question whether living in an oppressive state justifies overthrowing the regime or whether freedom in excess, "the land of do as you please," ultimately degenerates into a state of war. Should an oppressive political regime that has violated human rights through its use of force be replaced (Moore 2005)? And, although, the novel expounds on the injustices of an authoritarian regime, the question remains: is a violent revolution a means to recreating a social contract and bringing about a constitutional government – or, is it, instead, a means of doing away with the state altogether, given that Moore deems all governmental authority corrupt because it infringes on human freedom? And, what can this teach us about how we should react to abuses of power by governments in the real world?

To answer these questions, it will be necessary to consider a summary of *V for Vendetta* that reflects on how the Norsefire government oppressed its citizens and V's rebellion against its regime.

Summarizing *V for Vendetta*

V for Vendetta is set in a futuristic, postapocalyptic England where a tyrannical regime, known as Norsefire, took power after a nuclear war between the United States and Russia in the 1980s. The war destroyed Africa, continental Europe, and the crops in England's countryside leaving the country plagued by disease and hunger. Riots broke out throughout the country and gangs tried to seize power. When the Norsefire regime took power in 1992, it brought order to the country. It controlled power through surveillance cameras and enforcement officers who detained and tortured those who opposed the regime. Members of the state police, the Fingermen, arrested individuals, placed them into vans, and tortured them; this included the father of one of our protagonists, Evey Hammond, who was arrested for being associated with the socialist party, and V himself, who was arrested, tortured, and given hallucinogenic drugs. The Norsefire party utilized the Larkhill Resettlement Camp to experiment on prisoners; V was one of dozens of prisoners who were given chemical hormone treatments. In the end, only five prisoners survived the chemical hormone treatments, and only V survived the entire experiment. Because of the chemicals he was given – and the chemical fertilizers he was allowed to use on the vegetable garden and Roses he grew (because he was forced to feed those in charge of the Larkhill Resettlement Camp) – V gained great physical strength and mental capabilities. He used them to destroy the camp and flee.

The Norsefire regime conducts its surveillance by equating the components of the government to body parts. The Ear listens in on individual conversations to find what citizens are discussing. The Nose investigates terrorism and other major crimes. (Mr. Finch, a part of the Nose, is an important figure who investigates V throughout the novel.) The Eye captures images through surveillance cameras, which are installed throughout the country. The Mouth is the propaganda department whose broadcasters report on events, including the weather every night. The Finger is the law enforcement branch of the Norsefire government. And all of them work for the Head, Mr. Adam Susan.

In book I, we are introduced to V who, wearing a cloak and a Guy Fawkes mask, saves Evey Hammond from several Fingermen and then bombs the Houses of Parliament. After the bombing, the government puts out a broadcast through the "Voice of Fate" that the British people count on and trust for daily information. The "Voice of Fate," who is really Mr. Lewis Prothero, presents a convincing narrative to persuade individuals that the government intentionally caused the explosion. The coercion, however, depends on the individual belief in the "Voice." This is disturbed by the man in the Guy Fawkes mask who kidnaps and tortures Lewis Prothero by recreating a likeness of the "Larkhill Resettlement Camp." By subverting the government's attempt to dictate the narrative about the parliament bombing, we see the first violent attack on the Norsefire government and weakening its coercive power over its citizens.

It turns out that Mr. Prothero was a commander at the Larkhill Resettlement Camp where V was held and tortured. V, then, continues to isolate those who served at Larkhill; with Evey's help, V kills Bishop Lilliman – a pedophile clergyman who served as chaplain at Larkhill. Although Evey volunteered to help V, she was not aware that he was going to kill Bishop Lilliman, so she refuses to help V kill. Despite this, V continues to seek out those who served at Larkhill. In the end, V hunts down Dr. Delia Surridge, who conducted the chemical experiments on V. After killing Dr. Surridge, V starts to leave, when he encounters Derek Almond; although he is brandishing a gun, V quickly overpowers and kills him. He had been sent to Dr. Surridge's home by Detective Eric Finch who is investigating the terrorist bombings. Detective Finch had given Dr. Surridge a "Violet Carson" rose he found where V had kidnapped Mr. Prothero and the same uncommon hybrid rose in Bishop Lilliman's room. When Detective Finch finally arrives at the scene, he finds Dr. Surridge's diary, and connects the killings to the Larkhill Resettlement Camp.

In Book II, V shows Evey a rabbit trick, but instead of a rabbit in a top hat, it is in a cage. When Evey asks V to bring the rabbit back, V states, "But what if she is content where she is?" (Moore 2005, p. 94). When V brings the rabbit back, it no longer is in a cage but free. Then V sets Evey free by blindfolding her and abandoning her on a deserted street. The message, of course, is that the citizens of England, including Evey, are not free. On his way to the NTV Film Department where Roger Dascombe is monitoring the Norsefire government's reporting on terrorists' acts and food hoarding, V sees a poster with the words, "Strength through unity, purity through faith." He carves his symbol, which of course is a V (for "vendetta"), over the Norsefire government's motto. He enters the building and fights his way into Roger Dascombe's studio. He reveals that he is carrying explosives; V has one hand on his knife and the other on the detonator. In a video tape he hands to Dascombe to play, V addresses the people of England. He reminds them that the Norsefire regime is monitoring them. He shows pictures of Hitler, Stalin, and Mussolini and points out that these dictators were appointed and given power to make decisions over the people they ruled "without question" while its citizens had the power to stop them (Moore 2005 p. 117).

After the video, Detective Finch enters the studio and finds a man with a cape and Guy Fawkes mask lying dead on the ground. After his mask is removed, Detective Finch finds that it is Roger Dascombe's body. In a rage, Detective Finch yells and punches Mr. Peter Creedy who has replaced Derek Almond as head of the Finger. Detective Finch is furious that Mr. Creedy is treating V as if he were a normal human being. After the incident, Detective Finch is sent on vacation to Norfolk. He goes in search of what happened in the Larkhill Resettlement Camp. He believes finding out what happened at Larkhill will help him track down V and capture him.

Meanwhile, after being left by V, Evey has moved in with a gangster named Gordon. When he takes her to a club, Evey overhears a conversation between Gordon's friend Robert and Mr. Creedy. Robert tells him that his mother had been given an exemption from going into a home. Robert tells Mr. Creedy that they are not homes but gas chambers. Evey is horrified. When Robert goes to talk to Gordon, he expresses how "we shouldn't have to live like this!" and starts a fight (Moore 2005, p. 129). Gordon takes Evey out of the club. V is also outside watching Evey. After some time, Evey and Gordon are back at his place. He asks Evey to lock herself in the bathroom. Two men are outside the door asking for compensation to a deal that they had with Gordon. When he opens the door, one of the men stabs him with a sword. Seeking revenge, Evey takes Gordon's gun from a drawer. She returns to the club and sees two men speaking with the same accent as the ones who were outside the door. She immediately thinks these two men were the ones who killed Gordon. As the two men walk into the club, Evey points the gun ready to kill them; when suddenly, someone grabs her from behind.

In Chapter 10, we find Evey in a prison cell under a banner with the Norsefire slogan that reads, "Strength through purity, purity through faith" (Moore 2005, p. 148). After falling asleep, she wakes up to a guard outside her door. He blindfolds her and cuffs her wrists behind her. He takes her to a room where someone else interrogates her. She is shown a video of her propositioning a Fingerman. Evey is told she is "formally charged with the murder of Senior Officer, Peter Creedy" (Moore 2005, p. 152). She is tortured, her hair is shaved, and a guard wants her to sign a confession stating that she was tortured, brainwashed, and terrorized by V into committing the murders of Roger Dascombe, Derek Almond, Dr. Delia Surridge, and the Bishop Anthony Lilliman. When Evey refuses to sign the confession, the guard tells another to take Evey "out behind the chemical sheds and shoot her" (Moore 2005, p. 161).

Despite all this, Evey never gives up her integrity and refuses to sign the confession. The guard sets her free. She walks out and sees that the guard was V all along. He wanted to show her that she has "been in a prison all [her] life" (Moore 2005, p. 168). He has shown her what the Norsefire regime does to those who are imprisoned. Evey finally realizes that she has been living under a tyrannical, oppressive government. She is not free, but like all of England's citizens, she will have to decide for herself whether she wants to be free.

V has shown Evey what the Norsefire government does by recreating a prison cell in the "Shadow Gallery" as he recreated the "Larkhill Resettlement Camp" with Prothero. V has freed Evey from her metaphorical blindfold. At the end of Book II, Evey is ready to help V once again. During her time in prison, Evey read Valerie's story that she wrote while imprisoned in Larkhill. Valerie, an actor who was imprisoned in Larkhill, wrote about the roses she received from Ruth, her lesbian lover, before she was imprisoned. V was inspired by Valerie's story and placed her writings in the cell for Evey to read. He wanted her to pluck a rose from his garden in the "The Shadow Gallery" as revenge for the man that killed Gordon. (For V, roses symbolize revenge over the Norsefire regime.) Despite all of this, and learning what the Norsefire government does to those it imprisons, Evey continues to refuse to kill; V, on the other hand, thinks that the tyrannical Norsefire government needs to be toppled by any means necessary. V tells her that she will be needed at the end. He is preparing for "the finale."

Book III starts on Guy Fawkes' day, 1998. V's rebellion is not over. Evey asks V whether "something's going on" and he tells her "the ending is nearer than you think" (Moore 2005, p. 183). Next, V is standing on top of a roof with a score of Tchaikovsky's 1812 Overture. His hands wave into the air as if he is conducting the music as well as the destruction, while one building after the other explodes. V has toppled the old post office as well as Jordan Tower, the headquarters to both the Eye and the Ear, and has killed the head of the Ear, Mr. Etheridge. Mr. Conrad Heyer runs out of the Tower and states that citizens will not believe there has been another demolition. V has made certain that the government is left "blind and deaf and unable to speak" (Moore 2005, p. 186). The Leader, Adam Susan, wants to broadcast an explanation to reassure the citizens. But then V's voice is heard saying, "Her Majesty's government is pleased to return the rights of secrecy and privacy to you, its loyal subjects" (Moore 2005, p. 187). V tells them that in commemoration of Guy Fawkes day, the citizens will have three days of freedom; they will neither be watched nor listened to. They can do as they will.

V has freed the people and they are talking about the lack of microphones and cameras that moved as they walked and talked in the streets. He has "taken away the voice of fate" (Moore 2005, p. 189). While surveillance cameras and microphones are down, Rosemary Almond buys a gun from Alistair Harper, one of the gangsters who is responsible for Gordon's killing. Meanwhile, the Leader orders Mr. Creedy, who oversees the Finger, to double the manpower in the streets and have looters shot. Men in uniform march through the streets of London. V tells Evey that "a few [people] might take the opportunity to protest" (Moore 2005, p. 194). People are looting, a crowd is forming, and some are rioting. Police are calling for backup and requesting tear gas. Evey asks V if this is anarchy. V tells her that "anarchy means 'without leaders;' not 'without order'." "With anarchy comes ... true order, which is to say voluntary order ... This is chaos" (Moore 2005, p. 195).

We then learn that V has had control over the Fate computer from a downstairs room in the Shallow Gallery. Not only have people been rioting in London, but because of V's last broadcast, there have been riots in Manchester over food shortages (Moore 2005, p. 202). He has had control of the Fate computer from the start and has been posting leaflets throughout England. He has been using Fate to destroy government buildings and disrupt the Norsefire regime's control over its citizens. V's view is that oppressive states must be toppled, even if doing so leads to anarchy.

The Leader, Adam Susan, sits in his office as the citizens riot in the streets of London. He watches the Fate computer screen as people have their heads shaved, are "herded through the showers," and someone is hanged (Moore 2005, p. 196). The guards outside hear him proclaim that "anarchy is loosed upon the world" (Moore 2005, p. 196). Peter Creedy (who, recall, oversees the Finger) notices that the Head is weak and begins to recruit gangsters, like Alistair Harper. Helen Heyer is also maneuvering to have her husband – Conrad Heyer (who, recall, oversees the Eye) – overthrow the Leader; she pays Alistair Harper to betray Peter Creedy. And if that weren't complicated enough, Rosemary Almond, who was left without a pension from the Norsefire government after her husband was killed by V, is also intent on killing the Leader, Adam Susan. In the end it's the latter, Rosemary Almond, who shoots the Leader; she gets him while his motorcade is stopped on the way to give a speech to reassure the citizens that the Norsefire government was in control. It is Peter Creedy (the Finger), however, who takes over; he announces that he is the new Leader for the Norsefire regime, after the assassination. His rule as the Leader is not long lasting, however. Alistair Harper, the gangster paid to betray Peter Creedy by the wife of Conrad Heyer (the Eye), slashes his throat. But then Conrad Heyer is sent a video of his wife with Alistair Harper. He assaults Alistair Harper, and when it is over, both men are dead.

At the end of Book III, V has shown Evey where he kept the chemicals and instruction books on how to make explosives. V, then, takes her to a tunnel where there is a subway car. On the way, V asks Evey to carry a parcel with the high explosive gelignite. When Evey protests, V tells her "anarchy has two faces, both creator and destroyer" (Moore 2005, p. 222). Inside the subway car, V had been cultivating lilies and awaiting Detective Finch (who, recall, had been investigating V). When he reaches a closed Victorian station, he sees the train with the lilies. V surprises him and takes out a knife, wounding him; but Detective Finch takes out his gun and shoots V. As he dies, V tells him, "There's no flesh or blood within this cloak to kill. There's only an idea. Ideas are bulletproof" (Moore 2005, p. 236).

V reaches Evey before dying. He tells her the country's "old beliefs have come to rubble" (Moore 2005, p. 245). V has toppled the Norsefire government so "creators then can build a better world" out of the rubble (Moore 2005, p. 248). Evey, standing atop a roof wearing V's Guy Fawkes mask, hat, and cloak, addresses the crowd that was waiting to hear from the Leader. As V, Evey tells them that they have given away their power, and that they must choose whether to return to the same type of government or choose to free themselves of the chains. She then sends V's body off in the subway train that runs under Downing Street, thus, destroying the Head. But she had announced her plans in her speech, warning them before bombing the building. In the end, Evey has taken on V's role, but she will "help them build, ... [she'll] not help them kill" (Moore, 2005, p. 220). She has decided to take on the face as the creator not the destroyer.

The question, of course, is whether V's rebellion is justified. To answer this, I will dedicate a section to trying to answer four questions: First, is the Norsefire regime deserving of loyalty? Second, under what conditions is rebellion against a state justified? Third, what form should such rebellion take? And fourth, what would the state of nature, without government, really be like? Would it be better than what would be found under an oppressive regime?

Aristotle: Correct and Deviant Constitutions

In this section, I will use Aristotle's ideas to talk about whether the Norsefire regime deserves loyalty and whether the Leader, Adam Susan, falls short of promoting the nature of the citizens and how the political structure does not allow for the best life. I will first introduce how Aristotle thinks individuals are meant to live in political societies, and then how the constitution – its laws – and its ruler must possess certain attributes for individuals to flourish. I will outline the different types of political societies according to Aristotle to make the point that the type of regime that the Leader represents does not deserve the loyalty of the individuals living under the Norsefire government.

Aristotle tells us that it is part of being human to naturally form into societies (*Politics*, 1252a1–1253a4). His claim is that it is a natural development that evolves from household to villages to political societies. The emergence derives from the individual's need to live well; this is an individual's end. For individuals to perfect their end, they not only have to live in political societies, but they must live in a political society that will fulfill their end, that will perfect their nature. The political society needs to allow individuals to acquire the virtues of character in the full sense, that is in accordance with reason – practical intelligence. Reason is exclusively the nature of human beings, and by living in a political community, individuals will engage in practical deliberation. Thus, the political society emerges through the exercise of practical reason. It is what allows human beings in political communities to determine what is "just and unjust" because only human beings have speech that is connected to reason (*Pol.* 1253a8). It is through reason that individuals have the power to deliberate and discover what is right and wrong, just, and unjust. Therefore, a political community emerges naturally, but it also has its own nature, which must be perfected. Since the political community's good and the human good are intertwined, its perfection is the highest good for both. The way to achieve the highest good is through a political community's constitution, which is the nature of every political community.

Aristotle classifies political constitutions into three categories: the rule of the one (the monarchy), the few (the aristocracy), and the many (the polity). Two deviant forms of these constitutions are the rule by an oligarch and the rule of democracy. The best constitution is the one that lies between the two regimes: oligarchy, which is one of excess; ruled by the few wealthy and its opposite, democracy which is one of deficiency; ruled by the many, the poor (*Pol.*, III, 8 and IV, 9). The best constitution moderates its excesses and brings about justice by promoting and preserving the common good of the citizens. What does it mean to promote the common good? Aristotle says that each citizen must participate in the constitution, they must deliberate in politics (*Pol.*, 1332a32–8). By participating and deliberating in what is best, citizens will be disposed to aim for what is the common good of all. The participants constitute the virtue of justice by understanding their own good in relation to the good of all. The virtue of justice can only be found by living and participating in the political community.

With the best constitution, one in the interest of the citizens, the political regime will have the support and loyalty of its citizens. The deviant types of constitutions do not aim at the common good of their citizens and the ruler's aim is not living well (*Pol.*, 1280a31–32 and 1257b40–8a14). This type of ruler does not express the virtue of justice. The citizens, therefore, do not have (or owe) loyalty to the political regime or the ruler. The ruler must be able to enforce order and justice and to perceive and secure the common advantage of the citizens. Without justice, the enforcement of law and order is impossible. For Aristotle, the lack of loyalty is connected to constitutional injustices and ruling for the interest of the ruler. Justice is not understanding one's own good but that of the general good (*Nicomachean Ethics*, 129b25–7, 1140b7–11).

In Book III of *Politics*, Aristotle introduces the characteristic virtue of a good ruler: wisdom (1277b25–30). The ruler must also have other characteristics such as temperance, courage, and justice. It is the latter that qualifies him to rule over free men. This ruler has knowledge of the best constitution and is able to deliberate on how to enact policies that would best serve the interest of the people. The ruler will have already shown that he can deliberate well about what is good for himself, what is conducive to a good life. He has learned how to rule by obeying the constitution (*Pol.*, 1277b11-12). A ruler must have "a true and reasoned state of capacity to act with regard to the things that are good or bad for men in general" (*Nic. Ethics*, VI.5.1140b4–5; cf. 1140b20–21). Here is where the characteristic of temperance serves practical reason with regard to ruling. The ruler must act not on whatever he chooses but for what is reasonable and promotes the human good (*Nic. Ethics*, 140b16-20). For Aristotle, the ruler should have knowledge of what is morally good for the community, but only when the government is set up on the principle of equality and the citizens with equally rational capacities take turns in government participation (*Pol.*, 1279a9-10).

The ruler, like all human beings, has a "sense of good and evil, of just and unjust." But the ruler also has what is peculiar to him: the deliberative virtue of practical reason. This is the virtue of a ruler and it guides policy and the "power of speech ... which is a characteristic of man" along with a particular apprehension of the moral principles of what is advantageous and harmful and governs the moral practices of the community (*Pol.*, 1253a7-15). Aristotle emphasizes that if "the virtuous fill the offices in which virtue is needed" the political community will not fall into strife (*Pol.*, II. 8).

Aristotle and Plato on the Tyrant

Aristotle tells us that the ruler needs both practical wisdom and moral virtue. Without wisdom, the virtuous person would not necessarily know how to act, and without moral virtue, the clever person would not always pursue the appropriate ends (*Nic. Ethics*, 1144a24-35 p. 1807). The man who is a good person is harmonious in that he must be morally virtuous and (above all) courageous, moderate, and just in his dealings with others. Moreover, the ruler must have practical reason and reflect intelligently when making decisions. He must always consider practical rationality when making laws and for the creation of the constitution (*Pol.*, 1333a17-1334a15 p. 2115–6). His response should be an expression of intellectual virtue as well as character virtue because as a political leader he is concerned with the good of the community. The intellectual virtue is necessary for making decisions; however, Aristotle warns, there are men who instead of possessing practical reason are merely clever. In the *Nicomachean Ethics*, Aristotle argues that mere cleverness can be a corrupting factor in one's character. "Cleverness is not innately good because vicious people can achieve their goals through cleverness, [and] their cleverness is 'unscrupulous' or lacking moral standards" (1141a25-1141b7 and 1152a-12-14).

In describing bad character, Aristotle tells us of the type of man who is bereft of morality, whose actions reach "outside of the limits of vice" (*Nic. Ethics*, 1148b30-1149a21). Aristotle refers to the tyrant Phalaris as committing brutish acts that are beyond vicious; he is like a beast, Aristotle argues, and does not have the capacity to reason or of deliberative choice (1148b15-24). Consequently, he says, such men are like animals whose desires cannot be stopped thus whose behavior is pardonable. "In the most extreme cases, the tyrant becomes a beast, devoid of normative competence: he is incapable of recognizing moral norms, and unable to conform his conduct to moral knowledge" (Nielsen 2019, pp. 146–147). In "The Concept of Brutishness" however, philosopher Marcinkowska-Rosól argues that when "brutish behaviour [is] harmful to others [in] society," it must be punished through the legal system or other measures (Marcinkowska-Rosół 2018, p. 113). The cure is expulsion for the sake of the individuals in the political communities. Since these individuals lack the capacity to reason for the good of the community, punishment is justified in virtue of its social consequences. By removing these brutish men, the political community is free to form the best constitution and promote the best life.

In the *Republic*, Plato says that a tyrant is most distant from reason and also most distant from law and order (587a10-11 and c25-26). The tyrant, at first, appears the champion of the people; he is clever but lacks practical wisdom. For Aristotle, lawlessness is coincidentally associated with the tyrant's ruthless pursuit of pleasure and excessive greed. His desires for pleasure and power have become so that they make him unconcerned with acting ethically (*Pol.*, 1311a10-11 p. 2081). Aristotle attributes the lawlessness of the tyrant as bereft of morality because he is driven by desire and is unable to recognize virtuous actions. As we have seen in *V for Vendetta*, the Leader, Adam Susan, has shown that he is clever but not wise. He lacks the virtue of practical reason and is unable to resist falling into a trajectory of evil deeds.

The lack of capacity to listen to reason is ascribed to the Leader, and it implies why he lacks the fundamental restraints to pursue the aims that reason would dictate to rule for the good of the community. The Norsefire regime does not have its laws dictated by reason, and obeyance of the laws by the citizens depends on whether the laws are governed by reason. Because they lack the capacity to reason and are devoid of character virtues, there is virtually no limit to the devastation on the citizenry that the Leader and the Norsefire regime will bring – both in terms of individual happiness and the happiness of the community. They lack that which is necessary for the individual and the political community to flourish. For these reasons, it seems that Moore is right that the Norsefire regime does not deserve the loyalty of its citizenry – and, as we shall soon see, they are justified to rebel.

The Ties to Tyranny and the Source of Revolution

Plato claimed that morally evil acts relate to the agent's moral failure and the conflict within him, his self-interested desires. If unchecked, a morally deficient leader will enslave the whole city. In *V for Vendetta*, Adam Susan is a prime example of a pitiful individual who is totally enslaved to his overpowering lust for "Fate." It is this overpowering lust that enslaves the tyrannical man (*Republic*, 572e-575a).

The tyrannical leaders' desire for excess will lead to the city's degeneration, and for Aristotle these degenerate forms of government are the cause of revolutions. Perhaps this is a natural defect in some human beings who are unable to acquire the virtues, because as Aristotle writes, sometimes "nature ... produces bad men ... who cannot be educated and made virtuous" (*Pol.*, 13169a11). This means that at least some tyrants are men who are by nature vicious, a nature that can exist in any human being but in the tyrant is able to destroy the city-state and lead to the degeneration of its citizenry. Aristotle, who agrees with Plato, says that "their removal from society could be justified by the fact that they never actually belonged to it" (Marcinkowska-Rosół 2018, pp. 113–114).

Plato holds that both the unjust man and the unjust city are riven by dissension and at any point rebellion might break out (*Republic*, 562a4-566d2). The tyrant, he argues, comes into power from disobedience to the laws and unrest. Amid civil unrest, the tyrant is an opportunist; he appears as a champion of the people, but then takes over to become a tyrant. The tyrants are not loved and are not friendly even to themselves because they neither respect the humanity in others nor in themselves. Indeed, Moore describes the Leader, Adam Susan, as someone who has no friends, no love, not even for himself, and has no ability to reason on the basis of moral principles because the basis of morality within him is either absent or destroyed.

In referencing the tyrants and the corruption of the political institution, tyrants are much like those relationships where no friendship exists. Friendships are based on mutual respect and virtue. Tyrants have no friends because they lack the virtues of character, and the tyrant is always suspicious of conspiracies because there can be no friendship where there is cruelty, where there is disloyalty, where there is injustice. And in places where the wicked gather there is conspiracy only, not companionship: these have no affection for one another; fear alone holds them together; they are not friends, they are merely accomplices (Estienne de la Boétie 1942, pt. III).

In the Norsefire regime, government officials distrust each other, expelling and executing men and employing secret police and surveillance even on those who are faithful to the government. The reason for using surveillance is, for Adam Susan (the tyrant), to know what each of his subjects say or do. Aristotle tells us that "even friends of a tyrant will sometimes attack him out of contempt ... [and] the expectation of success is likewise a sort of contempt; the assailants are ready to strike, ... partly out of contempt and partly from the love of gain" (*Pol.*, 1312a6-16). Mr. Susan was assassinated by the contempt he bred in the widow Rosemary Almond. And Mr. Creedy, Derek Almond's successor, was ready to take his place.

In the above section, I have shown that the worst rule of government does not rule for the community but for its own interest. Alan Moore's depiction of the Norsefire regime is ruled by a ruler who shows absolute disregard for the interest of its citizens. Instead, the Norsefire regime has placed its citizens in fear because of the corruption of the degenerate Leader, Adam Susan, and its regime. They behave more like beasts, unable to recognize moral norms and possessing no concern for the good of the community. From the Leader to the members of the regime, the Norsefire regime does not understand that justice is for the good of the community and have only committed injustices and enslaved its citizenry.

John Locke

In the *Second Treatise* of Government, John Locke develops his account of the state of nature. It is a state of perfect freedom and equality where no one should have absolute power over another individual because the state of nature has a law of nature that governs over all of us. The law of nature prohibits taking the life, liberty, or possessions of another human being. Individuals do not have the moral liberty to harm another person. The law of nature forbids individuals from harming others and proscribes against them being harmed. And any transgressor could be punished because in the state of nature everyone is equal "where all the power and jurisdiction is reciprocal" (Locke 1689, ch. II, sect. 5). If any individual violates the natural law, he is unable or refuses to live by the law of reason, he places himself in a state of war against the individual whose rights he has violated. However, in the state of nature, men do not have a common judge. A violation of the natural law and no common judge is the reason people enter into political societies. This is the defining characteristic of the state of nature: it lacks an authority or impartial judge to punish those who violate the natural law.

Locke used the idea of the state of nature to inquire into the purpose of government. He stated that individuals were "quickly driven into society ... [because of] the inconveniences they are exposed to, ... and the uncertain exercise of the power every man has of punishing the transgressions of others" (Locke 1689, ch. IX, sect. 127). Without a government, individuals would be left to suffer the injustices and violence of others. Therefore, individuals decided to create a social contract "for the public good and safety" (Locke 1689, ch. VIII, sect. 110). Individuals enter into a social contract to establish a government for the protection of their natural rights to life, liberty, and property. Government, then, is restrained to the interest of the individuals it serves. Government is to promote the public good and safeguard individuals from interference with their natural rights. Individuals, through consent, place the legislative power in some person or body of people (Locke 1992, section 132). The legislative power is to dispense justice and "can never have a right to destroy, enslave, or designedly to impoverish the subjects" (Locke 1689, ch. XI, sect. 135). The law of nature proscribes that individuals should not give their consent to enslavement or the appropriation of their property.

Locke introduced the idea that government is by consent. He makes this claim because all people are free and only through their consent can government exist. According to modern philosopher John Simmons, however, the act of consent can bind individuals to unjust governments. When a government perpetrates acts of violence on innocent individuals, and an individual is given an opportunity to express dissent but remains silent, then that person has given their tacit consent to that unjust government (Simmons 1979, pp. 78–79). Simmons argues that, when governments behave this way, we have a duty not only to dissent but to fight – to fight the injustices of "autocratic and arbitrary forms of government" because fighting injustices "outweigh[s] any obligation we may have to respect its authority" (Simmons 1979, pp. 78–79).

When individuals enter into the social contract, they expect justice. When the government violates their rights, then the people have a right to replace the existing government with a new one. Locke argues that individuals always have the right to rebel against a government that violated their rights and use force unjustly. When government abuses the natural rights of the people, they have a right to revolution. In this case, the government is no longer the judge and has become the aggressor, thus placing itself in a state of war with its citizens. Individuals, because they have consented to the government, have a natural right to overthrow and replace any government that wishes to subordinate their citizens. Locke also affirms that the people have "*a supreme power to remove or alter*" the legislative power (Locke 1689, ch. XIII, sect. 149).

V's Rebellion and Why It Is Justified

The Norsefire government never had the rightful authority to govern the people. The people transitioned from a state of nature as Evey tells the story where, "everyone was waiting for the government to do something, but there wasn't any government" (Moore 2005, p. 28). When the Norsefire government took over, "it was all the fascist groups, the right-wingers" who "got together" and "called themselves Norsefire" (Moore 2005, p. 28). No one chose to subject themselves to the Norsefire government. Therefore, the Norsefire government was illegitimate the moment the people were under its subjection. A "social contract" was never created, and the people never consented to the terms of that society. A social contract with the Norsefire government would have protected the citizen's "natural rights" to life, liberty, and property. Again, according to Locke, such protections are the primary reason for leaving the "state of nature" (Locke 1689, ch. II). As V informed the citizens when he took over the Fate computer, they have a natural right to overthrow and replace any government that wishes to subordinate them. V's justified resistance comes from Locke's consent theory as the people were indefensibly subjected to the Norsefire government's strong-arm and arbitrary rules and never voluntarily subjected themselves to it. The Norsefire government had failed to protect their "natural rights" and, more importantly, a "social contract" cannot be created unless "the people are both at liberty to consent and have actually consented" (Locke 1689, ch. XVII, sect. 198). The conquest of the Norsefire regime that ruled only by ambition and whose rule did not conform to the natural law undermined the social contract and thus did not bind the people. The citizens, then, were sanctioned to rebel against and overthrow the government.

V made the point that, despite all this, by obeying the government and thus giving it the ability to command their lives and violate their liberty, they in fact had given their consent to the despotically unjust Norsefire government whose acts of violence violate the natural law. When it used its power to imprison, torture, and kill citizens, the people's decision to comply with the Norsefire government's actions was like so many before them who had given their consent to Stalin, Hitler, and the Fascist Mussolini. When groups of Pakistanis, Blacks, and homosexuals were taken away, the people decided to turn a blind eye. Only through the agreement of their mutual consent "without question" and their "nurtured bigotries" were the people willing members of the Norsefire government (Moore 2005, pp. 116 and 117). V reminded the people that the nonconsensual acquisition of power by the Norsefire regime rendered it illegitimate.

When V undermined the Norsefire government that counted on political obedience for its legitimacy by declaring "you could have stopped them" (Moore 2005, p. 117), the citizens understood, and the uncertainty of violence and persecution led to riots and protests. The regime, however, deployed armed men to kill protesters. And this gives rise to the next question: Must V's rebellion have been violent?

V's Right to a Violent Rebellion

As we have seen in *V for Vendetta*, the Norsefire government violated the natural rights of the citizens. The government imprisoned its citizens in the Larkhill Resettlement Camp and experimented on them. Dr. Delia Surridge's experiments were particularly vicious and violated the law of nature, which applies to all people. For Locke, all persons are equal based on

> being all the workmanship of one omnipotent and infinitely wise Maker ... here cannot be supposed any subordination among us, that may authorize us to destroy one another, as if we were made for one another's uses. (ch. II, sect. 6)

The regime's failure to secure the natural rights of its citizens, its attempts on the life and liberty of its citizens, and more importantly its abuse of power, placed the people in its absolute power (Locke 1689, ch. III, sect. 17). Who better to judge than V? When the Norsefire government, instead of preserving, attempted to destroy his life, his passive obedience would have exhorted the people to a quiet submission into the violent hands of the Norsefire regime (Locke 1689, ch. XIX, sect. 228 and 240). For Locke, the power to judge resides in the people who are justified in their rebellion against the government. V's call to rebellion was based on rational judgment, and when he warned the people of their consent to the violations of natural law, they were the best judges of their own situation and no longer accepted the oppressive power of the Norsefire regime.

V started by killing those members that served in the Larkhill Resettlement Camp. Knowing that the power of the government "hath no other end but preservation," V served as judge (Locke 1689, ch. XI sect. 135). He systematically put an end to the lives of those who served in the Larkhill Resettlement Camp either by driving Lewis Prothero insane or killing those officials who worked in the Camp. Although we do not know why V was placed in the Larkhill Resettlement Camp, where they took "Black people and Pakistanis" as well as homosexuals and socialists, the government violated V's life, liberty, and health by experimenting on V's mind and body. This gave V the justification for his violent rebellion (Moore 2005, p. 28).

Locke tells us that "the people have a right to overthrow the government," when the government employs its rule for destruction and not the preservation of the citizens (Locke 1689, ch. XIX, sect. 239). Elizabeth Frazer and Kimberly Hutchings have argued that John Locke was a proponent of fighting tyranny through violent civil disobedience of unjust laws. They claim that "when politics fails for whatever reason, violence comes into play as the alternative, default mode of getting things done; therefore, when "the ruler ... breaks his trust, ... acts so as to endanger the constitution, [he] has reverted to a state of war with the people" (Frazer and Hutchings 2009, p. 51). "Even though the state of nature is distinct from the state of war, Locke states 'there are men who are as if they are wild beasts'" (Locke quoted in Frazer and Hutchings 2009, p. 52). Thus, the rogue executive has made war upon the people and may be treated as "'beast of prey' and reverted to a state of nature" (Frazer and Hutchings 2009, p. 52). V's violence is justified because the

Leader has reverted the people into the state of nature where he placed the people into a state of war. Hence, the people are in a state of nature with respect to the wrongful violence and chaos associated with the Norsefire regime, but they are also in a state of war.

Locke's idea is to overcome the state of war and replace the illegitimate political regime with a legitimate one and reestablish the social contract. The idea is that violent revolution comes into play only when the people are bereft of resources and do not have legal access to overcome the tyrannical ruler. The Norsefire regime descended into what Frazer and Hutchings call "beast of prey" (2009, p. 52). If V had bargained with the tyrannical ruler, he would have "descend[ed] to [the] level of 'noxious beasts'" (Frazer and Hutchings 2009, p. 58). V refused "to give to any one, … an absolute arbitrary power over [his] person … and put a force into the magistrate's hand to execute his unlimited will arbitrarily upon them" (Locke 1689, ch. XI, sect. 137). At the end, V had "a right to destroy that which threatens [him] … and put[s] him in a state of war" (Locke 1689, ch. III, sect. 17).

Evey's Pacifist Rebellion

Evey finds the acts of killing people morally objectionable and refused to help V kill. In the end, V was willing to die knowing that ideas are not killed and knowing that he passed those ideas on to Evey. Before V dies, he tells Evey "This country is not saved, … But all its old beliefs have come to rubble, and from rubble may we build" (Moore 2005, p. 245). Evey's form of anarchy is that of a creator, whereas V's was that of a destroyer. In these last scenes, Moore treats Evey as a moral agent capable of guiding her behavior and limiting violence. Evey is capable of choosing autonomously her style of civil disobedience as a pacifist versus V's violent, revolutionary style. Evey's reason and restraint will allow her to choose a form of government that will provide protection for everyone in the state without the use of arbitrary force, while abstaining from killing. However, it was V's violent rebellion that allowed for Evey's pacifism.

V has handed his beliefs down to Evey, except that she has decided what must come next for her life: she will guide the people. Evey, wearing V's mask and cloak, speaks from atop a building and announces that the citizens "must choose what comes next. Lives of [their] own or return to chains" (Moore 2005, p. 258). During her speech, Evey warns the people that "tomorrow, Downing Street will be destroyed" (Moore 2005, p. 258). The next day, Evey places V's body, surrounded by lilies, into the train. She has given the people proper warning, to stay away from Downing Street. She sends the train with explosives off to destroy the Head. She states, "the age of killing is no more" (Moore 2005, p. 260). Her speech has given the citizens courage not to accept the ruling of the Norsefire regime and return to their chains. Those listening to her speech start fighting the enforcement officers. Evey has seemingly given the people a choice between anarchy or living under the arbitrary power of the Norsefire regime.

Rebuilding from the Rubble

But would the citizens be better off in a state of nature? Or would the Norsefire regime actually be preferable? The answer to this question seems to turn on what the state of nature is actually like.

As we saw above, according to John Locke, the state of nature was not so bad. Unfettered by government, people are basically good and mostly free. Despite its inconveniences, we enjoy broad liberty within it. None of us would agree to just anything – any government, no matter how repressive – to avoid it. So, if Locke is right, the state of nature would seem preferable to the Norsefire regime.

According to philosopher Thomas Hobbes, however, the state of nature was brutal. Human beings were equally vulnerable to being attacked and killed because no one is so strong or so intelligent that they cannot be overpowered. Therefore, in the state of nature, everyone is vulnerable to violence. People are in a state of "continual fear, and danger of violent death; and the life of man, [is] solitary, poor, nasty, brutish, and short" (Leviathan, Pt. I, Ch. 13, para. 9). The reasons for leaving the state of nature according to Hobbes is the violence, insecurity, and fear of threat. In essence, the state of nature is a state of war. We know we cannot survive in a state of war, so we want to leave it. It is the brutality of the state of nature and the fear of death that tell us, by the "general rule of reason," to get out of the state of nature, (Lev., I, 14, 4). Indeed, for Hobbes, rebellion against the state was never justified because, no matter how repressive a government is, living under it is not worse than living in the state of nature.

What is V's view? V's anarchist's claim is that no one has the authority to force individuals to join a government; he thus characterizes any regime as nonvoluntary and coercive, as something whose power must be opposed and eliminated. Government is never noncoercive and individuals are always bound by its authority. This is why the novel starts with V toppling the Houses of Parliament on the 5th of November. He wants to bring down the Norsefire regime so that the citizens can create a new society out of the rubble. Through his destruction, V hopes that the people would be free from government. And, he doesn't want another to arise because, according to V, only in anarchy is freedom preserved. Indeed, V places human freedom (especially freedom from government) as the central focus of anarchy. But V also thinks that humans have reason and the capacity to determine (and freely choose) what is good for the individual. So, according to V, anarchy brings voluntary order and individual freedom from the subjection of government control. As he puts it to Evey, anarchy means "without leaders," not "without order." It is both destruction and creation. Or as Evey puts it at the end of the novel, V has informed the people that "in anarchy there is another way" (Moore 2005, p. 258).

But what reason do we have to think that anarchy, the state of nature, would be the way V suspects it would be, instead of the way Hobbes described? If we think that the state of nature is not so bad, then why do some carry guns, or mace, or take other such protective measures even when there is a government? As Hobbes put it, we "lock our doors, when going to sleep." ... "and this...when [we] know there be laws, and public officers" (Lev., I, 13, 11). Isn't it because we feel the threat of other people – because we are in continual fear – even when we are protected by the social contract? How much more fearful would we be without that protection? After all, even Locke believed that the enjoyment of freedom in the state of nature is never certain; we are "constantly exposed to the invasion of others" (Locke 1689, ch. IX, sect. 123). That is part of the reason he thought people would enter the social contract.

In fact, Moore's novel itself presents reason to think V was wrong about how peaceful anarchy would be. Before the Norsefire government took over, people were rioting and gangs were "trying to take over" (Moore 2005, p. 28). Britain was without a government; people were free from external governmental control and no one was enforcing the law; the people were in a state of anarchy, and it was much more like Hobbes's account. Gangs were vying for power and the people lived in fear. Much like Hobbes theorized, the Norsefire regime came to power because no one felt safe; the people were in a state of war and were willing to accept anything to get out of it.

But none of this changes the fact that, under the regime, the natural rights of the people were violated and Norsefire became the aggressor that placed the people in a state of war where people are under the threat of violence and insecurity over the actions of the police (the Finger). And it certainly doesn't mean that V's rebellion was unjustified. What it does suggest is that Evey (as V), at the end of the novel, should encourage the reestablishment of a social contract that secures human rights. In other words, after the Norsefire is toppled, and people have recognized the importance of the natural law and human flourishing as the proper ends of political society, they have to make another choice: return to the state of nature or await a social contract to give legitimacy to a new political party. Given what the state of nature would probably be like, it seems they should opt for the latter (but also do everything they can to ensure that the new order protects their natural rights).

Conclusion: Real-World Connections

In *V for Vendetta*, Britain had been plagued by disease and the Norsefire government used the threat of the pandemic to limit freedom. In 2020–21, the novel coronavirus, SARS-CoV-2, spread almost everywhere in the world and governments justified limits to individual freedom in the name of protecting against it: restaurants and other businesses were closed, travel was restricted, city officials around the world called for lockdowns, and mask mandates (which required the wearing of masks in public spaces to help curb the spread of the disease) were common. The temptation to compare the real world to the world of *V for Vendetta* was undeniable, and such comparisons were not uncommon on social media.

Indeed, the government oppression suffered by lockdowns, temporarily closing businesses, and government forcing individuals to wear masks and socially distance caused some to try to justify a rebellion against the government. For example, at least six men decided to fight back against the actions of Governor Gretchen Whitmer of Michigan when she imposed an executive order forcing people into a lockdown in March of 2020. The men, angry over coronavirus control measures, plotted to kidnap the Governor. They performed surveillance on the Governor's vacation home and conducted field training to breach the Michigan Capitol with "tactical weapons" (Katkov, January 27, 2021). These men said they were affiliated with the Wolverine Watchmen, and later joined forces with an anti-government group that wanted to start a civil war "leading to a societal collapse" (Bogel-Burroughs et al., January 27, 2021). These men, like V, were willing to use unlawful force to topple the government, so that "instead of government and order," we would end up with "anarchy and confusion" (Locke 1689, ch. 18 sect. 201).

It doesn't seem, however, that the argument of *V for Vendetta* can be used to justify such actions. Yes, in the novel, the government uses the excuse of pandemic to restrict some freedoms; but the violations of freedom that justified V's rebellions had nothing to do with the pandemic specifically. Remember what he went through: along with many others, he was wrongly imprisoned and tortured. He was drugged and experimented on. Indeed, V was the only "lucky" one to survive. Temporarily being asked to wear a mask in public spaces, and stay a little further away from other people, pales in comparison. Yes, some businesses were forced to temporarily close, but part of the social contract (for both Hobbes and Locke) includes giving up some liberties in exchange for security and protection. Part of this is giving up the liberty to unnecessarily risk harm to others. Given that large groups in enclosed spaces guaranteed the spread of a disease that (in one year) killed more than 500,000 in the United States alone, taking actions to curb the spread didn't violate the social contract – it upheld it.

If we are looking for similarities to the kind of liberty violations suffered by V, and the actions of the Norsefire regime, consider the real-world events of protesters in Portland being rounded up by Federal Officers in unmarked vans. Or take the government separating immigrant children from their families and placing them in cages in the US/Mexico border, or the continued unjustified abuse and murder of persons (and more often black persons) at the hand of the police (Schwartz and Jahn 2020). These are much more similar to what happened to V, and it is without doubt that *protests* in response to such prolonged oppressions are justifiable. But is disobeying the law and engaging in rebellion, specifically in V type rebellion, or even doing away with the state, justified in the wake of such injustices?

Consider the mass protests that broke out in the United States in the Summer of 2020 after police were filmed on cell phones killing George Floyd, an unarmed black man who allegedly tried to pass off a counterfeit $20 bill. Black Lives Matter (BLM) protests grew across the United States and prompted protests in other countries. While most (93%) were peaceful (ACLED 2020), some resulted in riots; windows were smashed, some businesses were looted, and a few government offices were set on fire. In response, the Secret Service agency deployed surveillance in cities around the country to monitor Black Lives Matter protests (Crump, August 14, 2020).

Now, to be fair, the BLM protesters themselves were not necessarily the rioters. According to a Department of Homeland Security (DHS) internal memo, "most of the violence appears to have been driven by opportunists" (Kelly and Samuels, June 22, 2020). This was backed up by Seth G. Jones, director of the transnational threats project at the Center for Strategic and International Studies, whose research revealed that most of the violence was caused by "local hooligans, sometimes gangs, sometimes just individuals that are trying to take advantage of an opportunity" (Kelly and Samuels, June 22, 2020). In fact, some of those arrested in the riots were actually members of (the right-wing anti-BLM movement) "boogaloo," and the white nationalist group Identity Evropa was caught on Twitter, pretending to be run by antifa activists, and calling for violence at BLM protests (Kelly and Samuels, June 22, 2020).

Still, the DHS considers "anarchist and anti-government extremists [to] pose the most significant threat of targeted low-level, protest-related assaults against law enforcement" (Kelly and Samuels, June 22, 2020). Given the proximity of the riots to the BLM protests, and the abuses they were a response to, the question of whether such *V for Vendetta* type violence is a legitimate response to such government abuses is a legitimate one. Vicky Osterweil, "a self-described writer, editor and agitator," in an NPR interview said that the "riots are a space in which a mass of people has produced a situation in which the general laws that govern society no longer function" (Escobar, August 27, 2020). So, could the argument of *V for Vendetta* be used to justify riots in the face of police violence?

Simmons says that for Locke, individuals can be in the state of nature, war, while living under civil society. Simmons claims the legitimacy of the state is relational. The state is "partially illegitimate" for those who have suffered structural and historical injustices, and "the object of their disobedience is to defy or repair that wrong" (Simmons 2016, p. 1826). The Black Lives Matter movement and the riots were a consequence of a group of people living in the state of nature when those around them were not. "Rioters," Osterweil said, "who smash windows and take items from stores are engaging in a powerful tactic that questions the justice of 'law and order'" (Escobar, August 27, 2020). Violent disobedience arises from the structural and historical injustices of the state that does not rule for the good of all people. Locke's theory tells us that if people are disproportionately injured and have lost "legislative power" (how the law should be enforced) the people are justified in rebelling against the government (Locke 1689, sect. 176, 202, and 243). Rioting is a revolutionary type of activity used in order to repair the structural and historical wrongs. Indeed, it was the "Birmingham struggle of '63' that turned into a riot that caused the creation of the civil rights bill" (Escobar, August 27, 2020). The riots of 2020 were not about toppling the government *V for Vendetta* style; but they are about the injustices in the legal system and a government that infringes on human freedom. As such, and especially given that the Norsefire regime was run by right-wing fascists, if *V for Vendetta* was to be legitimately used as an analogy to justify anything that happened in 2020, it would seem to be the BLM protests against police violence and the riots that accompanied them.

References

ACLED. 2020. Demonstrations & political violence in America: New data for summer 2020. Bridging Divides Initiate. https://acleddata.com/acleddatanew/wp-content/uploads/2020/09/ACLED_USDataReview_Sum2020_SeptWebPDF_HiRes.pdf

Aristotle. 1984a. Nicomachean ethics. In *The complete works of Aristotle*, ed. Jonathan Barnes, 1729–1867. Princeton: Princeton University Press.

———. 1984b. Politics. In *The complete works of Aristotle*, ed. Jonathan Barnes, 1986–2129. Princeton: Princeton University Press.

Bogel-Burroughs, Nicholas, Shaila Dewan, and Gray Kathleen. 2021. F.B.I. Says Michigan anti-government group plotted to kidnap Gov. Gretchen Whitmer. *New York Times*, January 27. https://www.nytimes.com/2020/10/08/us/gretchen-whitmer-michigan-militia.html. Aaccessed 28 Feb 2021.

Crump, James. 2020. Secret service sought aircraft to protect Trump during Black Lives Matter protests outside White House: Agency asked for use of Black Hawk helicopter and surveillance plane to monitor demonstrators. *Independent*, August 14. https://www.independent.co.uk/news/world/americas/us-politics/secret-service-donald-trump-white-house-protests-george-floyd-black-lives-matter-a9671046.html. Accessed 2 Mar 2021.

Escobar, Natalie. 2020. One author's controversial view: 'In defense of looting'. *NPR*, August 27. https://www.npr.org/sections/codeswitch/2020/08/27/906642178/one-authors-argument-in-defense-of-looting. Accessed 2 Mar 2021.

Estienne de la Boétie. 1576. *The discourse of voluntary servitude*. Trans. Harry Kurz (1942). Indianapolis: Liberty Fund. https://oll-resources.s3.us-east-2.amazonaws.com/oll3/store/titles/2250/Boetie_Discourse1520_EBk_v6.0.pdf

Flood, Alison. 2019. "Alan Moore Drops Anarchism to Champion Labour against Tory 'Parasites.'" The Guardian, November 21, 2019. http://www.theguardian.com/books/2019/nov/21/alan-moore-drops-anarchism-to-champion-labour-against-tory-parasites

Frazer, Elizabeth, and Kimberly Hutchings. 2009. Politics, violence and revolutionary virtue: Reflections on Locke and Sorel. *Thesis Eleven* 97 (1): 46–63. https://doi.org/10.1177/0725513608101908.

Katkov, Mark. 2021. Suspect pleads guilty in plot to kidnap michigan governor, turns government witness. *NPR*, January 27. https://www.npr.org/2021/01/27/961215604/suspect-pleads-guilty-in-plot-to-kidnap-michigan-governor-turns-government-witne#:~:text=Garbin%20pleaded%20guilty%20to%20a%20single%20count%20of%20kidnapping%20conspiracy.,-Kent%20County%20(Mich&text=One%20of%20six%20defendants%20charged%20with%20plotting%20to%20kidnap%20Michigan,agreed%20to%20cooperate%20with%20investigators. Accessed 28 Feb 2021.

Kelly, Meg, and Elyse Samules. Who caused the violence at protests? It wasn't antifa. *The Washington Post*, June 22, 2020. https://www.washingtonpost.com/politics/2020/06/22/who-caused-violence-protests-its-not-antifa/

Killjoy, Margaret. "Mythmakers & Lawbreakers – Alan Moore on Anarchism." 2009 https://birdsbeforethestorm.net/2009/02/mythmakers-lawbreakers-alan-moore-on-anarchism

Locke, John. 1992. Second treatise of government. In *Classics of moral and political theory*, ed. Michael L. Morgan, 736–817. Indiana: Hackett Publishing.

Marcinkowska-Rosół. 2018. The concept of Brutishness (THĒRIOTĒS) in Aristotle's Nicomachean ethics. *Roczniki Humanistyczne* 66 (3): 81–117.

Moore, Alan. 2005. *V for Vendetta,* ed. Karen Berger, Jeb Woodard, and Scott Nybakken. Burbank: DC Comics.

Nielsen, Karen Margrethe. 2019. The tyrant's vice: Pleonexia and lawlessness in Plato's republic. *Philosophical Perspectives* 33: 146–169. https://onlinelibrary.wiley.com/doi/epdf/10.1111/phpe.12129

NPR. 2020. Federal officers use unmarked vehicles to grab people in portland, DHS confirms. https://www.npr.org/2020/07/17/892277592/federal-officers-use-unmarked-vehicles-to-grab-protesters-in-portland

Plato. 1997. Republic. In *Plato complete works*, ed. John M. Cooper, 971–1223. Indiana: Hackett Publishing.

Schwartz, G.L., and J.L. Jahn. 2020. Mapping fatal police violence across U.S. metropolitan areas: Overall rates and racial/ethnic inequities, 2013–2017. *PLoS One* 15 (6): e0229686. https://doi.org/10.1371/journal.pone.0229686.

Simmons, A. John. 1979. *Moral principles and political obligations*. Princeton: Princeton University Press.

———. 2016. Disobedience and its objects. *Boston University Law Review* 90(4): 1805–1831. https://www.bu.edu/law/journals-archive/bulr/documents/simmons.pdf

Asterios Polyp as Philosophy: Master of Two Worlds

93

Bradley Richards

Contents

Introduction	2066
The Story	2066
The Telling of the Story	2068
Ignazio as Narrator	2069
Perception and Self	2070
Universals and Particulars, the Concrete and the Abstract	2072
Plato and the Two Worlds	2073
The Hero's Journey	2075
Departure	2077
Initiation	2077
Return	2081
Conclusion	2082
References	2083

Abstract

The graphic novel *Asterios Polyp* uses the story of Asterios, a laughable "paper architect," who has never produced a building, to tackle the challenging topics of the abstract and the concrete, the universal and the particular. Asterios goes on a journey conforming with the Hero's Journey or Monomyth, but he arrives not at the rarified or transcendent, but the humble and concrete. Plato saw the sensible world of particulars as populated by imperfect imitations, and imitative art (like graphic novels) as even further removed from truth, *Asterios Polyp* cleverly uses pictures, their colors, lines, and other properties to illustrate its claims and vindicate and celebrate the particular, though not at the expense of the universal. We learn with Asterios that to live a good life and find peace in the world, we must integrate the abstract and the concrete, the universal and particular.

B. Richards (✉)
Department of Philosophy, York University, Toronto, ON, Canada
e-mail: tbrad.richards@torontomu.ca; bradrich@yorku.ca

© Springer Nature Switzerland AG 2024
D. K. Johnson et al. (eds.), *The Palgrave Handbook of Popular Culture as Philosophy*,
https://doi.org/10.1007/978-3-031-24685-2_101

Keywords

Asterios Polyp · Philosophy · Aesthetics · Depiction · Pictures · Metaphysics · Universals · Particulars · Abstract · Concrete · Monomyth · Hero's Journey

Introduction

Asterios Polyp shows that the seemingly arcane metaphysical topics of universals and particulars and the abstract and concrete can have practical relevance to how we conceive of our lives – and how we live them. The graphic novel exploits medium-specific properties to visually explore the tension between the transcendent other-worldly Platonic forms and the material world of concrete things. Asterios is sent on an archetypal Hero's Journey conforming with the monomyth, and his quest demands that he discover how to move from his detached, abstract life with his head in the clouds, to life in the concrete, temporal, world.

Content and form are expertly integrated in *Asterios Polyp*. Most, or perhaps all, of the claims and arguments presented in *Asterios Polyp* could be presented in a few well-chosen sentences. Yet this work is philosophically and artistically important. *Asterios Polyp* must exist in this form – it is only by presenting a story in this serial imagistic form that this work can be what it is and illustrate the points that it does. It cannot be translated without loss into a different medium because the illustrative examples would be lost, the artistry would be altered, the detail and particularity on which the claims depend would be changed – and they would no longer be convincing to the same degree (for better or worse).

The story must be presented as this concrete thing, this group of well-placed illustrations, apprehended in just the way it affords; and yet, paradoxically, the story is not identical to any particular concrete instance of *Asterios Polyp*, neither to my copy on my desk nor to your copy on yours. That is the profundity of the thing. The medium, the message, and the thing are knit together, through and through. This is a story about universals and abstractions, about their beauty, their necessity, their instability, and their near impossibility. All these things can be said about the concrete and particular too. They fit together like hand and glove, form and content, ink and illustration. We cannot hope to explain away the tension between the concrete and the abstract, to embrace one and abandon the other. We can, however, embark with Asterios on his Hero's Journey to see how they hang together, and find some peace in the profundity of the particular, and ease with our place in eternity, at least for a moment.

The Story

The story (or *fabula*) consists roughly of the chronological events as they occur in the fiction. This can be distinguished from the telling of the story (the syuzhet) (Erlich 1956). This section presents the fabula of *Asterios Polyp*. This is not just any story; it is an instance of the Hero's Journey or *Monomyth* (more will be said about this in the following). It is powerful partly because it is an instance of, or exemplifies, something more general (but it does this by being this story with all its warts and particularities).

The earliest events in the story concern the childhoods of Asterios and his future wife, Hana. Asterios's father is of Greek descent and the family surname was shortened when immigrating to the United States. Asterios was a precocious child who did things like disassemble a Swiss clock to learn how it works. He had a twin brother who was stillborn and whose name would have been Ignazio. (Ignazio narrates at least some of the story.) Asterios was a talented student who excelled in academia, ultimately earning a teaching position and professional respect as a "paper architect," meaning that, although he was well regarded, his drawings and architectural designs have never been realized as buildings.

We also meet Hana, who is similar in that she excels academically, and in that her pursuit of sculpture is like Asterios's study of architecture. Hana's father was German and her mother Japanese. Hana was raised in the shadow of her brothers and received very little recognition from her parents. Ultimately, Asterios and Hana meet while both are teaching at a college in Ithaca, NY. Asterios showers Hana with attention and wins her favor; however, he is self-absorbed and egotistical, and he doesn't really listen to her much. They have a long relationship with some charming and heartfelt moments, punctuated by intense conflict and distance. Ultimately, their relationship fails largely because of his egoism and the incompatibility of his cold and abstract rationalism with her warm, organic, and grounded perspective.

Sometime following the dissolution of the relationship, Asterios's apartment is struck by lightning. He is moping around his neglected apartment, watching videotapes of intimate moments in his relationship with Hana. The tapes are from a library of security camera-style recordings of every moment of his life, in every room in his apartment. Earlier when Hana discovers this collection, he explains that this archival doubling of his life has been part of his mechanism for dealing with his relationship with his deceased twin brother Ignazio.

The lightning strike causes a fire. Asterios flees the fire as his apartment and his video record of his life are destroyed. He descends into the train station and buys a ticket to the farthest point he can afford, a town called Apogee. In Apogee, he gets a job fixing cars. He doesn't know how to fix cars, so he has to fake it and learn what he can quickly. (This comes fairly easy to Asterios, as the story indicates early on that, even as a boy, "practically everything he read, he committed to memory.") He also moves in with the mechanic that employs him, "Stiff," and Stiff's family: his wife Ursula and son Jackson. We also meet Steven Drizzle in the local diner who is watching the sky, scanning for asteroids that could destroy Earth.

In Apogee, Asterios leads a practical life, getting his hands dirty fixing cars and living at a family pace. This is in stark contrast to his academic life and his egotism. After he has lived there for a while, Stiff presents him with a design drawing for a treehouse that he's planning to construct. Asterios proceeds to build the treehouse with Stiff. Asterios stays in town a little while longer, winds up getting hit in the head with a bottle while watching an acquaintance's band, the Radniks, at a local bar. He ends up hospitalized and comatose, or at least an unconscious state for a while. During that time, he has a confrontation with his brother Iganazio (in a dream or other worldly state).

When he awakens, he immediately finishes building a solar powered car that had sat, unfinished and abandoned, at Stiff's garage and begins a long journey across the country. The car breaks down and he finishes the journey on foot, through a blizzard. He finally arrives at Hana's house. When they reunite, they are sympatico; they relate better than ever before. However, we are shown that outside their building, there is an asteroid on a collision course with Earth.

That's a rough outline of the story events presented in chronological order. There is a separate issue of how the story is told and the order in which the events are actually presented to the reader (which is not chronological), both of which are indispensable to appreciating the philosophical significance of *Asterios Polyp*.

The Telling of the Story

The syuzhet (or the telling of the story) refers to the order in which the story events are presented to the reader. Most people are familiar with a variety of nonlinear or nonchronological storytelling forms from film and the powerful effects they can produce. For example, sometimes the film opens with an event near the end of the story before recounting how things got to that point, and consequently, the viewer is better able to understand where the action is going, and thus the storyteller can build tension and suspense.

Asterios Polyp begins with his apartment building being hit by lightning. From there, it continues forward following his trip to Apogee. In other words, it begins in the middle of the fabula. The color palette for the graphic novel is built around cyan, magenta, and yellow. These are the basic colors used in the subtractive CMYK printing and color mixing. This is significant because these three colors were used to print early comic books, and the various colors were created by overlapping, or mixing, those basic colors in different ways. This device is important for several reasons, but especially since the color use separates the graphic novel into several immediately recognizable sections that rely on distinctive combinations of only two of these three primary colors. These mark the transitions between the A, B, and C stories as well as a few vignettes. For simplicity, let's call the primary story the "A story." The A story begins with Asterios's apartment being struck by lightning and concludes with his reunion with Hana, and is told using only magenta and yellow (with the exception of last section). The "B story," which tells the backstory of Asterios's and Hana's lives (both apart and together), begins with the birth of Asterios and continues until the dissolution of his relationship with Hana sometime before his apartment is hit by lightning). This backstory is told primarily in magenta and cyan and does not use yellow.

The A and B stories are interwoven with a "C story" that is psychological, internal, or possibly otherworldly, and consists of a series of dream-like vignettes that occur between Asterios and Ignazio (Asterios's mysterious stillborn twin). This part of the story is told in *yellow* and magenta (in his case magenta is employed sparingly for accents, outlining and shading, as opposed to the *magenta* and yellow of the A story). Asterios is colored in yellow in this section, instead of magenta, or cyan. The exact metaphysical status of Ignazio is certainly open to interpretation, though there are textual hints that he is real, even if he is a purely psychological entity. We might think of Iganazio as Asterios's alter ego, in which case he is part of Asterios and these are psychological events, so it's a kind of memory or fantasy; alternately, we might think of Ignazio as a real denizen of another world that is psychologically accessible to Asterios, or perhaps he is a distinct person that also inhabits Asterios at a subconscious level.

In addition to these three visually distinct arcs in the telling of the story, there is an Orpheus story, where Asterios as Orpheus travels to the underworld to find Hana. This is colored entirely in magenta (dark purple in this case). There is also the psychological, flashback-style "I have a blister on my foot" chapter which is colored in the same way as the rest of the B story.

Distinguishing between these parts of the story visually with their unique color pallets is powerful because the B story provides insight into the problem that the A story resolves, in part through the C story (we will see that the A story reaches a sort of integrative visual crescendo (or is it a diminuendo?) bringing the color palates together). Simply put, Asterios has to change psychologically and come to terms with his past to reunite with Hana. When he reunites with her, the colors mix and the styles integrate. However, it is the nature of the change – relinquishing his staunch rationalism, abstraction, and commitment to simple dualities by finding a place in the world of particulars – that *Asterios Polyp* illustrates so well as it wrestles with the philosophical oppositions between universals and particulars and the abstract and concrete.

Ignazio as Narrator

Iganzio, Asterios's stillborn brother, is an explicit diegetic narrator (he tells the B story); he is also a character in the C story (he appears, very briefly, in the B story as a fetus). In addition to his explicit narration, Ignazio's perspective may be implicit in the visual representations. In his narrational role, he influences the interpretation of the story through his probing philosophical hypotheticals. Even the mere fact that Ignazio is the narrator brings into question the nature and objectivity of this part of the story. Is Ignazio just part of Asterios that is telling the story from his perspective, based on his memory? Or does Ignazio have another, perhaps objective view of these events? Can he tell us the truth of these events or just another biased perspective like that of Asterios? Ignazio draws attention to his puzzling and paradoxical status as narrator when he says at the beginning of the second chapter, "If it were possible for me to narrate this story, I'd begin here." Of course, on the one hand, it is possible for him to narrate the story, since he is narrating the B story, but on the other hand, the story doesn't begin here, since the A story begins in the first chapter.

The syuzhet begins, in the A story, with the forming of raindrops in the heavens (which we will see is the proper realm of the abstract and universal). We ride a lightning bolt thrown down from the sky to snap Asterios out of his torpor. There is no explicit narration here. There is no subjective perspective (Ignazio is present, if at all, only as a shadow). We are taken from the heavens to the gritty, dirty, fallen world of particulars: Asterios's squalid, derelict apartment and life, the filthy journey underground to the subway strewn with the suffering, homeless, sick, and lonely. This story is unfolding in the present. It is (at least apparently) immediate, not structured or rationalized, or presented by a mind. This story is concrete, in particular, in time. It is in the world, and the telling is more objective (less subjective) than the B story.

In contrast, the B story narrated by Ignazio is a story of the past, and so, if Ignazio is telling the B story (as a flashback) in the A story we see unfolding in the present, he cannot begin at the beginning (in the past). This may seem complex enough, but actually, there is an additional complication, since the narration of the B story starts with what seems like a window (a circular panel) into the A story. Asterios is depicted using yellow with a magenta background, standing in the rain, and Ignazio tells us he is, "right now, watching his home burn up." So he is in the present, and it seems natural to interpret his comment about where to start the story as referring to the backstory (saying he can't start with it because it is in the past), but there is the additional issue that he isn't in control of the bit of the A story that proceeds this (and so the A story is secured as more objective). Thus, there is a tension in the telling of the story, that Ignazio, whatever his ultimate nature, makes clear.

Perception and Self

Iganzio queries: What if reality (as perceived) were simply an extension of the self?

His idea is that the way each person experiences the world is determined by his or her self. Here "self" must be understood in the sense of the character, memory, and beliefs that the person has acquired over their life. This quote is in the "apple" chapter (the chapter preceded by a picture of a bunch of apples in different styles, or possibly the same apple depicted in a bunch of different styles). This foregrounds the central issue of universals and particulars, and how storytelling and depiction require taking a particular stance and concretizing the story told, or the apple depicted. Here this facet of artistic creation, that Plato criticized, is related to perception and the reality of the world perceived. (Plato and universals will be discussed in more detail in the next section.)

Ignazio's hypothetical is cleverly illustrated by showing the students and professors on a university campus depicted in different styles corresponding to illustrative conventions in their disciplines, or in a fashion that otherwise reflects their worldview. One person is a tangle of nerves, another blood vessels, corresponding to their life science worldviews. Others are subtly crosshatched in accordance with their well-integrated normal perception, and in contrast to still others who are depicted in a cubist perceptual multiplicity. Ignazio further muses:

> ...Maybe one person's construction of the world could influence someone else's. You would have to imagine that these constructions, whatever their origins, are not immutable. (Mazzucchelli 2009)

This is illustrated with Asterios lecturing. He is drawn as only a structure of hollow, cyan, three-dimensional solids; many, but not all, of the students in his class are depicted in the same style, suggesting that his view of the world is influencing their character and perspective. Finally, Ignazio adds: This would suggest it's possible for someone to freely alter his own perception of reality in order to overlap with that of another (Mazzucchelli 2009).

This is a non sequitur. This last thought does not follow from the earlier ones. The idea that your view could influence, or be influenced by, someone else's view seems true, but it does not seem voluntary, or at least not necessarily. The idea that you could freely alter your own perception of reality so you can choose to see things in the way that somebody does is very different from passively being influenced.

Whether or not Iganazio's views are philosophically defensible, or adequate to the interpretation of this work, they permeate many parts of the graphic novel. Asterios is characterized by the three-dimensional solid like cylinders and ellipses and very simple lines, and in contrast, Hana is shaded with a lot of subtlety and crosshatching. He is depicted in cyan, she in a sort of pinkish hot magenta. This establishes a convention that allows the world around Asterios to be depicted in a similar cool style, while the world around Hana is crosshatched, detailed, and pink. Especially in light of Ignazio's comments, this is taken to result from their characters influencing how they see the world.

These conventions are important because they allow us to see the worldview of the character, to see how they are influenced by others, and even to see how they are feeling, e.g., alone or connected, as a function of these illustrative conventions. For example, when their relationship is flourishing, the palette and illustrative conventions settle on a compromise or integration between the stylistic extremes, but when Hana and Asterios quarrel, she is again illustrated with pink hot magenta hatching, and he with simple cyan lines and geometric solids.

This clash of worldviews ultimately grounds the romantic story and integrates into the deeper philosophical problem. Emphasizing Iganzio's narrational signposts makes this seem like a purely psychological drama. It is a psychological journey, including changing perception, but it is also more. The metaphysical tension between universals and particulars and the abstract and concrete concerns not just how people see things, but how things actually are. It is this tension that makes resolving the issue of how we see things, and of synchronizing our perspectives, so pressing and so vexing. The tension between universals and particulars, the abstract and the concrete in general, and Plato's philosophy in particular, is a key to unlocking this story.

Universals and Particulars, the Concrete and the Abstract

At least since Plato, philosophers have reflected on the fact that we can find the same features or properties in many places at the same time: the one over the many. The very same shade of green is found in this leaf and in that one, so it appears that the very same green is in two places at once. This is a bit odd when you reflect on it; usually we think of things being limited to one place at a time. If I reported that my phone was in my pocket and also in my desk drawer, something would be amiss.

It is possible that my phone has two parts and one is in my desk drawer while the other is in my pocket. No problem. But that is not how it seems with the distribution of green things. Each one is wholly green (or has a part that is wholly green) – the green is not partly in each location, as if some of the green were missing. This point can perhaps be made more clearly with a different example. Suppose a bookstore has two copies of the same edition of the *Republic* by Plato. Each copy is a complete instance of Plato's *Republic*; it is clearly not the case that the *Republic* is partly in one copy and partly in the other.

Realists (like Plato or Bertrand Russell 1912) say properties like greenness are *universals*, and universals can be in many places at once. Each leaf has the property (or quality) of greenness. The two leaves from the earlier example (as well as emeralds and Granny Smith apples) are all green at the same time, but are in different locations, and are numerically distinct. This ability to be in more than one place at a time seems to be a special characteristic of universals. In contrast to each leaf's greenness, each leaf is a *particular* that must be in one place at a time.

It is useful to draw the distinction between universals and particulars, but it doesn't directly address the mystery of universals, of the one over the many. Plato thought that universals like green, or beauty, or goodness, are transcendent – that they exist outside space and time and independently of the concrete particulars that have them. Notice too, that this means they exist independently of any particular mind thinking them since psychological states are temporal (they have duration and happen "in" time). Some more contemporary philosophers (e.g., Russell 1912) endorse a view that is similar to Plato's in this respect; they treat properties (like greenness), as well as relations, numbers, and other mathematical entities like sets, as *abstract* (meaning that they exist outside space and time). Abstract entities are contrasted with concrete entities that exist in space and time, or at least in time, like the cedar tree in my yard, or your kitchen table.

Other philosophers acknowledge that universals exist, but treat them as immanent, which is to say that they exist only in the concrete particulars that have or exemplify them. David Armstrong (1997, p. 135ff) endorses this view. According to Armstrong's immanent realism, properties such as greenness exist only as nonspatial parts or aspects of actual physical things. This view acknowledges the reality of universals while refusing them transcendental status. However, the view may be unstable. It implies that greenness is scattered across the locations of all the particulars that exemplify it. Yet this leaves unaddressed the issue of how universals can be wholly present in more than one location, and how there can be a class of spatio-temporal entities that do not behave like particulars (Lowe 2002). Armstrong endorses universals but not abstract objects; others, like Quine (1964), accept some abstract objects (like sets) but reject universals.

In contrast to realists about universals, nominalists about universals deny the existence of universals; nominalists about abstract objects deny the existence of abstract entities outside of space and time (Rodriguez-Pereyra 2019). On some nominalist views, properties are taken to be *tropes* or property instances: the particular greenness of this leaf and the particular greenness of that leaf. This is in contrast to a universal which is wholly in both leaves, and may, at least for the transcendent realist, exist independently of both leaves. The tropist denies that both leaves are similar in having the universal green as a constituent. Instead, there are two distinct tropes: the greenness of leaf *a* and the greenness of leaf *b* (Orilia and Paolini Paoletti 2022). Trope theory avoids positing abstract or transcendent entities but loses the compelling explanation of the similarity and resemblance of particulars, like the two green leaves, in virtue of their shared universals. Another view, conceptualism, treats properties as mere concepts or ways of grouping things together; but this, like some versions of trope theory, seems to put the cart before the horse (what is it about the particular objects that makes us group them together?) (Orilia and Paolini Paoletti 2022).

There are many other subtle issues to explore here, but what should start to be clear is that neither taking properties to be real, transcendent universals nor treating them in some other way, as merely immanent, or as tropes, or concepts, is fully satisfying. Universals seem to be necessary, but not at home in the physical world, and particulars seem to be lost without them. This is especially clear in Plato's philosophy, which cleaves the world in two.

Plato and the Two Worlds

Plato discussed universals as *Forms* (in Hamilton and Cairns 1961, e.g., *Phaedo* 75c–d, *Symposium* 211e, *Republic* V.476c). Forms are transcendent and can be known directly, perhaps through reason, or as Plato claims, directly through acquaintance of the soul with the Forms before birth and embodiment. In contrast, particular things instantiate the Forms and are known through sense perception.

Beautiful things are beautiful, and we encounter the Form of beauty in each beautiful thing. But here's the catch: they are not perfect copies (so to speak) of the Form of beauty. They imperfectly instantiate the beautiful. Likewise for other things: for example, there is a Form of a bed, but no actual bed is adequate to the Form. This aspect of Plato's view and its legacy is an extreme version of the universal view in that it cleaves creation into two separate worlds: the eternal world of the Forms, reason, and abstraction, and the temporal world of imperfect, particular, concrete things, and also sensation and its illusions.

Plato distrusts sensation because sensation can mislead – it is changeable, and so any information based on sensation can only be temporarily or contingently true. This all makes Plato doubly suspicious of imitative art, since it imitates a sensible thing, which is itself an imitation, or imperfect instantiation, of the form, leading us further from the truth. Thus, getting back to *Asterios Polyp*, there are two points of interest here: first, Asterios, by virtue of his attitude and perspective, inhabits the world of the Forms and abstraction; it is a world free from illusion and error but detached from the concrete reality of particular things. He is a paper architect; his "buildings," such as the Akimbo Arms, have remained blueprints and designs, mere abstractions. They are perfect in that they are not marred by instantiation, but they also don't exist as concrete particulars at all! (It would seem to be a knock against a "perfect" apartment building, like the Akimbo Arms, that no one can actually *stay* in it.) To be perfect is to be uninstantiated, which captures that pervasive air of paradox. It is worth noting that Ignazio too inhabits this abstract world only. In contrast to Asterios, Hana very much occupies the sensuous world of detail, particularity, and imperfection. This is evident both in the detailed visual style in which she is depicted and also in her manner and sculptural work.

The second point of interest here is the relationship between the depictions and their subjects and between the form and content of the work more generally. This is raised explicitly by Ignazio and is evident throughout the work, starting from the volume's dust jacket that fails to conceal the book, the title (the letters of which are only discernible by the subtractive overlap, and negative-space magenta and cyan designs), and the binding pages, replete with line drawings of many types of flowers. Hana tells us that her name means "flower," and Asterios, in his pompous way, comments "Not coreopsis, or daisy? Not Tiger-Lily, or Jack-in-the-Pulpit?" This draws attention to the fact that these are all ways of being flowers; they are species of a genus, determinates under a determinable. Though there could be a universal for each species, as well as the genus, this foregrounds the fact that a concrete particular must be determinate. If there is to be a particular flower, it must be a daisy or lily; it cannot be simply a flower. Asterios is right that Hana's name is a poor fit, but for reasons that are opaque to him at the time. It is odd that Hana, who is organic, detailed, concrete, and particular, is named just flower (but maybe fitting that her parents, who ignored her particularities while focusing on her brothers, gave her that name).

This issue also arises for illustration, since illustrations must be particular in many respects; a drawing of a flower, if colored, will have a specific color, size, and contour. It will also be in a certain style. In this sense, imitative representations like drawings are more particular than, say, novels. In a novel, a character can smell "a flower," but in a graphic novel, the flower, if colored, must have visual features: a specific color and shape. These flowers and flower drawings may be imperfect flowers and flower illustrations, but a totally generic flower illustration would not depict a flower at all. This is highlighted in the apple chapter title illustration. We see 12 illustrations of apples, each in a different style. These could be understood as different ways of seeing or illustrating the same apple, but it is also reminiscent of all the different apples imperfectly instantiating applehood.

Asterios Polyp further explores the tension between these two worlds, that of the universal, abstract, and eternal on the one hand, and the particular, concrete, temporal, and imperfect on the other by placing it at the heart of a twisted version of the Hero's Journey, a narrative structure made explicit by Joseph Campbell in *The Hero with a Thousand Faces* (Campbell 1949/2008). The hero usually journeys from the mundane particularity of everyday life to the transcendent heavenly truths of universals. By contrast, Asterios must make an inverted journey from the perfect world of abstractions and universals to that of humble, concrete particulars.

Box 1 Joseph Campbell's Hero's Journey (Monomyth)

I. Departure
 1. Call to Adventure
 2. Refusal of the Call
 3. Supernatural Aid
 4. Crossing the Threshold
 5. Belly of the Whale
II. Initiation
 6. The Road of Trials
 7. Meeting with the Goddess
 8. Woman as Temptress
 9. Atonement with the Father
 10. Apotheosis
 11. Ultimate Boon
III. Return
 12. Refusal of Return
 13. Magic Flight
 14. Rescue from Without
 15. Crossing Return Threshold
 16. Master of Two Worlds
 17. Freedom to Live

The Hero's Journey

The Hero's Journey is a very powerful narrative structure that is evident in many stories, myths, and religions. It consists of the hero embarking on a journey that takes him away from his ordinary world, facing a series of trials, and ultimately undergoing a transformative ordeal resulting in a reward. Sometimes the reward is an item, often of profound or life-altering significance (such as an elixir of eternal life); at other times, it is deep or transcendent knowledge. The hero must then return to the ordinary world with their magical item or insight. Sometimes the Hero's Journey is a literal one, sometimes an inward psychological journey, and sometimes – like with Asterios's journey – it is both.

The journey consists of three major parts or acts: I. Departure/Separation; II. Descent/Initiation; and III. Return. Joseph Campbell (1949) divides the three acts into 17 stages, some of which fit *Asterios Polyp* very well (Box 1). Other authors have refined and simplified Campbell's stages (e.g., Vogler (2007) identifies 12 stages). This is a hint that it may be difficult to fit a given story exactly to any given version of this formal structure (another tension between the universal and particular). Nevertheless, stories of this kind are powerful because there is a confrontation with the deepest aspects of existence, like the mysteries of being, life, and death. As Campbell writes of the apotheosis stage, in which the hero achieves a deeper understanding:

> Those who know, not only that the Everlasting lives in them but that what they, and all things, really are *is* the Everlasting, dwell in the groves of the wish-fulfilling trees, drink the brew of immortality, and listen everywhere to the unheard music of eternal concord. (1949/2020, p. 190)

This achievement requires a dissolution of the hero's self, or ego, during the atonement with the father, as Campbell (1949) dramatically puts it:

> Atonement consists in no more than the abandonment of that self-generated double monster—the dragon thought to be God (superego) and the dragon thought to be Sin (repressed id). But this requires an abandonment of the attachment to ego itself, and that is what is difficult. (1949/2020, p. 154)

Asterios Polyp can be profitably interpreted in many ways, and treating it as a Hero's Journey is only one interpretation, and one that leaves much to the side, but it does provide some links to connect the philosophical themes of the work to its narrative structure.

Asterios's immediate problem is the loss of Hana, who complemented and completed him, and compensated in some way for the loss of Ignazio. Asterios's relationship with Hana failed largely because they occupied different worlds. He occupies the rational, binary, formally simplified, abstract, and eternal; she occupies the detailed, scalar, particular, concrete, temporal, and organic. Thus, the object of Asterios's quest is to return to Hana, but he cannot do this until he is transformed, until his personality dissolves – in other words, until he gains insight into the paradoxical relationship between universals and particulars, the eternal and the temporal, the abstract and the concrete. Asterios's Hero's Journey is inverted (at least superficially). His ordinary world is transcendent (at least as he conceives it), and thus, he must travel to the "lower" concrete world; in contrast, transformative religious insight is usually gained by shaking off the strictures of the material world and its particulars. Ultimately, though, the goal in both cases is to reconcile these two realms, and in that sense, Asterios's journey conforms. Moreover, in the ways discussed earlier, and in many others, *Asterios Polyp* wrestles with and exploits its own form and particularity. Thus, the tension between the abstract and concrete that structures his quest is palpable throughout the telling of the story. By discussing a few of the specific stages in his Hero's Journey, we will see how he achieves his goal.

Departure

For Asterios, the Call to Adventure (1) is when lightning strikes his apartment and in a very literal way his (record of) ordinary life – all his videotapes, as well as his curated furniture collection, and his apartment itself – are destroyed. He considers his video collection to be a video doppelganger of himself, and it is as if he is keeping this record as a surrogate for Ignazio. His apartment is also already a disaster, strewn with dirty pots and unpaid bills, so maybe he has Refused the Call (2) to address his character defects, and his relationship with Hana and Iganzio, for a while. The lightning strike sends him on his journey.

Asterios's journey begins with a descent into the train station, past various sick and destitute people. The descent status of this trip is made even clearer in the Orpheus chapter; Asterios takes a journey analogous to Orpheus' journey to the underworld to retrieve his wife Eurydice, and passes monsters and tortured souls. The journey in this chapter clearly visually mirrors Asterios's own descent into the train station.

As he descends, Asterios is accompanied by a shadowy, dotted-doppelganger, who seems clearly to be Ignazio. Ignazio may be a Supernatural Aid (3), or mentor, guiding Asterios at this point (although Asterios will have to resolve his conflict with Ignazio later). While the descent is sometimes located much later in the story structure, Crossing the Threshold (4) into the other, or magical world is clearly a descent in multiple senses in this story (although in this case he is crossing into the ordinary particular world – not the transcendent supernatural one – due to the inversion).

When Asterios arrives in Apogee and approaches Stiff and Ursula Major's house for the first time, it is surrounded by water. Stiff comments "We had some flooding." This seems to be the Belly of the Whale (5). The whale consumes, and entering is a kind of self-annihilation; Campbell likens the belly to the womb, and the temple, "Once inside he [the hero] may be said to have died to time and returned to the World Womb, the World Navel, the Earthly Paradise" (1949/2020, p. 108). This then is a life-renewing act. It is here – by living with Stiff, Ursula, and Jackson – that Asterios undergoes his transformation, one whereby he resolves the conflict between the universal and the particular, the eternal and the temporal, the abstract and the concrete.

Initiation

Stages 6–9 are not as important to the philosophical themes here (and also there are many valid interpretations that fit these stages). Nonetheless, there are still many aspects of Asterios's journey that conform to these stages. Asterios meets Ursula Major, who flatly says "While you're staying here, don't worry if you happen to fall in love with me, everyone does… I'm a goddess." Clearly, this is the Meeting with the Goddess (7) but also announces the Woman as Temptress (8). She seems to perform mainly the first role, providing wisdom, challenging Asterios's worldview, and urging him toward his transformation. For example, during their picnic by the giant asteroid crater, Ursula challenges Asterios's dualistic division between male and female and generalizes further "Well, y'know, in life, things are seldom either/ or." It is worth mentioning that Stiff is also clearly a mentor or helper: he gives Asterios shelter, guides him to the "temple" (his house), gives him a job, and ultimately provides him with the means of escape through magical flight (the solar car). In Vogler's (2007) version of the Monomyth, the stage before crossing the threshold is called "Meeting with the Mentor." In Campbell's version, the closest parallel is Supernatural Aid (3) (Stiff provides very natural, down-to-earth aid).

When Asterios leaves his burning apartment, he brings three items with him: his father's lighter, his first wristwatch, and a Swiss army knife Hana found on the beach while the two were together. These items structure his journey to some extent. He gives the watch to Ursula's son Jackson. In doing so, he sheds some of his personal history; the watch especially embodies his preoccupation with abstraction, systems, analogs, and conventions used to divide up the world into manageable parts (in this case, the day into hours, corresponding to wedges from a circle). The Swiss army knife he retains and employs the corkscrew tool to open a bottle of wine with Hana when they reunite. He still admires its design, (retaining his appreciation of the abstract), but he also puts it to practical use (in the concrete world).

His father's lighter is actually the first item he dispenses with; Asterios casually gives it to a former convict on the bus to Apogee. But that isn't the end of the matter. The Atonement with the Father (9) involves the dissolution of the self and the confrontation with the ultimate power in the hero's life, who holds power over life and death (Campbell 2020, p. 171ff). Parting with these items that are so closely tied to his personality, and in this case, his relationship with his father reflects Asterios's dissolution of character. Asterios's father also languished with Alzheimer's and other illness for years, while Asterios's mother struggled to make sense of the suffering and God's silence. When Asterios is on the train to Apogee, before he gifts the lighter, he recalls his father both as a powerful composed figure lighting a cigarette with the lighter and later as a helpless old man being spoon-fed. In addition to being his father, Asterios's father places him in direct contact with the Father, the incomprehensible nature of our fleeting earthly existence and the inscrutability of its divine or transcendent purpose.

> The problem of the hero going to meet the father is to open his soul beyond terror to such a degree that he will be ripe to understand how the sickening and insane tragedies of this vast and ruthless cosmos are completely validated in the majesty of Being...He beholds the face of the father, understands—and the two are atoned. (Campbell 2020, p. 171ff)

However, it seems that Asterios was not ready for the transition, and the glib gesture of giving the lighter away on the bus haunts him when the lighter-bearer reappears towards the end of the story and smacks Asterios in the face with a bottle, landing him in a coma (and blinding him in his left eye).

During the coma, Asterios bludgeons Ignazio, who has assumed Asterios's life and past in a dream-like scenario. Asterios feels that Ignazio has lived part of his life, that his own particular existence is contingent, and he even reflects, "If he had been the one to survive, would his life have followed exactly the path mine has?" (Mazzucchelli 2009, Terracotta Warriors chapter). Moreover, the bright yellow dream-world asides featuring Iganzio – the C story – punctuate the entire book. These are introduced with a psychological transition: Asterios is sleeping, or otherwise unconscious, before or after these scenes. Asterios is wrestling with several issues: with the fact that he survived instead of Ignazio (which includes Ignazio's claim on his life, or his type of life), with his own incompleteness or his sense that his life is unfulfilling, and with the loss of Ignazio. So, it seems reasonable to take this final conflict, and near-death experience, to complete Asterios's atonement.

The Apotheosis (10) is achieved when Asterios helps Stiff build a treehouse for Jackson. Stiff has scrawled a simple blueprint on a single sheet of paper, and when he shows it to Asterios, Asterios replies, "Looks Great." They immediately set to work building. The tree house – and Asterios's encouraging reaction to Stiff's crude blueprint – is so important because Asterios has been a "paper architect," which epitomizes his commitment to the abstract at the expense of the concrete. Following Plato, to create a concrete particular from the design or form, would be to make something imperfect: the thing will not live up to the idea. Moreover, Stiff's design is itself crude, but Asterios lauds it; in the past, he wittily insults his students design efforts, while inflating his own ego. Asterios has remained perfect, and received accolades, by staying out of the imperfect world of particulars, but he has comically remained an architect without buildings.

After finishing up with Stiff, Asterios shares with Ursula "that's the first house I ever built." It is perfect that his first actual building is a treehouse; so devoid of pretension, simple, and flawed, but also wonderful in its particularity. He has made a complete transition. Moreover, the treehouse also plays another significant role. In the final section of the graphic novel, Ursula and her family are all reposing in the treehouse together as an asteroid is hurtling toward the Earth. It doesn't matter that the treehouse is imperfect and humble. Their family has this incredible moment there together, which happened to be their last (there is a smidge of ambiguity here about their fate, and that is significant, especially in light of Asterios insights, and I will not seek to resolve it). Ronnie spots a shooting star, which is likely the asteroid. The final panel of that page is the sky and firmament viewed from earth, and the next page, the final page, is a title card of the asteroid viewed from the heavenly perspective with which we began the story. The heavenly transcendent and eternal has the last "word," but this doesn't undermine the tranquil moment.

When Asterios completes the treehouse, he has an aesthetic and religious experience that signals his realization. One kind of aesthetic experience, which we can call Proustian aesthetic experience, includes many features of a certain kind of religious experience: seeing the familiar in a novel way, an emphasis on formal properties (curves, angles, colors, and tones), a disinterested and not practical stance (Nanay 2016). The world is in slow motion as he is bathed in the formal properties of the particular world around him: the sun's warm rays on his cheek, the cricket's chirp, the fly's buzz, and the rustle of the tall grass. He doesn't even swat the fly on his cheek. He is not seeing the world in terms of practicality or simplifying abstractions; he is immersed in a flood of the simple formal properties in the immediate world around him. He is transformed. He sees the world around him now in its particularity, not just as abstractions. Again, his inverted journey is into the concrete and particular and away from the abstract, though, ultimately, he must unify them. He is now on his way to reuniting with Hana, but he must still return with this knowledge and master the two worlds. If this act of building the treehouse is not enough, he also captures his realization with a story he tells Ursula:

> There's a Shinto shrine in the town of Ise that's considered the most sacred shine in all Japan. It dates back to the fourth century, but since the late 800s it's been ceremonially razed and rebuilt every twenty years, using traditional techniques and materials. At any given time, no single piece of the structure is older than two decades... but the Japanese will tell you the shrine is about 2000 years old.

Ursula replies, "That makes perfect sense to me," and it seems that it now makes sense to Asterios too. This is a story about how a concrete, particular thing – a shrine – can have the permanence of an abstract universal. Ordinarily, particulars are perishable; this was exactly why Plato found them to be an inadequate source of knowledge and one reason why he believed that universal Forms were needed to explain any kind of permanence something might have. But the conclusion that Asterios and Ursula reach is that the shrine at Ise is the same, particular shrine despite every piece being destroyed and then replaced, all at once, every 20 years.

It is important to be clear that they don't mean that it's merely the same kind of shrine, but numerically the very same one, at least according to the story. So this is not merely a case of a universal – say shrine-ness, or even a certain specific style of Shinto shrine – being instantiated multiple times by different buildings in different places; this is the idea that the very same particular can persist through different material instantiations. The individual differences in constitution or material instantiation do not preclude the survival of the Ise shrine as a single, particular thing; that is, what makes the particular shrine what it is, consists in something other than the materials that it is made from, and yet it is a particular made from those materials. This suggests there is something like the "form" of an individual thing, though unlike a universal it cannot exist at two places at once.

On this view, the shrine does not have to be merely abstract to survive or to be eternal. Asterios finds resolution in this idea; he is able to bring together the abstract and concrete worlds and find some peace with death decay and eternity. Asterios's insight about shrines, or building in general, can be extended to the survival of persons over time and their place in eternity. (Swinburne 2019 argues that, at least for persons, survival does not depend on retaining other properties.) In the Hero's Journey, the hero must confront death – his own death – and here Asterios confronts, accepts, and transcends his own concrete material nature along with that of the whole fleeting material world. It is safe to realize a design as a particular building and to live in the material world.

This is a very metaphorical confrontation with his own mortality. Heroes often face a more literal death, or near-death and rebirth. Asterios is no exception, since he nearly dies when he is drunkenly bludgeoned by the man to whom he had earlier given his father's lighter. This incident occurs at the Radniks concert, after he has built the treehouse, and attained the insight and transformation necessary for reuniting with Hana. Arguably then, he has dwelled too long in Apogee and this incident is necessary to motivate his departure. Heroes often engage in a Refusal of the Return (12), doubting that their insight can survive the return journey, that it can be communicated, or just enraptured in the supernatural ecstasy (Campbell 1949/2020, p. 238). On the other hand, while he is unconscious, Asterios confronts Ignazio, so perhaps this is the final step necessary for his transformation and return and part of the Magic Flight (13). "If the trophy has been attained against the opposition of its guardian, or if the hero's wish to return to the world has been resented by the gods or demons, then the last stage of the mythological round becomes a lively, often comical, pursuit" (Campbell 1949/2020, p. 241). Perhaps Ignazio was not ready to see Asterios go.

When Asterios awakens in the hospital, he immediately asks Stiff if he can buy the solar car. Stiff gives it to him, and together they redesign the car. Once it is roadworthy, Asterios sets out on his return trip to meet Hana. A car powered by the sun might also qualify as a Magic Flight (13), and Stiff provides a kind of Rescue from Without (14) by these quasi-supernatural means.

Return

Returning to the ordinary world is not easy for the hero who must Cross the Return Threshold (15). As Campbell says, "he must survive the impact of the world" (Campbell 1949/2020, p. 268). The challenge is to return to the ordinary world with the insights he has gained. Asterios is making excellent progress on his return road trip, and this is apparent in the way his return is illustrated; the world around him is colored in soothing blends of the basic palette: greens, soft blues, and oranges. These are new color mixtures that have not occurred earlier in the story. His transition and transformation are evident. However, a blizzard covers his solar panels (and the road), cutting his journey short. He must make the rest of the journey on foot, through the snow, and exposed to the elements.

Finally, he reaches Hana, and is now Master of Two Worlds (16). The color blending is reaffirmed and intensified when he arrives at Hana's house. This is also a melding of the A, B, and C stories that have been told to that point, and of the periods with and without Hana. Interestingly, she has undergone a similar transition. They both now occupy the world of color mixtures (oranges, greens, fuchsias, browns, and soft blues) and share a more balanced visual style. Moreover, her new sculptures are of the five Platonic solids, forms crafted as particulars from a variety of materials. In the *Timaeus*, Plato (1961) hypothesizes that these solids are the corpuscles that constitute the elements of the physical world (Zeyl and Sattler 2022). Thus, as abstract mathematical objects that nonetheless have particular physicality, they are also sort of an interface between the abstract and the concrete. She too has integrated their disparate worldviews.

As Master of the Two Worlds Asterios is no longer constrained by his personal ambitions and idiosyncrasies and is able to enjoy Hana's company – and she his. He is able to relax and accept what comes to him. He can move easily between that material and the spiritual, the universal and particular, the concrete and abstract. The final step on the Hero's Journey is the Freedom to Live (17), which comes when the hero does not fear death (Campbell 1949/2020, p. 279ff). This freedom to live is exhibited in the final frames of the penultimate section where they sit quietly together as an asteroid hurtles toward them.

> He does not mistake apparent changelessness in time for the permanence of Being, nor is he fearful of the next moment (or of the "other thing"), as destroying the permanent with its change. (1949/2020, p. 284)
> But they don't get to live. Or rather, like the shrine, they don't get to go on living without being razed. They have the freedom to live, at peace in the particularity of those moments, and their place in eternity. Campbell writes, "one may invent a false, finally unjustified, image of oneself as an exceptional phenomenon in the world, not guilty as others are . . . The goal of the myth is to dispel the need for such life-ignorance . . . this is effected through a realization of the true relationship of the passing phenomena of time to the imperishable life that lives and dies in all." (1949/2020, pp. 280–281)

Asterios has escaped from his false self-image. He no longer insulates himself from others or the flaws and impermanence of the concrete world; he no longer hides in his perfect world of unrealized abstract designs. He has entered and accepted the concrete world, with its limitations, and perhaps dependence on the universal. But the concrete world is still not transcendent, universal, or abstract. It is temporal, changing, imperfect, particular, but beautiful. Like the lighting from above that started his journey, the asteroid from the immutable, eternal, and inscrutable heavens, ends it. Hana and Asterios are together, as are Ursula and her family in the treehouse, peaceful in the reality and wonder of that particular moment, below the heavens, and then, only sky.

Conclusion

In the graphic novel *Asterios Polyp*, we meet Asterios, who lives in a world of abstractions, holding himself above and apart from the concrete world. He is alone, doubly so because he is separated from his wife Hana. Illustrations bring us into his abstract world of universals while broadcasting their own determinate features and formal properties, which are inseparable from their content. We are constantly reminded in this way of the limitations of a simple focus on either the abstract or concrete, universals or particulars. The graphic novel is an instantiated concrete thing with determinate illustrations, but it is not identical to any copy; it conveys a profound message by exemplifying the Hero's Journey, but it is not just any Hero's Journey, it is Asterios's journey and, in some ways, an inverted journey into the everyday concrete world, not away from it.

Through his Hero's Journey, Asterios comes down from the lofty heights of academia, lives a family life, learns to maintain relationships, and enjoys the simple things. Among other things, he relinquishes his grip on his watch and its abstract representation of time; he resigns from the pretensions of his academic post to be an unassuming automotive mechanic; and he moves beyond mere conception and design and builds the treehouse for Ronnie and his family. Asterios is living and acting in the world. He is no longer struggling to define or sustain himself as something apart from the humdrum, or to justify his particular existence instead of Iganzio's. Instead, he finds himself in and among the mundane. He finds comfort in the thought that the shrine at Ise survives despite being razed. There is hope in the concrete world. He learns that he can't live exclusively in the world of abstractions and accepts the impermanence and imperfection of the world of concrete particulars. Plato is right that there are both universals and particulars, and even that the earthly is imperfect and impermanent, but Asterios learns (and *Asterios Polyp* shows us) that to properly understand our world and live our lives, we need both. Ordinary things are not merely imperfect forms. An architect without buildings is comical, but the lesson is about living not just architecture. Life cannot be lived in the abstract. Asterios's marriage, family relations, career, as well as his self, suffered when he limited himself to tidy abstraction. The abstract alone is lonely, hollow, cold, and empty, and can be misleading or harmful when it abstracts away from concrete particulars, simplifies continua, or ignores individuals. However, if we focus only on the particular and concrete, we miss the shared, the universal, and the eternal. *Asterios Polyp* is a call to those with their heads in the clouds to experience the beauty, detail, and diversity of the world and attend to the individuals around them. For those already earthly folks, it is a call to look to the heavens, and beyond the concrete.

References

Armstrong, D.M. 1997. *A world of states of affairs*. Cambridge, UK: Cambridge University Press.
Campbell, J. 1949/2020. *The hero with a thousand faces*, electronic edition. Joseph Campbell Foundation, Stillpoint Digital Press.
Erlich, Victor. 1956. Russian formalism: History – Doctrine. *Journal of Aesthetics and Art Criticism* 14 (4): 509–510.
Hamilton, Edith, and Huntington Cairns, eds. 1961. *Plato: The collected dialogues*. Princeton: Princeton University Press.
Lowe, E. Jonathan. 2002. *A survey of metaphysics*. Oxford, UK: Oxford University Press.
Mazzucchelli, D. 2009. *Asterios polyp*. New York: Pantheon Books.
Nanay, Bence. 2016. *Aesthetics as philosophy of perception*. Oxford, UK: Oxford University Press.
Orilia, F. and Paolini Paoletti, M. 2022. "Properties", *The Stanford Encyclopedia of Philosophy* (Spring 2022 Edition), Edward N. Zalta (ed.), https://plato.stanford.edu/archives/spr2022/entries/properties/
Plato and Bollingen Foundation. 1961. *The collected dialogues of Plato, including the letters*. New York: Pantheon Books.
Quine, W.V.O. 1964. On what there is. In *From a logical point of view*, 2nd ed., revised, 1–19. Cambridge, MA: Harvard University Press.

Rodriguez-Pereyra, Gonzalo. 2019. Nominalism in metaphysics. In *The Stanford encyclopedia of philosophy*, summer 2019 edition, ed. Edward N. Zalta. https://plato.stanford.edu/archives/sum2019/entries/nominalism-metaphysics/

Russell, Bertrand. 1912. *The problems of philosophy*. New York: Barnes & Noble.

Swinburne, Richard. 2019. *Are we bodies or souls?* Oxford, UK: Oxford University Press.

Vogler, Christopher. 2007. *The Writer's journey: Mythic structure for writers*. Studio City: Michael Wiese Productions.

Zeyl, Donald, and Barbara Sattler. 2022. Plato's Timaeus. In *The Stanford encyclopedia of philosophy*, summer 2022 edition, ed. Edward N. Zalta. https://plato.stanford.edu/archives/sum2022/entries/plato-timaeus/

Yes, Roya and Philosophy: The Art of Submission

94

Nathaniel Goldberg, Chris Gavaler, and Maria Chavez

Contents

Introduction	2086
Summarizing: Domination and Submission in *Yes, Roya*	2087
Domination and Submission in Comics Creation	2090
Domination and Submission in Philosophy	2093
Domination and Submission in Aristotle	2093
Domination and Submission in Kant	2095
Domination and Submission in Mill	2098
Conclusion: The Art of Submission	2099
End Notes	2100
References	2100

Abstract

Yes, Roya, a 2016 graphic novel written by C. Spike Trotman and illustrated by Emilee Denich, depicts Roya, a woman of color who writes and illustrates a comic strip; Joe, a white man who gave up his career after meeting Roya, who now publishes under his name; and Wylie, a young white man starting in the profession. Roya completely dominates Joe's career, making it hers. She also partly dominates Wylie's, acting as his mentor. Roya dominates Joe and Wylie personally too. She is their sexual dominant, and they are her submissives. Professionally and personally, moreover, Joe and Wylie each submit to Roya consensually. Further, though Roya both writes and illustrates her comic strip, often writer and illustrator differ. The former, creating the story, dominates the latter, illustrating the story after the fact – as Trotman and Denich themselves did consensually via a contract when creating their graphic novel. Hence *Yes, Roya*

N. Goldberg (✉) · C. Gavaler
W&L University, Lexington, VA, USA
e-mail: goldbergn@wlu.edu; gavalerc@wlu.edu

M. Chavez
Charlottesville, VA, USA

© Springer Nature Switzerland AG 2024
D. K. Johnson et al. (eds.), *The Palgrave Handbook of Popular Culture as Philosophy*,
https://doi.org/10.1007/978-3-031-24685-2_106

highlights domination and submission in comics creation and in sex. More than that, the graphic novel also presents both kinds of domination and submission as ethical. Because Aristotle, Kant, and Mill are the most influential ethicists in the Western tradition, this chapter investigates how each could accommodate such professional and personal dominant/submissive relationships in their philosophy.

Keywords

Aristotle · Comics · Consequentialism · Deontology · Domination and submission · Graphic Novel · Kant · Mill · Utilitarianism · Virtue ethics

Introduction

Yes, Roya, a 2016 graphic novel written by C. Spike Trotman and illustrated by Emilee Denich, depicts three people in the 1960s USA at different stages of their careers as comic-strip authors. Roya is a woman of color who writes and illustrates "Lil' Savage," a successful, mass-syndicated comic strip. Joseph ("Joe") Ahlstrom is a white man who gave up his career once he met Roya, who now publishes under his name, using Joe's white-male privilege to advance her career. Finally, as the story opens, Roya and Joe bring into the fold Wylie Kogan, a young white man trying to break into the profession but facing opposition from an editor with a grudge against Joe. Roya completely dominates Joe's career, making it hers. She also partly dominates Wylie's career, acting as his mentor. Roya dominates Joe and Wylie personally too. She is their sexual dominant, and they are her submissives. Professionally and personally, moreover, Joe and Wylie each submit to Roya consensually, because each makes the informed and uncoerced decision to do so. In their characters' professional and personal lives, Trotman and Denich therefore subvert the stereotype of women and people of color as submissive and men and white people as dominant. Perhaps emphasizing the subversion, Joe's and Wylie's last names are revealed but Roya's is not. Roya is so dominant that a first name suffices. Conversely, Roya is the only one to call Joe "Joseph," her only name for him. Joe is so submissive as to need his full first name when around Roya.

Hence *Yes, Roya* highlights domination and submission in comic-strip creation and in sex. Further, though Roya both writes and illustrates "Lil' Savage" – which ironically reflects traditional gender stereotypes – often writer and illustrator differ. The former, creating the story, dominates the latter, illustrating the story after the fact. Indeed, in a personal email exchange between Denich and an author of this chapter, Denich confirmed that this is how she and Trotman created *Yes, Roya*. Mixing intratextual and extratextual themes, therefore, *Yes, Roya* highlights sexual domination and submission, and graphic-novel and comic-strip writing and illustrating, as dominant/submissive relationships.

More than that, the graphic novel also presents both kinds of domination and submission as ethical. While dominants might be thought always to dominate, only the informed and uncoerced decision of submissives to comply empowers them. Joe and Wiley are letting Roya dominate them. As Philip Miller and Molly Devon, who write on sexual domination and submission, explain: "Power [...] flows from the bottom up" (4). That is why the informed and uncoerced decision of the submissive is key. And it is why Miller and Devin continue: "We call the consensual empowerment of a submissive by a dominant a power exchange." However, even then, the dominant's authority is not absolute. The submissive can revoke consent at any time. Further, in exchange for the devotion of the submissive, the dominant agrees to protect, care for, and in some cases mentor them.

Whether personally or professionally, once submissives do consent to domination, dominants generally hold power over them. Their relationship becomes unequal. Though the creation of *Yes, Roya* is evidence that Trotman and Denich's relationship is ethical, and the actions among Roya, Joe, and Wiley is evidence that their relationship is ethical also, how unequal relationships can be ethical may seem unclear. That could explain why the three main Western ethical theories lack straightforward analyses of them. Virtue ethics, famously advanced by Aristotle, urges cultivating dispositions that aim for the mean between two extremes. Yet dominating and submitting – in comics creation and sex – exemplify two extremes. Deontology, famously advanced by Immanuel Kant, prohibits any degree of domination of one person over another. Comics writers and sexual dominants do, however, dominate submissives and comics illustrators, respectively. Finally, utilitarianism, famously advanced by John Stuart Mill, maintains that actions are ethical only insofar as they maximize happiness, understood as pleasure and the absence of pain. But the point of certain sexual acts of domination is to cause submissives pain (dominants who hold this view are sadists, named after the Marquis de Sade, mentioned below), while writers routinely make unexpected, and to some extent even painful, demands on illustrators.

This chapter explores Roya's domination and Joe's and Wylie's submission in sex and writers' domination and illustrators' submission in comics creation.[1] It then determines how Aristotle's virtue ethics, Kant's deontology, and Mill's utilitarianism can accommodate unequal relationships as ethical.

Summarizing: Domination and Submission in *Yes, Roya*

Roya started her career as an artist in fetish magazines, publishing them under the masculine pseudonym "Rusty." As Rusty, she began a yearlong mail correspondence with Joe, an aspiring artist who admired her work and sought her advice. When they finally met and Roya revealed her true identity, she realized the benefit of having Joe as a submissive in two different ways. Roya offered Joe a deal allowing her to publish under his name, so Roya owns him professionally. Roya also lets Joe submit to her sexually, so she owns him personally. As Roya told Joe when they first met in person, "I want to take ownership of you," and that he had to "accept my ownership," in the form of double domination, which he did (Trotman and Denich 50, p. 51).

Wylie, the audience's point-of-view character, is a 19-year-old aspiring comic strip artist. After writing his own fan letter to Joe, Wylie is excited to have his work reviewed and critiqued by an established, award-winning comic-strip artist. Wylie, whom Joe invites to his home, doesn't realize that Joe's successes are due to Roya. The graphic novel's first image of sexual domination and submission appears in artwork when Wylie opens a folder of drawings in Joe's studio. Wylie stares at a depiction of Joe kneeling, hands bound behind him, with a bit in his mouth and the leash of a collar pulled tight by Roya, who is standing behind him with a high-heeled boot on his back (p. 9). Roya is grinning, and Joe's eyes are clenched.

Though Joe started his career drawing "[w]omen in rubber, captive men. That kind of thing" for "fetish magazines" because he "was already drawing it for free. That's just what I like," he later reveals to Wylie that Roya is "the one who drew it. Roya draws all of it" now (pp. 27, 28). Roya then explains to Wylie that Joe "lives with me in my house. And he takes credit for my work. He does this with my permission. This has made my success easier than it might be" (p. 29). This professional arrangement suggests that Joe has authority over Roya – he is legally the author of her work – but that her consent makes it equitable. Yet Roya entirely dominates Joe's career, as Joe has retired. Roya's artwork is also objectively better. An editor later observes that Joe's early work was "some of the worst comics this magazine ever published," but the work that he currently publishes (and that Roya actually produces) is "a slick little strip syndicated in every newspaper" (p. 95). As in their professional relationship, in their personal one too "Joseph complies with [Roya's] will completely" because "[s]ubmission is his natural state" (p. 30).

Joe gets a hint of Wylie's submissive proclivities when the drawing that Wylie saw in Joe's home studio goes missing. Later, when alone in his apartment, Wylie removes the now wrinkled paper from his jacket and masturbates while imagining Roya grabbing him by the throat (p. 17). During another visit, Roya asks Wylie if he is submissive like Joe, "Willing to serve a woman. Desirous of that. He thinks you are. He wouldn't have brought you home today otherwise" (p. 30). Questioning whether Wylie is indeed like Joe, Roya asks, "Do you want to leave? You're free to go" (p. 31). Everything, personally and professionally in the graphic novel, is consensual. Once Wiley makes the informed and uncoerced decision to stay, and he and Joe begin to have sex, Wylie looks to Joe for guidance. Roya counters, "Don't ask for his permission. He has no say in this" (p. 32). Later Roya asks Wylie why he obeyed her, since "[m]ost men would say no" (p. 53). Like Joe, submission is apparently Wylie's natural state too. Likewise, like Joe, Wylie is instructed to say only "Yes, Roya" when the three are intimate, which he does. The novel depicts them having sex in four separate scenes, the last three concluding each of the last three chapters. In each case, Roya gives commands, and Wylie and Joe obey.

Ultimately, Roya educates Wylie about sex and being a male submissive in a female-led relationship. She tells Wylie what she expects from his devotion. It should not be symbolic like Joe's self-inflicted "R" brand on his thigh. Rather, it should be about what she wants him to want. Wylie (and presumably Joe too) is to desire whatever Roya tells him to desire. She also shows Wylie how to please her sexually and expands his sexual horizons, directing his and Joe's sexual acts with one another and both of theirs with her. "There are *many* first times for that. Joseph only gave you *one*," she tells him after his very first sexual encounter, which was with Joe. "I'm going to give you another," Roya explains, and then proceeds to give him his first sexual encounter with a woman (p. 84).

Roya also mentors Wylie professionally. She starts by critiquing his illustrations: "You have a good sense of line. But it's not as confident as it needs to be" (pp. 9–10). She later provides guidance on how to create a comic strip that will appeal to his target audience even when he expresses reservations because he finds the approach inauthentic to his self-expression. "This comic is meant to be sold," she tells him, "and it's something you want to sell to men's magazines. So, your audience is young men of no great intellect or experience. And *that* joke is for *them*" (p. 79). Roya admits to Wylie that she created "Lil' Savage" to make a sustainable income that she would otherwise be unable to have because she is a woman of color. Her comic's humor would not be regarded as funny if the public knew that she was its creator: "When Wild Child wakes up, with her hair in [Lil' Savage's] fist. When he thinks he's beaten her. In every sense. And when she throws Savage into the bonfire, or freezes him in the snow and shatters him. When she feeds him to the lions. That's *my* punchline" (p. 82). As Roya had told Wylie earlier, "People like people who are most like them. It makes them comfortable" (p. 29). The only ones who know the truth are Joe and Wylie.

Those two forms of domination – professional regarding comics creation, and personal regarding sex – come together at the story's climax. Magazine editors Quincy Gabris and Walt Mayer warn Wylie about the suspiciousness of Joe's near-overnight transformation from a poor to a praiseworthy comic-strip creator. Mayer suggests that because he doesn't trust Joe, he may not trust Wylie either. Roya, realizing that Wylie will be blacklisted unless he breaks ties with Joe and therefore her, explains to Wylie that she doesn't want him to pay the consequences for her having dominated Joe's career. "Lying about my work wasn't my first choice, Wylie. It happened out of necessity, and I don't regret it. But the consequences of what I've done aren't yours to bear" (p. 100). She informs Wylie that if he wants to cut ties with her and Joe for the sake of his career, then she will understand. Hearing this, Wylie first responds angrily then breaks down melancholically when he realizes the choice before him. He begs Roya to keep him, as his relationship with her and Joe makes him feel that he is living his most authentic life. "I ... my life is okay," he explains.

> I grew up fine. But I wasn't ... ... I look back and it feels like I was *sleepwalking*. I would think, I'd say, maybe this is just how it goes? Everyone else does this. They're fine. They seem fine. So ... this is how I'm gonna be alive? ... Okay. But it wasn't. Meeting you and meeting Joe changed my life. It changed the *planet* for me. (p. 100)

Roya responds by explaining the reason that she chose him but empathizing about her own plight as a comic-strip creator. "I know what you want to be, Wylie. I wanted to be that, too. That's the only reason I offered" (p. 103). Nonetheless she reassures Wylie that she won't end her relationship with him. "You're mine. You're *always* mine. I'll protect you" (p. 103). Because Roya has accepted Wylie as her submissive, she is responsible for him. As Jay Wiseman, who writes on bondage, dominance, and sado-masochism, explains: "A dominant always has an ethical duty to act with concern for the submissive's wellbeing" (Wiseman p. 48). She therefore helps Joe, who comes up with the solution. Joe gets Mayer to back off by compelling him to admit that he had wanted Joe sexually when they first met (Trotman and Denich pp. 103, 113).

After the climax, when all three characters are relaxing and recharging at home, Wylie tells Roya that he wants what Roya wants him to do. Roya responds, "Then I want you to have what I can't. You're going to make something wonderful and tell the world it's yours, Wylie" (p. 122). Roya's guidance helps Wylie create a comic strip that's true to his self-expression, "[a] comic that says what I want it to say. But quietly. Between the panels, I guess" (p. 138). In Wylie's creation, Roya is cast as a wonder woman with a man under her heel, an acknowledgement to the original Wonder Woman's kinky roots.[2]

In the action of its characters, and over its developing narrative arc, *Yes, Roya* implicitly makes the case that the two different ways in which Roya dominates Wylie and Joe, and they submit to her, professionally and personally, are ethical. People threatening their relationship – Gabris and Mayer are the most explicit, but there are others, including the 1960s US society itself – are understood as ethically lacking. Similarly, the creation of *Yes, Roya* implicitly makes the case that the way in which Trotman dominates Denich, professionally, is ethical also. Though the reader is not presented with anyone who threatened their relationship, *Yes, Roya* was published by Iron Circus Comics, which Trotman founded in 2007 herself (Trotman). The US publishers hadn't been accepting of Trotman's earlier work. That she and Denich published *Yes, Roya* under Trotman's own press implies that those publishers were ethically lacking also.

Yes, Roya does not make its case explicitly, and neither do Trotman or Denich make theirs outside the text. They don't have to; implicit arguments are enough to make *Yes, Roya* philosophy. But philosophers have made explicit ethical arguments on issues surrounding unequal relationships. Those are considered next before determining how Aristotle, Kant, and Mill can accommodate unequal relationships – such as those within the graphic novel and between its creators – in their ethical systems.

Domination and Submission in Comics Creation

The dominant/submissive relationship in comics creation has not escaped the notice of philosophers or comics writers. Philosopher Christy Mag Uidhir describes the "assembly-line model" of "mass-art comics," which often includes a distinct writer, various artists, and others. He then distinguishes participants who should be considered authors, who dominate, from those who should not, who submit ("Comics" pp. 47–48). Mag Uidhir explains: "we regard the activities in which [assistants] engage, though complex and highly skilled, as being broadly directed by – or facilitating those activities directed by others" ("Minimal" p. 377). In fact, as philosopher Thomas E. Wartenberg explains: "The most obvious feature of an illustration is that it is *directed*.[...The illustration] stands in necessary relation to some other thing that [the illustration] is the illustration *of*. In most cases, what an illustration is an illustration of is a previously existing story," because "illustrations are ontologically dependent upon the text that they illustrate" (pp. 89, 90). In script-based comics, the activities of an artist are directed by the writer, making the artist more specifically an illustrator. The primary advantage of full scripts for writers, explains comics writer Dennis O'Neil, is that the "writer has full control of," and therefore dominance over, "the story" (p. 28).

Comics writer Michael Brian Bendis goes so far as considering writer and artist relationships "as intimate as dating" (p. 80). Comics writer-artist Will Eisner describes the potential dangers of such intimacy, likening the replacement of a writer's scripted dialogue with wordlessness as "the total castration of his words" (p. 133). Eisner's casting a writer's potential feeling of disempowerment in sexually negative terms follows since the writer, typically the dominant partner in the creative process, presumably would not have given informed and uncoerced consent to an artist's dominating and word-deleting creative choice. The same can apply to artists who typically dominate other artists who finish their illustrations. John Byrne expressed homophobic anxiety when artist Bob Layton inked his penciled artwork:

> I actually feel physically ill when I look at Bob's stuff. [...] It's like everything is greasy and slimy. [...] all his men are queer. They have these bouffant hairdos and heavy eye make-up and an upper lip with a little shadow in the corner which to me says lipstick. [...] I remember my father looking at [...] the finished inks [...] and my father said, "Well this guy's queer." No, he didn't look queer in the pencils, Dad. (Itkowitz 1980)

Uninformed of what it would look like, Byrne did not give his consent to what he experienced as Layton's alteration of his pencils' intended effects. Rejecting anything like Layton's homophobia, *Yes, Roya* nevertheless addresses both anxieties – male powerlessness and male homosexuality – through male characters who engage in both homosexual and heterosexual sex acts under the direction of a Black woman. All three are comics artists.

If the creation of *Yes, Roya* followed the "commercial, work-for-hire, freelance" process Bendis outlines, then Trotman herself first wrote a "full script," which Bendis identifies as the standard approach "in today's market" (p. 28). The approach is distinct from the so-called "Marvel Method" in which the artist is "co-writing" based only on the writer's general description or idea. Bendis admits

> writing Marvel Method scares the living crap out of me. It is the antithesis of what we teach ourselves as writers. It requires trust and sharing and believing in your partner – and he's a partner, not an artist here, just check the credits page – and trusting in the collaboration above all else. (pp. 53–54)

Bendis also assesses the potential disadvantages of the writer-dominating full-script approach:

> A full script, if overly descriptive, can stifle the artist's creativity, leaving him no room to fly. Even if only subconsciously, an artist, who, like yourself, is trying to do right by their collaborator and the company who is paying him, will follow the script to the letter. If the writer is not visually inclined, that can make for a very stifled storytelling experience. (p. 54)

Bendis is expressing a personal preference for a creative relationship where partners share power, neither dominating nor submitting to the other. Imbalance, however, still has advantages: "On the plus side, with full script, the artist has everything in front of them – a clear script with no guesswork involved" (p. 32).

Even if a full script can stifle the artist's creativity, the artist, as an illustrator of a writer's script, still needs to decide in an informed and uncoerced way to follow the writer's lead. And that can allow for the dominant/submissive relationship between writer and illustrator to become dynamic. Once the illustrator has drawn a draft of the comic, Bendis explains: "the writer, more often than not, has the opportunity to examine it and adjust his script accordingly.[...] Sometimes that ends up being the best writing you do" (p. 42). He does, however, add: "I have discovered that most of the time, artists do follow the script that was written just for them" (p. 37).

The *Yes, Roya* creative process followed the full-script approach. As Denich explained in that personal email exchange, Trotman initiated the script-focused collaboration, which Denich had to agree to of course, informed and uncoerced. "This was our first project together. I can't quite remember where [Spike] found my work, but she emailed me and asked if I wanted to work on an erotic graphic novel together, and I said of course!" Recalling Miller and Devon's observation that in submissive/dominant relationships power flows from the bottom up, here the power flowed from Denich to Trotman, enabling Trotman to dominate moving forward. Denich detailed their process:

> When we started work on *Yes, Roya*, Spike had a completed script ready to go for me. I would draw pages in batches of 10 [...] by first reading over the script and thumbnailing the 10 pages out. That then would be used as a springboard to sketch the pencils on top.
>
> This is a pretty standard way to do it. It's mainly to make sure I get the flow of action and conversation correct before I even start the pencils. Every step of the way I'd send what I was doing to Spike and get approval, so it went something like thumbs – approval – pencils – approval – inks – approval and then finally to grey tones and letters for the final approval. Spike is very easy to work with, so this approval process was super easy – mostly she'd say "Wylie's hair is too big and fluffy here" or something like that for fixing :) She generally let me make all the creative decisions! It went very smoothly.

By "all of the creative decisions," Denich presumably meant page layouts and the internal arrangements of the panel content described in Trotman's script. Denich appears to have been personally satisfied with the creative arrangement.

Domination and Submission in Philosophy

Domination and submission, professional and personal, have received increased philosophical attention. Contemporary social and political philosophers, inspired by Michel Foucault and others, focus on issues such as class, gender, power, race, and sex. The sexual sort had already piqued the interest of eighteenth-century French philosopher Donatien Alphonse François, better known as the Marquis de Sade, whose name is the source of the term "sadism." While there is much to glean from Foucault, de Sade, and more contemporary thinkers, ancient Greek philosopher Aristotle, eighteenth-century German philosopher Immanuel Kant, and nineteenth-century English philosopher John Stuart Mill are the most influential ethicists in the Western tradition. Though each had things to say about nonconsensual domination and submission especially in politics, they did not speak about consensual domination and submission in the form of comics writer/artist or sexual dominant/submissive. Since *Yes, Roya*, and Trotman and Denich themselves, present examples of these relationships that are ethical, how could Aristotle, Kant, and Mill accommodate them into their ethical system?

Each philosopher turns out apparently to hold one view that would render such relationships unethical and another that does not. Since the example relationships are ethical, it's useful to figure out how Aristotle's, Kant's, and Mill's views can each be made consistent.

Domination and Submission in Aristotle

Aristotle's chief ethical work is his *Nicomachean Ethics*, whose central theme is virtue. "Virtue," Aristotle explained,

> is a state that decides, consisting in a mean, the mean relative to us, which is defined by reference to reason, that is to say, to the reason by reference to which the prudent person would define it. It is a mean between two vices, one of excess and one of deficiency.[...] Some vices miss what is right because they are deficient, others because they are excessive, in feelings or in actions, whereas virtue finds and chooses what is intermediate. (p. 25 [1107a1–6])[3]

By a "state," Aristotle meant a way of being or, more specifically, because it is one "that decides," a way of acting. Virtue, or particular virtues, are such personal ways, or dispositions that inform decisions. Further, they are dispositions that are rational to have, as would be determined by someone who is prudent or rational concerning matters of practice. Those informed decisions would therefore be uncoerced and so ultimately consensual. Virtues are also intermediate between two extremes, or vices. Example virtues include bravery, the disposition informing decisions to respond to obstacles without rushing headlong into them (which would be brazenness) or fleeing from them (which would be cowardice). Bravery, as the mean, is a virtue between brazenness and cowardice, which as extremes are vices – of excess and of deficiency, respectively. Finally, virtues are means relative to the person being considered. A soldier's bravery may be closer to a civilian's brazenness, because what is a mean relative to a soldier might be an extreme (excess) relative to a civilian. A child's bravery may be closer to an adult's cowardice for reciprocal reasons.

It is unclear whether all virtues and vices fit Aristotle's schema. Aristotle himself acknowledged that "not every action or feeling admits of the mean" (p. 25 [1107a1–10]), though he might have had in mind virtues such as wisdom, which may lack excesses, rather than those of being a professional or personal dominant or submissive. Regardless, suppose that Aristotle can make his virtue ethics otherwise work. Accommodating professional and personal dominant/submissive relationships in it seems daunting. Rather than a mean, each member of each pair apparently chooses an extreme. The comics writer and sexual dominant lead, while the illustrator and submissive follow. Further, given the nature of their respective relationship, that seems to be what practical reason would determine them to do – even relative to themselves. Each seems therefore to opt not for a virtue but for a vice. Yet Trotman and Denich, and Roya and Wylie and Joe, are not vicious.

Worse, even if accommodating professional and personal dominant/submissive relationships is possible, doing so seems in tension with Aristotle's later (especially pp. 119–124 [1155a1–1157b5]) analysis of interpersonal relationships generally. Calling all such relations "friendships," Aristotle explored three kinds: friendships of utility, friendships of pleasure, and complete friendships. All three presumably require informed and uncoerced decisions on the part of all parties or they would not be "friendships." Only complete friendships, however, are what Aristotle considered friendships proper. Complete friendships are personal relationships engaged in for their own sake rather than for usefulness or gratification (physical or otherwise), as the other two, respectively, are. Though, Aristotle acknowledged, all three kinds of friendships overlap, and relations between people can change, the artist/writer friendship may be best characterized as one of utility. Each engages with the other because doing so is useful in producing a comic. Business relationships are characteristically those of utility. The dominant/submissive friendship may seem best characterized as one of pleasure, insofar as each engages with the other because doing so is gratifying. Because the sexual dominant also protects, cares for, and mentors the submissive, the relationship perhaps is better characterized instead as a complete friendship. Wylie's own relationship with Roya is just that. Regardless of how categorized, because Aristotle sanctions all three kinds of friendships, he could apparently sanction those of writer and artist, and of sexual dominant and submissive, respectively.

Hence, according to Aristotle's analysis of virtue, these relationships are vicious, while, according to his analysis of friendship, they are not. Aristotle did bring those analyses together when maintaining that friendship itself "is virtue, or involves virtue" (p. 119 [1155a4]). Because virtue is a state that decides, consisting in a mean, friendship itself then is, or involves, the same. But that seems only to exacerbate the problem. Comics writer and sexual dominant, and illustrator and submissive, occupy states that consist in extremes. If friendship is or involves virtue, then because these are vicious, they are not friendships.

Aristotle, however, also discussed unequal friendships:

> A different species of friendship is one that rests on superiority.[...] Now each does not get the same thing from the other, and must not seek it.[...] In all friendships that rest on superiority, the loving must also be proportional. (p. 127 [1158b1])

Inferiors must love their superiors more than their superiors love them. Besides what today are rightly regarded as problematic analyses of gender and political relations, Aristotle also offered as an example that children must love their parents more than their parents love them. This becomes less unpalatable if love is understood as involving emotional and physical dependence. In other ways, perhaps parents love their children as much if not more; though, in the specific sense of emotional and physical dependence, this may not be so. Regardless of how understood, Aristotle acknowledged that some friendships are unequal. If friendship is or involves virtue, then unequal friendships can be virtuous too. But how can that be reconciled?

Whether such unequal friendships, as "a different species," is a fourth to be added to Aristotle's other three kinds of friendships, or is orthogonal to them, is unclear. In the latter case, friendships of utility and pleasure, and complete friendships, can themselves be between unequal members. Either way, comics writers and illustrators, and sexual dominants and submissives, can engage in friendship. Using the model of love as involving emotional or physical dependence, Aristotle might be able to say that professional and personal submissives love their dominants (in that sense) more than their dominants love them. This understanding also admits of vices of excess and deficiency. The comics illustrator must depend more on the writer, and the sexual submissive more on the dominant, but not by too much or too little. Perhaps the illustrator needs to be able to take the initiative in filling out details not specified by the writer yet in a way that does not flout the writer's general aesthetic. Perhaps the sexual submissive needs to be able to act both without waiting on their dominant for orders to do anything at all and without challenging the dominant except when they exceed the terms of prior consent. Aristotle did not allow one to know ahead of time what counts as excessive or deficient in a relationship. That is the role of practical reason and relativity to the parties in the situation. But something like this gives reason to think that professional and personal relationships can be accommodated into his virtue ethics.

Domination and Submission in Kant

Kant developed his deontological ethics in his *Groundwork of the Metaphysics of Morals*, *Critique of Practical Reason*, and *Metaphysics of Morals*. (Besides the page number to the cited edition of *Practical Philosophy*, the authors follow custom and also cite parenthetically the volume followed by the page number to the German Academy Edition.) Deontology is the study of duty, and the most famous (and only absolute) duty that Kant's discussed is the Categorical Imperative. An imperative is a command that one is duty-bound to follow. What makes an imperative categorical, on Kant's view, is that it holds universally (or "categorically"). In the *Groundwork*, Kant presented different formulations of the Categorical Imperative, most famously the Formula of Universal Law and Formula of Humanity, respectively:

> [A]ct only in accordance with that maxim through which you can at the same time will that it become a universal law. (p. 73 [4:421], emphasis suppressed)
>
> So act that you use humanity, whether in your own person or in the person of any other, always at the same time as an end, never merely as a means. (p. 80 [4:429], emphasis suppressed)

The Formula of Universal Law makes central the role of maxims, subjective rules or principles of action. It requires that one act only in such a way that everyone could act on that same maxim. The maxim is then not merely subjective but, because it could become a universal law for everyone, in that sense also objective. Kant offered as an example the maxim that when one believes that they need money, they will borrow money and falsely promise that they will repay it. To determine whether this is ethical, one is to ask whether everyone could act on the maxim. Kant thinks not. Were everyone to try to do so, then everyone would be aware of the falseness of the promise. Since a promise requires the person to whom the promise is made accept it, and since that person – like all persons – would be aware of its falsity, the promise would never be accepted. Hence, though impossible, were everyone to falsely promise, then no one could falsely promise. Universalized, the maxim contradicts itself. The only way to act on the maxim would be to treat it as merely subjective, holding only for some rather than for all. But that violates the Categorical Imperative. So false promising is unethical.

Now consider the maxim on which a comics writer or illustrator, or sexual dominant or submissive, would act. The first member of each pair might act on the maxim that when one is in this relationship they will dominate the relationship's other member. The second member of each pair might conversely act on the maxim that when one is in this relationship they will submit to the other's domination. The question again is whether everyone could act on either maxim. Were everyone to try to dominate – or to submit – in a relationship, then there would be only writers or dominates, or illustrators or submissives. Since a comic book requires both a writer and an illustrator – and a sexual dominant/submissive act a dominant and a submissive – neither the comic nor the act would ever come about. Hence, though impossible, were everyone to write or dominate, or illustrate or submit, then no one could. Universalized, the maxim contradicts itself. The only way to act on the maxim would again be to treat it as merely subjective, again violating the Categorical Imperative. So, on Kant's view, it seems that comics writing or sexually dominating, or illustrating or submission, is unethical.

There is debate on how exactly Kant's Formula of Universal Law is meant to work. (See, e.g., Korsgaard, who argues that contradictions resulting from universalizing unethical maxims could be interpreted as logical, practical, or teleological.)

Though debate also surrounds the Formula of Humanity, its application is clearer. Yet its ethical verdicts regarding unequal relations seem in tension with the former formula's. Requiring that no one ever use a person merely as means requires that no person be taken advantage of or objectified. Using them always at the same time as an end requires respecting them as persons and so never violating their rights as such. It requires recognizing that they have their own projects and goals. Kant's use in the phrasing of the Formula of Universal Law of "merely" and "at the same time" is no accident. Just as Aristotle recognized that some friendships are of utility, Kant recognized that all relationships involve members each gaining something and in that sense using the other. The use, however, must be consensual. Kant would require that those deciding to enter into those relationships must be informed and not be coerced. It would never be "merely" use. The comics writer "uses" the illustrator to illustrate their work, but the writer also recognizes the illustrator's own projects and goals, specifically of illustrating the work. Because the illustrator makes the informed and uncoerced decision to illustrate the work, the writer at the same time treats the illustrator as an end. Likewise, the sexual dominant "uses" the submissive to order around, but the dominant also recognizes the submissive's own projects and goals, specifically of submitting. Because each relationship is consensual, each member ultimately treats the other as an end. Presumably, therefore, the Formula of Humanity permits both relationships.

One can release the tension between the two formulas by recognizing the element of consent in the maxim which needs to be universalized. Because the relationships are consensual, the comics writer and sexual dominant are better understood as acting on the maxim that when one is in their respective relationship they will dominate only if the other member of the relationship consents to it. Such consent would take the form of a contract, in professional relationships often an explicit one, as governed Trotman and Denich's own professional relationship. It would specify what each party agrees to regarding responsibilities and privileges of their position. The comics writer and illustrator agree to such things as expectations about how much or little is to be written or illustrated, deadlines when each is to be done, arrangements regarding marketing and profits, and ways to change all these terms. Consent between sexual dominants and submissives would also take the form of a contract, though likely an implicit one, as between Wylie and Joe on the one hand and Roya on the other. The sexual dominant and submissive agree to such things again as expectations only this time about behavior, deadlines perhaps in the sense of timing when the behavior will occur, financial and related arrangements, and as above ways to change all these terms.

If these relationships are consensual as suggested, then universalizing the maxim does not result in everyone trying to dominate or to submit overall, leaving no dominants or submissives – personal or professional. Instead, everyone would try to dominate only if they and the other member of the relationship consent to it. Because consent requires a dominant and a submissive – otherwise it would not be consent but a unilateral decision – universalizing the maxim does not result in a contradiction. The Formula of Universal Law therefore renders those relationships ethically permissible, aligned with the Formula of Humanity's result. Indeed, the Formula of

Universal Law and Formula of Humanity are meant to be equivalent. As Kant claimed, the former gives the form, and the latter the matter, of the Categorical Imperative (pp. 43–44 [4:336–37]). They should render the same result from a different perspective. The idea behind the universalization test of the first formula is that each person should act only in a way that each other person could act, *because* the idea behind the second formula is that all persons ultimately are ends in themselves and therefore should never be treated merely as means. Making the element of consent explicit in the above maxims recognizes that. So, though it initially seems that Kant would forbid dominant/submissive relationships, a better understanding of his arguments shows that he would, in the kinds of cases imagined here, permit them.

Domination and Submission in Mill

Mill's utilitarianism is a kind of consequentialism, the view that the ethically right thing to do is to cause the most overall good. The utilitarian specifies good as happiness. Hence, for them, the end of maximizing overall happiness justifies the means to it: "Utility, or the Greatest Happiness Principle, holds that actions are right in proportion as they tend to promote happiness, wrong as they tend to produce the reverse of happiness" (p. 10). And "by happiness," Mill specified, "is intended pleasure, and the absence of pain; by unhappiness, pain, and the privation of pleasure." Because such happiness is happiness not of any particular individual but overall, Mill was aware that utilitarianism could seem to sanction pain for the few to promote pleasure for the many. Thus, were comics writers painfully demanding of their artists, or sexual dominants of their submissives, yet society overall experienced a surplus of pleasure, then those acts would apparently be ethical.

There is more to say about Mill's Greatest Happiness Principle, however. Unlike Jeremy Bentham, the great utilitarian who came before him, Mill's utilitarianism recognized two kinds of pleasure: "higher," which tended to be social and intellectual, and "lower," which tended to be individual and physical. Mill also argued that other ethical views were subsumable under utilitarianism, including even Kant's (Mill p. 51). Virtues and duties were themselves explainable by appealing to Mill's own view. Relevant here, Mill insisted that the Greatest Happiness Principle had the resources to reject the conclusion that it could lead to pain (or at least significant pain) for some were the result pleasure for many. That is because, Mill maintained, considerations of justice follow from those of utility.

Mill explained: "justice is a name for certain classes of moral rules, which concern the essentials of human well-being more nearly, and are therefore of more absolute obligation, than any other rules for the guidance of life" (p. 57). Maximizing overall happiness requires elevating those moral rules protecting human well-being per se. Rules of justice amount to protections of basic human rights, including the right to consent. "[T]he claim we have on our fellow-creatures to join in making safe for us the very groundwork of our existence," though following from the Greatest Happiness Principle, "gathers feelings around it so much more intense than those concerned in any of the more common cases of utility, that the difference in degree [...] becomes a real difference in kind" (p. 53). Considerations of justice are a special case of considerations of utility, which the greatest happiness cannot come about without. Were justice overall not paramount, then though there would still be individual cases of happiness – the writer and dominant could get pleasure out of causing pain to the illustrator and submissive – overall happiness would not be maximized.

Hence, on a superficial understanding of utilitarianism, small amounts of pain seem justified if they return large amounts of pleasure. Maybe comics writers should keep their illustrators as prisoners, ruining their lives but with the greater good of having more comics issues and their readers consequently happier. Maybe sexual dominants should keep their submissives as prisoners, forcing them to cater to their every need and those of others without catering to any of the submissives' own. Were others, however, aware of not the mere submission but the full subjugation of a minority for the benefit of the majority, then those others would become fearful for their own safety. Were practices of imprisonment of the few for the enjoyment of the many generally known, then a good number of those many would rightly worry that their lives could be ruined for the enjoyment of others too. That is why, according to Mill, considerations of justice follow from considerations of utility, and so the Greatest Happiness Principle requires that all members of society join in making all other members of society safe. Maximizing overall happiness requires safeguarding individual rights. Though the majority can be made happy by subjugating the minority, the majority can be made happier by knowing that they will not be subjugated as part of any other minority themselves. And requiring that decisions be informed and uncoerced – and so requiring consent – between individuals is key.

All this has straightforward application to dominant/submissive relationships. Justice requires that personal and professional dominants and submissives feel safe in their own being. And utilitarianism requires justice. So comics writers and illustrators, and sexual dominants and submissives, to maximize overall happiness, should feel safe also. But then, comics writers can make painful demands on illustrators, and sexual dominants can cause pain to submissives. Neither is problematic, and indeed both can maximize overall happiness. All members of all relationships, dominant/submissive or otherwise, nevertheless need to feel secure in their persons. That is what justice demands, because that is what utilitarianism demands. So Mill can accommodate professional and personal dominant/submissive relationships into utilitarianism, by recognizing the rule of justice and so the importance of consent.

Conclusion: The Art of Submission

Yes, Roya, a graphic novel, contains the art of submission that Denich gave to Trotman based on the latter's script. The product of their collaboration, the illustrated script that is *Yes, Roya,* in turn depicts a young comics artist, Wylie, seeking advice from a well-established artist, Joe. Wylie soon learns that Joe submits professionally to Roya, as she uses his white-male identity to publish her own art. Joe also submits personally, as she uses him for her sexual pleasure. Wylie then joins Joe in the art of personal submission to Roya. He also joins Joe in the art of professional submission, accepting Roya's mentorship to inspire his own solo art that he hopes to submit elsewhere under his own identity.

Reading the graphic novel therefore raises the question of how art, and other acts, that are submitted – and ultimately how dominant and submissive relationships – can be accommodated by various ethical theories. Aristotle's virtue ethics privileges the mean between extremes, and domination and submission seem extremes. His ethics, however, can accommodate professional and personal domination and submission by appealing to how virtue functions in unequal friendships. Kant's deontology apparently prohibits domination and submission, which is why the Formula of Universal Law apparently cannot accommodate them. Nonetheless, if the domination and submission are consensual, then the Formula of Humanity can accommodate them, which is key to understanding why the Formula of Universal Law ultimately can as well. Finally, Mill's utilitarianism identifies right actions with those maximizing overall happiness, while professional and personal domination can yield unhappiness. Regardless, if domination and submission do not make individuals feel unsafe, and so do not violate the principles of justice, they can instead yield happiness, in which case Mill's utilitarianism can accommodate them also. Though each of these ethical theories may initially seem to have difficulty explaining how unequal relationships could be ethical, upon closer examination they can handle cases such as those within *Yes, Roya*'s characters and between its creators.

End Notes

1. Because graphic novels and comic strips both fall under the broader category of comics, when only one is meant it'll be called a "graphic novel" or "comic strip," respectively. When either or both are meant, they'll be called "comics."
2. See Lepore for those roots and Chavez, Gavaler, and Goldberg for a discussion of those roots in the context of the connection between sexual domination and submission and the ethics of care.
3. Besides the page number to the cited edition of *Nicomachean Ethics*, this chapters' authors follow custom and also cite parenthetically the Bekker number. Throughout the authors omit editorial paragraph numbers, notes, and bracketed interpolations.

References

Aristotle. 1999. *Nicomachean Ethics,* 2nd ed. Trans. Terence Irwin. Indianapolis: Hackett Publishing Company, Inc.

Bendis, Brian Michael. 2014. *Words for pictures: The art and business of writing comics and graphic novels*. Berkeley: Watson-Guptill.
Bentham, Jeremy. 1961. *An introduction to the principles of morals and legislation. 1789*. Garden City: Doubleday.
Chavez, Maria, Chris Gavaler, and Nathaniel Goldberg. 2017. Loving Lassos: Wonder woman, Kink, and care. In *Wonder woman and philosophy*, ed. Jacob M. Held, 188–197. Hoboken: Wiley Publishing.
Denich, Emilee. 2021. Personal email to Chris Gavaler, April 21, 2021.
Eisner, Will. 2008. *Comics and sequential art: Principles and practices from the legendary artist*. New York: Norton.
Foucault, Michel. 1975. *Discipline and punish*. New York: Vintage Books.
Itkowitz, Mitch, and J. Michael Catron. 1980. John Byrne: An X-tra special, four-star, flag-waving talk with the artist of *X-Men* and *Captain America*. The Comics Journal 57: 57–82, Summer.
Kant, Immanuel. 2002. Groundwork of the metaphysics of morals. 1785. In *Practical philosophy*, ed. Gregor. New York: Cambridge University Press.
Korsgaard, Christine. 1996. Kant's formula of universal law. In *Creating the kingdom of ends*, 77–105. New York: Cambridge University Press.
Lepore, Jill. 2015. *The secret life of wonder woman*. New York: Vintage Books.
Mag Uidhir, Christy. 2010. Minimal authorship (of sorts). *Philosophical Studies* 154 (3): 373–87.
———. 2012. Comics and collective authorship. In *The art of comics: A philosophical approach*, ed. Aaron Meskin and Roy T. Cook. Oxford: Wiley Blackwell.
Mill, John Stuart. 2001. *Utilitarianism. 1863*. Kitchener: Batoche Books Limited.
Miller, Philip, and Molly Devon. 1995. *Screw the Roses, send me the Thorns: The romance and sexual Sorcery of Sadomasochism*. Fairfield: Mystic Rose Books.
O'Neil, Dennis. 2001. *The DC comics guide to writing comics*. New York: DC.
Trotman, C. Spike. 2021. Iron Circus comics fact sheet. https://ironcircus.com/wp-content/uploads/2020/07/IronCircus-FactSheet.doc. Accessed 13 July 2021.
Trotman, C. Spike, and Emilee Denich. 2016. *Yes, Roya*. Chicago: Iron Circus Comics.
Wartenberg, Thomas E. 2012. Wordy pictures: Theorizing the relationship between image and text in comics. In *The art of comics: A philosophical approach*, ed. Aaron Meshkin and Roy T. Cook. Oxford: Wiley Blackwell.
Wiseman, Jay. 1992. *SM 101: A realistic introduction*. San Francisco: Greenery Press.

The Walking Dead as Philosophy: Rick Grimes and Community Building in an Apocalypse

95

Clint Jones

Contents

Introduction	2104
Plot Summary of *The Walking Dead*	2104
Analysis of The Walking Dead's Main Ideas	2108
Main Idea 1: Apocalypse	2108
Main Idea 2: Community	2110
Main Idea 3: Utopia	2111
Main Idea 4: Dystopia	2113
Main Idea 5: What Rules Should We Follow	2114
Conclusion	2116
References	2118

Abstract

To treat *The Walking Dead* as if it were only a zombie apocalypse story is to miss the deep and fundamental questions about society that the story raises. By looking past the immediacy of the zombie threat that drives the main narrative of the story – survival – it is possible to tease out important questions about community, social organization, leadership, utopian and dystopian world building, and, most importantly, morality. By focusing on the communities that come together in *The Walking Dead*, this chapter examines how societal questions of utopian and dystopian world building frame important questions about how society functions, how it ought to function, and what it will take to get us beyond the problems plaguing contemporary society.

Keywords

Dystopia · Utopia · Apocalypse · Zombies · Government

C. Jones (✉)
Plover, WI, USA

Capital University, Columbus, OH, USA

© Springer Nature Switzerland AG 2024
D. K. Johnson et al. (eds.), *The Palgrave Handbook of Popular Culture as Philosophy*,
https://doi.org/10.1007/978-3-031-24685-2_8

Introduction

The Walking Dead is an apocalyptic zombie story set in the near future and told in graphic novel format across four large compendiums. The focus is on a small group of survivors that traverse the American south and eastern seaboard in search of safety and a new beginning. More than being a mere zombie tale, however, the story is promoted as an attempt to answer the vital question built into the premise of the narrative, "In a world ruled by the dead, we are forced to finally start living." This leaves open several important philosophical questions (and probably more than a few not addressed below) but only if we put our emphasis on the latter half of the promotional claim. The primary agent through which this claim is analyzed and answered is the character Rick Grimes, whose centrality to the story makes him the prime candidate for study in this chapter.

Rick Grimes wakes up in a hospital after the apocalypse has begun and finds himself alone and unaware of what is going on. He stumbles from hospital to house and from house to city before beginning what will become an epic journey to find his family, rescue other survivors, and, ultimately, save civilization. Rick's relationships are the main point of view we have for trying to understand what the story means by "finally starting to live." This question is raised in all the primary media formats accepted as canon by having survivors deal with burgeoning dystopias and fledgling utopias. (The graphic novels are the first format for the story and though they can be found in graphic novel, chapbook, and collector edition volumes I am using the four volume compendiums. However, there are two television shows, novels, and video games that are all considered canon in *The Walking Dead* universe.) This raises questions of the Good and the Good Life. It also raises questions of what it means to be human and what it means to live in society with others. This latter question is especially important because in *The Walking Dead* the rules for society have been erased.

Plot Summary of *The Walking Dead*

The Walking Dead begins in a rupture of the idyllic when Sheriff's Deputy Rick Grimes and his partner, Shane, find themselves in a shootout in the countryside on the outskirts of Cynthiana, Kentucky. After Rick is shot during the gunfight, he lapses into a week's long coma only to wake up alone with no idea what is going on in the world. After waking, he stumbles through the hospital encountering the undead for the first time. Clumsily, and luckily, he escapes the hospital only to have to make his way on foot through the abandoned city that was once his home. Eventually, he arrives at his house where he meets another survivor, Morgan, and his son, Duane, who explain what happened and teach Rick how to kill the zombies. Morgan tells Rick that many people migrated to metropolitan areas that had been established as government strongholds against the outbreak. Learning that his own wife and son may have gone to Atlanta, Rick readies himself for a journey south.

Despite the death, devastation, and ruin that surround him on this trip, Rick strongly believes things will eventually return to normal.

This is evidenced first during Rick's preparations for his trip when he and Morgan plunder the Sheriff's office taking clothes, armaments, and squad cars. When they prepare to part ways, Rick admonishes Morgan to take care of the things he has taken from the police station as he will likely have to return them; he also asks Morgan to take care of his house until he returns. The second tell that Rick is committed to the idea that there is a fix for whatever is wrong happens after he arrives in Atlanta. Despite everything he has encountered on his journey south, everything he sees in Atlanta, and everything he learns from the survivors there, he persists in his thinking that the military or the government will soon be coming to the rescue.

Eventually, however, Rick and his small group of survivors come to grips with the hard truth that no one is coming to save them. Fearful of the oncoming winter and the increasing zombie menace, the group begins to discuss relocating. The decision to relocate is made for them after taking casualties in a zombie attack, so they decide to move from their encampment to somewhere more secure. This journey takes them first to a gated community; but they soon find out that it is filled with zombies so they have to abandon the safety of the brick walled community in search of a safer place. Moving farther afield in search of safety, the group stumbles upon a farm managed by Herschel Green and his family. Though the farm is only slightly safer than their original camp, it is better stocked with food and goods and offers plenty of room for the survivors to spread out. Unfortunately, Rick and Herschel do not see eye to eye regarding the walking dead; in fact, Herschel believes them to be afflicted with a curable illness despite some of the zombies shambling around his property missing whole chunks of their bodies and existing in various stages of rot. Rick cannot believe Herschel is serious about saving them and the rift between the two leads to Rick and his group leaving the farm to once again search for greener pastures.

After wandering and finding necessities such as food and gasoline to be scarce, the survivors hit what they believe is the jackpot – a prison! It is located well away from main thoroughfares and has a triple fence topped with concertina wire which provides defense against zombies and would-be marauders. The only drawback to the prison is the zombies lumbering around the prison yard; but Rick decides it is worth it to tackle the problem to secure a safe compound for themselves. They soon discover that what remained of the guards and the inmates, save four, are zombies and they are cleared out in short order. Eventually, Rick sends a team to retrieve Herschel and his family and relocate them to the prison. Rick makes an uneasy alliance with the remaining prisoners and everyone settles into shockingly mundane routines and begins the process of creating a semblance of normal life.

The prison paradise is soon threatened, however, by Woodbury, a nearby community, and the peaceful life is obliterated in a hail of gunfire, grenades, and carnage. The conflict with Woodbury ruins the prison's fence system and results in heavy casualties on both sides. This fundamentally alters the understanding of community for the remaining survivors going forward as well as their understanding of what is necessary to protect the ones they love. All that is known of the survivors as

Compendium One comes to a close is that they have been scattered in all directions as they fled the onslaught of the Woodbury militia.

Compendium Two opens with Rick and his son, Carl, in search of a safe place and a new direction given that they now believe they are alone in the world. Their meanderings bring them back into contact, first with fellow survivor and recent arrival to the prison, Michonne, then later several of their original group who have relocated back to Herschel's farm. The farm is more dilapidated from disuse and lack of upkeep, but the survivors have been trying to make upgrades to it. The newly reunited survivors are dealing with an increasing zombie threat when they encounter another group of survivors slowly making their way to Washington, DC. The newcomers make a persuasive case that not only is it unsafe to stay at the farm, but that one of their members is capable of helping (what is left of) the government in DC solve the crisis. With this newfound hope, Rick and his group decide they will join the newcomers on their trek to DC.

Most of the story in Compendium Two is made up of two parts once this decision is made. First, the trip itself requires quite a bit of narrative since the farm is located somewhere near the prison south of Atlanta. The journey requires them to travel north past Atlanta, east to South Carolina, and then north again through Appalachia to Maryland. This part of the story also includes a return trip to Cynthiana where Rick recruits Morgan to join his group and they pilfer what is left of the police station and the town. On the way back from Cynthiana, they meet another survivor, a priest named Gabriel, and recruit him to their group. Once they make it to what they believe to be Maryland, they encounter another survivor who, after some convincing, takes them to the community of Alexandria.

Alexandria is the second major focal point of the second compendium. The community of Alexandria lives in a walled neighborhood that runs on solar power and is stocked with ample dry goods. The community, it is revealed, was originally built to be a shelter for the Washington elite in the event of environmental or social collapse (but not for a zombie apocalypse...how could they have anticipated that?). The majority of the second compendium is the telling of how Rick and his fellow survivors integrate into, ultimately take over, and fundamentally reshape what Alexandria is and, for Rick, what it can be. Though the zombies remain an ever-present threat even at this stage of the story, it is clear that Alexandria is a narrative pivot away from zombies and on to the human survivors and *what it means to live*. The conclusion of Compendium Two introduces readers to a new character, Jesus, an emissary from the nearby Hilltop Community.

Through Jesus, in Compendium Three, Rick and his Alexandrian companions become aware of the Hilltop community and The Kingdom which make up a trade alliance with another group known as The Saviors. Soon Rick realizes that the trade pact is not mutually beneficial because the leader of The Saviors, Negan, enforces the pact through fear asymmetrically benefiting his group. In the arrangement between Negan, the Hilltop, and the Kingdom, the latter two groups produce or scavenge food and goods and turn over a portion to The Saviors in exchange for protection from the zombie hordes in the area. In other words, Negan's group provides protection in exchange for a hefty tax of food and supplies. Rick, upon learning of this arrangement, offers the groups the same deal at essentially a better rate, which brings Alexandria into conflict with The Saviors.

Because of the encroachment on what he sees as his domain, Negan seeks to put Rick in his place. This leads to an all-out war between Alexandria and The Saviors with the Hilltop and The Kingdom caught in the middle. Rick aligns with the other communities to bring an end to Negan's rule and establish a mutual trade pact between all the communities, including The Saviors. However, Rick has decidedly more in mind for the communities as he attempts to bring civilization back.

After winning the war against Negan and The Saviors, the storyline advances several years. During the elapsed time, Rick's vision of the world has come to fruition. Each community, those involved in the war with The Saviors as well as new communities brought into the fold, is a thriving little metropolis of farms, crafts, maintenance, and, most importantly, scouting parties that map the area and clear it of zombies. The mapping, clearing, and patrolling of the areas around and between the communities facilitates travel between locations and it allows the communities to expand and grow as more survivors join the various groups. During one of the scouting excursions from the Hilltop, the scouts encounter the most dangerous threat Rick and his companions have ever faced – a group known as the Whisperers.

The latter half of Compendium Three deals with the interactions between the two groups leading up to the Whisperer War. The Whisperers are a large group of people that have essentially gone feral. They make leather suits from the skin of the zombies and use those suits to blend in with the zombies as they move about the world. This allows them to scavenge for berries and small game without fear of being eaten by the undead. The primary belief of the Whisperer group is that they are living as God intended, a literal return to the real, as opposed to the broken ways of the pre-apocalyptic past. This difference is the hinge upon which the whole Whisperer War swings as both sides attempt to establish not only dominance over certain territory but also the right to determine *what the world should look like*. This theme also drove the conflict between Rick and Negan as each sought to bring civilization back according to their own vision.

Compendium Four, the final book in the series, begins with the Whisperer War but the war itself is quite different from the war with The Saviors because the Whisperers engage in asymmetrical and guerilla warfare. This forces the aligned communities under Rick's command to alter the way they think about inhabiting the world and subsequently the way they behave. During the Whisperer War, one of Rick's friends, Eugene, using a rebuilt radio, makes contact with another group of survivors. As the Whisperer War is winding down, Rick discovers Eugene's secret communications with the group known as The Commonwealth. The discovery once again alters how Rick thinks about his community's place in the world as they plan to meet.

The Commonwealth proves to be the largest community that Rick and his companions have encountered since the apocalypse began. The Commonwealth has numerous amenities Rick had thought lost forever from food stuffs to football games. The Commonwealth also has all the class tyranny of the pre-apocalyptic world as well as a lot of its racism, sexism, and violence – particularly police brutality. Rick again sees an opportunity for bettering his communities by challenging the established order of The Commonwealth; he does not wish to join their collective, but rather, to bring their communities into line with his view of the reconstituted world post-apocalypse. Rick's revolution suffers through tragedy and then sees success, and the final scenes of the graphic novel are of civilization on the rise: communities united, people working together for the greater good of humanity, the zombie menace nearly eradicated, and tranquility upon the land.

Analysis of The Walking Dead's Main Ideas

In *Apocalyptic Ecology and the Graphic Novel*, I argue that Robert Kirkman (co-creator of *The Walking Dead*) has delivered an epic tale of humanity that takes place after a super virus of some sort nearly wipes out humankind. While this is true, in that text I was concerned with representations of the apocalyptic world; here the questions I am concerned with are the philosophical questions that hide behind the fantastic storytelling of the zombie apocalypse. What makes a community, for instance, or what pre-apocalyptic rules should people still follow? What is a zombie is another key question, as is the question of when it is right or wrong to kill one.

These and other questions arise in the story only because the story begins with the downfall of humankind and civilization. One could ask, as Rick Grimes never does, what kind of society we should build if we are going to rebuild society? Rick only focuses on building a better version of what we had, but the question of what constitutes "better" is often unaddressed. In this chapter, I will focus on the communities Rick encounters and the ones he attempts to build, and assume that, in a post-apocalyptic world, all survivors would be attempting to build some form of utopia or dystopia regardless of whether they intend to do so or not. In the process of this analysis, I am going to explore a number of philosophical questions that are relevant to the overall analysis.

Main Idea 1: Apocalypse

Before surveying the communities that highlight the apocalypse in *The Walking Dead,* it is important to try to understand what an apocalypse is. Though everyone believes they know what constitutes an apocalypse, it is unlikely that many people have thought through the concept. Moreover, apocalypse has two distinct meanings which need to be separated prior to diving into the one we will be using. On the one hand, apocalypse has a religious meaning which means rapture and revelation. Though, for instance, Biblical apocalypses certainly entail destruction, the destruction is meant to be secondary to the outcome God pursues by bringing about divine destruction. Here we might consider Adam and Eve's expulsion from the Garden of Eden, the Great Flood, or even the Tower of Babel, where each represented a form of rapture, revelation, and destruction of the established order. Every religion has some form of apocalyptic belief either embedded in its history or ensconced in its beliefs about the future.

On the other hand, apocalypse in a secular sense also connotes destruction but without the aspect of divinity. This means that, while apocalypse can be revelatory, what it usually reveals is the frailty of the human condition in relation to the world at large rather than a grander divine plan. In this sense, we tend to think of major disasters – hurricanes Katrina and Sandy, the Fukushima nuclear plant meltdown in 2011, or the tsunami that rocked India in 2004 – but these actually do not compare to what is meant by apocalypse. An apocalypse is totalizing in its destruction; where the devastation of a hurricane is localized, in an apocalyptic event, the damage is everywhere. In Kirkman's story, we are confronted with a zombie *apocalypse* and a few things bear that out.

First, whatever causes the zombies to exist makes its way through humanity very quickly, at best a matter of weeks, and the result is that there are not only few survivors severely outnumbered by the zombies, but there are not enough people to manage basic infrastructures. Along these lines, if the infection could be spread so easily, there would be no way to contain it with quarantine or more drastic measures, thus ensuring that the apocalypse is totalizing and unavoidable. Second, the apocalypse is global in scope happening simultaneously everywhere. The reason for this speculation rather than assuming the apocalypse only happens in America is twofold. First, neither other counties nor the United Nations come to aid the survivors and, second, in the story *The Alien* – the only story written in this universe by someone other than Kirkman with his approval – the zombie apocalypse is occurring simultaneously in Spain. Finally, the experience the survivors have of the apocalypse is revelatory in relation to humanity – both in the form of the zombies and the survivors. While major disasters can often elicit similar responses on a local level, global disasters carry a different experience. This is because there is no way to avoid being caught up in an apocalypse and no one to save you from it.

This, of course, brings us to the instances of apocalyptic communities in *The Walking Dead*. What I mean by apocalyptic communities are those instances where the apocalypse reveals something about humanity, our understanding of it, or the role and importance of community generally as the concept is exposed through the experiences of the survivors. On his journey south from Cynthiana to Atlanta, Rick stops at a house in search of help and much needed supplies. What he discovers is the gruesome reality of the apocalypse: a family of suicides. The sad reality of an apocalyptic event is that many survivors would be alone and facing overwhelming odds for their own survival. While many might choose to make a go of it, others would not, and this scene contrasts Rick's earlier meeting with Morgan. This harsh fact is brought into stark relief for Rick as he resumes his journey through the desolate countryside anticipating what he will find in Atlanta.

The first apocalyptic community Rick encounters in a proper sense is the camp outside Atlanta where he discovers not only that his wife and son have survived, but that there is a small group of survivors with them. This encampment reveals the fragility of human response to major cataclysmic events. The camp is understocked and, save for one individual brave enough to risk stealth trips into Atlanta, there is no one that really knows how to provide for the group except through the vague notion of hunting; and even then, there is no evidence anyone in the camp actually knows *how* to hunt. The camp is poorly guarded despite the seriousness of the zombie threat and there is no effort to barricade the area where the campers congregate. An apocalyptic event would leave most survivors in just such a situation.

A second instance of apocalyptic community that Rick and his companions encounter is Father Gabriel and his church. Interestingly, this community is presented in two ways in the canonical telling of *The Walking Dead*. In the graphic novel, the church is a hideaway where Rick and his companions encounter cannibals. The cannibalistic community is run by a single leader but is a much smaller group than Rick's party. Cannibalism is always presented as the extreme in a dire situation and this is no different. In an apocalyptic scenario, we have to believe that there would be people who would resort to such things, but what makes the existence of cannibals significant is that there has to be an abandonment of traditional morality to make it possible. That question is a difficult question to tackle – when is it okay to abandon morality? The second use of the church is in the television show, and I address it here because it foregoes cannibals for a different moral quandary. In the show, Father Gabriel has locked himself in the church while people, presumably his congregants, begged for admittance and clawed to get in. The church bears the marks of their efforts, made presumably before his congregants were eaten within earshot of the good Father barricaded in the church. Gabriel claims he was too afraid to let them in which, true or not, raises an interesting question: in an apocalyptic event, are we morally required to save others? The moral nature of such questions is critical to our understanding of utopia and dystopia in *The Walking Dead* because morality exists in communities.

Main Idea 2: Community

Because *The Walking Dead* eradicates human society, the survivors are confronted with a twofold problem. One, they have to survive; this means working together, building trust so they can work together, and setting goals for what survival actually means beyond not getting bitten or eaten by zombies. Two, they have to organize themselves into a community of some sort in order to give shape and definition to concepts of leadership, success, fairness, and other political concepts that will – and do – dominate their discourse of survival. To better understand what a community is, let us detour to Aristotle prior to tackling questions of utopia and dystopia in *The Walking Dead* universe.

In the *Politics*, Aristotle argues that human society can take the form of one of six organizational models. There are two possibilities under the governing categories of the one, the few, and the many. Rule by the one entails either a monarchy or a tyranny, and a tyranny is the worst form of government and, therefore, the worst form of community. Rule by the few is either an aristocracy or an oligarchy. And, finally, there is rule by the many which is either a polity or a democracy. According to Aristotle, tyranny, oligarchy, and democracy are all corrupted versions of the governing categories. Here we may think of democracy as an odd choice to perceive as corrupt, but according to Aristotle, democracy is rule by the many only in favor of the poor, or needy, rather than everybody. In a polity, the many rule, but they do so for the betterment of everyone in the community – via the common interest. An aristocracy and a monarchy are preferable to their corrupt counterparts, but because they do not represent the interests of the entire political body, they are seen as less desirable to Aristotle. Because Aristotle shows us the basic governmental structures of human communities, we can use them as a template for identifying not only what communities are in *The Walking Dead* but how those communities are either utopian or dystopian.

If *The Walking Dead* is capable of showcasing a utopian society, it is clear that it ought to have the best form of government, a polity, and that should be our most basic standard for a utopian society. An aristocracy is rule by the few with the interests of the community as a guiding principle but fails to achieve the same level of goodness, or desirability, as a polity because only the wealthy leaders are determining what is the common good. In an oligarchy, the common interest is set aside for the interests of the ruling elite to the detriment of the community. In a monarchy, the community is guided solely by the interests of the monarch; so if that one person is degraded or debased at all, the community falls into tyranny and no one willingly lives in a tyrannical society.

Main Idea 3: Utopia

Though there are those that place the beginning of the concept of a utopia as far back as Plato's writing about the Kallipolis in *The Republic*, the term originates with Sir Thomas More's publication of *Utopia* in 1516. More plays with the Greek language to create a playful misnomer in the title of his book. Given the spelling and subsequent pronunciation, the title may mean either "good place" or it may mean "no place" and taken literally likely means "a good no place." More's writing about utopia detailed an island that was meant to be a sort of paradise compared to the England of his day. This distinction is necessary because More's Utopia includes slavery, war, and some invasive procedures that violate individual autonomy. But this raises a critical question for any utopian analysis, namely, what constitutes a utopia? This question is hard to wrestle with because it simultaneously asks us to think in universal terms while reckoning with the fact that our utopias reflect, as they did for More, criticisms of the culture we inhabit and individual notions of what is desirable.

A second difficulty is that what constitutes a utopia for one person is likely to be the incarnation of another person's dystopia. If we want to avoid this problem, we are left dealing with grand concepts like justice, peace, or equity, without being able to put substance into these ideas. This is the very problem of More's "good no place," namely, that it is purely imaginary and could not actually exist. However, this did not stop people from pursuing utopian community building in the eighteenth, nineteenth, and twentieth centuries, many of which met with disastrous results. However,

I would argue that the difficulty in pursuing utopian community building in practice is because there is not a blank canvas to work with as there would be in a post-apocalyptic setting. That is, we can observe the conditions of utopia as emergent properties of the various communities Rick Grimes encounters and attempts to build because the zombie apocalypse has removed the complications of civilizations preconceived notions of how society ought to be or, contrarily, existing society as a foil for a budding utopia to be compared against. While Rick Grimes and his adult companions may well remember and pine for what was lost with the arrival of the zombie apocalypse, the children and subsequent generations would have no ideas about what was; consequently, it should, theoretically, be possible to build a utopia from the ashes of an apocalyptic event.

Flashback to the original apocalyptic community Rick Grimes finds himself in at the outset of the story. A group of people lacking leadership, security, provisions, and a clear understanding of the apocalyptic threat. When Rick first arrives, he and his former partner Shane form the authoritative decision-making body for the group but they have no actual authority and the group might be better labeled a loosely anarchist community than anything else. This is important because over time not only does Rick assume command of the group, he does so with their consent. This establishes Rick in a monarchical role because his decisions are final, and early on he maintains a firm commitment to the common interest. As the group wanders, collecting more members and searching for safety, the structure of this community does not change adequately to justify understanding it differently than a monarchial government. However, the instability of such a community is put to the test when the survivors arrive at the prison compound.

The first utopian community, or attempt at utopian community building, is the prison the group inhabits during Compendium One. The prison is a utopia of confinement for the group, which seems like a contradiction – however, the group imprisons itself to isolate from and insulate against the external threat of the zombies they have not quite learned to manage. While the prison has enough space for a farm and recreation, as well as a kitchen, library, inmate attire for clothing, a laundry, and working showers, it also promises internal conflicts of interest between the existing inmates and Rick's group. The resolution of this problem follows Rick's murder of Dexter during an inmate revolt which highlights for the group that they no longer know what constitutes right and wrong. Another problem that arises from this conflict is that Rick has a mental breakdown from the strain of being the only person in charge and the group decides to relieve him of his responsibilities and establish a democracy; consequently, it remains an open question if the community in the prison represents a utopia. Life in the prison also produces murders and suicides as well as other day-to-day hardships, and part of what sparks the war with the Woodbury community is the desirability of the prison compared to other living arrangements – i.e., the insecurity of the Woodbury community. More importantly, the prison reshapes the community because of the safety the members believe they have against the external threat of the zombies.

Without barring the war with Woodbury for control of the prison, we could ask if a place that has murders and suicides and varying degrees of unhappiness could be a utopian place? These are, after all, generally thought to be the hallmarks of a utopia: general happiness, peace, individualism, a general lack of hardships, and laws that promote the overall welfare of the community. The prison seems to capture, at least in a rudimentary way, Socrates' early attempts to explain the perfect society in *The Republic* – the one that Glaucon indignantly referred to as a city of pigs. What Glaucon means is that the society Socrates describes is lacking in creature comforts necessary for a good life; but this, of course, misses the point that Socrates is making about what is necessary for the Good Life. The question of whether or not Rick and his companions could ultimately live a happy and good life within the confines of the prison is made moot by the Woodbury onslaught which ruins the prison for everyone.

The next utopian building attempt is when Rick works to bring Alexandria, the Hilltop, and The Kingdom together both to eliminate the threat represented by The Saviors and to increase the overall well-being of the communities individually and collectively. Here, I think, we have the best example of utopian building under Rick Grimes's leadership. Each community by itself represents a struggling attempt to build a safe and thriving community. The ability to thrive is stifled by The Saviors, obviously, but also by the limitations of the leadership in place. Alexandria is a self-sufficient aristocracy, built with solar power, reinforced steel walls, gardens, and an extensive pantry of scavenged dry goods. The leadership is somewhat domineering, but overall, the people seem to be happy and safe. The Hilltop has managed to produce industry and farming on a small scale along with high, but flimsy walls. Gregory, the leader, is incompetent at best and lives in fear of Negan and The Saviors which puts the Hilltop at risk. (His incompetence does not mitigate in any way his own tyrannical impulses.) The Kingdom is managed by Ezekiel and, though it is possible to generate ideas about the conditions similar in all respects to Alexandria and the Hilltop, The Kingdom is not given as much analysis in the graphic novel. Nevertheless, Ezekiel stands in stark contrast to Gregory; where Gregory is a failed tyrant, Ezekiel is a successful monarch. Still, the triumvirate of communities ultimately becomes a utopian-esque arrangement, with Oceania and The Savior compound, cultivating trade, movement among people, rudimentary currency, an increase in productivity, greater security, and overall increases in happiness for the citizens of each allied community.

Main Idea 4: Dystopia

The idea of a dystopia as the opposite of a utopia first entered popular discourse when John Stuart Mill used the construct to denounce England's Irish land policies. The word literally means "bad place" and is often characterized by dehumanization, tyranny, poverty, and misery. Often, as Gregory Claeys points out, dystopias tend to be failed utopias and that should guide our interrogation into dystopias because no one sets out to create a dystopia. Rick Grimes and his fellow survivors certainly encounter plenty of misery, poverty, and dehumanization on their travels, but these are especially highlighted in several of the communities they come across.

Though much of the focus on Rick Grimes throughout *The Walking Dead* centers on his attempts to bring people together and build communities within a utopian framing, there are dystopias scattered throughout the narrative as well. Although the focus on Woodbury is quite limited, it is the first dystopia readers encounter. Woodbury is governed by a despotic and cruel leader whose goal is power and control. So, even as the residents of Woodbury live in peace and have many of the same attributes as the prison occupied by Rick and his group, the Woodburians are living a lie. Not only is their life a façade for the cruelty of their leader and his inner circle, but they are lied to in order to keep them in line and, ultimately, to get them to go to war on behalf of their Governor.

The Saviors represent another dystopian group in the story. Not because of their domineering and parasitic relationship to the other communities, but because of how Negan runs the compound where they live. Individuals work, or more accurately, slave, for the group while certain members are freed from the laborious tasks that are necessary to keep the compound going. Worst among these is Negan himself, who accumulates wives by offering women the opportunity to get out of work by becoming an exclusive member of his harem. To fail to maintain this exclusivity results in the gruesome punishment of hot ironing the offender's face to scar them as a warning to others. The television show and the graphic novel tell similar, but ultimately different, versions of this dystopian community. Negan is, however, a good case study for the failed utopia. His rise to tyrant was not a straight line, but rather a series of false starts and hard losses during the apocalypse, and he genuinely believes he is doing the other communities a fair service for the pay they extract. The fact that Negan thinks he is bringing back civilization and creating utopia is underscored in his war with Rick Grimes when, after defeating Negan, Rick tells him, "I'm going to keep you alive…I'm going to make you watch what we become so that you can see how wrong you were…how much you were holding us back."

The Commonwealth is the largest and most organized of the communities Rick confronts throughout the story. While it presents as a utopia, or at least a budding utopia, the reality is far more sinister. The Commonwealth is structured around class biases and rigid division of labor and benefits. While there is the appearance of plenty, the lack of equality means that some of the citizens are actually impoverished while others have more than they need. The leader of The Commonwealth, while not as crazy as Woodbury's Governor or as savage as Negan, is a domineering authoritarian and fully expects to pull Rick and his communities into her scope of power and control. The biggest giveaway to the dystopian nature of The Commonwealth is the ease with which Rick is able to spark a rebellion and win over the majority of the citizens. I will return to the question of The Commonwealth below.

Main Idea 5: What Rules Should We Follow

In the event of an apocalypse, individuals would likely find themselves wondering what rules, if any, still applied. (The Telltale video game makes great use of this conundrum by using its unique choice making design drive the game narrative forward by asking players to make incredibly difficult decisions where pre-apocalyptic rules are no longer easy guides for what is right or wrong.) We can tackle this issue by considering some of the difficulties faced by survivors in *The Walking Dead*. Obviously, the first question that arises is whether or not we have obligations to other survivors. This problem is particularly hard, because most moral theories include a moral obligation to self-preservation, and in a world with limited resources, we may find ourselves not only hoarding resources but actively working in competition with others for those same resources. We see this concern (to what extent are we obligated to help others) in *The Walking Dead* several times as time passes in the story and each time the answer to the question is more difficult to give.

The first time we encounter a serious question of apocalyptic right and wrong is when Rick stumbles across Morgan and Duane after he escapes the hospital. Rick believes he is doing the right thing by giving Morgan access to the police department's stores of weapons and ammunition, including a police cruiser, but he also admonishes Morgan to take care of the things he takes as he will eventually have to return them. This position clearly speaks to the naïve nature of both Rick and Morgan in the early days of the apocalypse. Rick is clearly treating his fellow survivor along the lines of pre-apocalyptic rules with the expectation that those rules will soon reemerge as society recovers.

The relationship between weapons and survivors will change over time as Rick and his group undergo the travails of surviving in an apocalyptic world – for instance, who should be allowed to carry and use a gun. Defending one's self and others, however, is only one concern that dominates the moral discourse in Rick's communities; other serious concerns show up as well. First, at the prison, Carol asks Rick and Lori to marry her and form a triangular relationship – a throuple. While Carol's proposal is met with shock and disdain by Lori, Carol raises a key question about how things are going to go in the apocalyptic world implying, emphatically, that things *do not have to be the way they were before*.

This entanglement occurs while the group is struggling with what to do about someone who murders. Rick confidently claims, "You kill, you die" as a justification for executing the prisoner Thomas. This proposition is thrown out, however, when it comes to light that Rick, in order to defend his group and maintain control of the prison, killed Dexter, the leader of the prisoners. While there are numerous examples of the survivors attempting to build a rule structure for their new lives, the primary problem they face is that there is no enforcement behind the rules except for themselves and what they are willing to do or tolerate.

It is the notion of what they themselves are willing to do that motivates Rick to imprison Negan rather than execute him even though there are plenty of people advocating for his punishment. Rick will subsequently explain to Andrea that what makes him a good leader, what makes him better than the rest at being a leader, is that he is willing to do what the others are not. Killing Negan is the easy thing, but keeping him in prison is hard and the fact that it is *against the wishes of the people he leads* makes it harder still. We see Rick and his compatriots face a similar conundrum when Sebastian, son of Pamela Milton, Governor of The Commonwealth, is convicted of murder and the survivors have to choose to live up to Rick's example with Negan or go in a different direction.

This leads to the question of what counts as "better" in a post-apocalyptic society. How are we to know when a society is better than what came before? To answer this question, it is helpful to once again turn to Aristotle for guidance. Aristotle advanced a concept of *eudaimonia* to explain an individual's moral situation. Because, for Aristotle, a person could not be moral except in community with others, the concept of eudaimonia was meant to help people figure out if they were living their best life in the best possible community. The Greek word "eudaimonia" is typically translated as "happiness," but it is actually more akin to flourishing or what today we call thriving. What Aristotle means is that you are not merely happy with how your life is going but that your life is flourishing – enough money, good friends, family, opportunities, accolades, civic engagement, etc. – all of which combine to make a person genuinely happy. If people are flourishing, then, the thinking goes, so must be the community; but only one type of community can actually achieve such high aims and for Aristotle: the polity, a community ruled by the many with the common interest as its guiding principle. So, here we might say that a community is better than what came before it if that community is governed by the many, promotes the common interest, and provides for human flourishing.

Conclusion

Eudaimonia leads us back to The Commonwealth. The Commonwealth represents the manifestation of Rick's earliest ideas about the return of civilization. The community, on its surface, appears to be thriving and its denizens seem content – especially given the multitudes of trauma a person would undergo attempting to survive in an apocalypse. The Commonwealth is hierarchical, but this is explained as a necessary condition of rebuilding society where individuals are employed doing the tasks that they are best suited for, determined exclusively by what they did *before* the apocalypse. Though there are people employed in tasks that are irrelevant to their pre-apocalyptic lives, these are established as anomalies in the design and function of the community and are generally geared toward the accommodation of the elite class of citizens.

This is in stark contrast to what Rick and his confederacy of burgeoning communities has attempted to do in their own way of bringing civilization back. At one point, the Alexandrians and their allies plan, coordinate, and host a fair for their communities. It barely excels beyond what we might think of as a craft fair, or community festival, but it is a direct attempt to return to pre-apocalyptic normalcy. Having exceeded their primitive apocalyptic limitations, the Alexandrian coalition has, by the time they encounter The Commonwealth, built a mill to allow for the making of bread, planted an orchard to supplement their extensive agriculture, and developed communal ways of being that diverge from any of their previously held beliefs about the return of civilization. The language of civilization is curious in *The Walking Dead*, because it is used by Kirkman and his co-creators to specifically denote pre-apocalyptic life *and* to reinforce its desirability. Intentionally or not, this is a part of the narrative structure of *The Walking Dead*, and it buttresses for the reader the idea that pre-apocalyptic society – our society – was good and desirable.

Each member community of Rick's alliance is allowed to autonomously decide how they will organize and govern themselves. As long as they are contributing to the overall well-being of the alliance and ensuring their members are treated fairly, there is no evidence that Rick intervenes. In fact, he works in concert with the other leaders to ensure fair trade, that each community is contributing to the overall upkeep of their collective, and to facilitate developments and growth in the communities. The group that is the least capable and least integrated is The Saviors and the same volatile unrest that allows Rick to overthrow The Commonwealth exists, especially, in the leadership of this community. This highlights that eudaimonia is not the direct result of mere community inclusion.

For The Saviors, who inherited no small amount of indignation and derision thanks to Negan's behavior, there is a sense that the happiness others participate in is out of reach. No matter what they do, under Rick's thumb, they will never be able to thrive. In The Commonwealth, those outside the elite class, and specifically those who feel most used by the elites, harbor high levels of dissatisfaction even though they live in relative safety, amidst abundance, and with opportunities for advancement and recreation that are represented in no other community Kirkman showcases in *The Walking Dead*. Happiness in The Commonwealth is counterfeit, a façade used by the leadership to sell the community to survivors who come across it. Happiness in Rick's alliance seems more genuine, more capable of living up to the standards of utopian community building; in other words, Rick's narrative is clearly meant to be a utopian story arc.

This raises the most important question about community to emerge from *The Walking Dead*, namely, why does the society that ultimately emerges after the overthrow of The Commonwealth appear to be derivative of the communal hierarchies employed by The Commonwealth's leaders? After the revolution in The Commonwealth, the story again has a major jump forward in time, a decade and half at least, leaving the particulars of this question unaddressed. The society that has emerged is clearly one designed to reclaim what was lost even though the architects of that society passed through the sieve of apocalyptic moral discourse, changing and altering their desires and expectations as they went. Removing The Commonwealth's elite class, establishing a communal structure that would better reflect the eudemonic underpinnings of the Alexandrian alliance, and continuing the trajectory Rick had established prior to meeting The Commonwealth, should have borne out a social organism that was decidedly different from pre-apocalyptic civilization.

One wonders if something like The Commonwealth, the apocalyptic stand-in for pre-apocalyptic life, was not the ultimate goal of Rick – especially given the strength of his early commitment to society, its institutions, and his desire to see it rescued. But, if Rick is a dynamic character, capable of change, then the numerous moral quandaries he had to navigate, which clearly altered his character, should have likewise altered his desire to see "civilization" return. In fact, there is evidence in his dealings with his allied communities that this is what happened. Why, then, does the realization of his utopian vision end up being the rebuilding of pre-apocalyptic life? Perhaps, unlike Thomas More and other renaissance thinkers, who had half an unexplored globe to use as their canvas for utopian dreaming, utopia today is bound up in the totalizing forces of modern society. That is, maybe Rick's utopian aspirations had to succumb to more immediate practicalities and, in addressing those practical matters, the best, or most efficient means, was to draw upon what was best known – pre-apocalyptic life. If this is the case, though, then we can say confidently that the survivors of the zombie apocalypse have traded eudaimonia for a dystopian story arc, one where society must devolve into the toxic hierarchies on display in The Commonwealth prior to Rick's revolt.

Utopian and dystopian discourse is difficult, because it is incredibly easy to slip from one to the other. That is, what makes my utopia a good place might be dystopian to someone else. This difficulty makes it difficult to classify all but the most clear-cut examples as one or the other. For instance, it is entirely possible that some people enjoyed their place and their lives as one of The Saviors even though they had to do without certain things and often terrible things were expected of them. Or, even though the prison had its problems, it is possible that we can see the utopian potential of such an arrangement. The purpose of thinking about utopias and dystopias is because they provide us a lens to critique our society, our culture, and, ultimately, humanity. By interrogating Rick's decisions, actions, and beliefs, especially as they relate to the building of community, society, and civilization, we are able to achieve just such a critique.

References

Aristotle. 1984. *The complete works of Aristotle*, vols. I & II, ed. Jonathan Barnes. Princeton: Princeton University Press.
Claeys, Gregory. 2018. *Dystopia: A natural history*. Oxford: Oxford University Press.
Kirkman, Robert. 2009. *The walking dead, compendium one*. Portland: Image-Skybound.
———. 2012. *The walking dead, compendium two*. Portland: Image-Skybound.
———. 2015. *The walking dead, compendium three*. Portland: Image-Skybound.
———. 2019. *The walking dead, compendium four*. Portland: Image-Skybound.
More, Thomas. 2016. *Utopia: Five hundred year anniversary edition*. New York: Verso.

Index

A
Abberline, Frederick, 2016
Abduction, 766, 768
Absolute freedom, 1890, 1891, 1893–1895, 1902
Absolute free speech argument, 645, 654–659
  See also South Park
Absolute Pacifism, 317, 320
Abstract, 2066, 2069, 2071–2074, 2076, 2077, 2080, 2083
Absurd, 1209, 1992, 1993, 1997–1999, 2026, 2030, 2041
Absurd hero, 423, 424
Absurdity, 899, 906
ad Hitlerum, fallacy, 711
Adopted children, 292
Adorno, Theodor, 970, 971
Aesthetics, 164, 179, 182, 1171, 1587, 2079
Aesthetic transformation, 108
Afterlife, 4, 7–18, 20, 21, 597–600
Agamben, Giorgio, 95, 98, 100, 108, 110
Agonism, 76
"A Good Man Goes to War" (2011), 317, 327, 331
  See also Doctor Who
Ahab, *Moby Dick* character, 171, 172, 181
Ajax, *Deadpool* character, 969, 975, 976
Alcott, Louisa May, 1418, 1419
Aldiss, Brian, 1062, 1083
Alienation, 1670
  from activity of labor, 1674–1675
  Marx on, 1671–1672
  from the product of labor, 1673–1674
  and religion, 1680–1683
  from the self or species, 1676–1677
Aliens, 798, 1293
Allegory of the Cave, 754, 765, 1517–1518
Alliance, 261, 262, 264, 266–272, 274, 279

Allopathic catharsis, 1483, 1485
Alternative facts, 727
Altruism, 36
Altshuler, Roman, 323
America First, 735
Amici di cappello, 877–879, 885
Amicitia, 878, 881–883, 885
Amor fati, 904, 908
Anarchy, 2044, 2049
Ancient Greek Stoics, 1888
Ancient Stoicism, 51
Andersen, Elizabeth, 379
Anderson, Gillian, 520
Anderson, Thomas Paul (PTA), 1194
Androids, 455, 1812–1815, 1818, 1820–1829, 1831
Anger, 1472, 1480, 1487–1489
Animalism, 1296
Animal rights, 774, 779
Annas, Julia, 1031
Antagonism, 66
Anti-Defamation League, 437
Antifa, 713
Anti-feminine, 736
Anti-heroes, 171, 172, 179–181
Anti-Otherness jokes, 1628
Anti-rites, 1627
Anti-socratic sentiments, 530–534
Apathy, 1280, 1281, 1285
Apocalypse, 2108–2110
Aporia, 1781, 1783
Apotheosis, 100, 110
Appiah, Kwame Anthony, 1048
Aquinas, Thomas, 194, 219, 223, 552–553, 779
Architecture, 816
Arendt, Hannah, 103, 1844
Aries, 805
Aristotelianism, 943

Aristotle, 173, 193–194, 276, 277, 285, 288, 303, 567, 568, 577, 613, 615, 617, 624, 625, 803, 899, 903, 909, 913, 914, 918, 941, 943, 952, 1031, 1176, 1184, 1494, 1497, 1499, 1556, 1819, 1849, 1853, 1854, 1859–1861, 1897, 1902, 2087, 2090, 2093–2095, 2097
   human beings, 2051
   ideas, 2050
   Plato 2052–2054
   political community, 2051
   political constitutions, 2051
   societies, 2050
   theory of friendship, 953–955
   virtue, 2051
   virtue ethics, 911–913
Artifact theory of fiction, 2030, 2037–2039
Artificial consciousness, 1073–1075
Artificial intelligence (AI), 35, 36, 803, 1026, 1027, 1035–1037, 1062
   artificial consciousness, 1073–1075
   consciousness and ethics, 1076–1077
   emotions, 1077–1081
   measurement of intelligence, 1067–1068
   natural and artificial intelligence, 1066–1067
   natural consciousness, 1071–1073
   plot of, 1063–1066
   robotics, 1081–1086
   safety, 1070–1071
   simulation, intelligence and consciousness, 1075–1076
   technology, 1068–1070
Ash-bot, *Black Mirror* character, 480, 481
Ashley, Elizabeth, 409
Assimilation, 880, 893
Asterios Polyp, 2066, 2068
   departure, 2077
   Hero's Journey, 2075–2083
   Ignazio as narrator, 2069–2070
   initiation, 2077–2081
   perception and self, 2070–2071
   Plato and the Two Worlds, 2073–2075
   return, 2081–2083
   universals and particulars, concrete and abstract, 2072–2073
Asymmetry, 1428
Atheism, 585, 588, 604, 1441, 1452, 1459, 1683
Atheists, 69, 72, 83, 583, 585, 599, 605, 1438, 1439, 1441, 1442, 1447, 1450, 1455, 1458–1461

Atman, 18–20
Atwood, Margaret, 186, 189, 193, 203
Auden, Wystan Hugh, 227
Augustine, 858, 861, 864, 865
Authenticity, 1315–1316, 1319, 1322, 1608, 1697, 1804
Authoritarianism, 1113–1117
Autocracy, 367, 380
Autonomous individual selves, 107
Autonomy, 190–193, 297, 300, 303, 1026, 1031, 1033, 1035–1038, 1040, 1045, 1051–1053, 1055, 1057
   and language, 199–202
   and religion, 202–204
Ava, *Ex Machina* Character
   artificial intelligence, 1026
Avatar, 1290
   metaphysical thesis, 1292–1295
   summary, 1291, 1292
   switching bodies 1303
Avis, Krill deity in *The Orville*, 428, 430, 433–436, 441, 444, 445
Awakening, 1018–1022
Awareness, of present moment, 1013
   See also Meditation

B
Back-tracking counterfactual, 1344, 1345
Bad faith, 1316, 1317, 1319–1321, 1720, 1725–1727, 1729, 1731, 1733, 1736, 1737
"Bad Wolf" (2005), 314, 315, 328
   See also Doctor Who
Banality of evil, 1841
"Bandersnatch" (2018), 500
   See also Black Mirror
Bare life, 98–100, 106
Bar-Elli, Gilead, 1260, 1261
Barnett, Charlie, 408
Bash Explore and Acquire Drones (BEADs), 1390, 1400
   See also Don't Look Up
Bassham, Gregory, 220
Batman, 978, 1949–1967, 1988–1992, 1994–2000
"The Battle of Ranzkoor Av Kolos" (2018), 325
   See also Doctor Who
Battlestar Galactica (*BSG*)
   biopolitical inertia, 100–103
   phases, 95
   reconciliation and rebirth, 107–110
   television seasons, 94–97

Batty, Roy, *Blade Runner* character, 987–991, 996–999, 1001
Baudrillard, Jean, 766, 767, 1870, 1876–1880, 1925
"The Beast Below" (2010), 313, 323, 326, 329
　See also Doctor Who
Beauty, 1758, 1760, 1763, 1768
Beauvoir, Simone de, 342, 345–347, 358, 1152, 1277, 1284, 1286, 1413, 1495, 1496
　existentialism and freedom, 1733–1736
　vengeance, 1262–1263
Bein, Steve, 218, 230
Being and Nothingness, 1725, 1726
Being for-itself, 177, 1725
Being in-itself, 177, 1725
Belief, 1138–1141, 1156, 1157
Belief in God, 768, 769
Belliotti, Raymond A, 300
Benjamin, Walter, 1159
Bentham, Jeremy, 169, 788, 1747, 1924
Bergmann, Ernst, 724
Bergson, Henri, 1622
"Be Right Back" (2013), 480, 481
　See also Black Mirror
Berkeley, George, 414, 1870–1873, 1880
Better Call Saul, 171
Bible, 433, 442, 444, 602–604, 1442, 1444, 1446, 1447, 1926
Big Bang, 1442, 1444–1449, 1453
Big Blue, *X-Files* cryptid, 531
Big Data, 455, 463
Bigfoot, 1443, 1460
The Big Lebowski, 919–935
　"The Dude's virtues", 938–944
　masculinity, 935–938
　nihilism *vs.* Dude, 944–947
The Big Lie, 717–718, 728
　political tactic, 717–718
　Trump's election lie, 728–730
The Big Sleep, 918, 919, 942
Biodefense unit, 636
Biofeedback protocol, 97
Biologism, 1958
Biopolitics, 94, 98, 102, 1843
Biopower, 95, 101, 102, 107
Bioshock, 1898
Biotechnological power, 100
Bixby, Jerome, 1286
Black Lives Matter (BLM), 662, 2061, 2062
Black Mirror, 480, 481, 483–500
"Black Museum" (2017), 485, 489
　See also Black Mirror

Black Sails, 114
　democracy and equality, 125–129
　description, 114–116
　Hobbes, Thomas, 118–122
　justice, 131–132
　Locke, John, 118–122
　Rawls, John, 123–125
　Rousseau, Jean-Jacques, 122–123
　social contract theories, 118–125
　tolerance, 129–131
Black Shirts (in Italian fascism), 710, 731
Blade Runner, 984, 988
　characters, 992
　characters and basic story, 985
　messages, 985
　as philosophical film, 984
　philosophical significance of, 995
　set, 985
　significance, 984
　theatrical release of, 1001
Blinovitch, Aaron, 146
Blinovitch limitation effect, 146, 156
Block universe, 1337–1346
Blood-libel, 721, 722
Blow, Jonathan, 1772–1776, 1779, 1785
Bluebook, 1027
Blustein, Jeffrey, 295
Bluth, Lucille, *Arrested Development* character, 285, 289
Bodily resurrection, 598
Bolland, Brian, 1988, 1993, 1998
Bong Joon-ho, 774
Book, Shepherd, *Firefly* character, 263
Book of Job, 1163–1164
　See also Bible
Bootstrap paradox, 146, 147
Bordán, Irén, 419
Boredom, 1279–1283, 1285, 1895, 1896, 1900, 1902
Breath of the Wild (*BotW*), 1884–1899, 1901–1905
　See also "The Legend of Zelda: Breath of the Wild"
Bourdieu, Pierre, 1710
Brahman, 18–20
Breaking Bad, 164–166, 168–173, 175–182
Brennan, Jason, 380
Brenner, Ruth, 409
Brison, Susan, 299
British Broadcasting Cooperation (BBC), 1707, 1712, 1713, 1716
British colonization, 456
Brown shirts (in Nazi fascism), 710

Bruckman, Clyde, 531
  psychic "gift", 530
Bruno, Giordano, 504
Budapest, 420
Buddhism, 599, 693, 1803–1807
Buddhist monk, 5
Buddhist philosophy, 1006, 1537
Bundle theory, 599
Burke, Edmund, 1763–1764
Butler, Judith, 1843, 1845, 1846

C

The Cabin in the Woods, 1170–1173
  and caring, 1177–1180
  epistemic value and ethical complexity, 1173–1174
  ethical theory interlude, 1176–1177
  filmic counterexamples and philosophical theories, 1180–1182
  implicit theory of horror, 1182–1184
  philosophical engagement, 1188–1192
  utilitarianism, 1174–1176
  worthwhile horror, 1184–1188
Cady, Duane, 317–322, 338
Cameron, James, 1290, 1299
Camus, Albert, 423, 906–907, 946, 1209, 1766, 1993, 1998, 2026, 2030, 2041
Canavan, Gerry, 1182, 1183, 1186, 1188
Cancel culture, 660–662, 1553, 1559
Canons of honor, 565, 567
  See also Star Wars
Capability approach, 622
Capitalism, 874, 887, 888, 894, 1223, 1671, 1674, 1676, 1678, 1679
Capitalist hegemony, 1605, 1606
Caprica, 97–103
Caprica Six, 96, 107, 111
  See also Battlestar Galactica (*BSG*)
Cardinal virtues, 44, 45, 570
Care, 829, 835, 844
Care ethics, 575, 1818–1820, 1830
Carlin, George, 1512, 1514–1516
  beliefs, 1514
  "It's Bad for Ya", 1519–1526
  religious belief, 1515
  rhetorical strategies, 1514
  social commentary, 1513
Carrera, Cesare (Chez) Russian Doll character, 419
Cartoonists, 1966
"Cartoon Wars" Part I and II (2006), 637, 640, 642–646
  See also South Park

Caste, 1044, 1050, 1051, 1057, 1058
Categorical desires, 1281, 1282
Categorical imperative, 170, 1032, 1035, 1038, 1039, 1955
"Catering to Terrorism Creates More Terrorism" argument, 643, 645–646
  See also South Park
Catharsis, 1470, 1471, 1480, 1483, 1485–1487, 1489
Catholic Church, 1715
Catholic dogma, 1446
Catholic priest, 582
Causal loops, 1332, 1339, 1340
Cave allegory, 765
Censorship, 1550–1553, 1559
Certitude, 1136–1138, 1142
Chappelle, Dave, 1644
  color-blind racism, 1657–1664
  race and/as contradiction, 1647–1657
  use of stereotypes, 1644–1646
  work on *Chappelle's Show*, 1644
Character ethicists, 1031
Charlotte's Web, 227
Charlton Comics, 1970
Chelm
  citizens of, 1639
  jokes, 1639
  residents of, 1640
  Seinfeld as, 1640–1641
Chess, 819
Chesser, Zachary Adam, 641, 645, 655
Children of Dune, 675, 676, 678, 680, 682, 686, 689, 691, 693, 695, 699
Chinese Basketball Association (CBA), 660
Chivalry, 547–548
Choice, 1144–1147
  deliberate, 954
  matter of, 960
  one-on-one community, 956
  of presentation, 953
Choice-focused gameplay, 1890
Chomsky, Noam, 221
Christian, 70, 72, 691, 692, 694, 695, 697
  fundamentalism, 435
  humanists, 68
  morality, 1959
  nationalism, 437, 443
  nationalist ethos, 437
  persecution complex, 1439, 1440
Christianity, 685, 692–695, 769, 903, 1439, 1444, 1453, 1461, 1706, 1959
Civilized society, 1898
Clash of civilizations, 443, 444

Classic epistemology, 523, 535
Class inequalities, 1122
Clemens, Samuel, 1350
Clifford, William, 695–699, 770
Climate change, 1113, 1377, 1383–1387, 1395–1401
   See also Don't Look Up
Clyde Bruckman's Final Repose, 524
Cobb, Dom, *Inception* character 754–764, 769–771
Coen Brothers, 937, 944, 945
Cogito, 535, 1136
   See also Descartes, Rene
Cognitive development, 212
Cognitivism, 1155, 1156
Coincidence, 1200–1202
Collective catharsis, 1485, 1487–1489
Collectivist pacifism, 320
Collectivist-realist Pacifism, 324, 331–338
Colonial creep, 460
Colonialism, 454
   perpetrated by males, 457
   types, 458, 460
Coloniality, 456
Colonization, 454, 456, 457, 459, 460
   dehumanization, 469
   human bots, 470
   racial contract, 468
   robots, 467
   social construction, 468
   of space, 461, 462
   of time, 461, 462
The Colonization of Psychic Space, 462
Colonized, 454, 456, 459, 461, 462, 464–468, 470–474, 476
Colonizer, 454, 456–460, 462–468, 471–474, 476
Color-blind racism, 1645, 1657–1664
Columbus Day, 1589, 1601
Comedic philosophy, 1572
Comedy, 918, 934, 945, 1492, 1548, 1549, 1622, 1644, 1645, 1649, 1651, 1658, 1664, 1665
   and humor, 384
   philosophy and, 385, 1605, 1618
   political, 384
   sketch, 389
Comedy Central, 635, 638, 640–642, 645, 646, 650, 653, 663
Comet/climate change analogy, 1383–1387
   See also Don't Look Up
Commare, 878, 880, 882
Commonwealth, 271–275, 277–279

Community (*Harry Potter*), 260, 273, 275, 277, 278
   communion and, 956
   Death Eaters, 956
   friendship, 276, 277
   Gryffindor, 955
   Hogwarts houses, 955
   political, 961
   quidditch, 957
   Slug Club, 955, 960
   Slytherin, 956
   type of, 952
   Voldemort's, 962
   wider, 958
Comparaggio, 877, 878, 880–882, 885
Compari, 878, 882
Compassion, 323, 324, 329, 332, 335, 336, 338, 1013
Compatibilism, 1146, 1147, 1976–1977, 1980–1985
Compliance, 887
   See also Black Mirror
Concealing information, 1361, 1362, 1368
Concrete, 2066, 2069, 2071, 2072, 2074, 2076, 2077, 2079–2083
Confession, 166
Connors, Phil, *Groundhog Day* character, 410
Consciousness, 1028, 1087, 1298, 1304, 1306, 1812–1815, 1818, 1821–1824, 1827, 1828
   artificial, 1073–1075
   and ethics, 1076–1077
   natural, 1071–1073
   simulation and intelligence, 1075–1076
Consent, 2044, 2055
Consequentialism, 170, 787–789, 793, 1747, 1750, 2098
Conspiracy theories, 720–722, 734, 737
Conspiratorial thinking, 737
Constitutionalism, 1300, 1301
Constitution view, 1300
Consubstantiality, 1574–1577
Consumerism, 1224, 1225, 1230
Continuity, 1796, 2026–2029, 2031, 2032, 2041
Contractarians, 1031
Control, 613, 616–618, 623, 624
Cooke, Elizabeth, 226
Copley, Sharlto, 419
Corleone, Family from *The Godfather* 874–876, 880, 882, 887, 892–894
Corporate capitalism, 459
Corporate deception, 246
Corpus callosum, 1305, 1306

Cortright, David, 317, 321–323, 332
Cosmic ballet, 804
Cosmic war, 439, 446
Cosmological argument, 587
Cosmopolitanism, 58
Cosmos, 426
Costello, Peter, 222
Coughlin, Charles Edward (Father) (fascist radio personality), 725
  See also Father Coughlin (fascist radio personality)
Counterpart theory, 511, 2040
Courage, 173
  importance of, 955
COVID-19 pandemic, 1377, 1378, 1380, 1559, 1885
Co-writing, 2091
Cranston, Bryan, 165, 168
Crashing, 1720, 1721, 1727–1729, 1731, 1732, 1734
Creationism, 254
Creationist, 771
Crimefighter, 1952
Crime management, 877
Criminology, 1960
Critchley, Simon, 1470, 1476, 1481, 1489, 1628
Criteria of adequacy, 766, 768
Critical thinking, 191, 199, 208
Critique of Pure Reason, 768
Critique, philosophical meaning, 1621, 1625, 1630
Crockett Island, 582, 583
  See also Midnight Mass
Cultural critique, 1470
Cultural marketplace, 1550
Cultural norms, 1625
Cultural relativism, 507
Cultural shock, 814
Cultural theory, 1605, 1607, 1614
Culture industry, 490, 492, 499
Curb Your Enthusiasm, 1620, 1621, 1623–1630
CW-7, 1125
  See also Snowpiercer
Cybermen *Doctor Who* villain, 313, 314, 317, 325, 334–337
Cyberpunk 2077, 1790–1791
  posthumanism, 1799–1803
  problem of personal identity, 1795–1799
  transhumanism, 1791–1795
Cyborgs, 484
Cycle of violence, 1258
Cyclops, 813

Cylon attack, *Battlestar Galactica* (*BSG*), 94
Cylon models, *Battlestar Galactica* (*BSG*), 95, 102, 108, 109
Cynicism, 548–550
Cyrenaic school, 516

D
The Daily Beast, 1385
The Daily Rip, 1375, 1376, 1381, 1382, 1390, 1398, 1400, 1401
  See also Don't Look Up
Daleks, *Doctor Who* villians, 313–316, 318, 324, 326, 328, 330, 332, 334
Darwin, Charles, 1451, 1453, 1454
David, Larry, 1620–1630
Davros, *Doctor Who* villain, 313, 316, 317, 321–323, 327, 329, 331
Dawkins, Richard, 1448, 1449
The Dawn of Man, 800, 805
"The Day of the Doctor" (2013), 314, 322, 330, 332
  See also Doctor Who
"Day of the Moon" (2011), 316, 326
  See also Doctor Who
Dazzling, 1366
DC Comics, 1970
Deadpool, 968–971, 973–980
Deadpool Kills Deadpool, 2026, 2028, 2040
Deadpool Kills the Marvel Universe
  Deadpool as an anti-Sisyphean hero, 2030–2031
  Deadpool's master plan, 2029–2030
  fictional entities as artifacts, 2036–2039
  ontological status of possible worlds, 2034–2035
  possible worlds, trans-world identities and counterparts, 2031–2034
  synopsis, 2027–2029
Deadpool Killustrated, 2026, 2028–2030, 2035, 2038, 2039
Death, 597–599, 603, 997–999
  Deckard from, 988
  under penalty of, 986
"Death in Heaven" (2014), 313
  See also Doctor Who
Deception, 1350–1352, 1355, 1360, 1361, 1363, 1364, 1366–1369
Deckard, Rick, *Blade Runner* protagonist, 986, 990
Deep fakes, 717, 726
Dehumanization, 460, 469, 473
Deliverance from suffering, 1010, 1012, 1013, 1020, 1023

Deller, Ruth, 316
Democracy, 125–129, 362–365, 550, 551, 610, 613–625, 627–631, 678–681, 684, 691
Democratic decline, 368
Democratic systems, 679, 684
"Demon 79" (2023), 496–498
    See also Black Mirror
de Montaigne, Michel, 506
Deontologism (duty-based ethics), 325–328, 331
Deontologists, 1031
Deontology, 180, 181, 787, 793, 1392, 2087, 2096, 2100
Department of Homeland Security (DHS), 2062
Deplatforming, 660, 663, 664, 668
Derrida, Jacques, 767
Descartes, René, 33, 34, 535, 762, 765–768, 782, 990, 991, 1135–1138
Descriptive cultural vision, 882
Despair, 861, 868, 1321, 1322
Destiny, 892–894
Determinism, 1144, 1146, 1148, 1937, 1973, 1976–1981, 1983
Detroit Become Human (DBH), 1812–1816, 1818, 1821, 1822, 1825, 1827–1831
Developmental robotics, 1083–1084
Dialectic of Enlightenment, 490, 813
The Dibbuk, 1162
Dick, Philip K., 984
Dictators, 683, 684
Dictatorship, 675, 676
Digital Age, 480, 481
Dignity, 170, 1037
"Dinosaurs on a Spaceship" (2012), 316, 326
    See also Doctor Who
Diplomacy, 1117
Discipline, 1100, 1103
Discipline of desire, 564
Disco Elysium, 1866–1870
    semiological idealism, 1876–1879
    subjective idealism, 1870–1873
    transcendental idealism, 1873–1876
Discovery of identities and realities, 1909–1911
Discrimination, 235, 239
Disenchantment, 866, 867
The Disappearance of Childhood, 221
Distinctive hallucinations, 536
Django Unchained, 1243
The Doctor
    Eighth (McGann, Paul), 313, 322
    Eleventh (Smith, Matt), 313, 316, 323, 326–329, 331–334
    Fourth (Baker, Tom), 313, 330

Ninth (Eccleston, Christopher), 314, 324, 326, 327, 331, 333
    Ruth-Doctor/Ruth Clayton (Martin, Jo), 313, 317, 338, 339
    Seventh (McCoy, Sylvester), 313
    Tenth (Tennant, David), 313, 314, 316, 317, 322, 326, 329–334, 337
    Third (Pertwee, Jon), 313
    Thirteenth (Whittaker, Jodie), 313, 314, 325, 334, 337, 339
    Twelfth (Capaldi, Peter), 317, 325, 327, 330, 331, 334–338
    War Doctor (Hurt, John), 332, 333
"The Doctor Falls" (2017), 317, 325, 334, 335
    See also Doctor Who
The Doctor's pacifism, 321–325, 333, 335, 336
Doctor Who, 136, 140, 142–145, 147, 154, 156, 157, 312–314
    success of, 136
    time travel in, 135–162
"Doctor Who and the Silurians" (1970), 313
    See also Doctor Who
Dodge, Michael, 327
Domestic android, 1815
Domestic terrorism, 437, 731
Domestic workers movement, 1542
Domination, 2089
Domination and Submission, 2086, 2100
    Aristotle, 2093
    comics, 2090
    graphic novel, 2086
    Kant, 2095, 2096, 2098
    Mill, 2098, 2099
    personal, 2094
    philosophy, 2093
    sexual, 2088
Dominion voting systems (law suit), 725
Don Quixote, 168, 170–172
"Don't Capitulate, Reiterate" argument, 643, 646–651
    See also South Park
Don't Look Up, 1374–1379, 1381–1383, 1385, 1387–1399, 1401–1403
    criticism of the media, 1381–1383
Double consciousness, 1648
Douglas, Mary, 1625, 1627, 1628
Douglas, 1472, 1475, 1483
Dracula, 582
Dream problem, 766, 1135
Duchovny, David, 520
Dudeism, 940
    See also The Big Lebowski
Dune, 674, 675, 677, 678, 680, 682, 688–696, 699, 700

Dune Messiah, 675, 680, 686, 687, 697
Dussel, Enrique, 1587
Duties 291
    absolute/perfect, 319, 325
    actual, 319
    of affection, 285
    prima facie, 319, 327–328
Duty-based ethics (deontology), 325–328
Dystopia, 186, 188, 206, 2113–2114
Dystopian reality, 1834

E
Earth's atmosphere, 1111, 1128
Eastwood, Clint, 175
Ebert, Roger, 1198
Ecocriticism, 829
Economic inequality, 1121
Edo period of Japan, 456, 461
Education, 682, 694
Egalitarianism, 620
Eightfold path of Buddha, 1012, 1013
Einstein, Albert, 1338, 1340
Election denial, 658, 668
"The Eleventh Hour" (2010), 313, 328
    See also Doctor Who
Elliott, Chris, 410
Emotions, 1077–1078, 1627, 1758, 1762, 1763
    AI, robots, 1080–1081
    imprinting, 1079–1080
    love, 1078–1079
Emotivism, 180
Empiricism, 221
Empowerment, 621–624, 891
Emptiness, 1019
Enchantment, 831, 832, 842, 848, 849, 851
Endangered Earth, 1381
"The End of Time" (2009)
    Part 2, 317, 334
    See also Doctor Who
English, Jane, 297
Enlightened/rational egoism, 1430
Enlightenment, 1006, 1009–1012, 1015–1017
Entropy, 1330, 1334, 1340, 1346
Environment, 829, 831–833, 843
    crisis, 830, 849
    education, 850
    ethics, 847
    organization, 846
    philosophy, 828
    sensibility, 830
    values, 847
Epic, 164–169, 171, 173, 181

Epictetus, 45, 46, 48, 49, 57, 60, 63
Epicureanism, 939, 945
Epicurus, 938, 939
Epistemic access, 1536
Epistemic agnosticism, 1462
Epistemological relativism, 1785, 1786
Epistemology, 33, 628, 1153, 1154, 1351, 1357
Equality, 125–129, 617–621
Equal (sammā), 1013
Erikson, Erik, 213, 221
Ersatz realism, 2034
Erythropoietic protoporphyria (EEP), 584
"Escape Clause" (1959), 30
    See also Twilight Zone
Escape from Freedom, 490
Esposito, Roberto, 103
Eternalism, 155, 158, 412, 1972–1983, 1985
Eternal life, 1272, 1280
Eternal recurrence, 1888
Eternal return, 903–908, 914, 1888, 1889
Ethical norms, 1812
Ethical theories, 1031, 1829, 1830
Ethics, 5, 9, 11, 12, 19, 33, 67, 72–73, 80, 285, 376, 777, 846, 847, 1026, 1030–1031, 1036, 1499, 1503, 1505, 1746, 1750, 1751, 1753
    care, 330, 331, 575, 1177, 1178, 1180, 1182, 1184, 1188–1190
    consciousness, 1076–1077
    illusions, 1528–1530
    social, 86–89
The Ethics of Ambiguity, 345–348, 1231
The Ethics of Belief, 696
Etiquette, 1622, 1624, 1626
Etymology of comedy, 1594
Eudaimonia, 568, 569, 572, 577
Euthyphro, 439, 530, 1457
Evangelicalism, 433, 435, 437, 439, 444
Everett, Curtis, 1111
Everybody Draw Mohammed Day, 646
Evey's Pacifist Rebellion, 2058, 2059
    See also V for Vendetta
Evil, 892–894
    confronting with evil, 867–868
    confronting with oneself, 859–860
    demon, 762
    as inordinate desire, 864–866
    as phantom menace, 862
    pride and love of money, 862
Evil and Omnipotence, 594
Evolutionary lying, 1367, 1368
Evolved machines, 481–485

Existential crisis, 11, 12, 17, 19
Existentialism, 345, 899, 946, 947, 1210, 1231, 1232, 1420, 1697, 1724–1727, 1733, 1894
Existentialist themes, in *Fleabag* and *Crashing*, 1727–1731
Existential risk, 482–490, 493
Ex Machina, 1026, 1034
    Kant's position on lying, 1038–1040
    lying, 1029
    synopsis, 1027–1029
Experience machine, 765, 1526–1528
Expropriation contract, 460
Extended minds, 481–485
External incentivization, 1893
Extractive colonialism, 454, 458, 459
Extrinsic genoist, 1048, 1050
Extrinsic racist, 1048

F

Facticity, 1697, 1720, 1725, 1726, 1731, 1736
Fairness, 1645, 1647, 1649, 1651
Faith, 600–602, 1461, 1462
Fake news, 718, 726
False victimization narrative, 738
Famiglia, 877
Family, 876–878, 893
Family Guy, 640, 644
Family resemblance, 26, 734, 737
Fanaticism, 979
Fantasy, 831–833, 842, 849
Fantasy-prone personality, 529
Fascism, 706, 709–711, 720, 724, 727, 731–739
Fatalism, 1332, 1334–1337, 1341, 1342, 1344–1346
Fatalist attitude, 1343, 1345, 1346
Father Coughlin (fascist radio personality), 725
    See also Coughlin, Charles Edward (Father) (fascist radio personality)
Faust, 172
Favreau, Jon, 556
Fear, 1763–1765, 1768
Fear mongering, 718–720, 730–731
Femineity, 1495
Feminine mystique, 1495, 1499, 1501, 1506
Feminism, 1534, 1541–1543, 1548, 1550, 1554, 1555, 1559, 1736, 2010, 2015, 2016, 2018
Feminist movement, 1534
Fetus, 819
Feynman, Richard, 1340

Fiala, Andrew, 317
Fictionalism, 769
Fideism, 1461, 1462
Fidelity, 462
Fight Club
    evaluation, 1231–1234
    interpretation, 1222–1228
    moral of, 1229–1231
    summary, 1219–1222
Filial duty, 291, 301
Filial obligation, 285, 294, 297, 301
Film ambiguity, 761
Film-as-philosophy, xiv, xvii, 1171, 1173, 1188
Film noir, 919, 936
Filth theory, 591
Fincher, David, 1218
Finn, Huckleberry, 1350, 1353–1354
Firefly (Whedon), 260, 261, 266, 268–270, 272, 273
"The Fires of Pompeii" (2008), 323, 329
    See also Doctor Who
First Amendment, 646, 659, 660, 663, 668
Fission/fusion, 1796–1798
Fitting fulfillment, 1414, 1421, 1430
Fleabag, 1720–1724, 1727–1729, 1731, 1734, 1735
Flourishing, 568, 573, 577, 1888, 1902, 1903
Foot, Philippa., 1031
The Force, 856–859, 861, 862, 864, 865, 870–871
    See also Star Wars
Formula of humanity, 1033, 1038
Formula of Universal Law, 1032, 2096
Foucault, Michel, 67, 94, 98, 101, 102, 107–109, 441, 509, 1093, 1099–1106, 1998
Four-Dimensional Realism (4DR), 137, 154–156
Fox Comics, 1970
Fox News, 714–716, 725, 729–731
Frankfurt, Harry, 190, 191, 1342, 1343, 1817
Frankl, Viktor, 1470
Frederic, Wertham, 970
Freedom, 1092–1094, 1096, 1098, 1099, 1102, 1106–1108, 1695–1699, 1720, 1724, 1726, 1727, 1731–1737, 2044, 2045
Freedom and divine foreknowledge problem, 1344
"Freedom of Speech Isn't Free" argument, 644, 651–652
    See also South Park
Free speech, 659, 660, 663–668, 1550

Free will, 859, 1145, 1146, 1341–1344, 1814, 1822, 1823, 1827, 1970, 1976, 1978–1985
Free will defense, 1455, 1456
Freud, Sigmund, 1482
Friedan, Betty, 1494
Friendship, 246, 276, 940, 952, 1093, 1097, 1098, 1101, 1104, 1105, 1107, 2095
 beneficent, 957
 and community, 276, 277, 280
 maleficent, 957
 of pleasure, 289
 pleasure in HPCU, 957–960
 and trust, 277
 utility in HPCU, 960–963
 virtue in HPCU, 952–957
Frog and Toad Together, 228
From Hell, 2004–2006, 2008, 2009, 2011, 2012, 2014, 2017, 2022, 2023
Frontierism, 454
Frontier justice, 1238, 1239, 1247, 1248
Fry, Stephen, 1703–1704
 mania, 1716–1717
 social criticism, 1704–1705
"Fugitive of the Judoon" (2020), 313, 334, 338, 339
 See also Doctor Who
Fulfillment, 1421, 1425, 1427–1431
Fundamentalism, 434, 435
Fundamental project, 1729, 1730
 Futurama, 234, 235
 corporate deception, 246
 environmentalism, 244, 245
 freedom, 237
 friendship and suicide, 247, 248
 immortality, 252–254
 metaphysical lessons, 248
 peace and nonviolent waterfalls, 243
 robo-discrimination, 240, 241
 robots, 243, 244
 social-political themes, 236
 society, 237–239
 time-space, 248–251
 true meaning of life, 255
 war, 242

G
Gadsby, Hannah, 1470, 1471
 anger/justice, 1487–1489
 cultural critique, 1470
 humor/catharsis, 1481–1487
 jokes, problem with, 1478–1481
 self-deprecating humor, 1472–1478

Gallifreyan time machines, 140
Gameplay, 1812–1816, 1825–1828, 1830
Gamification, 1898
Ganon-Zelda-Link interaction, 1889
Garland, Alex, 1026, 1036
Gaslighting, 718, 720, 727–728
Gattaca
 genoism, 1047
 justice, 1055–1057
 life themes and an open future, 1051, 1054, 1055
 movie synopsis, 1045
 separate spheres, 1050, 1051
 valids and in-valids, 1045
Gattaca Aerospace Corporation, 1046
Gender, 682, 1505, 1646, 1648–1650, 1656
Genealogy as philosophy, 1098–1099
Genealogy of morals, 863
Generic fascism, 732
Generosity, 1859
"Genesis of the Daleks" (1975), 330
 See also Doctor Who
Genetic engineering, 1044, 1045, 1051, 1052, 1054, 1058
Genetic modification, 1801
Genoism, 1046, 1048–1051, 1053–1055, 1058
Genuine modal realism, 2026, 2034, 2035, 2037, 2039, 2040
Germ theory, 1453
Gervais, Ricky
 atheism, 1683
 comedy, 1670–1671
 critique of religion and religious belief, 1681
 Extras, 1675
 humanity, 1676
Gideon, Moff, villain from *Star Wars/The Mandalorian*, 558, 559
Gilligan, Carol, 330, 1819
Gilligan, Vince, 164–169, 173, 178, 179
The Girl with the Lower Back Tattoo, 1496, 1498
Global health security, 636
Global warming, 1113, 1385
Glossop, Ronald., 318
God, 408, 583, 585, 587, 588, 590, 593–597, 599, 600, 602, 603, 605, 858, 861, 862, 1321, 1323, 1459
Goddard, Drew, 1170
 ethical complexity, 1170
 ethics of care, 1177
 human condition, 1170, 1182
The God Delusion, 1448, 1449

The Godfather
  achievement, 874
  business, not personal, 887–888
  destiny and evil, 892–894
  honor, 883–887
  personal relationships, 877
  power, 890–892
  Sicilian, 888–890
  summarizing, 874–877
  undertaker, 880, 881
God of classical theism, 1933, 1934
God of War video game series
  determinism, 1937
  problem of prophecy, 1930–1932
God's Not Dead, 1435–1462
Godwin's Law, 710, 711
Golden Age piracy, 122, 132
Gold Train, 419
Good
  vs. evil, 857, 858, 862, 863
  life, 260, 278–280, 520, 533, 534, 539
The Good Place, 4–7, 10–14, 16–21
Government, 260, 263–266, 2104, 2110, 2111
Govier, Trudy, 1258
Goy's Teeth, 1162
Graham, Jacob, 218
Gramsci, Antonio, 1604–1608, 1611, 1617, 1618
The Grand Design, 1450
Grandfather paradox, 151, 152, 421, 1330, 1332, 1339, 1346
Graphic novel, 1950, 2086–2088, 2090, 2092, 2099
Gratitude, 285, 291, 294, 296, 297
Gravity, 1445, 1451
Graystone, Zoe, Battlestar Galactica character, 96, 97
Great Curtis Revolution, 1114
Greatest good, 1120, 1121, 1123
Greek trilogy, 1939, 1941
Grey, Meredith, *protagonist of Grey's Anatomy*, 342–344, 348–354, 356, 358, 359
Grey's Anatomy, 342
  Alzheimer's trial, 351–354
  bomb in a patient, 348–349
  immigration injustice and insurance fraud, 354–358
  PDR, 349–351
  summary and plot, 343–345
Gros, Frederic, 1092
Groundhog Day, 899–903, 908, 914
  amor fati, 904
  eternal return, 903
  hedonic treadmill, 911

  objective goods and intrinsic value, 909–910
  phenomenon, 410–417
  test of resolve, 903–904
  value in suffering, 904–905
Growing block (theory of time), 412, 1493, 1495, 1497, 1499, 1501, 1972, 1973, 1977

H
Habermas, Jurgen, 379
Hadot, Pierre, 229
HAL 9000, 813
The Handmaid's Tale, 187
  autonomy and religion, 202–204
  women's capacities in, 197–198
"Hang the DJ" (2017), 487, 488
  See also *Black Mirror*
Happiness, 898, 899, 909–911, 1010, 1121–1123, 1414, 1422, 1430
Happy Death Day, 417
Hardimon, Michael, 301
Harkness, Jack (Captain), *Doctor Who* character, 315, 316
Harm principle, 655, 664
Harry Potter Cinematic Universe (HPCU), 952, 964
Hasty generalization, 1438
The Hateful Eight, 1237–1239, 1247
Hawking, Stephen, 1451–1453
Headland, Leslye, 408
Hedges, Chris, 735
Hedonic calculus, 170
Hedonic treadmill, 911
Hedonism, 516, 910, 911, 913
Heidegger, Martin, 1319, 1322
Heisenberg, Werner, 165, 169, 171, 173, 174, 176, 178, 181
Held, Virginia, 330
Hell, 1094–1096, 1101, 1104–1107
"Hell Bent" (2015), 327
  See also *Doctor Who*
Herbert, Frank, 674, 675, 688–691
Hero, 167, 172, 175, 177, 676, 677, 919, 935
Heroic, 675–677
Hero's Journey, 2066, 2067, 2074–2083
Hesse, Herman, 1006
Heyd, David, 1260, 1261
Hiding the truth, 1361, 1364–1366, 1368
Hill, Thomas., 1031
Hinduism, 7, 18, 19, 21, 693

Hinge proposition, 1915–1918, 1923, 1924, 1926
Hitler, Adolf, 421, 707, 710–712, 717–719, 721–724, 726–728, 730–734, 738, 739
Hobbes, Thomas, 118–122, 260, 263–266, 268, 269, 275, 280, 375–379, 1119, 2059, 2060
   on vengeance, 1254–1255
Holoband technology, 95
   See also Battlestar Galactica
Hologram projection, 462
Holy Books, 602–604
Homeopathic catharsis, 1485
Homer's epics, 165
Homework assignment, 1220, 1224, 1230
Homo sacer, 100
   See also Agamben, Giorgio
Homosexual adoption, 1440
Honesty, 1499, 1500
Honor
   allegiance, 886
   canon of behavior, 884
   internalization, canon of behavior, 885
   notion of, 886
   personal identity, 886
   principle of redress, 885
   sense of belonging, 884
Honor code, 884–887
   See also The Godfather
Hope, 829, 830, 837, 846, 847, 849, 850, 1094, 1096–1098, 1101, 1106, 1108
Horkheimer, Max, 970–972
House of Cards, 362
   democracy in, 362–365
   as warning and opportunity, 380–381
Hoyle, Fred, 1445
The Human Condition (1958), 1846
Humanism, 67–69, 1894
   ethics, 72–73
   religion, 69–70, 81–86
   science/faith, 70–72
   secular humanism/agonism, 74–79
   and social ethics, 86–89
   virtue and character, 79–81
Humanity, 1110, 1127–1129, 1499
Humanoid robot technology, 1081–1082
Human-robot interaction, 1080
Humans, 1291, 1292
   bots, 470
   directed risks, 486
   downgrading, 491
   enhancement, 1792
   experience, 1492
   womb, 819

Hume, David, 219, 770, 1146
Humean Bads, 667
Hume's Problem of Induction, 1441
Humor, 228, 968, 969, 971, 973–978, 1493, 1497, 1499–1502, 1504, 1505
   and journalism, 394
Huxley, Aldus, 189
Hyper nationalism, 737
Hyperreality, 1876, 1878–1880, 1925
Hypertime, 140, 157
Hypnotherapist, 526, 527
Hyrule's geography, 1899

I
Idealism, 414
Identification, 1565–1566, 1568, 1575, 1578
Identity, 996, 1021, 1278, 1281, 1283, 1290, 1294
   ethnic, 1691–1695
   national, 1688–1691
   personal, 1695
   of reality, 1922
I Feel Pretty, 1493, 1502, 1504
Ikea nesting instinct, 1219, 1224, 1226, 1228
   See also Fight Club
The Iliad, 165
Imagination, 212, 216, 217, 220, 224, 226, 230, 231
Imitation game, 808, 1026
   See also Turing, Alan
Immigration, 894
Immoral art, 1559
Immortality, 4, 11, 12, 901–903, 908, 914
   curmudgeon, 1280
   desirability of, 1278–1279
   medical, 1276–1277
   models of, 1276
   Williams's argument, 1279–1282
"The Impossible Astronaut" (2011), 316, 326
   See also Doctor Who
Imposter syndrome, 1428
Imprinting, 1063, 1064, 1068, 1079–1080
   See also Artificial intelligence (AI)
Inception, 34, 754–758, 761–763, 771, 1328, 1335, 1336
   knowledge, 765–768
   leap of faith, 768–769
   reality, 766–767
   wager, 769–770
Inclusion, 965
Incongruity, 1622–1625, 1647–1650
Indebtedness, 285, 297, 299
Indicative meaning, 1429

Individualism, 893
Inflation Reduction Act, 1378, 1379, 1385
Inglourious Basterds, 1242
Inhumanity, 110
Inside Amy Schumer, 1493, 1496, 1497, 1505
The Inside Out Prison Exchange Program, 1557
Instrumental value, 909
Intelligence, 1066–1071
    See also Artificial intelligence (AI)
Intentional fallacy, 965
Interests, 955
    other-regarding, 956
    self-regarding, 955
International Space Station, 821
Interpersonal recognition, 97
Interrupt memory, 536
Intimacy, 292, 294, 305
"Into the Dalek" (2014), 317
    See also Doctor Who
Intrinsic genoism, 1057
Intrinsic racist, 1048
Intrinsic value, 909
Introductory philosophy, 28
Intuitions, 1156, 1157, 1165
The Invention of Lying, 1681
Islamophobia, 1693
"It's all or nothing" argument, 652–654
    See also South Park

J
Jackson, Frank, 1037
Jackson, Peter, 828–831, 834, 835, 838–841, 843
James, William., 213, 1925
Jeske, Diane, 292
Jecker, Nancy, 286
Jedi, 856, 859, 861–864, 866
    See also Star Wars
Jesus, 1437, 1461
Jewish, 932
    Chelm jokes, 1640
    epistemology, 1634–1636
    philosophy, 1635
    style of epistemology, 1632
Jews, 683, 691, 692
Jihad, 436
Jindal, Bobby, 1595, 1596
Jokalism
    concept of, 385
    definition, 396
    role of, 386
Joker, Batman villain 1988–1997
Joker problem, 1955–1957

Jokes, 1470, 1471, 1473–1481, 1621, 1627, 1628, 1630
"Jose Chung's From Outer Space" (1996), 524
    See also X-Files
Journalism
    advocacy, 395, 401
    humor in combination with, 394
    investigative, 385, 391
    objectivity in, 395
    satirical, 391
    training in, 392
Journey (game)
    analysis of, 1761–1762
    commentary, 1767–1768
    critical and commercial success, 1758
    and meaning, 1765
    and Sublime, 1762–1765
    summary of, 1758
    walking simulators, 1758
"Journey's End" (2008), 313, 316, 317, 321, 322, 330, 331
    See also Doctor Who
Judeo-Christian theology, 1157
Jung, Carl Gustav, 221
Jupiter Mission, 803
Justice, 12, 14–16, 106, 131–132, 173, 175, 314, 316, 322–324, 328, 329, 331, 336, 338, 617, 620, 628–630, 1045, 1049, 1051, 1055, 1058, 1237, 1238, 1240, 1249–1251, 1254, 1257–1259, 1263, 1264, 2051, 2054
    criminal, 1261
    legal, 1260, 1263
Just-war theory, 318
Juvenalian satire, 1706

K
Kafka break, 1158, 1165
Kafka, Franz, 1158
Kahler-Jex, 323, 328, 334, 335
Kahn, Yasmin (Yaz) *Doctor Who* character, 337
Kalam Cosmological argument, 1448
Kant, Immanuel, 8–10, 319, 320, 325–327, 330, 768, 780, 1026, 1031–1036, 1038, 1039, 1391–1393, 1395, 1396, 1749, 1750, 1763–1765, 1816–1818, 1821, 1955
Kantianism, 1818, 1819
Kantian philosophy, 1957
Keeping mum, 1359
"Kerblam!" (2018), 337
    See also Doctor Who

Kierkegaard, Søren, 768, 769, 1321, 1322,
    1894–1896, 1900, 1902
King, Martin Luther, 317, 322, 323, 338
King, Stephen, 1093
Kitcher, Philip, 1045, 1051–1055
Knowledge, 688, 1135–1138, 1392
    acquisition, 1779
    of reality, 765
Kohlberg, Lawrence, 224
Kondabolu, Hari
    album, 1585
    to Andy Warhol, 1593
    confronting white supremacy, 1600
    liberal hypocrisy, 1597
    liberalism, 1597
    meta-joke telling, 1593
    philosophy of liberation, 1589
    political comic forces, 1587
    proposal, 1586
    punchline, 1586
    rethinking comedy, 1591
    rethinking liberation, 1598
    revolutionary forms of liberation, 1601
    self-awareness, 1592
    Warhol's embarrassment, 1593
    work, 1584
Korean War Memorial, 652
Korsgaard, Christine, 1031
Kratos, *God of War* character, 1930, 1931, 1942
    attitude, 1937
    future, 1939
Kubrick, Stanley, 1062, 1065, 1076
Kuhn, Thomas, 1784
Kupfer, Joseph, 305

L
Labor, 1673–1675
Labyrinth, 811
Lacan, Jacques, 763
Lachesis (Greek goddess), 1938
Lamont, Corliss, 67
Language, 199–202
Language-game, 1918–1923, 1926
Larkhill Resettlement Camp, 2046, 2057
Last Fuckable Day, 1502
    See also Inside Amy Schumer
The Last of Us, 1742
    Joel, 1746–1751
    narratives, 1743–1746
    teleological particularism, 1751–1754
"Last of the Time Lords" (2007), 314, 316,
    317, 331
    See also Doctor Who

Last Week Tonight with John Oliver, 384, 390
Laughter, 1097, 1100, 1106–1108
Law and order, political motto, 736
Leaders, 105, 676–678, 680, 683, 684, 689
Leap of faith, 755, 757, 763, 768–769
The Leather Special, 1493, 1500, 1502, 1504,
    1508
    See also Inside Amy Schumer
Lee, Greta, 409
Legal justice, 1239, 1260, 1263
Legal retribution, 1238, 1247–1249, 1259,
    1262, 1263
The Legend of Zelda: Breath of the Wild,
    1883–1906
Lemaître, Georges, 1445, 1446
Lennox, John, 1451, 1452
Leone, Sergio, 175, 176
"Let's Kill Hitler" (2011), 326
    See also Doctor Who
Levitsky, Steven, 366, 368
Lewis, Courtland, 230, 313, 314, 316, 323, 324,
    328, 329, 331, 332, 338, 862
Lewis, David, 138, 147, 155, 510, 1339, 2026,
    2033–2037, 2039, 2040
Lewis, Sinclair, 366
Liberalism, 108
Liberation, 456, 463, 973, 976, 978, 980
    Kondabolu's comedy, 1588
    philosophy, 1587
Libertarianism (view on free will), 1341-1345
Libertarianism (political philosophy), 1555,
    1559, 1961–1964, 1976–1980,
    1982–1984
Liberty, 679
Liberty violations, 2061
"The Lie of the Land" (2017), 326
    See also Doctor Who
Life after death, 1307
    See also Afterlife
Life of needs, 331
    See also Lewis, Courtland
Liif app, 1382, 1400
    See also Don't Look Up
Linz, Juan, 380
Lipman, Matthew, 222
Live action role play (LARP), 455, 456, 458,
    472
Live at the Apollo, 1493, 1503, 1504, 1506
    See also Inside Amy Schumer
Live in Concert, 1604
    See also Richard Pryor
Live on the Sunset Strip, 1604, 1607, 1611–1613
    See also Richard Pryor

Livestock Management, 458
  See also Westworld
Locke, John, 118–122, 221, 260, 264–266,
  270–273, 280, 379, 550–552, 705, 767,
  2054, 2055
  on vengeance, 1255–1256
The Lone Gunmen, X-files Spin-off, 520
L'ordine della famiglia, 877–880, 882, 884,
  888, 895
Lord of the Rings (LOTR), 604, 769, 828–830,
  835–838
  assessing Jackson's argument, 847–851
  fantasy, enchantment and recovery of
    Middle-earth, 830–835
  relation to nature, 838–843
  shadow and struggle, 843–847
Louis C.K., 1534–1536, 1542, 1543,
  1546–1549, 1554, 1555, 1558, 1559
  accusations, 1543
  breakout episode of Louie, 1542, 1543
  fallout, 1544
  history, 1535
  philosopher, 1536–1542
  return of, 1546, 1547
Love, 235, 236, 861, 869, 952, 956, 1078–1079
Love for God, 861
Loyalty, 720, 723, 734, 1008
  to *Harry Potter*, 956
Lucas, George, 856
Lukey, Ben, 218, 230
Lying, 1350–1352, 1354–1357, 1359–1363,
  1367–1369
  Kantian prohibition of, 1038
  Kant's universal prohibition against, 1027
  Kant' view of, 1030
  movies about, 1029
  wrongness of, 1033
Lying acts, 1362, 1363
Lynch, David, 413
Lyonne, Natasha, 408
Lyotard, Jean-François, 767

M
MacDowell, Andie, 410
MacFarlane, Seth, 426, 427, 446
Machine consciousness, 482
MacIntyre, Alasdair, 27
Madness, 1989, 1990, 1995, 1998–2000
Madrine, 878
Magic(al) realism, 1199
"The Magician's Apprentice" (2015), 323, 331
  See also Doctor Who

Magic powers, 588
Magnesis Rune, 1892
  See also Legend of Zelda: Breath of the Wild
Magnolia, 1194, 1205, 1213
  characters and storylines, 1195–1196
  praise and criticism, 1194–1195
Mahayana Buddhism, 1012
Maieutic method, 1629
Mainstream American Comic, 1586, 1588,
  1596, 1602
Mainstream media, 714, 729
Make America Great Again (MAGA), 705,
  708, 711, 714–716, 720, 722, 724, 725,
  728–730, 732, 733, 737, 738
The Makropulos Case, 1276, 1279
The Master, *Doctor Who* villain, 313, 317, 323,
  325, 331, 334–336
  Missy (Michelle Gomez), 313, 331, 335,
    336
Malebranche, Nicolas, 195, 196
The Mandalorian, *Star Wars* character, 556
  personal motives, 573, 574
  primary virtue, 574–578
  Star Wars, 556, 558
  virtue ethics, 572
  virtue of care, 567
The Man from Earth, 1272–1275
  desirability of immortality, 1278–1279
  medical immortality, 1276–1277
  models of immortality, 1276
  as philosophy, 1285–1286
The Man in Black (MIB), *Westworld* character,
  457, 463, 465, 469, 472–475
Manichaeism, 858, 859
Manifest destiny, 461
Mann, Aimee, 1195
Man's Search for Meaning, 1470, 1482
Marcuse, Herbert, 1587, 1598, 1599
Marketplace of ideas, 656, 657
Maron, Marc, 1564
  comedy as equipment for living, 1577–1580
  consubstantiality and catharsis, 1574–1577
  identification, 1568, 1578
  philosophy of WTP, 1569–1573
  therapy, 1576, 1577
Maruki's cognitive distortion, 1925, 1926
  See also Persona 5 Royal
Marvel method, 2091
Marx, Karl, 1671–1672, 1674, 1678, 1682,
  1902, 1903
Marxist philosophy, 1605
Mary the Colorblind Neuroscientist thought
  experiment, 1037

Masculinity, 935–938, 1493, 1497, 1501, 1504, 1505
Masking, 1365, 1369
Mass Effect, 1813, 1815
Matthews, Gareth, 222–225, 227–229
Maxine, *Russian Doll* character, 409
May, Simon, 1116
"Mazey Day" (2023), 496, 497
  See also Black Mirror
McCain, Kevin, 327
McDonald, Nathaniel, 224
McDonald, Norm, x
McFarland, Margaret, 213, 221
McInster, Gerald, Snowpiercer character, 1114
McNeill, John, 735, 737
Mead, George Herbert, 226
Meaning, 998, 1014, 1194
Meaning in/of life, 899, 909, 1413, 1414, 1420
Meaninglessness, 1281
Meaning subjectivism, 907, 910
Mecha, 1064–1068, 1076, 1077, 1079–1081, 1085–1087
  See also Artificial intelligence (AI)
Media, 364, 371, 377, 379
Medical ethics, 344
Meditation, 18, 1013, 1020
Meditations on First Philosophy, 762
#MeToo movement, 1470
Memes, 715, 718, 719, 725, 726
Memory, 996
Memory confabulation, 528
Menippean satire, 1706, 1707
Meno, 1629
Mental Time Travel, 485
Meta-ethics, 1154
"Metalhead" (2013), 480, 483, 486, 487, 490, 495
  See also Black Mirror
Meta-Nav app, 1909
  See also Persona 5 Royal
Metaphysics, 33, 417–419, 421–422, 628, 1307
Mezzogiorno, 877–879, 895
Microaggression, 1552
Middle knowledge, 1935
Middle Path of Buddhism, 1010, 1011, 1014, 1018, 1019, 1021
Midnight Mass
  afterlife, 597–600
  faith, 600–602
  holy books, 602–604
  miracles, 588
  religion's origins, 584–588
  summary, 582–584
  supernatural, 590–593

Midwifery, 1629
Mill, John Stuart, 319, 379, 652, 655, 658, 664–666, 668, 1747, 1885, 1897–1899, 1902
Miller, Frank
  Batman, 1951–1952
  comics, 1950
  dark knight returns, 1950
  graphic novel, 1950
  personal philosophy, 1951
  problem, 1964–1966
Mimicking, 1363–1365, 1369
Minhaj, Hasan, 1686
  audacity of equality, freedom, and authentic identity, 1695–1699
  ethnic identity, 1691–1695
  national identity, 1688–1691
Minsu, Namgoong, *Snowpiercer* character, 1126
Miracles, 588, 590
Missy (Michelle Gomez)
  See also The Master
Mister Rogers' Neighborhood, 212, 223, 225, 226
  art, death and humor, 226–228
  origins of, 213–217
  professional philosophy, 228–229
Moby Dick, 168
Modal realism, 510
Modern Stoics, 43, 45, 48
A Modest Proposal, 1585, 1586
Modus operandi, 1621, 1629
Mohr, Eric J., 218, 219, 224, 226, 229, 230
Mohr, Holly K., 218, 219, 224, 226, 229, 230
Moksha, 18, 19, 21
Molinism, 1936
Monarchy, 545, 547, 552
Monolith, 803, 820
  See also 2001: A Space Odyssey
Monomyth, 2066, 2078
Moonwatcher, 800, 802, 806, 818, 820
  See also 2001: A Space Odyssey
"The Moonbase" (1967), 332, 338
  See also Doctor Who
Moore, Alan, 1988, 1992, 1998, 1999
Moral agency, 1813, 1816–1818, 1821–1824, 1828, 1830
  ambiguity, 343, 351, 354, 358
  character, 1556, 1849, 1853, 1854, 1858
  considerability, 1813, 1820
  corruption, 2013, 2014, 2017
  decision-making, 1819, 1820, 1829
  dimension of personhood, 104
  evil, 1456

existence model, 1152
imperative, 1391, 1393, 1395, 1396, 1401, 1405
improvement, 1474
integrity, 1500
nihilism, 862, 863
obligations, 1742, 1746, 1750–1755
patiency, 1813, 1816, 1820–1822, 1825, 1827, 1828
philosophy, 1742
reasoning, 1812–1814, 1816, 1818–1825, 1828–1831
status, 774, 777–779, 783, 784, 788, 1037
theory, 1178, 1189, 1190
virtues, 48, 49
Morality, 4, 7–14, 21, 72, 73
Moral justice, 1239
Moral knowledge
  description, 1155–1158
  ethics, epistemology and, 1154–1155
  fables and parables as, 1158–1165
  wisdom, 943
Morgan, Darin, 520, 524, 529, 533, 534, 539
Morgan, Tracy, 1592
  anti-Socratic message, 533
  non-verbal message, 532
Mormonism, 637
Morrison, Rachela, 984
Mostly Sex Stuff, 1499, 1504
  See also Inside Amy Schumer
Motif, 1614–1617
Motivation, 952, 953
  disposition, 954
  other-regarding, 956
  purpose-oriented, 953
  self-regarding, 953
  Slughorn's, 961
M-theory, 1451
Mudbone, 1613, 1614
  See also Richard Pryor
Mueller, Leilani, 219
Mueller, Nathan, 219
Mulder, Fox, X-Files Character, 520, 521, 524, 533, 534
  extraterrestrial hypothesis, 527
Multiverse theory, 511, 2026, 2031
Murphy, Annie, 419
Murray, Bill, 410
Music, 818
Muslims, 691–693
Mussolini, Benito, 709, 710, 731–733
Mysticism, 1809
"The Mystery Therefore Magic" fallacy, 588
Myth of Sisyphus, 423, 906–907, 1766

N
Nagel, Thomas, 1212
Nanette, 1470–1473, 1475, 1477–1482, 1485–1488
Nardole, *Doctor Who* character, 325, 326, 335, 336
National identity, 1688–1691
Natural Born Cyborgs, 484
Natural Born Killers, 1240
Natural consciousness, 1071–1073
Naturalism, 67
Natural rights, 264, 266, 278, 280
Natural selection, 1453, 1454
Nature does not jump rule, 1454
Nauert, Charles, 68
Na'vi, species from *Avatar*, 1293
Nazism, 705, 706, 709, 716, 721, 723, 724, 734
Near-death experiences, 598
"Nearer, my God, to Thee", 582, 584
Neil, Character from *Tenet*, 1328–1332, 1334–1340, 1342, 1345, 1346
Neoliberalism, 98, 111, 1844
Neo-Nazis, 734, 735, 739
Neo-Stoic theory, 1481
Neo-Talmudic thought, 1632, 1638
Netflix, 1544, 1552, 1555, 1556
Newsmax, 725, 729
Newspeak, 736
Newton's theory of gravity, 1441, 1445
New Yorker magazine, 1840
"The Next Doctor" (2008), 314, 316
  See also Doctor Who
Niccol, Andrew, 1044
"Nicola Tesla's Night of Terror" (2020), 314
  See also Doctor Who
Nicomachean Ethics, 1897
Nietzsche, Friedrich, 167, 182, 202, 523, 796, 863, 866, 899, 903–909, 913, 921, 933, 945, 1889, 1890, 1895, 1997, 1998
  radical perspectivism, 529
  on vengeance, 1256–1257
"Night of the Doctor" (2013), 313, 322
  See also Doctor Who
"Night Terrors" (2011), 313, 326
  See also Doctor Who
Nihilism, 903, 921, 933, 944–947
  galactic federation, 515
  hedonism, 516
  multiverse-switch instruments, 514
  superhuman order, 513
Nilsson, Harry, 409
Ninth Symphony, Beethoven's, 818
Nirvana, Buddhist concept, 1012

Noble, Donna, Doctor Who character, 323, 329, 337
Noble truths of Buddhism, 1012
Noddings, Nel, 576, 1176, 1179
Nolan, Christopher, 754, 759–763, 771, 1328, 1332–1336, 1338–1340, 1345, 1346
"Non, Je Ne Regette Rien", 760
Non-attachment, 1011, 1014
Non-cognitivism, 1156
Non-discriminatory wisdom, 1013, 1014
Non-dualism, 1786
Non-playable characters (NPCs), 1812, 1887
Non-self (anattā), 1012, 1021
No-platforming, 660
Normativity, 1030, 1031
Norns, sisters of fate, 1939, 1940
   See also God of War
Norse duology, 1939, 1940
Norsefire, 2060
   government, 2047–2049, 2056
   party, 2044
   regime, 2046, 2050, 2054, 2056, 2058, 2059
   slogan, 2047
North American Sartre Society conference, 4
No-self theory, 599
Nostalgia, 212, 230
Noumenal self, 1816, 1817
Noumenal world (Kantian concept), 768
Nozick, Robert, 765, 1264, 1526–1528
   argument against Rawls, 1125
   on vengeance, 1263
   See also Anarchy, State of nature, Utopia
Nussbaum, Martha, 1277, 1284, 1285

O
Objective
   goods, 909, 911
   knowledge, 1780, 1782
   meaning, 1423, 1428
   theories of life's meaning, 1414
   truth, 529, 530, 537, 538
Obligation(s), 286, 288, 303, 1742, 1746, 1750–1755
   of debt, 285
   to future generations, 207
Odysseus, 165, 168, 813
Okja
   animal liberation, 785
   deontological animal liberation, 790
   features, 774
   story, 775
Oldenquist, Andrew, 1259, 1260

Oligarchy, 372
Olympians, 1932
Om (sound), 1010
   See also Buddhism
Omerta, Mafia code of honor 893
Once Upon a Time in Hollywood, 1244, 1266
One America Network (OAN), 725
One Dimensional Man, 490
On Free Choice of the Will, 1538
On Humour, 1470, 1481
The Ood, Doctor Who monster/hero, 316, 331, 337
Open-world games, 1894
Operation American Savior, 1376
Oppression, 631, 890–892
Oppression Olympics, 1655
Orchestrating, 1121
Organic intellectual, 1604–1606, 1608, 1611, 1617
The Orville, 427–429, 1458
   identifying and critiquing, 430–439
   religion and morality, 439–441
   theocracy vs. democracy, 442–445
Origins of comedy, 1594
Origin of life, 1453
The Origins of Totalitarianism, 1841
Orthodox(y), 689, 692, 699, 700
Orwell, George, 188
Oswald, Clara, Doctor Who character 324, 327, 330, 332

P
Pacifism
   absolute, 317, 320
   collectivist, 320
   collectivist-realist, 332–338
   ecological, 321
   fallibility/epistemological, 320
   nuclear, 321
   pragmatic, 321
   technological, 321
   The Doctor, 321–324
Padrini, 878
Pain and suffering, 1011, 1017–1019
Pandemic guidelines, 1884–1885
Panopticism, 1093, 1102, 1103, 1105
Papers, Please
   anti-semitism, 1838
   attentive thinking, 1846
   definition, 1834
   empathy, 1841
   fundamental aspect, 1839

Index   2137

game, 1836
historical line, 1838
philosophical problems, 1845
player, 1836
power, 1837
racism, 1838
totalitarianism, 1838, 1840
totalitarian regimes, 1839
violence, 1839
Parabolic logic, 1159, 1164
Paradigms, 1783–1786
The paradox of Tolerance, 668–669
Paralipomena, 1899
Parallax, 591
Parerga, 1899
Parity principle, 484
Parsimony, 766
Partially illegitimate, 2062
Particulars, (Metaphysical concept), 2066, 2069–2073, 2076, 2077, 2082, 2083
"The Parting of the Ways" (2005), 314, 324, 331
    See also Doctor Who
Pascal, Blasé, 769
Pascal's wager, 769
Paternalism, 891
Patriarchal norms, 1493, 1499, 1500, 1503–1505
Patriarchy, 2004–2006, 2009–2011, 2013–2018, 2020–2022
Patriot news network, 1377, 1378
Paul, L.A., 306
Pauline principle, 868
PC adventure game, 1814
PC Principal, *South Park* character, 636, 662, 666, 667
PC principle, The, 663, 664, 666, 668
Peace, 313, 316, 318, 319, 321, 322, 324, 331–333, 335–338, 1019
    positive peace, 322, 338
Pediatric medicine, 522
Peirce, Charles Sanders, 226
Persona 5 Royal
    discovery of identities and realities, 1909, 1911
    hinge proposition, 1915, 1917
    identity of reality, 1922, 1924, 1925
    language-game, 1918–1920, 1922
    personal identity, 1908
    qualia, 1911–1913, 1915
Personal hinge propositions, 1916–1918
Personal identity, 285, 1308, 1695, 1795–1799, 1908, 1909, 1912, 1921, 1922

Personal submission, 2100
Personal *vs.* external time, 138, 140, 155
Personhood, 782, 790–792, 1026, 1033, 1036–1038
Perspectivism, 523, 526–530
Peschauer, Vera, *Russian Doll* Character, 419
Pezzonovanti, 883, 894
    See also The Godfather
Phenomenal world (Kantian concept), 768
Philia (Greek word for love), 941, 942
Philosophical wisdom, 1011
Philosophy, 214, 216, 217, 219, 220, 1742, 1743, 1751, 2071, 2073
    of childhood, 222–229
    of death, 1272, 1275, 1279, 1452
    of dialogue, 1806
    of liberation, 1587–1590
    of Time, 408
The Philosophy of Walking, 1092
Physiological continuity, 1796
Piaf, Edith, 760
Piaget, Jean, 222, 224
Picturephone, 821
The Plot Against America, 366
Pirates, 115–118, 120, 121, 125, 126, 129–131
Pittsburgh, 410
Planescape: Torment, 1848–1851
    development of virtue, 1859
    philosophical challenges to regret, 1860–1862
    Ravel's Question and nature of virtue, 1851–1854
    selfish, 1854–1857
"Planet of the Ood" (2008), 316, 331, 337
    See also Doctor Who
Planter colonialism, 458, 466
Plato, 25, 30, 31, 33, 193, 439, 570, 627, 628, 680–682, 685, 765, 1118, 1125, 1391–1393, 1395–1399, 1629, 1780, 1783, 1922, 1923, 2053, 2073
    Allegory of the Cave, 1001, 1517–1518
    critique of democracy, 371–375
    myth of the metals, 1118
    Republic, 369–371
    on vengeance, 1250–1252
"Playtest" (2016), 480, 481
    See also Black Mirror
Pleasure
    friendships for, 952, 955, 957–960
    and utility, 952
Pless, Deborah, 316, 334
Poehler, Amy, 408

Polanco, Dascha, 410
Policing, 721
Political correctness, 637, 661, 662, 666, 667
Political economic theories, 98
Political legitimacy, 542, 545, 548, 552
Political life, 98, 99
Political norms, 367
Political philosophy, 375, 385
Political society, 106
Politics, 677, 683, 686–689
Pollock, Jackson, 1028
Pond, Amy (Amelia), Doctor Who character, 323, 325–329, 331, 334
Pootie Tang, 1535
Popper, Karl, 669
Population control, 1111, 1120
Portable Automated Somnacin IntraVenous (PASIV) device, *Inception*, 754, 755, 758, 760
Positive Christianity (Nazi goal), 724
Possibility (as metaphysical concept), 1294–1295
Possible worlds, 2026, 2028, 2030–2036, 2038–2041
Postcolonial colonialism, 454, 458, 459, 462
Postdiction, 1447
Posthumanism, 1799
Postman, Neil, 221
Postmodernism, 899
Potts, Bill, *Doctor Who* character, 326, 327, 335, 336
Pragmatism, 1925
Precarious lives, 1843, 1845
  See also Butler, Judith
Prescriptive cultural vision, 882
Presentism, 155, 412, 1972, 1973, 1977
Primeval atom, 1445, 1446
Prison, 1092–1097, 1099–1105, 1107, 1108
The Prison Notebooks, 1605, 1607, 1617
Privacy, 1912, 1913, 1915
Procedural justice, 14, 16
Procreation, 96, 102
Projection, 728–730
Project Mayhem, 1218, 1221–1224, 1226–1228, 1231
  See also Fight Club
Prometheus Bound, 798
Prophet Mohammed, 637, 640
Proportionality (regarding just war), 877
"Proposition infinity" (2010), 239
  See also Futurama
Protagonist, 1328–1340, 1342, 1345
Prudence, as virtue, 173

Pryor, Richard, 1604, 1605, 1607–1615, 1617, 1618
Pryor Convictions, 1608
Psychological continuity, 1796
Psychological egoism, 1856, 1857
Psychological operations (PSYOP), 1366, 1367
Psychological survivor, 97
Public real world *vs.* private metaverse, 1913
Pulp Fiction, 1241, 1266, 1312, 1324
  case presentation, 1315–1317
  challenges, 1322
  story and narration, 1313–1315
Punxsutawney, 410
Putnam, Hilary, 1782–784
Pyroviles, *Doctor Who* villain, 329

Q
QAnon, 713, 722
"Quagmire" (1996), 524, 531, 533, 534
  See also The X-Files
Qualia, 1911–1915, 1918, 1921, 1923, 1926
Qualifications, 1627, 1628
Quantum computer system, 464
Quantum foam, 1449, 1450
Quantum mechanics, 768, 1340, 1445, 1447, 1448, 1452
Quantum reality, 173
Quaternary Ice Age, 1128
Quest for reality, 764–768, 770
  See also Inception

R
Race, 460, 464, 468, 469, 476, 1647–1657
Race-class, 476
Rachael, *Blade Runner* character, 987–989, 991, 992, 996, 998
The Racial Contract, book 467
Racial contract, concept 468
Racial minorities, 1439
Racism, 736, 1044, 1048, 1049, 1058
Racist jokes, 649–651, 654
Racnoss, *Doctor Who* villain, 317, 329, 338
Radical humor, 1671
Radicalizing effect, social media, 716
Rape culture, 1534, 1549, 1550, 1554, 1555
Rape jokes, 1555
Rationalism, 221
Rationality, 681, 1078, 1820, 1821, 1826–1828
Rawls, John, 14, 15, 123–125, 322, 332, 379, 1055–1058, 1119, 1120, 1124, 1125
Rawlsian test, 1058

Index

Reality, 754, 757, 759–764, 766–771, 1141–1144
  See also Inception and *The Matrix*
Reavers, *Firefly* villain, 262, 263, 268, 272, 274
Red Dead Redemption 2, 1884
Redemption, 167, 860–862
Regret, 1848, 1851, 1853, 1857–1863
Reitman, Jason, 1006, 1008
Relationships, 1007–1009, 1014, 1016–1018, 1021
  characters, 955
  Death Eater's, 963
  one-to-one, 955
  romantic, 959
  types of, 955
Relative goods, 909, 911
Religion, 69–70, 72, 73, 75, 81–86, 88, 90, 94, 582, 585–587, 591, 593, 597, 600, 602, 604, 605, 675–677, 686–695, 698, 699, 714, 720, 722–724, 734, 1515
  origins, 584–588
Religious, 675, 676, 678, 680, 686–700
  beliefs, 586, 587
  devotion, 442
  dictatorship, 675, 676
  fanatic, 686
  leadership, 678
  orthodoxy, 676, 695, 698
  terrorism, 438
  violence, 431, 435, 441
"Remaining Men Together"
  See also Flight Club, 1219
Repackaging (in Tom Sawyer), 1365, 1366
Repeatable pleasures, 1283
Repetition, 946, 947, 1888, 1889, 1895, 1896, 1900, 1902
Replacement theory, 738
Replicants (in Blade Runner), 986–992
  exactly like human beings, 994
  intelligence, 994
  recognition, 993
  utterly unlike human beings, 994
Reproductive freedom, 187
The Republic, 680, 682, 765
Research ethics, 1026
Reservoir Dogs, 1241
Respect, 1032, 1033, 1037, 1038, 1040
Retribution, 1237–1240, 1247, 1249, 1250, 1259, 1260, 1262, 1263
Retributive justice, 14, 16
"The Runaway Bride" (2006), *Doctor Who* episode, 316, 317, 329
Revenge, 876, 884, 885, 889, 1238, 1264

Reverse causation, 1332, 1340
Revolution, 979, 1111–1113, 1599
Reynolds, Malcom (Mal), *Firefly* character, 261–264, 266–269, 273, 274
Rhetoric act, 1565
Richards, Janet Radcliffe, 1049–1051
Rick & Morty
  alien culture, 506
  astronaut snake, 505
  cable box, 511
  citadel, 512
  counterpart theory, 511
  cultural phenomenon, 504
  cultural relativism, 506
  energy source, 508
  genetic makeup, 512
  human culture, 505
  Lewis' view, 511
  metaphysical assumption, 510
  metaphysical view, 511
  microscopic inhabitants, 507
  multiverse theory, 510
  nihilism, 504
  slavery, 509
  snake racism, 505
Rights, 2045, 2054, 2055
Riley's campfire theory, *Midnight Mass*, 585
Ring of Gyges, 1030
Ripper murders, 2004, 2007, 2011, 2013, 2016, 2018, 2022, 2023
Ritual, 687
Ritualism, 676
Robertson, Willie, 1437, 1438
Robo-discrimination, 239
Robotka (Czech word), 470
Robotic companions, 1077, 1080, 1082, 1083, 1087
Robots, 29, 31, 35, 36, 456, 458, 466, 467, 470
  developmental robotics, 1083–1084
  displacement of humans by robots, 1086
  and emotions, 1080–1081
  humanoid robot technology, 1081–1082
  real and artificial boys, 1084–1086
  robot pets, toys and companions, 1082–1083
  uncanny valley, 1084
"Robots of Death" (1977), 313
  See also Doctor Who
Rocky IV, 1461
Roddenberry, Gene, 66, 67, 70–72, 74–79, 83, 87, 88, 90
Rogers, Fred M., 212, 214, 216, 218
Role-playing game (RPG), 1890

Roles, 1743, 1746, 1751–1755
Rorty, Richard, 1137, 1141
Roslin, Laura, *BattleStar Galactica* character, 96, 101
Ross, William David, 319, 322, 327, 328
Roth, Phillip, 366
Rousseau, Jean-Jacques, 122–123, 213
Russell, Bertrand, 25, 28
Russian Doll, 408
    Groundhog Day Phenomenon, 410–417
    history of, 409–410, 419–420
    metaphysics, 417–419
    metaphysics of time travel, 421–422
    season one of, 409–419
    season two of, 419–423
Ryerson, Needlenose Ned, *Groundhog Day* character, 413
Ryle, Gilbert, 1912–1914

S
Sabotage actions, 1221, 1230
Sacred engine, 1115, 1119
    See also Snowpiercer
Sacrifice of Isaac, 1161
Saliency, 26–28, 30, 33
Sammon, Paul M., 984
Santayana, George, 68, 226
"The Satan Pit" (2006), 337
    See also Doctor Who
Sartre, Jean-Paul, 165–169, 171, 177, 178, 1093, 1094, 1096, 1098, 1102, 1104, 1316–1317, 1320, 1705–1707, 1891
    concept of, 389
    existentialism, 1724–1727
    fundamental element, 385
    paradigm, 386
    pool, 384
    purpose of, 384
    televised vehicles of, 384
Satirical epic, 166, 168, 171, 172, 176, 181
Savoir faire, 1626
Sawyer, Tom, 1350–1357, 1362, 1363, 1366–1369
Sayle, Alexei, 1702
Scalambrino, Frank, 224
Schelling, Friedrich Wilhelm Joseph, 869, 1875, 1876, 1880
Schick, Theodore, 528, 529, 536, 589, 591, 598, 766, 1351, 1450, 1457
Schopenhauer, Arthur, 1885, 1897, 1899–1903, 1905

Schumer, Amy
    absurdity, 1502
    comedy, 1501
    othering, 1498
    sex, 1503–1505
    social expectations, 1505–1507
    work, 1492–1493
Schumpeter, Joseph, 380
Scientific realism, 1775, 1782–1785
Scott, Ridley, 984–986, 989, 993
Scully, Dana, 520, 521, 524
The Second Sex, 1495, 1733, 1735, 1736
SEARCH method, 536
    See also criteria of adequacy
Searle, John, 1141, 1142
Second-order desires, 1817, 1823, 1831
Second Treatise of Government, 2054
Secular humanism, 67, 74–79
Seinfeld, Jerry
    observational humor, 1640
    as secular talmudist, 1636–1638
Self, 1012
    actualization, 903
    affirmation, 1219, 1222, 1226–1228, 1231–1234
    affirming exercise, 1219, 1223, 1225, 1226, 1230, 1232, 1233
    contradictory, 537
    deprecation, 1473–1477, 1481–1483, 1485, 1486, 1489
    determination, 1823
    improvement, 1476
    promotion, 1474
    reliance, 878
    satisfaction, 1474
Semiological idealism, 1876–1879
Sen, Amartya, 379
Sensationalized violence, 2011–2013
Sense-making stories, 1202–1204
Sentience, 788, 791, 792
Separate spheres society, 1050, 1051, 1055, 1057, 1058
Serenity, 260, 261, 263, 272–280
    See also Firefly
Serling, Rod, 24, 31
Settler colonialism, 454, 459, 460
Sevigny, Chloë, 419
Sexton III, Brenden, 417
Sexual dominant, 2096
Sexual harassment, 2006, 2021
Sexual identity, 1653
Sexuality, 101

The Shawshank Redemption, 1092, 1093,
    1107–1108
  amoral thought, 1104–1105
  freedom's hope and hell, 1094
  genealogy, 1098–1099
  hope, 1096–1098
  laughter and liberation, 1105–1107
  panopticism, 1102, 1103, 1105
  punish and discipline, 1099–1102
  silence and darkness, 1096
Sheikah Slate, *Legend of Zelda*, 1894
Shogunworld, 456, 461
  See also Westworld
Showing the false, 1361, 1363–1365, 1368
Sicilian, 888–890, 894
Sicilian family order, 877–880
Sider, Theodore, 140
Sidgwick, Henry, 285
Siler, R. Alan, 324
Silurians, *Doctor Who* villain, 313
Silver shirts (in American fascism), 731
Silver Streak, 1607
Simmons, A. John, 2055, 2062
Simulacrum, 1925
Simulation, 1361
Since I Found Serenity (SIFS) theory, 273–276,
    278–280
Singer, Peter, 785, 788, 790, 1031, 1391,
    1394–1396, 1820, 1821, 1825, 1826
Singularity, 482, 1791, 1792
Sisyphus, 167, 179
Sith, *Star Wars* villains, 856, 859, 862,
    864, 866
Skeptical problem, 762, 763, 765, 768
Skeptical theism, 596
Skinner, Burrhus Frederic, 221
Skithra, *Doctor Who* villain, 314
Skywalker, Luke, *Star Wars* hero, 172
Slasher films, 1170, 1172, 1185
Slippery Slope Fallacy, 653
Slote, Michael, 285, 576
SlutWalk movement, 1484
Smith, Carolyn Michelle, 420
Smith, David Livingstone, 469
Smithereens (2019), 492
  See also Black Mirror
Smithka, Paula, 314, 316, 317, 321, 323, 324,
    331
Snapshops, 806
Snowpiercer
  authoritarianism, 1113–1117
  humanity, 1127–1129

  justice, 1123–1127
  utilitarianism, 1120–1123
  well-ordered society, 1118–1120
Social classes, 1121, 1122, 1125, 1710, 1711,
    1713
Social contract theories, 118–125, 260, 263,
    265, 270, 273, 278, 550, 613, 1124, 2055
Social inequalities, 1124, 1125
Social justice, 314, 322, 324, 329, 331, 332,
    336, 337
Social ladder, 1124
Social norms, 1622
Social order, 1120
Socrates, 25, 28, 32, 439, 520, 530, 531, 537,
    538, 570, 1457, 1629, 1704–1705, 1780,
    1781, 1783
Solitary confinement, 1095, 1096, 1100, 1101,
    1104, 1105
Solitude, 1885, 1888, 1890, 1894–1905
Sony Playstation, 1814
Sophists, 1779, 1780
Sorority, 201
Soul making, 1455
Souls, 598, 1293, 1296–1297
South Park
  absolute free speech, 654, 656, 659
  freedom of speech argument, 651, 652
  history of "Blasphemy" on, 638
  "It's all or nothing" argument, 652
  as philosophy, 635–638
  terrorism, 645
2001: A Space Odyssey, 796–798, 813, 818,
    822, 1774
Space-time vortex, 140
  and time travel, 138–140
Spaemann, Robert, 229
Special obligations, 1176, 1179, 1181, 1190
Speciesism, 789, 1820
Spielberg, Steven, 1062
Spinoza, Baruch, 1860–1862
  on vengeance, 1252–1254
Spirit of seriousness, 343, 346, 347, 353, 354,
    357–359
Spock, *Star Trek* character 63
  career and personal development, 42
  modern Stoics, 43
  as *prokoptôn*, 56–62
  Stoic sagehood, 47–56
Spock, Benjamin, 213, 221
Spoken lies, 1351, 1352, 1354, 1356, 1357,
    1359, 1364, 1368
Spontaneous existential risks, 486

Squid Game, 610, 630
  myth of empowerment, 621–624
  myth of equality, 617–621
  myth of free choice, 613–617
  myth of the ideal, 627–630
  myth of transparency, 624–627
  myths of democracy, 613–630
Stand-up catharsis, 1478, 1480, 1485
Stand-up comedy, 1571, 1573, 1575, 1577, 1604, 1611, 1613, 1617
Stand-up comedy film, 1604–1607, 1609, 1612, 1613
Stanley, Jason, 735, 738
Star child, 815
  See also 2001: A Space Odyssey
Star gate, 818
  See also 2001: A Space Odyssey
Star Trek, The Next Generation (TNG), 426, 427, 443
  philosophy of humanism, 65–90
  preproduction work for, 78
  Space Fleet (*see also Black Mirror*)
Star Trek Original Series (TOS)
  recognitions, 42
  Spock as Stoic sage (*see* Spock)
Star Wars, 172, 524, 556, 557, 856, 859, 862, 870
Star Whale, *Doctor Who* hero, 323, 328, 329
State of nature, 263–265, 268, 631, 1119, 2054, 2056, 2057, 2059
State of war, 2058
Steady state theory, 1444, 1445
Stocker, Michael, 572
Stoicism, 44–46, 49, 51, 56, 57, 62, 563, 569, 860, 1197, 1537
Stoic virtues, 557
"The Stolen Earth" (2008), 321
  See also Doctor Who
"Stop climate change" campaign, 1387
Stranieri, 877–879
  See also The Godfather
"Striking Vipers" (2019), 492
  See also Black Mirror
Structural violence, 2004–2014, 2016–2019, 2021–2023
Subjective idealism, 1870–1873
Subjectivism, 537
Substance dualism, 1296–1297
Suffering, 596–597, 1012
  Buddist principles of, 1006, 1009, 1011
  cause of, 1012
  cessation of, 1012
  Suicide, 1211

"Super Best Friends" (2001), 641, 642, 651
  See also South Park
Superintelligence, 486
Superman, 1953–1955
Super Mario Odyssey, 1884
Supernatural, The, 590–593
Superstructure theory, 509
Supertoy, 1064, 1076, 1077, 1082–1084, 1087
  See also Artificial intelligence (AI)
Supertoys Last all Summer Long, 1062
  See also Artificial intelligence (AI)
Surveillance capitalism, 464
Swift, Jonathan, 1585, 1592
Switching bodies, 1296, 1303
  animalism, 1296
  brain hemisphere, 1305–1306
  brain patterns, 1304
  brains, 1306
  rewiring brains, 1298
  split brains, 1305
  substance dualism, 1296–1297
  transplanting brains, 1297
Sylvia, J.J., 331

T
Tacit consent, 271, 272
Tam, River, *Firefly* hero, 262, 268, 269
Tam, Simon, *Firefly* hero, 268
Tanner, Kathyrn, 972, 980
Tarantino, Quentin, 1236, 1312
  Death Proof, 1242
  Django Unchained, 1243
  filmography and argument for revenge, 1240–1245
  Inglourious Basterds, 1242
  Jackie Brown, 1241
  Once Upon a Time in Hollywood, 1244
  Pulp Fiction, 1241
  quest for vengeance, 1241, 1242
  Reservoir Dogs, 1241
TARDIS, *Doctor Who* time machine, 137, 140, 141, 312, 315, 326, 328, 332, 336–338
Targaryen monarchy, 544
Taylor, Charles, 866
Technological artifact, 98
Technological reason, 800
Technological singularity, 482, 1791
Technologies of the self, 108
Technopoly, 490
Teleological fine-tuning argument, 587
Teleological particularism, 1751–1754
Telltale games, 1815

Tenet, 1328–1332, 1335
  argument for fatalism, 1337–1341
  block universe, 1341, 1344, 1345
  nameless and emotionless Protagonist, 1336–1337
  Nolan's cinematic Sator Square, 1333–1335
Terrorism, 437, 438, 642, 643, 645, 668
The Testaments, 189, 201, 203–205
Theism, 70, 82, 1456, 1462
Theists, 1441, 1442, 1458, 1459
Theocracy, 442, 444, 715
Theodicy, 1715
"The Thong" (2001), 1624
  See also *Curb Your Enthusiasm*
Theories of justice, 1125
Theory of alienation, 1671
Therapy, 1565, 1576, 1577, 1579
Theravada Buddhism, 1012
"Thin Ice" (2017), 331
  See also *Doctor Who*
Thirteenth tribe of humanity, *Battlestar Galactica*, 96
Thompson, Emma, 1707–1709
Thorne, Kip, 139
Thornian time machine, 139
Thought experiments, 489
Thoughts and prayers (as political response), 716, 719
Thrasymachus, 370, 371
Thunberg, Greta, 1378
Thus Spoke Zarathustra, 167
Time, 998, 1092, 1094, 1096
Time inversion, 1328, 1329, 1332, 1336, 1340
Timelines, 415–417
Time Lord(s) character(s) from *Doctor Who*, 138, 312, 314, 316–318, 323–324, 330–334
"The Time of the Doctor" (2013), 333
  See also *Doctor Who*
Time machine, 137
Time paradox story, 146
Time portals, 408
"Time slip" stories, 139
Time travel, 137, 409
  and space-time vortex, 138–140
  in theory, 147–154
Time travelers, 144
Time Travel Law, 137
Time War, The 313–315, 318, 322, 330, 332
  See also *Doctor Who*
Titans, 1932
Tobolowsky, Stephen, 413
Tolerance, 129–131, 668

Tolkien, John Ronald Reuel, 828–835, 837, 838, 840–851
Totalitarian dictatorship, 614
Totalitarianism, 103, 104, 1838, 1839, 1841
Totalitarian measures, 96
"A Town Called Mercy" (2012), 323, 328, 334
  See also *Doctor Who*
Trainwreck, 1493, 1506, 1508
  See also *Inside Amy Schumer*
Transcendence, 1725, 1726, 1735
Transcendental idealism, 1873–1876
Transgender, 1653, 1654
Transhuman corporatism, 1805
Transhumanism, 100, 484, 485
Transitivity of identity, 1296
Transparency, 624–627
Transworld identification, 2033
Treasure Island, 114, 116
Treatise of Human Nature, 770
Trolley problem, 180
Trump, Donald, 705, 707, 711–716, 719, 721–735, 737–739, 1483, 1484
  attempted coup, 661
  Covid pandemic, 636
  election lies, 665
  Fox News opinion of, 662
  presidential candidacy, 636
Trumpism, 705, 706, 708, 709, 711, 714, 715, 725, 733–735, 737–739
  See also Make America Great Again (MAGA)
Turing, Alan, 806, 1026
Turing test, 808, 812, 1027, 1029, 1035, 1036, 1067, 1068
Tuskegee syphilis study, 462
Tuttle, Shea, 230
Twain, Mark, 1350–1352, 1354, 1356–1364, 1366–1369
"Twice Upon a Time" 2017, 322, 327, 338
  See also *Doctor Who*
Twilight Zone, 480
Twombly, Cy, 1593
Tyler, Rose, *Doctor Who* character, 315, 316, 324, 326, 331, 337
Tyrannical leaders, 2053
  See also Hitler, Adolf; Trump, Donald
Tyranny, 265, 274, 279, 370, 373, 375

U
Ubermenschen, 167
Ulysses, 168, 171
Uncanniness, 143
Uncanny valley, 1084

Unequal friendships, 2095
Uniacke, Suzanne, 1258, 1259
Unity/oneness, 1012
Universals,(metaphysical concept), 2066, 2069–2077, 2080, 2082, 2083
Up in the Air, 1006
   Ryan's story, 1006–1009
   Siddhartha's story, 1009–1011
"USS Callister" (2017), 487, 488
   See also Black Mirror
Utilitarianism, 169–171, 178, 180, 325, 329–330, 440, 788, 789, 791, 1120–1123, 1747, 1818, 1819, 1924, 1953, 1957, 2087, 2098–2100
Utilitarians, 1031, 1957
   ethics, 1154
   justice, 16
   moral principle, 1123
Utility
   economic, 960
   friendships for, 960
   mutual advantage, 962
   pleasure, 952, 953, 955, 957
   political, 960
   in relationships for, 960
   social, 960
   transactional, 962
Utopia, 2111–2113
Üubermensch, 904

V

Vacuum fluctuations, 1447, 1448, 1450, 1452
Vader, Darth, *Star Wars* villain 172
Vajrayana Buddhism, 1012
Value of philosophy, 26
Vampire, 582, 583, 593, 601, 604, 1277
Vaughn, Lewis, 536, 766
Veil of ignorance, 14–17, 332, 1055, 1124
Vengeance, 1238
   Beauvoir, Simone de, 1262–1263
   common arguments, 1245–1250
   definition, 1240
   historical arguments, 1250–1257
   Hobbes, Thomas, 1254–1255
   Locke, John, 1255–1256
   modern arguments, 1257–1266
   Nietzsche, Friedrich, 1256–1257
   Nozick, Robert, 1263
   Oldenquist, Andrew, 1260
   Plato, 1250–1252
   Spinoza, Baruch, 1252–1254
   Uniacke, Suzanne, 1259

V for Vendetta, 2045, 2053, 2057, 2060, 2062
Victimhood/oppositional identity, 736
Video games, 1742, 1754, 1773, 1777, 1779, 1783, 1812, 1813, 1828–1830
Vigilantism, 1265, 1953
Viking, 1896
Violation of categorical imperative, *see* Lying
Violence, 876, 1258, 2004–2014, 2016–2019, 2022, 2023
Virtue, 67, 72, 79–81, 167, 617, 624, 625, 879, 887, 938–944, 1849, 1853–1856, 1858, 1859, 1861, 1863, 2050
   of care, 557, 567
   courage, 955
   ethicists, 1031
   ethics, 173, 175, 180, 181, 624, 911–913, 1154, 1556, 1818, 1819, 1849, 2087, 2094, 2095, 2100
   friendships for, 952, 955–957
   inclusiveness, 956
   loyalty, 956
   theory, 4, 6, 9, 10, 13, 440, 1824
   of transparency, 626
Visual lyricism, 176
V-K test, 991
   See also Blade Runner
von Hessen, Philipp (Nazi prince), 723
von Leibniz, Gottfried Wilhelm, 510
Voting, 377, 379
Vulvokov, Lenora, *Russian Doll* character, 419
Vulvokov, Nadia, *Russian Doll* character, 408
V-world, 98
   See also Caprica and Battlestar Galactica

W

Waiting for 2042 (2014) 1584, 1585, 1592, 1597
   See also Kondabolu, Hari
"The Waldo moment" (2013), 492, 493
   See also Black Mirror
The Walking Dead, 2104–2108
   apocalypse in, 2108–2110
   community, 2110–2111
   dystopia, 2113–2114
   rules, 2115–2116
   Utopia, 2111–2113
Waller-Bridge, Phoebe, 1720
   Crashing, 1721
   female characters and appetite for transgressive women, 1722–1724
   Fleabag, 1721
   making choices and eliminating bad faith, 1731–1733

Wanton, 1817, 1822, 1825
  See also Detroit Become Human
War, 313–315, 317–323, 327, 331–335
Warhol, Andy, 1593
Warism, 317–319, 324
"War of the Coprophages" (1996), see The X-Files
  See also The X-Files
Warrior God, Christian concept, 428, 436, 438, 445
Wartenberg, Thomas, 222
Watchmen, 1950, 1970–1972, 1982, 1983, 1985
  determinism, 1980
  eternalism, 1980
  existence of free will, 1976–1980
  nature of time, 1972–1976
Weaponization of the federal government (political tactic), 729, 730
"The Wedding of River Song" (2011), 326
  See also Doctor Who
Weeping Angels, Doctor Who monster, 313
The Weimar Republic, 733
Wellsian time machine, 139
Westerns, 918, 919, 934
Whedon, Joss, 260, 1170
  aesthetic views on the genre, 1182
  DVD commentary, 1178
  goals, 1191
  philosophical meditation, 1187
  See also The Cabin in the Woods and Firefly
Whimsy, 220, 225, 226
Whitaker, David, 143
Whitechapel, 2005, 2007–2010, 2012, 2013, 2016, 2017, 2019–2022
White genocide (theory of), 738
White supremacists in policing, 716, 721, 731, 738
White supremacy, 721
White voice, 1609
White, Walter, Breaking Bad protagonist, 163–172, 181, 182
Wikipedia, 1351
Wildlings (in Game of Thrones), 546
Williams, Bernard, 1276, 1279–1282
Will to power, 863, 869, 870, 1957
Wisdom, 1006, 1020, 1022

"The Witch's Familiar" (2015), 323, 325, 327, 331
  See also Doctor Who
Witch hunt (as political dodge), 729
Withholding information, 1359–1362
The Witness, 1772, 1773, 1783–1786
Wittgenstein, Ludwig, 26, 734, 1621, 1628, 1630, 1913–1919, 1922
Wolf, Susan, 1413, 1421
Wolterstorff, Nicholas, 331
Wonder (in Tolkien), 828, 832, 833, 842, 847–849
Word-deleting creative choice, 2091
Workers (in Westworld), 468, 470
Workplace (as Hell), 2018–2023
"World Enough and Time" (2017), 335
  See also Doctor Who
Wormhole, 419, 420
Writer-dominating full-script approach, 2092
WTF philosophy, 1569–1573
WWII, 420, 705, 710, 728, 731, 733, 734, 739

X
Xenophobia, 429, 443, 444
The X-Files, 520–525, 527, 529, 530, 534, 536, 539

Y
Yoga, 18

Z
Zarathustra, 167
Zaveri, Alan, Russian Doll character, 408
Zen Buddhism, 1006, 1011–1013, 1023
Zen Buddhist philosophy, 1021
Zen meditation practice, 1020
Zeus, 423, 1931, 1932
Z-Eyes, 480, 481
  See also, Black Mirror
Ziblatt, Daniel, 366, 368
Zimmer, Hans, 760
Zombies, 2105, 2106, 2109, 2112
Zygon(s), Doctor Who villains, 330, 332–334